ดำเนิน - เสฐียรพงษ์

พจนานุกรมไทย - อังกฤษ

(ฉบับปรับปรุงใหม่)

ดำเนิน การเด่น J.D. (ฮาร์วาร์ด)
เสฐียรพงษ์ วรรณปก M.A. (เคมบริดจ์)

DOMNERN - SATHIENPONG

THAI-ENGLISH

DICTIONARY

(2nd Edition)

DOMNERN GARDEN
SATHIENPONG WANNAPOK

Amarin Printing and Publishing Public Company Limited
Bangkok, Thailand

Second Edition Revised 1999
First Edition 1994 (Ten Impressions)
Copyright © 1994, 1999 Domnern Garden and Sathienpong Wannapok
ISBN : 974-272-096-7

Printed in Thailand by
Amarin Printing and Publishing Public Company Limited
65/16 Chaiyapruk Road, Taling Chan, Bangkok 10170
Tel. (662) 882-1010 Fax (662) 433-2742, 434-1385

ฉบับปรับปรุงใหม่ พ.ศ. 2542
พิมพ์ครั้งแรก พ.ศ. 2537
(พิมพ์ซ้ำ 9 ครั้ง ในปี 2538, 2539, 2540, 2541, 2542)
11th Printing 1999   พิมพ์ครั้งที่ 11 พ.ศ. 2542
12th Printing 2000   พิมพ์ครั้งที่ 12 พ.ศ. 2543
13th Printing 2001   พิมพ์ครั้งที่ 13 พ.ศ. 2544

จัดจำหน่ายโดย
บริษัทอมรินทร์บุ๊คเซ็นเตอร์ จำกัด
65/60 - 62 ถนนชัยพฤกษ์ (บรมราชชนนี) เขตตลิ่งชัน กรุงเทพฯ 10170
โทรศัพท์ 882-1010 โทรสาร 434-1382, 434-1384

พิมพ์ในประเทศไทยโดย
บริษัทอมรินทร์พริ้นติ้งแอนด์พับลิชชิ่ง จำกัด (มหาชน)
65/16 ถนนชัยพฤกษ์ (บรมราชชนนี) เขตตลิ่งชัน กรุงเทพฯ 10170
โทรศัพท์ (662) 882-1010 โทรสาร (662) 433-2742, 434-1385
E-mail: info@amarin.co.th Homepage: http://www.amarin.co.th

สารบัญ

CONTENTS

ภาคผนวก

Appendices

คำนำ
สำหรับฉบับปรับปรุงใหม่

พจนานุกรมไทย - อังกฤษฉบับนี้ ได้แก้ไขปรับปรุงใหม่ จึงมีลักษณะ 7 ประการดังนี้

1. มีคำใหม่ๆ ที่ใช้สื่อสารกันโดยมากเพิ่มขึ้น รวมถึงสแลงที่ท่าทำจะอยู่นานพอสมควร

2. คำเดิมบางคำ ได้แก้ไขคำแปลใหม่ที่เห็นว่าสื่อความหมายดีกว่าเดิม เช่น ตกเขียว, เท่าทุน, คู่บ้านคู่เมือง, ชายอกสามศอก

3. การเรียงคำ ยังถือตามพจนานุกรม ฉบับราชบัณฑิตยสถานเป็นหลัก แต่ก็ไม่ทั้งหมด ลูกคำบางคำในพจนานุกรม ฉบับราชบัณฑิตฯ น่าจะใช้เป็นคำตั้ง เราก็นำมาเป็นคำตั้ง

4. การวางคำ ผู้จัดทำใช้วิธี "เดาใจ" ผู้ใช้ ว่าควรจะอยู่ใต้คำตั้งอะไร ก็ใส่ไว้ตรงนั้น เช่น ล้างผลาญ ควรจะอยู่ใต้คำ ล้าง หรือ ผลาญ แต่บางครั้งก็ตัดสินใจยาก จึงใส่ไว้ทั้งสองแห่ง เพื่อสะดวกแก่ผู้ค้นหาคำ

5. คำที่มีความหมายหลายนัย ทั้งความหมายเดิม และความหมายใหม่ บางครั้งก็ใส่ไว้ เฉพาะความหมายเดิม หรือความหมายใหม่ ในฉบับนี้ได้ปรับปรุงให้สมบูรณ์ขึ้น เช่นคำ บารมี กรรม

6. บางคำที่นักศึกษาไทยรู้สึกว่าแปลไม่ค่อยจะตรง เช่น หมั่นไส้ ใช้ว่า to be disgusted (with), disgusting เห็นว่าถูกต้องแล้ว จึงไม่แก้ไข ทั้งนี้ต้องดู ท่าที และบริบท ที่ใช้ด้วย จึงจะรู้ว่า คำนั้นๆ ใช้ถูกต้องหรือไม่

7. เพิ่มศัพท์ศาสนามากขึ้น เช่น ปัพพาชนียกรรม สังฆเภท พุทธพาณิชย์ นิคหกรรม

อย่างไรก็ดี พจนานุกรมฉบับแก้ไขปรับปรุงนี้ จุคำมากขึ้นกว่าเดิม มากพอที่จะเป็น เครื่องมือค้นคว้าของนักแปล นักศึกษา และประชาชนผู้สนใจ ทั้งไทยและเทศ ถ้ามีข้อเสนอแนะ ที่จะทำให้หนังสือเล่มนี้ถูกต้องสมบูรณ์ยิ่งขึ้นในโอกาสต่อไป ผู้จัดทำขอน้อมรับด้วยความยินดีและ ขอบคุณเป็นอย่างยิ่ง

ดำเนิน การเด่น
เสฐียรพงษ์ วรรณปก

กรุงเทพฯ
กันยายน 2542

Foreword to the Second Edition

During the past five years since first publication, many words have come into vogue like ลุ้น, แห้ว, จาบจ้วง, ฆ่าล้างเผ่าพันธุ์, ฟันธง and new words have been introduced like เศรษฐกิจฟองสบู่ for "bubble economy", หุ้นกู้แปลงสภาพ for "convertible debenture" and ครอบงำกิจการ for "business takeover". These have been added to the second edition. Many other words and expressions that had been left out of the first edition we felt should be included in the second like กระวีกระวาด "in a flurry", ลาภปาก "a real treat" and นานาจิตตัง "many men many minds". There are words which are technical but it would have been a shame not to have their English equivalents made available like อนุกรม "series", วงโคจรค้างฟ้า "geostationary orbit" and กระบวนทัศน์ "paradigm". In religious matters, we felt confident about including terms whose translations would not be easily found elsewhere like ปัพพาชนียกรรม "a drumming out ceremony", สังฆเภท "schism", โลกุตระ "supramundane". Where Thai sayings could be rendered reasonably well in English, they too have been included like สันหลังหวะ "to have a skeleton in the closet". In all, over a thousand words such as these have been added.

The appendices have been updated and, where appropriate, amended. For example, because of the commercial importance of identifying fish, we have been advised to include their scientific names. Thanks to Dr. Chavalit Vidthayanon we were able to do this.

For assistance in preparing the second edition, we wish to thank Ekachai Euataanpisit for his input on the nuances of words and painstaking amendment of the appendices and Theeraphon Khoomsap who keyed in the new entries, making many perceptive suggestions in the process. Also we are indebted to and thank the many others whose comments and suggestions helped along the way.

Domnern Garden
Sathienpong Wannapok

Bangkok
September 1999

คำนำ

พจนานุกรมไทย-อังกฤษฉบับนี้เรียงคำตามลำดับอักษรจาก ก ถึง ฮ ตามพจนานุกรม
ฉบับราชบัณฑิตยสถาน พ.ศ. 2525 แต่เลือกเอาเฉพาะคำที่มีใช้ทั่วไปเท่านั้น คำเก่าๆ และคำที่เป็น
ภาษาถิ่นส่วนมากจะไม่นำมารวมไว้ด้วย

การวางคำตั้งและลูกคำบางครั้งก็มิได้ยึดตามพจนานุกรม ฉบับราชบัณฑิตยสถานเสมอไป
บางคำมีความหมายหลายนัย ก็จะเลือกเอาเฉพาะความหมายที่ต้องการเท่านั้น

บางคำก็ได้ให้คำแปลพร้อมยกตัวอย่างประกอบด้วย เพื่อให้เข้าใจวิธีใช้ ตัวอย่างที่ยกมา
จะเป็นภาษาที่ใช้กันจริงๆ ในชีวิตประจำวัน มากกว่าภาษาหนังสือ

ภาษาแต่ละภาษามีภูมิหลังทางวัฒนธรรมแตกต่างกัน การจะแปลคำจากภาษาหนึ่งไปสู่
อีกภาษาหนึ่งตรงๆ นั้น บางทีก็มิได้สื่อความหมายอะไรเลย เพราะ "การแปล" มิได้หมาย
เพียงการถอดคำตรงตามตัวอักษรเท่านั้น ยกตัวอย่างเช่น "ง่ายเหมือนปอกกล้วย" ในภาษาไทย
เมื่อแปลเป็นภาษาอังกฤษตรงๆ ย่อมไม่สื่อความหมายอะไร จึงควรแปลให้ตรงกับวัฒนธรรม
ของเขา เช่น easy as falling off a log หรือ to be a lark หรือ a piece of cake.

อนึ่ง การแปลควรคำนึงถึงประเภทของคำด้วย เช่น คำภาษาวรรณคดี ภาษาเขียน
ภาษาปาก สำนวน สแลง คำไทยเป็นคำประเภทใด คำอังกฤษก็ควรเป็นคำประเภทนั้นด้วย ในที่นี้
จึงพยายามหาคำที่ "ตรงกัน" จากทั้งสองภาษานั้นให้มากที่สุดเท่าที่จะทำได้

ผู้จัดทำหวังว่าพจนานุกรมฉบับนี้ คงจะเป็น "ที่ปรึกษา" ที่ดีในการแปลภาษาไทยเป็น
ภาษาอังกฤษ สำหรับนักเรียนนักศึกษา นักแปล และผู้สนใจทั่วไป

กรุงเทพฯ   ดำเนิน การเด่น
24 มิถุนายน 2537   เสฐียรพงษ์ วรรณปก

FOREWORD

The DOMNERN-SATHIENPONG THAI-ENGLISH DICTIONARY is a dictionary of current Thai, literary and spoken, and its corresponding English. It is designed to assist the translation of books, newspapers, broadcasts, speeches, conversation and, of course, the usual classroom exercises. It gives equivalent words and expressions rather than definitions. It presupposes some knowledge of English syntax and grammar.

In trying to match the two languages, we have made an effort to give English equivalents which in meaning and register can be used to convey the sense, style and feeling of the Thai word. If there is no equivalent, the Thai word is defined.

While the Thai wordlist of the Royal Institute Thai Dictionary has generally been followed, words which are obsolete, rarely used or local dialect have been dropped. Where words have several meanings, only those meanings which are in common use have been rendered.

Once a key English word is located, additional information may be needed such as its part of speech, inflective forms, plural, definition and additional examples of correct usage. These are readily found in English language dictionaries such as *Oxford Advanced Learner's Dictionary, Longman's Dictionary of Contemporary English, the American Heritage Dictionary of the English Language, Merriam-Webster's Ninth New Collegiate Dictionary, Collins Cobuild English Language Dictionary* and the great American dictionary the *Webster's Third New International Dictionary (unabridged)* which we have depended on as a guide to spelling and usage. For best translation, use any of these or similar works as a companion to this dictionary.

Special lexicons of animal and plant names, names of Thai dishes, geographical names, military and police ranks and Thai government organs have been put together in appendices as a reference library.

Our special thanks go to all the kind people who helped us to find the "right" words and especially to Khun Smat Ruangnarong our fastidious and knowledgeable editorial supervisor, to Ms. Siriwan Tonthong our painstaking proofreader and to Ms. Dara Muenkaewthong, Ms. Sirima Markmanee and Ms. Nisakorn Koryanyong the admirable computer operators who managed so well to convert the manuscript into bilingual computer form.

Bangkok
June 24, 1994

DOMNERN GARDEN
SATHIENPONG WANNAPOK

EXPLANATORY CHART

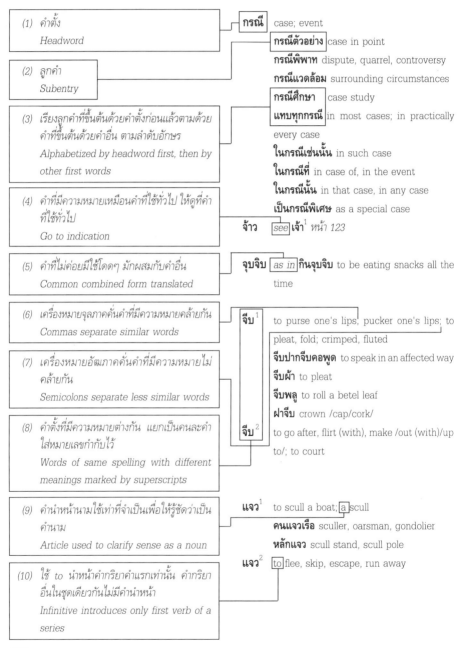

(1) คำตั้ง *Headword*	**กรณี** case; event
	กรณีตัวอย่าง case in point
	กรณีพิพาท dispute, quarrel, controversy
(2) ลูกคำ *Subentry*	**กรณีแวดล้อม** surrounding circumstances
	กรณีศึกษา case study
(3) เรียงลูกคำที่ขึ้นต้นด้วยคำตั้งก่อนแล้วตามด้วย คำที่ขึ้นต้นด้วยคำอื่น ตามลำดับอักษร *Alphabetized by headword first, then by other first words*	**แทบทุกกรณี** in most cases; in practically every case **ในกรณีเช่นนั้น** in such case **ในกรณีที่** in case of, in the event
(4) คำที่มีความหมายเหมือนคำที่ใช้ทั่วไป ให้ดูที่คำ ที่ใช้ทั่วไป *Go to indication*	**ในกรณีนั้น** in that case, in any case **เป็นกรณีพิเศษ** as a special case **จ้าว** $\boxed{see}$ **เจ้า**¹ หน้า *123*
(5) คำที่ไม่ค่อยมีใช้โดดๆ มักผสมกับคำอื่น *Common combined form translated*	**จุบจิบ** $\boxed{as\ in}$ **กินจุบจิบ** to be eating snacks all the time
(6) เครื่องหมายจุลภาคคั่นคำที่มีความหมายคล้ายกัน *Commas separate similar words*	**จีบ**¹ to purse one's lips; pucker one's lips; to pleat, fold; crimped, fluted
(7) เครื่องหมายอัฒภาคคั่นคำที่มีความหมายไม่ คล้ายกัน *Semicolons separate less similar words*	**จีบปากจีบคอพูด** to speak in an affected way **จีบผ้า** to pleat **จีบพลู** to roll a betel leaf **ฝาจีบ** crown /cap/cork/
(8) คำตั้งที่มีความหมายต่างกัน แยกเป็นคนละคำ ใส่หมายเลขกำกับไว้ *Words of same spelling with different meanings marked by superscripts*	**จีบ**² to go after, flirt (with), make /out (with)/up to/; to court
(9) คำนำหน้านามใช้เท่าที่จำเป็นเพื่อให้รู้ชัดว่าเป็น คำนาม *Article used to clarify sense as a noun*	**แจว**¹ to scull a boat; $\boxed{a}$ scull **คนแจวเรือ** sculler, oarsman, gondolier **หลักแจว** scull stand, scull pole
(10) ใช้ *to* นำหน้าคำกริยาคำแรกเท่านั้น คำกริยา อื่นในชุดเดียวกันไม่มีคำนำหน้า *Infinitive introduces only first verb of a series*	**แจว**² $\boxed{to}$ flee, skip, escape, run away

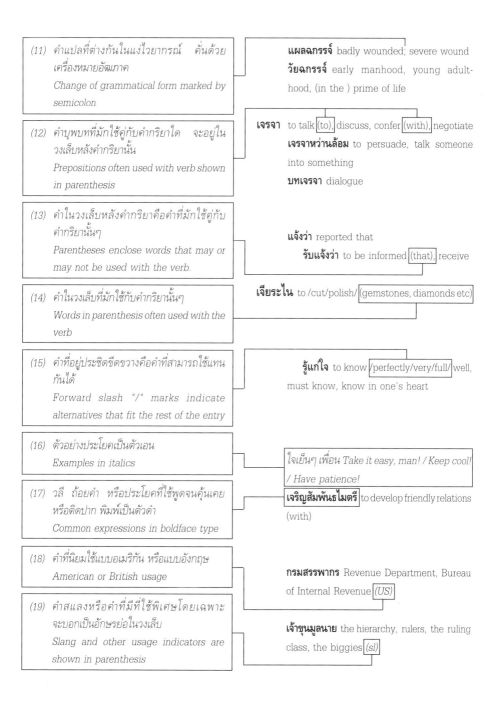

(11) *คำแปลที่ต่างกันในแง่ไวยากรณ์ คั่นด้วย*
เครื่องหมายอัฒภาค
Change of grammatical form marked by
semicolon

แผลฉกรรจ์ badly wounded; severe wound
วัยฉกรรจ์ early manhood, young adult-hood, (in the) prime of life

(12) *คำบุพบทที่มักใช้คู่กับคำกริยาใด จะอยู่ใน*
วงเล็บหลังคำกริยานั้น
Prepositions often used with verb shown
in parenthesis

เจรจา to talk (to), discuss, confer (with), negotiate
เจรจาหว่านล้อม to persuade, talk someone into something
บทเจรจา dialogue

(13) *คำในวงเล็บหลังคำกริยาคือคำที่มักใช้คู่กับ*
คำกริยานั้นๆ
Parentheses enclose words that may or
may not be used with the verb.

แจ้งว่า reported that
    รับแจ้งว่า to be informed (that), receive

(14) *คำในวงเล็บที่มักใช้กับคำกริยานั้นๆ*
Words in parenthesis often used with the
verb

เจียระไน to /cut/polish/ (gemstones, diamonds etc)

(15) *คำที่อยู่ประชิดขีดขวางคือคำที่สามารถใช้แทน*
กันได้
Forward slash "/" marks indicate
alternatives that fit the rest of the entry

รู้แก่ใจ to know /perfectly/very/full/ well, must know, know in one's heart

(16) *ตัวอย่างประโยคเป็นตัวเอน*
Examples in italics

ใจเย็นๆ เพื่อน Take it easy, man! / Keep cool! / Have patience!

(17) *วลี ถ้อยคำ หรือประโยคที่ใช้พูดจนคุ้นเคย*
หรือติดปาก พิมพ์เป็นตัวดำ
Common expressions in boldface type

เจริญสัมพันธ์ไมตรี to develop friendly relations (with)

(18) *คำที่นิยมใช้แบบอเมริกัน หรือแบบอังกฤษ*
American or British usage

กรมสรรพากร Revenue Department, Bureau of Internal Revenue (US)

(19) *คำสแลงหรือคำที่มีที่ใช้พิเศษโดยเฉพาะ*
จะบอกเป็นอักษรย่อในวงเล็บ
Slang and other usage indicators are
shown in parenthesis

เจ้าขุนมูลนาย the hierarchy, rulers, the ruling class, the biggies (sl)

EXPLANATORY NOTES

ARRANGEMENT

The Thai words are arranged alphabetically from ก to ฮ in accordance with the system of the Royal Institute Thai Dictionary (1982). The order of consonants and precedence of vowels is printed conveniently on the front and back inside covers with the page number on which a particular letter of the alphabet begins.

The main entry or headword appears in **boldface** type to the left of each column (1). Subentries including derivatives, compounds and common combinations are indented in **boldface** type (2). Those beginning with the headword are listed first followed by those in which the headword appears in a secondary position, for example, the headword **กลัว** is followed by subentries **กลัวบาป กลัวผี กลัวแพ้** in that order and then by the compound words **ขี้กลัว น่ากลัว** etc. (3). Many combined words are located under both the first word and the last word. For example, **ตกรถ** is listed under the headword **ตก** as well as under the headword **รถ**. **ชี้แจง** may be found under both **ชี้** and **แจง**. This makes it easier to find them.

Examples of a special use of adjectives may be found under the adjective itself, for example, **ขนมปังกรอบ** will be found under **กรอบ**.

Words which are so commonly used in combination as to be inseparable are listed under the first word, for example, **การเมือง** will be found under **การ**.

The indication *"see"* will direct the reader to where the word sought can be found, for example, **ตะเวน** *see* **ตระเวน** *หน้า 180,* **ถมถืด** *see* **ถมไป** *หน้า 321*

Words which are almost never used alone but rather in combination with another word are marked *"as in"* and are translated in their combined form, for example, **นิจ** *as in* **เนืองนิจ, เป็นนิจ** (5).

(12)

SENSE INDICATORS

Where several English words can be used for a single Thai word, those close in meaning are separated by a comma (6), those whose meanings are distinct enough to require special attention are separated by a semicolon (7), for example, "เก่ง smart, good (at something); easily, readily".

Where a Thai word has two separate meanings, each is shown as a headword marked with a superscript number, for example, "กรอบ[1] frame"

"กรอบ[2] crisp" (8)

USAGE INDICATORS

The articles "a", "an" and "the" are used where they form part of an expression or in rare cases like "หน้าม้า a shill; a claque" where the nouns are likely to be unfamiliar or "โดยมาก a majority" because without the article the word might be confused with the adjective "majority" (9).

Verbs are indicated by the infinitive "to" but only the first verb in a series separated by commas is so indicated (10). The semicolon is used to mark an otherwise unobvious change in grammatical form (11).

Prepositions or adverbs often used in combination with a verb to express the meaning of the Thai word are shown in parenthesis, for example, "agree (with); to be converted (to)" and "go (up, on, down)" (12).

The parenthesis is also used to enclose words that show how the verb is used (13) or that are frequently but not always used with the verb (14).

The forward slash without spaces indicates alternative words that can be used with the other words of the entry, for example, "to /inflate/raise/jack up/ the price" may be read : to inflate the price, to raise the price, or to jack up the price (15).

Examples of usage are shown in *italic* type, for example, "*คุณถืออะไรเป็นเกณฑ์ในการ ตัดสินว่าภาพดีหรือไม่ดี What's your basis for judging whether the painting is good or not?*" If more than one example is given, they are separated by a spaced forward slash, for example, *What's your basis...or not? / On what do you base your criticism of the painting?* (16).

Examples of usage which are themselves in common use such as proverbs and expressions are shown in **boldface** type as a sub-entry, for example, **บ้านแตกสาแหรกขาด** (17).

Spellings are those commonly used in the United States not because they are "correct" but rather because more Thais are exposed to American writing and usage than British or those of other English-using countries. In some cases, where words are special to Great Britain, they are tagged with the abbreviation *(Brit)* or where certain expressions are chiefly American, they are tagged *(US)* (18).

Ephemeral slang words have not been included but some slang expressions in such widespread use as to have become part of the mainstream of English have been included where they match their counterparts in Thai. They are marked *(sl)* (19).

ABBREVIATIONS USED

พหู = พหูพจน์ plural

พูด = ภาษาพูด colloquial

อี = อีสาน Northeast dialect, for example, "**กั้งจ้อง** to put up an umbrella *(อี)*" (p.22).

เอก = เอกพจน์ singular

abbr = abbreviation

etc = et cetera indicating that other words of the same sort may be used, for example, in the entry : "**ผู้บงการ** person who is /directing/running/ (an operation, etc)" (p.267), the "etc" indicates that words similar to "an operation" like "the show" or "the project" or "the enterprise" may be used instead.

fig = figurative to indicate the translation which follows is not the literal sense of the Thai word, for example, "กลืนไม่ลง *(fig)* I couldn't take it; I can't swallow." (p. 17). The translation appearing after the semicolon is the literal meaning.

Brit = British indicating usage special to British-English countries, for example, "ด้วยความนับถือ Yours faithfully *(Brit)*" (p. 159).

gr = grammar indicating the word is used in a technical sense in grammar, for example, "การันต์ [2] ending *(gr)*" (p.26).

sl = slang to indicate a slang word in English which might be appropriate to use in rendering the vernacular sense of the Thai, for example, "เจ้าขุนมูลนาย ...the biggies *(sl)*" (p.123).

US = United States and indicates the term is used particularly in the United States, for example, "กรมสรรพากร Bureau of Internal Revenue *(US)*" p.4.

คำชี้แจง

1. พจนานุกรมไทย-อังกฤษฉบับนี้ ผู้จัดทำประสงค์จะให้ใช้เป็นคู่มือในการแปลไทย
เป็นอังกฤษ หรืออังกฤษเป็นไทย จึงพยายามหาคำที่ "ตรงกัน" จากทั้งสองภาษาให้มากที่สุดเท่าที่
จะมากได้ โดยคำนึงถึงวัฒนธรรมเบื้องหลังภาษาทั้งสองนั้นเป็นสำคัญ คำไทยที่ใช้เป็นคำประเภทใด
เช่น ภาษาวรรณคดี ภาษาเขียน ภาษาปาก สำนวน สแลง คำอังกฤษก็เป็นคำประเภทนั้นด้วย ผู้ที่ใช้
พจนานุกรมฉบับนี้จะต้องเป็นผู้ที่มีความรู้ภาษาไทยและภาษาอังกฤษดีพอสมควรแล้ว ด้วยเหตุนี้
ผู้จัดทำจึงมิได้เขียนคำอ่านกำกับไว้ และมิได้บอกประเภทของคำไว้ด้วย

2. การเรียงคำ เรียงตามลำดับอักษร จาก ก ถึง ฮ ยึดตามพจนานุกรม ฉบับราชบัณฑิตย-
สถาน พ.ศ. 2525

3. คำตั้ง มิได้เอามาจากพจนานุกรม ฉบับราชบัณฑิตยสถานทั้งหมด คำเก่าที่ใช้น้อย
และเป็นภาษาถิ่น ส่วนมากจะตัดทิ้งไป

4. คำที่มีความหมายหลายนัย จะเลือกเฉพาะนัยที่มีที่ใช้ทั่วไปเท่านั้น

5. คำที่อาจแปลเป็นภาษาอังกฤษได้หลายสำนวน หรือมีวิธีพูดหลายอย่าง ใช้เครื่องหมาย
จุลภาค (,) คั่นในระหว่าง ถ้ามีความหมายไม่คล้ายกันนัก แต่ไม่ถึงกับต่างกันโดยสิ้นเชิง ใช้
เครื่องหมาย อัฒภาค (;) คั่นในระหว่าง เช่น เก่ง smart; good (at something); easily, readily

6. ลูกคำ (อนุพจน์) เรียงตามลำดับอักษรเช่นเดียวกับในข้อ 2. โดยเรียงคำที่ขึ้นต้นด้วย
คำเดียวกับคำตั้งไว้ก่อนลูกคำที่ขึ้นต้นด้วยคำอื่น เช่น (คำตั้ง) **กลัว** (ลูกคำ) **กลัวบาป กลัวแพ้... ขี้กลัว
น่ากลัว...**

7. คำที่ผสมขึ้นจากคำ 2 คำ อาจเปิดหาความหมายได้ที่คำแรก หรือคำสุดท้าย เช่น **ตกรถ**
เปิดดูที่คำ **ตก** หรือที่คำ **รถ** ก็ได้ **ชี้แจง** เปิดดูที่คำ **ชี้** หรือที่คำ **แจง** ก็ได้ ทั้งนี้เพื่อความสะดวกสำหรับ
ผู้ค้นหาคำนั้นๆ

8. คำตั้งเหมือนกันที่มีความหมายต่างกัน เก็บไว้ซ้ำกัน โดยใส่หมายเลขกำกับไว้ เช่น
กรอบ^1 **กรอบ**^{2}

9. ตัวอย่างของการใช้คำนั้นๆ ใช้อักษรตัวเอน เช่น *คุณถืออะไรเป็นเกณฑ์ในการตัดสินว่า
ภาพนี้ดีหรือไม่ดี What's your basis for judging whether the painting is good or not ?*

ถ้ามีวิธีพูดหลายอย่างจะใช้เครื่องหมาย / คั่นในระหว่าง เช่น *What's your basis for judging whether the painting is good or not? / On what do you base your criticism of the painting?*

10. ตัวอย่างที่ใช้แพร่หลาย เช่น คำพังเพย สุภาษิต หรือสำนวน ใช้อักษรตัวหนา เช่น **บ้านแตกสาแหรกขาด**

11. คำภาษาอังกฤษที่มีบุพบทกำกับเสมอ ใส่วงเล็บไว้ที่บุพบท เช่น agree (with), to be converted (to) คำที่ใช้กับหลายบุพบทในความหมายต่างกัน จะใส่เครื่องหมายจุลภาค (,) กำกับไว้ เช่น go (up, on, down)

12. คำที่ใช้กันทั่วไป จะให้คำนิยามไว้ ส่วนคำที่ไม่ค่อยมีใช้และมีความหมายเหมือนคำที่ใช้ ทั่วไป จะใส่ *see* หน้าคำที่ใช้ทั่วไปนั้น เช่น **ตะเวน** *see* **ตระเวน**, **ถมถืด** *see* **ถมไป**

13. คำที่มีความหมายในตัวเองแต่มักไม่ค่อยมีใช้โดดๆ มักผสมกับคำอื่น จะใส่ *as in* หน้าคำนั้น เช่น **นิจ** *as in* **เนืองนิจ, เป็นนิจ**

14. ชื่อนก สัตว์เลี้ยงลูกด้วยนม งู และสัตว์เลื้อยคลานอื่นๆ แมง แมลง พืช ปลา และ สิ่งมีชีวิตใต้น้ำอื่นๆ ชื่อภูมิศาสตร์ อาหารไทย ยศตำแหน่งต่างๆ ทางการทหารและตำรวจ ตลอดถึง ชื่อส่วนราชการไทย เก็บไว้เฉพาะที่สามัญทั่วไป นอกนั้นรวมไว้ในภาคผนวก

ก็ then, still, also; if; to be; well why not
ทำก็ทำ *Do it? Well why not.*

ก็ช่าง so what, never mind
เขาจะเป็นอย่างไร ก็ช่างเขา *Whatever he is, so what. / So what if he is.*

ก็ดี , ก็ตาม as well as, and, or.../all/both/
บิดาก็ดี มารดาก็ดี ย่อมรักบุตร *Fathers or mothers, they all love their children. / Father and mother, both love their children.*

ก็ได้ okay, all right; either...or
กินก็ได้ ทาก็ได้ *It can be taken either orally or applied to the skin.* คุณจะมาก็ได้ *It's okay for you to come.*

ก็ตามใจ please yourself
คุณจะทำอย่างนั้นก็ตามใจ *If that's what you want, please yourself.*

ก็ตามที whatever; up to /him/you/etc
เธอจะว่าอย่างไรก็ตามที ฉันไม่สนใจ *You can say whatever you like, it doesn't interest me.*
ฉันสั่งเขาแล้ว จะทำหรือไม่ทำก็ตามที *I've already told him. Whether he does it or not is up to him.*

ก็ถูก...แต่ it may be so, but

ก็แล้วกัน just

ก็แล้วแต่ it depends; it's up to you

ก็แล้วไป What's done is done., That's okay., never mind

ก็...แหละ that is, well, then
ถ้าอย่างนั้นก็ไม่ต้องสึกแหละ *Well, in that case, I better not leave the monkhood.*
ทำมากก็ได้มากแหละ *If you do a lot, well you get a lot.*
เด็กก็อย่างนี้แหละ *That's the way kids are.*

ละก็ boy!
คุณละก็ ชอบเป็นเสียอย่างนี้ *Boy, that's just like you!*

แล้วก็ and, and then
เขาพูดแล้วก็นั่งลง *He spoke and then sat*
down.

กก[1] to hug, embrace, hold in one's embrace, clasp to one's breast; to keep on one's person
กกกอด to hug, embrace, hold someone close
กกไข่ to brood, to sit on eggs, hatch, incubate eggs
กกนอน to cuddle, nestle
กกลูก to put one's arms around one's baby

กก[2] base, foot, bottom part
กกหู base of the ear

กก[3] sedge, reed

ก๊ก group, faction, clique; clan, tribe; race
แบ่งเป็นก๊กเป็นเหล่า *to split into factions / to form cliques*

กกุธภัณฑ์ regalia

กง rim; wheel; rib (of a boat)
กงการ business, concern, affair
กงเกวียนกำเกวียน to reap the consequences, get what one deserves
กงจักร a disk-shaped weapon
เห็นกงจักรเป็นดอกบัว *to mistake wrong for right*

ก่ง *see* **โก่ง** หน้า 42

ก๊ง to drink (alcohol); peg

กั๋ง grandfather

กั้งโค้ง to bend over, stoop /down/over/

กงเต็ก Chinese funeral ritual

กงสี firm, company; family
คุณกินกงสี ถึงเงินเดือนน้อยก็อยู่ได้ *Since you live off the family, you can get by on a low salary.*

กงสุล consul; consular
กงสุลใหญ่ consul-general
เจ้าพนักงานกงสุล consular officer
ตัวแทนกงสุล consular agent
รองกงสุล vice-consul
สถานกงสุล consulate

ก ข ค ฆ ง จ ฉ ช ซ ฌ ญ ฎ ฏ ฐ ฑ ฒ ณ ด ต ถ ท ธ น บ ป ผ ฝ พ ฟ ภ ม ย ร ฤ ฤๅ ล ว ศ ษ ส ห ฬ อ ฮ

กฎ   rule, regulation, law

     กฎกระทรวง ministerial regulation

     กฎเกณฑ์ principle, order, rule

     กฎข้อบังคับ by-law, rule, regulation

     กฎจราจร traffic regulation

     กฎทบวง /ministerial/agency/ regulations

     กฎทั่วไป general rule

     กฎเทศบาล municipal regulation; municipal ordinance

     กฎธรรมชาติ law of nature, natural law

     กฎธรรมดา law of nature, natural law, nature of things

     กฎบัตร charter

         กฎบัตรกฎหมาย the laws

         กฎบัตรสหประชาชาติ United Nations Charter

     กฎมนเทียรบาล royal family law

     กฎยุทธวินัย military code of conduct, code of military discipline

     กฎไวยากรณ์ grammatical rule

     กฎหมาย law, legislation, statute

         กฎหมายจารีตประเพณี customary law

         กฎหมายนานาประเทศ international law

         กฎหมายแพ่งและพาณิชย์ civil law

         กฎหมายระหว่างประเทศ international law

         กฎหมายลูก organic law, ancillary law

         กฎหมายอาญา penal law, criminal law

     กฎหมู่ mob rule

     กฎแห่งกรรม law of action, law of cause and effect, karmic law

     กฎอัยการศึก martial law

กฐิน   gift of robes presented to monks within a month after the end of the Buddhist Lent

     ทอดกฐิน to present robes to monks at the end of the Buddhist Lent

     ผ้ากฐิน robes for presentation

     รับกฐิน to receive robes at the presentation ceremony

กด   to press, push, hit

     กดกระดิ่ง to ring the bell

     กดขี่ to oppress, be oppressive, tyrannize, browbeat, persecute

     กดคอ to force

     กดดัน to be frustrated; tense, under stress, under strain

         ความกดดัน frustration, suppressed /desires/emotions/; tension, pressure

     กดท้อง to press the stomach

     กดปุ่ม to press the button

     กดราคา to force down the price

     กดลง to /press/push/ down, depress

     กดไว้ to hold back, suppress

     กดหัว to be kept down, intimidated

กตเวทิตา gratitude

กตเวที /grateful/appreciative/ person

     แสดงกตเวที to be grateful to, show gratitude (to, for)

     ด้วยกตเวที gratefully

กตัญญู gratitude, gratefulness, appreciation; good, dutiful

     เขาไม่มีความกตัญญู He is /ungrateful/ unappreciative/.

     ด้วยความกตัญญู gratefully, with gratitude, as an expression of gratitude

กติกา   rules

     กติกาสัญญา pact, treaty

         กติกาสัญญาแปซิฟิก Pacific Pact

     ตั้งกติกา establish rules, set up rules

กถา   discourse, talk, words

     ปาฐกถา talk, lecture

กถึก   as in ธรรมกถึก preacher

ก่น   to dig up; to persist, do nothing but, keep

     ก่นโคตร to revile (one's forebears)

     ก่นด่า to keep scolding

     ก่นแต่ร้องไห้ to do nothing but weep, keep crying

ก้น   bottom; buttocks, ass, fanny, behind

     ก้นกบ coccyx

ก้นกระเป๋า bottom of a pocket

ก้นกุฏิ factotum, majordomo

ก้นแก้ว bottom of a glass

ก้นขวด bottom of a bottle

ก้นครัว mistress, paramour

ก้นถ้วย bottom of a cup

ก้นทะเล bottom of the sea, depths of the ocean

ก้นบ่อ bottom of a well

ก้นบาตร bottom of a monk's bowl

ก้นบึ้ง bottom

ก้นบุหรี่ cigarette butt, cigarette stub

ก้นปอด flat buttocks

ก้นหนัก one who overstays; tiresome /talker/drinker/

ก้นหอย spiral, helical; finger whorl (skin-pattern on the finger)

ก้นอ่าง bottom of a basin

กนก gold

ลายกนก see กระหนก หน้า 11

กบ[1] to fill full; full (of), overflowing (with)

ข้าวกบหม้อ a potful of rice

เลือดกบปาก a mouthful of blood

กบ[2] frog

ลูกกบ tadpole

กบ[3] plane

กบไสไม้ plane

ขี้กบ plane shavings

ไสกบ to plane

กบฏ rebellion, insurrection, insurgency; sedition

เป็นกบฏ to be in revolt, be in /rebellion/ insurrection/; seditious

พวกกบฏ rebels, insurgents

กบดาน to go into hiding, be in hiding, hide out (in, at, somewhere)

จระเข้กบดาน to lie in wait

กบาล skull

เขกกบาล to give (someone) a little knock on the head

ตีกบาล to knock (somebody) in the head

กบี่ monkey

กบี่ธุช the king's military standard bearing the figure of Hanuman

ก.พ. Civil Service Commission

ก้ม to bend down, stoop; to bow

ก้มกราบ to bow down as a sign of respect

ก้มลง to bend down, bend over

ก้มศีรษะ to bow one's head, bow down

ก้มศีรษะให้ to nod in assent; to take off one's hat to someone, hand it to someone

ก้มหน้า to bow the head; to bear, suffer

ก้มหน้าทำมาหากิน to work hard to make a living / to keep one's nose to the grindstone

ก้มหน้าก้มตา to do (something) in earnest, do assiduously, make an effort, put one's mind to something

ก้มหน้าทนไป to endure with fortitude, bear patiently

ก้มหัวให้ see ก้มศีรษะให้

กมล lotus; heart

ดวงกมล heart

กร arm

ต่อกร to fight, take (somebody) on

ยอกรวันทา to join the hands in respect

กรกฏ Cancer

กรกฎาคม July

กรง cage

กรงไก่ chicken cage, chicken coop

กรงขัง cage; detention cell, prison cell

กรงทอง cradle; gilded cage

กรงนก birdcage

กรงเล็บ claws, talons

กรงสัตว์ animal cage

กรงเหล็ก jail

ลูกกรง bars; baluster, upright supports of a banister

กรณฑ์ root, surd

กรณฑ์สอง square root

ข ค ฆ ง จ ฉ ช ซ ฌ ญ ฏ ฎ ฐ ฑ ฒ ณ ด ต ถ ท ธ น บ ป ผ ฝ พ ฟ ภ ม ย ร ฤ ฤๅ ล ว ศ ษ ส ห ฬ อ ฮ

กรณฑ์สาม cube root

กรณี case; event

กรณีตัวอย่าง case in point

กรณีพิพาท dispute, quarrel, controversy

กรณีแวดล้อม surrounding circumstances

กรณีศึกษา case study

แทบทุกกรณี in most cases; in practically every case

ในกรณีจำเป็น in case of need

ในกรณีเช่นนั้น in such case

ในกรณีที่ in case of, in the event

ในกรณีนั้น in that case, in any case, where

ให้ผู้ประท้วงชุมนุมตามท้องถนนได้ในกรณีที่ไม่เป็นการกีดขวางการจราจร Protesters shall be allowed to demonstrate on roads where traffic is not impeded.

เป็นกรณีพิเศษ as a special case

ผู้สันทัดกรณี well-informed person

ไม่ว่าในกรณีใด in any event, no matter what the case

แล้วแต่กรณี as the case may be, depending on the circumstances

ศึกษาเฉพาะกรณี case study

กรณียกิจ business, activities, affairs

กรด acid

กรดกำมะถัน sulphuric acid

กรดเงิน silver nitrate

กรดดินประสิว nitric acid

กรน to snore

นอนกรน to snore in one's sleep

กรม department, bureau; regiment

กรมการขนส่ง Department of Transport

กรมการค้าต่างประเทศ Department of Foreign Trade

กรมการค้าภายใน Department of Internal Trade

กรมการเงินกลาโหม The Finance Department, Ministry of Defence

กรมการแพทย์ Medical Department

กรมการเมืองยุโรป Department of European Affairs

กรมการศาสนา Department of Religious Affairs

กรมจเร Inspector General Department

กรมเจ้าท่า Harbor Department

กรมชลประทาน Irrigation Department

กรมตำรวจ Police Department

กรมทรัพย์สินทางปัญญา Intellectual Property Department

กรมทหาร regiment; military installation

กรมทหารราบที่ 1 รักษาพระองค์ 1st Infantry Regiment, H.M. The King's Bodyguard

กรมทะเบียนการค้า Department of Commercial Registration

กรมประชาสงเคราะห์ Public Welfare Department

กรมประชาสัมพันธ์ Public Relations Department

กรมป่าไม้ Forest Department

กรมไปรษณีย์โทรเลข Post and Telegraph Department

กรมศิลปากร Department of Fine Arts

กรมศุลกากร Customs Department

กรมสรรพสามิต Excise Department

กรมสรรพากร Revenue Department, Bureau of Internal Revenue *(US)*

กรมสามัญศึกษา Department of General Education

กรมอัยการ Public Prosecution Department

กรมอาชีวศึกษา Vocational Education Department

กรมอุตุนิยมวิทยา Meteorological Department

กรมธรรม์ insurance policy

กรมธรรม์ประกันภัย casualty insurance policy, property insurance policy

กรรณ ear

พระกรรณ ear

กรรตุการก nominative case

กรรตุวาจก active voice

กรรไกร a pair of scissors, shears

ขากรรไกร jaw bone

กรรโชก to extort, blackmail

กรรโชกทรัพย์ to obtain property by /extortion/blackmail/

กรรม[1] Karma; action, deeds, volitional action

กรรมชั่ว bad deeds, unwholesome action

กรรมดี good deeds, wholesome action

ผลกรรม fruit of one's /action/deeds/, consequences of one's action

รับกรรม to suffer, suffer the consequences; to be the victim

กรรม[2] misdeeds, sins; misfortune

เป็นกรรมของผม It's my /karma/misfortune/.

กรรมตามสนอง You get what you deserve., the wages of sin

กรรมสนอง reckoning, (His) sins have caught up with (him).

ก่อกรรมทำเข็ญ to cause trouble, do terrible things

จองเวรจองกรรม to seek vengeance, be vengeful, vindictive

เจ้ากรรม unfortunate, ill-starred; damn

เจ้ากรรมนายเวร enemies from a former life; It must be something (I) did in a former life.

มีกรรม damned; luckless, hapless, ill-starred

เวรกรรม *see* **เวรกรรม** *หน้า 466*

กรรม[3] ceremony; work, activity

สังฆกรรม ceremony performed by the Sangha, Sangha ceremony

กรรมกร worker, laborer

กรรมการ committee member; director

คณะกรรมการ board of directors, committee, board, council

กรรมฐาน meditation

กรรมพันธุ์ inherited, congenital

โรคกรรมพันธุ์ congenital disorder

กรรมวาจก passive voice

กรรมวิธี process, procedure

กรรมสิทธิ์ title (to), ownership (of)

กรรมาชีพ work, labor

ชนชั้นกรรมาชีพ working class, proletariat

กรรมาธิการ commission

กรวด[1] gravel, pebbles

กรวด[2] to pour water

กรวดน้ำ to pour ceremonial water as a sign of dedication of merit to the departed

กรวย cone; funnel; covered receptacle for offerings

กรวยยาง road marker

รูปกรวย conical

กรอ to wind, reel; to grind

กรอกระสวย to wind a bobbin

กรอด้าย to wind a bobbin; to reel yarn

กรอฟัน to drill a tooth; to grind a tooth down

กรอก to fill, pour (into)

กรอกแบบฟอร์ม to fill /out/in/ a form, complete a form

กรอกน้ำ to fill a bottle with water, pour water into a bottle

กรอกหู to put something into someone's head, feed someone an idea; to say (something) persistently

พูดกรอกหูทุกวัน to keep saying the same thing everyday / keep after someone day after day

กรอง to filter, strain; to analyse, vet

เครื่องกรอง filter

สิ่งกรอง filtrate

กร่อน worn down, abraded, worn away, eroded

กรอบ[1] frame; confines (of), limitations (of)

กรอบเช็ดหน้า window frame

กรอบบ่าย late edition

กรอบรูป picture frame

อยู่ในกรอบ conventional; disciplined, con-

ข ค ฆ ง จ ฉ ช ซ ฌ ญ ฎ ฏ ฐ ฑ ฒ ณ ด ต ถ ท ธ น บ ป ผ ฝ พ ฟ ภ ม ย ร ฤ ฤๅ ล ว ศ ษ ส ห ฬ อ ฮ

trolled, well-behaved; to be within the confines (of /the family/society/etc)

กรอบ[2] crisp, brittle

   ขนมปังกรอบ biscuit, cracker, crisp bread, rusk

   ทอดกรอบ crispy fried, crisp-fried

กรอบ[3] completely, utterly

   จนกรอบ penniless

   ล้อมกรอบ attacked from every side; completely surrounded

กรอม to cover

   นุ่งกระโปรงกรอมเท้า to wear an ankle-length skirt / wear a skirt down to one's ankles / The skirt covered her ankles.

กร่อย brackish; dull, flat, lifeless, not much fun, vapid, insipid

   งานเมื่อคืนนี้กร่อย It was a dull party last night. / The affair last night was /pretty flat/dull/not much fun/.

กระ[1] freckles

   ตกกระ freckled

กระ[2] tortoise-shell

กระเง้ากระงอด petulant, crabby

กระจก glass

   กระจกเงา mirror, looking glass

   กระจกดูท้าย (รถ) rearview mirror

   กระจกรถ windshield, windscreen

กระจอก insignificant, of no importance, piddling, petty

   กระจอกข่าว cub reporter

   ข้าราชการชั้นกระจอก petty official

กระจอกงอกง่อย lowly, small-fry

กระจองอแง cranky

กระจ้อย, กระจ้อยร่อย tiny, tiny little, minute, diminutive, wee; puny, paltry

กระจะ distinctly, vividly

กระจัดกระจาย scattered, strewn about, spread around, sprinkled about, distributed around

กระจัดพลัดพราย to disperse, scatter in disarray

กระจ่าง bright; clear, understandable

   ทำให้กระจ่าง to clarify, make clear, clear up, make plain, elucidate, elaborate

   ฟ้ากระจ่าง clear sky

กระจาด shallow bamboo basket

กระจาย to broadcast, scatter, spread, decentralize, spread (about, around)

   กระจายคำ to decline (a noun), conjugate (a verb)

   กระจายแถว to spread ranks

   กระจายเสียง broadcast

กระจิด tiny, miniscule; puny

กระจิริด teensy

กระจุก tuft

   กระจุกตัว to crowd (at, around), bunch up (at, in)

   เป็นกระจุก in tufts, in bunches, in small groups, in a crowd

กระจุกกระจิก trifling, odds and ends (of), miscellaneous

   ของกระจุกกระจิก odds and ends, sundries, a variety of small things

   งานกระจุกกระจิก odd jobs, odds and ends (to do), miscellaneous things to do

กระจุ๋มกระจิ๋ม cute, cute little

กระจุยกระจาย scattered about

กระจู๋กระจี๋ cooing, to talk softly and intimately, billing and cooing

กระเจิดกระเจิง in disarray

   หนีกระเจิดกระเจิง to flee in all directions, scatter in disarray

กระเจี๊ยว pee-pee, wee-wee

กระโจน to spring (on, at), jump (on, at)

กระฉอก to splash, slosh (around)

กระฉ่อน widely talked about, rumored

   ดังกระฉ่อน talk of the town

   ลือกระฉ่อน widely rumored

กระฉับกระเฉง sprightly, active, lively

กระชับ tight, to tighten; to fit well

กระชาก to grab (away, out, from), yank

กระเช้า basket

    กระเช้าดอกไม้ basket of flowers

    กระเช้าไฟฟ้า cable car

    กระเช้าสวรรค์ ferris wheel

กระโชก to bark; to intimidate, threaten

    กระโชกกระชาก to snap (at someone), bark (at), be brusque, (to speak)/gruffly/crudely/

    กระโชกโฮกฮาก rough (in speech), gruff, rude, coarse

กระซิก to edge (up to, over to)

    กระซิกๆ sobbing

    กระซิกกระซี้ to flirt (with), banter amorously

กระซิบ to whisper

    กระซิบกระซาบ to speak in whispers, whisper

กระเซ็น to splash, spatter

กระเซ้า to tease, pull someone's leg, be joking

กระเซิง in disorder; disheveled

กระเซอะกระเซิง aimlessly, blindly

    วิ่งหนีกระเซอะกระเซิง

กระแซะ to press together

กระฎุมพี bourgeosie; man of wealth

กระดก[1] to bounce up, raise up, lift up

    กระดกลิ้น to flap the tongue, roll the tongue

กระดก[2] to tip up, teeter, seesaw

    ไม้กระดก seesaw

กระดัง threshing basket

กระดาก to be embarrassed (to), hesitant, timid, shy, bashful, feel diffident

กระดอ peter, cock, organ

กระดอน to bounce (up, back), rebound

กระด้าง hard, stiff

    กระด้างกระเดื่อง insubordinate

กระดาน board, plank

    กระดานดำ blackboard

    กระดานโต้คลื่น surfboard

    กระดานหก seesaw

    กระดานหมากรุก chessboard

    ฝากระดาน wall plank, wall board

กระดาษ paper

    กระดาษกรอง filter paper

    กระดาษก๊อบปี้ *see* **กระดาษคาร์บอน**

    กระดาษแก้ว tracing paper; cellophane

    กระดาษเขียนจดหมาย stationery, writing paper

    กระดาษแข็ง cardboard

    กระดาษไข stencil

    กระดาษคาร์บอน carbon paper

    กระดาษชำระ toilet paper, bathroom tissue

    กระดาษเช็ดปาก paper napkin

    กระดาษเช็ดมือ paper towel, paper napkin, paper handkerchief

    กระดาษเช็ดหน้า facial tissue

    กระดาษซับ blotting paper

    กระดาษทราย sandpaper, flint paper

    กระดาษปรู๊ฟ newsprint, proof paper

    กระดาษปอนด์ bond paper

    กระดาษพิมพ์หนังสือพิมพ์ newsprint

    กระดาษว่าว kite paper

    กระดาษสี colored paper

    กระดาษห่อของ wrapping paper

    กระดาษอัดรูป printing paper, photographic paper

    กระดาษอัดสำเนา duplicating paper

    กระดาษอาร์ต coated paper, art paper

กระดิก to flex, move, bend, budge, stir; to wag, waggle, shake

กระดิ่ง bell

กระดี้กระเดียม to be tickled; to tickle, tickling

กระดุกกระดิก to twitch, jerk, wiggle, move

กระดูก bone; mean, stingy

กระเด้า to make pelvic thrusts, bump; to pump away, screw, hump *(sl)*

กระเดือก[1] Adam's apple, larynx

    ลูกกระเดือก Adam's apple, larynx

กระเดือก^2 to swallow (with difficulty)

  กระเดือกไม่ลง inedible

กระโดกกระเดก unrefined, coarse; untrained; clumsy; awkward

กระโดด to jump; to skip

  กระโดดไกล to broad-jump

    การกระโดดไกล broad-jump

  กระโดดน้ำ to jump into the water, dive

  กระโดดโลดเต้น to jump with joy, be elated, overjoyed

กระได stairs, stairway; ladder

กระต๊อบ hut, shanty

กระต่าย^1 coconut grater, coconut shredder

กระต่าย^2 rabbit, hare

กระติก container; vacuum bottle; canteen

กระตือรือร้น in a hurry; anxious (to); enthusiastic, eager (to)

กระตุก to jerk, twitch

กระตุ้งกระติ้ง girlish, sissyish, effeminate

กระตุ้น to arouse, stimulate

กระเตาะกระแตะ to toddle (along)

กระเตื้อง to improve, get better, ameliorate

  อาการป่วยของเขากระเตื้องขึ้น His condition has improved.

กระโตกกระตาก to call attention (to something), make a stir (about), make a noise (about something), make a fuss; to cackle (on laying an egg (ไก่ร้อง))

กระถด to slide along on one's bottom

กระถาง pot, flowerpot

กระเถิบ to move (in, over, out, up, etc)

กระโถน spittoon, cuspidor

  ปากกระโถน foul-mouthed

กระทง^1 count, charge; issue

  กระทงความ count, charge; issue

  หมดถ้อยกระทงความ nothing more to say

กระทง^2 basket, little banana leaf receptacle

กระทง^3 cockerel

  รุ่นกระทง youth, juvenile, young adoles-

cent (boy), stripling

กระทบ to strike (against); hit; clack; to affect

  กระทบกระทั่ง to be hurtful, hurt someone's feelings, knock (someone or something); to affect

  กระทบกระเทียบ to be snide, invidious

    พูดกระทบกระเทียบ to make /an invidious /a snide/remark (about someone)/

  กระทบกระเทือน to affect

  กระทบกระแทก satirical, biting, caustic

กระทรวง ministry, department (US)

  กระทรวงกลาโหม Ministry of Defence

  กระทรวงการคลัง Ministry of Finance

  กระทรวงการต่างประเทศ Ministry of Foreign Affairs, Department of State (US)

  กระทรวงเกษตรและสหกรณ์ Ministry of Agriculture and Cooperatives

  กระทรวงคมนาคม Ministry of Transport and Communications

  กระทรวงพาณิชย์ Ministry of Commerce

  กระทรวงมหาดไทย Ministry of Interior, Department of the Interior (US)

  กระทรวงยุติธรรม Ministry of Justice

  กระทรวงแรงงานและสวัสดิการสังคม Ministry of Labor and Social Welfare

  กระทรวงวิทยาศาสตร์ เทคโนโลยี และสิ่ง-แวดล้อม Ministry of Science Technology and Environment

  กระทรวงศึกษาธิการ Ministry of Education

  กระทรวงสาธารณสุข Ministry of Public Health

  กระทรวงอุตสาหกรรม Ministry of Industry

กระท่อนกระแท่น haltingly; sketchy

  รู้ภาษาอังกฤษกระท่อนกระแท่น to have a sketchy knowledge of English

กระท่อม cabin, hut

กระทะ wok, frying pan

  กระทะล้อ wheel drum

กระทั่ง until

ข
ค
ฆ
ง
จ
ฉ
ช
ซ
ฌ
ญ
ฎ
ฏ
ฐ
ฑ
ฒ
ณ
ด
ต
ถ
ท
ธ
น
บ
ป
ผ
ฝ
พ
ฟ
ภ
ม
ย
ร
ฤ
ฤๅ
ล
ว
ศ
ษ
ส
ห
ฬ
อ
ฮ

กระทาย a small, round, woven-bamboo basket

กระทำ to do, commit, act, make; to arrange, conduct; to construct, erect, build

    กระทำการทดลอง to experiment, conduct a trial

    กระทำการร่วมกัน to act jointly

    กระทำตามหน้าที่ to act in the course of duty, act within one's authority

    กระทำตามอำเภอใจ to do as one pleases, self-willed

    กระทำผิดกฎหมาย to violate the law, act in violation of the law, do something against the law

    กระทำอัตวินิบาตกรรม to commit suicide

กระทืบ to stamp one's foot; to trample (on), stamp (on), stomp (on), beat (someone) up

    เขาถูกพวกวัยรุ่นรุมกระทืบ He was beaten up by a bunch of young hooligans.

กระทุง pelican

กระทุ้ง to ram, pound, batter

    ต้องเขียนกระทุ้งไม่อย่างนั้นเรื่องจะเงียบหาย I had to ram the message home, otherwise the thing would have been forgotten.

กระทุ่ม to splash

กระทู้ question, query; fence post

กระเท่เร่ lopsided, leaning

    เอียงกระเท่เร่ way off center, leaning to one side

กระเทียม garlic

    หัวเดียวกระเทียมลีบ to lead a solitary existence

กระเทือน to affect, disturb

    กระเทือนใจ affected, disturbed, shaken

กระแทก to strike, bump, hit, slam

    กระแทกกระทั้น to slam (something down, on); to be sarcastic, caustic

    กระแทกเสียง to snap (at), speak sharply

กระนั้น *as in*

    กระนั้นก็ตาม in spite of (that), even so, nevertheless

    ถ้ากระนั้น if so, in such case

    ถึงกระนั้น nevertheless, anyway

    แม้กระนั้น despite that, even so

กระนี้ this; like this

    กระนี้นี่เอง so that's why

กระบวน procession; procedure, proceedings

    กระบวนการ movement; process; *มักมีคำคุณศัพท์ "ing" เติมท้ายคำ*

    กระบวนการแก้ตัวแล้ว เขาเก่งที่สุด At making excuses, he's tops.

    กระบวนการยุติธรรม judicial process, judicial proceedings

    กระบวนความ (whole) story

    กระบวนทัศน์ paradigm

    กระบวนรถ procession, parade, cavalcade; train

    กระบวนแห่ procession, parade, cortege

    หนีไม่เป็นกระบวน to flee /in disorder/in disarray/

กระบวย dipper

กระบอก cylinder

    กระบอกตา eye socket

    กระบอกปืน gun barrel

    กระบอกไม้ไผ่ bamboo section

    กระบอกสูบ cylinder

    กระบอกเสียง mouthpiece, organ

    ทรงกระบอก cylindrical, tube-shaped, tubular

    หุ่นกระบอก puppet, marionette

กระบอง club, cudgel

กระบะ open box, bin

    รถกระบะ pickup truck

กระบาล *see* **กบาล** *หน้า 3*

กระบิ *as in* **ทั้งกระบิ** in its entirety

กระบิดกระบวน being difficult, devious; tricky

กระบี่กระบอง the martial art of stick fighting

กระบือ water buffalo

กระเบียดกระเสียร to economize

กระเบื้อง tile

กระแบะมือ palm (of the hand)

    น้อยนิดเท่ากระแบะมือ a small handful (of), tiny bit (of)

กระปรี้กระเปร่า active, lively, spry, energetic

กระป๋อง can, tin

    เครื่องกระป๋อง canned goods, canned food, tinned goods

    อาหารกระป๋อง canned food

กระปอดกระแปด chronic, on and off

    บ่นกระปอดกระแปด to be a chronic complainer

กระปุก pot, receptacle, box

    กระปุกเกียร์ gearbox, transmission

    กระปุกออมสิน coin bank, piggy bank

กระเป๋า bag; pocket

    กระเป๋าเงิน wallet *(แบบพับ)*, purse *(แบบถุง)*

    กระเป๋าเดินทาง luggage, baggage, suitcase

    กระเป๋าถือ handbag, pocketbook; hand luggage

    กระเป๋าเบา short (of money), strapped

    กระเป๋ารถเมล์ ticket taker, conductor, ticket /boy/girl/

    กระเป๋าเสื้อผ้า suitcase

    กระเป๋าหนัก flush, well-heeled, well-fixed

    กระเป๋าหิ้ว portable

กระเปาะ bulb; setting, mounting

กระโปก testicles, balls

กระโปรง skirt; hood

กระผม I, me

กระผีกริ้น tiny bit

กระพรวน round bell with a jinglet inside

กระพอง *see* ตะพอง หน้า 186

กระพี้ sapwood, alburnum; insubstantial

กระพือ to fan; to flap; to blow

    กระพือข่าว to make a big story (of something), blow up (a story, the news, etc) spread the news

    กระพือปีก to flap its wings

กระพือโหม blown up, fanned

กระพุ้งแก้ม cheek

กระพุ่มมือไหว้ to hold the hands pressed together in sign of respect

กระเพาะ pouch, bladder

    กระเพาะปลา fish maw

    กระเพาะปัสสาวะ bladder

    กระเพาะอาหาร stomach

กระเพื่อม to shake, bounce (up and down), bobble, ripple

    พุงกระเพื่อม potbellied, fat-bellied

กระฟัดกระเฟียด in a huff, petulant; to fly off the handle

กระมัง perhaps, maybe, to presume

    คุณเป็นคนที่นี่กระมัง You're from here, I presume.

กระมิดกระเมี้ยน hesitating; to hesitate out of shyness

กระยาจก beggar, pauper

กระยาหาร food, repast

กระยืดกระยาด sluggishly; to take one's time

กระรอก squirrel

กระไร what, how

    ช่างกระไร what a (cruel, marvellous, etc)

    ดีเสียนี่กระไร how good

    ดูกระไรอยู่ not quite right, to look /funny/ peculiar/, questionable

กระวนกระวาย anxious, uneasy, restless, impatient, perturbed, worried, distraught

กระวีกระวาด in a flurry, hurriedly; enthusiastically

กระษัตริย์ *see* กษัตริย์ หน้า 18

กระษาปณ์ coin, money

    โรงกระษาปณ์ mint

    เหรียญกระษาปณ์ coin

กระเษียร *see* เกษียร หน้า 37

กระสวย shuttle

    กระสวยอวกาศ space shuttle

กระสอบ gunny bag, sack

กระสัน to be sexually aroused; to lust (for, after),

crave

กระสับกระส่าย restless, uncomfortable, agitated, impatient, nervously

กระสาย portion; sampling

น้ำกระสาย dissolving spirits, liquid solvent

ยักกระสาย to change the subject, switch (to something else); to get around something

กระสือ a demoness that eats entrails and infants

กระสุน bullet, shot, pellet; bow for shooting pellets

กระสุนด้าน dud (shell or cartridge)

กระสุนปืน bullet, ammunition, cartridge

กระสุนวิถี trajectory

ลูกกระสุน bullet, cartridge, shot

หมดกระสุน to be spent, have shot one's wad

กระเส็นกระสาย bit (of), some; to shatter, fragment

กระเสาะกระแสะ sickly, ailing, in poor health

กระเสียร as in **กระเบียดกระเสียร** impecunious, in poverty; frugal

กระเสือกกระสน to struggle (to)

กระแส current, flow, stream; wave, tide, trend, fashion, vogue, sentiment of the day; movement, pressure

ผมไม่ทำตามกระแส I will not be pressured.
มีกระแสให้ถอนร่างกฎหมายเรื่องรัฐวิสาหกิจ There's pressure to withdraw the government enterprise bill. / There's a movement to get the government to withdraw the government bill.

กระแสกดดัน pressure on (someone to do or be something)

กระแสการเงิน circulation of money

กระแสข่าว stream of information, source (of news)

กระแสเงินทุน flow of capital

กระแสเงินสด cash flow

กระแสจิต thought waves

กระแสน้ำ stream, current, flow of water

กระแสพระราชดำรัส royal address

กระแสพระราชดำริ royal idea

กระแสไฟตรง direct current (D.C.)

กระแสไฟฟ้า electric current

กระแสรับสั่ง royal words

กระแสรายวัน (บัญชี) current account

กระแสลม air current, wind, breeze

กระแสสลับ (ไฟฟ้า) alternating current (A.C.)

กระแสสินธุ์ river

กระแสเสียง sound, tone

ต้านกระแส to go against the /trend/current/

สร้างกระแส to create pressure (for, to), bring pressure to bear (on)

สวนกระแส unconventional, unfashionable, non-conforming

กระหนก *as in* **ลายกระหนก** running scroll design

กระหนาบ to flank, press /in on both sides/against/

ตีกระหนาบ to flank, press against

กระหน่ำ to beat repeatedly, rain blows (on), pour blows (on); to devastate

กระหม่อม[1] crown of the head; fontanel

กระหม่อม[2] I; yes

กระหมิบ *see* ขมิบ หน้า 46

กระหมุบกระหมิบ *see* ขมุบขมิบ หน้า 47

ทำปากกระหมุบกระหมิบ to work the mouth silently, mumble inaudibly

กระหย่ง to stand on tiptoe

เดินกระหย่ง to tiptoe, walk on one's toes

นั่งกระหย่ง to squat

กระหยิ่ม glad, happy, pleased, proud; smug; to be pleased with oneself

กระหยิ่มยิ้มย่อง highly pleased, elated

กระหัง an offal and blood eating demon spirit

กระหาย to be thirsty; to be hungry (for), want, desire, to long for; eager (for), hunger (for), after), yearn (for), thirst (for)

กระหายใคร่ได้ to long for

กระหายเลือด bloodthirsty

กระหึ่ม roar, roaring, din

กระหืดกระหอบ panting, breathlessly, in a rush

ข ค ฆ ง จ ฉ ช ซ ฌ ญ ฎ ฏ ฐ ฑ ฒ ณ ด ต ถ ท ธ น บ ป ผ ฝ พ ฟ ภ ม ย ร ฤ ฤๅ ล ว ศ ษ ส ห ฬ อ ฮ

กระเหม็ดกระแหม่ thrifty, frugal, economical

กระเหม่น see เขม่น หน้า 65

กระเหี้ยนกระหือรือ to strain at the leash, be driven to do something

กระแหนะกระแหน sarcastic, cynical, satirical, to deride, mock

กระอ้อมกระแอ้ม without conviction; indistinctly

กระอัก to cough up (blood), be done for

กระอักกระอ่วน in a dilemma, in a quandary, unable to /decide/ choose/, hesitant, in a difficult position, uneasy

กระแอม to clear one's throat, cough

กรัก dye from the heart of the jackfruit tree

กรัง to be dried and stuck together, crust (of), crusted over with, caked (with)

เกรอะกรัง encrusted (with), caked (with)

กรับ claves

กรัม gram

กราก[1] as in แห้งกราก dry, dried out, parched

กราก[2] to approach

กรากเข้าไป to walk up (to), approach, go up to someone

เชี่ยวกราก rushing (current, stream, etc)

กร่าง brash, feisty; arrogant, puffed up

เดินกร่าง to swagger

กราด[1] indiscriminately, at random

ด่ากราด to abuse (people) indiscriminately, haul everyone over the coals

ยิงกราดเข้าไป to fire indiscriminately, shoot at random

กราด[2] as in กราดเกรี้ยว furious, enraged

กราน to prostrate oneself in sign of respect; to insist (on)

กราบกราน to kowtow, be submissive; to pay respect (to)

ยืนกราน to stand firm, see ยืนกราน หน้า 399

กรานกฐิน, กรานกฐิน to make and dye a robe for presentation to a monk at a Kathin offering

กร้าน rough (skin), hard

กราบ[1] gunwale

กราบ[2] to prostrate oneself (in sign of respect)

กราบเท้า to prostrate oneself at another's feet/before (someone)

กราบบังคมทูล to inform, report, tell (royal word)

กราบเรียน attention, Att:, to..., (I) beg to (inform, say, etc); Dear (Mr. President, Sir etc)

กราบลา to take leave (of a person)

กราม molar

ขบกราม to grind one's teeth

กราย to get too close

เยื้องกราย to walk /with grace/elegantly/; to walk in a way to catch the eye

กราว patter; roar

เกรียวกราว commotion; big news, headline news

ตบมือกราว /enthusiastic/good/ applause, to applaud enthusiastically

เสียงกราว patter, pattering, peppering noise

กร้าว hard, tough

แข็งกร้าว unyielding, tough, very firm

เสียงกร้าว to speak /vehemently/aggressively/

กราวรูด the whole lot

กรำ enduring, bearing, putting up with

กรำแดดกรำฝน to endure the elements

กริ่ง[1] to suspect, doubt, distrust

กริ่งเกรง to be doubtful (about)

กริ่ง[2] bell

กดกริ่ง to ring the bell

เสียงกริ่ง ringing

กริช dagger, kris

กริบ as in เงียบกริบ perfectly quiet, utterly silent, dead still, without a sound

กริ่ม as in ยิ้มกริ่ม to give a sly smile, smile slyly

กริยา[1] verb

กริยาวิเศษณ์ adverb

กริยา[2] see **กิริยา** หน้า 31
กริ้ว to get angry (with a person), become cross (with a person)
กรีฑา games, athletic events
　กรีฑาประเภทลาน field events
　กรีฑาประเภทลู่ track events
　กรีฑาสถาน sports arena, playing field, stadium
　นักกรีฑา athlete
กรีด[1] to scrape, slash
　กรีดยาง to tap a rubber tree
　กรีดเลือด to slash (one's arm etc), draw blood
กรีด[2] to walk in an affected manner
　กรีดกราย to walk /with grace/elegantly/; to walk in a way to catch the eye, strut; to put on an air of doing something
　กรีดนิ้ว to use the fingers daintily; to gesture with the fingers
กรีด[3] to shriek
　กรีดร้อง to scream
　ร้องกรีด to scream, shriek, screech
กรีธา to advance, move
　กรีธาทัพ to advance an army
　กรีธาพล to move troops
กรีน green
กรีนิช Greenwich (ออกเสียง เกร็นนิช)
กรุ[1] underground hiding place; /chamber/cavity/hole/repository/ inside a stupa
　กรุพระแตก a Buddha-image repository broken into
กรุ[2] to line, cover (with)
กรุง capital; city, metropolis, metropolitan
　กรุงเก่า old capital
　กรุงเทพฯ Bangkok
　ชาวกรุง city dwellers, city folk
กรุ๊งกริ๊ง tinkling, jingling
กรุณยฆาต, การุณยฆาต euthanasia, mercy killing
กรุณา compassion, kindness, mercy; please, kindly

กรุณาส่งให้เขาด้วย Kindly pass it to him.
　ทรงพระกรุณา graciously pleased
กรุ่น smouldering
　คุกรุ่น glowing
　หอมกรุ่น fragrant
กรุ้มกริ่ม to /have/make/bedroom eyes; happy-looking
กรุย to clear
　กรุยทาง to clear a way
กรุยกราย untidily; coquettish; philandering
กรู to run in a crowd
　วิ่งกรูเข้ามา /people/crowd/ rush in
กฤษฎาภินิหาร power of accumulated merit
กฤษฎีกา legislation; juridical
　คณะกรรมการกฤษฎีกา Juridical Council
กฤษณา eagle wood
กล trick, deception, artifice, ruse; conjuring; machine; method, like, similar, doubtful
　กลไก mechanism, device
　กลซ้อนกล to outsmart, turn the tables (on)
　กลมารยา cunning, craft
　กลเม็ด tip, trick, stratagem, art, artful, clever
เขามีกลเม็ดในการพูดจูงใจคน He is clever at convincing people.
　กลเม็ดเด็ดพราย wily, cunning
　กลยุทธ์ military stratagem, tactic, maneuver
　กลวิธี the way to (do, get etc. something)
　กลศาสตร์ mechanics
　กลศึก military tactics
　กลอุบาย trick, trickery, ruse, stratagem
　เล่นกล to play a trick (on someone), fool; to perform sleight of hand
　เล่ห์กล tricks, trickery
　หลงกล to fall for, be taken in (by), be fooled (by), duped
กลด long-handled umbrella; halo, ring around the /sun/moon/, penumbra
　ทรงกลด to have a /halo/penumbra/

กลั่น scattered about; abundant, plentiful

กลบ to cover over; to fill up
ฝ กลบเกลื่อน to cover up, hide (something)
ฝ กลบรอย to destroy the traces
ฝ กลบลบ to offset

กลม round, spherical
ฝ กลมกล่อม just right, perfect
ฝ กลมกลิ้ง slippery
ฝ กลมกลืน harmonious; to go well together
ฝ กลมเกลียว united, in harmony, to get along well together
ฝ กลมดิก perfectly round, in a ball
ฝ กลมรี oval, egg shaped, ovoid

กลวง hollow
ฝ โรงกลวง tin smeltery

กล้วย banana
ฝ กล้วยๆ to be /a lark/a piece of cake/a cinch

กล้วยไม้ orchid

กลอก to move around
ฝ กลอกตา to roll one's eyes
ฝ กลอกหน้ากลอกตา to look supercilious
ฝ กลับกลอก unreliable, fickle; slippery

กลอง drum

กล่อง case, box, carton
ฝ กล่องบุหรี่ cigarette case

กล้อง[1] to pound in a mortar
ฝ ข้าวกล้อง brown rice, unpolished rice

กล้อง[2] camera; pipe
ฝ กล้องจุลทรรศน์ microscope
ฝ กล้องดูดาว telescope
ฝ กล้องถ่ายรูป camera
ฝ กล้องโทรทรรศน์ telescope
ฝ กล้องบุหรี่ cigarette holder
ฝ กล้องยานัตถุ์ snuff tube
ฝ กล้องยาเส้น pipe
ฝ กล้องส่องทางไกล binoculars, field glasses, opera glasses, spyglass
ฝ กล้องสำรวจ theodolite
ฝ ลำกล้อง gun barrel, pipe stem; rod (sl)

กลอน[1] bolt; batten
ฝ ถอดกลอน to unbolt, unlock
ฝ ลงกลอน to bolt

กลอน[2] poem, verse, poetry, rhyme
ฝ กลอนสด extemporaneous rhyme
ฝ ว่าเป็นกลอนสด to speak extemporaneously, speak off the cuff

กล้อน tonsured, to cut very short, close-cropped

กล่อม to lull (a child) to sleep, sing a lullaby (to); to /charm/lull/ (someone into doing etc something), talk (someone) into (something)
ฝ กล่อมเกลา to train well; to bring up well
ฝ กล่อมเกลี้ยงเลี้ยงดู to bring (a child etc) up
ฝ กล่อมอารมณ์ to lull

กล้อมแกล้ม to /say/speak/ enough to get by; to bolt (one's food)

กลอยใจ sweetheart

กลัด to pin (on, together), fasten
ฝ กลัดกระดุม to button (one's coat)
ฝ กลัดกลุ้ม depressed, downhearted, upset, worried
ฝ กลัดมัน lusty; full of beans
ฝ กลัดหนอง to form pus, abscessed, purulent
ฝ เข็มกลัด safety pin; brooch, pin

กลั่น to distill, extract
ฝ กลั่นกรอง to select, cull, screen, vet
ฝ กลั่นกรองข้อมูล to verify data, analyze information
ฝ ต้มกลั่น to distill
ฝ น้ำกลั่น distilled water
ฝ โรงกลั่นน้ำมัน oil refinery
ฝ โรงกลั่นเหล้า distillery

กลั้น to repress, restrain, suppress, smother, hold back
ฝ กลั้นความรู้สึก to repress one's feelings
ฝ กลั้นใจ to hold one's breath
ฝ กลั้นใจตาย to hold one's breath unto death, die by holding one's breath
ฝ กลั้นโทสะ to suppress one's anger

กลั้นหัวเราะ to smother a laugh

กลั่นแกล้ง to do something out of spite; to provoke; to have it in for someone
เขาต้องออกจากงานเพราะถูกกลั่นแกล้ง He was fired out of spite. / He was fired because someone had it in for him.

กลับ to return, turn back, turn over, turn around, come back; back; whereas; instead
บางทีฝ่ายพูดตอบยาว คนแปลกลับแปลเสียสั้นจู๋ Sometimes the speaker makes a long reply whereas the translator comes out with a miniscule translation. / Sometimes instead of the long reply, you get a miniscule translation.

กลับกลอก unreliable, fickle; slippery

กลับกลาย to turn into, become

กลับกัน vice versa, conversely

กลับคำ to go back on one's word, break a promise, fail to keep one's word

กลับคืน to restore, return, give back, get back

กลับใจ to change one's mind; to have a change of heart; to turn over a new leaf, be reformed

กลับตะเข็บ to turn inside out

กลับตาลปัตร to become completely different, become the opposite

กลับเนื้อกลับตัว to turn over a new leaf, to get a hold of oneself, reform, mend one's ways

กลับบ้านเก่า to return to one's maker

กลับไปกลับมา vacillating, unreliable, off-again on-again

กลับลำ to reverse oneself, turn back (on, in respect of), do a turnabout

กลับหน้ามือเป็นหลังมือ to turn out to be just the opposite

กลับหลังหัน about face

กลับหัวกลับหาง inverted, upside-down, topsy turvy; sixty-nine *(sl)*

กลัว to fear, be afraid (of)
กลัวจนขี้ขึ้นสมอง scared stiff, scared shitless (sl)

กลัวเกรง to be in awe (of), fear, be in fear of; to obey

กลัวขาดทุน to be afraid of /taking a loss/ losing something/

กลัวเจ็บ to be afraid something is going to hurt, be afraid of the pain

กลัวตก to be afraid of falling

กลัวตาย to be afraid of /death/dying/, fear death

กลัวน้ำ (โรค) hydrophobia, rabies

กลัวบาป to feel something would be wrong, feel guilty (about)

กลัวเปื้อน to be afraid something will get dirty

กลัวผี to be afraid of ghosts

กลัวแพ้ to be afraid of losing

กลัวมาก to dread

กลัวไม่สำเร็จ to be afraid of /failure/failing/, be afraid (something or someone) might not succeed

กลัวลาน to be terrified

กลัวสอบตก to be afraid of /failing an examination/flunking/

ขี้กลัว timid, timorous, to lack self-confidence; easily startled

ความกลัว fear, (to have a) phobia (for)

น่ากลัว scary, fearful, frightening, terrifying

กลั้ว to mix, blend

กลั้วเกลี้ย almost finished; to mix with

กลั้วคอ to gargle

กลั้วปาก to rinse the mouth

กล้า[1] rice seedling

ตกกล้า to sow rice for seedlings

กล้า[2] bold, brave, fearless; not afraid (to), to dare (to), be willing (to), have the courage (to); adventuresome (of someone to do something); strong

คุณกล้าเดินผ่านป่าช้าคนเดียวตอนกลางคืนไหม
Would you dare to go past a cemetery alone at night?

กล้าแข็ง stalwart, strong, powerful, tough

กล้าได้กล้าเสีย to be willing to take a risk, courageous; easy come easy go

กล้าตัดสินใจ decisive; to be unafraid to make a decision

กล้าตาย to have the courage to die, death-defying, ready to die

กล้าทำ to /dare/have the courage/ to do something

กล้าเผชิญหน้า to dare to face

กล้าเสี่ยง to be willing to take a risk, dare

กล้าหาญ courageous, brave

กลาก ringworm

กลาง middle, center; intermediate; central; neutral

กลางเก่ากลางใหม่ neither old nor new, still in good condition, slightly used

กลางคน middle-aged

กลางคัน in the middle, in midstream

หยุดกลางคัน to interrupt

กลางคืน night, nighttime, at night, by night

กลางแจ้ง outdoors, in the open air, in the open, outdoor

กีฬากลางแจ้ง outdoor sports

กลางใจเมือง in the heart of /town/the city/

กลางแดด (out) in the sun

กลางถนน in the middle of the street

กลางทะเล in the middle of the sea, in the open sea, on the high seas

กลางทาง on the way

กลางทุ่ง in the fields

กลางน้ำ in midstream; in the water

กลางวัน day, by day, daytime

กลางวันแสกๆ in broad daylight

กลางหาว in midair

คนกลาง middleman, intermediary, medi-

ator

นอนกลางดินกินกลางทราย to rough it

เป็นกลาง neutral, impartial

กลาดเกลื่อน to be found all over, all over the place, strewn about

กล้าม coconut meat; muscle

กล้ามเนื้อ muscle(s)

กลาย to change, become, alter, transform, be converted (to)

กลายพันธุ์ to mutate; to lose its character, become inferior

กลายร่าง to be transformed (into), become

กล่าว to say, speak, state, express, mention, declare

กล่าวขวัญ to speak of, talk about, mention

กล่าวคือ that is to say, namely, i.e., viz.

กล่าวโดยย่อ in brief, briefly speaking, in summary

กล่าวตำหนิ to criticize, rebuke, reprove

กล่าวตู่ ascribe (something) falsely (to someone), misrepresent another's words

กล่าวตู่พุทธพจน์ to falsely ascribe (a doctrine, etc) to the Buddha

กล่าวถึง to speak about (a person or thing)

กล่าวเท็จ to prevaricate, lie

กล่าวโทษ to blame, accuse, charge (a person) with, reprimand (someone for something)

กล่าวร้าย to speak ill of (a person)

กล่าวสุนทรพจน์ to deliver a speech

กล่าวหา to accuse, allege, charge

คำกล่าวหา accusation, charge, complaint

กล่าวอ้าง to claim; to refer (to), cite

คำกล่าว statement, words, what was said

คำกล่าวนั้นเป็นเท็จ What was said is false.

กล้ำ to combine consonantal sounds

อักษรกล้ำ diphthong

กล้ำกราย to go too near, get too close, trespass

กล้ำกลืน reluctantly, whether one likes it or not, to put up with something

เขาแต่งงานกับหญิงที่เขาไม่รัก จำต้องกล้ำกลืน อยู่กับเธอไป Having married a girl he didn't love, he had to put up with it

กลิ้ง to roll

กลิ้งเกลือก to wallow (in mud or mire); to roll about; to flap around

ลูกกลิ้ง roller

กลิ่น smell, odor; flavor

กลิ่นตัว body odor

กลิ่นหอม fragrance, perfume, aroma

กลิ่นเหม็น bad smell, stench, stink

กลิ่นอาย atmosphere (of)

กลีบ petal

กลีบเมฆ cloud

กลีบส้ม section of an orange

กลียุค havoc (the last and most destructive of the four eras in Buddhism)

กลึง to turn (on a lathe)

เครื่องกลึง lathe

ช่างกลึง lathe operator, turner

กลืน to swallow

กลืนความขมขื่น to swallow one's bitterness

กลืนชาติ to swallow up the nation, swamp the country

กลืนน้ำลาย to swallow

กลืนไม่เข้าคายไม่ออก to be at an impasse, be caught in a personal dilemma

กลืนไม่ลง (fig) I couldn't /take it/accept it/; I can't swallow.

ถูกกลืน absorbed (by, into), swallowed up (by)

กลุ่ม group, bloc; cluster; ball of /string/thread/

กลุ่มด้าย ball of /string/yarn/thread/

กลุ่มดาว constellation

เป็นกลุ่มๆ in groups

เป็นกลุ่มเป็นก้อน a substantial amount

รวมกลุ่ม to form a group, assemble, get together, coalesce

กลุ้ม depressed, unhappy, bored

กลุ้มใจ to feel depressed, glum, feel awful, down in the dumps

แก้กลุ้ม to relieve boredom, cheer oneself up

กลุ้มรุม to gang up (on)

กเลวระ corpse, cadaver

กวด to chase

กวดขัน strictly, to be strict (with)

กวดทัน to catch up

กวดวิชา to coach; to /go for/take/ special lessons; intensive instruction (in)

กวน to bother, annoy, disturb, trouble; to stir

กวนตีน to be asking for it (sl)

กวนใจ to bother, disturb; vexatious, irritating

กวนตัว troublesome, bothersome

กวนน้ำให้ขุ่น to stir up something

อย่ากวนน้ำให้ขุ่น Don't stir anything up. / Don't muddy the water.

กวนประสาท to get on one's nerves, to drive one crazy, rile, be riled (by), irritating

กวนโมโห to rouse one's anger, to make one /angry/mad/

อย่ากวนเขา leave her alone / don't bother her

กวยจั๊บ boiled Chinese pasta squares

ก๋วยเตี๋ยว noodles

ก๋วยเตี๋ยวน้ำ Chinese noodles in soup

ก๋วยเตี๋ยวผัด fried Chinese noodles

ก๋วยเตี๋ยวแห้ง plain Chinese noodles

กวัก to beckon, signal

กวักมือเรียก to beckon

กวัดแกว่ง to swing, brandish

กวัดไกว see **กวัดแกว่ง**

กว่า more, over, -er (suffix as in richer, faster); by the time

กว่าจะ by the time

กว่าจะไปถึง การแสดงก็จะจบแล้ว The show will be over by the time we get there.

ก
ข
ค
ฆ
ง
จ
ฉ
ช
ซ
ฌ
ญ
ฎ
ฏ
ฐ
ฑ
ฒ
ณ
ด
ต
ถ
ท
ธ
น
บ
ป
ผ
ฝ
พ
ฟ
ภ
ม
ย
ร
ฤ
ฦ
ล
ว
ศ
ษ
ส
ห
ฬ
อ
ฮ

กว่าชั่วโมง more than an hour, over an hour

เกินกว่า more than

จนกว่า until

ดีกว่า better (than); instead

มากกว่า more than, more, (ประกอบคำว่า "อยาก") rather, prefer to

ฉันอยากพักผ่อนมากกว่า/*I prefer to/I'd rather/ take it easy. / I would more like to rest.*

กวาง deer, stag

　　เขากวาง antlers

กว้าง broad, wide, large

　　กว้างขวาง roomy, spacious, broad; popular, well-known

　　　　อย่างกว้างขวาง widely

　　กว้างใหญ่ vast, extensive, broad, spacious

　　ความกว้าง width, breadth

กวางตุ้ง Canton; Cantonese

กวาด to sweep

　　กวาดคอ to swab the throat

　　กวาดต้อน to be captured and herded

　　กวาดตา to look around, sweep เช่น *His eyes swept the room.*

　　กวาดบ้าน to clean the house

　　กวาดยา to swab the throat

　　กวาดล้าง to wipe out, clean out, eliminate, purge (someone or something of something)

　　ไม้กวาด broom

　　ยากวาด medicine used to swab the throat, linctus

　　ลูกกวาด hard candy, bonbon, pastille

กว้านซื้อ to corner the market, buy up

กว๊าน swamp; lake

กวี poet

　　กวีนิพนธ์ poetry

　　บทกวี poem

กษณะ moment

กษัตริย์ king, monarch; kshatriya; precious metal; pure (gold)

กษัย ending, termination; deterioration; adjuvant

กษัยกล่อน a wasting disease

กษาปณ์ money, a unit of currency

กษาย astringent taste; astringent medicinal /infusion/potion/

กสิ, กสิกรรม farming, agriculture

กสิกร farmer, peasant, agriculturist

กสิณ subject of meditation

กเฬวราก trash; trashy

กอ clump, thicket

　　กอไผ่ clump of bamboo, thicket of bamboo

ก่อ to build, construct, erect; to make, cause, start, originate, bring about; to set up, to establish, create

　　ก่อกรรมทำเข็ญ to cause trouble, do terrible things, do evil

　　ก่อกวน to stir up trouble, agitate, foment, create a disturbance

　　　　ผู้ก่อกวน troublemaker, agitator

　　ก่อการ to instigate, foment

　　　　ผู้ก่อการร้าย terrorist

　　ก่อกำเนิด to give birth to

　　ก่อความเดือดร้อน to cause discontent, make trouble, stir up things

　　ก่อความยุ่งยาก to make difficulties

　　ก่อตั้ง to establish, set up, form, create

　　ก่อพระเจดีย์ทราย to make a sand stupa

　　ก่อไฟ to light a fire, build a fire, kindle a fire

　　ก่อเรื่อง to start a fight, stir up trouble

　　เขาชอบก่อเรื่อง *He's a troublemaker.*

　　ก่อวินาศกรรม to sabotage

　　ก่อสร้าง to construct, build; construction, building

　　ก่อหวอด to foment, be fomented

　　การประท้วงก่อหวอดขึ้นที่โรงงาน *Protests were fomented in the factory.*

　　ก่อเหตุ to be the cause of the trouble, to start something, cause something to happen

　　ก่อให้เกิด to breed, engender, generate, give rise to, produce

ก่ออาชญากรรม to /commit/perpetrate/ a crime

ก่ออิฐ to lay bricks

ก๊อก[1] cock, faucet, tap, spigot

ก๊อกน้ำ water tap, faucet

น้ำก๊อก tap water

ก๊อก[2] cork

ก๊อก[3] knocking sound

ก๊อกก๊อก knock knock; knocking; clacking

ก๊อกแก๊ก knocking

ก๊อกๆ แก๊กๆ not much of anything

กอง to heap, pile (up), stack; to amass; group, multitude; mass, pile, heap, stack (of); division, bureau; troop

กองกลาง pot; midfielder (ฟุตบอล)

กองกลางตัวรับ defensive midfielder

กองกลางตัวรุก attacking midfielder

กองกำกับการ subdivision; command

กองขยะ pile of garbage, garbage dump

กองโจร guerillas

กองทัพ armed forces, troops

กองทัพน้อย corps

กองทัพบก army

กองทัพเรือ navy

กองทัพอากาศ airforce

กองทุน capital, fund

กองบัญชาการ (general) headquarters

กองเป็นภูเขาเลากา an enormous amount, a great heap, a vast pile (of)

กองพล division

กองพลน้อย brigade

กองพลใหญ่ division

กองพะเนิน pile (of)

กองพะเนินเทินทึก huge pile (of)

กองพัน battalion

กองพันสัตว์ต่าง Pack Squadron

กองฟอน ashes remaining after cremation; funeral pyre

กองฟาง haystack, pile of straw

กองฟืน woodpile

กองไฟ bonfire, campfire

กองร้อย company

กองเรือคุ้มกัน convoy

กองเรือรบ naval fleet

กองลำเลียง supply column, logistics unit

กองสลากกินแบ่ง Lottery Department

กองสัญญาณ signal corps

กองสารนิเทศ Information Office

กองหน้า vanguard; forward, attacker (ฟุตบอล)

กองหนุน reserve corps, reserves, reinforcements

กองหลัง rear guard; defender (ฟุตบอล)

กองอาสาสมัคร volunteer corps

ดีกว่าเป็นกอง /much/lots/ better, a lot better

มากมายก่ายกอง a whole lot, a great deal, an abundance (of)

ก้อง[1] echoing, resonant, resonating; loud

ก้องกังวาน resonant

ก้องโลก world famous, universally known

ก้อง[2] tribute

จิ้มก้อง to be a tributary (of)

กอด to hug, embrace, put one's arms around

กอดเก้าอี้ to hang on to one's office

กอดเข่า to be depressed

กอดคอ as in เพื่อนกอดคอกัน close friends

กอดจูบลูบคลำ to pet, neck, hugging and kissing

กอดรัด to hug, give a bear hug

กอดหมอนข้าง to be solitary

กอดอก to fold one's arms over one's chest

สวมกอด to throw one's arms around (her, her neck, shoulders etc.), embrace, hug

ก่อน first, before, prior (to), previous, former; for a while, for now

ก่อนกำหนด prematurely, before due, early

ก่อนเพื่อน before anyone else

ก่อนเวลา in advance, ahead of time, early

ก
ข
ค
ฆ
ง
จ
ฉ
ช
ซ
ฌ
ญ
ฎ
ฏ
ฐ
ฑ
ฒ
ณ
ด
ต
ถ
ท
ธ
น
บ
ป
ผ
ฝ
พ
ฟ
ภ
ม
ย
ร
ฤ
ฦ
ล
ว
ศ
ษ
ส
ห
ฬ
อ
ฮ

ก่อนหน้า beforehand

ก่อนหน้านี้ previously

ก่อนอื่น first of all

กินก่อน to eat first

คนก่อน former, previous (person, owner etc)

ครั้งก่อน see **ครั้งก่อน** หน้า 77

คอยก่อน wait a minute

คุณก่อน You first.

คุยกันก่อน let's have a talk first

แค่นี้ก่อน That's all for now.

เชิญก่อน After you.

เดี๋ยวก่อน just a moment, wait a minute.

แต่ก่อนนี้ formerly, in the past

แต่เก่าก่อน in former times, in the old days

นั่งก่อน sit down for a moment

พักก่อน take a rest, take a break

พูดก่อน speak first

เมื่อก่อนนี้ formerly, before

ยืมก่อน lend it to me for a while

ลาก่อน goodbye, so long

วันก่อน the other day

แวะก่อน stop by for a minute

หยุดก่อน stop

ก้อน piece, lump, chunk, mass, morsel

ก้อนกรวด pebble

ก้อนดิน clod

ก้อนเมฆ cloud

ก้อนเส้า stoverests

ก้อนหิน stone, rock

ก้อนอิฐ brick

ขนมปังก้อน loaf of bread

เงินก้อน substantial amount of money, a lump sum

น้ำตาลก้อน lump of sugar, cube sugar

กอบ[1] to scoop up (with the hands)

กอบกู้ to retrieve (the situation, financial position etc)

กอบโกย to amass, pile up, take everything

one can lay one's hands on

กอบ[2], **กอปร** consisting of, comprising; and in addition

เป็นกอบเป็นกำ solid, substantial, serious, something

เขาทำงานตั้ง 6 เดือน ยังไม่มีอะไรเป็นกอบ เป็นกำ He worked for 6 months and had nothing to show for it.

ก้อย the little finger, pinky; tails (reverse side of a coin)

ก้อยกุ้ง a prawn relish

เกี่ยวก้อย to go hand in hand; to link pinkies

โยนหัวโยนก้อย to /flip/toss/ a coin, heads or tails

ก้อร่อก้อติก flirtatious, cheeky

กะ to estimate, calculate; to guess, approximate; shift; with, and; to, for

กะการ to predict, estimate

มีกะใจ willing, considerate, generous, kind

ยังกะ like, as if

กะเกณฑ์ to conscript, force, compel

กะจิ๊ว gigolo, male parasite

กะแช่ fermented palm juice, toddy, rice liquor

กะดำกะด่าง uneven

สีกะดำกะด่าง uneven color

กะต๊าก to cackle, squawk

กะเตงๆ swinging, swaying, hanging

กะทอ a small wicker hamper

กะทัดรัด compact, trim; well proportioned, well fitting; handy; concise

กะทันหัน suddenly, all of a sudden, unexpectedly, on short notice

กะทิ coconut cream

หัวกะทิ pure coconut cream; (fig) the elite, the cream of the crop, the best

หางกะทิ thin coconut cream (from the second or third pressing)

กะเทย hermaphrodite; transvestite; androgenous;

effeminate

กะเทาะ to shell; chipped

กะบัง shelter, shield; weir

    กะบังลม diaphragm

    กะบังหน้า sunshade, sunvisor

    กะบังหมวก visor

กะบึงกะบอน peevish

กะปริดกะปรอย, กะปริบกะปรอย in dribs and drabs, on and off, slight and intermittent

กะปริบ to blink

กะปลกกะเปลี้ย worn out, exhausted, feeble

กะปิ shrimp paste

กะเผลก limping

    เดินกะโผลกกะเผลก to limp

กะพร่องกะแพร่ง defective, incomplete, imperfect

กะพริบ to wink, twinkle, blink; to flicker

    ชั่วกะพริบตา in a wink, in the blink of an eye

กะเพรา sweet basil

กะร่องกะแร่ง to be almost severed

กะรัต carat

    กะรัตหลวง carat (a unit of weight applied to gems equal to 20 centigrams)

กะรุ่งกะริ่ง tattered, in tatters, ragged

    เด็กบ้านนอกนุ่งกางเกงขาดกะรุ่งกะริ่ง The countrykid's pants were in tatters.

กะเร่อกะร่า oafish, like a /country bumpkin/ yokel/, looking awkward

กะเรี่ยกะราด a mess, messily; to be strewn about

กะล่อน a fast talker; an operator; slippery

กะล่อมกะแล่ม see **กล้อมแกล้ม** *หน้า 14*

กะล่อยกะหลิบ adroitly, dextrously

กะละมัง enameled basin

กะละแม rice caramel

กะลา coconut shell

กะลาสี sailor, seaman

กะลิ้มกะเหลี่ย longingly, to hanker (after, for)

    เด็กทำท่ากะลิ้มกะเหลี่ยอยากกินขนม The kid was obviously /longing to get/hankering for/ some candy.

กะเล่อกะล่า see **เล่อล่า** *หน้า 452*

กะโล่ dammared basker tray; pith helmet, topee

กะหนุงกะหนิง billing and cooing, amorous murmuring

กะหร่อง skinny

กะหร็อมกะแหร็ม sparse, scant

กะหรี่ curry; whore, tart, hooker

กะหรี่ปั๊บ curry puff

กะหล่ำ *as in*

    กะหล่ำดอก cauliflower

    กะหล่ำปลี cabbage

กะหลีกะหลอ to butter up (someone), flatter

กะหลุกกะหลิก to fidget, fidgety

กะหำแพะ a kind of eggplant

กะหือ groaning, moaning

กะหูด funnel trap for fish

กะเหรี่ยง Karen

กะเหลาะเปาะ nice and plump; nicely rounded

กะแหะ to laugh heh heh

กะโหลก coconut shell; skull, cranium

    ปวดกะโหลก a pain in the neck

กะออม native water dipper; native waterpot

กัก to shut up, confine, hold back, detain

    กักกัน to confine, restrict, detain

    กักขัง to imprison, incarcerate; to take into custody

    กักจดหมาย to intercept a letter; withhold a letter

    กักด่าน to confine for inspection; to quarantine

    กักตัว to detain

    กักตุน to hoard

    กักน้ำ to store water; to dam (a stream, source of water etc)

    กักบริเวณ to confine to a certain area

    กักรถ to stop vehicles at a checkpoint

    กักเรื่อง to hold back, delay (a matter, consideration, action etc)

กั๊กๆ chuckling

ก ข ค ฆ ง จ ฉ ช ซ ฌ ญ ฎ ฏ ฐ ฑ ฒ ณ ด ต ถ ท ธ น บ ป ผ ฝ พ ฟ ภ ม ย ร ฤ ล ว ศ ษ ส ห ฬ อ ฮ

ก๊ก half pint
    สี่ก๊ก intersection, four corners
    เสื้อก๊ก vest, waistcoat

กักขฬะ vulgar, coarse, crude
    คนกักขฬะสามหาว a crude bastard

กั้ง to keep (something or someone) back; to shelter, protect, shield
    กั้งจ้อง to put up an umbrella *(อี)*

กังขา to doubt, be doubtful, sceptical; (to have) doubts
    ไม่เป็นที่กังขาเลย It is /obvious/without doubt/.

กังฉิน corrupt, crooked, corruptible

กังฟู kung fu, martial arts

กังวล to be worried (about), troubled, anxious, concerned, nervous, on edge
    ความกังวล worry, care
    ไร้กังวล carefree

กังวาน resonant, sonorous

กังสดาล flat gong

กังไส Chinese pottery, china

กังหัน windmill, pinwheel *(ของเล่นเด็ก)*; turbine

กัญชา ganja, marijuana, Indian hemp, hashish, grass *(sl)*
    ต้นกัญชา cannabis

กัญญา[1] beautiful girl, beauty

กัญญา[2] roof
    เรือกัญญา roofed boat

กัณฑ์ sermon; chapter, portion, part, section
    ฉันโดนแม่เทศน์เสียหลายกัณฑ์ I got balled out at length by my mother. / My mother gave me a sermon.
    เครื่องกัณฑ์ offerings for the monk who delivers a sermon
    ติดกัณฑ์เทศน์ to add to the sermon offerings

กัด to bite; to strike *(งู)*; to corrode *(เคมี)*, eat away
    กัดกัน fighting; to be at odds; to snipe at one another

กัดฟัน to clench one's teeth; to make a determined effort
    กัดฟันทน to put up with (something), be patient, endure, support
    กัดฟันพูด to speak reluctantly
    กัดฟันสู้ to fight with determination

กัดไม่ปล่อย tenacious, to refuse to let go

กัดลาก seine

กัดวาง seine

กัดหางตัวเอง to talk in circles

ปลากัด fighting fish

กัตติกมาส twelfth lunar month

กัตติกา Pleiades

กัทลี banana

กัน[1] I, me

กัน[2] let's; they, it is; each other, one another
    สามีภรรยาช่วยกันทำงานบ้าน The husband and wife helped each other with the housework.
    กันเองน่า Take it easy!
    เขาลือกัน *(ว่า)*, they say, it is rumored that
    ไปกันเถอะ Let's go!

กัน[3] to prevent, bar, hinder; to protect (from), shield; to cut off, shelter from; to save, keep back
    กันกระแทก padded
        ซองกันกระแทก padded envelope
    กันความผิด to guard against error
    กันชน bumper; buffer
    กันชิด razor
    กันแดด to /protect/shield/ from the sun
        แว่นตากันแดด sunglasses
    กันตัว to /defend/protect/ oneself
    กันท่า to /stand/get/ in the way (of someone), frustrate
    กันน้ำ waterproof
    กันเป็นพยาน to hold back as a witness
    กันไว้ดีกว่าแก้ An ounce of prevention is worth a pound of cure.

กันสนิม rustproof

กันสะเทือน shock absorbing, shockproof

กันสาด cantilevered slab covering a walkway

กัน[4] to trim (one's hair with a razor)

กันคอ to shave the back of (my) neck

กันจอน to trim (my) sidebums

กั่น tang

กั้น to prevent, block, bar

กั้นกลด to shelter with an umbrella

กั้นกาง to bar the way

กั้นขันหมาก to prevent the bridegroom's gifts from entering the bride's home until some forfeit is paid

กั้นเขตแดน to form a boundary

กั้นคอก to fence in

กั้นถนน to set up a roadblock

กั้นม่าน to curtain off, hang a curtain; to screen

กั้นรั้ว to fence, put up a fence

กั้นห้อง to /partition/divide/ a room, put up a partition

กันไกร see **กรรไกร** หน้า 5

กันชีพ sash

กันแซง roof (on a /boat/cart/), hood

กันดาร deprived, hardship, arid, barren, remote

กันดารน้ำ arid

ทางกันดาร hard /road/way/, bad road

กันต์[1] to cut, shave

กันต์[2] beloved

กันไตร see **กรรไกร** หน้า 5

กันย์ Virgo

กันยา daughter, girl

กันยายน September

กันยารัตน์ virtuous girl

กันแสง to weep, cry, shed tears

กันหยั่น two-edged Chinese dagger

กับ[1] food eaten with rice, food to go with the rice

กับแกล้ม hors d'oeuvres, light dishes, something to go with the drinks

กับข้าว food (to be eaten with rice), dishes

จ่ายกับข้าว to do the marketing

กับ[2] with; on; at; and; from

ตรงกับ to correspond to, be the same as

ถึงกับ so

ฉันตกใจถึงกับเป็นลม I was so scared I almost fainted.

ยังกับ as if, like

เธอทำท่ายังกับเป็นนายฉันแน่ะ You act as if you were my master. / What do you think you are, my boss?

กับ[3] trap

กับดักหนู mousetrap

กับระเบิด landmine

กับ[4] book (of 800 palm leaves)

กัป eon

ชั่วกัปชั่วกัลป์ for /ages/eons/all time/

กัปตัน captain

กัปปาสิก cotton cloth, cotton

กัปปิย- appropriate, suitable

กัปปิยการก one who knows what to do to assist a bhikku; a monk's attendant

กัปปิยภัณฑ์ things allowable for monks

กัปปิยโวหาร language appropriate to monks

กัมปนาท loud, roaring, thundering

กัมปนี company

กัมประโด compradore

กัมพล woolen cloth

กัมพู[1] conch

กัมพู[2] gold

กัมมันตะ action

สัมมากัมมันตะ right action

กัมมันตภาพรังสี radioactivity

กัมมันตรังสี radioactive

กัลบก barber

กัลป-, กัลป์ eon, kalpa

กัลปพฤกษ์ wishing tree

กัลปาวสาน forever, eternally

ตลอดกัลปาวสาน for eternity, forever and ever

กัลปนา land given to a monastery; a deed dedicated to the dead

กัลปังหา coral

กัลเม็ด see กลเม็ด หน้า 13

กัลยา beautiful woman, lady

กัลยาณ- good, fine; beautiful

     กัลยาณคุณ virtue

     กัลยาณธรรม /virtuous/good/ action

     ผู้มีกัลยาณธรรม good person, fine man

กัลยาณมิตร /true/good/ friend

กัลยาณี beautiful woman, a beauty

กา[1] crow

กา[2] cross, to mark; to make a cross

อ่านถึงตรงไหนช่วยกาไว้ด้วย *Please mark the place where you leave off.*

     กาชาด Red Cross

ก๋า audacious

     ก๋ากั่น fast; forward, raffish, brash; pert

     เต้นก๋า ready for a /fight/confrontation/

ไอ้หมอนั่นเต้นก๋าออกมารับหน้าทีเดียว *The guy stalked out in a rage ready for a fight.*

กากี[1] double-dealing woman, adulteress, faithless woman, hussy

กากี[2] (สี) khaki

กาต้มน้ำ kettle

กาน้ำชา teapot

กาฝาก parasite

กาก refuse, residue, waste, dregs; roughage

     กากกะรุน emery, corundum

     กากข้าว paddy mixed in with milled rice

     กากเพชร diamond-point glass cutter; emery wheel; bort, diamond powder

     กากมะพร้าว coconut meat residue

     กากหมู crackling

     กากอุตสาหกรรม industrial waste

กากบาท cross; plus sign; multiplication sign, "x" mark

กากะเยีย folding wooden bookrest

กาง to spread, unfold, open, extend, stretch out

     กางขา to stretch the legs; to spread the legs

     กางแขน to /stretch/extend/ the arms

     กางใบ to /spread/unfurl/ the sail

     กางปีก to spead the wings

     กางมุ้ง to hang a mosquito net

     กางร่ม to open an umbrella

     ท้องกาง to have a swollen belly from eating a lot

     หูกาง protruding ears

ก้าง[1] fishbone

     ก้างขวางคอ (/someone/something/), in the way

     ก้างปลา fishbone

ก้าง[2] (ลาย) herringbone

กางเกง trousers, pants

     กางเกงขายาว long pants, slacks

     กางเกงขาสั้น shorts

     กางเกงใน briefs; boxer shorts, underpants (ชาย); panties (หญิง)

     กางเกงอาบน้ำ swim trunks

กางเขน cross

ก๊าซ, แก๊ส gas

     ก๊าซน้ำตา tear gas

     ก๊าซพิษ poison gas

กาญจน-, กาญจนา gold

กาน to ring a /tree/branch/, girdle a tree; to ring-bark a tree

ก้าน stem, stalk; rod

     ก้านขด decorative scroll design

     ก้านแข็ง a close-fitting bracelet

     ก้านคอ nape of the neck

     ก้านตอง exterior protective rib used on small boats

     ก้านต่อดอก a running foliage decoration

     ก้านบัว anklet, ankle bracelet

     ก้านแย่ง decorative design

ก้านสูบ connecting rod

กานดา beloved, sweetheart

กานต์ dear, beloved

กานท์ poem

กานพลู cloves

กาบ bract, spathe; sheath

กาบกล้วย leaf sheath (of the banana tree); half-round molding (concave or convex)

กาบเขียง coconut spathe

กาบปูเล fibrous covering of the areca made into small containers

กาบไผ่ bamboo bracts

กาบพรหมศร a post decoration

กาบมะพร้าว husk of a coconut; coir

กาพย์ poem

กาพย์กลอน poetical writings

กาเฟอีน caffeine (อ่าน แค ฟีน)

กาแฟ coffee

กาแฟดำเย็น iced black coffee

กาแฟดำร้อน black coffee with sugar

กาแฟผง instant coffee

กาแฟเย็น iced coffee with milk

กาแฟร้อน hot coffee with milk and sugar

กาม sexual desire, carnal desire, sex; sensual pleasure, sensual desire; sensuality

กามกรีฑา love games, lovemaking, sex games, the game of sex; voluptuous delights

กามคุณ /things/qualities/ evoking desire: form, sound, smell, taste, touch; sensual pleasures arising from sound, smell, taste and touch; the sources of sensual pleasure

กามฉันท์ desire for sensual pleasure, sensual excitement

กามตัณหา craving for sensual pleasure

กามตายด้าน impotence (ชาย); frigidity (หญิง)

กามเทพ Cupid, Eros, Love

กามภพ state of pleasure-seeking, sphere dominated by sensual pleasures

กามราคะ sensual passion, lust; lasciv-

iousness

กามโรค venereal disease

กามวิตก thoughts which dwell on pleasures

กามวิตถาร abnormal sex

กามวิปริต sexual perversion

กามารมณ์ libido, sexual desire

บ้ากาม sex-crazed, sex-mad

ก้าม claw, pincer

ก้ามปูนึ่ง steamed crab claws

กามา see กาม

กาเมสุมิจฉาจาร adultery

กาย body

กายกรรม calisthenics, gymnastics

กายทวาร orifices of the body

กายบริหาร physical exercise; to do exercise

กายภาพ physical

กายภาพบำบัด physical therapy

กายวิภาคศาสตร์ anatomy

กายสิทธิ์ magic, magical, miraculous

ก่าย to rest on

นอนเอามือก่ายหน้าผาก He was lying down with his hand resting on his forehead.

ก่ายกอง abundant, plenty of; more than enough

การ task, job, business, work, affair; authority; act, action, -ing, -tion

การกิน eating

การเกิด birth

การครัว cooking

เก่งการครัว good at cooking, a good cook

การคลัง finance; treasury affairs

การค้าขาย commerce, trade

การงาน work, job

การเงิน finance

การเงินไม่ดี My finances are in poor shape.

การจัดลำดับ permutations

การจัดลำดับหมู่ combination

การชลประทาน irrigation

การต้อนรับ reception, welcome

ข ค ฆ ง จ ฉ ช ซ ฌ ญ ฎ ฏ ฐ ฑ ฒ ณ ด ต ถ ท ธ น บ ป ผ ฝ พ ฟ ภ ม ย ร ฤ ฤๅ ล ว ศ ษ ส ห ฬ อ ฮ

การตาย death, dying, demise, extinction

การท่องเที่ยว tourism, touring

การทำนา farming

การแทรกซึม infiltration

การบ้าน homework

การบ้านการเมือง politics

การบ้านการเรือน housekeeping

การปกครอง government, public administration; authority, governing; guardianship

การปฏิบัติตามคำสั่งซื้อขายหลักทรัพย์ execution of a trading order

การประปา water supply, waterworks; Water Authority

การประมง fisheries

การปลูกถ่ายอวัยวะ organ transplant

การพิมพ์ printing

    พ.ร.บ.การพิมพ์ Press Act

การเพาะปลูก cultivation, agriculture

การไฟฟ้า electricity works; Electricity Authority

    การไฟฟ้าฝ่ายผลิต (กฟผ.) Electricity Generating Authority

การมีส่วนร่วม participation, participatory approach

การเมือง politics

    การเมืองน้ำ/คร่ำ/เน่า/ gutter politics

การรบ combat

การเรียน schooling; studying, learning; education

การเรือน housework, housekeeping

การเลี้ยงสัตว์ animal /husbandry/breeding/

การศึกษา education

การส่งเสริม promotion, encouragement, support, help

การสมโภช celebration

การสมรส marriage

การแสดง (the) show

การหนังสือพิมพ์ journalism

การหมั้น engagement, betrothal

การให้ giving; making of a gift

การก doer; case

    การกสงฆ์ officiating monks

    กรรตุการก nominative case

    กรรมการก accusative case

การณ์ event, circumstances, situation

    แถลงการณ์ official /announcement/statement/

    เป็นประวัติการณ์ a record (crowd, fight etc), notable

    สังเกตการณ์ to observe

        ผู้สังเกตการณ์ observer

การ์ด[1] card

    การ์ดแต่งงาน wedding /invitation/announcement

    แจกการ์ด to /send out/deliver/ invitations

การ์ด[2] guard

    บอดีการ์ด bodyguard

การ์ตูน cartoon

    นักเขียนการ์ตูน cartoonist

    พูดเป็นการ์ตูนไปได้ You're joking!

    หนังการ์ตูน cartoon, cartoon movie

    หนังสือการ์ตูน comic book

การบูร camphor

การันต์[1] sign indicating a silent consonant, " ์ "

การันต์[2] ending (gr)

การุญ, การุณย์ mercy, clemency; compassion, kindness

กาล time

กาลกิริยา death, demise

กาลเทศะ time and place

    เขาไม่รู้กาลเทศะ *He doesn't know how to behave. / His behavior was /out of place/ inappropriate/.*

    เขาพูดผิดกาลเทศะ *His remarks were out of place.*

กาลกรรณี, กาลกิณี bad luck, misfortune, evil

    เป็นกาลกิณี unlucky, inauspicious

กาลจักร the wheel of time; the wheel of fortune

กาลี a misfortune, an evil; witch; Durga, Kali
เป็นกาลี ill omened
เป็นกาลีบ้านกาลีเมือง ill omen for the nation

กาว glue, mucilage, adhesive
เทปกาว adhesive tape
มือกาว (to have) sticky fingers *(fig)*

ก้าว step; to step, take a step
ก้าวก่าย to interfere, meddle
ก้าวร้าว aggressive, belligerent, abrasive, antagonistic, bellicose
มีอาการก้าวร้าว aggressive nature
ก้าวล่วง to violate, offend against; to over-come, surmount
...เว้นแต่มีเหตุจำเป็นอันมิอาจก้าวล่วงเสียได้ ... *except in case of insurmountable necessity.*
ก้าวหน้า to advance, progress, develop, go forward; progressive; advanced, modernized

กาววาว flashy, gaudy
กาสาวพัสตร์ yellow robe
กาสิโน casino
กาหล trumpet horn; tumult
กาเหว่า blackbird
กาไหล่ to fill, cover with, filled
กาไหล่เงิน silver-filled
กาไหล่ทอง gold-filled

กาฬ death; black
กาฬปักษ์ period of the waning moon
กาฬปักษี nervous disease of new-born babies
กาฬโรค the plague, the black death
เหงื่อกาฬ cold sweat

กำ to clench, grasp; handful, bunch
กำมา a short cubit, distance between the elbow and clenched fist
กำมือ fist; handful; *(fig)* under one's thumb, under one's control, in one's clutches, in one's hands, in the palm of one's hand
เธอตกอยู่ในกำมือของผู้ร้าย The rogue had her in his clutches.

กำหมัด fist
ก่ำ[1] deep red
แดงก่ำ crimson, burgundy; bloodshot eyes (ตา)
ก่ำ[2] very, intensely
สุกก่ำ very ripe

กำกวม vague, obscure, ambiguous, unclear
กำกับ to superintend, oversee; to supervise, direct; to accompany
ผู้กำกับการตำรวจ police superintendant, police chief
ผู้กำกับการแสดง director
ผู้กำกับเวที stage director

ก้ำกึ่ง fifty-fifty, nearly the same; in the balance
แพ้หรือชนะยังก้ำกึ่งอยู่ There's only a fifty-fifty chance of winning.

ก้ำเกิน to trespass, infringe upon, offend
กำจร see **ขจร** หน้า 45
กำจัด eliminate, eradicate, get rid of, destroy
กำจาย see **กระจาย** หน้า 6
กำชับ to remind, reiterate, see that, insist; to admonish; to emphasize
กำชับลูกน้องของคุณด้วย ให้พูดจาสุภาพหน่อย See that your people use better language. /Remind/admonish/ your people to use better language.

กำซาบ to coat with; to penetrate
กำดัด adolescent, teenaged, young; blossoming
กำเดา (เลือด) epistaxis, nosebleed; (ไข้) a fever accompanying a cold
กำธร reverberating, resounding, roaring
กำนัน kamnan, chief of a tambon, head of a group of villages
กำนัล as in **นางกำนัล** maid of honor
ของกำนัล souvenir, memento, gift, present
กำเนิด birth, origin, source, to occur, happen, arise; to give birth (to), bear; to produce, generate, engender, bring into being; to establish, create

โดยกำเนิด by birth; innate, inborn
เป็นชาวพุทธโดยกำเนิด He was /born a Buddhist/a Buddhist by birth/.
ถือกำเนิด to be born (into, at, in), engendered, originated
มาแต่กำเนิด from the beginning, from birth
ให้กำเนิด to sire, give birth to
องค์กำเนิด reproductive organ, penis

กำบัง[1] spray of flowers; plant
กำบัง[2] to shelter, shield, screen; to hide, conceal
เขาหาที่กำบังฝน He looked for shelter from the rain. / He got out of the rain.
กำบังกาย to make oneself invisible

กำปั่น merchant ship; strong-box, safe
กำปั่นใบ sailing ship
กำปั่นไฟ steamship

กำปั้น fist
กำปั้นทุบดิน smart-alecky, smart, flip, fatuous

กำพร้า orphan
กำพร้าพ่อ, (แม่) fatherless, motherless, orphaned of a father (mother)
ลูกกำพร้า orphan

กำพืด background, stock, origins; to come from a line of (aristocrats, etc)

กำเพลิง flintlock

กำแพง wall
กำแพงมีหูประตูมีตา Even the walls have ears. / Watch what you do or say.
กำแพงแก้ว a low wall surrounding a shrine
กำแพงเขย่ง a walking-Buddha amulet
กำแพงเศียร large-combed hybrid fowl

กำมะถัน sulphur, sulfur

กำมะลอ fake, sham, phony, charlatan
ลายกำมะลอ Chinese style design in gold and color

กำมะหยี่ velvet

กำยาน gum benjamin, benzoin

กำยำ stout, strong, sturdy; muscular

กำราบ to subdue; to frighten, intimidate

กำเริบ[1] to get worse, become more serious; to recur, spread

กำเริบ[2] to become /presumptuous/demanding/
กำเริบเสิบสาน brash, impudent, insolent, presumptuous

กำไร profit, gain
กำไรงาม (to make) a handsome profit
กำไรสุทธิ net profit
ได้กำไร to profit, make a profit, make money, benefit (from), get something out of
ผลกำไร profit, benefit, outcome
ไม่ได้กำไร to make no profit

กำลัง[1] force, strength, power, energy
กำลังกาย physical force, bodily strength, energy
กำลังงาน energy
กำลังใจ enthusiasm, interest, spirit
หมดกำลังใจ My heart's not in it., to be fed up, lose heart, lose interest (in), be dispirited
กำลังเทียน candlepower
กำลังม้า horsepower
กำลังแรง power
กำลังวังชา vitality, energy
ใช้กำลัง to force, use /force/violence/
หมดกำลัง to be at the end of one's strength, exhausted, all in
ออกกำลัง[1] to exercise, /take/get/ exercise
ออกกำลัง[2] to use force; to exert oneself, use energy

กำลัง[2] power
กำลังสอง squared, to the power of two
2 ยกกำลัง 5 two to the fifth power, (2^5)

กำลัง[3] in the act of (*progressive auxiliary*)
กำลังเต้นรำ They /were/are/ dancing.
กำลังเย็น It is cool.
กำลังจะไป about to go, on the verge of going, on the point of going
กำลังประชุมอยู่ The meeting is in progress.

กำไล bracelet; anklet, ankle bracelet

กำสรด sad, sorrowful, unhappy

กำสรวล to lament, grieve; to weep (for)

กำแสง to cry, weep

กำหนด to prescribe, stipulate, fix, determine, set

    กำหนดกฎเกณฑ์ regulations

    กำหนดการ schedule, program

    กำหนดงาน to estimate work

    กำหนดตัว to select, choose (a person)

    กำหนดระยะทาง to fix the distance

    กำหนดราคา to /fix/set/ the price

    กำหนดวัน to fix the day

    กำหนดไว้ในใจ to have in mind

    กำหนดไว้ให้ assigned

    กำหนดหน้าที่ to allot work, assign a job

    กำหนดให้ to assign, prescribe

    เกินกำหนด overdue

    ถึงกำหนด, ครบกำหนด due, deadline

    พระราชกำหนด royal decree

    อาหารกำหนด diet

กำหนัด sensual excitement; pleasure

กำเหน็จ goldsmith's charge for workmanship

กำแหง strong; arrogant

กิก, กิ๊ก click

กิ่ง branch

    กิ่งก้อย the little finger, pinky

    กิ่งทองใบหยก going together like bread and butter

    กิ่งไม้ branch, twig

    กิ่งอำเภอ sub-district

กิ้งก่า chameleon

    กิ้งก่าได้ทอง a bumptious show-off

กิ้งกือ millipede

กิจ business

    กิจการ business, enterprise, affair, facility

        กิจการวิเทศธนกิจ(*ของธนาคารพาณิชย์*) BIBF, Bangkok International Banking Facilities

    กิจวัตร routine, regular practice

    เป็นกิจวัตร regularly

กิจจะลักษณะ official, formal, businesslike, in a businesslike manner; systematic; seriously

กิจจา report, account, written statement

    กิจจานุกิจ everything to be done, all the work

กิตติ reputation, renown

    กิตติกรรมประกาศ acknowledgements; repute; recognized virtues

    กิตติคุณ good reputation; virtue; goodwill

    กิตติมศักดิ์ honorary

        ดุษฎีบัณฑิตกิตติมศักดิ์ (to have) an honorary doctorate

    กิตติศัพท์ reputation; praises

กิน to consume, eat; to use, take; to occupy; to govern; to milk, exploit, take a cut

    มรดกของพ่อแม่ถูกลูกคนโตกินไปเกือบครึ่ง The eldest child milked the estate of almost half its assets.

    กินกันหลายทอด taking cuts down the line

    กินกัน to go together, harmonize, fit together, suit each other; to mesh; to wear away

        สายตาไม่กินกัน I /don't like/dislike/ him.

    กินกำไร to make easy profit; to pocket money (as a result of padding etc)

    กินขวา to pull to the right; to wear away on the right side

    กินขาด to be superior, much better, win hands down

    กินข้าว to eat, have /lunch/breakfast/dinner/ a meal/

    กินความ to include, cover, encompass, extend to

    กินจุ to eat a lot

    กินเจ, กินแจ to be a vegetarian, eat vegetarian food

    กินใจ to be /suspicious/wary/ of one another, (There was) something between

ก ข ค ฆ ง จ ฉ ช ซ ฌ ญ ฎ ฏ ฐ ฑ ฒ ณ ด ต ถ ท ธ น บ ป ผ ฝ พ ฟ ภ ม ย ร ฤ ฦ ล ว ศ ษ ส ห ฬ อ ฮ

(them).; to affect deeply, be moving, gripping

กินดอก to get interest; to live off the interest

กินดอง to feast at a marriage

กินดิบ to win hands down, win easily

กินได้ edible

กินตะกละตะกลาม to gorge oneself

กินตัว to fall into holes

กินตา to deceive the eyes; optical illusion

กินตามน้ำ to /get/take/ a rake-off

กินตำแหน่ง to hold the office/position/ of

กินโต๊ะ to have a Chinese dinner; to gang up (on someone)

กินแถว right down the line, everyone

กินทิ้งกินขว้าง to waste one's food, be wasteful of food

กินที่ to take up room

　ไม่กินที่ It takes up no room., It takes no space.

กินนอกกินใน to make money under the table (sl)

กินน้ำใต้ศอก to be a minor wife

กินน้ำมัน to take a lot of /gas/petrol/, a gas guzzler

กินน้ำลึก draft, draught

กินน้ำเห็นปลิง squeamish, uneasy

กินบนเรือนขี้บนหลังคา ungrateful

กินบ้านกินเมือง to rule the country

กินบุญเก่า to live off previously acquired wealth; He doesn't have to work for a living.

กินปูนร้อนท้อง defensive

กินเปล่า to get something for nothing

　เงินกินเปล่า tea money, key money, extra payment, under-the-table payment

กินผัว to have had two or more husbands who have died, be widowed two or more times

กินไฟน้อย It doesn't use much /power/ electricity/.

กินมัดจำ to forfeit a deposit

กินมือ to eat with the fingers

กินเมีย to have had two or more wives who have died, be widowered two or more times.

กินเมือง to govern; to rule

กินไม่ลง[1] not to like, be unable to bear *ปลาดิบ ฉันกินไม่ลง /I don't like/I can't bear/ raw fish.*

กินไม่ลง[2] to refrain from /winning/taking/

กินรังแตน scowling

กินแรง[1] to take a lot of /energy/force/

กินแรง[2] to use someone for something

กินลม to take the air; to catch the wind (ใบเรือ) *เดินกินลม to go for a walk*

กินลมกินแล้ง to gain nothing

กินล้างกินผลาญ extravagant, prodigal

กินลึก[1] to affect deeply

กินลึก[2] to have a deep draft (เรือ); to settle deeply in the water

กินเล็กกินน้อย to be slightly dishonest, take small amounts of money wrongfully

กินเลือดกินเนื้อ ferocious

กินวิบาก to have an /eating/drinking/ contest

กินเวลา see กินเวลา หน้า 467

กินสินบาตรคาดสินบน to be corrupt, take bribes

กินหญ้า to graze

กินหน้า to be nose-heavy (ว่าว)

กินหมาก to chew betel

กินหลัง to be tail-heavy (ว่าว)

กินหาง to lose its tail (ว่าว)

กินเหล็กกินไหล tough

กินแหนง to be on the outs, have something between (them, us)

กินอยู่พูวาย to have plenty, have an abundance

กินอาหาร to eat, have some food, have something to eat

กินนร mythological half-man half-bird

กินริน, กินรี mythological half-woman half-bird

กิมิชาติ worm

กิมิวิทยา helminthology

กิระดังได้สดับมา thus have I heard, so it has been told

กิริยา actions, manners, conduct, behavior, deportment

    กิริยาดี good manners

    กิริยาเลว bad manners

    เสียกิริยา impolite, unmannerly, rude, to show bad manners

กิเลน dragon-headed unicorn

กิเลส[1] desires, wanting, craving

กิเลส[2] defilements (พุทธศาสนา)

กิโลกรัม kilogram

กิโลเมตร kilometer

กิโลลิตร kiloliter

กิ่ว constricted, narrow

    ท้องกิ่ว My stomach is empty., I'm starved.

กี่[1] loom

กี่[2] how much, how many

    กี่คน how many people

    กี่ครั้ง how many times

    กี่มากน้อย how many, how much, what amount

    มีกี่มากน้อย How much have you got? / What amount do you have?

    กี่โมงแล้ว What time is it?

    ไม่กี่มากน้อย not so much, not much

    ไม่กี่วัน in a few days; a few days ago; a few days later

กี้[1] just past

    ก่อนกี้ in former times, in the old days

    เมื่อกี้นี้ a /moment/minute/ ago, just (left, came in, etc)

กี้[2] *as in* **เจ้ากี้เจ้าการ** a busybody; fusspot; meddlesome, officious

กี๋ tray; tea set on a tray

กีฎ insect

    กีฎวิทยา entomology

กีด to obstruct, impede, hinder, block

    กีดกัน to hinder, be kept from (doing something, keep someone from doing something), frustrate

    กีดขวาง to obstruct, impede, bar, bar the way, block, be a barrier

        เครื่องกีดขวาง barrier

    กีดหน้าขวางตา to /be/get/ in someone's way

กีตาร์ guitar

กีบ hoof

    กีบผา cloven hoof

กีรติ honor, distinction

กีฬา sport, sports, games

    กีฬากลางแจ้ง outdoor sports

    กีฬาในร่ม indoor sports

    กีฬาพระราชา the sport of kings, horseracing

    การกีฬา athletics, sports

    นักกีฬา athlete; sportsman

        น้ำใจนักกีฬา sportsmanship, sporting spirit

    เล่นกีฬา to play games, engage in sports

    สนามกีฬา stadium; playing field, sports field

กึก *as in*

    กึกก้อง resounding, very /loud/noisy/

    กึกกัก rattling sound, rattle

    หยุดกึก to come to a sudden stop; to stop /short/ abruptly/

    ม้าวิ่งมาเต็มฝีเท้า หยุดกึกอย่างกะทันหัน The galloping horse stopped short.

กึ่ง ครึ่ง half, middle; semi-

    กึ่งกลาง middle, center, heart

    กึ่งๆ กลางๆ (to do things) half-way

    กึ่งพุทธกาล half the Buddhist era

    กึ่งราชการ semi-official

    ก้ำกึ่ง in the balance; fifty-fifty; nearly the same

กึงกัง clunking sound

กึ๋น gizzard

    ถึงกึ๋น to the quick

กุ made up, unfounded, baseless, groundless

    กุข่าว to fabricate a news story, invent news, make up a story

    กุขึ้น to fabricate, invent, concoct, make out of whole cloth

กุก tap, tapping; knocking sound

    กุกกัก halting (speech)

กุ๊ก cook

กุ๊กกุ๊ก cluck cluck, clucking

กุก่อง shining, radiant, brilliant

กุกุธภัณฑ์ *see* กกุธภัณฑ์ *หน้า 1*

กุ้ง shrimp, crawfish, crayfish, prawn, lobster

    กุ้งก้ามกราม lobster; prawn

    กุ้งเต้น a small jumping insect resembling a shrimp

    กุ้งนาง a common shrimp

    กุ้งฝอย tiny freshwater shrimp

    กุ้งฟืด dried salted shelled shrimp

    กุ้งไม้ brochette of dried shrimp

    กุ้งส้ม pickled and salted shrimp condiment

    กุ้งหลวง big prawn

    กุ้งแห้ง dried shrimp; skinny *(fig)*

กุญแจ lock; key; wrench

    กุญแจเท้า fetters, legcuffs

    กุญแจปากตาย open end wrench, open spanner

    กุญแจผี skeleton key

    กุญแจมือ handcuffs, manacles

    กุญแจรหัส cipher

    กุญแจเลื่อน monkey wrench, adjustable /spanner/wrench/

    กุญแจเสียง clef

    ไขกุญแจ to unlock

    แม่กุญแจ lock; padlock

    ลั่นกุญแจ to lock, snap a lock shut

    ลูกกุญแจ key

    ใส่กุญแจ to lock, fasten a lock

กุญชร elephant

กุฎาคาร a building with a spire

กุมภพี *see* กระภูมพี *หน้า 7*

กุฏฐัง leprosy

กุฏิ,กุฎี monk's chambers, monk's dwelling

กุณฑล earring

กุณโฑ water jar, water pot

กุด to amputate, cut off; amputated, shorter than it should be, truncated, docked

    กุดหัว to behead, decapitate

กุดัง *see* โกดัง *หน้า 43*

กุดั่น jewelled ornament

    ลายกุดั่น decorative design

กุทัณฑ์ *see* เกาทัณฑ์ *หน้า 37*

กุน Year of the Pig

กุ๊น to edge, bind; to sew a binding on

กุนที stream, brook

กุบ a hat for working in the fields

กุบกับ clip clop, clattering

กุม to seize, hold, grasp, take hold of

    กุมขมับ to hold one's head in one's hands; to be worried

    กุมตัว to arrest, detain

    กุมมือ to /take/hold/ (her, his) hand

    กุมอำนาจ to seize power; to hold power

กุมภาพันธ์ February

กุมเหง *see* ข่มเหง *หน้า 46*

กุมาร boy, child

    กุมารแพทย์ pediatrician

    กุมารเวชศาสตร์ pediatrics

กุมารี girl

กุมุท lotus, water lily

กุ้ย[1] ghost, spirit

กุ๊ย[2] lout, tough guy, hooligan; boor

กุ้ยๆ mocking sound

กุยเล้ย a Chinese pointed hat

กุยเฮง a Chinese jacket

กุรุส *as in* เป็นกุรุส (by the) gross

กุรุพินท์ ruby

กุล lineage, family

    กุลธิดา good daughter

    กุลบุตร good son

    กุลสตรี lady, gentlewoman

กุลา[1] large bird-shaped kite

กุลา[2] hill tribe in northern Thailand

    กุลาขาว a European

    กุลาซ่อนผ้า children's circle game

กุลาหล chaotic; turmoil, chaos, tumult

กุลี[1] worker, coolie

กุลี[2] package containing twenty pieces of cloth

กุลีกุจอ energetically, with enthusiasm

กุศล wholesome, meritorious; intelligent

    กุศลกรรม meritorious action, right conduct

        กุศลกรรมบถ wholesome course of action

    กุศลจิต moral consciousness, meritorious thought

    กุศลเจตนา good intention, meritorious intention, right volition

    กุศโลบาย intelligent policy; meritorious policy

    การกุศล charity

        เพื่อการกุศล charitable, for charity

    สร้างกุศล to do good

กุสุม flower

กุสุมาลย์ flower

กุหลาบ rose

    ดอกกุหลาบ rose, roses

    ต้นกุหลาบ rose bush

กู I, me

กู[1] to call out to, halloo, shout

    กู่ไม่กลับ to be beyond reason, too committed to listen

กู่[2] chedi, stupa, temple

กู้[1] to raise, salvage, save, redeem

    กู้ชาติ to liberate; liberation

    กู้ชื่อ to restore one's reputation

    กู้ภัย to rescue

    หน่วยกู้ภัย rescue squad

    กู้บ้านกู้เมือง to save the country

    กู้เรือ to salvage a ship (boat)

    กู้หน้า to save face, /save/retrieve/a situation

กู้[2] to borrow, take a loan

    กู้เงิน to raise a loan, to borrow money (at interest)

    ขอกู้ to /apply for/ask for/make/ a loan

    เงินกู้ loan

    ให้กู้ to lend, loan

เก crooked; to play truant; to shirk (one's studies, work etc); be a shirker

    เกเข้าไป to raise the ante

    เกตาม to match (you, etc)

    เกทับ to match and raise (you, etc); to bluff

    เกโรงเรียน to play truant from school

    ขาเก twisted leg

    ฟันเก crooked teeth

เก๊ counterfeit, fake, false, spurious

เก๋ smart, smart looking, chic, cute, snazzy

เกก askew

    เขาเกก crooked horns

เก๊ก to put on airs, be stuck-up

    เก๊กหน้า/ท่า to pose, strike a pose

เก๊กซิม to feel /hurt/bad/, What a headache!

เกกมะเหรก hooligan, hoodlum; to act like a hooligan

เก๊กฮวย chrysanthemum

    น้ำเก๊กฮวย chrysanthemum tea

เก้กัง, เก้ๆ กังๆ awkward, ill at ease

เก็ง to guess, conjecture; to predict

    เก็งกำไร to speculate

    เก็งข้อสอบ to /guess/anticipate/predict/ foresee/ an examination question

    เก็งเหตุการณ์ to predict events, forecast, prognosticate

    ไพ่ตัวเก็ง winning card

    ม้าตัวเก็ง a winner เช่น *That horse is a winner.*

เก่ง smart; good (at something); easily, readily

เก่งกาจ fearless, audacious, daring

เก่งแต่ปาก ineffectual, all talk and no action

ปากเก่ง to be a sharp talker; loquacious

เป็นหวัดเก่ง to catch colds easily

พูดเก่ง to be a good talker

เรียนเก่ง to be good at school, learn quickly, smart

อวดเก่ง show off; brag

เก๋ง house with a Chinese style roof; /roof/ hood/ (of a boat, car, automobile); boat with a roof

เก้งก้าง awkward, ungainly, clumsy, unwieldy

เกจ, เก gauge

เก็จ crystal ornament

เกณฑ์[1] to conscript, compel, force

เกณฑ์ทหาร to conscript, draft (men into the armed forces), levy troops

ถูกเกณฑ์ทหาร drafted, conscripted; (to receive a) /conscription notice/draft call/

เกณฑ์[2] standard; requirement; basis

คุณถืออะไรเป็นเกณฑ์ในการตัดสินว่าภาพนี้ดี หรือไม่ดี *What's your basis for judging whether the painting is good or not? / On what do you base your criticism of the painting?*

ในการรับคนเข้าทำงานในบริษัท คุณมีเกณฑ์ อะไรบ้าง *What standards do you apply when hiring new people?*

เกณฑ์เงินสด cash basis

เกณฑ์สิทธิ์ accrual basis

เกด *as in* **ลูกเกด** raisin

เก็ต to get it *(sl)*

เขาไม่เก็ต *He doesn't get it at all.*

เกตุ flag; comet; falling star; the ninth planet

เกตุมาลา radiance emanating from the Buddha's head

เก็บ to collect, accumulate; to keep, preserve, maintain, store; to pick up; to gather; to put away, stow; *(sl)* to get rid of, do away with, waste

เก็บหมอนั่นซะ *Get rid of that guy!*

คนนั้นโดนเก็บ *The man was /put away/ done in/wasted/.*

เก็บกด to suppress

คนเก็บกด /withdrawn/suppressed/ person

ความเก็บกด suppressed feelings, frustration

เก็บกวาด to clean up

เก็บเกี่ยว to harvest

เก็บของ to put things away, tidy up

เก็บเข้าที่ to stow, put away

เก็บงำ to keep safely, put in a safe place, take good care of something

เก็บเงิน to collect money; The /bill/check/ please.

พนักงานเก็บเงิน bill collector

เก็บดอกเบี้ย to collect interest

เก็บตก to glean from others

เก็บตัว to /avoid/shun/ society; to keep to oneself; to go into training, go to training camp

เก็บโต๊ะ to clear the table

เก็บเบี้ยใต้ถุนร้าน to accumulate little by little

เก็บปากเก็บคำ to be reserved, discreet, mind one's tongue, be close-mouthed

เก็บภาษี to collect taxes

เก็บรักษา safekeeping

เก็บเล็กผสมน้อย to save up little by little

เก็บเล่ม to /gather/collate/ (sheet) sections; to put in book form

การเก็บเล่ม gathering

เก็บหอมรอมริบ to save up

เกม game

เกมตื้น ๆ a game easy to fathom, a shallow ploy

เกมแล้ว The game is over., to be final, be over

เกย[1] mounting platform for royalty
    เกยลา movable mounting platform for royalty
    ราชรถมาเกย unexpected good fortune, One's ship comes in.

เกย[2] to run up on, beach
    เกยตื้น to run aground
    เกยฝั่ง to beach; beached
    เกยหินโสโครก to run on the rocks
    เกยแห้ง to run aground, to /strand/ground/beach/ a boat

เกย์ gay

เกยูร necklace; bracelet

เกร่ to mosey around

เกรง to fear, be afraid
    เกรงกลัว to be in awe (of), fear, in fear of; to obey
    เกรงขาม to revere, hold in awe
    เกรงใจ to be reluctant to bother someone, show diffidence (towards), not to want to impose on someone; to feel obliged (to do something)
        ไม่เกรงใจ lacking consideration (for), inconsiderate, not afraid (to)
        อย่าเกรงใจ "Make yourself at home." (เฉพาะแขก); Don't be afraid to...., Don't hesitate to...., Don't stand on ceremony.
    เกรงว่า to be afraid, fear; lest, for fear that
    ยำเกรง to fear; to respect
    หวั่นเกรง to be apprehensive, fearful
    หวาดเกรง to dread, tremble (at, before); with trepidation

เกร็ง stiffened, rigid; tense, tensed
    เกร็งกล้ามเนื้อ to /tense/flex/contract/ a muscle, tighten a muscle

เกร็ด fragments; selection; anecdote
    เกร็ดพงศาวดาร historical tales
    ตำรายาเกร็ด pharmacological miscellany

เกรน grain (abbr gr.)

เกร่อ common; popular
    ชื่อสมศักดิ์มีใช้กันเกร่อ Somsak is a very common name.
    คนนิยมดื่มนมกันเกร่อ Everybody likes milk. /Milk is very popular.

เกรอะ[1] to filter, strain
    บ่อเกรอะ septic tank, cesspool

เกรอะ[2] crusted, dried out, caked
    เกรอะกรัง encrusted (with)

เกราะ[1] armor, armour
    เกราะอ่อน cuirass
    รถเกราะ armored car
    เรือเกราะ armored boat
    เสื้อเกราะ bulletproof vest

เกราะ[2] clapboard
    ตีเกราะเรียกประชุม to strike the clapboard to call (villagers) to meeting

เกริ่น to tell beforehand; to mention (something) briefly; to let on (that)
    บทเกริ่น foreword

เกรียง trowel

เกรียงไกร powerful, superior, mighty, almighty, imposing
    อานุภาพเกรียงไกร omnipotence

เกรียน very short, close cut
    หัวเกรียน having a crew cut

เกรียบ crisp, crispy; brittle
    ข้าวเกรียบ crispy rice flatcake, rice crisps
    ข้าวเกรียบปากหม้อ steamed ricecake filled with sweetmeats

เกรียม scorched, burnt

เกรียว all, all together; noisy, clamor, acclamation (ด้วยความยินดี)
    เกรียวกราว racket, din, clamor; noisy
    ขนลุกเกรียว My hair stood on end., hair-raising
    ข่าวเกรียวกราว news on everybody's lips, everybody's talking about, a brouhaha, big news

ก ข ค ฆ ง จ ฉ ช ซ ฌ ญ ฎ ฏ ฐ ฑ ฒ ณ ด ต ถ ท ธ น บ ป ผ ฝ พ ฟ ภ ม ย ร ฤ ฤๅ ล ว ศ ษ ส ห ฬ อ ฮ

โห่กันเกรียว to give an acclamation, a tumultuous acclaim

เกรี้ยว to be furious (with)

เกรี้ยวกราด enraged, infuriated; violently angry, in a rage

เกเร, เกเรเกตุง naughty (ใช้สำหรับเด็ก), wayward

    คนเกเรเกตุง troublemaker; rascal

    เด็กเกเร mischievous child; naughty kid, bad /boy/girl/, little rascal; juvenile delinquent, wayward child

เกล็ด scale; flake; slat

    เกล็ดปลา fish scale

    ขอดเกล็ด to scale a fish

    จับเกล็ด to make a dart

    ตีเกล็ด to tuck, sew tucks

    บานเกล็ด louvre, louvred, louvre window

    เป็นเกล็ด scaly

เกลอ close friend, comrade, chum, buddy

    เกลอแก้ว best friend

    เป็นเกลอกัน to be /pals/buddies/

    สามเกลอ manual pile driver

เกลา to finish, smooth; to polish

    เกลาสำนวน to polish the /writing/text/wording/

    เกลี้ยงเกลา smooth

        โกนหนวดเกลี้ยงเกลา clean shaven

    ขัดเกลา to polish, finish, refine, improve

เกล้า[1] head

    เกล้ากระผม I (subject), me (object)

เกล้า[2] to dress the hair

    เกล้าจุก to make a topknot

    เกล้าผม to put (one's) hair up

    เกล้ามวย to put one's hair up in a bun

เกลี่ย to even out, level, smooth

    ไกล่เกลี่ย to mediate, conciliate, get (people) to come to terms, bring (the parties) together

    ผู้ไกล่เกลี่ย mediator, conciliator

เกลี้ยกล่อม to persuade, induce, prevail upon, talk someone into doing something

เกลี้ยง smooth; used up, finished

    กินเกลี้ยง to eat up everything

    เกลี้ยงเกลา polished; spick and span

    โกนเกลี้ยง clean shaven

    ผิวเกลี้ยง clear complexion (ใบหน้า); smooth clear skin

    หมดเกลี้ยง all /gone/finished/, empty

เกลียด to hate, strongly dislike, detest, abhor

    เกลียดชัง to hate, loath, abominate

        การเกลียดชัง hatred

    เกลียดน้ำหน้า to detest

    ฉันเกลียดน้ำหน้าหมอนั่น I detest that guy. / That guy is detestable.

    น่าเกลียด ugly, awful, does not look good, not nice

เกลียว twisted together; screw, thread (of a screw); spiral

    เกลียวสัมพันธ์ close ties

    เกลียวหวาน stripped thread

    กลมเกลียว united, to get along well together, in harmony

    เป็นเกลียว spiral; twisted

เกลือ salt

    เกลือจิ้มเกลือ to repay in kind

    เกลือจืด gypsum

    เกลือเป็นหนอน treachery

    เกลือสมุทร sea salt

    เกลือสินเธาว์ rock salt

เกลือก to wallow; to roll about

    เกลือกกลั้ว to associate with, muck around with

    เกลือกกลิ้ง to tumble about

    เกลือกโคลน to wallow in mud

    เกลือกว่า if, provided that

เกลื่อน scattered about; all over the place, spread all over

    เกลื่อนกล่น in a mess

    เกลื่อนกลาด commonplace, to be found all over; all over the place; scattered everywhere

เกลื้อน ringworm

เกวียน[1] ox-cart, buffalo-cart

เกวียน[2] a measure of rice equal to 100 tang or 150 kilograms

　เกวียนหลวง a unit of volume equal to 2,000 litres

เกศ hair, strand of hair

　เกศธาตุ (a strand of) hair of the Buddha

เกศา, เกศี head; hair

เกษตร land; farmland; agriculture

　เกษตรกร farmer, agriculturist

　เกษตรกรรม agriculture, farming, cultivation

　เกษตรศาสตร์ agriculture

　การเกษตร farming, agriculture, cultivation

　พุทธเกษตร the land inhabited by the Buddha

เกษม happiness, felicity, happy, content; secure; contentment; security

　เกษมศานต์ happy, blissful, joyful

เกษียณ retirement, superannuation

　เกษียณอายุ retirement age; to retire

　ครบเกษียณอายุ to reach the age of retirement

เกษียน annotate; annotations

เกษียร milk

เกสร pollen

　ก้านเกสร stamen (ผู้), pistil (เมีย)

เกสรี lion

เก้อ abashed, embarrassed, disconcerted

　คอยเก้อ to wait for nothing, wait in vain

เก๊ะ drawer

　เก๊ะรถ glove compartment

เกะกะ messy, disorderly; obstructive, in the way

　คนเกะกะ a nuisance

　คนพาลเกะกะ hoodlum

เกา scratch

　เกาไม่ถูกที่คัน to bark up the wrong tree

　เกาสมอ to drag the anchor

เกาหลัง to scratch one's back

เก่า old, former, previous; antique, ancient; old fashioned, conservative; archaic

　เก่าเก็บ old and disused

　เก่าแก่ very old, age-old

　เก่าคร่ำคร่า ancient

　ของเก่า antiques; secondhand things

　คนเก่า, คนแก่ old, former (servant, employee, etc)

　เจ้าเก่า the original

　ดังเก่า as before, as of old

　ปีเก่า last year, the old year

　เพื่อนเก่า old friend

　ร้านขายของเก่า antique shop (ของเก่ามีค่า); secondhand shop (ขายของที่ใช้แล้ว)

　หัวเก่า of the old school, conservative, old fashioned

　อย่างเก่า as before, as formerly

เก้า nine

　เก้าสิบ ninety

　ที่เก้า ninth

เก๊า dog

เก๋า old hand (at), masterhand, virtuoso

เกาทัณฑ์ bow

　ลูกเกาทัณฑ์ arrow

เกาลัด chestnut

เกาหลี Korea

เกาเหลา Chinese soup without noodles

เก้าอี้ chair; position, office

　เก้าอี้นวม upholstered /chair/sofa/couch, easy chair

　เก้าอี้นอน chaise longue

　เก้าอี้ผ้าใบ deckchair

　เก้าอี้พับ folding chair

　เก้าอี้โยก rocking chair

　เก้าอี้หมุน swivel chair

　เก้าอี้หวาย rattan chair, wicker chair

　เก้าอี้เอน reclining chair

　ตกเก้าอี้ to lose one's job; to get sacked

ก ข ค ฆ ง จ ฉ ช ซ ฌ ญ ฎ ฏ ฐ ฑ ฒ ณ ด ต ถ ท ธ น บ ป ผ ฝ พ ฟ ภ ม ย ร ฤ ฦ ล ว ศ ษ ส ห ฬ อ ฮ

เกาะ[1] to perch (นก); to cling (to), adhere, stick (to)

    เกาะกิน to live at another's expense, be a parasite, sponge /on/off/someone

    เกาะแกะ to flirt

    เกาะแขน to take (his) arm

    เกาะถนน to hold the road

เกาะ[2] island

    เกาะหมาก Penang

    หมู่เกาะ archipelago

        หมู่เกาะฮาวาย the Hawaiian Islands

เกิด to be born; to arise, be, become, happen, occur; to cause, give rise to

    เกิดขึ้น to come about, happen, crop up, arise

    เกิดประโยชน์ to be useful

    เกิดผล to bear fruit, fruitful

    เกิดเรื่อง something has happened

    เกิดหึงหวง to become jealous

    เกิดเหตุ incident

        ที่เกิดเหตุ scene of the /incident/ accident/crime/ etc, the incident occurred at

    บ่อเกิด source, origin, wellspring, root

    บ้านเกิด birthplace, native /town/country/

    วันเกิด birthday

เกิน to exceed, surpass; over, more *เช่น เกินครึ่ง more than half*; excessive, inordinate, too, too much, too far, in excess of

    เกินกำลัง beyond one's strength

    เกินขนาด oversized, over-, too big, outsize; excessive; formidable

    เกินขอบเขต to go beyond the scope of one's authority; to go too far

    เกินความจริง exaggerated, overstated

    เกินคาด unexpected, more than one expects, beyond expectations

    เกินต้องการ beyond one's needs, more than enough

    เกินตัว beyond one's /ability/station/means/

เกินไป too much, too far, excessive; ridiculous

เกินเลย to behave improperly

เกินสมควร inappropriate, unseemly, improper

เกินอำนาจ beyond one's powers

เกินเอื้อม beyond reach

เกีย, เกียร์ gear

    เกียร์กระปุก floor gearshift

    เกียร์ต่ำ low gear

    เกียร์มือ manual gearshift

    เกียร์ว่าง in neutral, disengaged

    เกียร์สูง high gear

    เข้าเกียร์ to put in gear, go into gear; to engage the gears

    เปลี่ยนเกียร์ to shift gears

เกียกกาย[1] commissary of the army

เกียกกาย[2] to make a big effort (to), work hard (to)

เกี่ยง to argue (over), disagree (with), differ

    เกี่ยงงอน cross, petulant

    เกี่ยงราคา to haggle (over the price), bargain, dicker

เกียจคร้าน indolent, lazy, slothful

เกียดกัน to put obstacles in the way, keep someone from doing something, obstruct, thwart, frustrate

    ถูกเกียดกัน to be kept from doing something, obstructed, thwarted

เกียรติ, เกียรติ์ honor, distinction

    เกียรติคุณ good reputation, esteem; honor, merit, excellence

        ใบประกาศเกียรติคุณ certificate of /honor/ merit/excellence/, commendation, diploma

    เกียรตินิยม honorary; with honors, honors

    เกียรติประวัติ distinction

    เกียรติภูมิ prestige

    เกียรติยศ honors; honor, prestige; prestigious

ด้วยเกียรติยศ upon my honor

เกียรติศักดิ์ dignity, prestige, honor, reputation; distinction

ด้วยเกียรติของลูกผู้ชาย on my honor as a man

เพื่อเป็นเกียรติ in honor of

มีเกียรติ prestigious, honorable, respectable, distinguished, creditable

แขกผู้มีเกียรติ distinguished guests

ไม่มีเกียรติ common

รู้สึกเป็นเกียรติ I am honored to be (invited, welcomed etc)

เสียเกียรติ undignifed, demeaning

เสื่อมเกียรติ disgraced, in disrepute, degrading

ให้เกียรติ to show respect (for), do someone the honor (of)

ให้เกียรติกันบ้างสิครับ Don't be rude. / Show me some respect.

เกี่ยว[1] to hook, pull with a hook; to catch (on something), snag; to harvest

เกี่ยวก้อย (to go) hand in hand, link pinkies

เกี่ยวขอ to hook

เกี่ยวข้าว to harvest rice; reap the rice

เกี่ยวหญ้า to gather grass with a sickle

เกี่ยว[2] to pertain (to), be connected (with), be related (to), concern, relate (to)

คุณไม่เกี่ยว This doesn't concern you.

เกี่ยวกัน to be interrelated, concern one another

เกี่ยวกับ about, concerning, with respect to, pertaining to

เกี่ยวข้อง in connection with, concerning; concerned, related, connected

ที่เกี่ยวข้อง relevant

เกี่ยวดอง related by marriage

ไม่เกี่ยวดองกัน to have no relation (to), not related (to)

เกี่ยวเนื่อง pertaining to, relating to, connected (with)

เกี่ยวพัน to be involved (with)

เกี่ยวโยง to affect, have implications

คาบเกี่ยว overlapping; to extend to, related, pertaining to

ไม่เกี่ยวกัน unrelated, unconnected

เกี้ยว[1] Chinese-style palanquin

เกี้ยว[2] ornament for the head, topknot ornament

เกี้ยว[3] to woo, court, make advances; to go dating

เกี้ยวกันเล่น flirting

เกี้ยวพาราสี to court, make love, woo

เกี้ยวสาว to have a date, go out with a girl; to sweet-talk a girl

เกี๊ยว Chinese dumpling

เกี๊ยวน้ำ wonton soup

เกี๊ยะ wooden clogs

เกื้อ, เกื้อกูล to support, give financial aid; to help, give a hand (to), help out, assist

เกือก shoes, boots

เกือกเต้นรำ dancing shoes, pumps

เกือกแตะ slippers

เกือกนอก imported shoes

เกือกใน locally made shoes

เกือกม้า horseshoe

เกือบ about, almost, nearly, approximately

เกือบจะไม่ hardly, scarcely, almost did not

เกือบจะไปไม่ทันรถไฟ We almost missed the train. / I almost didn't make the train.

เกือบตาย to death

ทำงานเกือบตายได้เงินนิดเดียว I worked myself to death and got practically nothing for it.

เกือบไป to have a close shave, That was a close shave.

แก you, thou; he, him; she, her

แก่[1] to, for, in

แก่ใจ in (one's) heart

แก่[2] old, aged; strong; dark; ripe; too much

แก่กล้า strong; acute, sharp

แก่จัด very ripe

ก
ข
ค
ฆ
ง
จ
ฉ
ช
ซ
ฌ
ญ
ฎ
ฏ
ฐ
ฑ
ฒ
ณ
ด
ต
ถ
ท
ธ
น
บ
ป
ผ
ฝ
พ
ฟ
ภ
ม
ย
ร
ฤ
ฤๅ
ล
ว
ศ
ษ
ส
ห
ฬ
อ
ฮ

แก่ชรา very old, aged

แก่เฒ่า aged

แก่ดีกรี drunk, tipsy

แก่แดด cheeky, to /have/put on/ grown-up airs, be a whipper-snapper

แก่ตัว to get old, grow old

แก่เที่ยว to philander

คนแก่เที่ยว philanderer, roué, rake, womanizer

แก่บ่น to grumble too much, grouch

คนแก่บ่น complainer, grumbler, grouch

แก่ไป too strong, too concentrated; too old ชาแก่ไป ฉันกินไม่ได้ The tea is too strong for me.

แก่พอดี just right

แก่พูด talkative, garrulous

แก่แรด to be an /old bag/old hen/ (sl)

แก่เล่น playful

แก่วัด pretentious

แก่หง่อม very old, hoary, ancient

กาแฟแก่ strong coffee

สีแก่ dark color

แก้ to loosen, untie, undo, unwrap; to amend, change, alter; to revise, correct, better; to take off; to mend, repair; to solve, remedy, cure; to explain away

แก้กระหาย to quench one's thirst

แก้กลุ้ม to relieve boredom, cheer oneself up

แก้กันไป to cancel out

แก้เก้อ to make an excuse

แก้เกี้ยว to talk oneself out of an embarrassment, explain (something) away

แก้ขัด to give temporary relief, (do) in a pinch

แก้เขิน to relieve one's discomfort (by)

แก้ไข to make improvements, improve, repair; amend, revise

แก้ไข้ to reduce fever, cure an illness

ยาแก้ไข้ febrifuge, medicine for the relief of fever

แก้คดี to answer a case, put in a defense

แก้แค้น to get even (with someone), fix (someone for doing something), /take/get/ revenge, avenge มันฆ่าพ่อฉัน ฉันจะต้องแก้ แค้น I must avenge the death of my father.

แก้เงี่ยน to get sexual relief, let off (sexual) steam; to satisfy one's need

แก้เชือก to untie

แก้เซ็ง to do something for want of something better to do

แก้ตัว to make excuses, find an excuse; to redeem /oneself/one's losses/, make up for one's /losses/failure/

แก้ต่าง to represent a person in court; to speak for someone; to make excuses for someone else

แก้ต่างแทนจำเลย to represent the defendant

แก้บน to make a votive offering

แก้ปัญหา to solve a problem, find a solution, get over a difficulty (by)

แก้ผ้า to undress, disrobe, strip, take off one's clothes; naked, nude, in the nude

แก้เผ็ด to get even, get back at someone, retaliate

แก้ฝัน to interpret a dream

แก้มือ to have another go (at something), make up for (one's losses, defeat etc), have a return match

ผมขอแก้มืออีกสักครั้ง Let me have another go at it.

แก้เมื่อย to relax, for relaxation

นวดแก้เมื่อย a relaxing massage

แก้ไม่ตก insoluble

แก้รำคาญ to get rid of an annoyance

เด็กคนนั้นตื๊อขายลอตเตอรี่อยู่เรื่อย ฉันเลยซื้อ ทีเดียว 20 ใบ แก้รำคาญ The lottery kid *pestered me so much I bought 20 tickets just to get rid of him.*

แก้ลำ to retaliate, get back at someone

แก้หน้า to save face

แก้หิว to satisfy one's appetite, take the edge off one's appetite

แก้อรรถ to do an exegesis

แกง curry

แกงได to make a sign in place of a signature; a cross, mark

แกโซลีน gasoline, gas *(US)*, petrol *(Brit)*

แก่ง rapids; obstacle

ล่องแก่ง to shoot the rapids, do white-water /rafting/boating/

แก่งแย่ง to compete with no holds barred, vie for; to fight over something, pull and tug at something

แกน axis; pivot; shaft; spindle; center; hard inside part

แกนกลาง core

แกนโท minor axis (axes)

แกนนำ leader, leadership core, leading element

แกนนำพรรคฝ่ายค้าน the opposition party leadership

แกนเอก major axis (axes)

ทำแกนๆ to do something without one's heart being in it, half-heartedly, unwillingly

เป็นแกน containing abnormal hard areas, having granulation

ยิ้มแกนๆ to give a forced smile, force a smile

แก่น[1] core, heartwood; heart, essence, principles

แก่นเรื่อง theme

แก่นสาร, เป็นแก่นสาร meaningful, substantial; meaning, substance

ทำอะไรไม่เป็นแก่นสาร to act foolishly

พูดไม่เป็นแก่นสาร to babble, talk nonsense, prattle

ไร้แก่นสาร meaningless, without substance, inane

แก่น[2] mischievous; plucky

แก่นแก้ว full of mischief, naughty, mischievous

แก๊ป cap

แก๊ปปืน percussion cap

ปืนแก๊ป cap gun *(ของเล่น)*, musket

แกม mixed, blended (with)

โง่แกมหยิ่ง fatuous

ฉลาดแกมโกง crafty, sly

แก้ม cheek

แก้มตุ่ย puffed out cheek, bulging cheek

ยิ้มแก้มตุ่ย broad smile

แก้มยาง sidewall (of a tire)

แกรก scratching sound

แกร่ง hard, hardened, solid, tough, strong

แกร็น underdeveloped, dwarfed, stunted

แกร่ว to be stuck, have to hang around

เธอว่าจะมาก่อนเที่ยง บ่ายสามโมงแล้วยังไม่โผล่ ปล่อยให้เรามาแกร่วอยู่ตั้งสามชั่วโมง She said she'd be here before 12. /I've been stuck/ I've had to hang around/ here for three hours waiting for her.

แกล้ง to pretend to; to tease, pull one's leg; to do something just to annoy someone, make trouble for someone, give someone a hard time; to do on purpose, deliberately, intentionally; to do out of spite; to be provoking

ผมไม่ได้ทำผิดเลย เขาแกล้งใส่ร้ายผม I didn't do anything. He deliberately /told those stories about me/maligned me/.

แกล้งทำ to pretend to do

แกล้งทำเป็นโกรธ to feign anger, pretend to be angry

แกล้งทำเป็นดีใจ to feign delight, pretend to

be glad

แกลบ chaff, husk

   ม้าแกลบ pony

แกล้ม snacks, appetizers, hors d'oeuvres, side dishes

   มีอะไรแกล้มเหล้าบ้าง What have you got to go with the drinks?

แกลลอน gallon

   เป็นแกลลอน by the gallon

แกล้วกล้า brave, courageous, bold, audacious daring

แกละ tufts of hair left on a shaven head

แกว a Vietnamese; a tribe living in northeastern Thailand related to the Annamites and Chinese

แก้ว crystal; glass; precious, fine

   แก้วชิงดวง name of a decorative design

   แก้วตา lens of the eye; darling

   แก้วน้ำ water glass, tumbler

   แก้วผลึก milky quartz, rock crystal

   แก้วมรกต emerald

   แก้วสารพัดนึก magic crystal ball, wishing glass

   แก้วหิน quartz

   แก้วหู eardrum

   แก้วเหล้า liquor glass, whisky glass

   น้ำแก้วหนึ่ง a glass of water

แกว่ง to swing; to brandish

   แกว่งแขน to swing the arms

   แกว่งดาบ to brandish a sword

   แกว่งเท้าหาเสี้ยน to look for trouble

แก๊ส gas

   แก๊สน้ำตา tear gas

แกะ[1] sheep

   แกะดำ black sheep

   แกะตัวผู้ ram

   แกะตัวเมีย ewe (ออกเสียงว่า ยู)

   ขนแกะ wool, fleece

   คนเลี้ยงแกะ shepherd (ผู้ชาย), shepherdess

(ผู้หญิง)

   ทุ่งเลี้ยงแกะ sheep-run

   เนื้อแกะ mutton

   เนื้อลูกแกะ lamb

   ลูกแกะ lamb

   สุนัขไล่แกะ sheepdog

   หนังแกะ sheepskin

แกะ[2] to carve; to pry open delicately, separate

   แกะรอย to trace, follow clues

   แกะสลัก to carve; to engrave

   แกะสะเก็ด to pick off a scab

   เรื่องมันแล้วไปแล้ว อย่ามาแกะสะเก็ดให้เจ็บใจ อีกเลย It's over and done with. Why /pick at/open/ old wounds?

   ช่างแกะ carver, woodcarver, metal engraver; sculptor

   แกะออก to undo, open

โก้ smart, stylish; grand, rich; to look fine

   โก้เก๋, โก้หรูหร่าน see **โก้**

   โก้จริง! How grand!, How smart!, Very /snazzy/spiffy/!, You look like a million dollars!

   แต่งเล่นโก้ๆ dressing up for the fun of it

   เล่นโก้ๆ just for fun, for the hell of it

โก๋ Chinese flatcake

โกโก้ cocoa

โกง[1] to cheat, deceive, swindle; to trick

   โกงกิน to enrich oneself illegally, be a crook

   ขี้โกง a cheat, swindler, chiseler, crook, trickster; tricky, cheating

   คิดโกง disloyal, untrustworthy, crooked; to scheme, scheming

   ฉ้อโกง to defraud, cheat

   เล่นโกง to play dirty, to foul

โกง[2] bent, crooked

   หลังโกง humpbacked, hunchbacked, stooped over

     คนหลังโกง a hunchback

โก่ง to bend, flex, curve, arch; to raise; bent,

curved, arched

โก่งคอ to arch the neck

โก่งเป็นคันศร arched

โก่งราคา to /raise/put up/jack up/inflate/ the price, take advantage

โก่งศร to /draw/bend/ a bow

โก้งเก้ง spindly; rickety

โก้งโค้ง see **ก้งโค้ง** หน้า 1

โกณ as in **ตรีโกณมิติ** trigonometry

โกดัง warehouse, godown

โกดังศพ mortuary

โกดังสินค้า warehouse, godown

รถโกดัง truck (US), lorry (Brit)

โกทัณฑ์, เกาทัณฑ์ bow

โกน to shave

โกนผม to shave the head

โกนหนวด to shave

เครื่องโกนหนวด safety razor

เครื่องโกนหนวดไฟฟ้า electric razor

ใบมีดโกน razor blade

มีดโกน straight razor

วันโกน tonsure day for Buddhist monks

โกโนเรีย gonorrhea

โกมล[1] delicate, fine

โกมล[2] lotus

โกมุท red water lily

โกเมน garnet

โกเมศ lotus

โกย to scoop up, pile up

โกยแน่บ to flee

กอบโกย to pile up, amass, take everything one can lay one's hands on

โกรก[1] to rinse; to pour out, pour water over something

โกรก[2] continuously, steadily

ลมโกรก to blow gently, breezy; a breeze, draught

ไหลโกรก to gush

โกร่ง mortar

โกร่งกร่าง a hollow sound

โกรธ, โกรธา to be angry (with), get angry, mad (at), furious (with)

เธอโกรธฉันทำไม Why are you mad at me?

โกรธขึ้ง to be annoyed (with someone or at something), angry (with)

โกรธจนตัวสั่น to be in a rage, shake with anger

โกรธเป็นฟืนเป็นไฟ to throw a fit

ความโกรธ anger, ire

โกร๋น scanty, sparse, thinly scattered; bald, bare

หัวโกร๋น to have /thin/thinning/ hair, have little hair left, be balding

โกโรโกรก emaciated, anemic, wasted; rickety, run-down

โกโรโกโส dilapidated, shaky, ramshakle, falling into ruin, falling to pieces, decrepit

โกลน[1] stirrup

โกลน[2] to rough-hew (wood)

โกลน[3] to sketch

โกลาหล chaotic, turbulent; tumult, commotion, uproar

เหตุโกลาหล pandemonium

โกวิท scholar, expert

โกศ, โกษ[1] mortuary urn, funeral urn

โกศ, โกษ[2] treasury

โกศ, โกษ[3] sheath, scabbard

โกศล wise, clever, intelligent

โกสินทร์, โกสีย์ Indra

โกสุม flower

โกไสย silk

โกหก to lie, tell a /lie/tale/falsehood/, prevaricate

โกหกพกลม to be full of hot air

ขี้โกหก liar

ใกล้ near, close, nearby

ใกล้เข้ามา to near, approach, come /nearer/ closer/

ใกล้เคียง neighbouring, adjacent; approximate, close

ใกล้จะถึง approaching

ใกล้ชิด close, intimate

ใกล้ชิดกัน close to each other, intimate

ใกล้มือ at hand

สิบเบี้ยใกล้มือ A bird in the hand is worth two in the bush.

ใกล้สำเร็จแล้ว nearly complete, almost ready

ไก key

ไกปืน trigger

ลั่นไก to pull the trigger

เหนี่ยวไก to squeeze the trigger

ไก่ chicken, fowl; chick, broad *(sl)*

ไก่ขัน to crow

ไก่งวง turkey

ไก่เจี๊ยบ chick

ไก่แจ้ bantam; a dandy *(fig)*

ไก่ชน fighting-cock

ไก่ต่อ decoy

ไก่ต๊อก guinea fowl

ไก่ตอน capon

ไก่ตัวผู้ cock

ไก่ตัวเมีย hen

ไก่เถื่อน wild fowl

ไก่ทอด fried chicken

ไก่นา gullible *(fig)*

ไก่บ้าน domestic chicken

ไก่ป่า jungle fowl

ไก่ฟ้า pheasant

ไก่ย่าง grilled chicken

ไก่รองบ่อน a pinch-hitter *(fig)*

ไก่หลง streetwalker, hooker; chicken, easy chick

ไก่อบ roast chicken

ไก่อู a kind of game-cock

จับไก่ to pick up a girl

ปล่อยไก่ to make a faux pas, blunder, make a boo-boo *(sl)*, pull a boner

ลักไก่ to sneak something in, sneak a goal, slip /in/by/

ไก๋ to feign ignorance, pretend not to know, look innocent, play dumb

ไก๊ด์ guide

ไกรพ water lily

ไกรลาส, ไกลาส[1] Mount Kailasa, the name of Shiva's mountain abode.

ไกรลาส, ไกลาส[2] silver, silvery

ไกรศร, ไกรสิทธิ์ lion, king of the beasts

ไกรศรี a prosperous and successful person

ไกล distant, far, remote; long

ไกลกัน far from each other, widely separated

ไกลโขอยู่ very far away, a long way off

ไกลตา out of sight

ไกลบ้าน far from home

ไกลปืนเที่ยง remote, lawless

ไกลลิบลับ at the other end of the world *(fig)*

ไกลแสนไกล so far away, very distant

ไกลหูไกลตา out of sight; unsupervised

ตะวันออกไกล Far East

ทางไกล long way, long distance

โทรศัพท์ทางไกล *see* โทรศัพท์ทางไกล หน้า 228

มองการณ์ไกล farsighted, sagacious; to have foresight

ระยะไกล long distance

ไกล่เกลี่ย to mediate, reconcile, arbitrate, bring (the parties etc) together

ไกว to swing (ชิงช้า); to rock (เปล); to brandish (ดาบ)

ไกวัล[1] completely; all, every; in every respect

ไกวัล[2] paradise

ขงจื๊อ Confucius

ขจร to spread, be wafted

ขจรขจาย known far and wide, renowned

ขจัด to eliminate, remove, get rid of, dispose of

ขจาย see **กระจาย** หน้า 6

ขจิต decorated, embellished, adorned (with)

ขจี verdant

ขณะ moment, time

ขณะที่ while, at the /time/moment/instant/ จงรีบสร้างเนื้อสร้างตัวเสียขณะที่ยังหนุ่มแน่น *Make your way while still young and able.*

ขด coiled, curled up

ขดลวด coil of wire, wire coil

นอนขด to lie curled up

ขดาน see **กระดาน** หน้า 7

ขน[1] hair; feather

ขนแกะ fleece, wool

ขนไก่ chicken feathers

ไม้ขนไก่ feather duster

ขนคิ้ว eyebrow

ขนดก hairy, hirsute

ขนตา eyelash

ขนนก feather

ขนเพชร indestructible hair of Hanuman; pubic hair; special hairs

ขนลุก hair-raising, to make one's hair stand on end

ฉันเห็นแล้วขนลุก *The sight made my hair stand on end.*

ขนลุกขนพอง horrifying

ขนสัตว์ fur, bristles, hair of an animal

ขนหน้าแข้งไม่ร่วง It doesn't mean a thing to him., (to pay) without batting an eyelash, It is just a drop in the bucket (to him).

ขนหนู (ผ้า) Turkish towel, terry cloth

ขนหมู pig bristle

ขนหยอง scared

ขนอ่อน down

ขนอุย down

หญ้าขน Mauritius grass

ขน[2] to carry, transport

ขนของ to move (household goods etc); take things (out of, into, up, away, out), carry (packages, boxes, things etc)

พนักงานขนของ porter

ขนขึ้น to load, charge (a vessel)

ขนถ่าย to transfer

ขนลง unload, discharge (a cargo or vessel)

ขนส่ง to transport, carry

การขนส่ง transportation, carriage, cartage

ขัน thick, concentrated; viscid, sticky

ขันแค้น penniless, impoverished

ขนง eyebrows

ขนด coils of a snake

ขนดหาง base of a snake's tail

ขนบธรรมเนียม custom, tradition, usage, /customary/traditional/ ways

ขนม dessert, sweets, confectionery; candy; cakes; puddings; food not eaten with rice

ขนมเค้ก cake

ขนมจีน Thai vermicelli

ขนมปัง bread

ขนมปังปอนด์ a loaf of bread

ขนมปังปิ้ง toast

ขนมหม้อแกง custard

ขนอง back

ขนัด plot, parcel of farmland

ขนาด size; extent; how

ขนาดกลาง medium size

ขนาดจิ๋ว miniature

ขนาดเล็ก small size

ขนาดหนัก really

ขนาดใหญ่ big, large, large size

ขนาดไหน What size?, to what extent

เกินขนาด over-, oversized, too big, outsize; excessive; formidable

ถึงขนาด to the extreme, so far, to such an

ข ค ฆ ง จ ฉ ช ซ ฌ ญ ฎ ฏ ฐ ฑ ฒ ณ ด ต ถ ท ธ น บ ป ผ ฝ พ ฟ ภ ม ย ร ฤ ฤๅ ล ว ศ ษ ส ห ฬ อ ฮ

extent that, very, super

    ไม่ถึงขนาด undersized; not very; inadequate

    ไม่ได้ขนาด undersized, too small

ขนาน[1] group, kind, mixture

    ยาสองขนาน two kinds of medicine

ขนาน[2] to name, call; to give someone the name of

    ขนานนาม to give a name

        ได้รับขนานนาม given the name ..., named

ขนาน[3] parallel

    ขนานกัน to parallel each other, be parallel, run parallel to each other

    ขนานน้ำ a double boat landing

    เส้นขนาน latitude, parallel; parallel line

ขนาบ *see* **กระหนาบ** *หน้า 11*

ขนำ hut, shelter

ขนิษฐ์, ขนิษฐา younger sister

ขนุน jackfruit

ขบ to crack with the teeth, to bite; not fit together, overlap

    ขบเขี้ยวเคี้ยวฟัน to grind the teeth; to gnash the teeth, rage

    ขบคิด to wrestle with a problem, think over, ponder, think hard about something

    ขบฟัน to gnash the teeth, grind the teeth

    ขบสะเก็ด scabbed

ขบขัน funny, laughable

ขบเผาะ pubescent, nubile

    สาวขบเผาะ a nymphet

ขบถ *see* **กบฏ** *หน้า 3*

ขบวน train, procession

    ขบวนการ movement

    ขบวนรถไฟ train

    ขบวนแห่ procession

ขม bitter

    ขมขื่น to /feel/be/ bitter (about something), embittered

ข่ม to press down; to cow, browbeat, get the better of someone, put (someone) down; to

be one up on

ข่มขวัญ to frighten, intimidate

ข่มขี่ to oppress, tyrannize

ข่มขืน to rape, violate

    ข่มขืนใจ to compel, coerce

ข่มขู่ to threaten, put under duress, intimidate

ข่มเขาโคขืนให้กินหญ้า to put the screws to a person

ข่มความรู้สึก to suppress one's /feelings/ emotions/

ข่มใจ to control oneself, calm down, /repress/restrain/ oneself

ข่มท้อง to bear down on the abdomen to aid the giving of birth

ข่มเหง to bully, browbeat; to mistreat, abuse, persecute

    ข่มเหงคะเนงร้าย to be persecuted, oppressed

ตัดไม้ข่มนาม to cow, intimidate

ขมวด to knot, twist, curl

    ขมวดคิ้ว to frown, knit the brow

    ขมวดปม to tie up (a case etc)

    ขมวดผม to /do/put/ up the hair

ขมอง skull, head

ขม่อม *see* **กระหม่อม**[1] *หน้า 11*

ขมัง one who hunts by bow and arrow; powerful

ขมับ temple

    ปวดขมับ a headache

ขมา pardon, forgiveness

    ขอขมา to ask for forgiveness, apologize

        คำขอขมา apology

ขม้ำ to devour

ขมิ้น turmeric

ขมิบ to constrict, contract, make contractions, work, pulsate

ขมีขมัน enthusiastically, energetically; hurriedly, speedily

ขมิ่งทึ่ง *see* **ถมิ่งทึ่ง** *หน้า 209*

ขมุ tribe living in northern Thailand of Cambodian origin, Khamu

ขมุกขมัว overcast, dark

ขมุบขมิบ to /move /work/ one's lips silently

ขโมย robber, thief; to rob, steal

    ขโมยของเล็กๆ น้อยๆ to pilfer

ขย่ม to push up and down with one's whole weight

    เดินขย่มธรณี to bounce heavily along, have a heavy bouncing gait

ขยอก worm which feeds on rice plants; to gulp, swallow with difficulty

ขย้อน to retch; sickening, disgusting

ขยะ garbage, litter, refuse, rubbish, trash, swill; junk

    ถังขยะ garbage pail, litter bin

    รถขนขยะ garbage truck

    อาหารขยะ junk food

ขยะแขยง to be disgusted (by), feel disgust (for), to abominate, loathe

    น่าขยะแขยง disgusting, loathsome, repulsive, repugnant

ขยัก to save, leave the rest; to hold back, reserve for oneself, pocket

ขยักขย่อน to do in fits and starts, intermittently

ขยักขย่อน to feel queasy, nauseous; sickening

ขยัน hardworking, conscientious, industrious, diligent, persevering, sedulous; to work hard at something, energetic; to apply oneself

    ขยันเรียนหนังสือ to study hard, apply oneself to one's studies

ขยับ to move, move over, move /slightly/a little/, shift, change position, edge

    ขยับกรับ to play /castanets/claves/

    ขยับขยาย to enlarge, improve, expand; to move on to better oneself

    ขยับเขยื้อน to budge, stir, move
    มันไม่ขยับเขยื้อนเลย It doesn't budge.

ขยับเข้ามา to edge closer, move up to

ขยับตัว to /shift/change/ one's position

ขยับปีก to /flap/beat/ the wings

ขยับไปหน่อย to move over a bit

ขยาด to be afraid, fearful, in fear of, apprehensive

    ชักขยาด not dare to do something

ขยาย to enlarge, expand, extend, get bigger; to dilate (ของกลม); to divulge

    ขยายกิจการ to expand the /work/business/

    ขยายขนาด to magnify, enlarge (the size)

    ขยายเขต to extend the boundary

    ขยายเข็มขัด to loosen the belt

    ขยายความ to enlarge upon, spell out, elucidate

    ขยายความลับ to /divulge/reveal/ a secret

    ขยายตัว to expand, get bigger, enlarge

    ขยายแถว to spread ranks

    ขยายในทิศทางใหม่ to branch out

    ขยายบ้าน to enlarge a house

    ขยายใบเรือ to unfurl a sail

    ขยายรูป to enlarge a picture

    ขยายส่วน to enlarge, scale up

    ขยายเสียง to amplify

    ขยายห้อง to make a room bigger, enlarge a room

ขยำ, ขยำขยี้ to knead, squeeze; to crush, crumple up

ขย้ำ to bite

ขยิบ to blink

    ขยิบตา to wink (at); to blink

    ปากว่าตาขยิบ to dissemble

ขยิ่ม *see* **กระหยิ่ม** *หน้า 11*

ขยี้ to scrub, rub; to squeeze; to crush

    ขยี้ตา to rub one's eye

    ขยี้ผม to rub the hair

    ขยี้หัวใจ to break another's heart

ขยุกขยิก to be fidgety, restless; to fidget, squirm, wriggle

ข
ค
ฅ
ฆ
ง
จ
ฉ
ช
ซ
ฌ
ญ
ฎ
ฏ
ฐ
ฑ
ฒ
ณ
ด
ต
ถ
ท
ธ
น
บ
ป
ผ
ฝ
พ
ฟ
ภ
ม
ย
ร
ฤ
ฤๅ
ล
ว
ศ
ษ
ส
ห
ฬ
อ
ฮ

ลายมือขยุกขยิก /squiggly/unsteady/ hand-writing, scribbling; to scribble

ขยุกขยุย messy, in a mess, disorderly

ขยุบ quiver

ขยุบขยิบ to itch; itching to (say something)

ขยุ้ม to pick up with all five fingers

ขยุ้มตีนหมา a skin disease characterized by small bumps

ขยุ้มมือ amount able to be held by the five fingers, a handful

ขรม noisy, loud

เสียงขรม noisy, loud, clamor, hullabaloo, din

ขรรค์ double-edged knife

ขริว rich, wealthy; elder Buddhist monk; elderly person, old man

ขริวยาย grandmother of a prince or princess

ขริบ to trim; to cut the nails; to circumcise

การขริบ circumcision

ขรึม reserved; solemn, grave; grim

เคร่งขรึม serious, grave, solemn, sedate

ขรุขระ rough, uneven, bumpy, not smooth

ขลัง having supernatural powers, magic; sacred

ของขลัง amulet, talisman, charm; sacred objects; incantations (คำ)

พระขลัง a sacred Buddha image

ขลับ shiny, glossy, lustrous

ดำขลับ glossy black, jet black

ขลาด cowardly, pusillanimous, fainthearted, afraid

ขี้ขลาด cowardly; craven; timid, timorous, afraid of everything

ขลิบ to border, trim (with)

ขลุก busy (with), absorbed (in)

ขลุกขลัก to rattle, clatter; difficult, hard; not smoothly, roughly

ขลุกขลุ่ย absorbed in, occupied (with), busy

with; comfortably; cosily

ขลุ่ย flute

ขวด bottle, flask

ขวดยาขนาดเล็ก vial

ขวดโหล glass jar

ข่วน to scratch, scrape

ขวนขวาย to exert oneself, be energetic (in the pursuit of something), try hard

ขวบ year

เด็กอายุ 3 ขวบ a three year old child / a child three years old / a child three years of age

ขวย embarrassed, disconcerted, bashful, shy, sheepish, nervous

ขวยเขิน see ขวย

ขวยใจ to feel ashamed

แก้ขวย to /relieve/hide/ one's /nervousness/embarrassment/

ขวักไขว่ helter-skelter, to and fro, back and forth, milling around; busy

ขวัญ[1] hair that grows in a curl on the top of the head, cowlick

ขวัญ[2] /guardian/tutelary/ spirit; spirit, morale

ขวัญแขวน to be terrified

ขวัญใจ darling, sweetheart; favorite, beloved

ขวัญดี good spirits, good morale

ขวัญตา a beauty, something nice to /behold/look at/

ขวัญบิน see ขวัญหนี

ขวัญเสีย, เสียขวัญ low morale, disheartened, unnerved; to take fright, be frightened

After the attack, the platoon's morale was low. / The platoon was /disheartened/ scared/unnerved/.

ลงมาลูก แม่ขวัญเสียหมด Get down from the window, honey. You give me a fright.

ขวัญหนี to lose heart, lose self-confidence, have a sinking feeling; scared stiff, to quail

ขวัญหนีดีฝ่อ terrified, aghast

ขวัญหาย to be startled; frightened, scared

ขวัญอ่อน fearful, nervous; timorous, easily scared

ของขวัญ gift, present

ขู่ขวัญ to intimidate, cow, create fear

ไข่ขวัญ ceremonial boiled egg

ค่าทำขวัญ compensation, indemnity, amends

ทำขวัญ[1] to make amends, compensate, indemnify (for)

ทำขวัญ[2] see รับขวัญ

บำรุงขวัญ to boost morale, give encouragement, hearten

รับขวัญ to celebrate a recovery, return or survival; a ceremony to restore the spirits; to welcome back; to kiss

ขวัญข้าว[1] gratuity for a doctor

ขวัญข้าว[2] rice spirit

ทำขวัญข้าว to hold a rice celebration

ขวับ swish; quickly, fast, in a flash

หันขวับ to turn abruptly, a quick turn (of the head etc)

ขวา right, on the right

ขวาจัด rightist, reactionary

ขวาตกขอบ right extremist

ขวาหัน right face

ข้างขวา right-hand side, right side

ชกขวา to give a right (to the jaw)

ชิดขวา keep to the right

ถนัดขวา right-handed

มือขวา right hand; right-hand man

ระวังขวา Watch to the right!, Watch your right!

เลี้ยวขวา to turn to the right, turn right

ขวากหนาม barrier of spikes; obstacle

ขวาง to bar, obstruct, impede, block, thwart, get in the way, hinder

ขวางๆ รีๆ to be in the way

ขวางทาง to /bar/block/ the way

ขวางนัยน์ตา to dislike, irritating (to see)

ขวางโลก perverse, rebellious

คนขวางโลก a non-conformist, person at odds with society, a /contrary/perverse/ person

ขวางหน้า to bar the way; to block the view

ขวางหู not want to hear something, irritating (to hear)

ชอบพูดขวางหูเสียเรื่อย What he says is always so irritating.

ขวางหูขวางตา displeasing, irritating

กีดขวาง to obstruct, impede, block, bar, be a barrier

ขว้าง to throw, hurl, fling, cast, pitch

ขว้างปา to /hurl/throw/(something at something or somebody), pelt (someone with something)

ทิ้งขว้าง to be irresponsible, refuse to accept responsibility; to cast aside, throw away, abandon, dump, reject

ขวาน ax, axe, hatchet

ขวานผ่าซาก bluntly, outspoken, brutally frank, to make no bones about (something)

ขวานฟ้า a stone-age ax believed to have fallen from a thunderbolt

ขวิด to gore; to bat with the horns

ขอ[1], ตะขอ hook; gaff (ตะขอใช้ยกปลาขึ้นเรือ)

ขอเกี่ยว hook

ขอช้าง elephant goad

ขอ[2] to ask (for), request; to let one; please, may

ขอกาแฟแก้ว Let me have a coffee. / A cup of coffee please.

ขอเข้าห้องน้ำก่อน May I use the bathroom first.

ขอขมา to apologize, ask for forgiveness

ขอความกรุณา please

ขอความช่วยเหลือ to ask for /help/assistance/

ขอความเป็นธรรม to ask for justice

ขอความเห็นชอบ to ask for approval

ของ้อ to try to make up

ของานทำ to ask for a job

ขอเชิญ to request the pleasure of one's company at; to invite *You are invited to....*

ขอเดชะ by Your Majesty's leave

ขอตัว to excuse oneself, beg off

ขอทาง Excuse me, please., May I get /by/ through/.

ขอทาน to beg, ask for alms; beggar, mendicant

ขอที Please! (in the sense of stop), Do you have to? (sense of exasperation)

ขอโทษ to apologize, beg (another's) pardon, say one is sorry, excuse me.

    ขอโทษขอโพย to apologize profusely

ขอประทานกราบเรียน I should like to say (that), (แต่เวลากล่าวรายงานผู้ใหญ่ ไม่ต้องแปล มักขึ้นต้นด้วย title เช่น "Mr. President,....")

ขอไปที half-heartedly, for the sake of form, perfunctory

ขอผมก่อน Let me go first.

ขอผมพูดหน่อย Let me /speak/say/ something/.

ขอเฝ้า to ask for an audience, to ask to see (someone of high rank)

ขอยืม to borrow

ขอร้อง to request, ask; to implore, please! *ลูก ทำการบ้านเสียทีซิ แม่ขอร้อง Please do your homework. I'm asking you.*

ขอรับ yes, sir, yes ma'am

ขอแรง to ask for assistance, ask someone to lend a hand *ขอแรงหน่อยเถิด Please lend me a hand.*

    ทนายขอแรง court-appointed attorney, free legal counsel

ขอแสดงความนับถือ formal closing of a letter equivalent to "Very truly yours," "Yours truly," "Sincerely yours," *or* "Yours faithfully," *(Brit)*

ขออนุญาต to ask for permission *ขออนุญาตครับคุณครู Teacher, may I leave the room, please?*

ขออนุมัติ to ask for /approval/authorization/

ขออภัย to apologize, beg one's pardon, ask for pardon, ask forgiveness

ขอโหลิ to ask for forgiveness

แบบขอไปที slipshod; halfheartedly, indifferently

เหลือขอ incorrigible, impossible, beyond help

ข้อ[1] joint

ข้องอ elbow joint, pipe elbow

ข้อต่อ joint

ข้อเท้า ankle

ข้อนิ้ว finger joint, knuckle

ข้อมือ wrist

ข้อศอก elbow

ข้อ[2] clause, article, section, provision; point, item; question

ข้อติกา rule

ข้อกล่าวหา charge, accusation

ข้อแก้ตัว excuse, defence, justification

ข้อขัดข้อง problems, difficulties; certain objections

ข้อเขียน a writing

    สอบข้อเขียน to take a written examination

ข้อครหา a reproach, disparaging statement

ข้อความ text, wording, passage, statement *จดหมายฉบับนั้นมีข้อความว่า.... The letter reads....*

ข้อคิด thought, idea, point, something to think about, message

ข้อซักถาม questions, queries, interrogations

ข้อตกลง agreement, understanding, points of agreement

ข้อต่อรอง bargaining point, condition

มีข้อต่อรองว่า on condition that

ข้อติชม comments, commentary, criticism

ข้อโต้แย้ง argument against; objection, point in opposition, opposing view; disagreement, dispute

ข้อเท็จจริง fact

ข้อแนะนำ advice, suggestion

ข้อบกพร่อง defect, error, mistake, fault, (what is) wrong; weakness, flaw, short-coming

ข้อบังคับ regulation, bylaws, rules; obligation

ข้อปฏิบัติ instructions, rules, directions, practice, routine

ข้อผิดพลาด error

ข้อผูกพัน obligations, responsibilities, bonds

ข้อพิสูจน์ proof, evidence

ข้อมูล data, facts, information

ข้อแม้ proviso, condition

　โดยไม่มีข้อแม้ unconditional

ข้อยกเว้น exception

ข้อเรียกร้อง demand, claim, request

ข้อสงสัย question, doubt, doubts, suspicion

โดยไม่มีข้อสงสัย undoubtedly, without doubt, certainly, unquestionably

ข้อสอบ examination, exam, test, quiz, examination /questions/problems/

　ข้อสอบจับคู่ pairing exam

　ข้อสอบแบบปรนัย objective test, multiple choice exam

　ข้อสอบแบบอัตนัย essay /test/exam/

　ข้อสอบเลือกตอบ multiple choice exam

ข้อสังเกต comment, observation, remarks

ข้อสัญญา /term/clause/paragraph/(of an agreement)

ข้อเสนอ proposal, proposition, offer

ข้อเสีย defect, drawback

ข้อหา charge, accusation, allegation

ข้อใหญ่ใจความ the main point

ข้ออ้าง pretext, excuse; justification

ข้ออ้างอิง reference, citation

งัดข้อ to have a test of strength, arm-wrestle; to be at loggerheads

หัวข้อ subject, topic; heading, caption; item

ขอก boundary

ของ[1] things, stuff, possessions, article

ของกลาง a thing used in the commission of a crime and seized by the authorities

ของกำนัล present, gift

ของกิน edibles, something to eat

ของเก่า secondhand things; antiques;

ของขวัญ present, gift

ของแข็ง see **ของแข็ง** หน้า 69

ของคาว main course, main dishes, /meat/ fish/ dish

ของเค็ม salted food

ของเคียง a side dish

ของใครของมัน to each his own

ของโจร stolen goods

ของชำ groceries

　ร้านของชำ grocery store

ของชำร่วย gift, present, keepsake, memento, souvenir

ของใช้ articles, things, belongings; effects; equipment, utensils

ของใช้ส่วนตัว personal effects

ของดี of good quality; thing which has supernatural power; surprise; private parts อย่าอวดเก่งนัก ระวังจะเจอของดี *If you keep on like that, you'll be in for a surprise.*

ของดี ๆ nice things

ของตัวอย่าง sample

ของเถื่อน contraband, /smuggled/illegal/ goods

ของแถม a giveaway, premium, gift, an extra

ของแท้ genuine, real นาฬิกานี้ ของแท้หรือเปล่า *Is this watch genuine? / Is this watch the real thing?*

ข　ค　ฆ　ง　จ　ฉ　ช　ซ　ฌ　ญ　ฎ　ฏ　ฐ　ฑ　ฒ　ณ　ด　ต　ถ　ท　ธ　น　บ　ป　ผ　ฝ　พ　ฟ　ภ　ม　ย　ร　ฤ　ฦ　ล　ว　ศ　ษ　ส　ห　ฬ　อ　ฮ

ของเทียม artificial, synthetic

ของนอก something foreign, import, imported

ของประกัน collateral

ของปลอม counterfeit, fake, spurious article

ของปลอมราคาถูกกว่าของแท้ The counterfeits are cheaper than the genuine articles. / The spurious articles are cheaper than the genuine ones.

ของฝาก present, gift

ของมีค่า valuables

ของร้อน stolen article, hot goods *(sl)*

ของรักของหวง prized possession

ของลดราคา sale, goods on sale

ของลับ pudenda, private parts

ของเล่น toy, plaything

ของว่าง snack

ของสงวน bosom (not to be touched)

ของเสีย something /gone bad/spoiled/; bodily wastes; waste; rubbish

ของหนีภาษี contraband, smuggled goods

ของหลวง state property, public property

ของหวาน dessert, sweets, pudding *(Brit)*

ของเหลว liquid, fluid

ของแห้ง dried food

ขายของ to sell

ข้าวของ things, belongings, possessions

ซื้อของ to shop (for something), go shopping, buy things

สิ่งของ things

ห่อของ to wrap, pack

ของ[2] of, belonging to

ของเขา his; her, hers, their, theirs

ของใคร whose

ของฉัน my, mine

ของตัวเอง his own, their own

ของท่าน your own, of you

ของเรา our

ข้อง[1] vase-shaped basket-work creel

ข้อง[2] to be involved (in, with), connected (with, to), related (to), concerned (with); to get stuck

ข้องเกี่ยว to be concerned with, to be connected with, to have to do with

ข้องขัด difficulty, objection

ข้องใจ to doubt, suspect, be bothered (by something)

ข้องใจหรือเปล่า Do you have something on your mind? / What's bothering you?

ข้องแวะ to have something to do with

ไม่อยากจะข้องแวะ I don't want to have anything to do with (him, it, etc)

ขอด[1] to knot, knotted

ขอดผ้า to knot a piece of cloth

ขอด[2] running low, a little left at the bottom

ขอดคลอง The canal is /running low/almost dried up/

ขอดหม้อ The pot has a little left at the bottom., There is a little left to be scraped from the bottom of the pot.

ข้าวขอดหม้อ remainder of the rice at the bottom of the pot, not much rice left

ขอด[3] to scale, scrape

ขอดเกล็ด to scale a fish

ขอน[1], **ขอนไม้** log

ขอนดอก fragrant decomposed wood containing fungi used medicinally

ขอนสัก teak log

ขอน[2] a numerical qualifier for conch shells and bracelets

ข้อน to beat, strike, pound

ขอบ margin, edge, rim, periphery

ขอบข่าย parameters, scope (of), range

ขอบเขต boundary, limits, confines

ในขอบเขต (to keep) within bounds

ขอบตา edge of the eyelid

ขอบถนน curb, kerb *(Brit)*

ขอบบ่อ rim of the well

ขอบฟ้า horizon, edge of the sky

ขอบสระ edge of the pond

ขอบคุณ to thank (a person for something), to be /thankful/grateful/ (for)

ขอบคุณครับ Thank you /sir/ma'am/.

ขอบใจ to thank (a person for something), Thanks., Thank you.

ขอบใจมาก Thank you very much., Thanks a lot.

ขอม Khmer

ข่อย a shrub the bark of which is used to make paper

กระดาษข่อย handmade paper

ข้อย I, me

ขะมักเขม้น energetically, vigorously, enthusiastically, with determination, assiduously

ขะมุกขะมอม all dirty, dirty, soiled, to look a mess

ขัง to confine, imprison, cage, lock up, pen, shut up

ขังกรง to cage

ขังคอก to pen (หมู), to put into an enclosure

ขังคุก to imprison, jail, put in jail

กรงขัง cage; detention cell, prison cell

น้ำขัง stagnant water

ผู้ต้องขัง detainee, a person in confinement

ห้องขัง prison cell, detention cell, jail

ขัณฑ- part, section, piece

ขัณฑสกร saccharine

ขัณฑสีมา boundary, border, frontier

เป็นขัณฑ์ pieced together, of pieces

ขัด[1] to interrupt, obstruct, be contrary, go against, be at variance (with), at odds with; to attach, fasten

ขัดกระดุม to button, fasten a button

ขัดกระบี่ to /gird/attach/ a sword

ขัดกัน to be in conflict (with), at variance (with), not get along (with)

ขัดขวาง to hinder, impede, preclude (someone) from (doing something), frustrate, confound; to oppose, thwart

ขัดข้อง to object, dissent; not work properly, in difficulty, out of repair, out of order; to come up, inconvenient *ทำไม่ได้มีอะไรขัดข้อง I couldn't do it. Something came up.*

ไม่ขัดข้อง no objection, no problem

ขัดขืน to disobey; to resist

ขัดเขิน bashful, timid

ขัดแข้งขัดขา to undermine, trip someone up

ขัดคอ to contradict; to hinder (a person from doing something), cross, oppose, object

ขัดคำสั่ง to disobey an order

ขัดเคือง, โกรธเคือง to be angered

ขัดจังหวะ to interrupt, cut in (at a dance), break in upon someone

ขัดใจ to frustrate, cross; to be contrary, be disagreeable; frustrated; annoyed, dissatisfied

ขัดดอก to send a wife or child to work off interest

ขัดตา unsightly, ugly; not be able to bear the sight (of)

ขัดตาทัพ to send troops to gain time against an enemy; to stand in for (someone else); act as a seatwarmer (for)

ขัดตำนาน to give an introductory chant

ขัดแตะ interwoven strips of /wood/bamboo/ etc

ขัดบท to interrupt

ขัดเบา to have trouble urinating

ขัดยอก to feel creaky, stiff, muscular pain

การขัดยอก soreness, stiffness

ขัดแย้ง to be in disagreement, have differences, be in conflict (with), have conflicting interests, be at odds; to be contradictory, inconsistent

ข ค ฅ ง จ ฉ ช ซ ฌ ญ ฎ ฏ ฐ ฑ ฒ ณ ด ต ถ ท ธ น บ ป ผ ฝ พ ฟ ภ ม ย ร ฤ ฤๅ ล ว ศ ษ ส ห ฬ อ ฮ

ขัดศรัทธา to dampen another's good intentions

ขัดสน to be in want, needy, be in need (of), hard-pressed (for)

ขัดสมาธิ to sit cross-legged

ขัดหู jarring, to sound disagreeable, irritating

ไม่ขัดกับ in /accordance/line/ with, not against

ขัด[2] to polish, rub

ขัดเกลา to polish, finish, refine, improve (deportment)

ขัดเงา to give a glossy finish to something, burnish (ใช้สำหรับโลหะ), shine, polish; polished, glossy, shiny, burnished

ขัดถู to scrub, polish, rub

ขัดมัน to polish, wax; polished, waxed

ขัดรองเท้า to /polish/shine/ shoes

ขัดสีฉวีวรรณ to give oneself a beauty treatment

ขัตติย- king, monarch, sovereign

ขัตติยมานะ royal honor

ขัน[1] to tighten, screw tight

ขันก๊อก to turn the faucet off

ขันแข็ง as in อย่างขันแข็ง energetically, assiduously, enthusiastically

ขันชะเนาะ to twist (wire or rattan) tight by means of a lever

ขันสู้ plucky

ขันอาสา to volunteer

ขัน[2] dipping bowl

ขันโตก Northern style tray table for eating while sitting on the floor

ขันโตกดินเนอร์ Northern country style dinner

ขันลงหิน bronze bowl

ขันล้างหน้า bowl for washing the face

ขันหมาก traditional tray of gifts from the groom to the bride's family

ลงขัน to contribute, take up a collection

ขัน[3] funny, amusing

ขบขัน humorous

ความขบขัน humor

น่าขัน funny, comical; ridiculous, laughable

ขัน[4] to crow, coo

ขันจ้อ to keep on /crowing/cooing/

ขั้น stage, grade, step; rank, level

ขั้นกลาง intermediate stage, the middle

ขั้นต้น initial stage, the beginning

ขั้นตอน procedures, regular stages

ตามขั้นตอน following the procedures, step by step, in regular stages

ขั้นทดลอง in the experimental stage

ขั้นบันได step, stair

ขั้นปลาย /final/terminal/ stage, the end

ขั้นอันตราย critical stage, dangerous stage

เป็นขั้นๆ step by step, in stages

ขันติ forbearance, patience; tolerance, broadmindedness, willingness to listen

ขันที eunuch

ขันธ์ group, collection, aggregate; division

ดับขันธ์ to die

เบญจขันธ์ the five aggregates

ขับ[1] to drive away, expel, disperse, chase away

ขับขี่ to drive; ride (a bicycle, motorcycle)

ใบขับขี่ driver's license

ผู้ขับขี่ driver

ขับเคี่ยว to devote oneself (to), exert oneself to the utmost

ขับเคลื่อน powered (by), driven (by)

ขับเคลื่อนล้อหน้า front wheel drive

ขับรถ to drive

ขับไล่ to evict

ขับออกไป to excrete, expel

ขับ[2] to sing; recite, chant

ขับกล่อม to lull, sing soothing songs

ขับขาน to chant

ขับไม้ musical performance of three persons,

one singing, one playing a Thai fiddle and one beating rhythm

ขับเพลง to sing

ขับร้อง to sing

ขับร้องโดย Sung by....., Songs by.....

ขับเสภา to sing a long narrative of a particular style

ขัย end, expiration; life-span

อายุขัย life-span

ขั้ว pole; (battery) post, joint, connecting point; stem

ขั้วบวก anode

ขั้วไฟฟ้า electrode; electric socket

ขั้วแม่เหล็ก magnetic pole

ขั้วลบ cathode, negative pole

ขั้วโลก pole

ขั้วโลกใต้ South Pole

ขั้วโลกเหนือ North Pole

ต้นขั้ว stub, counterfoil

สุดขั้ว extreme

ขา[1] leg

ขากบ (ขาของว่าวจุฬา) the fishtail of one kind of kite; (ขาของกบ) frog's legs

ขากรรไกร jaw bone

ขาหยั่ง tripod, easel

ขาหยั่งพับได้ folding easel

ขาอ่อน thigh

คู่ขา partner; pal, buddy; lover

หว่างขา crotch, groin

ขา[2] leg, stage, phase

ขากลับ return, return trip, return leg of a voyage, on the way back

ขาขึ้น on the way up, outbound trip; ascent

ขาเข้า on the way in, incoming; imports (สินค้า)

ขาไป on the way, on the way out, when you go; outward leg (of a trip, journey etc)

ขาลง on the way down, when you come down, descent; return leg (of a trip, journey

etc), inward trip

ขาออก departure, outward; export (สินค้า)

ขา[3] guy, one, he, she; player

ขาจร casual customer

ขานั้น that guy, that one

ขานั้นเขาดี a good guy

ขาประจำ regular customer, good customer

ขาไพ่ card player, card partner

ข่า[1] mountain tribe of Cambodian and Mon stock

ข่า[2] wooden tongs used for holding fish over the fire

ข้า servant, slave; I, me

ข้าเก่า old servant

ข้าเก่าเต่าเลี้ยง old and trusted servant

ข้าไท servant

ข้าแผ่นดิน subject

ข้าเฝ้า royal attendants

ข้าพเจ้า I, me

ข้าราชการ government official, civil servant

ข้าราชการฝ่ายปกครอง administrative /official/officer/

ข้าราชการพลเรือน civil servant, civil official

ข้าศึก enemy, foe

ข้าหลวง provincial/ governor/commissioner

ข้าหลวงเดิม one who became a servant of a sovereign or high official before the elevation of his master to the throne

ข้าหลวงใหญ่ high commissioner, Governor-General

นางข้าหลวง lady-in-waiting

ขาก to hawk

ขากน้ำลาย to spit, expectorate, hawk up phlegm

ขาก๊วย Chinese-style shorts

ขาง flyspecks

ข่าง *as in* ลูกข่าง top

ข้าง[1] side

ข้าง²   side, ribs; next to, beside

ข้างๆ beside, alongside, next to

ข้างขวา to the right; right-hand side, right side

ข้างขึ้น period of the waxing moon

ข้างๆ คูๆ obstinately

ข้างเคียง adjoining, adjacent, next door, nearby, neighboring, beside

     คนข้างเคียง spouse

ข้างต้น /in/at/ the beginning, at the start, at the outset

ข้างถนน roadside; street, gutter

     เด็กข้างถนน guttersnipe

     ตายข้างถนน to die in the /gutter/street/

     หมาข้างถนน stray dog

ข้างท้าย toward the stern, abaft, toward the end; below

ข้างนอก out, outside, outdoors

ข้างน้อย minority

ข้างใน inside, indoors

ข้างบน above, on top, upstairs

ข้างมาก majority

ข้างแรม period of the waning moon

ข้างละสาม three to a side, three on each side

ข้างล่าง under, underneath, beneath; downstairs

ข้างหน้า in front (of); ahead

ข้างไหน which side, which way

ข้างหลัง to the rear (of), behind, in back (of)

     คนที่อยู่ข้างหลัง those who /remain/are left behind/, those in the back

เข้าข้าง to side with, take the part of someone, be biased (in favor of someone)

เคียงข้าง side by side, together, next to, beside

รอบข้าง on all sides

สีข้าง ribs, side

อยู่ข้างขี้เกียจ /rather/sort of/ lazy, lazyish

เอาข้างเข้าถู unreasonably argumentative

ขาด   to be torn; to break; to lack, want, be short (of), have a shortage (of), incomplete, deficient (in), to fall short (of); to be missing

ขาดคราว not to be found in the market

ขาดความเชื่อถือ unreliable, untrustworthy; to lose the respect of

     ทำให้ขาดความเชื่อถือ to cause a loss of reputation

ขาดความนับถือ to lose respect

พระที่ไม่สำรวม ทำให้ประชาชนขาดความนับถือ An unrestrained monk soon loses popular respect.

ขาดความมั่นคง to be insecure, lack security; to be unstable, lack stability

ขาดความรัก in need of love, unloved; deprived of /love/affection/

ขาดความรู้ unknowledgeable, ignorant

ขาดความสงบ in a state of unrest, restive, unpeaceful

ขาดความสุข to be unhappy, lack happiness, want happiness

ขาดความสุภาพ impolite

ขาดคอช้าง to be cut down from the back of an elephant

ขาดแคลน needy, in want; a shortage (of), lacking (in)

ขาดเงิน to be short of /money/cash/

ขาดใจ to stop breathing, expire, die, succumb

ขาดตกบกพร่อง shortcomings, deficiency, inadequacy, errors and omissions

ขาดตลาด out of stock

ขาดตัว (ราคาจำกัด) fixed price; final price

ขาดทุน to lose money, take a loss, sustain losses, have a deficit; to lose out, be at a disadvantage

ขาดประชุม to miss a meeting, be absent from a meeting

ขาดไป to be missing; to be short

ขาดผึ่ง to snap

ขาดพี่ขาดน้อง to sever one's family connections, disown one's brothers and sisters

ขาดเพื่อน to be friendless

ขาดมือ to be short (of), not have on hand

ขาดเรียน to be absent from /class/school/, to cut a class

ขาดลอย overwhelmingly, decisively

    ชนะขาดลอย overwhelming victory

ขาดเลือด to be anemic

ขาดวิ่น to be in tatters, tattered

ขาดเสียมิได้ indispensable, vital, essential, not be able to do without

ขาดเหลือ anything lacking, a shortage

คำขาด ultimatum, final word

    ยื่นคำขาด to give an ultimatum, serve notice (on someone)

เฉียบขาด decisive, rigorous, strict

ชี้ขาด to decide, make a final /decision/ determination/

    คำชี้ขาด an award, determination, judgment

เป็นอันขาด definitely, absolutely, (not /go/do/ etc/) under any circumstances

ผูกขาด to monopolize, corner the market

มิได้ขาด regularly, continually

โรคขาดอาหาร malnutrition, undernourishment

ส่วนที่ขาด deficiency

ขาน to answer, reply, respond; to call out

ขานไข to explain; to reply

ขานชื่อ to do a roll call

ขานตอบ to answer

ขานนาค the formal responses of a candidate for ordination

ขานรับ to answer, respond; to agree (with)

โจษขาน to be on everyone's lips, be talked about (/by everyone/everywhere/widely/)

ขาบ dark blue

ขาม to fear

ข้าม to cross over, cross, pass over, skip

ข้ามชั้น to skip a grade

ข้ามถนน to cross the street

ข้ามฟาก to cross (a river, street, etc), cross over to the other side

ข้ามรั้ว to /cross/go over/ a fence

ข้ามหน้า to give offence by bypassing someone; to be overlooked

    ข้ามหน้าข้ามตา to go over someone's head

ข้ามหัว to go over someone's head, go over the head of someone

ตรง (กัน) ข้าม to the contrary, conversely; opposite

    สิ่งตรงกันข้าม the opposite

มองข้าม to overlook

ขาย to sell, vend

ขายขาด to sell unconditionally; to sell as is, sell with no right of refund or exchange

ขายง่าย salable, readily salable; a fast-moving item

ขายเงินผ่อน to sell on the instalment plan, instalment sale

ขายชาติ to be a traitor, commit treason, betray one's country

    คนขายชาติ traitor

ขายเชื่อ to sell on credit

ขายดิบขายดี to sell like hotcakes, sell well

ขายต่อ to resell

ขายตัว to sell oneself, prostitute oneself

ขายตั๋ว to sell tickets

ขายทอดตลาด to auction, put up for auction, auction sale

ขายปลีก to retail, sell retail; to sell separately

ขายฝาก to sell with a right of redemption, make a conditional sale

ขายไม่ออก to be unsalable, hard to move; to be unable to get rid of something

ขายรุสต๊อค to clear out stock at reduced prices, clearance sale

ขายลดราคา a sale, on sale

ขายลดราคา20% Sale 20% off.

เสื้อตัวนี้เขาขายลดราคา I bought the shirt on sale.

ขายลดราคาครั้งใหญ่ big sale

ขายเลหลัง to auction

ขายส่ง to wholesale, sell wholesale

    ราคาขายส่ง wholesale price

ขายสด to sell for cash; cash sale

ขายสิทธิ์ to sell one's right

ขายเสียง to sell one's vote

ขายหน้า shameful, disgraceful, ashamed

    ทำให้ขายหน้า to be disgraced, disgrace someone

ขายเหมา to sell in a single lot, sell the lot

ค้าขาย (to be in) trade, commerce, business

ซื้อขาย buying and selling, trade

ผู้ขาย seller, vendor

ฝากขาย to sell on consignment, consign; consignment sale

เร่ขาย to peddle, hawk

ข่าย limit

    ขอบข่าย parameters, scope, range, limits; sphere

    เครือข่าย network

    ตาข่าย mesh, net

ขาล tiger

    ปีขาล the Year of the Tiger

ขาว white; bright; light; pure, clear, clean

    ขาวจั๊วะ dead white, pure white

    ขาวซีด pale

    ขาวนวล off-white, soft white, ivory

    ขาวโพลน all white

    ขาวสะอาด clean

    เขาชนะอย่างขาวสะอาด It was a clean victory for him.

    ตาขาว white of the eye; cowardly, pusillanimous

    ทองขาว nickel; platinum; distributor, contact points

    ปูนขาว lime; white cement

ข่าว news, report, story

    ข่าวกรอง intelligence

    ข่าวกระแสต่างๆ news from various sources, news in general

    ข่าวการเมือง political news

    ข่าวกีฬา sports news

    ข่าวคราว news

    ข่าวโคมลอย rumor, unfounded news, unsubstantiated report

    ข่าวโฆษณา advertisement

    ข่าวด่วน a newsflash

        ข่าวด่วนพิเศษ stoppress news

    ข่าวดี good news

    ข่าวต่างประเทศ foreign news

    ข่าวที่ว่า the /news/report/ that....

    ข่าวนำ lead story

    ข่าวในประเทศ local news, domestic news

    ข่าวบันเทิง entertainment news

    ข่าวพาณิชย์ commercial news

    ข่าวพาดหัว /headline/banner/ news, banner-headline news

    ข่าวพิเศษ special news

    ข่าวภาพ pictorial news, illustrated news

    ข่าวมรณกรรม obituaries

    ข่าวย่อย short news

    ข่าวร้าย bad news

    ข่าวล่า late news

        ข่าวล่าที่สุด latest news

    ข่าวลือ rumor

    ข่าววงใน inside /news/information/

    ข่าวสงคราม war news

    ข่าวสด fresh news

    ข่าวสาร news, information

ข่าวใหญ่ big news

ข่าวอกุศล vicious rumor; discreditable report

ข่าวอาชญากรรม crime news

ได้ข่าว (ว่า) It has been reported that..., to hear, get wind of, get news (of)

แถลงข่าว press release, communique; to report the news

นักวิเคราะห์ข่าว news analyst

นักวิจารณ์ข่าว news commentator

ผู้ส่งข่าว press officer, information officer

ผู้สื่อข่าว reporter, newspaperman

ภาพข่าว news /picture/photo/photograph/

รายงานข่าว a news report

ลงข่าว to publish, print

สรุปข่าว news summary

เสนอข่าว to present news

หัวข่าว headline

ข้าว rice; grain

ข้าวก้นบาตร the leftovers

ข้าวกล้อง brown rice, unpolished rice

ข้าวกล้า rice shoots ready for transplanting, rice seedlings

ข้าวเกรียบ rice crisps, crispy rice flatcake

ข้าวแกง rice and curry, Thai food

ข้าวของ things, possessions

ข้าวเจ้า rice

ข้าวซอย rice noodles in curry soup

ข้าวต้ม soft-boiled rice, rice porridge, rice gruel, congee

ข้าวต้มผัด, ข้าวต้มมัด glutinous rice wrapped in leaves and steamed

ข้าวตอก popped rice

ข้าวตัง crust of rice sticking to the bottom of a rice pan

ข้าวตาก dried cooked rice

ข้าวทิพย์ rice candy made ceremonially once a year

ข้าวนก wild rice

ข้าวนึ่ง parboiled rice; glutinous rice

ข้าวบิณฑ์ a rice offering wrapped in banana leaves

ข้าวเบา early rice

ข้าวเบือ pounded rice for addition to curries

ข้าวประดับดิน spirit offering of rice

ข้าวปลาอาหาร food, provisions

ข้าวปลูก paddy reserved for planting, seed rice

ข้าวเปลือก paddy, unmilled rice

ข้าวผัด fried rice

ข้าวแฝ coffee

ข้าวโพด maize, corn (US)

ข้าวฟาง millet; sorghum

ข้าวมัน rice cooked in coconut cream

ข้าวมันไก่ coconut cream rice with chicken

ข้าวเม่า unripe rice kernels roasted and pounded flat for eating; whole bananas deep fried in a coconut batter

ข้าวยากหมากแพง hard times

ข้าวยาคู a drink made of water extracted from unripe rice boiled with sugar

ข้าวเย็น supper, evening meal

ข้าวละมาน darnel, a kind of weed growing together with rice

ข้าวสวย boiled rice

ข้าวสาร rice

ข้าวสาลี wheat

ข้าวสุก cooked rice

ข้าวหนัก slow-growing rice, late rice

ข้าวหมาก sweet fermented glutinous rice

ข้าวหลาม glutinous rice roasted in a bamboo-joint

ข้าวเหนียว glutinous rice, sticky rice

ข้าวเหนียวแก้ว glutinous rice cooked with coconut cream and sugar

ข้าวเหนียวแดง brown glutinous rice cooked

ข ค ฆ ง จ ฉ ช ซ ฌ ญ ฎ ฏ ฐ ฑ ฒ ณ ด ต ถ ท ธ น บ ป ผ ฝ พ ฟ ภ ม ย ร ฤ ฦ ล ว ศ ษ ส ห ฬ อ ฮ

with coconut cream and palm sugar

กับข้าว food (to be eaten with rice), dishes

กินข้าว to eat, have /breakfast/lunch/dinner/ a meal/

ปลายข้าว broken rice

รวงข้าว ear of rice

หิวข้าว to be hungry

หุงข้าว to cook /food/breakfast/lunch/ supper/dinner/ etc; to cook rice

ข้าศึก enemy, foe

ขำ[1] handsome, /dark/dusky/ complexioned

คมขำ attractive; dark and handsome

งามขำ comely, dark and attractive

นางงามขำ a /dusky/handsome/ beauty

ขำ[2] amusing, humorous, funny

ขำขัน amusing, humorous

ขำจริงๆ very funny

คำขำ something witty

นึกขำในใจ to /recall/think of/ something with amusement

ขิง ginger

ขิงดอง pickled ginger

ขิงแห้ง dried ginger

ถึงพริกถึงขิง ferociously

ยุ่งขิง confused, mixed up, in confusion, in a state

ขิม Chinese dulcimer

ขี่ to mount, straddle; ride, drive

ขี่จักรยาน to ride a bicycle

ขี่หลังเสือ to ride /a/the/ tiger

กดขี่, ข่มขี่ to oppress, persecute

ขับขี่ to drive

ขี้[1] excrement (ของคนและสัตว์), feces (ของคน), manure, dung (ของสัตว์), droppings (ของนกและสัตว์) ; waste, discharge; to go to the toilet, have a bowel movement, defecate, shit (คำหยาบ)

ขี้กบ wood shavings

ขี้กลาก ringworm

ขี้เขม่า soot, lampblack

ขี้ครั่ง sticklac

ขี้โคลน mud, mire, muck

ขี้ไคล scurf, crud, dead skin

ขี้ตะกอน dregs, residue; sediment

ขี้เต่า underarm odor

ขี้เถ้า ashes, cinders

ขี้ปลาวาฟ plankton bloom, red tide

ขี้ปะติ๋ว trivial, trifling, piddling, insignificant, measly

ขี้เปียก smegma, cheese (sl)

ขี้ผง dust; rubbish; trash, nothing, trivial

ขี้ผึ้ง wax, beeswax; ointment, unguent, salve, pomade

ขี้มูก nasal mucus, snot (คำหยาบ)

ขี้มูก (ฉัน) ไหล My nose is running.

สั่งขี้มูก to blow one's nose

ขี้รังแค dandruff

ขี้ริ้ว not good-looking, homely, unattractive

ขี้ริ้วขี้เหร่ ugly

ผ้าขี้ริ้ว rag; tripe

ขี้เรื้อน mangy; leprous

ขี้เรื้อนกวาง itching skin disease of the foot

ขี้เล็บ dirt under the nails

เรื่องขี้เล็บ trivial, petty

ขี้เลื่อย sawdust

หัวขี้เลื่อย a blockhead

ขี้วัว cow manure, cow dung

ขี้สนิม rust; corrosive deposit

ขี้หดตดหาย scared shitless

ขี้หนู small capsicum, tiny fiery chili

ขี้หมูขี้หมา so simple

อย่างขี้หมูขี้หมา at the very least

ขี้หู earwax, cerumen

ขี้เหนียว stingy, tight, tight-fisted, niggardly

ขี้เหร่ ugly, unattractive, not good-looking, homely

ขี้[2] a combining word indicating natural bent, given to

ขี้เก๊ก affected; (คน) a poseur

ขี้เกรงใจ diffident, self-effacing

ขี้เกียจ lazy; not feel like doing something *ฉันขี้เกียจไป* I don't feel like going. / I feel too lazy to go.

ขี้โกง see **โกง**[1] หน้า 42

ขี้โกหก liar

ขี้ขลาด cowardly, craven; timid, timorous, afraid of everything

ขี้ขอ to sponge on someone

ขี้ข้า slave

ขี้คุก jailbird

ขี้ใจน้อย touchy, peevish

ขี้เซา a heavy sleeper

ขี้ตระหนี่ mean, miserly

ขี้ตืด miserly, stingy, a piker, niggardly

ขี้ตื่น excitable

ขี้ตู่ see **ตู่** หน้า 201

ขี้ทูด leprosy

ขี้เท่อ blundering, asinine; a fool, buffoon, jerk

    ขายขี้เท่อ to make a fool of oneself

ขี้บ่น given to complaining, always grumbling, fussy, irritable

ขี้ปด fibber; given to prevaricating

ขี้เมา drunkard, a drunk

ขี้โมโห short-tempered, irritable, truculent

ขี้ยา druggie, junkie, on drugs เช่น *ท่าทางเหมือนคนขี้ยา* He looks like he's on drugs.

ขี้แย whining

ขี้รำคาญ irritable

ขี้โรค unhealthy, sickly, ailing

ขี้ลืม forgetful, absentminded

ขี้เล่น playful, fun-loving; frisky; fond of joking

ขี้สงสัย suspicious, sceptical, doubting

ขี้สงสาร tenderhearted, compassionate, easily moved, to feel sorry for others; over-sympathetic

ขี้หลงขี้ลืม forgetful, absentminded

ขี้หึง jealous, possessive

ขี้เห่อ fad-mad, fashion-happy; to go for whatever is in vogue

ขี้อ้อน crybaby, given to crying

ขี้อาย bashful, shy, easily embarrassed

ขี้อิจฉา envious

ขี้โอ่ a show-off, braggart; boastful, boasting, bragging

ขีด to draw lines; to scratch; to write; a scratch; line; stroke, mark

ขีดขั้น to limit, to restrict, confine

ขีดเขียน to write

ขีดคร่อม to cross (a check)

ขีดคั่น to delimit, demarcate, draw the line

    ไม่มีขีดคั่น unlimited, no limit

ขีดฆ่า to delete, scratch out, cross out, strike out, cancel

ขีดไม้ขีดไฟ to strike a match

ขีดเส้นตาย to set a deadline

ขีดเส้นใต้ to underline, underscore

ขีดออก to cross out, strike out

ไม้ขีด match

รอยขีด scratch

ขีปนาวุธ guided missile

ขึง to make tight; to stretch, stretch out; put up, string

ขึงกั้น to curtain off

ขึงขัง serious; intimidating; robust

ขึงจอ to /put up/erect/ a movie-screen

ขึงตา to stare angrily, scowl

ขึงตาข่าย to put up a net

ขึงพืด to be spread-eagled on the ground

ขึงไม้ตีแบดฯ to string a badminton racket

ขึงสายโทรเลข to string a telegraph wire

ที่ขึง stretcher

ขึ้ง to be irritated, vexed, angry

ข ค ฆ ง จ ฉ ช ซ ฌ ญ ฏ ฏ ฐ ฑ ฒ ณ ด ต ถ ท ธ น บ ป ผ ฝ พ ฟ ภ ม ย ร ฤ ฦ ล ว ศ ษ ส ห ฬ อ ฮ

ขึ้น to go up, ascend, rise, mount; to get taller, grow; to have an erection (ใช้กับอวัยวะเพศ); to begin; combining word meaning to go, get, put, become, establish, -er; to hold in esteem, be popular; to depend on, be dependent (on); to be affiliated with

ขึ้นครู to experience for the first time, get one's first lesson (in sex, etc), make one's debut; to perform a ceremony to honor a teacher

ขึ้นคาน to become an old maid; to have no suitors

ขึ้นเงา to shine, take on a shine

ขึ้นเงิน to cash (a check), draw money

ขึ้นใจ to remember, learn by heart, commit to memory; to distinctly remember

ขึ้นชื่อ famous, noted, well known, renowned

ขึ้นเช็ค to cash a /check/cheque/

ขึ้นต้น to begin, commence, start (with, by, at)

   ขึ้นต้นใหม่ to begin again, recommence, start over again

ขึ้นต้นไม้ to climb a tree

ขึ้นทะเบียน to register, enroll, be registered

ขึ้นแท่น to put to bed (term used in printing)

ขึ้นบรรทัดใหม่ to begin a new line

ขึ้นบัญชี to enter in an account, charge, record, list; listed

ผมไม่มีจ่าย ขึ้นบัญชีไว้ก่อนก็แล้วกัน I'm short today, just charge it to my account.

   ขึ้นบัญชีดำ to blacklist

ขึ้นบันได to climb a ladder, mount the stairs, to go up the stairs, go upstairs

ขึ้นบ้านใหม่ to have a housewarming

ขึ้นปีใหม่ in the new year; to begin the New Year

ขึ้นมึงขึ้นกู to be nasty

ขึ้นรถไฟ to /board/get on/ a train

ขึ้นระวาง to be registered and assigned to a particular function

ขึ้นรา moldy

ขึ้นราคา to go up in price, increase the price

ขึ้นเรือน to go up into a house

ขึ้นโรงขึ้นศาล to go to court

ขึ้นเสียง to raise one's voice

ขึ้นหน้าขึ้นตา popular, well known; outstanding

ขึ้นหม้อ[1] famous, celebrated, noted; lucky; to be a favorite, favored

ขึ้นหม้อ[2] to be fluffy, fill the pot well

ขึ้นอยู่กับ to depend on; subject to

ข้างขึ้น period of the waxing moon

คนขึ้น popular, to have a big following *พระหมอดูองค์นั้นคนขึ้นมาก That monk who tells fortunes has a big following.*

ดีขึ้น better, to improve; to board, get on, mount, climb

ท้องขึ้น to have indigestion; flatulent

น้ำขึ้น The tide is /rising/coming in/; high tide, flood tide

พระจันทร์ขึ้น The moon is rising.

เพิ่มขึ้น to increase, grow

ยกมือขึ้น to raise the hand; "Hands up!"

ยืนขึ้น to stand up

ลุกขึ้น to get up, rise

มือขึ้น successful, to have success; adroit

เมืองขึ้น dependency, colony

ขืน to resist, oppose; to disobey; to compel, force; to persist

ขืนตัว to stiffen oneself

ขืนเรือ to steady a boat

ขืนสู้ to persist in /opposing/fighting/etc/

ขื่น[1] to taste very bitter

ขื่น[2] dismal, gloomy, depressed

ขื่นขม bitter

ขมขื่น bitter; hard to bear; embittered

ขืนใจ to force, constrain, compel, oblige; to force oneself (to)

อย่าขืนใจลูกซิ เขาไม่อยากไปก็ช่างเขาเถอะ
Don't force the kid, let him be.

ขืนใจทำ to do something against one's will, feel /constrained/forced/obliged/ compelled/ to do something

ขืนทำ to insist on doing something

ขื่อ[1] beam

ขื่อขวาง, ขื่อคัด collar beam

ขื่อคา tie-beam

ขื่อแป laws

ขื่อจมูก septum

ขื่อ[2] cangue

ขุก abrupt, sudden, immediate

ขุกเข็ญ catastrophe, sudden calamity

ขุกคิด to get an idea, have a sudden thought, be struck by an idea

ขุด to dig, excavate; grub, spade

ขุดค้น to make a dig, dig for something

ขุดคลอง to /dig/excavate/ a canal

ขุดคุ้ย to dig up, dig out, dig into

ขุดดินกินหญ้า to eke a living out of the land

ขุดทอง to dig for gold, find a fortune

คนไทยไปขุดทองที่ซาอุดีอาระเบียเป็นจำนวนมาก
A lot of Thai people go to Saudi Arabia to find their fortune. / Thai people have made a fortune out of Saudi Arabia.

ขุดบ่อ to dig a well

ขุดพบ to dig up, unearth; make a find by /digging/excavating/

ขุดเรือ to make a boat by hollowing out a log, make a dug-out

ขุดศพ to exhume, disinter

ขุดสนามเพลาะ to dig trenches

ขุดหลุม to dig a hole

ขุน ruler; leader; lowest civil title; king (in chess); to feed; large, great

ขุนเขา big mountain

ขุนคลัง minister of finance, lord of the treasury, treasurer

ขุนนาง, ขุนน้ำขุนนาง nobility, a member of the nobility, nobleman in government service; an official

ขุนพล /military/army/ commander, general

ขุนศึก military chief, warlord, general

ขุนหลวง archaic word for king

ลูกขุน jury

ขุ่น cloudy, murky, turbid; in a bad mood

ขุ่นข้องหมองใจ in a bad /mood/temper/; on bad terms (with)

ขุ่นคลั่ก muddy

ขุ่นเคือง irritated, displeased, annoyed

ขุ่นแค้น to resent, feel offended (by), take offense (at)

ขุ่นใจ moody, depressed, gloomy; vexed

ขุ่นมัว overcast, murky; in a /dark/bad/ mood, gloomy; frustrated

พูดเสียงขุ่น to snap (at)

ขุม pit, hole; source

ขุมขน pore

ขุมทรัพย์ buried treasure, treasure trove, goldmine (*fig*), source of wealth; natural resources

ขุมนรก abyss, hell

ย่างสามขุม to charge at someone

ขุย fine bits of earth piled up by ants or crickets

ขุยไผ่ tiny fruits of the bamboo which appear when the plant is dying

ขุยอินทรีย์ humus

เป็นขุย flaky

ขู่ to threaten, menace, intimidate; to growl at

ขู่กรรโชก to blackmail, extort

ขู่ขวัญ to intimidate, cow, scare

ขู่เข็ญ to coerce; force, compel

ข ค ฆ ง จ ฉ ช ซ ฌ ญ ฎ ฏ ฐ ฑ ฒ ณ ด ต ถ ท ธ น บ ป ผ ฝ พ ฟ ภ ม ย ร ฤ ฦ ล ว ศ ษ ส ห ฬ อ ฮ

ข่มขู่ to threaten, put under duress, intimidate

ขูด to scrape, scratch, grate

ขูดเค้น to torment (oneself or others)

ขูดรีด to exploit, gouge, squeeze, be rapacious

ขูดเลือด, ขูดเลือดขูดเนื้อ to overcharge, bleed

เข (เฉพาะตา) crossed

ตาเข cross-eyed, having a squint

เขก to /rap/knock/ with the knuckles

เข่ง a round open-work bamboo basket

เข่งปลาทู round bamboo tray for fish

ขนมเข่ง a steamed Chinese New Year confectionery

เข็ญ hardship, trouble

เข็ญใจ poverty-stricken

ก่อกรรมทำเข็ญ to cause trouble, do terrible things, do evil

ยากเข็ญ very hard

เข็ด[1] skein

เข็ด[2] to have learned one's lesson, dare not do something again; chastened

เข็ดขยาด to be afraid of doing something

เข็ดข้อ, เข็ดเขี้ยว, เข็ดลำ to be afraid to face someone again; to have learned one's lesson

เข็ดจนตาย I'll never do it again.

เข็ดฟัน to set one's teeth on edge

เข็ดหลาบ to be afraid to do something again; to have learned one's lesson, be chastened

เอาให้เข็ด to teach someone a lesson (he will never forget)

เขต boundary, border, frontier; limits; region, area, zone, district; field; ricefield, land, acreage

เขตก่อสร้าง construction area

เขตครอบครอง territory held in possession, one's territory

เขตคุ้มครอง protectorate, protected area

เขตแดน border, frontier

เขตเทศบาล municipality, municipal limits

เขตโทษ penalty zone

เขตปลอดทหาร demilitarized zone

เขตปลอดบุหรี่ no smoking zone, non-smoking area

เขตอำนาจ jurisdiction

ขอบเขต limits, confines, extent, boundary

เกินขอบเขต excessive, extreme, inordinate

นอกเขต outside the boundaries (of), outside, beyond the /bounds/area/

ในเขต inside, within the /bounds/area/

หมดเขต the time (for something) expires (on, at), deadline (for), final date

อาณาเขต territory, area

เขน shield worn on the forearm, buckler

เข็น to push, (ผลักไปข้างหน้า); to pull, draw (ลาก); to force

เข็นครกขึ้นภูเขา to be exceedingly difficult

เข็นไม่ขึ้น hopeless; unredeemable

เข็นรถ to push a car

รถเข็น cart, pushcart, trolly, hand cart (ใช้มือเข็น), baby carriage (ให้เด็กนอน), stroller (ให้เด็กนั่ง)

เข่น to beat, strike: to forge; to beat into thin sheets

เข่นเขี้ยว, เข่นเขี้ยวเคี้ยวฟัน to gnash one's teeth, grind one's teeth (in anger)

เข่นฆ่า to slay, murder

เข่นมีด to forge a knife

เขนย pillow

เข็ม needle; pile, piling

เข็มกลัด brooch, pin; safety pin

เข็มขัด belt

หัวเข็มขัด buckle

เข็มควัก crochet needle

เข็มฉีดยา hypodermic needle
เข็มทิศ compass
เข็มนาที minute hand
เข็มนาฬิกา hand (of a /clock/watch/)
เข็มยาว minute hand
เข็มเย็บผ้า needle
เข็มวินาที second hand
เข็มสั้น hour hand
เข็มหมุด pin
เข้าด้ายเข้าเข็ม at the crucial moment
งมเข็มในมหาสมุทร (like) looking for a needle in a haystack
ต้นเข็ม ixora
ตอกเสาเข็ม to put in piling; to drive a pile
ตั้งเข็ม to set one's course, aim (for, to be), direct oneself toward

เข้ม intense, strong; concentrated; dark
เข้มข้น rich, strong, thick; intense; serious, heavy, concentrated; at its height
    รสเข้มข้น sharp taste; flavorful, well seasoned
เข้มแข็ง strong, unyielding; industrious, assiduous
เข้มงวด strict, rigid, rigorous, harsh, austere, severe, stern
สีเข้ม dark color, /strong/intense/saturated/ color

เข็ม่ง to gaze (at), stare (at)
เข็ม่งเกลียว strained
เหตุการณ์เข็ม่งเกลียวเข้าทุกที The situation was becoming more and more strained.

เข็ม็ดแข็ม่ see **กระเหม็ดกระแหม่** หน้า 12

เขม่น to twitch; to find someone /unbearable/ annoying/, dislike, take a dislike to someone
เขม่นตา to have a twitch in the eye
ฉันเขม่นไอ้หมอนั่นจริงๆ That guy is unbearable. / I can't stand him. / He's so annoying.

เขม้น to stare at, gaze at, look closely at, peer at
เขม้นมอง to glare (at)

เขมร Cambodia, Cambodian, Khmer
เขมา a medicinal herb
เขม่า soot, lampblack; carbon (ในเครื่องยนต์)
เขมือบ to gulp; to eat greedily; to pocket
สมุห์บัญชีเขมือบเงินของบริษัทตั้งแสนเลยโดน ไล่ออก The accountant was fired for pocketing a hundred thousand of the company's money.

เขย son-in-law, brother-in-law
น้องเขย younger brother-in-law
น้าเขย, ลุงเขย, อาเขย uncle by marriage
พี่เขย elder brother-in-law
ลูกเขย son-in-law
หลานเขย nephew by marriage

เขยก limping
เขย่ง to tiptoe; to stand on ones toes; to hop
เขย่งก้าวกระโดด hop, skip and jump
เขย่งเก็งกอย a hopping game
เขย้อแขย่ง to strain to get a look (at)
เขย่า to shake
เขย่าขวัญ horrifying, grisly
เขยิน protruding
ฟันเขยิน buck teeth
เขยิบ to move over, move; to improve
เขยื้อน to move, shift, budge
ไม่เขยื้อนเลย It doesn't budge.
เขรอะ encrusted (with)
เขลง comfortably, happily
นอนเขลง to repose, lie peacefully
เขลา stupid, foolish, dull
โง่เขลา stupid, ignorant
เขว to deviate, stray
ไขว้เขว confused
    เข้าใจไขว้เขว to misunderstand, misapprehend
    ผมเข้าใจไขว้เขวมานาน เพิ่งรู้วันนี้เอง I

ข ค ฆ ง จ ฉ ช ซ ฌ ญ ฎ ฏ ฐ ฑ ฒ ณ ด ต ถ ท ธ น บ ป ผ ฝ พ ฟ ภ ม ย ร ฤ ฤๅ ล ว ศ ษ ส ห ฬ อ ฮ

misunderstood for a long time and just found out today.

ทำให้ไขว้เขว to mislead, misleading

เขษม *see* **เกษม** *หน้า 37*

เขฬะ saliva

เขา[1] hill; mountain, mount

เชิงเขา base of a /hill/mountain/, foot of a hill, foothills

ตีนเขา foot of a mountain

ทิวเขา mountain range

เทือกเขา mountain range

ยอดเขา peak, mountain top, summit

หุบเขา valley, vale

เขา[2] horn

เขากวาง antlers

เขากิ่ง antler, prong (of an antler)

เขา[3] he, him; she, her, they, them; I, me

เขาพูดกันว่า It is said that...., There is a saying...., They say....

เขาลือกันว่า It is rumored that...., They say....

ของเขา his, her, hers, their, theirs

เข่า knee

ขึ้นเข่า to knee someone, give a blow with one's knee

นักมวยคนนั้นขึ้นเข่าคู่ต่อสู้ชนะน็อคเอาท์ The boxer kneed a victory knockout.

คุกเข่า to kneel, kneel down

หัวเข่า knee, kneecap

เข้า to enter, go in, penetrate; to mix, blend, mingle, combine; to put in, insert; to form a group; to join, participate; to conform, fit in; to harmonize with; to fit together

เข้ากระดูกดำ deep-seated, deep-rooted, ingrained

เข้ากะ to work a shift

คุณเข้ากะไหน กะกลางคืน What shift do you work? I'm on the night shift.

เข้ากัน to get on well together, go

together, match, get along (with)

เข้ากันได้ congenial, compatible, to get along; to go well together

ความเข้ากันได้ compatibility

เข้ากับ to go with

เข้าเกณฑ์ to be up to standard, conform, fit

เข้าเกียร์ to put in gear, go into gear; to engage the gears

เข้าเกียร์สอง to /go/shift/ into second gear

เข้าใกล้ to approach, go near, get close (to)

เข้าขั้น up to the mark

เข้าขา to become a member of a group, become partners, affiliate (with), join

เข้าข้าง to side with, take sides

เข้าข่าย to meet requirements; qualified, suitable

เข้าแข่งขัน to compete, enter a competition

เข้าคิว to queue up, /get/stand/wait/ in line

เข้าเค้า right, reasonable; to fit, make sense

เข้าเจ้า to perform a ceremony to call a spirit to dwell in the body

เข้าใจ to understand, comprehend, see (what one means)

เข้าใจกันว่า It's understood that...., It is thought that....

เข้าใจผิด to misunderstand, mistake, make a mistake, be mistaken

เข้าใจว่าอย่างไร What do you make of that? / What do you understand by that?

ไม่เข้าใจ I don't understand., I don't get it., I don't see it.

เข้าฉาก to play a scene; to be on stage

เข้าชื่อ to petition, sign a petition

พนักงานเข้าชื่อกันขับไล่ผู้จัดการบริษัท The workers petitioned for the dismissal of the manager.

เข้าด้วย to join in, join with

เข้าด้ายเข้าเข็ม at the crucial moment, at the critical point

เข้าได้ to get in

เข้าได้ต้องมีเส้น You can't get in without /connections/pull/.

เข้าตรีทูต in a coma, comatose

เข้าตา to get into the eyes

ผงเข้าตา I got something in my eye.

> **เข้าตาจน** to be at a dead end, be in a bad fix, be at the end of one's rope; to be checkmated (หมากรุก)

เข้าตำรา typical, typically; not unexpectedly, as is usually the case; according to tradition

เข้าตู้ forgotten

ความรู้ที่เคยเรียนมาเข้าตู้ไปหมดแล้ว I don't remember anything of what I studied. / I've forgotten everything I learned.

เข้าไต้เข้าไฟ at dusk, twilight

เข้าถ้ำ double seam (ชื่อตะเข็บเย็บผ้า)

เข้าถือ to acquire

> **การเข้าถือหลักทรัพย์** acquisition of securities

เข้าทรง to be possessed

เข้าท่า, เข้าที *see* **เข้าท่า** *หน้า 227*

เข้านอกออกใน to have access (to), be on the inside, be an insider, be trusted

เข้านอน to retire, go to bed

เข้าเนื้อ to lose, to take a loss, suffer a loss, be affected (by), get worse off, disadvantaged

พูดให้เข้าเนื้อ He spoke to his disadvantage. ยิ่งพูดยิ่งเข้าเนื้อ The more he says, the worse off he gets.

เข้าแบบ to be /right/correct/

เข้าปก to bind

เข้าประจำที่ to take one's /place/position/

เข้าประเด็น to get to the point

เข้าปิ้ง to be unable to move, be driven into

a tight corner; to go to the slammer *(sl)*

เข้าไป to enter, go into, penetrate

เข้าผี to perform the ceremony of invoking a spirit to dwell in the body

เข้าผู้เข้าคน adaptable, to be able to adapt oneself to any situation; to get along with people, genial

เข้าฝัก to become experienced, master, acquire a mastery of

คนที่มีความรู้เข้าฝักแล้ว ไม่จำเป็นต้องเรียนอีก One who has mastered his subject need study no more.

เข้าฝัน to appear in one's dreams

เข้าเฝ้า to have an audience (with royalty)

เข้าเฝือก to apply a splint, put (one's arm, leg, etc) in a cast

เข้าพกเข้าห่อ to pocket (the money, proceeds, contributions etc)

เข้าพระเข้านาง to be romantic

เข้ามุม to get into a corner

เข้าร่วม to participate (in), take part (in)

เข้ารอบ to /make/be selected for/get into/ (the semi-finals, finals, etc), be a runner-up

เข้ารอย, เข้าร่องเข้ารอย to do what is expected of one, conform; to fall into place, act in the right way, move in the right direction; to behave oneself

> **เข้ารอยเดิม** to repeat itself, be just like before

เข้าร้าย (ตกอยู่ในฐานะไม่ดี) to be in trouble, driven into a corner, on the rocks

เข้ารีต to be converted

เข้ารูป to fit; to take shape

> **เข้ารูปเข้ารอย** to get into shape

เข้าเลือด to lose, suffer a loss, be affected

เข้าโลง to die, kick the bucket *(sl)*

เข้าว่า basically, primarily; prone to

การแก้ปัญหานี้ไม่ใช่ว่าจะใช้กำลังเข้าว่าได้ This

ข
ค
ฆ
ง
จ
ฉ
ช
ซ
ฌ
ญ
ฎ
ฏ
ฐ
ฑ
ฒ
ณ
ด
ต
ถ
ท
ธ
น
บ
ป
ผ
ฝ
พ
ฟ
ภ
ม
ย
ร
ฤ
ฤๅ
ล
ว
ศ
ษ
ส
ห
ฬ
อ
ฮ

problem cannot be solved primarily by force.

เขาเป็นคนใช้ความรุนแรงเข้าว่า He's a person prone to using force. / He's basically a brutal person.

เข้าแว่น to reach an age when spectacles are necessary, be time to wear glasses

เข้าสมาธิ to concentrate (on)

เข้าสุหนัต to be circumcised

เข้าไส้ really, great

มันเข้าไส้ great fun

เข้าหน้า to face, confront; to have a meeting with someone

> **เข้าหน้าไม่สนิท** to be hard to face someone, feel uncomfortable with someone

> **เข้าหน้าหนังสือ** to do page makeup; to paginate, do pagination

เข้าม้อ to forget what one has learned

เข้าหา[1] to go to see; to give oneself up, turn oneself in

เข้าหา[2] to steal into a woman's room to make love

เข้าหา[3] to, towards

เข้าหุ้น to go into partnership (with), team up (with someone)

เข้าหู to have heard, hear

> **เข้าหูซ้ายทะลุหูขวา** in one ear and out the other

> **พูดไม่เข้าหูคน** to be irritating, offensive, harsh

เขิน[1] lacquerware

เขิน[2] shallow, silted up

เขิน[3] embarrassed, self-conscious, to feel uneasy (about)

> **ทำให้เขิน** embarrassing

เขี่ย to brush /aside/away/, get rid of; to scrape off

ไก่เขี่ยดิน The chicken was scratching the

ground (looking for grubs).

เขี่ยขี้เถ้า to brush the ash away

เขี่ยบุหรี่ to flick the ash off a cigarette

> **ที่เขี่ยบุหรี่** ashtray

เขี่ยผง to extract a foreign body (from the eye)

ถูกเขี่ยออกจากตำแหน่ง to be kicked out of /office/one's job/, be /pushed out of/ removed from/ office

เขียง chopping /board/block/, cutting board

เขียงเท้า wooden shoe, clog

เขียงหมู a butcher

ขึ้นเขียง flayed; exposed to heavy criticism

เขียด small frog

เขียน to write; to draw, paint

เขียนจดหมาย to write a letter

เขียนชื่อ to write one's name; to fill in one's name

เขียนเช็ค to write a /check/cheque/

เขียนด้วยมือลบด้วยตีน to be insincere, hypocritical

เขียนตามคำบอก dictation, to take dictation

เขียนถึง to write about

เขียนไทย Thai dictation

เขียนบรรจง to print

เขียนแปลน to draw a plan

> **คนเขียนแปลน** draftsman

เขียนภาพ, เขียนรูป to draw a picture, paint a picture, make a drawing

เขียนหนังสือ to write

ตอนนี้คุณทำอะไร? เขียนหนังสือขายครับ What are you doing now? I am a writer.

เขียนหวัด handwriting, cursive writing

เครื่องเขียน stationery, writing materials

ช่างเขียน artist, painter; draftsman

นักเขียน writer, author

ภาพเขียน drawing, painting

วาดเขียน to draw, paint

เขียม thrifty, frugal, economical

เขียว green; blue

เขียวแก่ dark-green

เขียวไข่กา an old-time indigo-blue bowl

เขียวคราม indigo blue

เขียวสด bright green

เขียวอ่อน light-green

ตาเขียว a black eye; to glare, look /angry/ mad/

เธอมองฉันตาเขียวเชียว She glared at me. / She gave me an angry look. / She looked so mad.

สีเขียว green; blue

เสียงเขียว sharp tone

หน้าเขียว to be pale with anger, be blue in the face (with anger); to look green (in the face)

เหม็นเขียว smelly, rank

เขี้ยว fang, canine tooth, eye tooth

เขี้ยวแก้ว venom-tooth, fang

เขี้ยวตะขาบ double-spiked fastener used to join planks

เขี้ยวลากดิน wily old /rascal/parliamentarian/ etc

เข็ดเขี้ยว to be afraid to face someone again; to have learned one's lesson

เข่นเขี้ยว to gnash one's teeth, grind one's teeth (in anger)

ถอดเขี้ยวถอดงา to reform

มันเขี้ยว to feel like (punching someone in the nose, etc)

ไม่มีเขี้ยวเล็บ toothless, harmless

เขื่อง big, rather big, relatively big

คำเขื่อง big words

คุยเขื่อง big talk, He talks big.

เขื่อน dam, barrage; dike, embankment

แข the moon

แขก[1] guest, caller, visitor; stranger; person living elsewhere who comes to lend a hand

แขกผู้มีเกียรติ guest of honor, distinguished

guest

แขกเมือง official /visitor/guest/ state guest, visitor of state

พนักงานต้อนรับแขก receptionist

รับแขก to receive visitors, entertain guests, have /visitors/guests/

ลงแขก[1] (/neighbors/friends/) pitch in and help, have a (planting, house-building, etc) bee

ลงแขก[2] gang rape, gang bang (sl)

วัยรุ่นสามคนพาหญิงสาวไปลงแขก The girl was taken off and raped by a gang of three teenagers. / Three young guys grabbed the girl for a gang bang.

ห้องรับแขก living room, parlor, sitting-room; reception room

แขก[2] Indians, South Asians, North Africans

แขกขาว light-skinned Indians

แขกดำ dark-skinned Indians

แขกยาม Indian watchman

แขกอาหรับ Arabs

แข็ง hard; stiff, firm; strong; well

แข็งข้อ to defy, be defiant

แข็งขึ้น to harden, stiffen, get harder

แข็งใจ to steel oneself to do something, force oneself (to), do something unwillingly

แข็งตัว to freeze, congeal; to harden, stiffen, get hard

แข็งเมือง to assert independence; to become recalcitrant, defy the authority of the government

แข็งแรง strong, sturdy, robust; firm, solid; durable, lasting

กล้าแข็ง stalwart, strong, powerful, tough

ของแข็ง a solid; a stone wall, insurmountable barrier

พอเจอของแข็งก็ไม่กล้าสอบ The investigation came up against a stone wall and that

was it.

ขาแข็ง stiff legs

    เดินจนขาแข็ง to walk one's legs off

เข้มแข็ง resolute, tough, strong; industrious, assiduous

คอแข็ง a hard drinker; proud

มือแข็ง stiff (hand movements); to be a good hand at; uncourteous, unready to raise one's hands together in sign of respect

ไม่แข็ง not good (at), not well

ฉันว่ายน้ำไม่แข็ง I'm not good at swimming. / I don't swim well.

หัวแข็ง obstinate, stubborn, headstrong, non-conformist

แข่ง to compete, contest, vie (with someone for something); to rival

แข่งขัน to contend with, compete with, contest for, vie with, have a competition

    การแข่งขัน competition, contest, game, match

    แข่งขันฟุตบอล football match

แข่งบุญ to vie for merit

แข่งม้า horse racing, horse race

แข่งเรือ boat race, regatta, boat racing

แข่งวาสนา to compete for fortune

คู่แข่ง competitor, rival, opponent

ม้าแข่ง racehorse

วิ่งแข่ง to race, run a race; foot race, running race

แข้ง shin

แข้งขา legs

ด้วยลำแข้ง by one's own effort, self-made; to stand on one's own two feet

ฉันหากินด้วยลำแข้งของฉัน I earn my own living. / I make my own way.

แขน arm

    แขนขวา right arm; right-hand man *(fig)*

    แขนขา limbs

แขนซ้าย left arm

แขนเสื้อ sleeve

วงแขน shoulder girth; in one's arms; to encircle with one's arms

อ้อมแขน embrace, hug

แขนง twig; branch; sub-division

แขม, แขมร์ Khmer

แขม็บ to breathe faintly; to gasp, pant

แขม่วท้อง to pull in the stomach

แขย็ก ๆ (to climb a tree) with difficulty

แขยง to be disgusted, loathe, abhor, hate, be squeamish (about)

    แขยงแขงขน to feel revolted

แขย่ง with difficulty

แขวง district; sub-district, sub-division; region

แขวน to hang (up), suspend; to be left hanging *(fig)*; to depend on

    แขวนคอตาย to hang oneself

    แขวนนวม to retire from the ring, end (one's) boxing career

แขวะ to chide, taunt, snipe at, gibe (at), twit, be caustic, sarcastic, abusive

โข very

โขก to knock with the head, to head; to rip someone off, sting (someone), overcharge

    โขกสับ to scold, criticize sharply, lace into someone

โข่ง[1] snail

โข่ง[2] big

โขด hill; high land; mound, hillock, knoll

โขน masked /play/drama/

    สวมหัวโขน to play a role

โขนง eyebrow

โขม linen; silk; white cloth; lawn

โขมง[1] billowing

    ควันโขมง *see* **ควันโขมง** *หน้า 82*

โขมง[2] to be noisy

    โขมงโฉงเฉง boisterously, noisily

โขมด ignis fatuus, will-o'-the-wisp

โขยก to limp; to buck along

โขยกเขยก to wobble

โขยง a party (of people), company, band; a group; family; school (ปลา), herd (สัตว์), flock (นก), troop (ลิง), pack (หมาป่า); all, the whole lot

โขลก to pound, crush, pulverize

โขลง herd

    โขลงช้าง a herd of elephants

โขลน woman guardian of the palace

โขลนทวาร an arch made of branches at which two Brahmin priests asperge troops passing under going to battle

ไข[1] to disclose, reveal; to open, unscrew; to wind

    ไขก๊อก to quit (a job)

    ไขกุญแจ to unlock, open a lock

    ไขข่าว to spread the news

    ไขควง screwdriver

        ไขควงสี่แฉก Phillip's head screwdriver

    ไขความ to explain, elucidate

    ไขนาฬิกา to wind a /watch/clock/

    ไขน้ำ to turn on the water

    ไขลาน to get someone moving; to grease someone's palms

    ไขสือ to play dumb

ไข[2] fat

    ไขมัน fat

    ไขสันหลัง spinal cord

    เทียนไข (tallow) candle

    น้ำมันเป็นไข fat, grease

ไข่ egg; spawn (ปลา, กบ), roe (ในปลา), an egg-banana, a small variety of banana; to lay an egg

    ไข่ขาง fly-blow, fly specks

    ไข่ขาว the white of an egg, egg white, albumen

    ไข่คน scrambled egg

    ไข่เค็ม salted egg

ไข่เจียว omelet

ไข่ดก to be a good layer

แม่ไก่ที่เลี้ยงดี มักไข่ดก Well-fed chickens are usually good layers.

ไข่ดัน inguinal gland

ไข่ดาว fried egg, a sunny-side up egg

ไข่แดง yolk

    กินไข่แดง to deflower

    เป็นไข่แดง the odd /man/woman/ (in a group)

ไข่ต้ม hard-boiled egg

ไข่ตุ๋น steamed egg

ไข่ในหิน over-protected, coddled, molly-coddled

เลี้ยงลูกเหมือนไข่ในหิน He over-protects his child.

ลูกเป็นไข่ในหินของพ่อ He is mollycoddled by his father.

ไข่ปอก a peeled egg; alabaster, milky white

ไข่ปลา spawn, roe; caviar

ไข่เป็ด duck egg

ไข่พอก salted egg

ไข่มุก pearl

ไข่ยัดไส้ stuffed omelet

ไข่เยี่ยวม้า a hundred-year-old egg, an egg prepared by soaking in quicklime which turns the albumen green or black

ไข่ลม unfertilized egg, undeveloped egg

ไข่ลวก soft-boiled egg, scalded egg

ไข่ลูกเขย boiled egg fried in a sweet sauce

ไข่หวาน an egg poached in sweetened water

ฟักไข่ to /brood/incubate/hatch/ eggs

รังไข่ ovary

รูปไข่ oval, ovate, egg-shaped

วางไข่ to lay eggs, deposit eggs

ออกไข่ to lay an egg; egg-laying

ไข้ fever

ไข้กาฬนางแอ่น, ไข้กาฬหลังแอ่น meningitis; meningococcal

ไข้คอตีบ diphtheria

ไข้จับสั่น malaria

ไข้ใจ love-sickness, brokenhearted, downcast

ไข้ดำแดง scarlet fever

ไข้ทรพิษ, ฝีดาษ, ไข้หัว smallpox

ไข้มารยา feigned sickness, political illness

ไข้รากสาด typhoid fever

ไข้หวัด a cold with fever

    ไข้หวัดใหญ่ influenza, flu

ไข้หัว smallpox

ไข้อีสุกอีใส chicken pox

คนไข้ patient, sick person

    คนไข้นอก out-patient

    คนไข้ใน in-patient

จับไข้ to get sick, fall ill; to be getting a fever, be feverish

เจ็บไข้ได้ป่วย sick, ill, ailing; to get sick, fall ill

เป็นไข้, ป่วยไข้ to be sick, unwell, ill; to have a fever, be feverish

ฟื้นไข้ to recover, get better, convalesce, get over an illness

ไขว่ crossed; to place crosswise, be placed crosswise

ไขว่คว้า to grab (at); to try to catch hold of; to make an effort to get something, reach for; to seek

ไขว่ห้าง with legs crossed, to cross one's legs

นั่งไขว่ห้าง to sit with one's legs crossed

ไขว้ crossed, to place crosswise, be placed crosswise; to be interchanged; to be mismatched

ไขว้เขว to exchange; to pawn, hock

    เข้าใจไขว้เขว to misunderstand, be misunderstood; misunderstanding, misconception, confusion

นั่งไขว้ขา to sit with one's legs crossed

ไขสือ to feign ignorance (of), pretend not to know

คง[1] lasting, enduring; still

คงทน durable

คงที่ steady, static, stable; permanent, unchanging

คงเส้นคงวา constant, just as before; straightforward

คงเหลือ balance, remainder, still left

คงอำนาจ to have power, retain the power to

เงินคงคลัง treasury reserves

จะคง shall continue (to)

มั่นคง solid; strong; secure; stable, steady

คง[2] should, probably; I think

เจ้านายคงคอยเธออยู่ I think the boss is waiting for you.

คงจะ should, will probably, is likely to

คงจะเหลืออยู่บ้าง There should be something left.

คงจะดีขึ้น should get /better/improve/

คงได้ may get, may obtain, may achieve

คงกระพัน invulnerable

คงแก่เรียน learned, scholarly

คงคา water; river; sea

แม่คงคา Ganges River; river

คช elephant; bull-elephant

คชกรรม elephantmanship

คชนาม a first name beginning with ย, ร, ล or ว

คชลักษณ์ manual describing qualities of elephants as indicated by their appearance

คชศาสตร์ elephantology, study of elephants

คชสาร elephant

คชสีห์ fabulous lion with an elephant's trunk

คณ-, คณะ group, party, company, section เช่น *วัดมหาธาตุ คณะ 8 Wat Mahatat, Section 8.*

คณบดี dean

คณะกรรมการ committee, council, board,

board of directors, commission

คณะกรรมการเฉพาะกิจ ad hoc committee

คณะกรรมาธิการ commission

คณะทูต diplomatic corps

คณะเทศมนตรี municipal council, city council, town council

คณะผู้ก่อการ Coup Party

คณะผู้แทน mission

คณะผู้แทนทางทูต diplomatic mission

คณะผู้สำเร็จราชการ Regency Council

คณะมนตรีความมั่นคง Security Council

คณะรัฐมนตรี Council of Ministers, cabinet

คณะราษฎร์ People's Party

คณนา computation, calculation

คณาจารย์ body of teachers, faculty

คณิกา prostitute, harlot

คณิต computation, calculation; mathematics

คณิตศาสตร์ mathematics

พีชคณิต algebra

เรขาคณิต geometry

เลขคณิต arithmetic

คด bent, crooked, curved, not straight; devious, deceitful, crooked

คดโกง crooked, deceitful, cheating, perfidious

คดเคี้ยว winding, snaking, curving, meandering, tortuous, sinuous

คดในข้องอในกระดูก a real crook, deceitful

คดไปคดมา meandering

ถนนคด winding road

คดี story, account; course, procedure, operation; lawsuit, case, action

คดีธรรม religious matters

คดีแพ่ง civil /case/suit/action/

คดีโลก worldly matters

คดีอาญา criminal case

ต้องคดี to be prosecuted; accused, charged with; to be sued (ความแพ่ง), be involved in

ค ฆ ง จ ฉ ช ซ ฌ ญ ฏ ฐ ฑ ฒ ณ ด ต ถ ท ธ น บ ป ผ ฝ พ ฟ ภ ม ย ร ฤ ฦ ล ว ศ ษ ส ห ฬ อ ฮ

litigation

วรรณคดี literature

สารคดี non-fiction; feature story, article

อรรถคดี lawsuit, case, legal action, litigation

คติ principle, tradition; precept

คติธรรม moral saying, principle, teaching, maxim, wise saying; uplifting statement

คตินิยม tradition

คติพจน์ motto

ทัศนคติ, **เจตคติ** opinion, view, viewpoint; attitude

อุดมคติ ideal, principle

คทา baton, mace, rod, staff; scepter

คน[1] to stir, mix

ไข่คน scrambled egg

คน[2] human being, people, person, man, woman, girl, boy, fellow, chap, guy; thing

คนกลาง middleman, intermediary, mediator

คนเกียจคร้าน idler, lazy person, sluggard

คนโกง crook, cheat

คนโกหก liar, prevaricator

คนขนของ porter

    คนขนของที่สถานีรถไฟ railway porter, redcap (US)

คนขยัน /energetic/diligent/industrious/ person, hard worker

คนขับรถ chauffeur, driver

คนขายของ salesperson, salesman (ชาย), saleswoman (หญิง)

คนขายชาติ traitor

คนขายเนื้อ butcher

คนขายหนังสือ bookseller

    คนขายหนังสือพิมพ์ news vendor, newsagent

คนขายหมู butcher

คนข่าว reporter, newsman, newspaperman, correspondent

คนขี้เหนียว miser, stingy person, tightwad, penny pincher

คนไข้ patient, sick person

คนคด crook, cheat, dishonest person

คนครัว cook

คนงาน worker, workman, laborer

คนโง่ stupid person, fool, dunce, idiot; naive

คนจะกละ gourmand, big eater, greedy eater

คนเจ็บ patient, sick person; injured person, casualty

คนใจดำ a meanie; a heartless person

คนชั่ว bad person, bad guy, bad, wicked

คนชาติ national (of)

คนใช้ servant, household help, maid

คนเฒ่าคนแก่ old folks, elderly people

คนดับเพลิง fireman

คนดี good /man/woman/, fine person

คนดู spectator, audience, viewer, on-looker

คนเดินโต๊ะ waiter

คนเดียว alone, by oneself; one person, single person

เขาทำคนเดียว He did it by himself. / He did it alone.

คนโดยสาร passenger

คนตักน้ำ water-drawer

คนตัดฟืน woodcutter

คนต่างด้าว alien, foreigner

คนตาย deceased; deaths

มีคนตายเท่าไร How many deaths were there?

คนทรง medium, one to be possessed; witch

คนทั้งหลาย everyone, everybody, all

คนทั่วไป people in general

คนทำขนมปัง baker

คนไทย Thai, Thai people

คนนอก outsider, stranger, layman

คนนำทาง guide

คนนำร่อง pilot

คนใน insider

คนบัดซบ fool

คนบ้า a person who is /mad/insane/crazy/; madman, a nut

คนบาดเจ็บ injured person, casualty

คนใบ้ dumb person, a mute

คนประจบ flatterer, fawner

คนป่า savage, wild man; forest dweller

คนแปลกหน้า stranger, newcomer

คนโปรด favorite, pet

คนเฝ้าประตู porter, gatekeeper

คนพูดมาก someone who talks too much, blatherer; /loquacious/garrulous/ person

คนพื้นเมือง native, indigenous person

คนฟัง listener

คนรถ driver, chauffeur

คนรีดนม milker

คนรู้จักกัน acquaintance

คนล้วงกระเป๋า pickpocket

คนละ each, per, each one; different
แจกบัตรผ่านประตูคนละใบ One ticket per person. / Give each one a ticket.

> **คนละเรื่องเดียวกัน** a false analogy, a different kettle of fish

> **คนละอย่าง** a different thing

คนเล่นกล juggler

คนเลี้ยงแกะ shepherd

คนเลี้ยงควาย buffalo-boy

คนเลี้ยงเด็ก nursemaid, baby-sitter

คนเลี้ยงม้า horse-breeder

คนเลี้ยงสุนัข dog-raiser, dog-breeder

คนเลี้ยงหมู swineherd

คนสนิท confidant, close friend; aide-de-camp (ทหาร)

คนสวน gardener

คนสอพลอ flatterer, sycophant, bootlicker, toady

คนเสิร์ฟ waiter (ชาย), waitress (หญิง)

คนโสด bachelor (ชาย), spinster (หญิง), unmarried person

คนหนังสือพิมพ์ journalist, newspaperman, correspondent

คนใหญ่คนโต bigshot

คนใหม่ newcomer

ค้น to look for, search; to seek; to look (something) up

ค้นของ to look for something, search (for)

ค้นคว้า to research, do research; to search for, find out, investigate

ค้นคืน to retrieve

> **การค้นคืน** retrieval

ค้นพบ to discover, find; to uncover, find out

ค้นหา to look for, search for, seek, hunt for something

หมายค้น search warrant

คนโท long-necked water vessel

คนธ์, คันธ์ smell, odor

คนธรรพ์ an order of angels skilled in music; artist

คนธรรพวิวาห์ to become husband and wife without any formalities

คนธรรพศาสตร์ musicology

คเนจร to wander, roam, rove

คบ[1] torch; place where a branch joins the trunk of a tree

คบเพลิง torch

คบไม้ fork of a tree

คบ[2] to join

คบค้า to associate with, keep company with; go together, be friends with

คบคิด to be in complicity (with), to conspire

คบชู้ to have /a lover/paramour/, be adulterous, be unfaithful

คบหา to associate with, keep company with, go together, be friends, see each other

คม[1] cutting edge, sharp edge

คมมีด cutting edge

คม[2] sharp, keen; witty; astute, shrewd

คมกริบ quick-witted, keen-witted, sharp, astute, shrewd, razor-edged, very sharp

คมขำ attractive; dark and handsome

คมคาย witty; astute, apposite, shrewd, acute, keen-witted

คมในฝัก with a lot of potential, having latent qualities, of hidden virtue; judicious, wise, sagacious, discreet, careful about what one /says/does/; a person of hidden talents

    ตาคม bright-eyed; sharp

    ปากคม sharp-tongued

ครก   mortar

    ครกกะเบือ kitchen earthenware mortar

    ขนมครก soft rice cakes topped with coconut cream baked in covered recessions in an earthenware tray

    ปืนครก mortar

ครบ   complete, full; all

    คนครบหรือยัง Is everyone here?

    ของครบหรือยัง Do you have everything? / Is it all there?

    ครบครัน full, complete, perfect

    ครบเครื่อง whole, perfect, complete

    ครบชุด complete set

    ครบถ้วน in full, to be all there, complete with everything

    ครบบริบูรณ์ perfect, complete, full; everything

ครรภ์   womb, uterus

    ครรภ์แก่ advanced pregnancy

    ตรวจครรภ์ to have a prenatal check-up

    ตั้งครรภ์ to become pregnant, be with child, conceive

    ผดุงครรภ์ midwife

    ฝากครรภ์ to sign up for pre-natal care and delivery

    มีครรภ์ pregnant

ครรลอง (in the) right way

    ตามครรลอง duly in accordance with

ครรไล conveyance, vehicle; to go

ครวญ to lament, bemoan, bewail; to croon

    ครวญคราง to moan

    ครวญคร่ำ to moan, groan

    ครวญเพลง to croon

    โอดครวญ to bemoan, lament, lamentation, bewail; to complain

ครหา to criticize, find fault (with), malign, censure

    ถูกครหา to be criticized (for doing something)

ครอก[1] litter, brood

    ขี้ครอก slave

    ลูกครอก slave-child, offspring of a slave

ครอก[2] snoring; death rattle; menacing sound; to go off to sleep

ครอง[1] to rule, govern, hold sway over, reign over

    ครองแผ่นดิน to rule, reign

    ครองราชย์ to reign

ครอง[2] to maintain, keep, preserve

    ครองความเป็นโสด to remain single, preserve one's independence

    ครองความเป็นใหญ่ to maintain superiority, stay big

    ครองจีวร *see* **ครองผ้า** *หน้า 77*

    ครองใจ to control one's emotions, remain calm; constant, faithful

    ครองชีพ to make a living, support oneself

        การครองชีพ living, making a living

        ค่าครองชีพ cost of living

        มาตรฐานการครองชีพ standard of living

    ครองตน to lead the life of a (monk, farmer, good citizen etc); to exercise self-control

    ครองรัก to live together happily

    ขอให้คู่บ่าวสาวครองรักกันชั่วฟ้าดินสลาย May the bride and groom /have an everlastingly happy married life./live together in happiness forever./

คุ้มครอง to protect, watch over

ครอง[3] to wear, put on

　ครองผ้า to put on the yellow robe of a monk

ครอง[4] to own, possess

　คู่ครอง spouse, mate, husband and wife

　ยึดครอง to occupy, take possession (of)

ครอบ to cover; to put on; to impart knowledge to, teach; to take in charge, take charge of

　ครอบครอง to possess, be in possession (of), have in one's possession

　　สิทธิครอบครอง right of possession, possessory rights

　　อยู่ในครอบครอง under the control of; in the possession of

　ครอบครัว family

　　ครอบครัวขยาย extended family

　　ครอบครัวเดียว nuclear family

　ครอบงำ to dominate, control, have power over, overwhelm, overpower, keep under one's thumb; to take over

　　ครอบงำกิจการ business takeover(s); take over a business, do a takeover

　ครอบจักรวาล all embracing, covering everything, universal

　ครอบคลุม all-inclusive, exhaustive; to cover

　ฝาครอบ cover

คร่อม to straddle, bestride, be astride, bridge

　ขีดคร่อม to cross (a check)

ครั่ง lac

　ขี้ครั่ง stick lac

　ตัวครั่ง lac insect

ครั้ง time

　ครั้งก่อน formerly, previously, the time before, the last time

　ครั้งคราว occasionally

　ครั้งนั้น at that time, then

　ครั้งนี้ this time, now

　ครั้งแรก initial, the first time; at the outset

　　เป็นครั้งแรก for the first time, This is

the first time.

　ครั้งแล้วครั้งเล่า over and over again, again and again, time and again, time after time

　ครั้งหลัง the time after, next time, last time

　ครั้งใหญ่ momentous, major

　ทุกครั้ง every time, each time

　นานๆ ครั้ง once in a while

　บางครั้งบางคราว from time to time, now and then, occasionally, sometimes

　เป็นครั้งเป็นคราว periodically, from time to time, occasionally, once in a while

　เมื่อครั้ง when, at the time

　หลายครั้งหลายหน repeatedly

ครัน *as in* **นานครัน** so long a time

ครั่น to feel feverish, get a chill

　ครั่นคร้าม to feel a chill; to be apprehensive

　ครั่นตัว to feel feverish, have a chill

　ครั่นเนื้อครั่นตัว feverish

ครั้น when, at the time, then

ครับ[1] polite particle

　ขอทางหน่อยครับ Excuse me, please. / May I get through, please.

ครับ[2] (affirmative response) yes, *(พูด)* okay, right

ครับ[3] (polite attention-getter), sir, ma'am, mister, miss, please, excuse me, say

　ผู้จัดการครับ /sir/ma'am (หญิง)/

　พ่อครับ father / say dad

ครัว kitchen; family

　ครัวทาน things to be offered to monks

　ครัวไฟ kitchen

　ครัวเรือน household

　เครื่องครัว kitchen utensils, kitchenware

　เทครัว to take all the women of the family (widow and daughters) to wife

　พ่อครัว cook, chef

　แม่ครัว cook

　สวนครัว kitchen garden

ครา time

คร่า to drag (off, away), to carry off by force,

ก
ข
ค

abduct; to rape

คราก to be over-stretched; disjointed, dislocated

คราง to moan, groan; to whine

คราด rake, harrow

คร้าน to be fed up with, be apathetic, tired of doing something, what's the use
พูดยังไงก็ไม่รู้เรื่อง คร้านจะเถียง *You don't listen so what's the use of saying anything.*
เกียจคร้าน lazy, indolent, slothful

คราบ[1] slough, cast-off skin; clothing
คราบงู slough of a snake, cast-off snake skin
ผู้ร้ายในคราบนักบุญ a wolf in sheep's clothing
ลอกคราบ[1] to molt
ลอกคราบ[2] to reveal the true colors (of something); inside; to strip (of everything)
ลอกคราบสังคมไทย *inside Thai society*

คราบ[2] film (of); stain; incrustation, deposit
คราบน้ำ a deposit left after immersion in water, water stain
คราบน้ำมัน oil film, oil stain
คราบน้ำหมาก betel juice stain

คราม indigo plant

คร้าม to be scared, quail (at), be cowed (by), alarmed (at, by)
ฉันรู้สึกคร้าม ที่มาพูดต่อหน้าท่านผู้รู้ทั้งหลาย *I quail at the prospect of talking to such an audience.*

ครามครัน comparatively, somewhat, rather

คราว time
คราวก่อน the last time, before
คราวละ per time
คราวหน้า again, next time, later, afterwards,
เอาไว้คราวหน้าก็แล้วกัน *Save it for the next time.*
คราวหน้ามาใหม่นะคะ *Do come again.*
คราวหนึ่ง once, one time
คราวหลัง later, afterwards, again, next time
ข่าวคราว news

ชั่วคราว *see* ชั่วคราว *หน้า 139*

ทุกคราว every time

บางคราว sometimes, occasionally, once in a while

เป็นคราวๆ from time to time, periodically, intermittently

เมื่อคราว when, at the time

คร่าว[1] beam joining the corner posts of a house

คร่าว[2] indistinct, not clear; untidy, not well done, sloppy, sketchy, rough
อย่างคร่าวๆ roughly, rough

คร่ำ polluted water, stagnant foul water

คร่ำ amniotic fluid

คร่ำครวญ to lament, weep and wail, moan and groan, bemoan

คร่ำคร่า worn-out, dilapidated, shabby

คร่ำครึ ancient, antiquated, antediluvian, outdated, fuddy-duddy, old-fashioned

คร่ำเคระอะ dirty, filthy, soiled

คร่ำหวอด masterly, experienced, skilled, expert

คร่ำเคร่ง absorbed, engrossed (in), intent (on), preoccupied (with)

คริสต์ Christ
คริสต์มาส Christmas, Xmas
คริสต์ศักราช Christian era
คริสตัง Christian
ชาวคริสต์ Christian

ครีบ fin

ครีม cream, creme

ครึ old-fashioned, fuddy-duddy, behind the times; not with it

ครึกครื้น lively, fun (เช่น *a fun party*), merry, joyous, jolly

ครึกโครม noisy, boisterous; (เสียง) din, hubbub
ข่าวครึกโครม big news, news splashed over the media
เสียงครึกโครม clamor, tumult, din, uproar

ครึ่ง half
ครึ่งๆ กลางๆ half done, half-way, half-

hearted

ครึ่งต่อครึ่ง fifty-fifty; 100 percent (profit)

ครึ่งทาง half-way, midway

ครึ่งหนึ่ง half

คนละครึ่ง fifty-fifty, one half each

แบ่งกันคนละครึ่ง Let's divide it in half.

ครึ้ม[1] overcast, cloudy; gloomy; shady

ครึ้มฟ้าครึ้มฝน to look like rain

มืดครึ้ม cloudy, dark

ครึ้ม[2] happy, pleased; possessed

วันนี้นึกครึ้มอะไรขึ้นมา What possessed you to (dress up, etc) today? ก็นึกครึ้มขึ้นมา Just a whimsy.

ครึ้มอกครึ้มใจ elated; in high spirits

ครืด /scraping/dragging/ sound

ครืน, ครืนๆ waves of laughter; rumbling

ล้มครืน to topple with a thunderous crash

ครื้นครั่น resounding

ครื้นเครง merry, gay, animated, lively, full of fun

ครือ, ครือกัน just the same, no different, equal; to be square

ครุ[1] woven dammared bamboo bucket

ครุ[2] (เสียง, คำ) heavy sound

ครุภัณฑ์ durable goods

ครุวาร Thursday

ครุฑ Garuda, a mythical bird with a human body and head, wings and talons of an eagle

ครุฑพ่าห์ Garuda insignia

ครุ่น intent, rapt; continual

ครุ่นคิด to be thoughtful; ponder, contemplate; to brood (over)

ครุย[1] academic gown

ครุย[2] fringe

ครู teacher, instructor

ครูน้อย assistant teacher

ครูบาอาจารย์ teachers, the teaching profession

ครูประจำชั้น home room teacher

ครูฝึก instructor, trainer, coach

ครูมวย trainer

ครูใหญ่ headmaster, principal

ชั้นครู master

วิชาครู education

ครู่ instant, minute

รอฉันสักครู่ Wait for me. /I'll only be a minute./I'll be back in a minute./

ครู่หนึ่ง, ครู่เดียว a moment, a minute, an instant; for a while

ครู่ใหญ่ in a short while, after a while, for a while

ชั่วครู่ *see* **ครู่หนึ่ง**

ครูด to rub against something, scrape (along, against)

คฤหบดี well-to-do person, man of substance, householder, /rich/wealthy/ man

คฤหัสถ์ layman; lay disciple; head of the household, householder

คฤหาสน์ large house, fine house, residence, mansion

คลอ[1], **คล้อ** to accompany; to go side by side

คลอเคลีย to go together affectionately, show affection for one another

คลอ[2] to well up

น้ำตาคลอ Tears welled up in her eyes.

คลอก to burn, consume by fire

คล่อกแคล่ก to crackle, crackling

คลอง canal, waterway

คลองขุด canal

คล่อง easily, smoothly, deftly; quick; adept

คล่องคอ smooth, easy on the throat

คล่องแคล่ว active, nimble, spry, agile, brisk; experienced, skillful, expert

พูดคล่อง fluent; glib, to be a /smooth/good/ talker

คล้อง[1] to /hang/put/wear/ around the neck; to lasso; to hook

คล้องคอ to /wear/put/ around the neck

ค ฆ ง จ ฉ ช ซ ฌ ญ ฎ ฏ ฐ ฑ ฒ ณ ด ต ถ ท ธ น บ ป ผ ฝ พ ฟ ภ ม ย ร ฤ ฤๅ ล ว ศ ษ ส ห ฬ อ ฮ

คล้องช้าง to capture elephants

คล้องเชือก to loop a rope (over something)

คล้องพวงมาลัย to wear a garland around one's neck

คล้อง[2] to go together, harmonize (with), match, correspond in sound

คล้องจอง to rhyme (with)

คลอด to give birth (to), bear (a child), be born; to be realized, forthcoming

ร่างกฎหมายภาษีมรดก จนบานนี้ก็ยังไม่คลอด เลย The long overdue inheritance tax law has still not been realized.

คลอดลูก to have a baby, give birth

การคลอด delivery, childbirth

ช่องคลอด vagina

ทำการคลอด deliver a baby

หมอทำคลอด obstetrician

คลอน loose, unstable, unsteady, shaky

คลอนแคลน precarious, insecure; rickety (ของ)

ฟันคลอน a loose tooth

สั่นคลอน shaky, unstable

คล้อย[1] to pass downward; drooping

คล้อยคล้อย to go farther and farther

คล้อยตาม to go along (with), follow suit, acquiesce (in), accept, defer (to)

คล้อยหลัง just left, to have just gone off

คล้อย[2] afternoon

บ่ายคล้อย late afternoon

คละ mixed, assorted

คละกันไป mixed, assorted, miscellaneous

คละคลุ้ง stinking, malodorous, bad smelling, fetid; a stench

คลั่ก jammed, packed, jam-packed (with)

คนแน่นคลั่กที่สนามม้า The racecourse was packed (with people).

คลัง treasury; storehouse, warehouse

คลังข้อมูล database, data bank

คลังข้อมูลภาษา language corpus

คลังข้อสอบ item bank

คลังพัสดุ storeroom, storehouse, warehouse

คลังสินค้า warehouse, godown

คลังแสง *see* **คลังแสง** *หน้า 510*

คลังออมสิน savings bank

กระทรวงการคลัง Ministry of Finance

การคลัง finance, finances

ขุนคลัง minister of finance, lord of the treasury, treasurer

เงินคงคลัง treasury reserves

แผนกคลัง accounts department, treasury section, bursar's office (วิทยาลัย)

คลั่ง frantic, wild, hysterical; deranged, out of one's mind, demented, mad; to go wild about

คลั่งไคล้ infatuated (with), crazy about, besotted (by, with)

คลั่งดารา starstruck, star crazy

คลั่งรัก love-stricken; crazy about, mad about, madly in love (with), infatuated (with)

บ้าคลั่ง *see* **บ้าคลั่ง** *หน้า 274*

คลับ club, nightclub

คลับคล้ายคลับคลา vaguely, indistinctly; seem to

คลับคล้ายคลับคลาว่าผมเคยเจอคุณที่ไหนสักแห่ง I seem to remember having seen you before.

คลาคล่ำ to be full of; to have masses of

คลาไคล to fare, progress, go forth

คลางแคลง to doubt, have doubts, be suspicious

คลางแคลงใจ suspicious, sceptical

คลาด to miss

คลาดเคลื่อน inaccurate, incorrect, mistaken, off the mark

คลาดเคลื่อนจากความเป็นจริง erroneous

คลาดแคล้ว free from (peril etc); to escape

คลาดจากกัน to go separate ways

คลาดนัด to miss an appointment, fail to keep an appointment

คลาน to crawl, creep

คลาย to unravel, untwist; untie, loosen; to relax; to ease, abate, subside; to cool /off/ down/; to unravel (the mystery)

สถานการณ์คลายความตึงเครียด The tension was eased. / The situation became less critical.

เขาคลายความวิตกกังวล He was relieved. / He got over his worries.

คลายความสนใจ to lose interest

คลายทุกข์ to relieve suffering, alleviate distress

คลายนอต to loosen a bolt; to unscrew

คลายปม to unravel, be unravelled

คลายรัก to lose interest (in someone)

คลายอารมณ์ to relax, unwind

มิคลาย undying, everlasting

คล้าย, คล้ายคลึง nearly alike, almost alike, similar (to); such as, like; to resemble

คล้ายกับว่า like, as if, to seem like

เธอทำคล้ายกับว่าไม่รู้จักฉันเลย She acted /as if/like/ she didn't even know me. / She seemed like she didn't know me.

วันคล้ายวันเกิด birthday, anniversary

คลำ to feel about with the hands, fumble, grope

คลำดู to fumble around for, grope (for)

คลำทาง to feel one's way, grope for the way

คลำหา to grope (for)

ลูบคลำ to caress, fondle, *see* **ลูบคลำ** *หน้า 450*

คล้ำ swarthy, dark, dark-complexioned

ผิวคล้ำ dark complexioned, swarthy, dark skinned

สีคล้ำ dark; dull

คลิตอริส clitoris

คลี polo

ตีคลี to play polo

ผู้ตีคลี polo player

ผู้เล่นคลี polo player

ไม้ตีคลี polo mallet, polo stick

ลูกคลี polo ball

เล่นคลี to play polo

คลี่ to unfold, unroll; unfurl; to expand, extend, enlarge; to spread out, open; to stretch out

คลี่คลาย to improve, ease, develop positively, take a turn for the better

สถานการณ์คลี่คลาย The situation has eased. / The situation has improved.

คลี่ดอก to bloom, blossom; in blossom

คลี่ผ้า to /spread out/unfold/ a piece of material

คลึง to roll into a ball with the hand; to massage

คลึงเคล้น to stroke and squeeze; to caress, fondle

คลึงเคล้า to caress

คลื่น wave

คลื่นใต้น้ำ undertow, undercurrent

คลื่นยาว long wave

คลื่นลม sea weather

คลื่นสั้น shortwave

คลื่นเสียง sound wave

เป็นคลื่น wavy, undulating

เมาคลื่น seasick

คลื่นไส้ to feel sick to one's stomach, queasy, nauseous; to retch; disgusting, sickening

คลื่นเหียน disgusting, nauseating; to feel nauseous

คลุก to mix, blend, mingle, commingle; to close in (on)

คลุกคลี to go with, mix with, associate with, mingle with, make friends with

คลุกเคล้า to blend

คลุ้ง stinking, giving off a stench, badsmelling, odorous

คลุม to cover, envelop

คลุมเครือ ambiguous, vague, obscure, unclear

คลุมถุงชน an arranged marriage neither

ค ฆ ง จ ฉ ช ซ ฌ ญ ฎ ฏ ฐ ฑ ฒ ณ ด ต ถ ท ธ น บ ป ผ ฝ พ ฟ ภ ม ย ร ฤ ฤๅ ล ว ศ ษ ส ห ฬ อ ฮ

party knowing the other previously, blind marriage

คลุมโปง to cover (oneself) from head to foot, get under a blanket

คลุ้มคลั่ง deranged, demented, out of one's mind; crazy, mad; delerious; in a frenzy; to run amok

ควง[1] screw

ตะปูควง screw, woodscrew

ควง[2] to go together, date, go with

เพิ่งรู้จักกัน ก็ควงกันแล้ว They just met and already they're going together.

เดินควง to go together (with); to be seen together; to walk /arm in arm/hand in hand/

ควบ[1] to gallop

ควบม้า to gallop a horse

ควบ[2] coupled, double, together (with); to merge, amalgamate; to mount

สองบริษัทควบกัน The two companies merged. / There was a merger of the two companies.

ควบแน่น to condense *(วิทย์)*

ควบสองตำแหน่ง to hold two positions, double as

นายชวน หลีกภัยควบสองตำแหน่ง คือ นายก-รัฐมนตรี และรัฐมนตรีว่าการกระทรวงกลาโหม Mr Chuan Leekpai is doubling as prime minister and minister of defense.

ควบคู่กันไป together, simultaneously, at the same time, accompanied by, coupled with, in addition to, in parallel with

การควบกิจการ (business) merger

การควบและการซื้อกิจการ mergers and acquisitions (M & A)

หนังสองเรื่องควบ a double feature

ควบคุม to control, take charge of

ควบคุมดูแล to supervise; supervision

ใช้สิทธิควบคุมดูแล to exercise rights of

supervision

ควบคุมตัว to take someone into custody; to be detained

ควบคุมสติ to come to one's senses; control oneself, restrain oneself, keep calm

ควบคุมสถานการณ์ to control the situation

การควบคุม control

เจ้าหน้าที่ควบคุมความประพฤติ probation officer

ควย prick, cock

ควร should, ought to; to deserve, be worthy of; to be fit (to), suitably, appropriately, right, proper

ควรแก่การ to be worthy of, be fit to

ควรค่าแก่ to be worthy of

ควรจะ should, ought to

ควรจะกลับได้แล้ว /You/We/should be going.

ควรทำ ought to do, should do

ควรอยู่ ought to stay, should stay

มากเกินควร excessive, to excess, inordinately

อะไรที่มากเกินควรไม่ดี Anything done to excess is not good.

เห็นควร to agree, approve, okay; to /think/ feel/(something) should be (done etc)

เห็นควรเสนอไปตามขั้นตอน Approved for further action in the regular way.

ควัก to take out, scoop out, pull out, pluck out

ควักกะปิ to look awkward, be green; to fork out, pay

ควักตา to /gouge/pluck/ out the eye

ควัน smoke, fumes

ควันขึ้น to smoke

ควันโขมง smoke /billowing (from/)pouring (out)/, smoke-filled, smoky

ควันดำ smoky exhaust; black smoke

ควันบุหรี่ cigarette smoke

ควันไฟ smoke

ควันหลง aftermath (of), after-effects

ควั่น the node at which stem joins fruit; to cut around, make a circular incision; to girdle a tree

ควั่นจุก to shave the head so as to leave a topknot

ควั่นอ้อย to cut sugar cane into sections

อ้อยควั่น section of sugar cane

คว้า to snatch, grab, seize; to swoop down (on); to win; to get

หล่อนคว้าตำแหน่งรองนางงาม She grabbed second place in the beauty contest.

คว้าน้ำเหลว /(to do something)/(to be)/ in vain, fruitless

คว้าว่าว to put a kite into a nosedive

คว้าหมับ to snatch, grab

ไขว่คว้า see **ไขว่คว้า** หน้า 72

ควาก ripping noise

คว้าง to swing around, whirl around, swirl

เคว้งคว้าง adrift, drifting

ควาญ mahout, elephant /driver/keeper/

ควาน to fumble about, grope, feel about

ควานหา to grope (for something), feel for; to rummage (for, in)

คว้าน to scoop out with a circular motion

คว้านท้อง to eviscerate; to commit harakiri

คว้านผลไม้ to core, to pit (fruit)

ความ[1] subject, case, matter, story; gist, substance, message

กินความถึง to cover, encompass, include, extend to

ข้อความ text, wording; passage, statement

จำกัดความ to define

ใจความ substance, gist, essence, the heart of, the essentials

ได้ความ to understand, gather; to make sense; to be successful, get results

ตีความ to construe, interpret, define

การตีความ definition, nterpretation, construction

ไม่ได้ความ no good, not much good; nonsense, stupid

ย่อความ to summarize, abridge; (to/make/do/) an abstract, a digest, a summary, a precis

ความ[2] lawsuit, legal action, case

ค้าความ make a business out of going to court, champerty, ambulance chasing *(sl)*

คู่ความ parties (to an action), litigants

คำคู่ความ pleadings

เป็นความ to be involved in a lawsuit, engage in litigation (with)

ยอมความ to enter a settlement, settle a case, compromise

ความ[3] คำนำหน้ากริยาหรือวิเศษณ์ ในภาษาอังกฤษลงท้ายด้วย "ปัจจัย" ท้ายคำ เช่น -ness (happiness), -ity (ability), -th (width), -ment (excitement), -ance (tolerance), -tion (prevention), -tude (solitude), -ure (pressure), -y (honesty), -ery (robbery), -ship (friendship) เป็นต้น

ความกดของอากาศ air pressure

ความกดขี่ tyranny, oppression

ความกดดัน pressure; frustration

ความกล้าหาญ bravery, courage

ความเข้มข้น intensity; concentration

ความคิด idea, thought, thinking

ความคุ้นเคย familiarity

ความคุ้มกัน immunity

...ได้รับความคุ้มกันจาก... ...shall be immune from....

ความจริง truth, reality; in fact, actually

ความจริงผมไม่มีส่วนเกี่ยวข้องในเรื่องนี้เลย /Actually/In fact/In reality/ I had nothing to do with it.

ความจำ memory, recollection

ความจำเป็น necessity, need, needs, exigency

...โดยคำนึงถึงความจำเป็นของสถานทำการทาง

ค ฆ ง จ ฉ ช ซ ฌ ญ ฎ ฏ ฐ ฑ ฒ ณ ด ต ถ ท ธ น บ ป ผ ฝ พ ฟ ภ ม ย ร ฤ ฤๅ ล ว ศ ษ ส ห ฬ อ ฮ

กงสุล ...having regard to the needs of the consular post....

ความจุ capacity

ความเจริญ progress, prosperity, advancement, improvement

ความฉลาด cleverness, intelligence

ความเฉื่อย sluggishness, lethargy, torpor, inertia

ความชอบธรรม legitimacy

ความชั่ว evil, wickedness, badness, vice

ความชื้น humidity, damp

ความซื่อสัตย์ faithfulness, fidelity, integrity, honesty

ความดี virtue, the good, goodness

　　ความดีความชอบ merit, meritorious /work/service/action/, performance หัวหน้ามีหน้าที่พิจารณาความดีความชอบของลูกน้อง The department head has the duty to evaluate the /performance/ merits/ of his subordinates.

ความต่อเนื่อง continuity, (with) regularity

ความต้องการ desire, want, needs; demand

ความต้านทาน resistance

ความตึงเครียด tension, stress

ความตื่นเต้น excitement, agitation

ความเติบโต growth, expansion

ความถ่วง gravity

　　ความถ่วงจำเพาะ specific gravity

ความถี่ frequency

ความทุกข์ suffering, pain, misery, distress, anguish

ความน้อยใจ resentment; offence, feeling of being slighted

ความน่าจะเป็น probability

ความแน่น density

ความในใจ something in mind; concealed thoughts

ความเบื่อหน่าย boredom, ennui; disgust

ความประพฤติ conduct, behavior, deportment

ความปลอดภัย safety, security

ความเป็นกลาง neutrality, impartiality

ความเป็นมา history, background, origin; story

ความผิด guilt, culpability; offence; wrong, mistake, error, fault

ความฝัน dream, reverie

ความฝืด friction

ความพยาบาท ill will, malice; revenge, vengeance, vindictiveness, vengefulness

ความพอใจ what one likes; satisfaction ฉันให้เงินเธอ 100 บาท จะซื้ออะไรก็ได้ตามความพอใจ Here's a 100 baht. Buy what you like.

ความมั่นคง security

ความมานะ perseverance

ความมุ่งหมาย aim, object, purpose, intention

ความยากจน poverty, indigence

ความยืดหยุ่น flexibility, elasticity

ความระมัดระวัง caution, care, carefulness

ความรัก love, affection, fondness (for)

ความรู้ knowledge, understanding, learning, erudition; experience

ความเร็ว speed, velocity

ความเลื่อมใส faith, belief, trust (in); admiration, devotion (for)

ความสว่าง brightness, light, understanding, comprehension

ความสะดวก facilities

ความสามารถ ability, capacity

ความสำเร็จ success, successful completion, achievement, accomplishment

ความสุข happiness, felicity, bliss, contentment

ความหนักใจ concern, worry

ความหมาย meaning, sense; message

ความหย่อนยาน slackness; looseness; flabbiness, sagging, flaccidity

ความหลัง the past

ความหวัง hope, expectation

ความหวังดี good intentions, goodwill

ความหายนะ calamity, disaster, catastrophe, cataclysm

ความเห็น opinion, view, comment

ควาย water buffalo, carabao

ควายป่า wild buffalo

วัวควาย cattle

คว่ำ to turn upside down, capsize (เรือ), turn over, overturn

คว่ำบาตร to ostracize, boycott, excommunicate, shun; to reject

คว่ำมือ to turn the hand down

คว่ำรัฐบาล to overturn the government

คว่ำลง to lie face downward, prone; to turn down

ใจหายใจคว่ำ startled, My heart was in my mouth.

ถูกคว่ำ knocked down, overturned

นอนคว่ำ to lie prone, lie face downwards

ล้มคว่ำ to fall on one's face

ควินิน quinine

ค.ศ. A.D., Anno Domini, Christian era

คหกรรมศาสตร์ domestic science

คหบดี head of the household, householder; rich man, wealthy man, man of substance

คหปตานี mistress of the house; rich woman, wealthy woman, woman of means

คหัฐ layman

คอ neck

คอแข็ง silent, speechless; able to hold one's liquor

เจ้าหมอนั่นคอแข็งจริงดื่มเท่าไหร่ก็ไม่เมา That guy can really hold his liquor. Nothing makes him drunk.

คอคอด isthmus

คอเดียวกัน like-minded

คอตก downcast, crestfallen, dejected

คอต่อ nape of the neck

คอตั้ง high collar; tunic

คอทองแดง heavy drinker; one who holds his liquor well

คอปก turned-down collar; /shirt/blouse/ dress/ with a collar

คอเป็นเอ็น furiously; stubbornly

เธอเถียงเขาคอเป็นเอ็นเชียว She argued stubbornly.

คอพอก goiter

คอพับคออ่อน drowsy

คอเร้ง pen

คอสอง second voice in folk-singing

คอสูง having expensive taste; refined, discriminating

คอหนัง movie lover; leatherneck (US)

คอหอย throat

คอเหล้า a drinker, person fond of drinking, connoisseur of liquor, discriminating drinker

ติดคอ to get stuck in the throat

ถูกคอกัน compatible, get on well together, get along well with someone, like one another

ฝืดคอ to be hard to swallow; uninviting

ลอยคอ to float (with one's head above water)

คอก[1] enclosure, pen, fold (แกะ), corral (ม้า, ช้าง), coop (เป็ด, ไก่), sty (หมู); prison, jail, gaol,

คอกไก่ chicken coop

คอกควาย buffalo /corral/pen/

คอกพยาน witness-box, witness stand

คอกม้า stable; corral

คอกวัว cattle pen, stable

คอกหมู pig /sty/pen/

นอกคอก non-conformist, unconventional, eccentric, maverick, renegade; unruly

หญ้าปากคอก commonplace, simple, familiar

คอก[2] *as in* **แขนคอก** crippled arm

ค ฆ ง จ ฉ ช ซ ฌ ญ ฎ ฏ ฐ ฑ ฒ ณ ด ต ถ ท ธ น บ ป ผ ฝ พ ฟ ภ ม ย ร ฤ ฦ ล ว ศ ษ ส ห ฬ อ ฮ

คอด narrow, constricted; worn away; pinched

คอเต็บ Moslem preacher

คอน[1] perch, roost

คอน[2] to carry something on one end of a shoulder pole

ค่อน[1] as in **ค่อนขอด** to be sarcastic, slur, disparage, make a slighting remark, taunt, gibe (at)

    ค่อนแคะ see **ค่อนขอด**

ค่อน[2] more than half, almost full; less than half, almost empty

    เหล้าหมดไปค่อนขวดแล้ว The whiskey's almost gone. / There's not much left (in the bottle).

    ค่อนข้าง fairly, reasonably, sort of, comparatively, rather, more or less; -ish

        ค่อนข้างเปรี้ยว sourish

    ค่อนคืน most of the night

    ค่อนวัน most of the day

    ค่อนหม้อ an almost full pot (of rice), still plenty left in the pot

ค้อน[1] hammer; mallet (ทำด้วยไม้), gavel (สำหรับเคาะในที่ประชุม เช่น สภาผู้แทนราษฎร)

    ค้อนตอก punch

    ค้อนปอนด์ sledge hammer

ค้อน[2] to give someone a dirty look

    ค้อนควัก to glare at someone, scowl (at)

    ค้อนติง to be contrary, disapprove unreasonably, object blindly (to), oppose perversely

คอนกรีต concrete

    คอนกรีตเสริมเหล็ก reinforced concrete

คอนเสิร์ต concert

คอม commie (พูด)

คอม hunchbacked

ค้อม to bow the head, nod (at)

คอมมูนิสต์, คอมมิวนิสต์ communist

คอย to wait (for), await

    คอยเก็บคอยกวาด to pick up the pieces; to pick up after someone

    คอยจังหวะ to wait for the right moment

    คอยดูก็แล้วกัน just wait and see; I'll fix you.

    คอยท่า to wait (for), await

    คอยเฝ้าดู to keep an eye on, to keep watch

    คอยระวัง to be careful, take care, be on the alert (for, to), be on the lookout (for), vigilant

    คอยรับใช้ to wait upon someone, be at someone's service

    คอยเหตุ to watch for, keep watch, be on the watch for, be on the lookout for

    รอคอย to wait (for), await

    หอคอย watchtower, lookout

ค่อย slowly, gently, lightly, softly, easy, gradually, little by little; to be getting; leisurely; then

    ค่อยๆ คิด ค่อยๆ ทำ to do something step by step

    ค่อยดีขึ้น to be better, improve

    ค่อยๆ เดิน to walk /slowly/carefully/

        เดินค่อยๆ to walk /softly/lightly/

    ค่อยเป็นค่อยไป /to learn/get better/ /little by little/gradually/, slow but sure

    ค่อยพูดค่อยจา to discuss something

    อย่าใจร้อนน่า ค่อยพูดค่อยจากันก็ได้ Don't get excited. This can be discussed.

    ค่อยยังชั่ว to be better, That's more like it.

    ค่อยๆ หน่อย Take it easy.; (เสียงพูด) Pipe down., Not so loud

    ไม่ค่อย not so, not very

    ไม่ค่อยชอบ not care very much for something, not fond of something

    ทำแบบนี้ผมไม่ค่อยชอบ I don't care for that sort of thing very much.

    ไม่ค่อยดี not so good

คะ[1] คำถามอย่างสุภาพ ในภาษาอังกฤษมักมี would นำ a polite interrogative ending sometimes rendered by "would" เช่น ไปไหมคะ *Would you like to go?* บางครั้งออกเสียงสูงและยาว

กว่าธรรมดาหน่อย เช่น ดีไหมคะ *Is it good? Do you like it?*

คะ[2] คำเชื้อเชิญอย่างสุภาพ ในภาษาอังกฤษมักใช้ do หรือ yes นำหน้า *an emphatic terminal word used by women sometimes rendered in English by "do" or "yes"* เช่น เชิญนั่งซิคะ *Do sit down.* นั่นซิคะ *Yes, exactly. / Yes, that's right.*

คะ[3] ใช้หลังตำแหน่ง หรือเรียกร้องความสนใจ *a polite attention-getter used with titles not translated in English.* เช่น คุณนายคะ คุณคะ คุณลืมเงินทอน */Miss/Madame/Mister/Sir/, you forgot your change.* บางครั้งใช้ hey เช่น *Hey miss, you forgot your change!*

ค่ะ[1] คำท้ายประโยค ไม่มีคำแปลในภาษาอังกฤษ *a rhythmic terminal word not rendered in English*

ค่ะ[2] เป็นคำรับ ตรงกับ yes (*used emphatically and politely*), okay, right

คะคาน *as in* **เอาชนะคะคาน** to win an argument (with someone)

คะนอง spirited, high-spirited, mettlesome, wild
　　คะนองปาก to say things one shouldn't, irrepressible,
　　คะนองมือ to fool around (with the hand), have an itchy hand
　　คึกคะนอง lively, spirited, high-spirited
　　ฟ้าคะนอง thunder
　　วัยคะนอง teen-aged

คะน้า Chinese kale
　　คะน้าฝรั่ง California kale

คะนึง to think of, think about, ponder

คะเน to guess, estimate, approximate; to conjecture, surmise, speculate
　　คาดคะเน to estimate, expect, think, presume
　　　　ที่เป็นการคาดคะเน conjectured

คะแนน marks, score, grade, points; vote
　　คะแนนเต็ม full score, full marks, highest

/grade/mark/
　　คะแนนรวม total score, total number of votes
　　คะแนนเสียง votes; popularity
　　ทำคะแนน to score points; to gain popularity, win support
　　ลงคะแนน to vote, ballot
　　เสียคะแนน lose votes; lose favor
　　หัวคะแนน canvasser, vote-getter

คะมำ to pitch forward, take a tumble, fall on one's face

คะยั้นคะยอ to urge, insist, importune, press; to nag

คั่ง crowded, packed, congested, jammed; overdue, behind schedule, in arrears
　　คั่งค้าง overdue, behind schedule, in arrears; a backlog, a pile-up
　　คั่งแค้น to fume silently, be angry without showing it
　　คับคั่ง *see* **คับคั่ง** หน้า 88
　　เลือดคั่ง internal hemorrhage, congestion of the blood

คัด to select, choose, cull; to copy

คัดค้าน to object, oppose, disagree; protest, remonstrate
　　คำคัดค้าน opposition

คัดง้าง at loggerheads (with)
　　ในรัฐบาลชุดนี้ มีรัฐมนตรีสองคนคัดง้างกันเป็นประจำ *Two ministers in this government were often at loggerheads.*

คัดจมูก to have a stuffed nose, have nasal congestion

คัดฉาก to steer a boat, take the helm

คัดท้าย to be at the tail end

คัดไทย copying Thai

คัดเลือก to select, choose; selected
　　คัดเลือกทหาร to draft (men for service in the army), conscript
　　ไปคัดเลือกทหาร to present oneself for con-

ค ฆ ง จ ฉ ช ซ ฌ ญ ฎ ฏ ฐ ฑ ฒ ณ ด ต ถ ท ธ น บ ป ผ ฝ พ ฟ ภ ม ย ร ฤ ฤๅ ล ว ศ ษ ส ห ฬ อ ฮ

scription

คัดเลือด to stop the flow of blood, staunch bleeding

คัดสำเนา to copy, make a copy

คัดออก to reject, strike off, cull (from a list etc); drop (from), expunge (from)

คัน[1] handle, pole, rod

　คันฉ่อง mirror, looking-glass

　คันชัก plow handle; violin bow

　คันชั่ง scale beam

　คันชีพ cartridge belt; food pack

　คันไถ plow handle

　คันนา dike

　คันเบ็ด fishing rod, fishing pole

　คันร่ม bow

　คันเร่ง accelerator

　คันศร bow

คัน[2] to itch, /be/feel/ itchy; to have an /urge/ itch/ (to do something)

　คันตา My eye itches., I have an itchy eye.

　คันเท้า to have /an itch/an urge/ to kick someone

　คันปาก to have an urge to speak out, be itching to speak

　คันมือ to have an urge to do something, be itching to (sock someone, do something etc)

คัน[3] classifier for cars, spoons, forks and umbrellas

　ช้อนหนึ่งคัน a spoon

　รถสองคัน two cars

คั่น to separate, break, divide; to interpose, intervene

　คั่นกลาง in the middle, between

　คั่นรายการ to break the program (with some music, advertising, etc)

　คั่นหนังสือ to place a marker in a book

　　ที่คั่นหนังสือ bookmark

คั้น to squeeze

　คั้นกะทิ to squeeze coconut cream out of shredded coconut

　น้ำส้มคั้น fresh orange juice

คันถ- sacred writings of a religion, scriptures

　คันถธุระ scriptural studies

　คันถรจนาจารย์ author of sacred writings

คันธ- fragrance, perfume, scent, redolence

　คันธกุฎี abode of Lord Buddha

　คันธมาทน์[1] fragrant intoxicant

　คันธมาทน์[2] name of a mountain

คันธารราษฎร์ special Buddha image set out during the invocation of rain

คับ tight, too small

　คับขัน critical

　　เหตุการณ์คับขัน /tight/critical/ situation, crisis

　คับคั่ง congested, squeezed together, crowded, overcrowded, packed

　คับแค้น troubled, distressed, in distress, oppressed, down

　ชีวิตนี้คับแค้นเหลือเกิน This life is so oppressive. / This life has got me down.

　　คับแค้นใจ to feel frustrated

　　ช่างคับแค้นใจ frustrating

　คับแคบ narrow; tight, too small, unspacious, confined, not roomy, cramped

　คับใจ unhappy, distressed by something, to find something intolerable

คัพโภทร pregnancy

คัมภีร์ sacred writings of a religion, scriptures

　คัมภีรภาพ profound, subtle, deep; abstruse

คั่ว[1] to roast, roasted

　ข้าวโพดคั่ว popcorn

คั่ว[2] to be ready to /trump/pounce/(การพนัน)

คา[1] cangue

คา[2] in difficulty; to stick, stuck; to remain unfinished; to be left open; at

　คาที่ on the spot, then and there

　คามือ at the hand (of), by the hand of

คาหนังคาเขา in the act, red-handed

ค่า value, worth; price, cost, charge, expense

ค่ากิน food /expenses/costs/

    ค่ากินอยู่ living expenses, board and lodging

ค่าของเงิน value of money

ค่าขนส่ง freight charge, cost of transportation

ค่าครองชีพ cost of living

ค่าคุ้มครอง protection money

ค่าโฆษณา advertising expense

ค่าจ้าง wages, pay

ค่าชดเชย compensation, indemnification

ค่าเช่า rent, rental

ค่าใช้จ่าย expenses

    ค่าใช้จ่ายเบ็ดเตล็ด miscellaneous expenses

ค่าใช้สอย expenses

ค่าโดยสาร fare

ค่าตอบแทน remuneration, payment

ค่าตัว personal worth

ค่าไถ่ ransom

ค่าทดแทน compensation

ค่าทำขวัญ compensation, indemnity, amends

ค่าที่ land rent; land tax

ค่าธรรมเนียม fee, charge

ค่านา farm tax

ค่านายหน้า commission, brokerage

ค่าน้ำ fishing tax; water charge

    ค่าน้ำค่าไฟ cost of water and electricity, cost of utilities

    ค่าน้ำชา, ค่าน้ำร้อนน้ำชา tea money

ค่านิยม values

ค่าบริการ charges, service charge

ค่าบำรุง subscription, membership fee; donation

    ค่าบำรุงรักษา maintenance fee, maintenance expenses

ค่าบำเหน็จ emolument(s)

ค่าปฏิกรรม reparations

ค่าป่วยการ commission, service charge

ค่าปิดปาก hush money

ค่าผ่านประตู admission, entrance fee

ค่าพาหนะ travelling expenses, transportation

ค่าภาคหลวง royalty

ค่ารถ travelling expenses

ค่าระวาง freight

ค่าแรง labor, cost of labor; pay, wage

ค่าเล่าเรียน school fees

ค่าสัมบูรณ์ absolute value

ค่าเสียหาย damages, compensation

คุณค่า value, worth

มีค่า valuable, precious, worth something

มูลค่า cost, value; worth

ไร้ค่า worthless, valueless

หาค่ามิได้ invaluable, inestimable, priceless

ค้า to trade, do business, buy and sell

ค้าของหนีภาษี to trade in /smuggled goods/ contraband/

ค้าขาย (to be in) trade, commerce, business

ค้าความ to make a business out of going to court, champerty, ambulance chasing *(sl)*

ค้าประเวณี to engage in prostitution

การค้าทาส slave trade

พ่อค้า merchant, trader, businessman, storekeeper, shopkeeper, tradesman, dealer

แม่ค้า tradeswoman, woman vendor

ร้านค้า shop, store

ลูกค้า customer

สินค้า merchandise, goods, products, commodities, wares; cargo

คาง chin

คางเหลือง moribund; in a sorry state

สี่เหลี่ยมคางหมู trapezoid

คางทูม mumps

ค ฆ ง จ ฉ ช ซ ฌ ญ ฎ ฏ ฐ ฑ ฒ ณ ด ต ถ ท ธ น บ ป ผ ฝ พ ฟ ภ ม ย ร ฤ ฤๅ ล ว ศ ษ ส ห ฬ อ ฮ

ค่าง langur

ค้าง[1] to be left unfinished, pending, suspended, stuck; incomplete, hung up; in the middle (of)

เรากำลังคุยกันค้างอยู่ ก็มีคนมาขัดจังหวะ Some guy interrupted us in the middle of our conversation.

ค้างคืน to stay overnight, spend the night, pass the night

ค้างเติ่ง to get stuck; to be hung up, left undone

ค้างแรม to stay overnight, spend the night

ตกค้าง to be left over, remain; to be overlooked; to be left behind

ค้าง[2] overdue, outstanding, unpaid

ค้างค่าเช่า to be overdue in a rent payment

ค้างชำระ overdue, unsettled, unpaid, outstanding

ค่าเช่าที่ค้าง overdue rent, unpaid rent, outstanding rent

คางคก toad

ค้างคาว bat

ค้างถั่ว beanpole, stake

คาด[1] to fasten, bind; to gird, wear

คาดเข็มขัด to /put on/wear/ a belt

คาดเข็มขัดนิรภัย to fasten one's /seatbelt/ safety belt/

คาดคั้น to constrain, press, pressure

คาดคั้นคำตอบ to demand an answer

คาดบั้นเอว to tie around the waist, girdle the waist

คาดพุง to /tie/wear/ around the belly

คาดหมัด to bind the hands with rope for boxing

คาด[2] to expect, anticipate, guess

คาดการณ์ to foresee, anticipate

คาดคะเน *see* **คาดคะเน** *หน้า 87*

คาดคั้น to grill (someone)

คาดเดา to speculate

คาดโทษ to warn of punishment for further wrongdoing.

คาดไม่ถึง unexpected, unanticipated, unforeseen; (I etc) never dreamed (/it would happen/you would go/etc)

คาดว่า think, expect; to surmise

ผมคาดว่าเศรษฐกิจของประเทศเราจะดีขึ้น I think the economy of our country will soon improve.

คาดหน้า (ประมาทหน้า) to underrate, underestimate; to belittle, disparage

คาดหมาย to expect, plan, anticipate, estimate

ตามคาดหมาย as /planned/expected/anticipated/, according to expectations

คาดหวัง *see* **คาดหวัง** *หน้า 532*

เกินคาด beyond expectations, more than one expects

ผิดคาด below expectations; not as expected, surprising, disappointing

คาถา incantation; verse, stanza

คาถาพัน Jataka verses

คาถาอาคม incantation, magic spell, magic formula, mantra

ค่าที่ for, because, owing to

คาน[1] to counterbalance; to counter

คาน[2] beam, joist

คานดีด lever

คานเรือ cradle; drydock

คานหาม litter

ไม้คาน carrying pole, shoulder pole

ค้าน to protest, lodge a protest, oppose, be anti, object, remonstrate

ฝ่ายค้าน the opposition

คาบ[1] period

หนังสือพิมพ์รายคาบ periodical

คาบ[2] to /hold/carry/ in the mouth, grip with the teeth

คาบกล้อง to carry a pipe in one's mouth,

smoke a pipe

คาบเกี่ยว overlapping; to extend to, related, pertaining to

คาบข่าว to spread the news

คาบลูกคาบดอก uncertain, in the balance, borderline

คาบศิลา a flintlock (gun)

คาบสมุทร peninsula

คาบเส้น on the borderline; on the line

คาม village, settlement, hamlet

คามวาสี villagers, local folk

คาย to spit out, regurgitate

คายความลับ to divulge a secret

คายพิษ to secrete venom

ค่าย camp, encampment

ค่ายกักกัน place of detention, concentration camp

ค่ายกักเชลย prisoner-of-war camp

ค่ายทหาร military camp

ไปค่าย to go camping

คารม eloquence, verbal skill; wit

คารมคมคาย witty, clever; expressive

(คน) มีคารมคมคาย a good talker, an /astute/clever/ speaker

คารวะ to respect

มีสัมมาคารวะ deferential, respectful; well behaved

คาราคาซัง to hang fire, be left pending

คาว smell of fresh /fish/meat/; fishy taste

คาวปลา amniotic fluid

ของคาว main course, main dishes, /meat/ fish/ dish

ของสดของคาว something sexy *(fig)*

คำ[1] gold

คำ[2] word; a numerical designation for bites or mouthfuls

คำกล่าวหา accusation; allegation; charge

คำแก้ตัว excuse, alibi

คำขวัญ slogan, watchword, motto

คำขอ application, request

คำขอร้อง request; petition

คำขาด ultimatum, final word

คำคัดค้าน opposition

คำคู่ความ pleadings

คำจำกัดความ definition, meaning

คำชมเชย praise, compliment, commendation

เขาตั้งใจปฏิบัติงาน จนได้รับคำชมเชยจาก เจ้านาย His devotion to his work earned him the praise of his employer. / He was /praised/commended/ for his work.

คำชี้แจง explanation

คำเชิญ invitation

คำด่า an insult, invective, abuse, something bad said to a person

คำต่อคำ word for word

คำตอบ answer, reply

คำตักเตือน warning, word of caution

คำตัดสิน decision, judgment, verdict

คำตาย a word which cannot be inflected

คำโต้แย้ง counterstatement, counterargument

คำถาม question

คำแถลง statement, announcement, declaration; communique

คำท้าทาย a challenge

คำทำนาย prediction, prophesy

คำนำ preface, foreword, introduction

คำแนะนำ advice, instructions

คำบอกเล่า hearsay

คำปฏิญาณ oath, vow

คำประกาศ announcement

คำประท้วง protest, objection

คำประพันธ์ poetical writing, poetry

คำประสม combined word

คำปรารภ preface, introduction, preamble; statement, address

คำปราศรัย address, speech, talk

ค ฆ ง จ ฉ ช ซ ฌ ญ ฎ ฏ ฐ ฑ ฒ ณ ด ต ถ ท ธ น บ ป ผ ฝ พ ฟ ภ ม ย ร ฤ ฦ ล ว ศ ษ ส ห ฬ อ ฮ

คำเปรียบเทียบ analogy, comparison

คำแปล translation

คำผรุสวาท obscenity; abusive language, abuse

คำผวน spoonerism

คำพยากรณ์ forecast; prediction, prognostication

คำพังเพย saying, aphorism, adage, maxim

คำพิพากษา judgment, decision, verdict (คดีอาญา)

คำพูด word, words, what is said, speech, spoken word

ผมเชื่อคำพูดของเขา I believed what he said. / I believed him.

คำฟ้อง complaint, plaint

คำภาวนา prayer

คำมั่น promise, one's word

คำมั่นสัญญา promise, undertaking, pledge

คำเมือง Northern dialect

คำย่อ abbreviation

คำยินยอม consent

คำเยินยอ flattery

คำร้อง application, motion (กฎหมาย)

คำรับรอง recommendation, certification

คำเรียกร้อง demand; request

คำเล่าลือ rumor

คำสนอง acceptance

คำสั่ง order, instruction, direction, directive; program (คอมพิวเตอร์)

    คำสั่งสอน teaching, doctrine, exhortation

คำสาบาน oath

คำสุภาษิต proverb, maxim

คำเสนอ offer; tender

    คำเสนอซื้อหลักทรัพย์ tender offer to purchase securities

คำหยาบ a /coarse/dirty/obscene/lewd/ word, coarse language

คำหลวง a formal poetical writing

มหาชาติคำหลวง Epic of the Buddha-to-Be

คำหวาน sweet talk, blandishment

คำให้การ answer, reply, defense; statement

    คำให้การ (ในชั้นศาล) testimony (in court)

คำอวยพร greeting; blessing

คำอำลา farewell address, a goodbye

คำอุจาดลามก obscene language

คำอุทิศ dedication

กลับคำ, คืนคำ to go back on one's word, break a promise, fail to keep one's word

ชัดถ้อยชัดคำ distinctly, clearly, well enunciated; to speak emphatically

ถ้อยคำ words; wording, text; expression; declaration, statement

ค่ำ dusk, twilight; evening, day of the old lunar calendar

ตอนค่ำ at night, in the evening

มื้อค่ำ supper, evening meal, dinner

ย่ำค่ำ six o'clock in the evening, 6 p.m.

วันยังค่ำ all day long; anytime; all the time

หัวค่ำ early evening, dusk

หามรุ่งหามค่ำ day and night, from morn till night, arduously

อาหารค่ำ supper, evening meal, dinner

ค้ำ to support, hold up, prop, bolster, shore up

ค้ำเงิน to guarantee

ค้ำจุน to prop up, provide support (for)

ค้ำชู to support, sustain

ค้ำประกัน to guarantee, act as surety

    ผู้ค้ำประกัน guarantor, surety

    หนังสือค้ำประกัน guaranty, warranty

ค้ำฟ้า forever, eternally

ไม่มีใครอยู่ค้ำฟ้า No one lives forever.

คำนวณ to calculate, figure

คำนับ to bow (to), pay respect (to), salute

คำนึง to think of

    คำนึงถึง to think /of/about/; to take into account

โดยคำนึงถึง having in mind

คำเพลิง gun

คำรน to roar; to thunder, peal

คำรบ time
เขากล่าวคำเป็นคำรบสอง He spoke for the second time.

คำราม to roar; to thunder, peal

คำแหง bold, intrepid

คิกๆ to giggle, titter, tittering

คิด to think, have an idea; to calculate, figure; to charge (someone for something)
จะคิดเท่าไหร่ How much will you charge?

คิดการณ์ไกล make provision for; to be far-sighted, provident, sagacious; having foresight

คิดโกง disloyal, untrustworthy; crooked; to scheme, scheming

คิดคด perfidious, treacherous

คิดค้น to do some thinking about something; to do research, investigate

คิดจะ to plan to do something, think of doing something

คิดดอกเบี้ย to charge interest, take interest

คิดดูก่อน to think it over, reflect (on). Let me think about it.

คิดดูซิ Think of it!

คิดได้ to get an idea; to recollect, recall, remember; to become aware of (/something/an answer to a problem/etc)

คิดตก to find a solution, solve a problem, get it
ฉันคิดตกแล้วนะ I've got it!

คิดต่ำ to have a low mind

คิดถึง to think of; to miss someone, long for (someone or something)

> **คิดถึงคนึงหา** to yearn for someone
> **คิดถึงบ้าน** to be homesick, long for home

คิดทบทวน to review

คิดทรยศ to plan treachery, perfidious

คิดบัญชี to settle scores (with)

คิดเป็นอื่น to think otherwise

คิดไปคิดมา to think something over, ponder, ruminate

คิดมากไปเอง That's pretty far-fetched.; to attach too much importance to something

คิดมิชอบ to have /bad/wrong/ ideas

คิดมิดีมิร้าย to have immoral thoughts

คิดไม่ออก (I) can't think of it., (I) cannot /recall/remember/; to have no idea, be unable to think of anything

คิดร้าย ill-intentioned, malicious *see* **คิดร้าย** *หน้า 421*

คิดลึก to think /profoundly/deeply/, profound

คิดสกปรก to have dirty thoughts, have a dirty mind

คิดหนัก to give (something) a lot of thought, ponder, deliberate

คิดให้ดี to think carefully; Watch your step!

คิดออก to find a solution; have an idea

คิดอ่าน to understand

คิดอีกที to have second thoughts, on second thought

คิดเอาเอง to surmise, conjecture, suppose

ความคิด thought, idea, thinking

> **ความคิดเห็น** opinion, view, idea, thoughts

คิริ, คีรี mountain

คิลานปัจจัย medicine, drugs, pharmaceuticals

คิว queue, line, turn
ถึงคิวผมที่จะอภิปราย It is my turn to speak.

คิวรถ /taxi/motorcycle/ stand

เข้าคิว to queue up, get in line

แทรกคิว to cut in the line

คิ้ว[1] eyebrow

ขมวดคิ้ว to frown, show consternation

ยักคิ้ว to raise one's eyebrows

เลิกคิ้ว to raise one's eyebrows

ค
ฆ
ง
จ
ฉ
ช
ซ
ฌ
ญ
ฎ
ฏ
ฐ
ฑ
ฒ
ณ
ด
ต
ถ
ท
ธ
น
บ
ป
ผ
ฝ
พ
ฟ
ภ
ม
ย
ร
ฤ
ฦ
ล
ว
ศ
ษ
ส
ห
ฬ
อ
ฮ

คิ้ว[2] molding
คิ้วไม้ wooden molding

คี่ odd; single, one of a pair
คู่คี่ neck and neck, very close, a toss-up
เลขคี่ odd number
วันคี่ odd days, odd numbered days

คีตกวี composer

คีบ to take up (with /chopsticks/tongs/etc)
คีบบุหรี่ to hold a cigarette between the fingers

คีม tongs, pincers, pliers; forceps (ใช้ในการแพทย์)

คีย์แมน key man

คีรี mountain

คึก high-spirited, mettlesome; stimulated; excited, aroused
คึกคะนอง lively, spirited, high-spirited
คึกคัก animated, busy (with /people/ activity/etc), lively

คืน[1] night, evening
คืนก่อน a previous night
คืนนี้ tonight, this evening
คืนยังรุ่ง all night long, throughout the night
คืนส่งตัว bridal night

คืน[2] to return, give back; to return to the original /position/shape/, straighten
คืนคำ to go back on one's word, break one's promise, recant
คืนเงิน to refund, give a refund, return the /money/purchase price/
คืนชีพ to come back to life, be revived, be resurrected
การคืนชีพ resurrection, return to life
คืนดี to make up, be reconciled, get back on good terms, become friends again
คืนล้อ to straighten the wheels
คืนสติ to regain consciousness, come to
คืนให้ to return something to someone
เอาคืน to take something back, retrieve

คืบ[1] a span (a unit of length equal to one quarter of a meter)

คืบ[2] to inch along
คืบคลาน to creep up on
เขาป่วยหนัก ความตายคืบคลานเข้ามาทุกที He was gravely ill; death was creeping up on him.
คืบหน้า to advance, get along, come along, progress

คือ is, that is, namely, viz.
เขาคือใคร Who is he?
คือกัน see **ครือ** หน้า 79
คือว่า that is to say, I mean, that is, is that, i.e.
ก็คือ see **คือ** แต่บางครั้งไม่จำเป็นต้องแปล
กล่าวคือ that is to say, namely, i.e., viz.

คุ to smoulder; smouldering

คุก jail, gaol, prison
ขังคุก to imprison, put in jail, jail
ขี้คุก jailbird
ตัดสินจำคุก to be sentenced to imprisonment
แหกคุก to break out of jail, pull a jailbreak

คุกเข่า to kneel, kneel down

คุกคลาน to crawl, creep

คุกคาม to threaten, menace, endanger; to intimidate
การคุกคามทางเพศ sexual harassment

คุ้ง bend
คุ้งน้ำ river bend, bend in a river
เป็นคุ้งเป็นแคว (fig) at great length, interminably

คุณ[1] virtue, good; quality; benefit
คุณค่า value, worth
คุณงามความดี (the) good, virtue
คุณธรรม goodness, virtue, righteousness, fairness
คนมีคุณธรรม good man, /righteous/ moral/virtuous/ person

ไร้คุณธรรม unfair

คุณนาม adjective

คุณประโยชน์ benefit(s), utility, advantages; use

มีคุณประโยชน์ beneficial

คุณพระช่วย God help me!, My god!

คุณพระศรีรัตนตรัย the Triple Gem

คุณพิเศษ, คุณวิเศษ spiritual attainment

คุณภาพ quality

คุณลักษณะ character, attribute, characteristics, quality, property, traits

คุณวุฒิ qualification

ผู้ทรงคุณวุฒิ expert, qualified

คุณศัพท์ adjective

คุณสมบัติ qualifications; quality, characteristic, property, attribute; requirement

มีคุณ good, beneficial, valuable

ให้คุณ beneficial, of benefit, useful, positive

คุณ[2] you; Mister (Mr.), Misses (Mrs.), Miss (Ms.)

คุณครับ Sir!, Miss!, Madam!

คุณครู teacher

คุณนาย sir

คุณพ่อ father

คุณแม่ mother

คุณหญิง honorific title for a woman similar to "Lady"

ให้คุณ for you

คุณากร source of /goodness/virtue/

คุณูปการ benefit, support, patronage

ผู้มีคุณูปการ supporter, benefactor, patron

คุด to curl up

คุดคู้ to curl up; to cringe, shrink (from, away); curled up, in fetal position

หนวดคุด ingrown /whisker/hair/

คุดทะราด yaws

คุ้น to become accustomed (to), get used to; to be familiar with

คุ้นเคย to know someone, be familiar (with)

ความคุ้นเคย familiarity

คนคุ้นเคย acquaintance, someone you know, someone you are familiar with

คุ้นตา a familiar sight; to look familiar, recognize

คุ้นหน้าคุ้นตา to look familiar, have seen before, be no stranger

คุ้นหู to sound familiar, have heard of (it) before

รู้จักมักคุ้น to be acquainted with, know someone personally

คุม to control, direct, manage, operate, be in charge (of); to police; to detain, intern

คุมกันเข้า taken together

คุมกำเนิด to practice birth control

การคุมกำเนิด birth control

คุมเกม to control the game, exercise control, have control (over)

คุมขัง to jail, imprison

คุมแค้น to have a grudge against, harbor ill feelings against someone

คุมงาน to supervise, be in charge (of)

คุมแจ to keep a close eye on somebody, keep under close control

คุมเชิง to be wary, cautious, on the alert; to keep an eye on

คุมซ่อง to police a brothel

คุมตัว to detain, intern

คุมบ่อน to police a gambling den

ควบคุม to control; to take into custody

ภายใต้ความควบคุมของ under the control of

ผู้คุม jailer, gaoler, prison guard; guardian

คุ้ม[1] residence of princes in northern Thailand

คุ้ม[2] to protect; to cover

คุ้มกัน to give protection (to), guard; escort

คุ้มครอง to protect, watch over

การคุ้มครอง protection

ค ฆ ง จ ฉ ช ซ ฌ ญ ฎ ฏ ฐ ฑ ฒ ณ ด ต ถ ท ธ น บ ป ผ ฝ พ ฟ ภ ม ย ร ฤ ฤๅ ล ว ศ ษ ส ห ฬ อ ฮ

คุ้ม[3] to be worth

คุ้มค่า to be worth the expense, worthwhile, be value for one's money; justified

　คุ้มค่าเหนื่อย worth the effort

ได้ไม่คุ้มเสีย It is not worth it.

คุ้ม[4] to, until

คุ้มดีคุ้มร้าย unbalanced, temperamental, volatile, mercurial

คุย talk, have a talk, converse, have a conversation, chat

คุยเก่ง to be glib, voluble, be a good talker, be a good conversationalist

คุยโขมง to chat, have a discursive talk; to give a talkshow

　คุยโขมงโฉงเฉง to be a loudmouth; to brag

คุยโต to boast, brag, talk big

คุยฟุ้ง to crow (about), brag (about)

คุยโม้ to boast, brag, talk big

ขี้คุย to be a braggart, boaster, boastful

ช่างคุย talkative, affable

คุ้ย to grub, scratch (for)

คุ้ยเขี่ย to dig up, rake up, scrape up

ครุ teacher, instructor, tutor, guru

ครุภัณฑ์ heavy durable goods, furniture, heavy articles

ครุวาร Thursday

คูหา cave, cavern, grotto

คู[1] to coo

คู[2] ditch

คูคลอง canal

คูเมือง moat

คู่ even number; pair, couple, one of a pair

คู่กรณี party (to, in); person involved

คู่กัน paired, to make a pair

คู่ขา partner; pal, buddy; lover

คู่แข่ง rival, competitor, opponent

　คู่แข่งขัน competitor, contestant

คู่ครอง spouse, mate; husband and wife

คู่ควร compatible

　ไม่คู่ควร incompatible

คู่ความ parties (to an action), litigants

คู่คี่[1] neck and neck, very close, a toss-up

คู่คี่[2] gambling game of odds or evens

คู่เคียง[1] see **คู่ครอง** หน้า 77

คู่เคียง[2] officials who walk on either side of the royal vehicle in a procession, flanking attendants

คู่ใจ boon companion, someone close to one's heart, chum, trusted friend

คู่ฉบับ duplicate

คู่ฉีก bill of exchange

คู่ชก one of a pair of boxers, boxing partner; adversary, antagonist, nemesis

คู่ชีพ trusty; faithful

คู่ชีวิต constant partner, one's spouse, lifelong companion

คู่ซ้อม sparring partner

คู่ต่อสู้ opponent, rival, antagonist

คู่เต้นรำ (dancing) partner

คู่นอน bedfellow, bedmate

คู่บ้าน pride and joy of one's /home/village/ etc; the pride of one's /home/town/ etc, a /household/village/ treasure

　คู่บ้านคู่เมือง a national treasure, national icon, palladium

คู่บารมี court favorite, longtime supporter; symbol of authority

คู่บ่าวสาว the bride and groom

คู่ปรปักษ์ adversary, foe, enemy

คู่ปรับ enemy

คู่ผัวตัวเมีย married couple

คู่มือ[1] handbook, manual

คู่มือ[2] personal, one's own

คู่รัก boyfriend, girlfriend, lover, sweetheart, darling

　คู่รักคู่แค้น a couple whose love has turned to hate

คู่วิวาท disputant, parties to an argument

คู่สงคราม belligerent

คู่สมรส spouse

คู่สร้างคู่สม helpmate

คู่สวด monkly interrogator; the pair of monks who chant the ordination service

คู่สัญญา party to /a contract/an agreement/

คู่สัญญาณ (telephone) line

คู่สาย (telephone) line

คู่หมั้น fiancé (ชาย), fiancée (หญิง), person engaged to be married

คู่หู *as in* **เพื่อนคู่หู** confidant, /intimate/ close/friend, buddy, mate, pal

คู่อริ, คู่อาฆาต enemies, enemy, someone who has a grudge against another

    มวยคู่อาฆาต a grudge fight

จับคู่ to pair off, find a partner, a couple of

ทั้งคู่ both, both of them

คู้ to bend, folded up

คู้บัลลังก์ to sit cross-legged

คูณ to multiply

    คูณร่วมน้อย (ค.ร.น.) lowest common multiple (L.C.M.)

คูถ excrement

คูปอง coupon

คูหา cave, cavern, grotto; room, unit; carrel (ในห้องสมุด), cubicle, compartment

    ห้องแถวสี่คูหา a row house of 4 units

เค้เก้ clumsily

เค้น to squeeze, press; stress

    เค้นคอให้ตาย to /throttle/choke/ someone to death

    เค้นเอาความจริงออกมาให้ได้ to extract the truth

    เค้นหัวเราะ to force a laugh

เค็ม salty; *(fig)* hard, tough

    แม่ค้าคนนี้เค็มน่าดูเลย What a tough market monger she is!

    เค็มจัด[1] salty

เค็มจัด[2] grasping; mean, penny-pinching

น้ำเค็ม saltwater

เคมี chemistry

    เคมีภัณฑ์ chemicals, chemical supplies

    เคมีไฟฟ้า electrochemisty

      ทางเคมีไฟฟ้า electrochemical

เคย[1] baby shrimp, shrimp larvae, krill

เคย[2] have, used to, accustomed to; ever

    ฉันเคยอ่านแต่ในหนังสือ ไม่เคยทำ I've read about it in books but I have never done it.

    เคยชิน familiar, accustomed

    เคยตัว to get used to, habituated

    เคยไหม have you ever

    เช่นเคย as before, as usual

    ตามเคย once again, as usual

    ไม่เคย never, have not (haven't), never have, not before now

      ไม่เคยพบไม่เคยเห็น completely unknown

      ไม่เคยเลย never, never ever

      ไม่เคยทำเลย I have never ever done it.

    อย่างเคย as before, as usual

เคร่ง strict, severe; devout; restrained, serious; stern

    เคร่งขรึม serious, grave, solemn, sedate

    เคร่งครัด strictly

    เคร่งเครียด tense, strained

    พระเคร่ง a devout monk

เครดิต credit

    เครดิตฟองซิเอร์ credit foncier

เครา beard

เคราะห์ luck, fortune, fate, destiny; bad luck, misfortune

    เคราะห์ดี lucky, fortunate, good luck

    เคราะห์ดีที่ตำรวจมาทัน /Luckily/Fortunately/ the police came in the nick of time.

    เคราะห์ร้าย unlucky, unfortunate, bad luck

    เคราะห์หามยามร้าย in one's /misfortune/ misery/

ค ฆ ง จ ฉ ช ซ ฌ ญ ฎ ฏ ฐ ฑ ฒ ณ ด ต ถ ท ธ น บ ป ผ ฝ พ ฟ ภ ม ย ร ฤ ฤๅ ล ว ศ ษ ส ห ฬ อ ฮ

พ้นเคราะห์ to get over one's spell of bad luck, put paid to (one's) /bad luck/misfortune/

พ้นเคราะห์ไปที Thank goodness that's over!

สะเดาะเคราะห์ see สะเดาะเคราะห์ *หน้า 486*

เครียด tense, taut, tight; under strain, under stress

เคร่งเครียด tense, strained

ความเครียด strain, tension

ตึงเครียด tense, under stress; critical

เครือ[1] creeper, vine

เครือกล้วย a stem of bananas

เครือแย่ง a foliate decorative design

เครือ[2] lineage, pedigree, ancestry, family

เครือข่าย network

เครือจักรภพอังกฤษ British Commonwealth

เครือญาติ family tree, kindred, family, family line

ในเครือ of a group; affiliated

หนังสือในเครือ "มติชน" a publication of the "Matichon" group

วงศ์วานว่านเครือ family, family relations, origins

เครือ[3] shaky, tremulous, indistinct

คลุมเครือ vague, ambiguous, obscure, unclear

เสียงเครือ husky; shaky; hoarse (/sound/voice/)

เครื่อง machine, engine; contrivance, device, apparatus, equipment; ingredients; things; organ

เครื่องกรอง filter

เครื่องกระป๋อง canned goods, tinned goods, canned food

เครื่องกล machine, machinery

เครื่องกลึง lathe

เครื่องกัณฑ์ offering to the monk who gives a sermon

เครื่องกำเนิดไฟฟ้า generator, dynamo

เครื่องกิน a silver betel service

เครื่องแกง curry spices

เครื่องขยาย amplifier; enlarger

เครื่องขยายเสียง loudspeaker; amplifier

เครื่องเงิน lacquerware

เครื่องเขียน stationery, writing materials

เครื่องครัว kitchenware, kitchen utensils

เครื่องเครา things

เครื่องเงิน silverware

เครื่องจองจำ shackles, bonds

เครื่องจักร machinery, machine

เครื่องจักรไอน้ำ steam engine

เครื่องจักสาน basketry

เครื่องฉายหนัง projector

เครื่องฉายเอกซเรย์ X-ray /machine/apparatus/

เครื่องชูชีพ life-buoy, lifebelt (เข็มขัด), life-jacket (เสื้อ)

เครื่องใช้ utensil, implement, instrument, appliance, equipment

เครื่องใช้ไฟฟ้า electrical appliances

เครื่องซักผ้า washing machine

เครื่องเซ่น spirit offerings

เครื่องดนตรี musical instrument

เครื่องดองของเมา intoxicants

เครื่องดับเพลิง fire-engine; fire extinguisher

เครื่องดินเผา earthenware, pottery, ceramics

เครื่องดีดสีตีเป่า musical instruments

เครื่องดื่ม beverages, drinks

เครื่องดูดฝุ่น vacuum cleaner

เครื่องต้น things used or eaten by a king, royal habiliments and provisions

เครื่องตวง measure

เครื่องตอบแทน recompense; honorarium (เงิน), token of appreciation

เครื่องตัดกระดาษ paper cutter

เครื่องตัดหญ้า lawnmower, mowing-machine

เครื่องแต่งตัว wearing apparel, garb, clothing,

garments

เครื่องแต่งบ้าน home furnishings

เครื่องแต่งร้าน /shop/store/ fittings, store furnishings

เครื่องถม nielloware, niello

เครื่องถ่ายเอกสาร copier, copying machine

เครื่องทรง royal apparel

เครื่องทอผ้า loom

เครื่องทอง articles of gold

เครื่องทุ่นแรง laborsaving /machinery/ machine/device/equipment/

เครื่องเทศ spice, spices

เครื่องไทยทาน offerings for monks

เครื่องนุ่งห่ม clothing, garments, wearing apparel

เครื่องใน giblets (เฉพาะเป็ดไก่ซึ่งกินได้), viscera เช่น tripe, heart, liver, kidney, sweetbreads, gizzard

เครื่องบน roof members; votive objects

เครื่องบรรณาการ tribute

เครื่องบันทึกเสียง tape recorder, sound recorder

เครื่องบำเรอ luxuries, luxurious entertainment, things to gratify the senses, pleasurable things, a delight

เครื่องบิน aeroplane, airplane, aircraft

เครื่องบูชา altar offerings

เครื่องแบบ uniform

เครื่องประดับ ornaments, costume jewelry decorations, adornment

เครื่องประดาน้ำ diving equipment

เครื่องผูก structural members of a house tied in place with rattan

เครื่องพันธนาการ shackles

เครื่องพิมพ์ดีด typewriter

เครื่องพิสูจน์ proof, evidence, clear indication

เครื่องเพชรพลอย jewelry

เครื่องมือ tool, implement, instrument,

apparatus, appliance

เครื่องไม้เครื่องมือ equipment, everything one needs

เครื่องยศ insignia of rank

เครื่องยา medicinal substance, medicine, remedy, medicament

เครื่องร่อน glider, sailplane

เครื่องรับ receiving set, receiver

เครื่องรับฝากข้อความ answering machine

เครื่องรางของขลัง charm, amulet, talisman, fetish

เครื่องเรือน household articles, (home) furnishings

เครื่องลายคราม Chinaware, Chinese blue and white pottery

เครื่องเล่น toy, plaything; divertissement

   เครื่องเล่นจานเสียง phonograph

เครื่องว่าง snack

เครื่องวิทยุ radio, wireless

เครื่องส่งวิทยุ wireless transmitter

เครื่องสาย stringed instrument

เครื่องสำอาง cosmetics, perfumery

เครื่องสุขภัณฑ์ sanitary ware

เครื่องสูง regalia, emblems of high estate

เครื่องหมาย sign, mark, symbol, token

   เครื่องหมายการค้า trade mark, trademark

เครื่องอะไหล่ spare part

เครื่องอัดสำเนา duplicating machine

เครื่องอัดเสียง tape recorder

เครื่องอุปกรณ์ equipment, accessories

เครื่องอุปโภคบริโภค consumer goods

เครื่องไอพ่น jet engine

ช่างเครื่อง mechanic, fitter; engineer

ทรงเครื่อง savory, garnished

   แม่ม่ายทรงเครื่อง wealthy widow

น้ำมันเครื่อง engine oil, lubricating oil

เป็นเครื่องตอบแทน something given in return, to reciprocate with something

ห้องเครื่อง engine room; royal kitchen

ค
ฆ
ง
จ
ฉ
ช
ซ
ฌ
ญ
ฎ
ฏ
ฐ
ฑ
ฒ
ณ
ด
ต
ถ
ท
ธ
น
บ
ป
ผ
ฝ
พ
ฟ
ภ
ม
ย
ร
ฤ
ฤๅ
ล
ว
ศ
ษ
ส
ห
ฬ
อ
ฮ

เคล็ด[1] gimmick, trick, technique
　เคล็ดในการทำงาน technique used in one's work
　เคล็ดลับ trick (in, of, to, about)
เคล็ด[2] sprained; stiff
　เดินไกลจนขาเคล็ด My legs have got stiff from walking so far.
　ข้อเท้าเคล็ด sprained ankle
　คอเคล็ด stiff neck
เคล้น, คลึงเคล้น to knead
เคล้า to blend, mix together; to rub up against; to finger
　เคล้าคลึง to caress, fondle; to stroke; to embrace; to neck (sl)
　เคล้าเคลีย to fawn (on), rub against, brush against
เคลิบเคลิ้ม to forget oneself, be absorbed (in), enraptured, lost in thought
เคลิ้ม absent-minded, abstracted; carried away (by), euphoric; dozing, half asleep; to doze
　...เคลิ้มไปกับเสียงเพลงที่ไพเราะ...carried away by the heavenly song
　เคลิ้มฝัน to be daydreaming, have a reverie
เคลีย to caress
　เคล้าเคลีย, คลอเคลีย to fawn (on), rub against, brush against
　เดินคลอเคลีย to walk along fawning on one another
เคลียร์ to clear
　เคลียร์บัญชี to clear accounts
　เคลียร์พื้นที่ to clear an area
เคลื่อน to move, shift, drift
　เคลื่อนที่ mobile, moving; dislocated
　　ห้องสมุดเคลื่อนที่ mobile library
　การเคลื่อนไหว activity, movement
เคลือบ to enamel, glaze, coat; covered over (with), coated
　เคลือบคลุม vague, cryptic, equivocal, ambiguous

เคลือบแคลง doubtful, dubious, suspicious, sceptical, distrustful
เคลือบแฝง to explain vaguely; to give a fishy explanation
เคลือบสี to glaze in color, to apply a colored glaze, enamel
　กระเบื้องเคลือบ glazed tiles
　แก้วเคลือบ opal glass
　หม้อเคลือบ enamelled pot
เคว้ง to float /along/about/, unsettled
　เคว้งคว้าง adrift, drifting
เคอะ as in
　เคอะเขิน ill at ease, awkward, uneasy
　ท่าทางเคอะเขิน gauche, lacking in self-assurance
เค้า clue; vestige, trace, hint, sign
　เค้าโครง outline
　เค้าเงื่อน clue
　เค้ามูล source
　จับเค้า to get some idea (of), begin to understand; to detect
　ต้นเค้า root, source; prototype, precursor
　ตั้งเค้า to show signs (of), incipient
　มีเค้า to look like, resemble
　หน้าตาเขามีเค้าของปู่มาก He /resembles/looks like/ his grandfather.
เคารพ to respect; to observe, obey
　เคารพกฎหมาย to observe the law
　ทำความเคารพ to salute
　รูปเคารพ idol, object of worship/reverence
เคาะ to knock, tap, rap; to tease, speak playfully
　เคาะจังหวะ to beat time
　เคาะประตู to knock at the door
　เต้นรำเคาะเท้า tap-dance
เคียง side by side
　เคียงกัน close together
　เคียงข้าง side by side, together, beside, next to
　เคียงคู่ side by side, together; in tandem,

paired
เคียงบ่าเคียงไหล่ shoulder to shoulder
เคียดแค้น vengeful
เคียน to tie around the waist
เคียว sickle
เคี่ยว to simmer; without letup
    เคี่ยวขับ, ขับเคี่ยว to struggle with; to exert oneself
    เคี่ยวเข็ญ to urge, prod, press, insist on
        เคี่ยวเข็ญตัวเอง to force oneself (to do something)
เคี้ยว to chew, masticate
    เคี้ยวฟัน to gnash the teeth, grind the teeth
    เคี้ยวเอื้อง to ruminate, chew the cud
    ขบเคี้ยว to eat
เคือง to be annoyed, irritated (by, at), cross (with someone), vexed
    ขัดเคือง mad at, to feel resentful
แค่ up to, only as much as, only to
    แค่นั้น only that, up to there
    แค่นี้ this far, up to here
    ส่งผมแค่นี้ก็พอ This far will be fine.
    แค่นี้หรือ Is that all?
    แค่สองช้อนก็พอ Two spoonsful are enough.
    แค่ไหน how far, how much, to what extent
    แค่เอื้อม within reach, close at hand
แคน reed mouth organ, panpipe
แค่น to be constrained (to), feel obliged (to); grudgingly, reluctantly
    แค่นกิน to feel constrained to eat, force oneself to eat
    แค่นทำ to feel obliged to do something, do unwillingly
    แค่นเรียน to force oneself to study
แค้น to resent, take offense, feel angry; be bitter; to be vengeful
    แก้แค้น see **แก้แค้น** หน้า 40
    คับแค้น resentful, indignant, bitter

เป็นเดือดเป็นแค้น enraged, infuriated, furious (with someone)
    มีความแค้นในใจ vindictive
    แร้นแค้น in dire straits; poverty-stricken, destitute
    ล้างแค้น to /take/get/ revenge
แคบ narrow
    คับแคบ narrow; tight, too small, unspacious, confined, not roomy; cramped
    ใจแคบ narrow-minded
    ช่องแคบ narrows, straits; pass, gap
แคบหมู crackling, fried pork skin
แคม gunwale (ของเรือ); lip
    แคมนอก labia majora
    แคมใน labia minora
    เหยียบเรือสองแคม irresolute; undecided; to vacillate
แคร่ litter; a light /bed/seat/
    แคร่เครื่องพิมพ์ดีด carriage
แคระ dwarf; undersized, stunted
    คนแคระ midget; pygmy
แคลงใจ suspicious, to have one's doubts (about)
แคล้ว to miss; to escape
    แคล้วคลาด safe; to be safe, be kept safe
แคล่วคล่อง active, agile, brisk; skilful, experienced, expert
แคว tributary
แควก /ripping/tearing/ sound
แคว้น region, territory, area
แคะ[1] Hainanese
แคะ[2] to pick (at)
    แคะได้ to find fault (with someone), fault finding
    แคะจมูก to pick one's nose
    แคะเล็บ to clean one's nails
    แคะหู to clean one's ears
    ค่อนแคะ to criticize, mock, gibe at
โค cow (ตัวเมีย), bull (ตัวผู้)
    โคกระบือ cattle

ค ฆ ง จ ฉ ช ซ ฌ ญ ฎ ฏ ฐ ฑ ฒ ณ ด ต ถ ท ธ น บ ป ผ ฝ พ ฟ ภ ม ย ร ฤ ฦ ล ว ศ ษ ส ห ฬ อ ฮ

โคงาน work-ox
โคนม milk cow, dairy cow
โคบาล cowboy
โคมัย cow dung
โครส cow's milk

โคก highland, high ground, elevated area
โค่ง /older/bigger/ than usual
นักเรียนโค่ง big for his class
โค้ง to bend, curve, arch; curving, tortuous
โค้งคำนับ to bow (to someone)
โค้งให้ to bow to; to nod (/to/at/ someone)
ทางโค้ง winding road, curve
หัวโค้งถนน a bend in the road
โคจร to orbit; to travel
โค้ช coach
โคตร family, line, race
เจ็ดชั่วโคตร seven generations
ล้างโคตร to wipe out the whole family
ศึกล้างโคตร a vendetta
โคน foot (เช่น at the foot of a tree), base
ถอนรากถอนโคน to extirpate, eradicate, root out
โค่น to fell, cut down; to overthrow; to beat, overcome, topple, bring (someone) down
เขาเป็นแชมเปี้ยนที่เก่งมาก ไม่มีใครโค่นเขาได้ He's a real champion. No one can beat him.
โคม lamp, lantern
โคมไฟ lamp, lantern
โคมลอย hot air, nonsense; hot air balloon
ข่าวโคมลอย rumor, unfounded news, unsubstantiated report
โคม่า coma
เข้าขั้นโคม่า to be in a coma
โครก growling, rumbling (ท้อง)
ชักโครก flush toilet; to flush the toilet
ส้วมชักโครก flush toilet
โครง ribs; outline, sketch, model
โครงกระดูก skeleton
โครงการ plan, project, program, scheme

โครงการสิบปี ten year plan
โครงเรื่อง plot
โครงสร้าง structure, framework, skeleton; arrangement
โคร่ง[1] tiger
โคร่ง[2] big, large, huge
โคร่งคร่าง big and ungainly, unwieldy
โครม crash, sound of something falling, smashing sound
ครึกโครม noisy, boisterous; (เสียง) din, hubbub
โคลง[1] a form of verse; poetry
โคลง[2] to roll, rock; unsteady, shaky
โคลงเคลง rolling, unsteady
โคลน mud, mire, muck
ขี้โคลน mud
น้ำโคลน watery mud
บังโคลน mudguard, fender
ใคร who (subject), whom (object); anyone
ใครๆ anyone, anybody
ใครก็ตาม anyone, everyone
ใครคนหนึ่ง a certain person
ใครต่อใคร everyone, everybody
ตัวใครตัวมัน It's everyone for himself.
ทีใครทีมัน It's my turn now.; My turn will come.
นั่นใคร Who's there?
ไม่มีใคร There's no one.
ใคร่ to desire; wish, want, should like to
ใคร่จะ should like to
ความใคร่ desire, love
ไม่ใคร่ little, not much
รักใคร่ to be fond of, care for, like, love
ใคร่ครวญ to study, consider carefully
ไค้ as in แคะไค้ to pry
ไคล[1] as in ขี้ไคล dead skin, scurf, crud
ไคล[2] to loosen, unscrew
ไคล้ as in คลั่งไคล้ infatuated (with), crazy about
ไคลแมกซ์ climax

ฆราวาส household life; layman, householder; lay *มีแขกทั้งที่เป็นบรรพชิตและฆราวาส There were visitors, both clerical and lay.*

ฆ้อง gong

ฆ้องกระแต small gong

ฆ้องชัย victory gong

ฆ้องปากแตก blabber, tattler; to blab, tattle

ฆ้องวง an instrument consisting of tuned gongs set in a circular frame

ฆ่า to kill, slay, destroy; to cancel, cross out

ฆ่ากลิ่น to destroy an odor, deodorize

ฆ่าคนโดยความประมาท to cause death through negligence

ฆ่าคนโดยความอาฆาต to kill in revenge

ฆ่าคนโดยเจตนา premeditated murder, to kill intentionally, murder

ฆ่าคนโดยบังเอิญ to cause death by accident

ฆ่าคนโดยไม่เจตนา to kill unintentionally

ฆ่าคนเพื่อป้องกันตัว to kill in self-defence

ฆ่าตัวตาย to commit suicide, kill oneself, take one's own life

ฆ่าปิดปาก to kill someone to keep him from talking, silence (someone)

ฆ่าฟัน to slaughter, kill, slay

ฆ่าล้างเผ่าพันธุ์ ethnic cleansing

ฆ่าเวลา to kill time (by), while away the time

ขีดฆ่า to cross out, cancel

ฆาต killing, destroying, destruction

ฆาตกรรม homicide; murder

ฆาตกร murderer, killer

ปิตุฆาต patricide

เพชฌฆาต executioner

มาตุฆาต matricide

ถึงฆาต to die

เฆี่ยน to whip, thrash, flog; to speed; to defeat *เขา เฆี่ยนผู้สมัครพรรคตรงข้ามเสียยับเยิน He thrashed his political opponent.*

โฆษก announcer; spokesman, spokeswoman, spokesperson

โฆษณา to advertise, publish; to publicize, get publicity

โฆษณาชวนเชื่อ propaganda, to propagandize

โฆษณาตัวเอง to publicize oneself, blow one's own horn

ผู้พิมพ์ผู้โฆษณา publisher

แผนกโฆษณา advertising department

ลงโฆษณาในหน้าหนังสือพิมพ์ to advertise in the press, place an advertisement

ฆ
ง
จ
ฉ
ช
ซ
ฌ
ญ
ฎ
ฏ
ฐ
ฑ
ฒ
ณ
ด
ต
ถ
ท
ธ
น
บ
ป
ผ
ฝ
พ
ฟ
ภ
ม
ย
ร
ฤ
ฦ
ล
ว
ศ
ษ
ส
ห
ฬ
อ
ฮ

งก · **ง** · งอ

ก
ข
ค
ฆ
ง

งก[1] grasping, greedy; acquisitive

    งกเงิน covetous, greedy

    ขี้งก avaricious

งก[2] to tremble

    งกๆ to slave, toil

    งกงัน to shudder (ใช้กับความกลัว); beside oneself (with fear etc)

    งกๆ เงิ่นๆ to dodder; dodderingly, doddery

    ตัวสั่นงันงก to tremble, quake

งง perplexed, puzzled, mystified, bewildered, confused; not understand

    งงงวย baffled, nonplussed

    งงงัน stunned, dazed, stupefied

    งงเต็ก flabbergasted

    งงเป็นไก่ตาแตก dumbfounded, bewildered

งด to suspend, stop, halt, refrain (from), abstain (from); to drop, cancel, call off; called off

    งดสูบบุหรี่ *No smoking. / Refrain from smoking.*

    งดใช้สนาม Field Closed

    งดรับแขก to cancel appointments; no visitors

    งดเว้น to refrain from, abstain from

งดงาม superb, elegant, splendid, beautiful, handsome

    ชนะอย่างงดงาม to win handsomely, have a splendid victory (over)

งบ[1] to close (an account); to balance (an account), strike a balance

    งบจร contingent fund, non-recurring item

    งบดุล balance sheet

    งบประมาณ budget, budget estimate

งบ[2] a cake of sugar

    งบน้ำตาล a cake of palm sugar

    งบน้ำอ้อย a cake of cane sugar

งม to grope in the water, feel around in the water for something; fish around for something

งมโข่ง dumb

คุณไปงมโข่งอยู่ที่ไหน เรื่องนี้เขารู้กันตั้งนานแล้ว
You're so dumb. Everyone's known about it for /days/weeks/months/.

    งมงาย to believe in something blindly, credulous; dogmatic

        ความงมงาย credulity, blind faith, foolish belief in something

งวง trunk, proboscis; aerobridge, pier, rampway (อากาศยาน)

    งวงช้าง trunk of an elephant

    ไก่งวง turkey

ง่วง, ง่วงงุน sleepy, drowsy

    ง่วงนอน sleepy, to feel sleepy

    ง่วงเหงาหาวนอน drowsy, hardly able to keep one's eyes open

งวด[1] period, time; installment

    จ่ายเป็นงวด to pay in installments, periodic payments

    ลอตเตอรี่งวดหน้า the next drawing of the lottery

งวด[2] to dry up, almost dry

ง่วน to be absorbed (in), engrossed (in); to be preoccupied with; to busy oneself with something

งั้วน savoury

    งั้วนดิน savoury earth

    งั้วนผึ้ง ambrosia, honey

งวยงง *see* **งงงวย**

งอ bent, curved, arched; crooked, warped; to contract; to bend, flex

    งอก่องอขิง to be doubled up (/with pain/by a kick/etc); to cringe

    งอแขน to /flex/bend/ the arm

    งอมืองอเท้า lazy; submissive, passive, supine; gutless, without gumption

    งอหงิก[1] contorted; gnarled

    งอหงิก[2] angry looking; to look mad

    หน้างอ to scowl, look sullen, pout, look

angry

หัวเราะงอหาย to double up with laughter, guffaw

ง้อ, ง้องอน to mollify; to make up to someone

ไม่ง้อใคร to refuse to /kowtow/make up/ to anyone

งอก shoot, sprout; to grow, develop; germinate, sprout, bud

งอกงาม to grow, develop; to accrue (หมายถึงดอกเบี้ย); to multiply, flourish, bloom

งอกเงย see งอก

ถั่วงอก beansprout

หินงอก stalacmite

งอกแงก shaky, tottering, infirm, unsteady; feeble, frail

ง่องแง่ง[1] to totter, be unsteady

ง่องแง่ง[2] to bicker, squabble

งอแง finicky, hard to please; fretful; sulky

คนงอแง a difficult person

งอดแงด touchy, irritable; petulant

งอน[1] curved/bent/ up

งอน[2] to sulk

งอนตุ๊บป่อง to pout

ง่อน vertical projection of /land/rock/

ง่อนแง่น shaky, unstable, wobbly

งอบ a peasant's hat made of palm leaves shaped like a lampshade used for protection against the sun

งอม very ripe; over-ripe

งอมแงม utterly, terribly, inveterate เช่น คน ติดการพนันจนงอมแงม *an inveterate gambler / He was terribly stuck on gambling.*

งอมพระราม to a frazzle

ถูกคู่ต่อสู้ชกจนงอมพระราม *He was beaten to a frazzle.*

สุกงอม very ripe

ง่อย completely debilitated; crippled

งั่ง[1] a metal Buddha fashioned without upper clothing

งั่ง[2] stupid, ignorant

งัด to pry up, pull out; to lever; to pry open, break in

งัดข้อ to have a test of strength, arm-wrestle; to be at loggerheads

งัดแงะ to break in to steal something

งันงก trembling, shaking, quivering, shivering, shuddering

งั้นหรือ Oh?, Is that so?

งับ to shut, close; to nip, bite; to snap at

งับประตู to shut/close/ the door

งัว bull (ตัวผู้), cow (ตัวเมีย)

งัวเงีย sleepy, drowsy

งา[1] sesame, sesame seed

งาตัด sesame cake

น้ำมันงา sesame oil

งา[2] tusk; ivory

งาช้าง elephant tusk

สีงาช้าง ivory

งาแซง sharpened stakes implanted at an angle to fend elephants away from a stockade wall; spike fence

งาสาน (พัดยศ) a fan, originally of ivory, awarded to a monk master of meditation, ceremonial fan used by a high-rank monk

ช้างงา a tusked elephant, a tusker

ถอดเขี้ยวถอดงา to emasculate, tame, subdue

ง้าง to force (apart, out), pry apart

ง้างไก to squeeze the trigger

ง้างนก to cock the gun

งาน[1] a measure of land equal to 400 square meters, ngan

งาน[2] work, job, task; fair, festival; ceremony; celebration, party, function

งานก่อสร้าง construction work

งานการ work, business

งานโกนจุก top-knot cutting ceremony

งานฉลอง party, celebration; festival, fete

จ ฉ ช ซ ฌ ญ ฎ ฏ ฐ ฑ ฒ ณ ด ต ถ ท ธ น บ ป ผ ฝ พ ฟ ภ ม ย ร ฤ ฦ ล ว ศ ษ ส ห ฬ อ ฮ

งานเฉลิมพระชนมพรรษา royal birthday /celebration/festivities/

งานด้านปกครอง administration

งานตัวอย่าง sample; demonstration

งานเต้นรำ a dance, a ball

งานแต่งงาน wedding

งานในหน้าที่ duty, responsibility, job, function

งานบ้าน housework

งานเบ็ดเตล็ด odd jobs, odds and ends

งานเบา light work

งานปีใหม่ New Year's Celebration

งานพระเมรุ royal cremation ceremony

งานพิธี ceremony, official function

งานพิเศษ extra work, work on the side, special job

งานราษฎร์ private tasks

งานรื่นเริง party, celebration, festivities, entertainment

งานฤดูหนาว winter fair

งานล้น to be swamped (with work), overloaded (with work); The work is piling up.

งานละเอียด fine work

งานวัด temple /fair/festival/

งานวันเกิด birthday party

งานวันชาติ National Day celebration

งานวันแม่ Mother's Day celebration

งานวิจัย research, research work

งานวิจัยสนาม fieldwork

งานศพ cremation, funeral, obsequies

งานสมโภช celebration

งานสมรส wedding

งานสร้างสรรค์ creative work

งานส่วนตัว private business, personal affairs, private matter

งานหนัก heavy work

งานหยาบ rough work

งานหลวง state function, public work

งานอดิเรก hobby, avocation, pastime

งานออกร้าน fair

งานเอกสาร paperwork

ดำเนินงาน to carry out, execute, administer, manage

ดูงาน to /observe/inspect/study/activities, make a study trip

ได้งานทำ to get a job, find work

ตกงาน to be out of /work/a job/, lose one's job

แต่งงาน to marry, /get/be/ married, wed

ทำงาน to work; to run

เครื่องจักรกำลังทำงาน The machine is *running.*

ไม่ทำงาน out of order; not at work

นายงาน foreman, person in charge, chief

บริหารงาน to administer, manage, conduct the affairs (of)

ประสานงาน to coordinate (with), work together with

เป็นงานเป็นการ serious, businesslike, systematic, systematically

โรงงาน factory, plant

ว่างงาน unemployed, jobless

สำนักงาน office

หยุดงาน to stop work

เอางานเอาการ energetic, serious, industrious, conscientious

ง่าน   see งุ่นง่าน *หน้า 107*

งาบ ๆ   opening and closing slowly

งาม   beautiful, handsome; attractive; fine, good

งามขำ comely, dark and attractive

งามงอน beautiful, a beauty

งามจริง truly beautiful, exquisite

งามตา beautiful

งามผาด attractive at first, (to have) a superficial beauty

งามพิศ ever more beautiful

งามระยับ very beautiful

งามหน้า to be ashamed

งดงาม splendid, beautiful, enchanting

งอกงาม to flourish

โฉมงามนางหนึ่ง a beauty

ราคางาม good price

สง่างาม elegant; stately, majestic

สวยงาม beautiful, pretty, fine looking

เห็นดีเห็นงาม to commend, approve (of), applaud

ง่าม fork, crotch; slit

ง่ามถ่อ receding hairline at the temples

ง่ามเท้า the space between the toes

ง่ามมือ the space between the fingers

เป็นง่าม forked

ง่าย easy, simple, facile

ง่ายแก่ easy to

ง่ายดาย so easy, simple

ง่ายเหมือนปอกกล้วย easy as falling off a log

โดยง่าย easily, readily, without difficulty, smoothly

มักง่าย careless, slipshod, sloppy

ว่าง่าย see **ว่าง่าย** หน้า 460

ว่านอนสอนง่าย obedient, receptive, compliant

ง้าว curved-blade pike

งำ to conceal; to keep, take care of; to control

งำความ to put something under wraps

งำเมือง to govern, administer

เก็บงำ see **เก็บงำ** หน้า 34

เงื่อนงำ catch

ง้ำ protruding, jutting, projecting

หน้าง้ำ to scowl, pout

งิ้ว a Chinese play

งีบ to take a nap, nap; to doze off

หลับงีบหนึ่ง to take a nap

งึกๆ to bob, nod

งึมงำ mumbling, muttering

งุนงง puzzled, bewildered, perplexed; dazed

งุ่นง่าน to be irritated, aroused

งุบงิบ to whisper; to do surreptitiously, do something on the sly; do quietly

งุ้ม hooked, curved down

งุ่มง่าม clumsy, awkward; clumsily, to lumber (along)

งู snake, serpent, viper

งูๆ ปลาๆ a little bit, not much, rudimentary

งูสวัด herpes zoster, shingles

เงก wearisome, a hell of a

นั่งคอยเงก to wait a hell of a long time / to have a wearisome wait

เงย to look up, lift one's head

เงยหน้าอ้าปาก to hold one's own, stand on one's own feet, Things are looking up.

เงอะ, เงอะงะ green; bumbling, clumsy, cloddish

เงา[1] shadow; reflection; image

เงาๆ indistinctly

เงามืด in the shadows

เงาไม้ shade (of a tree, forest, etc)

กระจกเงา mirror, looking glass

เป็นเงาตามตัว inevitably; to reflect, follow

เงา[2] glossy, shiny, shining, lustrous

ขึ้นเงา polished, shiny

ชักเงา to shine, polish

น้ำมันชักเงา varnish

เป็นเงา polished, shiny, having a /sheen/ luster/, brilliant, glossy

เง้า annoyed, irritated, peeved

หน้าเง้า pouting, to pout, scowl, angry-looking, to wear a long face

เง้างอด sulking, to sulk

เงาะ[1] rambutan

เงาะ[2] Negrito

เงิน money; silver

เงินกองกลาง pot; common fund, pool

เงินกองทุนชั้นที่ 1 first-tier capital fund

เงินก้อน a lump sum, substantial amount of money

เงินกู้ loan, borrowing, money borrowed

ง
จ
ฉ
ช
ซ
ฌ
ญ
ฎ
ฏ
ฐ
ฑ
ฒ
ณ
ด
ต
ถ
ท
ธ
น
บ
ป
ผ
ฝ
พ
ฟ
ภ
ม
ย
ร
ฤ
ฤๅ
ล
ว
ศ
ษ
ส
ห
ฬ
อ
ฮ

ก
ข
ค
ฆ
ง

เงินคล่องมือ ready cash

เงินค่าลิขสิทธิ์ royalty

เงินค่าเลี้ยงดู maintenance, support

เงินค้าง unpaid balance, outstandings

เงินเชื่อ credit, on credit

เงินดาวน์ down payment

เงินเดือน salary

เงินได้ income, earnings

เงินตกเบิก deferred salary

เงินต้น capital

เงินตรา money, currency, lawful money

เงินตาย currency withdrawn from circulation; idle funds

เงินทอง wealth, money

เงินๆ ทองๆ money

    เรื่องเงินๆ ทองๆ money matters

เงินทอน change

เงินที่ชำระหนี้ได้ตามกฎหมาย legal tender for debts

เงินทุน capital, funds, money that is put up

    เงินทุนหมุนเวียน circulating capital

เงินบาท baht

เงินปลีก small /change/coins/bills/

เงินปันผล dividend

เงินปี annual stipend paid to members of the royal family

เงินผ่อน an installment (payment); in installments

    ซื้อเงินผ่อน to buy on the installment plan

เงินฝาก bank deposit

เงินเฟ้อ inflation

เงินมัดจำ deposit, down payment, earnest money

เงินสด cash

เงินสนับสนุน financial support

เงินหมุนเวียน circulating funds, revolving funds

เงินแห้ง credit

เงี่ยง barb; barbel; spine

เงี่ยน strong urge (for, to), to have a craving (for), need (someone); to be horny, randy, feel /sexy/lustful/, have the hots (for someone)

    เงี่ยนหมาก to have a craving for some betel

เงียบ silent, quiet; still, calm, placid, peaceful, tranquil

    เงียบกริบ utterly silent, without a sound, dead still

    เงียบขรึม reserved, silent, taciturn, solemn

    เงียบฉี่ dead silence

    เงียบเชียบ perfectly still; soundless

    เงียบสงบ peaceful, quiet

    เงียบๆ หน่อย quiet please, a little less noise please

    เงียบเหงา quiet and lonely; bleak; deserted

เงี่ยหูฟัง to strain to hear, listen /closely/attentively/, hearken (to)

เงื้อ to raise (a/fist/knife/etc) ready to strike

เงือก mermaid

เงื่อง, เงื่องหงอย sluggish, lethargic

เงือดเงื้อ *see* เงื้อ

เงื่อน knot; condition; clue

    เงื่อนไข condition, proviso

        โดยไม่มีเงื่อนไข unconditional, unconditionally

    เงื่อนงำ catch

    เงื่อนตาย a fast knot

    เค้าเงื่อน clue

เงื้อม projection

    เงื้อมผา overhanging rock, an overhang

    เงื้อมมือ to be in another's clutches, have in one's clutches, under one's thumb

    เขาอยู่ในเงื้อมมือของศัตรูแล้ว He's in the enemy's clutches.

แง[1] middle of the forehead

แง[2] sound of a child crying, wail

แง่ projection; corner, angle; trick, angle

แง่งอน to sulk

แง่มุม angle

เล่นแง่ crafty, tricky, devious

แง่ง[1] offshoot from the root of the ginger plant

แง่ง[2] snarling

แง่ง[3] squealing

แง่ง[4] chevron

แง้ม ajar

แงะ to pick; to pry (/up/open/off)

โง to raise the head

โงหัวไม่ขึ้น to be utterly defeated; addicted (to), inveterate

เขาติดการพนันจนโงหัวไม่ขึ้น He is an inveterate gambler. / He was a gambling addict.

โง่, โง่เง่า foolish, stupid, ignorant; to be a fool

โง่บรม, บรมโง่ idiotic; Idiot!

ให้โง่ would be stupid

ผมมีเรื่องกับเขาอยู่แล้วจะไปหาเขาให้โง่เหลอ!I've

got a quarrel going on with him so it would be stupid for me to go to his place.

โงก to nod drowsily

โงกเงก shaky, unsteady; to rock

โง้ง curled

หนวดโง้ง curled moustache

โงน about to fall; wobbling, to waver

โงนเงน tottering, reeling

ไง what; how; but; hi!; anything

เป็นไง How are things?, How are you?; And then what?

ยังไง anything; might as well

ยังไงก็มาแล้ว อยู่อีกสักพักซิ We got here so we might as well stay a while.

ยังไงก็ได้ I don't care, anything's all right with me.

แล้วไง So?, So what.; And then?

ว่าไง What did you say?, What did he say?

ให้แล้วไง But I've already given it to you.

ง
จ
ฉ
ช
ซ
ฌ
ญ
ฎ
ฏ
ฐ
ฑ
ฒ
ณ
ด
ต
ถ
ท
ธ
น
บ
ป
ผ
ฝ
พ
ฟ
ภ
ม
ย
ร
ฤ
ฤๅ
ล
ว
ศ
ษ
ส
ห
ฬ
อ
ฮ

จง should, ought to, be

จงเกลียดจงชัง to have it in for someone; to detest

จงใจ to /act/do/ intentionally, intend (to do something)

จงดี well, properly

จงทำดี Do good.

จงเป็นพลเมืองดี Be a good citizen.

จงรักภักดี loyal, faithful

จงกรม to practise a walking meditation, a walking exercise

จงกรมแก้ว an image of the Buddha standing under a decorative arch with left foot raised and hands crossed in front

จงกล lotus, lotus shaped candlestand

จงกลนี lotus

จงอาง king cobra

จงอยปาก beak

จด to touch, adjoin, abut; to mark, note, jot down

จดจ่อ to concentrate, be absorbed (in)

จดจ้อง[1] to hesitate, dither

จดจ้อง[2] to watch, observe closely

จด ๆ จ้อง ๆ to dither

จดจำ to remember, note

จดชื่อ to write one's name, make a note of someone's name, take down someone's name, list someone

จดบัญชี to charge to one's account; Charge it.

จดทะเบียน to register, record

จดไว้ to record, take down, note, jot down

จดหมัด to put up one's guard

จดหมาย letter

จดหมายแนะนำตัว letter of introduction

จดหมายลงทะเบียน registered letter

จดหมายเวียน circular

จดหมายเหตุ chronicle, gazette, record of events

จตุ four

จตุบท, จตุบาท quadruped

จตุปัจจัย the four requisites of a monk: clothing, food, shelter and medicine

จตุปาริสุทธิศีล fourfold observance to insure purity

จตุโลกบาล guardians of the four directions of the world

จตุร four

จตุรพิธพรชัย the four blessings: long life, beauty, happiness and health

จตุราริยสัจ the Four Noble Truths

จตุสดมภ์ the four ministers of the ancient government: Interior, Royal Household, Finance, Agriculture

จน[1] poor, needy; to be checkmated (เฉพาะ หมากรุก)

จนกรอบ penniless, flat broke

จนใจ to be /at a loss/at one's wit's end/; helpless

จนตรอก cornered, trapped, have no way out

จนแต้ม to be outsmarted, cornered

จนปัญญา to have run out of ideas, be unable to think of anything, stymied, baffled, at a loss

จนมุม cornered, stymied, checkmated

ยากจน poor, needy, in poverty, impoverished, indigent, hard up

ยากดีมีจน (whether) rich or poor

จน[2] until

จนกระทั่ง until, until finally

จนกระทั่งเดี๋ยวนี้ up to now, until now, right up to the present

จนกว่า until

จนตลอด from the beginning, continuously

จนตลอดชีวิต for life

จนตาย to death; until the day one dies

จนถึง up to, up until, until, to

จบ[1] จนถึงที่สุด until the very end
จนทุกวันนี้ until /today/now/, up to the present time
จนบัดนี้ until now, by now, up to now, yet
จนสุดความสามารถ to the best of one's ability
round, repetition; end, finish; to end, finish, terminate
จบกัน to finish, come to an end
จบกันที to be done with something
จบเห่ to be done for, the end
That was the end of me. / I was done for.

จบ[2] salute
จบของก่อนใส่บาตร to raise an offering to the head deferentially before giving it
ช้างจบนายควาญช้าง The elephant saluted his mahout.

จ.ม. letter

จม[1] to sink, founder, be buried, imbedded; to settle
จมน้ำ to drown, be drowned; to sink
จมปลัก to get stuck, be stuck in the mud
จมไม่ลง to be unable to adapt

จม[2] lots, millions (พูด)
กินจมไปเลย to eat like a horse / eat lots
คนจมไปเลย /millions/lots/ of people

จมูก nose, snout; nosing
จมูกข้าว germ (of the rice grain)
ถูกจูงจมูก to be led around by the nose
รูจมูก nostril

จร to go, proceed; to roam, wander; contingent
จรจัด vagrant, homeless, stray
เด็กจรจัด waif
หมาจรจัด stray dog
จรดล to travel (to)
จรยุทธ์ guerrilla tactics, hit and run strategy
จรลี to go
ขาจร casual customer
คนจร a passer-by
งบจร /non-recurrent/contingent/ budget

item

จรด to abut, touch, reach, contact
จรดกรรไกร to position the scissors before cutting a lock of hair
จรดพระนังคัล Ploughing Ceremony
ตั้งแต่หัวจรดเท้า from head to foot
หล่อนมองเขาตั้งแต่หัวจรดเท้า She looked him up and down.

จรรยา ethics, professional conduct, behavior
จรรยาบรรณ code of ethics, rule of /conduct/professional behavior/
จรรยาแพทย์ medical ethics
ผิดจรรยา to violate a code of ethics; to misbehave

จรรโลง to support, maintain, sustain
จรรโลงใจ to encourage

จรวด rocket, skyrocket

จระเข้ crocodile, alligator

จระนำ projecting bay at the rear of a temple

จระบี, จาระบี grease
อัดจระบี to grease (a car etc)

จรัส bright, shining; glorious, resplendent

จราจร traffic
จราจรคับคั่ง /heavy/congested/ traffic
จราจรติดขัด traffic jam
กฎจราจร traffic regulations
ตำรวจจราจร traffic police

จริง true; yes; very, truly, really, genuinely
จริงๆ really, truly
จริงๆ นะ really, honestly, truly
จริงจัง seriously
จริงใจ sincere; true to
จริงหรือ Really?, Is that so?
จริงอยู่ while, still, although
ใจจริง really, sincerely, truly
ดีจริง great, wonderful, truly good
เท่าตัวจริง lifesize, actual size
แท้จริง in reality, in fact; genuine, real, authentic

จ
ฉ
ช
ซ
ฌ
ญ
ฎ
ฏ
ฐ
ฑ
ฒ
ณ
ด
ต
ถ
ท
ธ
น
บ
ป
ผ
ฝ
พ
ฟ
ภ
ม
ย
ร
ฤ
ฦ
ล
ว
ศ
ษ
ส
ห
ฬ
อ
ฮ

เป็นจริง to come true, be realized; to materialize

พูดจริง to speak the truth; to mean what one says

ไม่รู้ว่าเขาพูดจริงหรือเปล่า I'm not sure he means what he says.

เสียจริง great

เห็นจริง perspicacious, discerning

อันที่จริง in fact, in reality, actually, as a matter of fact

เอาจริง to put one's heart into something, take (a job etc) seriously

จริต behavior, conduct, deportment, manner

จริย- morality

จริยธรรม morality

จริยศาสตร์ ethics

จริยศึกษา moral education

จริยา behavior, conduct, deportment; manner

จเร overseer, inspector

จเรตำรวจ police inspector

จลาจล unrest, disorder, riot

จลาจลต่อต้าน an uprising

การจลาจล a riot, rioting

จวก to stab, slash; to punch; to haul over the coals, censure

นายกสมาคม โดนสมาชิกจวกในที่ประชุมอย่างหนัก The meeting hauled the president over the coals. / At the meeting, the president was censured by the members.

จ้วง to stab; to /paddle/draw/ water with the full sweep of the arm

จ้วงจาบ insulting, insolent

จวน[1] governor's residence

จวน[2] almost, approximately, nearly, it won't be long, soon

จวนจะ to be about to

จวนเจียน almost; just about, on the verge of

จวนแจ with so little time; to have no time left; in the nick of time, just in time

จวนได้ที่ almost right

จวนตัว to have not enough time to react; at the critical moment, with no way out

เมื่อจวนตัวเข้า เขาก็กระโดดออกทางหน้าต่าง At the critical moment, he jumped out of the window.

จวนตาย almost dead, on the verge of death, moribund

จวนถึง approaching

จวนเวลา It is almost time.

จวนเสร็จ almost ready, just about finished

จวบ to meet; to join; to reach

จวบจน until

จวบเหมาะ right, appropriate

จวัก kitchen spoon

จอ[1] dog; the Year of the Dog

จอ[2] screen

จอแก้ว T.V. screen

จอเงิน movie screen, silver screen

ดาราจอเงิน movie star, film star

จ่อ to hold close to; to put to, press against

จ่อขมับ to press (a gun etc) against one's temple

จ่อคอหอย to /point at/press against/ one's throat

จ่อคิว waiting for attention

จ้อ as in **คุยจ้อ** to be garrulous, talkative, loqua-cious; to chat away, chatter

เขาพูดจ้อ จนเพื่อนไม่มีโอกาสพูด He talked so much, his friend couldn't get a word in edgewise.

จ๋อ monkey

จอก[1] small metal water cup; a little, a drop of

จอก[2] water lettuce

จ๊อก as in **ลูกจ๊อก** underling, flunkey

จ๊อกแจ๊ก noisy

เสียงจ๊อกแจ๊ก noise

จอง to fasten, tie; to book, reserve; to claim (land)

จองกฐิน to reserve a temple for offering gifts to monks at the end of the Buddhist Lent

จองจำ to imprison, jail

จองซื้อ to subscribe (to)

> **จองซื้อหุ้น** to subscribe to shares
>> **บัญชีจองซื้อหุ้น** share subscription account

จองตั๋ว to /book/reserve/ a ticket

จองที่ดิน to pre-empt land, lay a claim to land

จองที่นั่ง to /book/reserve/ a seat

จองล้างจองผลาญ to be bent on someone's destruction

จองแล้ว booked, reserved

จองเวร to be bent on revenge; to harbor ill feelings (towards someone), vindictive, vengeful

> **จองเวรจองกรรม** to hold a grudge (against)

จองหนังสือ to subscribe to a publication; to reserve a book

สั่งจอง to order, place an order (for), subscribe (to)

จ้อง to watch; to stare (at, into); to gaze (at, into); to watch and wait

> **จ้องเขม็ง** to fix with one's eyes; to watch, study; to glare (at)

> **จ้องจะเอาท่าเดียว** to be waiting to pounce

> **จ้องจับผิด** to find fault with someone

> **จ้องดู, จ้องมอง** to peer (at), stare (at), fix one's eyes on

จ๋อง meekly; forlornly

> **นั่งหน้าจ๋อง** to look forlorn

จองหอง proud; arrogant, haughty, contemptuous; to think a lot of oneself

จอแจ congested, crowded, bustling; noisy

จ้อแจ้ babbling

จอด to stop, halt; to park (รถ); to moor (เรือ)

> **ที่จอดรถ** parking, parking /place/space/lot/area/, garage

จอน sideburn

จอบ hoe

จอม top, summit, peak; head, arch, great; a royal consort

> **จอมทัพ** supreme commander of the armed forces

> **จอมบงการ** arch dictator

> **จอมปลวก** anthill

> **จอมปลอม** phony, fake

> **จอมพล** field marshal
>> **จอมพลอากาศ** Marshal of the Royal Air Force

> **ผู้ร้ายจอมโหด** arch fiend

จ้อย small, little; insignificant, trivial, trifling

จ๋อย downcast; subdued, depressed, low-spirited

จะ shall, will; would, should

> *จะไปไหน Where are you /going/headed/?*

> *จะทำอะไร What are you going to do? / What will you do?*

> *แล้วจะทำอย่างไร What should I do?*

จ๊ะ[1] yes

จ๊ะ[2] a polite informal ending used by superiors or intimates

จะงอย tip

> **จะงอยปาก** tip of the beak

จะจะ, จะแจ้ง clear

จะแล่ม clear, bright, radiant, beaming

จะปิ้ง a modesty shield of gold or silver for little girls

จะละเม็ด (ปลา) pomfret, butterfish

> **ไข่จะละเม็ด** green-turtle egg

จะละหวั่น see **จ้าละหวั่น** *หน้า 117*

จ๊ะเอ๋ Peekaboo!; to meet by chance

จัก[1] to split lengthwise; to pink (with a pinking shears)

> **จักตอก** to split bamboo into fine strips for /weaving/plaiting/tying/

> **จักสาน** to do basketwork
>> **การจักสาน** basketry, basketwork,

จ
ฉ
ช
ซ
ฌ
ญ
ฎ
ฏ
ฐ
ฑ
ฒ
ณ
ด
ต
ถ
ท
ธ
น
บ
ป
ผ
ฝ
พ
ฟ
ภ
ม
ย
ร
ฤ
ฤๅ
ล
ว
ศ
ษ
ส
ห
ฬ
อ
ฮ

ก
ข
ค
ฆ
ง
จ

wickerwork

ช่างจักสาน basketmaker

เป็นจักๆ serrated, saw-toothed

จัก[2] literary or formal form of **จะ**

จักขอบคุณยิ่ง (it) would be appreciated (if)

จักเป็นประโยชน์อย่างมาก would be of great benefit

จักๆ pattering of rain

จักขุ eyes; visual

จักขุประสาท seeing faculty

จักขุวิญญาณ eye-consciousness, visual perception

จักขุสัมผัส vision, seeing, eye contact

จักจั่น cicada

จักจี้, จั๊กจี้ to tickle; It tickles., tickling; to /feel/ sound/ funny

จักร, จักร- wheel; discus armed with knives used as a weapon; sphere, region

จักรพรรดิ emperor

จักรพรรดินิยม imperialist

ลัทธิจักรพรรดินิยม imperialism

จักรยาน bicycle

จักรยานยนต์ motorcycle

จักรเย็บผ้า sewing machine

จักรราศี planetary orbit

จักรวรรดิ empire

จักรวาล universe

เครื่องจักร machinery, machine

หัวจักร locomotive

จักรี, จักริน king, monarch

ราชวงศ์จักรี Chakri dynasty

จักษุ eye

จักษุแพทย์ oculist

จัง awfully, very, really, truly

จังหน้า full in the face, right in the face

คิดถึงจัง to really miss someone

ถูกจัง awfully cheap, truly inexpensive

หิวจัง starving, very hungry

จังก้า poised for action

ยืนจังก้า to strike an attitude of confrontation, confront belligerently, take a threatening stance

จังงัง stunned, stupefied, dazed; taken aback, surprised

จังหวะ[1] rhythm, tempo; phase; time, timing

จังหวะจะโคน good delivery

เขาพูดเป็นจังหวะจะโคน His delivery was excellent.

ขัดจังหวะ to interrupt, break in (on)

จังหวะ[2] speed; cycle

พัดลมสองจังหวะ two speed fan

เครื่องยนต์สองจังหวะ two /stroke/cycle/ engine

จังหวัด province; regional, provincial

จังหวัดแพร่ Phrae Province/ Province of Phrae

จังหัน food (for a monk)

จัญไร wicked, evil, loathsome, vile, abominable; calamitous; abomination

จัณฑ์ *as in* **น้ำจัณฑ์** liquor, spirits

จัณฑาล outcast

จัด[1] to arrange; to fix up; to put in order, tidy, straighten up; to organize

จัดการ to manage, direct

จัดแจง to prepare, make arrangements, get things ready

จัดตั้ง to set up, establish, form, organize

จัดโต๊ะ to lay the table, set the table, arrange the table

จัดสรร to allocate, apportion

บ้านจัดสรร housing development, housing estate

จัดห้อง to arrange the /room/ hall/ etc/; to make up the room, tidy up one's room

จัดหา to provide, acquire, find, procure

จัดให้ to supply, provide, /put/place/ at one's disposal

รัฐจะจัดพาหนะให้สำหรับการขนส่งที่จำเป็น The

state shall place at their disposal the necessary means of transport.

จัดใหม่ to re-arrange, revise, reorganize

จัด[2] extremely, very, intensly

จัดจ้าน brassy, outspoken; forward

จัดเจน experienced, an old hand (at), well versed in

ปากจัด sharp-tongued, biting, sarcastic

จัตวา four, fourth, quater

จัตวาศก any year of the old calendar ending in the number four

ชั้นจัตวา fourth /class/grade/

นายพลจัตวา brigadier general

จัตุ four, quadri-

จัตุบาท quadruped; quadrupedal

จัตุโลกบาล guardians of the four compass points of the world

จัตุสดมภ์ *see* **จตุสดมภ์** *หน้า 110*

จัตุร four

จัตุรงค์ four parts; four divisions of an army: (elephants, chariots, cavalry and infantry)

จัตุรัส square

จั่น trap

จันทน์ sandal tree

จันทน์เทศ nutmeg

ไม้จันทน์ sandalwood

จันทร์, จันทร- moon, lunar

จันทรคติ lunar calendar

จันทรคราส lunar eclipse

จันทรุปราคา lunar eclipse

จันทัน rafter

จันอับ a sweet star-shaped cake

จับ to catch, take, hold, take hold (of), grasp, grab, grip, get

จับกลุ่ม to gather

จับกุม to arrest, apprehend

จับขั้ว to form an alliance of political parties

จับเขม่า sooted, /covered/coated/ with soot

จับไข้ to get sick, fall ill; to be getting a fever, be feverish

จับความได้ to get the point, understand

จับคอน to perch

จับคู่ to pair off, find a partner; a couple of

จับเค้า to get some idea (of), begin to understand; to detect

จับจด shiftless; lacking in purpose, lackadaisical

จับจอง to claim, stake a claim (to), reserve

จับจ่าย to go shopping; expenses

จับจิต, จับใจ impressive; fascinating

จับเจ่า dejected

จับชีพจร to /feel/take/ one's pulse

จับต้นชนปลายไม่ถูก I cannot make head or tail of it.

จับต้อง to touch

จับตัว to catch someone

จับตา to catch the eye; to keep an eye on, watch

จับตาดู to keep watch

จับปลา to catch fish, go fishing

จับเป็น to catch alive

จับผิด to find fault with

จับพลัดจับผลู if luck would have it, Who knows?

สมัครผู้แทนเถอะน่า จับพลัดจับผลูคุณอาจได้เป็นรัฐมนตรีก็ได้ Throw your hat in the ring. Who knows? You may wind up being a cabinet minister.

จับมือ to shake hands; to hold someone's hand

    จับมือกัน to make up, become reconciled

    จับมือถือแขน to get familiar (with someone)

จับไม่ได้ไล่ไม่ทัน to be unable to keep up with someone

จับยาม to know, divine

จับรถ to catch a /bus/cab/ etc, grab a bus

จับเวลา to keep time, to check the time

จ
ฉ
ช
ซ
ฌ
ญ
ฎ
ฏ
ฐ
ฑ
ฒ
ณ
ด
ต
ถ
ท
ธ
น
บ
ป
ผ
ฝ
พ
ฟ
ภ
ม
ย
ร
ฤ
ฤๅ
ล
ว
ศ
ษ
ส
ห
ฬ
อ
ฮ

(it takes to do something)

จับสลาก to draw lots

จับหลัก[1] to be motionless; to perch on a pole

จับหลัก[2] to understand the principle (of), to /grasp/get/ the point (of)

จับกัง coolie, laborer (labourer)

จับฉ่าย[1] a Chinese multi-vegetable soup

จับฉ่าย[2] miscellaneous, assorted, all sorts of, a variety of, hodgepodge

จับปิ้ง see จะปิ้ง *หน้า 113*

จั่ว gable

จั่วไพ่ to turn up a card

จั่วหัว headline; to headline

จา see พูดจา *หน้า 355*

จ่า[1] a noncommissioned /military/police/ rank, a rank in the Royal Household Department

จ่ากลอง chief drummer of victory drums

จ่าตรี third petty officer

จ่าโท second petty officer

จ่านายสิบ sergeant-major

จ่าปี่ chief piper who accompanies the victory drums

จ่าฝูง herd leader, pack leader

จ่าศาล /clerk/registrar/ of the court

พันจ่า warrant officer

จ่า[2] to address

จ่าหน้า, จ่าหน้าซอง to address an envelope

จ้า very, strongly

แดดจ้า glaring (sun), bright sunlight

ร้องไห้จ้า to cry loudly, wail

จ๋า yes (spoken by a woman)

จาก[1] to separate, leave, depart, go away; from

จากกัน to separate

นอกจาก except, except for, apart from, excluding, but; unless

เนื่องจาก due to, owing to, because, as a result (of)

หลังจาก after

    หลังจากนั้น afterwards

จาก[2] atap, attap

หลังคาจาก atap roof

จาคะ donation, philanthropy, giving

จาง pale, diluted, insipid, weak, faint

เจือจาง diluted, faded, weak

โรคโลหิตจาง anemia

จ้าง to employ, hire, engage

จ้างทำของ to engage a person to /make/do/ something

จ้างแรงงาน to hire, take on workers, employ laborers

ค่าจ้าง wages, pay

นายจ้าง employer

รถรับจ้าง /car/truck/vehicle/ for hire; taxi

รับจ้าง for hire, to take employment, be /employed/hired/ (to do or for something)

    รับจ้างซักผ้า laundry service

    รับจ้างทำของ to do for hire, be employed (to /do/make/ something)

เรือจ้าง ferry boat, ferry, boat for hire

ลูกจ้าง employee, wage earner

ว่าจ้าง to employ, engage, hire

สินจ้าง pay, wages, remuneration

จาตุรงค์ see จัตุรงค์ *หน้า 115*

จาตุรงคสันนิบาต the first Buddhist Assembly marked by four events: the moon reached the star "Magha", 1250 priests gathered uninvited, all had been admitted to the monkhood by the Buddha and all of them were Buddhist saints. This is called Magha Puja Day.

จาตุรนต์, จาตุรันต์ ruler of the world

จาตุรนต์รัศมี the sun

จาน dish, plate, saucer

จานข้าว dinner plate

จานเชิง a footed dish

จานบิน flying saucer

จานผี flying saucer

จานเปล serving plate, platter

จานรอง saucer

จานสี palette

จานเสียง phonograph record

จ้าน *see* จัดจ้าน *หน้า 115*

จาบจ้วง to excoriate, affront

จาม[1] Cham

จาม[2] to sneeze

จาม[3] to strike with all one's force, bash, smash พูดมาก เดี๋ยวจามด้วยขวานชะเลย *If you don't shut your mouth, I'll bash your head in.*

จามจุรี, จามรี yak

จามร royal crest used in processions

จ่าย to distribute, supply, dispense, issue; to spend; to buy; to pay

จ่ายกับข้าว, จ่ายตลาด to do the marketing

จ่ายเกิน to overpay

จ่ายของ to go shopping

จ่ายเงิน to pay

จ่ายเงินเดือน to pay /wages/salaries/

จ่ายเช็ค to issue a check, pay by check

จ่ายล่วงหน้า to pay in advance, pay up front

จ่ายสินค้า to authorize the delivery of goods from a port warehouse

ใช้จ่าย to spend

รายจ่าย expenditure(s), expense(s)

จาร[1] to write, inscribe

จาร[2] spy

จารกรรม espionage

จารชน spy

จารบุรุษ spy

จาระไน to explain in detail, elaborate (on), expatiate

จาริก traveller, wayfarer; pilgrim

จารึก to inscribe, imprint, engrave

จารึกไว้ในดวงใจ to treasure

ศิลาจารึก stone inscription

จารีต good usage, common practice, good manners; convention, custom

จารีตประเพณี custom; customary

จ้าละหวั่น chaotic, confused; tumultuous

จาว pith inside some fruit

จาวมะพร้าว coconut heart

จ้าว *see* เจ้า[1] *หน้า 123*

จ่าหวัก *see* จวัก *หน้า 112*

จำ[1] to imprison, confine; to retain; to stay (at), remain; to have to, be /constrained/obliged/ compelled/ (to)

จำคุก to imprison, jail

จำจอง to put in chains; to fetter and imprison

จำจะต้อง to have to, must, under an obligation to

จำใจ to be obliged, constrained (to do something), do something against one's will

จำโซ่ to fetter, chain, shackle

จำทน to tolerate

จำพรรษา to stay in a single monastery during the rainy season

จำวัด to sleep (only for a monk), be resting

จำศีล to stay in a monastery to observe the Buddhist precepts

กบจำศีล an aestivating frog, a frog in aestivation

จำ[2] to remember, recall, recollect

จำขึ้นใจ to learn by heart, memorize

จำได้ to remember

จำไว้ Don't forget it.

จำหน้าได้ to recognize (someone)

ความจำ memory

จ้ำ to hurry, speed up; in haste

จ้ำจี้จ้ำไช to nag

เดินจ้ำ to hurry along, press /ahead/on/

จ๊ำ to connect (the line, wires)

จำกัด to limit, restrict; to confine; limited, confined, restricted, restrictive

จำกัดความ to define

จำกัดจำเขี่ย very limited

ข้อจำกัด limitation, restriction

จ้ำจี้ children's game

จ้าจี้จ้าไช to nag, keep reminding, harp (on something), keep after (someone)

จำเจ monotonous, repetitious, boring, humdrum

จำเดิมแต่ from then on, ever since

จำนง as in ความจำนง intention, aim, purpose; wish

จำนน to be defeated, vanquished, overcome (by)
ยอมจำนน to yield, give in; to surrender, admit defeat, give up

จำนรรจ์, จำนรรจา to talk; to be a good talker
ช่างจำนรรจ์ talkative

จำนวน amount, number, quantity
จำนวนจริง real numbers
จำนวนจินตภาพ imaginary quantities
จำนวนเชิงซ้อน complex numbers
จำนวนตรรกยะ rational numbers
จำนวนเต็ม integers
จำนวนนับ natural numbers
จำนวนอตรรกยะ irrational numbers
จำนวนร้อยละ percentage
เป็นจำนวน the amount of, to the amount of; to amount to, sum

จำนอง to mortgage
บังคับจำนอง to enforce a mortgage
ผู้จำนอง mortgagor
ผู้รับจำนอง mortgagee

จำนำ to pawn, pledge
จำนำพรรษา a yellow robe given to a monk during the rainy season of confinement
เจ้าจำนำ regular /customer/supplier/
ตั๋วจำนำ pawn ticket
ผู้รับจำนำ pawnbroker; pledgee
โรง (รับ) จำนำ pawnshop

จำเนียร long ago, a long time ago, in the days of yore

จำแนก to divide; to classify; to sort; to distribute

จ้ำบ๊ะ sexy show

จำปี pee pee (sl)

จำเป็น necessary, essential; must, have to, obliged to
ของจำเป็นจะต้องใช้ necessity, essential, a must
ธุระจำเป็น pressing business
มีความจำเป็นบางอย่าง to be under some pressure (to), have certain reasons (for)
ไม่จำเป็น unnecessary; don't bother
ไม่จำเป็นต้อง not necessary (to), no need (to)

จำเพาะ see เฉพาะ หน้า 131

จ้ำม่ำ chubby, roly-poly
อ้วนจ้ำม่ำ nice and fat, plump, chubby

จำรัส see จรัส หน้า 111

จำเริญ see เจริญ หน้า 122

จำเรียง to sing; to lull with song

จำลอง a model (of), mock-up; to copy; hypothetical
ท้องฟ้าจำลอง planetarium
แบบจำลอง model, scale model
รูปจำลอง model, mock-up, replica, reproduction
สถานการณ์จำลอง hypothetical situation

จำเลย defendant

จำแลง to turn oneself into, change into, disguise oneself (as)

จำหนับ mighty

จำหน่าย to distribute, dispose of, sell
จำหน่ายคดี to throw out a case, strike out a case
จำหน่ายหนี้สูญ to write off a bad debt
ผู้จำหน่าย dealer, distributor
ผู้แทนจำหน่าย distributing agent
พิมพ์จำหน่าย to publish

จำหลัก to carve

จำอวด clown, buffoon, comedian
เล่นจำอวด to play slapstick comedy; to clown

จิก to peck; to nose-dive; to /pinch/swipe/ something
จิกปีก to be dazed

จิกหัว to pull someone's hair

    จิกหัวใช้ to give someone a hard time

จิ๊ก to pinch, lift

จิ้งจก house lizard

จิ้งจอก fox

จิงโจ้ kangaroo, wallaby

    จิงโจ้น้ำ pond skater

จิ้งหรีด cricket

จิ้งเหลน skink

จิต mind, heart

    จิตใจ mind, sentiment, feeling

        จิตใจผ่องใส happy

        จิตใจบริการ service-minded, helpful

    จิตใต้สำนึก subconscious mind

    จิตแพทย์ psychiatrist

    จิตวิเคราะห์ psychoanalysis

    จิตวิญญาณ soul

    จิตวิทยา psychology

    จิตสำนึก conscious mind

    จิตหลอน hallucination

    ทางจิต mental

    มิตรจิต friendliness, cordiality, sociability, aimiability

    เมตตาจิต goodwill, loving kindness

    ไมตรีจิต see ไมตรีจิต หน้า 390

    โรคจิต mental disorder; neurosis

    สองจิตสองใจ undecided, of two minds

จิตร drawing, painting; beautiful, artistic

    จิตรกร artist, painter

    จิตรกรรม artistic work, drawing, painting, picture

    จิตรเลขา beautiful picture

จินดา imagination, thought

    จินดามณี wishing crystal

    จินดามัย success achieved through thought

จินต์ to think; to imagine

    จินตกวี imaginative poet

    จินตนา, จินตนาการ imagination

    จินตลีลา ballet

จิบ to sip

    ลองลักจิบซิ Have a sip.

จิปาถะ assorted, miscellaneous, sundry

    ของจิปาถะ sundries, a variety of things, odds and ends, a miscellaneous collection

จิ้ม to poke, pick out; to dip, dunk; to spear

    จิ้มพุง to stab in the belly

    จิ้มฟัน to pick one's teeth

    น้ำจิ้ม sauce; dip

    ไม้จิ้มฟัน toothpick

จิ้มก้อง to offer tribute to, secure the amity of another ruler

จิ้มลิ้ม dainty, lovely

จิรัง, จีรัง lasting, enduring

    ไม่จิรัง ephemeral

จิ๋ว tiny, diminutive, wee

    ตัวจิ๋ว small type (ตัวพิมพ์)

จี๋[1] jewelled pendant, brooch

จี้[2] to poke; to hold up

    จี้จุด to put (one's) finger on (something)

    จี้ไช to keep after someone to do something

    จี้เส้น to make someone laugh, be funny

    ถูกจี้ to be held up

    นักจี้ a holdup man

    บ้าจี้ ticklish; suggestible

จี๋ very, an adverb indicating high degree

    ด่วนจี๋ extremely urgent

    วิ่งจี๋ to race

จุ๋ด tiny, minute, teensie-weensie

จีน Chinese

    จีนคณะชาติ Nationalist China

    จีนแดง Red China

    จีนธิเบต Sino-Tibetan

    คนจีน, ชาวจีน a Chinese; the Chinese people

    ประเทศจีน China

    ภาษาจีน Chinese

    เมืองจีน China

จีบ[1] to purse one's lips, pucker one's lips; to pleat, fold; crimped, fluted

จ ฉ ช ซ ฌ ญ ฎ ฏ ฐ ฑ ฒ ณ ด ต ถ ท ธ น บ ป ผ ฝ พ ฟ ภ ม ย ร ฤ ฦ ล ว ศ ษ ส ห ฬ อ ฮ

ก
ข
ค
ฆ
ง
จ

จีบปากจีบคอพูด to speak in an affected way

จีบผ้า to pleat

จีบพลู to roll a betel leaf

ฝาจีบ crown /cap/cork/

จีบ[2] to go after, flirt (with), make /out (with)/up to/, play up to somebody; to court

จีบสาว to go after /a girl/the girls/, make up to a girl, sweet-talk a girl, dally with a girl; to go courting

ผมจีบสาวไม่เป็น I'm no good at going after girls. / I don't know how to make out with girls. / I'm not much good with girls. / I don't know how to flirt.

การจีบสาว dating

จีวร robe of a Buddhist monk

ไตรจีวร a monk's set of 3 articles of clothing

จึง, จึ่ง then; thus, so, because เป็นสันธาน บางครั้งไม่แปลในภาษาอังกฤษเช่น *เขาอยู่เมืองนอกนานไปหน่อยจึงไม่รู้ภาษาไทยดี* She spent so much time abroad, her Thai wasn't very good.

จึงจะ to be

ต้องเติมพริกป่นจึงจะอร่อย To be tasty, it needs some dried chili.

จืด tasteless, flat, bland, not sweet enough; dull, uninteresting; insipid

จืดจาง to fade, wane

จืดชืด dull, flat, unexciting

จืดตา uninteresting, dull

จืดไป not seasoned enough, too bland

แกงจืด unspiced soup (with vegetables, tofu, etc)

ใจจืด mean, unfeeling, unsympathetic, heartless

ดินจืด depleted soil

น้ำจืด fresh water

จุ a lot; filled (with)

จุใจ glad, thrilled

เขาพูดได้จุใจฉันจริงๆ I was thrilled to hear it.

กินจุ to eat a lot

คนกินจุ a big eater

ความจุ capacity

จุ๊ to fib

ไม่ได้จุ๊ I wasn't fibbing.

จุก topknot; bundle, bunch (of); cork, stopper, plug; to feel /bloated/colicky/; to be doubled up with pain

จุกขวด stopper

จุกไม้ก๊อก cork

จุกเสียด to have colic, a sharp pain in the stomach

ยืนจุกอยู่หน้าประตู to block the door

หัวจุก stopper; topknot

จุกจิก fussy, finicky; annoying, bothersome, irritating; trivial, petty ·

จุกจิกจู้จี้, จู้จี้จุกจิก fussy, pernickety, finical

ของจุกจิก odds and ends, all sorts of things

เรื่องจุกจิก petty irritations; trivia, petty matter

จุณ powder; bits

เป็นจุณ in powder; to bits เช่น *smashed to bits*

จุด[1] spot; dot; full stop, period

จุดไข่ปลา suspension points, ellipsis

จุดจบ the end, finish

ถึงจุดจบ to be finished, die

จุดเดือด boiling point

จุดบอด blind spot

จุดประสงค์ purpose, aim

จุดยอด vertex

จุดยืน stance, position, standpoint; principle

จุดรวม center, focus (of), focal point

จุดร่วม common aim; point of agreement

จุดลูกน้ำ comma

จุดวกกลับ turning point

จุดศูนย์กลาง center, hub; focus

จุดศูนย์ถ่วง center of gravity

จุดสุดยอด climax, orgasm

จุดหมาย aim, destination, objective, end,

goal, focus

จุดหมายปลายทาง ultimate goal, destination

จุดหักเห turning point

จุดอ่อน weak point

จุด[2] to light, ignite

จุดไต้ตำตอ get a nasty surprise; commit a faux pas, make an embarrassing blunder, make a boner

จุดเทียน to light a candle

จุดบุหรี่ to light a cigarette

จุดไฟ to light fire, to strike a match

จุติ to die, pass away

จุนเจือ to support, maintain, look after, to give patronage to

จุ้นจ้าน to meddle, to be meddlesome

จุนจู๋, จู๋ shrunken; miniscule, mini

จุนสี copper sulphate

จุ๊บ[1] sucking sound

จุ๊บ[2] tube

จุบจิบ as in **กินจุบจิบ** to be eating snacks all the time

จุ๊บแจง a marine gastropod

จุ่ม, จุ้ม to dip, immerse, dunk

จุมพิต to kiss

จุล small, little

จุลกฐิน a 24 hour community action of weaving, dyeing, sewing and presenting a set of yellow robes to a monk; something done in a rush

จุลชีพ microbe

จุลทรรศน์ microscope

จุลภาค comma

จุลศักราช the Thai minor era beginning March 21, 638 A.D.

จุลินทรีย์ microorganisms

จุฬา a bird-shaped kite

จุฬาราชมนตรี Sheikhul Islam, Adviser to the King on Islamic Religious Affairs

สำนักจุฬาราชมนตรี Office of the Sheikhul Islam

จุฬาลงกรณ์มหาวิทยาลัย Chulalongkorn University

จู่ to rush in, break in; directly to, straight to; unhesitatingly, without delay

จู่ๆ without warning, suddenly

จู่โจม to attack by stealth, attack without warning, assault, raid, take by surprise

หน่วยจู่โจม commando unit

จูง to lead

จูงจมูก to lead (a person) by the nose, lead a buffalo by the nose

จูงใจ to induce, motivate, persuade

จูงมือ to lead by the hand

จู้จี้ to fuss, be fussy, over-particular, finicky; meticulous

จู๋ pee pee

สั้นจู๋ peewee, very short

จู๋จี๋ affectionate chatting; billing and cooing

จูบ to kiss

เจ vegetarian

กินเจ to eat vegetarian food; be a vegetarian

เจ๊ older sister

เจ๊ก Chinese

เจ๊ง to flop, be finished; kaput, failed; to go bust, go broke

เจ๋ง cool, neat, spiffy

เจ็ด seven

ที่เจ็ด seventh

เจดีย์ stupa, chedi

เจดียสถาน a sacred Buddhist precinct

เจต mind; heart

เจตคติ attitude

เจตจำนง intention, intent

มีเจตจำนงอันแน่วแน่ we are determined to / we have a firm intention to

เจตนา intention, volition, will, motive; to mean to

เขาไม่มีเจตนาจะทำร้ายคุณ He didn't mean to harm you.

เจตนาบริสุทธิ์ pure intention, altruistic motive, to mean well

เจตนาร้าย malicious; with malice, ill will

เจตนารมณ์ intentions, objectives, aim; spirit

เจตนาแอบแฝง ulterior motive

ฆ่าด้วยเจตนา to murder, kill intentionally, to commit intentional manslaughter

เจตสิก mental; mental /state/activities/

เจติย see **เจดีย์** หน้า 121

เจโตวิมุติ deliverance from suffering through will-power

เจน experienced, accustomed to; familiar with, skilled, expert, proficient

เจนจบ versatile, an old hand (at), a master (of), widely proficient (in,at), to have extensive experience (in)

เจนจัด skillful; clever, cunning, wily, foxy

เจนใจ well remembered

เจนตา to be familiar; to well recall the sight of; to be able to visualize

เจนสนาม experienced

ชัดเจน very clear, distinct; obvious; precise, unequivocal

เจ็บ ill; to be hurt, injured; to hurt, be painful, sore

เจ็บไข้ to be ill, sick see **เป็นไข้** หน้า 72

เจ็บคอ to have a sore throat

เจ็บใจ to resent, be resentful, feel hurt

ความเจ็บใจ resentment, bitterness

เจ็บช้ำ to be bitter (about, over, at)

เจ็บช้ำน้ำใจ to be hurt

เจ็บตัว to get hurt

เจ็บท้อง to have labor pains

เจ็บปวด to be painful, hurt, sore, aching; pain, distress

เจ็บป่วย to be ill, sick

เจ็บแสบ bitter, embittered (by, over), rankled (by, over)

เจ็บหนัก seriously /ill/sick/

โรคภัยไข้เจ็บ sickness, illness, disease

ล้มเจ็บ to fall ill

หายเจ็บ to recover, get well, get over (a cold etc)

เจรจา to talk (to), discuss, confer (with), negotiate

เจรจาหว่านล้อม to persuade, talk someone into something

บทเจรจา dialogue

เจริญ to grow, develop, prosper, thrive, flourish, progress, advance, augment; to follow (in the footsteps of a person); to recite; to chant (a prayer); to practice

ความเจริญ development, prosperity, advancement, เวลาแปลเป็นอังกฤษมักไม่ใช้คำนาม เช่น ในถิ่นที่ความเจริญไปไม่ถึงประชาชนมีความเป็นอยู่อย่างสันโดษ In underdeveloped areas, people are generally undemanding.

เจริญก้าวหน้า prospering, flourishing, progressing

เจริญงอกงาม thriving

เจริญตา, เจริญใจ great, admirable, wonderful

เจริญเติบโต to grow

เจริญพร yes (used by monks)

เจริญพระพุทธมนต์ Buddhist chanting

เจริญรอยตาม to follow in the footsteps

เจริญวิปัสสนา to practice meditation

เจริญสัมพันธไมตรี to develop friendly relations (with)

เจริญอาหาร to give an appetite; to have a good appetite

เจว็ด figurine of a deity in a shrine, a figurehead

เจ๊สัว a wealthy Chinese

เจอ, เจอะ to meet, encounter, come upon; to find, come across

เจอบ่อย common; to meet someone often

เจ่อ to swell, swollen

เจ่าจุก dejected, forlorn, discouraged

เจ้า[1] a person of royal lineage, prince, royalty; king; owner; master (of)

เจ้ากรม director of a department, chief of /department/service/

เจ้ากรรม damn; unfortunate, ill-starred
พาแฟนไปดูหนังไปได้ครึ่งทาง รถเจ้ากรรมก็มาเสีย ซวยเป็นบ้าเลย I was taking my girl to the movies when, halfway there, the damn car broke down. What rotten luck!

เจ้ากรรมนายเวร see **เจ้ากรรมนายเวร** หน้า 5

เจ้ากลยุทธ master strategist

เจ้ากี้เจ้าการ meddler, busybody, officious person; bossy

เจ้ากู he, him (used for monks)

เจ้าเก่า the original

เจ้าของ owner, proprietor, to belong to
ใครเป็นเจ้าของรถคันนี้ To whom does this car belong? / Who is the owner of this car?

เจ้าของไข้ doctor in charge of a patient

เจ้าขา polite affirmative word used by a woman

เจ้าข้า affirmative word used for addressing a superior; word used by a public crier to call the attention of the people, like "Hear ye!"

เจ้าขุนมูลนาย the hierarchy, rulers, the ruling class, the biggies *(sl)*

เจ้าคุณ an appellation for the second highest rank of government official in olden times or a monk elevated to a rank requiring royal appointment

เจ้าจอม a royal minor wife

เจ้าจอมมารดา royal mother, a royal minor wife who has borne a child

เจ้าจำนำ regular /customer/supplier/

เจ้าชีวิต king, monarch, lord of life

เจ้าชู้ a wolf, philanderer, womanizer, Don Juan

เจ้าตำรับ pioneer, initiator, originator, leading exponent

เจ้าถ้อยหมอความ argumentative person
อย่ามาทำเจ้าถ้อยหมอความ Don't argue with me!

เจ้าที่ protecting spirit of a place

เจ้าทุกข์ injured party, complainant; victim

เจ้านาย boss, employer; one's superiors; ruling class, aristocracy

เจ้าเนื้อ chubby, plump, roly-poly

เจ้าบ้าน householder, house owner

เจ้าบ่าว bridegroom

เจ้าประคุณ honorific title used with one's benefactor or a respected person; introduction to an entreaty

เจ้าพนักงาน official, officer in charge (of), competent officer; employee

เจ้าพนักงานพิทักษ์ทรัพย์ receiver in bankruptcy

เจ้าพระยา Chao Phya, a title of the highest rank of government official in olden times

เจ้าพ่อ mogul; godfather

เจ้าฟ้า prince, princess; a local ruling prince

เจ้าภาพ host (ชาย), hostess (หญิง); sponsor

เจ้ามือ (เจ้ามือการพนัน) banker (in gambling games), (ผู้ตั้งต้นในวงไพ่) dealer (in card games); the host, one who pays, one who treats the others
วันนี้ใครเป็นเจ้ามือ Whose treat is it today?

เจ้าเมือง governor

เจ้าไม่มีศาล vagabond, unsettled person

เจ้ายศเจ้าอย่าง to be a snob, prig; imperious, pompous, snobbish, haughty; one who stands on ceremony, ceremonious, formal

เจ้ายุทธจักร the king (of)

เจ้าระเบียบ orderly person, /meticulous /methodical/ person

เจ้าเรือน disposition

เจ้าเล่ห์ cunning person, trickster, fox

เจ้าสาว bride

จ ฉ ช ซ ฌ ญ ฎ ฏ ฐ ฑ ฒ ณ ด ต ถ ท ธ น บ ป ผ ฝ พ ฟ ภ ม ย ร ฤ ฤๅ ล ว ศ ษ ส ห ฬ อ ฮ

เจ้าสำบัดสำนวน glib talker

เจ้าหน้าที่ official, officer, officer in charge, man in charge, authorities

   เจ้าหน้าที่ตำรวจ police officer

เจ้าหนี้ creditor; obligee

เจ้าหล่อน she, her

เจ้าอารมณ์ temperamental, emotional, testy

เจ้าอาวาส abbot

เจ้า[2] you; he, him

   เจ้าจะไปไหน Where are you off to?

   เจ้าหมอนั่น that /guy/fellow/

เจ๊า to end in a /draw/tie/; to call /it/something/ quits

เจาะ to bore, puncture, perforate, drill, pierce, punch a hole, penetrate

   เจาะจง to specify, designate

   เจาะรู to make a hole, perforate

เจ๊าะแจ๊ะ to pester

เจิ่ง to be full, overflowing, flooded, inundated
   น้ำเจิ่งทั่วบริเวณ The whole place was /flooded/under water/.

เจิดจ้า brilliant

เจิม to make auspicious marking

เจียด to spare a little, set aside

   เจียดเวลา to /spare/save/set aside/ some time (to, for), find time (to do something)

เจียน[1] to trim

เจียน[2] nearly, on the verge of, almost

   เจียนตาย almost dead, near death

เจี๊ยบ chirp, chirping

   ลูกเจี๊ยบ a chick; baby

เจียม modest, unassuming, self-effacing

   เจียมตัว humble

   เจียมเนื้อเจียมตัว to know one's place; to be modest

เจียระไน to /cut/polish/ (gemstones, diamonds etc)

   แก้วเจียระไน cut glass, crystal

   ช่างเจียระไน lapidary, gem cutter, gem

polisher

เจียว to render fat; to fry in oil, sauté

   ไข่เจียว omelet

เจี๊ยวจ๊าว boisterous; noisy

เจี๊ยะ to eat

เจือ to mix, blend, mingle, to put in, to add

   เจือจาง diluted

   เจือปน admixed, added; adulterated (with)

     สารเจือปน additive

เจือจาน to help, assist; to support; to lend a hand; to share with others

เจื่อน to be embarrassed, sheepish, discountenanced, discomfited, go pale

   ยิ้มเจื่อนๆ to give a sheepish smile

   หน้าเจื่อน embarrassed, disconcerted

เจื้อย smoothly, freely, fluently

   พูดเรื่อยเจื้อย garrulous, long-winded

แจ closely

   ติดแจ, ตามแจ to be inseparable, stay close together

แจ้ bantam

แจ่ an intensifier like /very/extreme/

   แดงแจ่ scarlet, bright red

   แดดแจ่ blazing sunlight, bright sunshine

แจก divide up, distribute, pass out, hand out; to classify, sort

   แจกจ่าย to disseminate, distribute widely

   แจกไพ่ to deal the cards

   แจกแว่น to punch in the eye, give someone a black eye

   แจกเสื่อ แจกหมอน to offer hospitality, warmly welcome

   แจกหมาก to punch in the mouth

แจกัน vase

แจง *as in*

   แจงสี่เบี้ย to elucidate, explain in detail, clarify

   จัดแจง to get things ready, prepare, make arrangements

แจกแจง to analyze, give an analysis (of)

ชี้แจง see **ชี้แจง** หน้า 144

แจ้ง[1] to tell, inform, report; to reveal, indicate, show, demonstrate; to know, understand

แจ้งความ to report, /make/lodge/ a report; to advertise, advertisement

แจ้งความตำรวจ to /lodge/file/ a police complaint; to make a police report

แจ้งความในหนังสือพิมพ์ to advertise, place an advertisement in the paper

แจ้งว่า reported that

รับแจ้งว่า to be informed (that), receive a report that

แจ้ง[2] bright, clear, light; distinct

แจ้งชัด perfectly clear, precise, lucid

โจ่งแจ้ง too openly; brazenly, blatant

ทุ่งแจ้ง open field

รู้แจ้งเห็นจริง see **รู้แจ้งเห็นจริง** หน้า 424

แจด, แจ๊ด an intensifier like /very/extremely/

แดงแจ๊ด bright red

เปรี้ยวแจ๊ด extremely sour

แจ้น in a hurry

วิ่งแจ้น to race

แจ่ม limpid, transparent; bright, clear; (sl) terrific, great

แจ่มแจ้ง perfectly clear

แจ่มชัด crystal clear

แจ่มใส bright

แจว[1] scull a boat; a scull

คนแจวเรือ sculler, oarsman, gondolier

หลักแจว scull stand, scull pole

แจว[2] to flee, skip, escape, run away

แจวอ้าว to take flight, take to one's heels

แจ้ว melodious, sweet, pleasant

แจ๋ว clear, bright; neat (as in neat websites)

แจ๋วไปเลย great, terrific, fantastic; superb

แจ๋วแหวว sparkling, bright and clear

ชัดแจ๋ว perfectly clear, as clear as anything (พูด)

โจก leader, chief, head, boss

โจ๊ก rice gruel, rice porridge

โจงกระเบน to wrap a long cloth around the waist, fan-fold the edges together then pass the folded portion between the legs and hitch it at the waist in back

โจ่งครึ่ม flagrantly

โจ่งแจ้ง too openly; brazenly, blatant

โจทก์ plaintiff (คดีแพ่ง); complainant, prosecutor (คดีอาญา)

โจทย์, โจท problem (in mathematics)

โจทย์ระคน miscellaneous factors

โจน to jump, leap, spring (into, onto, at, on)

โจม to rush (in, at), spring

โจมตี to attack; to criticize, lambaste

โจมทัพ elephant battalion

จู่โจม see **จู่โจม** หน้า 121

โจร bandit, brigand, gangster, highwayman, outlaw

โจรกรรม theft, burglary, robbery, larceny; banditry; to plunder, pillage

โจรผู้ร้าย criminal

โจรภัย robbery

โจรสลัด pirate; hijacker

โจรห้าร้อย gangster

โจษ rumored, reported; to spread by word of mouth

โจษจัน, โจษแจ to spread by word of mouth, rumored; to be talked about by everyone, to be spread around (that)

ใจ mind; heart; spirit

ใจกล้า courageous, brave; adventuresome

ใจกลาง center, middle, heart

ใจกว้าง broadminded, receptive; generous, magnanimous; forgiving

ใจเขาใจเรา feelings of others

ใจแข็ง unyielding, adamant, unmoved; resolute, firm

ใจคด traitorous, treacherous

ก
ข
ค
ฆ
ง
จ

ใจความ substance, gist, essence, the heart of, the essentials, meaning

ใจคอ character

ใจแคบ narrow minded, small minded; selfish, ungenerous

ใจง่าย agreeable to anything, easygoing, suggestible, to be a softy; easy to make, an easy make

ใจจดใจจ่อ absorbed (in), preoccupied (with) engrossed (in); attentively

    อย่างใจจดใจจ่อ with intense interest, very attentively

ใจจริง really, sincerely, truly

    ด้วยใจจริง sincerely, wholeheartedly, with all one's heart

ใจจืด mean, unfeeling, unsympathetic, unappreciative; heartless

ใจชื้น relieved, to have a sense of relief

ใจดำ selfish; mean, unkind, heartless

    ใจดำจัง You meany!

ใจดี good, good-hearted, kind, sweet, good-natured, decent

ใจเด็ด resolute, determined; fearless

ใจเดียว constant, faithful, steadfast

ใจตรงกัน like-minded, to share the same feelings

ใจต่ำ mean; base, low, vile

ใจเต้นไม่เป็นส่ำ one's heart misses a beat

เห็นเจ้าหนี้เดินเข้ามาเขาใจเต้นไม่เป็นส่ำ His heart missed a beat when he saw his creditor coming over.

ใจแตก to be spoiled, go astray, let oneself go, become dissipated

ใจโต lavish

ใจถึง tough; daring, up to it, ready-to-go, have the guts (to do something)

ใจทราม depraved; low-minded

ใจน้อย touchy, oversensitive, irritable

ใจนักเลง sporting

ใจบาป wicked

ใจบุญ, ใจบุญสุนทาน kindly, generous, charitable, benevolent, good

ใจบริสุทธิ์ innocent, ingenuous

ใจเบา credulous, easily convinced; gullible

ใจปลาซิว timorous, chickenhearted

ใจป้ำ venturesome; sporting

    คนใจป้ำ a real sport

ใจแป้ว agitated, to have one's heart in one's mouth

ใจฝ่อ scared

ใจเพชร resolute, determined, unshakable, strong-willed; to have a strong character

ใจมาร vicious

ใจไม้ไส้ระกำ unfeeling, hardhearted

ใจเย็น patient; even-tempered, cool, coolheaded

ใจเย็น ๆ calm down, be calm, take it easy

ใจเย็นๆ เพื่อน Take it easy, man! / Keep cool! / Have patience!

ใจร้อน impatient, hasty, impetuous; hotheaded

ใจรัก to like

    ทำด้วยใจรัก to put one's heart into something

    เห็นรูปปั้นก็รู้ว่าเขาทำด้วยใจรัก You can tell from the sculpture that /he liked doing it/he put his heart into it/.

    ผลงานทำด้วยใจรัก a labor of love

ใจร้าย mean, unkind; cruel, vicious, wicked

ใจร้ายจัง You are wicked!, How could you!

ใจเร็ว impetuous, hasty, impulsive

    ใจเร็วด่วนได้ impetuous

ใจลอย absentminded; daydreaming, abstracted, (my) mind was wandering; to have a vacant look

ใจสัตว์ beastly, vile, inhuman

    คนใจสัตว์ a beast

ใจสั่น to tremble; trembling, to have one's

heart in one's mouth, one's heart (is) beating fast; to have palpitations of the heart

ใจสูง highminded, fine

ใจเสาะ fainthearted, timorous, without gumption, not a fighter, unable to take it, chickenhearted

ใจเสีย disappointed, chagrined

ใจหวิว to skip a beat เช่น *His heart skipped a beat.*; to feel faint (with)

ใจหาย, ใจหายใจคว่ำ startled; My heart was in my mouth.; my heart sank, dismayed, aghast

ใจเหี่ยว dejected, gloomy, down in the dumps

ใจโหดร้าย cruel, brutal, ruthless, savage

ใจใหญ่, ใจใหญ่ใจโต openhanded, lavish; ostentatious; over-ambitious

ใจอ่อน softhearted; yielding, to give in, weaken

ผมเป็นคนใจอ่อน โดยเฉพาะกับผู้หญิง I'm a softy when it comes to women.

ใจอำมหิต cold-blooded, merciless, vicious, inhuman

ดวงใจ heart; sweetheart

ดังใจ as desired

ดีอกดีใจ delighted, so happy, elated

ตกใจ startled, frightened, alarmed

ตามใจ see **ตามใจ** หน้า *194*

ถอนใจ to sigh

ถึงใจ see **ถึงใจ** หน้า *214*

ถูกใจ to like

ทันใจ quick, fast

นอกใจ unfaithful, adulterous, inconstant

น้อยใจ offended, in a huff, fretting

เป็นใจ to favor, sympathize (with), side with; to be an accomplice (of), conspire (with), connive (with)

ผิดใจ to have a grudge (against), be on the outs (with someone); to displease

ใฝ่ใจ to be committed (to), take sides (with); to take an interest (in), absorbed in

พอใจ satisfied, happy (with)

ภูมิใจ proud (to, of)

มีแก่ใจ kind, considerate, obliging, generous, solicitous

มีใจเป็นธรรม fair, just, impartial, unprejudiced

    ไม่มีใจเป็นธรรม unfair, unjust, partial, prejudiced

ร้อนใจ anxious, impatient; worried, perturbed

รู้แก่ใจ to know /perfectly/very/full/ well, must know, know in one's heart

ไว้วางใจ to trust, have confidence in

สนใจ to be interested (in)

สองจิตสองใจ undecided, of two minds

สองใจ unfaithful, two-timing

สิ้นใจ to die, expire, breathe one's last

เสียใจ to be sorry, regret; to be disappointed

หดหู่ใจ miserable, depressed, despondent

หนักใจ worried, concerned, troubled, disturbed

หัวใจ heart; feelings; mind; cardiac

หายใจ to breathe

เห็นใจ to be sympathetic (with), understand, sympathize (with someone)

อย่างใจ as expected, as hoped for, as one would like

อึดอัดใจ to feel /uncomfortable/uneasy/ (about someone or something)

เอาใจ to go along with (someone); to please, make (someone) happy, humor (someone)

    เอาใจใส่ to pay attention (to), to take an interest (in), to be conscientious, care, put one's mind to (something)

เอาแต่ใจ to think only of oneself, willful, self-centered, inconsiderate

ไจ   ball (of string, thread etc)

ฉ six

ฉกษัตริย์ The Six Kings (title of a chapter of the Jataka tales)

ฉกามาพจร the six heavens

ฉศก the final number six in years of the minor era (Chulasakaraj)

ฉก to snatch, grab; to strike

ฉกฉวย to help oneself to something; to pocket, steal, take surreptitiously

ฉกชิงวิ่งราว to snatch, street-snatching

ฉกรรจ์ serious, severe, grave; dreadful; robust, strong, tough

ข้อหาฉกรรจ์ /serious/dreadful/ accusation; felony charge

ชายฉกรรจ์ able-bodied man; tough guy; young man

นักโทษฉกรรจ์ felon, prisoner under a heavy sentence

แผลฉกรรจ์ badly wounded; severe wound

วัยฉกรรจ์ early manhood, young adult-hood, (in the) prime of life

ฉกาจ formidable

ฉงน, ฉงนใจ puzzled; sceptical, dubious, doubtful

ฉงนฉงาย bewildered, perplexed

ฉนวน insulator, insulation

ฉบับ edition, issue (สำหรับนิตยสาร)

ไปซื้อหนังสือพิมพ์ฉบับเช้า ๓ ฉบับ *Get me 3 issues of the morning edition.*

ต้นฉบับ manuscript, copy; original

แบบฉบับ example, standard; exemplar, model, ideal; prototype

ฉมวก three-pronged fishing spear, trident

ฉลอง to celebrate; to show appreciation (for)

ฉลองพระเนตร glasses, spectacles (*royal word*)

ฉลองพระบาท shoes, slippers, boots (*royal word*)

ฉลองพระหัตถ์ spoon, fork, chopsticks (*royal word*)

ฉลอง (พระ) องค์ shirt (*royal word*)

ฉลองวันเกิด to celebrate one's birthday

งานฉลอง party, celebration; festival, fete

ฉลาก label

ฉลากยา drug label

จับฉลาก to draw lots

ฉลาด shrewd, astute, acute, sharp, bright, clever, smart, intelligent, ingenious

ฉลาดแกมโกง wily, cunning, full of guile, sly

ฉลาดแต่ไม่เฉลียว crafty but careless

ฉลาม shark

หูปลาฉลาม shark's fin

ฉลุ to perforate; to cut out; to carve, chase (metal)

ฉลุลาย to do scrollwork

เลื่อยฉลุ scroll saw, coping saw

ฉลู the Year of the Ox

ฉวย to snatch, seize, grab

ฉวยว่า in case, in the event

จงเตรียมข้อมูลไว้ให้พร้อม ฉวยว่าเจ้านายซักถาม จะได้ชี้แจงถูก *Get the data ready so you can give reasonable answers in case the chief asks.*

ฉวยโอกาส to seize the occasion, avail oneself of the opportunity, to take advantage of a situation

นักฉวยโอกาส opportunist

ฉวัดเฉวียน to wheel in the air, circling

ฉวี complexion

ฉวีวรรณ complexion

ขัดสีฉวีวรรณ to give oneself a beauty treatment

ฉ้อ to defraud (of), cheat (out of)

ฉ้อโกง to swindle

ฉ้อฉล to defraud

ฉ้อราษฎร์บังหลวง to embezzle public funds, be corrupt, engage in public corruption, misappropriate public /funds/property/

ขี้ฉ้อ crooked

    คนขี้ฉ้อ a crook

ฉอด, ฉอดๆ on and on, at great length

    ด่าฉอดๆ to let go a stream of abuse, vituperate

    พูดฉอดๆ to chatter away

ฉอเลาะ to coo, speak winningly

    ฉอเลาะกัน to bill and coo, converse affectionately

ฉะ to strike down (with a sword), attack; to devastate verbally; to eat up

    ผมฉะเจ้าหมอนั่นกลางที่ประชุมเลย ไม่กล้าเถียง ผมซักคำ I devastated him with my remarks to the whole assembly. He didn't dare say a word.

    อาหารอร่อยมาก ผมฉะชะสามจานเลย The dish was so good I ate up 3 helpings.

    ฉะฉาด clapping, slapping

    ฉะฉาน, ฉาดฉาน clearly, distinctly

ฉะนั้น therefore, consequently, so, thus

    มิฉะนั้น if not, otherwise, or else

ฉะนี้ this, this way, in this way, thus

ฉะอ้อน wheedle (something out of someone), cajole (someone into doing something); slender, lissome

ฉัตร[1] tiered umbrella

    ฉัตรมงคล coronation celebration

        วันฉัตรมงคล Coronation Day

ฉัตร[2] wooden separators in a circular set of tuned gongs

ฉัน[1] I (subject), me (object)

    ฉันเอง myself

ฉัน[2] to eat

    ฉันจังหัน to take the early morning meal

    ฉันเพล (of monks) to partake of the forenoon meal

ฉัน[3] like, as

    ฉันญาติพี่น้อง like a member of the family

    ฉันใด just as; whatever

ฉันใดก็ฉันนั้น just as...so

ฉันมิตร cordial, amicable, friendly, like friends

ฉันท์[1] pleasure, satisfaction (in doing something)

ฉันท์[2] a metrical composition

    ฉันทลักษณ์ versification

    ฉันทศาสตร์ prosody

ฉันทะ consent, authority

    มอบฉันทะ to authorize, give a /proxy/ mandate/authorization/ (to)

        ใบมอบฉันทะ proxy, mandate, authorization

ฉันทา to be partial to, biased in favor of, favor

    ฉันทาคติ bias, partiality, predilection, favor

    ฉันทานุมัติ authorization, mandate

    ฉันทามติ consensus

ฉับ abruptly, suddenly

    ฉับๆ briskly

    ฉับพลัน abruptly, all of a sudden; promptly, at once

    ฉับไว promptly, quick, fast

ฉัพพรรณรังสี six rays emanating from the head of Lord Buddha

ฉ่า, ฉ่าๆ sizzling, bubbling; splashing; intonation of a chorus by the sound "cha"

ฉาก[1] setting, stage set, scenery; scene; screen

    เปิดฉาก to raise the curtain (on something), commence, begin

    หลังฉาก behind the scene

    ออกฉาก to go onstage

ฉาก[2] T square; triangle

    ฉากหลบ to dodge

    ได้ฉาก perpendicular (to)

    ถอยฉาก to dodge

    มุมฉาก right angle

    หลบฉาก to slip /off/away/

ฉาง storehouse, granary, silo

    ฉางข้าว rice granary

ฉ ช ซ ฌ ญ ฎ ฏ ฐ ฑ ฒ ณ ด ต ถ ท ธ น บ ป ผ ฝ พ ฟ ภ ม ย ร ฤ ฤๅ ล ว ศ ษ ส ห ฬ อ ฮ

ฉาด slapping

ตบฉาด to give some slaps

เดี๋ยวตบซักฉาด I'll give you a good slap in a minute!

ฉาดฉาน see **ฉะฉาน** หน้า 129

ฉาตกภัย famine, starvation

ฉาบ[1] cymbals

ฉาบ[2] to paint, coat, cover (with), plaster (something with something)

ฉาบปูน to plaster, stucco; stuccoed

ฉาบหน้า to put up a front

ฉาบฉวย superficial; slipshod, shallow (person), carelessly done; coarse

ฉาย to radiate; to project; to reflect; to shine

ฉายเฉิด smart, elegant

ฉายแสง to shine; to treat with radiation, give a radiation treatment

ฉายหนัง to show a /movie/film/motion picture/, screen a film

เครื่องฉายหนัง projector

พระฉาย mirror; shadow

ไฟฉาย flashlight, torch, searchlight

ฉายา shadow; reflection, image, shade; a Pali name given to a monk on being ordained; epithet

ฉายาลักษณ์ royal photograph

ฉาวโฉ่ notorious, disreputable; smelly; to smell

ฉ่ำ[1] moist

ฉ่ำ[2] juicy; wet, rainy

สับปะรดลูกนี้ฉ่ำดี This pineapple is sweet and juicy. / The pineapple is nice and ripe.

หวานฉ่ำ juicy, sweet; sweet sparkling (eyes), doe-like (eyes)

ฉ่ำฉา raintree

ฉิ่ง small cymbals

ฉิบ before one knows it, on the spot; damn

เงียบฉิบ dead silent, damn quiet

เสียฉิบ damn, dammit

กำลังจะชนะอยู่พอดี โดนกินเสียฉิบ I was

about to win when, dammit, I got taken. / They took my damn /piece/card/ just as I was going to win.

ฉิบหาย[1] to be ruined, utterly destroyed

ฉิบหาย[2] damn

ฉิบหายแล้วซิ goddam!

เก่งฉิบหาย awfully good, damn good

ฉิว[1] to be annoyed, irritated, to get mad (at)

ฉิว[2] swiftly, like the wind; smoothly

รถคันนี้วิ่งฉิวเลย The car is running /very smoothly/like the wind/.

ลมพัดฉิว a steady breeze

ฉี่[1] sizzling, bubbling

ฉี่[2] to pee, piss, make wee-wee, take a leak

ฉี่ราด to wet /the bed/his pants/the floor/ etc

ฉีก to tear, rip

ฉีกขาด to be torn

ฉีกทิ้ง to tear up, throw away

ฉีกหน้า to humiliate, disgrace, shame

สมุดฉีก note pad, scratch pad

ฉีด to inject; to squirt; to spray

ฉีดยา to give an injection; (ผู้ที่ถูกฉีดยา) to /get/have/an injection, get a shot

ฉันจะไปหาหมอ ไปฉีดยา I'm going to see the doctor for an injection.

ฉีดยาฆ่าแมลง to spray (the room, cockroach, field etc) with insecticide

ยาฉีด injectable (preparation), injection

อัดฉีด to lubricate, grease; lubrication

ฉุ bloated, swollen; flabby, puffy

หน้าฉุ puffy face

ฉุก to occur instantaneously, happen instantly

ฉุกคิด to occur to /me/him/etc, pop into one's head; to suddenly recall

ฉันฉุกคิดขึ้นมาว่ายังไม่ได้ส่งจดหมายแสดง ความยินดีเลย It occurred to me I hadn't sent him a letter of congratulations at all.

ฉุกใจ to be seized with an idea; to call to

mind

ฉุกเฉิน emergency

   ภาวะฉุกเฉิน state of emergency

ฉุกละหุก in such confusion; precipitous, in great haste

ฉุด to pull, drag away, tow (เรือ); to carry off by force

ฉุดกระชาก to drag away violently

ฉุน strong, pungent; to be enraged, furious; to be annoyed

ฉุนเฉียว to lose one's temper, fly off the handle

ฉุนเฉียว irritable, cranky, quick-tempered

กลิ่นฉุน pungent

อารมณ์ฉุน annoyed, mad, irritated

ฉุย wafted; penetrating (odor)

กลิ่นฉุย pervasive smell

วิ่งฉุย to run smoothly

หอมฉุย redolent, beautiful smell

ฉู่ stinking, fetid; buzzing

ฉู่ฉี่ fish fried in a spicy sauce

ฉูด to shoot out, spurt; to run in a strong stream

   น้ำพุ่งฉูด The water spurted out.

ฉูดฉาด flashy, gaudy; vivid

เฉ not straight, to slant, deviate, be out of line; inclined; tilted; divergent

เฉไฉ to take one's time (about /doing something/going somewhere/), fool around

เฉก like, as, as would (a, the), just as

เฉโก cunning, crafty, foxy

เฉ่ง to pay, settle an account

เฉ่งเงิน to pay, settle an account

เฉ่งปี๋ to settle accounts (with someone) *เจ้าหมอนั่นทำฉันแสบ เดี๋ยวฉันจะไปเฉ่งปี๋มัน That damn fool did me a bad turn and I'm going to settle accounts.*

เฉด to shoo off, drive away, chase away

เฉดหัวไป to get rid of

เฉพาะ especially, specially, specifically, particularly (for), exclusively; only; special, particularly; limited, restricted

เฉพาะกาล provisional, temporary, transitory

เฉพาะกิจ special, ad hoc

เฉพาะตัว personal, private

เฉพาะหน้า short term, short run, immediate

เฉพาะอย่างยิ่ง especially, in particular

โดยเฉพาะ especially, particularly, in particular, specifically

เฉย to be indifferent (to), uninterested (in), unconcerned (with); reserved, easy going; I don't care.

เฉยเมย to take no heed (of), be indifferent; unresponsive

เฉยเลย without batting an eyelash

วางเฉย to be detached; to keep aloof (from)

หน้าเฉยตาเฉย expressionless, impassive

เฉยๆ passive, inactive, quiet, placid; to have no feelings one way or the other; easy going; I don't care.

คนเฉย ๆ phlegmatic, stolid

ให้เฉยๆ to give for no special reason, a simple gift

อยู่เฉยๆ to be quiet, keep still, keep quiet; to do nothing, be doing nothing, not do anything; Don't move!

เฉลย to answer

เฉลยปัญหา to solve a problem

เฉลว hex sign

เฉลา handsome, beautiful, fine

เฉลิม to celebrate; to increase, multiply; supreme, prestigious

เฉลิมพระเกียรติ to extol the king

เฉลิมพระชนมพรรษา to celebrate the King's birthday

วันเฉลิม (day of) celebration

เฉลี่ย to average, divide equally, share

เฉลี่ยเจือจาน to share

คิดเฉลี่ย on the average, an average of

ส่วนเฉลี่ย proportionate share, proportion

เฉลียง verandah, porch

เฉลียว to recall, be able to think of

เฉลียวใจ think of something, realize; to suspect, happen to think of something; to have second thoughts

เฉลียวฉลาด smart, clever, keen, intelligent

เฉวียง aslant

ห่มเฉวียงบ่า to wear aslant over one's shoulder

เฉอะแฉะ wet, slopping wet, soggy; muddy

เฉา to wither, withered, shriveled

เฉามือ to suffer from handling

เฉาก๊วย a Chinese black gelatin confection

เฉาะ to chop off, lop off; cut open

เฉาะๆ easy

เฉิด magnificent, splendid, gorgeous, majestic, grand

เฉิดฉาย magnificent, splendid, elegant

เฉิบ, เฉิบๆ rhythmical; peppy

รำเฉิบๆ rhythmical dancing

เฉียง diagonal, slanting, oblique, inclined

เฉียงไปทางตะวันออก to veer to the east

เดินเฉียง to slant

ตะวันออกเฉียงเหนือ northeast

เฉียด to almost hit, narrowly miss, come close (to); to brush against

เฉียบ very, exceedingly

เฉียบขาด decisive; rigorous, strict

เฉียบคม razor-sharp

เฉียบพลัน sudden, acute

เฉียบแหลม to be keen, clever, shrewd, sharp, astute, smart, acute

เฉียวฉุน to be enraged, furious, infuriated; ill-tempered, bad tempered

เฉี่ยว to snatch away in the beak; to graze, scrape

ถูกรถเฉี่ยว to be grazed by a car, scraped by a car

เฉือน to slice (off), shear; to trim, cut; to edge out

เฉือนคอ to slit someone's throat

แรงเฉือน shear

เฉื่อย, เฉื่อยๆ sluggishly, unenergetically

เฉื่อยแฉะ lethargic, indolent

เฉื่อยชา inert, lifeless, sluggish, lethargic, slow

แรงเฉื่อย inertia

ลมพัดเฉื่อยๆ gentle breeze

แฉ to reveal, disclose, expose

ข่าวแฉ an exposé

แฉโพย to reveal a secret, spill the beans

แฉก, แฉกๆ forked, pointed, having sharp projections

ดาวห้าแฉก five-pointed star

เป็นแฉกๆ pointed; jagged

แฉ่ง cheerful

ยิ้มแฉ่ง to give a broad smile

แฉลบ to go off course, to veer (from, off); to skim

เขาขับรถแฉลบไปชนต้นไม้ข้างทาง His car veered off the road and hit a tree.

แฉล้ม attractive, lovely, pretty

หน้าแฉล้ม healthy-looking, blooming

แฉะ[1] soggy, wet, sloppy

แฉะ[2] sluggish, lethargic

แฉะแบะ to sit idling away one's time; to be lethargic

โฉเฉ indecisive

โฉ่ disgraceful, distasteful, ugly

โฉ่ฉาว see ฉาวโฉ่ หน้า 130

โฉ่งฉ่าง clashing

เดินโฉ่งฉ่าง to swagger

ท่าทางโฉ่งฉ่าง cocky

พูดจาโฉ่งฉ่าง to talk without thinking

โฉด stupid, foolish

โฉดเฉา stupid, foolish

คนโฉด a dolt

โฉนด title deed, deed

    โฉนดที่ดิน land title deed

โฉบ to swoop down; to carry off

โฉม appearance, figure

    โฉมงาม beautiful figure

    โฉมฉาย strikingly beautiful

    โฉมเฉลา lovely

    โฉมตรู beautiful

    โฉมยง stunning

    โฉมศรี elegant, fine looking

    โฉมหน้า face

        บ่ายโฉมหน้า to head (to, towards)

    เสียโฉม disfigured

โฉลก fortune, luck, chance; way of telling one's fortune by casting lots

    โฉลกดี good luck, fortunate

    ถูกโฉลก auspicious, lucky, favorable

ไฉน[1] how, what, why

ไฉน[2] oboe

ไฉไล pretty, lovely; sparkling

ฉ
ช
ซ
ฌ
ญ
ฎ
ฏ
ฐ
ฑ
ฒ
ณ
ด
ต
ถ
ท
ธ
น
บ
ป
ผ
ฝ
พ
ฟ
ภ
ม
ย
ร
ฤ
ฤๅ
ล
ว
ศ
ษ
ส
ห
ฬ
อ
ฮ

ชก to strike, punch

   ชกต่อย to fight, have a fight

   ชกมวย boxing, fighting, prizefight

   ชกลม to shadow-box

ชง to infuse, steep

   ชงชา to make tea

   ชงนม to prepare milk

   ชงเองกินเอง to monopolize, do the whole works (to get all the credit)

ชฎา traditional pinnacled coronet; a high hairdo

ชฎิล one of a group of ascetics characterized by long hair bound in a high bun

ชดช้อย graceful, lissome

ชดเชย to compensate, substitute (for); to indemnify (for)

   ค่าชดเชย compensation, indemnification

   วันหยุดชดเชย substitute holiday

ชดใช้ to reimburse, pay, compensate, offset

   ชดใช้ค่าเสียหาย to pay damages

ชน[1] to collide (with), strike, bump (against, into), hit (against), run into; to meet, join, be up against; to last; to fight; to pit (against another)

   ชนแก้ว to toast, drink a toast (to)

   ชนไก่ to have a cockfight

   ชนขวบ for a full year

   ชนควาย to have a buffalo fight

   ชนช้าง to fight on elephantback

ชน[2] people

   ชนกลุ่มน้อย minority

   ชนชั้น class

      ชนชั้นกลาง middle class

   ชนชาติไทย the Thai nation, the Thai people

   ชนชาวต่างชาติ aliens, foreigners

   กลุ่มชน group, the people (who)

   ชุมชน community; assemblage, gathering

   ประชาชน the people, the public, populace

ชนก father

ชนนี mother

ชนบท rural area, country, countryside

ชนม-, ชนม์ birth

   ชนมพรรษา age

   วายชนม์ to die, deceased

ชนวน[1] slate

   กระดานชนวน slate

   หินชนวน slate

ชนวน[2] fuse

   จุดชนวน to light the fuse

   ดับชนวน to defuse (a situation, etc)

   ถอดชนวน to defuse

   เทียนชนวน candle used to light other candles

   เป็นชนวน to lead to, bring (something) on

ชนะ to win, beat, defeat, overcome; to be victorious

   ชนะคดี to win a case

   ชนะคะแนน to outscore

   ชนะใจ to win (someone) over, please

      ชนะใจตนเอง to control oneself

   ชนะตั้งแต่ในมุ้ง to be a sure winner

   ชัยชนะ victory, triumph, success

   เอาชนะ to beat, overcome, win; to get the better of (someone)

ชนัก harpoon; an elephant stirrup

   มีชนักปักหลัง to have a past

ชนิด kind, type, sort, class, variety; species (*วิทย์*)

   ชนิดที่ of a kind which

   ภาษีทางอ้อมชนิดที่อยู่ในราคาสินค้าแล้ว ...indirect taxes of a kind which are incorporated in the price of goods...

ชม to admire, compliment, praise, commend, esteem; to look (at,over), view

   ชมเชย to praise, extol, esteem, laud, honor, admire; to embrace

      รางวัลชมเชย honorable mention

   ติชม to comment, criticize

   น่าชม admirable, attractive

ชมดชม้อย *see* **ชดช้อย** *หน้า 134*

ชมพู pink, rose

    ชมพูทวีป India

    ชมพูนุท pure gold

ชมพู่ rose apple, rose apple tree

ชมรม group, club, circle

    ชมรมชาวพุทธ Buddhist group

    ชมรมนักกลอน poet's circle, poetry club

ชม้อย to glance (at someone) shyly

ชม้าย to cast a sidelong glance (at)

ชยันโต to sermonize, haul over the coals

    น้ำท่วมกรุงคราวนี้ ผู้ว่า กทม. ถูกชาวบ้านชยันโต
    กันทั่วเมือง As a result of the flooding, the
    Bangkok governor was hauled over the
    coals by everyone.

ชโย hurray, hooray, hurrah

ชรา old, elderly, aged, aging

    ชราภาพ old age; decrepitude

    วัยชรา old age; geriatric

ชล water

    ชลธาร river, waterway, watercourse, canal,
    stream, creek

    ชลธี sea, ocean

    ชลนัยน์ tears

    ชลนา tears

    ชลเนตร tears

    ชลประทาน irrigation

    ชลมารค by water

ชลาธาร well; pond

ชลาลัย sea; river

ชลี to press the hands together in respectful greeting

ชเล sea

ชโลทร river; sea, waters

ช่วง[1] part, section, stage, span, interval; sub;
stretch

    ช่วงครึ่งเปิด half-open interval

    ช่วงชก reach

    ช่วงชีวิตนี้ during this life, in this life

ช่วงตัว body length

ช่วงปิดเทอม during school vacation, in the
interval between terms

ช่วงยาว long interval, long stage; length

ช่วงล้อ wheelbase

ช่วงสั้น short interval, short stage; width

ช่วงล่าง suspension

ช่วงหลัง later, subsequently; more recently

จ้างช่วง to sub-contract

เช่าช่วง to sublet, sublease, sub-rent

ตัวแทนช่วง sub-agent, substitute

เป็นช่วง ๆ in stretches

    ถนนไม่ดีเป็นช่วงๆ The road is bad in
    stretches.

รับช่วง to get from someone else, take over
(something from someone)

ช่วง[2] to grab

    ช่วงชิง to grab, win

ชวด[1] rat, the Year of the Rat; great-grandfather (ชาย), great-grandmother (หญิง)

ชวด[2] to miss out (on something), lose /narrowly/
unexpectedly/, forego

    ฉันชวดดูหนัง I missed out on the movie.
    ชวดเรียน to forego one's studies / miss out
    on school

ชวน to invite, ask; to suggest, make one; to
persuade, induce

    ชวนหัว comic performance

    ชวนให้คิด It makes you think.; thought-
provoking, intriguing

    ชวนให้สงสัย to be suspicious

    โฆษณาชวนเชื่อ propaganda

    ชักชวน to invite ask; to induce, persuade

ช่วย to assist, help, aid, facilitate; to save;
please, do me a favor

    ช่วยรับโทรศัพท์ตอนที่ผมไม่อยู่ Please help by
    answering the telephone while I'm away.

    ช่วยกันทำ to pitch in, lend a hand, help

ช ฌ ญ ฎ ฏ ฐ ฑ ฒ ณ ด ต ถ ท ธ น บ ป ผ ฝ พ ฟ ภ ม ย ร ฤ ฤๅ ล ว ศ ษ ส ห ฬ อ ฮ

one another do something

ช่วยชีวิต to save another's life

ช่วยด้วย Help!

ช่วยไม่ได้ It can't be helped., Too bad., There's nothing to be done about it., It's no use. There is no help for it.

ช่วยหน่อย Please help me., Please give me a hand.

ช่วยเหลือ to assist, give /aid/assistance/, help out

รัฐมนตรีช่วยว่าการ assistant minister

ชวลิต resplendent, glorious

ชวเลข shorthand; stenography

นักชวเลข stenographer

ชวา Javanese, Java; double-reed pipe, a Javanese oboe

ชวาลา lamp, lantern

ช่อ cluster, bunch; spray, sprig, shoot

ช่อดอกไม้ spray of flowers, bouquet

ช่อฟ้า ornamental roof points shaped like serpents

ช้อกช้ำ to be bruised, wounded, hurt

ช้อกช้ำระกำใจ to be hurt to the quick, crushed, embittered

ช็อก shock

ตกใจช็อกไปเลย to be shocked (by, at)

ช็อกโกเลต, ช็อกโกแลต chocolate

ช่อง hole, aperture, window, opening, slot; channel; cavity; space; gap, pass; chance, opportunity, way, means

ติดต่อที่ช่อง 6 Go to window 6.

ช่อง 5 TV Channel 5

ช่องขายตั๋ว ticket window

ช่องคลอด vagina

ช่องแคบ narrows, straits; pass, gap

ช่องทาง way, means; opening, opportunity, chance

ช่องไฟ space

ช่องว่าง gap

ช่องว่างระหว่างวัย generation gap

ช่องโหว่ loophole; gap, hole

ชี้ช่อง to find an opportunity; to point the way, give practical advice

บ้านช่อง housing, house(s), home(s)

ช้อง wig, hairpiece

ชอน, ชอนไช to make its way into something, penetrate

ช้อน[1] to scoop, dip up; to raise, lift

ช้อนขึ้นมา to scoop up

ช้อนหุ้น to accumulate /shares/stocks/

ช้อน[2] spoon; a long-handled fishnet

ช้อนกลาง serving spoon

ช้อนชา teaspoon

ช้อนโต๊ะ tablespoon

ช้อนส้อม silverware, spoons and forks

ช้อนใส่รองเท้า shoehorn

ชอบ to be right, just, correct; to love, like, enjoy, be fond of, go for (someone)

ชอบกล tricky; appropriate, to sound /good/ right/; funny, queer, strange

ชอบใจ glad, be happy, to like something; to be delighted, pleased

ชอบด้วยกฎหมาย lawful, legal, in accordance with the law

ชอบที่จะ to be entitled to, be justified in, have the right to, warrant

ไม่ชอบที่จะรับจดทะเบียน is not registrable / does not warrant registration

ชอบธรรม lawful, rightful, legitimate; fair, right

ชอบนักชอบหนา to be crazy about (something), wild about (something), infatuated (with)

ชอบพอกัน to be fond of one another; to be friends, know each other

ความชอบ merit

ตามใจชอบ as one likes, freely

ผู้รับผิดชอบ person /responsible/in charge

(of)/

ใครเป็นผู้รับผิดชอบงานนี้ Who is in charge here? / Who is responsible for this?

ไม่เป็นการชอบ it is not right (for)

เห็นชอบด้วย to approve

เห็นผิดเป็นชอบ to take wrong for right

ชอล์ก chalk

ชะ to cleanse; to wash away, erode

ชะ ๆ, ชิชะ ha-ha, what the hell

ชะ ๆ หน้าอย่างมึงมาดูถูกกูได้! What the hell do you mean by that!

ชะง่อน overhanging rock, shelf

ชะงัก to stop short, be interrupted, get stuck; to come to a sudden halt

ชะงักงัน to come to a halt, stop

ชะงัด with accuracy, sure; miraculous; effective

ยาขนานนี้รักษาโรคได้ชะงัดนัก This is a sure cure, a miracle drug. / This medicine will surely do the trick.

ฝีมือชะงัดนัก highly skilled

ชะเง้อ to crane (one's neck)

ชะเง้อคอคอย to wait expectantly (for), long for (someone to return etc), yearn (for)

ชะแง้ to look up

ชะโงก to lean out

ชะโงกดูเงาตัวเอง Take a look at yourself in the mirror.

ชะโงกผา shelf, overhanging rock

ชะโงกหน้ามามอง to peer (at, out, over); to lean (out, over) and look

ชะดีชะร้าย in case, maybe

ชะตา fate, destiny

ชะตากรรม fate, lot

ชะตาขาด to die

ชะตาตกต่ำ to have fallen on bad times, suffer misfortune

ดวงชะตา horoscope

ถูกชะตากัน to hit it off, take to one another, get along well together

ชะนี gibbon

ชะเนาะ a wooden lever used to tighten a rope by twisting

ชะมด civet cat

ชะมัด, ชะมัดยาด fantastic, superb, super, exceptionally

ไอ้หมอนั่นเก่งชะมัด (ยาด) เลย That guy is fantastic! / The kid is exceptionally clever.

ชะรอย maybe, perhaps

ชะลอ to slow down, reduce speed, brake, retard; to move (something heavy) slowly and carefully

ชะลอการเกิด to slow down population growth; to space out the family, practice birth control

ชะลอม a plaited open-work bamboo produce basket

ชะล่าใจ to be complacent, overconfident, too sure of oneself; careless

เขาชะล่าใจเกินไปจึงแพ้การเลือกตั้ง Complacency led to his downfall in the election.

ชะลูด very tall, tall and slender

ชะแลง crowbar

ชัก[1] to pull, draw; to have convulsions

ชักโครก flush toilet; to flush the toilet

ชักเงา to shine, polish

ชักจูง to induce, lead, influence (someone to do something); to be influenced (by)

ชักจูงไปในทางเสียหาย to be led astray

ชักชวน to invite, ask; to induce, persuade

ชักช้า delay; to take one's time, be slow

โดยไม่ชักช้า without delay, promptly

ชักดาบ to refuse to pay

ชักตัวอย่าง to give an example, for instance

ชักธง to raise a flag, fly a flag

ชักธงชาติ to fly the national flag

ซ
ฌ
ญ
ฎ
ฏ
ฐ
ฑ
ฒ
ณ
ด
ต
ถ
ท
ธ
น
บ
ป
ผ
ฝ
พ
ฟ
ภ
ม
ย
ร
ฤ
ฦ
ล
ว
ศ
ษ
ส
ห
ฬ
อ
ฮ

ก
ข
ค
ฆ
ง
จ
ฉ
ช

ชักนำ to lead
ถูกชักนำในทางที่ผิด to be led astray
ชักปืน to draw a gun
ชักเย่อ tug of war
ชักใย to spin a web; to manipulate behind the scene
ชักว่าว to fly a kite; *(sl)* to jack off, jerk off, play with oneself
ชักหน้าไม่ถึงหลัง to be unable to make ends meet
ชักแหงกๆ to jerk, be jerking, have /spasms/ convulsions/

ชัก², **ชักจะ** getting, beginning to
ชักโกรธ getting angry, beginning to get mad
ชักจะร้อน getting hot
ชักเดือด to be aggravated, irritated, provoked
ชักเบื่อ getting bored
ชักหิว getting hungry

ชัง to dislike; to abhor, detest
จงเกลียดจงชัง to hate one's guts, loathe
ชิงชัง to hate, detest, abhor, loathe

ชั่ง Thai monetary unit equal to 80 baht; to weigh
ชั่งใจ to consider carefully, weigh the possibilities, think it over
ชั่งหลวง a unit of weight equal to 600 grams
คันชั่ง scale beam
เครื่องชั่ง scale, weighing machine

ชัชวาล bright, brilliant, splendorous; blazing
ชัฏ thick forest, dense forest, jungle
ชัด clearly, distinctly
ชัดๆ *as in* **ดูให้ชัดๆ หน่อย** to take a good look first
ชัดเจน very clear, distinct; obvious; precise, unequivocal
ชัดแจ้ง clear, precise
เห็นได้อย่างชัดแจ้ง to be very obvious,

apparent; to be clearly visible
อย่างชัดแจ้ง expressly, clearly
ชัดแจ๋ว perfectly clear, as clear as anything *(พูด)*
ชัดถ้อยชัดคำ distinctly, clearly, well enunciated, articulate clearly; (to speak) emphatically
แน่ชัด definite, certain, positive, definitely, clearly, without a doubt
พูดชัด to speak /clearly/distinctly
ภาพชัด clear picture
ลายมือชัด legible handwriting, writing that is clear
เห็นได้ชัด clearly visible; obvious

ชัน¹ dammar
ชัน² steep, precipitous; erect, standing on end
ชันคอ to raise one's head

ชั้น shelf, layer; storey, story, floor; class, rank, classification, degree, grade, order; stage, tier, level; section, part; class *(วิทย์)*
ชั้นจัตวา fourth /class/grade/
ชั้นเชิง craftiness, cunning; tricks, wiles; tactics
ชั้นต้น initial stage, primary stage, beginning
ชั้นตรี 3rd grade
ชั้นเตรียม preparatory stage
ชั้นโท 2nd grade
ชั้นนำ leading, outstanding
ชั้นใน inside, inner
เสื้อชั้นใน underwear, undershirt
ชั้นบน upstairs; on the top; top shelf; balcony *(โรงละคร)*
ชั้นประถม /elementary/primary/ (school, level, grade etc)
ชั้นผู้ใหญ่ highlevel, senior, high ranking (officer, official, guest etc)
ชั้นเยี่ยม excellent, top, first-class

ชั้นแรก in the first place, initially
ชั้นลอย mezzanine
ชั้นล่าง downstairs, orchestra *(โรงละคร)*
ชั้นเลิศ excellent
ชั้นเอก 1st grade
ทุนชั้นที่หนึ่ง first tier capital
ชันนะตุ seborrhea of the scalp
ชันษา age
ชันสูตร to verify; to inspect, investigate
ชันสูตรพลิกศพ to perform an autopsy, do a postmortem examination
ชัย victory, win, triumph
ชัยชนะ victory, triumph, success
ชิงชัย to conquer, win a victory
ชัยภูมิ location, situation; /good/favorable/ advantageous/ location
มีชัย to be victorious, successful
โชคดีมีชัยนะ Good luck and lots of success!
เส้นชัย finish line
ชั่ว[1] for, through, throughout
ชั่วกัปชั่วกัลป์ eternally, forever
ชั่วขณะ for a time
ชั่วคน generation
ชั่วคราว temporarily; for a time; ephemeral, temporary; for the time being, provisional
ชั่วครู่ for a /moment/minute/time/while/
ชั่วนาตาปี always, for years
ชั่วฟ้าดินสลาย eternally, forever
ชั่วโมง hour
ชั่วโมงละ per hour, an hour
ชั่วลูกชั่วหลาน for succeeding generations
ชั่วแล่น fleeting, momentary
ชั่วแวบเดียว (for, in) an instant
ชั่วอายุ (for the) lifetime (of)
ชั่ว[2] bad, no good, low
ชั่วเจ็ดทีดีเจ็ดหน You win some, you lose some. / Every cloud has a silver lining.
ชั่วช้า wicked, evil

ชั่วร้าย terrible
ชา[1] tea, tea plant
ชาดำเย็น iced tea without milk
ชาฝรั่ง black tea, Ceylon tea
ชามะนาว (hot or iced) tea with lemon
ชาเย็น iced tea with milk
น้ำชา tea
ใบชา tea leaves, tea
ชา[2] numb, insensitive; anesthetized, without sensation
ชาชิน to get used to, inured (to), accustomed (to), hardened (to)
ชาด้าน see ด้านชา *หน้า 162*
ชาเย็น, เย็นชา see เย็นชา *หน้า 401*
ยาชา local anesthetic
ฉีดยาชา to give a local anesthetic
เหน็บชา beriberi
ช้า long, slowly; inactively, lazily
ช้าก่อน Take it easy., Hold on., Calm down.
ชักช้า delay; to take one's time, be slow
โดยไม่ชักช้า promptly, without delay
อย่าชักช้านะ Don't be long!
ช่าง[1] one skilled in an art or craft, artist, craftsman, artisan, skilled workman, repairman
ช่างกล engineer
โรงเรียนช่างกล technical school
ช่างกลึง lathe operator, turner
ช่างก่อสร้าง builder, contractor, building contractor
ช่างก่ออิฐ mason, bricklayer
ช่างแก้นาฬิกา watchmaker
ช่างแกะ sculptor; carver, wood carver, metal engraver
ช่างเขียน artist, painter; draftsman
ช่างเครื่อง mechanic, fitter; engineer
ช่างเงิน silversmith
ช่างจักสาน basketmaker, matmaker, weaver of /mats/baskets/etc
ช่างชุบ electroplater, plater

ช่างเชื่อม welder

ช่างซ่อม repairman

ช่างต่อเรือ shipwright

ช่างตัดผม barber, hairdresser

ช่างตัดรองเท้า shoemaker, cobbler

ช่างตัดเสื้อ tailor (เสื้อผู้ชาย), dressmaker (เสื้อผู้หญิง)

ช่างถ่ายรูป photographer, cameraman

ช่างทอง goldsmith

ช่างทอผ้า weaver

ช่างทำผม hairdresser

ช่างนาฬิกา watchmaker

ช่างบัดกรี tinsmith

ช่างปั้น sculptor; potter; modeler, modeller

ช่างปั้นหม้อ potter

ช่างฟิต fitter, mechanic

ช่างไม้ carpenter, woodworker

ช่างยนต์ mechanic; machinist

ช่างย้อมผ้า dyer

ช่างเย็บ seamstress, sewer

ช่างเรียง compositor, typesetter

ช่างโลหะ metalworker, metalsmith

ช่างสลัก carver, woodcarver

ช่างแสง armorer

ช่างหล่อ caster, founder, molder

ช่างเหล็ก, ช่างตีเหล็ก blacksmith, ironsmith, ironworker

ช่างอ๊อก welder

ช่างอากาศ aircraft mechanic; aeronautical engineer

การช่าง craft, art

นายช่าง supervising engineer; chief mechanic, Chief

เรียกช่างมาทำ call the repairman

ช่าง[2] given to, fond of

ช่างคิด having good ideas, clever

   ช่างนึกช่างคิด intelligent, brilliant

ช่างคุย a good talker, fond of talking, affable

   ช่างพูดช่างคุย garrulous

ช่างเถียง argumentative, given to argument

ช่างสังเกต observant

ช่าง[3] as in

ช่างเขาปะไร never mind him

ช่างเถอะ never mind, forget it, don't pay any attention (to it)

ช่างปะไร What of it!

ช่างเป็นไร What difference does it make?, So what!

ช่างมัน Who cares!, Forget it., To hell with it.

ช่างหัวมันปะไร to hell with him

ช้าง elephant, pachyderm

ช้างค่อม pygmy elephant

ช้างงาเดียว one-tusked elephant

ช้างต้น state elephant, royal elephant

ช้างเถื่อน wild elephant

ช้างเท้าหลัง one's better half, helpmate

ช้างน้ำ hippopotamus

ช้างเผือก white elephant; the Order of the White Elephant

   ทางช้างเผือก Milky Way

ช้างพลาย male elephant, bull elephant

ช้างพัง cow elephant, female elephant

ช้างไม่มีงา tuskless elephant

ช้างสาร formidable elephant

ช้างสีดอ tuskless elephant

ชาญ skilled, skilful, experienced, expert, (in something), knowledgeable

ชาญฉลาด ingenious, resourceful

ชาด vermilion; rouge

ชาดก tales of the previous lives of Buddha, Jataka stories

ชาตรี powerful; traditional play of southern Thailand; musical accompaniment for a traditional play of southern Thailand

ชาตะ born

ชาตา fate, destiny; horoscope

ชาติ[1] life; birth; incarnation

ชาติก่อน former life, previous life; former incarnation

ชาติชั่ว low-life

ชาตินี้ in this life

ชาติหน้า next life, life to come; future incarnation

ชาติหมา a bastard, You bastard!, son of a bitch

ตลอดชาติ the rest of one's life, for one's whole lifetime, for life, for good

ตาปีตาชาติ year in year out, forever

ชาติ[2] country, nation, a people

ชาติไทย the Thai nation, the Thai people

ชาตินิยม nationalist

ชาติพันธุ์ ethnic

ชาติพันธุ์นิยม ethnocentrism

ชาติพันธุ์วรรณา ethnography

ชาติพันธุ์วิทยา ethnology

ข้ามชาติ multinational

ขายชาติ to be a traitor, betray one's country

คณะชาติ Nationalists

เชื้อชาติ parentage, origin; race

ต่างชาติ foreign, alien

ธงชาติ national flag

นานาชาติ international

ประจำชาติ national

ประเทศชาติ country

แปลงชาติ to be naturalized, acquire another nationality

ญวนแปลงชาติ a naturalized Vietnamese

เพลงชาติ national anthem

ระหว่างชาติ international

สัญชาติ nationality, citizenship

สันนิบาตชาติ League of Nations

องค์การสหประชาชาติ the United Nations

ชาน[1] open porch, deck

ชานชาลา platform

ชานเมือง outskirts, suburb

นอกชาน deck, open porch, terrace

ชาน[2] residue,

ชานหมาก chewed-out betel quid

ชานอ้อย bagasse, sugar cane pulp

ชาม bowl, dish

เช้าชามเย็นชาม lethargic, apathetic

ชาย[1] male, man, masculine

ชายโสด bachelor, single man

ชายหนุ่ม young man, youth

ชายอกสามศอก a real man, manly guy

กระทาชาย man

คบชู้สู่ชาย adulterous, wanton

ความเป็นชาย masculinity, manliness *เขา ไม่ค่อยมีความเป็นชายเท่าไหร่ He's not very /masculine/manly/.*

บุตรชาย son

ผู้ชาย man; men's, masculine

พวกผู้ชาย the boys, the menfolk, fellows

เพศชาย male, masculine; manhood; masculine gender

เพื่อนชาย boyfriend, buddy, pal

ลูกชาย son

ลูกผู้ชาย a real man, like a man, manly, manfully

เขายอมรับโทษอย่างลูกผู้ชาย He accepted his punishment /like a man/manfully/.

ไม่ใช่ลูกผู้ชาย contemptible

ไม่เป็นลูกผู้ชาย not very manly

ชาย[2] edge, end; fringe;

ชายกระเบน the tail of a long strip of cloth wound around the hips and tucked at the back

ชายกระเบนเหน็บ the small of the back

ชายคา eaves; roof, place

อยู่ชายคาเดียวกันไม่ค่อยได้พบกันเลย We live in the same place, yet never meet.

ชายแดน border, frontier

ชายตา to glance sideways

ชายผ้า selvage, edge of a piece of cloth

ชายฝั่ง bank, shore

ช ฌ ญ ฎ ฏ ฐ ฑ ฒ ณ ด ต ถ ท ธ น บ ป ผ ฝ พ ฟ ภ ม ย ร ฤ ฤๅ ล ว ศ ษ ส ห ฬ อ ฮ

ชายเมือง edge of town, fringe of a city

ชายเลน muddy coast, muddy bank

ชายหาด beach

ชายไหว an ornamental apron hanging from the waist

ชายา wife, consort

ชาลา open porch, terrace

ชานชาลา, ชานชาลาสถานี platform, station platform

ชาว group, people, folk, tribe; residents, inhabitants (of), denizens (of)

ชาวเกาะ islanders

ชาวเขา hill tribe, mountain dwellers, mountain folk, uplanders

ชาวดอย hill tribe, mountain dwellers, mountain folk, uplanders

ชาวตะวันตก westerner(s), Occidental(s)

ชาวตะวันออก easterner(s), Oriental(s)

ชาวต่างประเทศ foreigner(s)

ชาวทะเล seafolk, sea people *(พหู)*

ชาวนา farmer, peasant

ชาวบ้าน folks, villagers, local people, common folk, people, ordinary people *(พหู)*, ordinary person *(เอก)*

ชาวบ้านนอก country people, country dweller

ชาวประมง fisherman

ชาวป่า forest dweller

ชาวพารา townspeople, people, citizens

ชาวพื้นเมือง natives

ชาวเมือง city people, cityfolk, townspeople, urban dweller

ชาวยุโรป European

ชาวโลก the world

ชาววัง palace women; palace dwellers

ชาวสวน gardener, /fruit/vegetable/ growers, farmers

ชำ[1] to pot, plant as nusery stock

ชำ[2] *as in*

ของชำ groceries

ร้านของชำ grocery store

ช่ำ satisfied, fulfilled, delighted, to one's heart's content

คุยกันจนช่ำใจ We chatted to my heart's content.

ช้ำ to make a cutting; bruised, to be black and blue

ช้ำใจ to /be/feel/ hurt, embittered

ทำให้ช้ำใจ to embitter, hurt, deeply offend (someone)

ช้ำเลือดช้ำหนอง carbuncular

รอยช้ำ bruise, contusion, black and blue mark

ช่ำชอง to be expert, skilled (in, at), experienced, efficient, proficient, well versed (in)

ชำนัญ *as in*

ผู้ชำนัญพิเศษ specialist

ทบวงการชำนัญพิเศษ specialized agency

ชำนาญ to be experienced, have experience (in), expert, skilled, skillful, adept (at); quick-witted

ความชำนาญ expertise (in), mastery of

ผู้ชำนาญ expert, person skilled (in), specialist

ชำนิชำนาญ a master (of); having great skill (in), expert

ชำร่วย *as in* **ของชำร่วย** gift, present, keepsake, memento, souvenir

พิมพ์ชำร่วยในงานฌาปนกิจ Printed as a memento of the cremation.

ชำระ to wash, clean, cleanse; to pay, clear up; to revise, /do/make/ a recension

ชำระความ to try a case

ชำระใจ to purify one's mind, cleanse one's mind

ชำระเงิน to pay

ชำระดอกเบี้ย to pay interest

ชำระตัว to bathe, wash oneself

ชำระบัญชี to liquidate; to settle accounts

ชำระประวัติศาสตร์ to revise (the) history

(of)

ชำระพระไตรปิฎก to /revise/make a recension/ of the Tipitaka

ชำระสะสาง to cleanse

ชำระหนี้ to /pay/settle/ a debt, discharge one's /debt/obligation/, clear a debt; to fulfill an obligation

    ผ่อนชำระหนี้ to pay a debt in installments

    กระดาษชำระ toilet paper, bathroom tissue

ชำรุด damaged; defective, spoiled

ชำรุดทรุดโทรม to be dilapidated, ramshackle, worn out, in decay

ชำเรา to rape, ravish, violate; to have sexual intercourse (with)

ชำแรก to edge through (a crowd), shoulder a way through (a crowd etc), penetrate, infiltrate

ชำเลือง to look sideways (at), cast a sidelong glance (at)

ชำแหละ to butcher, cut up, carve up; to revise, scrutinize; to dissect; to dig into

    ชำแหละประวัติศาสตร์ to dig into the history (of)

ชิ, ชะ tush

ชิง to compete (for), scramble for; to win, get, seize

    ชิงชัย to conquer, win a victory

    ชิงโชค to participate in a /raffle/lucky draw/

    ชิงดีชิงเด่น to grab the honors, push oneself forward

    ชิงได้ to win; to seize, grab

    ชิงตำแหน่ง to compete for a /title/job/ position/office/

    ชิงทุน to win a /scholarship/grant/

    ชิงสุกก่อนห่าม to do something before it is time to do so, act prematurely, do something before the time is ripe

    ชิงไหวชิงพริบ to outsmart, outwit

    ชกชิงแชมป์โลก a world championship

/fight/bout/

ชิงชัง to hate, detest, abhor, loath

ชิงช้า swing

ชิด[1] *as in* **ลูกชิด** nipa palm fruit

ชิด[2] close, near; touching

    ชิดขวา keep to the right, keep right

    ชิดซ้าย keep to the left; not up to it, outdone

    ใกล้ชิด close, intimate

ชิน[1] to be accustomed (to), used to, familiar (with)

    ชินกับอากาศร้อน to get used to the /tropical climate/hot weather/

    ชินชา to be numb (to something), become indifferent (to)

    ชินตา to look familiar, have seen (some one, something) before

ชิน[2] pewter, alloy of tin and lead

    พระเนื้อชิน pewter Buddha amulet, Buddha amulet made of a tin and lead alloy

ชิ้น piece, section; lump, morsel; sheet; slice

    ชิ้นปลามัน choice (girl, job, bit, etc), prize

    เป็นชิ้นเป็นอัน substantial, serious, solid, real

    งานเป็นชิ้นเป็นอัน real work, substantial job

    ลูกชิ้นปลา fishball

ชิโนรส a disciple of the Buddha

ชิม to taste, sample

    ชิมลาง to see what will happen, try

ชิวหา tongue

ชี[1] a religious; Buddhist woman ascetic, a Buddhist (female) religious, nun

    ชีต้น Buddhist monk

    ชีปะขาว a lay ascetic

    ชีเปลือย sect of Jain naked ascetics

ชี[2] *as in* **ผักชี** coriander

ชี้ to point (at, to); to stretch out; to advise; to indicate, point out

    ชี้ขาด to decide, make a final /decision /determination/

        ผู้ชี้ขาด umpire

ช ฌ ญ ฎ ฏ ฐ ฑ ฒ ณ ด ต ถ ท ธ น บ ป ผ ฝ พ ฟ ภ ม ย ร ฤ ฦ ล ว ศ ษ ส ห ฬ อ ฮ

กรรมการผู้ชี้ขาดบนเวที referee

ชี้แจง to explain, make clear, make a statement, state a position

ชี้ช่อง to find an opportunity; to point the way (to do something), give practical advice

ผู้ชี้ช่อง (เรื่องการเงิน) finder

ชี้ตัว to identify

ชี้ทาง to show the way

ชี้นิ้ว to order others about

ชี้มือ to point (to)

ชี้หน้า to shake a finger at someone, point to someone in the face; to identify

ชี่ช้ำ to feel hurt (by)

ชีผ้าขาว, ชีปะขาว white moth

ชีพ life

ชีพจร pulse

จับชีพจร to take one's pulse

ครองชีพ see **ครองชีพ** หน้า 76

ดับชีพ to die

เลี้ยงชีพ to earn one's living

ชีว-, ชีวะ bio-, life, being, existence; soul, atman

ชีวเคมี biochemistry

ชีวจิต body and mind, holistic

อาหารชีวจิต health food

ชีวประวัติ life history, biography, resumé

ชีวภูมิศาสตร์ biogeography

ชีวโลก all living things, world of the living

ชีววิทยา biology

ชีวัน life; living things

ชีวา, ชีวี life

ชีวิต life

ชีวิตชีวา lively

ชีวิตักษัย death, demise

ชืด uninteresting; insipid, tasteless

จืดชืด see จืดชืด หน้า 120

เย็นชืด all cold

ชื่น cheerful, happy, merry, joyful, delighted, glad, happy; refreshing, beaming

ชื่นใจ refreshing; glad, delighted

เขาเป็นคนที่ใครคุยแล้วชื่นใจ She's a delightful person to talk to. / She's a delight to talk to.

ชื่นชม to admire

ชื่นบาน in a good mood, in good spirits, cheerful, lighthearted

ชื่นมื่น beaming, elated

ชื่นอกชื่นใจ delighted, elated, pleased as punch, jubilant

ชื้น wet; moist, damp; humid; not quite dry

ชื้นแฉะ wet

ความชื้น humidity, dampness

ความชื้นสัมพัทธ์ relative humidity

ใจชื้น relieved, to have a sense of relief

ชื่อ name, appellation, title; to be famous, well-known, have a reputation

ชื่อเดิม (เดิมชื่อ) formerly

มหาจุฬาลงกรณราชวิทยาลัย ชื่อเดิม (เดิมชื่อ) มหาธาตุวิทยาลัย Mahachulalongkorn Buddhist University (formerly Mahadhatu Vidhyalaya)

ชื่อตัว first name, personal name, Christian name

ชื่อแฝง alias, assumed named, pseudonym

ชื่อเล่น nickname

ชื่อว่า although, though; to be named, be called; to be termed, counted, regarded, considered; to be known (for,as), acknowledged /as/to be/

ชื่อสกุล family name, surname

ชื่อเสียง reputation, fame, renown, honor

ชื่ออะไร What is your name?; What is it called?

ขึ้นชื่อว่า to be known /as a/for/, have a reputation /for being a/as a/

ได้ชื่อว่า to be known as /a/for/, regarded as, gain a reputation /for being/as/

ตั้งชื่อ to name, give a name, call

ฝากชื่อ to establish one's reputation, get a good name (from or for something)

มีชื่อ famous, well-known, popular, noted; notorious

รายชื่อ names, list of names

เรียกชื่อ to call (someone) by name; to be called, named

ลงชื่อ to sign; to enter one's name, put down one's name; signed

ลือชื่อ famous, celebrated, renowned, well known, notorious

เสียชื่อ to get a bad name, be discredited, spoil one's reputation, look bad

ชุก abundant, plentiful, copious,

ชุกชุม plenty of, lots of, abounding (in, with)

ฝนตกชุก plenty of rain, abundant rainfall

ชุกชี masonry base for a principal Buddha image

ชุด qualifier for collections or sets; set; set of clothes, suite of furniture; act (ตอนหนึ่งของการแสดง)

นวนิยายเรื่อง เรือมนุษย์สองเล่มชุด "Reua Manoot", a novel in two volumes

ชุดเก่ง favorite outfit

ชุดนอน pyjamas

ชุดนักเรียน school uniform

ชุดรับแขก living room suite

ชุดราตรี evening dress, evening wear

ชุดลูกเสือ scout uniform

ชุดวันเกิด birthday suit

ชุดสากล coat and tie, suit, lounge suit, western dress

ชุน to darn

ชุบ to better, improve, care for; to restore the dead to life, bring the dead to life; to temper, harden; to dip (in), soak; to plate

ชุบโครเมี่ยม chromium-plated; to chromium-plate

ชุบเงิน silver-plated

ชุบชีวิต to better the life of someone; to bring back to life

ชุบตัว to better oneself

ชุบทอง gold-plated; to gold-plate, plate with gold

ชุบน้ำ to moisten, wet (with water), dip in water

ชุบมือเปิบ to take a free ride

ชุบเลี้ยง to bring up, raise, rear

ชุม to be abundant, plentiful, copious; to congregate, assemble, gather

ชุมชน community; assemblage, gathering

ชุมชนนิยม communitarianism

ชุมชนแออัด slum

ชุมทาง junction

ชุมทางรถไฟ railway junction

ชุมพล military staging area

ชุมสายโทรศัพท์ telephone exchange

ชุ่ม wet

ชุ่มคอ refreshing (to the taste)

ชุ่มชื่น refreshing; cheerful, happy, refreshed

ชุ่มปอด to one's heart's content

ชุมนุม congregation, gathering, assemblage, group, party

ชุมนุมชน /assembly/gathering/ of people

ชุมสาย a three-tiered umbrella

ชุ่ย, ชุ่ยๆ crappy, lousy; do in a slipshod way, to do carelessly; sloppy, slipshod, shoddy, half-baked

พูดชุ่ยๆ อย่างนี้ใช้ไม่ได้ He's shooting off his mouth. / It's a lot of crap.

อย่าทำอะไรชุ่ยๆ Don't do anything half-baked. / Don't be sloppy about what you do.

ชุ่ยส่ง sloppily, badly

ชุลมุน disorderly, in confusion, wild

ฝูงชนวิ่งหนีระเบิดกันชุลมุน At the sound of the explosion, the crowd took to their heels /fled/ in wild confusion.

ชุลมุนวุ่นวาย chaotic, turbulent

การชุลมุนต่อสู้ affray, brawl

ชุลี Thai style salutation (by pressing the

ซ ฌ ญ ฎ ฏ ฐ ฑ ฒ ณ ด ต ถ ท ธ น บ ป ผ ฝ พ ฟ ภ ม ย ร ฤ ฤๅ ล ว ศ ษ ส ห ฬ อ ฮ

ก
ข
ค
ฆ
ง
จ
ฉ
ช

hands together)

ชู to elevate, raise, lift up, uphold; to better, improve

ชูกำลัง stimulate, invigorate

    ยาชูกำลัง tonic

ชูคอ to look proud; to stretch one's neck

ชูใจ to make one feel good, hearten

ชูชีพ life preserver, lifesaver, life belt, life buoy, life jacket

ชูรส to enhance the /flavor/taste/; monosodium glutamate

ชู้ lover; adulterer, adulteress, adultery

ชู้สาว lovers

มีชู้ to have a lover

เช็ค[1] cheque, check

เช็คขีดคร่อม crossed /check(US)/cheque (Brit)/

เช็คเด้ง a bad check, to bounce

เช็คเด้งหรือเปล่า Did the check bounce? / Was it a bad check?

เช็คบิล to ask for the check (US), ask for the bill (Brit)/

เช็คไปรษณีย์ postal check

ตีเช็ค to write a check

เอาเช็คไปขึ้นเงิน to cash a check

เช็ค[2] to check; the check (บิลเก็บเงินในร้าน อาหารในสหรัฐ)

เช็คดูชิว่าถูกต้องไหม Could you check whether it's okay, please?

เช็คเอาไว้ to check it

เช้ง attractive, captivating, smart, chic; flashy, showy

เช้งวับ smashing

เช็ด to wipe, wipe off, clean

เช็ดก้น to wipe oneself; to wipe (a baby's etc) bottom

(ตาม)เช็ดขี้ to clean up the mess

เช็ดตัว to dry oneself; to give a bedbath

เช็ดน้ำ to pour off the excess water (when

boiling rice)

เช็ดน้ำตา to wipe one's eyes, wipe away one's tears

เช็ดปาก to wipe one's mouth

เช็ดหน้า to dry one's face, wipe one's face

เช็ดหม้อ see **เช็ดน้ำ**

เช็ดหน้า /door/window/ frame

เช่น for example, such as, like

เช่นเคย as usual, as before

เช่นใด whatever

เช่นนั้น like that, that, in that /way/manner/

เช่นนี้ for example; like this, this, in this way

เช่น...เป็นต้น for example, such as..., to give a few examples

เชย[1] to caress

เชยแก้ม to pat another's cheek

เชยคาง to chuck under the chin; to raise another's chin gently

เชยชม to praise, admire; to pet, caress, fondle

เชย[2], **เชยๆ** fuddy-duddy, outdated, not with it, unsophisticated, unstylish, not stylish, plain; to have no taste

เชยจัง so dull

เชยแหลก corny, sappy

เชลย prisoner, captive

เชลยศักดิ์ unofficial, amateur

เชษฐ-, เชษฐา elder brother

เชษฐบุรุษ elder statesman

เช่า to rent, lease, hire

เช่าช่วง to sublet, sublease, sub-rent

เช่าซื้อ to buy on the installment plan, buy by hire-purchase, buy by conditional sale

เช่าพระ to buy a Buddha image

ค่าเช่า rent, rental

รถเช่า rented car; rental car, car for rent

ให้เช่า for rent, to let, rent, lease

เช้า morning

เช้าตรู่ (at) dawn
เช้ามืด before dawn

เชาวน์ flair, gift (for); mental agility, quickness of mind

มีเชาวน์ quick (at, to), quick-witted; to have a flair (for something), be clever (at something), have a gift (for something)

เชิง[1] base, foot

เชิงกราน[1] portable earthen stove with a projecting foot

เชิงกราน[2] (กระดูก) pelvis

เชิงกลอน eave board

เชิงเขา foot of a hill, foothills, base of a /hill/mountain/

เชิงชาย eave board

เชิงเทียน candlestick, sconce

เชิง[2] trick, ploy, artifice, wile

เชิงชั้น see ชั้นเชิง หน้า 138

เชิงชาย masculine wiles

เสียเชิงชายหมด to be devastated

เชิงซ้อน complex; superimposed, composite

ภาพเชิงซ้อน superimposed photographs

เชิง[3] manner, sort, in the way of, aspect, -al, -istic, -ly

เชิงสัพยอก teasingly

ข้อเขียนเชิงขบขันเสียดสี satirical writings, writings in the satirical manner, writings of the satirical sort

ไม่เชิง not quite, not exactly

เชิงตะกอน crematory

เชิญ to invite, ask, bid; to convey, bring

เชิญก่อน After you.

เชิญเขาเข้ามา Please show him in.

เชิญเข้ามา Please come in.

เชิญครับ Please.

เชิญ เชิญ Come in, come in!; Please go ahead.; Please help yourselves.

เชิญตามสบาย Make yourself at home., Don't bother. I'm fine.

เชิญทางนี้ This way, please.

เชิญนั่ง Please take a seat.

เชิญรอประเดี๋ยว Please wait a moment., Just a moment, please., Hold the line, please. (โทรศัพท์)

คำเชิญ invitation

บัตรเชิญ invitation

รับเชิญ to accept (an invitation)

เชิด[1] to hold up, elevate, lift, raise; to pinch (something already borrowed); to use (someone), hold (someone) out (as)

เชิดเงินหนี to make off with the money

เชิดชู to extol, exalt, honor, praise

เชิดรถจักรยาน to pinch the bicycle

เชิดหน้าชูตา prestigious, (something) to be proud of

เชิดหุ่น to operate a /puppet/marionette/

คนเชิดหุ่น puppeteer, marionette operator

ถูกเชิด to be used, held out (as)

หุ่นเชิด puppet; (fig) strawman, figurehead, puppet; a front, front man

เชิด[2] the name of a kind of music to accompany fighting or long journeys used in the theater or boxing matches

เชิ้ต shirt

เชียร์ to cheer

เชี่ยนหมาก betel tray, betel box

เชียบ as in **เงียบเชียบ** dead still, dead silent

เชียว a word added for emphasis, right, really, indeed

ทำเดี๋ยวนี้เชียว Do it right now!

เชี่ยว[1] as in **เชี่ยวชาญ** experienced, expert, skilled

เชี่ยว[2] fast flowing, rushing

น้ำเชี่ยว rapids, fast flowing stream, fast current, rushing water

เชื่อ to believe, believe in, trust, have faith (in), rely on; to /get/take/ on credit

เชื่อเครดิต to trust (someone), to rely on (someone's) reputation

ช
ซ
ฌ
ญ
ฎ
ฏ
ฐ
ฑ
ฒ
ณ
ด
ต
ถ
ท
ธ
น
บ
ป
ผ
ฝ
พ
ฟ
ภ
ม
ย
ร
ฤ
ฤๅ
ล
ว
ศ
ษ
ส
ห
ฬ
อ
ฮ

เชื่อใจ to trust

น่าเชื่อใจ trustworthy, dependable, reliable

เชื่อถือ to believe in, trust, have confidence in, rely on; to respect

เชื่อถือได้ reliable, dependable, trustworthy

เชื่อฟัง to to be obedient, obey, listen (to), take heed

เชื่อมั่น to firmly believe (in, that), trust in, have confidence (in)

เชื่อมั่นในระบบรัฐสภา to trust in the parliamentary system

เชื่อมั่นในตัวเอง to have self-confidence

เชื่อว่า to be convinced (that), believe (that)

ขายเชื่อ to sell on credit, a credit sale

โฆษณาชวนเชื่อ propaganda

ซื้อเชื่อ to buy on credit

น่าเชื่อ believable, likely, credible

ไม่น่าเชื่อ unlikely, incredible, improbable, lacking in credibility

อย่างไม่น่าเชื่อ incredibly

แพงอย่างไม่น่าเชื่อ It is incredibly expensive.

เหลือเชื่อ unbelievable, incredible, preposterous

เชื้อ fuel, tinder, kindling; lineage, blood, family, ancestry, stock; yeast

เชื้อกษัตริย์ of royal blood

เชื้อชาติ parentage, origin, race

เชื้อเชิญ to invite, extend an invitation

คำเชื้อเชิญ invitation, formal invitation

เชื้อเพลิง fuel

เชื้อโรค germs, pathogen

อย่าเล่นกับหมา เดี๋ยวจะติดเชื้อโรค Don't play with the dog. You might catch something from it.

เชื้อสาย lineage, family, ancestry, stock

เชื้อหมัก yeast

ติดเชื้อ to catch a disease, become infected

(with), come down with

เชือก[1] rope, string, cord, twine

เชือก[2] numerical classifier for elephants

ช้างหนึ่งเชือก an elephant

ช้างสองเชือก two elephants

เชื่อง tame, domesticated; submissive

คนท่าทางเชื่องๆ a milquetoast, /unassertive /meek/ person

เลี้ยงไม่เชื่อง ungrateful; untameable, obstreperous

เชื่องช้า to take so long, move so slowly

เชือด to slice, cut, slit

เชือดคอ to /cut/slit/ someone's throat, slit the throat of

เชือดเฉือน to be cutting, make a cutting remark

เชือน as in **แชเชือน** to dawdle, dawdling

เชื่อม[1] syrup, preserve, to candy, cook with sugar

กล้วยเชื่อม candied bananas

น้ำเชื่อม syrup

เชื่อม[2] to connect, join, unite; to link; to weld

เชื่อมต่อ to join

รอยเชื่อมต่อ joint, junction

เชื่อมสัมพันธไมตรี to establish friendly relations

เชื่อมโยง to link, link up

เชื่อมเหล็ก to weld

ตัวเชื่อม mediator, intermediary (between)

แช่ to soak; to steep

แช่เย็น to refrigerate; to chill, put on ice, frozen; to be kept on ice, put in cold storage, shelved

แช่อิ่ม preserved (fruits etc)

แช่ง to curse, damn

แช่งชักหักกระดูก to call down curses (on someone), damn (someone)

แช่มช้อย captivating, charming, cute

แช่มชื่น cheerful, gay, happy

โชก soaking wet, drenched, soaked

โชกโชน old, veteran, experienced, to have /gone/been/ through a lot

นักชกผู้โชกโชน a veteran boxer / a boxer who's been through a lot

โชกเลือด covered with blood

เปียกโชก soaking wet, sopping wet, drenched

โชค luck, fortune

โชคชะตา luck, fortune

โชคดี good luck, good fortune

โชคร้าย bad luck, misfortune

ถือโชคถือลาง superstitious

เป็นโชคดี fortuitous, lucky

มีโชค fortunate, lucky, to be in luck

เสี่ยงโชค to try one's luck, take a chance

โช้กอัพ shock absorber

โชติช่วง bright, glowing

โชน blazing

ไฟลุกโชน the fire blazed up

โชย, โชยชาย to blow /gently/lightly/

ลมโชย breeze, /gentle/light/ breeze

ใช่ correct, right; yes

ใช่ไม่ใช่ is it or isn't it; did you or did you not

ใช่แล้ว that's right, correct, true

ใช่ไหม right?, Isn't that right?, Is it not so?

คุณไม่ชอบใช่ไหม You don't like it, do you?, Don't you like it ? *เขาไม่อยู่ใช่ไหม* He isn't in, is he?

ไม่ใช่ see **ไม่ใช่** หน้า 385

  ไม่ใช่อื่น nothing else but...., no one else but...

ใช้ to employ, use, apply, make use of, exercise; be used; to pay, repay

ไม่อาจใช้มาตรการการบังคับกับเจ้าพนักงานดังกล่าวได้ ...no coercive measure may be applied to the said officers.

ใช้การได้ in working condition, usable, serviceable

ใช้การไม่ได้ out of order, unserviceable, not working

ใช้กำลัง to force, use /force/violence/

ใช้คืน to repay

ใช้งาน working

  ความดันใช้งาน working pressure

ใช้จ่าย to spend

ใช้ได้ alright, good; it works, usable

ใช้บังคับ to enforce, come into force, take effect, impose upon, enforce against, govern

ใช้ใบ to unfurl a sail; to sail

ใช้ไม่ได้ unacceptable, no good; unusable, out of order

ใช้สอย to employ, use, make use of

ใช้สิทธิ to exercise rights (of), exercise one's right(s)

ใช้หนี้ to pay one's debt, repay; to satisfy an obligation

ใช้หัวคิด to use one's head

ใช้อำนาจในทางทุจริต to abuse one's authority, commit malfeasance

ใช้อุบาย to trick, use a trick; to use a /technique/device/

ของใช้ articles, things; belongings, effects; equipment, utensils

คนใช้ servant, household help, maid

เครื่องใช้ utensil, implement, instrument, equipment

บังคับใช้ to come into force, take effect

ประกาศใช้ to give notice of the coming into force (of), publish, promulgate

มีใช้ to have /some/enough/ample/

รับใช้ see **รับใช้** หน้า 417

สาวใช้ servant girl, maid

ไชชอน to bore (into), penetrate

ไชโย hurray, hurrah; hip hip hooray!

ช
ซ
ฌ
ญ
ฎ
ฏ
ฐ
ฑ
ฒ
ณ
ด
ต
ถ
ท
ธ
น
บ
ป
ผ
ฝ
พ
ฟ
ภ
ม
ย
ร
ฤ
ฦ
ล
ว
ศ
ษ
ส
ห
ฬ
อ
ฮ

ก
ข
ค
ฆ
ง
จ
ฉ
ช
ซ

ซก drenched (with sweat), dripping wet (with sweat, rain, etc)

ซด to sip

ซ.ต.พ.,(ซึ่งต้องพิสูจน์) Q.E.D. (quod erat demonstrandum)

ซน, ซุกซน mischievous, naughty; playful, lively
เด็กคนนี้ซนจริง What a mischievous kid!
เที่ยวซุกซน to run around, go out for a naughty time

ซ้น to be sprained
ข้อเท้าซ้น to have a sprained ankle

ซบ to rest one's head (on one's arms, another's shoulder or lap etc)
ซบเซา empty; quiet, dull

ซม lethargic, drowsy; helpless
เป็นไข้นอนซม drowsy with fever, in a sick torpor, laid low by illness

ซมซาน ignominiously

ซวดเซ to stagger; to teeter, wobble, be on the verge of falling, precarious

ซวนเซ to reel; to totter

ซวย unlucky, unfortunate; misfortune, Damn it!

ซอ fiddle
ซอด้วง soprano fiddle
ซออู้ alto fiddle
สีซอ to play a /violin/fiddle/
สีซอให้ควายฟัง to cast pearls before swine / I might as well be talking to the wind.

ซอก alley, narrow place, space, crevice, corner
ซอกซอน to go into concealment; to worm one's way
ทุกซอกทุกมุม every nook and cranny, all over, everywhere, high and low

ซอกแซก to probe, be nosy
ถามซอกแซก to be nosy, ask probing questions

ซอง envelope; stall; slot, narrow place; bamboo fishtrap
ซองบุหรี่ cigarette case

ซองมือ hollow of one's hand
ซองแว่นตา eyeglass case
ปืนลูกซอง shotgun

ซ่อง brothel; hiding place, den
ซ่องกะหรี่ whorehouse
ซ่องการพนัน gambling den
ซ่องโจร criminal association; hideout
ซ่องสุม to get together for wrongdoing
ซ่องโสเภณี brothel, house of prostitution

ซ่อน to hide, conceal, secrete, keep out of sight
ซ่อนคม to hide one's light under a bushel, be modest, unpretentious
ซ่อนเงื่อน insidious, cunning
ซ่อนหา hide-and-seek
ซุกซ่อน to hide

ซ้อน to lay on top of something; double up; to overlap, overlay, superimpose; double, multiple
ซ้อนกล to counter
ซ้อนท้าย to ride pillion

ซ่อม to repair, fix, renovate, restore
ซ่อมแซม to repair; to restore
ช่างซ่อม repairman, mechanic
โรงซ่อม repair shop

ซ้อม to practise, drill; to rehearse (โดยมากใช้กับละคร)
ซ้อมข้าว to mill rice by hand
ซ้อมความเข้าใจ to understand, to reach an understanding (about, over, as to), get (something) straight
ซ้อมผู้ต้องหา to give a prisoner the third degree, beat up the accused
ซ้อมมวย to train for a fight
ซ้อมมือ hand-milled (rice)
ซ้อมรบ to engage in military exercises, /hold/engage in/ maneuvers, hold war games; to have battle training
ซ้อมใหญ่ to hold a dress rehearsal
คู่ซ้อม sparring partner

ซอมซ่อ seedy, shabby, rundown

ซอย[1] to mince, chop up; to slice finely

ซอยเท้า to tap with the feet, mark time

ซอยผม to thin the hair

ซอยหอม to chop up an onion

ซอย[2] lane; branching

กลางซอย in the middle of the lane, down the lane

ซัก[1] to wash, launder; to question, interrogate, put questions to someone

ซักค้าน to cross-examine

ซักซ้อม to agree in advance, reach an understanding

ซักไซ้ to cross-question, grill, dig for answers

ซักถาม to interrogate, question

ซักผ้า to wash clothes, do the laundry

ซักฟอก to launder, wash; to interrogate

ผงซักฟอก detergent

ซักรีด to do the laundry, do the washing and ironing

ร้านซักรีด laundry

ซักแห้ง to dry-clean

ซัก[2], **สัก** only, just

จ่ายไปเถอะ มันจะซักกี่บาทกัน *It's just a few baht. Pay it!*

ซัง rice stubble; stringy pulp of the jackfruit; corncob; corner squares of a chessboard

ซังกะตาย to be constrained to do something; spiritless, listless, apathetic, lackadaisically

เขาทำงานซังกะตายไปวันๆ *They do their daily work lackadaisically. / They go about their daily work /listlessly/spiritlessly/. / Apathy marked their daily work.*

ซังกะบ๊วย useless, crummy

ซังตาย *see* **ซังกะตาย**

ซัด to douse; to throw; to hurl, fling; to implicate, put the blame on others

ซัดเซ to wander, roam

ซัดทอด to implicate, blame (someone else for something), put the blame on someone, put the finger on (somebody), pass the buck, point one's finger at someone

ซับ to blot, absorb; to mop up

ซับซ้อน to be complicated, complex, involved; having layer upon layer (of)

ซับใน lining

กระดาษซับ blotting paper

ซา to decrease, diminish, abate, subside, let up

ฝนซา *The rain has let up.*

ซ่า sound of a waterfall, splash, splashing; fizzy

ขนลุกซ่า to make one's hair stand on end, to get /gooseflesh/goosepimples/, be terrified, My hair stood on end.

ซาก remains; carcass, corpse

ซากดึกดำบรรพ์ fossil

ซากปรักหักพัง ruins

ซากศพ remains, corpse, body

งูตายซาก dried snake remains, dead dried-out snake

ซาง pampas grass; follicular pharyngitis

ซ่าน to diffuse, permeate, spread throughout

ซ่านเซ็น to be scattered, dispersed; to be routed

ซาบ to permeate

ซาบซ่าน to permeate the body, spread throughout the body; to be in ecstasy

ซาบซึ้ง to appreciate, be grateful (for); to be overwhelmed (by); heartfelt

ข้าพเจ้ารู้สึกซาบซึ้งในความกรุณาของท่าน *I deeply appreciate your /kindness/kind help/generosity/favor/.*

ซ้าย left

ซ้ายจัด extreme leftist, ultra leftist, left extremist

ซ้ายหัน left face

ซ
ฌ
ญ
ฎ
ฏ
ฐ
ฑ
ฒ
ณ
ด
ต
ถ
ท
ธ
น
บ
ป
ผ
ฝ
พ
ฟ
ภ
ม
ย
ร
ฤ
ฦ
ล
ว
ศ
ษ
ส
ห
ฬ
อ
ฮ

ก
ข
ค
ฆ
ง
จ
ฉ
ช
ซ

ด้านซ้าย left side, on the left, to the left

ถนัดซ้าย left-handed

ทางซ้าย to the left, on the left

ฝ่ายซ้าย the left

มือซ้าย left hand

เอียงซ้าย leftist, radical

ซาลาเปา steamed dumpling

ซาว to stir around with the hand

ซาวข้าว to rinse rice before cooking

ซาวเสียง to sound out, poll

ซ่าหริ่ม a sweet in coconut cream

ซ้ำ to repeat; to be alike; to have the same thing

ซ้ำชั้น to repeat a class, get left back

ซ้ำซ้อน to overlap, duplicate, be a duplication (of); overlapping, duplicated; repeated, multiple

หน่วยงานใหม่ไม่ซ้ำซ้อนกับที่มีอยู่แล้วหรือ Won't the new unit just be a duplication of what we already have?/ Will the new unit overlap the existing one?

ซ้ำซาก repetitious

ซ้ำ ๆ ซาก ๆ monotonous, over and over again

ซ้ำเติม to lay it on, add to another's woes, hit someone while he's down, make things worse for someone

ซิ an imperative particle often expressed by an exclamation point or the word "do"

ดูซิ Look at that! / Do look.

ซิก, ซิก ๆ perspiring, sweating, in a sweat

ร้องไห้ซิก ๆ to sob, sobbing.

เหงื่อแตกซิก to begin to perspire, sweat

ซิกข์ Sikh

ซิกซี้ to banter, teasing and giggling

ซิ่ง racing *(sl)*

ซิ่น traditional tube skirt

ซิบ to ooze, exude

เลือดไหลซิบ The blood is oozing out.

ซิว minnow

ซี *see* ซิ

ซี่ numerical designation for small elongate things; teeth, ribs, bars

ซี่โครง rib

ซี่โครงหมู spareribs

ซี้ to die

เพื่อนซี้ close friend, true friend

ซี้ซั้ว any old way, badly, slipshod

ซีก section, segment, part, piece, portion; half

ซีกไม้ a piece of wood

ซีกโลก hemisphere

เป็นซีก ๆ in pieces

พระจันทร์ครึ่งซีก half-moon

ซีด faded; pale, pallid, wan, ashen

ซีดเซียว wan, pallid

ซีดเป็นไก่ต้ม pale as a boiled chicken

ซีดเป็นผีตาย to turn deathly pale, blanch

ซีดเผือด to blanch, turn /white/ashen/

ซีดสลด to turn pale with distress

เท้าซีด pale feet

ปากซีด one's lips turn pale

มือซีด pale hands, hands turn /white/ashen/

หน้าซีด to blanch, turn pale, look pale

ซีอิ๊ว soy sauce

ซึ่ง who, that, which

นำมาซึ่งสันติภาพ to bring peace

ซึ่งกันและกัน each other, one another, reciprocal, mutual

ซึ่งหน้า in front of someone, face to face, openly

ผู้ซึ่ง who, one who

ซึ้ง deep, profound; to be impressed, touched

ซึ้งใจ moved, touched, deeply touched

ซึม to leak; to soak; to penetrate, seep, soak into; sleepy; dull, listless

ซึมกระทือ withdrawn, half-dead, spiritless, lifeless

ซึมซาบ to soak into, be absorbed (into, by),

seep into, permeate

ซึมเซา drowsy; lethargic

ซึมทราบ to know all about something, understand

ซึมเศร้า *see* **เศร้าซึม** *หน้า 471*

แทรกซึม to infiltrate, pervade

ปากกาหมึกซึม fountain pen

ซื่อ honest, faithful, loyal, true, upright; straight-forward, ingenuous, artless

ซื่อจนเซ่อ simple, naive; gullible; dumb

ซื่อตรง upright, true, honest, scrupulous, of integrity

ซื่อบื้อ nincompoop

ซื่อสัตย์ faithful, true, loyal, devoted (to); honest, upright

ทำเป็นซื่อ to be disingenuous, artful

พาซื่อ to take (someone) in, be taken in; naive, innocent, unsuspecting

พูดซื่อๆ to be forthright

เล่นซื่อๆ to be on the up and up, play by the rules

เว้าซื่อๆ to speak frankly, use plain language

ซื้อ to buy, purchase

ซื้อของ to shop (for something), go shopping, buy things

ซื้อขาย buying and selling, trade

สัญญาซื้อขาย contract of sale, purchase contract

ซื้อง่ายขายคล่อง readily salable

ซื้อเชื่อ to buy on credit

ซื้อปลีก to buy retail; to buy a small quantity

ซื้อเสียง to buy votes, /go/practice/ vote-buying

ซื้อหา to buy

ซื้อแล้ว sold

การซื้อกิจการ (business) acquisition

กว้านซื้อ to corner the market, buy up

เช่าซื้อ to buy by hire-purchase, buy on the

installment plan, buy by conditional sale

ผู้ซื้อ buyer, purchaser

รับซื้อ to buy

ซุก to hide, conceal; to insert (in, between), tuck (in, under), put (into)

ซุกซน *see* **ซน** *หน้า 150*

ซุง log; kite bridle

แพซุง log raft

ซุบซิบ to gossip; to whisper

ซุป soup

ซุปเปอร์มาร์เกต supermarket

ซุปเปอร์ไฮเวย์ superhighway

ซุ่ม to lie in wait (for); in private

ซุ่มซ่อน to go into hiding; to ambush

ซุ่มดักอยู่ to waylay, ambush

ซุ้ม arbor; archway

ซุ้มขาย booth

ซุ่มซ่าม clumsy, blundering

ซุย[1] *as in* **มีดซุย** a single-edged dagger

ซุย[2] friable, crumbly; rotten

ดินซุย light soil

ซู่ having /goose-flesh/goose pimples/

ซู่, ซู่ๆ sound of heavy rain

ซู่ซ่า to make a stir; sound of a heavy rain

ซูดซาด slurp

ซูบ drawn, haggard; rundown, wan

ซูบซีด wan, pale, sickly

ซูบผอม emaciated, wasted

ซูเอี๋ย to connive together

ซูฮก to hand it to (him, them, etc), give thumbs-up (to someone or something)

ไก่ย่างที่วิเชียรบุรีอร่อยขนาดที่ต้องยอมซูฮกให้จริงๆ You've really got hand it to them in Vichienburi for producing a grilled chicken as good as that.

เซ staggering; aslant; tottering

เซซัง staggeringly, unsteadily; aimlessly

เซหลุนๆ to stumble, trip, lose one's footing

เซ็ง to be bored, feel ennui, fed up; boring,

(sl) sucks

ฉันรู้สึกเซ็งชีวิต I'm bored to death. / Life sucks!

เซ็งตัวเองเหลือเกิน I hate myself!

เซ้ง to transfer for value, sell; to sublet; /shop/ leasehold/ for sale.

เซ้งร้าน Shop lease for sale., to sell rights to a shop

เซ็งแซ่ noisy; to make an uproar (about, over)

เซ็น to sign

เซ็นทราบ to sign by way of acknowledgement, initial

เซ็นไว้ก่อน to sign for something

เซ็นสัญญา to sign a /contract/agreement/, execute a contract

ลายเซ็น signature

เซ่น to make propitiatory offerings to spirits, offer food to spirits

เซนติกรัม centigram

เซนติเกรด centigrade

เซนติเมตร centimeter

เซนติลิตร centiliter

เซฟ to save

เซรุ่ม serum

เซลล์ cell

เซลล์วิทยา cytology

เซ่อ, เซอะ stupid, foolish, silly, lunkhead, blockhead, numskull

เซ่อซ่า clumsy, blundering; oafish, a clod

เซา to stop, abate, subside, let up; sleepy, drowsy

ขี้เซา sleepy

ซบเซา empty, quiet, dull

ซึมเซา drowsy; lethargic

เซ้าซี้ to insist (on), nag, keep after, pester

บอกว่าไม่กินก็ไม่กินสิเซ้าซี้อยู่ได้ I told you I don't want (to eat) it. Stop /pestering/ nagging/!

เซาะ to wear away, undermine, erode

เซิ้ง tousled

เซิ้ง a Northeastern music and dance jollification

เซิ้งกระติ๊บ Northeastern basket dance

เซียน saint; wizard

เซียนพนัน a gambling wizard, wizard at gambling

เซียนเหยียบเมฆ a corker, out of this world

เซียบ *as in* เงียบเซียบ (in) dead silence, utter quiet

เซียมซี fortune sticks; to tell one's fortune by shaking numbered sticks in a container the first to fall out indicating a similarly numbered printed fortune paper

เซียว pale, drawn, wan

เซื่อง sluggish, lethargic, lifeless

แซ่[1] clan; Chinese family name; Sae

แซ่[2], **เซ็งแซ่** tumultuous, noisy; uproar, shouting

แซ่ซ้อง to shout praises

แซง to overtake, pass, get ahead (of); to slip in between, to squeeze through a crowd; to scrape, graze

แซงคิว to jump the queue, cut into the line

แซงซ้าย to pass on the left, overtake on the left

แซงซ้ายแซงขวา to weave in and out of traffic

ขับรถแซง to /get ahead/cut in front/ of other cars

แทรกแซง to intervene (in); to interfere (with), meddle (with)

แซด buzzing, humming

ลือกันแซด to be buzzing with rumors

แซบ delicious, delectable, flavorsome, tasty, appetizing

แซบอีหลี great, wonderful (ใช้กับ food)

แซม to insert, thrust in between; to add in, to replace

แซมผม to stick into the hair

ซ่อมแซม to repair; to restore

แซยิด sixtieth birthday celebration

แซว to tease

แซ่ว *as in* **นอนแซ่ว** to lie helpless

แซะ to pry (up, away), lift with a spatula, unstick

แซะขนมครก to scoop out coconut pan-cakes

โซ[1] starving, haggard

ผอมโซ undernourished, gaunt

โซ[2] *as in* **โซเซ** unsteady.

เดินโซเซ, เดินโซซัดโซเซ to stagger (along), be unsteady on one's feet, reeling

โซ่ chain

โซ่ตรวน leg chains, shackles

ลูกโซ่ chain; link

โซก drenched

โซดา soda

โซดาไฟ caustic soda

น้ำโซดา soda, soda water, sparkling water

โซน zone

โซม to soak; to bathe; to smear, paint, coat; to be soaked, drenched; to perspire, sweat (เหงื่อ)

เหงื่อโซมกาย drenched in sweat

โซเวียต Soviet

สหภาพโซเวียต Soviet Union

ไซ a bamboo fishtrap

ไซ้ to dig, peck, root; to preen; to churn

ไซ้ขน to preen /its feathers/itself/

ซักไซ้ to cross-question, grill, dig for answers

ไซ่ง่อน Saigon

ไซบีเรีย Siberia

ไซปรัส Cyprus

ไซร้ know that, surely (ไม่นิยมแปล)

ถ้าคนเราไม่มีเมตตาต่อกันไซร้ โลกจะไร้สันติสุข /Surely/Know that/ unless we have loving kindness, the world will know no peace.

ฌาน ฌ เฌอ

ฌาน meditative absorption, meditation, a state of serenity attained by meditation

เข้าฌาน to be in a trance, lost in meditation; to go into a meditative trance, be in a state of deep meditation

ฌาปนกิจ to cremate; cremation

ฌาปนสถาน crematorium, crematory

เฌอ plant

ญ
ฏ
ฎ
ฐ
ฑ
ฒ
ณ
ด
ต
ถ
ท
ธ
น
บ
ป
ผ
ฝ
พ
ฟ
ภ
ม
ย
ร
ฤ
ฤๅ
ล
ว
ศ
ษ
ส
ห
ฬ
อ
ฮ

ญวน Vietnamese
ชาวญวน Vietnamese
ประเทศญวน Vietnam
ญัตติ proposition, motion
แปรญัตติ to propose (an) amendment, move to amend, /file/propose/ a motion to amend
เสนอญัตติ to move (an) amendment
ญาณ insight; sixth sense
ญาณทัศนะ enlightenment, intuitive illumination
ญาณวิทยา epistemology
ญาติ relative, family, kin, relation, cousin
ญาติดี to be partners (in gambling); to be reconciled

ญาติพี่น้อง relatives, family, kinfolk
ญาติมิตร friends and relatives
ญาติโยม family, kith and kin; laypeople
ญาติสนิท close /relation/relative/
ญาติห่าง ๆ distant /relation/relative/, distantly related
เครือญาติ family tree, kindred; family, family line
เป็นญาติกัน to be related (to), have an affinity with
ญี่ปุ่น Japanese
ชาวญี่ปุ่น Japanese
ประเทศญี่ปุ่น Japan
ภาษาญี่ปุ่น Japanese

ฎีกา[1] petition, appeal; an appeal to the Supreme Court
ศาลฎีกา Supreme Court
ฎีกา[2] an invitation to a monk; a solicitation for a

contribution; voucher; request for a treasury payment
ฎีกาเรี่ยไร solicitation
ฎีกา[3] sub-commentary

ฐาน base, foundation; basis, grounds
ถูกจับสึกฐานยักยอก defrocked on the grounds of embezzlement
ฐานกรณ์ place of articulation
ฐานทัพ military base
   ฐานทัพเรือ naval base
   ฐานทัพอากาศ air base
ถิ่นฐาน home, where one lives, home base
ฐานะ position, capacity, status, place, station, standing
ฐานะดี well-to-do, well-off, prosperous
ฐานะหน้าที่ capacity
ในฐานะหน้าที่ที่คล้ายกัน in other related capacities

ในฐานะ as, in one's capacity as
ปรากฏตัวในฐานะพยาน to appear as a witness
ตามฐานานุรูป in accordance with one's station in life
วิทยฐานะ academic /qualifications/ status/standing/, educational qualifications
   รับรองวิทยฐานะ to accredit
   กระทรวงศึกษาธิการรับรองวิทยฐานะโรงเรียนของเรา Our school was accredited by the Ministry of Education.
สมฐานะ as befits one's /status/position/place/
ฐานันดร order of precedence, rank
ฐานันดรที่สี่ Fourth Estate

ทราวิท Dravidian

เฒ่า old, elderly, aged
เฒ่าแก่ the Chinese /owner/boss/ (of a shop, enterprise, etc); elder go-between, distinguished person who formally presents

the prospective groom's suit
เฒ่าตัณหากลับ old lecher
เฒ่าหัวงู old goat, aging Lothario
ผู้เฒ่าผู้แก่ elders, old folk

ณ in, on, at, of
ประกาศ ณ วันที่ 6 มีนาคม Notice given the 6th March. / Published the 6th March.
ณ โรงละครแห่งชาติ at the National Theater
ณ วันนี้ today
ณ กาลครั้งหนึ่ง once upon a time
ณ ที่ใด wherever

ณ ที่นี้ on this occasion, at this time; herein, at this point
ณ บัดนี้ now, at this time
ณ อยุธยา of Ayuthia
ณรงค์ to battle, fight, engage in battle, campaign
เณร novice monk, samanera

ก
ข
ค
ฆ
ง
จ
ฉ
ช
ซ
ฌ
ญ
ฎ
ฏ
ฐ
ฑ
ฒ
ณ
ด

ดก   abundant, a lot of, fruitful, fecund

   ดกดื่น plenty (of)

   ขนดก hairy, hirsute

   ดอกดก heavy flowering

   ผมดก a good head of hair, thick hair

   ลูกดก prolific, fecund

ดง[1]   forest, jungle

   ดงดาน (in) the woods, wilderness, forested area

   ดงดิบ primary forest, jungle, rain forest

   ดงผู้ร้าย gangsters' hangout

   ดงหญ้า grassland

   ป่าดง heavy forest, jungle; uncultivated land in its natural state

ดง[2]   *as in* **ดงข้าว** to re-heat boiled rice after pouring off excess water

ดัน   to push forward

   ดั้นดั้น, ดั้นด้น to make one's way (into, to, through), penetrate

   ดันถอยหลัง to backstitch

   กลอนดัน free verse, extemporaneous verse

ดนตรี   music

   การแยกโน้ตดนตรี orchestration

   เครื่องดนตรี musical instrument

   นายวงดนตรี conductor, band leader

   โน้ตดนตรี music, score

     แยกโน้ตดนตรี to orchestrate

   เล่นดนตรี to play music, perform music

   วงดนตรี orchestra, band, ensemble

ดนัย   son

ดนุ, ดนู   I, me

ดม   to smell, sniff; to inhale

ดร.   Dr., doctor

ดรรชนี, ดัชนี index *(เอก)*, indices *(พหู)*; index finger

   ดรรชนีค้นคำ index

   ดรรชนีค้นเรื่อง subject index

   ดรรชนีชื่อผู้แต่ง author index

   ดรรชนีวารสาร periodical index

ดรุณ   child, youngster, youth, lad; young, juvenile, adolescent, teenage

ดรุณี   girl, lass; young, juvenile, adolescent, teenage

ดล   to reach, attain; to cause, create, give rise to, make

   อำนาจลี้ลับดลให้ฉันทำเช่นนี้ I was made to do this by a mysterious power

   ฉันไม่รู้ว่าอะไรดลให้ฉันทำเช่นนี้ I don't know what made me do it.

   ดลใจ to inspire

   ดลบันดาล to inspire (one with), engender, bring forth, give rise to, create

ดวง[1]   disc, ball, sphere, globe; spot, round mark; heart; mind

   ดวงจันทร์ the moon

   ดวงใจ heart; sweetheart

   ดวงดาว stars

     ไปไม่ถึงดวงดาว to fail to /achieve one's aim/realize one's aspirations/

   ดวงตรา seal, stamp, seals and stamps

     ดวงตราไปรษณีย์ postage stamp

   ดวงตา eye

   ดวงไฟ light; lamplight glow

   ดวงยิหวา darling, my beloved

   ดวงวิญญาณ soul

   ดวงสมร dearest

   ดวงอาทิตย์ the sun

   เป็นดวงๆ spotted

ดวง[2], **ดวงชะตา**   horoscope, luck, fate

   ดวงดี to have /a good horoscope/good luck/

   ดวงตก ill-starred, ill-fated, in a bad period

   ไปตามดวง to leave to fate; fatalistic

   แล้วแต่ดวง it's up to luck

   หมอดูดวง astrologer, fortune-teller

ด้วง[1]   caterpillar; beetle

ด้วง[2]   animal snare made from a joint of bamboo

ด้วง[3]   two-stringed bamboo fiddle

ดวด   to swill, guzzle

ไม่ทำอะไร เอาแต่ดวดเหล้าทั้งวัน *He doesn't do a thing but swill liquor the whole day long.*

ด่วน urgent, pressing; hasty, hurried
ด่วนจี๋ extremely urgent
ด่วนทันที for immediate action
ด่วนไป to hurry off
ด่วนมา to hurry back
ด่วนมาก very urgent, very pressing
ขายด่วน urgent sale, for quick sale
โดยด่วน urgently, expeditiously, without delay, quickly, rapidly
เป็นการด่วน urgently
รถด่วน express (train)
　รถด่วนสายเหนือ Northern Express
อย่าด่วนคิด don't be hasty

ด้วน amputated, truncated, cut short
ขาด้วน amputated leg, with a leg missing; leg stump
ต้นไม้ยอดด้วน a tree with a dead top, truncated tree
หางด้วน stump-tailed, a cropped tail

ด้วย with, by, through; also, too; please, kindly
ด้วยความนับถือ respectfully; Very truly yours *(US)*, Yours faithfully *(Brit)*
ด้วยความยินดี with pleasure, gladly
ด้วยความเสียใจ with regret
ด้วยใจ with pleasure, happily; with love
ด้วยซ้ำ not even
อย่าว่าแต่รักเลย แม้แต่หน้าฉันยังไม่อยากมอง ด้วยซ้ำ *Love, forget it; I don't even want to look at him.*
ด้วยดี without /difficulty/trouble/fuss/; amicably; well
ด้วยตนเอง by oneself, alone, oneself
ด้วยมือ by hand
ด้วยว่า because, owing to
ด้วยวิธี by...means
เขาแก้ปัญหาด้วยวิธีอันชาญฉลาด *He solved*

the problem /in a clever way/in a clever manner/by clever means/cleverly/.
ด้วยเหตุนี้ for this reason, therefor, thus; that is why
ได้รับแล้วตอบให้ทราบด้วย please acknowledge receipt, kindly acknowledge receipt

ดวล to duel

ดอก[1] flower, blossom; floral design, /round/floral/-figured; interest; a qualifier for flowers, corn, arrows and firecrackers
ดอกจอก water-lettuce
ดอกจัน asterisk
ดอกดาวเรือง marigold
ดอกบัว lotus; water lily
ดอกเบี้ย interest
ดอกฝิ่น opium flower
ดอกมะลิ jasmine
ดอกไม้ flower, blossom
　ดอกไม้จีน a Chinese flower used in cooking
　ดอกไม้เพลิง fireworks
　ดอกไม้ไฟ fireworks
ดอกยาง tread
ดอกลำดวน a Thai confection
ดอกลำโพง megaphone
ดอกเล็บ white spots under the fingernails

ดอก[2] an emphatic word, at all
ฉันไม่ว่าอะไรดอก *It's all right (with me); I don't mind at all.*
ดอกกระมัง probably, must be
ดอกทอง whore

ดอง[1] to pickle, steep, soak (in)
ดองยา to steep (in)
ดองเรื่อง to keep (it, the matter etc) on ice
ผักดอง pickled vegetable, kimchi, vegetable pickle
หมักดอง fermented; pickled

ดอง[2] related by marriage, relation by marriage; wedding

กินดอง to feast at a marriage

เกี่ยวดอง related by marriage

ดอง[3] *as in* **ห่มดอง** way of draping a monk's robe to leave the right arm uncovered

ดอด by stealth, stealthily; clandestinely, secretly, in secret, to steal (into, up, upon)

ชายหนุ่มดอดไปหาลูกสาวกำนัน The young man was seeing the kamnan's daughter clandestinely. / The boy met the kamnan's daughter in secret.

ดอน high ground, elevation, mound, knoll

ที่ดอน upland, highland, elevated land

ดอนเมือง Don Muang

ด้อม to bob

ด้อมๆ มองๆ to take a look (at), sniff around

ดอย mountain, mount, hill

ชาวป่าชาวดอย hillfolk, hill dwellers, hill people

ด้อย inferior; sunken

ด้อยคุณค่า to mean nothing, inferior, insignificant

ด้อยพัฒนา underdeveloped

ด้อยลง to decrease, diminish, decline

ด้อยศักดิ์ศรี undignified

ปมด้อย inferiority complex

ดะ indiscriminately, without control

กินดะ to be an avid eater, voracious, eat up everything

ตีดะ to strike at random, beat /indiscriminately/all over/

ฟันดะ to lash out indiscriminately with a /sword/knife/

ดัก[1] trap, snare; to lie in wait for, trap; to catch (someone)

ดักคอ to forestall, impede, thwart

ดักโจมตี to ambush

ดักฟัง to eavesdrop (on), listen in (on), bug

    ดักฟังโทรศัพท์ to /bug/tap/ a telephone

กับดัก trap

คอยดัก to wait

ดัก[2] *as in* **ดักดาน** stuck (in)

ดักแด้ pupa

ดั่ง[1], **ดัง** like, similar, analogous, alike

ดังกล่าว the, the said, aforementioned

    ดังกล่าวข้างบน as mentioned above, above-mentioned

    ดังกล่าวแล้ว as mentioned before, as said before

ดังกะไว้ as planned

ดังคาด as expected, as anticipated, as planned, as imagined

ดังจะแกล้ง /as if/like/ trying to make trouble

ดังเจตนา as intended

ดังใจ as desired, as one wanted, to one's liking

    ดังใจนึก as wished

ดังเดิม unchanged, without any change, the same as always, as before; (the) original; aboriginal

ดังตั้งใจ as intended

ดังแต่ก่อน as before, as /it/one/ used to be

ดังที่คิด as anticipated, as expected

ดังนั้น so, therefore, thus

ดังนี้ in this way, like this; as follows, the following

ดังฤๅ how; why

ดังว่า to be like that, as said to be

ดังหนึ่ง as if, like, as it were

ดัง[2] loud, making a noise, noisy; heard; in the public eye, talked about, famous

เดี๋ยวนี้ดังใหญ่แล้วนะ He's the talk of the town. / He's talked about everywhere.

ดังก้อง resounding, roaring

ดังจนหนวกหู deafening

ดังเป็นพลุแตก to /be/become/ a superstar

ดังลั่น earsplitting

พูดดัง to speak loudly, boom

    พูดดังๆ หน่อย speak up, speak louder

อยากดัง to want to be noticed, want to make a noise

ดั้ง[1] shield for the arm, buckler; king post; a boat used in a procession

ดั้ง[2] bridge (of the nose), nose

ดั้งเดิม olden times, originally, from the beginning, initially

ดัชนี *see* **ดรรชนี** *หน้า 158*

ดัด to shape; to bend; to straighten; to do body exercise

ดัดจริต to be affected, not natural, artificial, mannered; to put on airs

ดัดตน to do body exercise

ดัดแปลง to modify, alter, adapt

ดัดผม to have (one's) hair set; to get a /permanent/permanent wave/

ดัดสันดาน to reform, correct, train

โรงเรียนดัดสันดาน reformatory, reform school, training school

ดัดเสียง to disguise one's voice

ดัน to push, shove; to be stubborn, obstinate; to insist on doing something

ดันทุรัง mulish, pigheaded, bullheaded, stubborn

ดึงดัน stubborn, headstrong, pigheaded

ดุดัน fierce-looking, angry-looking; furious

แรงดัน pressure

ดั้น to pierce, go through, push through

ดั้นเมฆ to make one's way through the clouds

ดับ to extinguish, put out, quench, go out; to die, die out, go out; to disappear; to stop, quell, put down, come to an end, put an end to

ดับกระหาย to quench one's thirst

ดับกลิ่น to deodorize

ยาดับกลิ่น deodorant

ดับขันธ์ to die

ดับจิต to die, pass away, succumb

ห้องดับจิต mortuary

ดับชีพ to expire, die

ดับตะเกียง to put out the lamp

ดับทุกข์ to end suffering, put an end to suffering

ดับเทียน to blow out the candle, put out the candle

ดับโทโส to allay one's anger

ดับเพลิง to /extinguish/put out/a fire

ดับไฟ to put out a fire; to turn /out/off/ the light

ดับวูบ to go out all of a sudden

ดับสูญ to vanish, be extinguished

ความดับ extinction, end

แตกดับ to perish, be destroyed

ดัมพ์ dump

รถดัมพ์ dump truck

ดา *as in* **ดาหน้า** to advance in a body

ด่า to criticize, find fault with someone; to scold, chide, berate, tell someone off, attack (someone), malign, call (someone) down (for doing something); to swear (at), use abusive language

ด่าฉอดๆ to let go a stream of abuse, vituperate

ด่าทอ to have an /argument/altercation/; to berate, rail (at)

ด่าประจาน to ridicule in public

คำด่า an insult, invective, term of abuse; swear word

ดุด่า to berate, abuse, upbraid, chew out (someone), hurl abuse (at)

ด่าง alkaline, a salt; faded; discolored

ด่างดำ mottled

ด่างทับทิม potassium permanganate solution

ด่างพร้อย stained, spotted; tarnished, blemished, tainted

น้ำด่าง brine, alkaline solution; mordant, soda ash solution

ด
ต
ถ
ท
ธ
น
บ
ป
ผ
ฝ
พ
ฟ
ภ
ม
ย
ร
ฤ
ฤๅ
ล
ว
ศ
ษ
ส
ห
ฬ
อ
ฮ

ก
ข
ค
ฆ
ง
จ
ฉ
ช
ซ
ฌ
ญ
ฎ
ฏ
ฐ
ฑ
ฒ
ณ
ด

ดาด[1] to spread (with), line (with), lay; not steep, sloping
ดาดฟ้า deck; roof, flat roof, roof-deck

ดาด[2], **ดาดๆ** ordinary, common, simple, commonplace
คำพูดดาดๆ, สำนวนดาดๆ commonplace expression, simple talk

ดาน hard; compact
ดินดาน hardpan

ด่าน area, customs station; check point
ด่านกักสัตว์ animal quarantine station
ด่านตรวจคนเข้าเมือง immigration, station, port of entry
ด่านตรวจโรค health inspection station
ด่านภาษี customs post
เมืองหน้าด่าน border town, frontier /town /city/settlement/

ด้าน[1] side, face, direction; in, as, for, with regard to, in respect of, on, -wise; aspect
ปัญหาด้านกฎหมาย legal aspects of the problem
ด้านกลับ other side; reverse side
ด้านการปกครอง /in/in regard to/regarding /as for/ edministration
เขาเก่งด้านการปกครอง แต่ด้านการทูตเขาไม่รู้เรื่องเลย In administration he's clever but as for diplomacy, he doesn't know beans. / Administration-wise he's okay, but in diplomacy, zero.
ด้านขวา right side, on the right, to the right
ด้านข้าง side, lateral
ด้านซ้าย left side, on the left, to the left
ด้านธุรการ administrative
ด้านนอก outside, exterior
ด้านใน inside, interior
ด้านหน้า front, in the front
ด้านยุทธศาสตร์ strategically, with regard to strategy
ด้านวิชาการ technical

ด้านหลัง rear, back side, at the back, in the back
ในด้าน in the field of

ด้าน[2] hard, calloused; matte, dull; dud
ด้านชา unfeeling, cold
ดื้อด้าน obstinate, intractable
มือด้าน calloused hand, one's hand becomes calloused
ลูกกระสุนด้าน dud cartridge
หน้าด้าน tough-skinned, insensitive; shameless, brazen

ดาบ sword, saber, scimitar, rapier, cutlass
ดาบปลายปืน bayonet
ดาบสั้น short sword
ดาบสองคม to work both ways, cut both ways, double-edged
มีดดาบ dagger

ดาบส hermit

ดาม to brace; to patch (ปะยาง, ปะผ้า)

ด้าม handle, holder, barrel of a pen
ด้ามปากกา pen holder, barrel of a pen
ด้ามปืน stock, grip, handle (of a gun)
ใหม่ถอดด้าม brand-new

ดาย[1] to hoe, weed, cultivate
ดายหญ้า to hoe (a field), weed (a garden)

ดาย[2] intently, through; unconcernedly, indifferently; quite, very, only, easily, comfortably; singly, alone
กินดาย to eat greedily
ง่ายดาย so easy, simple, to be a snap
ดูดาย indifferent, unconcerned, without taking any interest
เดียวดาย all alone
สะดวกดาย to be very easy, simple; very convenient

ด้าย thread; yarn
ด้ายกลุ่ม skein of yarn
ด้ายสายสิญจน์ ceremonial thread
ด้ายหลอด spool of thread, thread in spools

ด้ายไหม silk thread, silk yarn

กรอด้าย to wind a bobbin; to reel yarn

เข้าด้ายเข้าเข็ม at the crucial moment, at the critical point

เส้นด้าย thread, sewing cotton

หลอดด้าย spool (of thread, for thread)

ดารา star, celebrity

ดาราทีวี T.V. star

ดาราภาพยนตร์ movie star, film star, film celebrity

ดาราศาสตร์ astronomy

ดาล see **เดือดดาล** หน้า 171

ดาว star, heavenly body

ดาวแกะผู้ Aries (ราศีเมษ)

ดาวคนคู่ Gemini (ราศีเมถุน)

ดาวคันชั่ง Libra (ราศีตุลย์)

ดาวโคผู้ Taurus (ราศีพฤษภา)

ดาวตก meteor, shooting star

ดาวตลก comedian

ดาวใต้ Southern Star

ดาวไถ Orion; regular sponger

ดาวเทียม satellite

ดาวธนู Sagittarius (ราศีธนู)

ดาวนพเคราะห์ planet

ดาวนางสาว Virgo (ราศีกันย์)

ดาวบริวาร satellite

ดาวประกายพรึก morning star

ดาวประจำเมือง evening star

ดาวปลา Pisces (ราศีมีน)

ดาวปู Cancer (ราศีกรกฏ)

ดาวโป๊ sex queen

ดาวพระเกตุ Neptune

ดาวพระพฤหัสบดี Jupiter

ดาวพระพิภพ Earth

ดาวพระพุธ Mercury

ดาวพระยม Pluto

ดาวพระศุกร์ Venus

ดาวพระเสาร์ Saturn

ดาวแพะ Capricorn (ราศีมังกร)

ดาวมฤตยู Uranus

ดาวแมงป่อง Scorpio. (ราศีพฤศจิก)

ดาวยั่ว sex bomb

ดาวร้าย villain, arch criminal

ดาวรุ่ง morning star, Venus

ดาวเรือง marigold

ดาวฤกษ์ fixed star; luminous star; portentous star

ดาวสิงโต Leo (ราศีสิงห์)

ดาวหม้อน้ำ Aquarius (ราศีกุมภ์)

ดาวหาง comet

ดาวเหนือ North Star

กลุ่มดาว constellation

เกี่ยวกับดาว, ของดาว stellar

หอดูดาว observatory

ด่าว as in **ด่าวดิ้น** dead

ยิงเสียด่าวดิ้น to shoot someone dead

ด้าว boundary, border; territory, area, region, foreign

คนต่างด้าว alien

ใบต่างด้าว alien registration /book/certificate/

ดาษ, ดาษดา everywhere, abundant, plentiful, copious, common

ดาษดื่น see **ดื่นดาษ** หน้า 166

ดำ[1] black, dark

ดำขลับ glossy black, jet black

ดำเขียว black and blue

ดำด่าง see **ด่างดำ** หน้า 161

ดำแดง tan

ดำตับเป็ด dark and sexy

ดำปี๋ very dark, pitch black

ดำปิ๊ด coal black

ดำปื๊ด very black

ดำมะเมื่อม glossy black, velvet black

ดำมิดหมี pitch dark

ดำ[2] to go into, put into

ดำดิ่ง to plummet

ดำดิน to go underground

ด
ต
ถ
ท
ธ
น
บ
ป
ผ
ฝ
พ
ฟ
ภ
ม
ย
ร
ฤ
ฤๅ
ล
ว
ศ
ษ
ส
ห
ฬ
อ
ฮ

ดำนา to transplant rice

ดำน้ำ to dive, go underwater

ดำเนิน to go, walk, proceed, advance; to conduct, to carry on, continue

ดำเนินการ to operate, carry on

ดำเนินคดี to conduct legal proceedings, go to court

การดำเนินคดี proceedings, prosecution

ดำเนินงาน to carry out, execute, manage, administer

ดำเนินชีวิต to lead a life of; to make a living; to live, conduct one's life

เป็นทางดำเนิน way of living; to go about something

ดำรง to uphold, maintain, sustain; to lead

ดำรงชีวิตอย่างแร้นแค้น to lead a life of hardship

ดำรงตำแหน่ง to hold the office of, occupy the position of

ดำรงวงศ์ตระกูล to maintain one's family

ดำรัส to say, state *(royal word)*

พระราชดำรัส royal words, royal speech

ดำริ to consider; to plan; to think

โครงการพระราชดำริ royal project

ดำฤษณา lust, lascivious desire

ดิก perfectly, exactly

กลมดิก perfectly round; in a ball

ตามดิก to follow on the heels of

ดิกๆ wagging; flapping

สั่นหัวดิกๆ to shake one's head

ดิค, ดิคชันนารี dictionary

ดิ่ง plummet, plumb bob; precise, exact; straight

ดิ่งนรก to crash

ดิ่งพสุธา to plummet to earth; parachuting, to parachute jump

จมดิ่งสู่ทางหายนะ to plunge to disaster

ถามดิ่ง re-direct examination

ลูกดิ่ง plumb, plumb bob, plummet; sounding lead

สายดิ่ง sounding line; plumb line

เส้นดิ่ง vertical

ดิฉัน I, me

ดิถี day, date

ดิน earth, ground, soil

ดินกาบ slate

ดินจืด depleted soil

ดินดาน hardpan

ดินดำ, ดินปืน gunpowder

ดินแดง rouge

ดินแดน land, country, territory

ดินทราย sandy soil

ดินนวล kaolin

ดินน้ำมัน plasticene

ดินน้ำลมไฟ the four elements : earth, water, air, fire

ดินปนทราย sandy loam

ดินประสิว saltpeter, niter, potassium nitrate

ดินโป่ง salt lick

ดินเผา pottery

ดินพอกหางหมู up to one's neck (in), piled up in

ดินฟ้าอากาศ weather; climate

ดินร่วน friable soil, loose /earth/soil/

ดินระเบิด dynamite

ดินเลน mud

ดินสอ pencil

ดินสอดำ lead pencil

ดินสอพอง white clay body-powder in cake or pellet form; white clay filler

ดินสอสี colored pencil

ดินสำลี guncotton

ดินเหนียว clay

ก้อนดิน clod of earth

จมดิน buried

ใต้ดิน underground; clandestine, secret; surreptitious

ที่ดิน land, plot, lot, property, real estate

น้ำมันดิน tar, shale oil

พื้นดิน ground; earth

ฟ้าดิน heaven and earth

ดิ้น[1] to squirm, writhe, wriggle; to struggle; ambiguous

ดิ้นได้ slippery, hard to pin down; ambiguous

กฎหมายดิ้นได้ The law is hard to pin down.

ดิ้นไม่หลุด to be unable to wriggle out of something

ดิ้นรน to struggle (to, for), strive (for)

ดีดดิ้น to play hard to get

ให้ดิ้นตายชิ I'll be damned (if)

ดิ้น[2] metallic thread

ดิ้นเงิน silver thread

ดิ้นทอง gold thread

ผ้าปักดิ้น brocade, /gold/silver/ brocade

ดิบ raw, unripe; uncooked

ขายดิบขายดี to sell like hotcakes, sell well

คนดิบ a person not yet become a monk

ดงดิบ primary forest, jungle, rain forest

ด้ายดิบ unbleached cotton thread, raw cotton yarn

ป่าดิบ primary forest, virgin forest

ผ้าดิบ unbleached cloth

ผีดิบ uncremated body; Frankenstein's monster, zombie, the living dead

ฝ้ายดิบ raw cotton

สุกๆดิบๆ half-cooked; half-ripe; superficial, half-baked

ดิบดี very well

ดิรัจฉาน animal; animals that walk; Beast!

ดี[1] good, well, okay, alright; to be reconciled

ดีๆ as usual; well; perfectly good; quietly, still; real; nicely

ดีกว่า better (than); instead

กินข้าวก่อนดีกว่า It would be better to eat first.

ดีกัน to be reconciled, make up

ดีขึ้น to improve, get better

ดีจริงๆ excellent, perfect, great, wonderful, very good, real good, how good!, fine

ดีใจ glad, happy, pleased

ดีเด่น outstanding

ดีที่สุด ideal, best, prime

ดีแท้, ดีนัก, ดีมาก splendid, excellent, very well, very good, jolly good *(Brit)*

ดีร้าย maybe, perhaps, it could be that

ดีละ, ดีแล้ว good, not bad, all right, okay, that's fine; all right for you

ดีอกดีใจ delighted, elated, so happy

จะดี better not

ถามดีๆ to ask nicely

ปากดี bigmouthed; loudmouthed

ผู้ดี fine person, gentleman, lady; upperclass people; highclass; well-mannered

มือดี able, fine, skilled; a crook

ไม่ดี bad, not good; poor

ยากดีมีจน (whether) rich or poor

รู้ดี to well know, understand well; to be so smart

ลางดี good omen, favorable sign

วันดีคืนดี one fine day

สนุกดี to be fun

สบายดี well, fine, comfortable

อยู่ดีกินดี to live well, be well off

ดี[2] bile, gall

ดีเกลือ epsom salts

น้ำดี bile

ถุงน้ำดี gallbladder

โรคดีซ่าน jaundice, hepatitis

ดี้ femme *(sl)*, lipstick lesbian *(sl)*, passive lesbian

ดีด to flick, fillip; to spring; to pluck; to kick (สัตว์เตะทางขาหลัง)

ดีดกลับ to spring back

ดีดดิ้น to play hard to get

ดีดนิ้ว to fillip; to snap the fingers; to flick with a finger

ด
ต
ถ
ท
ธ
น
บ
ป
ผ
ฝ
พ
ฟ
ภ
ม
ย
ร
ฤ
ฤๅ
ล
ว
ศ
ษ
ส
ห
ฬ
อ
ฮ

ดีดฝ้าย to card cotton

ดีดพิณ to pluck a lute, play a lute

ดีดลูกคิด to calculate on an abacus; to flip the beads of an abacus

    ดีดลูกคิดรางแก้ว to make a rosy calculation

ดีดสีตีเป่า to play music (by an orchestra)

ดีดออก to flick (away, off)

ดีดัก a long time

หลายปีดีดัก for a long long time, for years and years, for ages, many many years ago, ages ago, in the dim past

ดีบุก tin

ดึก late at night

ดึกดำบรรพ์ ancient, primeval

ดึกดื่น very late at night, after midnight

ดึกสงัด in the dead of night

ดึง to pull, draw, tug; to haul in

ดึงดัน to be stubborn, headstrong, pigheaded

ดึงดื้อ obstinate; to be dogged (in)

ดึงดูด to attract, arouse interest

    ดึงดูดจิตใจ appealing

ดึงเรื่องไว้ to hold back (an application, petition, etc)

ดื่น abundant, plentiful, copious, abounding, common

ดื่นดาษ abundant, plentiful, copious, in profusion, plenty of, full of, common, ubiquitous

ดื่ม to drink

ดื่มจัด to drink too much, drink a lot

ดื่มด่ำ to be moved (by)

ดื่มน้ำผึ้งพระจันทร์ to go on a honeymoon

ดื่มหัวราน้ำ to be a drunkard

เครื่องดื่ม beverages, drinks

ดื้อ stubborn, recalcitrant, obdurate, obstinate, contrary, headstrong, willfull

ดื้อๆ without any reason, willfully

ดื้อด้าน obstinate, intractable, wayward

ดื้อดึง obstinate; to be dogged (in)

ดื้อแพ่ง intransigent, obstinate, obdurate, cantankerous, contumacious

ดื้อยา drug resistant

ดื้อรั้น obstinate

หัวดื้อ stubborn, headstrong

ดุ to scold, rebuke, bawl out; savage, fierce, ferocious, brutal; irascible

ดุดัน fierce-looking, angry-looking; furious

ดุด่า to berate, abuse, upbraid, chew out (someone), hurl abuse (at)

ดุเด็ดเผ็ดมัน heated

ดุเดือด violent

ดุร้าย ferocious, fierce; pugnacious

คนดุ /irascible/testy/crusty/ person

ดุก as in **ปลาดุก** catfish

ดุกดิก to fidget, squirm, fiddle, wiggle

ดุจ, ดุจดัง, ดุจว่า like, as, as if

ดุน to emboss; to protrude; to push; to shove away

ดุ้น stick, piece

ดุ้นฟืน piece of firewood, log

ทั้งดุ้น the whole thing, entirely, in toto

ดุม button; hub

ดุมเกวียน hub of a buffalo cart

ดุมล้อ hub

รังดุม buttonhole

ดุ่มๆ intently, preoccupied, concentrating

    เดินดุ่มๆ อยู่กลางทุ่ง to walk in the field with an air of concentration

ดุริยะ musical instruments

ดุริยางค์ orchestra, band

    ดุริยางควิทยา musicology

    วงดุริยางค์ band, orchestra

ดุล[1] scales, balance; beam; an ancient weight of gold

    ดุลการค้า balance of trade

ดุล[2] equal

ดุลพินิจ discretion, judgment

ดุลภาค equilibrium, state of balance

งบดุล balance sheet

ดุลย์ balance; equality; equal; equivalent

ดุลยภาพ equality; balance

เสียดุลย์ to be off-balance

ดุษฎี pleasure, delight, delectation, joy, happiness, glee, rejoicing

ดุษฎีบัณฑิต doctor, holder of a /doctor's degree/doctorate/

ประสาทศิลปศาสตรดุษฎีบัณฑิต to confer a liberal arts doctorate (on someone)

รัฐศาสตรดุษฎีบัณฑิต Doctor of Political Science, Ph.D. in Political Science

ดุษฎีมาลา a medal given for academic distinction

ดุษฎีสังเวย verses for lulling elephants

ดุษณี, ดุษณีภาพ silent acceptance, quiet acquiescence

โดยดุษณี meekly; calmly

ดุสิต fourth of the six heavens

ดุเหว่า blackbird

ดู to look, see, behold, observe, view, look at, watch; to appear, seem; to foretell, prophesy, forecast

ดูก่อน Look here!, Look out!

ดูกีฬา to watch a sports event

ดูแคลน *see* **ดูหมิ่น**

ดูงาน to /observe/study/ inspect/activities, make a study trip

ดูใจ to keep a death watch; to see how (someone) /feels/reacts/

ดูดวง to check one's horoscope

ดูดาย indifferent, unconcerned, without taking any interest

ดูดู๋ sound indicating resentment

ดูถูก to look down on, belittle, disparage, insult, denigrate

ดูถูกเหยียดหยาม to hold in contempt

ดูเถิด Take a look!

ดูท่า it looks like, to look like, appear to be

ดูทีวี to watch television, look at T.V.

ดูเบา to regard lightly, to take (something or someone) lightly

ดูไม่ออก not understand, be puzzled by, difficult to /fathom/judge/understand/, cannot tell

เขาเป็นคนอย่างไร ฉันดูไม่ออก I can't tell what sort of person he is.

ดูฤกษ์ยาม to find the auspicious time

ดูละคร to go to the theater

ดูลาดเลา to size up the situation, make observations

ดูเล่น to look at something for the fun of it, casually

เลี้ยงสัตว์ไว้ดูเล่น to keep an animal as a pastime

ดูแล to take care of, look after, supervise, be responsible (for)

ดูแลให้ดี to take good care of

ผู้ดูแล superintendant, supervisor, person responsible

ดูหนัง to go to the /movies/pictures/cinema/

ดูหนังสือ to study; to be reading

ดูหมอ to check one's horoscope

ดูหมิ่น to insult, hold (someone) in contempt, disdain, look down on

ดูหมิ่นถิ่นแคลน to despise, hold in contempt, scorn

การดูหมิ่น contempt

ดูเหมือน to seem, like, appear, look as if

ดูเหมือนฝนจะตก It looks like rain.

ดูเหมือนว่า It seems..., It looks as if..., to appear to

ดูให้ดี to take a good look

ดูออก to understand, see, be able to tell; to see through (someone or something)

ค่าดู admission

ด
ต
ถ
ท
ธ
น
บ
ป
ผ
ฝ
พ
ฟ
ภ
ม
ย
ร
ฤ
ฤๅ
ล
ว
ศ
ษ
ส
ห
ฬ
อ
ฮ

คิดดู think about (something), think (something) over, consider

จ้องดู to stare (at), peer (at), fix one's eyes on

ตรวจดู to check, inspect; /have/take/ a look (at)

น่าดู attractive, worth seeing

เฝ้าดู to watch, keep an eye on, keep watch (on, over)

พอดู pretty; quite, rather, fairly

เพ่งดู to gaze; to stare (at), contemplate

มองดู to look (at)

ลองดู to try, give (something) a try, try out

แลดู to have a look (at), take a look

ส่องดู to peer (at), observe, watch

หมอดู fortune-teller

แอบดู to peep (at), peek (at), spy (on)

ดูด to suck; to draw in, attract; to absorb, soak up

ดูดซึม to soak (into, up), be absorbed (by, into); absorbent

ดูดดื่ม to be affected, be touched, be impressed

ดูดบุหรี่ to smoke

ไฟดูด to get an electric shock

หลอดดูด (drinking) straw

เด่ erect, upright, prominent

เด็ก child; infant; boy, girl; son; daughter; youngster; kid, novice, newcomer

เด็ก ๆ too easy, baby stuff (sl); playmate

เด็กกำพร้า orphan

เด็กเกเร see เด็กเกเร หน้า 36

เด็กเกิดใหม่ newborn baby

เด็กข้างถนน street urchin

เด็กคนใช้ servant /girl/boy/, houseboy

เด็กจรจัด waif

เด็กชาย Master, boy

เด็กดี good /boy/girl/

เด็กแดงๆ newborn baby

เด็กตาดำๆ a mere child, simple child

เด็กทารก infant

เด็กน้อย youngster

เด็กนักเรียน schoolboy (ชาย), schoolgirl (หญิง)

เด็กฝาก (somebody's) /boy/girl/, protegé
เด็กฝากของอธิบดี the director-general's /boy/girl/

เด็กฝาแฝด twins

เด็กเลี้ยงแกะ the boy who cries "wolf"; prevaricator, fibber

เด็กวัด temple boy

เด็กเส้น someone who owes his position to /pull/connections/, someone who got in by pulling strings, a fair-haired boy, someone's protegé

เด็กหญิง (คำนำหน้าเด็กผู้หญิงอายุไม่เกิน 14 ปี ไม่มีใช้ในภาษาอังกฤษ); girl

เด็กหนวด oldster

เด็กหนุ่ม youth, lad, young man

เด็กเหลือขอ young /scapegrace/reprobate/, problem child, bad kid

เด็กอกตัญญู ungrateful child, a young ingrate

เด็กอมมือ infantile

เด็กอ่อน infant, baby; small child

ทำเป็นเด็กไปได้ juvenile, puerile, childish

พวกเด็กๆ the children, kids

เดคากรัม decagram

เดคาเมตร decameter

เดคาลิตร decaliter

เด้ง to bounce, spring up

เช็คเด้ง a bad check, a check that bounces

เดินเด้งหน้าเด้งหลัง to stagger along

เดช, เดชะ power, might, authority

เดชะบุญ Thank God!, Thank goodness!, fortunately
หญิงสาวคนนั้นถูกพวกวัยรุ่นฉุดไปข่มขืน เดชะ บุญตำรวจช่วยไว้ทัน A gang of teenagers

were about to rape the girl but /thank goodness/fortunately/ the police turned up in time.

เดโช power, might

เดซิกรัม decigram

เดซิเมตร decimeter

เดซิลิตร deciliter

เด็ด[1] pinch off, pick, pluck

เด็ดชีวิต to take someone's life

เด็ดดอกไม้ to pick a flower

เด็ด[2] decisive, effective; resolute; bold; cool; deadly

เด็ดขาด absolutely, strictly, definitely, positively

ไม่ไปเด็ดขาด I will never go. / I am positive about not going. / I will definitely not go.

ห้ามเด็ดขาด to be strictly prohibited (to), absolutely forbidden (to)

เด็ดดวง smashing, fantastic, really great

เด็ดเดี่ยว resolute, determined, single-minded

ใจเด็ด resolute, determined; fearless

ไม้เด็ด stratagem, effective trick; to have clout

เดน leavings, rejects

เดนคน social outcast, pariah

เดนตาย stalwart, valiant,

กากเดน remains, trash

เด่น significant; superior, outstanding; distinct, clear; conspicuous, prominent, open, unconcealed

เด่นชัด distinct, very clear, vivid

ปมเด่น superiority complex

เดนมาร์ก Denmark

ชนชาติเดนมาร์ก Danish

ชาวเดนมาร์ก Dane

เดรฉาน, เดรัจฉาน animal

ไอ้เดรัจฉาน You beast!

เด๋อด๋า simple, artless; scatterbrained, flighty

เดา to guess, surmise, speculate

เดาสวด to guess; guessing, guesswork

เดาเอา to guess

เด้า *see* **กระเด้า** *หน้า 7*

เดาะ[1] to keep tossing and catching; to juggle

เดาะลูกบอล to bounce a ball; to keep tossing a ball

เดาะ[2] cracked

ซี่โครงเดาะ cracked rib

เดาะ[3] to dress up

เดาะชุดสากล to dress up in a coat and tie

เดิน to walk; to move, proceed, go; to march; to operate, run; to take steps to do something, proceed with something; to apply (gold, etc); to have /diarrhoea/loose bowels/

เดินแกว่งไปแกว่งมา to be at loose ends

เดินข้าม to walk across

เดินควง to walk /arm in arm/hand in hand/; to be seen together; to go together (with)

เดินเครื่อง to /run/operate/ (an /engine/ machine/)

เดินจ้ำ to hurry along, press /ahead/on/

เดินตลาด to go out on the market, go out to sell

พนักงานเดินตลาด (outside) salesman, traveling salesman

เดินต๊อกๆ to plug along

เดินตัดสนาม to walk across a field

เดินเตร่ to walk around aimlessly, wander about

เดินแต้ม to make a shrewd move, act shrewdly; to move

เดินโต๊ะ to serve at table

พนักงานเดินโต๊ะ waiter, waitress (หญิง)

เดินแถว to walk in line, march

เดินทอง to /block/stamp/ with gold

ปกแข็งเดินทอง gold-blocked hard cover

เดินทะเล seagoing; to make a sea voyage,

ด ต ถ ท ธ น บ ป ผ ฝ พ ฟ ภ ม ย ร ฤ ฦ ล ว ศ ษ ส ห ฬ อ ฮ

go to sea

เดินทัพ to move troops

เดินทาง to travel, voyage, make a journey, take a trip

    กระเป๋าเดินทาง baggage, luggage, suitcase

    ผู้เดินทาง traveller, voyager

เดินเท้า to go on foot

    เดินเท้าเปล่า to go barefoot

เดินไปเดินมา to walk to and fro; to pace back and forth

เดินพล่าน to dash around

เดินย้อน to retrace one's steps

เดินย่ำเท้า to march in place, mark time

เดินรถ transport; to operate a commercial vehicle

    บริษัทเดินรถประจำทาง bus company

    ระเบียบการเดินรถ /bus/truck/ operation regulations

เดินรี่ to rush (at, off, away, into)

เดินเรียงแถว to walk in line, walk in single file

เดินเรือ to navigate, to operate a /vessel/ ship/boat/

    บริษัทเดินเรือ shipping company, shipping line, maritime navigation company

เดินเรื่อง to follow up, handle (a matter), pursue (a matter); to carry the /story/plot/ forward

ในรามเกียรติ์พระลักษณ์กับหนุมาณเป็นตัวเดินเรื่อง In the Ramayana, the plot is carried forward by Lakshaman and Hanuman.

เดินลัด to take a shortcut

เดินเล่น to take a walk, stroll

เดินเลาะ to walk close /to/by/along/

เดินสวนกัน to pass in opposite directions

เดินสวนสนาม to march in review

เดินสะพัด current (account)

เดินสายไฟ to install electric wiring; to string an electric line

เดินหน้า to go forward, advance

เดินเหิน to be up and around; to get around; to walk

เดินอากาศ air navigation

    บริษัทเดินอากาศ airline

    บริษัทเดินอากาศไทย Thai Airways Co., Ltd.

เดิม originally, formerly previously, before, former, old, original, same as before

เดิมชื่อ formerly

เดิมที originally

เดิมพัน stake, stakes, ante

    เดิมพันด้วยชีวิต to stake one's life on something

    เป็นเดิมพัน at stake

ดังเดิม, เหมือนเดิม unchanged, without any change, as before; (the) original; aboriginal; the same as always

ตามเดิม as always

แต่เดิม at first, originally, /in/from/ the beginning, from before

บ้านเดิม hometown, old home

เดี้ยง out of action, lame; to be a lame duck

สิงห์เดี้ยง a lame duck

เดียงสา to know what is suitable and what is not; to know the situation thoroughly

    ไม่เดียงสา, ไร้เดียงสา innocent, childlike, naive; lacking discretion

เดียดฉันท์ to be dissatisfied with, dislike

เดียรดาษ all over, in profusion, plentiful

เดียรถีย์ cleric of another religion; heretic

เดียรัจฉาน *see* **เดรฉาน** *หน้า 169*

เดียว single, one; only

เดียวกัน the same

    ขณะเดียวกัน simultaneously, at the same time

คนเดียว alone, by oneself; one person, single

person

คนเดียวกัน the same person

คราวเดียวกัน of the same age; at the same time

คอเดียวกัน like-minded

ใจเดียว constant, faithful, steadfast

ใจเดียวกัน of the same mind

เที่ยวเดียว one way, single trip

บ้านเดียวกัน in the same house; of the same place

ปีเดียวกัน in the same year

โรงเรียนเดียวกัน /of/in/from/ the same school

วันเดียวกัน on the same day

อย่างเดียวกัน the same kind (of), of the same /kind/sort/

เดี่ยว single, solitary, lone; alone; solo

เดี่ยวขลุ่ย a flute solo

เดี่ยวโดด, โดดเดี่ยว all alone, solitary, isolated

เทนนิสประเภทเดี่ยว tennis singles

บินเดี่ยว to be on one's own; to go alone

มาเดี่ยว to come alone

เล่นเดี่ยว to play solo

เดี๋ยว instant, moment

เดี๋ยวก่อน just a minute, wait a minute

เดี๋ยวเดียว in a moment, for a moment, just a second

เดี๋ยวเถอะ! Just you wait!

เดี๋ยวนะ wait a moment

เดี๋ยวนี้ now, at present; immediately, at once, right now, right away

เดี๋ยวไป (we'll) go in a minute

เดียะ briskly

ตามเดียะ to tag (along, after), tail, follow on the heels of

ไต่เดียะๆ to climb briskly

เดือด to boil

เขาพูดเช่นนั้น ทำให้ฉันเดือดมาก What he said made me boil. / I got boiling mad at what he said.

เดือดดาล to be boiling (with anger etc), infuriated, furious, hopping mad

เดือดเนื้อร้อนใจ extremely upset, agitated

เดือดพล่าน boiling vigorously; furious, enraged, boiling mad

เดือดร้อน in trouble, in a fix; distressed, vexed, disturbed, worried, agitated; complaining

เดือน moon; month

เดือนก่อน last month, previous month

เดือนก่อนๆ some months ago

เดือนขึ้น the rising of the moon; moonrise; waxing moon

เดือนดับ the setting of the moon

เดือนที่แล้ว last month, ultimo, ult.

เดือนนี้ this month, instant, inst.

เดือนเพ็ญ full moon

เดือนมืด moonless night

เดือนยี่ second lunar month

เดือนหงาย moonlit night, to have moonlight

เดือนหน้า next month, proximo, prox.

เดือนอ้าย first lunar month

รายเดือน monthly, per month

รายสองเดือน bimonthly

แรมเดือน for months, for months and months, for months on end

แสงเดือน moonlight

เดือย cockspur; spindle, pin, rod, shaft

แด heart, mind

แดดาล to affect, move

แดดิ้น to be tormented

แดยัน to almost die

ดวงแด the heart; sweetheart, beloved

แด่ to

แด่นางผู้เป็นที่รัก to my beloved

แดก[1] to gorge oneself; to eat greedily; to eat

แดกห่า to stuff oneself

แดก[2] to provoke, taunt

แดกดัน to be sarcastic, use sarcasm; to be

cutting, provocative, taunting

แด็กๆ *as in* **ชักแด็กๆ** to /writhe/squirm/jerk/ convulsively

แดง red

แดงก่ำ bloodshot eyes (ตา); crimson, burgundy

แดงแจ๋ scarlet

แดงแจ๊ด bright red

แดงฉาน pool of red, bathed in red

แดงแช็ด brilliant red, flashy red

แดงแปร๊ด shiny red

แดงเรื่อ rose

แดงโร่ vivid red

เรื่องแดง (of a secret) to leak out, come to light

ลูกเล็กเด็กแดง babies, infants

สีแดง red

หน้าแดง flushed, red-faced, to blush

แดด sunlight, sun, sunshine

แดดกล้า strong sunlight

แดดจ้า bright sunlight, glaring (sun)

แดดแจ๋ blazing sunlight, bright sunshine

แดดเปรี้ยง (in the) hot sun, strong sunlight

แดดร่มลมตก at sundown

แดดออก the sun comes out

กลางแดด (out) in the sun

แก่แดด *see* **แก่แดด** หน้า 40

นาฬิกาแดด sundial

บังแดด to /shade/shield/block/from the sun

ผึ่งแดด to sun, put (something) out in the sun

สุกแดด sun-ripened

แสงแดด sun, sunlight, sunshine, sun's rays

อาบแดด to sunbathe, take a sunbath

แดน territory; boundary; frontier; province, region, area; compound, sector, section

แดนห้า Compound Five

เขตแดน border, frontier

ชายแดน border, frontier

ดินแดน land, country, territory

พรมแดน frontier, boundary

แด่ว, แด่วๆ to contort, writhe, jerk

แดะแด๋ to be affected, affect manners, put on airs

โด่ erect; prominent

โด่เด่ sticking up

โดกเดก unpolished, unrefined; swaying, unsteady

โด่ง to rise high, soar

โด่งดัง famous, renowned, well-known, noted

จมูกโด่ง pointed nose

โดด[1], **กระโดด** to jump, leap, spring

โดดน้ำตาย to drown oneself

โดดร่ม to parachute; to play hooky

โดด[2] alone, single; singly

โดดเดี่ยว all alone, isolated, solitary

ลูกโดด single shot

โดน to strike, hit, touch, bump against, collide with; to get, be affected, caught; to be punished, get it in the neck; to be hit *เตะบอลไปโดนกำแพง The ball was kicked against the wall.*

โดนกักบริเวณ to get confined to quarters

โดนจับ to get arrested

โดนใจ touching

โดนดี to get what one is asking for, get it

โดนตี to get a /spanking/whipping/beating/

โดนใบสั่ง to get a ticket, be slapped with a /ticket/summons/

โดนมือ to hit one's hand

โดนออกจากงาน to get /sacked/fired/

โดม dome, cupola

โดย[1] to follow; to attend, accompany; by, with

โดยสาร to ride (with, by), go (by); to take part in, join in

ผู้โดยสาร passenger

โดยเสด็จ to attend a royalty (the king, queen, prince etc)

โดยเสด็จพระราชกุศล to contribute to a

royal charity

โดย² by, with

โดยกำเนิด by birth; innate, inborn

โดยคำนึงถึง having regard to

โดยง่าย easily, readily, without difficulty, smoothly

โดยเฉพาะ particularly, especially, in particular, specifically

โดยชอบ lawful, legal, rightful

    โดยชอบธรรม honestly, rightfully

โดยด่วน see **โดยด่วน** หน้า 159

โดยดี amicably, without /difficulty/trouble/ argument/, willingly

โดยตนเอง by oneself

โดยตรง directly

โดยตลอด the whole time, from the beginning, throughout, all along, consistently

    โดยตลอดรอดฝั่ง from beginning to end, in every way

โดยตำแหน่ง ex officio, by virtue of one's office (as)

โดยทั่วไป generally, in general

โดยทางบก by land

โดยทางน้ำ by water

โดยทางรถไฟ by rail

โดยทางอากาศ by air

โดยทุจริต wrongfully, dishonestly

โดยบังเอิญ to happen, accidentally, by accident, by chance, fortuitously

เมื่อวานนี้ฉันพบเพื่อนเก่าโดยบังเอิญที่สยาม สแควร์ Yesterday I happened to meet my old friend in Siam Square.

โดยปราศจากเงื่อนไข unconditionally

โดยปริยาย indirectly, by implication, in a sense

โดยเปิดเผย openly, publicly

โดยพยัญชนะ literally, word for word

โดยพลการ arbitrarily, on one's own, without asking, officiously; without /authorization/ authority/

โดยพลัน prompt, promptly

เตรียมพร้อมและปฏิบัติการโดยพลัน Be prepared and /take prompt action/act promptly/.

โดยมาก mostly, generally, for the most part, a majority

โดยไม่คำนึงถึง regardless of, without regard to; not to speak of

โดยไม่คิดมูลค่า free of charge, gratis

โดยไม่ปริปาก without complaining

โดยไม่ยาก easily, without difficulty, smoothly

โดยไม่รู้ตัว unaware, not to realize something, without one's knowledge

โดยรอบ around, in circumference

โดยเรียบร้อย smoothly, well, without any problem

โดยลำดับ respectively, in order

โดยลำพัง alone, by /oneself/itself/

โดยวิธีทางการทูต through the diplomatic channel

โดยสวัสดิภาพ safe and sound, safely, good *เช่น I hope you have a good trip.*

โดยสิ้นเชิง entirely, utterly, completely; absolutely

โดยหน้าที่ as part of one's job, to be one's duty

โดยเหตุที่ due to, because of

โดยอรรถ in effect, in substance; to mean

โดยอาศัย by means of, relying on, using, through

ใด what, which; any

ใดๆ everything; whatever

คนใด anyone

คำใดคำหนึ่ง any word, either word, any one of several words

เท่าใด how much, how many, to what

ก
ข
ค
ฆ
ง
จ
ฉ
ช
ซ
ฌ
ญ
ฎ
ฏ
ฐ
ฑ
ฒ
ณ
ด

extent; whatever

ผู้ใด anyone (who), whosoever, whoever

เพียงใด how much, how

เหตุใด why, for what reason, because of what

อย่างหนึ่งอย่างใด one, either one, any one; something

ได้ to obtain, get, have, make; to win; to attain, reach; to achieve; may be, can, to be able; an auxilliary verb indicating past tense

ได้กลิ่น to smell something

ได้กัน to become husband and wife; to live together

ได้การ effective, to work, it works

ได้กำไร to profit, make a profit, make money; to benefit (from), get something out of, profitable

ได้แก่ that is, namely, is, are

ได้ข่าว It has been reported that..., to hear (that), get wind of, get news (of), heard (that)

ได้ความ to make sense; to be successful, get results

    ได้ความว่า to understand (that), gather, it appears

ได้คิด to come to one's senses, realize

ได้คืน to get back

ได้งานทำ to get a job, find work

ได้เงิน to get (money), make money

    เขาได้เงินค่าขนมวันละ 10 บาท He gets 10 baht a day for snacks.

    ได้เงินเป็นพัน He made thousands.

    เขาได้เงินเท่าไร How much did he make?

ได้ใจ to be overconfident

ได้ช่อง to get a chance to, get an /opening/ opportunity/

ได้ชื่อว่า to be regarded as, be known as, gain a reputation /for being/as/

ได้ซิ certainly, no problem, sure

ได้ดิบได้ดี to be in clover, have done well for oneself, have it made

    ไม่ได้ดิบได้ดีอะไรเลย not get anything out of (something)

ได้ดี to make good, do well

ได้ทราบ to learn, understand

ได้ที to get the upper hand

ได้ที่ at the right point, when ready, at the right moment, to get (something) right

ได้เปรียบ to be at an advantage, have an advantage, outmatch

ได้ผล to work, be effective, get results, fruitful

ได้มาโดยชอบ to get /honestly/fairly/in good faith/

ได้มาโดยมิชอบ to get /dishonestly/unfairly /in bad faith/

ได้ยิน to hear

ได้รับ received

    ได้รับการศึกษา to be educated

    ได้รับความเห็นชอบ to meet with approval, get approval, approved

    ได้รับแต่งตั้ง (He) was appointed

    ได้รับทราบว่า (I) have learned that, (I) understand that

    ได้รับบาดเจ็บ (He) was injured

    ได้รับรางวัล to be rewarded, get a prize

ได้ฤกษ์ at the auspicious time

ได้เวลา to be time to (do something)

ได้สติ to become conscious of wrongdoing, come to one's senses; to regain consciousness

ได้ส่วน in the right proportion; to fit, be right

ได้เสีย to have been intimate, have sexual relations

ตีได้ to vanquish, overcome

ไปได้ (You) can go now., Let's /go/leave/.

ผลพลอยได้ by-product, incidental benefit

เผื่อจะได้ in order to, so that

ไม่ได้ no, to be unable to, cannot

   ไม่ได้ความ no good, not much good, lousy; nonsense, stupid

   ไม่ได้ไม่เสีย to come out even

รายได้ income, revenue; proceeds

ไว้ใจได้ trustworthy, reliable, dependable

สอบได้ to pass (an exam)

หาได้ to find

หาไม่ได้ to be unable to find

เห็นแก่ได้ to think only of profit, grasping, avaricious, greedy

อยากได้ to want something

อาจจะได้ (you) might be able to, to be possible

ก
ข
ค
ฆ
ง
จ
ฉ
ช
ซ
ฌ
ญ
ฎ
ฏ
ฐ
ฑ
ฒ
ณ
ด
ต

ตก to fall, drop, abate, diminish, decline, decrease, be not so good as before; to sow; to sag; to fish; to fade, run; to be about; to be missing, omitted, left out; to be overlooked; to come to; to meet, arrive

ตกกระ freckles, freckled

ตกกระไดพลอยโจน to be compromised, get embroiled, be an innocent victim

ตกกระป๋อง to be out of favor, have a downfall, become a has-been, suffer a misfortune

เหตุการณ์วันที่ 14 ตุลาคมทำให้นายกรัฐมนตรีตกกระป๋อง The 14th October uprising caused the downfall of the prime minister.

ตกกระแส to be out of vogue, do what is unfashionable, be out of step

ตกกล้า to sow rice for seedlings

ตกกลางคืน at nightfall

ตกเก้าอี้ to lose one's position, be put out of office

ตกขอบ ultra, egregious

ตกขาว to have leukorrhea

ตกข่าว to miss a news item

ตกข้าว, ตกเขียว to advance money against a growing crop, take a future contract on a rice crop; to sell a child (in one's care) for future delivery into prostitution, marriage or labor; to pay now for future delivery on a promise

ตกไข่ to lay an egg

ตกคลัก fish concentrated in a drying pond; (a crowd of people) jammed together

ตกค้าง to be left over, remain; to be overlooked; to be left behind

ตกงาน to be out of /work/a job/, lose one's job

ตกใจ to be startled, frightened, alarmed

ตกดิน to set

ตกตะกอน to settle, to have sediment

ตกตะลึง to be amazed, surprised; stupefied, taken aback, electrified

ตกต่ำ to take a fall, suffer a decline; to diminish; to be reduced (to)

ฐานะเขาตกต่ำลงมาก His standing was sharply reduced.

เศรษฐกิจเดี๋ยวนี้กำลังตกต่ำ The economy is now /in a state of depression/depressed/in recession/.

ตกแต่ง to decorate, adorn, embellish, beautify

ตกถังข้าวสาร to hit the jackpot, luck out, be in clover

ตกทอด inherited, handed down; to devolve (on), passed on (to)

ตกที่นั่งลำบาก to be caught in a difficult position

ตกทุกข์ได้ยาก to fall on hard times, be in difficulty

ตกนรก to go to hell, be in hell

    ตกนรกทั้งเป็น to suffer hellishly, experience hell on earth

ตกใน internally

    น้ำตาตกใน to grieve, be tormented, cry silently to oneself

    เลือดตกใน to bleed internally, have /internal bleeding/an internal hemorrhage/

ตกเบ็ด to fish, go fishing; to lure, entice; female masturbation

ตกประหม่า abashed, stunned, flabbergasted

ตกปลา to fish, catch fish, angle

ตกปากตกคำ to agree to do something, promise, undertake, give one's word

ตกเป็นของ to devolve on; to become the property of, come to belong to

ตกเป็นจำเลย to become a defendant

ตกผลึก crystallized, to crystallize

ตกพุ่มม่าย to be a widow, widowed

ตกฟาก to be born

ตกมัน to be in /must/musth/, in rut

ตกมืด at nightfall

ตกยาก to fall on hard times; to be impoverished; to suffer misfortune, in adversity

ตกรถ to miss a /train/bus/

    ตกรถไฟ to miss the train

ตกร่อง to get stuck, keep repeating, be a broken record

ตกรอบ to be eliminated, lose (the semifinals, etc), fail to make the grade, fail to qualify, be out of the running

ตกราง to be derailed

ตกรางวัล to give a /prize/reward/(to)

ตก (ราว) to come to (about)

ราคาของตกราว 500 บาท The price comes to about 500 baht.

ตกรุ่น dated

ตกลง to agree, come to terms; okay, agreed; so, after all; in conclusion

ตกลงจะไปไหม So, are you coming along?

ตกลงไปด้วย Okay, I'm coming.

ตกลงได้ลงน้ำหรือเปล่า Did you go into the water after all?

ตกลงใจ to make up one's mind (to), decide

ตกลูก to give birth to, foal (ม้า), calve (วัว ควาย ช้าง), drop a litter (สัตว์ที่ออกลูก ครั้งละหลายๆ ตัว)

ตกเลือด to have excessive menstruation; to have a miscarriage

ตกว่า in short, that is to say

ตกสะเก็ด scab; to form a scab

ตกหนัก to get it in the neck; to pile up on someone, shoulder (the burden, responsibility, etc)

ตกหลุมพราง to fall into a trap, be duped, be taken in, have been had, be tricked into doing something; be made a fool of

ตกหลุมรัก to fall in love

ตกอับ to be down in one's luck, fall on hard times; to be out of favor

แก้ตก to find a solution

ของที่สั่งตกมาแล้ว The things (you) ordered have just arrived.

คอตก crestfallen, dejected, downcast, disappointed

ทำตก to drop something, knock something down

ปลงตก *see* **ปลงตก** *หน้า 299*

พลัดตก to fall down (from)

มือตก to lose one's touch, go downhill

ยิงตก to shoot (something) down, hit

เลือดตกยางออก with great hardship, exceeding difficulty

สีตก to run; to fade (of colors, dyes, paint)

เสียงตก to decline in popularity; to lose one's voice

ตง   joist; a kind of thick bamboo

ต่ง   to take a rake-off, discount winnings

ตงฉิน upright, righteous, of high integrity, straight as an arrow

ตงิด, ตงิดๆ slightly, a little

    ฉันชักโมโหตงิดๆ แล้วนะ You're getting my dander up a little, you know that?

ตด   fart (ไม่สุภาพ); to fart, pass wind

ตถาคต the Accomplished One, the Thus Gone, the Truth-Getter, an epithet of the Lord Buddha

ตน   oneself, self; body; man, person; numerical designation for demons

ตนเอง oneself, self

ครองตน to lead the life of a (monk, farmer, good citizen etc); to exercise self-control

ปกครองตน to look after oneself

ลืมตัวลืมตน to forget oneself, lose one's self-control

วางตน to be, conduct oneself, comport oneself

ต
ถ
ท
ธ
น
บ
ป
ผ
ฝ
พ
ฟ
ภ
ม
ย
ร
ฤ
ฤๅ
ล
ว
ศ
ษ
ส
ห
ฬ
อ
ฮ

ก
ข
ค
ฆ
ง
จ
ฉ
ช
ซ
ฌ
ญ
ฎ
ฏ
ฐ
ฑ
ฒ
ณ
ด
ต

ต้น[1] beginning, original, first, primary, initial; source; principal; numerical designation for trees

ต้นกำเนิด progenitor, origin

ต้นขั้ว stub, counterfoil

ต้นคอ nape of the neck

ต้นคิด inventor, author, one who first got the idea to do something, originator

ต้นเค้า root, source; prototype, precursor

ต้นฉบับ manuscript, copy; original

ต้นตระกูล forefathers

ต้นตอ root, origin, originator

ต้นตำรับ originator, initiator

ต้นทุน capital, investment; cost

ต้นน้ำ water source

ต้นเพลิง, ต้นไฟ source of a fire

ต้นมือ in the beginning, at first, initially, at the outset

ต้นเรื่อง original (file, application, submission etc), the /cause/start/ of something
ใครเป็นต้นเรื่อง Who started it?

ต้นสังกัด one's affiliation, one's /organization/service unit/

ต้นเสียง precentor, cantor, lead voice

ต้นเหตุ cause, root; culprit

ต้น[2] stem; trunk; plant, tree

ต้นกล้า rice seedling

ต้นข้าว rice plant

ต้นไม้ tree, plant

ต้นไม้ยืนต้น a perennial

ต้นไม้ล้มลุก an annual

ลำต้น trunk; stem, stalk

ลืมต้น aged fruit, ripened off the tree

ต้น[3] a person in a position of trust

ต้นกล first engineer

ต้นเครื่อง chief cook in the royal kitchen

ต้นเรือ first mate

ต้นหน second mate, deck officer

ต้นห้อง personal caretaker

ตบ to slap, swat; to pat; to extort

ตบตา to deceive, trick, beguile, mislead, delude

ตบตูด to round off with

ตบแต่ง to beautify; improve the appearance (of); to marry off one's daughter

ศัลยกรรมตบแต่ง plastic surgery, cosmetic surgery

ตบทรัพย์ to extort /money/property/ (from someone)

ตบท้าย to wind up (with), end

ตบเท้า to march (into, out of); to stomp (out); to goose-step

ตบแผะ, ตบแผละ pat-a-cake

ตบมือ to applaud, clap (one's hands)

ตบมือข้างเดียวไม่ดัง It takes two to make a fight.

ตบหัวลูบหลัง to offend and then mollify

ตม mud, mire

เป็นตม muddy

ต้ม to boil; to take (someone) in, take (someone) for a ride, swindle; to be taken in, swindled, cheated (out of some- thing)

ต้มกลั่น to distil

ต้มข่า (chicken, etc) coconut soup flavored with gingery galingale

ต้มเค็ม /meat/fish/ soup with salt and sugar

ต้มโคล้ง salted fish soup with tamarind and onions

ต้มเปรต spicy eel soup

ต้มยำ /fish/meat/ soup flavored with lemongrass and kaffir lime

ต้มยำกะทิ /fish/meat/ soup made with coconut cream and flavored with lemongrass and kaffir lime

ต้มส้ม fish soup with ginger

ต้มหมู to cheat (/at cards/in gambling/)

ถูกต้ม to be duped, swindled (out of something), taken in (by)

ถูกต้มสุก to be stripped clean, completely deceived (by)

ตรง straight; accurate, impartial; upright (person, seatback, etc); the same; at, in, particularly at, for

ฉันรักคุณตรงที่นิสัย I like you for your character.

ตรงกลาง in the /middle/center/

ตรงกัน identical, the same, corresponding

  ตรงกันข้าม opposite; to the contrary, conversely

ตรงกับ to correspond to, be the same as

ตรงเดียะ perfectly straight

ตรงต่อเวลา on time, punctual; accurate

ตรงเป้า to the point, to hit the nail on the head

ตรงไปตรงมา frank, straightforward, forthright

ตรงรี่ straight ahead

ตรงเวลา on time, punctual; accurate

ตรงหน้า in front (of)

ซื่อตรง upright, true, honest, scrupulous, of integrity

ตามตรง frankly, in reality

ทางตรง direct route; straight road

ที่ตรงนี้ here

บอกตรงๆ to tell the truth, frankly speaking, to speak frankly

เวลาห้าโมงตรง 5 o'clock sharp, exactly 5 o'clock, 5 o'clock to the dot

ตรม to grieve, sorrow

ตรมใจ, ตรอมตรม anguish, grief, grieving, broken-hearted, sorrowful, sorrowing

ตรรก logic, reasoning, logical reasoning, thought, reflection

ตรรกวิทยา, ตรรกศาสตร์ logic

ด้าน (ทาง) ตรรกะ logical

ตรวจ to inspect, examine, check; to investigate

ตรวจการณ์ to patrol

ตรวจข้อสอบ to mark examination papers

ตรวจค้น to search

ตรวจดู to check, inspect; /have/take/ a look (at)

ตรวจต้นฉบับ to copyread

ตรวจตรา to inspect; check carefully, to patrol

ตรวจทาน to verify

ตรวจปรู๊ฟ to proofread

ตรวจพล to review the troops

ตรวจราชการ to make an official inspection

ตรวจโรค to examine, have a medical examination, have a check-up

ตรวจลงตรา to issue (a) visa(s)

ตรวจเลือด to have a blood test

ตรวจสอบ to check, inspect, verify, audit

การตรวจประเมิน auditing (an industry, etc)

จุดตรวจ check point

นายตรวจ inspector, supervisor; conductor (รถไฟ)

ใบตรวจ /examination/inspection/ certificate

ตรวน fetters, leg chains, shackles

ตรอก lane, alley, narrow passage

ตรอกคดเคี้ยว winding lane

ตรอกตัน blind alley, cul-de-sac, dead end

จนตรอก cornered, trapped, have no way out

ตรอง to reflect, consider; meditate (on), contemplate, ponder, think deeply about, cogitate

ตรองดูก่อน to think it over

ตรอม, ตรอมตรม despondent

ตระกอง embrace

ตระการ beautiful; wonderful, amazing; fantastic; various, diverse

ตระการตา spectacular, marvelous

ตระกูล family, lineage, race, stock

ตระกูลมูลชาติ (of) good /family/lineage/

ตระเตรียม to prepare, make ready

ตระบัด to misappropriate, embezzle

ต
ถ
ท
ธ
น
บ
ป
ผ
ฝ
พ
ฟ
ภ
ม
ย
ร
ฤ
ฤๅ
ล
ว
ศ
ษ
ส
ห
ฬ
อ
ฮ

ตระบัดสัตย์ to go back on one's word, break a promise

ตระโบม to caress; to embrace

ตระพัง well; pool, pond

ตระเวน to patrol, go around looking, make the rounds

    พลตระเวน patrolman

    ลาดตระเวน to patrol, cruise, scout

        เรือลาดตระเวน cruiser

ตระหง่าน prominent, lofty, towering

ตระหนก to be afraid, scared, apprehensive, feel afraid

    ตระหนกตกใจ startled, fearful

      ความตระหนกตกใจ fears

ตระหนัก to be conscious of, concerned about, aware of, realize

    โดยตระหนักว่า realizing

ตระหนี่ stingy, miserly, tight

    ตระหนี่ถี่เหนียว niggardly, mean, a skinflint

ตรับฟัง, สดับตรับฟัง to listen /closely/attentively/ (to), pay attention (to)

ตรัย three, triple, tri-

ตรัส to speak, state (royal word)

ตรัสรู้ to /be/become/ enlightened

ตรา[1] seal, stamp, chop; mark, brand; sign; coat-of-arms

    ตราประจำชาติ national coat-of-arms

ตรา[2] to promulgate, enact, pass; to note, take note of, remember; to tie

    ตรากฎหมาย to /promulgate/enact/ a law

    ตราจอง document of possessory rights to land

    ตราชู balance, scales

    ตราตั้ง letter of appointment

    ตราบาป remorse, sense of guilt, deep-rooted feeling of wrongdoing

    ตรายาง rubber stamp

      รัฐมนตรีตรายาง a rubber-stamp minister

    ตราสัง to bind a body (after death)

ตราหน้า to label, brand

เงินตรา currency, lawful money, legal tender

ตรวจตรา to inspect, check carefully; to patrol

ตีตรา to seal, stamp, chop

ประทับตรา see **ประทับตรา** หน้า 294

สารตราตั้ง credentials, letter of credence

ตรากตรำ to /endure/undergo/suffer/ (physical) hardship

ตราบ until, up to

    ตราบจนวันตาย until death, as long as one lives, until the day one dies, until one's dying day

    ตราบใดที่ as long as

    ตราบเท่า, ตราบท้าว until, up to ; so long as

ตรำ see **ตรากตรำ**

ตริตรอง see **ไตร่ตรอง** หน้า 207

ตรี[1] trident

ตรี[2] three, triple, tri-, ter

    ตรีโกณ triangle

      ตรีโกณมิติ trigonometry

    ตรีคูณ threefold, triple

    ตรีทูต in extremis

    ตรีมูรติ having three forms: Brahma, Vishnu, and Siva

    ชั้นตรี third grade

    นายพลตรี major general

    ไม้ตรี third tone sign (๋)

ตรึก as in **ตรึกตรอง** to consider, think (something) over, think about (something), reflect, ponder

ตรึง to tighten, make tight, make taut, put under tension; to pin down, peg, hold down; to stabilize; to tie up, bind; to besiege

    ตรึงข้าศึก to pin down the enemy

    ตรึงใจ fascinating, captivating; deeply impressed

    ตรึงตรา to tighten, make tight, make taut

ตรึงราคาข้าว to stabilize the price of rice; to hold down the price of rice

ตรุ jail, prison

ตรุณ youngster, youth

ตรุษ New Year

ตรุษจีน Chinese New Year

ตรุษฝรั่ง the New Year

ตรุษสงกรานต์ Songgran Festival

ตรู[1] *as in* **โฉมตรู** beautiful, pretty

ตรู[2], **กรู** to sweep (in, forward), rush forward in a body, swarm in; to overwhelm, inundate *ตำรวจตรูเข้าไปจับนักการพนัน The police swept in and arrested the gamblers.*

ตรู่ dawn

เช้าตรู่ (at) dawn

ตฤณ grass

ตฤณชาติ Graminae, the grass family

ตฤณมัย turf

ราชตฤณมัยสมาคม Royal Turf Club

ตลก funny, comical, ridiculous; queer

ตลก ๆ comical

ตลกคะนอง to be a /joker/comedian/

ตลกคาเฟ่ slapstick, low comedy

ตลกแดก to sponge (on someone); to get something under false pretenses

ตลกบริโภค *see* **ตลกแดก**

ตลกแบบถ่อย ribald

ตลกโปกฮา roistering, reveling; coarse merriment

ตลกฝืด a joke that falls flat

คนเล่นตลก comedian

ไม่ตลก serious, not funny

เล่นตลก to play a trick (on someone), pull a fast one, be devious

ตลบ[1] to throw back over; to turn down; to snare by enveloping in a net

ตลบตะแลง deceitful, untruthful; crafty, tricky

ตลบนก to snare a bird in a net

ตลบมุ้ง to tidy up a fastened mosquito net by gathering and throwing the bottom portion over the canopy

ตลบหลัง to betray; to attack from behind

กลิ้งหลายตลบ to roll over several times

อ่านหนังสือหลายตลบ to read (a book etc) over several times, read over and over

ตลบ[2] pervasive, permeating

กลิ่นตลบ pervasive /perfume/scent/ fragrance/, a good smell which permeates

ตลอด through, throughout; including, inclusive of; all the time, always, from beginning to end

ตลอดกัลปาวสาน forever, eternally, for eternity

ตลอดกาล perpetually, forever; for the whole time

ตลอดคืน throughout the night, all night long

ตลอดจน as well as, including

ตลอดชาติ the rest of one's life, for one's whole lifetime, for life, for good

ตลอดชีพ for life, throughout one's life, life, lifetime

ใบขับขี่ตลอดชีพ lifetime driver's licence

สมาชิกตลอดชีพ life member

ตลอดชีวิต for life, throughout one's life

ตลอดถึง as well as, including

ตลอดปี throughout the year, the whole year

ตลอดไป forever; always, all the time

ตลอดรอดฝั่ง the whole way, all the way

ตลอดวัน all day long, the whole day

ตลอดเวลา the whole time, all the time, continuously, incessantly, perpetually, always

ตลอดศก forever

ตลอดอายุ for the life of (something); throughout one's life, lifetime

โดยตลอด the whole time, from the beginning, throughout, all along, consistently

ต
ถ
ท
ธ
น
บ
ป
ผ
ฝ
พ
ฟ
ภ
ม
ย
ร
ฤ
ฤๅ
ล
ว
ศ
ษ
ส
ห
ฬ
อ
ฮ

มีมาตลอด enduring

เลี้ยวซ้ายผ่านตลอด left turn always permitted, left turn on red signal permitted

ตลับ small box; compact, case

ตลับเทป tape cassette

ตลับลูกปืน ball bearing

ตลับยา pillbox

ตลาด market, bazaar, marketplace

ตลาดเงิน money market

ตลาดดอกไม้ flower market

ตลาดทอง gold market

ตลาดทุน capital market

ตลาดนัด occasional market, morning market, Sunday market

ตลาดนัดจตุจักร Chatuchak Weekend Open Market

ตลาดน้ำ floating market

ตลาดมืด black market

ตลาดรอง secondary market

ตลาดรองสินเชื่อที่อยู่อาศัย secondary mortgage market

ตลาดสด fresh-food market

ตลาดหลักทรัพย์,ตลาดหุ้น stock market, stock exchange

ขาดตลาด out of stock

จ่ายตลาด to go marketing, do the marketing

ชาวบ้านร้านตลาด everybody

ปากตลาด coarse-mouthed, vulgar

ภาษาตลาด vernacular, colloquial, vulgar /speech/language/

ราคาตลาด market price, going price

ตลิ่ง bank

ตวง to measure out

ตวงข้าว to scoop up rice by the measure, measure out rice

ตวน satin

ตวนกู tungku

ต้วมเตี้ยม sluggishly; unsteadily

เดินต้วมเตี้ยม to toddle

ตวัก, จวัก coconut-shell ladle

ตวัด to whip back

ตวัดคอ to grab around the neck

ตวัดผ้า to throw (the end of a scarf etc) over the shoulder

ตวัดแส้ to whip, flick with a /whip/switch/

ตวาด to snap (at someone), /yell/shout/(at someone)

พูดดีๆ ก็ได้ ทำไมต้องตวาดด้วย Why do you have to /snap/yell/shout/ at me?

ตอ stump

ตอม่อ footing, foundation post

ตอไม้ tree stump

ต่อ[1] hornet

ต่อ[2] to extend; to renew; to continue, keep on, go on, go back to; to lengthen, add, enlarge; to join, connect; to bargain; to build, make, construct; to bet; to decoy, lure; to telephone, dial; extension (ย่อ Ext.) เช่น *โทร. 2349000 ต่อ 21 Tel. No. 2349000 Ext. 21;* to be next (to), adjacent; from; by

ต่อกร to put up a fight, fight (with someone)

ต่อกัน to follow, run in succession; to be joined

ต่อกิ่งไม้ to graft (a branch)

ต่อจากนั้นมา from then on, thereafter

ต่อจากนี้ไป from now on

ต่อจากหน้า 1 continued from page 1

ต่อฉบับหน้า continued next issue

ต่อเดือน per month, a month, monthly

ต่อตา bud grafting

ต่อต้าน to fight against, oppose, resist, counter, combat

ต่อแต้ม dominoes

ต่อแท็กซี่ to then /take/continue in/ a taxi

ต่อนี้ไป from now on

ต่อเนื่อง continuing, continuous, sustained, regular, unabated

ต่อปาก pass on by word of mouth; to argue

ต่อปากต่อคำ to argue (with), squabble (with), have /a spat/an altercation/

ต่อปี per year, a year, per annum

ต่อไป next; then; to continue to

ดังต่อไปนี้ as follows, the following

ต่อมา later, afterwards, subsequently

ต่อมาไม่ช้า not long after, a little later, shortly afterwards, before long

ต่อมาสักครู่ a moment later (*see also* **ต่อมาไม่ช้า**)

ต่อเมื่อ when; on condition that

ต่อรอง to bargain, negotiate, dicker

ต่อเรือ to build a boat

ต่อล้อต่อเถียง to argue, be argumentative, talk back

ต่อโลง to make a coffin

ต่อวัน per day, a day, per diem

ต่อว่า to complain (to someone about something); to reproach, rebuke

ต่อว่าต่อขาน to complain strongly, reproach (someone for something)

ต่อสัญญา to /renew/extend/ a contract

ต่อสัปดาห์ per week, a week, weekly

ต่อสัปดาห์หน้า continued next week

ต่อสู้ to fight, combat, battle (with); to struggle

ต่อหน้า before, in front of, in the presence of

ต่อหน้าต่อตา before one's very eyes, right before one's eyes, in one's presence, in front of

ต่อหน้าธารกำนัล in public

ต่อหน้า 8 continued on page 8

ต่อให้ to give a handicap (to)

ต่ออายุ to renew; to extend one's life (of government service, as a musician, etc)

คำต่อคำ word by word

ตัวต่อตัว hand to hand; privately

ทำงานต่อ to go back to work, keep on working

นอนต่อ to go back to sleep,

เป็นต่อ to be favored, have the odds in one's favor, the odds are on...

พูดต่อ to go on to say

มากต่อมาก great, enormous

เล่นต่อ to keep on playing

สองต่อ two times, twice, double; two /bus/train/etc/ connections

สองต่อหนึ่ง two to one

หัวเลี้ยวหัวต่อ critical point, turning point, period of transition

อ่านต่อ to go on reading

ต้อ　corneal ulcer; dumpy; squat; roly-poly

ต้อกระจก cataract

ต้อเนื้อ pterygium

ต้อหิน glaucoma

ตอก[1]　to pound, hammer, drive in; to pop

ตอกหน้า to attack, assail; to insult

ตอกเหล้า to throw the drinks back, drink heavily

ตอก[2]　strip of bamboo

จักตอก to split bamboo into fine strips for /weaving/plaiting/tying/

ต๊อก　*as in* **ย่ำต๊อก** to hoof it; to scurry along; to be walking the streets

ตอง　banana leaf; Thai playing cards; three of a kind

ต้อง[1]　must, have to, is to be

ผมต้องไปแล้ว I have to go now.

ต้องการ to want, desire, need, require, must have

ต้อง...แน่ๆ definitely, bound to (go, do, etc)

ไม่ต้อง Don't bother., It's not necessary., It's alright., You don't have to.

ไม่ต้อง ผมจ่ายเอง That's alright. I'll take care of it.

ต้อง[2]　to touch; to catch; to get, be; to be in accordance with, in line with, in conformity

ต

ถ
ท
ธ
น
บ
ป
ผ
ฝ
พ
ฟ
ภ
ม
ย
ร
ฤ
ฤๅ
ล
ว
ศ
ษ
ส
ห
ฬ
อ
ฮ

with; consistent (with)

ต้องขัง held in custody, confined

ต้องคดี to be prosecuted; accused, charged with; to be sued (ความแพ่ง), be involved in litigation

ต้องใจ to like, take a liking to, be fond of; to catch one's fancy; to move one

ต้องด้วย to agree with, conform to, correspond with, square with

ต้องตา to catch one's eye, be attractive, captivating

ต้องตามตำรา orthodox; classic, typical

ต้องโทษ to be imprisoned

ต้องนับว่า must be regarded as

ใครเอาชนะเจ้าหมอนี่ได้ ต้องนับว่าเก่ง Whoever can lick this guy deserves a medal. / Whoever can beat this guy must be regarded as being pretty good.

ต้องพายุ to be caught up in a storm

ต้องลม to catch the wind

ต้องหา to be charged with, be accused

   ผู้ต้องหา the accused, person charged with an offense

ต้องห้าม forbidden, prohibited, taboo; untouchable

ต้องอาบัติ to commit a religious offense

ต่องแต่ง swinging, oscillating

   ห้อยต่องแต่ง to dangle, hang down loosely

ตองเหลือง, ผีตองเหลือง Kha Tong Luang, Yumbri, Mrabri, Mlabri, a Mon forest tribe

ตอด to nibble

   พูดตอดเล็กตอดน้อย to snipe at someone, make /cutting/stinging/ remarks; to have a sharp tongue

ตอน[1] to castrate, geld, neuter, spay, sterilize; to divide, cut

   ตอนกิ่งไม้ to propagate a plant by /marcottage/air layering/

   ตอนควาย to geld a buffalo

ตอน[2] part, section; period; episode; installment; stage

ตอนกลาง in the middle, middle

ตอนกลางคืน at night, during the night

ตอนกลางวัน in the daytime, during the day

ตอนจบ ending; last installment

ตอนเช้า in the morning

ตอนดึก late at night

ตอนต้น at the beginning, early period

ตอนใต้ in the south

ตอนท้าย at the end; in the back

ตอนเที่ยง at noon, noontime

ตอนบ่าย in the afternoon

ตอนปลาย at the end, last stage

   ชั้นมัธยมศึกษาตอนปลาย senior high-school

ตอนไพ่ to cut a deck of cards

ตอนเย็น in the evening

ตอนสาย late, late morning, late in the morning

ตอนหลัง later on, subsequently

ตอนไหน when; which part

ทีละตอน section by section, one part at a time

ในตอนนี้ at this time, at present

เป็นขั้นเป็นตอน methodically, systematically

เป็นตอนๆ in parts; in installments, in /sections/stages/

ต้อน to drive, herd (along, in)

ต้อนเข้าคอก to drive into an enclosure

ต้อนเข้ามุม to corner

ต้อนเข้าห้อง to motion into a room

ต้อนรับ to welcome, greet, receive

   ต้อนรับขับสู้ to entertain warmly, welcome heartily

   ต้อนรับแขก to receive guests, welcome guests, greet visitors

ต้อนพยาน to keep at a witness; to trap a

witness

ต้อนหมู to outsmart

กวาดต้อน to be captured and herded

ตอบ[1] to reply, answer, respond; to repay

ตอบโต้ to retaliate

ยิงตอบโต้ to shoot back

ตอบแทน to repay, return; reciprocate, in consideration for; to get even

ตอบแทนบุญคุณ to repay a kindness

ตอบรับ to acknowledge, respond

ตอบสนอง to respond, answer, reciprocate, requite

ค่าตอบแทน payment, compensation, honorarium

ตอบ[2] sunken, hollow

แก้มตอบ /sunken/hollow/ cheeks

ตอม to settle (on); swarm (over, on, at, around)

เขาเป็นดารายอดนิยม สาวๆ ตอมกันมากมาย
A great pack of girls swarmed over the super-star.

ต่อม gland

ต่อมน้ำลาย salivary gland

ต่อมทอนซิล tonsils

ต่อม plop

หายต๋อม to vanish

ต่อย to punch, box, strike; to hit; to sting, bite

ต่อยปาก to punch in the mouth

ต่อยมวย to box

ชกต่อย to fight, have a fight

พูดเป็นต่อยหอย to chatter away, prattle

ต้อย short, small, little

ต้อยต่ำ inferior

ต้อยๆ close behind, on the heels of

เดินตามต้อยๆ to follow on the heels of someone / to follow like a puppy dog / to tag after (someone)

ตอแย to hound, hassle, bug; to make a nuisance of oneself (by); to have anything to do with someone

เขาเป็นคนปากมาก ไม่มีใครกล้าไปตอแยด้วย
He's such a bigmouth, nobody dares to have anything to do with him.

ตอร์ปิโด torpedo

เรือตอร์ปิโด torpedo boat

ตอแหล to tell lies lie, make something up, fib

คนตอแหล dirty liar; fibber

อีตอแหล You liar., that liar

ตะกร้อ sepak-takraw; a rattan ball; fruit-picker made of a wicker scoop fixed to a long handle

ตะกร้อขดลวด a stent

ตะกรัน *as in* **ขี้ตะกรัน** scale

ตะกร้า basket

ตะกรุด tiny rolled metal amulet inscribed with magic words

ตะกรุม adjutant stork

ตะกรุมตะกราม greedy, gluttonous, voracious

ตะกละ, ตะกละตะกลาม greedy, gluttonous, voracious

ตะกวด monitor

ตะกอ teenage, young cock

ตะกอน sediment, sludge; dregs, lees, settlings

ตะกั่ว lead

สีตะกั่วตัด steel blue

ตะกาย to climb; to scratch (at), paw; to claw (at)

ตะกุกตะกัก haltingly

พูดตะกุกตะกัก to speak haltingly, falter, stammer, stutter

ตะกุย to scratch (at), dig up

ตะกุยตะกาย to scramble (up, away), clamber

ตะเกียกตะกาย to struggle (to attain something), exert oneself

ตะเกียง lamp, lantern

ตะเกียงเจ้าพายุ pressure lantern

ตะเกียงรั้ว barn lantern

บานตะเกียง plenty, more than enough

ไส้ตะเกียง wick; mantle

ตะเกียบ chopsticks

ตะเกียบรถ fork (of a motorcycle, bicycle, etc)

ตะแก he, that guy

ตะแกรง sieve, screen

ตะโก้ gelatin topped with coconut-cream; monsoon

ตะโกน to shout, yell, to call out in a loud voice

ตะโกนเรียก to shout /for/to/ someone

ตะไกร scissors, shears

ปากตะไกร caustic

ตะขอ hook; gaff (ตะขอใช้เกี่ยวปลาขึ้นเรือ)

ตะขาบ centipede

ตีนตะขาบ caterpillar tread

รถตีนตะขาบ caterpillar tractor

ตะขิดตะขวง to hesitate (to), be reluctant (to do something), be embarrassing

รู้สึกตะขิดตะขวงที่จะเอ่ยปากขอความช่วยเหลือจากเขา It's embarrassing to ask him for help.

ตะเข้ crocodile, alligator; a rafter

ตะเข็บ seam

ตะครั่นตะครอ feverish

ตะคริว, ตะคิว cramp

เป็นตะคิว to /get/have/ a cramp

ตะครุบ to seize, grab; to pounce (on)

ตะคอก to /shout/yell/ at someone; raise one's voice; shout menacingly

ตะคุ่ม shadowy, indistinct

ตะเครียว net bag with a drawstring, reticule

ตะเคียน Malabar ironwood, thingan

ตะแคง on one's side; to tilt to one side; to list (สำหรับเรือ)

นอนตะแคง to lie on one's side

ตะไคร่ moss, lichen

ตะไคร่น้ำ algae

ตะไคร้ lemon grass

ตะเม่ two-wheeled handcart, barrow

ตะบอง club, truncheon, cudgel; billy, nightstick (สำหรับตำรวจ)

ตะบัน[1] tubular mortar and pestle for pounding betel

ตะบัน[2] to punch, pierce, poke, to penetrate; to pound

ตะบันหน้า to give someone a punch in the nose

ตะบัน[3] stubbornly, unremittingly; without restraint, non-stop

เถียงตะบัน to argue /unremittingly/stubbornly/

เที่ยวตะบัน to play around /non-stop/all the time/

ตะบี้ตะบัน pigheaded

รู้ว่าตัวเองผิดยังตะบี้ตะบันเถียงอยู่ได้ He knows he's wrong, but keeps on with his pigheaded argument. / Though he knew he was wrong, he argued pigheadedly.

ตะบึง right (to, off, away, in), straight away, straight (to, in, away, back, etc)

ควบม้าตะบึงไป to gallop right off / to ride off at full tilt

ตะเบ็ง to shout, yell

ตะเบ็งเสียง to shout, yell, call out in a loud voice, bellow

ตะแบง cantankarous, contrary

ตะแบงมาน, ตะเบ็งมาน a way of wearing a scarf crossed over the bosom and tied at the back of the neck, a scarf worn halter-fashion

ตะโบม to caress

ตะไบ file (ถูเหล็ก), rasp (ถูไม้)

ตะปบ to grab, slap down; to catch in flight

เสือตะปบเหยื่อ The tiger pounced on his prey.

ตะปุ่มตะป่ำ bumpy; warty; uneven, rough, rutted

ถนนตะปุ่มตะป่ำ bumpy road, rutted road

ตะปู nail

ตะปูควง screw, woodscrew

ตะพด walking-stick, cane; stick

ตะพอง frontal protuberances of an elephant's head

ตะพัง reservoir, pond

ตะพัด regularly, a lot, all the time

ตะพาน *see* **สะพาน** *หน้า 487*

ตะพาบ, ตะพาบน้ำ soft-shelled turtle

ตะพาย[1] hole in the nose of a /bull/buffalo/

    สนตะพาย to put a cord through the nose of a /bull/buffalo/; to lead (a person) around by the nose *(fig)*

    สายตะพาย cord passed through the nose of a /bull/buffalo/

ตะพาย[2] to wear over the shoulder

    ตะพายแล่ง to wear slung over the shoulder; down across the chest

ตะพึด continually, constantly, all the time

    ตะพึดตะพือ continually, constantly, incessantly, without a letup

ตะเพิด to chase away, drive /away/off/

ตะโพก hips, rump

    เนื้อตะโพก /rump/round/ cut of meat, /rump/round/ steak

ตะโพน a tuned two-faced drum

ตะราง jail, gaol, prison

    ขี้คุกขี้ตะราง jailbird

    ติดตะราง to be put in jail

ตะล่อม to gather up, pile up

    พูดตะล่อม to lead to the point; to persuade, induce

ตะลีตะลาน in great haste, frantically

ตะลึง, ตกตะลึง astonished, aghast, astounded

    ตะลึงงัน speechless, stunned

    ตะลึงพรึงเพริด stupefied, petrified

ตะลุง shadow-play puppet

ตะลุ่ม footed tray

ตะลุมบอน a free-for-all /fight/combat/, brawl, scrimmage, wild battle

ตะลุย through; persistently

ตะแลงแกง execution ground

ตะไล[1] firework pinwheel

ตะไล[2] steamed cupcake

ตะไล[3] tiny china cup

ตะวัน the sun

    ตะวันขึ้น sunrise

    ตะวันตก west; occident; sunset

    ตะวันยอแสง twilight, dusk

    ตะวันออก east; orient

        ตะวันออกกลาง Middle East

ตะเวน *see* **ตระเวน** *หน้า 180*

ตะหลิว spatula

ตะแหมะแขะ dumpy, squat, dwarfish

ตัก[1] to draw, scoop up; to help oneself (to)

    กับข้าวพร้อมแล้ว เชิญตักเลยครับ The food's ready. Do help yourselves.

    ตักข้าว to help /oneself/others/ to rice; to dish out the rice

    ตักตวง to amass; to help oneself (to something)

    ตักบาตร to make a food offering to a monk

ตัก[2] lap

    นั่งตัก to sit on one's lap

ตักกะ *see* **ตรรก** *หน้า 179*

ตักเตือน to warn, caution; to admonish, put (someone) on notice

ตั๊กแตน grasshopper

ตั่ง stool

ตั้ง[1] to place, set, put; to erect, set on end; to be based (on), be built (on); to establish, set up, found, organize; to begin, start, commence

    ตั้งกฎเกณฑ์ to set rules

    ตั้งข้อรังเกียจ to take a dislike to someone, find fault with someone

    ตั้งข้อสังเกต to notice, observe, make an observation, comment, make a comment

    ตั้งเข็ม to set one's course, aim (for, to be), direct oneself toward

    ตั้งไข่ begin to stand

    ตั้งครรภ์ to be pregnant, be with child, conceive

    ตั้งคำถาม to /put/pose/ask/ a question,

ต.
ถ
ท
ธ
น
บ
ป
ผ
ฝ
พ
ฟ
ภ
ม
ย
ร
ฤ
ฦ
ล
ว
ศ
ษ
ส
ห
ฬ
อ
ฮ

query, question

ตั้งเค้า to show signs (of), incipient

ตั้งใจ to intend (to), mean to, set one's mind on something; intentionally; attentively, with determination, assiduous

ตั้งใจฟัง to pay attention (to)

ตั้งชัน to stand on end; be erect

ตั้งชื่อ to name, give a name, call

ตั้งโด่ to have a hard-on, have an erection

ตั้งต้น to begin, commence, start

ตั้งตัว to establish oneself; to come up in the world, to improve oneself

ตั้งตัวได้ to establish oneself, become well off

ตั้งตาคอย to look forward to

ตั้งแต่ since, from

ตั้งแต่เด็ก /from/since/ childhood, since one was small

ตั้งแต่นั้นมา from then on, ever since

ตั้งแต่นี้ไป from now on

ตั้งแต่วานนี้ since yesterday

ตั้งโต๊ะ to set the table; to put food on the table

ตั้งถิ่นฐาน to settle down

ตั้งแถว to form ranks, get in line

ตั้งท้อง to become pregnant

ตั้งท่า to be poised (to)

สมศักดิ์ตั้งท่าเข้าตำแหน่งเลขาฯ แทนเสริม Somsak is poised to replace Serm as secretary-general.

ตั้งนานแล้ว for a long time, since a long time ago, since long ago, long ago

ตั้งนาฬิกา to set a /clock/watch/

ตั้งประเด็น to determine an issue; the issue one wishes to /address/talk about/; to /identify/focus on/ an issue

ตั้งปีแล้ว since last year, for a whole year now

ตั้งภูมิลำเนา to settle down (in), take up

residence (in), become domiciled (in)

ตั้งมั่น to be firmly established (in); to be firm (in one's /belief/course of action/), unwavering

ตั้งรกราก to make one's home (in, at), settle down (in), establish oneself (at, in)

ตั้งรับ on the defensive

ตั้งราคา to /set/fix/establish/ a price

ตั้งศพ to hold funeral rites

ตั้งสติ to compose oneself, regain one's composure, recover one's self-possession, pull oneself together; to be careful

ตั้งหน้าตั้งตา to apply oneself (to), devote oneself (to), concentrate (on)

ตั้งหน้าเรียน to study hard

ตั้งหลัก to get set; to gather oneself together

ตั้งหลักไม่ทัน to be flurried, unprepared

ตั้งหลักฐาน to establish oneself

ตั้งอกตั้งใจ to concentrate, be determined to; with concentration

ตั้งอยู่ situated, located; standing; established

ตั้งอยู่ในศีลในธรรม moral, ethical; imbued with moral principles

ติดตั้ง to install, put in

แต่งตั้ง to appoint, name

ที่ตั้ง location

เลือกตั้ง to elect

สารตราตั้ง letters of credence, letter of appointment

ตั้ง[2] time

สักตั้ง once

ลองดูสักตั้งซิ Give it a try. / Try once anyway.

ตั้ง[3] many, much, a lot of, as many as, as much as

มาตั้งแปดคน As many as 8 came.

ขอตั้ง 2000 บาท He asked for as much as 2000 baht.

ตั้งกระบุง an awful lot (of)

ตั้งบาน a lot, much, a heap (of)

ตั้งมากมาย an enormous amount, so much

ตั้งหลายเดือน many months ago, for many months

ตั้ง[4]   pile

หนังสือตั้งหนึ่ง a pile of books

ตังเม[1] taffy, toffee

ตังเม[2] stingy, miserly, tight

ตัณหา desire, craving, passion

ตัด[1] to cut, cut off, sever

    ตัดกัน contrasting

    ตัดกางเกง to have /trousers/pants/slacks/ made

    ตัดขาด to have nothing more to do with someone, sever a relationship, break off; to disown

    ตัดคอ to behead

    ตัดคะแนน to lose points; to downgrade, lower one's marks

    ตัดคิว to jump a line, cut in

    ตัดเงินเดือน to cut one's salary

    ตัดใจ to put something out of one's mind, to get over something, drop

    ตัด...จาก to preclude (someone) from

ไม่ควรตัดคนไทยในต่างแดนจากการเลือกตั้ง Thai nationals abroad should not be precluded from voting.

    ตัดญาติ to sever one's family ties

    ตัดต้นไม้ to fell a tree, cut down a tree

    ตัดต่อ to edit

    ตัดตอน to abridge; abridged

    ตัดถนน to make a road

    ตัดทอน to cut, pare

    ตัดทาง to preclude one from a chance to make a living; to take a short cut; to make a short cut; to make a way through, cut a path

    ตัดบท to cut (someone) off, cut short, /conclude/end/(a discussion etc) abruptly

    ตัดผม to get a haircut, have one's hair cut; to give a haircut, cut someone's hair

    ตัดพ่อตัดลูก to disown, be disowned; to disinherit

    ตัดพ้อ to complain, reproach, express one's resentment

    ตัดไฟต้นลม to nip (something) in the bud

    ตัดไมตรี to break off a friendship, sever friendly relations, become estranged

    ตัดรอน to break off a friendship, stop seeing one another

    ตัดรัก to break off, withdraw one's love (from), stop loving

    ตัดราคา to cut the price

        ขายตัดราคา to sell at cut price, cut-rate sale

    ตัดรายจ่าย to cut expenses

    ตัดสัมพันธ์ to sever relations

        ตัดสัมพันธ์ทางการทูต to sever diplomatic relations

    ตัดสิทธิ to deprive someone of a right, deny someone the right to do something

    ตัดสิน to judge, pass judgment, decide, give a verdict

        ตัดสินใจ to decide, make up one's mind

    ตัดเสื้อ to have clothes made

    ตัดหนทาง to deprive someone of his livelihood

    ตัดหน้า to cut in front (of); to /cut/edge/ someone out, get the jump on someone; to get the first word; to get in first

    ตัดหัว to behead, decapitate

    ตัดอกตัดใจ *see* **ตัดใจ**

    ตัดออก to cut off, cut out, take out; to take something out; excise; to delete; to expunge

    คู่ตัดเชือก semifinalists

    รอบตัดเชือก semifinals

ตัด[2] to dial

ต ถ ท ธ น บ ป ผ ฝ พ ฟ ภ ม ย ร ฤ ฤๅ ล ว ศ ษ ส ห ฬ อ ฮ

ตัด 9 ก่อน First dial nine, then....

ต้น[1] solid, not hollow; blocked; stopped up; blind; without a future

ตรอกตัน blind alley

ท่อตัน blocked pipe

ทางตัน dead end road, to have no future

ไส้ตัน appendicitis, inflamed appendix

อกตัน tough, sturdy

ต้น[2] ton

ตันตระ tantra

ตันติ classic

ตันติภาษา classical language; Pali

ตับ[1] liver

ตับแข็ง cirrhosis of the liver

ตับบด liver pate

ตับเหล็ก pig's spleen

ตับอ่อน pancreas

ตับ[2] bamboo fish-tongs

ตับ[3] set, row, series, string; skewer; arrangement (of)

ตับจาก piece of atap thatching

เป็นตับ in sets; in waves; large groups (of)

ตัว body; thing; self; character; classifier for animals and things; you (familiar)

ตัวกลั่น outstanding, super, leading

ตัวกลาง medium

ตัวการ principal; instigator, prime figure

ตัวเก็ง favored to win

ตัวเก่ง favorite

ตัวเขาเอง he himself, even he

ตัวคูณ multiplier

ตัวใครตัวมัน It's every man for himself.

ตัวเงิน money

ตัวเงินตัวทอง drawing card, money-maker; euphemism for **เหี้ย** see หน้า 548

ตัวจำนำ hostage

ตัวโจ๊ก joker

ตัวฉันเอง I myself, even I

ตัวชูโรง principal player, lead

ตัวเชิด front man, straw-man, puppet

ตัวเชื่อม link, bridge

ตัวดี the very one

ตัวตน soul; the self; personal

มีตัวตน to be a real person

พระเจ้ามีตัวตน personal god

ตัวตลก clown, comedian, funny guy, comic, buffoon

ตัวต่อตัว hand to hand; privately

ตัวตั้ง augend (บวก), minuend (ลบ), multiplicand (คูณ), dividend (หาร)

ตัวตั้งตัวดี person responsible, organizer, originator, promoter

ตัวถ่วง counterweight, counterbalance; a drag (on)

ตัวถัง body

ตัวท่านเอง you yourself, even you

ตัวทำละลาย solvent

ตัวแทน agent, representative, attorney

เป็นตัวแทน representing

ตัวนำ lead

ตัวบท text; theorem

ตัวบทกฎหมาย the law, legal text, letter of the law

ตัวบุคคล individual; person

เพื่อป้องกันการประทุษร้ายต่อตัวบุคคล to prevent any attack on their person

ในตัวบุคคล personal

ความละเมิดมิได้ในตัวบุคคล personal inviolability

ตัวประกอบ supporting /actor/actress/ character/; factor (คณิต)

ตัวประกัน hostage, surety

ตัวเป็นเกลียว to the extreme; to a frazzle, knock oneself out (to get something done)

ทำงานหนักตัวเป็นเกลียว He worked himself to a frazzle. / He knocked himself out doing it.

ตัวเปล่า empty-handed, without anything;

to be single

ตัวแปร variable

ตัวผู้ male, masculine

ตัวพิมพ์ type, print; printing

ตัวมาร obstacle, hindrance; troublemaker

ตัวเมีย female

ตัวเมือง town, city proper

ตัวแมลง insect, bug

ตัวยง star, popular

ตัวร้อน to have a fever, be feverish

ตัวเราเอง we ourselves; even we; I myself; even I

ตัวละคร actor (ชาย), actress (หญิง), player, character

ตัวเลข number, numeral; figure

ตัวสะกด final pronounced letter

ตัวสั่น to shiver, tremble, shake

ตัวแสดง performer, actor; indicator

ตัวแสบ troublemaker, bum

ตัวหนอน worm, caterpiller

ตัวหนังสือ letter(s), lettering

ตัวไหม silkworm

ตัวอย่าง example, instance, specimen

ของตัวอย่าง sample

ตัวอ่อน larva

ตัวอักษร letter, alphabets

ตัวเอก principal /player/speaker/character/ etc/, leader

ตัวเอง oneself

คำตอบอยู่ที่ตัวคุณเอง The answer is in you yourself.

กลับตัว to turn over a new leaf, reform oneself

กลิ่นตัว body odor

ขยายตัว to expand, enlarge

ขอตัว to excuse oneself, decline, regret not to be able to do something

คงตัว steady, stabilized

เคยตัว to get in the habit (of), get used to

จับตัว to arrest, catch (someone)

เจ้าตัว he, she

เจียมตัว to be unassuming, modest; deferential

ตายตัว fixed; immutable, unalterable

เต็มตัว real, whole, complete

ถือตัว to be aloof, distant; haughty; proud; to think a lot of oneself

ไม่ถือตัว informal, modest, friendly, readily accessible

ทั้งเนื้อทั้งตัว all

ทำตัว to behave, act (like)

เขาทำตัวเขาเอง He did it to himself. / He's suffering the consequences of his own action.

เท่าตัว twice as much, double

ประจำตัว personal; particular

บัตรประจำตัว identity card

ลำตัว trunk, body

ลืมตัว to forget oneself

เล่นตัว to play hard to get, be standoffish, be difficult

ส่วนตัว private, personal

หมดตัว destitute, to have lost everything

หลวมตัว to be committed, plunge into something, do something /ill-advisedly/ imprudently/

หายตัว to disappear

อยู่ตัว stable, established, settled

ออกตัว to apologize (for)

อิ่มตัว saturated, gorged (with), plethora (of)

หนังสือแนวบู๊ล้างผลาญถึงจุดอิ่มตัวแล้ว There is a plethora of blood and thunder books. / The market is saturated with them.

ตั๋ว ticket, note, bill

ตั๋วคูปอง coupon

ตั๋วเงิน bill, note; commercial paper

ตั๋วจำนำ pawn ticket

ต
ถ
ท
ธ
น
บ
ป
ผ
ฝ
พ
ฟ
ภ
ม
ย
ร
ฤ
ฤๅ
ล
ว
ศ
ษ
ส
ห
ฬ
อ
ฮ

ตั๋วชานชาลา platform ticket

ตั๋วโดยสาร (bus, train, boat) ticket

ตั๋วไป one-way ticket

ตั๋วไปกลับ round-trip ticket

ตั๋วรถไฟ ticket

ตั๋วละคร theater ticket

ตั๋วแลกเงิน bill of exchange

ตั๋วสัญญาใช้เงิน promissory note

คนเก็บตั๋ว ticket taker

คนขายตั๋ว ticket seller

ตี๋ตั๋ว to buy a ticket

ห้องขายตั๋ว ticket /booth/window/

ตั๋วโผ impresario

ตา[1] eye; node; knot; square, check; turn

ถึงตาฉัน *It's my turn.*

ตาขอ hook

ตาข่าย net; network, grid

ตาขาว white of the eye; cowardly, pusillanimous

ตาขุ่นตาเขียว angry-looking, to glower

ตาเข cross-eyed, having a squint

ตาแข็ง sleepless, insomniac, unable to get to sleep

ตาคม keen; sharp-eyed

ตาค้าง unblinking eyes; eyes open

(เข้า) **ตาจน** to be checkmated; to be at an impasse, at bay, have no way out

ตาแฉะ /watery/rheumy/ eyes

ตาชั่ง scale, steelyard, balance, pair of scales

ตาดำ iris; pupil

(เด็ก) **ตาดำๆ** a mere child, a kid, an innocent child

ตาดี fortunate; good eyesight

ตาเดียว (ปลา) sole, turbot

ตาแดง conjunctivitis, pink eye; bleary-eyed, red-eyed

ตาตั๊กแตน crystal clear

ใสเหมือนตาตั๊กแตน crystal clear, limpid

ตาต่อตา ฟันต่อฟัน an eye for an eye a tooth

for a tooth

ตาตาราง checkered

กระดาษตาตาราง graph paper

ตาตุ่ม ankle bone, astragalus

ตาเต็ง steelyard, lever scales

ตาโต beady eyes, beady-eyed, greedy looking

ตาถั่ว failing eysight; blind, not being able to see the nose in front of one's face; fool

ตาทัพ /army/troop/ movements

ขัดตาทัพ to send troops to gain time against an enemy; to stand in for (/someone/ else), act as a seatwarmer (for)

ตาน้ำ spring

ตาบอด blind, sightless; undiscerning, blind (to)

ตาบอดตาใส blind without a physical sign of blindness

ตาปรือ half-closed eyes, heavy eyes; drowsy; dreamy, dreamy-eyed; ecstatic

ตาปลา corn, bunion

ตาปลาดุก slant-eyed; small slanting eyes

ตาปี throughout the year, the whole year

ตาปีตาชาติ year in year out, forever

ตาเป็นมัน to look hungrily (at), have a hungry look; yearning eyes

ตาฝาด to be mistaken about what one sees

ตาฟาง to have poor /vision/eyesight/; clouded vision, eyes clouded over

ตาราง square

ตารางเวลา timetable, schedule

ตารางสอน class schedule

ตาร้าย adversity; unfortunate

ตาลอย to have /glazed eyes/a glazed look/ a vacant look/; dreamy, to have a dreamy look

ตาลาย to have eyes that are swimming, be unable to see straight, dizzy

ตาลุก with popping eyes

ตาไว quick-eyed, sharp-eyed

ตาหวาน sweet eyes

　ทำตาหวาน to /look/gaze/ (at someone) /sweetly/lovingly/doe-eyed/

　แม่ตาหวาน sweetheart, darling

ตาเหล่ cross-eyed, to have a squint

ตาเหลือก with eyes rolled up; frantic

ตาแหลม sharp-eyed, perspicacious

ตาเอก cross-eyed, astigmatic

แก้วตา lens of the eye

ขนตา eyelashes

ติดตาติดใจ impressed (by); impressive

ติดหูติดตา clear in one's mind, memorable

ถลึงตา to give (someone) a hard look

ทันตาเห็น soon

ทำตาปริบๆ to blink; helplessly

นัยน์ตา eyes

น้ำตา tears

บังตา blind

บางตา scanty, sparse

บาดตา repugnant sight, ugly

เบิกตา to open one's eyes wide

เป็นหูเป็นตา to be one's eyes and ears, keep a watch over, oversee

เปลือกตา eyelid

ผิดตา unusual, to look odd

พริบตา an instant

มองเป็นตาเดียว to all look together

มีหน้ามีตา respectable; of substance

ไม่วางตา to stare (at)

ลวงตา deceptive, illusory

ลับตา to close one's eyes

ลานตา abundance (of), profusion (of), plethora (of)

ลืมตา to open one's eyes

ลูกตา eye, eyeball

แว่นตา spectacles, eyeglasses

แววตา a /twinkle/sparkle/ in one's eye

สะดุดตา striking

สายตา eyesight; view, point of view

หนาตา abundant, ample, plenty (of), numerous

หน้าตา appearance

　หน้าตาดี goodlooking

หมอตา eye doctor

หมายตา to have one's eye on (/something /someone/)

หลับตา to close one's eyes

หูตาสว่าง to learn the truth, know what is going on

หูป่าตาเถื่อน ignorant, uncivilized

ตา[2] maternal grandfather

ตาแก่ old man

ตาสีตาสา simple folk

ปู่ย่าตายาย forebears, ancestors; grandparents

พ่อตา father-in-law

อีตาคนนั้น that /guy/old boy/

ตาก to dry, to expose to the air, hang out; to endure, to put up with; sun-dried

ตากแดด to sun, put out in the sun; to sun oneself, take a sunbath

ตากฝน to get wet in the rain, go out in the rain

ตากลม to take the air, be out in the air

　นั่งตากลม to sit out in the open air

ตากอากาศ to take the air, go to the country, take a vacation

ไปตากอากาศที่ชายทะเล to take a vacation at the seaside / go to the beach for a change of air / take the air at the seaside

กล้วยตาก sun-dried banana

ต่าง[1] pack, packsaddle

ลาต่าง pack donkey

สัตว์ต่าง pack animal

ต่าง[2] each; other; different, diverse, various; instead of, in place of; on behalf of, for

ก
ข
ค
ฆ
ง
จ
ฉ
ช
ซ
ฌ
ญ
ฎ
ฏ
ฐ
ฑ
ฒ
ณ
ด
ต

ต่างๆ different, diverse, various

　ต่างๆ นานา all sorts of, a variety of, an assortment of, assorted

ต่างกัน to be different, distinct

ต่างกับ different (from)

ต่างคนต่างใจ each to his own taste

ต่างชาติ foreign, alien

ต่างด้าว alien, foreign

　คนต่างด้าว alien, foreigner

　ใบต่างด้าว alien identification book

ต่างประเทศ foreign; abroad; other countries

　ชาวต่างประเทศ foreigner, person from another country

　ไปต่างประเทศ to go abroad

ต่างภาษา a different language, another language

ต่างเมือง a different place, another place

ต่างว่า if, suppose

ต่างหน้า as a memento, (something) to remember someone by

ฝากรูปไว้ดูต่างหน้า *I give you this picture to remember me by.*

ต่างหาก separate, extra, to boot; it is just that, it is, what...is, where...is etc

ฉันไม่ได้พูดกับเธอ ฉันพูดกับเขาต่างหาก *I wasn't talking to you. It was he I was talking to.*
ไม่ใช่ว่าฉันไม่ชอบ ฉันไม่หิวต่างหาก *It isn't that I don't like it. It's just that I'm not hungry.*
ฉันหมายถึงกินข้าวต่างหาก *What I meant was eating.*

　คิดค่าส่งต่างหาก postage extra

ผลต่าง difference (in, between)

ว่าต่าง to represent

ต่างหู earring, eardrop

ตาด silk shot with /gold/silver/, brocade

ต้าน to resist, withstand, oppose

　ต้านทาน to resist, thwart, check

　　ความต้านทาน resistance

　ต้านลม to withstand the wind

ต่อต้าน to fight against, combat, oppose, counter, resist

ตานขโมย a children's malady caused by worms characterized by emaciation and a bloated stomach

ตาเบ๊ะ to salute

ตาปู *see* ตะปู *หน้า 186*

ตาม[1] to follow; to accompany; to send for; in accordance with, according to; along

　ตามกฎหมาย in accordance with the law, according to the law, under the law, legally

　ตามกล่าว as aforesaid

　ตามกว้าง crosswise, widthwise, transversal

　ตามควร reasonable, appropriate, as may be /appropriate/proper/, befitting; appropriately, reasonably

　ตามเคย once again, as usual

　ตามจริง in fact, in truth; frankly

　ว่ากันตามจริงแล้ว *frankly speaking*

　ตามแจ to shadow, stick close to; to be hot on the heels of

　ตามใจ to go along with, as you like; to give in to; to please, indulge

　　ตามใจคุณ as you like, do what you like

　　ตามใจตัวเอง self-indulgent; headstrong

　　ตามใจนึก as one pleases; as anticipated

　　ตามใจสมัคร at will

　ตามฐานะ befittingly, in accordance with one's means

　ตามตรง frankly, directly

　ตามตัวอย่าง as per sample

　ตามตัวอักษร literal, literally

　ตามตำรา classic

　ตามติดแจ to follow close behind, to tail

　ตามแต่จะได้ whatever it is it's alright

　ตามแต่จะให้ to give whatever one likes

　ต้องการเท่าไหร่ ตามแต่จะให้ *How much is it? /As you like./Give whatever you like./*

　ตามแต่โอกาส when the opportunity presents

itself, if one gets a chance, whenever one can

ตามถนน along the road

ตามทาง along the way

ตามทางการ officially

ตามที่ as; what; with reference to, regarding

ตามที่คุณพูดมานั้น ผมเห็นด้วย I agree with what you said.

ตามธรรมดา ordinarily, usually, normally

ตามน้ำ downstream; with the current

    กินตามน้ำ to /get/take/ a rake-off

ตามบุญตามกรรม to let nature take its course; naturally; left to one's fate, neglected

ตามปกติ ordinarily, usually; normally, as usual

ตามโผ as prelisted, as expected

ตามพฤติกรรม in practice

ตามมีตามเกิด within one's means; whatever there is; to make do (/with what there is/ with what one has/)

ตามยาว lengthwise

ตามรอย to follow in the footsteps (of); to track

ตามรายงาน as reported

ตามเรื่อง as things are; to follow up; as the story goes

ปล่อยมันไปตามเรื่อง Let it take its course. / Forget it. / Hang it!

พูดไปตามเรื่องอย่างนั้นเอง (He) is just talking. / It's just talk.

ตามลม with the wind, downwind

    ตามลมตามแล้ง fatalistically

ตามลำดับ respectively; in order, seriatim; progressively

    ตามลำดับชั้น through official channels, through proper channels, up the line; according to rank

ตามลำพัง alone; on one's own

ตามสบาย *see* **ตามสบาย** *หน้า 477*

ตามสมควร as is appropriate

    ตามสมควรแก่กรณีย์ appropriately

    ตามสมควรแก่ฐานะ according to one's means

ตามสมัย fashionable, to follow the fashion

ตามส่วน proportionately, in proportion

ตามอย่าง to follow, imitate, copy

เขียนตาม to take dictation

จะตามให้ I'll follow up; I'll get /it/him/etc/ (for you)

ติดตาม to accompany; to follow; to keep an eye on something, follow (something) up

ติดสอยห้อยตาม to go everywhere with (someone); to cling (to)

เป็นเงาตามตัว inevitably

เป็นไปตาม to be as

มองตาม to gaze after (someone), watch

ว่าตาม to repeat after (someone)

ให้ไปตาม to fetch; to send (someone) for (someone)

ตาม[2] to light

    ตามโคม to light a lantern

    ตามไฟ to kindle a fire

ตาย[1] to die, pass away, succumb; to expire; to stop; to be motionless, paralysed; to be out of order, dead, fail, not work; to keep turning up; never turning up (of/numbers/ devices/in gambling); to be at low tide; deathly

    ตายคาที่ to die instantaneously, be killed outright, die on the spot

    ตายใจ to trust, have complete /confidence/ faith/ (in someone), fall for something implicitely

    หลอก(ทำ)ให้ตายใจ to fool someone into /believing/trusting/ one

    ตายซาก dried remains (of a dead body)

    ตายด้าน impotent

    ตายตัว to be fixed; inevitable

ต
ถ
ท
ธ
น
บ
ป
ผ
ฝ
พ
ฟ
ภ
ม
ย
ร
ฤ
ฤๅ
ล
ว
ศ
ษ
ส
ห
ฬ
อ
ฮ

ตายตาไม่หลับ to be unable to rest in peace

ตายทั้งกลม to die while pregnant

ตายในสนามรบ to die in battle

ตายในหน้าที่ to die in the line of duty, die in the course of duty

ตายฝอย wither away, shrivel up and die

ตายพราย to die before bearing fruit

ตายละซิ heavens!

ตายละวา oh damn

ตายเลย oh no!; it will be the end of me

ตายหมู่ to die en masse

ตายโหง to die a violent death

ตายอนาถ to die tragically

กระโดดน้ำตาย to drown oneself

กุญแจปากตาย wrench, spanner

คนตาย deceased, dead person

ความตาย death

คำตาย word ending in a short vowel; syllable with a short vowel sound arising from the use of two consonants without a vowel sign

ฆ่าคนตาย to kill, slay; (การ...) homicide

จมน้ำตาย to drown, be drowned

จับตาย to catch dead

ตกน้ำตาย to be drowned

แทบตาย to knock oneself out (doing something), almost died

ทำงานแทบตาย I almost died doing that job.

ผู้ตาย deceased, victim

ไม้ตาย trump card

รถตาย the car went dead

ตาย[2] Oh!; Damn!, Hell!

ตายจริง Oh!, Goodness!, My god!

ตายละทีนี้ I'm in for it!

ตายแล้ว Jesus!, uh oh!, Damn!

ตายห่า Shit!, Goddam!, Damn it!, Oh damn!

ต๊ายตาย Oh la la!; Oh my goodness!

อุ๊ยตาย Oh my!

ตาย[3], จะตาย badly, so much, too

จะตายอยู่แล้ว unbearably, infinitely, extremely, as one can be เช่น I am poor as I can be.

เดี๋ยวผมถูกเจ้านายเล่นงานตาย I'll get it in the neck from my boss. / My boss will give me hell.

หนาวจะตายอยู่แล้ว already too cold

ออกจะตาย awfully, terrifically

ตาล sugar palm

ต้นตาล sugar palm

น้ำตาล sugar

ตาลปัตร ceremonial fan

กลับตาลปัตร to be just the opposite, utterly different

ตำ to pound, beat; to pierce, puncture, prick, stick

ตำข้าว to husk rice by pounding

ตำตา before one's very eyes

ต่ำ low, inferior, base

ต่ำช้า base, low, ignoble, vile

ต่ำต้อย inferior

ต่ำสุด lowest, minimum; nadir

อักษรต่ำ any of the 24 low consonants in Thai

ตำนาน chronicle; legend; account, traditional history, tradition

ตำบล district, township, tambon

ตำแย fever-nettle

หมอตำแย midwife

ตำรวจ policeman, police

ตำรวจจราจร traffic police

ตำรวจนครบาล city police, metropolitan police

ตำรวจภูธร provincial police

ตำรวจหลวง palace police

กรมตำรวจ Police Department

นายตำรวจ police officer

ผู้กำกับการตำรวจ police commander

พลตำรวจ policeman

ตำรับ recipe; text; prescription
　　ตำรับตำรา textbook; books
ตำรา book, textbook, handbook
ตำลึง a monetary /unit/weight/ of silver equal to /four baht/60 grams/
ตำหนัก princely residence, palace
ตำหนิ[1] defect; blemish; scar
　　เป็นตำหนิ to have a /scar/marking/
　　มีตำหนิ to have a slight defect, be slightly damaged
ตำหนิ[2] to blame, censure, criticize
ตำแหน่ง location, place; rank; position, post, office
　　ชิงตำแหน่ง to /vie/compete/ for a /position/title/
　　ดำรงตำแหน่ง to hold the office (of), hold office (as)
　　สมัยนั้นเขาดำรงตำแหน่งอธิบดีกรมตำรวจ He was then the director-general of the Police Department. / He then held the office of director-general.
　　อยู่ในตำแหน่ง to hold office, occupy the position (of)
ติ to blame, censure, find fault (with), reprove, criticize
　　ตินินนินทา to backbite, gossip maliciously
　　ติชม to comment, criticize
　　ติติง to reprove, admonish
　　ติเตียน to criticize, reprove, reproach; to denounce
　　ติเพื่อก่อ to give constructive criticism
　　ติเพื่อทำลาย to denigrate
ติ๊ต่าง supposing; let's suppose
ติ่ง excrescence, growth
　　ติ่งหู earlobe
　　ไส้ติ่ง appendix
ติงต๊อง nutty
ติ๊งต่อง dingdong
ติ๋ง, ติ๋งๆ drip, dripping
ติด to stick; to get stuck, be stuck, be unable to proceed, bogged down; to attach, fix; to light; to kindle, make, (a fire); to adjoin; to be addicted (to); to bear (fruit); to fall in love with, become attached (to); to be close to; to owe, be owed

ติดๆ closely, one after another, on top of one another
ติดกระดุม to button
ติดกัณฑ์เทศน์ to make an offering to a preaching monk
ติดกัน next, adjoining, next to each other; attached (to); stuck together
ติดกับ to be trapped
ติดกาว to paste, glue (something to something)
ติดเก้ง to get stuck while mating (of dogs)
ติดขัด out of order; to be stuck; trouble, difficulty
ติดคอ to /stick/be stuck/ in one's throat
ติดค้าง to owe, have an outstanding amount to be paid, owing
ติดคุก to be jailed, go to jail, be imprisoned
ติดเครื่อง to start an engine
ติดเครื่องโทรศัพท์ to install a telephone
ติดงาน to have work to do
ติดเงิน to owe
ติดใจ to like, fancy, love, be taken with, be fond of; to be impressed (by, with); to be interested (in); to doubt, question
ติดฉลาก to label
ติดชะงัก to be interrupted, get stuck
ติดตลก to be joking
ติดต่อ[1] contagious, infectious
ติดต่อ[2] to associate (with), see; to communicate with, contact, get in touch (with); continuous
ติดต่อเขาให้ผมหน่อย Get in touch with him for me, will you?
ติดต่อไม่ได้ I can't /reach/contact/ him.

ต
ถ
ท
ธ
น
บ
ป
ผ
ฝ
พ
ฟ
ภ
ม
ย
ร
ฤ
ฤๅ
ล
ว
ศ
ษ
ส
ห
ฬ
อ
ฮ

ยังติดต่อกันอยู่หรือเปล่า Are you still in touch? / Do you still see each other?

การติดต่อ communication, contact, intercourse, connection

ติดตะราง to be put in jail

ติดตั้ง to install, put in, set up

ติดตัว with one, on one

บาปติดตัว sins on one's head

ติดตาติดใจ unforgettable

ติดตาม to accompany, follow, go with someone; to follow up, look after, track, keep track (of)

การติดตาม tracking

ติดธุระ to be busy, tied up, engaged, occupied, not available

ติดบุหรี่ to be a smoker, have the smoking habit

ติดเบ็ด to be hooked

ติดป้าย to put up a sign

ติดปีก to get one's wings (on graduation from flight training); to fly away

ติดผู้หญิง to be stuck on a girl

ติดพัน to be concerned with; to be taken with, stuck on, be involved (with); unfinished, still going on; to be unable to stop

ติดฟัน to get stuck in the teeth

ติดไฟ to catch fire; to light a fire; to /install/ put in/ electricity

ติดยศ to wear insignia of rank

ติดยา to be addicted, be drug-dependent

ติดรถ to go along in someone's car

ติดราชการ to be occupied with official duties, on government service

ติดแร้ว ensnared

ติดโรค to get sick, get infected, catch a disease

ติดลบ negative; deficit

ติดลม to catch the wind; to get caught up in (one's work, train of thought, etc)

พูดติดลม to be long-winded, get caught up in what one is saying

ติดศัพท์ to get stuck on a word, not know the meaning of a word

ติดสอยห้อยตาม to stick close (to someone), follow everywhere

ติดสัด in heat, in rut

ติดสำนวน to use flowery language, eloquent

ติดสินบน to bribe, give a bribe

ติดแสตมป์ to stamp, put on a stamp

ติดหมัด all at once

ติดหูติดตา memorable, imprinted in one's mind, unforgettable

ติดเหล้า to be an alcoholic

ติดอกติดใจ to love (something)

ติดอ่าง to be tongue-tied, stammer, stutter; without a let-up, like a broken record

ติดอาวุธ to carry a weapon, armed

ติดแอร์ to put in air-conditioning; air-conditioned

ติรัจฉาน animal, beast

ตี to beat, strike; to attack, fight; to thrash, whip; to define, interpret; to draw; to beat (gold); to beat (eggs); to fix, appraise

ตีกรรเชียง, ตีกระเชียง to row; backstroke

ตีกรับ to /clap/beat/ claves together

ตีกลอง to beat a drum

ตีกลับ to return; to reject

ตีกิน to take advantage, grab (it, something); to throw down the winning card

ตีไก่ to have a cock-fight

ตีขลุม to grab (for oneself)

ตีขวา to keep to the right, get over to the right

ตีไข่ to beat eggs

ตีไข่แตก to get out of the doldrums, do something

ตีความ to construe, interpret, define

ตีคู่ to be neck and neck

ตีจาก to distance oneself (from someone), desert

ตีฉิ่ง to have lesbian sex

ตีชิง to rob, mug

ตีซ้าย bear to the left

ตีตนก่อนไข้ to cross one's bridges before coming to them, act prematurely

ตีตรวน to shackle, put in chains

ตีตรา to seal, stamp, chop

ตีตัวออกห่าง to distance oneself (from)

ตีตั๋ว to buy a ticket

ตีตื้น to improve, get better

ตีทะเบียน to register

ตีท้ายครัว to go in through the backdoor; to use another's wife to advantage

ตีบทแตก to play a role convincingly

ตีปีก to jump for joy, get all excited (over something)

ตีแผ่ to unfold; to reveal, expose

ตีฝีปาก to be glib, fancy-talking

ตีพิมพ์ to print, publish

ตีโพยตีพาย to kick up a fuss (about something), get excited (about), make a commotion (over, about)

ตีไม่แตก invincible; to be unable to vanquish; to be unable to solve a problem

ตีรันฟันแทง to brawl with weapons

ตีรั้ว to fence

ตีราคา to appraise, estimate the /value/ price/, give an estimate; to set a price

ตีลังกา to somersault, turn over

ตีสกัด to cut-off, block

ตีสนิท to get on familiar terms (with), get close (to), play up to (someone), befriend (for ulterior motives)

ตีสองหน้า hypocritical, to be two-faced, double-dealing, duplicitous; wily; to dissemble

ตีสำนวน to play with words

ตีเสมอ to even the score; to behave without regard to one's (inferior) position, act insolently, be presumptuous

ตีเสียว่า to say, suppose

ตีหน้า to wear an expression (of); to feign; to pretend (to be), act (sad, stupid, etc)

    ตีหน้าตาย to look blank, be impassive

    ตีหน้าทะเล้น to make a face

ตีหม้อ to screw *(sl)*

ตีเหล็ก to forge (iron)

ตีอวน to lay a seine

ตี่ต่าง supposing, let's suppose

ตีน foot; base, bottom, foot

    ตีนกบ fins

    ตีนกา crow's-feet

    ตีนเขา foothills, base of a mountain

    ตีนตะขาบ caterpillar tread

       รถตีนตะขาบ caterpillar tractor

    ตีนติดดิน down-to-earth

    ตีนเปล่า barefoot

       หมอตีนเปล่า barefoot doctor

    ตีนผี hot-rod driver

    ตีนแมว cat burglar

    ตีนโรงตีนศาล (ทนาย) ambulance chaser

ตีบ constricted; vestigial

    ตีบตัน constricted

    โรคคอตีบ diphtheria

ตึก building, brick building

    ตึกระฟ้า skyscraper

    ตึกรามบ้านช่อง buildings

ตึกๆ throbbing, beating, ticking

ตึ้กตั้ก *see* ตึกๆ

ตึง[1] tight, strained, stretched, taut

    ตึงเครียด tense, under stress; critical

    หน้าตึง tight-skinned; to look displeased, look tense

ตึง[2] to be sullen; to feel discontented

    บึ้งตึง sullen, cross

ต
ถ
ท
ธ
น
บ
ป
ผ
ฝ
พ
ฟ
ภ
ม
ย
ร
ฤ
ฤๅ
ล
ว
ศ
ษ
ส
ห
ฬ
อ
ฮ

มึนตึง cold

หูตึง hard of hearing

ตึง[3] thud, with a thud

ตึงตัง thumping

ล้มตึง to fall with a thud

ตึงๆ as in ลมพัดตึงๆ a stiff breeze, strong wind

ตืด tapeworm

ขี้ตืด tight, to be a skinflint

ตื่น to wake up, be awake; to be excited, agitated

ตื่นข่าว to become excited (about some news)

ตื่นคน skittish

ตื่นตระหนก to get panicky

ตื่นตัว to awake (to), become aware (of)

ตื่นตาตื่นใจ impressed, excited

ตื่นตูม to be panic-stricken

ตื่นเต้น to be excited; exciting

ตื่นนอน to wake up

ตื้น shallow, not deep, superficial; choked up, speechless

ตื้นเขิน silted up

ตื้นตัน overwhelmed, moved, touched (by)

ตื้นตันใจจนบอกไม่ถูก inexpressibly moved (by gratitude)

ตื้อ thick-headed

มืดตื้อ pitch dark

อิ่มตื้อ gorged, very full

ตื้อ to keep after (someone to do something); to pester (someone for something); be persistent

ตุ, ตุๆ smelly, odorous

เหม็นตุๆ to begin to smell

ตุ as in เป็นตุเป็นตะ convincingly

ตุ๊[1] chubby

ตุ๊[2] monk

ตุ๊กแก gecko

ตุ๊กตา doll; model; hypothetical /situation/case/; bearing; reflection in an eye

ตุ๊กตาหน้ารถ a front-seat doll, babe for show

ตุ๊กตุ่น plastic or rubber mini-doll

ตุกติก cunning, foxy, crafty; to play dirty, do funny business, do a fiddle

มีการเล่นตุกติกในการแข่งกีฬาครั้งนี้ There was some funny business going on in the competition this time.

ตุง bulging

กระเป๋าตุง bulging /wallet/pocket/

ตุ้งติ้ง pendant earring; affected, prissy, girlish

ตุ๊ด fairy, fruit, fag, gay queen, a tootsie

ตุ๊ต๊ะ roly-poly; corpulent, very fat

ตุน, กักตุน to store, put aside; to hoard

กักตุนสินค้า to hoard goods, hold back goods from the market

ตุ่น mole; bamboo rat

ตุ๋น[1] to swindle

ต้มตุ๋น to be /conned/screwed/

ตุ๋น[2] to steam

เป็ดตุ๋น steamed duck

ตุบ thump

ตุบๆ throbbing, beating

ตุบตับ thumping, sound of blows

ตุปัดตุป่อง to make a great show of (annoyance, sulking etc)

ตุปัดตุเป๋ unsteadily

เดินตุปัดตุเป๋ to stagger (along)

ตุ่ม jar, mosquito-bite, bump, swelling

ตุ้ม spherical, roundish; impediment (to)

ตุ้มหู earring

ลูกตุ้ม pendulum; clock-weight; weight

ตุ้ม, ตุ้มต่อม plop

ตุ่ย swollen, puffed up

แก้มตุ่ย puffed out cheek, bulging cheek

ตุ้ย swollen, puffed out

ตุ้ยๆ as in เคี้ยวตุ้ยๆ to chew with gusto

ตุ้ย to punch, sock (in); to improvise

ตุลา balance, scales

ตุลาการ judge, justice

ตุลาการศาลรัฐธรรมนูญ a justice of the Constitutional Court

ตุลาคม October

ตุหรัดตุเหร่ aimlessly, wandering about, roaming around

ตู myself; I, me, we, us

ตูข้า myself, ourselves

ตู่ to claim falsely another's property is one's own

ตู่ตัว to mistake one /person/letter/for another, take (someone) for (someone else)

ขี้ตู่ to be a fibber; to be a crook

ตู้ cupboard, cabinet, closet

ตู้กระจก glass cabinet, cabinet with a mirror; glass enclosure; fish tank, aquarium

ตู้กับข้าว food cupboard

ตู้จดหมาย letterbox

ตู้แช่แข็ง freezer

ตู้แช่เย็น refrigerated case

ตู้โชว์ showcase

ตู้เซฟ safe

ตู้ถ้วยชาม china cabinet

ตู้โทรศัพท์ pay station

ตู้น้ำแข็ง cold chest; icebox

ตู้นิรภัย safe; vault

ตู้ ป.ณ. PO Box *see* **ตู้ไปรษณีย์**

ตู้ไปรษณีย์ letter-box, mailbox, post-office box

ตู้ยาม guardhouse, sentry box

ตู้เย็น refrigerator

ตู้เลี้ยงปลา fish tank

ตู้เสื้อผ้า wardrobe, clothes closet

ตู้หนังสือ bookcase

ตูด anus, ass, behind

ตูดหนัก to have lead in one's ass

ตูบ[1] hut, cabin

ตูบ[2] hanging, drooping

หูตูบ floppy-eared, drooping ears

ตูม[1] budding, in bud, unopened

ตูม[2], **ตูมตาม** boom, booming

เต่ง firm, tight

เต่งตึง firm and ample, gorgeous

เต็งหาม for sure

เต้น to dance; to be excited; to beat, throb, palpitate, pulsate

เต้นระบำ to dance in /a chorus/an ensemble/, give a dance performance

เต้นรำ to dance

เต้นแร้งเต้นกา to jump with joy; to get excited about something, become agitated

กระโดดโลดเต้น to be elated, jump with joy, overjoyed

ใจเต้น to be excited

ตื่นเต้น exciting; to be excited

วิ่งเต้น to pull strings, use /pull/influence/; to run around, rush around (to get something done)

เต็นท์ tent

เต็ม full, complete, filled up; unabbreviated

เต็มกลั้น unbearable

เต็มกำลัง awfully; at full capacity; to one's utmost, as hard as possible, with all one's strength

เต็มแก่ unbearably

หิวเต็มแก่ starved

เต็มแกน with extreme difficulty

เต็มขั้น full-fledged

เต็มคราบ stuffed, full up, to stuff oneself

ผมล่อซะเต็มคราบ I'm /stuffed/full up/.

เต็มใจ to be willing (to), happy to do something; wholeheartedly

เต็มตัว completely, wholly, all over; devoted completely to something

ภาพถ่ายเต็มตัว full length photograph

เต็มตา (to sleep) sufficiently; (to see) distinctly

เห็นเต็มตา to get a good look (at), see distinctly

ต
ถ
ท
ธ
น
บ
ป
ผ
ฝ
พ
ฟ
ภ
ม
ย
ร
ฤ
ฤๅ
ล
ว
ศ
ษ
ส
ห
ฬ
อ
ฮ

เต็มตื้น to be choked up

เต็มเต็ง as in ไม่เต็มเต็ง nutty, crackbrained, having a screw loose

เต็มทน intolerable, unbearable, unendurable, awful

เบื่องานเต็มทนแล้ว I am /awfully/unbearably/ fed up with my job. / I find my job unbearable.

เต็มที extremely; terrible, awful, rotten, too bad

เต็มที่ full; hard; to capacity, extremely, as can be, as possible

　โตเต็มที่ full grown / fully grown

เต็มปาก[1] with conviction; to assure, with assurance

เต็มปาก[2] mouthful (of)

เต็มประดา see เต็มที

เต็มประตู completely, absolutely

คุณผิดเต็มประตู You are /completely at fault/absolutely wrong/. / There is no excuse for what you did.

เต็มเปี่ยม brimming (with)

เต็มไปด้วย full of, filled with

เต็มฝีเท้า at full speed

เต็มมือ to have one's hands full (with work etc)

ผมมีงานเต็มมือ I have my hands full of work. / I am up to my ears in work.

เต็มเม็ดเต็มหน่วย perfect, excellent, up to expectations, fulfilled, complete, at full capacity

　ไม่เต็มเม็ดเต็มหน่วย disappointing; under capacity, inadequate

เต็มยศ full dress

เต็มแรง with full force

เต็มวัน the whole day, full time

เต็มเวลา full time; the whole time

เต็มเหนี่ยว with full force

เต็มอก full well

เต็มอัตรา (in, at) full strength

เต็มเอี้ยด packed; fully booked

เตร่ to wander, roam, rove, drift

เดินเตร่ to amble about

เตร็ดเตร่ see เตร่

เที่ยวเตร่ to play around, go here and there, roam about, wander around

เตรียม to prepare, make ready

เตรียมการ preparatory

เตรียมตัว to prepare oneself, get ready

เตรียมพร้อม to be prepared, ready, on the alert; ready for action, in a state of preparedness

เตละ sesame

เตลิด to disperse, go in all directions, run off

เตลิดเปิดเปิง to take off, flee; scattered

เตอร์กี, ตุรกี Turkey

เต่อ as in สั้นเต่อ mini, brief

เตอะ as in หนาเตอะ thick

เตะ to kick, boot

เตะจมูก pungent; to get a whiff (of)

เตะโด่ง to be kicked upstairs

เตะตา noticeably; striking, eye-catching

เตะถ่วง to hold back, delay

เตะโทษ to get a free kick

เตะปี๊บ to kick up one's heels, have a fling

เตะฝุ่น to be jobless

เตา stove, brazier

เตาผิง heater, stove; fireplace

เตาเผา kiln

เตาฟู่ pressure stove

เตาไฟ stove

เตารีด iron

　เตารีดไฟฟ้า electric iron

เตาอบ oven

เต่า tortoise, turtle, terrapin

เต่ากระ hawk turtle

เต่าตนุ sea turtle

เต่าทอง ladybug, ladybird

เต้า[1] breast, udder (นมสัตว์เช่นแพะ); breast-shaped

เต้าปืน cap-hole, touch-hole, fuse-hole

เต้าปูน red lime container

เต้า[2] as in **ลูกเต้า** children, offspring, progeny

เต๋า dice *(พหู)*, die *(เอก)*

เต๋าเขย่า a gambling game played with three dice

เต้าเจี้ยว soy sauce

เต่าตุ่น as in **โง่เง่าเต่าตุ่น** utterly stupid, a clod

เต้าหู้ tofu, soybean curd

เต้าหู้ยี้ fermented soybean sauce

เต้าฮวย bean curd and ginger syrup

เตาะแตะ toddling

เดินเตาะแตะ to toddle

เติ่ง as in **ค้างเติ่ง** to get stuck; to be hung up, left undone

เติบ big, large

เติบโต, เติบใหญ่ to grow up, mature

มือเติบ extravagant, spendthrift

เติม to add, augment, put in, insert

เติมคำในช่องว่าง to fill in the blanks / to insert the right word in the blank spaces

เติมน้ำตาลในกาแฟ to put some sugar in the coffee / add sugar to the coffee

เพิ่มเติม to add, supplement; additional, in addition, extra

เตี่ย father

เตี้ย short; low; dwarf

เตี้ยอุ้มค่อม the halt leading the blind

เตียง bed, bedstead

เตียงคนไข้ hospital bed

เตียงคู่ double bed

เตียงเดี่ยว single bed

เตียงผ้าใบ camp bed, cot

เตียงแฝด twin beds

เตียงลา stands

เตียงเหล็ก metal bed

เตียน cleared, bare, clean, smooth, leveled; all

consumed; removed

เตี่ยว short pants knotted at the waist; loincloth

เตือน to remind; to warn, admonish, caution, forewarn; to advise, counsel

เตือนใจ to recall to mind, remind

คติเตือนใจ maxim

เตือนตา to be inviting to look at, attractive

เตือนภัย danger signal

เตือนสติ to caution, warn, give a warning (to)

แต่[1] since, from, at

แต่ก่อน before, formerly, previously

แต่ก่อนนี้ formerly, in the past

แต่กาลก่อน since the days of old, a long-time ago, in ancient times

แต่เช้า early in the morning

แต่เช้าจนค่ำ from morning till night

แต่เช้าตรู่ at dawn

แต่ดึกดำบรรพ์ from time immemorial, since the earliest times

แต่เด็ก from childhood

แต่เดิม at first; originally; /in/from/ the beginning, from before

แต่ต้นจนจบ from beginning to end

แต่นี้ไป from now on

แต่นั้นมา ever since, from that time on, from then on

แต่โบราณกาล from olden times, from ancient times

แต่มืด before dawn

แต่แรก in the beginning

แต่แรกเริ่ม at the commencement, from the beginning

แต่แรกเห็น at first sight

แต่เล็กแต่น้อย since one was small, from childhood

แต่วัน early

แต่ไหนแต่ไรมา always; never; since long ago, heretofore

ต
ถ
ท
ธ
น
บ
ป
ผ
ฝ
พ
ฟ
ภ
ม
ย
ร
ฤ
ฤๅ
ล
ว
ศ
ษ
ส
ห
ฬ
อ
ฮ

แต่[2] but, however; only

แต่ทว่า however, but

แต่ประการใด in any way, whatsoever, at all

ไม่เป็นความจริงแต่ประการใด not at all true / completely untrue / to have no truth whatsoever

แต่ผู้เดียว exclusive, sole

แต่เพียง only, just

แต่ลำพัง alone, on one's own

แต่ว่า but

แต่อย่างใด in any way

แม้แต่ even, not even

ล้วนแต่ all

แล้วแต่ depending on, it depends; as you like, to be up to (someone)

แล้วแต่จะโปรด as it may please (the court etc)

เว้นแต่ unless, except, on condition that, if not

สุดแท้แต่ as; who knows

หากแต่ but, however

แต่[3] *as in* **แต่ละ** each

แต่ละท่าน each person

แต่ละประเทศ each country

แต่ละปี each year

ไม่เว้นแต่ละวัน day in day out, every day without exception

แตก[1] to be separated, separate; to be broken, break, shattered; to germinate, sprout; to appear; to break up

แตกกระจาย scattered, shattered, broken into pieces

แตกกลุ่ม to go one's own way, go separate ways; to divide up

แตกกัน to split, break up, separate, divide

แตกกิ่ง to sprout

แตกกิ่งก้านสาขา to branch out, have ramifications, develop

แตกแขนง to have ramifications, branch out

แตกคอ to split, break up, have a falling out, quarrel

แตกเงิน to get change, to break (a bill)

ขอแตกเงินสักร้อยหน่อย Can you give me change of a hundred?

แตกฉาน to be well-versed (in), be knowledgeable (in, about), have a profound knowledge (of); to be dispersed, scattered

แตกดับ to, perish, be destroyed

แตกต่าง to differ, be different (from)

แตกต่างกัน differing

แตกตื่น to panic; to be agitated; to flee in terror; excitedly

แตกแถว to get out of line

แตกทัพ to be routed

แตกเนื้อสาว pubescent, to reach puberty

แตกใบ to bud

แตกฝูง to go off alone, separate from the herd; unconventional, contrary

แตกพวก to break off from one's group

แตกฟอง to foam, froth, frothy

น้ำลายแตกฟอง to talk away, talk up a storm, talk non-stop

แตกแยก divided, disunited, broken apart

แตกร้าว to divide over conflicting opinions

แตกสลาย to go to pieces, crumble, break (up, apart), dissolve

แตกหัก decisive

ขั้นแตกหัก crucial, final

ถังแตก broke

แตก[2] proficiently, clearly, well

แตกฉาน skilled, experienced, expert, well-versed

เขามีความรู้แตกฉาน He has a thorough knowledge (of)

แตง melon, fruit of a vine

แตงกวา cucumber

แตงไทย musk melon

แตงโม watermelon

แต่ง to arrange; to appoint; to decorate, adorn, ornament; to dress; to embellish; to finish, retouch, trim, touch up; to govern; to put on make-up; to write, compose

แต่งกลอน to write poetry

แต่งกาย to dress, get dressed

    การแต่งกาย dress, attire

    แต่งกายชุดสากล coat and tie, lounge suit

แต่งขาว to wear white

แต่งโคลง to write poetry

แต่งงาน to marry, /get/be/ married, wed

แต่งดำ to wear black, wear mourning

แต่งตั้ง to appoint, name

แต่งตัว to dress, get dressed, put on some clothes, wear

    แต่งตัวไว้ทุกข์ to wear mourning

แต่งเต็มยศ to wear full dress; in full dress; all dressed up

แต่งทนาย to appoint /counsel/a lawyer/an attorney/

แต่งทูต to send an envoy

แต่งบ้าน to furnish a house

แต่งผม to dress the hair, go to the hair-dressers

แต่งแผล to dress a wound, put on a dressing

แต่งไม้ to finish a piece of wood

แต่งร้าน to decorate a shop

แต่งเล็บ to have a manicure, manicure

    ช่างแต่งเล็บ manicurist

แต่งหน้า to put on make-up, wear make-up

แต่งหนังสือ to write

แต้จิ๋ว Teow Chao

แตด clitoris

แตน hornet

แต้ม[1] to daub, paint, mark; to anoint

แต้มสี to retouch; to color

แต้ม[2] square; stratagem, tactic, move; point

แต้มคู tactics, strategy, maneuver

แต้มหัก futile stratagem; foiled

จนแต้ม to be outsmarted, cornered

เดินแต้ม to make a shrewd move, act shrewdly; to move

ต่อแต้ม dominoes

เสียแต้ม to lose points

ห้าแต้ม (do) something foolish, (commit) a faux pas

แตร bugle, trumpet, horn; klaxon

แตรงอน trumpet

แตรรถยนต์ horn

แตรวง brass band

แตะ[1] to touch; to hit

แตะต้อง to touch

แตะต้องไม่ได้ untouchable, sacrosanct

ห้ามแตะต้อง Do not touch.

แตะ[2] as in รองเท้าแตะ slippers, sandals, thongs, scuffs, flip-flops

โต big, large

โตขึ้น bigger, getting bigger, enlarging; growing up

โตแค่ไหน How big is it?

โตเต็มที่ full-grown, mature

โตนัก imposing

โตเป็นสาว to be grown up, to be a young lady

โตเป็นหนุ่ม to be grown up, to be a young man

โตแล้ว to be grown up, adult; fully grown

คุยโต to boast, talk big, brag

เป็นใหญ่เป็นโต to become a bigshot

หน้าใหญ่ใจโต openhanded, munificent, lavish

ใหญ่โต big, huge; powerful, formidable

โต้ to object, make a rejoinder; to attack, oppose, counter; to answer, reply, respond, retort; to resist, withstand

ต
ถ
ท
ธ
น
บ
ป
ผ
ฝ
พ
ฟ
ภ
ม
ย
ร
ฤ
ฦ
ล
ว
ศ
ษ
ส
ห
ฬ
อ
ฮ

โต้คลื่น to go surfing

โต้คารม to argue

โต้ตอบ to correspond; to carry on a /dialogue /conversation/; to answer, retort; to argue; to retaliate, strike back

  การโต้ตอบ retaliation

  จดหมายโต้ตอบ correspondence

โต้เถียง to argue, dispute

โต้แย้ง to dispute, raise an objection, object, argue, refute, rebut, oppose, contest; to answer, maintain

  ข้อโต้แย้ง argument against, objection, point in opposition, opposing view; dispute, disagreement

  คำโต้แย้ง counterstatement

โต้รุ่ง all-night

  ร้านอาหารโต้รุ่ง all-night food shop

โต้ลม to go against the wind; stand up to the wind, /resist/withstand/ the wind

โต้วาที to debate, have a debate

โต๋เต๋ to roam around, go gallivanting

โต้โผ kingpin

โตก footed tray

โต้ง lead cock, cock of the walk

โต้งๆ with one's own eyes

โตงเตง dangling, hanging, pendant, swinging

โตมร lance, javelin, spear

โต๊ะ table

  โต๊ะเขียนหนังสือ desk

  โต๊ะเครื่องดื่ม buffet, bar

  โต๊ะเครื่องแป้ง dressing table

  โต๊ะจีน Chinese food

  โต๊ะทำงาน desk; worktable

  โต๊ะบูชา altar table, altar

  โต๊ะเรียน desk

  กินโต๊ะ to have a Chinese dinner; to gang up (on someone)

  ตั้งโต๊ะ to set the table; to put the food on the table

  ผ้าปูโต๊ะ tablecloth

  ร่วมโต๊ะ to sit at the same table (with)

โต๊ะอิหม่าม imam

ใต้ under, beneath, below; south

  ใต้ดิน underground; clandestine, secret; surreptitious

  ใต้ถุน under the house; area under a raised dwelling

  ใต้เท้า your highness; your honor

    ใต้เท้ากรุณา your excellency

  ใต้น้ำ underwater, submarine

    เรือใต้น้ำ submarine

  ใต้ฝ่าละอองธุลีพระบาท Your Majesty

  ใต้ฝ่าละอองพระบาท Your Royal Highness

  ใต้ลม in the path of the wind

  ขีดเส้นใต้ to underline, underscore

  ตะวันตกเฉียงใต้ southwest

  ทิศใต้ south

  ปักษ์ใต้, ภาคใต้ the south

  ภายใต้ under, subject to

ไต kidney; wen (เนื้อแข็ง); a cyst

  ไตปลา fish maw

ไต่ to walk; to climb

  ไต่คู้, ไม้ไต่คู้ the tonal mark " ็ "

  ไต่เดียะ to scramble up, climb nimbly

  ไต่เต้า to make one's way up, climb

  ไต่ถาม to inquire (of someone), make an inquiry

  ไต่ลวด to tightrope walk

  ไต่สวน to hold an inquiry, inquire (into), conduct a hearing, investigate

ไต๋ (to have) something up one's sleeve

  เผยไต๋ to show one's cards

ไต้ torch

  ขี้ไต้ tinder

  เข้าไต้เข้าไฟ twilight

  ผีพุ่งไต้ shooting star, meteor

ไต้ก๋ง captain of a Chinese junk

ไตร three, triple, tri-, threefold

ไตรจีวร a set of three yellow robes

ไตรทวาร the three /doors/avenues/ of action: body, speech and mind

ไตรปิฎก Tipitaka, the Pali Canon, the Triple Basket (the three divisions of the Buddhist canon: Vinaya, Suttanta, and Abhidhamma)

ไตรเพท the three vedas

ไตรภพ the Three /Worlds/Spheres/

ไตรภูมิ *see* ไตรภพ

ไตรยางค์ trifold; three classes of Thai consonants

ไตรรงค์ the tricolor, three colors of the Thai flag: blue, white and red

ไตรรัตน์ the Triple Gem

ไตรลักษณ์ the three characteristics of existence : impermanence, incompleteness and non-self

ไตรสรณคมน์ the three refuges: the Buddha, the Dharma, and the Sangha

ไตรสิกขา the threefold method of training in morality, concentration, and wisdom

ไตร่ตรอง to consider, think (something) over, mull over, ponder, reflect (on)

ต
ถ
ท
ธ
น
บ
ป
ผ
ฝ
พ
ฟ
ภ
ม
ย
ร
ฤ
ฤๅ
ล
ว
ศ
ษ
ส
ห
ฬ
อ
ฮ

ก
ข
ค
ฆ
ง
จ
ฉ
ช
ซ
ฌ
ญ
ฎ
ฏ
ฐ
ฑ
ฒ
ณ
ด
ต
ถ

ถก to pull up, hitch up, raise; to discuss
เรื่องนี้ต้องมาถกกันก่อน That's something we'll have to /talk about/discuss/.

ถกเขมร to hitch up a wrap-around cloth in the form of a breech clout

ถกแขนเสื้อ to push up one's sleeves

ถกเถียง to discuss, debate; to be under discussion, in dispute

ถกปัญหา to discuss

ถดถอย to lessen, weaken, fade, recede, be in recession; to regress

ถนน road, street, avenue, way

ถนนคอนกรีต concrete road

ถนนยุทธศาสตร์ strategic road

ถนนราดยาง asphalt road, paved road, macadam road

ถนนโรยหิน gravel road

ถนนลูกกระนาด corduroy road

ถนนหนทาง roads, ways

ถนนหลวง public road, public thoroughfare

ตามท้องถนน in the middle of the road; /along/in/ the road

ปากถนน at the beginning of the /street/ road/, upper end of the road

มุมถนน corner

ริมถนน by the side of the road, roadside

หัวถนน end of the road, corner

หมากลางถนน stray dog; homeless wretch

ถนอม to take care of, treat with care, cherish, nurture, conserve

ถนอมกาย to take care of one's health

ถนอมกำลัง to conserve one's energy

ถนอมน้ำใจ to be solicitous (of); to spare someone's feelings

ถนอมอาหาร to preserve food, food preservation

ทะนุถนอม *see* **ทะนุถนอม** *หน้า 224*

ถนัด skillful, good at, handy (at), up one's alley;

clearly; easily
ผมถนัดด้านการช่าง I'm good at mechanical things.

ถนัดขวา right-handed

ถนัดใจ to feel right about

ถนัดถนี่ perfectly, clearly

ชกถนัดถนี่ to /sock/punch/ someone with full force

เห็นถนัดถนี่ to see perfectly clearly

ถนัดปาก to feel right about /speaking/ saying/

ถนัดมือ handy, easy to handle

ตามถนัด as (one) likes, as it suits (one), whichever way is easier

ผิดถนัด to be all wrong, clearly wrong; of course not

ไม่ถนัด not good at, not one's cup of tea

จับไม่ถนัด to be unable to get a good grip

พูดไม่ถนัด to find it difficult to /say/ speak/

ฟังไม่ถนัด not hear very well, to be indistinct

ถนิม ornament

ถนิมสร้อย delicate, frail, fragile

ถม[1] to fill

ถมดิน, ถมที่ to fill /the land/a plot of land/ (with earth)

ถมถืด *see* **ถมไป**

ถมเถ *see* **ถมไป**

ถมไป loads (of), lots (of), plenty (of), more than enough

ดินถม (ที่) earth fill

ทับถม to pile up; to be overwhelmed (by); to make something worse (by), pile it on

ถม[2] *as in* **เครื่องถม** nielloware, niello

ถ่ม to spit

ถ่มน้ำลาย to spit, expectorate

ถ่มน้ำลายใส่ to spit at someone

ถมึงทึง sullen, dour, lowering, angry looking

ถลก to hitch up, push up; to peel

    ถลกกระโปรง to hitch up the skirt

    ถลกหนัง to skin, peel back the skin

        โดนถลกหนัง to be fleeced

    ถลกศีรษะ to scalp

ถลกบาตร cloth sling for a monk's bowl

ถลน to protrude, stick out, bulge

    ตาถลน popping eyes

ถล่ม to collapse, cave in, subside

    ถล่มด้วยปืนใหญ่ to destroy by artillery fire

    แผ่นดินถล่ม earthquake

    ภูเขาถล่ม landslide

ถลอก to be excoriated, skinned, abraded, scraped

    ถลอกปอกเปิก lacerated

    หัวเข่าถลอก The knee is /skinned/ scraped/.

    หัวถลอก The head is /excoriated/ scraped/.

ถลัน to force one's way, push one's way in, enter stubbornly

ถลา to trip; to fall (/forward/backward/ etc), to slip

ถลำ to take a false step, make a mistake; to break into, intrude

    ถลำตัว to go too far (to extricate oneself)

    ถลำลึก to be deeply involved (in)

ถลึง, ถลึงตา to glare (at), glower (at)

ถลุง to smelt, refine; to give a drubbing

    ถลุงเงินพ่อแม่ He went through his parent's money like water. / to waste one's patrimony.

    เขาถลุงคู่ต่อสู้จนหมอบ He gave his opponent a drubbing.

ถ่วง to weight; to slow, delay, retard; to sink (by weighting)

    ถ่วงความเจริญ to retard progress

    ถ่วงดุล to balance; to offset

    ถ่วงน้ำ to /drown/sink/ by weighting

    ถ่วงน้ำหนัก to weight

    ถ่วงเรื่อง to stall, put something on hold

    ถ่วงล้อ to balance a wheel

    ถ่วงเวลา to stall, play for time

    ถ่วงอำนาจ balance of power

    ความโน้มถ่วง gravity

    แรงโน้มถ่วง gravity

    ลูกถ่วง weight

ถ้วน all; in all, only

    หนึ่งร้อยบาทถ้วน one hundred baht only

    ถ้วนถี่ carefully, thoroughly, scrupulously

    ถ้วนหน้า everyone, one and all

    ครบถ้วน in full, to be all there, complete with everything

    นับไม่ถ้วน countless, innumerable, incalculable

ถ้วย cup

    ถ้วยแก้ว glassware; glass cup

    ถ้วยชา teacup

    ถ้วยชาม crockery, dishes

    ถ้วยรางวัล cup, trophy

ถวาย to offer, present

    ถวายตัว to offer oneself to a king or prince, to go into the service of a king

    ถวายน้ำพระพิพัฒน์สัตยา to drink an oath of allegiance

    ถวายบังคม to pay homage (to the /king/ queen/)

    ถวายพระพร May it please Your /Grace/ Majesty/.

    ถวายพระเพลิง to cremate (a king)

    น้อมเกล้าฯ ถวาย humbly to offer (something to a king)

ถวิล to think of, miss, long for, yearn for (someone)

ถ่อ punting pole; to punt; to make an effort (to)

    ถ่อกาย to make an effort (to), struggle

    ถ่อกายมาถึงนี่ to /make an effort/struggle/ to get here

ถ
ท
ธ
น
บ
ป
ผ
ฝ
พ
ฟ
ภ
ม
ย
ร
ฤ
ฤๅ
ล
ว
ศ
ษ
ส
ห
ฬ
อ
ฮ

ก
ข
ค
ฆ
ง
จ
ฉ
ช
ซ
ฌ
ญ
ฎ
ฏ
ฐ
ฑ
ฒ
ณ
ด
ต
ถ

ถ่อสังขาร *see* **ถ่อกาย** *หน้า 209*

ถ่อเรือ to /punt/pole/ a boat

ถอก to draw back the foreskin; circumcised

ถอง to elbow, poke with one's elbow

ถองเหล้า to drink heavily,

ถ่อง *as in* **ถ่องแท้** true, genuine, real, clear, thorough

เขาเข้าใจเรื่องราวได้ถ่องแท้ *He has a /clear/ thorough/real/ understanding of the situation.*

ถอด to take off, remove, doff (หมวก), divest; to reproduce, make a copy; re-, de-

ถอดกลอน to unbolt, unlock

ถอดเขี้ยวถอดงา to reform

ถอดความ to paraphrase, give the gist (of), summarize

ถอดจากตำแหน่ง to dismiss, discharge; remove from office

ถอดด้าม *as in* **ใหม่ถอดด้าม** brand new

ถอดถอน to dismiss, discharge

ถอดแบบ to reproduce, copy; to take after (someone)

ถอดรหัส to decode

ถอดรองเท้า to /take off/remove/ one's shoes

ถอดสลัก to defuse

ถอดเสื้อ to take off one's /shirt/coat/

ถอดเสื้อผ้า to undress

ถอดหมวก doff one's hat, take one's hat off; to tip one's hat

ถอน to withdraw; to retract; to uproot, pull out; to extract, pluck

ถอนขน to pluck (a chicken, hair's, etc)

ถอนขนห่าน to milk dry

ถอนคดี to withdraw a case

ถอนคำพูด to retract, take back what one has said

ถอนคำสั่ง to /cancel/rescind/revoke/ an order

ถอนเงิน to draw money, make a with-

drawal

ถอนใจ to sigh

ถอนใจใหญ่ to give a big sigh, heave a sigh

ถอนฉุน to get mad, become irritated, get worked up

ถอนชื่อ to withdraw support; to expunge a name, strike (from)

ถอนตะปู to pull out a nail

ถอนตัว to withdraw, decline

ถอนทุน to recoup one's investment

ถอนใบอนุญาต to revoke a license

ถอนพิษ to counteract a /poison/ bad effect/

ถอนฟ้อง to withdraw /a complaint/an action/

ถอนฟัน to pull a tooth, extract a tooth, have an extraction

ถอนรากถอนโคน to eradicate, extirpate, root out

ถอนสมอ to weigh anchor, raise an anchor

ถอนสายบัว to curtsy

ถอนหงอก to call (a senior person) to task, embarrass (an elder)

ถอนหมั้น to break off an engagement

ถ่อม *as in* **ถ่อมตัว** to be modest, unassuming, self-effacing, humble

ถอย to retreat, draw back, withdraw; to weaken; to back up; to move; to decrease, diminish; to be discouraged

ถอยกรูด to flee, retreat in disarray

ถอยกลับ to retreat

ถอยกำลัง to weaken, lose strength

ถอยฉาก to dodge, evade cunningly

ถอยทัพ to withdraw /troops/forces/an army/, order a retreat

ถอยเท้า to step back

ถอยรถ to back up (a car); to buy a new car

ถอยร่น to /retreat/withdraw/ in disarray

ถอยหน้าถอยหลัง vacillating; to move backwards and forwards

ถอยหนี to flee, run away (from something), retreat

ถอยหลัง to back up, go in reverse; to regress, go backwards

ถอยหลังเข้าคลอง reactionary, retrograde, retrogressive

ถ่อย low, vile, base, coarse, crude

ไอ้ถ่อย You shit!

ถ้อย word

ถ้อยความ contents, text, wording

ถ้อยคำ words, wording, text; expression(s); declaration, statement

ถ้อยคำเท็จ false statement

ถ้อยแถลง statement, declaration

ถ้อยทีถ้อยอาศัยกัน reciprocal, mutually dependent, dependent upon one another

ชัดถ้อยชัดคำ clearly, distinctly, well enunciated, articulate clearly; (to speak) emphatically

หมอถ้อยหมอความ a glib talker, fast talker; know-it-all

ถัก to plait, braid; to crochet; to knit

ถักเปีย to braid, make braids

ถักลูกไม้ to crochet

ถักเสื้อ to knit (a sweater)

เย็บปักถักร้อย sewing, needlework

ถัง barrel, tank, cylinder; bucket, tub, pail; drum; a unit of measurement of about 20 litres

ถังเก็บน้ำ cistern

ถังแก๊ส gas cylinder

ถังขยะ garbage pail

ถังซีเมนต์ concrete pipe

ถังแตก broke

ถังน้ำ water tank

ถังน้ำมัน gas tank

ถังผง dustbin, trash basket

ถังเมล์ nightsoil bucket

ถังออกซิเจน oxygen cylinder, cylinder of oxygen

ตกถังข้าวสาร to hit the jackpot, luck out, be in clover

ตัวถัง body

ถัด[1] to slide along on one's bottom

ถัด[2] following, next, succeeding

ถัดจากนั้น after that, then; thereafter

ถัดไป next, succeeding

ถัน breast, bosom

ถัว to average

ถัวเฉลี่ย on the average

ค่าอาหารเลี้ยงแขก 100 คน ถัวเฉลี่ยตกหัวละ 20 บาท For 100 guests, the average food cost per head would be 20 baht.

ถั่ว bean, pea; a gambling game played with cowries

ถั่วเขียว green chick-pea

ถั่วงอก beansprout

ถั่วดำ black bean

อัดถั่วดำ to bugger, have anal sex, sodomize

ถั่วตัด peanut brittle

ถั่วทอง yellow gram, yellow chick-pea

ถั่วแปบ hyacinth bean

ถั่วฝรั่งเศส haricot, stringbean

ถั่วฝักยาว stringbean

ถั่วพร้า jack bean

ถั่วพู winged bean, princess bean

ถั่วเพาะ beansprout

ถั่วแระ pigeon pea

ถั่วลันเตา sugar pea, green peas; snow peas

ถั่วลิสง peanut, ground nut

ถั่วเหลือง soya bean, soybean

ตาถั่ว to be blind, fail to see

ฝักถั่ว pea pod

ส.ส. ฝักถั่ว yes-man parliamentarian

ถ้า if, although, provided; suppose

ถ
ท
ธ
น
บ
ป
ผ
ฝ
พ
ฟ
ภ
ม
ย
ร
ฤ
ฦ
ล
ว
ศ
ษ
ส
ห
ฬ
อ
ฮ

ถ้าผมไม่ไปคุณจะว่ายังไงไหม Suppose I don't go, would you say anything?

ถ้ากระนั้น if so, in such case

ถ้าจะ if

   ถ้าจะว่าไป when it comes to that, after all, on second thought

   ถ้าจะว่าไป (แล้ว) เขาก็ไม่เลวนัก After all, he's not all that bad.

ถ้าเป็นเช่นนั้น if so, if such is the case, if that's the way it is

ถ้าเป็นเช่นว่า if so

ถ้าผมเป็นคุณ if I were you

ถ้าแม้ว่า even if

ถ้าไม่ if not

   ถ้าไม่อยู่ if (someone is) /not in/out/

ถ้าว่า, ถ้าหากว่า if, in case, provided, supposing

ถ้าอยู่ if /in/there/present/

ถาก to hoe; to trim, shape; to chip away; to graze

   ถากถาง to be sarcastic, cutting, biting

ถาง to clear; to weed

   ถางทาง to pave the way for

   ถางป่า to clear a forest, clear land

   ถางพง to clear of weeds

      หักร้างถางพง to clear land for farming

   ถางไร่ to clear a field

   ถางหญ้า to clear of grass

   แผ้วถาง to clear a way (for); to clear land

ถ่าง to spread, open wide

   ถ่างตาดูบ้างซิ Open your eyes!

ถาด tray

ถาโถม to push one's way in; to rush in, sweep in

ถาน monk's toilet

ถ่าน charcoal

   ถ่านคุ live coals

   ถ่านโค้ก coke

   ถ่านเถ้า ashes, cinders

ถ่านไฟ ember

   ถ่านไฟเก่า an old flame

   ถ่านไฟฉาย flashlight battery

   ถ่านไฟแช็ก flint

ถ่านมอด dying ember

ถ่านมอเตอร์ carbon brush

ถ่านหิน coal

ไม่เอาถ่าน lazy, hopeless

ถาม to ask; to examine, question

   ถามข่าว to ask (about someone or something), inquire (after, about)

   ถามค้าน to cross-examine

   ถามซอกแซก to be inquisitive, nosey

   ถามถึง to ask about

   ถามไถ่ to ask (about), inquire (after, about)

   ถามติง to do a re-direct examination

   ถามนำ to ask a leading question, lead a witness

   ถามหา to ask for, look for

   คำถาม question

      เครื่องหมายคำถาม question mark

   ซักถาม to question, interrogate

   ไต่ถาม to inquire (of someone), make an inquiry

   ยื่นกระทู้ถาม to file an interrogatory

   เรียนถาม to ask, inquire

   สอบถาม to inquire, make an inquiry, ask, question

ถ่าย to change; to decant, pour out; to discharge, to take out, to remove, to throw away, pour out; to reproduce, copy, photograph

   ถ่ายท้อง to have a bowel movement

   ถ่ายทอด to transfer, transmit; relay; to broadcast

      ถ่ายทอดสด to broadcast live, cover live

         การถ่ายทอดสด live coverage

      ถ่ายทอดเสียง to broadcast

   ถ่ายทำ to film; filming

   ถ่ายทุกข์ to go to the toilet, relieve one self

ถ่ายเท to ventilate, ventilated; to circulate

ถ่ายน้ำ to change the water

ถ่ายน้ำมันเครื่อง to change the oil

ถ่ายแบบ to make a copy (of); to /make/ take/ fashion photographs

ถ่ายปัสสาวะ to urinate, go to the bathroom

ถ่ายภาพ to take a /picture/photograph/

ถ่ายภาพยนตร์ to take a motion picture, to film (a scene etc), shoot a movie

ถ่ายยา to take a laxative

ถ่ายรถ to change /trains/buses/

ถ่ายรูป to take a picture, have one's picture taken, photograph

ถ่ายเลือด to have a blood transfusion

ถ่ายหนัง *see* ถ่ายภาพยนตร์

ถ่ายอุจจาระ to move one's bowels, have a bowel movement, pass a stool, defecate

ถ่ายเอกสาร to photocopy; make a photocopy, reproduce a document

ยาถ่าย laxative, physic, cathartic

รูปถ่าย photograph, picture

ถ่ายเดียว, โดยถ่ายเดียว only, exclusively, solely

ถาวร permanent, fixed, enduring, lasting

ถาวรวัตถุ permanent structure

ถ้ำ cave, cavern, grotto

ถ้ำชา tea-caddy

ถ้ำมอง peep-show

นักถ้ำมอง peeping Tom; to peep (at)

ถิ่น location; locality, territory, region; residence, home

ถิ่นฐาน home, where on lives, home base

ถิ่นที่อยู่ residence

ถี่ close together, frequent, in quick succession, one right after the other

ถี่ถ้วน carefully, scrupulously; stingy, miserly

ถี่ยิบ very /fine/close/; in rapid succession, very frequently

เขียนถี่ยิบ fine writing, close writing

ผ้าทอถี่ยิบ /finely/closely/ woven material

ยิงถี่ยิบ rapid fire

ความถี่ frequency

หายใจถี่ๆ rapid breathing

ถีบ to kick, boot, push with the foot

(หนู) ถีบจักร to /operate/run/ a /treadmill/squirrel cage/

ถีบจักรยาน to /ride/pedal/ a bicycle

ที่ถีบจักรยาน pedal

ถีบจักรเย็บผ้า to treadle, work the treadle

ถีบตัว to climb

ถีบรถ to ride a bicycle

ถีบหัวส่ง to get rid of someone

ถึก *as in* โคถึก a prime bull

ถึง[1] to reach, arrive (at), attain, to the extent of; enough, until; to, toward; although, even if; then

ถึงกัน to be in close /contact/touch/

ถึงกับ so

เขาป่วยถึงกับลุกไม่ขึ้น He was so sick he couldn't move. / He was far too sick to get up.

ถึงกำหนด to be due; to be time (for, to)

ถึงแก่กรรม to die

ถึงแก่พิราลัย to die (of a lord)

ถึงแก่มรณภาพ to die (of a monk or novice)

ถึงแก่อนิจกรรม to die (of a Phya)

ถึงแก่อสัญกรรม to die (of a Chao Phya)

ถึงขนาด to the extreme, so far, to such an extent that; very, super

ถึงขนาดนั้นเชียวเรอะ As far as that?

ไม่ถึงขนาดนั้นหรอก We didn't go /as far as that/so far/.

ถึงแค่นี้ up to here

ถึงจะ even if; only then

ถ้าคุณพูด เขาถึงจะฟัง If you talk to him only then will he listen. / He'll listen only to you.

ถึงจะเอาเงินล้านวางต่อหน้าฉันก็จะไม่เปลี่ยนใจ Even if you offer me a million, I won't

ถ
ท
ธ
น
บ
ป
ผ
ฝ
พ
ฟ
ภ
ม
ย
ร
ฤ
ฤๅ
ล
ว
ศ
ษ
ส
ห
ฬ
อ
ฮ

change my mind.

ถึงใจ, สะใจ to one's liking, just the way one like's something; to like, great!

ถึงตา one's turn

ถึงตาคุณแล้ว It's your turn.

ถึงที่ตาย to be doomed to die

ถึงพร้อม replete (with), endowed (with)

ถึงพริกถึงขิง hotly

ถึงเพียงนี้ so; so far

ถึงมือ to reach, get to someone, come to hand

ถึงแม้ว่า although, even though

ถึงไหม Can you reach it? Does it reach?

ถึงอย่างไรก็ดี nevertheless, nonetheless; what- ever the case may be, no matter what

ไปถึง to reach, arrive (at, in)

ไม่ถึง less than, short of; not even; not to reach, not to get (to)

หมายถึง to mean; to refer to; to imply

อ้างถึง to refer (to), cite; with reference to, Ref.

เอ่ยถึง to mention, talk about, speak of

ถึง[2] to accept, trust in

ถึงพระพุทธเจ้าเป็นที่พึ่ง to accept the Buddha as one's guide / trust in the Buddha

ถือ to hold; to hold oneself; to believe in, trust in, profess; to regard, deem, treat (as), hold, consider; to keep, observe, attach importance (to); to mind, take something seriously

ถือกำเนิด to be born (into, at, in), engendered, originated

ถือโกรธ to bear a grudge

ถือเคร่ง to observe strictly, to be strict (in a religious practice)

ถือโชคถือลาง superstitious

ถือดี arrogant, proud; to think a lot of oneself; how dare you..., who do you think

you are (to)

ถือตัว aloof, reserved; proud, to have a high opinion of oneself

ถือท้าย to steer, take the helm

ถือที่ดิน to hold land

ถือโทษ to blame

ถือน้ำพระพิพัฒน์สัตยา to drink an oath of allegiance

ถือบวช to observe religious rules

ถือปูน to do cement work

ถือเป็น to be treated as

    ถือเป็นความลับ confidential; to be treated as /confidential/secret/

    ถือเป็นอารมณ์ to take to heart

ถือผิว racist; to attach importance to race

ถือพวก, ถือพรรคถือพวก partisan, cliquish; to stick together

ถือพวงมาลัย to have one's hands on the wheel, steer

ถือยศ lordly, self-important; to pull one's rank (on someone)

ถือว่า regard, consider, assume; to think of oneself as

ถือวิสาสะ to think someone would not mind one's doing something (because of friendship or familiarity), take the liberty (of doing something), be presumptuous

ผมถือวิสาสะหยิบหนังสือของคุณไป I hope you don't mind my taking your book. / I took the liberty of taking your book.

ผมถือวิสาสะเขียนถึงท่าน I am taking the liberty of writing to you....

ทำไมเขาถือวิสาสะเขียนจดหมายถึงฉัน Why was he so presumptuous as to write to me?

ถือศีล to /keep/observe/ the rules (of religion), observe the precepts

ถือสา to mind

    ไม่ถือสา not to mind, not to be bothered by something; to be alright

ถือหาง to bet on (someone); to take sides with, support

ถือไหม Do you mind?

ถืออาวุธ to carry a weapon

ถือโอกาส to take the opportunity (to)

กระเป๋าถือ handbag, pocketbook; hand luggage

จับมือถือแขน to get familiar (with someone)

มือถือสากปากถือศีล hypocritical

    คนมือถือสากปากถือศีล hypocrite

ถุง pouch, bag

ถุงกระดาษ paper bag

ถุงเครื่องมือ tool bag, tool kit

ถุงเงิน moneybag

ถุงทางทูต diplomatic /bag/pouch

ถุงเท้า socks (สั้น), stockings (ยาว), hosiery

ถุงน่อง stocking; panty hose

    ถุงน่องพยุงขา support panty

ถุงน้ำ blister

ถุงน้ำดี gallbladder

ถุงพลาสติก plastic bag

ถุงมือ gloves

ถุงยา medicine bag

ถุงยางอนามัย condom

ถุงย่าม shoulder bag

ผ้าถุง tube skirt

ถุน to take a nip (of liquor/opium drink/)

ถุย to spit

ถู to rub, polish; to clean

ถูตัว to rub oneself (with something)

ถูเนื้อถูตัว to scrub oneself

ถูบ้าน to clean the house

ถูมือ to rub one's hands together (with pleasure)

ถูลู่ถูกัง forcibly

พอถูไถ enough to get by on, it's not easy

สบู่ถูตัว toilet soap

ถูก[1] to be (expressing passive voice)

ถูกกระทำ to be put under a spell, hexed

ถูกขโมย to be robbed

ถูกจับ to be arrested, caught, apprehended, seized

ถูกจำ to be jailed, imprisoned

ถูกต้ม to be duped, taken in (by), swindled (out of something)

ถูกถอด to be removed, ousted

ถูกทอดทิ้ง to be abandoned, neglected forsaken

ถูกปรับ fined

ถูกวางยา to be poisoned

ถูกหลอกลวง to be duped

ถูก[2] right, correct

ถูกกฎหมาย lawful, legal

ถูกต้อง right, correct, true, authentic; precisely

    ตัวบทที่ถูกต้อง authentic text

    รับรองคำแปลถูกต้อง certified true translation

ถูกทำนอง in the right way, proper

ถูกทีเดียว right-on; certainly, absolutely

ถูกแล้ว yes, that's right, sure

ผิดถูก right or wrong

ไม่ถูก *see* **ไม่ถูก** *หน้า 386*

ถูก[3] to touch

ถูกคอกัน compatible, to get on well together, get along well with someone, like one another, hit it off

ถูกใจ to like; to one's liking

ถูกชะตา to hit it off; appealing, attractive

ถูกเนื้อต้องตัว to have physical contact (with), touch

ถูกโรค to be effective; to work; inviting

ถูกลอตเตอรี่ to win a lottery

ถูกเส้นกัน to get along (with), like, have a lot in common

ยิงถูก to hit

ถูก[4] cheap, inexpensive

ซื้อได้ถูก to get (something) cheap

ถ
ท
ธ
น
บ
ป
ผ
ฝ
พ
ฟ
ภ
ม
ย
ร
ฤ
ฤๅ
ล
ว
ศ
ษ
ส
ห
ฬ
อ
ฮ

ราคาถูก low-priced, cheap, economical

เถน /loose/wanton/ monk

เถร-, เถระ a senior monk

    เถรภูมิ senior rank (of the Sangha)

    เถรานุเถระ Buddhist monks in general, monks of all ranks

เถรี senior nun

เถลไถล to loiter, dawdle, dillydally, waste time, linger on the way

เถลิง to ascend, mount; to start

    เถลิงศก to start the new year

    เถลิงถวัลยราชสมบัติ to ascend the throne

    เถลิงอำนาจ to come to power

เถลือกถลน to be frantic

เถอะ an auxiliary expressing decision or agreement

    เถอะน่า come on

    เถอะน่าดอรีน ดิ้นกันเถอะ Come on Doreen, let's dance.

    ช่างเถอะ forget it, don't pay any attention (to it).

    เชิญเถอะ Go /ahead/along/!

    ไปกันเถอะ Let's go!

    เมินเสียเถอะ No way!

    เอาเถอะ Okay!

เถา[1] vine, liana; line, family, pedigree

    เถาวัลย์ liana, vine, creeper

    เทือกเถา clan, origins

    ไม้เถา vine, climber

เถา[2] graded series

    ปิ่นโต 2 เถา two-tiered tiffin carrier

เถ้า[1] *see* **เฒ่า** *หน้า 157*

    เถ้าแก่ *see* **เฒ่าแก่** *หน้า 157*

เถ้า[2] ash

เถาะ the Year of the Rabbit

เถิก with receding hairline; exposed, opened up

เถิด an auxiliary verb indicating agreement or decision

ลืมเสียเถิด Forget it!, Forget about it!

เอาเถิด Let's do it!, Go for it!

เถิดเทิง bottle drum, tall drum shaped like a bottle

เถียง to argue, dispute, bicker

    เถียงกัน to wrangle

    เถียงดื้อๆ to argue /stubbornly/obstinately/

    เถียงไม่ขึ้น indisputable, inarguable, incontrovertible; to argue without success, be unpersuasive

    ตำรวจมีหลักฐานแน่ชัดว่าคุณทำผิด จะเถียงยังไงก็เถียงไม่ขึ้น The police's evidence of your guilt is so clear as to be incontrovertible.

    ต่อล้อต่อเถียง to argue, be argumentative, talk back

    โต้เถียง to argue, dispute

    ถกเถียง to discuss, debate; to be under discussion, in dispute

เถือ to cut up, slice up

เถื่อน unlawful, illicit, smuggled; wild, savage, primitive; barbaric

    ของเถื่อน contraband, /smuggled/illegal/ goods

    ช้างเถื่อน wild elephant

    ป่าเถื่อน barbarous, savage

    ฝิ่นเถื่อน illicit opium

    หมอเถื่อน unlicensed doctor, village healer; quack doctor

    หูป่าตาเถื่อน simpleton, ignorant

    เหล้าเถื่อน illicit liquor, bootleg liquor, moonshine

แถบ section, side, piece; region, zone, area; stripe, strip

    แถบกางเกง stripe

    แถบนั้น somewhere there, around there

    แถบนี้ somewhere here, around here

    แถบร้อน torrid zone

    แถบอบอุ่น temperate zone

    เป็นแถบๆ in stripes, in rows; a block (of),

large number (of)

ผ้าแถบ breast cloth

ภูมิภาคแถบนี้ this region

แถม to give something extra, give in addition; besides

แถมท้าย to add at the end, wind up with

แถมพก to give a premium, give something special

แถมยังอวดดีนัก and arrogant besides

แถลง to give an account (of), inform, tell; to narrate, relate, report

แถลงการณ์ communiqué

แถลงการณ์ร่วม joint communiqué

แถลงข่าว press release, communiqué; to report the news

แถว row, line; area

แถวกลาง middle row

แถวนั้น over there, in that direction

แถวหน้า front row; in the forefront (of)

แถวหลัง back row

เข้าแถว to line up, get in line

เดินแถว to walk in line, march

ตรวจแถว to review (the troops, guard of honor, etc)

ต่อแถว to get at the end of the line

ตั้งแถว to /form/make/ a line

แตกแถว to get out of line

เป็นแถว one after the other, down the line; in lines, in rows

ลูกแถว rank and file, subordinate

ห้องแถว row house, shophouse

หัวแถว /head/front/ of the line; leader

โถ[1] covered earthen pot with wide mouth and small bottom

โถเครื่องแป้ง toilet set

โถส้วม toilet bowl

โถ[2] what a pity, oh dear

โถ ไม่น่าอายุสั้นเลย /What a pity/Oh dear/, *such a short life.*

โถง open; hall

โถม to push one's way in, rush in abruptly

โถมกำลัง to go all out

โถมทับ to overwhelm

โถมนาการ admiration (for), admiring, praising, lauding

ไถ to plough; to ask for something brazenly

ไถคู่ to plough with a team, plough double

ไถเงิน to ask for money, beg some money

ไถดะ to plough for the first time

ไถเดี่ยว to plough with a single /buffalo/ ox/, plough single

ไถแปร to plough for the second time

คันไถ plow handle

ไถ่ to redeem; ransom; to atone (for)

ไถ่ถอน to redeem

ไถ่ถาม, ถามไถ่ to ask (about), inquire (after, about)

ไถ่โทษ to atone (for)

ไถ่บาป to redeem (one's) sins; redemption

เยซูเป็นผู้ไถ่บาป Jesus is the redeemer of our sins.

ค่าไถ่ ransom

ไถ้ moneybelt, moneybag

ไถล to skid, slip, slide; to loiter, dawdle, linger on the way; to speak evasively

ถ
ท
ธ
น
บ
ป
ผ
ฝ
พ
ฟ
ภ
ม
ย
ร
ฤ
ฦ
ล
ว
ศ
ษ
ส
ห
ฬ
อ
ฮ

ทกล้า, ทแกล้ว the brave; warrior, trooper, soldier

ทชี, ธชี sadhu

ทด to repay, return; to add to, increase; to dam; to channel water, carry water (to); to carry (เลข)

    ทดแทน to substitute, replace; to repay, compensate

    ทดน้ำ to dam; to /channel/carry/ water

    ทดรอง to advance, pay in advance

        เงินทดรองจ่าย advance payment, disbursement

    ทดเลข to carry (a number)

ทดลอง to try; to experiment, test, give (something) a trial, try out something

    การทดลอง experiment, trial, experimentation

    ห้องทดลอง laboratory

ทดสอบ to test

ทน to put up with, tolerate, bear, stand, endure; to last

    ทนแดดทนฝน to be tough, hardy; to withstand the elements, hold up under the weather, weather

    ทนทาน lasting, durable; sturdy; hardy

    ทนทายาด to have great /stamina/staying power/; very durable

    ทนทุกข์ to suffer, bear hardship

    ทนพิษบาดแผลไม่ไหว to succumb

    ทนไฟ fireproof, fire resistant, refractory

    ทนไม่ไหว unbearable intolerable; to be unable to stand (/someone/something/) *ทนไม่ไหวแล้ว I can't bear it anymore.*

    ทนหิว to put up with hunger, stand being hungry

    เต็มทน unbearable, unendurable, awful *ฉันเบื่อเต็มทน I am unbearably /bored/fed up/.*

    เหลือทน unbearable, intolerable, insupportable, insufferable

ผู้หญิงคนนี้ปากร้ายเหลือทน She's an insufferable shrew.

ทนต์ tooth; tusk

ทนโท่ obvious, conspicuous, plain *เห็นอยู่ทนโท่ ยังจะถามอะไรอีก /It's so obvious./It's as plain as the nose on your face./It's right before your eyes./ What makes you keep asking?*

ทนาย royal officer; a master's representative

    ทนายความ lawyer, attorney at law, attorney, counselor at law, solicitor, barrister

    ทนายจำเลย defendant's /attorney/counsel/, attorney for the defendent

    ทนายโจทก์ plaintiff's /attorney/counsel/, attorney for the plaintiff

    ทนายหน้าหอ spokesman; majordomo

ทบ. army

ทบ to fold up, fold over; to add; to compound

    ทบทวน to revise, review, go over (something) again, recapitulate

    ทบทุน to put in more money; increase /a fund/the capital/

    ดอกเบี้ยทบต้น compound interest

ทบวง government /bureau/agency/, ministry

    ทบวงการ government bureau

    ทบวงการชำนัญพิเศษ specialized agency

    ทบวงการเมือง political bureau

    ทบวงมหาวิทยาลัย Ministry of University Affairs

ทมิฬ Tamil; vicious, savage, brutal

ทโมน dominant; assertive; monkey king; like a monkey; vast

ทยอย gradually, to do /bit by bit/in installments/a little at a time/

    แขกทยอยกันมา The guests /drifted in./ came a few at a time./

ทแยง diagonal, slanting, aslant

    ทแยงมุม diagonal

ทรกรรม torture, torment

ทรง[1] form, shape, figure, style; to sustain, support; to have; to remain

ทรงกลด to have a halo, with a halo

ทรงคุณวุฒิ qualified

ทรงเครื่อง to be appareled, attired, decked out; garnished

    เต้าหู้ทรงเครื่อง garnished tofu

    แม่ม่ายทรงเครื่อง wealthy widow

ทรงเครื่องใหญ่ to have a haircut *(royal word)*

ทรงจำ memory, recollection

ทรงตัว to remain the same, stable, hold one's own; to balance oneself

ทรงบาตร to place an offering in a monk's bowl

ทรงผม hairstyle, hair-do

ทรงพลัง powerful, mighty

ทรงไว้ซึ่ง to be, be endowed with
*ผู้พิพากษาคนนี้เป็นผู้ทรงไว้ซึ่งความยุติธรรม
This judge is a /just/fair/ person.*

ทรงศักดิ์ grand; honored; powerful

ทรงศีล devout, religious, moral, virtuous

ผู้ทรงเกียรติ honorable, your honor

ทรง[2] to be; a complement to verbs indicating royal action

ทรงเป็นประมุข to be the head of state

ทรงพระนาม to be named

ทรงพระสรวล to laugh

ทรงพระอักษร to write; to read

ทรงมีพระราชดำรัส to say (to)

ขอทรงพระเจริญ Long live the King!

ทรชน evildoer, wicked man; criminal

ทรชาติ wicked race

ทรพิษ smallpox

ทรพี brass ladle; ungrateful

ทรมาน to torture, punish, torment, mistreat

    การทรมาน mistreatment, torture

    ความทรมาน suffering, agony

ทรยศ to betray, stab someone in the back; traitorous, treacherous, perfidious

    คนทรยศ traitor

ทรยุค evil times

ทรรศนะ view, opinion, viewpoint

ทรราช tyrant

    ระบบทรราช tyranny

ทรลักษณ์ lacking good qualities, mongrel

ทรวง bosom, breast, chest

ทรวดทรง shape, form, appearance; figure

    ทรวดทรงดี a good figure

ทรหด tough, to be able to /take/stand up to/ punishment

ทระนง independent, self-confident; arrogant

ทรัพย์ property, possessions, wealth

    ทรัพย์จาง as in **โรคทรัพย์จาง** financial anemia

    ทรัพย์สมบัติ possessions, property, wealth

    ทรัพย์สิน property

        ทรัพย์สินทางปัญญา intellectual property

    ขุมทรัพย์ buried treasure, treasure trove, goldmine *(fig)*, source of wealth; natural resources

    โภคทรัพย์ consumer goods, consumables

    สินทรัพย์ assets

    หลักทรัพย์ security, collateral; securities

ทรัพยากร resources

    ทรัพยากรธรรมชาติ natural resources

    ทรัพยากรบุคคล individual resources; resource person

    ทรัพยากรมนุษย์ human resources

ทราบ to know, be aware of, learn, understand, hear (of)

    ทราบเกล้าทราบกระหม่อม to know, understand (used when speaking to royalty)

    ทราบดี to well know, realize

    ทราบว่า to learn, understand, hear

    จึงเรียนมาเพื่อทราบ for your information (ในภาษาอังกฤษมักไว้ต้นข้อความ)

    แจ้งให้ทราบ to inform, notify

    รับทราบ acknowledged; to acknowledge,

ท
ธ
น
บ
ป
ผ
ฝ
พ
ฟ
ภ
ม
ย
ร
ฤ
ฤๅ
ล
ว
ศ
ษ
ส
ห
ฬ
อ
ฮ

be informed, note

ทราม deteriorating, degenerating, decadent; bad, inferior; tender, soft

  ใจทราม depraved; low-minded

  โรคจิตทราม psychopathic, degenerate

  เลวทราม abominable, detestable; vicious, wicked

ทรามวัย girl

ทราย sand

  กระดาษทราย sandpaper, flint paper

  ดินทราย sandy soil

  ดินปนทราย sandy loam

  ทะเลทราย desert

  น้ำตาลทราย granulated sugar

  ผ้าทราย emerycloth

  หาดทราย beach; sandy bank

ทรุด to subside, settle, sink; to drop (down, into); to worsen, get worse, deteriorate *อาการมีแต่ทรงกับทรุด He is barely holding his own. / His condition is unstable.*

  ทรุดกาย to sink down, go down

  ทรุดโทรม dilapidated, worn (down, out), run down, in poor condition

  ทรุดลง to collapse, drop; to sink, down, get worse; take a turn for the worse

ทฤษฎี theory

ทลาย to collapse, tumble down, fall down; to be shattered

ทวง to ask for the return of something

  ทวงถาม to /demand/call for/ payment

  ทวงบุญคุณ to demand something in return for past favors

  ทวงสัญญา to claim on a promise

  ทวงหนี้ to demand payment of a debt

ท้วง to remind; to raise an objection (to), object

  ท้วงติง to advise against, dissuade

ท่วงท่า bearing, comportment

ท่วงที manner, deportment, bearing

ท่วงทีวาจา manner of speaking

ทันท่วงที timely, in time, just in time, in the nick of time

ท่วงทำนอง tone (of), way of /speaking/acting/etc/

ทวด great-grandfather, great-grandmother

ทวน[1] lance; a gold-smith's holder, collet; end-piece of a Thai fiddle

ทวน[2] against, go against, counter; to review, go over, run over (something) again

  ทวนกระแส to go against the /stream/current/, swim against the tide, go counter to (popular opinion, the fashion, what is /popular/in vogue/etc/)

  ทวนเข็มนาฬิกา counter clockwise

  ทวนคำ to repeat

  ทวนน้ำ up-stream, against the current

  ทวนลม against the wind

  ทวนสาบาน to break a vow

  ทบทวน to revise, review, go over (something) again, recapitulate

ท่วม to flood, inundate; to cover; to overflow

  ท่วมท้น overwhelming *ชนะด้วยคะแนนท่วมท้น to win by a landslide*

  น้ำท่วม flood, to be flooded

    น้ำท่วมทุ่ง empty talk, rubbish *พูดจาน้ำท่วมทุ่ง to talk nonsense / talk a lot and say nothing*

    น้ำท่วมปาก tongue-tied

  หนี้สินท่วมตัว to be overwhelmed by debt

ท้วม plump, stout

ทวย group, company (of)

  ทวยเทพ all the /devas/gods/, company of angels

  ทวยราษฎร์ the people, citizenry

ทวาย a tribe of Burmo-Tibetan stock

ทวาร gate, entry; entrance, orifice, opening

  ทวารบาล gatekeeper, doorkeeper, guardian of the entrance

  ทวารหนัก anus

ทวิ two, bi, bis

ทวิชาติ bird; Brahmin

ทวิบาท, ทวิบท biped, two-footed animal

ทวิภาค two /parts/sections/

มาตรา 8 ทวิ section 8 bis.

ทวี two; to increase, multiply, grow

ทวีคูณ doubled, twofold, double, twice, two times; exponential; to multiply; in multiples of

งานเพิ่มขึ้นทวีคูณ There's twice as much work as before. / The workload has doubled. จะต้องจองซื้อขั้นต่ำเป็นจำนวนเงินสิบล้าน และ ทวีคูณของหนึ่งล้านบาท ...are required to buy at least ten million and in multiples of one million,....

ทวีป continent

ทศ ten

ทศชาติ ten lives, ten rebirths

ทศทิศ the ten directions

ทศนิยม decimal system, decimal

ทศพล Bearer of the Ten Powers (a title of the Buddha)

ทหาร soldier

ทหารช่าง Army Engineers

ทหารแตร bugler

ทหารปืนใหญ่ artillery

ทหารผ่านศึก war veteran

ทหารม้า cavalry, cavalryman

ทหารยาม sentry, sentinel

ทหารราบ infantry; infantryman

ทหารราบอากาศ paratrooper

ทหารเรือ navy; sailor, navyman

ทหารสื่อสาร Signal Corps; member of the Signal Corps

ทหารใหม่ new recruit

ทหารอากาศ air force man

ทหารอาสาสมัคร militia

กรมทหาร regiment; military installation

กองทหาร a military force

ข้าราชการทหาร military personnel

ทแกล้วทหาร soldiers, troops, men

นายทหาร officer

นายทหารชั้นสัญญาบัตร commissioned officer

นายทหารบก army officer

นายทหารเรือ naval officer

นายทหารอากาศ air force officer

ผู้บัญชาการทหาร commander in chief

ราชการทหาร military service

ทอ[1] to weave

ทอผ้า to weave

ช่างทอผ้า weaver

ทอ[2] to cast; to shine

ทอแสง to cast light, shine

ท่อ pipe, conduit, tube, duct, main

ท่อแตก The /main/pipe/ is broken.

ท่อน้ำ waterpipe

ท่อประปา waterpipe, water main

ท่อยาง rubber /hose/pipe/

ท่อรั่ว The pipe is leaking.

ท่อเสีย The pipe is no good.

ท่อใหญ่ water main

ท่อไอเสีย exhaust pipe

ฝังท่อ to /bury/lay/ pipes

วางท่อ to lay pipes, lay a pipeline

ท้อ discouraged, disheartened

ท้อถอย discouraged; dispirited; to give up

ท้อแท้ dejected

ย่อท้อ daunted, discouraged, disheartened; intimidated

ทอง gold

ทองขาว nickel; platinum; distributor contact points

ทองคำ gold

ทองคำขาว white gold

ทองคำเปลว gold leaf

ทองเค fine gold

ท
ธ
น
บ
ป
ผ
ฝ
พ
ฟ
ภ
ม
ย
ร
ฤ
ฤๅ
ล
ว
ศ
ษ
ส
ห
ฬ
อ
ฮ

ทองแดง copper

ทองทึบ gold cladding

ทองแท่ง gold ingot, gold bar

ทองนพคุณ pure gold

ทองบรอนซ์ bronze

ทองใบ gold foil

ทองปลายแขน gold bracelet

ทองแป ancient gold currency

ทองไม่รู้ร้อน complacent, unconcerned, unmoved

ทองรูปพรรณ gold ornaments, gold jewelry

ทองแล่ง gold thread

ทองสัมฤทธิ์ bronze

ทองหมั้น betrothal gage of gold, gift of gold to seal an engagement to marry

ทองเหลือง brass

กะไหล่ทอง, กาไหล่ทอง gold-filled

ช่างทอง goldsmith

ชุบทอง gold-plated

เดินทอง gold-blocked, gold-stamped

ทำเป็นทองไม่รู้ร้อน to pay no attention to something; not to care (about), completely indifferent (to), smug, complacent

ปิดทอง to gild, apply goldleaf; gilt

เป็นทองแผ่นเดียวกัน united by marriage

ท่อง[1] to take a trip, tour; to walk; to wade

ท่องเที่ยว to travel, take a trip, tour

นักท่องเที่ยว tourist

สำนักงานท่องเที่ยว tourist office, /tourist/ travel/ agency

ท่องน้ำ to wade

ท่อง[2] to memorize, learn (something) by heart

ท่องขึ้นใจ to learn (something) by heart, commit (something) to memory

ท่องจำ to commit to memory, remember

ท่องหนังสือ to study; to learn by rote

ท้อง stomach, abdomen, belly; womb; to be pregnant, expecting; area, expanse; open

ท้องกาง distended stomach, stuffed belly

ท้องแก่ about ready to give birth, expecting at any time, far advanced pregnancy

ท้องขึ้น flatulent; to have indigestion

ท้องแขวน famished, starving

ท้องเดิน to have diarrhea, have loose bowels

ท้องตรา ministerial /order/directive/

ท้องตลาด the market

หาซื้อได้ตามท้องตลาดทั่วไป It's on sale everywhere. / It's being marketed all over. / It can generally be found in the market.

ท้องถิ่น local, regional; native; locality

อากรทั้งปวงของชาติหรือท้องถิ่น all national or regional taxes

ท้องทะเล open sea

ท้องที่ local; locality, district

ตำรวจท้องที่ local police

ท้องทุ่ง fields, open fields

ท้องน่อง calf

ท้องแบน flat-bottomed (เรือ), flat-bellied

ท้องผูก constipated

ท้องพระคลัง treasury

ท้องพระโรง throne room, throne hall

ท้องพอง bloated

ท้องฟ้า sky, heavens

ท้องเฟ้อ flatulent; to have indigestion

ท้องมาน abdominal dropsy

ท้องร่วง to have diarrhea, have loose bowels

ท้องเรือ hull, bottom of a boat

ท้องเรื่อง story

ท้องไร่ท้องนา (in) the fields; country, countryside

ท้องสาว first pregnancy

ท้องเสีย to have indigestion, have an upset stomach

ท้องแห้ง to be starved, famished, have an empty stomach

ท้องอืด to feel bloated, feel gassy, have

indigestion

แน่นท้อง to have indigestion

ปวดท้อง to have a stomachache

ฝีในท้อง tuberculosis

แพ้ท้อง to have morning sickness

มีท้อง pregnant, expecting

ลงท้อง *see* **ท้องร่วง** *หน้า 222*

สุดท้อง youngest, last

หายใจไม่ทั่วท้อง anxious, worried

หงายท้อง to roll over, turn belly up, take a tumble; to be finished

อุ้มท้อง to carry a baby

ทองม้วน rolled wafer

ทองหยอด eggdrop sweet

ทอด[1] to fry

ทอดปลา to fry a fish

ทอดมัน fried /fish/shrimp/ patty

ปลาทอด fried fish

ทอด[2] to discard, throw away; to throw, cast; to lay down, lie down; to span

ทอดกฐิน *see* **ทอดกฐิน** *หน้า 2*

ทอดขา to stretch the legs

ทอดตลาด to auction, sell by auction

    ผู้ขายทอดตลาด owner (of goods sold at auction)

    ผู้ทอดตลาด auctioneer

ทอดตา to look around, cast one's eyes about

ทอดเต๋า to throw dice

ทอดทิ้ง to abandon, neglect, forsake

ทอดน่อง take a stroll, stroll, (walk) leisurely

ทอดผ้า to place a ceremonial offering of cloth

    ทอดผ้าป่า to make an off-season offering of robes and other needs to monks

ทอดพระเนตร *(royal word)* to look (at), see, /have/take/ a look (at)

ทอดยอด to sprout, put forth a new shoot

ทอดรวง to form a spike (of rice grains)

ทอดสมอ to drop anchor, cast an anchor

ทอดสะพาน to make things easy (for someone to do something), show willingness; to /throw/build/ a bridge (over), to bridge

ทอดเสียง to drawl, speak in a drawn out way

ทอดหญ้า to give (an animal) grass to eat

ทอดหุ่ย to lie blissfully, stretch out and relax

ทอดแห to /throw/cast/ a net

ทอดอาลัย to lose hope, be in despair, despondent

ขายทอดตลาด to auction, put up for auction, auction sale

เดินทอดน่อง to take a stroll, stroll, amble (along), saunter (along)

ตกทอด handed down, inherited; to devolve (on), passed on (to)

ทอด[3] section, stretch

ขึ้นรถสองทอด to take two buses; to (take a bus and) pay for two stretches

เป็นทอดๆ from hand to hand; in stretches, in stages, at intervals

ทอน to cut; to shorten

ทอนกำลัง to weaken

ทอนเงิน to give change

ทอนอายุ to shorten one's life

ตัดทอน (ข้อความ) to excise, cut

ท่อน section, segment, length, piece, part; movement (เพลง); passage

ท่อนไม้ log (ใหญ่กลม); piece of wood

ทอนซิล tonsil

ทอม tomboy; butch

ทอมดี้ lesbian

ท่อมๆ intently; to walk for no special reason

ทอย to pitch, fling

ทอยกอง penny-pitching game

ทะนง to be self-confident, cocky

ท
ธ
น
บ
ป
ผ
ฝ
พ
ฟ
ภ
ม
ย
ร
ฤ
ฤๅ
ล
ว
ศ
ษ
ส
ห
ฬ
อ
ฮ

ทะนงตัว proud of oneself

ทะนงศักดิ์ lordly; haughty

ทะนาน coconut-shell measure for rice; an old measure of capacity

ทะนานหลวง old measure equal to one liter

ทะนุถนอม to maintain, keep up, preserve; to cherish; to be considerate (of another's feelings), not to hurt (another's) feelings

ทะนุบำรุง to support, take care of, look after; to improve

ทะเบียน register, record

ทะเบียนบ้าน house registration

ทะเบียนรถ car registration

ทะเบียนสมรส marriage register

ทะเบียนสำมะโนครัว see **ทะเบียนบ้าน**

ขึ้นทะเบียน to register, record; registered, recorded

จดทะเบียน to register, record

นายทะเบียน registrar, recorder, register

ลงทะเบียน to register, record

จดหมายลงทะเบียน registered letter

ทะมัดทะแมง energetic, lively

ทะมื่น looming, large, awesome, towering

ทะแม่ง, ทะแม่งๆ something wrong (in, about), not right; suspicious

คำพูดของเขาฟังดูทะแม่งๆ ชอบกล There was something suspicious about what he said. / There was something wrong in what he said.

ทะยาน to jump, leap, spring; to climb

ทะยานใจ presumptuous, emboldened

ทะยานอยาก craving (for)

โลดโผนโจนทะยาน adventurous

ทะเยอทะยาน ambitious (to, for); to want to get ahead; to desire strongly

ทะลวง to pierce, penetrate, make a /passage /hole/ through

ทะลัก to gush, pour (out, in, into)

เลือดไหลทะลัก The blood gushed (forth, out, up).

ไส้ทะลัก The guts were hanging out.

ทะลาย cluster (of coconuts, areca nuts etc)

ทะลึ่ง to shoot up, spring up; to be impudent, fresh, cheeky

ทะลึ่งตึงตัง badly behaved, impolite

เด็กทะลึ่ง a fresh kid, imp

ต้นข้าวทะลึ่งน้ำ The rice plants shot up to clear the water.

ทะลุ perforated, to have a hole; to go through

ทางนี้ทะลุไหมคะ Can you tell me please if this is a through road?

ทะลุกลางปล้อง to butt in, interrupt

ทะลุปรุโปร่ง thorough

ทะเล sea, marine

ทะเลทราย desert

ทะเลบ้า stormy sea

ทะเลเพลิง sea of flames

ทะเลสาบ lake

ทะเลหญ้า sea of grass

ชายทะเล seaside, beach, seashore

ปลาทะเล seafish, saltwater fish

ฝั่งทะเล coastal, seacoast, seashore, seaside

โพ้นทะเล overseas

เรือเดินทะเล oceangoing /vessel/ship/, seagoing ship

ลมทะเล sea breeze

ทะเล้น to bulge; protrude, stick out; to make a face (at someone); to be cheeky, impudent

จอมทะเล้น a joker; fresh guy

หน้าทะเล้น impish /face/look/

ทะเล่อทะล่า see **เล่อล่า** หน้า 452

ทะเลาะ to quarrel, squabble, wrangle, argue, have an argument, have a fight

ไม่อยากทะเลาะด้วย I don't want to /quarrel /get into a quarrel/ with you.

ทะเลาะเบาะแว้ง to bicker; to be fighting all the time

ทะเลาะวิวาท to have /an altercation/a fight/

ชอบทะเลาะ quarrelsome

ทะวาย off-season

ทัก to greet; to address; to caution, warn against danger, give a warning, signal possible danger, caution; to protest

ทักท้วง to call (someone's) attention to (something), remind; to caution, admonish, give (someone) one's advice; to protest, remonstrate, oppose

ทักทาย to address; to greet

ทักทายปราศรัย to exchange greetings

ทักษิณ, ทักษิณา right; south

ทักษิณานุประทาน offering dedicated to the deceased

ทักษิณาวรรต circling to the right, clockwise

ทักษิโณทก water poured into a /hand/ vessel/ as a token of an offering

ทั่ง anvil

ทั้ง all, entire, the whole of, and together with

ทั้งกายและใจ body and soul

ทั้งขึ้นทั้งล่อง going and coming, no matter what, either way

ทั้งคืน all night long

ทั้งคู่ both, both of them

ทั้งชั้น the whole class, entire class

ทั้งชาติ forever

ทั้งดุ้น the whole thing, completely

ทั้ง...ทั้ง both, including both

ทั้งหญิงทั้งชาย both sexes, both men and women

ทั้งที่, ทั้งๆ ที่ although, even though, despite, in spite of

ทั้งๆ ที่หัวหน้าเตือนแล้วเขาก็ยังขึ้นทำ He did it despite the boss's warning. / Even though his chief warned him, he did it anyway. / In spite of the warning from the department head, he went ahead and did it.

ทั้งนั้น all, everything, the whole lot

ทั้งนี้ this by this; in this respect, in this regard, here

ทั้งนี้และทั้งนั้น on the whole, all in all; be that as it may, anyway, that being said; all the same

ทั้งเนื้อทั้งตัว all one has (to one's name)

ทั้งเนื้อทั้งตัวผมมีอยู่ 50 บาท All I have to my name is 50 baht.

ทั้งบ้าน the whole house

ทั้งประเทศ the whole country

ทั้งปวง all

ทั้งเป็น alive

ทั้งเพ the whole /lot/thing/, entirely, from beginning to end

ทั้งมวล all, in (its, their) entirety; entirely

ทั้งเมือง the whole /town/country/

ทั้งแม่ทั้งลูก both mother and /child/ children/

ทั้งรู้ๆ knowing, although aware (that)

ทั้งโลก the whole world, everyone

ทั้งสอง both

ทั้งสิ้น all, at all; whatsoever

อยู่เฉยๆ ห้ามทำอะไรทั้งสิ้น No activities for you. You will do nothing /at all/ whatsoever/.

ทั้งหมด all; total

ทั้งหลาย all, everyone

คนทั้งหลาย everyone, everybody

ท่านทั้งหลาย all of you; my (distinguished) friends

สุภาพบุรุษและสุภาพสตรีทั้งหลาย ladies and gentlemen

พร้อมทั้ง together with

รวมทั้ง including, as well as

ร้อยทั้งร้อย everybody, a hundred out of a hundred (มักใช้ ten out of ten)

ร้อยทั้งร้อยจะต้องบอกว่าอาหารร้านนี้อร่อย Everybody says the food at that restaurant is terrific.

ทัณฑ์ punishment, penalty

ทัณฑกรรม punishment, imposition of a

ท
ธ
น
บ
ป
ผ
ฝ
พ
ฟ
ภ
ม
ย
ร
ฤ
ฤๅ
ล
ว
ศ
ษ
ส
ห
ฬ
ฮ

penalty

ทัณฑฆาต (ˋ) mark indicating a silent letter

ทัณฑ์บน (to give) a bond of good behavior

ทัณฑสถาน prison

ภาคทัณฑ์ probation, to be put on probation, put on probation

ลงทัณฑ์ to put under a bond of good behavior

วิทยาทัณฑ์ scholastic probation

นักศึกษาวิทยาทัณฑ์ student on probation

ทัด[1] to place behind one's ear

ทัดดอกไม้ to /stick/wear/ a flower behind one's ear

ทัด[2] *as in* **ทัดทาน** to try to stop (someone from doing something), warn against; to resist

ทัด[3] *as in* **ทัดเทียม** equal, comparable

ทัน in time; to have time (to); to catch, catch up with

ทันกิน *as in* **ไม่ทันกิน** to miss out

มัวแต่เหนียมอายไม่กล้าบอกรักสักทีเลยไม่ทันกิน He was so shy about saying he loved her, he missed out.

ทันควัน immediately, then and there, on the spot, promptly, in the nick of time

ทันใจ fast, quick

ไม่ทันใจ slow, so slow

ทันใด at that /moment/instant/; as soon as

ทันตาเห็น to be apparent, become manifest, visible

ทันท่วงที in time, timely, just in time, in the nick of time

ทันที, ทันทีทันใด immediately, instantaneously, right away, at once, all at once; at that moment, thereupon

ทันเวลา in time

ทันสมัย modern, up-to-date, fashionable

ไม่ทัน to miss

ไปไม่ทันรถ I missed the /bus/train/ etc./

ยังไม่ทัน even before, hardly

ยังไม่ทันว่าอะไรเลย ก็โกรธเสียแล้ว I hardly said a word when he got a fit.

ไล่ทัน to catch up (to, with), overtake

ไหวทัน to sense something; to move first, anticipate

ทันต์ tooth; (งาช้าง) tusk

ทันตแพทย์ dentist, dental surgeon

คณะทันตแพทยศาสตร์ Faculty of Dentistry

ทับ[1] to lay on top (of), to pile (up); to be on top (of), to put on top; cover

ทับกัน on top of one another, to overlay; to cover

ของวางทับกัน The things were /on top of each other/overlaid/.

หมาทับกัน The male dog covered the bitch. / The dogs were mating.

ทับถม to pile up; to be overwhelmed (by); to make something worse (by), pile it on

ทับศัพท์ transliteration

นอนหลับทับสิทธิ์ to lose a right by default

ทับ[2] living quarters

ทับ[3] stroke (*as in* 156/55)

ทับทิม pomegranate; ruby, ruby red; a confection looking like pomegranate seeds

ทับหลัง lintel

ทัพ army, troops

ทัพบก army

ทัพหน้า spearhead

ทัพหนุน reinforcements, reinforcing army

ทัพหลัง rear guard

กองทัพ armed forces, troops

กองทัพบก army

กองทัพเรือ navy

กองทัพอากาศ air force

แม่ทัพ commander

ทัพพี ladle

ทัพสัมภาระ building materials; equipment; gear, stuff

ทั่ว all over, throughout; everyone, everything, everywhere

    ทั่วกัน all, everybody

    ทั่วถึง well distributed; comprehensive, broad; to everyone

    ทั่วทุกแห่ง everywhere

    ทั่วประเทศ throughout the country, all over the country

    ทั่วไป, ทั่วๆ ไป in general, generally; common; everywhere, all over

    ทั่วโลก worldwide, all over the world

ทัศ ten

ทัศน-, ทัศน์ opinion, view, viewpoint; attitude

    ทัศนคติ opinion, view

    ทัศนวิสัย visibility

    ทัศนศาสตร์ optics

    ทัศนศิลป์ visual arts

    ทัศนศึกษา educational tour

    ทัศนาจร to go sightseeing

ทัศนียภาพ view, scenery; panorama; perspective

ทา to coat, paint, apply

    ทาเนย to butter

    ทาปาก to /put on/wear/ lipstick; to coat the lips

    ทายา to apply medicine

    ทาสี to paint

ท่า[1] landing; dock, pier; port

    ท่าเทียบ (อากาศยาน) ramp

    ท่าน้ำ boat landing, dock

    ท่าเรือ port; boat landing, pier, wharf

    ท่าอากาศยาน airport

    เมืองท่า seaport, port

ท่า[2] position; posture; carriage; appearance, mien; pose; situation; means, method

    ถ่ายกี่ท่า How many poses do you want to take?

ท่าจะดี It looks good., It may be good., a good idea

ท่าเดียว only, exclusively, nothing but, all. ..is *เอาแต่กินท่าเดียวไม่ทำงานเลย He does nothing but eat and never works. / All he does is eat, never any work.*

ท่าทาง appearance, manner, bearing, mien

ท่าที look, attitude, manner; appearance

ท่านั้นท่านี้ this, that and the other thing; fussing around

มัวแต่พูดท่านั้นท่านี้อยู่ตั้งนานกว่าให้มา He went on and on about this, that and the other thing before finally /forking/handing/ it over.

ท่าบังคับ prescribed exercise *(ยิมนาสติก)*

ท่าไม่ดี It doesn't look so good.

เข้าท่า pretty good, perfect, great; to the point, apt

ดูท่า it looks like; to look like, appear to be

พลาดท่า to muff (something), bungle; to miss the chance (to do something), lose the opportunity; to be taken in (by)

มีทีท่า it looks like; the outlook (is /good/ bad/bleak/etc/)

ไม่เข้าท่า senseless; idiotic; gauche; ill-timed; inappropriate

ไม่เป็นท่า in disarray; lousy; to be nothing

เห็นท่า to seem, look like, appear

ให้ท่า to give (someone) an opening, give encouragement (to), invite advances, give (someone) the glad eye, appear willing, make overtures

ท่า[3] *as in* **คอยท่า** to await, wait for

ท้า to challenge; to defy (someone to do something), dare

คุณท้าผมเรอะ Is that a dare?

ท้าต่อย to /challenge/dare/ (someone) to fight

ท้าทาย challenging, daring; to provoke; provocative; defiant

ท
ธ
น
บ
ป
ผ
ฝ
พ
ฟ
ภ
ม
ย
ร
ฤ
ฤๅ
ล
ว
ศ
ษ
ส
ห
ฬ
อ
ฮ

เป็นงานที่ท้าทายมาก It's a challenge. / It's a very challenging/assignment/task/. / It's a very daring project.

ท้าพนัน to challenge to a bet

ทาก land leech

หอยทาก land snail, garden snail, slug

ทาง[1] road, street, passage; trail; direction, way; opportunity, occasion, chance; means; side; by; course

ทางกาย physically, in body

ทางการ officially, formally

ทางไกล long distance, long

   โทรศัพท์ทางไกล long-distance call; to call long distance, make a long distance call

   เดินทางไกล to make a long trip, travel a long way

ทางขนาน frontage road, service road

ทางขวา to the right, on the right

ทางเข้า entrance, entry; opening, in

ทางแคบ narrow way, narrow road

ทางโคจร orbit

ทางใจ mentally; in mind; inward; spiritual

ทางช้างเผือก the Milky Way

ทางซ้าย to the left, on the left

ทางด่วน expressway, throughway

ทางดำเนิน way of; to conduct; the conduct (of)

ทางเดินข้างถนน sidewalk, footpath

ทางเดี่ยว one-way road

ทางได้ advantage, benefit

งานนี้ไม่มีทางได้เลย มีแต่ทางเสีย To do that will not be to your benefit; you can only lose by doing it.

ทางตรง direct route; straight road

   ไปทางตรง to go straight

ทางตัน dead end, no thoroughfare, blind alley

ทางใต้ southern; (in, to) the south

ทางถูก the right way

ทางทุจริต corruptly, crookedly

ทางเท้า footpath, sidewalk

ทางโท the /street/road/ having to /yield/give way/

ทางธรรม (in) the way of the dharma; religiously; spiritual

ทางนั้น that way, that direction

ทางน้ำ by water; waterway, water route

ทางนี้ this way, this direction

ทางบก by land, land route

ทางบ้าน one's family; at home; the people at home

ทางเบี่ยง diversion

ทางไปรษณีย์ postal, by /post/mail/

ทางผ่าน passage, passage way; through road; a place one passes through; on the way

ทางผิด the wrong way

ทางภาคพื้น by surface

ทางม้าลาย zebra crossing

ทางแยก corner, intersection, branch in the road, junction

   ทางแยกต่างระดับ interchange, flyover

ทางรถไฟ railway; by train

ทางรถยนต์ motorway; by car

ทางร่วม merging road; junction

ทางราชการ in government service; official

ทางเรือ by sea, by boat

ทางลัด a shortcut

ทางโลก worldly, temporal, mundane

ทางวิทยาศาสตร์ scientific

ทางสามแพร่ง fork in the road

ทางสุจริต honestly, righteously

ทางเสีย disadvantage; way to lose

   ไม่มีทางเสีย there is no way to lose

ทางหน้า in the front, the front way

ทางหนีไฟ fire escape

ทางหลวง highway, state highway, public

road

ทางหลัง behind, in the back; the back way; by the back door

ทางเหนือ in the north, to the north, northward; the north

ทางไหน which way

ทางออก exit, way out

การลาออกมิใช่ทางออกที่ดี Resignation is not a good way out.

ทางอ้อม detour, roundabout way, indirect route; in a roundabout way, indirectly

    ให้ผลทางอ้อม to give an indirect benefit

ทางอากาศ by air

ทางอาญา criminal

ทางเอก the /street/road/ having right-of-way (over)

ตามทางที่กำหนด on course; to follow the prescribed course

ในทางอื่น otherwise

ให้ทาง yield *(จราจร)*

ทาง[2] qualifier for palm leaves

ทางมะพร้าว coconut-palm leaf stalk

ใบมะพร้าวสองทาง two coconut palm leaves

ทาน[1] donation, charity; gift

ทานกัณฑ์ third of the thirteen sections of the story of Vessantara Jataka

ทานมัย almsgiving, charitable deed

พระราชทาน to give, confer; royally conferred; granted, given by the king, royal

ให้ทาน to give charity, give alms, donate

ให้เป็นทาน to give as charity, to treat as a gift; to chalk it up to experience

ทาน[2] to withstand, bear, resist, stand

ทานกำลัง to resist (a force)

ทานน้ำหนัก to bear a load, stand up under the weight

ความต้านทาน resistance

ทนทาน lasting, durable; sturdy; hardy

ทัดทาน to try to stop (someone from

doing something), warn against; to resist

ทาน[3] to proofread, check with the original

สมเกียรติ คัด/ทาน copied/checked by Somkiat

ทาน[4] *(พูด)* to eat, have, take /food/a meal/; to drink

ทานข้าวหรือยัง Have you eaten yet? / Have you had /lunch/supper/dinner/ yet?

ทานกาแฟไหม Would you like some coffee? / Have a cup of coffee?

ทาน[5] shortened form of **ประทาน**

ทานโทษ excuse me, pardon me, I beg your pardon.

ท่าน you

ท่านทั้งหลาย friends, all of you, all who are here

ท่านผู้ฟังทั้งหลาย one's /listeners/audience/, all of you who are listening

ท่านผู้หญิง Than Puying, Lady *(a title)*

บางท่าน some, some people, some of you

ฯพณฯ (ท่าน) your excellency, excellency

ทาบ to put /place/lay/ on top (of), overlay

ทาบทาม sound (someone) out, ask in advance

ท่ามกลาง among, amidst, in the middle (of)

ทาย to predict, prophesy, divine; prognosticate; to guess, make a guess

ทายใจ to guess what is in (someone's) mind

ทายดูสิ guess

เสี่ยงทาย to tell one's fortune by lots

ท้าย rear, back; end; tail, stern *(เรือ)*

ท้ายครัว the little woman, wife

    เข้าท้ายครัว to approach through /his/ /the/ wife

    ตีท้ายครัว to have an affair with someone's wife

ท้ายโต่ง the extreme end

ท้ายทอย nape of the neck

ท

ธ

น

บ

ป

ผ

ฝ

พ

ฟ

ภ

ม

ย

ร

ฤ

ฤๅ

ล

ว

ศ

ษ

ส

ห

ฬ

อ

ฮ

ก
ข
ค
ฆ
ง
จ
ฉ
ช
ซ
ฌ
ญ
ฎ
ฏ
ฐ
ฑ
ฒ
ณ
ด
ต
ถ
ท

ท้ายเรือ stern

นายท้าย helmsman, steersman

บั้นท้าย hips, buttocks, behind, bottom

พ่วงท้าย added at the end, added on, appended

รั้งท้าย to bring up the rear, be the last

ลงท้าย to end, finish (with, by)

ให้ท้าย to spoil (a child, servant etc); to egg (someone) on

ทายก giver, donor, patron

ทายาด as in **ทนทายาด** tough; unyielding

ทายาท heir; descendant

รัชทายาท royal heir, heir to the throne

ทายิกา giver, donor, patroness

ทารก baby, infant

ทารกำนัล see **ธารกำนัล** หน้า 245

ทาริกา little girl

ทารุณ heartless, cruel, brutal, vicious; inhuman, tough; to mistreat, maltreat, be cruel (to)

ทารุณกรรม cruelty, torture, brutality

ท้าว chief, head, leader; king, monarch; title of a woman palace attendant; title of a prince or high-ranking official

ท้าวพระยา, ท้าวพญา king, monarch

ทาส slave

ทาสการพนัน slave to gambling, addicted to gambling, an inveterate gambler

ทาสเชลย captive

ทาสน้ำเงิน one who sells himself into slavery; a slave who has himself redeemed from his master; one who sells himself to another (for gain)

ทาสในเรือนเบี้ย children of a slave

ทาสปัญญา inferior intellect, low intelligence; intellectual slave

คนไทยส่วนมากเป็นทาสปัญญาของฝรั่ง Most Thais are the intellectual slaves of the foreigners.

ทาสี female slave

ทำ to do, make; perform, act; to work; to operate; to pretend, feign; to do something to someone

ทำ ณ กรุงเวียนนาเมื่อวันที่ _ Done at Vienna this _ day

แกทำเขาหรือเปล่า Did he do something to her?

ทำกับข้าว to prepare the food, make a meal

ทำการ to do, operate

ทำการค้นคว้า to do research

ทำการค้า to do business, to trade

ทำการบ้าน to do homework

ทำการรบ to fight, battle

ที่ทำการ office

รัศมีทำการ range

ทำไก๋ to pretend not to know, look innocent, feign innocence

ทำขวัญ to make amends, compensate, indemnify (for)

ค่าทำขวัญ compensation, indemnity

ทำครัว to cook, do the cooking, prepare the food

ทำครึ่งๆ กลางๆ to do something halfway, leave something unfinished

ทำคลอด to assist at childbirth

หมอทำคลอด midwife, accoucheur

ทำความเข้าใจ to come to an understanding

ทำความเคารพ to salute

ทำความผิด to do something wrong, make a mistake

ทำความสะอาด to clean, clean up, to wash

ทำคุณ to cast a spell

ทำงาน to work; to run

เครื่องจักรกำลังทำงาน The machine is running.

ทำงานง่วน to be absorbed in work, busy oneself (with); to be busy (with), preoccupied (with)

ทำงานหนัก to work hard, do heavy work, carry a heavy load

ไม่ทำงาน out of order; not at work

ทำเงิน to make money; profitable, money-making

ทำจริงๆ to do seriously, do in earnest, really do

ทำเจ็บ, ทำเสียเจ็บ to hurt

ทำใจ to accept; manage one's /emotion/ feeling/; to come to terms with it; to adjust to (the situation, etc), make the best of (it, a situation, etc); to put up with

อยู่กรุงเทพฯสมัยนี้ลำบาก รถก็ติดมลพิษก็มาก งานก็หายาก ต้องทำใจ *These days life in Bangkok is hard what with the traffic, pollution, scarcity of jobs but you have to put up with it.*

ทำใจได้ to be stoical (about)

ทำใจเย็น ๆ ไว้ be patient

ทำชั่ว to do (something) /bad/wrong/, commit a /misdeed/sin/, do evil

ทำด้วย made of

ทำด้วยมือ to be made by hand, handmade

ทำดี to do good; well-made, well-done

ทำดีที่สุด to do one's best

ทำได้ลงคอ How could /he/she/etc/ do it?

ทำตัว to act, behave

ทำตาปริบๆ to look on helplessly

ทำตาม to follow

ทำตามคำสั่ง to follow orders

ทำตามใจชอบ to do as one /likes/pleases/

ทำตามแบบ to follow the pattern, follow an /example/style/etc/

ทำตามอย่าง to copy, imitate

ทำถูก to do the right thing; do something /right/correctly/; to act well

ทำท่า to act (like); to be acting, strike a pose; to look like

ฝนทำท่าจะตก *It looks like rain.*

ทำที to pretend (to)

ทำแท้ง to have an abortion

ทำโทษ to punish, penalize

ทำนา to work in the ricefield; to be a rice farmer; to farm

ทำนาบนหลังคน to exploit

การทำนา rice farming

ทำในประเทศ to /make/produce/ domestically, domestic, locally-made

ทำในประเทศไทย made in Thailand

ทำบาป to sin, do bad

ทำบุญ to make merit, do good, perform good deeds, do an act of charity, give to charity

ทำเป็น expert, skilled; to pretend, feign

ทำเป็นเด็ก to act like a child, childish

ทำเป็นทองไม่รู้ร้อน to feign indifference, appear unconcerned

ทำเป็นไม่เห็น to close one's eyes to something, pretend not to see

ทำไปทำมา finally, after a time, in due course

ทำผิด to do wrong, make a mistake, commit an offense

ทำผิดกฎหมาย to break the law, commit a violation, disobey the law

ทำผิดๆ ถูกๆ to do ineffectively; to do badly, bungle

ทำพินัยกรรม to make a will

ทำพิษ to have a bad effect; to cause trouble

ทำฟัน to go to the dentist

ทำมาหากิน to make a living

การทำมาหากิน life, livelihood, way of earning a living

ทำร้าย to harm, injure, hurt, do violence to

ทำร้ายร่างกาย to assault, commit bodily harm

ทำรายงาน to make a report

ทำเรื่อง to /cause/create/ trouble; to submit the matter

ท
ธ
น
บ
ป
ผ
ฝ
พ
ฟ
ภ
ม
ย
ร
ฤ
ฤๅ
ล
ว
ศ
ษ
ส
ห
ฬ
อ
ฮ

ทำไร่ to farm; to work in the field

ทำลิงทำค่าง to act like a monkey

ทำเล่นๆ to be playing; to do something for fun

ทำวัตร to hold a service; to pay respect to a senior monk

ทำเวร to be on duty

ทำเวลา to make time, make good time, make up for lost time; to catch up, to make up time; to get somewhere in time *จาก บ้านไปสถานีรถไฟผมทำเวลา 20 นาทีพอดี I made it from my house to the station in exactly 20 minutes.*

ทำศึก *see* ทำสงคราม

ทำสงคราม to wage war, make war, be at war (with)

ทำสวน to fruitfarm, have an /orchard/fruit farm/garden/; to work in the /orchard/ garden/

    คนทำสวน gardener

ทำสอพลอ to curry favor (with), curry up to (someone)

ทำสัญญา to /make/enter/ a contract

ทำสาว to do a (vaginal) repair

ทำเสน่ห์ to charm (someone); to use a love-/philtre/potion/

ทำเสีย to spoil something, ruin; to break

ทำเสียงดัง to make noise, be noisy

ทำหก to spill

ทำหน้าที่ to perform one's duty, to do one's job

ทำหนี้สิน to get into debt, incur debts

ทำหมัน to sterilize, be sterilized

ทำหูทวนลม to pay no attention (to), pretend not to hear

ทำเหตุ to be the cause; to get into trouble

ทำเหลวไหล to misbehave; to let someone down; to be unreliable

ทำให้ to make, cause; to be; to do (something) for (someone)

    ทำให้เกิด to generate, engender, give rise to, create

    ทำให้ขายหน้า to be /disgraced/humiliated; disgraceful

    ทำให้เข้าใจผิด to cause a misunderstanding, mislead

    ทำให้แน่ใจ to ensure

    ทำให้เป็นเรื่อง to make a big to do (/about/over/ something), make a mountain out of a molehill

ทำอะไรไม่ถูก to be flustered

ทำอะไรไม่ได้ helpless; useless

ทำอันตราย to harm, endanger

ทำเอง self-made

ทำเอา to cause, make, do

เดินบุกป่าฝ่าดงทั้งวัน ทำเอาแย่ไปเลย The full day's push through the jungle did me in.

ทำนบ dam, weir

ทำนอง[1] style, vein, pattern, way

    ทำนองเดียวกัน similarly, in the same vein

    ตามทำนองคลองธรรม in the accepted way, in the right way; uprightly, morally

ทำนอง[2] melody, tune, music, mode of chanting; theme

    ทำนองเพลง music, melody

    ทำนองเสนาะ tonal recitation

ทำนาย to predict, foretell, read, prophesy

    ทำนายฝัน to interpret a dream

ทำนุบำรุง to support; to maintain, take care of

ทำเนียบ residence, official residence; official record (of)

    ทำเนียบรัฐบาล Government House

ทำเนียม custom, practice, tradition, convention

ทำไม why, what for; what

ทำลาย to destroy, demolish, pull down, ruin

    ทำลายขวัญ demoralize, discourage

    ทำลายสถิติ to break a record, record-breaking

ทำเล location; district, area

ร้านขายก๋วยเตี๋ยวนี้ ทำเลดีมาก It's an excellent location for that noodle shop.

ทิ้ง to abandon, walk away from, forsake, desert, dump; to throw away, discard; to drop; to relinquish; to /hang/drape/ well (ผ้า)

ทิ้งขว้าง to be irresponsible, refuse to accept responsibility; to cast aside, throw away, abandon, dump, reject

กินทิ้งกินขว้าง to waste one's food

ทิ้งงาน to neglect one's work; to stop work; to /abandon/walk away from/ a job

ทิ้งจดหมาย to mail a letter, drop a letter in the mailbox

ทิ้งทวน to give a parting shot

ทิ้งไพ่ to discard

ทิ้งร่องรอย to leave /tracks/traces/a clue/

ทิ้งระเบิด to drop a bomb

ทิ้งลาย to lose one's touch

ทิ้งไว้ to leave behind; to leave undone

ทิ้งสมอ to anchor

ทิ้งหลุดลุ่ย to be way out in front, leave far behind

ทิฐิ view; prejudice, obstinacy, intellectual arrogance

ทิฐิมานะ opinionated

ทิพย์ celestial, divine; magic, supernatural

ตาทิพย์ clairvoyant; all-seeing eye

หูทิพย์ sharp ears; magic hearing

อาหารทิพย์ ambrosia

ทิ่ม to stab, pierce, prick; to thrust (something) in; to fall headlong

ทิ่มตำ to castigate, heap abuse (on)

ทิ่มแทง to hurt; to be sarcastic, caustic

ทิว range, row, line

ทิวเขา mountain range

ทิวแถว row

ทิวทัศน์ scenery; panorama

ทิวไม้ /row/line/ of trees

ทิวงคต to die, succumb (royal word)

ทิศ direction, point of the compass

ทิศตะวันตก west

ทิศตะวันออก east

ทิศใต้ south

ทิศเหนือ north

เข็มทิศ compass

คนละทิศ in different directions

ที [1] time, occasion; by

ทีนี้ here, now, as to this

ทีเดียว this instant, at once, instantly; once, one time; quite, really, very

ทีแรก at first, initially

ทีละ at a time, ...by...

ทีละขั้น step by step

ทีละคน one by one, one at a time, one person at a time

ทีละคำ word by word, one word at a time

ทีละเล็กละน้อย gradually, little by little

ทีละอย่าง one thing at a time

ทีหน้าทีหลัง again, in the future, the next time

ทีหน้าทีหลังอย่าทำอย่างนี้ Don't do that again. / In the future, don't do that.

ทีหลัง later; next time; some other time

ที [2] as in

ทีเด็ด clincher, trump card; a certain something

ทีท่า to look like, appear to be

ทีเล่นทีจริง half-seriously

เข้าที good, a good idea; attractive, just what (one) wants; right, appropriate

ได้ที to get the upper hand

ตามที see ก็ตามที หน้า 1

เต็มที terrible, awful, extremely; rotten, too bad

ท่วงที manner, deportment, bearing

ท่าที attitude, manner; look, appearance

ท

ธ
น
บ
ป
ผ
ฝ
พ
ฟ
ภ
ม
ย
ร
ฤ
ฤๅ
ล
ว
ศ
ษ
ส
ห
ฬ
อ
ฮ

รู้ที่ to know

เสียที for once, now, to be high time (to)

พักนานแล้ว ไปทำงานเสียที You've had a long break. /It's high time you got back to work./Get to work for once./Now go to work/.

ที่ [1] which, that; what is

ที่แย่กว่านั้นคือ ...what is worse is that...

ที่ร้ายคือชนแล้วรถหนี What is bad is that he fled after the collision.

ที่สมมติขึ้น conjectured

ที่ [2] position, location, place, spot, locality; land, room; at

ที่กัน barrier

ที่เก็บ place (for something), storage /place/ area/ เช่น closet, cabinet, drawer

ที่เกิด birthplace

ที่เกิดเหตุ scene of the /crime/accident/etc/, the place in question

ที่ขายตั๋ว ticket counter, ticket window; box office (โรงหนัง), ticket office (สำนักงาน)

ที่เขี่ยบุหรี่ ashtray

ที่แขวน hook

    ที่แขวนเสื้อ coathook

ที่จริง in reality, in fact, actually

ที่จอดรถ parking, parking place, parking space; garage, parking lot

ที่แจ้ง in the open

ที่เชื่อถือได้ reliable, trustworthy

ที่ซ่อน hiding place, hideout (สำหรับคน), cache (สิ่งของ)

ที่ซึ่ง place where, place (at, to, in) which

ที่ดอน upland, highland, elevated land

ที่ดิน land, plot, lot, property, real estate

ที่ตั้ง location, seat, site, situs

ที่ตากอากาศ resort

ที่ทาง position, location

ที่ทำการ office

    ที่ทำการไปรษณีย์ post office

ที่ทำงาน office; place of work; work site

ที่เที่ยว sight, place of interest, tourist attraction, fun spot

ที่นอน bed; place to sleep; berth (ในเรือ หรือรถไฟ); mattress; bedding

ที่นั่ง seat, place to sit

ที่นั่น there

ที่นา ricefield

ที่นี่ here

ที่บ้าน at home

ที่ประกาศ notice board, bulletin board

ที่ประชุม meeting, meeting place

ที่ปรึกษา adviser, consultant, counselor

ที่ปลอดภัย safe place, place of safety; haven, shelter

ที่เผาศพ crematorium, crematory

ที่ฝังศพ cemetery, burial ground

ที่พัก resting place; residence, home, house, place where one is staying

    ที่พักแรม resting place, stopover, lodging

    ที่พักอาศัย dwelling, house, housing

ที่พำนัก residence, dwelling, lodging, where one is /staying/living/, domicile

ที่พึ่ง supporter; benefactor, backer; refuge, help

ที่มั่น stronghold

ที่มา origin, source

ที่รกร้าง undeveloped land, wasteland

ที่รัก dear; beloved, sweetheart, honey, darling

ที่ราบ plain, flatland, flat area

    ที่ราบสูง plateau

ที่ไร่ที่นา farmland

ที่ล้างหน้า lavatory, washbasin, sink

ที่ลุ่ม lowland, low-lying land, depression

ที่แล้วก็แล้วไป let bygones be bygones

ที่ว่าการ office

ที่ว่าง room, a place, space; vacant place, /unoccupied/vacant/ land, /unoccupied

/empty/ place, empty spot

ที่ว่างเปล่า uncultivated land, idle land, vacant land

ที่สุด the end; finally; -est, most; extremely; the breaking point

ที่สุดท้าย last

เร็วที่สุด fastest

ที่หมาย destination, objective, end, goal, target

ที่หลบภัย shelter

ที่ไหน where

ที่ไหนได้ ironically; unfortunately

ที่เหลือ the remainder, the rest, the balance

ที่อยู่ place to live, place; address; accommodation, living quarters; habitat, habitation

ที่อยู่อาศัย residence, dwelling

สำหรับใช้ในที่อยู่อาศัย for household use

ที่อื่น elsewhere, other places

ไม่มีที่อื่น nowhere else, not found anywhere else

เนื้อที่ area, space

ไม่มีที่วางของ there's no room for anything

สถานที่ place, site, spot; building, premises; location, area

ที่ [3] as in ที่หนึ่ง the first

ที่ [4] qualifier for places

ที่นั่ง 3 ที่ three /seats/places/

ทึกทัก to assume, jump to a conclusion

ทึ่ง to be impressed (by), very interested (in), surprised (by, at)

น่าทึ่ง interesting, striking, fascinating, impressive

ทึ้ง to yank (at, out), pull out

ทึ้งผม to yank (one's) hair

ทืนทึก as in สาวทืนทึก spinster

ทึบ dense; opaque; solid, without an opening

ทึบแสง opaque

ความทึบแสง opacity

ปัญญาทึบ dense, slow-witted

ป่าทึบ dense forest

สมองทึบ thick-headed, dim-witted

ทื่ม dumbbell, blockhead

ทื่อ, ทื่อๆ blunt, dull

แข็งทื่อ stiff

พูดทื่อๆ to speak crudely

ทุก each, every, all, entire

ทุกคน everyone, everybody; every person, each person

ทุกครั้ง every time, each time

ทุกคืน nightly, every night

ทุกชนิด every kind, a wide variety (of)

ทุกชั่วโมง every hour, hourly

ทุกชาติ all nations

ทุกซอกทุกมุม every nook and cranny, every corner

ทุกทิศทุกทาง in every direction, everywhere, all over

ทุกที every time

ทุกเที่ยวเมล์ every mail

ทุกประการ in every /respect/way/, completely, entirely, all

ทุกภาษา every language

ทุกเมื่อ at all times, at any time, always

ทุกฤดูกาล for every season, for all seasons, throughout the year

ทุกวันทุกคืน day in day out, day and night, always

ทุกวันนี้ now-a-days, today, at present, in these times

ทุกเวลา at all times, at any time

ทุกสิ่งทุกอย่าง everything, all

ทุกหนทุกแห่ง every place, everywhere

ทุกหย่อมหญ้า everywhere, all over, high and low

ทุกหัวระแหง every corner, every inch

ทุกแห่ง everywhere, at every place

ทุกอย่าง *see* ทุกสิ่งทุกอย่าง

ท
ธ
น
บ
ป
ผ
ฝ
พ
ฟ
ภ
ม
ย
ร
ฤ
ฦๅ
ล
ว
ศ
ษ
ส
ห
ฬ
อ
ฮ

ทุกโอกาส at every occasion, at every op- portunity, whenever one can

ทุกข์ suffering, pain, conflict, woe, trouble, distress, misery

ทุกข์กาย /physical/bodily/ suffering, physical illness

ทุกข์ใจ mental suffering, sorrow, anguish

ทุกข์ร้อน to be distressed (by something), troubled (by), in trouble; to have a problem

ทุกข์สุข news, state of wellbeing, how one is

เจ้าทุกข์ injured party, complainant; victim

ทนทุกข์ to suffer, bear hardship

ปรับทุกข์ to talk /about/over/(one's) problems; to complain (to)

เป็นทุกข์, เป็นทุกข์เป็นร้อน to be worried, troubled, distressed, upset

ร้องทุกข์ to complain, /lodge/file/ a complaint, make a complaint

ไว้ทุกข์ to wear mourning

ทุกขลาภ hard-earned reward

ทุกขเวทนา painful feelings, suffering

ทุกรกิริยา self-mortification

ทุคติ realm of woe

ทุ่ง field

ทุ่งแจ้ง open field

ทุ่งนา ricefield see **ท้องนา** หน้า 253

ทุ่งพระเมรุ Pramane Ground

ทุ่งราบ plain

ทุ่งหญ้า grassland, grassy field

ลูกทุ่ง country, hillbilly (music)

ไปทุ่ง to relieve oneself

ทุจริต dishonest, corrupt, crooked

ถูกจับในข้อหาทุจริต arrested on a charge of /malfeasance/dishonest conduct/

ทุจริตคิดมิชอบ dishonest, corrupt

ทุจริตต่อหน้าที่ to be corrupt, guilty of /mis- conduct/a corrupt practice/, misfeasance,

malfeasance

ทุด Disgraceful!

ทุน capital, fund, funds, investment; schol- arship, grant, stipend

ทุน ก.พ. Civil Service Commission /grant/ /scholarship/

ทุนการศึกษา scholarship, fellowship, educa- tional grant

ทุนชั้นที่หนึ่ง first tier capital

ทุนเดิม original capital; foundation

ทุนทรัพย์ capital

ทุนนอน fixed investment

ทุนรอน circulating capital, funds avail- able, money available

ทุนส่วนตัว private funds

ทุนสำรอง reserve, reserve fund, back-up fund

ขาดทุน see **ขาดทุน** หน้า 56

เงินทุน capital, funds, money that is put up

นักเรียนทุน scholarship student

นายทุน capitalist, financial backer

ลงทุน to invest, put /in/up/ money

ทุ่น[1] buoy; float

ทุ่นเบ็ด float

ทุ่นระเบิด mine

ทุ่น[2] to save

ทุ่นเงิน to economize, save money (by), cut down /expenses/costs/

จ่ายเฉพาะค่าเดินทาง ที่อยู่ฟรี ทุ่นเงินไปเยอะ You pay only transportation, lodging is free. That will save a lot.

ทุ่นแรง labor-saving

ทุ่นเวลา time-saving, to save time

ทุนิยม pessimism

ทุบ to hammer, pound, beat, punch

ทุบโต๊ะ to pound the table

ทุบหม้อข้าวตัวเอง to cut off one's nose to spite one's face

ทุบอก to beat one's chest

ทุพพลภาพ to be disabled, crippled, incapacitated

ทุพภิกขภัย famine

ทุ่ม[1] to strike, beat (the time)

    ทุ่มหนึ่ง 19 hours, 7 p.m.

ทุ่ม[2] to throw down into

    ทุ่มเงิน to lavish money (on), spend unstintingly (on, for)

    ทุ่มตลาด to flood the market (with)

    ทุ่มเถียง to have an argument, have a row, quarrel, have an altercation

    ทุ่มเท to lavish; unstinting; to dedicate (oneself to something), dedicated

    ทุ่มน้ำหนัก shot put; to /throw/put/ a shot (in a shot-put event)

    ทุ่มเวลา to spend much time, to lavish time (on)

ทุ้ม bass; deep-toned, alto

ทุย round; having misshapen horns; water buffalo

ทุรกันดาร remote, inaccessible; poor; arid

ทุรน *as in* **ทุรนทุราย** to be agitated, very disturbed

ทุรัง *as in* **ดันทุรัง** mulish, pigheaded, stubborn

ทุเรศ awful, shocking, dreadful, god-awful; pitiful; obscene

ทุเรียน durian

ทุลักทุเล painful, with difficulty, difficult

ทุเลา to abate, lessen; to alleviate, mitigate; to get better, improve; to reduce, remit

    ทุเลาการบังคับคดี to suspend the execution of a judgment

ทู่ blunt, dull

    ทู่ซี้ to persist, persistent; to hang on

ทูต envoy, minister; representative; messenger, delegate

    ทูตการค้า commercial attaché

    ทูตทหาร military attaché

        ทูตทหารบก military attaché

        ทูตทหารเรือ naval attaché

        ทูตทหารอากาศ air attaché

ทูตผู้มีอำนาจเต็ม minister plenipotentiary

ทูตานุทูต diplomatic corps

การทูต diplomacy

    ความสัมพันธ์ทางการทูต diplomatic relations

    นักการทูต diplomat

ราชทูต diplomatic representative, envoy; embassy

สถานทูต embassy, legation

อัครราชทูต minister

เอกอัครราชทูต ambassador

ทูน to place on the head, carry on the head

    ทูนหัว dear

        พ่อ (แม่) ทูนหัว godfather, godmother

ทูล to tell, inform, speak with *(royal word)*

    ทูลกระหม่อม Your Royal Highness

    ทูลถาม to ask, inquire of

    กราบทูล to inform /His/ Her/ Royal Highness

    กราบบังคมทูล to inform /His/Her/ Majesty

เท to pour out, spill out, empty, discharge

    เทกระเป๋า to spend everything, empty one's pockets

    เทขาย to sell off

    เทครัว to take all the women of the family (widow and daughters) to wife

    เทน้ำเทท่า *as in* **ขายดีเป็นเทน้ำเทท่า** to sell like hotcakes / sell extremely well

เท่ elegant, smart

    แต่งตัวเท่ to be a smart dresser; be elegantly dressed, wear smart clothes

เทคนิค technique

เทคโนแครต technocrat

เท้งเต้ง floating about, drifting

เท็จ false, untrue

    ข้อเท็จจริง fact

    พูดเท็จ to lie, prevaricate

    ให้การเท็จ to commit perjury, perjure oneself, give false testimony, make a false statement

ท
ธ
น
บ
ป
ผ
ฝ
พ
ฟ
ภ
ม
ย
ร
ฤ
ฤๅ
ล
ว
ศ
ษ
ส
ห
ฬ
อ
ฮ

เทพ god, deity, divinity, divine being; angel
    เทพเจ้า god, deity, divinity
    เทพดา god, deity, divinity
    เทพธิดา goddess, divine female
    เทพนิยาย fairy tale
    เทพบุตร god, deity, divinity; angel; prince charming; prince (of a /man/boxer/etc./)
    เทพพนม representation of a deity with hands pressed together in a gesture of respect
เทพย- god, deity
    เทพยดา angel; god, deity, divinity, celestial being
เทพารักษ์ guardian angel
เทพี goddess of the Ploughing Ceremony; queen, beauty queen
    เทพีสงกรานต์ queen of the Songkran festival
เทริด a pointed crown-like headdress
เทว-, เทวา god, deity, divinity, celestial being, angel
    เทวธิดา see **เทพธิดา**
    เทวนาครี Devanagri script
    เทวนิยม theism
    เทวรูป /figure/statue/ of a /god/deity/, idol
    เทวโลก celestial world, heaven
    เทววิทยา theology
    เทวสถาน, เทวาลัย temple
เทวดา angels, gods and goddesses, deities, divinities, celestials, celestial beings, heavenly hosts
เทวี queen; angel, goddess
เทศ country, land; municipality; foreign, alien
    เทศกาล season, festival
    เทศบัญญัติ municipal ordinance
    เทศบาล municipality, municipal government, local government
        เขตเทศบาล municipality, municipal limits
        เจ้าหน้าที่เทศบาล municipal officer

        โยธาเทศบาล municipal works department
    เทศมนตรี municipal councillor, member of a municipal council
        คณะเทศมนตรี municipal council
        นายกเทศมนตรี mayor
    เครื่องเทศ spice, spices
เทศน์ to preach, give a sermon; sermon; give a dressing down
    โดนพ่อเทศน์ my father /gave me a sermon/preached to me/gave me a dressing down/.
    ฟังเทศน์ to listen to a sermon
เทศนา preaching; sermon
    พระธรรมเทศนา sermon
เทศะ as in **กาลเทศะ** that which is fitting
เทหวัตถุ body
เท่อ as in **ขี้เท่อ** dunce, blockhead, dumbbell
เทอญ amen, so be it, ipsi dixit
เทอม term
    ค่าเทอม term fee
เทอะทะ shapeless, ill-proportioned, dumpy, clumsy-looking, bulky
เทา[1] as in **สั่นเทา** to quake, shiver, tremble (with)
เทา[2] gray, grey
    สีเทา gray, grey
เท่า as much as, the same as, equal (to), equivalent (to); time
    เท่ากัน equal
        เท่ากันทุกอย่าง equivalent in all respects (to), exact equivalent (of)
        เท่ากันพอดี exactly the same size
    เท่ากับ to be equal to, make; the same as, means
    สองบวกสองเท่ากับสี่ two plus two makes four เธอพูดเช่นนี้เท่ากับไม่ให้เกียรติฉันซิ What you said means (that) you don't trust me.
    เท่ากับว่า to mean

ทำอย่างนี้เท่ากับว่าไม่รักตัวเอง To do that means you don't care about yourself.

เท่าใด how much, how many, to what extent; whatever

เท่าตัว equal to itself; the same amount

สองเท่าตัว two times the amount / twice as much

ได้กำไรเท่าตัว to make a 100 percent profit

   รูปขนาดเท่าตัว actual size

เท่าที่ทราบ as far as one knows

เท่าที่นึกออก as far as one /recalls/remembers/; all one can think of

เท่าทัน *as in* **รู้เท่าทัน** to understand what someone is up to, fathom (another's /game/course of action/etc/), to know exactly what the situation is

เท่าที่พูด as much as one said, as many as one said

เท่าที่มี as much as one has, as much as there is

เท่าที่เห็น as far as one sees, from what can be seen

เท่าทุน the same as the original investment

เท่าเทียม equal (to), on a par (with), equivalent (to)

เท่านั้น that much, only, just

   เท่านั้นหรือ Is that all?

   เท่านั้นแหละ That's all., That's all there is to it.

เท่านี้ this much

   เท่านี้หรือ Is this all?, What a surprise?

เท่าไร how much (นับไม่ได้), how many (นับได้)

สองเท่า, สามเท่า double, twice as much; triple, three times as much, treble

หลายเท่า several times, many times, a mulitple of

เท้า[1] to rest

เท้าแขน arms, armrest; corbel, bracket; to

rest one's arms (on something)

เท้าคาง to rest one's chin on one's hand

เท้าโต๊ะ to lean on the table

เท้าเอว with arms akimbo

ไม้เท้า cane, walking stick, staff

เท้า[2] foot

เท้าเจ็บ My foot hurts.

เท้าเปล่า barefoot

เท้าระบม (to have) a sore foot

เท้าหน้า forelegs, front legs

เท้าหลัง hind legs

กราบเท้า to prostrate oneself /at (another's) feet/before someone/

ข้อเท้า ankle

ช้างเท้าหลัง (one's) better half, helpmate

เดินเท้า to go on foot

ใต้เท้า your highness; your honor

นิ้วเท้า toe(s)

ฝ่าเท้า sole (of the foot)

ฝีเท้า speed; footstep

ย่ำเท้า to mark time

รองเท้า shoes *see* **รองเท้า** *หน้า 408*

รอยเท้า footprint

ส้นเท้า heel

สัตว์สี่เท้า quadruped, four-legged animal

เทิดทูน to uphold; to extol, revere

เทิดทูนพระมหากษัตริย์ to uphold the monarchy, revere the king

เทิน[1] knoll, mound, rise

เทิน[2] to carry on one's head

เทิ้ม *as in* **สั่นเทิ้ม** to tremble, shake all over, quake

เที่ยง[1] noon, twelve o'clock

เที่ยงคืน midnight

เที่ยงวัน midday, noon

ก่อนเที่ยง before noontime, before twelve, a.m. (ย่อจาก ante meridian)

เวลาเที่ยง at noon, at twelve o'clock

หลังเที่ยง after twelve, p.m. (ย่อจาก post

ท
ธ
น
บ
ป
ผ
ฝ
พ
ฟ
ภ
ม
ย
ร
ฤ
ฤๅ
ล
ว
ศ
ษ
ส
ห
ฬ
อ
ฮ

meridian)

อาหารเที่ยง lunch, luncheon, dinner

เที่ยง[2] accurate, certain; permanent, unchanging, immutable; steady

เที่ยงตรง impartial, just

เที่ยงแท้ certain, sure; permanent

เที่ยงธรรม unbiased, impartial, dispassionate, fair, righteous; upright

เทียน candle, taper

เทียนขี้ผึ้ง beeswax candle

เทียนไข (tallow) candle

เชิงเทียน candestick, sconce

ราวเทียน candlestand

แรงเทียน candlepower; watt

แสงเทียน candlelight

หลอดเทียน candle bulb

เทียบ to compare, liken; to check

เทียบเคียง to compare

เทียบเท่า equal (to), comparable (to), equivalent (of)

เทียบเรือ to dock, come alongside

เทียบเวลา to check the time

จอดเทียบ to stop /in front of/alongside/at/

เปรียบเทียบ to compare

เทียม[1] to compare, liken; to yoke

เทียมบ่าเทียมไหล่ to keep pace (with), keep up with, be equal to

เทียมรถ to harness a carriage

เทียมหน้า not to be outdone, keep up with

เท่าเทียม equal (to)

เทียม[2] artificial, synthetic

ดาวเทียม satellite

ทำเทียม to synthesize, make something artificially

เนยเทียม margarine

ฝนเทียม artificial rain

เพชรเทียม synthetic diamond

ยางเทียม synthetic rubber

เที่ยว[1] to come and go

เที่ยวไปเที่ยวมา to go back and forth (between)

เที่ยว[2] very, really, awfully *หมู่นี้เงียบไปเทียวไม่เห็นหน้าเลย You're keeping /very/awfully/ quiet these days. I haven't seen you at all.*

เที่ยว[1] to go out (for /enjoyment/pleasure/); to go around; to visit

เที่ยวซุกซน to play around, go gallivanting

เที่ยวเตร่ to play around, go here and there, roam about, wander around

เที่ยวถามหา to go around asking (about, for)

เที่ยวบอก to go around telling

เที่ยวไป to tour; to wander, roam

เที่ยวผู้หญิง to go whoring

เที่ยวสนุกๆ to go out for fun, have fun; to go for the fun of it; a pleasure trip

เที่ยวหา to go around looking for, search (for)

ท่องเที่ยว to travel, take a trip (to), tour

ที่เที่ยว a sight, tourist attraction, place of interest, fun spot

ไปเที่ยว to go out; to take a trip (to); to take a walk

ผู้นำเที่ยว guide, tour leader

มาเที่ยว to visit

เที่ยว[2] trip, journey, run

เที่ยวกลับ return trip

เที่ยวขึ้น /outward/upward/ trip

เที่ยวเดียว single trip; one way ticket

เที่ยวนี้ this time, this trip

เที่ยวบิน flight

เที่ยวไป single /trip/ticket/

เที่ยวล่อง /inward/downward/ trip

เที่ยวเรือ voyage

เที่ยวหน้า, เที่ยวหลัง next time, next trip

เทือก row, range, line

เทือกเขา mountain range

เทือกเถา lineage, line

    เทือกเถาเหล่ากอ ancestry

อะไรเทือกนั้น and so forth, that sort of thing

แท้ genuine, true, real; pure
แท้จริง in reality; real, genuine, authentic
แท้ที่จริง in reality, in fact
เที่ยงแท้ certain, sure; permanent
เนื้อแท้ in essence, in reality
พันธุ์แท้ purebred

แท้ๆ really, genuinely, truly, totally
งามแท้ๆ /truly/really/genuinely/ beautiful

แท็กซี่ taxi
แท็กซี่บุคคล privately owned taxi

แทง to stab; to puncture, pierce; to prick; to record, enter; to gamble, play
แทงใจดำ to wound
แทงบัญชี to record, enter, make an entry
แทงบัญชีสูญ to write off
แทงบิลเลียด to play billiards
แทงม้า to bet on a horse, play the horses
แทงหวย to play the lottery

แท่ง wedge; bar, piece
ทองแท่ง gold ingot, gold bar
ทั้งแท่ง through and through
ชายทั้งแท่ง a man through and through, whole man, real man, he-man

แท้ง to abort, have a miscarriage, miscarry
โครงการนี้ยังไม่เริ่มดำเนินการก็แท้งเสียก่อน The project /miscarried/aborted/ even before work got started.
การแท้งลูก abortion; miscarriage

แทน to represent; to substitute (for), replace (หมายถึงแทนที่); in place of, instead (of); on behalf of, for
แทนคุณ to repay a kindness
แทนที่ instead, in place of, as a substitute (for)
แทนที่จะ instead of
ตอบแทน to repay, return; reciprocate, in consideration for; to get even

ตัวแทน agent, representative, attorney
ทดแทน to substitute, replace; to repay, compensate
ใบสำคัญแทน replacement certificate
ผู้แทน representative, delegate
รักษาการแทน acting

แท่น seat; platform; bench; base
แท่นตัดกระดาษ paper cutting machine
แท่นบูชา altar
แท่นพิมพ์ printing press
ขึ้นแท่น to be in the running (for top place)
นั่งแท่น to hold the position (of)

แทบ almost, nearly, practically
แทบจะ, จนแทบจะ so.../almost/practically/
เขาเดินมาไกลมากจนแทบจะหมดแรง He walked so far he was practically exhausted.
แทบตาย almost dead, practically dead
ทำงานแทบตาย to work oneself to the bone
หาเงินแทบตาย to kill oneself /making a living/to find the money/; to knock oneself out (to /do/get/ something)
แทบเท้า at one's feet
แทบเป็นบ้า outrageously
แทบไม่เชื่อ could not believe, unbelievable

แทรก to insert; to push, through; to shoulder one's way through, edge one's way through (a crowd); to infiltrate; to interrupt
แทรกซ้อน complication
ปัญหาแทรกซ้อน a complication, intervening problem
แทรกซึม to infiltrate, permeate
แทรกแซง to intervene (in); to interfere (with), meddle (with)
การแทรกแซง interference, intervention
แทรกแผ่นดินหนี to be swallowed up

แทะ to gnaw; to nibble, to brouse
แทะโลม to flirt (with)

ท
ธ
น
บ
ป
ผ
ฝ
พ
ฟ
ภ
ม
ย
ร
ฤ
ฤๅ
ล
ว
ศ
ษ
ส
ห
ฬ
อ
ฮ

โท two, second

ชั้นโท second /grade/class/, grade two

นายพลโท lieutenant general

ปริญญาโท master's degree

ไม้โท the second tone mark (˝)

เสียงโท falling tone

โท่ as in **ทนโท่** obvious, conspicuous; manifest

ความผิดเห็นทนโท่อย่างนี้ คุณยังจะเถียงอีกรึ How can you argue /when the fault is so obvious/when you are so obviously in the wrong/?

โทง ๆ as in

แก้ผ้าวิ่งโทง ๆ to run around naked

โทน only; single

กระเทียมโทน garlic having a single clove

ลูกโทน an only son

โทนโท่ see **โท่**

โทมนัส grieving, grief, sorrow; mental displeasure; mental suffering, sad-mindedness; heartache

โทร. Tel.

โทร- a prefix equivalent to "tele"

โทรจิต thought waves

โทรทัศน์ television

โทรพิมพ์ teletype; telex

โทรภาพ telefax, telefacsimile

โทรเลข telegram, cable

โทรศัพท์ telephone; to telephone

โทรศัพท์กลับ to call back; return one's call

โทรสาร telefax, fax, telefacsimile

โทรม[1] to deteriorate, decline, be run down;

ทรุดโทรม dilapidated, worn (down, out), run down, in poor condition

โทรม[2] to commit gang rape

วัยรุ่นสามคนถูกจับ ข้อหาโทรมหญิงสาว The three teenagers were arrested and charged with gang rape.

โทษ[1] harm, detriment; harmfulness, /bad/harmful/ effects (of), offense; punishment, penalty; sentence

โทษทัณฑ์ penalty, punishment

โทษเบา light penalty

โทษประหาร to carry the death penalty

โทษหนัก heavy penalty

โทษานุโทษ the offenses

กล่าวโทษ to accuse see **กล่าวโทษ** หน้า 16

ขอโทษ to beg (another's) pardon, apologize, say (one) is sorry, Excuse me.

ขออภัยโทษ to apply for a pardon

คนโทษ prisoner, convict

คาดโทษ to warn of punishment for further wrongdoing

ทำโทษ to punish, penalize

นักโทษ prisoner, convict

บทลงโทษ penalty, penalty /clause /provision/

มหันตโทษ heavy /sentence/penalty/; felony

มีโทษ noxious, bad, have a bad effect; harmful; to carry a penalty (of)

ยกโทษ to pardon, forgive

ลงโทษ to penalize, punish, chastise

ลหุโทษ light /sentence/penalty/; misdemeanor, petty offense

สำเร็จโทษ to execute, put to death, carry out an execution

ให้โทษ detrimental, harmful

ให้อภัยโทษ to pardon

โทษ[2] to blame

โทสะ, โทโส anger, hate, hatred, rage, wrath; ill will, animosity

โทสาคติ bias arising from ill will

บันดาลโทสะ to fly into a rage, become /enraged/infuriated/, get angry

ไท, ไท้ chief, leader; ruler, king; independent, free

เป็นไท free

ไทย[1] Thai

ไทยมุง *see* มุง *หน้า 381*

ไทย² Thailand

คนไทย Thai

ชาติไทย the Thai /people/nation/

ประเทศไทย Thailand

ภาษาไทย Thai

เมืองไทย Thailand

อ่าวไทย Gulf of Thailand

ไทยทาน offering

ไทยธรรม offering

ไทร banyan tree

ธ you; he

ธง[1] flag, standard, banner, pennant, colors, ensign

   ธงชัย house flag, standard

   ธงชาติ, ธงประจำชาติ national flag

   ชักธง to raise a flag, fly a flag

      ชักธงขึ้นเสา to raise a flag

      ชักธงลง to lower a flag

      เชือกชักธง halyard

   นายธง flag captain

   ประดับธง to decorate with flags, deck with flags

   เรือธง flagship

   เสาธง flagstaff, flagpole

ธง[2] limits, bounds

ธนบัตร bank note, bill, paper money

ธนาคาร bank

   ธนาคารพาณิชย์ commercial bank

   ธนาคารเลือด blood bank

   การธนาคาร banking

ธนาณัติ postal money order

ธนู arrow; Sagittarius

   แข่งขันยิงธนู archery

   คันธนู bow

   นายขมังธนู archer

   ลูกธนู arrow

ธรณี earth, land, ground; threshold, doorsill

   ธรณีวิทยา geology

   ธรณีสงฆ์ monastery /land/property/

   แม่ธรณี mother earth, earth goddess

ธรรม[1] Dharma, the Doctrine, the Buddha's teaching, the Law

   ธรรมกถึก preacher of the Dharma, sermon-giver

   ธรรมคุณ /virtue/benefits/ of the Dharma

   ธรรมจักร the Wheel of the /Dharma/Law/

   ธรรมจักษุ enlightenment, the Eye of Wisdom

   ธรรมบท an article of the Dharma, verses on the Dharma

   ธรรมยุต Dhammyuttika, a sub-sect of the Thai Theravada school of Buddhism

   พระธรรม Dharma

      พระธรรมเทศนา sermon

ธรรม[2] good, righteousness, virtue, morality; law, principle, justice; mental state, mind-objects, idea, mental factor; condition; qualities

   ธรรมจริยา virtue, ethical conduct, morality

   ธรรมราชา righteous king

   ธรรมศาสตร์ moral science; jurisprudence, law

   ชอบธรรม lawful, legitimate, rightful; fair, right

   เที่ยงธรรม unbiased, impartial, fair, righteous, upright

   เป็นธรรม fair, just, equitable

      ไม่เป็นธรรม unfair, unjust, inequitable

   มนุษยธรรม humanity, compassion

   ยุติธรรม justice; fair, just, equitable

   วัฒนธรรม culture

   อารยธรรม civilization

ธรรมดา ordinary, common, usual, normal; undistinguished

   กฎธรรมดา law of nature, natural law, nature of things

   ของธรรมดา natural, normal, ordinary, common; undistinguished

   ตามธรรมดา ordinarily, usually, normally

   เป็นธรรมดา to be natural (for); common, naturally, normally, in the nature of things

   ผิดธรรมดา unusual, exceptional, abnormal, extraordinary, out of the ordinary

   อย่างธรรมดา regular, ordinary, plain

ธรรมนูญ basic law, charter, statute

   ธรรมนูญศาลยุติธรรมระหว่างประเทศ statute of the International Court of Justice

   รัฐธรรมนูญ constitution

ธรรมเนียม custom, practice, tradition, convention

ขนบธรรมเนียม custom, tradition, usage, /customary/traditional/ ways

ค่าธรรมเนียม fee, charge

ตามธรรมเนียม as usual, in the usual way; to be customary (to), as is customary; traditionally

ธรรมภิบาล good governance

ธรรมรัฐ good governance

ธวัช flag, standard, banner

ธัญญาหาร food; cereals, grains

ธันวาคม December

ธาตุ element, essence, elements (earth, water, air, fire); remains, relics; stupa containing relics, reliquary

ธาตุแท้ true nature, innate quality; intrinsically, inherently, essentially

ไฟธาตุ digestion

ยาธาตุ digestive preparation, stomachic

แยกธาตุ to do a chemical analysis, analyze

แร่ธาตุ minerals, mineral supplement

ธานี town, city

ธาร water, course, stream, brook, creek

ลำธาร stream, brook

ธารกำนัล public; forum

ต่อหน้าธารกำนัล in public

ธำมรงค์ ring

ธำรง to uphold, support, maintain

ธิดา daughter

ธุ *กร่อนจาก* **สาธุ** amen; salute (in the Thai way) *(an imperative used for small children)* *ธุคุณลุงเสียลูก Salute your uncle, darling (in the Thai way).*

ธุดงค์ austerity practice; to travel on foot shunning society

เดินธุดงค์ to go on a pilgrimage usually on foot

ธุระ business, affairs, work, something to do

ธุรกรรม transaction

ธุรการ administrative /service/work/, administration

ด้านธุรการ administrative

ธุรกิจ business, affairs

ธุระปะปัง business, affair

ธุระไม่ใช่ Mind your own business., It's none of your business.

ธุระร้อน something urgent, urgent business

ธุระส่วนตัว personal /business/matter/affair/

ธุระอะไร What business is it of /yours/ mine/his/etc/; What brings you here?

ติดธุระ to be busy, be tied up, engaged, occupied, not available

ไปธุระ to have some business to do, have something to do

มีธุระ busy, to have something to do *มีธุระอะไรกับผมรึเปล่า Is there something you want to see me about?*

ไม่มีธุระ free, unoccupied

เอาธุระ concerned, responsible, serious

ไม่เอาธุระ indifferent (to); to have nothing to do with something

ธุลี dust

ธูป joss stick, incense

กระถางธูป joss stick pot

กลิ่นธูป incense, smell of incense

ก้านธูป joss stick, incense stick

เธอ you; he, him, she, her, they, them

โธ่, โธ่เอ๋ย Oh!, Really!, Oh dear!, What a pity!

นก bird; hammer (of a gun)

    นกรู้ a know-it-all

    ขึ้นนก to cock a gun

    นางนกต่อ decoy

    หลับนก to doze

นกเขา [1] dove

นกเขา [2] one's thing, peter, cock *(หยาบ)*

นกหวีด whistle

นคร city, metropolis

    นครบาล *as in* ตำรวจนครบาล metropolitan police

    นครโสเภณี courtesan

    นครหลวง capital

นงคราญ girl; beautiful girl, pretty maid, fair maiden

นงนุช girl, young lady

นงพะงา *see* นงคราญ

นงเยาว์ girl, young lady

นที river

นบ to salute by raising the arms and pressing the palms together

นพ new; nine

    นพเก้า a ring with a tiered setting containing jewels of nine colors

    นพคุณ pure gold

    นพเคราะห์ nine celestial bodies: Sun, Moon, Mars, Mercury, Jupiter, Uranus, Venus, Saturn and Neptune; planets

นภ sky; air

    นภดล sky, the heavens, firmament

นภา sky

    นภาลัย sky, heavens, firmament

นม breast; udder (นมสัตว์เช่นวัว, แพะ), breast-shaped object; milk

    นมกระป๋อง /canned/tinned/ milk

    นมข้น condensed milk

        นมข้นหวาน sweetened condensed milk

    นมคืนรูปขาดมันเนย reconstituted skim milk

    นมเต่งตึง firm breasts, firm-breasted

    นมเปรี้ยว sour cream

    นมผง powdered milk

    นมยาน /pendant/hanging/ breasts

    นมวัว cow's milk

    นมสด fresh milk, milk

    นมหนู nipple; nozzle

    นางนม, แม่นม wet nurse

    รีดนม to milk

        เครื่องรีดนม milking machine

    วัวนม milk cow

    หย่านม to wean, weaned

    หัวนม nipple

นมัสการ to pay respects to; Your Reverence, Venerable Sir; to salute by raising the arms and pressing the palms together

นมนาน /in/for/ a long time

นโยบาย policy

น.ร. pupil, student

นรก hell, purgatory; hellish

นรี woman

    นรีเวชวิทยา gynecology

นฤมิตกรรม creative art

นว- new, novel; nine, nona.

นวนิยาย novel

นวโลหะ a metal-casting alloy composed of iron, mercury, copper, silver, gold, a silvery-green metal(?), zinc, tin and lead

นวด to massage, give a rubdown; to knead; to thresh

    นวดข้าว to thresh rice

    นวดฟั้น to massage

    บีบนวด to massage

    หมอนวด masseur (ชาย), masseuse (หญิง)

นวม [1] padded; upholstered

    เก้าอี้นวม upholstered /chair/sofa/couch/, easy chair

    ผ้านวม quilt

    เสื้อนวม padded jacket, quilted jacket

นวม [2] boxing gloves

    แขวนนวม to retire from the ring, end

(one's) boxing career

นวม[3] (tea) cozy

น่วม soft

นวยนาด to strut, swagger

นวล cream color; creamy-complexioned, fair skinned; beautiful, pretty

   นวลนาง fair lady

   นิ่มนวล see **นิ่มนวล** *หน้า 260*

   แสงนวล soft /light/lighting/, subdued lighting

   หน้านวล to look radiant, glowing complexion

นวัตกรรม innovation

น.ส. Miss

นอก out, outside, beyond, outer, external; out of, extra; foreign

   นอกกฎหมาย illegal, unlawful, illegitimate, illicit

      ลูกนอกกฎหมาย illegitimate child

   นอกเขต outside the boundaries (of), outside, beyond the /bounds/area/

      นอกเขตเทศบาล outside municipal limits

   นอกครู recalcitrant, willful

   นอกคอก non-conformist, unconventional, eccentric, maverick, renegade; unruly

   นอกจาก except, except for, apart from, excluding, but; unless

      นอกจากนี้ in addition, besides, apart from this

   นอกจากว่า unless

   นอกใจ unfaithful, adulterous, inconstant

   นอกชาน raised deck (of a house), open /porch/veranda/

   นอกตำรา unconventional, not in any book, outlandish

   นอกถนน in the street

   นอกประเด็น irrelevant, beside the point, not pertinent, not germane, inapposite

   นอกเมือง out of town

   นอกรีต untraditional, unconventional; heretical

      คนนอกรีต heretic

   นอกเรื่อง off the subject, irrelevant

   นอกลู่นอกทาง to deviate (from), unconventional

      คนนอกลู่นอกทาง nonconformist

   นอกเวลา overtime, outside working hours

   นอกศาสนา as in **คนนอกศาสนา** unbeliever, infidel, heathen

   นอกหน้าที่ not one's job

   นอกเหนือจาก apart from, beyond, over and above

   นอกอำนาจ beyond one's /authority/ powers/, unauthorized, outside the scope of one's authority, ultra vires

   ข้างนอก out, outside, outdoors

   คนนอก stranger, outsider, layman

   นักเรียนนอก someone who is studying abroad, foreign-educated, educated abroad

   บ้านนอก provincial, country, in the country; country, rural area, up-country

   ไปนอก to go abroad

   ภายนอก outside, exterior, external

   เมืองนอก abroad, foreign country

   รอบนอก outside, outer, outlying; periphery (of)

   ส่วนนอก outside (of), outer part

   เสื้อนอก jacket, suitcoat, coat

   หัวนอก foreign-educated, educated abroad, foreign-oriented, westernized

   ออกนอกหน้า to show

น็อค knock

   ถูกน็อค to be knocked out

นอง to be flooded, inundated, covered with (/water/blood/etc/)

   นองเลือด bloody; with much bloodshed

   น้ำนอง to flood, inundate

 น
บ
ป
ผ
ฝ
พ
ฟ
ภ
ม
ย
ร
ฤ
ฤๅ
ล
ว
ศ
ษ
ส
ห
ฬ
อ
ฮ

ก
ข
ค
ฆ
ง
จ
ฉ
ช
ซ
ฌ
ญ
ฎ
ฏ
ฐ
ฑ
ฒ
ณ
ด
ต
ถ
ท
ธ
น

ไหลนอง to flood, stream (out, along, from, forth); swollen (river, etc)

น่อง calf

ทอดน่อง to take a stroll, stroll, (walk) leisurely

น้อง younger /brother/sister/; friend; miss, young lady (หญิง), young fellow (ชาย); dear; I, me, you, he, him

น้องๆ almost, almost the same as, second to; younger /brothers/sisters/

น้องเขย brother-in-law

น้องชาย younger brother; young fellow, young man

น้องเมีย brother-in-law, sister-in-law

น้องร่วมท้อง a full younger /brother/sister/; younger /brother/sister/ of the same mother

น้องสะใภ้ sister-in-law

น้องสามี the younger brother or sister of one's husband, /brother/sister/-in-law

น้องสาว younger sister

น้องสุดท้อง the youngest /brother/sister/

น้องใหม่ freshman, freshie, newcomer

พี่น้อง relatives brothers and sisters, family members; fellows, folks, my friends

ลูกน้อง (one's) /boys/men/people/henchmen/, followers, a subordinate

ลูกพี่ลูกน้อง cousin

นอต [1] bolt; nut

นอต (ตัวผู้), ตัวนอต bolt

นอต (ตัวเมีย), หัวนอต nut

นอตหลวม to have a screw loose; to be out of control

หัวนอต nut

นอต [2] knots

นอน to lie, recline; to go to bed

นอนก้น to settle; sedimentation, sediment

นอนกลางดินกินกลางทราย to live a simple life

นอนก่ายหน้าผาก to lie despondent (with his hand resting on his forehead)

นอนกิน not have to work for a living, have an income without working

เสือนอนกิน free rider; someone who makes an easy living, someone who gets something for nothing

นอนขด to lie curled up

นอนคว่ำ to lie prone, lie face downward

นอนคู้ to sleep curled up

นอนใจ complacent; trusting, unquestioning

นอนซม to lie helpless

นอนดึก to go to bed late

นอนตะแคง to lie on one's side

นอนตาไม่หลับ to be sleepless, worried, unable to get to sleep

นอนตาหลับ to feel secure (in one's own bed), be at peace

นอนแบ็บ to lie in a feeble condition

นอนแผ่ to lie sprawled out

นอนพังพาบ to lie /prone/on one's stomach/ face down/

นอนไม่หลับ to be sleepless เช่น to pass a sleepless night, unable to get to sleep, have insomnia

โรคนอนไม่หลับ (to have) insomnia

นอนราบ to lie flat

นอนลง to lie down

นอนลืมตา to lie with one's eyes open

นอนเล่น to take a rest, lie down, lie about, repose

นอนแล้ว to have gone to bed

นอนหงาย to lie on one's back, lie face upwards, supine

นอนหรือยัง Are you ready for bed?

นอนหลับ to sleep, go to sleep, be sleeping

นอนหลับตา to lie with one's eyes closed

นอนหลับๆ ตื่นๆ to sleep fitfully

นอนหลับทับสิทธิ์ to fail to exercise one's right to vote

นอนหัวค่ำ to go to bed early

นอนเหยียดยาว to lie stretched out

นอนเอากำลัง to sleep to gather strength

นอนเอาแรง to gather strength, take a rest

เข้านอน to retire, go to bed

ง่วงนอน sleepy, to feel sleepy

ตื่นนอน to wake up, get up

เตียงนอน bed

ที่นอน bed; place to sleep; berth (ในเรือ หรือรถไฟ); bedding; mattress

บ้านเกิดเมืองนอน birthplace, native land

เวลานอน bedtime; when sleeping

ห้องนอน bedroom

หัวนอนปลายตีน background, origins, who (one) is

ไม่รู้หัวนอนปลายตีน to not know (someone) from Adam / know nothing about one's background / not know anything about who one is

นอบ to bow down, show deference

นอบนบ, นบนอบ to bow (to); to make an obeisance, bow and salute in Thai style

นอบน้อม to show respect (to), be respectful, deferential

น้อม to bow, stoop, bend down

น้อมเกล้าน้อมกระหม่อม humbly, with humility

น้อมใจ humbly

น้อมนำ to lead

อ่อนน้อม deferential, respectful, gentle, unassertive, mild-mannered

น้อย little; small, diminutive, not much; few, not many

น้อยกว่า less (than), fewer (than)

น้อยใจ to feel slighted; resentful, take offense; to be hurt, have hurt feelings; offended, in a huff, fretting; indignant; annoyed

สนั่นไม่มีสิทธิน้อยใจ Sanan has no right to be annoyed.

น้อยอกน้อยใจ bitter, resentful, deeply hurt

น้อยที่สุด least, smallest

น้อยเนื้อต่ำใจ to feel slighted, be resentful, indignant, offended

น้อยมาก very little, negligible; rarely

น้อยราย few, in rare cases

น้อยลง to get/less/smaller/, decrease, decline, lessen, diminish, abate; depleted

เราพึ่งพิงทุนต่างประเทศน้อยลง We are less dependent on foreign capital.

น้อยหน้า to be outdone, feel inferior (to)

น้อยหรือ dammit

ผู้น้อย junior, subordinate, inferior, underling; person of small importance, a little guy

มักน้อย modest, undemanding, easily satisfied, content with what one has; frugal

มีน้อย /there is/to have/ a little

เมียน้อย minor wife, mistress

ไม่น้อย a lot (of), not a small /amount/ number/ of, quite a few

ไม่มากก็น้อย more or less, to some extent

ลักเล็กขโมยน้อย petty thievery; to be a petty thief, pilfer

ส่วนน้อย minority, a small /part/portion/

หนูน้อย little child, kid, littleshaver

อย่างน้อย at least; minimum

นอแรด rhinoceros horn

นะ do, please; okay?; right?

ไม่ดีนะ That's not good, right?

ไม่เอาน่ะ Don't! / Stop it!

นะ ? isn't it; now, then, okay

ใครนะ ส่งของมาให้ Now who could have sent that?

ดีจริงนะ It's wonderful, isn't it?

ตกลงไปด้วยกันนะ Let's go, okay?

วันนี้ อากาศดีจริงนะ The weather's perfect isn't it?

น
บ
ป
ผ
ฝ
พ
ฟ
ภ
ม
ย
ร
ฤ
ฤๅ
ล
ว
ศ
ษ
ส
ห
ฬ
อ
ฮ

นัก[1] expert, one skilled (in),-er; fancier

นักกฎหมาย lawyer

นักการ messenger

นักการทูต diplomat

นักการพนัน gambler

นักการเมือง politician

นักการศึกษา educator, educationalist, educationist

นักกีฬา athlete, sportsman

นักข่าว reporter, newsman, correspondent

นักเขียน writer, author

นักเขียนการ์ตูน cartoonist

นักคำนวณ mathematician

นักเคมี chemist

นักชีววิทยา biologist

นักดนตรี musician

นักดื่มสุรา heavy drinker, alcohol fancier

นักเต้นรำ dancer

นักแต่งเพลง songwriter, composer

นักท่องเที่ยว tourist

นักเทศน์ preacher, sermon giver

นักโทษ prisoner, convict

    นักโทษการเมือง political prisoner

    นักโทษเด็ดขาด a prisoner with a confirmed sentence of imprisonment

นักธุรกิจ businessman

นักธรรม dharma scholar

นักธรรมชาติวิทยา naturalist

นักบวช a religious; monk, priest, bhikku, nun

นักบิน pilot, aviator (ชาย), aviatrix (หญิง), flyer

    นักบินอวกาศ astronaut

นักบุญ saint

นักโบราณคดี archaeologist

นักประพันธ์ writer, author

นักประวัติศาสตร์ historian

นักปราชญ์ sage, philosopher

นักผจญภัย adventurer

นักพรต an ascetic, recluse, a religious

นักพฤกษศาสตร์ botanist

นักพูด orator, good speaker

นักฟันดาบ swordsman

นักฟุตบอล football player

นักภาษา linguist

นักมวย boxer, pugilist, fighter

นักแม่นปืน sharpshooter

นักรบ warrior

นักร้อง singer

นักเรียน student, pupil

    นักเรียนชาย schoolboy, male student

    นักเรียนนายร้อย cadet

    นักเรียนนายเรือ naval cadet

    นักเรียนหญิง schoolgirl, female student

นักเลง tough guy, hooligan, hoodlum, ruffian, rogue; bighearted person; sporting; lover, collector; big

    นักเลงโต bully, ruffian

    นักเลงผู้หญิง womanizer

    นักเลงหนังสือ booklover; book collector

    นักเลงหัวไม้ tough, hooligan, rowdy, ruffian

    นักเลงเหล้า big drinker

นักเล่นนก bird fancier

นักวาดเขียน artist; draughtsman

นักวิจารณ์ critic, commentator

นักวิชาการ academic(s)

นักวิทยาศาสตร์ scientist

นักวิทยาศาสตร์การแพทย์ medical technician

นักศึกษา student, scholar

นักสวด chanter

นักสืบ detective, sleuth

นักหนังสือพิมพ์ newspaperman, journalist, reporter

นักอ่านหนังสือ avid reader

นัก[2] really, so much, very

งานนี้ฉันอยากทำนัก I would really like to get that job. / That job is right up my alley.

นักต่อนัก plenty
เรื่องอย่างนี้ ฉันเห็นมานักต่อนักแล้ว I've seen plenty of that sort of thing.

นักหนา excessively, very, so
ชอบนักชอบหนา to be crazy about (something), love
อะไรกันนักหนา What's the big fuss?, Why all the fuss?

นักขัตฤกษ์ festival, seasonal festivity

นักษัตร star, the constellations

นั่ง one's woman

นั่ง to sit
นั่งกินนอนกิน to have an easy life
นั่งขัดสมาธิ to sit cross-legged
นั่งไขว่ห้าง to cross one's legs (while sitting)
นั่งคร่อม to straddle, sit astride
นั่งคอย to wait (for), sit and wait
นั่งคิดนอนคิด to ruminate (on), ponder
นั่งโงก to doze, sit dozing
นั่งทาง to lie in wait (for); to keep a lookout (for)
นั่งทางใน to go into a trance
นั่งเทียนเขียน to make up (a story)
นั่งแบบผู้หญิง to /sit/ride/ sidesaddle
นั่งปรก to consecrate by concentration
นั่งพัก to take a rest, sit and rest
นั่งพับเพียบ to sit on the floor with one's legs tucked back
นั่งเมือง to govern, administer
นั่งยองๆ to squat, sit on one's haunches
นั่งร้าน scaffolding
นั่งลง to sit down
นั่งเล่น to sit down and relax
นั่งสมาธิ to practice a sitting meditation
นั่งห้อยขา to /sit/ride/ sidesaddle
นั่งห้าง to keep watch on a hunting platform
ม้านั่ง bench, stool
ห้องนั่งเล่น sitting room, living room, lounge; study, den

นัด time; shot, round
ยิงหนึ่งนัด to fire /a single shot/one round/

นัด to schedule, make an appointment, make a date; /fix/set/ a time; to load (a gun)
นัดกระชับมิตร /friendly/friendship/ match
นัดแขก to make an appointment (for someone to visit)
นัดแนะ to fix a rendezvous
นัดประชุม to schedule a meeting
นัดหมาย to date, make an appointment
นัดหยุดงาน to strike
ตลาดนัด occasional market, morning market, Sunday market
ผิดนัด to miss an appointment, fail to keep an appointment, fail to appear, not show up; to default, be in default
มาตามนัด to keep an appointment, appear at the appointed time
มีนัด to have /an appointment/a date/
เวลานัด (at the) appointed time, on time

นัด to sniff
นัดยานัตถุ์ to take a sniff of snuff

นัดดา grandson

นั่น that
อ้ายหมอนั่น that guy
นั่นไง there it is, over there
นั่นซิ a word indicating agreement or approval, That's right!, How right you are., I see., I get it., So!, Exactly
นั่นซี *see* **นั่นซิ**
นั่นแน่ How about that!
นั่นแหละ That's it., That's the way it is., just so, indeed, yep (แทน yes)
นั่นอะไร What's that?
นั่นเอง himself, herself, itself, themselves; just, only, merely
ที่นั่น there

นั้น that, the
นั้นๆ those

น
บ
ป
ผ
ฝ
พ
ฟ
ภ
ม
ย
ร
ฤ
ฦ
ล
ว
ศ
ษ
ส
ห
ฬ
อ
ฮ

นั้นแล the end

นั้นเอง /the/that/ very, that, the same

แค่นั้น only that; up to there

เช่นนั้น like that, in that /way/manner/, that

ดังนั้น therefore, thus, so

ตรงนั้น there, over there; at that point

ทั้งนั้น all, everything, the whole lot

เท่านั้น that much, only, just

    เท่านั้นแหละ That's all., That's all there is to it.

ในวันนั้นเอง on /that/the very/ day, on that same day

บัดนั้น at /the/that/ time, at that moment, then

บุคคลนั้นๆ those, these, the

ผมเองนั้น as for me I, I myself

ผมเองนั้น ไม่ชอบเดินทางโดยรถไฟ As for me, I don't like to go by train.

ยิ่งกว่านั้น moreover, more than that

อย่างนั้น that, like that; that's right, correct

นับ to count, enumerate; to regard, consider, deem

นับได้ว่า, นับว่า /is/may be/should be/ considered, regarded as, deemed; to be tantamount to

นับตั้งแต่ counting from

นับแต่นั้นมา ever since, from that time on

นับไม่ถ้วน innumerable, countless, incalculable

นับถือ to respect, hold in high regard, look up to (someone); to believe in, profess

คุณนับถือศาสนาอะไร What is your religion? / What religion do you /believe in/profess/?

ด้วยความนับถือ Yours truly, Very truly yours, Sincerely yours, Yours faithfully *(Brit)*

...ที่นับถือ Dear...

นับหน้าถือตา respected, esteemed, highly

regarded

นัย sense, meaning

นัยว่า it means; it appears; it seems

พูดเป็นนัยๆ to intimate, hint, imply, insinuate

มีนัยสำคัญ meaning, significance

อีกนัยหนึ่ง in a sense, in another sense, in other words, on the other hand

นัยน์ eye

นัยน์ตา eye

กวนนัยน์ตา irritating, annoying, obnoxious, offensive

นัยน์เนตร eye

นัยนา eye

นัว confused

วัยรุ่นยกพวกตีกัน ไม่รู้ใครเป็นใคร ล่อกันนัว The teenage gangs clashed in a confused melee.

นัวเนีย to mill about; in confusion

นา[1] farmland, field, ricefield, paddy field

นาเกลือ saltfield

นาดำ transplanted ricefield

นาบุญ wellspring of merit

นาปรัง an off-season ricefield

นาปี an in-season ricefield

นาหว่าน broadcast ricefield

ชาวนา, ชาวไร่ชาวนา farmer; peasant

ทดน้ำเข้านา to irrigate a field

ท้องนา, ท้องไร่ท้องนา ricefield, farm; in the fields, on the farm, in the country

ทำนา to farm, grow rice

ทุ่งนา *see* **ท้องนา**

โรงนา a shelter in a field

ไร่นา farmland, farm

หน้านา planting season

นา[2] (an emphatic word) boy, man, no way, I tell you

จะมาว่าผมไม่ได้นา You can't blame me, no way.

มันมิใช่ของง่ายนาคุณ I tell you it's not easy. / It's not that easy, boy.

น่า -ful, - able, - y, - ing, good for

น่ากลัว frightening, scary, fearful, terrifying

น่ากอด cuddlesome, huggable

น่ากิน appetizing, tempting, inviting, delectable; to look delicious

น่าเกลียด ugly, awful, does not look good, not nice, unseemly

น่าขัน funny, comical; ridiculous, laughable

น่าคิด interesting

น่าคลื่นไส้ revolting

น่าเคารพ worthy of respect, admirable, estimable; venerable

น่าจะ ought to, likely to

น่าจะเป็น probable, plausible

น่าจะเป็นไปได้ feasible, possible

น่าใจหาย dismaying; terrifying; breathtaking

น่าชม admirable, attractive

น่าเชื่อ credible, believable

น่าดีใจ should be glad, gladdening

น่าดื่ม inviting, to look delicious, delectable

น่าดู worth seeing, attractive

น่าเดินเล่น inviting, good for a stroll

น่าเดือด irritating, vexing

น่าเตะ abrasive, provocative

น่าทึ่ง remarkable, striking, fascinating, amazing

น่าทุเรศ detestable, shameful

น่านอน good for sleeping

น่านับถือ respectable, worthy of respect, admirable, estimable

น่าบัดสี disgraceful, shameful, indecent

น่าเบื่อ boring, tiresome, tedious

น่าประหลาด astonishing, amazing, strange

น่าฟัง sensible, interesting, worth, listening to, listenable

น่ารัก lovely, nice, attractive, cute, lovable,

adorable, sweet, endearing, likeable

น่ารังเกียจ offensive, objectionable, repugnant, disagreeable

น่ารำคาญ annoying, irksome, bothersome, a nuisance

น่ารู้ interesting

น่าละอาย indecent, shameful

น่าวิตก worrisome, alarming

น่าไว้ใจ trustworthy, reliable, dependable

น่าเศร้า sad

น่าสงสัย suspicious, doubtful, questionable

น่าสงสาร *see* **น่าสงสาร** *หน้า 474*

น่าสนใจ interesting

น่าสนุก fun, to look like fun

น่าสยดสยอง gruesome, horrifying, terrifying, ghastly, grisly

น่าเสียใจ too bad, sad

น่าเสียดาย What a pity!, it's a shame, regrettable, unfortunately, too bad

น่าเสียวไส้ terrifying, horrifying, gruesome

น่าหัวเราะ laughable, comical, funny; ridiculous, ludicrous

น่าอดสู shameful

น่าอภิรมย์ enjoyable, delightful, blissful

น่าอยู่ comfortable, cozy, livable

น่าอับอายขายหน้า ignominious

น่าอัศจรรย์ marvelous, amazing, spectacular

น่าอ่าน worth reading, interesting

น่าอึดอัด uncomfortable, disquieting

น่าเอ็นดู lovely, adorable, cute, sweet

ไม่น่าเชื่อ unreliable; unbelievable; incredible, extraordinary

ไม่น่าเลย Oh no!, How awful!, /You/he/etc/ should not have done it.

น้า aunt; uncle

คุณน้า sir; ma'am

นาก otter; alloy of gold, silver and copper

นาค fabulous serpent, Naga; elephant; postulant, candidate for ordination

น
บ
ป
ผ
ฝ
พ
ฟ
ภ
ม
ย
ร
ฤ
ฤๅ
ล
ว
ศ
ษ
ส
ห
ฬ
อ
ฮ

นาคปรก a figure of a sitting Buddha canopied by a seven-headed Naga

นาง woman, lady; female; she, her; Mrs., misses; female role; female lead

นางงาม beauty queen

นางเงือก mermaid

นางชี nun

นางนม wet nurse

นางนวล seagull

นางใน lady of the bedchamber

นางแบบ model

นางผดุงครรภ์ midwife, accoucheuse

นางพญา queen, noblewoman

นางพยาบาล nurse

นางพระกำนัล lady of honor, lady of presence

นางฟ้า fairy, goddess

นางไม้ wood sprite

นางระบำ dancer, dancing girl

นางละคร actress

นางโลม courtesan

นางสนองพระโอษฐ์ lady-in-waiting

นางสาว Miss; unmarried woman

นางสาวไทย Miss Thailand

นางห้าม royal concubine

นางเอก leading actress, the leading lady, female lead; star, heroine

นาฏกรรม drama, play

นาฏดนตรี musical drama

นาฏศิลป์ theatrical arts, performing arts

นาที minute

นาทีทอง golden opportunity; precious moment

เข็มนาที minute hand

นาน long, a long time, sustained, lasting

นานเกินควร too long

นานๆ ครั้ง once in a while

นานทีปีหน once in a blue moon, rarely, once in a great while

นานเท่าไร how long

ไม่นานเท่าไร not too long, not very long, not so long, not for long

นานนม long ago, since long ago, for a long long time

นานไป too long

นานพอดู quite a while, fairly long

นานวัน as time passed, in time

นานแสนนาน forever

นานเหลือเกิน ever so long

มิช้ามินาน shortly, soon; not long ago, in not so long

ยืนนาน long-lasting, enduring

น่านน้ำ territorial waters

น่านฟ้า territorial airspace

นานัปการ diverse, various, a variety of

นานา different, various, a variety of

นานาจิตตัง many men many minds

นานาชนิด different kinds (of), heterogeneous

นานาชาติ international

นานาประการ diverse, different, various, a variety of

นานาประเทศ international

กฎหมายนานาประเทศ international law

นานาพรรณ variegated, motley

นานาสังวาส of a separate sect; a sect which does not permit itself to participate in rites performed by other sects of the same religion; group having its own ideas

นาบ to press down, press, to flatten; to iron; to lay (a girl)

นาม noun; name

นามกร name

นามธรรม abstract, subjective

นามบัตร card, name card, visiting card, business card

นามปากกา pen name, nom de plume

นามแฝง alias, pseudonym

นามสกุล surname, family name

นามานุกรม dictionary of proper names

นามาภิไธย royal name

ชื่อเสียงเรียงนาม reputation

รายนาม names, list of names

    รายนามผู้บริจาค contributors, donors

    รายนามผู้แสดง cast

ลงนาม to sign; signed

เลื่องชื่อระบือนาม famous, renowned; widely known; popular

นาย Mr., Mister, Sir; master; owner, employer; chief, boss; superior; you

    นายกอง commander

    นายจ้าง employer

    นายงาน foreman, person in charge, chief

    นายช่าง chief mechanic; supervising, engineer, chief

    นายตรวจ inspector, supervisor; conductor (รถไฟ)

    นายตำรวจ police officer

    นายทหาร officer

        นายทหารชั้นประทวน warrant officer

        นายทหารชั้นสัญญาบัตร commissioned officer

        นายทหารบก army officer

        นายทหารเรือ naval officer

        นายทหารอากาศ air force officer

    นายทะเบียน registrar, recorder, register

    นายท้าย helmsman, steersman

    นายทุน capitalist; financial backer

    นายนาวา naval commander

        นายนาวาตรี lieutenant commander

        นายนาวาโท commander

        นายนาวาเอก captain

    นายประกัน guarantor, surety, bailor

    นายไปรษณีย์ postmaster

    นายพราน hunter

นายก president, chairman

    นายกเทศมนตรี mayor

    นายกรัฐมนตรี prime minister, President of the Council of Ministers, premier

        สำนักนายกรัฐมนตรี Office of the Prime Minister

นายพล general

    นายพลจัตวา brigadier general

    นายพลตรี major general

    นายพลโท lieutenant general

    นายพลเอก general

นายพลตำรวจ police general

    นายพลตำรวจตรี police major general

    นายพลตำรวจโท police lieutenant general

    นายพลตำรวจเอก police general

นายพลเรือ admiral

    นายพลเรือตรี rear admiral

    นายพลเรือโท vice admiral

    นายพลเรือเอก admiral

นายพัน colonel

    นายพันตรี major

    นายพันโท lieutenant colonel

    นายพันเอก colonel

นายพันตำรวจ police colonel

    นายพันตำรวจตรี police major

    นายพันตำรวจโท police lieutenant colonel

    นายพันตำรวจเอก police colonel

นายแพทย์ Dr., doctor, physician, M.D., medical doctor

    นายแพทย์หญิง Dr., M.D., woman doctor

นายร้อย junior officer

    นายร้อยตรี second lieutenant

    นายร้อยโท first lieutenant

    นายร้อยเอก captain

นายเรือ captain, skipper

    นายเรือตรี ensign

    นายเรือโท lieutenant, junior grade

    นายเรือเอก lieutenant, senior grade

นายเวร duty officer

นายสถานี station master

นายสิบ non-commissioned officer

    นายสิบตรี private, first class

น
บ
ป
ผ
ฝ
พ
ฟ
ภ
ม
ย
ร
ฤ
ฤๅ
ล
ว
ศ
ษ
ส
ห
ฬ
อ
ฮ

นายสิบโท corporal
นายสิบเอก sergeant
จ่านายสิบ master sergeant, sergeant major
นายหน้า broker, commission agent
นายห้าง business manager; big boss; Mr. Manager
นายเหนือหัว one's boss
นายอำเภอ district officer, Nai Amphur; sheriff
นายิกา president, chairlady, chairwoman
ท่านนายิกา madame president
นารายณ์ Narayana
นารี woman
น้าว to draw, bend
โน้มน้าว see โน้มน้าว หน้า 265
นาวา ship, boat, vessel
รัฐนาวา ship of state
นาวิกโยธิน marine
นาวี boat, ship, vessel; navy
พาณิชยนาวี merchant marine, merchant fleet
ราชนาวี Royal Navy
นาสา, นาสิก nose; nasal, rhin-, rhino-
นาฬิกา clock; watch; o'clock, hours
นาฬิกาข้อมือ wristwatch
นาฬิกาแขวน wall clock
นาฬิกาแดด sundial
นาฬิกาตั้ง grandfather clock
นาฬิกาทราย hourglass, sandglass
นาฬิกาน้ำ clepsydra, water clock
นาฬิกาปลุก alarm clock
นาฬิกาพก pocket watch
กี่นาฬิกา? What time is it?
เข็มนาฬิกา hand of a /watch/clock/
ไขนาฬิกา to wind a /clock/watch/
ชั่วนาฬิกา an hour
ช่างแก้นาฬิกา watchmaker, watch repairer
ยี่สิบสองนาฬิกา twenty-two hours, ten p.m.
สองนาฬิกา two o'clock
สองนาฬิกาครึ่ง half past two, two thirty
สองนาฬิกาสิบนาที ten past two, two ten,

ten after two
สองนาฬิกาสิบห้านาที a quarter past two, two fifteen
อีกสิบนาทีสองนาฬิกา ten to two, one fifty
อีกสิบห้านาทีสองนาฬิกา a quarter to two, one forty-five
หน้าปัดนาฬิกา face (of a /clock/ watch/) dial
หอนาฬิกา clock tower

นำ to lead, conduct; to head; principal; to bring, take; to escort; to introduce, begin
นำเข้า to import
นำทาง to show the way, guide
นำเที่ยว to guide, to take (a person) around, lead a tour
นำพา to care (about), be concerned (about), pay attention (to), take care of
นำมา to bring, lead
นำมาใช้ to apply, use, utilize
นำมาใช้ได้ applicable
นำมาซึ่ง to lead to, bring, bring about, give rise to
นำร่อง to pilot (a ship)
การศึกษานำร่อง pilot study
โครงการนำร่อง pilot project
นำสมัย modern, fashionable
นำสืบ to adduce evidence, prove; to go forward with the evidence
นำแสดงโดย starring
นำหน้า to lead, be in the forefront
คำนำ preface; foreword
ตัวนำ[1] principal /actor/actress/character/ etc, lead /actor/actress/, star
ตัวนำ[2] conductor
แนะนำ to introduce; present; to advise
บทนำ introduction
ผู้นำ head, leader; elite

น้ำ water; liquid, fluid, juice; aquatic
น้ำกรด acid
น้ำกร่อย brackish water

น้ำกระด้าง hard water
น้ำกระเพื่อม ripple
น้ำกระสาย aqueous adjuvant
น้ำกลั่น distilled water
น้ำก๊อก tap water
น้ำกะทิ coconut cream
น้ำกาม semen, sperm
น้ำกิน drinking-water, potable water
น้ำเกลือ saline solution
น้ำขาว rice wine
น้ำข้าว boiled rice water
น้ำขึ้น high tide, flood tide; The tide is /rising/coming in/.
    น้ำขึ้นให้รีบตัก Make hay while the sun shines. / Get while the getting is good.
น้ำแข็ง ice
    น้ำแข็งป่น shredded ice
    น้ำแข็งเปล่า ice water
    น้ำแข็งหลอด ice cube
    น้ำแข็งแห้ง plain ice cubes; dry ice
น้ำคร่ำ polluted water, stagnant pool of putrid water
น้ำคร่ำ amniotic fluid
น้ำค้าง dew
น้ำคาวปลา lochia, postpartum vaginal discharge
น้ำคำ words, what one says
น้ำเค็ม salt water
น้ำโคลน mud
น้ำเงิน blue
น้ำจัณฑ์ liquor, spirits
น้ำจิ้ม sauce; dip
น้ำจืด fresh water
น้ำใจ spirit, heart, feelings; goodwill, thoughtfulness, helpfulness
    น้ำใจอันกว้างขวาง generous
    เจ็บช้ำน้ำใจ to be hurt
    มีน้ำใจ helpful, kind, generous (person)
    ไม่มีน้ำใจ ungenerous; unfeeling, unkind

ไม่ให้เสียน้ำใจ to not want to /discourage/disappoint/ someone
น้ำชา tea
น้ำเชื่อม syrup
น้ำซาวข้าว rice rinsing water
น้ำดิบ unboiled water, untreated water
น้ำดี bile
น้ำดื่ม drinking water
น้ำตก waterfall, cascade
น้ำตา tears
    น้ำตาคลอ tears welling up in one's eyes
    น้ำตาเทียน candle drippings
น้ำตาล sugar
    น้ำตาลแดง brown sugar
    น้ำตาลโตนด palm sugar, jaggery
    น้ำตาลทราย granulated sugar
    น้ำตาลปึก palm sugar in soft cakes
    น้ำตาลมะพร้าว coconut sugar
    น้ำตาลเมา toddy
    น้ำตาลสด sugar palm sap
    น้ำตาลไห pot of palm sugar
น้ำเต้า bottlegourd
น้ำทรง still water
น้ำท่วม flood, to be flooded
    น้ำท่วมปาก tongue-tied
    น้ำท่วมทุ่ง garrulous
น้ำทะเล seawater
น้ำท่า water
น้ำนม milk
น้ำนวล beaming, radiant, glowing
น้ำนิ่ง still water, (of water) to be still, calm
    น้ำนิ่งไหลลึก Still water runs deep.
น้ำเน่า polluted water, dirty water; junk, trashy, cheap
    ละครน้ำเน่า soap opera
    นวนิยายน้ำเน่า pulp fiction
น้ำบ่อ well water
น้ำบาดาล artesian well water
น้ำประปา piped water, water supply

น
บ
ป
ผ
ฝ
พ
ฟ
ภ
ม
ย
ร
ฤ
ฤๅ
ล
ว
ศ
ษ
ส
ห
ฬ
อ
ฮ

น้ำประสานทอง soldering flux

น้ำปลา fish sauce, fish soy

น้ำเปล่า plain water

น้ำเปลี่ยนนิสัย joy juice (liquor, beer), joy water (hard liquor, not beer)

น้ำผลไม้ fruit juice

น้ำผึ้ง honey

น้ำฝน rain water

น้ำพระพิพัฒน์สัตยา water of allegiance

น้ำพริก hot shrimp-paste sauce

น้ำพักน้ำแรง by the sweat of one's brow, by one's effort, through the efforts (of)

น้ำพุ fountain; spring

น้ำมนตร์ holy water, lustral water

น้ำมะกรูด kaffir lime juice

น้ำมะนาว limeade, lime juice

น้ำมะเน็ด lemonade; limeade

น้ำมะพร้าว coconut milk

น้ำมัน oil

   น้ำมันกระเบา chaulmoogra oil

   น้ำมันก๊าด kerosine, kerosene

   น้ำมันเขียว cajeput oil

   น้ำมันเครื่อง engine oil, lubricating oil

   น้ำมันงา sesame oil

   น้ำมันชักเงา lacquer

   น้ำมันชักแห้ง linseed oil

   น้ำมันเชื้อเพลิง fuel oil

   น้ำมันโซลา diesel fuel

   น้ำมันดิน tar, shale oil

   น้ำมันดิบ crude oil

   น้ำมันตับปลา cod-liver oil

   น้ำมันเบนซิน gasoline, gas (US), petrol (Brit)

   น้ำมันปาล์ม palm oil, palm olein

   น้ำมันพราย oil melted from the chin of a corpse and applied to induce love or madness

   น้ำมันพืช vegetable oil

   น้ำมันมวย rubbing oil

น้ำมันมะกอก olive oil

น้ำมันมะพร้าว coconut oil

น้ำมันยาง dammar oil

น้ำมันระกำ oil of wintergreen

น้ำมันแร่ mineral oil

น้ำมันละหุ่ง castor oil

น้ำมันล้างเครื่อง flushing oil

น้ำมันวัว beef fat

น้ำมันสน turpentine

น้ำมันสลัด salad oil

น้ำมันใส่ผม hair oil; pomade

น้ำมันหมู lard

น้ำมันหล่อลื่น lubricating oil

น้ำมือ handiwork, hand

บริษัทนี้ล้มเหลวเพราะน้ำมือผู้จัดการ The company went downhill at the hand of the manager. / The failure of the firm is the manager's handiwork.

น้ำมูก nasal mucus

เช็ดน้ำมูกสิลูก Wipe your nose, darling.

น้ำเมา intoxicating beverages

น้ำย่อย digestive juice, gastric juice

น้ำยา spicy sauce put on Thai vermicelli; solution

   ไม่มีน้ำยา impotent, powerless, ineffectual, to carry no weight

น้ำเย็น ice water, cold water

น้ำร้อน hot water

   ค่าน้ำร้อนน้ำชา tea money

น้ำรัก lacquer

น้ำแร่ mineral water

น้ำลด low tide, ebb tide

น้ำลาย saliva, sputum, spit

   น้ำลายแตกฟอง to be carried away by one's /talk/speech/etc, talk and talk

   น้ำลายหก to drool (over), slaver; mouth-watering

   น้ำลายไหล one's mouth is watering (for something); to salivate

บ้าน้ำลาย raving

น้ำเลี้ยง sap; lifeblood; aqueous humor

น้ำวน eddy; whirlpool, maelstrom

น้ำส้ม vinegar; orange drink, orangeade, orange juice

   น้ำส้มคั้น fresh orange juice

   น้ำส้มสายชู vinegar

น้ำสุก boiled water

น้ำเสีย wastewater

น้ำเสียง tone (of voice)

น้ำใส clear water, limpid water

   น้ำใสใจจริง sincerely, truly, genuinely, from the bottom of one's heart

น้ำหนวก aural discharge

น้ำหนัก weight; load

คำพูดของเขาไม่มีน้ำหนัก His words carried no weight.

น้ำหนักสี chiaroscuro *(ศิลปะ)*

น้ำหน้า likes (of)

น้ำหน้าอย่างเอ็ง ใครเขาจะเชื่อ Who would believe the likes of you?

   สมน้ำหน้า It serves (you) right.

น้ำหนึ่ง of the first water; fine

   น้ำหนึ่งใจเดียว in solidarity

   เพชรน้ำหนึ่ง diamond of the first water

น้ำหมาก betel juice

น้ำหมึก ink

น้ำหวาน sweet drink, soft drink

น้ำหอม perfume, scent, lotion, toilet water, eau de Cologne

น้ำเหลือง lymph

น้ำไหล the water /runs/flows/, running water

   น้ำไหลบ่า torrent

   พูดเป็นน้ำไหลไฟดับ to chatter away; to speak non-stop

น้ำอดน้ำทน endurance, stamina

น้ำอบ scented water, toilet water

น้ำอสุจิ semen

น้ำอ้อย molasses

น้ำอัดลม aerated waters, carbonated beverages, soft drink

บ่อน้ำ well; pond

ปั้นน้ำเป็นตัว to make something out of nothing; make (something) up out of whole cloth, fabricate

ปากน้ำ mouth of a river, estuary

ฝั่งน้ำ bank (of a river)

พูดเป็นน้ำ to speak in a steady stream, talk fluently, loquacious

ฟองน้ำ sponge

แม่น้ำ river

สัตว์น้ำ aquatic animal

หม้อน้ำ boiler; radiator; waterpot

ห้องน้ำ bathroom, lavatory, restroom, men's room, ladies' room

หิวน้ำ thirsty

อาบน้ำ to bathe, take a bath

ไอน้ำ steam, vapor

นิกร group, company

นิกาย sect, school

นิคม settlement

นิคหกรรม penalty prescribed by the /Sangha/ Buddhist Order/

   กฎนิคหกรรม Sangha rules of disciplinary action, penal code of the Buddhist Order

นิ่ง still, quiet, silent; motionless, steady

   นิ่งๆ still; be still, keep still

      คนนิ่ง ๆ quiet type

   นิ่งเงียบ to keep quiet

   นิ่งเฉย indifferent (to); to remain silent

   นิ่งแน่, แน่นิ่ง unconscious; to pass out

   นิ่งเสีย Be still., Keep quiet.

   นิ่งอึ้ง to be speechless, struck dumb

   นั่งนิ่ง to sit still, sit quietly

   น้ำนิ่ง still water, (of water) to be still, calm

      น้ำนิ่งไหลลึก Still water runs deep.

   ภาพนิ่ง still picture

   ยืนนิ่ง to stand still

น
บ
ป
ผ
ฝ
พ
ฟ
ภ
ม
ย
ร
ฤ
ฤๅ
ล
ว
ศ
ษ
ส
ห
ฬ
อ
ฮ

นิจ   as in **เนืองนิจ, เป็นนิจ** regularly, constantly

นิด   small, little

    นิดเดียว small; tiny; a little bit, a little, just a bit

    นิดหน่อย not much, a little

นิตย์   see **นิจ**

    นิตยสาร magazine, periodical

นิติ   law; legal, juristic

    นิติกร legal officer

    นิติกรณ์ legalization

    นิติกรรม juristic act, legal act

    นิติธรรม legal principle

    นิตินัย legally, de jure

    นิติบัญญัติ legislation

        สภานิติบัญญัติ legislature

        อำนาจนิติบัญญัติ legislative power

    นิติบุคคล juristic person, legal entity

    นิติภาวะ legal age, majority

        บรรลุนิติภาวะ to attain one's majority, be of legal age, become of age

    นิติศาสตร์ law

นิทรา   sleeping

นิทาน   story, fable, tale

    นิทานเรื่องนี้สอนให้รู้ว่า This story teaches that

    เล่านิทาน to tell a story

นิเทศ   to supervise, oversee

    นิเทศการสอน to /supervise/oversee/ teaching

    นิเทศศาสตร์ communication arts

    สารนิเทศศาสตร์ information science

นิธิ   treasure

    มูลนิธิ foundation

นินทา   to talk about (someone), gossip (about); to backbite, say mean things about someone

นิพนธ์   work, writing; composition, dissertation; to compose, write

    พระราชนิพนธ์ royal literary work

    วิทยานิพนธ์ thesis

    วิทยานิพนธ์ปริญญาเอก doctoral dissertation

นิพพาน   nirvana, enlightenment, extinction of all defilements and sufferings, final deliverance from suffering

    บรรลุนิพพาน to attain /enlightenment/ nirvana/

นิ่ม   soft; tender; smooth; yielding

    นิ่มนวล gently, softly, mildly, delicately; with finesse, smoothly, diplomatically

    นุ่มนิ่ม soft

    ปัญญานิ่ม nitwit, dummy, soft in the head

นิมนต์   to invite (a monk)

นิมิต   sign; omen; indication

    เป็นนิมิตหมายอันดี a /good/encouraging/ sign

นิยม   ...ism,...ist; to be interested in, like; to admire

    ค่านิยม values

    จักรวรรดินิยม imperialist

    ชาตินิยม nationalism

    พวกนี้เป็นนักชาตินิยม They are nationalists.

    เป็นที่นิยม popular; fashionable

    รสนิยม taste, preference

นิยาม   definition; law of nature, norm

นิยาย   story, fable, tale

    เอานิยายอะไรกับเธอไม่ได้หรอก She can't be taken seriously.

    นิยายอิงประวัติศาสตร์ story based on history, historical novel

    นวนิยาย novel

นิรเทศ see **เนรเทศ** หน้า 263

นิรโทษกรรม amnesty, general pardon

นิรนาม anonymous, nameless, unknown

    ทหารนิรนาม unknown soldier

    นักเขียนนิรนาม anonymous author

นิรภัย safety, safe, danger-free

    เขตนิรภัย safety zone

    ตู้นิรภัย safe

    ห้องนิรภัย vault, strongroom

นิรมล pure, immaculate, spotless

นิรมิต *see* **เนรมิต** *หน้า 263*

นิรันดร forever, eternally, for eternity, always
รักเธอชั่วนิรันดร I will love you /for eternity/ forever/.

นิราศ travels
นิราศภูเขาทองของสุนทรภู่ Suntorn Poo's "Travels to the Golden Mount"

นิรุกติ word
นิรุกติศาสตร์ etymology

นิรุตติ *see* **นิรุกติ**

นิโรธ complete extinction, nirvana

นิล black, jet black; dark blue; dark green; onyx
ไอ้นิล blackie

นิ่ว[1] calculus, stone

นิ่ว[2] contorted, screwed up (with pain etc); to frown, scowl
หน้านิ่ว face contorted with pain; scowling

นิ้ว finger; inch
นิ้วกลาง middle finger
นิ้วก้อย little finger, pinkie
นิ้วชี้ index finger, forefinger
นิ้วเท้า toe(s)
นิ้วนาง ring finger
นิ้วโป้ง thumb
นิ้วฟุต inch
นิ้วมือ finger
นิ้วหัวแม่มือ thumb
กระเบียดนิ้ว a quarter of an inch
ทุกกระเบียดนิ้ว every inch
ข้อนิ้ว knuckle, finger joint
ดีดนิ้ว to fillip; to snap the fingers; to flick with a finger
ยกนิ้วให้ to think something great; give (someone) credit for (something), appreciate
ฝีมือทำกับข้าวของเธอผมยกนิ้วให้เลย I think your cooking is great, darling. / I give you credit for your cooking.

นิวเคลียร์ nuclear

นิวรณ์ hindrances, obstacles to the attainment of goodness: lust, ill will or malice, sloth or indolence, anxiety and doubt or uncertainty

นิวัต, นิวัตน์ to return

นิเวศ, นิเวศน์ house; estate, housing development
นิเวศวิทยา ecology
ราชนิเวศน์ palace

นิสัย habit, disposition, character
นิสัยใจคอ disposition, temperament, character
นิสัยเสีย bad, (to get into, have) bad habits
น้ำเปลี่ยนนิสัย *see* **น้ำเปลี่ยนนิสัย** *หน้า 258*
ประพฤติจนเป็นนิสัย to become habituated (to), get in the habit of
อบรมบ่มนิสัย character training, character building

นิสิต student, undergraduate
นิสิตเก่า alumnus *(เอกพจน์ชาย)*, alumni *(พหูพจน์ชาย)*, alumna *(เอกพจน์หญิง)*, alumnae *(พหูพจน์หญิง)*, graduate (of)

นิสิตา woman undergraduate, co-ed

นี่ this; hey
นี่กี่โมงแล้ว Hey, what time is it?
นี่แน่ะ Look here!; Take this!
นี่ยังไง here it is
นี่ยังไงกัน What's the meaning of this?, What's going on?
นี่แหละ you see
แล้วก็บอกว่านี่แหละเผด็จการมันดี Then he said, "You see, dictatorship is not bad."
นี่หว่า dammit, for god's sake
เขาเถียงคอเป็นเอ็นว่า "ผมไม่ได้ทำนี่หว่า" "I didn't do it, for god's sake."
เอ็งทำแบบนี้ใช้ไม่ได้นี่หว่า "Dammit, that sort of thing just doesn't go around here!"
ที่นี่ here

นี้ this, the
คืนนี้ tonight, this evening
เช่นนี้ for example; like this, this, in this way

น
บ
ป
ผ
ฝ
พ
ฟ
ภ
ม
ย
ร
ฤ
ฤๅ
ล
ว
ศ
ษ
ส
ห
ฬ
อ
ฮ

เช้านี้ this morning, in the morning

ดังนี้ in this way, like this; as follows, the following

แต่นี้ from now on

พรุ่งนี้ tomorrow

เย็นนี้ this evening, in the late afternoon

วันนี้ today

วานนี้ yesterday

หมู่นี้ nowadays, lately, these days

อย่างนี้ like this

นีออน fluorescent light

นึก to think of, recall

นึกกลัว to feel afraid, scared; become fearful

นึกเกลียด to take a disliking (to)

นึกขัน to be amused

นึกขำในใจ to laugh to oneself (at, over, about)

นึกฉงน to wonder (at, about, whether)

นึกดูก่อน to think something over first

นึกดูให้ดี to think carefully, give careful consideration (to)

นึกได้ to recall, remember; to think (of)

นึกฝัน to imagine, dream (of)

นึกไม่ออก to be unable to /recollect/recall/, cannot think of

นึกย้อน to think back (to)

นึกรัก to take a /liking/fancy/to someone

นึกว่า to think

นึกสงสัย to feel suspicious, feel uneasy (about)

นึกเห็นภาพ to visualize, imagine

นึกอยาก to feel like, want, need

นึกออก to recollect, remember, recall, think of something

นึกอาย to feel embarrassed

นึกเอา to think

หวนนึก to think back (to), recall

นึ่ง to steam

นึ่งข้าวเหนียว to steam sticky rice

ปลานึ่ง steamed fish

นุง confused, in confusion

นุงถุง entangled; jumbled, mixed up

นุงนัง tangled, in a mess, in disorder

นุ่ง to wear, put on, be clad in

นุ่งกระโจมอก to wear a skirt-cloth knotted above the chest

นุ่งลมห่มฟ้า to wear (one's) birthday suit, be stark naked, nude

นุ่งห่ม to wear

เครื่องนุ่งห่ม clothing, garments, wearing apparel

ผ้านุ่ง panung, a dhoti-like garment, breeches draped from a single hip cloth

นุช younger sister

นุ่น kapok

นุ่ม soft; smooth; yielding, plastic; tender, gentle

นุ่มนวล sweetly, gently, smoothly

นุ่มนิ่ม soft, pliant; gentle in manner

เนื้อนุ่ม tender; soft to the touch

อ่อนนุ่ม soft; spongy

นุ้ย chubby, plump

ตุ้ยนุ้ย roly-poly

นูน to bulge; embossed; convex; bulging; raised

กระจกนูน convex mirror

พิมพ์ตัวนูน to emboss, embossed printing

นู่น over there, yonder

เนคไท necktie

เน็ต net

เนตบอล netball

เนตร eye; guide

เนตรนารี Girl Guide

พระเนตร eye (royal word)

ทอดพระเนตร (royal word) to see, look at, /have/take/a look (at)

เนติ law; example; convention

เนติบัณฑิต law graduate, bachelor of laws

เนติบัณฑิตยสภา Bar Association

เน้น to emphasize, accent, stress, underline,

highlight, accentuate

เน้นตัวอักษร emphasized letters

เน้นเสียง to speak emphatically

พูดเน้น to emphasize, stress

เนย butter

เนยแข็ง cheese

เนยเทียม margarine

เนยใส ghee

เนรคุณ ungrateful

เนรเทศ to banish, exile, deport, expel

เนรนาด in a shambles, on top of one another, all over the place; strewn about

เนรมิต to create, conjure up

เน้อ a sound used for emphasis เช่น boy, man, don't forget, okay

เนา[1] to baste

เนา[2] to live, dwell

เนา[3] as in **วันเนา** the day on which the sun travels between Pisces and Aries marking the old Thai New Year's Eve about April 14.

เน่า rotten, spoiled, decayed, decomposed, corrupted

เน่าเปื่อย spoiled; to get spoiled, deteriorate

เน่าเฟะ putrid

เน่าเหม็น putrid

ไข่เน่า rotten egg

น้ำเน่า trashy, see **น้ำเน่า** หน้า 257

เนิน hill, mound, knoll, rise

เนินเขา foothill

เนินดิน hill

เนินทราย sand dune

เนินสวรรค์, เนินสวาท pubic mound, mound of Venus

เป็นเนิน, เป็นโคก hilly

เนิ่น early, beforehand

เนิ่นๆ well in advance

เนิ่นนานมาแล้ว a long time ago, in early days

มาเนิ่นๆ come early

เนิบ, เนิบๆ slowly, sluggishly, ponderously, in slow motion

พูดเนิบๆ to drawl, speak slowly

เนิบนาบ see **เนิบ**

เนียน neatly; fine

ผิวเนียน fine complexioned, having fine skin

เนื้อ flesh, meat; beef; substance

เนื้อๆ theme

เนื้อกระป๋อง /canned/tinned/ beef

เนื้อกวาง venison

เนื้อแกะ mutton, lamb

เนื้อความ meaning, substance, material

เนื้อควาย buffalo meat

เนื้อคู่ a perfect match; a husband and wife destined for one another, to be meant for one another, made for each other

เนื้อเค็ม salted beef

เนื้องอก tumor

เนื้อเงิน silver

เนื้อซี่โครง short ribs

เนื้อตะเข้ rumpsteak

เนื้อตัว body, I, you, etc

น้ำไม่อาบ เนื้อตัวสกปรกหมด You are filthy dirty and haven't taken a bath.

เนื้อตาย dead tissue

เนื้อถ้อยกระทงความ text, wording

เนื้อทอง gold

เนื้อที่ area, space

เนื้อแท้ heart of the matter; in essence, in reality, in fact, the fact is...

เนื้อน่อง shank

เนื้อใบบัวใน flank

เนื้อผ้า texture, body, weave

ตามเนื้อผ้า truthfully, justly; calling a spade a spade, (saying something) the way it is

เนื้อเพลง melody, theme

เนื้อม้า horsemeat

น
บ
ป
ผ
ฝ
พ
ฟ
ภ
ม
ย
ร
ฤ
ฤๅ
ล
ว
ศ
ษ
ส
ห
ฬ
อ
ฮ

เนื้อไม้ wood

เนื้อเยื่อ tissue

เนื้อเยื่อวิทยา histology

เนื้อร้อง lyrics, words

เนื้อร้าย cancer, malignant tumor

เนื้อเรื่อง plot, story

เนื้อวัว beef, veal (เนื้อลูกวัว)

เนื้อสด fresh meat; female flesh

เนื้อสัน loin

เนื้อสันกลาง rib set

เนื้อสันกลางถอดกระดูก rib eye

เนื้อสันคอ chuck

เนื้อสันนอก sirloin

เนื้อสันใน tenderloin

เนื้อสะโพก round, round steak

เนื้อหมู pork

เนื้อหอม in demand, popular, pop

ดาราเนื้อหอม pop star

เนื้อหา gist, essence; substance; subject matter

เป็นเนื้อเดียวกัน blended together, combined; homogeneous, uniform

หมดเนื้อหมดตัว penniless, to lose everything, be wiped out

เนื่อง, เนื่องๆ regulary, often, frequently

เนื่องนอง to pour in

เนื่องนิตย์, เนื่องนิจ regularly, constantly

เนื่องแน่น crowded

เนื่อง connected with, due to, related to; since, as, as a result (of)

เนื่องจาก due to, owing to, because, as a result (of)

เนื่องด้วย as, since, due to, because of

สืบเนื่อง as a consequence of, consequential

เรื่องสืบเนื่อง to be the consequence (of), result (of), ramification

เนือย, เนือยๆ tired; listless, enervated, spiritless; apathetic, indifferent

เนือยลง to become tired, lose steam, lose

one's pep

แน่ certain, sure, definite; smart, expert, big

แน่กว่า stronger, better

แน่แก่ใจ to be positive, convinced, know in one's heart

แน่ใจ sure, certain, confident

แน่จริง to have what it takes, have the guts

ถ้าเอ็งแน่จริง ก็อย่าหนีซีวะ If you've got/what it takes/the guts/ face up to me, man!

ไอ้หมอนี่ ไม่แน่จริงนี่หว่า There's nothing to that guy.

แน่ชัด definite, certain , positive, definitely, clearly, without a doubt

แน่แท้ definitely, absolutely

แน่นอน definitely, for sure, certainly

แน่นิ่ง still, dead still, motionless; unconscious

แน่แน่ว steadfast, constant

แน่ละ for sure

แน่ละซิ definitely, absolutely

แน่หรือ Really?, Are you sure?, Is it certain?; Let's see how good you are, wise guy.

เป็นแน่, เป็นแน่แท้ absolutely, definitely

ไม่แน่ uncertain, not certain, not definite; I'm not so sure., doubtful, maybe

แน่น tight; fast; constricted; firm; dense, compact; to be crowded, congested, packed

แน่นขนัด packed

แน่นปึ้ก, แน่นเปรี๊ยะ solid; very tight

แน่นแฟ้น firm, solid, close, established

แน่นหนา strong, solid, firm

แน่นหน้าอก to feel /constricted/a tightness in the chest/

หนักแน่น steady, stable, solid

หนาแน่น crowded, packed, congested, heavily (populated, etc)

แนบ to overlay; to press against; to attach, be attached (to); to cling (to), hold close to; to press against

แนบกาย to hold (someone) close
แนบข้าง to lie beside
แนบติด to attach
แนบเนียน to fit snugly; to be acceptable
  อย่างแนบเนียน acceptably
แนบเนื้อ to cling (to), clinging
แนบแน่น constant; binding
  ความแนบแน่น consistency
ที่แนบ attached
หลักฐานที่แนบ attached evidence
แนม as in **สอดแนม** to spy (on), reconnoiter, gather intelligence
แนว line, row
  แนวความคิด thinking, idea, philosophy, line of thought, way of thinking
  แนวตั้ง vertical
  แนวทแยง diagonal
  แนวทาง way
  แนวที่ห้า fifth column
  แนวเทียบ analogy
  แนวนอน horizontal
  แนวโน้ม trend, tendency
  แนวป่า line of the forest
  แนวรบ front line, line of battle
  แนวร่วม front
  แนวหน้า front, front line; vanguard
  แนวหลัง rear, behind the lines
แน่ว straight; unwavering, composed, concentrated
  แน่วแน่ steady, firm, steadfast, constant, single-minded
  ตรงแน่ว straight (to)
แนะ to advise, counsel; to indicate; to hint, suggest
  แนะนัด to make an appointment, make arrangements (to, for)
  แนะนำ to advise, recommend; to guide, direct; to introduce
    แนะนำตัว to introduce oneself (to)

    แนะนำให้รู้จักกัน to introduce (someone to another person)
    รายการอาหารแนะนำ recommended dishes
  แนะแนว to give guidance, give counselling, to counsel
    แนะแนวการศึกษา educational /guidance/counselling/
แน่ะ hey!; see!; jesus!
โน swollen; a bump
  หัวโน to have a bump on the head
โน้ต note
  โน้ตเพลง music; score
  จดโน้ต to take notes
  ฟุตโน้ต footnote
โนน hill, rise, high land
โน่น there; that one; over there
  ทำโน่นทำนี่ this and that, busy with this and that; pottering around
โน้น over there, way over there, yonder
  ชายคนโน้น that man over there
  อย่างโน้นอย่างนี้ this and that, a whole lot of things
โน้ม to bend down, bow down
  โน้มน้าว to convince, persuade, induce, incline (someone to do something), influence (someone to do something), work on (someone)
  พูดโน้มน้าวจิตใจจนเขายอมสารภาพผิด His words so worked on her that she confessed. / What he said induced her to confess.
  โน้มถ่วง see **ความโน้มถ่วง** *หน้า 209*
โนมพรรณ see *รูปโฉมโนมพรรณ หน้า 425*
โนรา, มโนราห์ Manorah; a folk drama
ใน in, on, at; inner, internal
  ในขณะนี้ now, at present; for the time being, at this time
  ในใจ to oneself; private
  ในฐานะ as

น
บ
ป
ผ
ฝ
พ
ฟ
ภ
ม
ย
ร
ฤ
ฤๅ
ล
ว
ศ
ษ
ส
ห
ฬ
อ
ฮ

ปรากฏตัวในฐานะพยาน to attend as a witness

ในตอนนี้ at this time, now, at this point

ในตัว ipso facto, in itself

ในทาง /in a/the/ way (which); - ly

    ในทางทุจริต unlawfully, dishonestly

    ในทางเศรษฐกิจ economically

ในที่สุด at last, finally; in the long run, in the end

ในปัจจุบัน at present

ในพริบตาเดียว in the wink of an eye

ในภายหลัง later, subsequently, afterwards; in the future

ในเมื่อ since, as, when

ในไม่ช้า before long, shortly, soon

ในร่ม in the shade; indoor

ในระดับหนึ่ง to /some/a certain/ extent

ในระยะ while, during, when; in, within

ในระหว่าง during; between, among

ในราว about, approximately, around

ในเร็วๆ นี้ soon, coming soon

ในเรื่อง in the matter of, in regard to, with respect to, in this case, in this regard

ในวันพรุ่ง by tomorrow, tomorrow

ในวันหน้า later on, in the future, some other day

ในวันไหน which day

ในเวลา at (night etc), when (speaking etc), during (office hours etc)

ในสมัยก่อน formerly, in former times

ในไส้ blood, natural, by consanguinity

ในหลวง the King, His Majesty

ในอันที่จะ in order to; which will

ในโอกาส on the occasion (of)

คนใน insider

เครื่องใน giblets (เฉพาะเป็ดไก่ซึ่งกินได้), viscera เช่น tripe, heart, liver, kidney, sweetbreads, gizzard

บ่ not, no
หาค่าบ่มิได้ invaluable, priceless

บ.ก. editor; headquarters

บก land, terrestrial
กองทัพบก army
ขึ้นบก to land, go ashore
ทหารบก soldier
ทางบก by land, land route
ลมบก land breeze
สัตว์บก terrestrial animal

บกพร่อง defective, faulty, wrong, not right; shortcoming, error, mistake
บกพร่องต่อหน้าที่ misfeasance; to perform badly, do one's job poorly
ข้อบกพร่อง defect, error, mistake fault, (what is) wrong; weakness, flaw, shortcoming
ขาดตกบกพร่อง shortcomings, deficiency, inadequacy, errors and omissions

บ่ง to indicate, show; to specify; to extract with a needle; to lance (บ่งหนอง)
บ่งเฉพาะ distinctive
บ่งถึง to indicate, point to, refer (to)
บ่งบอก to evince, manifest, reveal, exhibit
บ่งหนาม to extract a thorn with a needle

บงกช lotus

บงการ to direct, run, dictate
จอมบงการ arch dictator
ผู้บงการ dictator; person who is /directing/ running/ (an operation, etc)

บด[1] to crush, pulverize; to roll; to screen, block out
บดขยี้ to crush, smash, destroy
บดถนน to roll a road
รถบดถนน road roller, steam roller
บดบัง to block
บดยา to grind up a medicine, prepare a medicine by grinding

บด[2] as in **เรือบด** small boat

บท chapter, section, clause; article; script, text, lines; role; time
บทกลอน poem
บทกวีนิพนธ์ poetry, poem
บทความ article; editorial; feature
บทคัดย่อ abstract
บทจร to walk, go on foot
บทจะ when it comes time (for something); when one wants to do something
บทจะทำก็ทำ บทจะเลิกก็เลิก When he wants to work he works and when he wants to quit he quits.
ทำงานมาหลายอย่างไม่ประสบความสำเร็จเลย พอหันมาร้องเพลงก็ดังเป็นพลุ ชีวิตเราไม่แน่ บทจะรุ่งก็รุ่งง่ายๆ He tried a lot of things without success. But when he turned to singing, he rocketed to the top. Life is uncertain. When it comes time for glory, it comes so easily.
บทเจรจา dialogue
บทเฉพาะกาล transitory provisions
บทที่ 1 Chapter One
บทนำ leader, editorial
บทบรรณาธิการ editorial
บทบัญญัติ law, legal provision; legislation
บทบาท role
บทประพันธ์ article, story, work, writing
บทพิสูจน์ theorem (math); proof
บทเพลง lyrics
บทเรียน lesson
บทลงโทษ penalty, penalty /clause/ provision/
บทละคร play; script
บทสนทนา dialogue
ตัดบท to cut (someone) off, cut short, /conclude/end/ (a discussion etc) abruptly
บอกบท to prompt, cue, tell someone /what to /say/do/
เล่นนอกบท to play offside, underhanded;

unseemly, unconventional, unusual to say
the least

บน[1], **บนบาน** to make a votive prayer

แก้บน to make a votive offering

บน[2] on, on top of, over, up, upper

ข้างบน above, on top; upstairs

ชั้นบน upstairs; on the top; top shelf

เบื้องบน those on high, the higher
authorities, higher-ups, powers that be

บ่น to complain, grumble (about), beef (about),
grouse (about)

บ่นถึง to ask after, enquire after; to talk
about (someone) fondly

บ่นพร่ำเพรื่อ to be always grumbling

บ่นหา to keep asking for (someone) to come

บ่นอุบอิบ to mutter

ขี้บ่น given to complaining, always
grumbling, fussy, irritable

คนขี้บ่น a fusspot, complainer

บพิตร Your Highness (used by a monk)

บพิตรพระราชสมภาร see **มหาบพิตร**

มหาบพิตร Your Majesty (used by a monk)

บ่ม to heat-ripen; to train

บ่มผิว to avoid getting sunburned, preserve
the paleness of one's skin, protect one's
skin from the elements

อบรมบ่มนิสัย to train, cultivate

บรม supreme, most excellent, highest; sublime

บรมโง่ sublimely stupid

บรมธาตุ relic of Buddha

บรมวงศานุวงศ์ royal family

บรรจง to do painstakingly, with care, carefully

บรรจงเขียน to write neatly, write with care

เขียนบรรจง to print

ตัวบรรจง printed letters, block letters

บรรจบ to meet, join; make up, come to; to complete
(a cycle)

บรรจุ to fill, pack, load; to contain

บรรจุขวด to bottle, fill a bottle

บรรจุตำแหน่ง to appoint to a post, fill a
position; to be permanently appointed, get
a permanent appointment (to a position)

บรรจุปืน to load a gun

บรรจุ 1 ลิตร Contents 1 liter

บรรจุศพ to place an enshrouded body in a
coffin

บรรจุหีบห่อ packaged, packed

บรรจุอัฐิ to deposit ashes in a /stupa/wall/
etc

ถังบรรจุน้ำมัน gasoline drum

บรรณ book; leaf; wing

บรรณพิภพ, บรรณโลก world of books,
bookworld

บรรณาการ gift of friendship, tribute

บรรณาธิการ editor

บรรณานุกรม bibliography

บรรณารักษ์ librarian

บรรณารักษศาสตร์ library science

บรรณสาร papers; archives

บรรดา all, entire, whole

บรรดาแขกเหรื่อทั้งหลาย all the guests

บรรดามี all, the whole (of)

บรรดาศักดิ์ rank, title, dignity

บรรทม to lie down; to sleep

บรรทัด line

บรรทัดฐาน norm, standard; precedent
(เช่น คำพิพากษาฎีกา)

บรรทัดฐานของสังคม social norm

ตัวอย่างบรรทัดฐาน guideline example

ตีบรรทัด to rule, draw a line

ไม้บรรทัด ruler, straightedge

เว้นบรรทัด to skip a line

บรรทุก to load; loaded with, carrying

ค่าระวางบรรทุก freight

รถบรรทุก truck, lorry (Brit), van

เรือบรรทุกสินค้า freighter, cargo /vessel/
ship/

บรรเทา to relieve, give relief; to abate, alleviate,

assuage, reduce; to subdue; to quiet

บรรเทาทุกข์ to rescue, provide relief, /alleviate/relieve/ distress

บรรเทาเบาบาง to become less serious, eased

บรรเทาลง to get better, alleviated, relieved

การบรรเทาภาระ relief (from)

บรรพ, บรรพ์ primitive, ancient

บรรพกาล in /olden/ancient/ times, in the early days, originally

บรรพบุรุษ ancestors, forebears, antecedents, forefathers

ดึกดำบรรพ์ ancient, primeval

บรรพชา ordination

บรรพชิต clerical; cleric, the ordained; monk, a religious

บรรพต mountain

บรรยากาศ atmosphere, air

บรรยาย to lecture, give a /lecture/talk/; to explain, narrate

บรรยายธรรม to preach, expound the dharma

บรรยายสรุป to brief (someone /on/about/)

ผู้บรรยาย commentator

บรรลัย disaster, calamity, destruction, annihilation; to die, be destroyed

ซวยบรรลัย calamitous, disastrous

บรรลุ to attain, achieve, reach

บรรลุธรรม to attain enlightenment

บรรลุนิติภาวะ to come of age, reach one's majority, be of legal age

บรรลุผล to succeed, work; successful, accomplished

บรรเลง to play, perform

บรรเลงเพลง to play music, perform, give a musical performance

บรรษัท corporation

บรั่นดี brandy

บริกร service /personnel/person/, attendant, waiter *(ชาย)*, waitress *(หญิง)*

บริการ to serve, give service; service

มีอาหารและเครื่องดื่มบริการตลอดงาน refreshments served throughout

บริการไม่ดี bad service, poor service

บริการส่งถึงที่ home delivery

หญิงบริการ service girl

บริขาร, อัฐบริขาร the eight requisites for monks: foodbowl, lower garment, outer robe, shoulder scarf, razor, needle, girdle and water filter

บริคณห์ loan contract secured by an indenture agreement

บริคณห์สนธิ memorandum of association

สินบริคณห์ common property, community property

บริจาค to donate, contribute, give to charity, make a charitable gift (of money, clothing etc)

บริบท context

บริบาล guardian, one who takes care of; to keep, maintain, take care of, attend to, bring up

บริบาลทารก child care, infant care

บริบูรณ์ plentiful, abundant, plenty (of), complete, lacking nothing

จบบริบูรณ์ complete, completed, completely finished; the end

บริพาร *see* **บริวาร**

บริภาษ to be irate (with); to blame, censure, reprove, reproach

บริโภค to eat, partake (of); to use, consume

บริโภคนิยม consumerism

เครื่องบริโภค food, foodstuffs, comestibles

ผู้บริโภค consumer

บริวาร entourage, followers, adherents, people, men, attendants, retinue, household, staff; satellite

บริเวณ area, zone, sector; grounds, compound; vicinity, environs

บริษัท company; assembly

บริษัทจำกัด limited company (Co., Ltd.)

 บ
ป
ผ
ฝ
พ
ฟ
ภ
ม
ย
ร
ฤ
ฤๅ
ล
ว
ศ
ษ
ส
ห
ฬ
อ
ฮ

บริษัทในเครือ affiliate, affiliated company, subsidiary

บริษัทบริวาร entourage

บริษัทมหาชน public company limited, public limited company, (plc.)

บริษัทแม่ parent company

บริสุทธิ์ pure; flawless, immaculate; altruistic; innocent, guiltless, blameless; virgin

บริสุทธิ์ใจ honest, sincere, ingenuous, straightforward; altruistic

ทองบริสุทธิ์ pure gold, 24 karat gold

เพชรบริสุทธิ์ flawless diamond

บริหาร to manage, administer; to govern; management

บริหารงาน to administer, manage, conduct the affairs (of)

บริหารธุรกิจ business administration

กายบริหาร physical exercise; to do exercise

บริษัทบริหารสินทรัพย์ asset management company

ผู้บริหาร executive, administrator, director

อำนาจบริหาร executive /power/authority/

บลั๊ฟ to bluff

บวก to add; positive, plus

เครื่องบวกเลข adding machine, calculator

แง่บวก positively, optimistically

ผลบวก sum

เลือดบวก positive blood reaction

บ่วง noose, loop, snare

บ่วงบาศ lasso

ไม่มีบ่วงผูกคอ unattached

บวงสรวง to make an oblation (of, to), give a sacred offering

บวช to ordain; to be ordained, enter the monkhood

บวชชี to become a nun

บวชหน้าไฟ to be ordained for a short period at the cremation of a parent or a senior relative

จับบวช to be forced to become a monk; to religicize a word

คำว่าวัดมักถูกจับบวชว่ามาจากวัตร The word "wat" is sometimes religicized by attributing the Sanskrit "watra" as its derivation.

ถือบวช to observe religious rules; to be a monk

นักบวช a religious; monk, priest, bhikku, nun

บ้วน to spit, spit out

บ้วนน้ำลาย to spit, expectorate

บ้วนปาก to rinse (one's) mouth, gargle

ยาบ้วนปาก mouthwash

บวม to swell, swollen

ปอดบวม pneumonia

บวร excellent, splendid

บ่อ well; fish pond; pit, mine

บ่อเกิด source, origin, wellspring, root

บ่อเงินบ่อทอง gold mine, bonanza

บ่อถ่านหิน coal mine, coal pit

บ่อทอง gold mine

บ่อน้ำ well; pond

บ่อน้ำมัน oil well

บ่อน้ำร้อน hot spring

บ่อปลา fish pond

บ่อเพชร diamond mine

บ่อเพาะพันธุ์ปลา fish hatchery

บ่อแร่ mine

น้ำบ่อ well water

บอก to tell, state, say (to); to prompt

บอกกล่าว to announce, state; to give notice

บอกข่าว to tell the news, have news for someone

บอกแขก to give word (of something to friends, neighbors, etc); to call on neighbors for help

บอกบท to prompt, cue, tell (someone) what to /say/do/

บอกบุญ to solicit a contribution (for religious

or charitable purposes); to invite to participate in merit-making

บอกบุญไม่รับ unfriendly, cold, unsympathetic

บอกใบ้ to give the high sign (to someone), use sign language, let someone know something surreptitiously, hint (at something)

บอกปัด to reject, refuse; to put (someone) off; to disclaim responsibility (for); to pass the buck

บอกไม่ถูก can't say, don't know, be unable to put one's finger on it

บอกยี่ห้อ to label (as), indicate, bespeak (the /nature/origin/ of /someone/something/)

บอกล่วงหน้า to tell in advance

บอกเล่า to relate, tell

    คำบอกเล่า hearsay, something heard (from someone else); narration

บอกเลิก to cancel, rescind; revoke

    บอกเลิกสัญญา to give notice of termination (of a contract), /rescind/ cancel/ a contract

บอกแล้ว I told you., I told you so.

    บอกแล้วนะ You heard me!

    บอกแล้วไหมล่ะ I told you so., You see?

บอกศาลา to say goodbye, say good riddance (to a person, job etc)

บอกหนทาง to put a person who is near death in mind of spiritual matters; to show an opportunity, show the way (to)

บอกให้รู้ to tell, inform, to let (someone) know

บ้อง bamboo section

    บ้องกัญชา water pipe

    บ้องตื้น nitwit, fool, idiot, ass

    บ้องไฟ *see* **บั้งไฟ** *หน้า 272*

    บ้องหู ear

เดี๋ยวตบบ้องหูซะเลย I'll box your ears for you.

บ๊อง, บ๊องๆ wacky, crackpot, nutty, nuts, crazy

บ๊องแบ๊ว *as in* **หน้าบ๊องแบ๊ว** innocent-looking
    ทำหน้าบ๊องแบ๊ว to look so innocent

บอด blind

    บอดสี color-blind

    คนตาบอด blind /woman/man/person/, sightless person

    นมบอด inverted nipple

    ลูกกระสุนบอด blank cartridge; dud cartridge

    หัวเทียนบอด bad spark plug

บอน restless, busy; itchy

    ปากบอน to tattle, talk too much, blabber; gossipy, bigmouthed, talebearing

    มือบอน to have itchy fingers, roving hands

บ่อน[1] place for gambling

    บ่อนการพนัน gambling den

    บ่อนไก่ cockpit

    โรงบ่อน gambling /house/den/

บ่อน[2] to undermine, sap

    บ่อนแตก to be put in disarray; disarrayed, kaput

        ทำให้บ่อนแตก to throw a monkey wrench into (the plans, works, etc), cause (a plan etc) to fall apart

    บ่อนทำลาย to subvert, undermine

    หนอนบ่อนไส้ spy, infiltrator, fifth column; subversive (person, element etc)

บอบช้ำ bruised, sore; battered

บอบบาง fragile, delicate; flimsy, tinny; vulnerable

บอบแบบ limply, exhausted

บ้อม to lambaste, drub

    ถูกบ้อม to get lambasted, get a drubbing

บอมบ์ bomb

บ่อย often, frequently, regularly; in quick succession

บ๋อย boy, waiter, bellhop, bellboy, room attendant
บ๋อย ขอกาแฟถ้วยหนึ่ง Waiter, a coffee please.

บ
ป
ผ
ฝ
พ
ฟ
ภ
ม
ย
ร
ฤ
ฤๅ
ล
ว
ศ
ษ
ส
ห
ฬ
อ
ฮ

ก
ข
ค
ฆ
ง
จ
ฉ
ช
ซ
ฌ
ญ
ฎ
ฏ
ฐ
ฑ
ฒ
ณ
ด
ต
ถ
ท
ธ
น
บ

บอล ball

งานบอล a ball

บ๊ะ oh, eh

บ๊ะ คุณกล้าขนาดนั้นเชียวเรอะ Eh, do you think you're tough enough?

บะหมี่ Chinese egg noodles

บัก[1] a title prefixed to the name of a man of equal or inferior station

บัก[2] cock

บักโกรก emaciated, wasted, spent

บักอาน exhausted, worn out, dead beat, sore and spent

บัง to hide, conceal, screen, shield; to obstruct, get in the way (of), block

บังโคลน mudguard, fender

บังแดด to /shade/shield/block/ from the sun

บังตา blind

บังมืด to block the light

บังหน้า as a cover (for), under cover of, as a guise

เบียดบัง to misappropriate, embezzle

ปิดบัง to conceal, cover up, hide, keep secret

บังเกิด to be born; to originate, occur, happen; to cause, produce, realize, materialize, give rise to, bring about

บังคน excrement *(royal word)*

บังคนเบา urine *(royal word)*

บังคนหนัก feces *(royal word)*

บังคม to salute the king in Thai style

กราบบังคมทูล to address His Majesty the King

ถวายบังคม to pay homage (to the /king/ queen/)

บังควร appropriate, fitting, proper, as behooves

มิบังควร to be inappropriate (to, for), unseemly, improper

บังคับ[1] power, jurisdiction

บังคับ[2] to force, enforce, compel, coerce; to order, command; to oblige, constrain, control, make (someone do something); required

บังคับการ to command

กองบังคับการ command, headquarters

ผู้บังคับการ commander

บังคับคดี to /enforce/execute/ a judgment

การบังคับคดี execution

บังคับบัญชา to be in command

ผู้บังคับบัญชา commander, superior officer

เครื่องบินบังคับวิทยุ radio-controlled aircraft

ท่าบังคับ prescribed exercise *(ยิมนาสติก)*

บีบบังคับ to coerce, force, put pressure on (someone to do something), compel

มาตรการบังคับ coercive measure

วิชาบังคับ required /subject/course/

บั้งไฟ sky rocket

บังสุกุล monk's robes dedicated to a deceased person; to perform the ceremony of dedicating robes to a deceased person

ผ้าบังสุกุล robes offered to monks at a cremation

บังเหียน bridle, reins

กุม (ถือ) บังเหียน to hold the reins, be in control (of)

สายบังเหียน reins

บังอาจ wantonly, wrongfully; to dare (to), have the audacity to; purposely

บังเอิญ accidentally, by accident, by chance, unexpectedly, to happen (to)

บัญชา order, instruction, command; to order, instruct, command, direct

บัญชาการ to command

กองบัญชาการ (general) headquarters

บัญชี account; list; register *(ทะเบียน)*

บัญชีกระแสรายวัน current account

บัญชีการค้า trading account

บัญชีเงินฝาก deposit account

บัญชีเงินสด cash account
บัญชีดำ blacklist
บัญชีเดินสะพัด current account
บัญชีผี phoney /account/list/
บัญชีพัสดุ inventory, stock account
บัญชีรายชื่อ list of names
บัญชีลูกหนี้ account receivable
บัญชีสะสม savings account, thrift account
บัญชีสินค้า /goods/merchandise/stock/ account
บัญชีออมทรัพย์ thrift account
การบัญชี bookkeeping; accounting
ขึ้นบัญชี to charge to an account, enter in an account
คิดบัญชี to strike an account; to /give/ render/make out/ a bill, give a statement of account; to settle accounts; to settle scores (with)
งบบัญชี financial statement
ปิดบัญชี to close an account
เปิดบัญชี to open an account
สมุดบัญชี account book
หักบัญชี to debit (an account), put to (one's) account

บัญญัติ enactment, provision, rule, regulation; to enact, prescribe, legislate
บัญญัติกฎหมาย to legislate, enact a law
นิติบัญญัติ see **นิติบัญญัติ** หน้า 260
บทบัญญัติ law, legal provision, legislation
พระราชบัญญัติ act

บัณฑิต graduate; scholar, pundit, learned man, sage; highly skilled person
ดุษฎีบัณฑิต doctor, holder of a /doctor's degree/doctorate/
เนติบัณฑิต law graduate, bachelor of laws
มหาบัณฑิต master (of), holder of a master's degree
ราชบัณฑิต Fellow of the Royal Institute

บัด time, moment, instant

บัดดล instantaneously, immediately
บัดเดี๋ยว just a moment
บัดนั้น at /the/that/ time, at that moment, then
บัดนี้ now, at this time

บัดกรี to solder
บัดซบ stupid, idiotic, asinine
บัดสี, **บัดสีบัดเถลิง** disgraceful, shameful, disgusting, sickening
น่าบัดสี disgraceful, shameful, indecent

บัตร card; ticket, coupon
บัตรเครดิต credit card
บัตรเงินฝาก certificate of deposit
บัตรเชิญ invitation
บัตรดี /good/valid/ ballot
บัตรประจำตัวข้าราชการ official identification card
บัตรประชาชน identity card
บัตรผ่านประตู pass; ticket
บัตรพลี offerings to deities
บัตรลงคะแนน ballot
บัตรสนเท่ห์ anonymous letter, poison-pen letter, anonymous accusation
บัตรสมนาคุณ gift coupon, gift certificate
บัตรเสีย /spoiled/invalid/ ballot
บัตรหมาย official order
　ที่ส่งบัตรหมาย address for service
บัตรอนุญาต pass
กฎบัตร charter
　กฎบัตรกฎหมาย the laws
นามบัตร card, name card, visiting card, business card
ประกาศนียบัตร diploma; award, certificate, certificate of recognition
ไปรษณียบัตร postcard
ลงบัตร to ballot, vote
วุฒิบัตร certificate of proficiency (in English etc)
หย่อนบัตร to drop a ballot (in a ballotbox),

บ
ป
ผ
ฝ
พ
ฟ
ภ
ม
ย
ร
ฤ
ฤๅ
ล
ว
ศ
ษ
ส
ห
ฬ
อ
ฮ

cast a ballot

บั่น to cut up, chop

บั่นทอน to affect, sap, debilitate; to shorten

บั้น half; section, part, group

บั้นท้าย hips, buttocks, behind, bottom

บั้นปลาย later, /towards/at/ the end

ใน**บั้นปลาย**ชีวิต in later life, towards the end of one's life

บั้นหลวง unit of volume equal to 1000 liters

บันดาล to create; give rise to

บันดาลโทสะ see **บันดาลโทสะ** หน้า 242

ดล**บันดาล** to inspire (one with), engender, bring forth, give rise to, create

แรง**บันดาลใจ** inspiration

บันได ladder; stairs, stairway, staircase

บันไดเชือก rope ladder, Jacob's ladder (บนเรือ)

บันไดรถ step (of a bus, train etc)

บันไดลิง[1] rope ladder

บันไดลิง[2] liana

บันไดเลื่อน escalator

บันไดเวียน spiral staircase

ราว**บันได** banister, handrail

หัว**บันได** /head/top/ of the stairs

บันทึก note, memorandum; to note, take notes; to record; to save (คอมพิวเตอร์)

บันทึกการสอน lecture notes

บันทึกการให้ถ้อยคำ to take a statement

บันทึกความเข้าใจร่วมกัน memorandum of understanding, MOU

บันทึกคำให้การ affidavit, sworn statement

บันทึกช่วยจำ aide memoire

บันทึกภาพ to take /photographs/pictures/ (of); photographic record

บันทึกรายงานการประชุม minutes of a meeting

บันทึกเสียง to make a sound recording, record (sounds)

เครื่อง**บันทึกเสียง** tape recorder, sound recorder

บันเทิง entertainment

บันเทิงคดี light entertainment

บันเทิงใจ happy

ผู้สื่อข่าว**บันเทิง** entertainment reporter

วงการ**บันเทิง** entertainment circles, world of entertainment

หน้า**บันเทิง** entertainment page

บันเบา as in ไม่**บันเบา** not a little, not bad

เรื่องการค้าขายแล้ว เขาเก่งไม่บันเบาทีเดียว In business, he's not bad at all.

บันยะบันยัง in moderation, to not overdo

บันลือ to make a loud noise; to spread widely; to roar

ข่าว**บันลือโลก** earthshaking news

บัลลังก์ throne; seat; lap; bench; courtroom

นั่งคู่**บัลลังก์** to sit cross-legged, sit in lotus position

นั่ง**บัลลังก์** to sit on the bench, preside

ราช**บัลลังก์** throne

บัว lotus, water lily

บัวไม่ให้ช้ำ น้ำไม่ให้ขุ่น to handle (a situation etc) adroitly

กอ**บัว** a clump of lotus

ดอก**บัว** lotus

สาย**บัว** lotus stem

บัวบก Asiatic pennywort

บัวลอย a Thai confection; a song

บ่า[1] shoulder

เคียงบ่าเคียงไหล่ shoulder to shoulder

เหลือบ่ากว่าแรง beyond (one), too much (for one), too hard, more than (one) can handle

บ่า[2] rushing, torrential

น้ำไหล**บ่า** torrent, rushing waters

บ้า mad, insane, crazy, out of one's mind, nuts; to be mad (for, about)

บ้าคลั่ง deranged, maniacal, berserk, to go berserk; crazed

บ้างาน a workaholic

บ้าจี้ ticklish; compliant

บ้าดารา star-crazy

บ้าดีเดือด maniacal; in a frenzy, frenzied

บ้าน้ำลาย raving

บ้าๆ บอๆ crazy, screwy, nutty

บ้าบิ่น reckless

บ้ายศ vainglorious, hoity-toity; to like to act big

บ้ายอ to love to be flattered

บ้าระห่ำ hot-tempered; wild, fanatical, frenzied

    การกระทำที่บ้าระห่ำ savagery

บ้าเลือด blood-crazed

บ้าหนังสือ bibliomaniac, book-crazy; a bookworm

บ้าหมู epilepsy

บ้าอำนาจ megalomaniac, power-mad, to have megalomania

คนบ้า a person who is /mad/insane/ crazy/; madman, a nut

หมาบ้า mad dog, rabid dog

อ้ายบ้า You must be mad!, Jerk!, You jerk!

บาก to incise, make a cut, chip away

บากท่า to suggest, intimate, hint

บากบั่น to persevere (in), make an unflagging effort (to); to overcome difficulty

บากหน้า (to go to someone) /humbly/ meekly/, swallow one's pride in going to someone for help

บาง¹ waterway, a settlement along a waterway

บาง² some

บางขณะ on some occasions

บางคน some people

บางครั้งบางคราว now and then, from time to time, occasionally, sometimes

บางตัว some

บางท่าน some of /you/them/, some people

บางที perhaps, may be; sometimes, at times

บางประการ in some respects, in certain ways, some

บางเวลา sometimes, at times

บางส่วน some parts (of), in part, certain parts

บางสิ่งบางอย่าง certain things, something

บางหน sometimes, at times

บาง³ thin; slender; weak

บางตา thin, sparse, scarce, rare; to dwindle

บางเบา to subside, fall off, lessen, grow less, diminish, ease off, thin out

เยื่อบาง membrane

วิสกี้บาง a weak whiskey

บ่าง flying lemur

บ่างช่างยุ busybody, scandalmonger

บ้าง some; partly, somewhat

บ้างก็นอน บ้างก็นั่ง Some were lying down, some were sitting around.

ขอผมบ้าง Can I have some?, / Is there some for me?

จริงบ้าง เท็จบ้าง partly true partly false

เป็นยังไงบ้าง How are things?, How are you doing?, How are you?

มีอะไรบ้าง What do you have?

เห็นเขาทำก็ทำบ้าง to do what someone else does too

อย่างนั้นบ้าง อย่างนี้บ้าง some of this and some of that, some of each

บาด to cut, slice; to wound

บาดแก้วหู deafening, strident, piercing

บาดคอ raw, sharp

บาดเจ็บ injured, wounded

    คนบาดเจ็บ casualty, injured person

    ได้รับบาดเจ็บ to be injured

    ทหารบาดเจ็บ wounded soldier, casualty

บาดใจ to be hurt, hurt one's feelings, offended, incensed; offensive, intolerable, disgusting

บาดตา dazzling, glaring; garish; sexy, flashy; offensive, intolerable, disgusting

บ
ป
ผ
ฝ
พ
ฟ
ภ
ม
ย
ร
ฤ
ฦ
ล
ว
ศ
ษ
ส
ห
ฬ
อ
ฮ

เห็นภาพบาดตา to see a /disgusting/ offensive/ sight, disgusting to see

บาดหู strident, deafening, raucous, irritating

มีดบาด to /get/have/ a cut (with a knife), knife /wound/cut/

บาดทะยัก tetanus

บาดแผล wound, cut, laceration

บาดแผลเหวอะหวะ gaping wound

ทนพิษบาดแผลไม่ไหว to succumb

บาดหมาง to be at odds (with); be on bad terms, fall out, have a rift (with); to have one's differences, have hard feelings (towards)

บาดาล the nether world, subterranean land of the Nagas

น้ำบาดาล artesian well water

บ่อบาดาล artesian well

บาตร alms bowl

คว่ำบาตร to ostracize, boycott, excommunicate, shun; to reject

ใส่บาตร, ตักบาตร to make a food offering (in a monk's bowl)

อำนาจบาตรใหญ่ (to use) force, coercion, arbitrary power, authority

บาท[1] foot

บาทวิถี sidewalk, pavement, footpath

บาท[2] baht

ไม่เต็มบาท to be not all there, cracked

บาท[3] line, cadence

โคลงบทหนึ่งมี 4 บาท Each verse of a "Klong" has four lines.

บาทหลวง priest

บาน[1] a numerical designation for some flat things: doors, windows, mirrors etc

บานกบ window frame

บานเกล็ด louvre

ประตูบานเกล็ด louvred door, door with louvres

บานกระจก window pane, pane of glass

บานประตู door, leaf (of a door)

บานแผนก table of contents

บานพับ hinge

บาน[2] to bloom, blossom, open, spread; to flare, flared

บานปลาย to escalate, get out of hand, snowball

กางเกงขาบาน bell-bottom /trousers/pants/

ชื่นบาน in a good mood, in good spirits, cheerful, lighthearted

เบ่งบาน blooming, in full bloom

เบิกบาน in high spirits, cheerful, joyful, exuberant

หน้าบาน beaming, delighted, to look happy

บาน[3] lots of

บานเบอะ, บานตะไท loads, tons, masses (of)

มีผลไม้บานเลย tons of fruit

บาน[4] *as in* สุราบาน drink, liquor

บ้าน house, home; settlement, community, village; domestic

บ้านเกิด birthplace, native /town/country/, home town

บ้านจัดสรร housing development, housing estate

บ้านช่อง housing, house(s), home(s)

บ้านเดิม hometown, old home

บ้านแตก broken home

บ้านแตกสาแหรกขาด broken home, forced separation; families /broken up/torn asunder/

บ้านนอก the country, rural area, up-country

เด็กบ้านนอก country boy

บ้านนา farmhouse

บ้านผีสิง haunted house

บ้านพัก house, residence, rest house, housing

บ้านพักนักเรียน boarding house for students, students' lodging house

บ้านเมือง country

บ้านรับรอง guest house

บ้านเรือน houses, dwellings, buildings

บ้านไร่ farmhouse

บ้านว่าง vacant house

บ้านให้เช่า house for rent

กลับบ้าน to go home, return home

การบ้าน homework; housework

คู่บ้านคู่เมือง national, identified with the nation; national /treasure/heritage/

เจ้าของบ้าน owner, house owner, home owner, landlord, householder

ชาวบ้าน folks, villagers, common folk, people, ordinary people *(พหู)*, ordinary person *(เอก)*

ตามบ้าน from house to house; household

ที่บ้าน at home, at the house; the wife

นอกบ้าน out, outside

ในบ้าน at home

บนบ้าน in the house, at home

ไปบ้าน to go home

พ่อบ้าน head of the family, head of the house; my husband

เพื่อนบ้าน neighbor, next-door neighbor; neighborhood

แม่บ้าน housekeeper, housewife; matron

ย้ายบ้าน to move (to a new house), change (one's) address

แยกบ้าน to live apart

รวมบ้าน to live together

รั้วบ้าน (house) fence

หน้าบ้าน in front of the house, (at the) front door

หมู่บ้าน village, hamlet; house group

หลังบ้าน /behind/in back of/ the house; through the backdoor

บาป unwholesome deed, wrong action, demerit, a wrong; sin

บาปกรรม wicked, sinful, bad thing to do, not right; to suffer from one's previous wrongdoing

บาปหนา wicked, burdened with sin

ทำบาป to wrong someone; to do a wrong, commit a sin

ฉันทำบาปกับเขามาก I wronged him terribly.

พิธีล้างบาป baptism

ยกโทษบาป to give absolution; to get absolution (from one's sins)

รู้บาปบุญคุณโทษ to know right from wrong

บายศรี ceremony of welcome or encouragement

บ่าย[1] afternoon

บ่ายคล้อย late afternoon

บ่ายสองโมง 2 p.m., two in the afternoon

ตกบ่าย, เวลาบ่าย in the afternoon

ตะวันบ่าย afternoon

บ่าย[2] to turn, face

บ่ายเบี่ยง to be evasive, equivocate, dodge (an issue etc), tergiversate

บ่ายหน้า to head for

บารมี moral authority, majesty, charisma, greatness, stature; power, influence; the Ten Perfections: liberality, morality, renunciation of the world, wisdom, perseverance, forbearance, truth, determination, loving kindness and equanimity

ชมพระบารมี to behold the royal presence

พระบารมีปกเกล้า (by) the grace of His Majesty

บาร์ bar

บาร์เดี่ยว singles bar

บาร์คู่ couples bar

บาลี Pali

ภาษาบาลี Pali

เลี่ยงบาลี to justify oneself

บ่าว servant; young man

บ่าวไพร่ servants, retinue; menials, peons

คู่บ่าวสาว the bride and groom

เจ้าบ่าว bridegroom

บาศก์ *as in* **ลูกบาศก์** cube, cubic; square

บำนาญ pension

ข้าราชการบำนาญ pensioned official

เบี้ยบำนาญ (monthly) pension

บำบัด to treat, cure, remedy, alleviate, relieve

บำบัดน้ำเสีย to treat wastewater, wastewater treatment

กายภาพบำบัด physical therapy

การบำบัด treatment, therapy

บำเพ็ญ to accomplish, carry out, do, perform

บำเพ็ญกุศล to make merit, do charitable deeds

บำเพ็ญตน to behave, conduct oneself, act

บำเพ็ญบารมี to perfect a virtuous action, practice paramita

บำเพ็ญบุญ to make an act of merit, do good

บำเพ็ญภาวนา to meditate

บำราบ *see* ปราบ *หน้า 297*

บำราศ *see* ปราศ *หน้า 298*

บำรุง to take care of, look after, care for, tend; to nourish; to keep, maintain; to preserve; to support; to beautify

บำรุงกำลัง to strengthen, fortify (oneself)

บำรุงขวัญ to give encouragement, hearten, boost morale

บำรุงครรภ์ to /get/have/ prenatal care

บำรุงรักษา to preserve, take care (of), maintain

บำรุงเลี้ยง to look after, support

ค่าบำรุง subscription; membership fee; donation

ยาบำรุงกำลัง tonic

บำเรอ to wait on, serve; to please, delight; to worship

นางบำเรอ entertainer, pleasure-girl; girl employed for pleasure, geisha, courtesan

บำเหน็จ reward, remuneration; gratuity, bonus

เงินบำเหน็จ severance pay, retirement benefit, retirement bonus

ปูนบำเหน็จ to reward; to promote; bonus, reward

บิ to pinch off

บิณฑบาต to receive food offerings

พระออกบิณฑบาต The monks were making their rounds for food offerings.

ขอบิณฑบาต to ask as a favor

บิด[1] dysentery

บิด[2] to twist, distort; to wring; to be sprung, warped; to dawdle

บิดขี้เกียจ to stretch lazily

บิดคอ to wring the neck

บิดจะกูด, บิดตะกูด to drag one's feet, procrastinate

บิดเบือน to distort

บิดเบือนความจริง to /distort/twist/ the truth, be mendacious

ที่บิดเบือน distorted, mendacious

บิดผัน to falsify

บิดผ้า to wring (the clothes, shirts, towels, etc)

บิดพลิ้ว to fail to act, put off doing something

บิดไส้ to cast a spell to wring one's bowels

บิดหู to twist one's ears

ลูกบิดประตู door knob

บิดร father

บิดา father

บิดามารดา parents, mother and father

บิน to fly

บินขึ้น to take off

บินเดี่ยว to solo

บินผาดโผน to do stunt flying, /perform/do/ aerobatics

บินร่อน to hover, glide

บินว่อน to swarm

บินเวียน to fly in circles, circle

การบิน aviation, flying, aeronautics, aeronautical

สายการบิน airline

ขวัญบิน terrified; panicky

เครื่องบิน airplane, aircraft; aeroplane *(Brit)*

เครื่องบินขับไล่ fighter plane, fighter-interceptor, pursuit plane, pursuer (P)

เครื่องบินทิ้งระเบิด bomber

เครื่องบินบรรทุก cargo carrier

เครื่องบินบรรทุกเชื้อเพลิง kerosene carrier (KC)

จานบิน flying saucer

นักบิน pilot, aviator *(ชาย)*, aviatrix *(หญิง)*, flyer

บิ่น nicked, chipped

มีดบิ่น nicked knife

บิหลั่น muezzin

บี้ to crush, mash, squash

บี้มด to squash an ant

บีฑา to harass, harry; trouble, harm

บีบ to press, squeeze

บีบคั้น to press, exert pressure (on someone), force (someone to do something)

บีบน้ำตา to force out tears, weep crocodile tears

บีบบังคับ to coerce, force, put pressure on (someone to do something), compel

ถูกบีบ to be compelled (to), put under pressure, forced, obliged to

เขาถูกบีบให้ลาออก He was /forced/compelled/obliged/put under pressure/ to resign.

บึกบึน tough; strapping

ร่างบึกบึน muscular, powerfully built

บึง swamp, marsh

บึ่ง to speed; to go directly, right away, with all haste

พอได้รับข่าว ผมก็บึ่งมานี่เลย As soon as I got the news, I came right away.

บึ้ง sulky, sullen, cross

บึ้งตึง glowering, scowling

หน้าบึ้ง sullen, sulky, to look /cross/cranky/, grumpy-looking

บื้อใบ้ *as in* **เป็นบื้อใบ้** woodenly

บุ to hammer into shape; to sheath, cover

(with); to line (with)

บุก to invade; attack; to intrude, trespass; to penetrate

บุกเข้าไป to push forward

บุกทลาย to raid

บุกบั่น to persevere, overcome hardships, make one's way

บุกเบิก to clear land (for farming); to be a pioneer (in), open the way (to, for)

บุกเบิกตลาด to pioneer the market

บุกป่าฝ่าดง to make an arduous journey

บุกรุก to trespass, intrude, invade

การบุกรุก intrusion, invasion; trespass

ผู้บุกรุก intruder, invader, trespasser

บุ๊ก, บุ๊ค to book (a seat/ticket/etc)

บุคคล person

บุคคลที่ไม่พึงปรารถนา persona non grata

บุคคลสาธารณะ public figure

นิติบุคคล juristic person, legal entity

ส่วนบุคคล private

บุคลากร personnel

บุคลาธิษฐาน personification

บุคลิก personality

บุคลิกภาพ personality, character

บุคลิกลักษณะ personality

บุญ merit, meritorious deeds, boon, good

บุญคุณ benefit, favor, help

ไม่อยากเป็นหนี้บุญคุณใคร I don't want to be /beholden/indebted/obligated/ to anyone (for something).

เป็นหนี้บุญคุณ to be indebted to someone (for/help/support/encouragement/etc), / owe a lot to someone, / be grateful (to someone for something)

เขามีบุญคุณต่อผมมาก He has done much for me. / He has helped me a lot.

บุญธรรม adopted, foster

บุตรบุญธรรม adopted /son/daughter/, fosterchild

บ
ป
ผ
ฝ
พ
ฟ
ภ
ม
ย
ร
ฤ
ฤๅ
ล
ว
ศ
ษ
ส
ห
ฬ
อ
ฮ

ก
ข
ค
ฆ
ง
จ
ฉ
ช
ซ
ฌ
ญ
ฎ
ฏ
ฐ
ฑ
ฒ
ณ
ด
ต
ถ
ท
ธ
น
บ

ใจบุญ kindly, generous, charitable, benevolent, good

ทำบุญ to make merit, do good, perform good deeds, do an act of charity, give to charity

นักบุญ saint; pious person

บอกบุญ to solicit a contribution (for religious or charitable purposes), invite to participate in merit-making

เป็นบุญ blessing; good, fortune

ผู้แสวงบุญ pilgrim

บุตร son, child, children, offspring

บุตรา son

บุตรี daughter

บุถุชน common man, common folk, ordinary /person/people/

บุบ dented

บุบง่าย easily dented

บุบสลาย damaged

ไม่บุบสลาย durable; undamaged

บุปผชาติ flowers, floral

บุปผา flower, blossom

บุพ- prior, previous, former, first; original, initial; eastern

บุพกรรม previous karma

บุพการี parents; ascendants

บุพบท preposition

บุพเพสันนิวาส to be meant for each other, be predestined to marry, a preordained marriage; cohabitation

บุ๋ม dimpled; dented

แก้มบุ๋ม dimpled cheek

บุ่มบ่าม rash, precipitous; hot-tempered

บุ้ย to make a lip gesture, pucker the lips

บุ้ยใบ้ to give a high sign with the lips

บุ้ยปาก to signal with the lips

บุรพ- former, first, original

บุรพคดี Oriental studies

บุรพทิศ east

บุริมสิทธิ preferential right, prior right; preference

หุ้นบุริมสิทธิ preference share, preferred stock

บุรี town, city

บุรุษ man, male; person

บุรุษที่หนึ่ง first person

บุรุษไปรษณีย์ postman

บุรุษพยาบาล male nurse

รัฐบุรุษ statesman

โรคบุรุษ venereal disease

วีรบุรุษ hero

สุภาพบุรุษ gentleman

บุโรทั่ง dilapidated, rickety, ramshackle

รถบุโรทั่ง old jalopy

บุษบา flower

บุษราคัม topaz

บุหรี่ cigarette, cigar

ขี้บุหรี่ ashes

คอบุหรี่ heavy smoker

จุดบุหรี่ to light a cigarette

ซองบุหรี่ pack of cigarettes, cigarette pack

ที่เขี่ยบุหรี่ ashtray

บู้ dented

บู้บี้ crumpled

บู๊ action-packed, blood and thunder

คนบู๊ pugnacious guy

ดาราบู๊ action-movie star

หนังบู๊ an action-packed film, action movie, blood and thunder movie, thriller

บูชา to worship, revere, venerate, adore

บูชายัญ to sacrifice

แท่นบูชา altar

บูด rancid, sour, spoiled; wry

บูดบึ้ง sour

บูดเบี้ยว sour-faced; grimacing, contorted

หน้าบูด to make a wry face, sour looking, sullen

เหม็นบูด rancid, rank, to go bad

บูติก boutique

บูรณะ to repair, maintain, improve, keep up

บูรณปฏิสังขรณ์ to restore, repair

การบูรณปฏิสังขรณ์ restoration

บูรณภาพแห่งอาณาเขต territorial integrity

บูรณาการ integration

บูรพา east

เบ้ wry; twisted

ทำหน้าเบ้ to screw up one's face (in pain etc)

หน้าเบ้ weepy face

เบ่ง to strain, force out (by muscular effort)

เบ่งกล้าม to flex one's muscles

เบ่งลูก to bear down (during childbirth)

เบ่งเสียง to raise one's voice, shout

เบ่งอุจจาระ to force a bowel movement, strain at stool

เบญจ- five, fifth, penta-

เบญจกัลยาณี a fivefold beauty (having beauty of hair, red lips and gums, teeth, skin and aging)

เบญจขันธ์ the five aggregates: corporality, sensation, perception, mental properties, and consciousness

เบญจพรรณ mixed forest

เบญจเพส the age of twenty-five

เบญจม- five, fifth, quinque

เบญจมาศ chrysanthemum

เบญจรงค์ polychrome chinaware; five basic colors: black, white, green, red, and yellow

เบญจศีล the five precepts

เบญจางค์ five parts of the body: head, two hands and feet

เบญจางคประดิษฐ์ prostration in which the head, hands and feet touch the ground, a kowtow

เบ็ด fishhook

คันเบ็ด fishing rod, fishing pole

ตกเบ็ด to fish, go fishing; to lure, entice; female masturbation

สายเบ็ด fishing line

เบ็ดเตล็ด odds and ends, sundry, miscellaneous

การแสดงเบ็ดเตล็ด skit; variety show

ของเบ็ดเตล็ด sundries, odds and ends, variety of things, potpourri (of)

งานเบ็ดเตล็ด odd jobs, odds and ends of things to do, little things to do

เรื่องเบ็ดเตล็ด miscellanies, miscellaneous matters

เบ็ดเสร็จ total, all together, all included, general, comprehensive

คิดเบ็ดเสร็จ all included it comes to, total price

ภาษีเบ็ดเสร็จ general duties (except the rice export tax)

สงครามเบ็ดเสร็จ total war

เบน to turn, veer (to)

เบนความสนใจ to distract

เบนหัวเรือ to change the direction of a boat, veer a boat (to, away from), head (to the left etc)

เบี่ยงเบน to deviate; to distract, divert

เบนซิน gasoline, gas, petrol, benzine

เบอร์ number

เรียงเบอร์ (list of) prize-winning numbers

หวยเบอร์ private lottery; lottery number

เบ้อเร่อ huge, enormous, gigantic, humongous

เบอะ[1] gaping, severe

ปากหนาเบอะ to have thick lips, thick-lipped

เบอะ[2] plenty, loads

บานเบอะ plenty (of), more than enough, loads (of)

เบะ see **เบ้**

เบา[1] to urinate, pass water, relieve oneself, go to the bathroom

เบา[2] light; insubstantial; softly, lightly; slowly; easy

เบาๆ slowly; gently, softly

เบาความ frivolous, shallow, unthinking

เบาเครื่อง to slow down (the /car/engine/

 บ
ป
ผ
ฝ
พ
ฟ
ภ
ม
ย
ร
ฤ
ฤๅ
ล
ว
ศ
ษ
ส
ห
ฬ
อ
ฮ

etc)

เบาใจ relieved; to feel /easy/easier/, be rest assured

เบาบาง lighter, less serious, to become less, lessen, subside

เบาปัญญา foolish, brainless, lightminded, dim-witted

เบามือ light; to go easy, gently

เบาแรง to require less effort, make easier

เบาลง to weaken, diminish, wane, on the wane

เบาหวาน diabetes

เบาโหวง light as a feather, weightless

ความหนักเบา weight, seriousness (of)

แบ่งเบา to help, make things easier, unburden, relieve, give relief (to)

ผ่อนหนักผ่อนเบา flexible, accommodating, conciliatory; to compromise, make concessions

ย่องเบา to commit a burglary, burgle, burglarize, housebreak

    นักย่องเบา burglar, housebreaker

หูเบา credulous, ready to believe anything (one) hears, suggestible, easily influenced

อย่างเบาที่สุด lightest; as /gently/softly/ lightly/ as possible

เบ้า crucible; socket

    เบ้าตา eye socket

    จมเบ้า to be fixed to (one's) place for a long time, stuck in one's seat

เบาะ[1] cushion, seat

    เบาะหลัง back seat

เบาะ[2], **เบาะๆ** lightly, softly, delicately, gently

เบาะแส information

    รู้เบาะแส to have information (that, about, on, in regard to); getting to the bottom

เบิก to open; to widen; to draw, requisition; to present (someone) to a king

    เบิกของ to /draw/requisition/ goods (from

/stock/a warehouse/etc)

เบิกความ to testify, give testimony, give evidence

เบิกเงิน to draw money, make a withdrawal

เบิกตา to open one's eyes

เบิกทาง to clear the way, insure free passage

เบิกทูต to present an envoy to the king

เบิกนักโทษ to produce a prisoner, take a prisoner outside

เบิกบาน in high spirits, cheerful, joyful, exuberant

เบิกพยาน to introduce a witness (to the court), call up a witness

เบิกพระเนตร to make the eyes of a new Buddha image

เบิกโรง opening /performance/dance/ play/; debut

เบิกโลง rites performed before putting a body into a coffin

ใบเบิก requisition

    ใบเบิกทาง laissez-passer, road pass

เบิ่ง to gaze, look

เบิ้ม big

    พี่เบิ้ม boss; big brother

เบิ้ล double

เบี้ย cowrie; money

เบี้ยกันดาร hardship supplement

เบี้ยน้อยหอยน้อย of small means, impecunious

เบี้ยบ้ายรายทาง incidental expenses

เบี้ยบำนาญ (monthly) pension

เบี้ยบำเหน็จ retirement compensation

เบี้ยประกัน insurance premium

เบี้ยประชุม meeting fee

เบี้ยล่าง subject to the control of; at a disadvantage; under someone's thumb, under the thumb (of)

เบี้ยเลี้ยง daily allowance, expenses

เบี้ยหวัด military pension

ดอกเบี้ย interest

ไล่เบี้ย to have recourse (to a person for something); to be subrogated (to); to take (something) out on (someone else); to pass on liability

สิทธิไล่เบี้ย right of subrogation

เบี่ยง to avoid, evade, dodge, sidestep

เบี่ยงบ่าย, บ่ายเบี่ยง to be evasive, equivocate, dodge (an issue, etc), tergiversate; to be devious

เบี่ยงเบน to deviate; to distract, divert

ทางเบี่ยง detour, diversion

เบียด to crowd, (off, out, in), press against; to push (through a crowd); to take a wife

เบียดกรอ frugal, mean

เบียดบัง to misappropriate, embezzle

เบียดเบียน to harm, molest; to oppress; to trouble

เบียดเสียด to crowd (together, against one another), crowded together, /pushing /pressing/ (against one another, through), jostling

เบียร์ beer

เบียร์ดำ stout

เบี้ยว crooked, distorted, twisted, lopsided; to default, fail to (/keep one's promise/appear/ do something expected/etc), default, go back on one's word

เบี้ยวค่าแรง to fail to pay, default on payment of wages

ชอบเบี้ยว to be a deadbeat

เบือ multitude, droves, large number (of)

ตายเป็นเบือ to die in droves, a multitude of deaths

เป็นเบือ a slew of

เบื่อ[1] *as in* ยาเบื่อ poison

เบื่อ[2] tired (of), be fed up (with), bored (with, by); disgusted (with), cannot stand (someone or something)

เบื่อไหม Have you had enough? / Are you tired of it? / Do you find it /tiresome/ tedious/?

เบื่อจะตาย to be bored to death

เบื่อฟัง tired of listening (to)

เบื่อโลก to be tired of living, fed up with everything, world weary

เบื่อหน้า not to care for someone; cannot stand someone, irritated (by someone)

เบื่อหน่าย to be fed up, disgusted (with), so bored (with, by), tired (of), to have had enough (of)

ความเบื่อ boredom, ennui, tedium

ทำให้เบื่อ boring, tedious, tiresome

เหม็นเบื่อ disgusted (with), fed up to one's ears (with, by); bored stiff (with)

เบื้อ dumb

นั่งเป็นเบื้อ to sit like a dummy

เบื้อง side, part

เบื้องต้น elementary, primary; introductory; initially, at the outset

เบื้องบน those on high, the higher authorities, higher-ups, powers that be

แล้วแต่เบื้องบนจะสั่ง It depends on those on high. / Whatever the powers that be say.

เบื้องปลาย the end

เบื้องล่าง below

เบื้องหน้า in the future; ahead (of), before, in front (of)

เบื้องหลัง inside story, more than meets the eye, one's past; behind

เบือน *as in* เบือนหน้า to turn away (from)

แบ to spread, open out

แบกะดิน to spread goods out on the ground for sale

แบไต๋ to divulge

แบเบาะ infancy

แบมือ to hold out one's hand; to ask for a handout

 บ
ป
ผ
ฝ
พ
ฟ
ภ
ม
ย
ร
ฤ
ฤๅ
ล
ว
ศ
ษ
ส
ห
ฬ
อ
ฮ

แบกมือขอ to ask for a handout

แบกหลา sprawled out

แบก to shoulder, bear

แบกปืน to shoulder a gun

แบกภาระ to shoulder responsibility, be saddled with, be burdened (with), bear responsibility (for)

แบกหน้า eat humble pie, make a humiliating supplication

แบกหาม to carry; tote, transport, porter; porterage; unskilled labor, coolie-work

แบกอาวุธ to carry a weapon; to shoulder /arms/a gun/, armed

แบ่ง to divide; separate; to allot, allocate, apportion, share

แบ่งเบา to help, unburden, relieve, make things easier, give relief (to)

แบ่งปัน to share

แบ่งเป็นสองส่วน to divide in two

แบ่งภาค incarnated; to have only two hands, cannot be two people at the same time

สอนก็จะให้สอน ประชุมก็จะให้ประชุม ผมแบ่งภาคไปไม่ได้หรอก They want me to teach, they want me to go meetings. I can't be two people at the same time.

โน่นก็จะให้ทำ นี่ก็จะให้ทำ ใครมันจะแบ่งภาคได้วะ That one wants one thing this one wants something else. It's crazy, I've only got two hands.

แบ่งแยก to separate, divide (into), segregate

แบ่งรับแบ่งสู้ to give a partial confession, admit in part and deny in part; noncommittal, wary

แบ่งสันปันส่วน to apportion, share (between, among)

สลากกินแบ่ง lottery, government lottery

ส่วนแบ่ง share, part, portion, quota, division

แบตเตอรี่ battery

แบน[1] flat; plane

แบนแต๊ดแต๋ flat as a pancake, flattened

แบน[2] to ban

เพลงเสียดสีผู้นำถูกแบน The song satirizing the head of the government was banned.

แบบ plan, scheme; example, model; style, way; pattern; form

แบบจำลอง model, scale model

แบบฉบับ example, standard; model, ideal; prototype

แบบไทยๆ Thai style

แบบนี้, แบบนั้น this type (of); like /this/that/

ไม่ให้ทำแบบนี้จะให้ทำแบบไหน If you don't want me to do it /like this/this way/ how do you want me to do it?

อย่าพูดแบบนั้น Don't talk like that. / Don't say that.

แบบบาง fragile, delicate

แบบแปลน plans

แบบแผน usage, customs, the way things are done , regulations

แบบฝึกหัด /exercise/drill/ book; exercise, drill

แบบพิธี formalities; ceremony, rite

แบบพิมพ์ printed form

แบบพื้นๆ plain, simple, everyday

แบบฟอร์ม form

แบบเรียน textbook, schoolbook

แบบสากล western; international

แบบเสื้อ pattern

แบบอย่าง example, model, exemplar

เครื่องแบบ uniform

ตามแบบ to copy; to emulate, follow the example (of), do as someone else does

ถอดแบบ to reproduce, copy; to take after (someone)

ถ่ายแบบ to make a copy (of); to /make/ take/ fashion photographs

นางแบบ model

ไม้แบบ wooden forms

แบล็คเมล์ to blackmail

แบะ to be separated; to separate; to be broken; to break, be split, split

    แบะแฉะ to hang /on/around/, be stuck (/in place/to one's seat/etc)

    แบะท่า to hint (at)

    แบะปาก to make a face

    แบะอก to open (one's shirt)

    ถูกตีหัวแบะ to get a bloody blow to the head

    เสื้อคอแบะ open at the collar

โบ bow

    โบแดง blue ribbon

โบ้, โบ๋ sunken, hollow

    กางเกงขาดเป็นรูโบ๋ pants with a /gaping hole/ big rip/

    ตาโบ๋ hollow-eyed, sunken eyes

    สะดือโบ๋ recessed navel

โบก to wave; to flap; to blow; to coat (with)

    โบกธง to wave a flag, signal with a flag

    โบกปูน to plaster

    โบกมือ to wave (one's hand)

        โบกไม้โบกมือ to wave vigorously; waving of hands

โบนัส bonus

โบย to beat, lash, flog, whip, thrash; to fly

    โบยบิน to fly (off, away, about, etc), wing

โบราณ ancient, antique, archaic

    โบราณกาล ancient times, olden days

    โบราณคดี archaeology

    โบราณชีววิทยา paleontology

    โบราณวัตถุ historical object, antique, antiquity, archaeological /object/find/

    โบราณสถาน historical /site/monument/, ruins

    คนโบราณ people of old

    คำโบราณ old saying; archaic word

    โบร่ำโบราณ ancient

    สมัยโบราณ in ancient times

โบสถ์ temple

    ไปโบสถ์ทุกอาทิตย์ to go to church every Sunday / to go to the temple every week

    โบสถ์แขก mosque

    โบสถ์ฝรั่ง church

    โบสถ์ยิว synagogue, temple

ใบ leaf; sheet; sail; a numerical designation for vessels, fruits and sheets

    ใบกำกับสินค้า, ใบเรียกเก็บหนี้ invoice

    ใบขับขี่ driver's licence

    ใบจักร propeller

    ใบจับจอง pre-emption certificate

    ใบแจ้งการซื้อ-ขายหลักทรัพย์ contract note

    ใบแจ้งความ police report receipt

    ใบแจ้งหนี้ bill

    ใบชา tea leaves, tea

    ใบฎีกา solicitation letter, invitation to participate in merit-making

    ใบตรวจโรค medical certificate

    ใบตอง banana leaf

    ใบต่างด้าว alien registration /book/ certificate/

    ใบแทรก insert, supplement

    ใบบอก official report from the provinces

    ใบบุญ (in one's) grace

    ใบเบิก requisition

        ใบเบิกทาง laissez-passer, road pass

    ใบปก book jacket, dust cover

    ใบประกอบโรคศิลป์ a license to practice medicine

    ใบปลิว leaflet, handbill, handout, flyer, throwaway; tract

    ใบปะหน้า cover sheet

    ใบปิดหนัง movie poster

    ใบพลู betel pepper leaf

    ใบพัด fan blade, propeller, propeller blade

    ใบมีดโกน razor blade

    ใบไม้ leaf

    ใบยา tobacco leaf

บ
ป
ผ
ฝ
พ
ฟ
ภ
ม
ย
ร
ฤ
ฤๅ
ล
ว
ศ
ษ
ส
ห
ฬ
อ
ฮ

ก
ข
ค
ฆ
ง
จ
ฉ
ช
ซ
ฌ
ญ
ฎ
ฏ
ฐ
ฑ
ฒ
ณ
ด
ต
ถ
ท
ธ
น
บ

ใบยืนยันการปฏิบัติตามคำสั่งซื้อ/ขายหลักทรัพย์ Report of Execution of Trading Order

ใบรับ receipt

    ใบรับประกัน guarantee, warranty

    ใบรับรอง certificate

    ใบรับสินค้า bill of lading

ใบลา request for leave of absence

ใบลาน palm leaf

ใบเลี้ยงเดี่ยว monocotyledon

ใบเลี้ยงคู่ dicotyledon

ใบส่งของ delivery order

ใบสมัคร application (form)

ใบสั่ง ticket, police summons

    ใบสั่งของ purchase order

    ใบสั่งจ่าย payment voucher

    ใบสั่งยา prescription

ใบสำคัญ certificate

    ใบสำคัญคู่จ่าย duplicate

    ใบสำคัญแสดงสิทธิที่จะซื้อหุ้น warrant

ใบสุทธิ school-leaving certificate, testimonial; monk's identification card

ใบเสร็จ receipt

ใบหน้า features, face, visage

ใบหุ้น share certificate

ใบหู ear

ใบอนุญาต licence, permit, authorization

    ใบอนุญาตส่งสินค้าออก export licence

เรือใบ sailboat; sailing vessel

แล่นใบ to sail, be under sail

ใบ้ dumb, mute

คนใบ้ dumb person, a mute

บอกใบ้ to give the high sign (to someone), use sign language, let someone know something surreptitiously, hint (at something)

บุ้ยใบ้, บุ้ยบ้าย see **บุ้ยใบ้** *หน้า 280*

เป็นใบ้ to be mute, dumb

ไบ bisexual

ไบเบิล bible

ปก cover; collar
ปกแข็ง hard-cover
ปกคอเสื้อ collar
ปกหน้า front cover
ปกหลัง back cover
ปกอ่อน soft-cover, paperback
ปกครอง to take care of, oversee; to govern, rule, administer
การปกครอง government, public administration; authority, governing; guardianship
ข้าราชการฝ่ายปกครอง administrative /official/officer/
ในความปกครอง under the /jurisdiction/authority/guardianship/ of
ผู้ปกครอง parent, guardian; ruler, governor
ปกคลุม to cover; to be covered (with), shrouded (by, in)
ปกติ normal, regular, usual, ordinary
ตามปกติ ordinarily, usually; normally, as usual
เป็นปกติ normal
ผิดปกติ unusual, different, out of the ordinary, queer, odd, strange, abnormal
ยามปกติ in normal times, in peacetime
ปกป้อง to protect, shield (from), defend; to /stick up/stand up/ for (somebody or something)
ปกปักรักษา to take care (of), preserve, maintain
ปกปิด to hide, conceal, cover up, be covered up
ปกปิดความจริง to hide the truth, lie (about), keep something from somebody
ปกิณกะ miscellaneous
ปฏิกรณ์ reactor
ปฏิกรรมสงคราม war reparations
ปฏิการ (to give a) token of /appreciation/gratitude/
ปฏิกิริยา reaction
ปฏิกิริยาลูกโซ่ chain reaction
ปฏิกูล garbage, refuse, waste; offensive matter, offal; scum; foul, disgusting

ขนถ่ายสิ่งปฏิกูล nightsoil disposal
ปฏิคม greeter, receiver
กรรมการปฏิคม /welcoming/greeting/reception/ committee
ปฏิญญา charter; solemn promise
ปฏิญาณ to take an oath (of allegiance etc), swear (by), pledge
ปฏิญาณตัว to be sworn in, take an oath of office
ปฏิทิน calendar
ปฏิบัติ to do, perform, act, put into practice; to practice, follow, handle; to behave
ปฏิบัติการ to act, work, perform; to operate; service
ปฏิบัติการเชิงรุก to take the initiative, be pro-active
ห้องปฏิบัติการ laboratory; operations room
ปฏิบัติต่อกัน to treat one another (with)
ปฏิบัติตาม to act accordingly, comply (with), execute
ปฏิบัติตามสัญญา to /execute/perform/ a contract, observe an agreement
การปฏิบัติตามคำสั่งซื้อขายหลักทรัพย์ execution of a trading order
ปฏิบัติธรรม to practice the dharma
ปฏิบัติบิดามารดา to /look after/serve/wait upon/ one's parents
ปฏิบัติราชการ to act officially, on government service, in service, to perform official /duties/functions/
ปฏิบัติราชการแทน acting
การปฏิบัติ performance
การปฏิบัติหน้าที่ทางทูต the performance of diplomatic acts
ข้อปฏิบัติ instructions, rules, directions, practice, routine
นำมาปฏิบัติ to apply, put into practice, implement

ป
ผ
ฝ
พ
ฟ
ภ
ม
ย
ร
ฤ
ฤๅ
ล
ว
ศ
ษ
ส
ห
ฬ
อ
ฮ

ปฏิปทา way, path; deportment; way of life

    มีปฏิปทาน่าเลื่อมใส to have an inspiring way of life, (to be a person) of admirable deportment

ปฏิปักษ์ opponent, enemy, adversary, foe; hostile

ปฏิพัทธ์ to love, have affection (for)

ปฏิภาค proportion

ปฏิภาณ quick-witted, adroit, ready, smart; acumen

    ปฏิภาณกวี ready poet, improvisatore

ปฏิมา Buddha /image/figure/

ปฏิมากร see **ปฏิมา**

ปฏิรูป to reform

    ปฏิรูปที่ดิน land reform

ปฏิโลม conversely; in reverse order

ปฏิวัติ to revolt; to drastically reform

    การปฏิวัติ revolution

        การปฏิวัติวัฒนธรรม cultural revolution

ปฏิเวธ penetration, comprehension, realization

ปฏิสนธิ conception

ปฏิสังขรณ์ restoration, repair, renovation

ปฏิสันถาร to greet; to converse (with)

ปฏิสัมพันธ์ interaction; relation (with)

ปฏิเสธ to refuse, decline (to), say no (to); to deny, negate; to reject

    ปฏิเสธข่าว to issue a denial

    ปฏิเสธความจริง to deny reality, refuse to admit the truth

    การปฏิเสธ denial; refusal

ปฐพี earth, ground

ปฐม first, original; elementary, primary

    ปฐมกษัตริย์ the founder of a dynasty

    ปฐมทัศน์ premiere, first showing

    ปฐมนิเทศ orientation /meeting/session/

    ปฐมพยาบาล first aid

    ปฐมภูมิ primary

        ข้อมูลปฐมภูมิ primary source

    ปฐมยาม the early night watch, evening from six to nine

ปฐมวัย childhood, youth

ปฐมศึกษา see **ประถมศึกษา** *หน้า 293*

ปฐวี see **ปฐพี**

ป.ณ. P.O. (post office)

    ป.ณ.ก. G.P.O. (general post office), C.P.O. (central post office)

ปณาม see **ประณาม** *หน้า 292*

ปณิธาน resolve, resolution, dedication

ปด to lie, fib, tell a /lie/fib/

    คนขี้ปด fibber; liar, one who tells lies

ปถวี see **ปฐพี**

ปทัสถาน see **บรรทัดฐาน** *หน้า 268*

ปทานุกรม dictionary

ปทีป see **ประทีป** *หน้า 294*

ปทุม lotus; breast

ปน to be mixed, blended; to mix, blend, mingle, combine

    ปนกันยุ่ง all mixed up

    ปนเป mixed up, in disorder

    ใช้ปนกัน to use in common, share

    ดินปนทราย sandy loam

ป่น ground, pulverized

    ป่นปี้ ruined, destroyed, shattered; damaging, vicious

    เกลือป่น granulated salt

    พริกป่น ground chili

ปม knob, bump, protuberance; knot; knotty problem; complex; case

    ปมเขื่อง, ปมเด่น superiority complex

    ปมเงื่อน problem

    ปมด้อย inferiority complex

    ปมประสาท nerve center; a sore spot

    ปมสังหาร murder case

ปรก[1] to cover, shield, protect

    ผมปรกบ่า hair worn down to the shoulders, shoulder-length bob, pageboy (bob)

    พระนาคปรก Buddha figure sheltered by a Naga

ปรก[2] *as in* **นั่งปรก** to perform a silent incantation

ปรกติ *see* **ปกติ** *หน้า 287*

ปรนนิบัติ to serve, wait upon (someone), take care (of)

ปรนปรือ to well look after (someone), nurture, do everything for someone

ปรนเปรอ to indulge, pamper, gratify, please (someone) in every way

ปรนัย objective

    ลัทธิปรนัยนิยม objectivism

ปรบ to clap; to flap

    ปรบปีก to flap its wings

    ปรบมือ to applaud, clap (the hands), give (someone) a hand

        ปรบมือให้ to applaud (an action, effort etc)

ปรปักษ์ opponent, enemy, foe; adverse, hostile

    การครอบครองปรปักษ์ adverse possession

ปรมัตถ์ ultimate truth

ปรมาจารย์ past master (at, of), great teacher

ปรมาณู atom; atomic, nuclear

    พลังงานปรมาณู atomic energy

    ระเบิดปรมาณู atomic bomb

    สงครามปรมาณู atomic warfare

ปรมาภิไธย name (of a king)

ปรโลก afterworld

ปรวนแปร changeable, changing, uncertain, variable

    อารมณ์ปรวนแปร fickle, capricious, mercurial

ปร๋อ swiftly

    วิ่งปร๋อ to run swiftly

ปรองดอง on good terms, in harmony, in agreement; to compromise, settle one's differences, come to terms, reconcile one's differences; be reconciled

ปรอท mercury, quicksilver; thermometer

    วัดปรอท to take (somebody's) temperature

ปรอย sad; in a drizzle

    ตาปรอย sad, downcast, down in the mouth, woebegone

    ฝนปรอย to drizzle; light rain, a drizzle

ประ to strike; to touch; to add; to attack; to pat on

    ประคารม to have an altercation, argue, have a row

    ประแป้ง to powder

    ประวิสรรชนีย์ to add the vowel sign " ะ "

    ประหมัด to punch

ประกบ to tail, shadow, keep; under surveillance; to cover; to sidle up to someone; to join, splice

    ประกบตัว to cover; to tail, shadow, keep under surveillance

ประกวด to enter a /contest/competition/; to compete; to show; to bid

    ประกวดนางงาม (to hold a) beauty contest

    ประกวดประขัน to compete, keep up with the Joneses

    มีรถคันเล็กๆ พอไปไหนได้สะดวกก็พอแล้ว ไม่ต้องการประกวดประขันกับใคร A small car easy to get around in is enough for me. / I don't need to compete with anybody. / I don't have to keep up with the Joneses.

    ประกวดราคา tender

        ใบประกวดราคา bid

    ประกวดสุนัข dog show

ประกอบ to do, engage in, carry on, perform; to assemble, put together; to make; to be composed of, comprising, consisting of

    ประกอบคุณงามความดี to do good, lead a virtuous life, be virtuous

    ประกอบเครื่องยนต์ to assemble engines

    ประกอบด้วย to consist (of, in); made of, consisting of, comprising, composed of

    ประกอบเป็น to form

    ประกอบยา to compound medicine

    ประกอบอาชีพ to carry on an occupation, make a living

ป ผ ฝ พ ฟ ภ ม ย ร ฤ ฤๅ ล ว ศ ษ ส ห ฬ อ ฮ

ท่านประกอบอาชีพอะไร What is your occupation? / How do you make your living?

ประกอบอาหาร to make food

ตัวประกอบ supporting /actor/actress/character/; factor (คณิต)

ตัวอย่างประกอบ illustration, example

ภาพประกอบ illustration

สมประกอบ perfect

ส่วนประกอบ part, component, constituent, element, ingredient

องค์ประกอบ element; requisite; factor; constituent

ประกัน to guarantee, secure, warrant; to insure; to put up bail; bail, security, guaranty

ประกันชีวิต life insurance

ประกันตัว to obtain the release (of someone) on bail, bail out

ประกันตัวเอง to bail oneself out

ประกันภัย casualty insurance

กรมธรรม์ประกันภัย insurance policy

ประกันรถยนต์ to insure one's automobile, take out automobile insurance; car insurance

ประกันอัคคีภัย to insure against fire, take out fire insurance

การประกันสังคม social security

ค้ำประกัน to guarantee, act as surety

ตัวประกัน hostage, surety

นายประกัน guarantor, surety

ใบประกัน guaranty, warranty

รับประกัน to insure; to guarantee, assure

รับประกันตลอดอายุการใช้งาน lifetime guarantee

หลักประกัน security, assurance, guarantee

ประกับ splint, spline; ceramic coin

ประกาย sparkle, shine; sparks, flash

ประกายพรึก morning star

ประกายไฟ spark

ตามีประกาย sparkling eyes, eyes that /sparkle/shine/

ประการ kind, sort, thing; point

ประการใด what; whatever, whatsoever, *ไม่รู้จะทำประการใด I don't know what to do. ไม่มีมูลความจริงแต่ประการใด There is no truth (to the accusation) whatsoever. / It is completely /false/untrue/.*

ประการใดประการหนึ่ง of some sort, in some way; either one, one or the other; in any respect, in any way whatsoever, anything

ประการต่อไป next

ประการแรก in the first place, firstly, initially

ประการสำคัญ the important thing is, essential (point, action etc)

ประการสุดท้าย lastly

ด้วยประการฉะนี้ therefore

ทุกประการ in every /respect/way/, completely, entirely, all

บางประการ in some respects, in certain ways, some

เป็นประการสำคัญ principal, main (/consideration/point/issue/etc)

อีกประการหนึ่ง furthermore, besides, in addition, moreover

ประกาศ to announce, proclaim, declare, give notice; to promulgate, publish; to post *ประกาศ ณ วันที่ 1 มกราคม 2537 /published/given/proclaimed/announced/ the 1st January 2537*

ประกาศกฎอัยการศึก to declare martial law

ประกาศโฆษณา to advertise

ประกาศใช้ to give notice of the coming into force (of), publish, promulgate

ประกาศเป็นกฎหมาย to promulgate

ประกาศภาวะฉุกเฉิน to declare a state of emergency

ประกาศเรียก to page

ประกาศว่า to announce

ประกาศสงคราม to declare war

ประกาศอิสรภาพ to declare independence

ป้าย (ที่) ประกาศ signboard

ปิดประกาศ to post a notice, put up /an announcement/notice/

ประกาศนียบัตร diploma; certificate, award, certificate of recognition

ประกาศิต order, command, commandment

ประคด sash, belt

ประคบ to apply a compress

ประคบประหงม to raise with care, take good care of

ประคอง to sustain, support; to prop up, keep from falling, hold; to carry carefully

ประคับประคอง to support, sustain, shore up, prop (up)

ประคับประคองสถานการณ์ to stabilize the situation

ประคำ rosary

ประคุณ as in **เจ้าประคุณ** Your Holiness, His Holiness, Your Grace, His Grace

ประเคน to hand (something) to a monk; to sock, sock it to (someone), punch

ประโคม to play an overture; to play a lively tutti

ประโคมข่าว to splash (a story, news, information etc), make big news of

ประจง see **บรรจง** หน้า 268

ประจญ see **ผจญ** หน้า 322

ประจบ[1] see **บรรจบ** หน้า 268

ประจบ[2] to flatter, fawn (on, over), adulate; to blandish, ingratiate oneself (with someone); to please, humor

ประจบประแจง to flatter, to fawn (on, over)

การประจบประแจง flattery, blandishment

ประจบสอพลอ to be a sycophant

คนขี้ประจบ flatterer

หมาขี้ประจบ dog that likes to fawn on people

ประจวบ in addition to, plus; fortuitous

ประจวบเหมาะ timely, opportune

ประจ๋อประแจ๋ to charm, beguile

ประจักษ์ clear, distinct, evident, obvious

ประจักษ์พยาน eyewitness

เห็นประจักษ์ to see; to realize; clearly visible

ประจัญ to fight, battle

เรือประจัญบาน battleship

ประจันหน้า to confront

ประจาน to humiliate publicly, disgrace, shame; to ridicule, hold up to /ridicule/contempt/

พูดประจาน to put someone to shame, ridicule, humiliate, disparage publicly

ประจำ in at; regular

ประจำการ in service

ประจำชาติ national

ประจำทาง /fixed/regular/ route

ประจำเดือน monthly; (menstrual) period, menstruation

มีประจำเดือน to be having one's period

ประจำตัว personal

บัตรประจำตัว identity card

ประจำปี yearly, annual

ประจำวัน daily

ประจำสัปดาห์ weekly

ขาประจำ regular customer, good customer

นักเรียนประจำ boarding student

รถเมล์ประจำทาง bus

โรงเรียนประจำ boarding school

ประจิม west

ประจิ้มประเจ๋อ to show off; bumptious

ประจุ to load, charge; to pack

ประจุไฟฟ้า electric charge

ยาประจุ purgative

ประเจิดประเจ้อ in public, public, (too) exposed, exposed to view, too conspicuous

ประแจ key

ประแจจีน a Chinese decorative design

ประชด to mock, ridicule, deride, treat con-

ป
ผ
ฝ
พ
ฟ
ภ
ม
ย
ร
ฤ
ฤๅ
ล
ว
ศ
ษ
ส
ห
ฬ
อ
ฮ

temptuously; to spite

ฆ่าตัวตายประชดสามี She /killed herself/ commited suicide/ to spite her husband.

ประชดสังคม to hold society in contempt, contemptuous of society; antisocial

ประชวร to be sick, ill *(royal word)*

ประชัน to compete (with one another); to hold a contest

ประชา people

ประชากร population

ประชาคม community

ประชาคมเศรษฐกิจยุโรป European Economic Community

ประชาชน the public, the people, populace

ประชาชนพลเมือง people

ประชาชาติ nation

ประชาทัณฑ์ to lynch, take the law into one's own hands; mob-inflicted punishment

ประชาธิปไตย democracy

ระบอบประชาธิปไตย democratic /system/form of government/

ประชาบาล rural government

โรงเรียนประชาบาล rural primary school, local elementary school

ประชาพิจารณ์ public hearing

ประชามติ public opinion

ประชาราษฎร์ subjects, people, population

ประชาสงเคราะห์ public welfare

ประชาสัมพันธ์ public relations

ประชิด to be close to, /move/come/up to

ประชุม to meet, hold a meeting, assemble, congregate; collection, assemblage; collected

ประชุมบทความทางวิชาการ collected essays (on history, microbiology etc)

ประชุมพงศาวดาร annals, chronicles

ประชุมเพลิง to light a funeral pyre

ประชุมลับ closed meeting

ประชุมสุดยอด summit meeting

การประชุม meeting, conference; session

การประชุมสามัญ ordinary meeting

การประชุมใหญ่ general meeting

การประชุมใหญ่วิสามัญ extraordinary general meeting

การประชุมใหญ่สามัญ ordinary general meeting

ที่ประชุม meeting, meeting place

เรียกประชุม to call a meeting, convene a /meeting/session/

ห้องประชุม meeting room, assembly hall, auditorium

ประเชิญ to collide, clash; to hit, strike; to meet, encounter, face, confront

ไม่อยากประเชิญหน้า I do not want to face him. / I don't want a confrontation.

ประณต to bow and salute in Thai style

ประณม see **ประนม** หน้า 294

ประณาม to condemn (for, as), denounce (for, as), accuse (of)

ประณิธาน see **ปณิธาน** หน้า 288

ประณีต good, excellent, careful, neat, fine; subtle; scrupulous

ประณีตศิลป์ fine arts

ศิลปะประณีต fine artwork

อาหารประณีต /fine/carefully prepared/ food, gourmet cooking

ประดักประเดิด disconcerted, embarrassed, rattled, discombobulated

ประดัง to pour in, flooded (with)

งานประดังเข้ามาจนทำไม่ทัน I was unable to handle all the work that poured in. / I was so flooded with work, I couldn't keep up.

ประดับ to decorate, ornament, embellish, adorn; decorative

ประดับประดา decorated (with)

เครื่องประดับ ornaments; costume jewelry, decorations, adornments

ไม้ประดับ ornamental plant

ประดา[1] all; every bit (of), the entirety

ฉันเบื่อเต็มประดา I'm thoroughly fed up.

ประดามี everything there is

ประดา[2] to dive and stay under water

ประดาน้ำ expert diver, skilled diver, frogman

ประดิดประดอย to embellish, beautify, make beautiful

ประดิษฐ์ invent, create; to fabricate, make up

ประดิษฐกรรม invention

ประดิษฐาน to establish, introduce; located

ประดิษฐานพระพุทธศาสนา to /introduce /establish/ Buddhism (in)

การประดิษฐ์ invention

นักประดิษฐ์ inventor

ประดุจ, ประดุจดัง like, as, as if

ประเด็น issue, question, point, problem, subject

ประเด็นนี้ผมเห็นด้วย On that question, I agree. / I accept on that issue.

ขอให้เข้าประเด็นหน่อย Please come to the point. / Please address the issue.

นอกประเด็น irrelevant, beside the point, not pertinent, not germane, inapposite, immaterial

พูดไม่ตรงประเด็น not to the point

ประเดิม, เผดิม to begin, start, open, commence, inaugurate, be the first (to do something)

ประเดิมการสู้ราคา to open the bidding

ประเดี๋ยว instantly; in an instant; just a moment, momentarily

ประเดี๋ยวก่อน just a minute, wait a minute, hold your horses

ประเดี๋ยวเดียวก็เสร็จ to be /ready/done/ finished/ in a moment, ready in a jiffy

ประเดี๋ยวประด๋าว ephemeral

ประติมากรรม sculpture, sculptural work

ประตู door, doorway, gate, entrance, opening, portal; goal; shot

ประตูกล self-opening door, automatic door

ประตูชัย arch of triumph, victory arch

ประตูน้ำ watergate, lock

ประตูผี charnel gate, the gate of a walled town through which corpses may be removed

ประตูฟุตบอล goalkeeper

ประตูเลื่อน sliding door

ประตูหน้า front door

ประตูหลัง back door

ค่าผ่านประตู price of a ticket, admission, admission fee

ชนะเต็มประตู to win on all counts, have a solid victory

บัตรผ่านประตู pass, ticket

บานประตู door, leaf of a door

ราคาประตูละ 500 บาท 500 baht a shot

สู้ทุกประตู to avail (oneself) of every defense, fight by every means

ประถม primary, elementary, first

ประถมศึกษา /primary/elementary/ education, primary schooling

ชั้นประถม /elementary/primary/(school, level, grade, etc)

โรงเรียนประถม /elementary/primary/ school

ประท้วง to protest

เดินขบวนประท้วงรัฐบาล to march in protest against the government

ประทวน ministerial certificate of appointment

ประทวนสินค้า warehouse receipt

นายทหารชั้นประทวน warrant officer

ประทักษิณ right side, righthand side

เดินประทักษิณ 3 รอบ to circumambulate clockwise thrice, circle to the right 3 times

เบื้องประทักษิณ to the right (of), at the right (of), at the right side (of)

ประทัง sustain, maintain, support

พอประทังชีวิต enough to keep body and soul together, enough to survive

ประทัด firecracker

ประทับ[1] *(royal word)* to be in residence, reside; to sit

ประทับแรม to spend the night

ประทับอยู่ในวัง to be in residence at the palace

ประทับ^2 to make an impression (on); impress; to imprint, stamp, affix

    ประทับใจ impressive; to make an impression (on)

    ประทับตรา to seal, chop, affix a /stamp/ seal/; sealed, L.S. (ย่อจาก locus sigilli = place for the seal)

ประทาน to give, bestow

    ประทานโทษ excuse me, pardon me

    ขอประทานเสนอ allow me to (/propose/offer /submit/etc.), may I...

ประทีป lamp, lantern, flame-light

ประทุน hood, top, covering

ประทุม see ปทุม หน้า 288

ประทุษร้าย to do harm (to), assault, attack, injure, do violence (to), commit an act of violence (on, against someone by doing something)

ประเทศ country

    ประเทศชาติ nation, country

    ประเทศมหาอำนาจ great power

    ประเทศร้อน tropical country

    ประเทศราช protectorate, dependency

    ต่างประเทศ foreign

    นอกประเทศ outside the country, foreign, external

    ในประเทศ inside the country, domestic, internal

    ภูมิประเทศ landscape, scenery, countryside; geography

    ระหว่างประเทศ international

        กฎหมายระหว่างประเทศ international law

ประเทือง to improve, better, enhance

ประธาน chairman, president, chief, leader

    ประธานกรรมการ chairman of the board (of directors); committee chairman

ประธานบริษัท president of the company

ประธานรัฐสภา president of the national legislature

ประธานสภาผู้แทนราษฎร speaker of the House of Representatives

ประธานองคมนตรี President of the Privy Council

เป็นประธาน to preside (over), be chairman

ประธานาธิบดี president

    รองประธานาธิบดี vice-president

ประนม to make a gesture of respect by pressing the palms of the hands together at the chest

ประนอมหนี้ to reach a compromise with creditors, compound with creditors

ประนีประนอม to compromise, reconcile differences, reach a settlement

ประปราย sparsely, thinly; not /much/many/; scant, occasional

ประปา water supply

    ก๊อกประปา hydrant

    การประปา waterworks, water authority

    ท่อประปา water pipe

    น้ำประปา piped water, water supply

ประเปรียว lively, spirited, animated

ประพรม to asperge; to sprinkle

ประพฤติ to behave, act, conduct oneself, do

    ประพฤติตนดี to behave well, act properly, be good

    ความประพฤติ behavior, conduct

ประพันธ์ to write, compose

    นักประพันธ์ writer, author

    บทประพันธ์ article, story, work, writing

ประพาส to travel (to, in, around), tour, take a trip

ประพิมพ์ประพาย appearance

    ประพิมพ์ประพายคล้ายพ่อ He takes after his father. / He /resembles/looks like/ his father.

ประเพณี custom, tradition, usual practice, the

way things are done

ประเพณีนิยม customary, traditional

ประเพณีปฏิบัติ usages, practices

ประภาคาร lighthouse, beacon

ประเภท class, category; type, kind

ประมง fishery, fishing

การประมง fishery, fishing

ชาวประมง fishermen, fisherfolk

เรือประมง fishing boat

ประมวล to collect, compile, gather, organize; to codify

ประมวลกฎหมาย code of laws

ประมวลกฎหมายแพ่ง civil code

ประมวลการสอน course /outline/survey/

ประมวลรัษฎากร revenue code

ประมาณ to estimate, approximate; about, approximately

งบประมาณ budget, budget estimate

พอประมาณ reasonable, moderate, reasonable amount (of), some

เหลือประมาณ inconceivably

ประมาท negligent, careless, imprudent; to underestimate

ทีมญี่ปุ่นประมาทเรา The Japanese team underestimated us.

ประมาทเลินเล่อ negligent

ประมาทหน้า to belittle, disparage, treat contemptuously, libel

สบประมาท to insult, affront

ฟ้องหมิ่นประมาท to sue for /defamation/ slander/libel/

ประมุข head, chief

ประมุขประเทศ head of state

ประมูล to tender, bid, bid at an auction

เปิดประมูลราคา to call for /tenders/bids/

ผู้ดำเนินการประมูล auctioneer

ประเมิน to assess; to estimate; to appraise, value

ประเมินผล to evaluate

ประเมินภาษี to assess a tax, make a tax

assessment

ประเมินราคา to /give/make/ an estimate, appraise, make an appraisal, give a valuation

ประยุกต์ applied, adapted

วิทยาศาสตร์ประยุกต์ applied science

ประโยค sentence; grade, level

ประโยคมัธยม secondary school level

เปรียญ ๓ ประโยค holder of a third level certificate of Pali studies

ประโยชน์ utility, usefulness; benefit, good, advantage; use

ประโยชน์มหาศาล tremendous benefit

ประโยชน์ส่วนรวม common good

ก่อให้เกิดประโยชน์ beneficial; to benefit, do good (for)

คุณประโยชน์ benefit(s), utility, advantages; use

ได้ประโยชน์ to gain, benefit, profit

เป็นประโยชน์ useful, advantageous

เปล่าประโยชน์ useless, of no use, worthless, unprofitable, disadvantageous, futile; nugatory

ผลประโยชน์ interest (in), benefit (from); income

เพื่อประโยชน์ in the interest of, for the benefit of, for the sake of

มีประโยชน์ useful, valuable, helpful; usable; wholesome, nutritious

ไร้ประโยชน์ worthless, useless, futile, fruitless

สาธารณประโยชน์ (in the) public interest, (for the) public benefit

แสวงหาผลประโยชน์ to seek /gain/profit/ (from), turn to account, make gains

ประลอง to practise; to test

ประลองยุทธ์ to stage maneuvers, hold /wargames/field exercises/

ประโลม to cheer up, make (someone) feel good

ประโลมใจ to comfort, soothe; to console

ป
ผ
ฝ
พ
ฟ
ภ
ม
ย
ร
ฤ
ฦ
ล
ว
ศ
ษ
ส
ห
ฬ
อ
ฮ

นวนิยายประโลมโลก romantic /novel/fiction/

ประวัติ history; record; resumé, curriculum vitae

ประวัติการณ์ record

ชนะท่วมท้นเป็นประวัติการณ์ *a record landslide victory*

ประวัติศาสตร์ history

ประวัติศาสตร์ซ้ำรอย *history repeats itself*

มีประวัติ to have a past, have a past record

ประวิง to delay, hold back, defer

ประวิงเวลา to delay, put off, stall

ประเวณี sexual intercourse; fornication

ผิด (ล่วง) ประเวณี to have illicit sexual intercourse, fornicate, (engage in) sexual misconduct

ร่วมประเวณี to have sexual intercourse

ประสงค์ to wish, desire, want

ประสงค์ร้าย ill-will, ill-intentioned, malevolent, malicious

ความประสงค์ intention, purpose; wish, desire

จุดประสงค์ purpose, aim, goal, objective

ประสบ to meet, encounter, come up against; to be

ประสบการณ์ experience

ประสบความสำเร็จ to do well, meet success, be successful, make good

ประสม to combine, mix, blend; to add,

ประสมประสาน to accumulate little by little, save up

ประสมประเส to join in

ประสมพันธุ์ to breed

ประสมโรง to join in, take part (in)

ประสา way, manner

ประสาเด็ก like children, childlike, juvenile

ประสาผู้ใหญ่ maturely, in an adult way

ประสามิตร amicably, in a friendly way

ตามประสา as (they) do, in (their) own way, as is (their) wont

พวกเด็กๆ ก็คุยกันตามประสา *The children were chatting away as children do.*

นับประสาอะไร what can (you) expect?

อธิบดีตำรวจยังถูกขโมยขึ้นบ้าน นับประสาอะไร กับคนอย่างเรา *What can folks like us expect when even the police chief's house gets burgled?*

ไม่ประสา innocent, simple, unsophisticated, naive

รู้ประสา to know what's what, have sense; mature

ประสาท[1] nerve, neuro-; nuts

ประสาทพยาธิวิทยา neuropathology

ประสาทพิการ impaired nerve, neurasthenia

ประสาทไว sensitive

กวนประสาท to get on (one's) nerves, drive (one) crazy, rile, be riled (by), irritating

โรคประสาท nervous /disease/disorder/; neurosis

เส้นประสาท nerve

โสตประสาท auditory nerve

ประสาท[2] to bestow, confer, give

ประสาทปริญญา to confer a degree

ประสาทพร to bless, bestow a blessing (on)

ประสาน to cohere; to heal; to join together, unite (in); to weld (together)

ประสานงา to lock horns (with, over)

ประสานงาน to coordinate (with), work together with

ประสานมือ to clasp one's hands

ประสิทธิ์ effectiveness, fruitfulness, success

ประสิทธิ์ประสาท to impart knowledge (of), teach

ประสิทธิผล productivity

ประสิทธิภาพ efficiency, effectiveness

ประสิว *as in* ดินประสิว saltpeter, niter

ประสีประสา mature, knowing

ไม่ประสีประสา naive, simple, innocent, unworldly; immature

ประสูติ birth

ประเสริฐ superb, excellent; fine, splendid, decent; sublime

ประหนึ่ง as though, as if, like, appear (as if, like, as though, etc)

ประหม่า to be nervous; to have /stage fright /buck fever/

ตกประหม่า abashed, stunned, flabbergasted

ประหยัด to economize, save, be thrifty, be careful (about, in); economical

ประหยัดค่าใช้จ่าย to cut down expenses, save on expenses, economize on costs

ประหยัดปาก to be taciturn

อย่างประหยัด sparingly, economically

อยู่กินอย่างประหยัด to live modestly, economize

ประหลาด strange, odd, unusual, extraordinary, astonishing, amazing, outlandish

ประหลาดใจ surprised

น่าประหลาด extraordinarily, unusually, oddly

แปลกประหลาด peculiar, odd, wierd, uncanny, amazing, astonishing

ประหวัด to recall, be reminded of, call to mind

ประหวั่น apprehensive; to dread, be in dread of, fearful

ประหัต to slay, destroy

ประหัตประหาร to slay, destroy

ประหาร to slay, kill

ประหารชีวิต to execute

รัฐประหาร (to make a) coup d'etat, to overthrow a government

ปรัก *as in* **ปรักหักพัง** in ruins

ปรักปรำ to malign, slander; to go heavy (on someone), put the blame on

ปรัชญา philosophy

ปรัชญาชีวิต philosophy of life

ปรัชญาเมธี philosopher

ปรับ[1] to tell

ปรับทุกข์ to talk /about/over /one's problems; to complain (to)

ปรับ[2] to adjust; to tune; to correct; to level, smooth, even; to fine

ปรับความเข้าใจ to reach an understanding (/with someone about/as to something/), clear up a misunderstanding, be reconciled, effect a reconciliation

ปรับตัว to adjust, adapt

ปรับโทษ to sentence, impose a penalty

ปรับปรุง to improve; to adjust; to revise

การปรับปรุงโครงสร้างหนี้ debt restructuring

ปรับยอด to update (the balance, the account, one's passbook, etc)

ปรับอากาศ air-conditioned; to air-condition

เครื่องปรับอากาศ air-conditioner

ปรัมปรา traditionally; ancient

นิยายปรัมปรา ancient tale

ปรัศนี question mark; questioner

ปร่า untasty, unsavory; indistinct

รสปร่า untasty, a taste which is not right

เสียงปร่า strained /voice/sound/

ปรากฏ to appear, show, be visible, apparent

ปรากฏการณ์ phenomenon, occurence

ปรากฏชัด to be clear

ปรากฏตัว to attend, appear

ปรากฏว่า it /appears/happens/ that

ปราการ wall

ปราง cheek

ปรางค์ tall stupa

ปราจีน east

ปราชญ์ sage, learned man, authority, wise person

ปราชัย defeat

ปราณ breath

ลมปราณ breath

วายปราณ to expire, pass away, breathe (one's) last

ปราด fast, swiftly, quickly, rapidly

ปราดเปรื่อง brilliant, sharp, quick-witted

ปรานี to have mercy, be merciful, compassionate, kind

ปราบ to control, suppress, exterminate; to tame,

ป
ผ
ฝ
พ
ฟ
ภ
ม
ย
ร
ฤ
ฤๅ
ล
ว
ศ
ษ
ส
ห
ฬ
อ
ฮ

subdue, overpower

ปราบกบฏ to put down a rebellion

ปราบปราม to suppress, wipe out

ปราบดาภิเษก coronation achieved through conquest

ปราม to impede, obstruct; to forbid

ปรามาส to insult

ปราโมช, ปราโมทย์ happiness, pleasure

ปราย to scatter, strew, cast about

ปรายตา to cast one's eyes (on, at)

ปรารถนา to want, desire, wish for

พึงปรารถนา desirable, attractive

สมปรารถนา see **สมปรารถนา** หน้า 478

ปรารภ to say; to mention (see **คำปรารภ** หน้า 91)

ปรารมภ์ to reflect (on), meditate (on); to ruminate, muse; to be anxious, be worried

ปราศ, ปราศจาก free (of), without, devoid of

ปราศจากน้ำมัน oil-free

ปราศจากความลำเอียง impartial, just, fair; without prejudice, unbiased

ปราศจากชีวิต devoid of life, inanimate

ปราศจากเชื้อโรค sterile

ปราศรัย to speak, address, give /a speech/an address/a talk/

คำปราศรัย address, speech, talk

ปราสาท castle

ปริ to part, split, open slightly; bursting, popping (out, open)

ปริปาก to open (one's) mouth, mention (to)

อย่าปริปาก Keep your mouth shut. / Don't mention a word (of this).

ไม่ได้ปริปาก I didn't say a word.

เสื้อปริ a /shirt/dress/coat/blouse/ bursting at the seams

ยิ้มแก้มปริ broad smile

ปริญญา degree

ปริญญากิตติมศักดิ์ honorary degree

ปริญญาตรี bachelor's degree

ปริญญาโท master's degree

ปริญญาบัตร diploma

ปริญญาเอก doctor's degree, doctorate

ปริทัศน์ review

ปรินิพพาน total extinction; the death of the Buddha

ปริบ, ปริบๆ blinking; dripping; helplessly

ทำตาปริบๆ (to /stand by/look on/sit there/ etc) helplessly

ปริ่ม brimming; gleeful

ปริ่มเปรม brimming with good spirits

ปริมณฑล circumference; environs

นุ่งห่มให้เป็นปริมณฑล (of monks) to be properly habited

ปริมาณ quantity, amount

เชิงปริมาณ quantitative

ปริมาตร volume

ปริยัติ study of the Buddhist scriptures

ปริยัติธรรม dharma to be studied

ปริยาย as in **โดยปริยาย** indirectly, by implication; in a sense

ปริวรรต to exchange; to transliterate

ปริวรรตจากอักษรขอมเป็นอักษรไทย transliteration from Khmer to Thai script

ปริวรรตเงินตราต่างประเทศ foreign exchange

ปริวาส to do penance

ปริวิตก to be worried, worry

ปริศนา question, puzzle, riddle, paradox

ปริศนาธรรม koan, dharmic paradox

ปริศนาอักษรไขว้ crossword puzzle

ปรี่ to trickle; brimming, full to the brim, almost overflowing; to dash (at), rush (at); straight

ปรีชา proficient, skilled; learned, intelligent

เป็นผู้มีปรีชาสามารถ He is a person of great intelligence and ability.

ปรี๊ด rapidly, in a jet; whistling, tweet

น้ำพุ่งปรี๊ด The water spurted out. / He ejaculated.

ปรีดา to be glad, happy, delighted, pleased

ปรึกษา to consult, confer, to take counsel

ที่ปรึกษา adviser, consultant, counselor

ปรือ drowsy

ตาปรือ half-closed eyes, heavy eyes, drowsy; dreamy, dreamy-eyed; ecstatic

ปรื๋อ fast, quickly, rapidly

ปรุ[1] perforated; to perforate

ปรุกระดาษไข to cut a stencil

เครื่องปรุกระดาษ stencil /cutter/maker/

ปรุ[2] thoroughly, through

ปรุโปร่ง open, unobstructed, clear

ปรุง to season; to prepare, combine

ปรุงแต่ง to touch up, dress up, polish; to concoct; to prepare

ปรุงยา to compound medicine, fill a prescription

ปรุงอาหาร to cook, prepare food, make a dish; to season food, make food tasty

ปรูด, ปรู๊ด rapidly

พุ่งปรู๊ด to spurt

วิ่งปรู๊ด to dash

ปรู๊ฟ proof

ปลก, ปลกๆ repeatedly (of saluting)

ไหว้ปลกๆ to salute repeatedly

ป.ล. P.S. (*ย่อจาก* postscript)

ปลง to put down; to resolve; to agree, decide; to consider

ปลงใจ to resolve, come to a decision, make up one's mind

ปลงใจรัก to make up one's mind to love

ปลงชีวิต to kill

ปลงตก to be resigned (to), resign oneself (to), accept (one's situation, predicament, condition etc)

ปลงผม to shave the head (of a monk)

ปลงพระชนม์ to commit regicide

ปลงศพ to cremate; to perform a burial

ปลงอนิจจัง to realize the impermanence of all things

ปลงอาบัติ to confess and atone for an infraction of the discipline

ปลด to remove, detach; to free, release

ปลดเกษียณ to be superannuated, reach retirement age

ปลดคนงาน to lay off workers

ปลดจากตำแหน่ง to dismiss, discharge, remove from office

ปลดทุกข์ to relieve, give (someone) relief, help; to relieve oneself

ปลดปล่อยทหาร to demobilize

ปลดเปลื้อง to relieve (of), free (from), release (from); to shed, get rid of, divest (oneself of)

ปลดหนี้ to discharge a debt, release a debt

ปลดอาวุธ to disarm

ปลดแอก to unyoke; to liberate

ปล้น to rob; to plunder, pillage

ปล้นสะดม to pillage, sack, plunder, commit gang robbery

นักปล้น robber

ปลวก termite, white ant

ปลอก collar, band, ferrule; condom

ปลอกกระสุน casing

ปลอกแขน vambrace

ปลอกคอ collar

ปลอกมีด ferrule

ปลอกมือ thimble

ปลอกหมอน pillowcase

สวมปลอก to /use/put on/ a condom

ปล่อง hole; chimney, flue, funnel (*เรือ*),

ปล่องควัน, ปล่องไฟ smokestack, chimney; funnel, smoke vent

ปล่องภูเขาไฟ crater

ปล่องรถไฟ smokestack

ปล้อง section; rings (of /fat/wrinkles/etc) around the neck

ปลอด free (of, from), clear (of), without; all

ปลอดโปร่ง clear; safe

ปลอดภัย safe

ปลอดภัยไว้ก่อน safety first

ไม่ปลอดภัย dangerous, risky, unsafe

ป
ผ
ฝ
พ
ฟ
ภ
ม
ย
ร
ฤ
ฤๅ
ล
ว
ศ
ษ
ส
ห
ฬ
อ
ฮ

ขาวปลอด all white

เขตปลอดทหาร demilitarized zone

ปล้อน to spit out; to take /out/off/ (seeds, rind, peel, etc)

ปล้อนมะพร้าว to husk a coconut

ปลอบ, ปลอบโยน to cheer (someone) up, comfort; to mollify, soothe, pacify; to solace, console

ปลอบขวัญ to give encouragement (to), raise morale

ปลอบใจ to console, cheer up, commiserate with

ปลอบใจตัวเอง to console oneself

รางวัลปลอบใจ consolation prize

ปลอม to forge, counterfeit, fake; counterfeit, spurious, fake, forged

ปลอมตัว to disguise oneself

ปลอมปน adulterated

ปลอมแปลง to falsify, counterfeit; to disguise

ปลอมแปลงเอกสาร to forge, falsify (a letter, document etc)

ปล่อย to free, release, drop, let go, let loose; to untie; to give rein to, spoil, pamper, let someone have his own way

ปล่อยเกียร์ว่าง to leave the gear in neutral, disengage the gear

ปล่อยแก่ to kick up one's heels, act younger than one's age

ปล่อยไก่ to make a fool of oneself, make a /gaffe/faux pas/

ปล่อยข่าว to spread /a story/the news/

ปล่อยตัวตามสบาย to take things easy

ปล่อยตามเรื่อง to let (something) take its course, let things happen

ปล่อยตามลำพัง to leave (someone) alone

ปล่อยปละละเลย to neglect

ปล่อยไป to set free

ปล่อยไปตามยถากรรม to leave to one's fate, let things take their course

ปล่อยมือ to withdraw, let go

ปล่อยเลยตามเลย to let go as is; do nothing (about something), acquiesce, allow to happen

ปล่อยให้ to allow, permit

ปลัก wallow, mire

จมปลัก to be mired (down, in), sucked down (in), to get stuck, be stuck in the mud

ปลั่ง shining, beaming, glowing

เปล่งปลั่ง radiant, beaming, shining, glowing

สุกปลั่ง lustrous, shining

ปลัด deputy, lieutenant

ปลัดกระทรวง undersecretary

ปลัดจังหวัด deputy provincial governor

ปลัดอำเภอ assistant district officer

ปลัดขิก phallic amulet

ปลา fish

ปลากระป๋อง tinned fish, canned fish

ปลากัด fighting fish

ปลาเค็ม salted fish

ปลาร้า a condiment of fermented fish

กัดปลา fishfight

ก้างปลา fish bone

ข้าวปลาอาหาร food, provisions

งูๆปลาๆ a little bit, not much, rudimentary

ชิ้นปลามัน choice (girl, job, bit etc), prize

น้ำปลา fish sauce, fish soy

ปลาบ twinge

ปลาบปลื้ม gleeful; overjoyed

เสียวปลาบ (to feel a) sharp pain, twinge, stab of (pain, fear etc), stabbing pain, pang

ปลาย end; top, tip

ปลายข้าว broken rice

ปลายแถว underling

ปลายทาง end of the /road/way/

ปลายน้ำ mouth of a /river/stream/

ปลายนิ้ว fingertip

ปลายปากกา pen; nib

ปลายปี end of the year, year-end

ปลายมือ in the end, at the end of the day,

in the long run
ปลายลิ้น tip of the tongue
ปลายแหลม pointed
จุดหมายปลายทาง goal, objective, ultimate aim
เสมอต้นเสมอปลาย steady, constant, genuine; consistent, unchanging
หัวนอนปลายตีน origins, background, who (one) is
ปลาสนาการ to flee, run away
ปล้ำ, ปลุกปล้ำ to wrestle (with); to horse around (with someone); to assault, molest
มวยปล้ำ wrestling
ปลิง leech
ปลิงทะเล sea slug
ปลิด to pick, pluck
หายเป็นปลิดทิ้ง to vanish (without a trace)
ปลิ้น to turn inside out; to expose; to peel; to swindle, deceive, dupe
ปลิ้นปลอก, ปลิ้นปล้อน slippery, tricky
ปลิว to float (in the air); to be blown away, fly away; to wave
ปลิวว่อน flying around; to fill the air, float around in the air
ใบปลิว leaflet, handout, handbill, flyer, throwaway; tract
ปลี banana /blossom/flower spike/
ปลีน่อง calf
แตกปลี to put forth a flower spike
หัวปลี banana blossom
ปลีก to separate, be separated
ปลีกตัวออก to separate oneself (from), hold oneself aloof (from); to get away, go off
ปลีกย่อย small, minor, subsidiary; details
ปลีกวิเวก to /make/do/ a retreat
ปลีกเวลา to find time (to), spare the time (to, for), set aside some time
ข้อปลีกย่อย detail(s)
ขายปลีก to retail, sell retail; to sell separately

เงินปลีก small change
ซื้อปลีก to buy retail; to buy a small quantity
ปลิ้ม delighted, ecstatic, overjoyed
ปลุก to awaken, to wake up (someone); to arouse, excite; to encourage, embolden; to endue with magical power
ปลุกใจ to encourage, rouse
ปลุกใจเสือป่า erotic
ปลุกปล้ำ to assault, molest; to horse around (with someone)
ปลุกปั่น to incite, stir up
ปลุกผี to resurrect; to rouse a spirit
ปลุกระดม to organize, rouse, stir up
ปลุกเสก to consecrate, recite incantations; to endue with supernatural power
นาฬิกาปลุก alarm clock
ปลูก to plant, grow; to build, construct, erect
ปลูกถ่าย to transplant
การปลูกถ่ายอวัยวะ an organ transplant
ปลูกฝัง to instill, cultivate; to marry off
ปลูกฝี to vaccinate, (get) vaccinated, have a vaccination
ปลูกสร้าง to build, construct, erect
สิ่งปลูกสร้าง structure, building
เพาะปลูก to cultivate, plant, raise, grow
ปวกเปียก limp, flaccid; spent, worn out; spineless weak
ปวง all
ปวงชน people, public
ทั้งปวง all
ปวด to ache, hurt, be painful
ปวดตุบ ๆ, ปวดหนึบ ๆ throbbing pain
ปวดท้อง to have a stomachache
ปวดท้องเบา to have to /urinate/pass water/
ปวดแปลบ ๆ /sharp/piercing/ pain
ปวดฟัน to have a toothache
ปวดมวน to have bowel cramps, griping pains
ปวดร้าว to suffer, be tormented (by); to be

ป
ผ
ฝ
พ
ฟ
ภ
ม
ย
ร
ฤ
ฤๅ
ล
ว
ศ
ษ
ส
ห
ฬ
อ
ฮ

deeply hurt (by), crushed, shattered, deeply wounded, embittered

ปวดศีรษะ *see* **ปวดหัว**

ปวดแสบปวดร้อน to feel a burning pain; to burn

ปวดหลัง to have a backache

ปวดหัว to have a headache; to be a headache

ปวดหู to have an earache

เจ็บปวด to be painful, hurt; sore, aching; pain, distress

ป่วน   to be confused, in confusion, in a turmoil; to have an upset stomach

ป่วนใจ upset, agitated, distracted, overwrought

ป่วนปั่น turbulent; in confusion

ป้วนเปี้ยน to hang around

ฉันเห็นคนท่าทางไม่น่าไว้ใจป้วนเปี้ยนอยู่หน้าบ้าน *I saw a suspicious character hanging around in front of my house.*

ป่วย   sick, ill, unwell, ailing

ป่วยกระเสาะกระแสะ ailing, sickly

ป่วยการเมือง to be sick for political reasons

ป่วยไข้ to be sick

ป่วยเป็นโรคหัวใจ to have /heart trouble/a heart disease/

เจ็บไข้ได้ป่วย to get sick

ล้มป่วย to fall ill, get sick

ลาป่วย to take sick leave, request sick leave

ป่วยการ useless, to be of no use, waste of time

ป่วยการพูดกับคนไม่รู้เรื่อง *It's a waste of time to talk to an ignoramus.*

ค่าป่วยการ commission, service charge

ปเวณี *see* **ประเวณี** หน้า 296

ปศุสัตว์ animal husbandry; domestic animals, livestock

ปอ   hemp, jute

ปอกระเจา jute, hemp

ปอก   to peel

ปอกลอก to fleece, mulct, skin

ปอง   to intend, aim, direct

ปองรัก to fall in love (with), direct one's affections (toward)

ปองร้าย to be malicious, intend to harm, have ill-will (towards somebody), malevolent

หมายปอง object of (one's) /desire/affection/

ป่อง   swollen, distended

ป่องๆ piqued, petulant

พุงป่อง potbelly, potbellied; distended /tummy/belly/

ป้อง   to protect, shield, screen

ป้องกัน to protect (against, from), prevent; to defend

การป้องกัน prevention (of)

ป้องกันตัวเอง self-defense, to protect oneself against, defend oneself; to justify oneself, (in, as, by way of) self-justification

ป้องหน้า to shield (one's) eyes

ป้องหู to cup (one's) ear to hear better

ปอด[1]   lung, pulmonary

ปอดชื้น pulmonary congestion

ปอดบวม pneumonia

ผายปอด to give artificial respiration

โรคปอด lung trouble, pulmonary disease

ปอด[2]   afraid, scared

ปอดลอย afraid

ปอดแหก scared to death, scared stiff; chicken

ปอน   seedy, shabby, scrubby

แต่งตัวปอน to dress shabbily, wear shabby clothes, look seedy

เปียกปอน soaking wet, soaked

ป้อน   to feed, spoon-feed; to supply, provide

ป้อนข้าว to feed

ป้อนข้อมูล to supply information, provide with data

ปอนด์ pound

ป้อแป้ weak, feeble; spent, bushed; weakly, sickly

ป้อม citadel, fortress; plump, chubby
ป้อมตำรวจ police box
ป้อมบังคับการ bridge
ป้อมปืน pillbox
ป้อมปืนกล machine gun /nest/ emplacement/
ป้อมยาม sentrybox

ป๋อม plop
ป๋อมแป๋ม splashing; to splash about

ปอย tuft; skein
ปอยผม /tuft/lock/ of hair

ป้อย repeatedly
คลำหัวป้อย to massage (one's) head, rub (one's) head repeatedly

ป้อยอ to flatter, adulate

ปะ[1] to meet, come upon, encounter; to see
พบปะ to meet, get together
พบปะสนทนา to have a get-together, have a /meeting/social gathering/

ปะ[2] to patch
ปะหน้า to attach (in front, on the cover, on top, etc)
ใบปะหน้า cover sheet
รอยปะ patch
มีรอยปะ in patches, patched

ปะการัง coral
หินปะการัง coral

ปะขาว white-clad devout /layman/laywoman/

ปะติดปะต่อ to piece (something) together, pieced together, be a patchwork (of)

ปะติ๋ว insignificant, trifling; tiny, small
ขี้ปะติ๋ว trivial, trifling, petty, insignificant, measly

ปะทะ to clash, collide, bump, strike; to confront
การปะทะ collision; clash, battle, fight; confrontation
แรงปะทะ impact

ปะทะปะทัง to sustain, prop, bear; to keep (something or someone) going
กินข้าวรองท้องพอปะทะปะทังทั้งชีวิต to take a little sustenance / eat enough to keep himself going/

ปะทุ to burst, pop (out)

ปะปน to mingle (with), mix; to be mixed (with)

ปะปัง as in ธุระปะปัง business, affair
ธุระปะปังอะไรของคุณ It's none of your business. / What business is it of yours?

ปะรำ pavilion
ปะรำพิธี ceremonial pavilion, ceremony stand, (covered) dais

ปะไร, เป็นไร an emphatic ending
ช่างหัวมันปะไร ฉันไม่สน (ใจ) To hell with it, I don't care.

ปะแล่ม ปะแล่มๆ mild, mildly

ปะเหลาะ to wheedle, cajole; to butter up someone
ปะเหลาะแม่อยากได้ของเล่น to wheedle his mom into giving him a toy / wheedle a toy from his mother

ปัก to stick (something in), stab; to plant, implant; to embroider
ปักเขต to demarcate
ปักใจ to resolve (to), make up one's mind (to), be determined (to); to be convinced
ปักดำ to plant (a ricefield)
ปักเต็นท์ to put up a tent
ปักผม to stick into the hair
ปักหลัก to take a /stand/position/, hold firm; to settle down, stay; to plant a marker
ปักหลักสู้ to make a stand
ปักหลักอยู่กับที่ to stay in place
ปักหัว to dive
ลงหลักปักฐาน to settle down

ปักเป้า[1] as in ปลาปักเป้า puffer, blowfish, globefish

ปักเป้า[2] as in ว่าปักเป้า Pak Pao kite, a small diamond-shaped attack kite

ปักษ์ fortnight
ปักษ์ใต้ the south

ป
ผ
ฝ
พ
ฟ
ภ
ม
ย
ร
ฤ
ฦ
ล
ว
ศ
ษ
ส
ห
ฬ
อ
ฮ

ก
ข
ค
ฆ
ง
จ
ฉ
ช
ซ
ฌ
ญ
ฎ
ฏ
ฐ
ฑ
ฒ
ณ
ด
ต
ถ
ท
ธ
น
บ
ป

รายปักษ์ fortnightly, biweekly

ปัง[1] *as in* **ขนมปัง** bread

ปัง[2] bang; bang on the mark

ปังตอ cleaver

ปัจจัย factor, requisite; necessaries; money, wherewithal

    ปัจจัยสี่, จตุปัจจัย the four requisites of life: food, clothing, shelter and medicine

ปัจจุบัน the present, today; now; current

    ปัจจุบันทันด่วน all of a sudden

    ปัจจุบันพยาบาล first aid

    ในปัจจุบันนี้ today, now, at present, currently

    แพทย์แผนปัจจุบัน practitioner of modern medicine, medical doctor

    โรคปัจจุบัน sudden illness, acute /illness/ disease/

    โรคลมปัจจุบัน sudden attack

    สมัยปัจจุบัน modern times, at present

ปัจเจก personal, individual

    ปัจเจกบุคคล individual

    ปัจเจกพุทธะ silent Buddha, private Buddha

    ปัจเจกภาพ individuality

ปัจฉิม west; post, final

    ปัจฉิมนิเทศ concluding session, farewell

    ปัจฉิมลิขิต postscript (P.S.)

    ปัจฉิมวัย old age, last years

ปัญญา intelligence, wisdom; knowledge, insight

    ปัญญาชน intellectual

    สติปัญญา intelligence

    หมดปัญญา to have no further idea, be at a loss, be at (one's) wits'end, not be able to think of anything; to be unable (to)

ปัญหา problem, question; difficulty, trouble

    ปัญหาเรื้อรัง /chronic/persistent/ problem

    ปัญหาโลกแตก conundrum, insoluble problem

    ปัญหาอยู่ที่ไหน What's the /trouble/problem/?

    แก้ปัญหา to solve a problem, find a solution,

get over a difficulty (by)

    ตัดปัญหา to get around a problem, put an end to (the /problem/difficulty/dispute/ difference/etc), get rid of a problem (by)

    ไม่มีปัญหา no problem, easy, to be okay; trouble-free

    หมดปัญหา The problem is solved; that does it, to be all right

ปัด[1] to brush /away/off/, to dust; to reject

    ปัดกวาด to clean

    ปัดขึ้น to up

    ปัดแข้งปัดขา to fawn (on, over), curry favor (with)

    ปัดที่นอน to dust the bed

    ปัดเป่า to work a cure, sweep away difficulties, clear up (a problem), alleviate

    ปัดฝุ่น to dust, dust off

    ปัดรังควาน to exorcise evil spirits

    ปัดเศษ to /throw out/discard/disregard/ the remainder, to round off

    ที่ปัดน้ำฝน windshield wiper

    บอกปัด to reject, refuse; to put (someone) off; to disclaim responsibility (for); to pass the buck

ปัด[2] *as in* **ลูกปัด** bead

ปัดๆ furiously; convulsively, jerking about

ปัน to divide, allot, apportion; to give

    ปันผล to pay a dividend

        เงินปันผล dividend

    ปันส่วน to ration; to apportion, share

    ขอปัน to /ask for/buy/ a portion; to ask (someone) to spare something

    คุณมีที่อยู่ตั้งหลายไร่ ขอปันสักไร่ได้ไหม You have plenty of land. Can you spare me a rai?

ปั่น to spin; to turn

    ปั่นจักรยาน to pedal a bicycle

    ปั่นต้นฉบับ to turn out /a manuscript/copy/ a story/an article/etc

ปั่นป่วน to be in a state of /confusion/ /commotion/chaos/, confused, mixed up

ปั่นฝ้าย to spin cotton

ปั่นหัว to indoctrinate, brainwash

ปลุกปั่น to incite, stir up, arouse

หัวปั่น to make one's head spin เช่น *There was so much to do, my head was spinning*.; to be snowed under (with work), overwhelmed with work

ปั้น[1] lump; to model, mold, sculpture; to make

ปั้นจิ้มปั้นเจ๋อ to show off

ปั้นน้ำเป็นตัว to make something out of nothing, make up (something) out of whole cloth, fabricate

ปั้นปึ่ง aloof, unsociable, haughty

ปั้นสีหน้า to dissemble, make a show of, feign

ปั้นให้เป็นดารา to make a star

ช่างปั้น sculptor; potter; modeler, modeller

รูปปั้น statue, sculpture; model, molded figure

หมายมั่นปั้นมือ to be ambitious (to), determined (to), be set on (doing etc)

ปั้น[2] teapot

ปั้นจั่น crane

ปั๊บ in a flash, instantly

ทำเสร็จปั๊บ เขาก็ไป The instant work was over, he left. / When he finished, he left in a flash.

ปั๊บเดียว in a second

ปัพพาชนียกรรม Sangha ceremony to /banish/ drum out/ a recalcitrant monk

ปั๊ม pump

ปั๊มน้ำมัน gas station *(US)*, petrol station *(Brit)*, filling station, service station

เครื่องปั๊มน้ำ water pump

ปัสสาวะ urine; to pass water, urinate

กระเพาะปัสสาวะ bladder

สวนปัสสาวะ to do a urinary catheterization

การสวนปัสสาวะ urinary catheterization

ป่า to throw, fling, cast, hurl

ป่าเข้าไป already, as (...) as

กว่าหนังจะเลิกก็ป่าเข้าไป 5 ทุ่มแล้ว ยังจะไปต่อที่อื่นอีกหรือ By the time the movie is over it will /be as late as/already be/ eleven o'clock. Will you really want to go someplace else? อายุป่าเข้าไปตั้ง 40 แล้ว ยังไม่คิดจะมีครอบครัวอีก You are /already 40/as old as 40/ and still not thinking about having a family.

ขว้างป่า to /hurl/throw/ (something at something or somebody), pelt (someone with something)

ป่า forest, woods; overgrown area, overgrowth; wild

ป่าคอนกรีต concrete jungle

ป่าช้า cemetery, burial ground

ป่าชายเลน, ป่าเลน mangrove forest

ป่าดง heavy forest, jungle; uncultivated land in its natural state

ป่าดิบ primary forest, virgin forest

ป่าเถื่อน barbarous, savage

ป่าเบญจพรรณ mixed forest

ป่าโปร่ง open forest

ป่าพง wooded area, woods, wood

ป่าพรุ peat swamp forest

ป่าไม้ forest, woods

ป่าละเมาะ grove, wood, scrub forest

ป่าสงวน forest reserve

ป่าสัก teak forest

ป่าสูง forest

ป่าเส็งเคร็ง degraded forest

ป่าเสื่อมโทรม denuded forest

ไก่ป่า jungle fowl

ไข้ป่า malaria, jungle fever

คนป่า savage, wild man; forest dweller

ผีป่า forest spirit

ไฟป่า forest fire

ลมป่า an ill wind

ป
ผ
ฝ
พ
ฟ
ภ
ม
ย
ร
ฤ
ฤๅ
ล
ว
ศ
ษ
ส
ห
ฬ
อ
ฮ

สัตว์ป่า wild animal

หูป่าตาเถื่อน a simpleton, ignorant

ฮาป่า to boo, jeer, heckle

ป้า aunt

ป๊า papa, daddy

ป๊าของอีหนู sugar daddy

ปาก mouth; entrance; orifice

ปากกระบอกปืน muzzle (of a gun)

ปากกล้า outspoken

ปากกา pen

ปากกาเขียนปาก lip ink

ปากกาลูกลื่น ballpoint pen

ปากกาหมึกซึม fountain pen

ด้ามปากกา penholder; barrel of a pen

นามปากกา pen name, nom de plume

ปากแข็ง not talking, uncooperative, to refuse to talk, recalcitrant, obdurate

ปากคม sharp-tongued

ปากคัน loose-tongued, gossipy

ปากคำ testimony, statement

ให้ปากคำ to testify, give a statement

ปากคีบ pincers, tweezer

ปากจัด sarcastic, biting, sharp-tongued, acerbic, shrewish

คนปากจัด a shrew

ปากดี bigmouthed; loudmouthed

ปากตรอก mouth of a lane, entrance to a lane

ปากตลาด coarse-mouthed, vulgar

ปากต่อปาก from mouth to mouth, by word of mouth

ปากตะไกร sharp-tongued, cutting

ปากถนน at the beginning of the /street/ road/, upper end of the /street/road/

ปากทาง /mouth/end/entrance/ (of a /road/ path/way/etc)

ปากน้ำ mouth of a river, estuary

ปากบอน to tattle, talk too much, blabber; gossipy, bigmouthed, talebearing

คนปากบอน tattletale, gossip, blabber-mouth

ปากเบา to learn quickly to speak; to speak without restraint, have a ready tongue; to speak without thinking

ปากแบะ having thick lips; to be on the verge of tears

ปากเปราะ to tattle; talkative, affable; caustic, biting; to bark all the time, yapping

ปากเปราะเราะราย argumentative, quarrelsome

ปากเปราะเราะร้าย foul-mouthed

ปากเปล่า extemporaneously

สอบปากเปล่า to take an oral examination

ปากเปียกปากแฉะ /say/tell/ over and over again

สอนจนปากเปียกปากแฉะ ไม่รู้จักจำ I've taught this to you over and over again. Why can't you get it into your head?

ปากโป้ง indiscreet; outspoken; to shoot off (one's) mouth

ปากมาก bigmouthed; talkative; to talk too much, shoot off one's mouth; querulous

ปากไม่มีหูรูด to be a blabbermouth

ปากร้าย malicious; sharp-tongued, bitchy

ปากร้ายใจดี bad-mouthed but good-hearted

คนปากร้าย a scold

ปากสว่าง to blab, be a blabbermouth, spill the beans, talk too much

ปากเสีย not nice (to say), (to have) a big mouth

ปากเสียง to quarrel, dispute, squabble

เป็นปากเสียง to have an argument, squabble, quarrel

ปากหนัก[1] reserved, temperate (in speech); silent, closemouthed, taciturn

ปากหนัก[2] slow to speak

ปากหวาน smooth, honey-tongued; to use

soft words, blandish, honey up (to someone)

ปากหอยปากปู to backbite; backbiting

ปากเหยี่ยวปากกา dangers, perils

ปากแหว่ง cleft palate, harelip

ปากอ่าว mouth of a /bight/bay(เล็ก)/gulf (ใหญ่)/

    ล่มปากอ่าว to have a premature ejaculation

ขึ้นปาก to be on everyone's lips, talk (of), to be talked about, *เช่น The boss was the talk of the office. / He was talked about by everyone.*

คันปาก to have an urge to speak out, be itching to speak

ต่อปากต่อคำ to argue (with), squabble (with), have a /spat/altercation/

ติดปาก to be on (one's) lips

เต็มปาก[1] mouthful (of)

เต็มปาก[2] with conviction; to assure, with assurance

    พูดได้เต็มปาก I can assure you

บ้วนปาก to rinse (one's) mouth, gargle

ปริปาก *see* **ปริปาก** *หน้า 298*

เป็นปากเป็นเสียง to be a spokesman (for someone), speak for (someone)

ผิวปาก to whistle

ฝีปาก *see* **ฝีปาก** *หน้า 337*

มุมปาก corner of the mouth

เม้มปาก to purse the lips, compress the lips

รับปาก to promise, agree (to do something)

ริมฝีปาก lip

ลมปาก words, talk, what (someone) says

ลั่นปาก to give (one's) word, make a commitment, commit oneself

ออกปาก *see* **ออกปาก** *หน้า 561*

อ้าปาก to open one's mouth

เอ่ยปาก to speak, mention, say something (about)

ปาง[1] time; when

    ปางก่อน formerly, in olden times

    ปางบรรพ์ from ancient times, from time immemorial

    ปางหลัง the past, days of old

    พระพุทธรูปปางลีลา walking Buddha

ปาง[2] almost, virtually

    ปางตาย almost dead, almost died, close to death, in critical condition, moribund

ปาง[3] camp

ปาฏิหาริย์ miracle

    อย่างปาฏิหาริย์ miraculously

ปาฐก lecturer

ปาฐกถา lecture, talk

ปาด to slice off; to level, smooth

    ปาดซ้ายปาดขวา to weave in and out (of traffic, etc)

    ปาดหน้า to cut in front

    ขับรถปาดหน้า He cut in front of me (with his car).

    ปาดเหงื่อ to wipe the sweat away

ปาติโมกข์ code of monastic precepts

    สวดปาติโมกข์ to recite the code of monastic precepts

    โอวาทปาติโมกข์ the fundamental teaching (of the Buddha)

ปาเต๊ะ batik

ปาท่องโก๋ fried popover

ปาน[1] birthmark, nevus

ปาน[2] like, similar

    ปานกลาง moderate, medium, average, mean

        ระดับน้ำทะเลปานกลาง mean sea-level

    ปานกัน as, equally, about the same

    สองพี่น้องนี้ขี้เกียจปานกัน The older brother was as lazy as his younger brother. / The brothers were equally lazy.

    ปานฉะนี้ like

    ปานใด no matter how (big/clever/etc)

    ปานนี้, ป่านนี้ to such an extent, as (/good/

ป

ผ
ฝ
พ
ฟ
ภ
ม
ย
ร
ฤ
ฤๅ
ล
ว
ศ
ษ
ส
ห
ฬ
อ
ฮ

ก
ข
ค
ฆ
ง
จ
ฉ
ช
ซ
ฌ
ญ
ฎ
ฏ
ฐ
ฑ
ฒ
ณ
ด
ต
ถ
ท
ธ
น
บ
ป

bad/etc) as this; by now; so late

ป่าน flax; hemp, jute

กระสอบป่าน burlap bag, gunny /bag/sack/

เชือกป่าน hemp rope

ผ้าป่าน fine ramie cloth, lawn

ป๊าบ, ป้าบ smack, slap; bop

ป่าย, ป่ายปีน to climb, clamber up, scramble up; to swing (one's /leg/arm/) over

ป้าย[1] signboard, sign

ป้ายถนน street sign

ป้ายบอกทาง road sign

ป้ายราคา price tag, price sign

ป้ายหยุดรถ bus stop

ป้ายห้ามจอด no-parking sign

ป้าย[2] to daub; to smear; to coat, paint

ป้ายสี to smear (someone)

ปาราชิก cardinal offences entailing expulsion from the monkhood: fornication, theft, killing, and falsely claiming sainthood

ปาริชาต erythrina; a mythological tree enabling one to recall former lives

ปาล์ม palm

ป่าว to publicize, proclaim

ป่าวประกาศ to proclaim, advertise

ป่าวร้อง to publicize, announce publicly, advertise

ป่าวๆ shouting

ปาหี่ as in **เรื่องปาหี่** vaudeville

ป้ำ as in **ใจป้ำ** venturesome, daring; sporting

ป้ำเป๋อ absentminded; not all there, dotty, gaga

ปิกนิก picnic

ปิ้ง to grill, broil, toast

ขนมปังปิ้ง toast

ปิงปอง ping-pong

ปิฎก Buddhist scriptures

พระไตรปิฎก Three Pitakas, Pali canon

ปิด to shut, close; to cover; to turn off; to stick, affix

ปิดข่าว news deadline; to suppress the

news

ปิดข่าวไม่เกินเที่ยง The deadline for late news is noon.

ปิดความ to suppress, hush up (an affair)

ปิดฉลาก to label, put a label on

ปิดตา to close one's eyes, be blind (to something)

ปิดทอง to gild, apply gold leaf; gilt

ปิดทองหลังพระ to do good without ostentation

ปิดบัง to conceal, cover up, hide, keep secret

ปิดบัญชี to close an account; to close the books

ปิดประกาศ to post a notice, put up an /announcement/notice/

ปิดประชุม to close a meeting

ปิดประตูใส่หน้า to slam the door in (one's) face

ปิดป้อง to cover oneself

ปิดปาก to close (one's) mouth; to hush up; to keep someone quiet, gag

ค่าปิดปาก hush money

ฆ่าปิดปาก to kill someone to keep him from talking, silence (someone)

ปิดป้าย to put up a sign

ปิดไฟ to switch off the light, turn /off/out/ the light

ปิดภาคเรียน to /end/close/ the term

ปิดม่าน to lower the curtain, draw the curtains; to close a blind

ปิดล้อม to besiege, blockade, cordon off

ปิดแสตมป์ to stamp a letter, put on a stamp, affix a stamp

ปิดอากร to affix a tax stamp

ปิตุฆาต patricide

ปิตุภูมิ fatherland, native land

ปิ่น hairpin; top, summit

ข้าวปิ่นแก้ว a fine variety of rice

ปิ่นโต food-carrier, tiffin-carrier
ปิ่ม, ปิ้ม almost, nearly
ปิระมิด, พีระมิด pyramid
ปิ๋ว to miss out
เธอไปประกวดนางงามโลก ผลปรากฏว่า ปิ๋ว She entered the Miss World competition but the upshot was that she missed out.
ปี year
　ปีกลาย last year
　ปีก่อน year before last; past years
　ปีการศึกษา /academic/scholastic/ year
　ปีเกิด year of birth
　ปีละ annual, yearly
　ปีแล้วปีเล่า year after year
　ปีหน้า next year
　ปีใหม่ New Year, the new year
　　ขึ้นปีใหม่ in the new year; to begin the New Year
　　งานวันปีใหม่ New Year's celebration
　　พรปีใหม่ New Year's greetings
　เป็นปี years, for years
　รายปี annual, yearly, per year
　แรมปี for years
　หัวปี firstborn, eldest
ปี่ oboe
　ปี่พาทย์ Thai orchestra
　ปี่สกอต bagpipes
　เป็นปี่เป็นขลุ่ย in complete harmony, in accord, like peas in a pod
ปี้ to copulate
ปี๋ very
　ดำปี๋ very dark, pitch black
　หลับตาปี๋ (with) eyes closed tight
　อิ่มปี๋ very full, stuffed
ปีก wing, side, flank
　ปีกกล้าขาแข็ง full-fledged, strong enough to go it alone
　ปีกกา flank; brackets
　ปีกนก projecting roof below the gable

ปีกไม้ outside slabs cut from a log
ปีติ rapture, delight, joy, pleasure; ecstasy, bliss
　รู้สึกปีติยินดี to be delighted, overjoyed
ปีน to climb
　ปีนเกลียว to strip the thread, jump a thread; (fig) to clash, not get along together
　ปีนขึ้น to climb up
　ปีนป่าย to clamber, scramble up
ปีบ, ปี๊บ tin, can
　ตีปี๊บ to advertise oneself
　เตะปี๊บดัง to display sexual prowess, be a rooster
ปีศาจ demon
ปึก pile, sheaf (of paper, documents, etc); lump, mass; solid; a qualifier designation for a pile of sheets
　น้ำตาลปึก palm sugar in soft cakes
　เป็นปึกแผ่น solid, stable; well established
ปึง boom, bang
　ปึงปัง noisy
ปึ่ง sullen, ill-tempered
　ปึ่งชา frosty, unfriendly
ปึ้ง twang
ปื้ด as in **ดำปื้ด** very dark, inky black
ปืน gun, firearms, gun barrel
　ปืนกล machine gun
　ปืนครก mortar
　ปืนคาบศิลา flintlock
　ปืนเดี่ยว single-barreled shotgun
　ปืนต่อสู้อากาศยาน anti-aircraft gun
　ปืนเถื่อน unregistered gun, illegal firearm
　ปืนผาหน้าไม้ weapons, arms
　ปืนแฝด double-barreled shotgun
　ปืนพก pistol, handgun
　ปืนยาว rifle
　ปืนลูกซอง shotgun
　ปืนสั้น pistol
　ปืนใหญ่ cannon; artillery

ป
ผ
ฝ
พ
ฟ
ภ
ม
ย
ร
ฤ
ฦ
ล
ว
ศ
ษ
ส
ห
ฬ
อ
ฮ

ปืนใหญ่สนาม field gun

กระบอกปืน gun barrel

กระสุนปืน bullet, ammunition, cartridge

ไกปืน trigger

ซองปืน holster

ดาบปลายปืน bayonet

ด้ามปืน stock, grip, handle (of a gun)

ดินปืน gunpowder

นกปืน hammer (of a gun)

บรรจุปืน to load a gun

ปากกระบอกปืน mouth of a gun

ยิงปืน to shoot, fire a gun

เรือปืน gunboat

ลูกปืน cartridge, bullet, shell; ball bearing

ศูนย์ปืน gunsight

หอกปลายปืน bayonet

อาวุธปืน firearms

ปื้น¹ split plank

ปื้น² qualifier for saws

ปื้น³ rash; welt

ปุก as in เท้าปุก clubfoot, clubfooted

ปุกปุย fluffy, curly-haired, bushy

ปุ้งกี๋ scoop basket

ปุจฉา question

ปุด, ปุดๆ simmering, bubbling

ผมรู้สึกเดือดปุดๆ I was /seething/ simmering/ (with /anger/rage/etc).

ปุถุชน worldly person; ordinary person, common man

ปุบ, ปุ๊บ in a flash, instantaneously

ปุบปับ abruptly; without warning, all of a sudden, just like that

เมื่อวานนี้ยังคุยกันอยู่เลย ปุบปับตายเสียแล้ว We were talking together just yesterday, and /now, all of a sudden, he's dead./he died just like that./

ปุ่ม knob; boss, bump, button

ปุ่มป่ำ covered with bumps, warty; rough

ปุย fluff

ปุยฝ้าย cotton; cotton candy

ปุ๋ย fertilizer, manure

ปุ๋ยคอก manure

ปุ๋ยธรรมชาติ organic fertilizer

ปุ๋ยหมัก compost

ปุโรหิต Brahman adviser on customary law

ปู¹ crab

ปูจ๋า crabmeat baked in a shell

ปูทะเล sea crab

ปูนา field crab

ปูเสฉวน hermit crab

ปู² to lay, spread, put (sheets, tablecloth, mat, etc) on (the bed, table, floor etc)

ปูกระดาน to lay a plank

ปูโต๊ะ to lay the table

ปูทาง to pave the way (for)

ปูที่นอน to make a bed

ปูพรม to lay a carpet

ปูพื้น to lay a floor; to lay the way (for)

ปูเสื่อ to spread a mat; to welcome

ปู่ (paternal) grandfather

ปู่ทวด great-grandfather

ปู่ย่า (paternal) grandparents

ปู่ย่าตายาย grandparents; forebears, ancestors

ปูชนียบุคคล person worthy of /esteem/respect/; reverential, venerable

ปูด swollen; to leak

ความลับปูดออกมา The secret leaked.

ปูน¹ cement

ปูนขาว lime; white cement

ปูนฉาบ stucco, plaster

ปูนซีเมนต์ cement

ปูนปั้น decorative /cement/plaster/ work, stucco-work

ปูนสอ mortar

ฉาบปูน to plaster, stucco, stuccoed

ช่างปูน mason, bricklayer

ถือปูน to do cement work

หินปูน limestone, lime; tartar

ปูน[2] to distribute, give

    ปูนบำเหน็จ to reward; to promote; bonus, reward

ปูน[3] as, like, such

    แก่ปูนนี้แล้วจะทำอะไรได้ How much can he do at /his age/such an age/?

    อายุปูนพ่อ to be as old as one's father / old enough to be one's father

ปูม astrological almanac

ปู้ยี่ปู้ยำ to destroy, ruin; to ravish

เป้ backpack

เป๋ off to one side; to lose (its) bearings, lose (its) balance; to totter

    เป๋ไปเป๋มา to reel

    ขาเป๋ lame

เป็ก[1] thumbtack,

เป็ก[2] peg

เป็ก[3] as in **แข็งเป็ก** hard as a rock

เป่ง very swollen, bloated

เป้ง, เป้งๆ big, large

    ข้าราชการตัวเป้งๆ ทั้งนั้นที่โดนจับ Of those picked up, there was no one who was not a big man in the government.

เป๋ง right (at, on, to), directly; exactly, precisely

    จ้องตาเป๋ง to stare right at something

    ตรงเป๋ง right on time; perfectly straight

    เที่ยงเป๋ง twelve o'clock sharp

เป็ด duck

    เป็ดไก่ poultry

        หมูเห็ดเป็ดไก่ meat; plenty of food, substantial food

    เป็ดย่าง roast duck, grilled duck

เป็น[1] live, living, existing

    เป็นๆ alive

    เป็นอยู่ live

เป็น[2] to be; to appear; to happen, occur; to be able, know how (to); to; in

    เป็นกบฏ to be in /rebellion/revolt/, rebel

เป็นกระจุก in bunches, tufts

เป็นกระเซิง tangled, touseled, disheveled

เป็นกระบวน in droves; in order

    ไม่เป็นกระบวน in disorder

เป็นกระสาย an enhancer, a complement

เป็นกลาง neutral, impartial

เป็นกลุ่มเป็นก้อน substantial; in a body

    พวก NGO's รวมกันเป็นกลุ่มเป็นก้อนเพื่อสร้างพลังต่อรอง The NGO's joined together in a body to strengthen their bargaining power.

เป็นกอง a lot (of), heaps (of)

    เป็นกองสองกอง lots and lots of

เป็นก้อน in lumps

เป็นกอบเป็นกำ lots of, a lot of; flocculated

เป็นกันเอง to be friendly, informal, not stand on ceremony, relaxed; to feel at home, feel at ease

เป็นการชั่วคราว temporarily; provisional

เป็นการด่วน urgently

เป็นการเป็นงาน formally

เป็นการยาก to be difficult (to)

เป็นการใหญ่ on a large scale; to a great extent

เป็นกำลัง extremely, exceedingly, intensely, very much, really

เป็นเกลียว twisted; helical, spiral, screw

    ทำงานตัวเป็นเกลียว to work very hard

เป็นเกียรติ to be an honor; to honor

เป็นขน hairy

เป็นของ to belong to

    เธอเป็นของเขาแล้ว You have already been his. / You belong to him now.

เป็นของตาย to be a sure thing, always dependable

เป็นขั้นๆ step by step, in stages

เป็นข่าว to be news; to get publicity

เป็นไข้ to be sick, unwell, ill; to have a fever, be feverish

    เป็นไข้ใจ to be heartsick

เป็นคนอย่างนั้นเอง That's just the way he is.

เป็นครั้งเป็นคราว periodically, from time to time, occasionally, once in a while

เป็นครั้งแรก for the first time

เป็นคราวๆ from time to time, periodically, intermittently

เป็นควัน smoky, smoking; vigorously

ปฏิเสธเป็นควัน to deny on the spot, deny vigorously

เป็นความ to be involved in a lawsuit, engage in litigation (with)

เป็นคุ้งเป็นแคว at great length

เป็นคุณ to be beneficial

เป็นคู่ๆ in pairs

เป็นงวดๆ in installments

เป็นง่อย crippled

เป็นงาน to know the job; to know what to do, skilled

เป็นงานเป็นการ serious, businesslike, systematic, systematically

เป็นเงา see เป็นเงา^2 หน้า 107

เป็นเงินเป็นทอง to be money; valuable

เป็นจริงเป็นจัง in earnest

เป็นจำนวน the amount of, to the amount of, to amount to, sum

เป็นจุดๆ dotted, spotted, speckled

เป็นเจ้าหัวใจ to have a claim on someone

เป็นใจ to favor, sympathize (with), side with; to be an accomplice (of), conspire (with), connive (with)

เป็นชนวน to lead to, bring (something) on

เป็นชั้นๆ in levels

เป็นชิ้นเป็นอัน serious, solid, substantial, real

เป็นชู้ to commit adultery; to be having an affair with someone, be lovers

เป็นเชิง to the effect (that), impliedly

พูดเป็นเชิง to suggest, indicate, imply, say in effect (that)

เป็นได้ to be possible

เป็นต้น for example, such as

เป็นต้นว่า for example, such as, like

เป็นต่อ to be favored, have the odds in one's favor, the odds are on...; to have the upper hand

เป็นต่อยหอย volubly

พูดเป็นต่อยหอย to gab, chatter, (talk etc) volubly

เป็นตับ in a mass; great numbers (of)

เป็นตัว to be unbroken (ข้าว); to be formed

เป็นตัวเป็นตน to become somebody, become what one is; real

เป็นตัวหนังสือ in writing

เป็นตา with checks, checkered (pattern, design)

เป็นตายเท่ากัน in critical condition

เป็นตายร้ายดี no matter what happens

เป็นตายร้ายดีอย่างไร no matter what happens; what has befallen (someone)

เป็นตุเป็นตะ with all the details, realistically

เป็นแต่ simply, only, merely

เป็นแถบ in stripes; block of, large number (of)

เป็นแถว one after the other, down the line; in lines, in rows

เป็นทอดๆ from hand to hand; in stretches, in stages, at intervals

เป็นท่า as in ไม่เป็นท่า inept, foolish, stupid

เป็นทางการ official

เป็นที่ in place; permanent address, a home

เป็นที่เป็นทาง in order, neatly

วางของเป็นที่ to put things in place

อยู่เป็นที่ to have a permanent address, have a home

เป็นที่ทราบกันว่า as you know, as everyone knows

เป็นที่นิยม popular; fashionable

เป็นที่พอใจ satisfactory, happy (with),

acceptable

เป็นที่เรียบร้อย well done; already; all right; duly; in order

เป็นที่สุด final; utterly

เป็นโทษ harmful

เป็นไท free, independent

เป็นธรรม fair, just, equitable

เป็นธรรมดา to be natural (for); common; naturally, normally, in the nature of things of course

เป็นนักเป็นหนา inordinately, excessively

เป็นน้ำ liquid, fluid; fluently

    พูดเป็นน้ำ speak fluently

เป็นนิจศีล routinely, regularly, habitually

เป็นนิตย์ regularly

เป็นเนื้อเดียวกัน blended together, combined; homogeneous, uniform

เป็นแน่ definitely

เป็นบ้า fantastically; extremely; to be mad *เขาเก่งเป็นบ้า He's extremely clever.*

เป็นบุญ blessing; good fortune

เป็นเบี้ยล่าง subordinate; to be at a disadvantage; to be under someone's thumb

เป็นเบื้อ in silence

    นั่งเป็นเบื้อ to sit like a bump on a log

เป็นแบบ model, style

เป็นใบ้ mute, dumb

เป็นปกติ normal

เป็นปฐม initial, inaugural, primary

เป็นปม in a knot; problem, riddle

เป็นประจำ regularly, all the time

เป็นประธาน to preside over

เป็นประวัติการณ์ history-making, a record

เป็นปากเสียง to have an argument, squabble, quarrel

เป็นปีๆ years, for years

เป็นปึกแผ่น well established; solid, steady

เป็นไป to go on, proceed, move

    เป็นไปได้ possible, feasible

โดยเร็วที่สุดเท่าที่จะเป็นไปได้ at the earliest possible moment

    ความเป็นไปได้ feasibility

เป็นไปตาม to follow, be in accordance with

เป็นไปไม่ได้ impossible

เป็นผล effective, fruitful

    เป็นผลดี beneficial, desirable, gain

    เป็นผลสำเร็จ to be successful, succeed

    เป็นผลเสีย detrimental; loss, damaging, harmful

เป็นผื่น to have a rash

เป็นผู้เป็นคน to be somebody

เป็นฝักเป็นฝ่าย in factions, factionalized, disunited

เป็นฝั่งเป็นฝา to be established, be settled down, have a family

เป็นฝ้า clouded; to have a film (of something on it); freckled

เป็นพยาน to be a witness

เป็นพวง bunch, cluster (of), in /bunches/ clusters/

เป็นพักๆ sporadically, occasionally, from time to time; in fits and starts

เป็นพิเศษ especially, specially, particularly; special

เป็นพิษ *see* **เป็นพิษ** *หน้า 353*

    เป็นพิษเป็นภัย dangerous

เป็นพืด to be webbed; packed solidly

เป็นพื้น as a /basis/foundation/

เป็นเพื่อน to keep someone company; to be a friend, one's friend

เป็นฟืนเป็นไฟ enraged, infuriated

เป็นไฟ like anything

พูดเป็นไฟ to speak like anything

เป็นมัน oily (skin); /glittering/eager/(eyes), shiny, glossy, shining

เป็นมั่นเป็นเหมาะ definitely, firmly, positively

ป
ผ
ฝ
พ
ฟ
ภ
ม
ย
ร
ฤ
ฤๅ
ล
ว
ศ
ษ
ส
ห
ฬ
อ
ฮ

เป็นเมือก slimy

เป็นแม่นมั่น surely, verily, certainly

เป็นโมฆะ void

เป็นรอง to have the odds against one, be unfavored, the underdog

เป็นระนาว all, a large number (of), in large numbers

เป็นระเบียบ systematically; in order, neat, well arranged

เป็นระยะๆ at intervals, periodically

เป็นรายตัว individually, one by one

เป็นริ้วๆ striped, in strips

เป็นริ้วรอย lined; scratched; in strips; in rows

เป็นรู in holes

เป็นรูปเป็นร่าง to materialize, take shape, become a reality, be realized

เป็นแรมเดือน for months and months

เป็นโรค diseased, sick

เป็นไรเป็นกัน I don't care what happens.

เป็นลม to swoon, faint

เป็นลายลักษณ์อักษร in writing, written

เป็นลำดับ respectively

เป็นล่ำเป็นสัน good เช่น to have a good job; good business

เป็นเล่น playing, joking

พูดเป็นเล่น You must be joking.

เป็นวรรคเป็นเวร unconsolably, nonstop, endlessly

เป็นว่าเล่น lightly, like it is a game

เป็นส่วนมาก for the most part

เป็นสัดเป็นส่วน well arranged

เป็นสุข happy, to have contentment

เป็นเสียงเดียวกัน (to speak) with a single voice, with one accord, to say the same thing, unanimous

เป็นโสด single, unmarried

เป็นหนี้ to owe, be indebted (to, by), be in debt

เป็นหนี้บุญคุณ see **เป็นหนี้บุญคุณ** หน้า 519

เป็นหมัน to be sterile; futile, fruitless, to come to nothing, of no avail, in vain

เป็นหม้าย widow, widowed

เป็นหมู่ in a group, in groups

เป็นหย่อมๆ in clusters

เป็นหลักแหล่ง permanent, fixed

เป็นห่วง to worry (about), be worried (about)

เป็นหวัด to have a cold

เป็นหูเป็นตา to keep an eye on things (for someone), take charge (for someone), act as another's /representative/surrogate/

เป็นเหตุให้ to cause, be conducive to, generate

เป็นใหญ่ in charge, to be the head, be on top, topdog

เป็นไหนๆ far, so much

กินส้มสดดีกว่าน้ำส้มปั่นเป็นไหนๆ Fresh oranges are /far/so much/ better for you than orange frappes.

เป็นอนุสรณ์ in memory of; to commemorate

เป็นอย่างๆ each by itself; one thing at a time; sorted

เป็นอย่างดี well, carefully

เป็นอริกัน to be enemies, hostile

เป็นอะไร What's wrong?; What happened?, What is it?

    เป็นอะไรไป What's got into you?; What's the matter?

เป็นอันขาด definitely, absolutely, (not /go/ do/etc) under any circumstances

เป็นอันดี well, happy

เป็นอันตราย dangerous (to)

เป็นอันมาก very much, many, a lot of, most

เป็นอันว่า so, it means

เป็นอันหนึ่งอันเดียวกัน united, to be one, as one, one and the same

เป็นอาจิณ regularly, always, constantly

เป็นอาชีพ professional

เป็นอาทิ for example, and so on, et cetera

เป็นอารมณ์ to take to heart

เป็นอื่น unfaithful; otherwise

เป็นเอกฉันท์ unanimously

เป็นเอง I myself, you yourself, he himself, they themselves; naturally

เปยยาล *see* **ไปยาล** *หน้า 321*

เปรต ever-hungry ghoul

เปรม[1] to be happy, glad

เปรม[2] love, affection

    เปรมปรีดิ์ to be overjoyed, rejoice, be delighted

เปรย to remark, say

    เปรยปราย to make general remarks; to greet everyone

    พูดเปรยๆ to remark, speak in general, say out of the blue, make a casual remark

เปรอะ dirty; messy, in a mess

เปราะ fragile, brittle, frangible

    เปราะบาง fragile, delicate

    ปากเปราะ to tattle; talkative, affable; caustic, biting; to bark all the time, yapping

เปรี้ยง crash, thunder; strong

    แดดเปรี้ยง (in the) hot sun, strong sunlight

เปรียญ graduate in Pali studies, holder of a certificate in Pali studies from the third to the ninth level

เปรียบ to compare

    เปรียบข้อแตกต่าง to contrast

    เปรียบเทียบ to compare

    เปรียบเปรย to be snide, make an invidious comparison

    เปรียบมวย to pair boxers

    ได้เปรียบ to be at an advantage, have an advantage, outmatch

    เสียเปรียบ to be at a disadvantage, lose, be prejudiced (by)

    หาที่เปรียบมิได้ incomparable

เอาเปรียบ to take advantage (of), exploit, get the better of (someone)

เปรียว untamed, wild; lively, quick, spirited; vivacious, sprightly, animated

เปรี้ยว sour, tart

    เปรี้ยวปาก to have an urge to /eat/say/ something in particular

    แต่งตัวเปรี้ยว to dress stylishly

    ผัดเปรี้ยวหวาน sweet and sour

    ออกเปรี้ยว tart

เปรื่อง to be expert, sharp

    เปรื่องปราด brilliant, learned

เปล cradle

    เปลญวณ hammock

    เปลหาม stretcher

    จานเปล serving plate, platter

เปล่ง[1] bright, shining, beaming

    เปล่งปลั่ง radiant, beaming, shining, glowing

เปล่ง[2] to project, sound forth

    เปล่งวาจา to say, speak (out)

    เปล่งเสียง to call out, project one's voice, raise one's voice; to announce; to make a noise

    เปล่งเสียงดัง to be noisy; to shout

    เปล่งอุทาน to exclaim, cry out,

เปลว[1] flame

    เปลวควัน outpouring of smoke

    เปลวเพลิง flames

    เปลวไฟ flame

    ทองคำเปลว gold leaf

เปลว[2] fat

    เปลวมัน lard

    เปลวหมู lard

เปล่า[1] empty, void; no; free, for nothing; alone

    เปล่าๆ free, for free; alone, without anything else

        ดีกว่าอยู่เปล่าๆ It's better than doing nothing.

    เปล่าประโยชน์ useless, of no use, worthless,

ป
ผ
ฝ
พ
ฟ
ภ
ม
ย
ร
ฤ
ฤๅ
ล
ว
ศ
ษ
ส
ห
ฬ
อ
ฮ

unprofitable, disadvantageous; futile; nugatory

เงินกินเปล่า key money, tea money, extra payment, under-the-table payment

ได้เปล่า to get (something) /for nothing/ free/

ตาเปล่า (with the) naked eye

เท้าเปล่า (to go, be) barefoot

    หมอเท้าเปล่า barefoot doctor

ปากเปล่า extemporaneously

มือเปล่า emptyhanded

ว่างเปล่า uncultivated; vacant, unoccupied

เสียเปล่า in vain, unproductive, useless, for nothing

เปล่า[2] to be lonesome, feel lonely

เปล่าเปลี่ยว lonely, lonesome, feel neglected

เปลาะ stage, step, section, part

แก้ปัญหาได้เปลาะหนึ่ง One part of the problem has been solved.

เปลี้ย palsied; paralysed, weak

ง่อยเปลี้ยเสียขา lame, crippled

เปลี่ยน to change, alter, vary, fluctuate

เปลี่ยนเกียร์ to shift gears

เปลี่ยนใจ to change one's mind

เปลี่ยนบรรยากาศ to change the /atmosphere/mood/

เปลี่ยนแปลง to change, alter

เปลี่ยนมือ change hands; to transfer; to negotiate

    เปลี่ยนมือได้ negotiable

เปลี่ยนยางรถ to change a tire

เปลี่ยนเวร to change shifts

เปลี่ยนสี to be a turncoat; to adapt oneself; to change (the) color

เปลี่ยนเสียง to change one's attitude, sing another tune

จุดเปลี่ยน turning point

ผลัดเปลี่ยน to change, exchange places, take over

แลกเปลี่ยน to exchange, change

เปลี่ยว hump; young; lonely; forlorn; solitary, isolated, empty; remote

เปลี่ยวใจ to be forlorn, feel lonely; dispirited

ควายเปลี่ยว young buffalo

เปล่าเปลี่ยว *see* เปล่าเปลี่ยว

อารมณ์เปลี่ยว have a certain longing (for sex), to feel sexy, have desire (for), have a (sexual) need, be sexually aroused

เปลือก bark; rind; shell; skin; husk; peel

เปลือกตา eyelid

เปลือกนอก appearances, the outside

ดูแต่เปลือกนอก ไม่รู้หรอกว่าเขาเป็นคนดีหรือ ไม่ You can't tell from appearances whether he's good or not.

ข้าวเปลือก paddy, unmilled rice

ปอกเปลือก to peel, skin

เปลือง to waste, be wasteful (of), inefficient, /consume/use/ a lot of something

เปลืองเงิน extravagant, wasteful

เปลืองตัว to waste oneself (on somebody); to get involved

เปลืองที่ to take up room; to waste space

เปลืองเวลา to waste time; to take time

หมดเปลือง to cost; to spend; to consume; to waste, be wasted

เปลื้อง to strip off, take off, remove

เปลื้องผ้า to undress, take off one's clothes

ปลดเปลื้อง to relieve (of), free (from), release (from); to shed, get rid of, divest (oneself of)

เปลือย naked, nude, stripped; uncovered, bare

เปลือยกาย nude, in the nude, naked, undressed; to strip, undress

เปลือยเปล่า naked

เปอร์เซ็นต์ percent

เป๋อเหลอ stupid-looking, vacuous

เป๊ะ sharp, exactly

11 นาฬิกาเป๊ะ 11 o'clock sharp. / Exactly at eleven.

เป๊ะ ๆ exactly right, right on the mark

เปะปะ aimless; haphazard, without a plan, disorganized

พูดเปะปะฟังไม่รู้เรื่อง to ramble, speak in a disorganized way

เป่า to blow; to play

เป่าขลุ่ย to play a flute

เป่านกหวีด to blow a whistle

เป่าลูกโป่ง to blow up a balloon

เป่าหู to insinuate, whisper in someone's ear

เป้า[1] target; mark

เป้าเคลื่อนที่ moving target

เป้านิ่ง stationary target

เป้าหมาย purpose, target, aim, object

ยิงเป้า to fire at a target, to do /target shooting/target practice/; to execute by shooting

สนามเป้า rifle range, pistol range

เป้า[2] crotch, groin; rise; gusset

เป้ากางเกง rise

เปาะ as in **ชมเปาะ** to pay steady compliments (to)

เปาะเหลาะ to fawn (over, on)

เปิง to be demolished, devastated

โดนด่าเสียเปิง to be devastated by criticism

เปิด to open, turn on; to open up; to flee, run away

เปิดกล้อง to start shooting

เปิดก๊อกน้ำ to open the tap, turn on the water

เปิดความลับ to divulge a secret

เปิดฉาก to raise the curtain (on something), commence, begin

เปิดทาง to give (someone) an /opportunity/ chance/ (to do something), open the way

เปิดแน่บ to flee at top speed, fly

เปิดบัญชี to open an account

เปิดประชุม to open a meeting, call a meeting

to order

เปิดป้าย to unveil a signboard

เปิดเปิง aimlessly, helter-skelter

เปิดโปง to tell, divulge, reveal (a secret etc)

เปิดผนึก unsealed

จดหมายเปิดผนึก open letter

เปิดเผย openly, frankly, candidly, with candor; to disclose

คนเปิดเผย straightforward, open, /frank /candid/ person

เปิดไฟ to /turn/switch/ on the light

เปิดสะพาน to open a bridge

เปิดหนี to take flight, disappear

เปิดหูเปิดตา to open one's eyes, /learn/see / something new; to go sightseeing, go for a change

เปิดอก to be frank, candid, open with someone, speak frankly

เปิดโอกาส see **เปิดทาง**

เปิ่น gauche, funny

เปิบ to put rice into the mouth with the fingers

เปีย braid(s), pigtail, queue

ถักเปีย to braid the hair, make /a braid/ braids/

ผมเปีย to wear (one's) hair in a braid, have braids; pigtail, queue

ไว้เปีย to wear braids

หางเปีย pigtail, braid

เปียก wet, soaking; limp

เปียกโชก soaking wet, sopping wet, drenched

ข้าวเปียก gluey rice

ปากเปียกปากแฉะ see **ปากเปียกปากแฉะ** หน้า 306

เปี้ยก small, little; tiny

เปียแชร์ to put in a bid for a chit fund

เปี๊ยบ extremely, exactly, positively, quite

เหมือนกันเปี๊ยบเลย exactly the same

เปี่ยม brimming, full to the top, full (of), replete

ป
ผ
ฝ
พ
ฟ
ภ
ม
ย
ร
ฤ
ฦ
ล
ว
ศ
ษ
ส
ห
ฬ
อ
ฮ

ก
ข
ค
ฆ
ง
จ
ฉ
ช
ซ
ฌ
ญ
ฎ
ฏ
ฐ
ฑ
ฒ
ณ
ด
ต
ถ
ท
ธ
น
บ
ป

(with), abounding (in), to abound (with); almost overflowing, to fill the banks

เปี่ยมไปด้วย full of, replete with

เปี้ยว *as in* **วิ่งเปี้ยว** to run a relay race

เปือกตม mud, mire

เปื้อน soiled, dirty

แปดเปื้อน soiled, dirty; sullied, stained

ผ้ากันเปื้อน apron

เปื่อย falling apart, disintegrating; soft, tender

เปื่อยเน่า decomposed, in a state of decay, rotten

คอเสื้อเปื่อย frayed collar

เนื้อเปื่อย boiled beef

แป[1] horizontal roof beam; ridgepost; purlin

แป[2] *as in* **มือแป** paralysed hand

แป้ง flour; talcum powder, talc

แป้งกันหมัด, แป้งทาหมา flea powder

แป้งทำขนม cake flour

แป้งนม powdered milk

แป้งนวล cake of white face powder

แป้งเปียก paste

แป้งผัดหน้า face powder

แป้งมัน tapioca flour

แป้งร่ำ perfumed face powder

แป้งหมี่ wheat flour

แป้งเหล้า yeast

โต๊ะเครื่องแป้ง dressing table

ผัดหน้าทาแป้ง to get dressed up

แปด[1] eight

แปดด้าน completely, utterly

มืดแปดด้าน very bleak, hopeless; to be up a blind alley, see no way out

แปดสาแหรก the great-grandparents

ผู้ดีแปดสาแหรก blueblood, aristocrat

แปดสิบ eighty

แปด[2] soiled

แปดเปื้อน *see* **แปดเปื้อน**

แป้น potter's wheel; plate, base plate, cover plate; base

นั่งแป้น to be appointed to play the role (of director, prime minister etc)

ยิ้มแป้น to smile broadly, grin

แป๊บ (water) pipe

แป๊บเดียว in a jiffy, it will just take a second, just a /second/moment/

แปร to turn, (into), change (to, into), convert, become

แปรญัตติ to propose an amendment, move to amend, /file/propose/ a motion to amend

แปรธาตุ to transmute (base into precious metal); to convert

แปรปรวน changeable, variable, changing; to be unstable; change

แปรผัน to vary

การแปรผัน variation

การแปรผันตรง direct variation

การแปรผันผกผัน inverse variation

การแปรผันรวม joint variation

แปรพักตร์ to be disloyal, go over to the other side, be a /turncoat/renegade/

แปรรูป to convert, transform; to transfigure

ไม้แปรรูป lumber, (timber) conversion

แปรอักษร to do card stunts (with flipcards or mosaic cards), do letter stunts

ที่แปรอักษร mosaic stand

ตัวแปร determinant, determining factor

ผันแปร to alter, turn (to, into), become; vicissitude; fickle, changeable

แปรง brush; to brush

แปรงปัดผม hairbrush

แปรงฟัน brush one's teeth

แปรงลบกระดาน (blackboard) eraser

แปรงสีฟัน toothbrush

แปร่ง with an accent; changed, strange

แปร่ง ๆ off

แปร่งปร่า strange (taste)

พูดแปร่ง to speak with an accent; to sound strange

เสียงแปร่ง accent; off pitch, out of tune, to not sound right

แปร๊ด exceedingly; vivid, brilliant, flashy

แปร๋น trumpeting (ช้าง); shrill

แประ to the gunwales

เพียบแประ loaded to the gunwales

เมาแประ dead drunk, completely soused

แปล to translate, interpret; to mean

แปลตามเนื้อความ free translation

แปลตามพยัญชนะ word-for-word translation, literal translation

แปลเป็นไทยว่า which means in Thai, which translated into Thai means, in Thai is

คำแปล translation

ผู้แปล translator

แปล้ overloaded; full

อิ่มแปล้ stuffed, full

แปลก changed; different; strange, queer, odd, unusual, uncharacteristic (of someone to do something)

แปลกจริง very strange, fantastic

แปลกใจ surprised; puzzled

แปลกตา strange-looking; (to look) different

แปลกประหลาด peculiar, odd, weird, uncanny, amazing, astonishing

แปลกปลอม foreign; disguised

แปลกๆ funny

แปลกหน้า unfamiliar, unknown

คนแปลกหน้า stranger, newcomer

ไม่แปลก not unusual, characteristic, normal, I'm not surprised

แปลกแยก alienated

ความแปลกแยก alienation

ความรู้สึกแปลกแยก feeling of alienation

แปลง[1] plot, piece, lot, parcel

แปลงผัก vegetable patch

ที่ดิน 2 แปลง two lots / two /pieces/plots/ parcels/ of land.

แปลง[2] to transform, change, alter; to be different; to transmute

แปลงกาย to transform oneself (into)

แปลงสัญชาติ to become naturalized, acquire another nationality

แปลงเพศ to change one's sex, have a sex change

การแปลงสินทรัพย์เป็นหลักทรัพย์ securitization

ดัดแปลง to modify, alter, adapt

ปลอมแปลง to falsify, counterfeit; to disguise

เปลี่ยนแปลง to change, alter

แปลน plan

แบบแปลนบ้าน house plan

แปลบ sharp, piercing, stabbing

เสียวแปลบ sharp pain, stab of pain, twinge

แปลบปลาบ flashing

แปะ to stick something onto something, affix

แป๊ะ old Chinese man

แป๊ะเจี๊ยะ tea money

แป๊ะซะ steamed fish served with vinegar sauce and vegetables

โป๊ indecent; revealing; scantily dressed; nude, in the nude; blue, risqué

แต่งตัวโป๊ to wear a revealing dress; to be dressed indecently

ภาพโป๊ nude picture

หนังโป๊ blue movie, x-rated film

โป๊ก a knock, knocking (sound)

โป๊กเกอร์ poker

โปกฮา see ตลกโปกฮา *หน้า 181*

โปเก junky, junk

โปง *as in* **คลุมโปง** to cover (oneself) from head to foot, get under a blanket

โป่ง[1] inflated

ลูกโป่ง balloon

โป่ง[2] salt lick

โป่งดิน salt lick

โป่งน้ำ spring

ดินโป่ง salty earth

ป
ผ
ฝ
พ
ฟ
ภ
ม
ย
ร
ฤ
ฦ
ล
ว
ศ
ษ
ส
ห
ฬ
อ
ฮ

โป้ง bang, report
    นิ้วโป้ง thumb
    ปากโป้ง indiscreet; outspoken; to shoot off (one's) mouth
    ยิงโป้ง to shoot with a bang

โปน *as in* **ตาโปน** bulging eyes, popping eyes

โปรแกรม program

โปร่ง clear; spaced out, thin
    โปร่งใจ relieved
    โปร่งตา transparent
    โปร่งแสง translucent
    โปร่งใส transparent
    ปลอดโปร่ง clear; safe
    ผ้าโปร่ง see-through material, diaphanous fabric, netting
    ฟ้าโปร่ง clear sky
    สมองโปร่ง clearheaded, to have one's mind clear

โปรด please; to like, favor; to have compassion for, help
    โปรดเกล้า graciously
    โปรดตอบ R.S.V.P. (ย่อจาก Répondez s'il vous plaît.)
    โปรดปราน favor, like, have a liking for, prefer
    โปรดพลิก please turn over (P.T.O.)
    โปรดสัตว์ to be compassionate towards all beings; to go to receive food offerings
    ของโปรด favorite
    ขอได้โปรด please, I beg you
    คนโปรด favorite, pet

โปรตีน protein

โปรย to scatter, strew, sow broadcast
    โปรยปราย to blandish
    โปรยยิ้ม to smile at everyone
    ฝนโปรยลงมา a light drizzle; to drizzle

โปลิโอ polio, poliomyelitis

โปะ to plaster, coat (something with mud, filler, etc); to give something extra

โป๊ะ weir, fish stake; pontoon
    โป๊ะตะเกียง lampshade

ไป to go, move; too
    ไปก่อน to go on ahead; I'm leaving (now), so long
    ไปดูหนัง to go to the movies
    ไปได้ go; how can /you/he/they/ *ใครๆ ก็รู้ทั้งนั้น ทำเป็นไงไปได้* Everybody knows it. How can you pretend not to.
    ไปถึง to reach, arrive (at, in)
    ไปทุ่ง *see* **ไปทุ่ง** หน้า 236
    ไปเที่ยว to go out; to take a trip (to); to take a walk
    ไปนอก to go abroad
    ไปนอน to go to bed, lie down
    ไปบ้าน to go home
    ไปโบสถ์ to go to /church/temple/
    ไปพบ to go to /see/meet/, meet, see
    ไปพลาง in the meantime, meanwhile; while
        ไปพลางก่อน for the time being, in the meantime, meanwhile
    ไปมา to have been
    ไปๆ มาๆ eventually, in the end; to go from time to time, keep in contact
    ไปไม่ถึง to fall short (of), not get somewhere
        ไปไม่ถึงดวงดาว to fail to realize one's /aspirations/dreams/, fail to /achieve/fulfil/ one's ambition
    ไปร่วมงาน to take part (in), participate
    ไปรับ to get
    ไปโลด to zip (away, ahead, off)
    ไปวัด to go to the /monastery/wat/
    ไปหา to go and see, visit; towards
    ไปให้พ้น Get out!
    ไปไหน Where are you going?; Hi there!, Where are you off to?, How are you doing?
        ไปไหนมา Where have you been?; Hi there!

Left margin letters: ก ข ค ฆ ง จ ฉ ช ซ ฌ ญ ฎ ฏ ฐ ฑ ฒ ณ ด ต ถ ท ธ น บ **ป**

ถมไป loads (of), lots (of), plenty (of), more than enough

ถัดไป next, succeeding

ทั่วไป in general; generally, common; everywhere, all over

นอกไปกว่านั้น in addition to, apart from that

บางไป too thin

เป็นต้นไป starting, from

เป็นไป to go on, proceed, move

ผ่านไป to pass

เผลอไป to make a slip, overlook (something), make a mistake

พ้นไป after

มุ่งไปสู่ to head for; aiming at

ร่ำไป repeatedly, incessantly, continually frequently, always

ลงไป to go down; to have (done)

ล่วงไป in the past

สืบไป from now on, henceforth

หมดไป gone, finished

ห่างไป too far, not close enough

หายไป lost, disappeared, vanished

ออกไป to go out, leave; Get out!

เอาไป to take (away); to take along, bring

ไปยาล "ฯ" et cetera (etc)

ไปยาลใหญ่ "ฯลฯ" et cetera et cetera (etc, etc)

ไปรษณีย์ post

ไปรษณีย์กลาง /General/Central/ Post Office, G.P.O., C.P.O.

ไปรษณียบัตร postcard

ไปรษณียภัณฑ์ postal matter

ไปรษณียากร postage stamp

ไปรษณีย์อากาศ airmail

ตราไปรษณีย์ postmark

ที่ทำการไปรษณีย์ post office

นายไปรษณีย์ postmaster

บุรุษไปรษณีย์ postman

พัสดุไปรษณีย์ parcel post

เรียนทางไปรษณีย์ to take a correspondence course

ป
ผ
ฝ
พ
ฟ
ภ
ม
ย
ร
ฤ
ฤๅ
ล
ว
ศ
ษ
ส
ห
ฬ
อ
ฮ

ก
ข
ค
ฆ
ง
จ
ฉ
ช
ซ
ฌ
ญ
ฎ
ฏ
ฐ
ฑ
ฒ
ณ
ด
ต
ถ
ท
ธ
น
บ
ป
ผ

ผกผัน to be turned upside down; unpredictable; inverse

ผง dust; powder

    ผงขาว heroin

    ผงชูรส monosodium glutamate, MSG

    ผงซักฟอก detergent

    ขี้ผง dust; trash, rubbish; trivial, nothing

        เรื่องขี้ผง /trivial/small/ matter, a nothing

    นมผง powdered milk

    เป็นผง powdery, in powder form

ผงก to raise; to look up

    ผงกศีรษะ to look up, raise one's head; to nod (at someone)

ผงะ to start, stop short

ผงาด prominent, towering, giant, formidable

ผจง to do painstakingly

    ผจงแต่งบทกวี a poem written with painstaking care, painstakingly written poem, painstaking poem

ผจญ to fight, struggle, battle

    ผจญภัย to venture (into), have an adventure

        นักผจญภัย adventurer

ผด prickly heat

ผดุง to take care of, maintain, uphold, support, bolster

    ผดุงครรภ์ midwife

        การผดุงครรภ์ midwifery

        นางผดุงครรภ์ midwife

    ผดุงความยุติธรรม to /maintain/uphold/ justice

ผนวก to add (to), supplement

    ภาคผนวก annex, appendix, exhibit, addendum, supplement, attachment

ผนวช to be ordained, enter the monkhood

ผนัง wall; partition

    ผนังห้อง wall

    ฝาผนัง wall

ผนึก to seal, glue together; to consolidate

ผนึกกำลัง to consolidate forces

ผนึกซอง to seal an envelope

    จดหมายเปิดผนึก open letter

ผม[1] hair

    ผมกระเซิง disheveled (hair)

    ผมจุก topknot

    ผมดก a good head of hair, thick hair

    ผมดัด waved hair, permanent, permanent wave

    ผมปลอม wig, hairpiece, toupee

    ผมเปีย see **เปีย** หน้า 317

    ผมไฟ hair present at birth

    ผมม้า bangs

    ผมยาว long hair

        ผมยาวประบ่า shoulder-length hair

    ผมยุ่ง /tousled/tangled/ hair

    ผมร่วง falling hair

    ผมสั้น short hair

    ผมสีแดง red hair, auburn hair, redhead

    ผมสีทอง blond hair

    ผมสีน้ำตาล brown hair, brunette

    ผมหงอก gray hair

    ผมหยักศก curly hair

    ผมหยิก curly hair; frizzy hair, kinky hair

    เกล้าผม to put (one's) hair up

    ช่างตัดผม barber, hairdresser

    ช่างทำผม hairdresser

    เซ็ทผม to have (one's) hair set

    ดัดผม to have (one's) hair set; to get a /permanent/permanent wave/

    ทรงผม hairstyle, hair-do

    แบบผม hairstyle, hair-do

    ม้วนผม to curl (one's) hair

    มวยผม to a put (one's) hair up in a bun

    ไรผม hairline

    เสยผม to brush back (one's) hair, run /(one's) fingers/a comb/ through (one's) hair

ผม[2] I, we; me, us

ผมด้วย I too, me too

ผมเอง I myself

ผยอง[1] to buck; to prance; to caper

ผยอง[2] overbearing

    หยิ่งผยอง arrogant, self-important, ego-centric

ผรุสวาท coarse language, abuse, obscenity, obscene language

ผล effect, result, consequence, fruit; gain; interest; profit; product

    ผลกรรม fruit of misdeeds, punishment

    ผลกำไร profit, return (on an investment, etc)

    ผลข้างเคียง side effect

    ผลงาน (one's) work(s); record; achievement; something to show, results

    ผลเฉลี่ย average

    ผลได้จากทุน capital gains

    ผลที่สุด after all

    ผลบวก sum

    ผลปฏิบัติ practical result; treatment

    ผลประโยชน์ interest (in), benefit (from); income

    ผลผลิต output, production

    ผลพลอยได้ by-product, incidental benefit

    ผลพวง consequence, result

    ผลไม้ fruit

        ผลไม้กระป๋อง canned fruit, tinned fruit

        ผลไม้กวน fruit preserve

    ผลย้อนหลัง retroactive effect

    ผลร้าย dire consequence, /bad/harmful/ effect, negative consequences

    ผลลบ negative /consequences/effect/, detrimental; remainder

    ผลลัพธ์ total, sum, result; product

    ผลสะท้อน consequence, result, after-effect, secondary effect

    ผลสำเร็จ accomplishment, success, achievement

    ผลสุดท้าย the upshot, the final result

    ผลเสียหาย damage, detriment

    ได้ผล to work, be effective, get results, fruitful

    บรรลุผล to succeed, work; successful, accomplished

    บังเกิดผล effective, to have an effect; to be successful

    ประสิทธิผล effectiveness

    ปันผล to pay a dividend

    เป็นผลดี good, useful, worthwhile

    พืชผล produce, crops, yield

    มีผล effective, productive; to bear fruit, produce results, take effect, have consequences, result in

    ยังผลให้ to result in, cause, have as a consequence, give rise to

    ไร้ผล useless, ineffective, nugatory; futile, vain, empty

    สัมฤทธิผล achievement; to achieve success

    เหตุผล reason, justification

    ออกผล to bear fruit, be fruitful, produce results, bring dividends

ผล็อย suddenly, abruptly

    หลับผล็อย to drop off to sleep

ผละ to separate, part, split

    ผละหนี to run /off/away/, take off, skedaddle

    ผละออกไป to split away, part company, walk out, separate, leave

ผลัก to push

    ผลักดัน to push, pressure, press; to exert pressure (on someone), force; to induce

    ผลักไส to drive someone out, get rid of, kick someone out

ผลัด to change; to shed; shift

    ผลัดกัน to take turns

    ผลัดเช้า /morning/early/ shift

    ผลัดใบ to shed (its etc) leaves; deciduous

ก
ข
ค
ฆ
ง
จ
ฉ
ช
ซ
ฌ
ญ
ฎ
ฏ
ฐ
ฑ
ฒ
ณ
ด
ต
ถ
ท
ธ
น
บ
ป
ผ

ผลัดเปลี่ยน to change, exchange places, take over

ผลัดไป to postpone, put off

ผลัดผ้า to change one's clothes

ทำงานเป็นผลัด to work in shifts

วิ่งผลัด relay race

ผลาญ to destroy, devastate

ผลาญชีวิต to annihilate

ผลาญสมบัติ to squander (one's fortune or property)

ล้างผลาญ to ravage, lay waste (to); to waste

ผลิ to bud

ผลิใบ to bud, put forth new leaves

ฤดูใบไม้ผลิ spring

ผลิต to produce, make, manufacture; to blossom, bloom, put forth

ผลิตกรรม production

ผลิตผล product

ผลิตภัณฑ์ product, manufacture

ผลีผลาม to be hasty, rush (into)

ผลึก crystal

ตกผลึก to crystallize, form crystals

ผลุนผลัน in a rush, in great haste

ผลุบ to dive (into), pop (into, up, out, in); plop (into); to duck; to close up (เช่น ร่ม); to bob

ผลุบผลับ excitedly, hurriedly, in a hurry

ผลุบโผล่ to bob up and down, appear and disappear; irregularly, in fits and starts, fitful, casual

ผวน to reverse, invert

คำผวน spoonerism

ผันผวน see **ผันผวน** หน้า 325

ผวา to be startled; to be scared, terrified; to rush into (his, her, each other's etc) arms, rush up and embrace

ผวากอด to rush up and embrace, give a big hug

ผวาตื่น to awake with a start

ผสม to mix, mix in, add (to), combine

ผสมเทียม (to give) artificial insemination

ผสมผสาน mixed, blended, composite

ผสมพันธุ์ to breed, reproduce; to mate

ผสมโรง to join in, take part

ของผสม mixture, combination, compound

คำผสม combining word; combined word

พันธุ์ผสม hybrid, mixed breed, mongrel

รัฐบาลผสม coalition government

ส่วนผสม ingredient, component, constituent, contents

ผอง all

ผ่อง bright, happy; pure

ผ่องใส bright, beaming, happy

ขาวผ่อง pure white

ผุดผ่อง radiant, clear, unblemished

ผ่อน to slacken; loosen; to abate, lessen

ผ่อนชำระหนี้ to pay a debt in installments

ผ่อนใช้ to pay back in installments

ผ่อนปรน to be lenient, soften (the terms, penalty etc), go easy (on someone)

อัตราที่ผ่อนปรน favorable rate

ผ่อนผัน to make an exception, be indulgent, give someone a break, make an allowance for, give a dispensation

ผ่อนลมหายใจ to breathe lightly

ผ่อนสั้นผ่อนยาว to bargain

ผ่อนหนักผ่อนเบา flexible, accommodating, conciliatory; give and take, to compromise, make concessions

ผ่อนหนี้ to pay in installments

เงินผ่อน in installments; an installment (payment)

ซื้อเงินผ่อน to buy on the installment plan

ผอบ a cup with a foot and tapering lid

ผอม thin; lean

ผอมกะหร่อง skinny

ผอมเกร็ง lean, sinewy

ผอมโซ emaciated, gaunt

ผอมลง to grow thin, lose weight

ผอมแห้ง gaunt, scrawny; emaciated, wasted

ผ็อย *see* **ผล็อย** หน้า 323

ผัก vegetable

ผักกาดเขียว Chinese mustard

ผักกาดหอม lettuce

ผักกาดหัว turnip

ผักชี coriander

ผักชีฝรั่ง parsley

ผักชีโรยหน้า window-dressing

ผักดอง pickled vegetable, kimchi, vegetable pickle

ผักตบชวา water hyacinth

ผักบุ้ง morning-glory

ผักบุ้งฝรั่ง a kind of morning-glory

ผักสด fresh vegetable; raw vegetable

ผัง plan, layout; marking stakes

ผังเมือง town plan

ผัด[1] fried, stir-fried

ผัดเปรี้ยวหวาน sweet and sour (pork, fish etc)

ข้าวผัด fried rice

ผัด[2] to powder

ผัดหน้า to powder one's face

ผัดแป้ง to powder

ผัด[3] to postpone, put off

ผัดนัด to postpone /a meeting/an appointment/, put off an appointment

ผัดเพี้ยน to put off (doing something); dilatory

ผัดวันประกันพรุ่ง to procrastinate, be dilatory, put (something) off

ผัดผัน to oscillate

ผัน to change, shift, turn; to modulate

ผันแปร to alter, turn (to, into), become; vicissitude; fickle, changeable

ผันผวน to fluctuate, variable, in flux, in a state of flux, destabilized, unstable, turbulence, in turmoil; to /suffer/meet with/ reverses

ผันผาย to proceed

ผันอักษร to recite the tonal paradigm of a consonant

ผัว husband, man

ผัวเดียวเมียเดียว monogamous

ผัวเมีย husband and wife, spouses

ผิดผัวผิดเมีย to be unfaithful, commit adultery, have an extramarital affair

พ่อผัว father-in-law

แม่ผัว mother-in-law

ผา rock, rock face

เงื้อมผา overhanging rock, an overhang

ชะง่อนผา crag

หน้าผา cliff, precipice

หินผา rock

ผ่า to split, split open, cleave, cut in two; to slice, make an incision; to operate

ผ่าตัด to operate, perform an operation

การผ่าตัด surgery

การผ่าตัดเล็ก minor surgery

การผ่าตัดใหญ่ major surgery

ห้องผ่าตัด operating room

ผ่าฟืน to chop firewood; to split kindling

ผ่าเหล่า to be a mutation, mutate, be a sport; to be different

ผ้า cloth, material, fabric, textile

ผ้ากระสอบป่าน burlap

ผ้ากันเปื้อน apron

ผ้ากาสาวพัสตร์ monk's yellow robes

ผ้าขนสัตว์ woolen cloth

ผ้าขาวม้า wrap-around cloth, a utilitarian usually checked cloth often used as a male lower garment, sash or shawl

ผ้าขี้ริ้ว rag; chitterlings, tripe

ผ้าคลุมเตียง bedspread

ผ
ฝ
พ
ฟ
ภ
ม
ย
ร
ฤ
ฦ
ล
ว
ศ
ษ
ส
ห
ฬ
อ
ฮ

ผ้าเช็ดตัว towel
ผ้าเช็ดมือ napkin, serviette
ผ้าเช็ดหน้า handkerchief
ผ้าซิ่น traditional tube skirt
ผ้าดิบ unbleached cloth
ผ้าไตร a set of monk's robes
ผ้าถุง tube skirt
ผ้าแถบ breast cloth
ผ้านวม quilt
ผ้าน้ำมัน oilcloth
ผ้านุ่ง panung, a dhoti-like garment, breeches draped from a single hip cloth
ผ้าบังสุกุล robes offered to monks at a cremation
ผ้าใบ canvas, sail cloth
ผ้าป่า robes offered to monks after the Kathin season; the ceremony of making such an offering
ผ้าปูโต๊ะ tablecloth
ผ้าปูที่นอน sheet, bedsheet
ผ้าโปร่ง gauze
ผ้าผวย blanket
ผ้าผ่อน clothing, clothes
ผ้าผูกคอ necktie
ผ้าฝ้าย cotton, cotton cloth
ผ้าพันคอ shawl, scarf, neckerchief, muffler
ผ้าพันแผล bandage
ผ้าพื้น plain cloth
ผ้าแพร silk; rayon
ผ้าโพกหัว turban
ผ้าม่วง silk panung, silk hip cloth for draping into a kind of breeches
ผ้ามัสลิน muslin
ผ้ายีน blue denim
ผ้าเย็บที่นอน ticking
ผ้าลินิน linen
ผ้าลูกฟูก corduroy
ผ้าสำลี cotton flannel
ผ้าห่ม blanket

ผ้าเหลือง yellow robe
ผ้าอ้อม diaper
ผ้าอาบ monk's bathing cloth
ร่มผ้า covered areas (of the body)
เสื้อผ้า clothes, clothing, wearing apparel, garments
ห่มผ้า to wear clothes, clothed

ผาก as in แห้งผาก parched, dried out, sere

ผาง slap

ผาด, ผาดๆ to go quickly, move swiftly, speed; on the surface, superficially, unclearly, indistinctly, vaguely
ผาดโผน daredevil, daring, wild; frisky
มองผาดๆ to glimpse, get a glimpse (of), glance (at)

ผ่าน to pass, go through, traverse, cross, transit; to get past (something); through
ผ่านเข้าออก to go in and out, pass through
ผ่านฉลุย to sail through
ผ่านไป to pass
ผ่านพ้นไป to be over
ผ่านมา to pass by, be passing
ผ่านร้อนผ่านหนาว through thick and thin
ค่าผ่านประตู admission, entrance fee
เดินผ่าน to cross, pass through, transit
ทางผ่าน passage, passage way; through road; a place (one) passes through, on the way
บอกผ่าน to jack up the price, overstate the price, overcharge
บัตรผ่านประตู pass; ticket
สอบผ่าน to pass (an examination)

ผ่านๆ as in อ่านผ่านๆ, ดูผ่านๆ to skim (over)

ผาย to open; to spread; to release
ผายปอด to give artificial respiration
ผายผัน to go, proceed
ผายลม to break wind
สะโพกผาย broad hips

ผ่ายผอม to grow thin, lose weight

ผ่าว *as in* **ร้อนผ่าว** burning, scorching, intensely hot

ผาสุก *as in* **ความผาสุก** happiness, contentment
อย่างผาสุก happily, contentedly

ผิ provided that
ผิว่า if; provided that

ผิง[1] a plain cookie baked on a firepot

ผิง[2] to bake; to warm
ผิงแดด to warm oneself in the sun, sun oneself
ผิงไฟ to warm oneself by a fire
เตาผิง heater, stove; fireplace

ผิด wrong, erroneous, incorrect, mistaken, untrue
ผิดกฎหมาย illegal, unlawful, against the law
ผิดกติกา not playing the game, not abiding by the rules
ผิดกัน to differ, be different, not the same
ผิดกับ different from, unlike
ผิดคาด unexpected, not as expected, surprising
ผิดจังหวะ to be off beat; to be ill-timed, wrong timing
ผิดจารีต to commit a transgression, misbehave
ผิดใจ to have a grudge (against), be on bad terms, be on the outs (with someone); to displease
ผิดตา unusually; to look different
ผิดถนัด to be all wrong, clearly wrong; of course not
ผิดถูก right or wrong
ผิดท่า to make a wrong move; to get in a wrong position; to go wrong
ผิดที่ to be in the wrong place, out of place; to be in a strange place
ผิดที่หมาย to miss the target, fall wide of the mark

ผิดธรรมดา unusual, exceptional, abnormal, extraordinary, out of the ordinary
ผิดนัก if things go wrong
ผิดนัด to miss an appointment, fail to keep an appointment, fail to appear, not to show up; to default, be in default,
ผิดปรกติ unusual, different, out of the ordinary; queer, odd, abnormal
ผิดประเพณี unconventional, contrary to custom; wrong, immoral
ผิดเป็นครู to learn from one's mistakes
ผิดไปแล้ว It's my fault, I'm sorry., What's done is done., I admit I'm in the wrong.
ผิดผัวผิดเมีย to commit adultery
ผิดผี to violate., a convention, do some thing morally wrong
ผิดแผก different (from); to deviate, vary, differ (from)
ผิดฝาผิดตัว to be mismatched
ผิดๆ พลาดๆ (to do something) badly, mess (something) up; to keep making mistakes, bungle
ผิดเพี้ยน inaccurate, off, at variance with, not in line with, irregularly, deviating
ผิดระเบียบ to be against the rules, not allowed
ผิดรูป misshapen, deformed
ผิดสังเกต noticeably, remarkably, unusually; not look right, to look funny
ผิดสัญญา to commit a breach of contract, violate a contract, break a /promise/ contract/
ผิดหวัง disappointed
 ทำให้ผิดหวัง to disappoint (someone), fail (someone)
ผิดหูผิดตา noticeably, markedly, remarkably; to seem different
เข้าใจผิด to misunderstand, mistake, make a mistake, be mistaken

ผ
ฝ
พ
ฟ
ภ
ม
ย
ร
ฤ
ฤๅ
ล
ว
ศ
ษ
ส
ห
ฬ
อ
ฮ

ความผิด guilt, culpability; offence; wrong, mistake, error, fault

   ความผิดพลาด blunder, mistake

ผู้ผิด wrongdoer, guilty person, offender

มีความผิด to be guilty (of), be at fault, (in the) wrong, to have done something wrong

ยอมรับผิด to admit (one's) /guilt/mistake/fault/

รับผิด to confess, admit (one's) /fault/guilt/responsibility/

   รับผิดชอบ to be responsible (for), take responsibility (for), accept liability (for)

หลงผิด mistaken, misled, misguided; to misunderstand

เห็นผิดเป็นชอบ to take wrong for right

ผิน to turn one's head

   ผินหน้าเข้าหากัน to put ones' heads together, get together, cooperate; to make up

ผินหลังให้ to turn one's back (on)

ผิว complexion; skin, rind, peel, outer layer, surface

   ผิวกาย skin

   ผิวขาว fair-skinned, light /skin/complexion/

      คนผิวขาว white /man/person/

   ผิวคล้ำ dark-complexioned, swarthy, dark-skinned

   ผิวดำ dark-skinned

   ผิวน้ำ surface of the water

   ผิวบาง delicate

   ผิวเผิน superficially, on the surface

   ผิวพรรณ complexion, skin

   ผิวโลก /surface/crust/ of the earth

   ผิวส้ม orange peel

   ผิวหนัง skin, epidermis

   การถือผิว racism, racial discrimination

ผิวปาก to whistle

ผี ghost, spirit, ghoul, spook, specter, apparition; the dead, deceased

ผีเข้า to be possessed (by a spirit)

ผีเข้าผีออก erratic

ผีดิบ uncremated body; Frankenstein's monster, zombie, the living dead

ผีดุ heavily haunted; evil spirit

ผีตากผ้าอ้อม twilight

ผีตายโหง ghost of one who died a violent death; person who dies a violent death

ผีบุญ one who claims to have supernatural powers, messiah, faith leader

ผีพุ่งไต้ meteor, shooting star

ผีไม่มีศาล vagabond

ผีเรือน guardian spirit of a house

ผีสิง haunted, possessed

ผีเสื้อ butterfly; moth (ไม่พับปีก)

ผีหลอก to haunt; to be scared by a ghost

ผีอำ to be constricted by a ghost

ยาผีบอก spirit-revealed remedy

ผึ่ง to dry, expose to the sun; to stretch out, spread out

   ผึ่งแดด to sun, put (something) out in the sun

   ผึ่งผาย imposing, dignified, grand; smart

ผึ้ง bee

   ผึ้งงาน worker, worker bee

   ผึ้งตัวผู้ drone

   ผึ้งนางพญา queen bee

   ขี้ผึ้ง wax, beeswax; ointment, unguent, salve, pomade

   น้ำผึ้ง honey

      น้ำผึ้งพระจันทร์ honeymoon

   รวงผึ้ง honeycomb

   รังผึ้ง beehive; radiator; perforated earthen grate

ผืน piece; classifier for mats or pieces of cloth

   ผ้าเช็ดหน้า 2 ผืน two handkerchiefs

   ผืนดิน ground, earth

   ผืนนา ricefield

   ผืนน้ำแผ่นฟ้า expanse of sky and water

ผื่น a rash

ผุ rotten, decayed; rusted; disintegrating

    ผุพัง falling to pieces, crumbling; in a state of decay, in ruins; dilapidated

    ฟันผุ caries, cavity, tooth decay

ผุด to emerge, rise up, crop up

    ผุดผ่อง see **ผุดผ่อง** หน้า 324

    ผุดผาด lovely

    ผุดลุกผุดนั่ง agitated

ผุยผง dust; powder

ผู้ male; one who, equivalent to English suffixes "-or" "-er"

    ผู้กระทำ doer, actor

        ผู้กระทำผิด wrongdoer, offender, culprit

    ผู้กล่าวหา complainant, accuser

    ผู้ก่อกรรมทำเข็ญ trouble-maker

    ผู้ก่อการ a promoter of the revolution of B.E. 2475; revolutionary

        ผู้ก่อการร้าย insurgent; terrorist, bandit

        ผู้ก่อการจลาจล rioter

    ผู้กำกับการ superintendent; head

        ผู้กำกับการแสดง director

    ผู้กู้ borrower

    ผู้ไกล่เกลี่ย mediator, conciliator

    ผู้ขับ, ผู้ขับขี่ driver, chauffeur

    ผู้ขาย seller, vendor

        ผู้ขายทอดตลาด seller at auction

    ผู้เขียน writer, author

    ผู้คงแก่เรียน learned (person)

    ผู้คน people

    ผู้ค้นคว้า researcher

    ผู้ค้ำประกัน guarantor, surety

    ผู้คุม jailer, gaoler, prison guard; guardian

    ผู้จัดการ manager

    ผู้จ้าง employer

    ผู้จำนอง mortgagor

    ผู้จำนำ pledgor

    ผู้จำหน่าย dealer, distributor

        ผู้จำหน่ายปลีก retailer

    ผู้จำหน่ายเหมา wholesaler

    ผู้ชนะ victor, winner

    ผู้ช่วย assistant

        ผู้ช่วยแพทย์ medical attendant

    ผู้ชาย man; men's, masculine

    ผู้ชำนาญ person skilled (in), expert, specialist (in)

    ผู้เช่า tenant, lessee

    ผู้เชี่ยวชาญ expert, specialist

    ผู้ซื้อ buyer, purchaser

    ผู้เซ็นสัญญา signatory, signer, signed by

    ผู้เฒ่า aged person, old man; venerable

    ผู้ดี fine person, gentleman, lady; upperclass people; highclass, mannered

        ผู้ดีแปดสาแหรก person of good family; patrician, aristocrat; highfalutin' person

    ผู้ดู spectator, viewer

        ผู้ดูแล superintendent

    ผู้เดินทาง traveller, voyager

    ผู้เดียว alone, the only person, the one person, sole

    ผู้โดยสาร passenger

    ผู้ใด whosoever, whoever, anyone (who)

    ผู้ตรวจการณ์ inspector

    ผู้ต้องสงสัย suspect

    ผู้ต้องหา the accused, person charged with an offense

    ผู้ตัดสิน referee, umpire, judge

    ผู้ตาม follower

        ผู้ตามเสด็จ royal entourage

    ผู้ตาย the deceased, decedent, dead person

    ผู้ติดตาม entourage, retinue, escort; attendant, aide

    ผู้แต่ง author, writer

    ผู้ถาม questioner

    ผู้ถือ bearer

        ผู้ถือจดหมาย bearer of a letter

        ผู้ถือสาร courier

        ผู้ถือหุ้น shareholder

ผ ฝ พ ฟ ภ ม ย ร ฤ ฤา ล ว ศ ษ ส ห ฬ อ ฮ

ผู้ทรง holder

ผู้ทรยศ traitor

ผู้ทอดตลาด auctioneer

ผู้ที่ไว้ใจ someone who can be trusted, confidant, confidante (ผู้หญิง)

ผู้แทน representative, delegate

    ผู้แทนจำหน่าย distributing agent

    ผู้แทนจำหน่ายแต่ผู้เดียว sole distributor

    ผู้แทนราษฎร representative of the people, member of the legislature, M.P., member of parliament, elected representative

    ผู้แทนหนังสือพิมพ์ press representative

ผู้น้อย subordinate, junior, inferior, underling; person of small importance, a little guy

ผู้นำ leader

    ผู้นำทาง guide

ผู้บงการ dictator; person who is /directing/ running/ (an operation, etc)

ผู้บรรยาย commentator

ผู้บริจาค donor

ผู้บังคับการ commander

ผู้บังคับบัญชา superior, boss

ผู้บัญชาการทหาร commander in chief

    ผู้บัญชาการทหารสูงสุด supreme commander

ผู้ปกครอง guardian, parent; ruler, governor

ผู้ประสบภัย victim, casualty

ผู้ประสาธน์การ rector

ผู้ประสานงาน coordinator

ผู้ป่วย patient

    ผู้ป่วยนอก out-patient department, OPD

ผู้แปล translator

ผู้ผิด wrongdoer, guilty person, offender

ผู้เผด็จการ dictator

ผู้ฝักใฝ่ adherent, partisan; sympathizer

ผู้ฝากเงิน depositor

ผู้พิทักษ์สันติราษฎร์ police, protector of the people

ผู้พิพากษา judge, justice, magistrate

ผู้แพ้ loser, the defeated

ผู้ฟัง listener, audience

ผู้มอบ transferor

ผู้มาติดต่อ visitor

    ที่จอดรถผู้มาติดต่อ visitor parking

ผู้มีเกียรติ distinguished (person, guests, visitors etc)

ผู้มีความรู้ learned person, someone who knows, expert

ผู้มีตระกูลสูง person of high birth

ผู้มีอันจะกิน well-to-do, person of /means/ substance/, solid citizen

ผู้มีอาวุโส senior, ranking

ผู้มีอำนาจ powerful person, boss; authorized, competent

เจ้าหน้าที่ท้องถิ่นผู้มีอำนาจเต็ม competent local authorities

    ผู้มีอำนาจเต็ม plenipotentiary

ผู้มีอิทธิพล influential person

ผู้มีอุปการะ benefactor

ผู้ยิ่งใหญ่ big man, person of consequence, powerful person, personage

ผู้เยาว์ minor, infant; youth, youngster

ผู้ร้อง petitioner, claimant,

    ผู้ร้องขัดทรัพย์ intervener

    ผู้ร้องทุกข์ complainant

ผู้รอดชีวิต survivor

ผู้รักชาติ patriot

ผู้รักษาเวลา timekeeper

ผู้รับจ้าง employee, hired person

ผู้รับจำนอง mortgagee

ผู้รับจำนำ pawnbroker; pledgee

ผู้รับประโยชน์ beneficiary

ผู้รับมอบ transferee

ผู้รับหนังสือพิมพ์ subscriber

ผู้รับเหมา contractor

ผู้รับเหมาก่อสร้าง building contractor

ผู้ร้าย criminal, perpetrator, wrongdoer, offender, culprit

ผู้ร้ายฆ่าคน killer, murderer

ผู้ริเริ่ม pioneer, trailblazer, originator

ผู้เรียบเรียง compiler; adapter

ผู้ล่วงลับ the deceased, departed, the late (Mr...., husband etc)

ผู้ลากมากดี high-class person, (a member of) the upper crust

ผู้ลี้ภัย refugee

ผู้ว่าการธนาคารชาติ governor of the Bank of Thailand

ผู้ว่าราชการจังหวัด provincial governor

ผู้วิเศษ magician, sorcerer; wizard, wonderworker

ผู้ส่งข่าว messenger

ผู้สมรู้ร่วมคิด conspirator

ผู้สมัคร candidate, applicant

ผู้สร้างภาพยนตร์ producer

ผู้สร้างโลก the Creator

ผู้สั่งจ่าย drawer

ผู้สัญจรไปมา passers-by

ผู้สันทัดกรณี well-informed person, authority, specialist

ผู้สำเร็จราชการ regent

ผู้สื่อข่าว reporter, correspondent, newspaperman, journalist

ผู้สู่ขอ suitor

ผู้สู้ราคา bidder

ผู้เสียสละ one who sacrifices (his life etc); martyr

ผู้หญิง woman, girl, female; women's; feminine

ผู้หญิงหากิน prostitute

ผู้หลักผู้ใหญ่ person of importance

ผู้หวังดี well-wisher, friend

ผู้ให้กู้ lender

ผู้ใหญ่ adult, older person; responsible person; /senior/top/ people, senior /person/ officer/executive/people/etc, big man, bigwig; dignitary

ผู้ใหญ่บ้าน village headman

ผู้อพยพ evacuee, refugee

ผู้อยู่ใต้บังคับ subordinate

ผู้ออกแบบ designer

ผู้อ่าน reader

ผู้อารักขา protector, bodyguard

ผู้อำนวยการ director

ผู้อื่น stranger, someone else

ผู้อุปการะ benefactor, patron, supporter, person who looks after someone else

ตัวผู้ male, masculine

เป็นผู้เป็นคน to be somebody

ไม่เป็นผู้เป็นคน a nobody, a nothing, a nonentity

ผูก to tie, fasten, secure, bind, knot; to make; to be bent on, be determined to

ผูกขาด to monopolize, corner the market

ผูกคอตาย to hang oneself

ผูกเงื่อน to knot, tie a knot

ผูกเชือก to tie with /string/cord/rope/

ผูกดวง to cast a horoscope

ผูกพยาบาท vindictive, vengeful, to harbor resentment, be bent on revenge

ผูกพัน to be bound (to), have ties with, be linked (to), have an obligation (to); to be concerned (with), interested (in); to have ties of affection

ข้อผูกพัน obligation, duty

ผูกมัด to incriminate; to be conclusive (of); to bind, obligate, commit

ข้อผูกมัด commitment, duty, binding obligation; condition

ไม่มีข้อผูกมัด no strings attached, unconditional

ผูกมิตร to make friends (with)

ผูกไมตรี to establish friendly relations,

establish a friendship (with), secure the friendship of, cultivate (someone)

เผง direct, straight

ตรงเผง exactly right; perfectly straight; completely honest

ถูกเผง right on the nose

เผชิญ to meet (with), be confronted with, confront, face

เผชิญหน้า to meet, face, face up to (someone or something), confront

เผ็ด hot, pungent, sharp, peppery

เผ็ดร้อน hot, heated, fiery, peppery, acrimonious

แก้เผ็ด to get even, get back at someone, retaliate

แกงเผ็ด hot curry

เผด็จ to eliminate, destroy

เผด็จการ dictatorial, autocratic

จอมเผด็จการ arch dictator

ผู้เผด็จการ dictator

ลัทธิเผด็จการ dictatorship

เผด็จศึก to win a battle, be victorious; to take (a girl etc)

เผด็จสวาท to violate, take (a girl etc) forcibly

เผดิม to start off

เผ่น to leap, spring, bound

เผ่นเข้าใส่ to spring at, leap on

เผ่นหนี to flee, run away, take to one's heels, skip

เผย to reveal, disclose, divulge; to expose

เผยความลับ to /reveal/divulge/ a secret

เผยแผ่ see **เผยแพร่**

เผยแพร่ to spread, propagate, disseminate, publicize

เผยวาจา to speak

เผยอ to open slightly

เผยอหน้า to show off; to put oneself forward

เผล่ as in **ยิ้มเผล่** broad smile; to smile broadly

เผล็ดผล to bear fruit

เผลอ to forget, make a mistake, be careless, overlook (something)

เผลอตัว to forget oneself, make a misstep

เผอเรอ careless, negligent; forgetful

เผอิญ accidentally, by accident, by chance, fortuitously

เผา to burn, cremate, to set fire (to); to warm up; to bake; to consume

เผาขน at close range

เผาถ่าน to make charcoal; to burn charcoal

เผาทั้งเป็น to be burnt alive

เผาผลาญ to waste, squander; to ravage, devastate

เผาไฟ to burn, burn (something) up; to set fire (to something)

เผาศพ to cremate, hold a cremation

เผาอิฐ to /burn/bake/ bricks

การเผาไหม้ combustion

เตาเผา kiln

น้ำพริกเผา mild roasted chili paste

เผ่า tribe, ethnic group

เผ่าพันธุ์ lineage, stock, family

เผ้า as in **ผมเผ้า** hair

เผินๆ on the surface, superficially, shallow; slight

เผื่อ for; if, in case (of), extra

เผื่อแผ่ to be generous

เผื่อเรียก on call

เผื่อว่า in case, if

เผื่อไว้ก่อน tentative; in advance

นัดเผื่อไว้ก่อน a tentative appointment

เผื่อเหลือเผื่อขาด extra

เผือก[1] taro

เผือก[2] albino, white

ช้างเผือก white elephant

เผือด to turn pale; gloomy; pallid; faded

หน้าซีดเผือด pallid, pale

แผ่ to spread (out), extend

แผ่กุศล to dedicate merit

แผ่ซ่าน to spread

แผ่เมตตา to extend loving kindness to all, be compassionate

แผ่แม่เบี้ย to spread (its) hood

แผ่รังสี to radiate; radiation

แผ่หลา stretched out, at full length, sprawled out; to sprawl

แผ่อาณาเขต to extend one's territory, enlarge the frontiers

แผ่อำนาจ to /spread/extend/ one's authority

แผ่อิทธิพล to influence, dominate

แผก *as in* **ผิดแผก** different (from); to deviate, vary, differ (from)

แผง plaited screen

แผงลอย street stall, stand

แผงหนังสือ bookstall

แผด *as in*

แผดเสียง to shout, scream, yell; to trumpet

แผดแสง to blaze

แผน plan, scheme, plot

แผนการ plan, scheme, plot, design

แผนที่ map, chart

แผนโบราณ old, traditional, old style

แผนปัจจุบัน modern, new style

แผนผัง plan, drawing, layout, sketch (of)

แผนภูมิ chart

แผนใหม่ modern, new

แผ่น a numerical designation for sheets or flat things

แผ่นกระจก pane of glass

แผ่นกระดาน plank, board

แผ่นดิน land, earth; state, country, kingdom, government; reign

    งบประมาณแผ่นดิน state budget estimates

    พระเจ้าแผ่นดิน king, monarch, sovereign

แผ่นตะกั่ว lead sheet, lead foil

แผ่นป้าย signboard

แผ่นเสียง phonograph record, platter

แผนก division, section, department

แผนกเครื่องสำอาง perfumery department

แผล scar, wound, lesion; defect, crack, mark

แผลกดทับ bedsore

แผลฉีก a split wound

แผลเป็น scar

บาดแผล wound, injury, cut

เป็นแผล to have an /injury/wound/cut/; to have a /defect/mark/crack/

แผลง to display, show, exercise; to modify, convert; to shoot

แผลงฤทธิ์ to display magical power; to act up, be acting up, have a fit, go haywire

แผล็บ in a flash, momentarily; to flick out

แผล็ว swiftly, in an instant

แผ่ว softly, faintly, quietly

แผ่วลง to fade; fading

แผ้ว to clear

แผ้วถาง to clear a way (for); to clear land

แผ้วพาน to trouble, disturb

โผ¹ to rush (at, into), dash (in, to, at); to rush into someone's arms

โผเข้าใส่ to rush at

โผผิน to circle about in the air

โผ² forecast, advance list, proposed list

ตามโผ as /expected/forecast/

หลุดโผ dropped

หลุดโผท็อปเท็น dropped from the top-ten forecast

โผเผ spent, worn out, pooped

โผน to jump on, leap (on), spring, bound

โผนทะยาน to spring forward

ผาดโผน daredevil, daring, wild; frisky

    บินผาดโผน to do aerobatics, daredevil flying

ผ ผ พ ฟ ภ ม ย ร ฤ ฦ ล ว ศ ษ ส ห ฬ อ ฮ

โลดโผน adventurous, daring, daredevil; fancy, extraordinary, spectacular

โผล่ to emerge, crop up, surface, appear; to stick out, stick up, show

โผล่หน้า to appear, turn up

ไผ่ bamboo

ฝน[1] rain; year

  ฝนตก to rain; it is raining

    ฝนตกพรำๆ to drizzle, to be drizzling; a light rain, a steady rain

    ฝนตกหนัก to rain hard; a heavy rain, downpour

  ฝนตั้งเค้า to look like rain

  ฝนเทียม artificial rain

  ฝนฟ้าอากาศ weather

  ฝนลงเม็ด to begin to rain

  ฝนแล้ง to be dry, have a dry spell, /no/ little/ rain, drought condition

  ปีนี้ฝนแล้งไม่ได้ทำนา It was too dry for rice this year.

  ฝนสั่งฟ้า the last rain of the rainy season

  น้ำฝน rainwater

  พลอยฟ้าพลอยฝน to get sucked in, get mixed up in something

  พายุฝน rainstorm

  ฤดูฝน rainy season

  หน้าฝน rainy season

  หยาดฝน raindrop

ฝน[2] to sharpen, grind

  ฝนมีด to sharpen a knife; to /strop/sharpen/ a razor

  ฝนยา to rub off, grind off

ฝรั่ง[1] foreigner from /Europe/America/, Westerner, European, white man

  ฝรั่งกังไส delftware

  ฝรั่งมังค่า white people, white man, European

  คนฝรั่ง *see* **ฝรั่ง**[1]

  พูดฝรั่ง to speak /English/a European language/

  ภาษาฝรั่ง English, a European language

ฝรั่ง[2] guava

ฝรั่งเศส Frenchman, French, Gallic

ฝ่อ withered, dried out; stunted, rudimentary

  ขวัญหนีดีฝ่อ terrified, aghast

  ใจฝ่อ scared

ฝอย[1] fibers, filaments; directions for the use of a medicine

  ฝอยทอง sweet egg-serpentine, a boiled confection

  กุ้งฝอย tiny freshwater shrimp

  เป็นฝอย shredded, shreds of, fibrous; fine hair; threadlike

  มูลฝอย rubbish, trash, garbage, refuse

  รากฝอย hair root, rootlet

  เหล็กฝอย steel wool

ฝอย[2] to gas, prattle, talk nonsense

  แกจะฝอยมากไปแล้ว He's talking nonsense.

ฝัก sheath, scabbard (เฉพาะดาบ); pod; testicle

  ฝักถั่ว pea pod, bean pod; yes-man

  ฝักบัว shower head; watering can, sprayer

  ฝักฝ่าย group, side, faction

  ฝักใฝ่ to be a supporter (of), side with, be a sympathizer, be pro, be for

  ออกฝัก to have pods

ฝัง to bury, inter; buried; to inset, implant

  ฝังใจ deeply, strongly, indelibly

  ฝังทั้งเป็น buried alive

  ฝังเพชร set with diamonds, diamond-studded

  ฝังรกราก to settle, settle down (in), put down roots (in)

  ฝังราก to be rooted (in)

  ฝังศพ to bury the dead, hold a burial

  ฝังหัว dogmatic, opinionated

  ฝังอยู่ใน to be embedded in

ฝั่ง bank; shore; coast; side

  ฝั่งขวา right bank; right side

  ฝั่งซ้าย left bank; left side

  ฝั่งทะเล coastal, seacoast, seashore, seaside

  ฝั่งแม่น้ำ river bank

  เกยฝั่ง to beach, beached

ฝ
พ
ฟ
ภ
ม
ย
ร
ฤ
ฦ
ล
ว
ศ
ษ
ส
ห
ฬ
อ
ฮ

ก
ข
ค
ฆ
ง
จ
ฉ
ช
ซ
ฌ
ญ
ฎ
ฏ
ฐ
ฑ
ฒ
ณ
ด
ต
ถ
ท
ธ
น
บ
ป
ผ
ฝ

ขึ้นฝั่ง to go ashore

เป็นฝั่งเป็นฝา to be established, be settled down, have a family

ฝัด to winnow

ฝัน to dream; a dream

ฝันกลางวัน to daydream

ฝันถึง to dream of someone

ฝันเป็นตุเป็นตะ to have a realistic dream

ฝันเปียก to have a wet dream

ฝันร้าย to have a nightmare

ฝันลมๆ แล้งๆ empty dream; to build castles in the air

ฝันว่า to dream that

ฝันหวาน to be a dreamer

แก้ฝัน to interpret a dream

เคลิ้มฝัน to be daydreaming, have a reverie

นึกฝัน to imagine, dream (of)

ใฝ่ฝัน see ใฝ่ฝัน หน้า 338

ฝา lid, cover; valve (ฝาหอย); wall

ฝากระดาน wooden wall; Thai house of wood

ฝากั้นห้อง partition, dividing wall

ฝาขัดแตะ mat partition

ฝาครอบ cover

ฝาครอบล้อ hubcap

ฝาจีบ crown cap, crown cork

ฝาชี food cover

ฝาผนัง wall

จิตรกรรมฝาผนัง mural, mural painting

ฝาห้อง wall (of a room)

ฝ่า[1] palm (มือ); sole (เท้า)

ฝ่า[2] to disobey, violate, /act/go/do/ contrary to; to overcome, prevail (against, over), surmount, /go/get/ through; to go against

ฝ่าบาท you (for princes of the rank of Serene Highness (Mom Chao))

ฝ่าฝืน to disobey, violate, contravene, disregard, go against, break

ฝ่าฝืนระเบียบ to break the rules

ฝ่าฟัน to /surmount/overcome/ difficulties

ฝ่ามรสุม to get through a storm, brave a storm

ฝ่าอันตราย to overcome /perils/dangers/

ฝ้า film; clouded; ceiling; melasma

กระจกฝ้า frosted glass, translucent glass, opal glass

เป็นฝ้า clouded; to have a film (of something on it); freckled

ฝาก to deposit; to put under the care of someone, place for safekeeping, entrust (to someone), put something in, hand over (something), leave (with)

ฝากข้อความ to leave a message

ฝากของ to leave something with someone, entrust something to someone

ฝากขาย to sell on consignment, consign; consignment sale

ฝากครรภ์ to sign up for pre-natal care and delivery

ฝากความระลึกถึง Please remember me to..., Give my regards to...

ฝากเงิน to deposit money, make a deposit, put money in the bank

ฝากซื้อ Buy...for me.

ฝากผีฝากไข้ to depend on someone; to look after one in /extremity/old age/

ฝากฝัง to entrust to, place under the care of

ฝากรถ to entrust one's car (to), leave one's car with; to park; parking

ฝากรัก to give one's heart (to), declare one's /love/affection/ for someone, confess one's love, let someone know you love /him/her/

ฝากลวดลาย to make one's mark

ฝากไว้ to leave (something or a thought with someone); consign (to), deposit (with)

ฝากหน่อยนะ Keep an eye on (it, this, her,

etc) for me.

รับฝากของ consignments

รับฝากรถ parking

ฝาง sappanwood

ฝาด[1] astringent

เลือดฝาด health; complexion

อมเลือดอมฝาด healthy-looking, to look healthy

ฝาด[2] as in **ตาฝาด** blind; to be seeing things

ฝาน to slice

ฝาแฝด twin, twins, Siamese twins (ติดกัน)

ฝ่าย side, group, part, party

ฝ่ายขาย sales

ฝ่ายค้าน the opposition

ฝ่ายชาย men, male

ฝ่ายซ้าย the left

ฝ่ายเดียว only; alone; ex parte, one-sided

ฝ่ายใดฝ่ายหนึ่ง either /party/side/

ฝ่ายตรงข้าม the opposition, the other side, the opposite side, opponents

ฝ่ายธุรการ administration

ฝ่ายวิชาการ technical office, studies department, academic administration

ฝ่ายเสนอ affirmative side

ฝ่ายหญิง ladies, female

ฝ่ายหนึ่ง on the one side, of the one part

ทั้งสองฝ่าย both /parties/sides/

อีกฝ่าย the other /party/side/

ฝ้าย cotton

ฝ้ายดิบ raw cotton

ปั่นฝ้าย to spin cotton

ปุยฝ้าย cotton; cotton candy

ฝิ่น opium

ฝิ่นเถื่อน illicit opium

ดอกฝิ่น opium poppy

ติดฝิ่น to be addicted to opium

สูบฝิ่น to smoke opium

ฝี[1] boil, pustule, abscess, carbuncle

ฝีดาษ smallpox

ฝีประคำร้อย tubercular cold abscess

ฝีมะม่วง bubo, mango abscess (lymphogranuloma venerium)

ปลูกฝี to vaccinate, (get) vaccinated, have a vaccination

ฝี[2] skill, ability

ฝีจักร speed, velocity

ฝีตีน see **ฝีเท้า**

ฝีเท้า speed; footstep

ฝีปาก verbal skill; /glib/smooth/ talk

เด็กคนนี้ฝีปากไม่เลว That kid is a good talker.

ตีฝีปาก to be a windbag; loquacious, bombastic, grandiloquent; to use empty words, engage in empty talk, give (someone) a line

ฝีพระหัตถ์ (royal word) see **ฝีมือ**

ฝีพาย oarsman, paddler, rower

ฝีมือ workmanship, craftsmanship; work, handiwork, skill, ability

ฝีไม้ลายมือ ability, capability

ลูกน้องผมคนนี้ เป็นคนมีฝีไม้ลายมือทีเดียว My assistant here is /very capable/a really capable fellow/.

ฝึก to practice, drill; train

ฝึกปรือ well trained

ฝึกฝน to practice

ฝึกสอน to practice teaching

ฝึกหัด to train

วิทยาลัยฝึกหัดครู Teachers' Training College

ฝืด to stick; tight; stiff; hard going, with difficulty

ฝืดคอ hard to swallow

ฝืดเคือง hard up, hard-pressed, short of money, impecunious

ความฝืด friction

ฝืน to disobey; to act contrary (to), do something against (the law, one's will etc); to force oneself

ผ
พ
ฟ
ภ
ม
ย
ร
ฤ
ฤๅ
ล
ว
ศ
ษ
ส
ห
ฬ
อ
ฮ

ฝืนความรู้สึก to go against the grain, distasteful

ฝืนใจ to force oneself (to do something), do something unwillingly, go against the grain

ฝืนธรรมชาติ unnatural; to go against one's nature

ฝืนยิ้ม to force a smile *see* ฝืนยิ้ม *หน้า 398*

ฝุ่น dust; powder

ฝุ่นจับ to be covered with dust, dusty; dust is settling (on something)

ฝุ่นตลบ full of dust; clouds of dust; dust kicked up (by a passing car etc)

ฝุ่นละออง dust, fine dust, particulate matter

ปัดฝุ่น to dust, dust off

ฝูง crowd, group, herd, flock, pack, troop

ฝูงแกะ flock of sheep

ฝูงชน crowd, throng, mob, mass of people

ฝูงนก flock of birds

ฝูงบิน flight

ฝูงปลา /shoal/school/ of fish

ฝูงแพะ /flock/herd/ of goats

ฝูงลิง troop of monkeys

ฝูงวัว herd of cows

เพื่อนฝูง friends

หลงฝูง a stray; to stray

เฝ้า to watch; to tend, take care of; to keep watch, keep guard; to attend, have an audience (with)

เฝ้าไข้ to nurse (someone who is ill)

เฝ้าดู to watch, keep an eye on, keep watch (on, over)

เฝ้าปรนนิบัติ to wait upon, serve

เฝ้ายาม to keep watch

เฝ้าระวัง to guard against, be on the alert (for)

เฝ้าแหน to be in attendance, watch over

การเฝ้าดูผล monitoring

เข้าเฝ้า to have an audience (with royalty)

เฝือก splint; cast

เข้าเฝือก to apply a splint; to put (one's arm, leg etc) in a cast

เฝื่อน queer, off (taste), bitter; to be in bad taste; leave a bad taste in the mouth; disconcerted

แฝก elephant grass

แฝง to hide, conceal, secrete

เคลือบแฝง to explain vaguely; to give a fishy explanation

นามแฝง alias, pseudonym

อำนาจแฝง invisible /power/influence/

แฝด twin, double, coupled, paired

คู่แฝด twin, double

ฝาแฝด twin, twins, Siamese twins (ติดกัน)

ยาแฝด love philter

ใฝ่ to aim (at, for), hope (to), aspire (to); to be concerned with

ใฝ่ใจ to be committed (to), take sides (with); to take an interest in, absorbed in

ใฝ่ฝัน to dream of (being, becoming, going, etc), aspire to, have an ambition to, ambitious (for)

ใฝ่สูง ambitious, to aim high

ฝักใฝ่ to be a supporter (of), side with, be a sympathizer, be pro, be for

ไฝ mole, beauty spot

พก to carry, have on one's person
    พกปืน to carry a gun, have a gun on him
    พกพาอาวุธ to carry a weapon
    พกมีด to carry a knife

พง brush, underbrush; tall grass
    หักร้างถางพง to clear land for farming

พงพี forest, jungle

พงศ์ family, stock, lineage
    พงศ์พันธุ์ member of a family, relation

พงศาวดาร annals, historical record, chronicle

พจน์ word, words, speech; number
    สุนทรพจน์ address, speech, oration

พจนานุกรม dictionary
    พจนานุกรมศาสตร์ lexicography

พญา king, ruler; lord, Phya; leader, chief
    พญาช้าง great elephant, lordly elephant, king elephant
    พญามาร Mara, the Evil One

ฯพณฯ H.E. (His Excellency)
    ฯพณฯ นายกรัฐมนตรี H.E. the Prime Minister

พณิชย์ *see* **พาณิชย์** *หน้า 350*

พ.ท. Lt. Col.

พธู woman, beauty; beloved

พ่น[1] to spray, squirt, emit, spit
    พ่นควัน to smoke, emit /smoke/exhaust/ fumes/
    พ่นน้ำ to squirt water
    พ่นน้ำลาย to spit (at, in, out)
    พ่นพิษ to be venomous
    พ่นไฟ to breath fire; to be a blowtorch
    พ่นสี to spray paint

พ่น[2] to blow, chatter
    อย่าพ่นนักเลย ขี้เกียจฟัง /Cut the blowing!/ Go easy on the chatter./ I don't want to listen.

พ้น to go beyond, pass, pass by, get /by/ through/, clear (an obstacle); to escape
    พ้นกำหนด late, out of time, after the due date, after the appointed time
    พ้นเคราะห์ *see* **พ้นเคราะห์** *หน้า 98*
    พ้นตา out of sight
    พ้นภัย out of danger
    พ้นวิสัย beyond one, impossible (for); unfeasible
    พ้นเวลา out of time, late; after a certain time; to exceed a time limit
    พ้นสมัย old fashioned, out of date, antiquated
    พ้นหูพ้นตา to get out of my sight
    พ้นอันตราย out of danger
    ไปให้พ้น Get out!, Get out of my sight!
    รอดพ้น to be saved (from)
        ความรอดพ้น salvation
    หลุดพ้น to be free (of, from), be released (from), escape (from), get out (of)

พนม[1] mountain

พนม[2] to press the hands together in respect

พนัก backrest
    พนักเก้าอี้ back of a chair

พนักงาน official, officer, agent *(US)*, employee, /man/person/ in charge (of)
    พนักงานขับรถ driver, chauffeur
    พนักงานขาย salesperson, salesclerk
    พนักงานทำความสะอาด cleaning person, sweeper
    พนักงานโทรศัพท์ operator
    พนักงานบริการ service /personnel/person/
    พนักงานพิมพ์ดีด typist
    พนักงานเสิร์ฟ waiter(*ชาย*), waitress(*หญิง*)
    เจ้าพนักงาน officer, official in charge (of), competent officer

พนัน to gamble, wager, bet
    พนันกันไหม You want to bet?
    พนันขันต่อ gambling
    การพนัน gambling
    นักการพนัน gambler
    บ่อนการพนัน gambling den, casino

พ ฟ ภ ม ย ร ฤ ฦ ล ว ศ ษ ส ห ฬ อ ฮ

เล่นการพนัน to gamble

พเนจร wandering, to wander

พบ to meet, encounter, come upon; to see, find

    พบกัน to meet

    พบจุดจบ to meet (one's) end

    พบปะ to meet, get together

    พบพาน to meet, see; to come across, come upon, run into

    พบว่า to find, discover, learn, see

    พบหน้า to see somebody

    ขุดพบ to dig up, unearth, make a find by /digging/excavating/

    เข้าพบ to meet, see, have a meeting (with)

    ค้นพบ to discover, find; to uncover, find out

    ไปพบ to go to /see/meet/, see, meet

พม่า Burmese; Burma, Myanmar

พยศ fractious

พยัก to nod

    พยักเยิด to nod in agreement

    พยักหน้า to nod (in assent)

พยัญชนะ consonant, letter of the alphabet

พยับ gloomy weather

    พยับแดด haze, hazy

    พยับฝน overcast, rainy weather

พยากรณ์ to predict, forecast, foretell, prognosticate, prophesy

พยากรณ์อากาศ (to give a) weather forecast, to forecast the weather

พยางค์ syllable

    พยางค์เดียว monosyllabic, one syllable

    สองพยางค์ bisyllabic, two syllables

    สามพยางค์ trisyllabic

    หลายพยางค์ multisyllabic

พยาธิ sickness, disease; patho-; parasite, worm

    พยาธิตัวแบน flatworm

    พยาธิปากขอ hookworm

    พยาธิวิทยา pathology

    นักพยาธิวิทยา pathologist

    โรคาพยาธิ sickness, disease

พยาน witness; evidence

    พยานเท็จ /perjured/false/ witness

    พยานบอกเล่า hearsay evidence

    พยานปากเอก principal witness

    พยานผู้เชี่ยวชาญ expert witness

    พยานรัก child, children

    พยานหลักฐาน evidence

    พยานเอก principal witness

    พยานเอกสาร documentary evidence

    ประจักษ์พยาน eyewitness

    วัตถุพยาน physical evidence

    สักขีพยาน witness

พยาบาท to be vengeful, vindictive

    ความพยาบาท illwill, malice; revenge, vengeance; vindictiveness, vengefulness; vendetta

    ถือพยาบาท to bear a grudge (against); be vindictive

    ผูกพยาบาท vindictive, vengeful, to harbor resentment, be bent on revenge

พยาบาล to nurse, take care of, tend the sick

    นางพยาบาล nurse

    บุรุษพยาบาล male nurse

    ปฐมพยาบาล first aid

    รถพยาบาล ambulance

    โรงพยาบาล hospital

พยายาม to try, make an effort (to), endeavor, strive (to), attempt (to)

    ความพยายาม effort(s), endeavor, attempt, try; perseverance

พยุง to support, hold up, sustain; to maintain, keep (something) going, take care of

พร blessing; benediction; good wishes, congratulations

    พรปีใหม่ New Year's greeting

    พรสวรรค์ gift, talent

    ให้พร to bless, give one's /blessings/good

wishes/congratulations/

พรต *as in* **นักพรต** an ascetic, recluse, a religious

พ.ร.บ. act

พรม[1] carpet, rug

พรมน้ำมัน linoleum

ไหมพรม knitting /wool/yarn/

พรม[2] to sprinkle (with)

พรมน้ำมนต์ to asperge, sprinkle with holy water

พรมแดน frontier, boundary

พรรค party, group

พรรคการเมือง political party

พรรคพวก group, followers; friends, band, gang

พรรค์ kind, sort (of)

ผู้หญิงพรรค์นั้น that kind of woman

พรรณ complexion; kind, type (of)

พรรณไม้ plants, trees; kind of tree

ผิวพรรณ complexion, skin

พรรณนา to describe, elaborate, narrate

พรรษา rainy season; Rainy Season Retreat, Buddhist Lent; year

เข้าพรรษา to /enter/begin/ the Rainy Season Retreat/Buddhist Lent/

ออกพรรษา to end the /Rainy Season Retreat/ Buddhist Lent/

พรวด precipitately, all of a sudden, headlong

พรวดๆ at full tilt, headlong

พรวดเดียว in a jiffy

พรวดพราด abruptly, precipitately, in great haste

เผ่นพรวด to clear out at top speed

พรวน[1] to loosen the soil, harrow, cultivate

เครื่องพรวนดิน harrow

รดน้ำพรวนดิน to cultivate the soil

พรวน[2] troop (of)

ตามมาเป็นพรวน to troop after

พรหม Brahma; sublime

พรหมจรรย์ chastity; holy life

เสียพรหมจรรย์ to lose one's /virginity/ chastity/, be deflowered

พรหมจารี virginity, chastity

สาวพรหมจารี virgin, chaste maiden

พรหมลิขิต to be predestined, preordained; destiny, fate; divine providence

ทุกอย่างเป็นไปตามพรหมลิขิต Everything is /predestined/preordained/.

พรหมวิหาร the sublime states of mind: loving kindness, compassion, sympathy, and equanimity

พร่อง lacking, low (on, in); to be short (by), missing

พร่องไขมัน low-fat

พร้อม ready, set; prepared; together, at the same time

พร้อมกัน together, at the same time, simultaneously

พร้อมกันนี้ at this time

พร้อมๆ กัน at one and the same time, all together

พร้อมกับ, พร้อมด้วย, พร้อมทั้ง together with, including

พร้อมใจ all together, in accord, of one accord, in concert

พร้อมที่จะ ready to, prepared to, happy to

พร้อมพรัก in unison, in harmony, all together; rich in, everything (for)

พร้อมพรั่ง *see* **พร้อมพรัก**

พร้อมเพรียง *see* **พร้อมพรัก**

พร้อมมูล in full, with everything, complete (with)

พร้อมแล้ว ready, all set

พร้อมหน้ากัน everyone, all (here), all together

ความพร้อม preparedness

เตรียมพร้อม to be prepared, ready, on the alert; ready for action, in a state of preparedness

พร้อย highly figured, overly designed

พ
ฟ
ภ
ม
ย
ร
ฤ
ฦ
ล
ว
ศ
ษ
ส
ห
ฬ
อ
ฮ

ลายพร้อย a busy design, fancy figuration, highly figured pattern

พระ monk, priest; title for kings or princes; hero in a play; Phra, a royal service title above "Luang"; prefix indicating sanctity or royal connection; a small Buddha image

พระคลังข้างที่ privy purse

พระคุณ beneficence, grace

    ขอบพระคุณ Thank you.

พระคุณเจ้า you, second personal pronoun used for a highly respected monk

พระเคราะห์ planet

พระเครื่อง a small Buddha image used as an amulet; (เครื่องเสวย) food *(royal word)*

พระจันทร์ the moon

พระเจดีย์ stupa, chedi

พระเจ้า god, deity, lord; title for kings

    พระเจ้าอยู่หัว king, His Majesty

พระเดชพระคุณ /your/his/ grace; /your/his/ reverence

พระทัย heart, mind

พระที่นั่ง throne; throne hall; palace

    หน้าพระที่นั่ง in the royal presence

พระนคร capital city

พระนอน reclining Buddha

พระนาง Her Majesty; Her Royal Highness; princess

    พระนางเจ้า queen

พระบรมธาตุ relic of the Buddha

พระบรมมหาราชวัง The Grand Palace

พระบรมราชโองการ royal command

พระบรมราชานุญาต by appointment of His Majesty

พระบรมราชินี the Queen

พระบรมวงศานุวงศ์ the Royal Family

พระบรมศพ royal remains

พระปรมาภิไธย royal signature; (in the) name of the king

พระประธาน principal Buddha image in a temple

พระปรางค์ stupa

พระปรีชาญาณ royal wisdom, intelligence

พระเป็นเจ้า god

พระผู้เป็นเจ้า god

พระพาย wind

พระพุทธเจ้า the Buddha

พระพุทธเจ้าข้า formula of assent used in speaking with a king, like "Yes, Your Majesty."

พระพุทธปฏิมากร Buddha image

พระพุทธรูป /figure/statue/sculpture/image/ of the Buddha

พระพุทธไสยาสน์ reclining Buddha

พระเพลิง fire

พระโพธิสัตว์ bodhisattva

พระภิกษุ bhikku, Buddhist monk

พระภูมิ guardian spirit

    พระภูมิเจ้าที่ guardian spirit of the land

พระมหากรุณาธิคุณ His Majesty's /kindness/ graciousness/

พระยา Phya, a royal service title above "Phra"

พระรัตนตรัย the Triple Gem

พระราชกฤษฎีกา royal decree

พระราชกำหนด royal enactment

พระราชฐาน palace; royal premises

พระราชดำรัส royal words

พระราชบัญชา royal command

พระราชบัญญัติ act

พระราชลัญจกร royal seal

พระราชวินิจฉัย royal decision

พระราชสวามี Prince Consort

พระราชสำนัก court

พระราชสาส์น king's letter, royal letter, royal message

พระราชเสาวนีย์ the queen's words

พระราชหฤทัย royal mind; royal heart; royal

/wish/desire/

พระราชหัตถเลขา royal /missive/writing/

พระราชูปถัมภ์ royal patronage

พระศรีรัตนตรัย The Triple Gem

พระสงฆ์ the Buddhist Order, Sangha

พระองค์ a numerical designation for Buddhas, god, kings and princes; he

พระอาทิตย์ the sun

พระเอก male lead, leading actor, star, hero

พรักพร้อม assembled; ready, prepared

พรั่งพร้อม rich in, replete with

พรั่งพรู to pour forth; to throng into, crowd into

พรั่น scared, afraid

พรั่นพรึง terrified

พร่า to ruin, waste, ravage; diffused, blurred (vision), indistinct

พร่ามัว filmed over, clouded over, blurred, indistinct

พร่าเวลา to waste time

ตาพร่า blurred /vision/sight/

เสียงพร่า husky voice, hoarse /voice/ sound/; out of tune, indistinct

พร้า machete

มีดพร้า machete

พราก to take (someone) away

พรากผู้เยาว์ child abduction

พลัดพราก *see* **พลัดพราก** *หน้า 345*

ไหลพราก copious flow (of tears etc)

พราง to disguise, mask, dissemble, camouflage

พรางตา to camouflage

พรางแสง to shield a light

หลุมพราง pitfall, trap

    ตกหลุมพราง to fall into a trap

พราน hunter

พรานล่าผู้หญิง wolf, womanizer

นายพราน hunter

พราย elf; air bubbles; sparkling, glittering, brilliant; luminous

พรายทะเล Saint Elmo's fire

พรายน้ำ luminescence, phosphorescence

พรายแพรว glittering sparkling, shining, dazzling

พราว glossy, glittering; full of

พราวแพรว glittering, shining, brilliant, dazzling

พราหมณ์ Brahman

พรำ to drizzle, fall lightly

ฝนพรำ light shower, a drizzle; to drizzle

พร่ำ continually, repeatedly; frequently, often

พร่ำเพรื่อ all the time, continually, repetitious, over and over again, the same old thing, ad nauseum

พร่ำสอน to exhort; to teach well

พริก chili, hot pepper, capsicum

พริกกับเกลือ a condiment of chili and salt

พริกขิง a seasoning of chili and ginger

พริกขี้หนู bird pepper; tiny but powerful

พริกชี้ฟ้า goat pepper

พริกเทศ imported long dried pepper

พริกไทย pepper, black pepper

พริกหยวก green pepper, red pepper, sweet pepper

พริกแห้ง dried chili

ถึงพริกถึงขิง hot, peppery

น้ำพริก chili sauce

พริ้ง gorgeously, dazzlingly

พริ้งพราย dazzling

พริ้งเพริศ resplendent

เพราะพริ้ง beautiful, sweet, melodious

สวยพริ้ง dazzlingly beautiful, gorgeous, stunning

พริบ *as in* **ไหวพริบ** quick, adroit, sharp-witted

พริบตา to blink, wink

    ชั่วพริบตา in a wink, in an instant

พริ้ม sweet

พริ้มพราย sweetly captivating

พริ้มเพรา charming, bewitching, captivating

พ
ฟ
ภ
ม
ย
ร
ฤ
ฤๅ
ล
ว
ศ
ษ
ส
ห
ฬ
อ
ฮ

ก
ข
ค
ฆ
ง
จ
ฉ
ช
ซ
ฌ
ญ
ฎ
ฏ
ฐ
ฑ
ฒ
ณ
ด
ต
ถ
ท
ธ
น
บ
ป
ผ
ฝ
พ

นอนหลับตาพริ้ม to sleep sweetly

พรึบ suddenly; quickly, swiftly

ไฟลุกพรึบ the flame(s) shot up, to blaze up

พรืด scraping; all over, a lot of

พรืดๆ /dragging/scraping/ sound

พรุ่ง tomorrow

ผัดวันประกันพรุ่ง to procrastinate, be dilatory, put (something) off

พรุ่งนี้ tomorrow

พรุ่งนี้เช้า tomorrow morning

พรุ่งนี้เย็น tomorrow evening

พรุน full of holes, holed, perforated

พรู in great numbers; flowing

พฤกษ์ plant; tree

พฤกษชาติ plants, trees; vegetable king-dom

พฤกษศาสตร์ botany

พฤกษา tree

พฤติ conduct, behavior, action, activity

พฤติกรรม action, behavior; conduct

พฤติการณ์ circumstances, course of /events/conduct/

ในพฤติการณ์เช่นนั้น under the circum-stances

พฤตินัย de facto, in fact

พฤศจิกายน November

พฤษภาคม May

พฤหัสบดี Jupiter; Thursday

พล strength, force, power; private, soldier; forces, troops; ordinary, general

พลการ force, strength

โดยพลการ without /authorization/ authority/, unauthorized, without right; officiously; on one's own, willfully, by force

พลความ unimportant matter, minutiae, trivialities

พลตระเวน patrolman

พลตำรวจ police private, policeman, police

constable

พลทหาร private

พลโท lieutenant general

พลเมือง population, inhabitants, people; citizen

พลร่ม paratrooper, paratroops

พลเรือตรี rear admiral

พลเรือน civilian; civil

ข้าราชการพลเรือน civil servant, civil official

พลศึกษา physical education

พลอากาศ air force general

พลเอก general

กองพล division

ขุนพล /military/army/ commander, general

จอมพล field marshal

นายพล general

รี้พล army, troops, armed forces

พลบ dusk

พลบค่ำ dusk, just before dark

พลอง boy scout staff

พลอด to talk

พลอดรัก to flirt (with), court, make love (to), romance

พลอย[1] gem, precious stone, jewel

เพชรพลอย gems, gemstones, precious stones, jewels

พลอย[2] to join, go along (with)

เจ้าก็พลอยเป็นกะเขาด้วยรึ You too?

พลอยติด to get embroiled

พลอยฟ้าพลอยฝน to get sucked in, get mixed up in

ผลพลอยได้ by-product, incidental benefit

พล่อย thoughtlessly, heedlessly

พูดพล่อยๆ to /speak/say/ thoughtlessly, speak without thinking

อย่าพูดพล่อยๆ นะ Mind what you say!

พละ[1] strength, energy; force; power

พละ[2] Phys. Ed., physical education

พลั่ก to spurt, gush; punching sound

    ออกพลั่กๆ to gush out, spurt (out, forth)

พลัง energy; power, force, strength

    พลังงาน energy

        พลังงานปรมาณู atomic energy

    มีพลังแรง high-powered, powerful

    เสริมพลัง tonic, invigorating

พลั้ง to blunder, make a mistake

    พลั้งปาก to make a slip, blunder

    พลั้งเผลอ by accident, by mistake

พลัด to fall from, to slip off; to go astray, stray from

    พลัดกัน to get lost, get separated

    พลัดคู่ to lose one's mate, be separated from one's mate

    พลัดตก to fall down (from)

    พลัดถิ่น displaced

        คนพลัดถิ่น displaced person

        รัฐบาลพลัดถิ่น government in exile

    พลัดพราก to be parted (from), go away (from), be separated (from), taken (from)

พลัน swiftly, rapidly, instantly, immediately, suddenly; abruptly

    ฉับพลัน abruptly, all of a sudden; promptly, at once

    เฉียบพลัน acute, sudden

    เร็วพลัน quickly, at top speed

พลับพลา royal pavilion

พลั่ว shovel, spade

พล่า savory raw /meat/shrimp/ salad

พลาง at the same time, simultaneously, while, meanwhile, in the meantime

    พูดพลางเดินพลาง to talk and walk, talk while walking

    ไปพลางก่อน for the time being, in the meantime, meanwhile,

    ไปพลางๆ in the meantime, for the time being

พลาด make a mistake, err, be inaccurate, slip; to trip, make a false step; to fall wide of the mark, miss

    พลาดจังหวะ to miss one's timing, lose an opportunity

    พลาดท่า to muff (something), bungle; to miss the chance (to do something), lose the opportunity; to be taken in (by)

    พลาดพลั้ง to make a /mistake/misstep/

    พลาดเวลา to miss the time

    พลาดโอกาส to miss an opportunity, lose the chance (to)

    ผิดพลาด to make a mistake, err

        ความผิดพลาด mistake, error

พล่าน in confusion, in disorder

    เดือดพล่าน boiling vigorously; furious, enraged, boiling mad

    พลุกพล่าน crowded (with), swarming (with), teeming (with), congested, busy

    วิ่งพล่าน to run around /in confusion/ wildly/, to run helter-skelter

พล่าม endlessly, incessantly, tediously

    พูดพล่าม to prattle, talk nonsense, be garrulous, gabble

พลาสติก plastic

พลิก to turn over

    พลิกตัวตื่น to wake up

    พลิกแผ่นดิน to /overturn/overthrow/ a government; (to look) high and low, leave no stone unturned

    พลิกพลิ้ว to dodge artfully

    พลิกแพลง to modify, vary, make changes, use variations; to twist, contort; wily, unprincipled

    พลิกศพ to determine the cause of death, make a postmortem (examination)

พลิ้ว to flap

    บิดพลิ้ว to fail to act, put off doing something

พลี worship, religious offering; to sacrifice

    พลีกรรม religious offering

พ
ฟ
ภ
ม
ย
ร
ฤ
ฦ
ล
ว
ศ
ษ
ส
ห
ฬ
อ
ฮ

พลีชีพ to sacrifice one's life

พลุ skyrocket, signal rocket, flare; Roman candle

พลุกพล่าน crowded (with), swarming (with), teeming (with), congested, busy

พลุ่ง furiously, vigorously; to roil

เดือดพลุ่ง to boil /vigorously/furiously/

พลุ้ย protruding, bulging

พุงพลุ้ย pot belly, fat tummy, fat-bellied, paunchy

พลู betel, betelvine

หมากพลู prepared betel, betel and betel nut

พวก group, party, band, company, gang; people; things

พวกพ้อง relatives; friends, companions, colleagues

พวกเรา we, us, we all, all of us

เล่นพรรคเลือกพวก to play favorites, practice favoritism, be partial to one's own people

พวง bunch, cluster

พวงกุญแจ key ring; bunch of keys

พวงมาลัย garland; steering wheel

พวงมาลา garland, string of flowers, wreath

พวงหรีด wreath

เป็นพวง bunch, cluster (of), in /bunches/ clusters/

แก้มเป็นพวง rounded cheeks, nice chubby cheeks

พ่วง to attach; to be attached; to trail, trailing

พ่วงท้าย added at the end, added on, appended

รถพ่วง trailer

เรือพ่วง barge; children

พ่วงพี stout, sturdy

พวย spout; to pour out, spout

พวยกา spout

พวยพุ่ง to stream out, shoot /forth/out/, pour out

รัศมีพวยพุ่ง beam of light, radiance

พ.ศ. B.E. (abbr. of Buddhist Era)

พสกนิกร citizens, subjects, people

พสุธา earth

ดิ่งพสุธา to plummet to earth; parachuting, to parachute jump

พหูพจน์ plural

พหูสูต learned

พอ enough, sufficient, adequate; to suffice; just; on

พอกันที to have had enough (of someone or something), enough is enough

พอๆ กัน on a par, just about the same

พอกับความต้องการ sufficient to meet the demand, as much as one needs, adequate

พอควร enough, moderately, reasonably
กินแต่พอควร ชีวิตจะสบาย Eat moderately, live happily.

พอจะ can, to be able (to); just when

พอจะทำได้ to be able to do something, can do

พอใจ satisfied, happy (with)

เป็นที่พอใจ satisfactory, to one's satisfaction

พอใช้ fair, reasonable

ดีพอใช้ fairly good, fair

พอดี just (at, on, in), just right; just enough; just in time; to fit well

ไม่พอดี ill-fitting, not right

พอดีพอร้าย could be

พอดู pretty; rather, fairly, quite

ไกลพอดู /pretty/rather/fairly/ far off

พอได้ when, on

พอได้ยินว่า /when/on/ hearing (that)

พอตัว adequate, suitable, about right; fairly

พอถึง on arriving, on arrival, on getting there

พอทำเนา adequate

พอที enough, lay off, hold it

พอประมาณ reasonable, moderate, reasonable amount (of), some

พอเป็นพิธี perfunctory, token, cursory, for show; formal, for form's sake

พอเพียง enough, sufficent, adequate

พอฟัดพอเหวี่ยง well-matched, about even

พอแรง quite, very

พอแล้ว enough, stop; Stop it!

พอสถานประมาณ reasonable

พอสบาย in reasonable comfort

พอสมควร reasonable, moderate

พอสิ้น at the /close/end/ (of), just as

พอหอมปากหอมคอ enough to get a taste (of something)

พอเหมาะ good, just right; appropriate

พออยู่พอกิน enough to get by

พออายุได้ on reaching the age of, at the age of, when (he was three) years old

ไม่พอ insufficient, not enough, inadequate

พ่อ father, dad, daddy

พ่อขุน king, prince

พ่อครัว cook, chef

พ่อค้า merchant, businessman, dealer, trader, tradesman, shopkeeper, storekeeper

> **พ่อค้าเพชรพลอย** jeweller
>
> **พ่อค้าม้า** horse dealer
>
> **พ่อค้าย่อย** petty tradesman, small merchant, retailer
>
> **พ่อค้าเร่** hawker, peddler
>
> **พ่อค้าหมู** pork seller, butcher
>
> **พ่อค้าเหมา** wholesaler

พ่อคุณ a title of entreaty; my good man; for God's sake

พ่อตา father-in-law

พ่อทูนหัว godfather

พ่อบ้าน head of the family, head of the house; my husband

พ่อมด sorceror, wizard

พ่อม่าย widower

พ่อเมือง governor

พ่อแม่ parents

พ่อเลี้ยง stepfather, foster father; provincial personage, squire

พ่อสื่อ matchmaker

พ่อหนุ่ม young man, my boy, lad

พอก to plaster; apply (something) to, daub; to coat (with); to pile up, swollen

> **พอกพูน** to pile up, augment, accumulate
>
> **พอกหนี้** to /pile up/accumulate/ debts
>
> **คอพอก** goiter

พอง to swell, blister; swollen, inflated, raised; haughty, stuck-up, conceited, puffed up

> **พองขน** bristling; haughty, puffed up
>
> **พองตัว** to expand, be enlarged
>
> **ข้าวพอง** crispy rice cake
>
> **ดินสอพอง** white clay body-powder in cake or pellet form; white clay filler
>
> **ตาพอง** popping eyes
>
> **เป็นพุพอง** inflamed, abscessed

พ้อง synonymous; consistent, consonant

> **พ้องกัน** to rhyme; to be the same
>
> **พ้องพาน** to confront; to meet, come upon
>
> **เห็นพ้อง** to agree, go along, subscribe to, think the same

พะงาบ to gasp

พะเน้าพะนอ to flatter, adulate, fawn on

พะเนิน sledge hammer; towering

> **พะเนินเทินทึก** enormous pile
>
> **กองเป็นพะเนิน** towering pile, pile of (work, books, etc)

พะแนง a thick curry without vegetables

พะยูน manatee, dugong

พะเยิบพะยาบ to flap, flapping

พะรุงพะรัง messy; a mess of

> **หอบของพะรุงพะรัง** to carry a whole mess of stuff

พะวง to be anxious, be worried about, worry

ก
ข
ค
ฆ
ง
จ
ฉ
ช
ซ
ฌ
ญ
ฎ
ฏ
ฐ
ฑ
ฒ
ณ
ด
ต
ถ
ท
ธ
น
บ
ป
ผ
ฝ
พ

(about); edgy

พะวงถึง to be concerned (about)

พะวักพะวน perplexed, in a quandary, in a state of confusion

พะว้าพะวัง distraught, overwrought, apprehensive, in a turmoil

พะอืดพะอม hard to deal with; in a difficult situation, squeamish (about); to feel squeamish

พัก to stay (at, over); to rest, take a rest, take a break, stop for a while; a time, sometime

พักแถว at ease

พักผ่อน to rest, take a rest, take a vacation

พักพิง to stay, take shelter

พักฟื้น to convalesce

พักรบ truce

พักราชการ to be suspended from service

พักแรม to stay overnight, spend the night (with, at, in), stay over

พักสมอง to take a break, rest one's brains, have a diversion

พักหนึ่ง for a while

พักอยู่กับ to stay with

ที่พัก resting place; residence, home, house, place where one is staying

บ้านพัก house, residence, rest house, housing

บ้านพักรับรอง guest house

เป็นพักๆ sporadically, occasionally, from time to time, in fits and starts

โรงพัก police station

ลาพัก to take leave

สักพัก for a while

หยุดพัก to take a break, stop for a rest; intermission

ห้องพัก room

หอพัก dormitory, dorm, hostel

พักตร์ face

พัง ^{1} broken down, tumbled down, broken,

collapsed, destroyed, in ruins, ruined

พังเข้าไป to force open, break open

พังทลาย to fall apart, be destroyed, demolished

พังบ้าน to wreck a house

พังประตู to force open the door, break down the door

พังราบ to be razed to the ground

พังหมด to be completely destroyed, a total loss

ผุพัง dilapidated; falling to pieces, crumbling; in a state of decay, in ruins

พัง ^{2} *as in* **ช้างพัง** cow elephant, female elephant

พังผืด membrane, fascia

พังพอน mongoose

พังพาบ face down, prone

นอนพังพาบ to lie /prone/ on one's stomach/ face down/

พังเพย *as in* **คำพังเพย** adage, saying, aphorism maxim

พัฒนา to develop, advance, progress, evolve, improve

พัฒนากร development officer

พัฒนาการ development

พัด fan; to fan; to blow

พัดกระโชก to be gusty

พัดขนนก feather fan

พัดฉิว to blow steadily

ลมพัดฉิว A steady breeze is blowing.

พัดโบก royal longhandled fan

พัดลม electric fan

ใบพัด fan blade, propellor, propellor blade

รำพัด to play cards; fan dance

ลมพัด wind, breeze, windy; The /wind/ breeze/ is blowing.

พัทธสีมา the consecrated precinct of a temple; temple marker

พัน ^{1} thousand; colonel, lieutenant colonel, major

พันจ่า warrant officer
พันตรี major
พันโท lieutenant colonel
พันปี royal mother
พันเอก colonel
กองพัน battalion
นายพันตรี major

พัน[2] to wind around, wrap around, bind
พันพัว to be involved, get mixed up (with, in)
เกี่ยวพัน to be involved (with)
ผ้าพันคอ shawl, scarf, muffler, neckerchief
ผ้าพันแผล bandage
ผูกพัน see **ผูกพัน** หน้า 331

พันตู to be engaged in a pitched battle
พันทาง hybrid, cross-bred
พันธะ obligation
ไม่มีพันธะ to have no family; to be without obligations
ไม่มีพันธะที่จะ not obliged to

พันธกรณี obligation
พันธนาการ imprisonment
เครื่องพันธนาการ fetters, shackles

พันธบัตร bond
พันธุ-, พันธุ์ species; breeding stock; seeds, seedlings, nursery plants; lineage, family, family stock; inherited
พันธุกรรม inherited, hereditary
พันธุ์ผสม hybrid, mixed breed, mongrel
ผสมพันธุ์ to breed, reproduce; to mate
สืบพันธุ์ to have offspring, reproduce, procreate; to inherit
สูญพันธุ์ extinct
หมดพันธุ์ extinct, to die out

พับ to fold, double over, roll up; to write off
พับแขนเสื้อ to roll up one's sleeves
พับจดหมาย to fold a letter
พับได้ folding
พับไป to call (something) quits; to col-

lapse; no claims (for costs, expenses etc), claims (for costs) disallowed
พับเพียบ to sit on the floor with legs tucked back to one side
ข้อพับ joint
คอพับ (with a) turned-down collar
บานพับ hinge
ผ้าเป็นพับ bolt of /cloth/material/
มีดพับ pocket knife, jack knife
ล้มพับ to collapse

พัลวัน entangled, tangled up with
พัลวันพัลเก tangled together, tangling in disorder

พัวพัน related (to), connected (with); involved (with, in), implicated, linked (to)

พัวะ slapping sound
ตบพัวะ to slap

พัศดี warden, jailer, gaoler

พัสดุ supplies, things, stores; land
พัสดุไปรษณีย์ parcel post
คลังพัสดุ storeroom, storehouse, warehouse
บัญชีพัสดุ inventory, stock account
ส่งทางพัสดุ to mail parcel post

พัสตร์ cloth, material

พัสถาน possessions, property
สมบัติพัสถาน wealth, riches, possessions, property

พา to take, lead, conduct; to guide
พากลับบ้าน to take (someone) home
พากัน to do (something) together, join in, all
พากันหัวเราะ they all laughed, joined in laughing, The laughing was contagious.
พาซื่อ to take (someone) in, be taken in; naive, innocent, unsuspecting
พาไปดูหนัง to take (someone) to the movies
พาไปเที่ยว to take (someone) out

พ
ฟ
ภ
ม
ย
ร
ฤ
ฤๅ
ล
ว
ศ
ษ
ส
ห
ฬ
อ
ฮ

นำพา to care (about), be concerned (about), pay attention (to), take care (of)

ลักพา to elope; to kidnap

พากเพียร to apply oneself (to), persevere (in); persevering, industrious, diligent, unflagging

พากย์ version, narration, narrative

พากย์โขน recitative accompanying a traditional masked play

พากย์ไทย Thai version

พากย์หนัง to dub a /film/movie/motion picture/

ผู้พากย์ film dubber

พาชี horse

พาณิช merchant, trader, businessman

พาณิชย์ commercial; commerce, trade, business

กระทรวงพาณิชย์ Ministry of Commerce

พาด rest on, lean (on, against), hang on

พาดบ่า to throw over the shoulder, wear over the shoulder

พาดพิง to refer (to), involve, implicate, allude (to); to refer (to someone) in a derogatory way, impugn

พาดหัว headline

พาน[1] footed tray

พาน[2] on the verge of, almost, going to, about to

พานจะเป็นลม about to faint, on the verge of fainting, almost fainted, to feel dizzy

พาน[3] as in **แตกพาน** to reach puberty, at puberty

พาน[4] as in **พบพาน** to see, meet; to come across, come upon, run into

พานท้ายปืน stock

พาย paddle

พายเรือ to paddle (a boat), row

พายเรือในอ่าง to get nowhere

ฝีพาย oarsman, paddler, rower

ไม้พาย paddle, oar

เรือพาย paddle boat

พ่าย as in **พ่ายแพ้** to be defeated, vanquished, beaten, lose, lose out

พายัพ northwest

พายุ storm

พายุจัด heavy storm, tempest, very stormy

พายุโซนร้อน tropical storm

พายุฝน rainstorm

พายุฟ้าคะนอง thunderstorm

พายุหมุน cyclone, tornado

พายุหิมะ snowstorm

กินเป็นพายุ voracious, to eat up a storm

ขับเป็นพายุบุแคม to drive like wildfire

ลมพายุ windstorm

พารา[1] city

พารา[2] as in **ยางพารา** Para rubber

พาราโบลา parabola

พาล[1] bad, troublemaking, mean; wicked, vicious

คนพาล a rowdy, bully, tough, bad guy

อันธพาล bad guy, ruffian see **อันธพาล** หน้า 566

พาล[2] to /stir up/make/ trouble, find fault

พาลหาเรื่อง to look for trouble; to bully

อย่าพาลหาเรื่อง Watch your words., Cut it out., Are you looking for trouble or something?, Get off my back.

พาโล to make a baseless accusation; to pull a tantrum (to get something)

พาหนะ vehicle, carrier, means of transport, conveyance

ยานพาหนะ vehicle, conveyance, carrier

สัตว์พาหนะ riding animal, draft animal, beast of burden

พาหะ, พาหะของโรค carrier, vector

พำนัก to reside, stay, dwell

พำนักอาศัย to reside

ที่พำนัก residence, dwelling, lodging, where one is /staying/living/, domicile

พิกล unusual, peculiar, not normal, queer, odd,

strange, funny

พิกลพิการ having a physical defect, handicap

เงียบพิกล strangely quiet

ท่าทางพิกล something /not quite right/ funny/ about someone; odd

พิกัด schedule

พิกัดอัตรา tariff

พิกัดอัตราภาษีศุลกากร customs tariff

ของต้องพิกัด dutiable /goods/article/

พิการ crippled; defective; disabled

คนพิการ /handicapped/disabled/crippled/ person, a cripple

พิเคราะห์ to consider, examine, analyse, scrutinize, study

พิฆาต to kill, slay, destroy

เรือพิฆาต destroyer

พิง to lean against, lean on; to place against

พิจารณา to consider, think about, examine; consideration, investigation; trial

พิจารณาคดี to try a case

พิจารณาเห็นว่า in one's opinion; to understand, find

โดยพิจารณาว่า considering

รับไว้พิจารณา under consideration, to take into consideration

เสนอมาเพื่อโปรดพิจารณา for (your) consideration

พิชิต to conquer, vanquish, defeat, subdue

พิณ one stringed instrument with a gourd as a resonator; harp, lyre

พิณพาทย์ classical Thai orchestra

พิถีพิถัน careful, meticulous, particular, painstaking, fastidious

พิทักษ์ to protect; watch over, care for, guard

พิทักษ์ทรัพย์ to place property in receivership

พิทักษ์รักษา to safeguard

ผู้พิทักษ์สันติราษฎร์ police, protector of the people

พิธี ceremony, rite, ritual; formality

พิธีกร master of ceremonies, host

พิธีกรรม ceremony, service, rite, ritual

พิธีการ protocol

พิธีโกนจุก topknot-cutting ceremony

พิธีขึ้นบ้านใหม่ house-warming ceremony

พิธีเฉลิมฉลอง celebration

พิธีฌาปนกิจ funeral /service/ceremony/ rites/

พิธีแต่งงาน see **พิธีสมรส**

พิธีบวช ordination

พิธีฝังศพ funeral, funeral service

พิธีรีตอง ceremony, formalities; fuss

พิธีสมรส wedding, wedding ceremony

พิธีสวด prayer service

พิธีสาร protocol

งานพิธี ceremony, official function

ประกอบพิธี to perform a ceremony

พระราชพิธี royal ceremony

พอเป็นพิธี perfunctory, token, cursory, for show; formal, for form's sake

พิโธ่, พิโธ่เอ๋ย oh!, oh dear; gee, by golly; damn, jeez

เห็นคุยว่าเก่งอย่างโน้นอย่างนี้ ที่แท้ก็แค่นี้เอง พิโธ่เอ๋ย For someone who talks so big, this is damn little. Jeez!

พินอบพิเทา deferential, attentive; obsequious, to bow and scrape, kowtow (to), fawn /on/ over/ someone, fuss over someone, be over-attentive

พินัยกรรม will, testament

ตายโดยมิได้ทำพินัยกรรมไว้ to die intestate

ทำพินัยกรรม to make a will

ผู้ทำพินัยกรรม testator

พินาศ to be destroyed, ruined; destruction, ruin

ใครคิดร้าย จงพินาศ Down with those who would do us harm!

พินิจ to consider, examine; to investigate; to inspect

พ
ฟ
ภ
ม
ย
ร
ฤ
ฦ
ล
ว
ศ
ษ
ส
ห
ฬ
อ
ฮ

พินิจพิเคราะห์ to scrutinize; to /consider/ examine/ carefully, study thoroughly; to deliberate

พินิจพิจารณา to consider carefully, on careful examination, after careful study

สถานพินิจเด็ก training school, reformatory

พิบัติ disaster, calamity

ภัยพิบัติ disaster, calamity, tragedy

พิพากษา to judge, adjudge, /give/render/ a judgment

คำพิพากษา judgment

ผู้พิพากษา judge, justice, magistrate

พิพาท to dispute, have a dispute, quarrel

กรณีพิพาท dispute, quarrel, controversy

ข้อพิพาท disputed point, matter in dispute, issue

พิพิธภัณฑ์ museum

พิพิธภัณฑสถานแห่งชาติ National Museum

พิภพ world

บรรณพิภพ literary world

พิมพ์ to print; to type

พิมพ์เขียว blueprint

พิมพ์ใจ to impress, be impressed (by); attractive, impressive

พิมพ์ดีด typewriter; to type

พิมพ์ดีดกระเป๋า portable typewriter

พิมพ์ดีดไฟฟ้า electric typewriter

พนักงานพิมพ์ดีด typist

พิมพ์เดียวกัน cut from the same cloth, of the same stamp

พิมพ์ที่ printed by

พิมพ์แบบจิ้ม to hunt and peck; the hunt and peck system

พิมพ์ผิด to misprint; to mistype; a misprint, typing /error/mistake/

พิมพ์โรเนียว to duplicate

พิมพ์ลายมือ to fingerprint

พิมพ์สัมผัส touch-typing

พิมพ์หนังสือ to publish; to print a book

ตัวพิมพ์ type, print; printing

แท่นพิมพ์ printing press

ผู้พิมพ์ printer

ผู้พิมพ์ผู้โฆษณา publisher

แม่พิมพ์ printing block; matrix, die, mold; teacher

เรียงพิมพ์ to set type, compose

โรงพิมพ์ printing press, press, printing /establishment/house/

สำนักพิมพ์ publisher, publishing house

หนังสือพิมพ์ newspaper, journal

พิมเสน borneol; a kind of mango

พิราบ pigeon

พิรี้พิไร to dawdle, dillydally

พิรุณ rain

พิรุธ suspicious, suspect, fishy

ท่าทางพิรุธ to arouse suspicion, look suspicious, behave suspiciously

พิเรน eccentric, deviant

พิโรธ to be infuriated, enraged, in a rage

พิลึก queer, odd, funny, weird, bizarre, peculiar

พิลึกพิลั่น weird, queer, outlandish, very strange, peculiar

พิศ to examine, peer at

พิศวง surprised, amazed, astonished

พิศวงงงงวย stupefied, dumbfounded; perplexed, bewildered

น่าพิศวง amazing, surprising, astonishing

พิศวาส to delight in, be taken with (someone), love

พิศวาสฆาตกรรม passion slaying

น่าพิศวาส attractive

ไม่น่าพิศวาส unattractive

ไม่เห็นมีอะไรน่าพิศวาส I can't see anything attractive there.

พิเศษ specific, particular; special, extraordinary, exceptional

ชั้นพิเศษ special grade

เป็นพิเศษ especially, specially, particularly; special

ลักษณะพิเศษ special characteristic, distinctive feature, uniqueness

สิทธิพิเศษ privilege, prerogative, perquisite

พิษ poison, venom, toxin

พิษไข้ fever

พิษงู snake venom

พิษรัก bitterness of love, harm that comes of loving

พิษสง dangerous, vicious; destructive power

ไม่มีพิษสงอะไร (he is) harmless

งูพิษ /poisonous/venomous/ snake

ทำพิษ to cause trouble; to have a bad effect

เป็นพิษ poisonous, toxic, noxious, deleterious; spoiled

มีพิษ poisonous, venomous, toxic

ยาแก้พิษงู anti-venin

ยาพิษ poison

ลมพิษ hives

ไอพิษ poison gas; toxic fumes

พิสดาร extensive, amplified; detailed; in full, comprehensive

ข้อความพิสดาร comprehensive /text/story/article/, in full

โดยพิสดาร in detail, comprehensive

วิจิตรพิสดาร elaborate, exquisite, amazingly beautiful; fantastic, marvelous

พิสมัย engaging beauty; to be attracted (to)

น่าพิสมัย appealing, lovely, attractive

พิสูจน์ to prove, show, demonstrate

พิสูจน์อักษร to proofread

ข้อพิสูจน์ proof, evidence

เครื่องพิสูจน์ proof, evidence, clear indication

พี่ older /brother/sister/; I, he, she, you; my husband; please

ชิดซ้ายหน่อยพี่ Move to the left, please.

พี่แก he

พี่เขย older brother-in-law

พี่ชาย older brother

พี่น้อง relatives, brothers and sisters, family members; fellows, folks, my friends

พี่เบิ้ม big boss

ประเทศพี่เบิ้ม superpower

พี่เมีย older /brother/sister/-in-law

พี่เลี้ยง big brother; nurse, nursemaid, governess; baby-sitter; trainer; escort; chaperone

พี่สะใภ้ older sister-in-law

พี่สาว older sister

คุณพี่ honey, darling; sir, ma'am

ลูกพี่ boss; big shot

ลูกพี่ลูกน้อง cousin

พีชคณิต algebra

พึง ought to, should

พึงเข้าใจว่า should understand that

พึงใจ pleased (with), satisfied (with), content (with), satisfactory

พึงปรารถนา desirable, attractive

บุคคลไม่พึงปรารถนา persona non grata, undesirable person

ไม่พึงปรารถนา undesirable

พึงสังวร should take care, should be careful (to, that)

พึ่ง[1] just

เขาพึ่งมาถึง He just arrived.

พึ่ง[2] to rely on, depend on

พึ่งตนเอง to rely on oneself, self-reliant, to stand on one's own feet

พึ่งพา to depend on, lean on, rely on, count on

พึ่งพาอาศัย to depend on, be dependent on

พึ่งพาอาศัยกัน to help one another, be interdependent

พึ่งพิง to be dependent on

พึ่บ abruptly, in an instant

พึ่บพึ่บ lustily, vigorously, full of vigor

พ
ฟ
ภ
ม
ย
ร
ฤ
ฤๅ
ล
ว
ศ
ษ
ส
ห
ฬ
อ
ฮ

พึม, พึมพำ to mutter

    บ่นพึมพำ to grumble, fret, grouse

พืช plant, vegetation

    พืชผล crops, produce, yield

    พืชพันธุ์ seed; plant stock

    พืชเมืองร้อน tropical plants

    พืชยืนต้น perennial

    พืชไร่ field crop

    พืชล้มลุก annual

    น้ำมันพืช vegetable oil

    เมล็ดพืช seeds

พืด chain, line, strip (of), webbed

    ติดกันเป็นพืด webbed; chain (of); array (of), mass (of)

พื้น surface; floor; ground; basic, fundamental, superficial, simple, common; background, foundation

    พื้นกระเบื้อง tile floor

    พื้นดิน ground; earth

    พื้นที่ area

    พื้นน้ำ surface of the water

    พื้นบ้าน floor; folk

        ศิลปะพื้นบ้าน folk art

    พื้นเพ background

    พื้นเมือง native, homemade; domestic, indigenous

    พื้นรองเท้า sole (of a shoe)

    พื้นราบ plain

    พื้นเสีย to get angry; be annoyed, cross, in a bad mood, in a bad temper

    พื้นหิน stone floor

    ผ้าพื้น plain/unfigured/ cloth

พุ to gush up, spout

    พุพอง inflamed

    น้ำพุ fountain, spring

พุง stomach, belly; viscera

    พุงกระเพื่อม fat-bellied, potbellied

    พุงป่อง distended stomach; round tummy

    พุงพลุ้ย pot belly, fat tummy; paunchy, fat-

bellied

    ลงพุง to get fat, have a potbelly, potbellied, get paunchy, develop a paunch

พุ่ง to throw, hurl; to ejaculate, spurt, spew (forth, out); to shoot

    พุ่งตัว to shoot (up, out, forward)

    พุ่งพรวด to take off *(กิจการ)*, shoot up

    พุ่งแหลน to throw a javelin

    พวยพุ่ง to stream out, shoot out/forth/, pour out

    รบพุ่ง to fight a pitched battle, battle

พุทธ Buddha

    พุทธกาล the time of the Buddha

    พุทธคุณ, พระพุทธคุณ /qualities/virtues/ of the Buddha

    พุทธบริษัท Buddhists, followers of the Buddha

    พุทธพาณิชย์ commercialized Buddhism

    พุทธมามกะ Buddhist

    พุทธรูป, พระพุทธรูป Buddha image, /statue/ figure/representation/ of the Buddha

    พุทธศักราช Buddhist era

    พุทธศาสนา, พระพุทธศาสนา Buddhism, Buddhist religion

    พุทธศิลป์ Buddhist art

    พุทธองค์, พระพุทธองค์ the Buddha; He, Him

พุทธิ wisdom, knowing

    พุทธิปัญญา intellect

พุทโธ่ Oh my!, Oh dear!

    พุทโธ่เอ๋ย What a /shame/pity/!; For goodness sake!

พุธ Mercury; Wednesday

พุ่ม[1] bush; /floral/waxen/ cone-shaped offering; burning bush firework

    พุ่มเทียน cone-shaped candle

    พุ่มไม้ bush, shrub, shrubbery

    เป็นพุ่ม bushy, full

พุ่ม[2] *as in* **พุ่มม่าย** widowhood

    ตกพุ่มม่าย to be widowed, be a /widow

หญิง/widower ชาย/

พุ้ย to paddle briskly; to shovel food into the mouth

พุ้ยข้าวเข้าปาก to shovel rice into one's mouth (with chopsticks)

พุ้ยน้ำ to paddle water

พู section (of some fruits)

พู่ tassel

พู่กัน paintbrush

พูด to say, speak, talk

ฮัลโลแดงพูด Hello, this is Dang speaking.

พูดกระซิบ to whisper, talk in whispers

พูดกระทบ to make disparaging remarks, cast aspersions (on), have a sharp tongue

พูดกลับกลอก to blow hot and cold, fickle

พูดกันได้ not serious; to be able to talk (about something), discussible

พูดกับ to speak to, talk to, say to

    พูดกับตัวเอง to say to oneself

พูดคนเดียว to speak alone, be the only one to speak, be the /sole/only/ speaker

พูดคล่อง fluent; glib, to be a /smooth/good/ talker

พูดความจริง to tell the truth

พูดค่อยๆ to speak softly

พูดคำตอบคำ uncommunicative

พูดง่ายๆ in short; in simple terms

พูดง่ายทำยาก easier said than done

พูดง่ายฟังยาก subtle, hard to grasp

พูดจ้อ talkative, loquacious, voluble

พูดจา to talk, speak, have a talk (with someone)

    พูดจาประสาซื่อ to speak plainly, plain talk

    พูดจาหลักแหลม to speak intelligently, be articulate

    พูดจาเหลวไหล to talk nonsense

    พูดจาอ่อนหวาน soft-spoken; to speak sweetly

พูดโดยทั่วไป generally speaking, in general

พูดตลก to joke, be joking, kid, be kidding

พูดต่อ to say further

พูดตะกุกตะกัก to speak haltingly, falter, stammer, stutter

พูดติดอ่าง to stammer, stutter

พูดถึง to speak of, talk of, mention

พูดทองแดง to speak with a Southern (Thai) accent

พูดทับ (in talk) to outdo, go one up on (someone)

พูดทีเล่นทีจริง to be half-serious, half-joking, speak with tongue in cheek

พูดเท็จ to lie, prevaricate

พูดโทรศัพท์ to telephone; to be on the phone

พูดบ้านนอก to /have/speak with/ a provincial accent

พูดแบบขวานผ่าซาก to be blunt

พูดปรักปรำ to lay it on; to reproach unjustly, jump on (someone)

พูดเป็น to know how to talk, be a clever talker; to know how to speak

    พูดเป็นต่อยหอย to chatter away, prattle

    พูดเป็นน้ำ to speak in a steady stream, talk fluently, loquacious

    พูดเป็นน้ำไหลไฟดับ to chatter away; to speak non-stop

    พูดเป็นวรรคเป็นเวร to talk too much (about)

พูดเปรยๆ to remark, speak in general, say out of the blue, make a casual remark

พูดแปร่ง to speak with an accent; to sound funny

พูดไปสองไพเบี้ย นิ่งเสียตำลึงทอง Silence is golden.

พูดพล่อยๆ to speak thoughtlessly, speak without thinking

พ
ฟ
ภ
ม
ย
ร
ฤ
ฦ
ล
ว
ศ
ษ
ส
ห
ฬ
อ
ฮ

พูดเพ้อ to rave, be delirious

    พูดเพ้อเจ้อ to jab, jabber, ramble; to speak vacuously, talk /nonsense/ rubbish/, speak foolishly, talk through one's hat

    เพ้อเจ้อ foolish, nonsensical

พูดมาก to talk too much

พูดไม่เข้าเรื่อง to speak beside the point; irrelevant

พูดไม่จริง insincere; untruthful

พูดไม่รู้เรื่อง to speak unintelligibly; to be dense

พูดไม่ออก to be speechless, stunned; not know what to say; to be unable to bring oneself to /speak out/say anything/, tongue-tied, What could I say?

พูดยืดเยื้อ to be /long-winded /long drawn out/

พูดล้อ to tease, make fun of someone, joke, be joking

พูดลอยๆ to toss (something) out, say something out of the blue, mention casually

พูดเล่น to speak in fun, jest, joke, be joking, not serious

พูดแล้วก็แล้วกัน forget it

พูดวิทยุ to speak over the radio, broadcast

พูดสกปรก use /obscene/dirty/ language

พูดสามหาว to speak coarsely, use coarse language

พูดสาย to telephone, speak (with)

พูดเสียดสี to be sarcastic

พูดห้วนๆ to be curt, be short with someone

พูดหว่านล้อม to cajole, talk someone into doing something

พูดให้ดี to speak nicely; Watch what you say!, Mind your words!

พูดให้แน่ to say for sure

พูดอย่างคร่าวๆ roughly speaking

พูดอย่างตรงไปตรงมา frankly speaking, to be frank, to be honest, candid, plain-speaking

พูดอ้อมค้อม to beat around the bush, be evasive, use circumlocutions, say indirectly

พูดอะไรเป็นนั้น to be as good as one's word

พูดเอ็ดตะโร to shout

พูดเอาใจ to be ingratiating, be pleasing, say what somebody wants to hear

คนช่างพูด good talker

คนดีแต่พูด one who pays only lip service; impractical person

คนพูดมาก someone who talks too much, blatherer; /loquacious/garrulous/ person

คำพูด word, words, what is said, speech, spoken word

    เครื่องหมายคำพูด quotation mark

    รักษาคำพูด to keep one's word

ช่างพูด talkative

พูน to heap up, pile up; to accumulate, add (to)

ตักข้าวพูนจาน to fill up a plate with rice

พอกพูน to pile up, augment, accumulate

    พอกพูนหนี้ to pile up debts, accumulate debts

พู้น yonder, way over there

เพ่ง to concentrate (on), contemplate; to look intently (at something), gaze (at, on, into)

เพ่งกสิณ to fix one's mind on an object, contemplate an object of meditation

เพ่งเล็ง to watch, suspect, keep an eye on someone; to be directed at, be aimed at

เพชฌฆาต executioner

เพชร diamond; adamantine

    เพชรตัดเพชร It takes a diamond to cut a diamond.

เพชรน้ำค้าง crystal

เพชรน้ำหนึ่ง diamond of the first water

เพชรนิลจินดา precious stones, jewels

เพชรพลอย gems, gemstones, precious stones, jewels

ช่างเพชร jeweler

แหวนเพชร diamond ring

เพ็ญ full

จันทร์เพ็ญ full moon

วันเพ็ญ day of the full moon

พระจันทร์วันเพ็ญ full moon

เพ็ดทูล to speak (to, with), address (royalties)

เพดาน ceiling

เพดานเงินเดือน salary ceiling, top salary

เพดานปาก hard palate

เพทุบาย trick, cunning

เพ่นพ่าน to roam; to intrude, interlope, trespass

เพราะ[1] beautiful, harmonious, melodious, pleasing to the ear, sweet

เพราะพริ้ง beautiful, heavenly

เพราะ[2] because, because of, for, for the reason (that)

เพราะฉะนั้น therefore, hence, for that reason

เพราะว่า because, for the reason that

เพราะเหตุนั้น for that reason

เพราะเหตุไร for what reason, why

เพริศแพร้ว radiantly beautiful, gorgeous

เพรียก to screech; to call out

เพรียกพร้อง a medley of calling

เพรียบ see เพียบ หน้า 359

เพรียว wild, untamed; active, spry; slender, slim, slightly built, slinky

เพรียวลม streamlined, sleek

เพรื่อ see พร่ำเพรื่อ หน้า 343

เพล lunchtime for monks (11.00 a.m.)

ฉันเพล (of monks) to partake of the forenoon meal

เพลง music, song, melody; dance

เพลงกล่อม lullaby

เพลงฉ่อย responsive folk singing accompanied by clapping

เพลงชาติ national anthem

เพลงเต้นรำ dance music

เพลงไทย Thai music

เพลงยาว love poem, madrigal

เพลงสรรเสริญพระบารมี royal anthem

เพลงสวด hymn

เพลงสากล popular /song/music/, Western-style music

แต่งเพลง to /compose/write/ music

ทำนองเพลง melody, music

เนื้อเพลง melody, theme

บทเพลง lyrics

ร้องเพลง to sing

หีบเพลง harmonica, mouth organ; accordion

เพลา (เพ-ลา) time

เพลา[1] axle; shaft

เพลา[2] to abate, slowdown, ease up

เพลามือ to let up, go easy, take it easy

เพลาะ[1] to sew edges (of material) together; to piece together

เพลาะ[2] as in สนามเพลาะ trench

เพลิง fire, flames

คบเพลิง torch

เชื้อเพลิง fuel

น้ำมันเชื้อเพลิง fuel oil

ดอกไม้เพลิง fireworks

ดับเพลิง to /put out/extinguish/ a fire

รถดับเพลิง fire truck, fire engine

เปลวเพลิง flames

พระราชทานเพลิง royally sponsored cremation

วางเพลิง to set fire (to), commit arson

เพลิดเพลิน to have fun, take pleasure (in), enjoy, happily absorbed (in)

เพลิน absorbed (in), engrossed (in), to enjoy

พ
ฟ
ภ
ม
ย
ร
ฤ
ฦ
ล
ว
ศ
ษ
ส
ห
ฬ
อ
ฮ

เพลินใจ delightful, enjoyable

อ่านหนังสือเพลิน to be /absorbed/engrossed/ in one's book; to enjoy a book

เพลีย exhausted, weak, tired, worn out, fatigued; weary

เพลียใจ dejected, dispirited, in the dumps

อ่อนเพลีย weak, spent, worn out, pooped, tired out, weary

เพลี้ย aphid, plant louse

เพลี่ยง *as in* **เพลี่ยงพล้ำ** to blunder, err, make a mistake

เพศ gender; sex; -hood

เพศชาย masculine, male; manhood; masculine gender

เพศศึกษา sex education

เพศสมณะ, สมณเพศ monkhood, monk's condition, monk

เพศหญิง feminine, female, womanhood; feminine gender

เพศอ่อนแอ the weaker sex, the gentle sex

เพื่อนต่างเพศ friend of the opposite sex

ทางเพศ sex, sexual

อาชญากรรมทางเพศ sex crime

ร่วมเพศ to have sexual intercourse, have sex

เพ้อ to be delirious

เพ้อเจ้อ foolish, nonsensical *see* **พูดเพ้อเจ้อ** *หน้า 356*

เพาะ to grow, plant; to breed

เพาะชำ to plant as nursery stock

โรงเพาะชำ plant nursery

เพาะปลูก to cultivate, plant, raise, grow

เพิกเฉย to take no interest (in), pay no attention (to), ignore (a demand, request, etc), be indifferent (to), unresponsive (to)

ถูกทวงหนี้หลายครั้ง เขาเพิกเฉยเสีย Our demands for payment were ignored.

เพิกถอน to withdraw, cancel, rescind, revoke

เพิง projecting roof, shed, shelter

เพิงหมาแหงน roof sloping backwards; a lean-to

เพิ่ง just

เพิ่งมาถึง just arrived

เพิ่ม to add, increase, augment, enlarge, enhance

เพิ่มกำลัง to reinforce

เพิ่มขึ้น to increase, grow

เพิ่มเติม to add, supplement; additional, in addition, extra

มีอะไรเพิ่มเติมไหม Do you have anything to add?

แก้ไขเพิ่มเติม to amend, revise

เพิ่มพูน to add to, further; to multiply

เพิ่มพูนความรู้ to add to one's /knowledge/expertise/, for further study, further one's studies

ได้ความรู้เพิ่ม to learn a lot of new things, learn something /new/extra/

เพียง only, just

เพียงแค่ merely

เพียงแค่นี้ even, all

เพียงแค่นี้ยังทำไม่ได้ งานใหญ่กว่านี้จะทำได้ยังไง If you can't even handle this, how can you expect to do bigger things? / If this is all you can do, what's the use of giving you more important jobs?

เพียงแต่ only, just

ไม่เพียงแต่ not only

เพียงนั้น that much

เพียงนี้ this much, to such

ดีถึงเพียงนี้เชียวรี How good!

เพียงพอ enough, sufficient, adequate

เพียงไร to what extent, how much, however much

เพี้ยง verbal reinforcement for a wish rather like "So may it be" or "Amen"

เพี้ยน irregular, aberrant; crazy, odd, peculiar,

off; at variance with, to vary (from)

ผิดเพี้ยน inaccurate, off, at variance with, not in line with, irregularly, deviating

เพียบ to be filled to overflowing, heavily loaded

เพียบแประ loaded to the gunwales

เพียบพร้อม in abundance; fully equipped (with)

เพียบพร้อมด้วย replete with, abounding in, have an abundance of

เพียบหนัก in critical condition, gravely ill

อาการเพียบ in critical condition

เพียร assiduously, diligently, persistently, to persevere, apply oneself (to)

ความเพียร perseverance, diligence, assiduity, persistence, industry, industriousness, application to

พากเพียร to apply oneself (to), persevere (in); persevering, industrious, diligent, unflagging

เพื่อ for, for the purpose of; in

เพื่อจะ to, in order to, for

เพื่อตัวเอง for one's own sake, in one's own interest, for oneself

เพื่อประโยชน์แก่ for the benefit of, in the interest of, for the sake of

เพื่อเป็นเกียรติ in honor of; to grace

เพื่อเป็นที่ระลึก in commemoration of, in memory of, as a /souvenir/memento/ of

เพื่อเป็นพยานแก่การนี้, เพื่อเป็นหลักฐาน in witness whereof

เพื่อว่า so that

เพื่อเห็นแก่ for the sake of

เพื่อให้ for

เพื่อน friend, companion, buddy, fellow; others

ไปกันเถอะเพื่อน Let's go you guys.

เพื่อนกิน fair-weather friend, false friend

เพื่อนเก่า old friend

เพื่อนคู่หู confidant, bosom pal

เพื่อนเจ้าบ่าว best man

เพื่อนเจ้าสาว bridesmaid

เพื่อนชาย boyfriend, buddy, pal

เพื่อนซี้ buddy, intimate friend

เพื่อนเดินทาง traveling companion, fellow traveler

เพื่อนโดยสาร fellow passenger

เพื่อนตาย close, friend, bosom pal

เพื่อนนักเรียน schoolmate

เพื่อนบ้าน neighbor, next-door neighbor; neighborhood

เพื่อนมนุษย์ fellow man

เพื่อนยาก true friend

เพื่อนร่วมงาน colleague, co-worker, fellow worker

เพื่อนร่วมชั้น classmate

เพื่อนร่วมชาติ fellow countryman

เพื่อนร่วมโรงเรียน schoolmate

เพื่อนร่วมโลก fellow inhabitants of the world, all fellow beings

เพื่อนเล่น friend, playmate

เพื่อนสนิท close friend, dear friend, pal

เพื่อนหญิง girlfriend

แพ raft; a numerical designation for joss-sticks and bananas fried in batter

แพซุง log raft

แพยนต์ car ferry

เรือแพ floating house, houseboat

ล่องแพ to ride a raft, travel on a raft

แพ้ to lose, be defeated, be beaten, be overcome

แพ้เขา to be outdone, defeated, lose out

แพ้ความ to lose a case

แพ้คะแนน to lose on points

แพ้ท้อง to have morning sickness

แพ้เปรียบ to be at a disadvantage, have the odds against one

แพ้ผม to be balding; to be prematurely gray

แพ้ผัว to have had two or more husbands die

แพ้พิษ to be allergic (to), sensitive (to); to succumb (to)

แพ้ภัยตัว to get oneself into trouble, dig one's own grave

แพ้ยา to be allergic (to a drug)

พ่ายแพ้ to lose, be defeated, be beaten, vanquished

ยอมแพ้ to surrender, give up, give in (to), yield (to), admit defeat

แพง expensive, dear, costly, pricey

แพงขึ้น to go up in price, become more expensive

แพงหูดับ fantastically expensive

แพ่ง civil

กฎหมายแพ่ง civil law

คดีแพ่ง civil /case/suit/action/

ศาลแพ่ง Civil Court

แพทย์ doctor, physician; medical

แพทย์แผนโบราณ /traditional/herbal/ doctor, practitioner of traditional medicine

แพทย์แผนปัจจุบัน practitioner of modern medicine, medical doctor

แพทยศาสตร์ medicine, medical science

จรรยาแพทย์ medical ethics

จิตแพทย์ psychiatrist

ทันตแพทย์ dentist, dental surgeon

นายแพทย์ Dr., doctor, physician, M.D., medical doctor

วิชาแพทย์ medicine

ศัลยแพทย์ surgeon

สัตวแพทย์ veterinarian, veterinary, doctor of veterinary medicine

แพ่นกบาล to bash one's head in

แพร silk; rayon

แพร่ to spread; to publish; to propagate, publicize, circulate

แพร่พันธุ์ to multiply, breed, propagate

แพร่สะพัด to spread like wildfire, circulate,

spread widely

แพร่หลาย well-known, popular, widely known

ข่าวนี้รู้กันแพร่หลาย Everyone knows it.

เผยแพร่ to propagate, spread, disseminate, publicize

แพร่ง *as in* **ทางสองแพร่ง** a /fork/branch/ in the road; two possibilities, alternatives

แพร่งพราย to reveal, divulge, leak (out); to let someone in on something

แพรวพราย scintillating, resplendent, shining, glittering

แพรวพราว *see* **แพรวพราย**

แพลง sprained, twisted

ข้อเท้าแพลง to have a sprained ankle

พลิกแพลง to modify, vary, make changes, use variations; to twist, contort; wily, unprincipled

แพลม to stick out; to come out

แพศย์ Vaisya

แพศยา prostitute, harlot, whore, streetwalker

แพะ goat

แพะรับบาป scapegoat

โพก to tie around the head

โพกหัว to wear a turban, wear as a turban

โพธิ enlightenment

โพธิญาณ enlightenment

โพธิสมภาร king's grace

อาศัยร่มโพธิสมภาร to find a haven under the king's grace, take shelter under royal protection

โพธิสัตว์ bodhisattva

โพธิ์ bodhi

ต้นโพธิ์ bodhi tree, pipal

โพ้น yonder

โพ้นทะเล overseas

ไกลโพ้น far far away, very distant

โพนทะนา to criticize; accuse (of), malign,

calumniate

โพย[1] list, record

    โพยหวย list of lottery customers

โพย[2] danger, harm

    โพยภัย danger, peril

โพย[3] *as in* **ตีโพยตีพาย** to kick up a fuss (about something), get excited (about), make a commotion (over, about)

โพรก loose; having little meat

    หลวมโพรก too loose, baggy, oversized; capacious

โพรง cavity, hole, hollow

    โพรงใต้ดิน burrow

    โพรงไม้ hollow of a tree

โพล poll

โพลง bright

    ขาวโพลง all white; bright white

    ลืมตาโพลง to be wide awake; eyes wide open

    สว่างโพลง bright

โพล่ง thoughtlessly, carelessly, heedlessly

โพล้เพล้ dusk, twilight

ไพ่ playing cards

    ไพ่ข้าวหลามตัด diamonds

    ไพ่ดอกจิก clubs

    ไพ่ตอง Thai cards

    ไพ่ตาย trump card, winning card

    ไพ่นกกระจอก mah jong

    ไพ่โพธิ์ดำ spades

    ไพ่โพธิ์แดง hearts

    ไพ่ไฟ phony ballot

    ไพ่หนึ่งสำรับ a deck of cards

    กินไพ่ to take a card

    ขาไพ่ partner

    ตัดไพ่ to cut the /cards/deck/

    ถือไพ่เหนือกว่า to hold a trump card; to be one up (on someone)

    เล่นไพ่ to play cards, get up a card game

    วงไพ่ cardgame, card players

ไพฑูรย์ cat's-eye

ไพบูลย์ abundance, spaciousness

ไพร forest, woods

    นักนิยมไพร woodsman; forest conservationist

    สมุนไพร herb, medicinal plant

ไพร่ commoner; churl, boor, riffraff

    ไพร่ฟ้า subjects, people; serf, villein, common folk

    บ่าวไพร่ servants, retinue; menials, peons

ไพเราะ sweet, beautiful, sweet-sounding, harmonious melodious; to sound/pleasant/sweet/

    ไพเราะหู pleasant sounding, good to hear

ไพล่ instead

    บอกให้รีบๆ ทำ แต่ไพล่ไปนอนหลับเสีย งานเลยไม่เสร็จ I told him to get on with it but he went to sleep instead and so the work is not finished.

    ไพล่หลัง to clasp one's hands behind one's back

ไพลิน sapphire

ไพศาล enormous, vast, immense

พ
ฟ
ภ
ม
ย
ร
ฤ
ฤๅ
ล
ว
ศ
ษ
ส
ห
ฬ
อ
ฮ

ฟก bruised
ฟกช้ำ bruised; contused, to have a contusion
ฟกช้ำดำเขียว black-and-blue

ฟอก to wash, clean, cleanse; to bleach
ฟอกเงิน to launder money
การฟอกเงิน money laundering
ฟอกผ้า to scrub clothes clean; to bleach
ฟอกหนัง to tan leather, dress a hide
โรงฟอกหนัง tannery
ซักฟอก to launder, wash; to interrogate, grill
ผงซักฟอก detergent
น้ำยาฟอกขาว bleach

ฟอง foam, bubbles, froth, lather; a numerical designation for eggs
ฟองน้ำ sponge
ฟองสบู่ suds, soapsuds, lather
ฟองอากาศ air bubble
ตกฟอง to lay an egg
แตกฟอง to foam, froth; frothy
น้ำลายแตกฟอง to talk away, talk up a storm, talk non-stop

ฟ่อง high, conspicuously, in full view
ลอยฟ่อง to float /up/high/; to have a head (of foam)

ฟ้อง to sue, file legal proceedings, prosecute; to accuse, complain to someone about someone else
ฟ้องแพ่ง to bring a civil action
ฟ้องแย้ง to counterclaim
ฟ้องร้อง to sue, take legal action, file legal proceedings, file a court case, bring suit (against someone)
ฟ้องเรียกค่าเสียหาย to sue for damages
ฟ้องหย่า to sue for divorce
ฟ้องอนาถา to sue in forma pauperis
ฟ้องอาญา to bring a criminal action, file a criminal /suit/case/

คำฟ้อง complaint, plaint
ถอนฟ้อง to withdraw /a complaint/an action/
ถูกฟ้อง to be sued
ยกฟ้อง to dismiss a /case/complaint/, case dismissed
ยื่นฟ้อง to bring legal action (in, against), institute legal proceedings, sue, file a /complaint/case/ (in, against)
สั่งไม่ฟ้อง to give a no-prosecution order, nolle pros, give a nolle prosequi

ฟ่อน sheaf, bundle

ฟ้อน to dance
ฟ้อนรำ to do Thai dancing

ฟัก[1] to hatch, incubate
ฟักไข่ to /brood/incubate/hatch/ eggs
ฟักตัว to be coming on, hatching, developing, growing

ฟัก[2] squash
ฟักทอง pumpkin

ฟัง to hear, listen (to); to obey
ฟังขึ้น reasonable, sound, credible, tenable, to hold water, make sense, sound reasonable
ฟังดนตรี to listen to music
ฟังได้ plausible, reasonable
ฟังเทศน์ to listen to a sermon
ฟังไม่ขึ้น unreasonable, untenable, unsound, not credible, ill-founded
ฟังเสียง to listen (to)
ฟังหูไว้หู to reserve judgment, be circumspect, be skeptical
ฟังออก to understand, follow (the meaning etc)
กรุณาฟังทางนี้ Attention please., May I have your attention.
เครื่องดักฟัง sound detector, (electronic) eavesdropper, eavesdropping equipment
เงี่ยหูฟัง to strain to hear, listen attentively
เชื่อฟัง to be obedient, obey, listen (to),

take heed

ได้ยินได้ฟัง to have heard

ตั้งใจฟัง to pay attention

ไม่ตั้งใจฟัง inattentive

น่าฟัง sensible; interesting, worth listening to, listenable

ว่าไม่ฟัง obstinate, recalcitrant; naughty, disobedient

สดับตรับฟัง to listen /closely/attentively/ (to), pay attention (to)

หูฟัง earphone

ฟัด to horse around (with), knock about (with)

ฟัดกัน to have a rough-and-tumble

ฟัน[1] tooth, teeth, dental

ฟันกระทบกัน (His) teeth are chattering.

ฟันกราม molar

ฟันคุด wisdom tooth

ฟันน้ำนม milk teeth

ฟันปลอม false tooth, false teeth, denture

ฟันปลา serration, saw-tooth design

ฟันผุ caries, cavity, tooth decay

ฟันฝ่า to overcome, get through, surmount

ฟันเฟือง cog, tooth

ฟันเลื่อย sawtooth design, tooth of a saw

ฟันหนู diacritical mark comparable to the umlaut (¨)

ฟันหลุด to fall out เช่น *My tooth has fallen out.*

ฟันเหยิน buckteeth, projecting teeth

กัดฟัน to clench one's teeth; to make a determined effort

ขี้ฟัน dental detritus

เข็ดฟัน to set one's teeth on edge

จิ้มฟัน to pick one's teeth

ไม้จิ้มฟัน toothpick

ปวดฟัน to have a toothache

แปรงฟัน to brush one's teeth

ยาสีฟัน dentifrice, toothpaste, tooth powder

ยิงฟัน to show one's teeth; to grin

ไรฟัน gumline

หมอฟัน dentist

ฟัน[2] to chop, slash, cut

ฟันดาบ sword fighting, to fight with swords

ฟันธง to declare with finality, make a /decision/determination/

ฟันฝ่า to overcome

ฆ่าฟัน to slaughter, kill, slay

ฟั่น to twist (together)

ฟั่นเชือก to make a /rope/cord/ (by twisting)

ฟั่นเทียน to roll a candle

ฟั่นเฝือ confused, tangled; complicated, complex, involved

ฟั่นเฟือน of unsound mind, demented, not all there

ฟ้า sky; air, weather; heaven, celestial, heavenly

ฟ้าคะนอง thunder

ฟ้าดิน heaven and earth

ฟ้าผ่า lightning, thunderbolt; to be struck by lightning

ฟ้าร้อง thunder

ฟ้าแลบ lightning, flash of lightning

ฟ้าสาง dawn

ขอบฟ้า horizon, edge of the sky

ดาดฟ้า deck, roof, flat roof, roof-deck

ท้องฟ้า sky, heavens

ลมฟ้าอากาศ weather

สวรรค์ชั้นฟ้า heaven, celestial world

สายฟ้า lightning

สีฟ้า light blue, sky blue

สุดหล้าฟ้าเขียว at the other end of the world, far, far away

ฟ้าทลายโจร creat (Andrographis paniculata)

ฟาก[1] strips of split bamboo flooring

ตกฟาก to be born

ฟาก[2] side, bank, shore

ฟากนี้ this side

ฟากโน้น that side

ข้ามฟาก to cross (a river, street, etc), cross

over to the other side

ฟาง[1] straw

กระดาษฟาง straw paper

หมวกฟาง straw hat

ฟาง[2] blurred vision

ตาฟาง to have poor /vision/eyesight/; clouded vision, eyes clouded over

ฝ้าฟาง overcast

ฟ้าง *as in* **ข้าวฟ่าง** millet; sorghum

ฟาด to strike, knock (against); to punch, bash; to eat

ฟาดเคราะห์ to forestall calamity by experiencing a smaller misfortune

ฟาดฟัน to battle (with)

ฟาดหัว to give a sop เช่น *Give him an extra hundred thousand as a sop and he'll sign.*

ฟ่าม flabby; spoiled

ฟาร์ม farm

ฟาร์มโคนม dairy farm

ฟิด sneezing; sniffing

ฟิต fit

ฟิตปั๋ง in top form, very fit

ฟิตรถ to repair a car

ช่างฟิต fitter, mechanic

ฟิล์ม film

ฟิล์มกรองแสง (tinted) window film

ฟิวส์ fuse

ฟิวส์ขาด to blow a fuse, The fuse has blown.

ฟืน firewood

คนหาฟืน wood-cutter

ดุ้นฟืน piece of firewood, log

ฟื้น to recover; to regain consciousness, come to; to wake up

ฟื้นไข้ to recover, get better, get over an illness, convalesce

ฟื้นความจำ to recall, refresh one's memory

ฟื้นความหลัง to recall the past, recollect

ฟื้นตัว to improve; recover, get better,

take a turn for the better

ฟื้นฟู to revive, recover, rehabilitate

การฟื้นฟูกิจการ business reorganization

ยุคฟื้นฟูวัฒนธรรม renaissance

ฟีม reed

ฟุ้ง to spread, diffuse; to fill the air, blow around

ฟุ้งกระจาย to fill, spread about, permeate

ฟุ้งซ่าน to be distracted, flighty, scatter-brained; to have wild thoughts; be unfocussed

ฟุ้งเฟ้อ extravagant, lavish

ฟุ้งเฟ้อเห่อเหิม puffed up, conceited

ฟุ้งเฟื่อง to spread, be widespread; genius-like, extraordinary

คุยฟุ้ง to boast, talk big, gab

ฟุต foot

ฟุตบอล soccer

การแข่งขันฟุตบอล soccer match

ลูกฟุตบอล soccer ball, football

อเมริกันฟุตบอล football

ฟุตปาท footpath, sidewalk, pavement

ฟุบ to collapse, fall, slump (down, over)

ฟุบลง to crouch down, prostrate oneself

ฟุ่มเฟือย luxury, luxurious, extravagant; unnecessary

ชีวิตฟุ่มเฟือย a life of luxury

มีชีวิตอย่างฟุ่มเฟือย to live /in luxury/ extravagantly/

สินค้าฟุ่มเฟือย luxury goods

ฟู to be inflated, swell; to rise; to be light

แป้งฟู baking powder

ฟื้นฟู to revive

ฟู่ blowing sound

ฟู่ฟ่า extravagant, flamboyant

เตาฟู่ pressure stove

ฟูก mattress

ฟูมฟัก to bring up, raise

ฟูมฟาย in tears, bathed in tears, weeping, tearful;

grieving

เฟ้น to select, choose, pick out, pick and choose, look for

    นวดเฟ้น to massage

    เลือกเฟ้น to select; selected, carefully selected

เฟ้อ inflated

    เงินเฟ้อ inflation

    ท้องเฟ้อ flatulent; to have indigestion

    ฟุ้งเฟ้อ extravagant, lavish

เฟอร์นิเจอร์ furniture

เฟะ, เน่าเฟะ rotten, decomposed, putrid; decadent

เฟือ *as in* **เหลือเฟือ** more than enough, plenty, ample

เฟือง gear, cogwheel

    เฟืองท้าย differential gear

เฟื่องฟู prospering, prosperous, thriving, flourishing

เฟื้อง a Thai monetary unit equivalent to twelve stang

เฟื้อย *as in* **ยาวเฟื้อย** /very/exceedingly/miles/ long; elongated

แฟง ash-pumpkin

แฟชั่น fashion

    เป็นแฟชั่น to be in fashion

แฟน fan; wife; husband; boyfriend, girlfriend

    เป็นแฟนกัน going /together/steady/

แฟบ deflated, flattened, flat, depressed

แฟ้ม file, folder

แฟรนไชส์ franchise

ไฟ fire; power

    ไฟฉาย flashlight, torch, searchlight

    ไฟแช็ก lighter

    ไฟดับ to have a power failure, the lights go out

    ไฟท้าย taillight

    ไฟธาตุ digestion

    ไฟนรก hellfire

    ไฟนีออน neon light

ไฟบรรลัยกัลป์ Armageddon

ไฟป่า forest fire

ไฟฟ้า electricity

    ไฟฟ้าหลอดยาว fluorescent light

ไฟมอด dying fire

ไฟสัญญาณ traffic light, signal light

ไฟหน้า headlight

ไฟไหม้ fire; burning

กองไฟ bonfire, campfire

ก่อไฟ to light a fire, build a fire

ควันไฟ smoke

ค่าน้ำค่าไฟ cost of water and electricity, cost of utilities

เครื่องทำไฟ generator

โคมไฟ lamp, lantern

จุดไฟ to light a fire; to strike a match

ช่องไฟ space

เชื้อไฟ tinder, fuel

ดวงไฟ light; lamplight glow

ดับไฟ to put out a fire; to turn /out/off/ the light

ต้นไฟ the start of a fire

ติดไฟ to catch fire; to light a fire; to /install /put in/ electricity

เตาไฟ stove

ทนไฟ fireproof, fire resistant; refractory

ปล่องไฟ chimney, smokestack, funnel

ปิดไฟ to turn /off/out/ the light, switch off the light

เปลวไฟ flame

เปิดไฟ to /turn/switch/on the light; to turn on the power

รถไฟ train, railway, railroad

เรือไฟ steamboat

ลนไฟ to heat over an open flame

ไวไฟ inflammable; hot, sexy

ส่องไฟ to shine a light (on, at)

แสงไฟ light; firelight

อยู่ไฟ postpartum lying-in by a fire

ฟ
ภ
ม
ย
ร
ฤ
ฤๅ
ล
ว
ศ
ษ
ส
ห
ฬ
อ
ฮ

ก
ข
ค
ฆ
ง
จ
ฉ
ช
ซ
ฌ
ญ
ฏ
ฏ
ฐ
ฑ
ฒ
ณ
ด
ต
ถ
ท
ธ
น
บ
ป
ผ
ฝ
พ
ฟ
ภ

ภพ world; existence

จักรภพ empire

เครือจักรภพ commonwealth

ภมร bee, carpenter bee

ภยันตราย danger, peril, calamity

ภยาคติ /prejudice/bias/ caused by fear

ภรรยา wife

ภรรยาน้อย minor wife

ภรรยาหลวง legal wife, major wife

ภราดร brother

ภราดรภาพ fraternity, brotherhood

ภราดา brother

ภริยา wife

ภวังค์ (in a) trance, reverie

ภวังคจิต the subconscious mind

ภักษา, ภักษาหาร food, sustenance

ภัณฑ์ products, things, supplies

ภัณฑารักษ์ curator; caretaker

ครุภัณฑ์ heavy durable goods, furniture, heavy articles

เคมีภัณฑ์ chemicals, chemical supplies

ผลิตภัณฑ์ product, manufacture

ยุทธภัณฑ์ war material, armaments, military equipment

เวชภัณฑ์ pharmaceuticals, medical supplies, drugs

ภัตตาคาร restaurant

ภัตตาหาร food

ภัย danger, peril

ภัยทางอากาศ perils of the air, danger of flying

ภัยธรรมชาติ natural peril

ภัยพิบัติ disaster, calamity, tragedy

ภัยอันตราย danger, harm

ที่หลบภัย safety shelter

ประกันภัย casualty insurance

ปลอดภัย safe

เป็นภัย dangerous, harmful, hazardous

ผจญภัย to venture (into), have an adventure

โพยภัย danger, peril

โรคภัย sickness, illness, disease

เสี่ยงภัย to risk, take a risk, take a chance, adventure (into)

หลุมหลบภัย bunker, air raid shelter

ภัสดา husband

ภาค part, section, sector, portion; side; time, session

ภาคกลาง central (part of)

เขามีภูมิลำเนาอยู่ภาคกลาง He lives in central Thailand. / He lives in the central part of Thailand.

ภาคทัณฑ์ probation, to be put on probation, put (someone) on probation

ภาคผนวก appendix, annex, exhibit, addendum, supplement, attachment

ภาคพื้นยุโรป (in) Europe

ภาครัฐบาล government sector

ภาคเรียน term, semester

ภาคเสธ to deny in part and admit in part

ภาคหลวง royalty

ภาคเอกชน private sector

ภาคภูมิ grand, majestic, imposing, impressive

ภาคภูมิใจ to be proud (of)

ภาคยานุวัติ accession

ภาคยานุวัติสาร instrument of accession

ภาคี party, member

ภาคีสมาชิก associate member

ภาคีสัญญา signatory, party to a treaty

ไตรภาคี tripartite

ภาชนะ container

ภาพ picture; state, quality, condition

ภาพข่าว news photo

ภาพเขียน drawing, painting

ภาพถ่าย photograph, photo

ภาพนิ่ง still picture

ภาพนู้ด nude

ภาพประกอบ illustration

ภาพเปลือย nude (picture, painting)

ภาพฝาผนัง mural, fresco

ภาพพจน์ image; figure of speech

ภาพพิมพ์สี colored print

ภาพยนตร์ motion picture, film, movie

   โรงภาพยนตร์ cinema, the movies, movie /theater/house/, motion picture theater

ภาพร่าง sketch

ภาพลวง mirage

ภาพล้อ caricature

ภาพลักษณ์ image

ภาพวาด painting, drawing

ภาพสีน้ำ a watercolor

   ภาพสีน้ำมัน oil painting

ภาพหน้าปก cover picture

ภาพหลอน hallucination, illusion

ภาพหุ่นนิ่ง still life

เจ้าภาพ host (ชาย), hostess (หญิง); sponsor

ช่างภาพ photographer

ถ่ายภาพ to take a /picture/photograph/

รูปภาพ picture

วาดภาพ to /paint/draw/a picture; to portray, depict

ห้องภาพ studio

ภาย place; side; time

ภายใต้ under, subject to

ภายนอก outside, exterior, external

ภายใน inside; within, interior, internal; among /ourselves/themselves/

   ภายในประเทศ internal, domestic, within the country

   ภายในไม่กี่วัน /in/within/ a few days, soon

   ภายในระยะเวลา within a period of

   เป็นการภายใน confidential, private, internal

ภายหน้า in the future, later on, next time

ภายหลัง after; subsequently, afterwards, later (on); post-

   ภายหลังที่ after, following

ภาร load, burden, weight, heavy task, obligation duty, job, responsibility; burdensome

ภารกิจ business, task, work, job, mission

ภารโรง caretaker, janitor

ภาระ obligation, responsibility, job; burden

   ภาระจำยอม servitude (กฎหมาย)

   แบกภาระ to shoulder responsibility, be saddled with, bear responsibility (for), be burdened (with)

   แบ่งเบาภาระ to share responsibility (for), relieve (someone) of a burden, unburden

   เป็นภาระ to be obligated (to do something), take the responsibility (to do something); to be a burden

ภาวนา to pray; to cultivate

   ขอภาวนาให้เขาปลอดภัย I pray he's safe.

   ภาวนาพึมพำ to murmer mantras

ภาวะ state, condition, status

   ภาวะการเงิน financial /status/condition/

   ภาวะคับขัน critical state

   ภาวะเงินเฟ้อ inflation

   ภาวะฉุกเฉิน state of emergency

   นิติภาวะ legal age, majority

      บรรลุนิติภาวะ to attain one's majority, be of legal age, become of age

ภาษา language, speech, tongue

   ภาษากลาง universal language; Mandarin

   ภาษาคน human speech

   ภาษาตลาด vernacular, vulgar /speech/ language/, marketplace language

   ภาษาต่างประเทศ foreign language

   ภาษาท้องถิ่น dialect, local speech

   ภาษาปัจจุบัน modern language

   ภาษาพื้นเมือง native language

   ภาษาพูด spoken language, colloquial/ speech/language/

   ภาษามนุษย์ human speech

   ภาษาศาสตร์ linguistics

ภ
ม
ย
ร
ฤ
ฤๅ
ล
ว
ศ
ษ
ส
ห
ฬ
อ
ฮ

ภาษาศาสตร์สังคม sociolinguistics
ภาษาหนังสือ literary language
พูดไม่รู้ภาษา thickheaded, dense, so stupid
ภาษิต saying, proverb, maxim, aphorism
ภาษี[1] tax, duty, impost
ภาษีการค้า business tax
ภาษีขาเข้า import duty
ภาษีขาออก export duty
ภาษีเงินได้ income tax
ภาษีที่ดิน land tax
ภาษีมูลค่าเพิ่ม value-added tax, VAT
ภาษีศุลกากร customs duty
ภาษีเสริม surtax
ภาษีหัก ณ ที่จ่าย withholding tax
ภาษีอากร taxes and duties
เก็บภาษี to collect tax
ขึ้นภาษี to /raise/increase/ a tax
โรงภาษี customs house
เสียภาษี to pay tax
อัตราภาษี tax rate
ภาษี[2] advantage
มีภาษีเหนือกว่า to have an edge (on), have the advantage (over)
ภิกษุ Buddhist monk, bhikku, bonze
ภิกษุณี Buddhist nun
ภิญโญ surpassing, supreme
ภู่ carpenter bee
ภูเขา mountain; hill
ภูเขาไฟ volcano
กองเป็นภูเขาเลากา a mountain (of), enormous pile (of)
ภูตผีปีศาจ demons, evil spirits
ภูผา rocky mountain
ภูมิ earth, land; status; level; background, qualifications
ภูมิความรู้ education, academic background, educational level
ภูมิประเทศ landscape, scenery, countryside; geography

ภูมิภาค region, provinces, area
ส่วนภูมิภาค provincial
ภูมิลำเนา domicile
มีภูมิลำเนา domiciled
ภูมิศาสตร์ geography
ปิตุภูมิ fatherland
มาตุภูมิ motherland
ไม่สมภูมิ unworthy (of), disappointing; undignified, inappropriate
ดอกเตอร์เขียนบทความห่วย ๆ อย่างนี้ไม่สมภูมิเลย It was unworthy of that Ph.D to write such trash.
สมรภูมิ battlefield, battleground
เสียภูมิ degrading, discreditable, demeaning
อมภูมิ modest, to conceal one's abilities, hide one's lights under a bushel, keep what one knows to oneself, not forthcoming
ภูมิคุ้มกัน, ภูมิต้านทาน immunity, resistance
ภูมิใจ proud (to, of)
ภูมิฐาน grand, elegant, smart
แต่งตัวภูมิฐาน dressed up, well-dressed, smartly /dressed/apparelled/
ภูมิแพ้ allergy
ภูมิหลัง background, past, history
เภทภัย various dangers, different perils
เภทุบาย divisive maneuver
เภสัช pharmaceutical, drug, medicine, remedy
เภสัชกร pharmacist
เภสัชกรรม pharmacy
เภสัชวิทยา pharmacology
เภสัชศาสตร์ pharmacy
โภค riches, wealth, goods; to use, consume
โภคภัณฑ์ commodity
โภคยทรัพย์ consumer goods, consumables
เครื่องบริโภค food, foodstuffs, comestibles
เครื่องอุปโภคบริโภค consumer goods
บริโภค to eat, partake (of); to use, consume
อุปโภค to use, utilize, consume

โภชนา food, food consumption

    มนตรีโภชนา Montri's Restaurant.

    โภชนาการ nutrition

        โภชนาการบำบัด therapeutic nutrition,

        nutritional therapy

    โภชนาหาร food

    การกล่าวอ้างทางโภชนาการ nutrition claim

ภ
ม
ย
ร
ฤ
ฤๅ
ล
ว
ศ
ษ
ส
ห
ฬ
อ
ฮ

มกราคม January

มกุฎ crown
    มกุฎราชกุมาร crown prince

มคธ Bihar
    ภาษามคธ Pali

มงกุฎ crown; coronet
    สวมมงกุฎ crowned

มงคล auspicious, favorable, propitious
    ด้ายมงคล auspicious fillets
    เป็นสิริมงคล propitious, auspicious
    พิธีมงคลสมรส wedding
    ไม่เป็นมงคล inauspicious, a bad thing (to say, do, etc)

มณฑป square structure with a spire

มณฑล administrative area, division
    มณฑลทหาร military circle

มณี precious stone, jewel, gem
    แก้วมณี gem, jewel

มด ant

มดลูก uterus, womb

มติ resolution, decision; opinion, view, sense
    มติคณะรัฐมนตรี resolution of the Council of Ministers
    มติมหาชน public opinion
    ที่ประชุมมีมติว่า The meeting has /decided/ resolved/ that...; It is the sense of the meeting that...
    ลงมติ to resolve, pass a resolution, decide, come to a decision

มท. (มหาดไทย) Ministry of Interior

มน[1] rounded; round

มน[2] as in **มืดมน** bleak, hopeless; dark, obscure

มนต์, มนตร์ spell, magic formula, incantation; prayer; chant
    น้ำมนต์ holy water, lustral water
    เวทมนตร์ spell, magic incantation
    สวดมนต์ to pray; to chant

มนตรี minister; councillor
    คณะมนตรีความมั่นคง Security Council

    คณะรัฐมนตรี Council of Ministers, cabinet
    เทศมนตรี municipal councillor, member of a municipal council
    นายกรัฐมนตรี prime minister, president of the council of ministers, premier
    รัฐมนตรี minister, secretary
    องคมนตรี privy councillor

มนเทียร royal household
    มนเทียรบาล administration of the royal household, Royal Household Department officer

มนุษย์-, มนุษย์ man, human being
    มนุษยชาติ humanity, mankind
    มนุษยธรรม humanity, compassion
    มนุษยนิยม humanism
    มนุษยโลก this world, the earth
    มนุษยศาสตร์ humanities
    มนุษยสัมพันธ์ human relations, social relations; personality
    มนุษย์อวกาศ astronaut
    เพื่อนมนุษย์ fellow man

มโน heart, mind
    มโนคติ concept; idea, thought
    มโนทัศน์ concept
    มโนธรรม conscience
    มโนภาพ imagination, vision

มโนสาเร่ trivial, petty, insignificant
    คดีมโนสาเร่ petty case

มรกต emerald

มรณ-, มรณ์, มรณะ death, demise, decease
    มรณบัตร death certificate
    มรณภัย fear of death
    มรณภาพ to die, pass away; death, decease, demise

มรดก inheritance, legacy
    มรดกตกทอด inherited, handed down; inheritance by right of representation
    กองมรดก estate
    รับมรดก to inherit, receive a legacy

ก
ข
ค
ฆ
ง
จ
ฉ
ช
ซ
ฌ
ญ
ฎ
ฏ
ฐ
ฑ
ฒ
ณ
ด
ต
ถ
ท
ธ
น
บ
ป
ผ
ฝ
พ
ฟ
ภ
ม

      ผู้รับมรดก heir, legatee

มรรค, มรรคา path, way

      มรรคนายก spiritual guide

      ไม่เป็นมรรคเป็นผล unproductive, ineffectual, fruitless

มรรยาท, มารยาท conduct, behavior, manners, etiquette

      ตามมรรยาท as a matter of etiquette

      ไม่มีมรรยาท impolite, rude, ill-mannered, uncouth, discourteous

ม.ร.ว. M.R. (*abbr. of* Mom Rachawong)

มรสุม monsoon

      ลมมรสุม monsoon

      หน้ามรสุม monsoon season

ม.ล. M.L. (*abbr. of* Mom Luang)

มลทิน blemish, stain, tarnish, impurity

      พ้นมลทิน to be exonerated, cleared, absolved

      มีมลทิน to have a bad record, have a tarnished reputation, have a black mark against one's name

มลพิษ pollution

มลภาวะ pollution

มลายู Malay, Malayan; Malaysia, Malaya

      แหลมมลายู Malay Peninsula

ม่วง[1] purple, violet, lavender

      ผ้าม่วง silk panung, silk hip cloth for draping into a kind of breeches

      สีม่วง purple, violet, lavender

ม่วง[2] boat with a curved stem and stern

มวน to roll (a cigarette)

      บุหรี่หนึ่งมวน a cigarette

ม้วน to roll, reel, wind, coil; a numerical designation for rolled things

      ม้วนตัวกลม to roll oneself into a ball, curl up

      ม้วนไปม้วนมา to be bashful; to act coyly

      ม้วนผม to curl one's hair, roll up one's hair

      ม้วนเสื่อ to roll up a mat

มวย[1] boxing

      มวยปล้ำ wrestling

      มวยล้ม a phony, put-up job, /fixed/rigged/ fight

      มวยสากล international-style boxing, Western-style boxing

      ชกมวย boxing, fighting, prizefight

      เวทีมวย boxing ring, prize ring

      สนามมวย boxing stadium

มวย[2] *as in* **มวยผม** to put (one's) hair up in a bun; a bun

ม่วย Chinese girl; younger sister

มวล all

      ทั้งมวล all, in (its, their) entirety; entirely

มวลชน mass

มวลสาร mass

มหรสพ entertainment

      โรงมหรสพ theater

มหันต์, มหันต- great

      มหันตโทษ heavy penalty/sentence/; felony

      มหันตภัย great danger

มหัศจรรย์ miraculous; amazing, astounding, astonishing

มหา great, major; title given to a monk who has passed the third of nine grades of Pali studies

      มหาชน public, masses

      มติมหาชน public opinion

      มหาบัณฑิต master (of), holder of a master's degree

      มหาบุรุษ great man

      มหาประลัย hazardous

      มหาภัย great danger; calamity

      มหายาน Great Vehicle, Mahayana

      มหาราช the Great

      มหาวิทยาลัย university

      มหาศาล fantastic, enormous

      มหาเศรษฐี millionaire, very wealthy person

      มหาสมุทร ocean

      มหาอำนาจ /great/major/ power

ม
ย
ร
ฤ
ฦๅ
ล
ว
ศ
ษ
ส
ห
ฬ
อ
ฮ

ประเทศมหาอำนาจ /major/great/ power

มหาชาติ the last life of the Bodhisattva

เทศน์มหาชาติ to recite the last life of the Bodhisattva

มหาดไทย Interior Department, Ministry of Interior

กระทรวงมหาดไทย Ministry of Interior, Department of the Interior (US), Home Department (Brit)

มหาดเล็ก royal page

มหึมา gigantic, immense, huge, mammoth, colossal, gargantuan, prodigious

มเหสี queen

มโหรี a traditional Thai orchestra with singing

มโหฬาร magnificent, splendid, grand; stupendous, prodigious, vast

อย่างมโหฬาร with great pomp, grandly

มอ mooing

มอ ๆ drab

มอง to look (at), see, glance (at), cast one's eyes on; to take someone for a
อย่ามองฉันเป็นคนโง่ *Don't take me for a fool.*

มองกระจก to look in the mirror

มองกราด to look around, cast one's eyes (about, around)

มองการณ์ไกล farsighted, sagacious; to have foresight

มองขวา to look to the right

มองข้าง ๆ to look to the side, look over one's shoulder

มองข้ามไป to overlook

มองดู to look (at)

มองตากัน to gaze into each other's eyes

มองตาม to follow (someone) with one's eyes

มองในแง่ร้าย to be pessimistic, look at the dark side (of things etc), take a disparaging view (of)

มองไม่เห็น invisible; unable to see

มองสบตา eyes met

มองหน้ากันไม่ติด to have a mutual /antipathy/dislike/, be on the outs

มองหา to look for, search for

มองเห็น to see, notice, catch sight of, perceive

มองเห็นไรๆ indistinct, vague; to see indistinctly

จ้องมอง to stare (at)

จับตามอง to keep an eye on, watch, observe

เหลียวมอง to look around, look over one's shoulder

เหลือบมอง to glance (at), look up

มอซอ shabby, seedy; dejected

แต่งตัวมอซอ /badly/shabbily/dressed; shabby, ill-kempt; to look seedy

มอญ Mon

มอด[1] wood borer, weevil

มอด[2] to die out, go out, be extinguished

ม่อต้อ stocky, chunky; dumpy

มอบ to give (to), hand over something to someone, deliver; to submit; to turn over

มอบฉันทะ to give a /proxy/mandate/ authorization/ (to)

ใบมอบฉันทะ a proxy, mandate, authorization

มอบตัว to give oneself up, surrender; to hand (someone) over (to); to report (for duty, work etc); to enroll, present oneself

มอบไว้ to deposit (with), place in another's care

มอบสมบัติ to bequeath; to distribute one's property on one's deathbed; to name a successor to the throne

มอบสิทธิ์ to /transfer/assign/ a right

มอบหมาย to authorize, assign, delegate, appoint, entrust

มอบให้ to give, present

มอบอำนาจ to empower, authorize, give a power of attorney (to), delegate authority

(to)

    ใบมอบอำนาจ power of attorney, proxy

ส่งมอบ to deliver, hand over, transfer

มอม to /dirty/blacken/ one's face; dirty, black

    มอมเมา to mislead, brainwash, drug

    พวกทรราชพยายามมอมเมาประชาชนว่าการเมือง

    เป็นเรื่องสกปรก The tyrants tried to /mislead/

    brainwash/drug/ the people into thinking

    politics is dirty.

    มอมแมม filthy, dirty, dirty-looking

    มอมเหล้า to get someone drunk

ม่อย to doze; doze off, be half-asleep

    หน้าม่อย crestfallen, downcast, to /pull/ wear/have/ a long face

ม่อลอกม่อแลก *as in* **เปียกม่อลอกม่อแลก** drenched, sopping wet; bedraggled

ม่อฮ่อม indigo, indigo-dyed; peasant-style

มะกรูด kaffir lime

มะกอก olive

มะเกลือ ebony

มะขาม tamarind

    มะขามเทศ Manila tamarind

มะขามป้อม emblic myrobalan

มะเขือ eggplant, aubergine

    มะเขือเทศ tomato

    มะเขือเผา toasted eggplant; flaccid, limp, ineffectual

มะงุมมะงาหรา to fumble around

มะเดื่อ fig tree

มะตูม bael fruit, bel fruit, Bengal quince

มะนาว lime

    น้ำมะนาว limeade; lime juice

มะปราง marian plum

มะพร้าว coconut

    มะพร้าวห้าว ripe coconut

    เอามะพร้าวห้าวมาขายสวน to take coals to Newcastle

    มะพร้าวอ่อน young coconut

    กะลามะพร้าว coconut shell

    ทางมะพร้าว coconut-palm leaf stalk

    น้ำมะพร้าว coconut milk

    เปลือกมะพร้าว coconut husk

    ลูกมะพร้าว coconut

มะเฟือง carambola, star fruit

มะม่วง mango

    มะม่วงมัน green-delicious mango

    มะม่วงหิมพานต์ cashew, cashew nut

    ข้าวเหนียวมะม่วง mango and sticky rice

มะเมีย the Year of the Horse

มะแม the Year of the Goat

มะยม star gooseberry

มะรืน the day after tomorrow

มะรุมมะตุ้ม a turmoil, confusion of (problems, fighting etc)

มะเร็ง cancer

มะเรื่อง two days after tomorrow

มะโรง the Year of the Dragon

มะละกอ papaya

มะลิ jasmine

    ดอกมะลิ jasmine

มะเส็ง the Year of the Snake

มะเหงก a gesture of contempt

    มะเหงกแน่ะ So what!

มัก to like, prefer

    มักคุ้น to be familiar with, be intimate with

    มักง่าย careless, slipshod, sloppy

    มักจะ often, usually, would, to like to

    มักได้ greedy, grasping, avaricious

    มักน้อย modest, undemanding, easily satisfied, content with what one has; frugal

    มักมาก to be greedy (for), insatiable

    มักใหญ่ใฝ่สูง ambitious, over-ambitious

มัคคุเทศก์ guide

มั่ง to be rich, wealthy

    มั่งคั่ง well-off, well-to-do, rich, wealthy

        มั่งคั่งสมบูรณ์ rich, affluent

    มั่งมี wealthy, affluent, well-off, well-to-do

        มั่งมีขึ้น to get rich

ม
ย
ร
ฤ
ฤๅ
ล
ว
ศ
ษ
ส
ห
ฬ
อ
ฮ

มังกร dragon; Capricorn

มังคุด mangosteen

มัจจุ death

มัจจุราช King of Death, the Great Reaper

มัจฉริยะ stinginess, niggardliness, parsimonious-ness

มัจฉะ, มัจฉา fish

มัจฉาชาติ fish

มัชฌิม-, มัชฌิมา middle, moderate

มัชฌิมาปฏิปทา the Middle Way, Middle Path

มัณฑนศิลป์ interior decoration, decorative arts

มัด to bind, tie up, bundle, tie in bunches; a numerical designation for bundles and bunches

มัดจำ deposit

เงินมัดจำ deposit, down payment, earnest money

วางมัดจำ to give a deposit, make a down payment

มัดมือมัดตีน to bind hand and foot, render helpless

ผูกมัด to incriminate; to be conclusive (of); to bind, obligate, commit

ข้อผูกมัด binding, obligation, duty, commitment; condition

มัธยม secondary, middle

มัธยมศึกษา /secondary/high school/edu-cation

มัธยมศึกษาตอนต้น junior high school

มัธยมศึกษาตอนปลาย senior high school

ครูมัธยม secondary school teacher

ชั้นมัธยม secondary school level

ชั้นมัธยมบริบูรณ์ high school, secondary school

มัธยัสถ์ economical, thrifty, sparing, frugal

มัน[1] glossy, shiny, polished; oily, rich

มันขลับ polished, having a luster

มันย่อง oily

มันวับ gleaming, shiny

มันวาว shining, glittering

กระดาษมัน glazed paper, coated paper

กระดูกขัดมัน tightfisted, miserly

ข้าวมัน rice boiled with coconut cream

เป็นมัน oily (skin); /glittering/eager/(eyes), shiny, glossy, shining

มัน[2] tuber

มันแกว turnip

มันเทศ sweet potato

มันฝรั่ง potato

มันสำปะหลัง tapioca, cassava

มัน[3] it, he, she, him, her, guy

มันคนละเรื่อง irrelevant, altogether different, It's another matter.

มันจะเป็นอะไรไป What does it matter?

มันยุ่ง troublesome, bothersome; too com-plicated, too much trouble

ของใครของมัน to look after yourself; (to take) one's own, to each his own

ช่างมัน Who cares?, Forget it., To hell with it.

ทีใครทีมัน Just you wait!; It's my turn now.

มัน[4] to feel like (doing something),/itching/ stewing/(to do something); to be fun; to like, enjoy

มันเขี้ยว to feel like (punching someone in the nose, etc)

มันมือ to get a kick out of (doing something), be having fun, enjoying

มั่น certain, sure, positive, confident, firm, solid

มั่นคง solid, strong; stable, steady

มั่นใจ certain, sure, confident; convinced, positive

เชื่อมั่น to be confident, strongly believe

เชื่อมั่นในตนเอง to have self-confidence

ตั้งมั่น to be firmly established (in); to be firm (in one's /belief/course of action/), unwavering

ยึดมั่น to be attached to, adhere to, hold

fast to, believe firmly in

หมายมั่นปั้นมือ to be determined (to), resolved (to), be set on (doing etc)

มัว[1] gloomy; indistinct, obscure; dim; dizzy, crazy about, absorbed in; clouded, overcast (ฟ้า)

มัวซั่ว to mess around (with); in a confused way, messy

มัวเมา addicted (to), intoxicated (by), blinded (by), be crazy about

มัวหมอง under a cloud, in disgrace, tarnished, tainted

ขุ่นมัว frustrated; overcast, murky; in a /dark/bad/ mood, gloomy

พร่ามัว filmed over, clouded over, blurred

มืดมัว dark, gloomy, overcast; indistinct

มัว[2] so, to insist on

มัวชักช้า to take so much time, be so slow; to insist on being so slow

มัวแต่ to do nothing but..., be so caught up in (work, thinking about something, etc), so busy *มัวแต่ดูทีวีเพลินเลยไม่ได้ยินเสียงโทรศัพท์ I was so busy watching TV, I didn't hear the telephone ring.*

มัวโอ้เอ้ to be blithely dallying

มั่ว, มั่วๆ undiscriminating; in a mess, a jumble (of), mixed up; indiscriminately, haphazardly; chaotic, erratic, quirky *อาหาร ถ้าสั่งดีๆ เป็นไม่แพง สั่งมั่วๆ ก็มักจะแพง If you order carefully it's not expensive but if you order indiscriminately it is expensive. คอมพิวเตอร์ก็มั่วได้ A computer can also be erratic.*

มั่วสุม to mix with, associate with, hang around together, hang out (with)

ทำมั่วๆ to do any old which way *ข้อสอบง่ายมาก ทำมั่วๆ ก็ถูก The questions are so easy. You can do it any old which way and you'll be right.*

มัสยิด mosque

มา to come; ...ing *ผมโทรศัพท์มา...I am calling to...*

มาครับ Here., Yes, sir., Aye aye sir (ทหารเรือ)

มาจากไหน Where are you from? Where do you come from?

มาซิ Come on., Come along.

มาตามนัด to keep one's appointment, come /at the time appointed/on time/

มาแต่ from

   มาแต่กำเนิด inborn, innate, congenital

   มาแต่เดิม from the beginning

มาถึง to arrive (at), reach

   การมาถึง arrival

มาเถอะ Come on., Come along.

มาทัน to come in time

มาทำไม? Why did you have to come?, What are you here for?

มานี่ Come here., Come over here.

   มานี่แน่ะ Come here.

มาเยี่ยม to visit, come to visit

มาแล้ว already; He (it etc) is here.

มาสาย to be late (for school etc)

มาหรือยัง? Has he (it etc) come yet?

มาหา to call on, come to see

ม้า horse; trestle; stool; knight; speed *(sl)*

ม้ากาบกล้วย cockhorse

ม้าแกลบ pony

ม้าแข่ง racehorse

ม้าใช้ mounted messenger; flunkey

ม้าดีดกะโหลก tomboyish; hoyden

ม้าตัวผู้ stallion

ม้าตัวเมีย mare

ม้าต่าง packhorse

ม้าเทศ horse

ม้าน้อยเพศผู้ colt

ม้าน้อยเพศเมีย filly

ม้านั่ง bench, stool

ม
ย
ร
ฤ
ฦ
ล
ว
ศ
ษ
ส
ห
ฬ
อ
ฮ

ม้าน้ำ seahorse

ม้ามืด dark horse

ม้ายาว bench; horse, trestle

ม้าโยก rockinghorse

ม้ารองเท้า footstool

ม้าเร็ว mounted messenger

ม้าลาย zebra

ม้าหมุน merry-go-round, carrousel

กำลังม้า horsepower

เกือกม้า horseshoe

ขี่ม้า mounted, equestrian; to ride a horse, ride horseback

แข่งม้า horse racing, horse race

ควบม้า to gallop a horse

รถม้า horse carriage

แรงม้า horsepower

เล่นม้า to play the horses, bet on horses

สนามม้า race course, race track

หน้าม้า a shill; a claque

อานม้า saddle

มาก many, much, a lot

มากๆ a lot of, much, many

มากกว่า more than, more *see* **มากกว่า** หน้า 18

มากเกินไป too much, too many, excessive

มากขึ้น more, increasing

มากที่สุด most

มากนัก very /much/many/,so /much/many/

มากมาย a great many, a whole lot of, more than enough, abundant, plentiful, copious

มากมายก่ายกอง an enormous amount (of), plenty (of), a pile (of)

มากมายหลายชนิด a great variety of

กี่มากน้อย *see* **กี่มากน้อย** หน้า 31

ข้างมาก majority

โดยมาก mostly, generally, for the most part, a majority

ปากมาก bigmouthed, to talk too much, be a blabbermouth, shoot off one's mouth

เป็นจำนวนมาก a large number (of)

เป็นอันมาก very much

มักมาก to be greedy (for), insatiable

มันจะมากไปแล้ว That's going too far.; to be intolerable

รู้มาก to show off; to take advantage (of)

มาฆบูชา Magha Puja, Buddhist puja on the day of the full moon in the third lunar month to commemorate the great assembly of the Buddha's disciples

มาด[1] manner, style, the impression one gives; pose

มาดเขาดี (to have) presence, fine bearing, good style

มีมาด to have presence

วางมาด to pose, be overbearing

มาด[2] *as in* มุ่งมาด to aim to,intend (to); to desire

มาตร[1] meter

มาตร[2] *as in* มาตรว่า even if, no matter (if, how)

มาตรการ measure(s)

ห้ามจอดรถระหว่าง 8.00 ถึง 10.00 น. เป็น มาตรการอย่างหนึ่งในการแก้ไขปัญหาจราจร The prohibition of parking between 8 and 10 is a measure taken to solve the traffic problem.

มาตรฐาน standard, up to standard; specification

มาตรฐานการครองชีพ standard of living

มาตรฐานสินค้า industrial standards

สินค้ามาตรฐาน standard /product/goods/, product of recognized quality

มาตรา section, clause, article, paragraph; meter

มาตราชั่ง scale

มาตราทองคำ gold standard

มาตราเมตริก metric system

มาตราส่วน scale

อนุมาตรา subsection, subparagraph

มาตุภูมิ motherland, homeland, native land, birth place

ม่าน curtain, drapery, blind

ม่านตา iris

ม่านบังตา a blind

ม่านรูด motel with curtained parking spaces

ม่านหน้าต่าง window curtain (ผ้า), window blind, window shade (ม้วนได้)

ม่านเหล็ก Iron Curtain

กั้นม่าน to curtain off, hang a curtain; to screen

ปิดม่าน to lower the curtain, draw the curtains; to close a blind

เปิดม่าน to open a /curtain/blind/, raise the curtain

แหวกม่านประเพณี to flout convention, break with tradition; unorthodox

ม้าน to grow pale with shame

มานพ young man

มานะ perseverance, persistence, diligence; pride, self-regard

มานุษยดุริยางควิทยา ethnomusicology

มานุษยวิทยา anthropology

นักมานุษยวิทยา anthropologist

ม้าม spleen

ม่าย widow (ผู้หญิง), widower (ผู้ชาย); divorced

พ่อม่าย widower

แม่ม่าย widow; grass widow (ม่ายผ่อร้าง), divorcee

แม่ม่ายทรงเครื่อง wealthy widow

มายา tricky, crafty, cunning, scheming, deceit; illusion, maya

มายากร conjurer, magician

มาร Mara, The Evil One, The Tempter, devil

มารคอหอย spoiler

มารผจญ hindrance

มารสังคม a blight on society

มารหัวขน baby born out of wedlock, bastard child

มารดร, มารดา mother

มารยา tricky, crafty, cunning, disingenuous, scheming

มารยาท, มรรยาท manners, conduct, behavior; etiquette

คนดีมีมารยาท well-mannered person, gentleman, refined person

ไม่มีมารยาท bad-mannered, impolite, discourteous, rude

เสียมารยาท (it is) bad manners, impolite; unprofessional

มาราธอน marathon

มารุมมาตุ้ม to be piling up; a mess of (problems, work etc)

มาลัย garland, string of flowers

พวงมาลัย garland, string of flowers; steering wheel

มิ not, no

มิฉะนั้น otherwise, or else, if not

มิชอบ wrong, wrongful, unlawful; bad, reprehensible, immoral

มิช้ามินาน before long, shortly

มิดีมิร้าย (for) immoral purposes, (to do) an immoral act, (to do) something bad (to a woman)

มิได้ no, not so, no sir

หาที่เปรียบมิได้ incomparable

มิได้ขาด regularly, regular (in doing something)

มิได้ห้ามไว้ not prohibited

มิน่า what a shame; I'm not surprised., It's not surprising., It's no surprise.

มิน่าล่ะ so that's why

มิน่าเล่า no wonder, it's no surprise

มิไย despite

มิหนำซ้ำ as if it were not enough, besides

มิคสัญญี violence and turmoil, calamity, doomsday; calamitous

มิ่งขวัญ beloved; a joy (to); auspicious (for); glory (of)

มิจฉาชีพ /wrongful/unlawful/ occupation, unlawful way of making a living, wrongful livelihood

ม
ย
ร
ฤ
ฤๅ
ล
ว
ศ
ษ
ส
ห
ฬ
อ
ฮ

เหล่ามิจฉาชีพ criminals, gangsters, malefactors, the criminal element

มิจฉาทิฏฐิ wrong /idea/view/, misconception

มิด concealed, covered over, out of sight; tightly, completely; sealed

    มิดชิด entirely concealed, hidden (under, in), completely covered over

    มิดเม้น to conceal

    จมมิด completely immersed, buried

    บังจนมิด to obscure, block out, screen

    ปิดอย่างมิดชิด tightly concealed, kept completely secret; tightly /closed/sealed/

มิตร friend

    มิตรจิต friendliness, cordiality, sociability, aimiability

    มิตรภาพ friendship, amity

    มิตรสหาย friends, companions, comrades

    มิตรสัมพันธ์ friendly relations, amicable relations

    ญาติมิตร friends and relatives

    ผูกมิตร to make friends (with)

    สัมพันธมิตร ally

มิติ dimension

มิถุนายน June

มิลลิกรัม milligram

มิลลิบาร์ millibar

มิลลิเมตร millimeter

มิลลิลิตร milliliter

มี to have; to consist of, comprise; to be; there is, there are; rich, wealthy

    มีกระสุน to be loaded

    มีกลิ่น to smell (of), have a smell; smelly; fragrant

        มีกลิ่นคาว to have a /fishy/meaty/ smell; to smell of (blood, raw meat etc)

        มีกลิ่นแรง to have a strong odor, smell strongly (of)

        มีกลิ่นเหล้า to smell of liquor

    มีกังวล worried, disturbed, to have worries

มีกำไร profitable, to yield profit, make money

มีเกียรติ prestigious, honorable, respectable, distinguished, creditable

มีแก่ใจ generous, solicitous, considerate, kind, obliging

มีข้อสงสัย to be dubious; (it raises) questions, questionable

มีขึ้น to happen, occur, take place

มีคนจองแล้ว to be taken, reserved, booked

มีครอบครัว to be married, have a family

มีความทรงจำดี to have a good memory

มีความผิด to be guilty (of), be at fault, (in the) wrong, to have done something wrong

มีความยินดี to be pleased, take pleasure in, glad

มีความรู้มาก to know a lot, learned, experienced

มีความสนใจ to be interested (in), take an interest (in)

มีความหมาย to mean something (to), have meaning (for), to be meaningful, significant

มีความห่วงใย to be concerned (about), worried (about)

มีความเห็นว่า to be of the opinion (that)

มีค่า valuable, precious, worth something

มีคุณ beneficial, good, valuable

มีเงิน rich, wealthy, (person) of means, to have money

มีเจ้าของ to have an owner, to belong to, proprietary

มีชีวิต alive, living

มีชื่อ famous, well-known, popular, noted; notorious

มีชื่อว่า named, called, to bear the name of

มีชื่อเสียง well-known, famous, eminent, celebrated

มีชู้ to have a lover

มีโชค fortunate, lucky, to be in luck

มีใช้ to have /some/enough/ample/

มีต่อ to be continued

มีถมไป a lot (of), plenty (of)

มีทรัพย์ to be well-to-do, well-off, wealthy, opulent

มีท้อง pregnant, expecting

มีทาง possible

มีท่าว่า to appear, look like, seem to

มีทิฐิ opinionated, prejudiced

มีทีเด็ด to have a /trump/clincher/

มีโทษ harmful, noxious, bad, have a bad effect; to carry a penalty (of)

มีธุระ busy, to have something to do

มีนามว่า called, named

มีประโยชน์ useful, valuable, helpful; usable; wholesome, nutritious

มีปัญญาดี bright, intelligent, to have a good mind

มีผล effective, productive, to bear fruit, produce results, take effect, have consequences, result in

มีผลใช้บังคับ to enter into force

มีผลงาน to show results; to get the credit (for something)

มีผู้คนหนาแน่น crowded, congested

มีฝีมือ skilled, capable, proficient, adept (at), skillful

มีพิษ poisonous, venomous, toxic

มีมลทิน sullied, tarnished, to have something against one, have a black mark against one's name

มีรส tasty, delicious, flavorsome, to taste good

    มีรสมีชาติ juicy, exciting

มีระดับ classy, to have class

มีระเบียบ orderly, well-organized, methodical, systematic; neat

มีรากฐาน to have a (/solid/sound/good/ etc) foundation

มีราคามาก to be worth a lot

มีลาภ fortunate, lucky

มีลูก to have children; to bear fruit

มีเลศนัย (there is) something between the lines, having /a hidden/an ulterior/ meaning; (there is) something suspicious (about)

มีวิชา educated

มีแวว see มีแวว *หน้า 468*

มีศรัทธา to have confidence (in)

มีสง่า dignified

มีสตางค์ well-heeled, moneyed

มีสภาพ to be, have the nature of, be in a (liquid, solid, etc) state

มีส่วน to have a share (in), take part in, be part of, be partly responsible (for)

    มีส่วนร่วม to participate, take part (in), have a share (in, of)

มีส่วนได้ส่วนเสีย to have an interest (in), have a stake (in)

มีสิทธิ์ authorized, to be entitled, have the right (to); possibly, within the realm of possibility, (there is) a good chance

    มีสิทธิ์มีเสียง to have a voice, be entitled (to)

    มีสีสัน colorful; attractive, having panache

มีเส้น to have /pull/influence/connections/

มีเสน่ห์ charming, personable, attractive, appealing, alluring, to have charm

มีเสรี (ที่จะ) to be free (to)

มีหน้ามีตา to be a /somebody/personage/, be someone, respected, esteemed

มีหนี้สินรุงรัง to be heavily in debt

มีหวัง hopeful, there is hope; to be possible

มีหัวใจ to have feelings, kind, sympathetic, compassionate, thoughtful

    ไม่มีหัวใจ to be unfeeling, heartless, thoughtless, insensitive

มีไหวพริบ see ไหวพริบ *หน้า 553*

มีเหตุผล sensible, reasonable

ม
ย
ร
ฤ
ฤๅ
ล
ว
ศ
ษ
ส
ห
ฬ
อ
ฮ

มีเหย้ามีเรือน to have a family, be married

มีอย่างหรือ to be the limit

มีอันจะกิน well-to-do, well-off, prosperous, well-heeled

มีอันเป็น to be struck by misfortune

มีอาวุโส senior

มีอำนาจ powerful; to have the power (to), be empowered, authorized

มีอิทธิพล influential, to have influence, powerful

มีโอกาส to have the /opportunity/chance/ (to)

มีชัย condom *(sl)*

มีด knife

มีดโกน straight razor

มีดตัดเล็บ nail clippers

มีดโต้ bush knife, machete

มีดปังตอ butcher's knife

มีดผ่าตัด scalpel

หินลับมีด whetstone

มีนาคม March

มึง you *(vulgar)*

มึน tipsy; giddy, dizzy; in a daze

มึนงง groggy, dazed

มึนชา numb, cold, distant

มึนตึง to be cool (to), (to be or look) irritated, annoyed

มึนเมา drunk, inebriated

มึนหัว dopey, dazed, woozy

มืด dark, obscure

มืดค่ำ nightfall, dusk; nighttime, at night

มืดตื้อ pitch dark

มืดแปดด้าน to be in a /hopeless/bleak/ situation, see no way out, be completely stymied

มืดฟ้ามัวฝน to be overcast, look like rain

มืดมน bleak, hopeless, dark, obscure

มืดมัว dark, gloomy, overcast

เช้ามืด before dawn

หน้ามืด see **หน้ามืด** หน้า 517

มือ hand

มือกาว light-fingered, sticky-fingered

มือเก่า old hand (at)

มือขวา right hand; right-hand man

มือขึ้น to improve, be improving

มือใครยาวสาวได้สาวเอา up for grabs

เวลานี้บ้านเมืองอยู่ในสภาพมือใครยาวสาวได้สาวเอา At present the country is in a condition where everything is up for grabs.

มือขั้นไหน How good is he?

มือซ้าย left hand

มือดี able, fine, skilled; a crook

มือตก to lose one's touch, go downhill

มือเติบ extravagant, spendthrift

มือถือ handle; mobile phone

มือถือสากปากถือศีล see **มือถือสากปากถือศีล** หน้า 215

มือที่สาม third party, outsider, outside intervention

มือบอน to have itchy fingers, have roving hands

มือปืน gunman

มือเปล่า emptyhanded

มือผี ghostwriter; one asked to fill in at cards as a dummy

มือไพล่หลัง hands clasped behind one's back

มือมืด unknown hand

มือไม่ถึง not /skilled/experienced/ enough, not up to it

มือไว light-fingered; free with one's hands

มือสะอาด clean, uncorrupt

มือหนึ่ง first rate, top, tops

มือใหม่ novice; to be new at something

มืออาชีพ professional

แก้มือ to have another go (at something), make up for (one's loss, defeat etc), have a return match

ข้อมือ wrist

ขาดมือ not have on hand, to be short (of)

คันมือ to have an urge to (do something), be itching to (sock someone, do something etc)

คามือ red-handed; before one's very eyes

คู่มือ[1] handbook, manual

คู่มือ[2] personal, one's own

เครื่องมือ tool, implement, instrument, apparatus, appliance

เงื้อมมือ see เงื้อมมือ *หน้า 108*

จับมือ to shake hands; to hold someone's hand

เจ้ามือ see เจ้ามือ *หน้า 123*

ต้นมือ in the beginning, at first, initially, at the outset

เต็มมือ to have one's hands full (with work etc)

ถนัดมือขวา right-handed

ถนัดมือซ้าย left-handed

ถนัดสองมือ ambidextrous

ถึงมือ to come to hand, reach, get to someone

ถุงมือ glove

น้ำมือ see น้ำมือ *หน้า 258*

นิ้วมือ finger

แบมือ to hold out one's hand; to ask for a handout

โบกมือ to wave (one's hand)

ปรบมือ to applaud, give (someone) a hand, clap (the hands)

ฝ่ามือ palm (of the hand)

ฝีมือ skill, ability, work, handiwork; workmanship, craftsmanship

ลงมือ to begin, start, commence

ลงลายมือ to sign; signature

ลายมือ handwriting; lines on the fingers and palm of the hand

ลูกมือ helper, assistant

อยู่ในมือ in hand

มื้อ mealtime; meal

มื้อกลางวัน lunch, midday meal

มื้อค่ำ dinner, evening meal, supper

มื้อเช้า breakfast, morning meal

กินข้าวมื้อเดียว to eat once a day, take one meal a day

อดมื้อกินมื้อ to live from hand to mouth

มุ intensively, with concentration

มุก pearl oyster; mother-of-pearl

ไข่มุก pearl

ฝังมุก inlaid with mother-of-pearl

มุกดา, มุกดาหาร pearl; opal

มุข[1] face, visage; mouth; entrance; balcony, porch, portico

หน้ามุข balcony; porch, verandah

มุข[2] angle, twist; trick; joke; turn of expression

มุขตลก gag, joke, comic twist, humorous twist, funny angle of the story

มุขเศร้า sad twist

มุขปาฐะ oral literature, oral tradition

มุง[1] to roof, cover with a roof (of grass, thatch, shingles etc)

มุงกระเบื้อง to roof with tiles, tile-roofed

มุงจาก atap-thatched

มุงสังกะสี to roof with corrugated iron, tin-roofed

มุง[2] to crowd around (to look at something)

ไทยมุง curious spectators, on-looker, gawkers

ยืนมุง to gather around to watch; to gawk (at something)

มุ่ง to aim, intend

มุ่งมั่น determined (to), firmly intend (to)

มุ่งมาด to aim to, intend (to); to desire

มุ่งร้าย to bear ill will, ill-disposed (toward someone); malicious, to have malicious intent

มุ่งหน้า to head (for, to, towards)

ม

ย

ร

ฤ

ฦ

ล

ว

ศ

ษ

ส

ห

ฬ

อ

ฮ

มุ่งหมาย to intend (to), plan (to, on), aim (to, at); purpose, intention, design, aim

มุ่งหวัง to hope (for, to), expect to; aim, purpose, objective

มุ้ง mosquito net

มุ้งลวด screen, screening

กางมุ้ง to put up a mosquito net

เรื่องในมุ้ง family affair

มุด to crawl under; to burrow (into the ground); to dive under

มุดหัว to be hiding, lie low

มุทะลุ hot-tempered, aggressive, pugnacious, truculent

มุทิตา sympathetic joy (over the success of others)

แสดงมุทิตาจิต to congratulate

มุ่น *as in* **มุ่นผม** to put one's hair up in a bun

มุบมิบ to whisper; secretly, surreptitiously

มุม angle; corner

มุมกลับ to the contrary; reflex angle

มุมฉาก right angle

มุมถนน corner

มุมปาก corner of the mouth

มุมป้าน obtuse angle

มุมมอง point of view, view, angle

มุมมืด dark corner

มุมเรขาคณิต angles

มุมแหลม acute angle

จนมุม cornered, stymied

ต้อนเข้ามุม to drive into a corner, corner

หลบมุม to find a discreet corner, stay out of sight

มุ่ย *as in* **หน้ามุ่ย** to scowl, look cross, pout, have a sour face; to look unhappy, out of sorts

มุสา lying, false

มุสาวาท falsehood, lie; to lie, tell a lie

คนมุสา liar

มูก *as in* **น้ำมูก** nasal mucus

น้ำมูกไหล to have a running nose

สั่งน้ำมูก to blow one's nose

มู่ทู่ rounded, bulbous; blunt

มูล[1] basis, source, origin; grounds (for /believing /conviction/etc); fund; cost

มูลความจริง factual basis

มูลค่า cost, value; worth

มูลค่าหุ้น par value

มูลฐาน basic, fundamental

มูลเหตุ origin, basic cause, grounds, real reason

ข้อมูล data, facts, information

คดีมีมูล prima facie case, case with grounds (for trial)

เค้ามูล source

มีมูล to have a basis, have grounds, prima facie, substantiated

    ไม่มีมูล baseless, no grounds, unsubstantiated

มูล[2] excrement, dung; detritus

มูลโค cow dung

มูลฝอย rubbish, trash, garbage, refuse

มูลนิธิ foundation

มู่ลี่ blinds

เมฆ clouds

ก้อนเมฆ cloud

มีเมฆมาก cloudy

หายเข้ากลีบเมฆ to vanish into thin air

เม็ด seed, pip, grain, bead, granule; a numerical designation for grains, seeds, etc

เม็ดเงิน money, funds

เม็ดทราย grain of sand

เม็ดบัว lotus seed

เม็ดฝน raindrop

เม็ดละมุด clitoris

เม็ดโลหิต corpuscle

เต็มเม็ดเต็มหน่วย *see* **เต็มเม็ดเต็มหน่วย** *หน้า 202*

เป็นเม็ด pimply; granular, granulated

ฝนซาเม็ด to stop raining, It has stopped raining.

ก
ข
ค
ฆ
ง
จ
ฉ
ช
ซ
ฌ
ญ
ฎ
ฏ
ฐ
ฑ
ฒ
ณ
ด
ต
ถ
ท
ธ
น
บ
ป
ผ
ฝ
พ
ฟ
ภ
ม

เมตตา loving kindness, goodwill, friendliness; to be kind (to)

เมตร meter, metre

เมตริกตัน metric ton

เมถุน sexual intercourse

เม่น porcupine; hedgehog

   ขนเม่น quill

เม้ม to hem

   เม้มเงิน to pocket money

   เม้มปาก to purse the lips, compress the lips

เมรัย fermented alcoholic beverage, beer, wine

เมล์ mail

เมล็ด seed, bean, grain

   เมล็ดกาแฟ coffee bean

   เมล็ดข้าว grain of rice, rice kernel

   เมล็ดพืช seeds

เมษายน April

เมา intoxicated, drunk, inebriated, tipsy

   เมาคลื่น seasick

   เมาค้าง to have a hangover

   เมามัน *as in* อย่างเมามัน wild, wildly

   เมามาย to be dead drunk

   เมายา dopey, woozy, intoxicated

   เมารถ carsick

   เมาหมัด reeling, punch-drunk, dazed

   เมาหัวราน้ำ tight

   เมาเหล้า drunk, intoxicated, inebriated

   เมาอำนาจ to be drunk with power

   ขี้เมา drunkard, a drunk, a lush

   มัวเมา addicted (to), intoxicated (by), blinded (by), be crazy about

เมิน to turn away, look away; to spurn, be indifferent (to)

   เมินเฉย(ต่อ) to shrug off

   เมินเสียเถิด Not on your life!, Fat chance!

   เมินหน้า to turn away

เมีย wife; mistress; female

   เมียเก็บ mistress

   เมียน้อย minor wife, mistress

   เมียหลวง principal wife

   ตัวเมีย female

เมียงมอง to peek (at, around, in)

เมี่ยง tidbits wrapped in leaves

เมื่อ time; when; at

   เมื่อแก่ when old, when one is old, in one's old age

   เมื่อคืนนี้ last night

   เมื่อคืนวานนี้ the night before last

   เมื่อตะกี้ a moment ago

   เมื่อนั้น at that time, then

   เมื่อแรกเห็น at first sight

   เมื่อไร when, whenever

      เมื่อไรก็ได้ anytime, at any time, whenever (you like)

   เมื่อวันก่อน the other day

   เมื่อวานซืนนี้ the day before yesterday

   เมื่อวานนี้ yesterday

เมือก slime; mucus

เมือง world; country, land, province; town, city, urban

   เมืองขึ้น colony, dependency

   เมืองท่า seaport, port

      เมืองท่าปลอดภาษี free port

   เมืองไทย Thailand

   เมืองนอก abroad, foreign country

   เมืองผี spirit world

   เมืองพัทยา Pataya City

   เมืองร้อน tropical country

   เมืองหลวง capital

   เมืองอุตสาหกรรม industrial town; industrialized country

   การเมือง politics

   แขกเมือง state visitor, official /visitor/guest/

   คนต่างเมือง foreigner, outsider, stranger

   คู่บ้านคู่เมือง national, identified with the nation, treasured by the nation

   ชานเมือง outskirts, suburb

ม
ย
ร
ฤ
ฤๅ
ล
ว
ศ
ษ
ส
ห
ฬ
อ
ฮ

ก
ข
ค
ฆ
ง
จ
ฉ
ช
ซ
ฌ
ญ
ฏ
ฐ
ฑ
ฒ
ณ
ด
ต
ถ
ท
ธ
น
บ
ป
ผ
ฝ
พ
ฟ
ภ
ม

ชาวเมือง city people, cityfolk, townspeople, urban dweller

บ้านเมือง country

พลเมือง population, inhabitants; citizen, people

พื้นเมือง native, homemade, domestic, indigenous

เมื่อย tired, stiff

เมื่อยเนื้อเมื่อยตัว aching all over

เมื่อยปาก tired of talking

เมื่อยล้า tired, exhausted, worn out

แม่ mother, mom; female; river

แม่กุญแจ lock, padlock

แม่ไก่ hen

แม่ครัว cook

แม่ค้า tradeswoman, woman vendor

แม่คุณ a flattering term of address for a woman, my dear lady

แม่งาน person in charge

แม่ทัพ commander in chief, commanding general

แม่ทูนหัว godmother; darling

แม่ตาหวาน sweetheart

แม่นม wet nurse

แม่น้ำ river

แม่บท basic steps, basic /positions/poses (of Thai dance), basic /text/law/source/ scales/etc; model /law/work/etc

แม่บ้าน housekeeper, housewife; matron, mistress of a house, lady of the house

แม่เบี้ย hood (of a snake)

แม่แบบ model, pattern

แม่ผัว mother-in-law

แม่พิมพ์ teacher (see **แม่พิมพ์** หน้า 352)

แม่มด witch, sorceress

แม่ม่าย widow

แม่ม่ายทรงเครื่อง wealthy widow

แม่ยาย mother-in-law

แม่เรือน housewife, mistress of a house,

lady of the house

แม่แรง (lady) organizer

แม่เล้า brothel keeper, madam, mamasan

แม่เลี้ยง stepmother, foster mother

แม่สี primary color

แม่สื่อ matchmaker

แม่เหล็ก magnet

แม่เหล็กไฟฟ้า electromagnet

แม่ใหญ่ grandmother

แม้ although, though, if, even if; even; irrespective of

แม้กระทั่ง even

แม้กระนั้น even so

แม้แต่ even; not even

แม้แต่น้อย not in the least, not even a little

แม้ว่า if, even if, even though, no matter

แมกไม้ tree, branch

แมง insect, bug; Arachnida

แมงกะพรุน jellyfish

แมงดา pimp, procurer

แมงดาทะเล horseshoe crab

แมงทับ scarab beetle

แมงป่อง scorpion

แมงมุม spider

แมน manly, masculine, man

แม่น exact, accurate, precise; right, correct

แม่นกฎหมาย to know one's law

แม่นยำ (to remember) accurately

ความจำแม่น good memory

ยิงแม่น to be a sharpshooter, shoot accurately

แม้น even though, even if; like, resembling

แมลง insect, bug

แมลงปอ dragonfly, darning needle

แมลงภู่ carpenter bee

แมลงวัน fly, housefly

แมลงสาบ cockroach

ยาฆ่าแมลง insecticide

แมว cat

    แมวคราว big cat

    แมวตัวผู้ tomcat

    แมวน้ำ seal

    แมวมอง scout; talent scout

แม้ว Hmong hill tribe, a member of the Hmong tribe

โม่ hand ricemill, grinder

    โม่แป้ง to grind into flour

โม้ to boast, brag, talk big

    ไอ้หมอนี่ โม้สะบัดช่อ What a /braggart/ blowhard/!

โมฆะ void

โมฆียะ voidable

โมง o'clock, hours

    โมงเช้า seven in the morning, 7 a.m., 7 o'clock; from 7 a.m. to 11 a.m.

    กี่โมง What time is it?; at what time

    ชั่วโมง hour

    บ่ายโมง one in the afternoon, 1 p.m., 1 o'clock in the afternoon, 13 hours; from 1 p.m. to 5 p.m.

โม่ง hooded bandit

โมเม to surmise, be just guessing

โมลี topknot

โมหจริต delusion; ignorance

โมหะ delusion, ignorance

โมโห angry (with), mad (at) to get /angry/mad/

ไม่ not, no, un-, in-, im-, -less, dis-

    ไม่กลัวตาย fearless; daredevil

    ไม่กล้า timid, not dare (to do something), be afraid (to do something)

    ไม่กินเส้นกัน not get along together, not on good terms

    ไม่โก้ not smart, unfashionable, inelegant

    ไม่ขาดสาย continually, uninterruptedly, regularly, in a steady stream

    ไม่ขึ้นแก่ใคร independent

    ไม่เข้าข้าง impartial, neutral

ไม่เข้าใครออกใคร neutral, independent, impartial, one's own man

ไม่เข้าใจ do not understand, do not see, to fail to understand

ไม่เข้าที inappropriate, unseemly, unbecoming, out of place, unsuitable

ไม่เข้าเรื่อง irrelevant, beside the point; nonsense

ไม่ค่อยได้ความ not so hot, so-so, not amount to much

ไม่คู่ควรกัน unsuited to one another, unsuitable

ไม่เคย never, not before now, have not (haven't), never have

ไม่แคร์ I don't care.

ไม่ง่ายเลย tough, not easy at all, hard

ไม่จำกัด unlimited

ไม่ชอบ unlawful, wrongful; to dislike

    ไม่ชอบด้วยกฎหมาย unlawful, illegal

    ไม่ชอบธรรม unfair, unjust; illegitimate

    ไม่ชอบมาพากล dubious, fishy

    ไม่ชอบหน้า to dislike (someone); I can't stand him.

ไม่ชักช้า to lose no time (in going, getting, etc), promptly

ไม่ช้าก็เร็ว sooner or later

ไม่ชำนาญ inexperienced, unskilled, inexpert

ไม่เชิง not exactly, not quite, hardly, cannot say (he's clever, it's difficult etc)

ไม่เชื่อหู can hardly believe one's ears, unbelievable, incredible

ไม่ใช่ no, not at all; not that, that's not it

    ไม่ใช่เช่นนั้น no, not so, it is not like that, on the contrary

    ไม่ใช่แต่เพียงเท่านั้น not only that

    ไม่ใช่เพราะ not because

    ไม่ใช่หน้าที่ It's not my job.

ไม่ซื่อสัตย์ disloyal; unfaithful, untrue (to);

ม
ย
ร
ฤ
ฦ
ล
ว
ศ
ษ
ส
ห
ฬ
อ
ฮ

dishonest

ไม่เดือดร้อน not to affect, not to /worry/ bother/

เขามีรายได้มากมาย จะซื้อของแพงหน่อย ก็ไม่ เดือดร้อน With an income like that, a little extra on the price wouldn't bother him.

ไม่ได้ cannot, unable (to), no

    ไม่ได้ความ no good, not much good, lousy; nonsense, stupid

    ไม่ได้ตั้งใจ It was unintentional.; not deliberate, unintended

    ไม่ได้นึกฝัน unexpected, I never dreamt (/I would meet you/it would happen to me/ etc)

    ไม่ได้บอกสักหน่อย didn't say anything

    ไม่ได้ผล ineffective, it didn't work, useless, in vain, the result was negative

    ไม่ได้ไม่เสีย to come out even

    ไม่ได้เสียอะไร not to cost one anything (to); to have nothing to lose (by)

ไม่ต้อง Don't bother., It's not necessary., You don't have to., It's alright.

ไม่ต้อง ฉันจะทำเอง It's alright. I'll do it myself.

ไม่ต้องการ unwanted, I don't /want/need/ it., to not want to /go/do/have/etc

ไม่ติดใจ to not care; to waive *(กฎหมาย)*

ผมไม่ติดใจเอาเรื่อง I don't care to press the matter.

ไม่ติดใจเรียกร้องค่าเสียหาย The plaintiff waives damages.

ไม่ติดต่อกัน interrupted; out of touch

ไม่เต็มใจ to be reluctant (to), unwilling (to), half-hearted (about)

ไม่ถึง less than, short of; not even; not reach, not get to

ไม่ถือโทษโกรธใคร forgiving; kindly

    ไปไม่ถึง not get as far as, I never got there.

มือไม่ถึง not /skilled/experienced/ enough, not up to it

เอื้อมไม่ถึง out of reach, unreachable

ไม่ถูก wrong, incorrect, not right, improperly

    ตัดสินใจไม่ถูก I can't make up my mind., I don't know how to decide., It's hard (for one) to decide.

    บอกไม่ถูก I don't know., It's hard to say.

    พูดไม่ถูก I can't say., I don't know how to say it., not know what to say

    ไม่ถูกกาลเทศะ out of place, The timing was wrong., gauche, inappropriate

    ไม่ถูกชะตากัน not to get on well together, not on good terms

ไม่ทันรู้ตัว unawares, without warning

ไม่ทันสังเกต I didn't notice.

ไม่ทางใดก็ทางหนึ่ง somehow, in one way or another, in some way

ไม่เท่าไรหรอก not much, not so very

ไม่เที่ยง impermanent; inaccurate; unsteady

ไม่น้อย a lot (of), not a small /amount/ number/ of, quite a few

ไม่นับ not counting, not counted, apart from เช่น This is not counted.

บ้านหลังนี้เสียค่าซ่อมไปหนึ่งแสน ค่าจัดสวน ญี่ปุ่นไม่นับ It cost a hundred thousand to redo the house /not counting the Japanese garden./apart from the Japanese garden./ the Japanese garden not counted./

ไม่นับถือ not to respect, to have no respect for

ไม่น่าจะ not likely (to), unlikely (to)

ไม่น่าเชื่อ unreliable, unbelievable; incredible, extraordinary

ไม่น่าดู unsightly; inappropriate (to, for), not nice

ไม่นานเกินรอ before long; not too long to wait

ไม่น่าเป็นไปได้ improbable, unlikely

ไม่น่าพิศวาส unattractive

ไม่น่าเลย Oh no!, How awful!, /You/he/ etc/ should not have done it.

ไม่นำพา indifferent

ไม่นึกเลย (I) never /expected/thought/, totally unexpected

ไม่นึกอยาก not to feel like (doing, going etc)

ไม่แน่ใจ (I'm) not sure, uncertain

ไม่แน่นอน changeable, undependable, uncertain

ไม่แน่นัก not so sure

ไม่บริสุทธิ์ not pure (intentions, motives, etc), ulterior; impure, not clean; unchaste

ไม่ประสงค์จะออกนาม anonymous

ไม่ปะติดปะต่อ disjointed, incoherent

ไม่ปิดบัง openly, without concealing anything

ไม่เป็นแก่นสาร insubstantial, without substance

ไม่เป็นตัวของตัวเอง (I'm) not free (to), (he's) not (his) own man; spineless, to have no mind of one's own

ไม่เป็นที่ clumsily, gracelessly

ไม่เป็นมวย to be green, inexpert

ไม่เป็นรองใคร second to none

ไม่เป็นระเบียบ disorderly, messy, untidy, not in order

ไม่เป็นเรื่อง rubbish; nonsense, nonsensical; no good

ไม่เป็นไร never mind, it's nothing, don't mention it, that's alright, forget it, it doesn't make any difference

ไม่เป็นอันกินอันนอน to be worried to death (about)

ไม่เปลี่ยนแปลง not to change, steady, unchanging, constant, stable

ไม่แปลก not unusual, characteristic, normal; I'm not surprised.

ไม่ไปก็อย่าไป If you don't want to go then don't go.

ไม่พอ not enough, insufficient, inadequate

ไม่พอใจ dissatisfied (with), displeased, irritated (by), disgruntled

ไม่พึงปรารถนา non grata; unwelcome, undesirable

ไม่เพราะหู dissonant, discordant; unpleasant

ไม่เพียงพอ insufficient, inadequate

ไม่ฟังเสียง not to listen (to); obstinate

ไม่มี without, not to have, no, free (of), zero

ไม่มีกำหนด indefinitely

ไม่มีกิริยา unmannerly, crude

ไม่มีแก่ใจ hard, ungenerous, unfeeling

ไม่มีใคร there is no one, nobody, no one

    ไม่มีใครนอกจาก I have no one except....

    ไม่มีใครเล่นด้วย No one will play ball with (him)., Nobody will go along with that.

    ไม่มีใครสู้ incomparable, peerless

ไม่มีงานทำ jobless, unemployed; to have nothing to do

ไม่มีเงิน poor, broke, to have no money, be without funds, strapped (for money)

ไม่มีชีวิต lifeless, dead; inanimate

ไม่มีทาง there is no way, hopeless, useless

    ไม่มีทางทราบ There is no way to know., How could (I) know?

    ไม่มีทางเลี่ยง unavoidable

    ไม่มีทางเลือก inevitable, to have no choice

ไม่มีที่ติ flawless, perfect

ไม่มีที่เปรียบ incomparable, unparalleled, without parallel, matchless

ไม่มีที่มาที่ไป dubious, of unknown origin

ไม่มีที่อยู่ to have no place to live, homeless

ไม่มีใบ leafless

ไม่มีผิด faultless; innocent, guiltless

ม
ย
ร
ฤ
ฦๅ
ล
ว
ศ
ษ
ส
ห
ฬ
อ
ฮ

ไม่มีฟัน toothless

ไม่มีเม็ด seedless

ไม่มียางอาย shameless, brazen

ไม่มีเยี่ยงอย่าง unprecedented, no precedent (for)

ไม่มีระเบียบ disorganized, lacking in organization

ไม่มีศาสนา to have no religion

ไม่มีหาง tailless

ไม่มีอะไรเลย There is nothing at all.

ไม่มีอะไรใหม่ในโลกนี้ There is nothing new under the sun.

ไม่มีอันตรายอะไร completely safe, no danger whatsoever

ไม่มีอำนาจอะไร to have no /authority/power/

ไม่ยกเว้น without exception

ไม่ย่อท้อ unflagging, tireless

ไม่ยอม to refuse, not to allow, no, don't

    ไม่ยอมฟังเหตุผล unreasonable, not to listen to reason

    ไม่ยอมรับ to deny, refuse to admit; to refuse

    ไม่ยอมเสี่ยง to take no risk, play it safe, take no chance

    ไม่ยอมให้ไป not to /permit/allow/ another to go

ไม่ยัก at all

ไม่ยักรู้ it's news to /me/her/etc (that), to be unaware (of, that)

ไม่ยักรู้ว่าสุพรรณมีหัตถกรรม It's news to me that Suphanburi has handicrafts.

ไม่ยาก not difficult, not hard, easy, simple

ไม่ยำเกรง to have no respect (for)

ไม่ยิ่งหย่อนกว่า no less...than

ไม่ยินดียินร้าย indifferent (to), unconcerned, could not care less (about); with equanimity

ไม่ยี่หระเลย I don't care., not give a damn (about)

ไม่แยแส to be unconcerned (with, about),

indifferent (to), take no interest (in)

ไม่รังเกียจ I don't mind.

ไม่รับผิดชอบ irresponsible

ไม่รับรู้ to ignore, refuse responsibility

    ไม่รับรู้ด้วย It's not my business., I don't want to know about it.

ไม่รีบร้อน in no hurry, not urgent

ไม่รู้ I do not know., to be unaware (of, that)

    ไม่รู้จักจบ unending, interminable, perpetual, endless

    ไม่รู้จักเมื่อย tireless, indefatigable

    ไม่รู้จักอิ่ม insatiable

    ไม่รู้ไม่ชี้ unresponsive; I don't know anything.

    ไม่รู้ร้อน complacent, to remain unconcerned

    ไม่รู้หัวนอนปลายตีน not to know anything about someone, of obscure origin

    ไม่รู้อิโหน่อิเหน่ to know nothing at all (about something), not to know anything

ไม่เร่งร้อน to be in no hurry, not in a hurry

ไม่ลงตัว does not fit; does not come out, does not work

ไม่ลดละ relentless, unremitting

ไม่ลดลาวาศอก to make no concession (to)

ไม่ลำเอียง impartial, unbiased, fair

ไม่เล่นด้วย nothing doing

ไม่เลือกหน้า indiscriminately, without distinction

ไม่วันใดก็วันหนึ่ง sooner or later, one day

ไม่ว่าเวลาใด at any time

ไม่เวลาใดก็เวลาหนึ่ง some time or other

ไม่ไว้วางใจ no-confidence

ไม่ไว้หน้าใคร (he) does not spare anybody; to have no regard (for anyone)

ไม่สนใจ not interested (in), uninterested, take no interest (in)

ไม่สบาย unhappy; unwell, not to feel well,

to feel bad

ไม่สบายใจ unhappy; to be bothered about something

ไม่สมบูรณ์ imperfect; incomplete

ไม่สวย not beautiful, not pretty, not good-looking, not nice-looking, unattractive; not nice

ไม่สะดวก inconvenient

ไม่สะดวกใจ to be difficult (to)

ไม่สามารถ incapable, unable

ไม่สู้จะ not so....

ไม่เสียภาษี tax-free; duty-free; not to pay taxes

ไม่ไหวติง motionless, still

ไม่อยาก not to want (to do something), not to feel like (doing something); I don't feel like it.

ไม่อย่างใดก็อย่างหนึ่ง either...or, it is either one or the other, (this) or else (that)

ไม่อยู่ absent, not in, out

ไม่อยู่กับร่องกับรอย changeable, erratic; inconsistent

ไม่อินังขังขอบ to take no notice of, couldn't care less (whether, about), not to give a hang (whether, about)

ไม่เอา no, not interested

ไม่เอาใจกันเลย not to go out of one's way to please (someone), pay /no/little/ attention (to someone)

ไม่เอาใจใส่ to take no interest (in something or someone), uninterested; careless

ไม้[1] wood, timber; stick; plant; a numerical designation for bolts of cloth and things on sticks

ไม้กระดาน plank, board

ไม้กระดานหก seesaw

ไม้กระบอง quarterstaff

ไม้กลัด wooden /pin/fastener/

ไม้กวาด broom

ไม้กางเขน cross

ไม้ขีดไฟ match

ไม้แข็ง hard xylophone hammer; tough approach; (to exert) heavy pressure, (to take) strong action, (to be) tough (with), (to deal) aggressively (with), play hardball

ไม้แขวนเสื้อ (clothes) hanger, coat hanger

ไม้แคะหู earpick

ไม้จริง wood other than bamboo, true wood

ไม้จันทน์ sandalwood

ไม้จิ้มฟัน toothpick

ไม้ซุง log

ไม้ดอก flowering plant

ไม้ตาย trump card

ไม้ตีกลอง drumstick

ไม้ถ่อ punting pole

ไม้เถา vine, climber

ไม้เท้า walking stick, cane, staff

ไม้แทงบิลเลียด cue

ไม้นวม padded xylophone hammer; soft approach, gently

ไม้บรรทัด ruler, straightedge

ไม้ป่าเดียวกัน of the same sort; men who prefer men, on the same team

ไม้ไผ่ bamboo

ไม้พาย paddle, oar

ไม้พุ่ม bush, shrub

ไม้เมตร measuring stick

ไม้ยืนต้น perennial, tree

ไม้เรียว switch, rod

ไม้เลื้อย creeper, climber, vine, ivy

ไม้วา two-meter stick

ไม้สั้น short end (of the stick)

ไม้หมอน sleeper

ไม้หึ่ง a children's game of knocking sticks about

ไม้อัด plywood

กอไม้ thicket

กิ่งไม้ branch, twig

ม
ย
ร
ฤ
ฦ
ล
ว
ศ
ษ
ส
ห
ฬ
อ
ฮ

ช่างไม้ carpenter, woodworker

ต้นไม้ tree, plant

ท่อนไม้ piece of wood, log (ใหญ่กลม)

เนื้อไม้ wood

ใบไม้ leaf

ป่าไม้ forest, woods

เปลือกไม้ bark

ผลไม้ fruit

มือไม้ hands

ยอดไม้ crown (of a tree or bush), treetop; shoot (of a plant)

ร่มไม้ shade (of a tree)

เรือนไม้ wooden house

ลูกไม้ lace; fruit; trick

เสี้ยนไม้ splinter

หน่อไม้ bamboo shoot

ไม้[2] tone sign; vowel

ไม้จัตวา fourth tone sign (ˇ)

ไม้ตรี third tone sign (˜)

ไม้ไต่คู้ short vowel sign (็)

ไม้โท second tone sign (้)

ไม้มลาย a vowel with the sound "ai" (ไ)

ไม้ม้วน a vowel with the sound "ai" (ใ)

ไม้ยมก repeat sign (ๆ)

ไม้หันอากาศ a vowel with the sound "ǎ" (ั)

ไม้เอก first tone sign (่)

ไม้[3] as in

จะมาไม้ไหนกัน *What's he getting at?/ What's he up to. / What has he got up his sleeve?*

ไม้ตาย trump card

ลูกไม้ trick

    มีลูกไม้เยอะ cunning, crafty, tricky

ไมโครเมตร micrometer (a unit of length equal to one millionth of a meter)

ไมตรี friendship, friendliness, amity, goodwill

ไมตรีจิต (in) friendship, friendly spirit, friendly disposition, goodwill (towards), cordially

สำหรับคุณ..ด้วยไมตรีจิต *To.. with /best wishes/cordial best wishes/*

กระชับไมตรี to strengthen friendly relations

ตัดไมตรี to sever friendly relations, break off a friendship, become estranged

ผูกไมตรี to establish friendly relations, establish a friendship (with), secure the friendship of, cultivate (someone)

สัญญาพระราชไมตรี treaty of /friendship/ amity/

สันถวไมตรี goodwill, friendship

สัมพันธไมตรี /friendly/cordial/ relations, amity

ไมล์ mile

ไมล์ทะเล nautical mile

ยก[1] to raise, lift; to move; to give, put forward; to exempt (from); to remit (punishment); to reject, dismiss

ยกกำลัง to the power (of); to move forces, proceed to battle

ยกครู to do honor to a teacher and pay the school fee

ยกตนข่มท่าน conceited, overbearing

ยกตัวอย่าง for example, for instance; to give an example

ยกตัวเอง to brag, be self-important, (practice) self-aggrandizement

ยกทรง brassiere

ยกทัพ, ยกพล to move /an army/forces/troops/

ยกพลขึ้นบก to land troops

ยกโทษ to forgive, pardon

ยกประโยชน์ให้จำเลย to give the defendant the benefit of the doubt

ยกป้าย to put up a sign

ยกพวก to come in force; to act in a body, gang up

ยกฟ้อง to dismiss a /case/complaint/, case dismissed

ยกมาพูด to bring (something) up, raise (a question, issue, point, etc)

ยกเมฆ to make (something) up, fabricate (a story, event etc)

ยกมือไหว้ to pay respect by raising the hands pressed together

ยกยอ to flatter, praise

ยกยอด to carry over a balance; to take care of remaining work

ยกระดับ to elevate; to upgrade

ยกลูกสาวให้ to give one's daughter in marriage (to), marry one's daughter to someone

ยกเลิก cancel, repeal, rescind

ยกเว้น to except, excluding, not including, with the exception of; to exempt (from)

การยกเว้นจากการเก็บภาษี exemption from taxation

ยกไว้ to suspend, put aside, hold in abeyance

ยกหนี้ให้ to forgive a debt

ยกหางตัวเอง to crow (about); to blow one's own horn, blow one's own trumpet *(Brit)*; self-aggrandizing

ยกให้ *see* **ยกให้** *หน้า 552*

ยกให้ว่า to admit, concede; grant

ยกใหญ่ a lot, big, extremely

ยก[2] round; page size, format of type for printing pages of a book; piece

ผ้าไหม 1 ยก one piece of silk

มวยชก 10 ยก a 10 round fight

หนังสือ 8 หน้ายก octavo (size book), *ย่อ* 8 mo, 8°

หนังสือ 16 หน้ายก sixteenmo (size book), *ย่อ* 16 mo, 16°

ยงโย่ to bend over with the hands touching the ground

ยถากรรม fate, destiny

ปล่อยไปตามยถากรรม to leave to one's fate, let things take their course

ย่น to shorten, abbreviate, abridge; to shrink; wrinkled, crinkled

คอย่น to draw in one's neck

หน้าย่น wrinkled face, to have wrinkles; to frown; to wrinkle one's brow

ยนต์, ยนตร์ engine, motor

เครื่องยนต์ engine, machine, motor

จักรยานยนต์ motorcycle

ช่างยนต์ mechanic, machinist

แพยนต์ motor ferry

ภาพยนตร์ motion picture, film, movie

ยานยนต์ motor vehicle

รถยนต์ automobile, car, motorcar

เรือยนต์ motorboat, motor vessel, launch

หุ่นยนต์ robot, a form endued with life by incantation, zombie

ยม god of the underworld, Hades, Pluto

ยมทูต messenger of death, guide to the underworld

ยมบาล guardian of /hell/the underworld/; torturer of the dead

ยมราช god of the underworld, Pluto, Hades

ยมโลก Hades, world of the Dead

ยมก double

ไม้ยมก repeat sign (ๆ)

ยวง pulp, flesh; pure silver

ยวงขนุน /pulp/flesh/ of the jackfruit

เป็นยวง blob (of)

ยวดยาน vehicles, cars, conveyances

ยวดยิ่ง extremely, to the highest degree, top

ยวน[1] Ionian

ยวน[2] to tempt, allure, entice, invite; to charm; to annoy, rile, irritate

ยวนใจ to captivate, fascinate; to provoke, annoy, irritate, bother

ยวนตา inviting, charming, enticing; annoying; to bother

ยวนยี provocative, exciting

ยวบ soft; spongy; to give, sagging

ยวบ ๆ springy, resilient

ยวบยาบ to walk heavily

ย้วย crooked, askew, warped, out of shape

ยศ rank, title, insignia of rank

เกียรติยศ honors; honor, prestige; prestigious

เครื่องยศ insignia of rank

เจ้ายศเจ้าอย่าง to be a snob; imperious, haughty; one who stands on ceremony, formal

ถือยศ lordly, self-important; to pull one's rank (on someone)

เพื่อเป็นเกียรติยศ in honor of; to grace

ยโส arrogant, haughty, insolent, overbearing, disdainful

ยอ[1] to flatter, praise; to hold in high /esteem/regard/

ยอแสง to fade เช่น *The sunlight is fading.*

ตะวันยอแสง twilight, dusk

ยกยอ to flatter, praise

ลูกยอ compliment

ยอ[2] a dip net (for fishing)

ยกยอ to raise a dip net

ย่อ to make shorter, shorten, abbreviate, abridge, summarize; to reduce in size

ย่อความ to summarize, abridge; (to /make/do/) an abstract, a digest, a summary, a precis

ย่อตัว to bow down

ย่อท้อ daunted, discouraged, disheartened; intimidated

ย่อมุม to recess

ย่อหน้า indent, to make a new paragraph

ย่อหย่อน decreasing, diminishing, reduced

โดยย่อ briefly, in short, in summary

พจนานุกรมฉบับย่อ abridged dictionary, condensed dictionary

อย่างย่อ ๆ in brief, briefly

ยอก (to feel a) stabbing pain; to pierce, prick

ขัดยอก muscular pain; to feel creaky, stiff

ยอกย้อน involved, circuitous, complicated

ยอง ๆ in a squatting position; to crouch (down)

นั่งยอง ๆ to squat

ย่อง to walk stealthily, sneak (in, up on)

ย่องเบา to burgle, burglarize, housebreak, commit a burglary

นักย่องเบา burglar, housebreaker

ยองใย filaments; beaming

ยอด top, summit, peak; crown; tip; best (of); great!, superb, excellent, top-notch, champion; balance; shoot

ยอดเขา peak, mountain top, summit

ยอดชาย best of men, great guy

ยอดบัญชี balance, total

ยอดไม้ crown (of a tree or bush), treetop; shoot (of a plant)

ยอดยกมา balance carried over

ยอดเยี่ยม best, top, superb

ยอดรัก dearest, darling, my beloved

ย้อน to retrace, go back; to reverse

ย้อนตอบ to talk back (to)

ย้อนนึกถึง to recall, think back (to when)

ย้อนไปที่ to go back to, turn back to, revert to

ย้อนรอย to retrace one's steps; to retaliate, get back (at someone)

ย้อนหลัง retroactive

ยอบ to stoop, bow down, lower one's head; running /down/out/, getting less

ยอบแยบ at a low ebb, run down, depleted

ยอม to yield, give in, submit; to allow, consent (to), permit; to agree

ยอมความ to enter a settlement, settle a case, compromise

ยอมจำนน to yield, give in; to surrender, give up, admit defeat

ยอมตาม to consent, comply (with), go along (with)

ยอมตาย I'll never give in.; to lay down one's life (for)

ยอมผูกพันตน to agree to be bound

ยอมแพ้ to surrender, give up, give in (to), yield (to), admit defeat

ยอมยกให้ว่า to admit, recognize, grant

ยอมรับ to admit, concede, agree; to confess

ยอมรับได้ acceptable

ยอมรับไม่ได้ unacceptable

ยอมรับสารภาพ to confess

ยอมให้ to permit, allow

ยินยอม to consent, agree, permit, allow

ย่อม[1] small, little, smallish

ราคาย่อมเยา low-priced, inexpensive, cheap, bargain price

ย่อม[2] can; as a rule, it is natural (for someone to do something)

ย่อมจะ can, to be possible (to)

ย่อมได้ can (do something), to be a possibility; generally, naturally

ทุกคนย่อมรู้ everyone knows

ย้อม to dye, tint

ย้อมใจ to stimulate

ย้อมแมวขาย to sell (someone) a bill of goods, dupe

ช่างย้อมผ้า dyer

ย่อย to digest; to pulverize, crush, break into small parts; subordinate, sub-, ancillary; small

ย่อยยับ totally destroyed, devastated, ravaged; devastating

ย่อยสลายได้ degradable

เงินย่อย change; small bills, small change

น้ำย่อย digestive juice, gastric juice

แบ๊งค์ย่อย small bills

ขอแลกแบ๊งค์ 100 สัก 1,000 บาท May I have change of a thousand, please, in 100 baht bills.

ปลีกย่อย small, minor, subsidiary; details

ไม่ใช่ย่อย downright, pretty

เขาเก่งไม่ใช่ย่อย He is pretty clever. / He is a downright clever man.

ย้อย to hang down; pendulous; to drip

ก้นย้อย /heavy/fat/ bottom

หินย้อย stalactite

ยัก[1] to move up and down; to stick with its spines

ยักกระสาย to change the subject, switch (to something else); to get around something

ยักคิ้ว to raise one's eyebrows

ยักท่า to make things difficult (for)

ยักยอก to misappropriate, embezzle

ยักย้าย to remove, get rid of, put (something)

ย

ร

ฤ

ฤๅ

ล

ว

ศ

ษ

ส

ห

ฬ

อ

ฮ

out of reach (of)

ยักไหล่ to shrug (one's shoulders)

ยัก[2] *as in* **ไม่ยัก** not...too much; not happen (to), surprisingly, strangely enough

ไม่ยักชอบ I don't happen to like (him). / I don't like (him) too much.

ยักแย่ยักยัน (to walk) painfully, awkwardly.

ยักษ์ giant, ogre, demon

ขนาดยักษ์ giant, giant-size

ยักษิณี giantess, ogress

ยัง[1] to cause, give rise to, bring about, result in; to have; to be

ยังความเสียใจให้ to cause /regret/sorrow/ disappointment/ (to)

ยังชีพ to sustain life; to make a living

ยังผลให้ to result in

ยัง[2] still, yet, to remain

ยังคง still, yet; to remain

ยังไงก็ดี at any rate

ยังชั่ว that's better, to get better

   ค่อยยังชั่ว that's a relief; getting better

ยังดี still good

ยังเด็ก still a child

ยังมี still there, still have some, remaining, There is still some left.

ยังมีชีวิตอยู่ to be still alive, remain alive

ยังมีต่อ to be continued

ยังมีตัวอยู่ to be still /available/around/

ยังมีหน้า still dare to

ยังไม่เกิด unborn; it hasn't happened yet

ยังไม่ทัน not have a chance (to do, speak etc), even before (I could say, do etc), hardly

ยังไม่ทันว่าอะไรเลยก็โกรธเสียแล้ว I hardly said a word when he got a fit.

ยังหรอก not yet

ยังเหลืออยู่ to be left, still some left, still remains

ยังอยู่ to be still there, still alive, remaining

ยังอยู่ในความทรงจำ still remember

ยั้ง to go easy, pull one's punches, hold back; to curb, restrain

ยั่งยืน sustained, long-lasting, long-lived, enduring, to last a long time; sustainable

ยัด to stuff (in, with), cram (in, with), stuffed (with)

ยัดเยียด crowded, crammed (up, together); to press; to force (an opinion, gift etc on someone), insist on giving

ยัดห่า to stuff oneself

ไข่ยัดไส้ stuffed omelet

ยัน[1] to push (against); to prop (up); to lean (something) against (something) for support

ยืนยัน to confirm, affirm, assure

ยัน[2] to, up to, until; again and again, non-stop

ยันป้าย doggedly; always, forever; (fight) to the end

ยั่น scared; high on betel (*ยั่นหมาก*)

ยับ wrinkled, crushed; totally

ยับยั้ง to stop (from), check, veto, put a halt to, block

ยับเยิน utterly, completely, totally, radically

ยัปปี้ yuppy, yuppies

ยั่ว provocative; to provoke; to arouse, entice

ยั่วโทสะ to irritate, rile, anger, make (someone) mad, provoke

ยั่วยวน provocative, sexy; seductive; to arouse desire, tempt, seduce

ยั่วเย้า to tease, make fun of, rag

ยั่วอารมณ์ provocative

   ยั่วอารมณ์เพศ to arouse sexual desire

ยั้ว, ยั้วเยี้ย crawling mass (of), pullulating, teeming (with), swarming

ยา[1] drug, medicine, pharmaceutical, medicinal /preparation/compound/

ยากวาดคอ linctus, medicine used to swab the throat

ยาแก้พิษ antidote, anti-venin (*แก้พิษงู*)

ยาขับปัสสาวะ diuretic

ยาขับลม carminative, anti-flatulence preparation

ยาขับเหงื่อ diaphoretic, sudorific

ยาขี้ผึ้ง ointment, salve

ยาฆ่าเชื้อโรค germicide, antiseptic, disinfectant

ยาฉีด injectable (preparation), injection

ยาช่วยย่อยอาหาร digestive

ยาชา local anesthetic, desensitizing preparation

ยาดม inhalant, smelling salts

ยาดอง medicated spirits, medicinal substances steeped in spirits

ยาดำ *as in* **แทรกเป็นยาดำ** to be a pill

ยาแดง mercurochrome

ยาถ่าย laxative, physic, cathartic

ยาทา ointment, cream, salve, liniment, pharmaceutical for topical application

ยาธาตุ digestive preparation, stomachic

ยาน้ำ potion, liquid medicine

ยาบ้า amphetamine, speed *(sl)*

ยาบำรุง tonic

    ยาบำรุงผม hair tonic

ยาฝิ่น opium

ยาพอก poultice

ยาพิษ poison

ยาเม็ด pill, tablet

ยาระงับความรู้สึก anesthetic

ยาระงับปวด analgesic, pain-killer

ยาระบาย laxative

ยารักษาโรค pharmaceuticals

ยาสมุนไพร herbal /remedy/medicine/

ยาสลบ anesthetic

ยาสามัญประจำบ้าน common household remedy

ยาสั่ง drug which induces a fatal reaction to some food

ยาสูบ tobacco

ยาเสน่ห์ love-potion, philter

ยาเสพย์ติด narcotic, habit-forming drug, addictive drug

ยาอม lozenge, pastille, troche, cough drop

ยาอายุวัฒนะ elixir, elixir of life

กินยา to take (one's) medicine

ฉีดยา *see* **ฉีดยา** *หน้า 130*

ทายา to apply (medicine to the skin), rub (on, in)

ใบสั่งยา prescription

ร้านขายยา pharmacy, drugstore, chemist's shop

ยา^2 compound, preparation, substance

ยากันยุง mosquito repellant, mosquito coil

ยาขัดรองเท้า shoe polish

ยาฆ่าแมลง insecticide

ยาชา local anesthetic

ยาดับกลิ่น deodorant

ยานัตถุ์ snuff

ยาเบื่อ poison

ยาเรือ to caulk (a boat)

ยาสีฟัน dentifrice, toothpaste, tooth powder

ลงยา enamelled, cloisonné

ย่า   paternal grandmother

ย่าทวด paternal great-grandmother

ปู่ย่าตายาย grandparents; forbears, ancestors

ยาก   to be difficult, hard (to do, say, make etc), not so easy, to be inconvenient

ยากแค้น in dire poverty, impoverished, penniless

ยากจน poor, needy, impoverished, in poverty, indigent, hard up

ยากจนค่นแค้น poverty-stricken, destitute

ยากดีมีจน (whether) rich or poor

ยากเย็น very difficult, almost impossible, arduous

ยากไร้ underprivileged

โดยยาก with difficulty

ย
ร
ฤ
ฤๅ
ล
ว
ศ
ษ
ส
ห
ฬ
อ
ฮ

ก
ข
ค
ฆ
ง
จ
ฉ
ช
ซ
ฌ
ญ
ฏ
ฎ
ฐ
ฑ
ฒ
ณ
ด
ต
ถ
ท
ธ
น
บ
ป
ผ
ฝ
พ
ฟ
ภ
ม
ย

ตกยาก to fall on hard times, suffer misfortune, in adversity

เป็นการยาก it is difficult (to)

ยุ่งยาก hard, difficult, troublesome, too complicated

ว่ายาก stubborn, intractable, headstrong

หายาก hard to find, scarce, rare

ยาง rubber; rubber tree; sticky substance; resin, sap, latex, tar

ยางแตก to have a flat tire, have a blowout

ยางเทียม synthetic rubber

ยางนอก tire, tire casing

ยางใน inner tube

ยางบอน oozing

ยางแบน (to have a) flat tire, The tire has gone flat.

ยางพารา Para rubber

ยางมะตอย asphalt

ยางไม้ resin

ยางรถ tire

ยางรัด rubber band

ยางลบ rubber, eraser

ยางล้อ tire

ต้นยาง rubber tree; yang tree

ถุงยางอนามัย condom

น้ำมันยาง dammar oil

ไม้ยาง yang wood (Dipterocarpus alatus)

ราดยาง to asphalt, surface with asphalt; asphalted, macadamized

ย่าง[1] to broil, grill

ย่างสด to burn alive

ไก่ย่าง /grilled/broiled/ chicken

เนื้อย่างน้ำตก /grilled/broiled/ beef with spices basil and mint leaves

ย่าง[2] to be going on, approach; to step, stride; to stalk (along, up, on, out, in)

ย่างกราย to approach; to involve oneself (in, with)

ย่างเข้าห้าสิบ to be going on fifty, approa-

ching fifty

ย่างเท้า to step, take a step

ย่างสามขุม to advance aggressively, three advancing steps of a /swordsman/boxer/

ยาจก beggar, mendicant

ยาน[1] sagging, drooping, hanging down, pendant

ยานคาง to draw out (one's words), speak deliberately

ยาน[2] vehicle

ยานพาหนะ conveyance, vehicle, carrier

ยานยนต์ motor vehicle

ยานอวกาศ spacecraft

ยวดยาน vehicles, cars, conveyances

รถจักรยาน bicycle

รถจักรยานยนต์ motorcycle

อากาศยาน aircraft, airplane, aeroplane

ย่าน district; area, quarter

ย่านการค้า businese district

ย่านคนจีน Chinese quarter

ย่านความถี่ band (*สื่อสาร*)

ย่านชุมชน populated area

ยาม watch; watchman, sentry, guard; time

ยามคับขัน critical period, emergency

ยามค่ำ evening

ยามเช้า morning

ยามดึก (at) night; late at night

ยามทุกข์ in adversity, difficult period, hard time, time of distress

ยามปกติ in normal times, in peacetime

ยามยาก hard times

ยามเย็น late afternoon

ยามรักษาการณ์ guard, sentry

ยามวิกาล improper time; at night

ยามสงคราม wartime

เข้ายาม to go on guard duty

ทหารยาม sentry, sentinel

ฤกษ์งามยามดี auspicious time (to, for), right moment (to, for)

อยู่ยาม to be on /duty/watch/guard duty/

ย่าม[1] shoulder bag

ย่าม[2] *as in* **ย่ามใจ** to feel one can get away with something, overconfident, complacent

ยาย maternal grandmother; maternal/gran-daunt/great-aunt; appellation for an old woman or girl

    ยายแก่ old woman

    ยายชี lay religious (woman)

    ยายทวด maternal great-grandmother

    ยายหนู little girl, she

ย้าย to move, transfer, shift

    ย้ายงาน to move to a new position; change one's job

    ย้ายบ้าน to move (to a new house), change (one's) address

    แยกย้าย to go off in different directions, disperse, split

    สั่งย้าย to transfer

ยาว long, wise

    ยาวเฟื้อย /very/exceedingly/miles/ long; elongated

    ยายยืด at length, overlong, protracted

    ยาวรี tapering

    ยาวเหยียด longline (of), stretching a long way

    เข็มยาว minute hand

    ความยาว length

    ตามยาว lengthwise

    ปืนยาว rifle

    ม้ายาว bench; horse, trestle

    สายตายาว farsighted, farsightedness

    อายุยืนยาว long-lived

ยำ to mix, blend; to maul; spicy salad

    ยำเกรง to fear; to respect

    ยำใหญ่ potpourri, mishmash, hodgepodge, melange; spicy seafood and pork salad with garlic and peanut sauce

ย่ำ to mark time; to trample, trod

    ย่ำค่ำ six o'clock in the evening, 6 p.m.

ย่ำต๊อก to hoof it; to scurry along; to be walking the streets

ย่ำเท้า to mark time

ย่ำยี to oppress, harass, step on (someone)

ย่ำรุ่ง six in the morning; early morning, daybreak

ย้ำ to repeat, stress, emphasize, to reiterate, underline, confirm

    ย้ำคำ to reiterate, stress, repeat

    ย้ำหัวตะปู to sink a nail home; to give emphasis (to)

ยิกๆ repeatedly, over and over again

ยิง to shoot, fire

    ยิงตก to shoot (something) down, hit

    ยิงตาย to shoot (someone) dead

    ยิงปืนนัดเดียวได้นกสองตัว to kill two birds with one stone

    ยิงเป้า to fire at a target, do /target shooting/ target practice/; to execute by shooting

    ยิงฟัน to show one's teeth; to grin

    ยิงสลุต to fire a salute

    ยิงหนังสติ๊ก to shoot a slingshot

    ระดมยิง to fire away (at), fire in volleys, concentrate one's fire power (on), shoot in concert

ยิ่ง exceedingly

    ยิ่ง...ยิ่ง... the more...the more

    เด็กคนนี้ยิ่งบอกยิ่งดื้อ This kid, the more you say to him, the more stubborn he becomes.

    ยิ่งมากยิ่งดี the more the better

    ยิ่งกว่านั้น more than that, moreover

    ยิ่งขึ้น more and more, increasingly

    ยิ่งๆ ขึ้นไป ever greater, increasing

    ยิ่งดีใหญ่ so much the better

    ยิ่งนัก exceedingly; supremely, greatly

    ยิ่งแน่ใจ even more sure, more certain than ever

    ยิ่งไปกว่า much more than, not only that, in addition

ย
ร
ฤ
ฤๅ
ล
ว
ศ
ษ
ส
ห
ฬ
อ
ฮ

ก
ข
ค
ฆ
ง
จ
ฉ
ช
ซ
ฌ
ญ
ฎ
ฏ
ฐ
ฑ
ฒ
ณ
ด
ต
ถ
ท
ธ
น
บ
ป
ผ
ฝ
พ
ฟ
ภ
ม
ย

ยิ่งยง great

ยิ่งยวด extremely, superbly, best

ยิ่งเร็วยิ่งดี the sooner the better

ยิ่งใหญ่ great, important, momentous

เฉพาะอย่างยิ่ง especially, specially (for)

ไม่ยิ่งไม่หย่อนกว่า neither more nor less

ยิน to hear

ยินดี glad, pleased (to), be happy (for, to)

ยินดีที่ได้รู้จัก glad to meet you, it is a pleasure to know you

ยินดีรับใช้ to be glad to be of service

ขอแสดงความยินดี congratulations (on), to congratulate

ยินยอม to consent, agree, permit, allow

ยินยอมพร้อมใจกัน with complete accord, in unison

โดยความยินยอมของ by permission of, with the consent of

ไม่ยินดียินร้าย indifferent (to), unconcerned, could not care less (about); with equanimity

ยิบ as in ถี่ยิบ หน้า 213

ยิบๆ blinking; shimmering; tingling

ยิ้ม to smile

ยิ้มกริ่ม to look pleased with oneself

ยิ้มกว้าง to smile broadly, give a broad smile

ยิ้มกะเรี่ยกะราด to smile sheepishly; to grin foolishly

ยิ้มเก่ง to have a ready smile

ยิ้มค้าง (to /wear/have/) a fixed smile

ยิ้มเจื่อนๆ to give a sickly smile

ยิ้มแฉ่ง to give a /broad/beaming/ smile

ยิ้มตอบ to smile back, return a smile

ยิ้มแต้ to beam (at), give a beaming smile

ยิ้มน้อยยิ้มใหญ่ to be gleeful, smile gleefully

ยิ้มไม่ออก to not find (something) funny; cheerless

ยิ้มย่อง to smile contentedly

ยิ้มเยาะ to smirk, smile smugly, scoff (at)

ยิ้มแย้ม cheerful

ยิ้มละไม to smile sweetly, give a beautiful smile

ยิ้มแสยะ to smirk

ยิ้มหัว to giggle

ยิ้มแห้งๆ to smile drily, give a /dry/empty/ smile

ยิ้มแหยๆ a shamefaced grin; to look sheepish, smile sheepishly, give an embarrassed smile

โปรยยิ้ม to smile at everyone

ฝืนยิ้ม to /give/wear/ a forced smile, force a smile, wear a smile, give a tight smile

แสยะยิ้ม derisive smile, sneer, smirk, grin

อมยิ้ม to have an amused look, smile to oneself

ยียวน to aggravate, vex, provoke, irritate

ยี่ two, second

ยี่ปั๊ว middleman, wholesaler

ยี่เก a form of popular theater, traditional melodrama

พูดเป็นยี่เก You must be joking.

ยี่สิบ twenty

ที่ยี่สิบ twentieth

ยี่หระ as in ไม่ยี่หระ unmoved, unperturbed

ยี่หร่า fennel

ยี่ห้อ brand, tradename; reputation, name

ทำอย่างนี้เสียยี่ห้อหมด It's going to spoil our good name. / It will ruin your reputation.

ยึกยัก to hold back

ยึกยือ icky, slimy, squiggly

ยึด to seize, capture; to take hold of, take over; to be attached (to); to follow, hold (to), believe in; to keep (to, in)

ยึดเกาะ to latch onto

ยึดครอง to occupy, take possession (of)

ยึดคืน to repossess

ยึดได้ to seize, take over

ยึดถือ to believe in, put one's faith in

ยืดทรัพย์ to /seize/attach/impound/ property

ยืดเป็นอาชีพ professional, make a living (at, by)

ยืดมั่น to be attached to, adhere to, hold fast to, believe firmly in

ยืดเลนขวา to keep in the right lane

ยืดไว้ to hold on to, distrain, impound

ยืดหน่วง to retain, withhold

   สิทธิยืดหน่วง right of retention

ยืดหลัก to base (something) on, /observe/ uphold/hold to/ the principles of

ยืดอำนาจ to seize power

ยืด to expand, stretch, prolong

ยืดเข้ายืดออก elastic

ยืดแข้งยืดขา to stretch one's legs

ยืดยาด see **ยืดเยื้อ**

ยืดยาว long drawn-out

ยืดเยื้อ protracted, interminable, lasting a long time, overly long, at great length

ยืดเวลา to prolong; to extend the time (for doing something), give an extension (of time)

ยืดเส้นยืดสาย to stretch

ยืดหยุ่น flexible; elastic; accommodating

ยืน to stand, get on one's feet; long; firm

ยืนกระต่ายขาเดียว to stick to one's guns, maintain one's position

ยืนกราน to stand firm, be unyielding, resolute, steadfast

ยืนขวางหน้า to stand in one's way

ยืนขึ้น to stand up

ยืนเขย่ง to tiptoe

ยืนจังก้า to be planted (on, at, by), plant oneself

ยืนจังงัง to be stupefied, stunned, dazed

ยืนต้น perennial; dead tree

ยืนตรง to stand straight; to stand at attention

ยืนตัวตรง to stand straight, stand erect

ยืนตากแดด to stand in the sun

ยืนตากฝน to stand in the rain

ยืนแถว to stand in line

ยืนนิ่ง to stand still

ยืนบัง to stand in the way

ยืนพัก to stand at ease

ยืนพิง to lean against

ยืนพื้น to remain the same

ยืนยง to last, endure

ยืนยัน to confirm, affirm, assure

ยืนยาม to stand watch

ยืนโรง actor who always plays the same part; fixture (at, in), mainstay (of)

ยืนหยัด to stand fast, stand firm, unyielding

พิพากษายืน Judgment sustained.

ยั่งยืน sustained; long-lasting, long-lived, enduring, to last a long time

ล้มทั้งยืน to fall to the ground, fall over, topple over, collapse

ยื่น to project, stick out; to hand; to offer; to present, hand in, submit, file, lodge, turn in

ยื่นคำขาด to give an ultimatum, give one's /final/last/ word

ยื่นคำร้อง to /file/submit/lodge/ a request; to file a motion

ยื่นจมูก to poke one's nose into (another's affairs), meddle

ยื่นต่อ to file with

ยื่นใบลาออก to submit one's resignation

ยื่นใบสมัคร to apply, submit an application

ยื่นฟ้อง to file a /case/complaint/(in, against), bring legal action (in, against), institute legal proceedings, sue

ยื่นรายงาน to /submit/file/turn in/hand in/ a report

ยื่นหน้า to interfere, meddle; to push oneself forward

ยื่นหมูยื่นแมว to swap, give a quid pro quo on the spot, exchange (one thing) for

ย
ร
ฤ
ฦ
ล
ว
ศ
ษ
ส
ห
ฬ
อ
ฮ

(another thing)

ยืม to borrow; to lend
　ขอยืม to borrow
　ให้ยืม to lend

ยื้อ to seize, snatch away, grab; to take away by force
　ยื้อยุด forcibly grab

ยุ to incite, urge, egg (someone) on, coax
　ยุยง to incite, stir up, provoke, instigate, foment
　　ผู้ยุยง instigator, provocateur
　ยุแหย่ to create dissension, cause friction
　ยุให้แตกแยก to incite /friction/rivalry/
　ยั่วยุ to provoke, foment
　ยิ่งว่ายิ่งยุ The more warning the more daring., to be counterproductive

ยุค time; period, age, epoch, era
　ยุคกลาง middle ages
　ยุคเข็ญ age of calamity, time of disaster
　ยุคต้น early period, the beginning
　ยุคทอง golden age
　ยุคหิน stone age
　ยุคใหม่ new era, new age
　ไม่ตกยุค timeless, always in vogue

ยุคล pair, two
　ยุคลบาท the two feet; His Majesty
　ดำเนินตามรอยยุคลบาท to follow His Majesty's example, follow in His Majesty's footsteps

ยุง mosquito
　ยุงก้นปล่อง Anopheles mosquito

ยุ่ง to get mixed up (with); to be in disorder, tangled; to interfere, meddle; to make a stir; to fool with, fool around (with); troublesome, bothersome
　ยุ่งเกี่ยวกับ to mess (with), fiddle (with), tamper (with); to have an affair (with), fool around (with); to be involved (with), have something to do with (someone or

something)
　ยุ่งขิง confused, mixed up, in confusion, in a state
　ยุ่งใจ upset, troubled, anxious, bothered (about something)
　ยุ่งด้วย to interfere, get involved, get tangled up (with)
　ยุ่งมาก hectic; troublesome
　　พักนี้งานยุ่งมาก Right now, the work is hectic.
　　การพิมพ์พจนานุกรมสักเล่มเป็นเรื่องยุ่งมาก Getting a dictionary to press is troublesome.
　　การติดต่อหน่วยราชการบางครั้งบางคราวก็ยุ่งมาก Occasionally, dealing with the bureaucracy is troublesome.
　　หมอนี่ยุ่งมาก That guy is troublesome.
　ยุ่งไม่เข้าเรื่อง meddlesome, officious; to be aggravating
　ยุ่งยาก hard, difficult, troublesome, too complicated
　ยุ่งยิ่ง very involved, in a mess
　ยุ่งสมอง disturbing, bothersome, irksome
　ยุ่งเหยิง tangled up; to be in a muddle, confused, in a state of confusion, in disorder
　อย่ายุ่ง Leave /it/me/ alone!, Don't interfere., Don't trouble yourself., Don't /mess/fool/ with (someone or something).

ยุ้ง granary; silo

ยุด to hold back, restrain; to pull

ยุติ, ยุตติ over, ended, stopped, finished, to stop, cease
　เรื่องยังไม่ยุติ It's not over yet.

ยุติธรรม justice; fair, just, equitable
　กระทรวงยุติธรรม Ministry of Justice

ยุทธ war
　ยุทธการ tactical; battle, warfare
　ยุทธภัณฑ์ armaments, war material, military supplies and equipment

ยุทธภัย war risks, perils of war

ยุทธภูมิ battlefield, battleground

ยุทธวิธี tactics

ยุทธศาสตร์ strategy; science of war

ยุทธหัตถี fight on elephant back

กลยุทธ์ military stratagem, tactic, maneuver

ประลองยุทธ์ to stage maneuvers, hold /war games/field exercises/

ยุทธจักร warfare, feud; circle, fraternity

ยุทธจักรดงขมิ้น the fraternity of the yellow robe

ยุทธนาการ battle, fight

ยุทธศึกษา warfare studies

ยุทโธปกรณ์ war material

ยุบ to settle, subside; sink; to collapse; to abolish; to dissolve; to melt (something) down

ยุบยับ into pieces, total wreck

ยุบสภา to dissolve the /legislature/house/

ยุบยิบ over-detailed, full of trivia

ยุพราช crown prince

ยุ่มย่าม to meddle, get in the way, intrude, fuss around

ยุ่ย friable, crumbling, disintegrating

ยุ้ย chubby, plump, well-rounded

ยุว young man, young, juvenile

ยุวชน young people, the youth, youngsters

ยุวราช crown prince

ยู่ to be crumpled

ยู่ยี่ wrinkled, rumpled creased; sour-looking

เย้ skewed, slanting

โย้เย้ crooked, askew, skewed

เยซู Jesus

เย็ด to fuck

เย็น evening, late afternoon; cold, cool, chilly

เย็นเจี๊ยบ chilled, iced, icy cold

เย็นใจ relieved, to feel relief, have a load off one's mind; carefree; peaceful, composed

เย็นเฉียบ ice cold, frozen

เย็นชา, ชาเย็น frigid, frosty, chill (reaction, response, reception etc); indifferent, unfeeling

เย็นชืด all cold

เย็นตา attractive, pleasing, cool-looking, refreshing

เย็นเป็นน้ำแข็ง frigid, icy

เย็นวาน yesterday evening, last evening

เย็นเยียบ chill

เย็นเยือก frosty

เย็นไว้ chill it (sl), ease off, calm down

เย็นหู pleasing (to hear), pleasant, mellow, fine

กาแฟเย็น iced coffee with milk

ข้าวเย็น supper, evening meal

ชาเย็น iced tea with milk

แช่เย็น see **แช่เย็น** หน้า 148

ตู้เย็น refrigerator

น้ำเย็น ice water, cold water

ยากเย็น very difficult, almost impossible, arduous

ร่มเย็น shady, cool and pleasant; happily

อยู่เย็นเป็นสุข to be well and happy

อาหารเย็น dinner, supper

เย็บ to sew; to string, stitch, to pin; to staple

เย็บปักถักร้อย sewing, needlework

เย็บผ้า to sew

เย็บเสื้อ to sew a shirt; to sew a blouse (สำหรับผู้หญิง), make clothes

ช่างตัดเย็บ seamstress; tailor

ช่างเย็บผ้า dressmaker (หญิง), tailor (ชาย)

ตัดเย็บ to make (clothes), to sew

ที่เย็บกระดาษ stapler

เย้ย to deride, mock; to ridicule

เย้ยหยัน to sneer; to scoff (at)

เย่อ to pull back and forth, tug back and forth

เยอรมนี เยอรมัน German, Germany (ประเทศ)

เย่อหยิ่ง haughty; puffed up

ย
ร
ฤ
ฤๅ
ล
ว
ศ
ษ
ส
ห
ฬ
อ
ฮ

เยอะ, เยอะแยะ plenty (of), a lot (of), lots (of), an abundance (of), any amount (of)

เยา low

    ราคาย่อมเยา low priced, inexpensive, cheap, bargain price

เย้า as in **เย้าแหย่** to tease

เยาว์ young, youthful, juvenile

    ผู้เยาว์ minor, infant; youth, youngster

เยาวชน youth, young people, youngsters, juveniles

เยาะ to laugh at (someone), mock, taunt

    เยาะหยัน to mock

    เยาะเย้ย to ridicule, deride, taunt

    หัวเราะเยาะ to make fun of someone, laugh at someone, mock

เยินยอ to praise, laud, speak highly (of)

เยิ่นเย้อ tedious, long-winded, long drawn-out

เยิบ ๆ flapping

เยิ้ม to ooze, exude

    นัยน์ตาเยิ้ม glowing eyes, liquid eyes

เยี่ยง model, example; similar to, comparable to, like

    เยี่ยงอย่าง example, exemplar

เยียบ ice-cold

เยี่ยม[1] superbly; beautifully, first rate, excellently, great, tops

    ชั้นเยี่ยม excellent, top, first-class

    ยอดเยี่ยม best, top, superb

เยี่ยม[2] to visit, call on, go to see (someone)

    เยี่ยมไข้ to pay a sick call, visit (someone) in the hospital

    เยี่ยมคำนับ to pay a courtesy call (on)

    เยี่ยมตอบ to return a visit

    เยี่ยม ๆ มอง ๆ to spy (on), keep an eye on

    เยี่ยมเยียน, เยี่ยมเยือน to visit

เยี่ยว urine, to urinate, make water, piss, pee

    เยี่ยวราด to wet (the bed, one's pants, the floor etc)

เยียวยา to treat (an illness); to remedy, cure, correct; to ameliorate, improve

เยื่อ membrane, tissue; marrow

    เยื่อกระดาษ paper pulp

    เยื่อเคย shrimp paste

    เยื่อพรหมจารี hymen

    เยื่อใย residual attachment, some ties, remaining affection, leftover sentiment

เยื้อ to last long, endless

เยือก chilling

    เยือกเย็น calm, not easily moved; nice and cool, cool, imperturbable

    เย็นเยือก freezing cold, /biting/penetrating/ cold

เยื้อง diagonally opposite; to walk with style

    เยื้องกราย to walk with /grace/elegantly/; to walk in a way to catch the eye

    เยื้องอย่าง to walk with style

    ยักเยื้อง to shift (an approach, viewpoint, analysis, meaning etc); to be evasive

เยือน to visit, pay a visit (to)

แย่ in trouble; bad, no good, awful; to suffer, affect

    เธอทำไม่ดี ทำให้ฉันแย่ไปด้วย Your doing badly has affected me too. / What you did wrong is making me suffer too.

    แย่จริง damn, dammit; how awful; terrible, appalling

    แย่มาก ๆ lousy

    แย่ว่ะ Oh great!

    ที่แย่หนักไปอีก what is worse

    ย่ำแย่ in a tough situation, Oh great!; in a bad way; hard-up

แยก to separate, split, divide, be separated, spread apart

    แยกเขี้ยว to bare one's teeth, snarl (at someone)

    แยกทาง to go separate ways, part, split (with)

    แยกธาตุ to do a chemical analysis, analyze

    แยกประเภท to classify, categorize

แยกไม่ออก indistinguishable; inseparable

แยกย้าย to go off in different directions, disperse

แยกแยะ to analyze, give a breakdown, itemize

แตกแยก to split up, break up, separate

ทางแยก corner, intersection, branch in the road, junction

สามแยก fork (in the road), three-way intersection

สี่แยก corner, intersection, crossroads

แยง to insert, put in, stick in; to pick; to probe

แยงหู to pick one's ear

แย่ง to grab, snatch, get hold of, scramble for; to vie, compete (for)

แย่งกรรมสิทธิ์ to grab title (to), get hold of title; to vie for/ ownership/title/; make competing claims to ownership

แย่งกัน to compete (for), grab (away, for); to scramble for

แย่งชิง to snatch, grab (something *or* someone) away (from)

แย่งที่ to scramble for a /place/seat/; to grab a /place/seat/, take another's place

แย่งสมบัติ to fight over property, try to get hold of (something)

แก่งแย่ง to compete with no holds barred, vie for; to fight over something, pull and tug at something

แย้ง to be contradictory (to), inconsistent (with); to oppose, contradict, oppose, conflict (with)

แย้งกัน to be contradictory, be inconsistent; in conflict

ขัดแย้ง to be in disagreement, have differences, be in conflict (with), have conflicting interests, be at odds; to be contradictory, inconsistent

โต้แย้ง to dispute, raise an objection, object, argue, refute, rebut, oppose, contest; to answer, maintain

คำโต้แย้ง counterstatement, counter-argument

มุมแย้ง alternate angles

แยบคาย sharp, acute, ingenious, shrewd, penetrating

แยบยล cunning, clever, wily, smart

แย็บ to jab, give a jab

แยม jam

แย้ม to open slightly; to give a hint (of), intimate; to bloom

แย้มพราย to give a hint (of), give an inkling (of), intimate

แรกแย้ม first bloom (of youth)

แยแส to pay attention to, take an interest (in), be concerned (with)

ไม่แยแส to be unconcerned (with, about), be indifferent (to), take no interest (in)

แยะ plenty, lots, tons (of)

เยอะแยะ *see* **เยอะ** *หน้า 402*

โย้ slanting, aslant, askew; wobbly

โย้เย้ crooked, aslant; out of kilter; loose

โยก to wobble, shake, be loose, rock, teeter; to weave *(มวย)*

โยกย้าย move, remove

โยกเยก to swing, rock, sway

โยกโย้ to beat about the bush, be evasive

โยง[1] to string, link

โยงเรือไว้กับหลัก to tie up a boat

เรือโยง tugboat

โยง[2] permanently, the whole time

อยู่โยง to hold the fort, take care of things, be there the whole time

โย่ง lanky, gangly, spindly

โยธา works, construction work; work done by physical labor

กรมโยธา Public Works Department

โยน[1] to throw, toss

ย
ร
ฤ
ฤๅ
ล
ว
ศ
ษ
ส
ห
ฬ
อ
ฮ

โยนกลอง to pass the buck; to /refuse/ evade/ responsibility

โยนทิ้ง to throw away, discard, get rid of

โยนหัวโยนก้อย to /toss/flip/ a coin, heads or tails

โยนให้ to toss to, throw to

โยน,[2] **โยนก** Ionian; northern Thai people

โยนี vagina, female genitals

โยม appellation used by a monk for his parents persons of similar age or folks in general

โยมอุปัฏฐาก one who supports a monk, patron of a monk

ญาติโยม relatives

โยเย to be a crybaby; abrasive, provocative, annoying

โย้เย้ unsteady; shaky; crooked, aslant, out of kilter

โยโส conceited, puffed up, self-important

ใย filament, fiber, thread

ใยแก้ว fiber glass

ใยฟ้า gossamer

ใยแมงมุม spider web, cobweb

ใยลวด filament

ใยสังเคราะห์ synthetic fiber

ไย why

ไยดี concerned (about, with), to care (about), take an interest (in), have concern (for)

ไม่ไยดี to take no interest (in), be indifferent (to), not care (about)

รก[1] messy, in disorder, cluttered, untidy; overgrown (with), tangled

   รกใจ annoying, awful

   รกชัฏ overgrown, dense, impenetrable

   รกร้าง vacant and overgrown

   รกรุงรัง in a mess, cluttered, untidy, messy

   รกหูรกตา annoying

รก[2] placenta

   รกราก origins; birthplace, old home

      ตั้งรกราก to settle down (in), establish oneself, make one's home (in, at)

รง gamboge

รงค์ color, chrome

รจนา to compose, write; beautiful

รชตะ silver; money

รณรงค์ to campaign (for, against), fight (to, for, against)

รด to water, pour

   รดน้ำคู่บ่าวสาว to pour lustral water at a wedding ceremony

   รดน้ำต้นไม้ to water /the plants/the garden/

   รดน้ำมนตร์ to sprinkle with holy water, asperge

   รดน้ำศพ to perform the funeral bathing ceremony

   รดน้ำสังข์ to pour the nuptial water

   ลายรดน้ำ gold appliqué on black lacquer

รถ car, wagon, cart, carriage, carrier

   รถกระบะ pickup truck

   รถเก๋ง car, automobile; sedan

   รถเกราะ armored car

   รถโกดัง truck (US), lorry (Brit)

   รถเข็น cart, pushcart, trolley, hand cart; baby carriage, stroller

   รถแข่ง racing car

   รถจักร locomotive

   รถจักรยาน bicycle

      รถจักรยานยนต์ motorcycle

   รถจี๊บ jeep

รถเช่า rented car; rental car, car for rent

รถซิ่ง hot rod

รถด่วน express train

รถดับเพลิง fire truck, fire engine

รถดีเซลราง diesel railcar

รถโดยสาร bus, coach

รถถัง tank

รถแท็กซี่ taxi, cab, taxicab

รถนอน sleeping car, pullman

รถบดถนน road roller, steam roller

รถบรรทุก truck, lorry (Brit), van

รถประจำทาง bus

รถเปิดประทุน a convertible

รถพยาบาล ambulance

รถพระที่นั่ง royal car

รถพ่วง trailer

   รถพ่วงข้าง sidecar

รถไฟ train, railway, railroad

   รถไฟใต้ดิน underground, subway

รถม้า horse carriage

รถเมล์ bus

รถยนต์ car, motorcar, automobile

รถรับจ้าง /car/truck/vehicle/ for hire; public carrier; taxi

   รถรับจ้างไม่ประจำทาง non-regular route public carrier

รถรา cars, motor vehicles, traffic

รถราง trolley car, streetcar, tram

รถลาก rickshaw

รถวิบาก off-road vehicle

รถศพ hearse

รถสองแถว jitney, taxi-bus, a small bus with bench seating along the sides

รถสามล้อ tricycle taxi, samlor, trishaw

รถสินค้า freight train

รถสิบล้อ ten-wheeled truck, ten wheeler

รถเสบียง restaurant car, dining car

รถเสีย The car is dead., (My) car has broken down.

ร
ฤ
ฦ
ล
ว
ศ
ษ
ส
ห
ฬ
อ
ฮ

รถหวอ police car; ambulance; fire /engine /truck/

กระบวนรถ procession, parade, cavalcade; train

ขบวนรถ train; train of cars

ขับรถ to drive

ขึ้นรถ to /board/get on/ (a bus, train), get in (a car)

ค่ารถ travelling expenses

จับรถ to catch a /cab/bus/ etc, grab a bus
จับรถไฟไปเชียงใหม่ to catch a train for Chiang Mai

เดินรถ *see* **เดินรถ** *หน้า 170*

ตกรถ to miss a /train/bus/

ทะเบียนรถ car registration

ป้ายจอดรถ bus stop

ยางรถ tire

รางรถ tracks

อู่รถ garage

ร.น.   R.N. (Royal Navy)

รน   to be restless, agitated, anxious

รนหาที่ to do oneself in, look for trouble, ask for /trouble/it/

ดิ้นรน to struggle (to, for), strive (for)

ร้อนรน worried, full of anxiety, agitated, disturbed, anxious

ร่น   to press back, retract, pull back

ร่นเข้า to shorten; to move up

ร่นเวลา to shorten the time, compress the time, expedite

ร่นออก to move forward; to lengthen; to move farther apart

รั้น   *as in* **กระตือรือร้น** in a hurry; anxious (to); enthusiastic, eager (to)

รบ   to fight, battle

รบทัพจับศึก to engage in battle, war with

รบพุ่ง to fight a pitched battle, battle

รบรา to fight, battle

รบเร้า to keep asking, importune, pester

(someone for something or to do something)

ซ้อมรบ to hold military exercises, /hold/ engage in/ maneuvers, hold war games; to have battle training

แนวรบ front line, line of battle

พักรบ truce

เรือรบ warship, man-of-war

สนามรบ battlefield, battleground

สู้รบ to fight, battle, engage in combat

รบกวน to disturb, bother, trouble

รปภ. (รักษาความปลอดภัย) Security

รม   to smoke

รมควัน to smoke; smoked

รมยา to fumigate

ร่ม   shade; shelter; umbrella, parasol

ร่มชูชีพ parachute

ร่มผ้า covered parts of the body

ร่มไม้ shade (of a tree)

ร่มเย็น shady, cool and pleasant; happily

โดดร่ม to parachute; to play hooky

ในร่ม indoor, in the shade

พลร่ม paratrooper, paratroops

ร.ม.ต. minister

รมย์   *as in* **รื่นรมย์** *หน้า 423*

ร.ร.   school

รวก   a kind of light thornless bamboo

รวง   cluster; ear, spike; beehive

รวงข้าว ear of rice

รวงผึ้ง beehive

ตกรวง to form ears

ร่วง   fall (from, out, off), drop off, shed

ร่วงโรย worn-out; wilted, drooping, lifeless; haggard

โรคท้องร่วง diarrhea

ฤดูใบไม้ร่วง fall, autumn

รวด[1]   all at one time, single; stretch

รวดเดียว in a single stretch, without stopping

รวด[2]   quick, rapid, speedy

รวดเร็ว fast, quickly, rapidly, speedily, swiftly

รวน[1] to sear, pan-fry

รวน[2] crooked, askew; to give trouble, be a lemon; to look for trouble, pick a fight; provocative, exasperating

รวนเร undecisive, uncertain, wishy-washy, fickle

ตีรวน to make trouble, be a troublemaker, quarrelsome

ร่วน[1] friable, loose

ดินร่วน friable soil, loose /earth/soil/

ร่วน[2] as in **หัวเราะร่วน** to laugh heartily, happy laughter

รวบ to gather (up, together); to arrest, catch, seize

รวบตัว to capture, arrest

รวบผม to gather up one's hair

รวบยอด to total, add together

รวบรวม to compile, collect, gather

รวบรัด to cut (something) short; compress, abbreviate; to expedite

รวบหัวรวบหาง to conclude in a peremptory way

รวบอำนาจ to centralize /power/authority/ in oneself, build a power base

รวม to total, add together; to mix; to join; to collect, marshal; altogether, in all

รวม 7 ประเทศ altogether 7 countries, 7 countries in all

รวมกลุ่ม to group, form a group, combine, join together

รวมกัน (put, do etc) together

รวมกำลัง to pool resources

รวมเข้าด้วยกัน to amalgamate, combine, merge

รวมความว่า in short, in summary, to sum up, summarize

รวมทั้ง including, as well as

รวมทั้งหมด altogether

รวมพล to marshal forces

รวมห่อ wholesale book distribution

รวมหัว to put ones' heads together, conspire, act in collusion

จุดรวม center, focus, focal point

ส่วนรวม public, common, general

ร่วม[1] to live together, join, associate (with), participate (in), pool; joint, co-

ร่วมกัน jointly, mutual, common, to join, participate, get together, cooperate, take part (in), collaborate

ร่วมคิด to have the same /idea/thoughts/ as someone else; to put (their) heads together, pool ones' thoughts

ร่วมงาน to collaborate, work together

เพื่อนร่วมงาน co-worker

ร่วมใจ to be united

เพื่อนร่วมใจ true friend

ร่วมชายคา under the same roof, to /live/ work/ together

ร่วมชีวิต to share another's life, be married, cohabit

ร่วมท้องเดียวกัน born of the same mother, having the same mother

ร่วมทุกข์ร่วมสุข to share one's joys and sorrows, for better or worse

ร่วมประเวณี to have /sex/sexual intercourse/, have sexual relations

ร่วมเพศ to have sexual intercourse, have sex

ร่วมภาคี to take part, become a party (to something)

ร่วมมือ to cooperate, help, join hands (with)

ร่วมรัก to make love

ร่วมเรียงเคียงหมอน to live together

ร่วมแรง to unite, be united (in), join together, pool one's efforts

ร่วมวง to join (in), participate (in), co-

ร่วมสายโลหิต of the same /family/line/

ร
ฤ
ฤๅ
ล
ว
ศ
ษ
ส
ห
ฬ
อ
ฮ

ร่วมหอลงโรง to live together

ร่วมหัวจมท้าย to stick together

เข้าร่วม to join

แถลงการณ์ร่วม joint /statement/communiqué/

ทางร่วม junction; merging road

พี่น้องร่วมชาติ fellow countrymen

เพื่อนร่วมชั้น classmate

เพื่อนร่วมชาติ fellow countryman

มีส่วนร่วม to have a /share/part/ (in), participate (in)

ร่วม^2 almost, nearly, about

ร่วมปี almost a year

รวย rich, well off, to have money

รวยขึ้น to get richer, prosper

รวยรัก rich in /love/lovers/

ร่ำรวย rich, wealthy

รวิ sun

รวิวาร Sunday

ร.ศ. Rattanakosin Era (date from the founding of Bangkok)

รส taste, flavor; mood, sensation

รสชาติ taste, flavor

รสนิยม taste, preference

ลิ้มรส to taste, try, experience

ออกรส to taste; to be tasty; stimulating, exciting, delightful

ออกรสหวาน to taste sweet, have a sweet taste, sweetish taste

โอชารส fine tasting, delicious, to taste great

ร.ส.พ. E.T.O. (ย่อจาก Express Transport Organization)

รหัส code, password; combination

รหัสตู้นิรภัย combination (of a safe)

รหัสนักศึกษา student's code number

รหัสไปรษณีย์ postal code

ถอดรหัส to decode, decipher

รโหฐาน private; sumptuous

รอ to wait (for, at, in, on), await; to look

forward to; to suspend, hold in abeyance

รอการพิจารณา to await trial; pending

รอการลงอาญา to suspend sentence

รอคอย to wait (for), await

รอคำสั่ง to await /instructions/orders/

รอจดหมายแฟน to look forward to a letter from one's /girlfriend/boyfriend/

รอจังหวะ to wait for the /right time/chance/ opportunity/

รอช้า to delay

รอดูก่อน to wait and see, temporize

รอท่า see รอคอย

รอเวลา to wait for the time; to take time

รอโอกาส to bide one's time, wait for the /chance/opportunity/

รั้งรอ to delay, hold back, wait a long time

รีรอ to hesitate, delay

รอก pulley

ชักรอก to pull up by a pulley

รอง to put something under (something else), place underneath; next below, secondary; vice-, deputy

รองจ่าย to advance, pay (money) in advance

รองทรง graduated short cut for men, schoolboy cut

รองท้อง to have a snack to eat

รองเท้า shoes, footwear

รองเท้าแตะ slippers, sandals, thongs, scuffs, flip-flops

รองเท้าผ้าใบ canvas shoes, sneakers, tennis shoes

รองเท้าฟุตบอล football shoes

รองเท้าส้นสูง high-heel shoes

รองเท้าหุ้มข้อ boots, high shoes

รองเท้าหุ้มส้น shoes

รองนางสาวไทย runner-up for Miss Thailand

รองนายกรัฐมนตรี deputy prime minister

รองน้ำ to collect water

รองน้ำฝน to collect rainwater

รองบ่อน to belong to a gambling house
  ไก่รองบ่อน house cock
รองประธาน vice-chairman, vice-president
รองประธานาธิบดี vice-president
รองปลัดกระทรวง deputy undersecretary
รองผู้บัญชาการทหารบก deputy commander in chief of the army
รองพระบาท shoes
รองพื้น to prime, undercoat (with)
  สีรองพื้น primer, undercoat
รองรับ support, supporting, back up, underpin; to be a basis (for)
รองอธิการบดี vice-rector
จานรอง saucer
ชั้นรอง second to, next below; second /rate/grade/
ตลาดรอง secondary market
ต่อรอง to bargain, negotiate, dicker
เป็นรอง to have the odds against one, be unfavored, the underdog
พระรอง supporting actor

ร่อง ditch, furrow, channel, groove; hole; path, way; slit
  ร่องน้ำ channel
    ร่องน้ำลึก deepwater channel; thalweg
  ร่องรอย clue, trace, trail, track, mark (of), sign (of)
ร่องแร่ง to dangle; dangling

ร้อง to call; to cry; to sing; to appeal, claim, petition, request
  ร้องกรีด to scream, shriek, screech
  ร้องขอ to request, appeal (for), petition
    ร้องขอความช่วยเหลือ to /ask/appeal/ for help
  ร้องคำราม to growl, roar
  ร้องทัก to greet
  ร้องทุกข์ to complain, /file/lodge/ a complaint, make a complaint, file charges (against, at)

ร้องเป็นเสียงเดียว to sing in unison; to sing the same tune, be of one mind
ร้องเพลง to sing
ร้องเรียก to call (to); to call out to
ร้องเรียน to complain, make a complaint
ร้องลั่น to scream, bellow
ร้องส่ง to sing alternatively with music
ร้องห่มร้องไห้ to weep and wail, sob uncontrollably, cry and cry
ร้องหา to cry out for, call for
ร้องให้ช่วย to call for help
ร้องไห้ to cry, weep, sob, shed tears
  ร้องไห้สะอึกสะอื้น to sob
ร้องโฮ to wail
กบร้อง to croak
การ้อง to caw
แกะร้อง to bleat
ขับร้อง to sing
เขียดร้อง to croak
คำร้อง motion, request, petition
ช้างร้อง to trumpet
นกเค้าแมวร้อง to hoot
นกพิราบร้อง to coo
นกร้อง to sing, chirp, twitter
เนื้อร้อง lyrics, words
ป่าวร้อง to publicize announce, publicly, advertise
เป็ดร้อง to quack
ฟ้องร้อง to sue, take legal action, file legal proceedings, bring suit (against someone), file a court case
ฟ้าร้อง thunder
ม้าร้อง to neigh, whinny
แมวร้อง to mew
เรียกร้อง to demand, claim, make demands (for)
ลาร้อง to bray
ลิงร้อง to chatter, hoot
วัวตัวผู้ร้อง to low, moo

ร
ฤ
ฤๅ
ล
ว
ศ
ษ
ส
ห
ฬ
อ
ฮ

วัวร้อง to low, moo

สุนัขร้อง to squeal, yelp

หนูร้อง to squeak

หมูร้อง to grunt, squeal

ห่านร้อง to honk

โห่ร้อง to cheer, hail, acclaim

รอด[1] floor joist, briding

รอด[2] to be safe, out of danger

รอดชีวิต to survive, escape death, be saved

รอดตัว to save oneself, get out of (a predicament, fix etc)

รอดตาย to survive, escape death

รอดไป to escape, go free

รอดพ้น to be saved, liberated, freed (from)

ความรอดพ้น salvation

รอดสายตา to escape notice

รอดอย่างหวุดหวิด narrowly escape, to have a narrow escape

จนแล้วจนรอด in the end

โดยตลอดรอดฝั่ง all the way, right to the end

เอาตัวรอด to save one's own skin, come out all right, get out of (a predicament etc); to get by

รอนๆ nearly, almost; fading

ร่อน to sift, sieve; to brandish, flourish (เช่น ร่อนดาบ); to sail, glide; to fling (เช่นร่อน กระเบื้อง)

ร่อนทอง to pan for gold

ร่อนเร่ to wander, roam, drift (from place to place)

ร้อน hot; agitated, anxious; urgent, pressing; uncomfortable

ร้อน ๆ piping hot; instant, ready; hot

ฉันชอบกาแฟร้อน ๆ I like my coffee piping hot.

ร้อนเงิน to be hard pressed, pressed for money, short (of money)

ร้อนจัด very hot, broiling, roasting; torrid

ร้อนจี๋ burning, extremely hot

ร้อนใจ worried, troubled, agitated, upset

ร้อนตัว to feel guilty, have a guilty conscience, feel the heat, feel menaced, nervous

ร้อนถึง to affect, have repercussions (on), involve, cause trouble (for someone)

ร้อนใน internal heat

ร้อนเป็นไฟ blazing hot

ร้อนผ้าเหลือง uncomfortable in the yellow robe, to feel the strain of being a monk

ร้อนผ่าว scorching

ร้อนรน worried, full of anxiety, agitated, disturbed, anxious

ร้อนระอุ intensely hot, sizzling hot, stifling (อากาศ)

ร้อนรุ่ม (ใจ) to be agitated

ร้อนแรง passionate, heated

ร้อนวิชา to be an academic show-off

ร้อนอกร้อนใจ to be worried, upset

ร้อนอบอ้าว sweltering, sultry, muggy, suffocating (heat, weather)

ขี้ร้อน to feel the heat

ใจร้อน impatient, hasty, impetuous; hot-headed

ทุกข์ร้อน to be distressed (by something), troubled (by), in trouble; to have a problem

เผ็ดร้อน hot, fiery, heated, peppery, acrimonious

รีบร้อน in a big hurry

เร่าร้อน sexy, torrid, sultry, passionate; tormented troubled, afflicted

ฤดูร้อน summer, hot season

เลือดร้อน hot-tempered

สดๆ ร้อนๆ fresh, hot (news, out of the oven, off the press, etc)

รอนแรม to sleep out; to travel making overnight stops

รอนสิทธิ์ to prejudice one's right, be detrimental

รอบ round, time

รอบๆ around; ambient

รอบคอบ careful, thorough, prudent, circumspect

รอบจัด high-speed; fast; cunning

รอบชิงชนะเลิศ final match, cup final

รอบด้าน on every side, in every /way/ respect/

รอบนอก outside, outer, outlying; periphery (of)

รอบปี year

รอบรู้ well-informed, expert

รอบโลก around the world

เข้ารอบ /to make/be selected (for)/get into/ (the semi-finals etc), be a runner-up

โดยรอบ in circumference, around

ตกรอบ to be eliminated, lose (the semi-finals, etc), fail to make the grade

ในรอบ during the course of

ล้อมรอบ to surround, encircle, surrounded (by), all around

หมุนรอบ to rotate, revolve, spin around

รอมชอม to compromise, come to an agreement, make up

รอมร่อ almost, nearly, narrowly, on the threshhold (of), on the verge of

รอย trace, mark, track

รอยต่อ seam

รอยตำหนิ flaw, defect, mark, scar, disfigurement

รอยแตก crack

รอยไถ furrow

รอยเท้า footprint

รอยเปื้อน stain, spot

รอยแผลเป็น scar

รอยพระพุทธบาท Buddha's footprint

รอยพระพุทธบาทจำลอง model footprint of the Buddha

รอยพับ crease

รอยเย็บ stitch mark, stitching

รอยร้าว crack, fracture, fissure

รอยเลือด blood stain

รอยสัตว์ animal track

เข้ารูปเข้ารอย to fall into place, turn out well, come together nicely, be running well

เจริญรอยตาม to follow in the footsteps (of)

ตามรอย to follow in the footsteps (of); to track

เป็นริ้วรอย lined

ย้อนรอย to retrace one's steps, repeat; to retaliate, get back at someone

ร่องรอย mark (of), sign (of), clue, trace, trail, track

สะกดรอย to trace, track (down), trail

ร้อย[1] to string (เช่นร้อยดอกไม้)

ร้อยกรอง to compose, write

ร้อยแก้ว prose

ร้อย[2] hundred

ร้อยตรี second lieutenant

ร้อยเท่า a hundred times, hundredfold

ร้อยโท first lieutenant

ร้อยแปด a hundred and one (things to do etc), a myriad (of)

ร้อยละ percent, per hundred

ร้อยเอก captain

ร้อยเอ็ด a hundred one

ร้อยเอ็ดเจ็ดหัวเมือง everywhere, all over (the country)

ร่อยหรอ to be gradually consumed, diminished, grow less and less

ร่อแร่ in a critical condition, almost dead, moribund

หายใจร่อแร่ to breathe feebly, breathe one's last

ระกา the Year of the Chicken

ระกำ to be bitter, hurt, suffering, sorrowful

ระกำใจ to be bitter, embittered, hurt, resentful

ระเกะระกะ in disorder, messily, in a clutter; helter-skelter, higgledy-piggledy

หนังสือวางระเกะระกะอยู่บนโต๊ะ There is a clutter of books on the table. / The table is cluttered with books.

ระคน mixed, mingled, combined (with)

ระคาย irritating

ระคายผิว irritating, coarse

ระคายหู harsh, unpleasant

ระแคะระคาย hint, trace, (to have an) inkling, (have an) intimation (of)

ระฆัง bell

ระฆังหมดยก the bell at the end of the round

ตีระฆัง to strike a bell, ring a bell

หอระฆัง bell tower, belfry

ระงม noisy, clamorous, to make a clamor

ระงับ to stop, halt, discontinue, suspend, put an end to; to quell; to abate, allay

ระงับความรู้สึก to allay, suppress one's feelings

ระงับใจ to control oneself, calm down, /restrain/suppress/ (one's emotions, feelings, desires, etc)

ระดม to marshal, muster, gather, pool, mobilize

ระดมข้อมูล to marshal /files/facts/

ระดมความคิด to brainstorm

ระดมพล to mobilize, marshal forces

ระดมยิง to fire away (at), concentrate one's fire power (on), fire in volleys, shoot in concert

ระดับ level, grade

ระดับดิน ground level

ระดับน้ำ water level

ระดับน้ำทะเล sea level

ระดับสายตา (at) eye level

ระดับสูง high level; high, superior

ระดับเสียง pitch

ในระดับหนึ่ง to some extent

มีระดับ classy, to have class

ระดู menses, menstruation

ระดูขาว leukorrhea, leucorrhoea

ระทดระทวย dispirited

ระทดระท้อ disheartened

ระทม to be brokenhearted, suffer, in sorrow, grieving, distressed

ระทมใจ to be suffering, brokenhearted

ระทมทุกข์ to be grief-stricken

ระทึก to pound, thump, be pounding, go pit-a-pat, beat rapidly

ระทึกขวัญ shocking

ระนาด xylophone

ระนาดแก้ว metal xylophone

ระนาดทุ้ม alto xylophone

ระนาดเหล็ก xylophone with metal bars

ระนาดเอก lead xylophone

ระนาบ level, flat

ระนาว line, row, in lines, in rows

เป็นระนาว in droves

ระเนระนาด on top of one another, every which way, a jumble (of)

ระแนง roof batten, lath

ระบบ system, organization; manner, mode, way

คนละระบบ different way of doing things

ระบม bruised, sore, aching, contused

ระบมไปทั้งตัว to be sore all over

ระบอบ model; custom, customary way; form, system

ระบอบการปกครอง /form/system/ of government, regime

ระบอบประชาธิปไตย democratic form of government, democracy

ระบอบราชาธิปไตย monarchical form of government

ระบอบสมบูรณาญาสิทธิราชย์ absolute monarchy

ระบอบสังคมนิยม socialist form of government

ระบัด newly sprouting (grass), young (grass)

ระบาด widespread, spreading; epidemic

    ระบาดวิทยา epidemiology

    โรคระบาด epidemic

ระบาย to paint, draw in color; to release; to vent, unload, get (something) out

    ระบายความคิด to express one's /thoughts/ ideas/

    ระบายความในใจ to speak one's mind, unburden oneself, get something off one's chest, vent one's feelings

    ระบายท้อง to have a bowel movement

    ระบายน้ำ to release the water

        ประตูระบายน้ำ sluice gate, water gate

    ระบายสี to paint

    ระบายอากาศ to ventilate

    ยาระบาย laxative

ระบำ ballet, dance /ensemble/troupe/

    ระบำโป๊ striptease dance, stripdance, fan dance

    เต้นระบำ to dance in /a ballet/an ensemble/

    นางระบำ ballet dancer, ballerina; chorus girl

ระบิล affair, matter; accepted way

    ระบิลเมือง law and customs

ระบือ spread far and wide, widely known

ระบุ to specify, indicate, name

    ระบุชื่อ to name, identify

    โปรดระบุ please indicate, please /fill in/ insert/

ระเบิด to explode, blow up, erupt; burst; to blow one's top

    ระเบิดขมอง to blow one's brains out

    ระเบิดขวด bottle bomb

    ระเบิดทำลาย high-explosive bomb

    ระเบิดปรมาณู atomic bomb

    ระเบิดเพลิง incendiary bomb, fire bomb

    ระเบิดมือ hand grenade

    ระเบิดเวลา time bomb

    ระเบิดอารมณ์ to explode

    ระเบิดไฮโดรเจน hydrogen bomb

    ดินระเบิด dynamite

    ทิ้งระเบิด to drop a bomb

    ทุ่นระเบิด mine

    ลูกระเบิด bomb

ระเบียง veranda, porch; balcony; gallery (surrounding a temple), portico (of a temple)

    ระเบียงบ้าน veranda, porch, deck

ระเบียน register, record

    ระเบียนสะสม cumulative (scholastic) record

ระเบียบ order; regulations, rules; organisation

    ระเบียบการ procedure, rules and regulations

    ระเบียบจัด meticulous; formalistic

        คนระเบียบจัด a stickler for the rules; a meticulous person

    ระเบียบวาระ agenda

    ระเบียบวินัย rules; disciplinary

        อยู่ในระเบียบวินัย well-disciplined

    เป็นระเบียบ systematically; in order, well-arranged, neat

    มีระเบียบ neat, well-organized, orderly, methodical, systematic

ระมัดระวัง to be careful, cautious, take care

ระย่อ in a funk, discouraged

ระยะ interval; distance; stage; space; bar (in music)

    ระยะใกล้ short range

    ระยะไกล long range

    ระยะทาง distance

    ระยะเวลา space of time, during the /time/ period/, for a period (of)

    ระยะสายตา visible; range of sight

    ระยะห่าง clearance

    ชั่วระยะ for a time, in the space of (an hour etc)

    ในระยะ while, during, when; in, within

    เป็นระยะๆ at intervals, periodically

ระย้า pendant, hanging ornament, hanging spray (of flowers etc); to hang, overhang

โคมระย้า chandelier

ตุ้มหูระย้า pendant earring

ห้อยเป็นระย้า to hang in profusion; tassels (of)

ระยำ low, base, vile, damn

ไอ้ระยำ You bastard!, That /bastard/ lowlife/!

ระยิบระยับ glittering, sparkling, twinkling, dazzling

ระโยงระยาง a /profusion/mess/ of (lines, streamers, wires etc)

ระรวย gentle, soft, faint

หายใจระรวย to breathe faintly

ระรัว beating

สั่นระรัว trembling, shivering

หัวใจเต้นระรัว his heart was beating (with fright, love etc)

ระราน to make trouble (for), annoy, bother

ระริก giggling

สั่นระริก to quiver

ระรื่น happy; delightful, refreshing

ระเริง overjoyed, ecstatic

หลงระเริงอยู่ในโลกียวิสัย enamoured of worldly pleasures

ระลอก wave, ripple, in waves

มาเป็นระลอก in waves

ระลึก to think of; recollect, remember, recall

ระลึกชาติ to recall a previous life

ของที่ระลึก souvenir, remembrance, memento

พิมพ์เป็นที่ระลึก printed /in remembrance/ as a souvenir/ (of the wedding etc of...)

วันที่ระลึก memorial day

ระวัง to take care (of), be careful (of), guard against, beware (of), watch, watch out (for)

ระวัง! Watch out!

ระวังของแตก fragile

ระวังของหาย watch your things, keep an eye on your belongings

ระวังตัว to be careful, watch out for oneself

ระวังสุนัขดุ beware of the dog

ระวังหัว/ศีรษะ Watch your head!

คอยระวัง to be careful, take care, be on the alert (for, to), be on the lookout (for), vigilant

ระมัดระวัง to be careful, cautious, take care

ระวาง hold

ระวางขับน้ำ displacement, tonnage

ค่าระวาง freight charge, freight

ระแวง to be wary, suspicious, mistrustful; to suspect, distrust

ต่างฝ่ายต่างระแวงกัน They were wary of one another.

ระแวดระวัง to be very careful, extremely cautious, wary

ระส่ำระสาย in disarray, in confusion; disintegrating, chaotic, in turmoil

ระหกระเหิน vagrant

ระหง tall, slender, willowy

ระหว่าง between, among; during, while; (in the) interval, at /this/that/ time

ระหว่างกลาง in the middle (of)

ระหว่างชาติ international

ระหว่างประเทศ international

กฎหมายระหว่างประเทศ international law

ระหว่างเวลา while, during (เช่น while walking, during the walk)

ในระหว่างกันเอง as between themselves

ระหองระแหง antagonistic, contentious, always at odds, estranged

ระหัด treadmill for raising water

ระเห็จ to flee

ระเหย to evaporate

ระเหระหน to drift, wander; vagabond; nomadic, itinerant

ระเหิด to sublime

ระแหง /crack/fissure/ in the ground

แตกระแหง to be /fissured/cracked/

ทุกหัวระแหง everywhere, all over

ระโหย feel tired, weary, worn out

ระอา to be tired (of), bored (with), dispirited, disheartened

เอือมระอา to be fed up (with), disgusted

ระอุ hot, heated; torrid; smouldering

รัก[1] to love, like, be fond of

รักใคร่ to be fond (of), care (for), love, like

รักชาติ to love one's country; be patriotic

   ความรักชาติ patriotism

   ผู้รักชาติ patriot

รักชีวิต to love life, have a will to live

รักซ้อน to two-time, have a secret love

รักเดียว to be true (to)

รักตัวเอง to love oneself

รักแรก first love

รักแรกพบ love at first sight

รักสามเส้า the eternal triangle, love triangle

คู่รัก boyfriend, girlfriend, lover, sweetheart, darling

ที่รัก dear; darling, beloved, honey, sweetheart

น่ารัก lovely, nice, attractive, cute, lovable, adorable, sweet, endearing

นึกรัก to take a /liking/fancy/ to someone

ฝากรัก to give one's heart (to); to tell someone you love her, declare one's /love/ affection/ for someone, confess one's love, let someone know you love /him/her/

พิษรัก bitterness of love, harm that comes of loving

ไฟรัก burning love, fire of love

ยอดรัก dearest, my darling, my beloved

หลงรัก to be infatuated (with), fall for someone, be crazy about, head over heels in love (with)

รัก[2] lacquer

ลงรักปิดทอง to lacquer and gild

รักบี้ rugby

รักแร้ armpit

รักษา to care for; to maintain, preserve; observe; to protect; to defend; to take care of, treat, cure remedy, heal

รักษากฎหมาย to abide by the law, uphold the law

รักษาการ on duty, in charge (of); acting

รักษาคำพูด to keep (one's) word

รักษาคำมั่นสัญญา to keep one's /promise/ word/

รักษาประโยชน์ to protect one's interests

รักษาระเบียบ to observe the rules and regulations

รักษาโรค to treat (an illness, a disease etc)

รักษาศีล to observe the precepts

รักษาหน้า to maintain (one's) reputation; to avoid embarrassment

รัง nest

รังไข่ ovary

รังดุม buttonhole

รังแตน a running hexagonal design; wasps' nest

รังนก bird's nest

รังผึ้ง beehive; radiator; perforated earthen grate

รังมด ants' nest

รังไหม silkworm cocoon

รั้ง to hold back, restrain

รั้งเจ้าอาวาส acting abbot

รั้งท้าย to bring up the rear, be the last

รังเกียจ to mind, dislike, have an aversion for

น่ารังเกียจ offensive, objectionable, repugnant, disagreeable

รังแก to bother, annoy, bully, mistreat

รังควาน to harass, molest; to keep disturbing, trouble, bother

รังแค dandruff

รังแต่ to do nothing but

รั้งรอ to await, wait

รังรอง splendor (of), splendorous

รังวัด to survey, measure

ร
ฤ
ฤๅ
ล
ว
ศ
ษ
ส
ห
ฬ
อ
ฮ

รังสฤษดิ์ to create

รังสี rays, beam, /ray/beam/ of light, radiation

    รังสีแพทย์ radiologist

    รังสีวิทยา radiology

    กัมมันตภาพรังสี radioactivity

    กัมมันตรังสี radioactive

รัชกาล reign

รัชชูปการ poll-tax, capitation

รัชดาภิเษก royal silver jubilee

รัชทายาท heir to the throne

รัญจวน to yearn (for), be lovesick

รัฐ state, country, government

    เจ้าหน้าที่ของรัฐ state official, government officer

    สหรัฐ the United States

รัฐธรรมนูญ constitution

รัฐนาวา ship of state

รัฐนิยม State Convention

รัฐบาล government

    รัฐบาลกลาง central government

    รัฐบาลท้องถิ่น local government, local authorities

    รัฐบาลผสม coalition government

    รัฐบาลพลัดถิ่น government-in-exile

    ทำเนียบรัฐบาล Government House

    โรงเรียนรัฐบาล state school, public school (US)

    องค์การรัฐบาล government organization

รัฐบุรุษ statesman

    รัฐบุรุษอาวุโส elder statesman

รัฐประศาสน์ public administration

    รัฐประศาสโนบาย public policy

รัฐประหาร (to make a) coup d'etat, to overthrow a government

รัฐมนตรี minister, secretary

    รัฐมนตรีช่วยว่าการ deputy minister

    รัฐมนตรีว่าการ minister, secretary

    คณะรัฐมนตรี Council of Ministers, cabinet

รัฐวิสาหกิจ state enterprise

รัฐศาสตร์ political science

รัฐสภา legislature, parliament, national assembly, congress; council of state

รัด to bind, tie up, strap; to squeeze, constrict, constrain; to fasten

    การเมืองรัดกันอยู่ constrained by politics

    รัดกุม concise, succinct, terse; watertight, comprehensive, tightly written; tight-fitting

        แต่งตัวรัดกุม safely attired, properly outfitted

    รัดเกล้า fillet

    รัดของ to strap

    รัดตัว tight, constrictive

    รัดรึง to tie tightly, bind firmly; to hug firmly; to implant, imprint (in one's mind etc)

    รัดรูป to mold the figure; skintight, close-fitting

    กอดรัด to hug, embrace

    กะทัดรัด compact, trim; well-proportioned, well-fitting; handy; concise, succinct

    ยางรัด rubber band

    รวบรัด to cut (something) short, compress, abbreviate; to expedite

    เร่งรัด to press (someone for something); urgent, pressing

รัตน์, รัตน- precious stone, gem, jewel

    รัตนโกสินทร์ Rattanakosin, another name for Bangkok

    รัตนตรัย the Triple Gem

รั้น stubborn, obstinate, bullheaded, recalcitrant

รันทด to be deeply distressed, dismayed, saddened

รับ to receive, take, get; to bear, suffer; to accept, agree; to admit; to answer; to meet.

    รับกับใบหน้า to go with her face, suit (her/him/ etc)

    รับขวัญ see **รับขวัญ** *หน้า 49*

    รับแขก to receive a guest, entertain, look

after a guest

รับความเสียหาย to suffer a loss, suffer damage

รับความเห็นชอบ to get the approval of, be approved

รับคำ to promise, give one's word

    รับคำสั่ง to /receive/get/ an order

รับเคราะห์ to be the victim, suffer (for something); to get the blame; to be affected

รับเงินเดือน to get paid, receive one's /salary/wages/

รับจ้าง for hire, to take employment, be /employed/hired/(to do or for something)

รับเชิญ to accept (an invitation)

รับใช้ to serve, work for (someone), be at (another's) disposal

    รับใช้ประเทศชาติ to serve one's country

    คนรับใช้ servant, attendant, retainer, help, assistant, a domestic

    ทหารรับใช้ orderly, batman *(Brit)*

รับซ่อม to repair; repairs ในป้ายโฆษณา เช่น *ที่นี่รับซ่อมนาฬิกา Watch Repairs*

รับซื้อ to buy

รับทราบ acknowledged, to acknowledge, be informed, note

รับทำ to agree to do; to do, make

รับทุกข์ to suffer

รับโทษ to receive punishment, be penalized

รับบาป to take the blame (for), suffer the consequences (of misdeeds)

    แพะรับบาป scapegoat

รับประกัน to insure; to guarantee, assure

รับประทาน to eat, dine, take, have

    รับประทานอาหารกลางวัน to lunch, have lunch, take lunch

    รับประทานอาหารเช้า to breakfast, have breakfast, eat breakfast

    รับประทานอาหารเย็น to dine, have dinner, have supper

    รับประทานอาหารว่าง to have a /snack /light meal/light refreshment/tea/ etc

รับปะยาง Tire Repairs., Flat Tires Fixed

รับปาก to promise, agree (to do something)

รับเป็นสัตย์ to confess, admit

รับผิด to admit (one's) /fault/guilt/responsibility/

    รับผิดชอบ to be responsible (for), take responsibility (for), accept liability (for)

รับผู้โดยสาร to accept passengers, take passengers

    ไม่รับผู้โดยสาร no passengers

รับฝากเด็กอ่อน infant care center

รับฝากรถ car park

รับพร to receive a blessing

รับฟังได้ to accept

รับภาระภาษี to bear the tax

รับมรดก to inherit, receive a legacy

รับมือ to withstand; to compete with; to deal with, handle

รับไม่ได้ unacceptable, inadmissable

รับรอง to confirm, certify; to recognize; to give an assurance, vouch for; to ententain

    ใบรับรอง certificate

รับราชการ to enter government service, be in government service

    รับราชการทหาร to be in military service

รับรู้ to acknowledge, be informed, know; to take cognizance (of), take note (of), perceive

รับเลือก elected, chosen

รับไว้พิจารณา under consideration, to take into consideration

รับศีล to affirm observance of the precepts

รับศึก to engage in battle, battle; to rise to a challenge

รับสั่ง to say

รับสารภาพ to confess

    การรับสารภาพ confession

รับสินบน to take a bribe

รับเสด็จ to wait upon the /king/queen/

รับหลักการ to accept in principle

รับเหมา to do contract work; to contract (to do a job etc), be hired (to), be a contractor

ผู้รับเหมา contractor

รับไหว้ to return a greeting; to accept a token of a bride's and bridegroom's respect

รับอาสา to volunteer

ขานรับ to answer, respond; to agree (with)

เข้ารับตำแหน่ง to take office, assume a position

เครื่องรับวิทยุ radio, radio receiver

ได้รับ received

ต้อนรับ to welcome, greet, receive

ตอบรับ to reply, answer; to accept

ตั้งรับ to make a stand

ใบรับเงิน receipt

ยอมรับ to admit, concede, agree; to confess

รองรับ supporting, to support, back up, underpin; to be a basis (for)

รัว roll (of a drum), ratatat (of a gun), rapid firing; trilling; tremorous (voice); kind of Thai music; indistinct

รัวกระสุนใส่ to fire rapidly (at), fire a hail of bullets (at)

รัวลิ้น to speak fast

รั่ว to leak

รั่วไหล to leak out, get to be known

รั้ว fence; hedge

รั้วของชาติ defenders of the nation

รั้วต้นไม้ hedge

รั้วบ้าน fence (around a house)

กั้นรั้ว to fence, put up a fence

ล้อมรั้ว to fence (in), put a fence around

รัศมี ray; light, halo, radiance; radius

รัศมีทำการ range of operation

รัษฎากร revenue

รา[1] mold, fungus

ขึ้นรา moldy

รา[2] to subside, break off, slacken; to give up, stop

ราข้อ to back off, withdraw, retreat

ราปีก to glide

ราไฟ to lower a fire

รามือ to take it easy, go easy; to give /in/ up/, stop

ราก[1] root; foundation

รากแก้ว taproot

รากฐาน basis, foundation, base

รากตึก building foundation, piling

รากที่สอง square root

รากที่สาม cube root

รากฝอย fibrous root, rootlet

รากฟัน root (of a tooth)

รากศัพท์ root (of a word)

รากเหง้า roots, origins

ฝังราก to settle down, berooted (in)

รกราก origins; birthplace, old home

ราก[2] to throw up, vomit, retch

รากแตก to throw up, vomit

ราคะ lust

ราคา price, value, worth

ราคาขาดตัว bottom price, lowest price, best price

ราคา 12 บาทขาดตัว 12 baht is the best I can do.

ราคาขาย selling price

ราคาขายปลีก retail price

ราคาขายส่ง wholesale price

ราคาขายสด cash price

ราคาซื้อ purchase price, cost price

ราคาตลาด market price, going price

ราคาถูก low-priced, cheap, economical

ราคาเป็นกันเอง moderate price, reasonable price, /moderately/reasonably/ priced

ราคาแพง dear, high-priced, expensive

ราคาย่อมเยา low-priced, inexpensive

กดราคา to force down the price

เกี่ยงราคา to haggle (over the price), bargain, dicker

โก่งราคา to /raise/jack up/put up/inflate/ the price

ขายลดราคา see **ขายลดราคา** หน้า 58

ขึ้นราคา to go up in price; increase the price

ต่อ (รอง) ราคา to bargain

ตั้งราคา to set a price, put a price (on)

มีราคา to be worth something, valuable, costly, precious

ลดราคา to /reduce/lower/the price, go down in price, give a /discount/price reduction/; to put on sale

เสื่อมราคา to depreciate in value

ราคี defiled

ราง[1] rail, track; channel, groove, trough; gutter

รางน้ำ gutter; water trough

รางรถไฟ railroad tracks

รางหญ้า manger

รางหมู pig trough

ลำราง waterway, ditch

ราง[2] as in **รางๆ** indistinctly, faintly, vaguely

ร่าง figure, form, outline, shape; body; draft; to draft, sketch, outline

ร่างกาย body

ร่างทรง medium

ร่างพระราชบัญญัติ bill, draft law; to draft a bill

ร่างร้าน scaffold

ร่างแห net, mesh

พลอยติดร่างแห to get /enmeshed/ embroiled/involved/, be implicated

ต้นร่าง first draft

รูปร่าง appearance, look; figure, shape, form; physique

เรือนร่าง body

ร้าง deserted, abandoned, vacant

รกร้าง vacant and overgrown

เริดร้าง to be separated, go their separate ways

วัดร้าง deserted monastery

รางวัล prize, award; reward

รางวัลชมเชย honorable mention

ราช- king, royal

ราชการ government service, official

ราชการทหาร military service

ราชกิจจานุเบกษา Government Gazette

ราชครู Brahman chief of ceremony

ราชดำเนิน to proceed

ราชทัณฑ์ correction (department), penitentiary (department)

ราชทินนาม title conferred by the king

ราชทูต diplomatic representative, envoy; embassy

ราชธานี capital; royal palace

ราชธิดา royal princess

ราชนาวี Royal Navy

ราชนิกุล a royal descendant, members of a royal family, person of royal blood

ราชบัณฑิต Fellow of the Royal Institute

ราชบัณฑิตยสถาน Royal Institute, Royal Academy

ราชภัฏ as in **สถาบันราชภัฏ** teachers training institution, former normal schools

ราชไมตรี friendly relations, friendship (of a kingdom)

ราชวงศ์ dynasty, royal house

เช่น house of Windsor

ราชวงศานุวงศ์ members of the royal family

ราชวัง royal palace

ราชสำนัก court

ราชสีห์ lion-king

ราชหัตถเลขา royal letter

ราชอาณาจักร kingdom

ราชโองการ royal /order/command/

ราชา king, monarch, rajah

ราชาคณะ a title of ranking monks

ราชาภิเษก coronation

ราชาศัพท์ royal word

ร
ฤ
ฤๅ
ล
ว
ศ
ษ
ส
ห
ฬ
อ
ฮ

ราชินี queen

ราชินูปถัมภ์ patronage of H.M. the Queen

ราชูปถัมภ์ royal patronage

ราชูปโภค royal article of use

ราโชวาท royal address

ราด to pour (something) on (something else); topping

    ราดน้ำ to pour water (on, over)

    ก๋วยเตี๋ยวราดหน้า noodles with a topping (of pork, chili-fried chicken etc), noodles with (pork etc)

    ข้าวราดแกง rice topped with curry, rice with curry

    เยี่ยวราด to wet (the bed, one's pants, the floor etc)

ราตรี evening night

ราน to prune

    รุกราน to invade, attack, commit an act of aggression against

ร่าน flirtatious

ร้าน shop, store; stall, booth; scaffolding, platform

    ร้านกาแฟ coffee shop

    ร้านขายของ store, shop

    ร้านขายเครื่องกระป๋อง grocery store

    ร้านขายเครื่องเขียน stationers, stationery /store/shop/

    ร้านขายปืน gun shop

    ร้านขายผัก vegetable /stall/shop/

    ร้านขายยา drugstore, pharmacy, chemist's shop *(Brit)*

    ร้านขายรองเท้า shoestore

    ร้านขายเสื้อผ้า clothing store

    ร้านขายหนังสือ bookstore

    ร้านค้า store, shop

        ร้านค้าของเก่า antique shop; second-hand shop

        ร้านค้าย่อย retail /shop/store/

    ร้านชำ grocery store, the grocer's

    ร้านซักรีด laundry

    ร้านดอกไม้ florist's, flower shop

    ร้านตัดผม barber shop, the barber's

    ร้านตัดเสื้อ dressmaking shop, the dressmaker's

    ร้านทำผม hairdresser's, hair stylist, hairdressing salon

    ร้านผลไม้ fruit store

    ร้านเพชรพลอย jewelry /store/shop/

    ร้านสหกรณ์ cooperative store, cooperative, co-op

    ร้านเหล้า liquor store

    ร้านอาหาร eating place, foodshop, restaurant

    ชาวบ้านร้านตลาด everybody

    ห้างร้าน businesses, commercial establishments, stores, shops, stores and shops

    ออกร้าน to set up stalls (foodstalls, bookstalls, merchandise stalls etc)

ราบ flat, level, plain, even; smooth

    ราบคาบ subdued, pacified; crushed, utterly defeated

    ราบรื่น smoothly, untroubled

    ราบเรียบ smooth

    ทหารราบ infantry

    ที่ราบ plain; flatland

        ที่ราบสูง plateau

    ทุ่งราบ /level/flat/ field

    พื้นราบ plane surface, flat area

    สงบราบคาบ peaceful, pacified

รามเกียรติ์ Ramayana

รามัญ Mon

ราย list; particular, individual, item, case; edition; per; a numerical designation for things in series

    รายการ list; item; particulars; program; transaction

        รายการการแสดง number

        รายการอาหาร menu, fare

รายงาน report, to report

    รายงานการประชุม proceedings, minutes

    รายงานข่าว news report, news item, report

    รายงานตัว to report (to), present oneself (to), appear before (a committee, commanding officer etc)

รายจ่าย expenditure(s), expense(s)

รายชื่อ names, list of names

รายเดือน monthly, per month

รายได้ income, revenue; proceeds

    อันมีรายได้ gainful, income-producing

รายทาง along the way

รายนาม names, list of names

รายบุคคล individual, personal; one by one

รายปักษ์ fortnightly, biweekly

รายปี annual, yearly, per year

รายรับ income, receipt, credit account

รายละเอียด particulars, details

รายวัน daily

รายสัปดาห์ weekly

เป็นรายๆ individually, in particular cases

ร่าย a kind of free verse

ร่ายมนต์ to murmur incantations

ร่ายยาว to be long-winded, go on and on

ร่ายรำ to brandish, flourish

ร้าย bad, evil, malicious; vile; ferocious; malignant; wicked, terribly good, great

ร้ายกาจ terrible; formidable, fantastic, extraordinary

ร้ายแรง serious, grave

คิดร้าย to plot against, to harbor /ill will/ animosity/ (towards), be spiteful, malicious, ill-intentioned

คุ้มดีคุ้มร้าย unbalanced; temperamental, volatile, mercurial

เคราะห์ร้าย unlucky, unfortunate, bad luck

ใจร้าย mean, unkind, heartless

ดุร้าย ferocious, fierce; brutal, savage

ทำร้าย to injure, harm, hurt, do violence to

ปองร้าย to be malicious, intend to harm, have ill will (to wards somebody), malevolent

ผลร้าย dire consequence, /bad/harmful/ effect, negative consequences

ผู้ก่อการร้าย insurgent; terrorist, bandit

โรคร้าย malignant disease

สัตว์ร้าย ferocious animal, predator

ใส่ร้าย to slander, vilify, malign, say bad things about someone

ร่าเริง cheerful, happy, in good spirits, gay

ราว[1] handrail, banister, clothes pole, clothesline; row, line, strip (of); rack, bar

ราวบันได handrail, banister

ราวป่า line of trees, strip of/woods/forest/; edge of a forest

เรื่องราว story, matter, what happened, case

ราว[2] about, around

    ราวหกโมง about six o'clock, around six

    ในราว about, around, approximately

ราวกะ, ราวกับ like, as if, as though

    ราวกับว่า like, as if, as though

    เธอใช้เงินราวกับเศรษฐี You spend /like/as though/ you were a millionaire.

ร้าว to be cracked, fissured

ร้าวฉาน at odds, in disagreement, in discord

ร้าวราน to disunite

ก้าวร้าว aggressive, belligerent, abrasive, antagonistic, bellicose

แตกร้าว to divide over conflicting opinions

ปวดร้าว to suffer, be tormented (by); to be deeply hurt (by), crushed, shattered, deeply wounded, embittered

ราวี to attack, beleaguer

ศัตรูมาราวี the enemy attacks

ราศี measurement of the zodiac equal to 30 degrees; sign of the zodiac, house (of), constellation; radiance

ราศีกรกฎ Cancer

ร
ฤ
ฤๅ
ล
ว
ศ
ษ
ส
ห
ฬ
อ
ฮ

ราศีกันย์ Virgo

ราศีกุมภ์ Aquarius

ราศีตุลย์ Libra

ราศีธนู Sagittarius

ราศีพฤษภ Taurus

ราศีพิจิก Scorpion

ราศีมังกร Capricorn

ราศีมีน Pisces

ราศีเมถุน Gemini

ราศีเมษ Aries

ราศีสิงห์ Leo

ใบหน้ามีราศี to have an inward /glow/ radiance/, have presence

ราษฎร์, ราษฎร population, people

ทวยราษฎร์ the people, citizenry

ทะเบียนราษฎร์ civil register

ผู้แทนราษฎร representative of the people, member of the legislature, elected representative, M.P., member of parliament

โรงเรียนราษฎร์ private school, public school (Brit)

สภาผู้แทนราษฎร National Assembly, House of People's Representatives

สมาชิกสภาผู้แทนราษฎร member of the National Assembly, national assemblyman, member of parliament

รำ[1] rice bran

รำ[2] to dance

รำเท้า to do ballroom dancing; to kick

รำพัด to play cards; fan dance

รำแพน to strut

รำวง ramwong, a Thai couple-dance

เต้นรำ to dance

ฟ้อนรำ to do Thai dancing

ร่ายรำ to dance

ร่ำ to keep (doing something); constant, continual, over and over again, prolonged; persistent

ร่ำไป repeatedly, incessantly, continually

frequently, always

ร่ำร้อง constant begging (for something), to keep asking (someone for something), ask persistently

ร่ำเรียน to study hard, apply oneself to one's studies

ร่ำลา to say a prolonged goodbye, take leave (of someone) interminably, say goodbye over and over again

ร่ำไห้ to wail, sob, make lamentations

รำคาญ to be annoyed, irked

รำคาญใจ annoyed, irritated, vexed

แก้รำคาญ see แก้รำคาญ หน้า 40

น่ารำคาญ annoying, irksome, bothersome, a nuisance

รำพัน to speak at length

รำพึง to think (about), muse; to ponder

รำเพย (to blow) gently, softly, /light/gentle/ (breeze)

รำไพ beauteous

รำมะนาด pyorrhea

ร่ำรำ nearly, almost, on the verge of, about to

ร่ำรวย rich, wealthy

รำไร indistinctly, vaguely, a little (of)

ร่ำไร to be slow, take one's time

รำลึก to think (of), recollect, recall

ริ to begin (to), start

ริเริ่ม to initiate, begin, start, commence, be the first (to do something)

ริอ่าน to plan

ริก, ริกๆ as in สั่นริกๆ vibrating, shaking; beating fast; shivering, trembling (with cold etc)

ริดสีดวง hemorrhoids

ริดสีดวงจมูก rhinitis

ริดสีดวงตา trachoma

ริดสีดวงทวาร hemorrhoids, piles

ริน[1] to pour; gradually, in a trickle; gently, softly

ไหลริน to trickle; to flow gently, run (down, along)

ริน[2] *as in* **ทองริน** gold of less than 9.6 carats

ริ้น gnat

ริบ to confiscate; to be forfeited

    ริบทรัพย์ to confiscate property

    ถูกริบ forfeited, confiscated, seized

ริบหรี่ almost extinguished, faint, dim

ริม edge, rim

    ริมถนน by the side of the road, roadside

    ริมทาง roadside, wayside

    ริมน้ำ water's edge

    ริมฝีปาก lip

ริ้ว mark, streak, stripe, line

    ริ้วรอย sign, trace, evidence

ริษยา envy, jealousy, envious, jealous

รี tapering; oval

    วงรี oval, ovoid

รี่ to rush in, dash in, go straight in

    เดินรี่เข้าไป go straight in, dash in

รี้ *as in* **รี้พล** armed forces, troops, army

รีด to squeeze; to wring, put through a /wringer/roller/; to draw, roll; to iron, press

    รีดเงิน to squeeze money (out of someone), extort money

    รีดไถ to squeeze (someone for something), put the squeeze on someone

    รีดนม to milk

    รีดนาทาเร้น to extort (something from someone)

    รีดผ้า to iron (clothes), do the ironing; to press, have (a suit etc) pressed

    รีดภาษี to extract taxes

    รีดลูก to have an abortion

    รีดเลือดกับปู *as in* **อย่ารีดเลือดกับปู** You can't get blood out of a turnip.

รีต custom, tradition

    เข้ารีต to be converted (to)

        ผู้เข้ารีต a convert

    นอกรีต heretical

รีบ pressing, urgent, hurried, in a hurry, without

delay; to rush

    รีบทำ to do in a hurry; do promptly

    รีบไป to hurry, rush off

    รีบร้อน in a big hurry

    รีบรุด to dash (over, away), rush over (to); to speed

    รีบเร่ง to hurry, hasten, go quickly

รีๆ รอๆ to hesitate, waver, vacillate; indecisive, unable to make up one's mind, to dither

รี้รัก giggle

รื่น happy, pleased, refreshing

    รื่นรมย์ to be happy; pleasant, refreshing

    รื่นเริง cheerful, gay, jolly, lighthearted

        งานรื่นเริง party, celebration, festivities, entertainment

รื้อ to pull down; dismantle, undo, take apart; to re-do; to revive, bring up, raise

    รื้อถอน to remove, take (something) down, raze

        ค่ารื้อถอน cost of removal

    รื้อฟื้น to revive, resuscitate, bring up again

รุ to throw away, discard, dispose of; to dismiss, get rid of

    รุทิ้ง to throw away, get rid of, dispose of, discard

    รุสต๊อค stock clearance

รุก to advance; to trespass, intrude; to attack; to be aggressive, active; to put in check

    รุกคืบ invasive

    สังคมชนบทได้ล่มสลายจากความเจริญรุกคืบแล้ว Rural society has already been disintegrated by invasive development.

    รุกฆาต to checkmate

    รุกราน to invade, attack, commit an act of aggression against

        ผู้รุกราน aggressor, invader

    รุกล้ำ to trespass, intrude

    บุกรุก to trespass, invade, intrude

    หมากรุก chess

ร
ฤ
ฤๅ
ล
ว
ศ
ษ
ส
ห
ฬ
อ
ฮ

รุกขชาติ the vegetable kingdom

รุ่ง bright, shining, brilliant, glorious; dawn
รุ่งขึ้น the next day, following day
รุ่งเช้า dawn, daybreak; the following morning
รุ่งเรือง prosperous, thriving, flourishing
รุ่งโรจน์ glorious, brilliant, resplendent; highly advanced
รุ่งสาง break of dawn
รุ่งอรุณ (at) dawn, daybreak
ใกล้รุ่ง at the approach of dawn, before dawn
คืนยังรุ่ง the whole night long
ดาวรุ่ง morning star, Venus
ตลอดรุ่ง throughout the night, until dawn
ย่ำรุ่ง six in the morning; early morning, daybreak
หามรุ่งหามค่ำ from morn till night, day and night, arduously

รุ้ง rainbow; iridescence; curved; arched, vaulted
รุ้งพราย iridescence
รุ้งร่วง sparkle
สายรุ้ง rainbow
เส้นรุ้ง latitude

รุงรัง messy, unkempt; disorderly, untidy, in disorder
ผมเผ้ารุงรัง disheveled hair, tousled (hair)
รกรุงรัง in a mess, cluttered, messy, untidy

รุด to speed (up, along, forward), hurry
รุดหน้า to make progress

รุ่น model; batch, lot; shipment; version; class; generation; adolescent, young, teenaged
รุ่นกระเตาะ pre-teen, youngster
รุ่นกระทง stripling, young adolescent (boy)
รุ่นกำดัด budding girl, young adolescent (girl)
รุ่นจิ๋ว mini; little youngsters
รุ่นตะกอ entering puberty

รุ่นราวคราวเดียวกัน of the same age; of the same period, contemporary
แรกรุ่น pubescent
วัยรุ่น youth, adolescence; teenagers, youngsters, adolescents
อนุชนรุ่นหลัง younger generation, future generations

รุม to gather around, crowd (around, against, up on); to gang up on
รุมกินโต๊ะ to gang up (on someone); to join the feast, pounce on the spoils
รุมล้อม to crowd around
รุมเร้า to overwhelm

รุ่มร่าม baggy, loose fitting, sloppy

รุ่ย to unravel, slipping
รุ่ยร่าย hanging /out/down/about/

รู hole, burrow; perforation
รูรั่ว a leak
เจาะรู to perforate, make a hole
เป็นรู in holes, full of holes, perforated

รู้ to know, understand, be aware of
รู้กล to see through
รู้กัน to have an understanding, they know, known
รู้แก่ใจ to know /perfectly/very/full/ well, must know, know in one's heart, realize
รู้แกว to have an inkling (of); to be in the know, know what's what
รู้ความ to understand (things)
รู้คุณ grateful, to know the meaning of gratitude; to appreciate (the value of), be appreciative
รู้จัก to know, be acquainted (with)
   รู้จักคิด clever, smart
   รู้จักมักจี่ to know (someone) personally, be familiar with, be close to, be on intimate terms (with)
รู้แจ้งเห็นจริง to realize, comprehend, be enlightened, have a profound understanding

(of), have an insight into the true nature of things

รู้ใจ to understand (someone)

รู้เช่นเห็นชาติ to know (someone) inside out

รู้ดี to well know, understand well; to be so smart

รู้ตัว to know /in advance/beforehand/; to recognize, identify; to be aware (of, that), conscious (of)

รู้เต็มอก to know full well

รู้ทัน to see through, (someone or something), know another's game, be up to (someone or to another's scheme etc); know what's what, perceptive

รู้ที to know what another is up to

รู้เท่า to know as much as another; to be perceptive

> **รู้เท่าไม่ถึงการณ์** through ignorance, not knowing what one is doing, blindly, innocently

รู้แน่ to know for sure

รู้เบาะแส to have information (that, about, on, in regard to); getting to the bottom

รู้ภาษา to understand; to have horse sense

รู้มาก to take advantage (of); to show off

รู้ไม่จริง does not really know

รู้รอบ to know all about (something), have a comprehensive knowledge (of)

รู้เรื่อง to understand; to be informed, aware, know what is going on, be au fait

รู้แล้วรู้รอด to /be/have/done with it; to get (something) over with

รู้ไว้ไม่เสียหลาย It doesn't do any harm to know.

รู้สำนึก to be penitent, contrite, conscience-stricken, have (something) on one's conscience, feel sorry (about, for)

รู้ไส้รู้พุง to see through someone

รู้เห็นเป็นใจ to connive (with, at), abet, be

in collusion (with), give encouragement (to)

ความรู้ knowledge, understanding, learning

น่ารู้ interesting

ไม่รู้ *see* ไม่รู้ *หน้า 388*

> **ไม่รู้จบ** *see* ไม่รู้จักจบ *หน้า 388*

รับรู้ to acknowledge, be informed, know; to take cognizance (of), take note (of)

เรียนรู้ to learn how; to understand

ล่วงรู้ to have foresight, know in advance, anticipate

สอดรู้สอดเห็น nosy, prying

อยากรู้อยากเห็น curious

รูด   to slide, pull, draw, strip

รูดทรัพย์ (จากคน) to strip the body of valuables

รูดม่าน to slide a curtain, draw a curtain

รูดแหวน to slide a ring (on, off)

รูป[1]   picture; image; shape, figure, form appearance, outline; body, visible object

รูปการ situation, the way things have shaped up, the overall picture

รูปแกะ carving, carved figure; sculpture

รูปเขียน drawing, painting

รูปไข่ oval, ovate, egg-shaped

รูปคดี the case

รูปความ the way a /case/affair/ has developed

รูปจำลอง model, mock-up, replica, reproduction

รูปโฉมโนมพรรณ overall appearance

รูปถ่าย photograph, picture

รูปทรง shape, form, figure

รูปบูชา idol; object of worship

รูปประกอบ illustration

รูปปั้น statue, sculpture, model, molded figure

รูปพรรณ description, appearance; /gold/ silver/ articles

ร
ฤ
ฤๅ
ล
ว
ศ
ษ
ส
ห
ฬ
อ
ฮ

ก
ข
ค
ฆ
ง
จ
ฉ
ช
ซ
ฌ
ญ
ฎ
ฏ
ฐ
ฑ
ฒ
ณ
ด
ต
ถ
ท
ธ
น
บ
ป
ผ
ฝ
พ
ฟ
ภ
ม
ย
ร

ทองรูปพรรณ gold /ornaments/jewelry/
รูปภาพ picture
รูปร่าง appearance, look; form, shape, figure; physique
รูปลักษณะ *see* **รูปร่าง**
รูปสมบัติ physical beauty
รูปสลัก carving, sculpture
รูปสามเหลี่ยม triangle
รูปสี่เหลี่ยม square, quadrilateral
รูปหล่อ pretty as a picture, handsome
รูปหุ่น dummy, mannequin, manikin
ถ่ายรูป to take a picture, have one's picture taken, photograph
ในรูป in the form of
เป็นรูปเป็นร่าง to materialize, take shape, become a reality, be realized
แปรรูป to convert, transform; to transfigure
พระบรมรูป a royal statue
พระพุทธรูป /figure/statue/sculpture/image/ representation/ of the Buddha
ล้างรูป to develop a picture
สำเร็จรูป finished, ready-made, ready-to-wear, prepared, prefabricated
อัดรูป to make a print (from a film); to develop pictures, have pictures developed
รูป² numerical designation (for monks)
รูปธรรม concrete, corporeal, material, real, objective
รู้สึก to feel, sense, have a feeling (of, that)
รู้สึกกลัว to feel afraid, be scared, fearful, frightened
รู้สึกผิด to feel guilty
รู้สึกร้อนๆ หนาวๆ to feel feverish; to be apprehensive, worried
รู้สึกละอายใจ to feel ashamed (at, for, by)
รู้สึกสงสาร to feel sorry for; to feel pity (for)
รู้สึกเสียใจ to be sorry (for, about), to apologize, be apologetic, feel sorry
ความรู้สึก feeling
ความรู้สึกแปลกแยก alienation

เร่ to go about, roam, wander, travel from place to place
เร่ขาย to peddle, hawk
เร่ร่อน to wander, roam; a vagrant
พ่อค้าเร่ peddler, pedlar, hawker, itinerant vendor
เรขาคณิต geometry
เร่ง to hurry, accelerate, expedite, step on it, speed up, press
เร่งเครื่อง to step on the gas
เร่งด่วน urgent
เร่งมือ to speed up, do something more quickly
เร่งร้อน to be in a hurry, rushed, in a rush, rush-job
เร่งรัด to put pressure on (someone to do something), press (someone for something), insist; urgent, pressing
เร่งเร้า to urge, insist (on)
คันเร่ง accelerator
เรดาร์ radar
เร้น *as in* **หลีกเร้น** seclude oneself, secrete oneself
เรรวน changeable, unreliable
จิตใจเรรวน inconstant, fickle, capricious
เร็ว fast, rapid, swift, speedy; soon; hurriedly, hastily, urgently
เร็วๆ as soon as possible; as fast as you can; hurry up
เร็วทันใจ quick
เร็วไป premature; too soon, too fast
ความเร็ว speed, velocity; celerity
ใจเร็ว impetuous, hasty, impulsive
โดยเร็ว fast, quickly; very soon
โดยเร็วที่สุด at the earliest moment
เมื่อเร็วๆ นี้ recently, not long ago
ไม่ช้าก็เร็ว sooner or later
รถเร็ว rapid (train)
รวดเร็ว fast, speedily, rapidly, quickly, swift

อัตราความเร็ว velocity, rate of speed

เรอ to belch, burp

เร่อร่า awkward, clumsy

เรา we, us, you

เราทั้งคู่ we both, both of us

เราทั้งหมด all of us, we all

ของเรา our, ours

คนเรา we, people, nobody, no one, everybody, everyone

พวกเรา we, all of us, we all

เร่าๆ *as in* **เต้นเร่าๆ** to /shake/tremble/ (with anger, eagerness, joy etc), jump up and down

เร้า to excite, stimulate, encourage, urge, rouse, stir up, incite

เร้าใจ to excite, rouse, encourage

รบเร้า to importune, pester (someone for something or to do something)

เร่งเร้า to hurry, urge to, press

เร่าร้อน sexy, passionate, torrid, sultry; tormented, troubled, afflicted

ความเร่าร้อน excitement (of)

เราะ to look for a way (out, in, through); to knock (out, off)

เราะรั้ว to look for a way through a fence

เราะราย sarcastic; to knock (someone or something)

เราะสนิม to knock rust off

เริด *as in* **เริดร้าง** parted, separated (from); foresaken (by)

เริม nettle rash; shingles, herpes /zoster/simplex/

เริ่ม to begin, start, commence, initiate

เริ่มก่อตั้ง to promote

ผู้เริ่มก่อตั้ง promoter

เริ่มชีวิตใหม่ to start a new life

เริ่มด้วย to begin (by, with)

เริ่มต้น to begin, start

เริ่มต้นใหม่ to make a fresh start, begin again

เริ่มตรงไหน Where do we start?

เริ่มแรก originally, in the beginning, at the outset

เรี่ย to skim, be almost touching, be down (to)

เรี่ยดิน to skim the ground; to be down to the ground

พุ่มไม้ใบเรี่ยดิน The leaves of the bush grew down to the ground.

เรี่ยราด all over the place

เรียก to call; to demand, call for; to name, call

เรียกกลับ to recall

เรียกเก็บ to levy, collect

เรียกขวัญ to invoke the indwelling of a guardian-spirit, perform a heartening ceremony

เรียกเงิน to demand payment; to want เช่น *How much does he want for the car?*, ask เช่น *How much is he asking for the car?*

เรียกชื่อ to call (someone) by name; to be called, named

เรียกได้ว่า can be regarded as, can be said to be, that's what I call (a brilliant statement etc)

เรียกตัว to send for, summon, call

เรียกประชุม to call a meeting, convene a /meeting/session/

เรียกประชุมรัฐสภา to convoke the legislature

เรียกประมูล to call for tenders

เรียกผิด to mistake another's name

เรียกร้อง to demand, claim, make demands (for)

ข้อเรียกร้อง demand, claim, request

เรียกว่า called, named

เรียกหา to call for

หมายเรียก summons

เรียง to line up, arrange, list, sort; arrayed; to compose, write; adjoining, connecting; in

ร
ฤ
ฤๅ
ล
ว
ศ
ษ
ส
ห
ฬ
อ
ฮ

order

เรียงกันเป็นแถว to be lined up, lines of, rows of

เรียงความ to compose, write a composition; essay

เรียงคิว to line up, queue up; to gang-rape

เรียงตามตัวอักษร (arranged) in alphabetical order

เรียงแถว to line up, in ranks

เรียงเบอร์ list of winning lottery numbers

เรียงเป็นหน้ากระดาน lined up, in a solid line

เรียงพิมพ์ to set type, typeset, compose

เรียงราย to be spaced out, placed (around, along, about, throughout), spread (along, around, about, all over); strewn about, strewn with (bodies etc), scattered around; to line, be lined (with)

เรียงลำดับ (to put or arrange) in order (from youngest to oldest, best to worst etc), in sequence

เรียน to learn, study; to practise, take lessons, take a course (in); to inform, tell; to address; *ในจดหมายคำว่า เรียนนาย ก To Mr. A; Dear Mr. A,*

เรียนเก่ง to be good at school, learn quickly, smart

เรียนขับรถ to take driving lessons

เรียนด้วยตนเอง to learn by oneself, do a self-study course

เรียนทางไปรษณีย์ to take a correspondence course

เรียนปฏิบัติ to seek one's advice; obtain the benefit of one's counsel (to)

เรียนรู้ to learn how; to understand

เรียนหนังสือ to go to school, study, schooling
  การเรียนหนังสือ schooling, education

เรียนให้ทราบ to inform, tell

กราบเรียน *see* **กราบเรียน** *หน้า 12*

การมาเรียน school attendance

ขาดเรียน to miss school, be absent (from /class/school); to cut a class

คงแก่เรียน learned, scholarly

บทเรียน lesson

ร้องเรียน to complain, make a complaint

โรงเรียน school

เล่าเรียน to go to school, schooling; to study learn

เรียบ smooth, even; level; flat; to arrange evenly, spread, lay

เรียบกระดาน to lay floorboards

เรียบเรียง to compose; to adapt, make an adaptation

เรียบวุธ Order arms!; the lot, the works *เขาล่อเสียเรียบวุธ He ate the works!*

เรียบ ๆ quietly; plain, simple

เรียบร้อย well-mannered, polite; well done, well arranged, in good order; neat, tidy; peaceful; all done, all finished, all okay

เรียม I, me

เรี่ยม immaculate; splendid, superb

เรี่ยมเร้ gorgeous; natty

เรี่ยราย strewn, spread, scattered (about, around, all over)

เรี่ยไร to take up a collection, solicit contributions

เรียว tapering

เรียวหนาม thorny tip of a bamboo stalk

ไม้เรียว switch, cane, rod

เรี่ยวแรง strength; force

เรือ boat, ship, vessel

เรือกรรเชียง rowboat

เรือกลไฟ steamer, steamboat

เรือกวาดทุ่นระเบิด minesweeper

เรือกำปั่นใบ sailing ship

เรือกำปั่นไฟ steamship

เรือค้าขาย merchant /ship/vessel/

เรือจับปลา fishing boat

เรือจ้าง ferry, ferryboat, taxi-boat, boat for hire

เรือจูง tugboat

เรือแจว sculling boat

เรือด่วน express boat

เรือดำน้ำ submarine

เรือเดินทะเล oceangoing /vessel/ship/, seagoing ship

เรือเดินสมุทร oceangoing /ship/vessel/

เรือตอร์ปิโด torpedo boat

เรือแตก shipwreck

เรือทิ้งทุ่นระเบิด minelayer

เรือธง flagship

เรือนำร่อง pilot boat

เรือบด small boat

เรือบรรทุกเครื่องบิน aircraft carrier

เรือบรรทุกสินค้า freighter, cargo /vessel/ship/

เรือบิน aeroplane, airplane, seaplane

เรือใบ sailboat, sailing /vessel/ship/

เรือประจัญบาน battleship

เรือประมง fishing boat

เรือปืน gunboat

เรือพ่วง barge; children

เรือพาย paddle boat

เรือพิฆาต destroyer

เรือเมล์ mail boat, packet boat

เรือยนต์ motorboat, motor vessel, launch

เรือโยง tugboat, towboat

เรือรบ warship, man-of-war, naval vessel

    เรือรบหลวง H.M.S. (His Majesty's Ship)

เรือเร็ว speedboat; fast patrol boat

เรือลากอวน trawler

เรือลาดตระเวน cruiser

เรือลำเลียง lighter

เรือสำปั้น a small wooden boat with elevated stem and stern

เรือสำเภา junk

เรือสินค้า freighter

เรือหาปลา fishing boat

เรือเหาะ aircraft, airplane; airship (เบากว่าอากาศ)

ต่อเรือ to build a boat

ช่างต่อเรือ shipwright; boatbuilder, boat-maker

อู่เรือ drydock; boatyard; dockyard; boathouse

เรื่อ light, pale

เรื้อ as in

    เรื้อรัง chronic, persistent

        ปัญหาเรื้อรัง /chronic/persistent/ problem

        แผลเรื้อรัง chronic /sore/wound/

    เรื้อเวที to lose one's touch (over time)

เรือกสวน garden, orchard

เรือง glittering, shining, bright

    เรืองนาม famous, famed, celebrated

    เรืองรอง splendorous

    เรืองแสง iridescent

    เรืองอำนาจ in power

เรื่อง story, record, account, matter; event; affair

    เรื่องเก่าเล่าใหม่ old story retold, old wine in new bottles

    เรื่องของเรื่อง problem, trouble, the real story, the heart of the matter

    เรื่องจุกจิก petty irritations; trivia, petty matter

    เรื่องโจษจัน scandal; the talk of the town

    เรื่องแดง (of a secret) to leak out, come to light

    เรื่องเบ็ดเตล็ด miscellanies, miscellaneous matters

    เรื่องประโลมโลกย์ romance

    เรื่องผี ghost story

    เรื่องไม่เป็นเรื่อง nonsense

    พูดเรื่องไม่เป็นเรื่อง He's making something out of nothing

    เรื่องย่อ synopsis

    เรื่องรักใคร่ love story; love affair

    เรื่องราว story, matter, what happened, case; details

ร
ฤ
ฤๅ
ล
ว
ศ
ษ
ส
ห
ฬ
อ
ฮ

เรื่องเล็ก small matter, bagatelle

เรื่องสั้น short story

เรื่องใหญ่ big event, important matter

    ทำเป็นเรื่องใหญ่ to make a big issue of (it, something, etc)

เรื่องอ่านเล่น fiction

เรื่องอื้อฉาว scandal

แก่นเรื่อง theme

เค้าเรื่อง outline

โครงเรื่อง outline; plot

เนื้อเรื่อง plot, story

ไม่ได้เรื่อง unsuccessful; unhelpful; punk

ไม่เป็นเรื่อง There is nothing to it! nonsensical

เอาเรื่อง to press charges, to make a to-do, press the matter

เรือด bedbug

เรือน[1] house, home, dwelling; style; setting; a numerical designation for watches and clocks

เรือนกาย physique, build, body

เรือนแก้ว bell jar

เรือนจำ jail, gaol, prison

เรือนชั้นเดียว bungalow, one story house

เรือนเบี้ย child of a debt-slave

เรือนผม hairdo, coiffure, hairstyle

เรือนแพ floating house, houseboat

เรือนไฟ kitchen

เรือนไม้ไผ่ bamboo house

เรือนร่าง body

เรือนสองชั้น two-story house

เรือนหอ newlywed's new home

เรือนแหวน setting

บ้านเรือน houses, dwellings, buildings

มีเหย้ามีเรือน to have a home

แม่เรือน mistress of the house, housewife

เรือน[2] amount, amounting to

เป็นเรือนแสน in the hundred thousands, in six figures, amounting to /six figures/the hundred thousands/

เรื้อน as in **โรคเรื้อน** leprosy

เรื่อย gently, softly; regularly, often

เรื่อยๆ as usual, nothing special; at a steady pace

เรื่อยเจื้อย garrulous, rambling

    พูดเรื่อยเจื้อย to ramble

เรื่อยเฉื่อย indolent, lazily

เรื่อยเปื่อย aimlessly; without much thought

แร่[1] mineral; ore

แร่ดีบุก tin ore, cassiterite

แร่ตะกั่ว lead ore, galena

แร่ทองแดง copper ore

แร่ธาตุ minerals, mineral supplement

แร่พลวง antimony ore, stibnite

แร่แมงกานีส manganese ore, psilomelane, hollandite

แร่โมลิบดินั่ม molybdenum ore, molybdenite

แร่ใยหิน asbestos

แร่วุลแฟรม tungsten ore, wolfram, wolframite

แร่เหล็ก iron ore

น้ำแร่ mineral water

สินแร่ ore

เหมืองแร่ mine

แร่[2] to rush

วิ่งแร่เข้าไป to rush at

แรก beginning, commencement, start; original, first, initial; prior

แรกเกิด newborn

แรกแย้ม first bloom (of youth)

แรกรุ่น pubescent

แรกเริ่มเดิมที (at) the very beginning

ข้อแรก in the first place, point one; first /point/paragraph/

ขั้นแรก at the outset; initially, the first step

ครั้งแรก the first time, initial; in the beginning

ชั้นแรก first floor, ground floor; at the outset,

initially

ตอนแรก in the beginning, at the start

แต่แรก from the /beginning/start/

ทีแรก at first, firstly

รักแรก first love

เริ่มแรก initially, to begin with

แร็กเกต racket

แรง strength, force, energy, power, strong, powerful

แรงกระแทก impact

แรงขับทางเพศ sexual drive

แรงคน man-power

แรงงาน labor

แรงเฉื่อย inertia

แรงดัน pressure

แรงเทียน candlepower; watt

แรงบันดาล inspiration

แรงผลักดัน incentive, driving force

แรงม้า horsepower

แรงเหวี่ยง centrifugal force

เต็มแรง with full force

ทุ่นแรง laborsaving

เบาแรง to require less effort, make (the work etc) easier

ผ่อนแรง to go easy; to save one's strength

ร่วมแรงร่วมใจ *see* **ร่วมแรง** หน้า 407

เรี่ยวแรง strength, force, might

สิ้นแรง exhausted, worn-out

หมดแรง spent

หัวเรี่ยวหัวแรง main force, mainstay

อ่อนแรง to weaken, get tired

เอาแรง to recover one's strength, rest

แร้ง vulture

อีแร้งทึ้ง old hag

แรเงา to shade

แรด rhinoceros

แร้นแค้น in dire straits, poverty-stricken, destitute, impoverished

แรม[1] *as in* **ข้างแรม** period of the waning moon

แรม[2] to spend the night, stay overnight

แรมคืน to spend the night

ที่พักแรม *see* **ที่พักแรม** หน้า 234

แรม[3] extended period

แรมเดือน for months, for months and months, for months on end

แรมปี for years, for years and years, for years on end

แรมรา to part, go separate ways

แรมโรย to long for

แร้ว snare

แระ footing support

โร่ sharp, vivid; fast

แดงโร่ vivid red

วิ่งโร่ to race, dash

โรค disease, sickness, illness, disorder

โรคกระดูกอ่อน rickets

โรคกลัวน้ำ hydrophobia, rabies

โรคคอตีบ diphtheria

โรคจิต mental disorder, neurosis

โรคจิตทราม psychopathic, degenerate

โรคติดต่อ contagious disease

โรคท้องร่วง diarrhea

โรคแทรกซ้อน complication

โรคบิด dysentery

โรคบุรุษ venereal disease

โรคประสาท neurosis

โรคปัจจุบัน acute disorder

โรคผิวหนัง skin disease

โรคภัยไข้เจ็บ sickness, illness, disease

โรคมะเร็ง cancer

โรคระบาด epidemic

โรคร้าย malignant disease, malignancy

โรคเรื้อน leprosy

โรคโลหิตจาง anemia

โรคศิลปะ medicine

โรคเส้นประสาท nervous, disorder

โรคเสื่อมสมรรถภาพ penile dysfunction

โรคไส้ตัน appendicitis

ร
ฤ
ฤๅ
ล
ว
ศ
ษ
ส
ห
ฬ
อ
ฮ

ก
ข
ค
ฆ
ง
จ
ฉ
ช
ซ
ฌ
ญ
ฎ
ฏ
ฐ
ฑ
ฒ
ณ
ด
ต
ถ
ท
ธ
น
บ
ป
ผ
ฝ
พ
ฟ
ภ
ม
ย
ร

โรคหัด measles

โรคห่า plague

โรคหืด asthma

โรคเอดส์ HIV positive; AIDS

    เป็นโรคเอดส์ to be HIV positive; to have AIDS

โรคา disease, malady

    โรคาพยาธิ sickness, illness

โรง building, house, hall; shed; factory; a numerical designation for theatrical companies and amusements

    โรงกลั่นเหล้า distillery

    โรงกษาปณ์ mint

    โรงเก็บ(อากาศยาน) hanger

    โรงเก็บรถ garage

    โรงเก็บเรือ boat house

    โรงเก็บศพ mortuary; morgue

    โรงครัว cook-house, kitchen

    โรงฆ่าสัตว์ slaughterhouse, abattoir

    โรงงาน workshop; factory, plant, mill

        โรงงานอุตสาหกรรม (industrial) factory, plant

    โรงจำนำ pawnshop

    โรงต้มกลั่น distillery

    โรงตีเหล็ก smithy, forge

    โรงเต้นรำ dancehall

    โรงเตี๊ยม inn

    โรงทหาร barracks

    โรงทาน almshouse

    โรงทำเครื่องกระป๋อง cannery

    โรงทำน้ำตาล sugar refinery, sugar factory

    โรงทำเบียร์ brewery

    โรงน้ำแข็ง ice plant

    โรงบ่อน gambling /house/den

    โรงปูน cement factory

    โรงโปเก secondhand shop

    โรงพยาบาล hospital

        โรงพยาบาลกลาง Central Hospital

        โรงพยาบาลเด็ก Children's Hospital

        โรงพยาบาลโรคจิต Mental Diseases Hospital

        โรงพยาบาลโรคติดต่อ Contagious Diseases Hospital

        โรงพยาบาลเสนารักษ์ Military Hospital

        โรงพยาบาลหญิง Women's Hospital

โรงพลศึกษา gymnasium

โรงพัก police station

โรงพิมพ์ printing press, press, printing /establishment/house/

โรงไฟฟ้า power station, power plant, electric works

โรงภาพยนตร์ movie theater, movie house, motion picture theater, cinema

โรงภาษี customs house

โรงมหรสพ theater

โรงม้า stable

โรงรถ garage

โรงเรียน school

    โรงเรียนกฎหมาย law school

    โรงเรียนกินนอน boarding school

    โรงเรียนเก่า old school, alma mater

    โรงเรียนช่างกล technical /school/college/institute/

    โรงเรียนตำรวจ Police Cadet School

    โรงเรียนเทศบาล municipal school

    โรงเรียนนายร้อย Military Cadet School

    โรงเรียนนายเรือ Naval Academy

    โรงเรียนประจำ boarding school

    โรงเรียนประถมศึกษา /elementary/primary/ school

    โรงเรียนป่าไม้ school of forestry

    โรงเรียนผู้ใหญ่ school for adults

    โรงเรียนฝึกหัดครู Teachers' Training College, normal school

    โรงเรียนพาณิชยการ commercial school

    โรงเรียนเพาะช่าง School of Arts and Crafts

    โรงเรียนมัธยมศึกษา secondary school

โรงเรียนรัฐบาล government school, public school (US)
โรงเรียนวัด monastery/temple/ school
โรงเรียนสาธิต demonstration school
โรงเรียนอนุบาล kindergarten
โรงเรียนอาชีวศึกษา vocational training school
โรงเรือน building
 ภาษีโรงเรือน building tax
โรงแรม hotel
โรงละคร theater
 โรงละครสัตว์ circus
โรงเลี้ยงเด็ก orphanage
โรงเลื่อย sawmill
โรงสี mill
 โรงสีข้าว ricemill
โรงสูบฝิ่น opium den, opium parlor
โรงแสง arsenal
โรงหนัง cinema (Brit), movie /theater/house/
โรงหมอ hospital, clinic
โรงหล่อ foundry
โรงหลอม foundry
โรงหัตถกรรม crafts, factory
โรจน์ see รุ่งโรจน์ หน้า 424
โรมรัน to fight a pitched battle
โรมัน Roman
 โรมันคาทอลิก Roman Catholic
โรย[1] haggard; withered; exhausted; let out, release /slowly/little by little/; to sprinkle
 โรยรา to lessen, decrease; to deteriorate
โรย[2] to sprinkle, strew, scatter
 โรยกรวด to pave with gravel, spread gravel
 ผักชีโรยหน้า window dressing, facade
ไร[1] how; what; when
 เท่าไร how much, how many
 เป็นไร what's the matter?; how about
 เมื่อไร when, whenever

ไร[2] mite, fowl louse
ไร[3] as in **ไรๆ** for away, off in the distance
 ไรผม hairline
 ไรฟัน gumline
ไร่ farm; field; measurement of land equal to 1,600 square meters, rai
 ไร่นา farmland, farm
 ไร่ฝ้าย cotton field, cotton plantation
 ไร่องุ่น vineyard
 ชาวไร่ชาวนา farmer
 ทำไร่ to farm, grow field crops
 ที่ไร่ที่นา farmland
 พืชไร่ field crop
ไร้ without, -free, un-, -less; destitute of;
 ไร้การศึกษา uneducated
 ไร้เกียรติ without honor, undistinguished
 ไร้ความคิด thoughtless
 ไร้ความสามารถ incompetent
 ไร้ความหมาย meaningless
 ไร้ค่า worthless, valueless
 ไร้จุดหมาย aimless
 ไร้ญาติขาดมิตร alone (in the world), without family or friends
 ไร้เดียงสา see **ไร้เดียงสา** หน้า 170
 ไร้ที่พึ่ง to have no one to turn to
 ไร้เทียมทาน peerless
 ไร้น้ำยา impotent, ineffective
 ไร้ประโยชน์ useless
 ไร้ผล futile
 ไร้เพศ neuter; asexual, sexless
 ไร้มารยาท lacking in manners, unmannerly, impolite
 ไร้สติ witless, foolish; unconscious
 ไร้สมรรถภาพ impotent
 ไร้สารตะกั่ว unleaded, lead-free
 ไร้สาระ silly, nonsensical, empty, foolish, without substance

ร
ฤ
ฤๅ
ล
ว
ศ
ษ
ส
ห
ฬ
อ
ฮ

ฤกษ์ auspicious /time/moment/, propitious time

ฤกษ์งามยามดี at the auspicious time; at the right time, one fine day

ได้ฤกษ์งามยามดี auspicious time

ฤคเวท Rigveda

ฤชา fee

ฤชากร revenue from fees; /fee/tax/ stamp

ฤดี pleasure, delight

ฤดู season; period

ฤดูกาล season

ฤดูใบไม้ผลิ spring

ฤดูใบไม้ร่วง autumn, fall

ฤดูฝน rainy season

ฤดูร้อน hot season; summer

ฤดูแล้ง dry season

ฤดูหนาว cold season, winter

ฤทธิ์ supernatural power; power, strength; potency

อิทธิฤทธิ์ /magical/supernatural/ power

แผลงฤทธิ์ to display magical power; to act up, be acting up, have a fit, go haywire

มีฤทธิ์ effective, powerful, potent

ออกฤทธิ์ effective, active

สารออกฤทธิ์ active ingredient

ฤทัย heart, feeling, mind

ฤษี hermit, anchorite

ฤๅ or; not; really?, oh?

ฤๅษี hermit, anchorite

ฤๅษีแปลงสาร an inverted-order cipher

ลง to go down, descend; to dismount, get off; to put (in), contribute; to write down, note, enter, put down, post; to bring oneself to (do something)

แพงไป ฉันซื้อไม่ลงหรอก It's too dear; I just cannot bring myself to buy it.

ลงกลอน to bolt

ลงขัน to contribute, take up a collection

ลงข่าว to print /a story/the news (of)/, report

ลงแขก (/neighbors/friends/) pitch in and help, have a (planting, house-building etc) bee; *see* **ลงแขก** *หน้า 69*

ลงคอ[1] without compunction, without a qualm

ทำได้ลงคอ How could (he) do such a thing? / He did it without /compunction/ any qualms/.

ลงคอ[2] to infect the throat; to get stuck in the throat

    หวัดลงคอ (to have) a sore throat, laryngitis

ลงคะแนน to vote, ballot

ลงชื่อ to sign; to enter one's name, put down one's name; signed

ลงแดง dysentery; to have withdrawal symptoms

ลงดิ่ง to plummet

ลงตัว to come out /right/even/, balance; to fall into place

ลงท้อง to have diarrhea

ลงทะเบียน to register, record

    จดหมายลงทะเบียน registered letter

ลงทัณฑ์ to put under a bond of good behavior

ลงท้าย to end, finish (with, by)

ลงทุน to invest, put /in/up/ money

    ลงทุนลงแรง to put money and effort into (something), invest one's money and effort in (something)

ลงโทษ to punish, penalize, chastise

    บทลงโทษ penalty, penalty /clause/ provision/

ลงนวม to spar

ลงนอน to lie down

ลงนาม *see* **ลงชื่อ**

ลงบัญชี to post; charge it, put it on (my) account

ลงบันได to /go down/descend/ the stairs

ลงแป้ง to starch

ลงพระปรมาภิไธย to affix the royal signature

ลงพื้น to apply a / ground/primer/

ลงพุง to develop a paunch, get paunchy

ลงมติ to resolve, pass a resolution; decide, come to a decision

ลงมา to come down, descend

ลงมือ to begin, start, commence

ลงยา enamelled, cloisonné

ลงรถ to get out (of the car), get down (from the car), get off (the bus, taxi etc)

ลงรอย to come to terms, agree; to get on well together

ลงรัก to lacquer

ลงรายการ to enter in the books, record, post

ลงเรือ to embark, board a ship, get on a boat

ลงแรง to contribute /labor/personal effort/

ลงโรง to begin a play

ลงศอก to elbow

ลงสรง to bathe

ลงหุ้น to take a partnership interest; to invest with partners

ลงอาชญา to punish, penalize

ลงเอย be concluded, end up, finish up (with), wind up

ก้าวลง to step down

แก่ลง to age

ขาลง inward trip, return leg (of a trip, journey, etc)

ล
ว
ศ
ษ
ส
ห
ฬ
อ
ฮ

ค่ำลง to get dark

จบลง to end, finish

จมลง to sink, get bogged down

ช้าลง to slow down, decelerate

ตกลง to agree, come to terms; okay, agreed

เบาลง to become lighter

เย็นลง to get colder

ล้มลง to fall (down, over)

เลวลง to worsen, deteriorate, get worse, grow worse

สงบลง to become /quiet/peaceful/; to calm down

อ่อนกำลังลง to weaken

ลด to lower, reduce, decrease, lessen, decline, go down; to settle; to discount

ลดค่าจ้าง to /reduce/lower/cut/ wages

ลดตัว to/lower/demean/oneself; demeaning

ลดธงครึ่งเสา to lower a flag to half-mast, fly a flag at half-mast

ลดน้อยลง to lessen decrease, diminish, abate

ลดราคา to /reduce/lower/ the price, go down in price, give a /discount/price reduction/; to put on sale

ลดลง to go down, abate, subside

ลดละ to relent, ease off

ลดเลี้ยว to take a circuitous shortcut, go in a roundabout way, winding, circuitous, meandering

ลดหย่อน to bring (the price etc) down, reduce, abate, lighten; to allow a deduction

ลดหลั่น in descending order; progressively

ลดให้ to reduce

ลดอาวุธ to disarm, arms reduction

ลน to heat over a fire

ลนไฟ to heat over an open flame

ลนลาน to scurry (off, into, away); to make a frantic effort

ล้น to overflow; excessive, awash (with), over-

ล้นเกล้าล้นกระหม่อม Your Most Gracious Majesty

ล้นค่า priceless

ล้นพ้น overwhelming

ล้นมือ more than enough, too much to handle, to be swamped, overloaded

งานล้นมือ to have more than enough work, too much work to do, to be swamped with work, overloaded with work

ล้นหลาม vast number (of), multitude (of), myriads (of); overflowing; overwhelming

ล้นเหลือ superabundant, too /many/ much/, more than enough

ลบ to erase, rub out; to wear away; to subtract, deduct; negative; minus

ลบคม, ลบเหลี่ยม to outdo (someone), outsmart (someone), get one up (on somebody), undercut (someone), bring (someone) down a peg

ลบชื่อ to expunge (a name); to rub someone out (sl)

ลบมุม to bevel, chamfer

ลบล้าง to erase, remove, eradicate

ลบเลือน faded, obliterated, faint

ลบศักราช to change calendars

ลบหลู่ to disparage, insult, show disrespect (for), be disrespectful (to), treat (someone) with disrespect

ลบหลู่สิ่งศักดิ์สิทธิ์ to commit a sacrilege

ลบเหลี่ยม to bring (someone) down a peg, put (someone) to shame

ลบออก minus, to subtract; to erase, expunge

ขั้วลบ cathode, negative pole

แปรงลบกระดาน (blackboard) eraser

ยางลบ eraser, rubber

ลม wind, breeze, air; breath

ลมๆ nonsensical, full of wind

ลมกระพือ The wind is blowing.

ลมขึ้น indigestion, to be gassy

ลมเงียบ still air, The wind has died down.

ลมจัด strong wind

ลมจับ about to faint, about to have a fainting spell

ลมเฉื่อย breeze

ลมชัก *as in* เป็นลมชัก to have a /convulsion/ fit/

ลมเซิง westerly wind

ลมตะโก้ northwest wind

ลมตะเภา southeasterly wind

ลมตึง strong steady /breeze/wind/, stiff breeze

ลมทะเล sea breeze

ลมบก land breeze

ลมบ้าหมู epilepsy

ลมปราณ breath

ลมปาก words, talk, what (someone) says

ลมฝน rain-bringing wind

ลมพัด wind, breeze, windy; the /wind/ breeze/ is blowing.

ลมพัดหลวง northwest wind

ลมพัทยา southwest breeze

ลมพายุ windstorm, storm, tempest, squall

ลมเพลมพัด fickle, disorganized

ลมฟ้าอากาศ weather

ลมมรสุม monsoon

ลมไม่ดี out of sorts, in a bad humor, moody

ลม ๆ แล้ง ๆ empty, vain, futile

ลมว่าว northerly wind

ลมสลาตัน southwesterly wind, southwest monsoon

ลมสินค้า trade wind

ลมเสีย out of sorts, in a bad humor, moody, irritable

ลมหนาว cold wind, winter wind

ลมหายใจ breath

ลมอ่อน ๆ light breeze, faint wind

ล่ม to sink; to capsize

ล่มจม ruined, wiped out, sunk; to fail, collapse

ล่มปากอ่าว to have a premature ejaculation

ล่มสลาย to disintegrate, collapse

ล่มหัวจมท้าย (to join with someone) for better or worse, cast one's lot in with someone, throw in one's lot with someone, give a total commitment

ล้ม to fall over, topple, collapse; to fell; to slip; to kill; to die

ล้มกลิ้ง to fall and roll over

ล้มคว่ำ to fall face down

ล้มเจ็บ to fall ill

ล้มตะแคง to fall on one's side

ล้มตัวลงนอน to go to bed

ล้มตาย to die

ล้มตึง to fall flat (on one's /face/back/side/ head/)

ล้มทั้งยืน to fall to the ground, fall over, topple over, collapse

ล้มพับ to collapse

ล้มฟาด to fall against (something), crash (to the floor, down against a chair, etc)

ล้มยักษ์ giant-killing

ล้มละลาย to go bankrupt be wiped out, ruined

    คดีล้มละลาย bankruptcy /action/case/

ล้มล้าง to wipe out, destroy, eliminate, do away with

ล้มลุก balancing, pop-up, to fall over and get up again

    ล้มลุกคลุกคลาน to struggle

    ไม้ล้มลุก an annual

ล้มเลิก to cancel; call off; to pull out (of a deal etc)

ล้มหงาย to fall on one's back

ล้มหมอนนอนเสื่อ laid up, bedridden

ล้มหายตายจาก to disappear

ล้มเหลว to fail, be a failure

ล

ว

ศ

ษ

ส

ห

ฬ

อ

ฮ

หกล้ม to fall down, take a fall, trip (over something), take a tumble

ลวก to burn, singe, scorch; to scald; to parboil, blanch; careless, perfunctory, slipshod; superficial, rough

ลวกๆ carelessly, roughly, in a /perfunctory/ cursory/ way, slipshod (work etc), slapdash

ไข่ลวก soft-boiled egg, scalded egg

น้ำร้อนลวก to scald, scalded; to parboil, blanch

ไฟลวก to burn, singe, scorch

ลวง to deceive, fool, delude

ลวงตา deceptive, illusory

ลวงไป to lure (away, into)

ลวงโลก to fool everyone, deceive the public

ล่อลวง to lure, fool (someone into doing something), seduce (into)

หลอกลวง to deceive, delude; defraud, cheat

ล่วง to pass; over, to go beyond, exceed; to trespass, violate, infringe

ล่วงเกิน to go too far (with someone), take liberties (with someone), trespass (against someone), commit a transgression

ล่วงประเวณี to commit adultery

ล่วงไป to pass (on, by), lapse

ล่วงรู้ to have foresight, know in advance, anticipate

ล่วงละเมิด to violate

ล่วงลับ to be dead, pass away; to set

ล่วงล้ำ to trespass, intrude

ล่วงเลย to expire, pass

ล่วงหน้า in advance, beforehand

ล่วงหน้าไปก่อน to go ahead, go beforehand, precede

ล่วงหน้ามาก่อน to come ahead, come beforehand, precede

ลุล่วง accomplished, achieved, fulfilled, completed, finished, done

ล้วง to fish (out, for), draw out, extract

ล้วงกระเป๋า to pick a pocket; to put one's hand in one's pocket; to /fish/take/ out of a /bag/pocket/etc

นักล้วงกระเป๋า pickpocket

มือล้วงกระเป๋า with one's hand in one's pocket

ล้วงถาม to elicit (an answer from), draw (someone) out, extract an answer; to probe

ล้วงเอาความลับ to elicit a secret, /discover/ uncover/ the truth

ลวด wire

ลวดตาข่าย wire fencing

ลวดลาย decorative design; style; tricks

ลวดหนาม barbed wire

ขดลวด coil of wire, wire coil

ไต่ลวด to tightrope walk

มุ้งลวด screen, screening

ล้วน all, solid, completely

ล้วนๆ all, only, without exception; pure, solid

ลวนลาม to annoy; to molest; to go too far (with)

ลหุ *as in*

ลหุโทษ light /sentence/penalty/; misdemeanor, petty offense

คดีลหุโทษ petty offense case, misdemeanor case

ความผิดลหุโทษ petty offense, misdemeanor

ล่อ[1] mule

ล่อ[2] to tempt, entice, lure

ล่อใจ to tempt

ล่อลวง to lure, fool (someone into doing something), seduce (into)

ล่อแหลม precarious, perilous

เหยื่อล่อ bait, lure

ล้อ[1] to tease, kid, make fun (of someone)

ล้อเล่น to joke, be joking, be fooling, be teasing, pull (someone's) leg

ล้อเลียน to mimic, ape; to mock, ridicule; to parody

ภาพล้อ caricature

หยอกล้อ to tease, kid around (with someone), joke (with), play a joke (on someone)

ล้อ[2] wheel

ล้อรถ wheel

ล้อเลื่อน vehicle

ลูกล้อ wheel

สามล้อ trishaw, pedicab, samlor; tricycle; three-wheeled

ห้ามล้อ brake, to brake, put on the brakes

ลอก to skin; to flay; to peel, strip; to copy; to plagiarize

ลอกข้อสอบ to copy exam answers, copying

ลอกคราบ see **ลอกคราบ** หน้า 78

ลอกคู to deepen a /ditch/stream bed/

ลอกแบบ to copy; make a copy (of a drawing, form, design etc)

ลอกหนังสือ to copy, make a copy (of a writing, book, etc); to plagiarize

ลอกออก to peel off

ขุดลอก to dredge

ปอกลอก to fleece, mulct, skin

หนังลอก (the skin, one's hand etc is) peeling

ลอกแลก furtive, agitated

มองลอกแลก furtive looking, shifty-eyed, to look furtive

ล็อก lock

ล็อกคิว to reserve (something) for (someone); to put (someone) down for (something)

ลอง to try, give (something) a try, attempt, experiment; to test, sample

ลองกำลัง to try one's strength

ลองคิดดู think it over, think about it

ลองใจ to test (someone)

ลองเชิง to test (one's adversary, etc), spar (with)

    คู่ลองเชิง sparring partner

ลองดี to test, try, see how far one can go; to challenge

ลองดู to try, give (something) a try, try out

ลองภูมิ to test someone out

ลองมือ to try one's hand (at something)

ล่อง an outlet in the floor; to go downstream, go down a /river/stream/, descend a /river/ stream/, go downwind

ล่องแก่ง to ride the rapids

ล่องซุง to float a log-raft down a river

ล่องแพ to go rafting

ล่องเรือ to take a boat down a /river/stream/

ล่องลม to go with the wind

ล่องลอย floating, drifting

    ล่องลอยไป to float away

ล่องหน to vanish, disappear, be gone

ขาล่อง return, return /trip/leg/, downward leg (of a journey)

เที่ยวล่อง downward trip, return trip

ลอด to duck under

ลอดหูลอดตา to /be/get/ overlooked

เล็ดลอด to escape, leak out, slip out, wriggle out

ล็อตเตอรี่ lottery

ลอน wavy; corrugated part, portion, section; to wave, set

ลอนผม curl, wave

เป็นลอน wavy, curly

ล่อน to come off easily, easily /stripped/peeled/

ล่อนจ้อน bare, naked, unclothed

ลอบ[1] bamboo fishtrap

ลอบ[2] (to do something) slyly, on the sly, covertly, undercover, secretly

ลอบกัด to backbite, attack (someone) behind his back, attack from behind

ลอบเข้าไป to steal into

ลอบจับ to trap

ลอบทำร้าย to ambush, waylay

ลอบมอง to peep (at), peek (at, in, into), spy (on someone)

ลอบยิง to shoot from hiding, assassinate

ล
ว
ศ
ษ
ส
ห
ฬ
อ
ฮ

ลอบวางระเบิด to plant a bomb

ลอบหนี to elope

ลักลอบ to smuggle; clandestinely, in secret, on the sly

ลักลอบได้เสียกัน to have an affair in secret, fool around on the sly

ล็อบบี้ยิสต์ lobbyist

ลอม to pile up

ล้อม to surround, encircle, ring, in a /circle/ring/

ล้อมกรอบ see **ล้อมกรอบ** หน้า 6

ล้อมคอก to pen, fence in

ล้อมจับ to round up

ล้อมเมือง to /besiege/beleaguer/ (a town or city); to /surround/encircle/ring/ (a town or city)

ล้อมรอบ to surround, encircle, surrounded (by), all around

ล้อมรั้ว to fence (in), put a fence around

ล้อมวง to form a protective /circle/ring/ (around)

ล้อมหน้าล้อมหลัง surrounded (by one's attendants, devotees, etc), to crowd around, hem in

ปิดล้อม to besiege, blockade, cordon off

แวดล้อม surroundings

สถานการณ์แวดล้อม (surrounding) circumstances

หว่านล้อม to cajole someone into (doing or agreeing to something), prevail (upon someone to do something), win someone over

พูดหว่านล้อม to coax

ห้อมล้อม surrounded (by), /mobbed (by)/ beseiged (by)/ (admirers, reporters, etc)

ลอย to float; exposed; in blank

ลอยกระทง Loi Kratong Festival, a festival centered on the floating of little baskets containing flowers, a candle and incense

ลอยแก้ว (fruit) in syrup

ลอยขึ้น to float up

ลอยคอ to float (with one's head above water)

ลอยชาย casually

ลอยนวล to /go/get off/get away/ scot-free, go unpunished, to get away with (it, a misdeed, etc); (to make a) clean getaway

ลอยน้ำ to float (in the water)

ลอยแพ to set adrift, float on a raft, to lay off

ลอยแพคนงาน to lay off workers

ลอยฟอง to float /up/high/; to have a head (of foam)

ลอยฟ้า sky, floating in the air; superb

ภัตตาคารลอยฟ้า sky restaurant

ลอยหน้า to waggle one's head

ลอยอยู่ในน้ำ floating in the water

ลอยอยู่ในอากาศ to float in the air

ข่าวโคมลอย rumor, unfounded news, unsubstantiated report

ใจลอย absentminded, daydreaming, (My) mind was wandering

ตาลอย to have /glazed eyes/a glazed look/ a vacant look/; dreamy, to have a dreamy look

ปอดลอย afraid

พูดลอยๆ to toss (something) out, say (something) out of the blue, mention casually; to speak in general

เลิศลอย superb, tops

สลักหลังลอย to endorse in blank, endorsement in blank

สายเดินลอย exposed wiring

ลออ fair and silky

ละ[1] give up, quit, stop (doing something); to omit

ละทิ้ง to abandon, renounce, abandoned

ละพยศ to behave oneself, stop throwing tantrums, stop being belligerent

ละมือ to put aside

ละลด to cut down (on something)

ละเลย to neglect (to), fail (to); to overlook

ละวาง to give up, quit

ละเว้น to refrain (from), fail (to), neglect to; to abstain (from), eschew; to renounce; to exempt

ละ[2] per, to, by

ข้างละ 5 คน five to a side

คนละทิศละทาง every which way

ครั้งละ per time, a time

ทีละขั้น 2 ขั้น step by step

ใบละพัน (bills) of 1,000 each

ปีละ per /annum/year/, each year, annually

ร้อยละ percent, per hundred

วันละ daily, per day, each day, a day

ละ[3] a word to give emphasis

ดีละ okay

ถูกละ that's right

เอาละ okay, very well

ละคร a play, theatrical performance, show

ละครตลก a comedy

ละครใบ้ mime show

ละครพูด a play

ละครเพลง a musical

ละครรำ dance-drama

ละครสัตว์ circus

บทละคร script

เล่นละคร to /perform/act/ in a /play/show/; to playact, be playacting, pretend, make believe

ละม่อม *as in* **โดยละม่อม** without /resistance/a fight/, easily, smoothly

ตำรวจจับโจรได้โดยละม่อม The police arrested the bandits without /resistance/a fight/.

ละม้าย resembling, similar (to)

ละม้ายคล้ายคลึง to resemble

ละมุน soft, tender, smooth, gentle

ละมุนละม่อม smooth, gentle

ละมุนละไม tender, gentle

พูดละมุนละไม soft-spoken

อ่อนละมุน tender, soft

ละเมอ to sleepwalk; to talk in one's sleep; to murmur

ละเมาะ grove, a wood

ละเมิด to violate, infringe, disobey, go against

ละเมิดกฎหมาย to /break/violate/ the law

ละเมิดมิได้ inviolable

ละโมบ covetous; avaricious, greedy, gluttonous

ละไม sweet

งามละไม beauteous, comely, sweet-looking

ยิ้มละไม /gentle/sweet/soft/ smile, winsome smile

ละลาบละล้วง to pry (into), be prying

ละลาย to melt; dissolve

ละล้าละลัง (with, in) frantic indecision, in desperate hesitation

ละล่ำละลัก to sputter

ละเลง to smear (something on), spread around; to twist (the /facts/information/data/etc)

ละเลียด to pick at one's food

ละแวก neighborhood, around

ในละแวกนี้ around here, hereabout, in this neighborhood

ละแวกบ้าน vicinity

ละโว้ Lawo, old name of Lopburi

ละหมาด the performance of divine worship five times a day

ละห้อย to dejected; sad, mournful, sorrowful

ละหาน a broad water, broad lake, broad part of a river

ละหุ่ง castor-oil plant; castor bean

ละเหย (ระเหย) to evaporate

ละเหี่ย dispirited, weary

ละเหี่ยใจ dejected, depressed, down in the dumps

ละออง powder, dust; mist, droplets

ละอองดาว the twinkle of a star

ละอองน้ำ mist, spray

ล
ว
ศ
ษ
ส
ห
ฬ
อ
ฮ

ละอองฝน mist, droplets of rain

ละอ่อน greenhorn, novice; infant

ละอาย to /be/feel/ ashamed, feel shame

ละเอียด fine, delicate, pulverized, powdered; meticulous, careful, thorough

ละเอียดลออ neat, careful, thorough, paying attention to details, meticulous; fair-skinned, fair complexioned, having a creamy complexion

ละเอียดอ่อน sensitive; delicate, subtle

โดยละเอียด in detail

รายละเอียด details, particulars

ลัก to steal, rob; to do surreptitiously

ลักไก่ to steal in, slip in; to sneak (in, by, through, around); to bluff (การเล่นไพ่)

ลักทรัพย์ to steal, commit /theft/larceny/

ลักพา to elope; to kidnap

ลักเพศ to /dress/behave/ like the opposite sex; homosexual, gay

ลักยิ้ม dimple

ลักลอบ to smuggle; clandestinely, in secret, on the sly

ลักลั่น incompatible, incongruous; ill-fitting, at odds

ลักเล็กขโมยน้อย petty thievery, to be a petty thief, pilfer

ลักหนี to /sneak/steal/ away

ลักปิดลักเปิด scurvy; half-concealed

ลักลั่น incompatible, mismatched, incongruous; ill-fitting; skewed

ลักษณะ character, characteristics, nature, form, appearance

ลักษณะคล้ายกัน similar

ลักษณะด้อย recessive characteristic

ลักษณะเด่น dominant characteristic

คุณลักษณะ character, characteristic, attribute, quality, property, trait

บุคลิกลักษณะ personality

รูปลักษณะ appearance, look; form, configu-

ration

ลัคนา auspicious time; sign (of the zodiac) under which one was born

ลัง wooden box, case, crate

ลังไม้ crate

ลังกา Ceylon, Sri Lanka

ลังเล hesitant, undecided, to hesitate, demur, waver, dither

ลังเลใจ hesitant, undecided, unable to make up one's mind

ความลังเลใจ hesitation, indecision

อาการลังเล (to /show/give) signs of / indecision/hesitation/wavering/

ลัด[1] to /take/make/ a shortcut

ลัดนิ้วมือ in an instant

ลัดเลาะ to take a shortcut

ทางลัด a shortcut

ลัด[2] as in ลัดใบ to sprout leaves

ลัทธิ ideology, -ism; doctrine, sect, creed

ลัทธิคอมมิวนิสต์ Communism

ลัทธิจักรพรรดินิยม imperialism

ลัทธิชาตินิยม nationalism

ลัทธินายทุน capitalism

ลัทธินีโอนาซี neo-Naziism

ลัทธิประชาธิปไตย democracy

ลัทธิเผด็จการ dictatorship

ลัทธิสังคมนิยม socialism

ลั่น to sound; to fire, pull the trigger; to burst (out)

ลั่นกลอน to bolt (a door, etc)

ลั่นกุญแจ to lock, to snap a lock shut

ลั่นไก to pull the trigger

ลั่นฆ้อง to sound a gong

ลั่นดาล to bolt

ลั่นนก to pull the trigger

ลั่นปาก, ลั่นวาจา to give (one's) word, make a commitment, commit oneself

ทำปืนลั่น to fire a gun, make a gun /go off /fire/, The gun went off.

ลับ[1] to sharpen, hone, whet
ลับใบมีดโกน to hone a razor
ลับมีด to sharpen a knife

ลับ[2] hidden, secret, closed; invisible
ลับ-เฉพาะ confidential
ลับตา out of sight
ลับลมคมใน cunning, sly, crafty
ลับๆ ล่อๆ furtive, sneaky, secret
ลับลี้ mysterious, hidden, secret, arcane
ลับแล screen, blind, stone /blockage/ blind/
ลับหลัง behind one's back
ลับหู-ลับตา far off
ความลับ secret
เคล็ดลับ trick (in, of, to, about)
เมียลับ mistress
ลี้ลับ surreptitious, secretive; mysterious; suspicious
ลึกลับ secret, hidden; mysterious; mystery (story)
สายลับ spy, informer

ลัพธ์ *as in* **ผลลัพธ์** result

ลา[1] donkey, ass

ลา[2] to say good-bye, take leave, depart
ลาก่อน goodbye, farewell
ลาคลอด to take maternity leave
ลาป่วย to take sick leave, request sick leave
ลาพัก to take leave
ลาโลก to depart from this world, say goodbye to the world, take leave of this world
ลาสิกขา to leave the monkhood
ลาหยุด to take leave of absence
ลาออก to resign, hand in one's resignation, quit

ล่า[1] to retreat
ล่าถอย to fall back, withdraw, retreat, retire
ล่าทัพ to retreat, withdraw, retire

ล่า[2] to hunt, stalk, pursue, hunt (someone or something) down

ล่าลายเซ็น to hunt for autographs
ล่าสัตว์ to hunt

ล่า[3] late
ล่าสุด latest, hottest, most up-to-date

ล้า tired, fatigued
ล้าสมัย out-dated, dated, out of date, outmoded, old-fashioned
ล้าหลัง backward, outmoded, underdeveloped, lagging behind
เมื่อยล้า sore, aching, stiff (with fatigue)

ลาก to pull, draw, drag, tow, tug
ลากจูง to tow
    เรือลากจูง tugboat, towboat
ลากรถ to tow a car
ลากเส้น to /draw/make/ a line
ลากเสียง to drawl, speak with a drawl

ลาง[1] omen, portent, sign
ลางดี good omen, favorable sign
ลางร้าย /bad/evil/ omen
ลางสังหรณ์ premonition, presentiment
ถือโชคถือลาง superstitious
เป็นลาง to be a /sign/omen/portent/, ominous

ลาง[2] some
ลางที sometimes
ลางเนื้อชอบลางยา One man's meat is another man's poison. / Each to his own taste.

ล่าง underneath, under, below, lower; space under the house
ข้างล่าง downstairs, under the house, below
ชั้นล่าง downstairs, lower floor

ล้าง to clean, cleanse, wash; wash away, purge; to destroy, get rid of, liquidate, kill
ล้างแค้น to /take/get/ revenge
ล้างซวย to get rid of one's bad luck
ล้างถ้วยล้างชาม to do the dishes
ล้างบาง to wipe out the lot
ล้างบาป to baptize
ล้างผลาญ to ravage, lay waste (to); to waste

ล
ว
ศ
ษ
ส
ห
ฬ
อ
ฮ

ล้างฟิล์ม to develop (a film or pictures), have a film developed

ล้างมือ to take no further responsibility (for something), wash one's hands (of)

ล้างรูป to develop pictures

ล้างโลก to /destroy/annihilate/ the world

ล้างสมอง to brainwash (someone)

ล้างหน้า to wash one's face, get cleaned up

ล้างอาย to recover face

กวาดล้าง to round up, get rid of

ชะล้าง to erode

ทำลายล้าง to destroy

ลบล้าง to cover up

ล้มล้าง to overthrow

ลาญ *as in* **แหลกลาญ** demolished, razed, flattened

ลาด[1] to spread; to unroll and lay (a carpet etc)

ลาดตระเวน to patrol, cruise, scout

　　เรือลาดตระเวน cruiser

ลาดพระบาท royal carpet

ลาด[2] to slope, incline

ลาดเขา mountain slope

ที่ลาด slope, sloping land, an incline; a ramp

ลาดเลา a lead

ลาน[1] open space; lawn; ground, field

ลานจอดรถ parking lot

ลานจอด (อากาศยาน) apron, ramp

ลานนวดข้าว threshing floor

ลานบ้าน yard

ลานบิน airfield, landing field

　　ทรงลานบิน crew cut, flattop

ลาน[2] coil spring

ลานขาด broken spring, The spring /is broken/has snapped/.

ลานนาฬิกา watch spring

ไขลาน to wind the spring, wind a /watch/ clock/

หมดลาน wound down

ลาน[3] petrified; dazzling, shimmering, glittering

ลานตา dazzling; dizzying

ลาน[4] book palm

ใบลาน palm leaf

ล้าน[1] million

เศรษฐีเงินล้าน millionaire

ล้าน[2] bald, bare

หัวล้าน baldheaded

ลาบ spiced minced meat

ลาภ fortune, luck, stroke of good fortune, windfall; gain

ลาภปาก unexpected treat

ลาภมิควรได้ unjust enrichment

ลาภยศ high position, dignity

ลาภลอย windfall

ได้ลาภ to have a stroke of luck, get a windfall

มีโชคมีลาภ lucky, fortunate

มีลาภ fortunate, to have good fortune, have fortune shine on one

ลาม to spread; to be contagious; to be presumptuous, be overfamiliar

ลามทุ่ง *as in* **ไฟลามทุ่ง** to spread like wildfire

ลามปาม to be presumptuous, be over-familiar; to drag someone else in (by reference when berating or arguing)

ล่าม[1] interpreter

ล่าม[2] to tether, tie up

ล่ามเชือก to tie up

ล่ามโซ่ to chain

ลามก obscene, dirty, lewd, smutty

ความลามก pornography; licentiousness

สิ่งพิมพ์ลามก pornography

หนังลามก blue movie, pornographic film

ลาย design, figure; striped, patterned

ลายก้างปลา herring bone design

ลายคราม blue and white china; classic; veteran, old seasoned

ลายเซ็น signature

ลายตา dizzying, to make one dizzy

ลายแทง cryptic writing, cipher

ลายน้ำ watermark

ลายมือ lines on the fingers and palm of the hand; handwriting

การอ่านลายมือ palmistry, chiromancy, palm reading

ลายมือชื่อ signature

ลายไม้ grain (of wood); wavy lines of watered silk (ที่ปรากฏบนผ้าไหมบางชนิด)

ลายลักษณ์ writing; mark

ลายลักษณ์อักษร in writing, written

ลายสือ letters

ลายเสือ tiger stripes; prowess

ออกลายเสือ to show one's stripes, be up to one's old tricks; to show one's ability

ดูลายมือ to do palm reading, have one's palm read

ลวดลาย design, figuration; designing, scheming, full of tricks, devious; not aboveboard, guileful, disingenuous

ลาว Laos

คนลาว Laos, Laotian

ประเทศลาว Laos

ภาษาลาว Laos

สาธารณรัฐประชาธิปไตยประชาชนลาว Lao People's Democratic Republic

ลาวก reaper (of rice)

ลำ trunk; pole, a numerical designation for things long and round, and boats

ลำกระโดง feeder /canal/channel/

ลำกล้อง gun barrel; pipe stem; rod (sl)

ลำแข้ง shin, lower leg

ด้วยลำแข้ง see **ด้วยลำแข้ง** หน้า 70

ลำแขน arm

ลำคลอง canal

ลำคอ neck

ลำต้น stalk, stem; trunk

ลำตัว trunk

ลำตาล trunk of a palm tree

ลำธาร stream, brook, creek

ลำน้ำ waterway

ลำไผ่ culm, bamboo stem, bamboo pole

ลำห้วย creek

ล่ำ stocky, sturdy, muscular, brawny, heavy-set, solid

ล่ำสัน robust, sturdy, solid

เป็นล่ำเป็นสัน solid, established

อ้วนล่ำ chunky

ล้ำ[1] to trespass

ล้ำเส้น to cross the line, overstep, transgress

รุกล้ำ to intrude, encroach (on, upon), trespass, invade, make an incursion

ล่วงล้ำ to impinge (on)

ล้ำ[2] surpassing, superior

ล้ำเลิศ excellent, superior, surpassing, superb

ลำเค็ญ hard, tough, arduous, difficult

ชีวิตลำเค็ญ hard life, life of (grinding) poverty

ลำดับ series, order; to arrange (in order), marshal, organize (step by step), list seriatim; rank

ลำดับอาวุโส order of seniority

โดยลำดับ in order, by order

ตามลำดับ respectively; seriatim, in order, in that order

ตามลำดับชั้น through /official/proper/ channels, up the line

ลำตัด racy folk banter and song show

ลำเนา line, edge; domicile

ลำเนาป่า edge of a forest, line of a forest

ภูมิลำเนา domicile

ลำบาก troublesome, difficult, hard

ตกอยู่ในความลำบาก to be in a bind

เป็นอยู่ลำบาก life is hard

อยู่ในฐานะลำบาก to be in a difficult position

ลำพอง to be overconfidant, be puffed up

ลำพัง alone, by oneself

ลำพังคนเดียวทำไม่ได้ I cannot do it /on my own/by myself/unaided/.

ลำพังแต่ alone, by oneself

ลำพังแต่ฉันเองผ่อนบ้านไม่ไหว Alone I

ล
ว
ศ
ษ
ส
ห
ฬ
อ
ฮ

couldn't make the payments on the house. / I couldn't meet the house installments by myself.

โดยลำพัง alone, on one's own

ตามลำพัง alone, by oneself

ลำแพน *as in* **เสื่อลำแพน** woven bamboo mat

ลำโพง loudspeaker

ลำไพ่ extra income, money on the side, supplement to one's income

เขาเป็นข้าราชการ กลางคืนก็ขับแท็กซี่หาลำไพ่ *He's a government official but at night he drives a taxi to /supplement his income/ make some money on the side/get extra income/.*

ลำไย longan

ลำลอง informally, casually

ชุดลำลอง casualwear, casual clothes, sportswear

ลำลึก *see* รำลึก หน้า 422

ลำเลิก to bring up one's past favors to demonstrate ingratitude

ลำเลิกบุญคุณ indirectly to complain of ingratitude by mentioning past favors

ลำเลียง to transport, carry

การลำเลียง transportation, carriage

เรือลำเลียง lighter, barge

ลำไส้ intestine

ลำไส้เล็ก small intestine

ลำไส้ใหญ่ colon

ลำเอียง partial, biased, prejudiced

ลิเก a musical folk drama, traditional melodrama

ลิขสิทธิ์ copyright

ลิขิต writing, writings, letter; to write

ปัจฉิมลิขิต postscript

สมณลิขิต letter of a monk

ลิง monkey, monkeylike

ลิงลม slow loris

ลิงค์ gender

นปุงสกลิงค์ neuter gender

ปุงลิงค์ masculine gender

อิตถีลิงค์ feminine gender

ลิงโลด to jump with joy, overjoyed, jubilant, gleeful, ecstatic

ลิด to prune; to pick off, trim

ลิดใบ to pick off leaves, trim leaves (from a plant, bush etc)

ลิดรอน to chip away (at), impinge (on), encroach (on), undermine

ลิตร liter

ลิ้น tongue; valve

ลิ้นไก่ uvula

พูดลิ้นไก่สั้น to speak in a drunken slur

ลิ้นชัก drawer

ลิ้นทอง silver-tongued, eloquent

ลิ้นทูต diplomatic

ลิ้นปี่ reed; xiphisternum, bottom of the breastbone

ลิ้นห้อย lolling tongue, exhausted

เข้าลิ้น mortised, having a tongued joint, tongue-and-grooved, mortise-and-tenoned, dovetailed

ลิ้นจี่ lychee

ลินิน linen

ลิบ very, exceedingly, vastly

ลิบๆ far /off/away/

ลิบลิ่ว far far away

ไกลลิบ very far, a vast distance away

สูงลิบ very high, sky-high

ลิปดา minute

ลิปสติก lipstick

ลิ่ม wedge, quoin; ingot; clotted (blood)

ลิ้ม to taste

ลิ้มรส to taste, try, experience

ลิลิต mixed poetical composition

ลิ่ว very, exceedingly, vastly

ลิ่วล้อ one's /boy/man/, henchman, one's people, follower

ลี้ to take refuge; to flee, avoid

ลี้ภัย to take refuge, seek asylum

   ผู้ลี้ภัย refugee

ลี้ลับ surreptitious, secretive; mysterious; suspicious

ลีบ atrophied, degenerated, arrested in development; sterile

ลีลา way, style (of doing something), flow, cadence; elegant bearing, gracefulness

ปางลีลา walking (Buddha)

ลีลาศ dance, dancing

งานลีลาศ dance, ball

ลึก deep, profound, abstruse

ลึกซึ้ง profound, deep, penetrating

ลึกลับ secret, hidden; mysterious; mystery (story)

ลึกล้ำ profound

ลึงค์ gender; lingam

นปุงสกลึงค์ neuter noun, neuter gender

ปุงลึงค์ masculine

อิตถีลึงค์ feminine

ลื่น slippery, slick; smooth, free

ลืม to forget; to open

ลืมต้น aged fruit, ripened off the tree

ลืมตัว to forget oneself, lose one's self-control

ลืมตา to open one's eyes

ลืมเลือน forgotten

ลืมสนิท to completely forget, be a blank

ลืมเสียเถิด Forget it!, Forget about it!

ขี้ลืม forgetful, absentminded

ขี้หลงขี้ลืม absentminded, to have a poor memory, forgetful

ไม่รู้ลืม unforgettable

ลือ to be rumored

ลือกันว่า It is rumored that..., they say

ลือชา widely known

ลือชื่อ famous, celebrated, renowned, well known, notorious

ลือนาม renowned, illustrious, celebrated

ข่าวลือ rumor

ลื้อ[1] a northern Thai tribe

ลื้อ[2] you

ลุ to reach, attain, arrive at

ลุแก่โทษ to confess seeking clemency

ลุแก่โทสะ to be beside oneself with anger, uncontrollably angry

ลุแก่อำนาจ to abuse one's authority

ลุล่วง done, finished, achieved, accomplished, fulfilled, achieved

ลุก to stand, get up, rise; to flare up, blaze; to have an erection, get a hard-on

ลุกขึ้น to get up, rise, stand up

ลุกขึ้นยืน to stand up

ลุกเป็นไฟ to burst into flame; to become infuriated; to become inflamed, in turmoil

ลุกไป to get up and go, go away

ลุกโพลง to blaze

ลุกลน nervously, in a hurry, in a flurry, in a rush

ลุกลาม to spread, be contagious

ลุกลี้ลุกลน see **ลุกลน**

ลุกไหม้ to burn, catch fire

ลุกฮือ to rise up

ขนลุก hair-raising, to make one's hair stand on end

ผุดลุกผุดนั่ง agitated, anxious, restless, to have ants in one's pants

ล้มลุกคลุกคลาน to struggle

ลุง uncle; sir, my good fellow, friend

ลุ้น to back, support; to cheer, root for, plug; to look forward eagerly (to); to win, have a good chance (to)

ลุ้นตั๋วชมภาพยนตร์พรีวิวเรื่อง "Message in the Bottle" Win free tickets to the preview of "Message in the Bottle".

โทรศัพท์เข้ามาลุ้นโชคกับเราสิคะ Telephone in to win a prize.

ล
ว
ศ
ษ
ส
ห
ฬ
อ
ฮ

ลุ่ม low-lying, low, depressed

ลุ่มๆ ดอนๆ uneven; to have (one's, its) ups and downs, vicissitudes

เศรษฐกิจในขณะนี้ลุ่ม ๆ ดอน ๆ ไม่ควรลงทุนทำธุรกิจ With the economy having its ups and downs, investment in business is not advisable.

ลุ่มน้ำ basin

ที่ลุ่ม lowland, low-lying land, depression

ลุ่มลึก deep

ลุ่มหลง infatuated (with), head over heels in love, mad about, besotted (by, with), obsessed (with)

ลุย to wade (in, into), /walk/go/ through

ลุยข้ามน้ำ to ford (a river, stream etc), walk through (a puddle etc)

ลุยโคลน to go through the mud

ลุยงาน to get through (the work, job etc), forge ahead (with), wade into (the pile of work etc)

ลุยไฟ to walk through a fire; fire-walking ceremony

ลุยเลย (go) full steam ahead

ลุ่ย to fall apart; to slip off; to unravel

หลุดลุ่ย to unravel, come undone; badly *แพ้หลุดลุ่ย* to lose badly

ลู่ lane

ลู่ทาง way, chance

ลู่ลม to bend with the wind

ลูก child, offspring; fruit; a numerical designation for fruits and ball-like things

ลูกกรง bars; baluster, upright supports of a banister

ลูกกรอก mummified fetus said to bring good luck

ลูกกระดุม button

ลูกกระเดือก Adam's apple, larynx

ลูกกระโปก balls; underling

ลูกกระสุน bullet, cartridge, shot

ลูกกลอน a moist pill, bolus

ลูกกลิ้ง roller

ลูกกวาด hard candy, bonbon, pastille

ลูกกะโล่ henchman, minion

ลูกกำพร้า orphan

ลูกกุญแจ key

ลูกแก้ว crystal ball

ลูกแกะ lamb

ลูกไก่ Pleiades; chick

ลูกข่าง top

ลูกขุน jury

ลูกเขย son-in-law

ลูกครึ่ง person of mixed parentage, part (American, etc) part (Thai, etc), person of mixed descent, Eurasian; hybrid

ลูกความ client

ลูกค้า customer, client

ลูกคิด abacus

ลูกคู่ chorus

ลูกจ๊อก flunky

ลูกจ้าง employee, wage earner

ลูกเจี๊ยบ chick; baby

ลูกช้าง calf of an elephant; I, me, your humble servant

ลูกชาย son

ลูกชิ้น/เนื้อ/ปลา/ meatball, fishball

ลูกโซ่ link, chain

ลูกดอก dart

ลูกดิ่ง plumb, plumb bob, plummet; sounding lead

ลูกดุม button

ลูกเดียว just, (do) nothing but (work, etc) and only (work, etc)

ลูกแดงๆ newborn baby

ลูกโดด single shot; bullet, slug

ลูกตะกั่ว (lead) bullet, ball

ลูกตา eyeball

ลูกตุ้ม pendulum, clock-weight; weight (สำหรับชั่งของ); impediment (to)

ลูกเต้า children, offspring, progeny

ลูกเต๋า die, dice (พหู)

ลูกแถว rank and file, subordinate

ลูกทุ่ง country, hillbilly

    แบบลูกทุ่ง in /simple/folksy/ style, like countryfolk

    เพลงลูกทุ่ง /country/hillbilly/ music

ลูกโทษ free kick *(ฟุตบอล)*

ลูกน้อง, ลูกสมุน (one's)/boys/, men, /people/ henchman/, followers; fellows, folks, my friends

ลูกน้ำ mosquito larva

ลูกนิมิต consecrated stone-ball marker buried under a temple

ลูกบอล ball

ลูกบ้าน villager, local people

ลูกบาศก์ cube, cubic; square

    ลูกบาศก์เมตร cubic meter

ลูกบิด doorknob

ลูกบุญธรรม foster child, adopted child

ลูกประคำ rosary

ลูกประสม, ลูกผสม hybrid

ลูกปัด bead

ลูกปา confetti

ลูกปืน cartridge, bullet, shell; ball bearing (สำหรับเครื่องจักร)

ลูกโป่ง balloon

ลูกผู้ชาย man, manly

    อย่างลูกผู้ชาย like a man, manfully

ลูกผู้หญิง woman, womanly

ลูกแฝด twins

ลูกพี่ boss; big shot

ลูกพี่ลูกน้อง cousin

ลูกฟูก tufted compartment of a mattress; corrugated

    ผ้าลูกฟูก corduroy

ลูกไฟ spark

ลูกมือ assistant, helper

ลูกแมว kitten

ลูกโม่ roller; grinder; revolver chamber (ของปืน)

ลูกไม้ lace; fruit; trick

ลูกยอ compliment

ลูกโยน clay missile for chasing birds

ลูกรอก pulley; egg-drop

ลูกระเบิด bomb

ลูกรัง laterite

ลูกเรือ crew, crewman, sailor

ลูกลม tumbleweed

ลูกล้อ wheel

ลูกเล็กเด็กแดง little children

ลูกเล่น trick; improvisation

ลูกเลี้ยง stepson, stepdaughter, stepchild, foster child

ลูกโลก globe

ลูกไล่ stooge, flunky, lackey, underling

ลูกศร arrow

ลูกศิษย์ student, pupil; boy

ลูกสมุน one's /boy/man/, the boys, henchman, follower, gang

ลูกสวาท lover boy, pleasure boy

ลูกสะใภ้ daughter-in-law

ลูกสาว daughter

ลูกสุดท้อง last child, youngest (child)

ลูกสุนัข puppy, pup

ลูกสูบ piston

ลูกเสือ boy scout; tiger cub

ลูกหญิง daughter

ลูกหนัง football

ลูกหนี้ debtor, obligor

ลูกหนู string-running rocket; tonsils

ลูกหม้อ old (Thammasart, Ministry of Interior etc) /man/woman/, one of the old /boys/ girls/ (of)

ลูกหมา puppy, pup

ลูกหลง stray bullet

ลูกหลาน offspring, descendants, younger generation, children and grandchildren

ล
ว
ศ
ษ
ส
ห
ฬ
อ
ฮ

ลูกหัวปี oldest child, firstborn

ลูกหิน marble

ลูกเห็บ hail, hailstone

ลูกแหง่ calf; mamma's boy

ลูกอม hard candy; troche, lozenge, cough-drop

ลูกอ่อน baby, infant

ลูกอัณฑะ testicle

ลูกอุกกาบาต meteorite

ออกลูก to give birth (to a boy, girl etc), have a baby

ลูบ to stroke, rub; to wipe

ลูบคม to insult

ลูบคลำ to fondle, caress; to familiarize oneself (with a subject, etc), get familiar (with a job, etc)

ลูบตัว to have a rub (with water)

ลูบไล้ to rub on, pat on

ลูบหน้า to /wipe/rub/ one's face

ลูบหน้าปะจมูก to hold back for fear of treading on someone's toes

ลูบหน้าลูบหลัง to give a hug of /approval/ affection/, give (someone) a pat on the back

เล็ก small, little, diminutive, insignificant, minor

เล็กกะจิริด, เล็กกะจ้อยร่อย tiny, teensy-weensy, teeny, miniscule

เล็กน้อย slight

เล็กๆ น้อยๆ minor, trivial, trifling

เล็กพริกขี้หนู small but feisty

เล็กมาก very small, minute, diminutive

การผ่าตัดเล็ก minor surgery

เลข figure, number, numeral; arithmetic

เลขคณิต arithmetic

เลขคิดในใจ mental arithmetic

เลขคี่ odd number

เลขคู่ even number

เลขโดด digit

เลขท้าย last numbers

เลขที่ number

เลขไทย Thai numerals

เลขบ้าน house number

เลขประจำตัว one's identification number

เลขฝรั่ง Arabic numerals

เลขยกกำลัง power number

เลขโรมัน Roman numerals

เลขเศษส่วน fraction

เลขหมาย number

เลขอารบิค see เลขฝรั่ง

คิดเลข to calculate

เครื่องคิดเลข calculator

โจทย์เลข arithmetic problem

ตัวเลข number, numeral; figure

ทดเลข to carry (a number in adding)

เลขา secretary; letter, writing, drawing; pretty as a picture

เลขาธิการ secretary-general

เลขาธิการ ก.พ. Secretary-General of the Civil Service Commission

เลขานุการ secretary

เลขานุการิณี (female) secretary

เล็ง to aim (at), take a bead on; to observe, see

เล็งผลเลิศ optimistic, sanguine

เล็งเห็น to observe, foresee

เพ่งเล็ง to suspect, keep an eye on someone

เล็ด to come out, ooze, exude, well up (ใช้กับ น้ำตา)

เล็ดลอด to slip out, leak out, escape, wriggle out

เลน mud

เล็น louse, lice

เล่น to play; to deal (in, with)

เล่นกล to perform sleight of hand; to play a trick (on someone), fool

เล่นกล้าม to practise body-building

เล่นการพนัน to gamble

เล่นการเมือง to engage in politics

เล่นคำ to play on words, pun

เล่นงาน make trouble (for), find fault (with), attack make it hot for (someone), deal with (someone) harshly, make things tough for (someone)

เล่นชู้ to have an affair (with), commit adultery

เล่นซ่อนหา to play hide-and-seek

เล่นดนตรี to play music, perform music

เล่นตลก to trick, pull a fast one, be devious

เล่นตัว to play hard to get, be difficult

เล่นตา to ogle

เล่นน้ำ to go swimming, play in the water

เล่นเนื้อ to smoke pot *(sl)*

เล่นพวก to play favorites, be partial to one's own people, practice favoritism

เล่นเพื่อน (for women) to have a gay relationship, have lesbian sex, sleep together

เล่นไพ่ to play cards

เล่นม้า to play the horses; to take speed *(sl)*

เล่นไม่ซื่อ not play straight

เล่นแร่แปรธาตุ to practice alchemy

เล่นละคร to /perform/act/ in a /play/show/; to playact, be playacting, pretend, make believe

เล่นลิ้น to play with words

เล่นว่าว to go kite-flying

เล่นสกปรก to play dirty

เล่นสนุก to play

    เล่นไพ่สนุก ๆ to play (cards) for fun

เล่นสวาท to have sex

    การเล่นสกปรก skulduggery

เล่นหัว to joke around, play around

เล่นหุ้น to play the stock market

เล่นหูเล่นตา to make eyes at someone

เล่นเอาเถิด to fool around (with a job, work, problem etc)

ของเล่น toy, plaything

ขี้เล่น playful, fun-loving; frisky; fond of joking

ชื่อเล่น nickname

นั่งเล่น to sit down and relax, sit pleasantly

    ห้องนั่งเล่น sitting room, living room, lounge, study, den

พูดเล่น to speak in fun, jest, joke, be joking, not serious

เพื่อนเล่น friend, playmate

ไม่ใช่เล่น pretty, very

สมัครเล่น amateur

อ่านเล่น to read for pleasure

เลนส์ lens

เล็บ nail; claw, talon

    เล็บขบ ingrown /toenail/fingernail/

    เล็บเท้า toenail

    เล็บมือ fingernail

    หมดเขี้ยวเล็บ emasculated, rendered harmless

เล็ม to hem; to trim; to nibble, graze

เล่ม a numerical designation for books, candles, knives, sickles

    เข้าเล่ม to bind

    เย็บเล่ม to staple together; to bind, make a (spiral, plastic etc) binding; to sew into book form

เลย further, beyond, too much; at all, definitely; so

    ทำอย่างนี้ไม่ดีเลย That's no good at all. / It's definitely bad.

    เลยบ้านนี้ไปเป็นบ้านผู้จัดการบริษัท The manager's house is beyond this one.

    วันนี้ไม่สบายเลยไม่ไปทำงาน I didn't feel well today so I didn't go to work.

    เลยตามเลย to leave alone, let (something) go, never mind, let things take their course

    เลยเถิด too far, excessive, inordinate

    เลยธง immoderate, too much

    เลยเวลา after hours; late, overdue

เลว[1] base, vile, not good, bad, low, inferior

    เลวทราม abominable, detestable; vicious,

ล
ว
ศ
ษ
ส
ห
ฬ
อ
ฮ

wicked

เลวลง to worsen, deteriorate, get worse, grow worse

คนเลว a bad (character, egg, guy), villain, scoundrel

คุณภาพเลว /bad/poor/inferior/ quality

ไม่เลว not bad, pretty good

เลว^2 common, common soldier, foot soldier, rank and file

เลศนัย ulterior /motive/purpose/, something behind (it, what one says or does)

เล่ห์ trick, intrigue

เล่ห์กระเท่ห์ wiles, scheming

เล่ห์กล ruse, trick

เล่ห์เหลี่ยม tricks, craftiness, wily, cunning, crafty; foxy; intrigue

เจ้าเล่ห์ schemer, tricky (person etc)

เลหลัง to auction

เลอ superior, superlative, surpassingly, indescribably

เลอโฉม indescribably beautiful, surpassingly beautiful, superlative beauty

เลอเลิศ exceedingly fine, superlative

เล่อล่า foolishly, stupidly, like a dolt; to do (something) out of ignorance; discountenanced; to look foolish

เลอะ dirty, soiled; messy; unsound, not all there, senile

เลอะเทอะ messy; filthy, dirty, soiled; nonsensical, incoherent, to make no sense

เลอะเลือน forgetful, mixed up

ทำเลอะ to make a mess (of something); to dirty, soil

เละ decomposed, rotten; crushed, mushy, runny; badly run, a failure, a mess

เละเทะ see **เลอะเทอะ**

เลาๆ roughly, vaguely

เล่า^1 to tell, relate, narrate; to recite

เล่าขาน to tell (of), it has been said

เล่านิทาน to tell a story

เล่าเรียน to study, learn; to go to school, schooling

เล่าเรื่อง to tell (about something), narrate

เล่าลือ rumor, hearsay; they say

เล่าให้ฟัง to tell, relate

บอกเล่า to relate, tell

คำบอกเล่า hearsay

เล่า^2 an emphatic intensifier

ครั้งแล้วครั้งเล่า time and again, over and over again, again and again, time after time

มิน่าเล่า I'm not a bit surprised., Wouldn't you know it.

อนึ่งเล่า moreover

เล้า enclosure, pen, coop

เล้าไก่ chicken coop

เล้าหมู pig sty, pig pen

เล้าโลม to caress, fondle, pleasure (someone)

เลาะ to skirt, go along the edge (of); to cut off; to rip out (ตะเข็บผ้า)

เลาะตะเข็บผ้า to /rip out/undo/ a seam

เลาะริมฝั่ง to go along the bank, skirt the bank

เลิก to raise, lift; to stop, end, cease, give up; to separate, divorce, break up; to rescind, terminate; to abolish

เลิกสูบบุหรี่ to give up smoking

เลิกกัน to end, separate, break off, call (something) quits; to break up, be divorced, separate

เลิกกิจการ to wind up (a business), end operations, dissolve (a business, company etc)

เลิกเกี่ยวข้อง to stop having anything to do with (someone or something)

เลิกคิด to put something out of one's mind, stop thinking (about)

เลิกคิ้ว to raise one's eyebrows

เลิกจ้าง to discharge

เลิกแถว to fall out

เลิกทัพ to disband an army

เลิกทาส to abolish slavery

เลิกพูดกัน not on speaking terms; to stop talking (about); old hat, dated

เลิกร้าง to divorce, separate

เลิกล้ม to give up, abandon

เลิกล้มความพยายาม to abandon the effort

เลิกลั่ก to look /furtive/disconcerted/

เลินเล่อ careless, negligent

เลิศ excellent, superb, the best, optimum

เลิศลอย superlative, supreme

ชนะเลิศ to win first prize.

เล็งผลเลิศ optimistic, sanguine

เลีย to lick, lap

เลียแข้ง to flatter, fawn (on, over), toady (to)

เลียแข้งเลียขา to curry favor (with someone), be an apple polisher

เลียตีน to be a bootlicker

เลี่ยง to evade, avoid, get around

เลี่ยงกฎหมาย to get around the law

เลี่ยงความรับผิดชอบ to avoid responsibility

เลี่ยงเมือง to bypass; as in ทางเลี่ยงเมือง a bypass

การเลี่ยงรัษฎากร tax /evasion/avoidance/

เดินเลี่ยงไปทางอื่น to slip /away/off/ (in another direction)

เลี้ยง to feed, treat (someone) to a (meal, lunch, dinner etc), entertain (to dinner etc); to raise, rear, support, bring up; to keep from falling, sustain

เลี้ยงกลางวัน to treat (a person) to lunch; to give a luncheon

เลี้ยงแขก to entertain guests

เลี้ยงชีพ to earn one's living

เลี้ยงดู to look after, support; to bring up

    ค่าเลี้ยงดู maintenance

เลี้ยงดูปูเสื่อ to entertain warmly

เลี้ยงต้อย to raise someone from small and then marry /him/her/

เลี้ยงตัวเอง to support oneself

เลี้ยงน้ำชา to serve tea

เลี้ยงปากเลี้ยงท้อง to make a living

เลี้ยงพระ to provide a meal for monks

เลี้ยงไม่เชื่อง ungrateful; untameable, obstreperous

เลี้ยงลูก to raise one's child

เลี้ยงสัตว์ to keep animals

เลี้ยงส่ง to give a farewell party (for someone)

เลี้ยงเหล้า to treat to drinks, serve drinks

เบี้ยเลี้ยง daily allowance, expenses

พ่อเลี้ยง stepfather, foster father; a provincial personage, squire

พี่เลี้ยง big brother; nurse, nursemaid, governess, baby-sitter; trainer; escort; chaperone

แม่เลี้ยง stepmother, foster mother

ลูกเลี้ยง stepson, stepdaughter, stepchild, foster child

สัตว์เลี้ยง domestic animal; pet

เลียน to imitate, copy; to mimic

เลียนแบบ to imitate, copy

ล้อเลียน to mimic, ape; to mock, ridicule; to parody

เลี่ยน[1] glossy

ผ้าเลี่ยน plain glazed silk

เลี่ยน[2] greasy, fatty, oily; rich; saccharine, syrupy (letter, speech, manner, etc)

รสเลี่ยน /oily/rich/ taste

เลียบ to go along the edge (of), skirt

เลียบเคียง to beat around the bush, be circumspect (in speaking)

เลียบเมือง to go in procession around the /city/town/

เลี่ยม to edge (with), frame (/with/in/ metal), encase (in)

เลี่ยมเงิน to edge with silver, encase in

ล
ว
ศ
ษ
ส
ห
ฬ
อ
ฮ

ก
ข
ค
ฆ
ง
จ
ฉ
ช
ซ
ฌ
ญ
ฎ
ฏ
ฐ
ฑ
ฒ
ณ
ด
ต
ถ
ท
ธ
น
บ
ป
ผ
ฝ
พ
ฟ
ภ
ม
ย
ร
ฤ
ฦ
ล

silver

เลี่ยมทอง to edge with gold, encase in gold

เลี่ยมพระ to frame a Buddha image (in gold, silver etc)

เลี่ยมฟัน to encase a tooth in gold

เลี้ยว to turn

เลี้ยวกลับ to turn back, make a U-turn

เลี้ยวขวา to turn to the right, turn right

เลี้ยวลด serpentine, winding, snaking; to snake (along, through, by), meander

หัวเลี้ยว corner, curve, turn (in a road)

หัวเลี้ยวหัวต่อ turning point, critical point, period of transition (age, time etc), crucial period

เลือก to choose, pick, select, elect; elective, optional

เลือกคู่ to select a mate, find a wife (or husband)

เลือกตั้ง to elect

    การเลือกตั้ง election, elections

เลือกที่รักมักที่ชัง partial, biased, to play favorites

เลือกปฏิบัติ discriminatory; to discriminate (against)

    การเลือกปฏิบัติ discrimination

เลือกเป็น discriminating

เลือกเฟ้น to select; selected, carefully selected

เลือกมาก choosy

เลือกสรร to select

เลือกเอา to take your choice, have the pick of the lot, choose

คัดเลือก to select, choose; selected

โดยไม่เลือกหน้า without discrimination, impartially

ได้รับเลือกเป็น to be elected (chairman, president etc), chosen to be (the prophet, guinea pig etc)

ทางเลือก option

เผื่อเลือก for selection

วิชาเลือก an elective, /elective/optional/ course

เลื่องชื่อ renowned, famous

เลื่องลือ widely known, famous, notorious; rumored, it is well known (that)

เลือด blood

เลือดกำเดา nosebleed, epistaxis

เลือดขึ้นหน้า to be red in the face (with anger)

เลือดเข้าตา in a rage, infuriated

เลือดดำ venous blood

เลือดเดือด boiling mad, seething with anger

เลือดแดง arterial blood

เลือดตาแทบกระเด็น excruciatingly

เลือดเนื้อเชื้อไข flesh and blood

เลือดฝาด (healthy) complexion

เลือดฝาดดี in fine color / Your color is good today.

เลือดเย็น cold-blooded, unfeeling

เลือดร้อน hot-tempered, hot-blooded, impetuous

เลือดออก bleeding, to bleed

เลือดอาบ covered with blood, blood-soaked

ก้อนเลือด blood clot

กินเลือดกินเนื้อ to eat someone up *เช่น He was so mad he looked like he was going to eat me up.*

เจาะเลือด to take a blood /sample/ specimen/, take a blood test

ตรวจเลือด to have a /blood check/blood test/

นองเลือด bloody, with much bloodshed, a bloodbath

บ้าเลือด blood-crazed

เม็ดเลือดขาว white blood cell, leukocyte

เส้นเลือด blood vessel, artery, vein

หน้าเลือด bloodsucker, bloodsucking, extortionate

ห้อเลือด bruise, contusion, black and blue (spot), subcutaneous hemorrhage
ให้เลือด to give blood, give a transfusion

เลือน blurred, vague, indistinct, unclear
เลือนลาง faint, indistinct

เลื่อน[1] to postpone, defer, put off; to move, slide; to rearrange
เลื่อนขั้น to be promoted, get a raise, get a promotion
เลื่อนขึ้น to move up
เลื่อนตำแหน่ง to be promoted (to another position), be moved up (to the position of)
เลื่อนที่ to advance in rank; to move over
เลื่อนนัด to postpone /the/our/your/*etc*/ appointment
เลื่อนประชุม to /postpone/defer/ a meeting
เลื่อนไป to put off
เลื่อนยศ to be promoted in rank
เลื่อนลอย groundless, unfounded, baseless; blank (look), absently; to be vague, indefinite
เลื่อนออกไป to defer
ประตูเลื่อน sliding door

เลื่อน[2] sledge
เลื่อมใส to be devoted (to), have faith (in), believe in, be a devotee (of)

เลื่อย saw, to saw
ขี้เลื่อย sawdust
หัวขี้เลื่อย blockhead, dumbell
ฟันเลื่อย sawtooth design, tooth of a saw
โรงเลื่อย sawmill

เลื้อย to crawl, slither, creep; to climb
ไม้เลื้อย creeper, climber, vine, ivy

แล[1] to see, look, take a look (at), watch
แลดูกัน to gaze at one another
แลเห็น to see, sight, observe; visible
ดูแล to take care (of), look after, supervise, be responsible (for)
ไม่เหลียวแล to be irresponsible, fail to take care (of), neglect

แล[2] a word used for emphasis, very, you bet
ดีนักแล You bet it's good!

แล่ to slice

แลก to exchange, barter
แลกเงิน to get change; to change money
รับแลกเงิน money changer
ตั๋วแลกเงิน bill of exchange
แลกเปลี่ยน to exchange, change
แลกเปลี่ยนความคิดเห็น to exchange ideas
แลกเปลี่ยนสินค้า to barter
อัตราแลกเปลี่ยน rate of exchange

แล้ง dry season, dry; little, paucity (of rain, spirit etc)
แล้งน้ำใจ selfish, mean, ungenerous, unkind
ฝนแล้ง to be dry, have a dry spell, a paucity of rain, /no/little/ rain, drought condition
ปีนี้ฝนแล้งไม่ได้ทำนา It was too dry for rice this year.
หน้าแล้ง dry season
แห้งแล้ง arid, very dry

แลน monitor

แล่น to move, go, run, sail (along, by)
แล่นฉิว to zip along
แล่นใบ to sail (along)
แล่นเรือ to sail, go on a boat, run a boat
ชั่วแล่น fleeting, momentary

แลบ to stick out, project
แลบลิ้น to stick out one's tongue (at)
ฟ้าแลบ lightning, flash of lightning

แล้ว finished, completed; already; then; now; so
แล้วสิ่งที่ควรสังเกตต่อไปคือ Now what you should take note of is....
แล้วจะทำยังไงล่ะ So, what do we do?
แล้วก็ and then
แล้วก็แล้วกันไป Let bygones be bygones., Forget it., to call (something) off
แล้วกัน For Pete's sake!, Really!

ล
ว
ศ
ษ
ส
ห
ฬ
อ
ฮ

ก็แล้วกัน to settle on; just (go ahead, do it etc)

เอาอย่างนี้ก็แล้วกัน Let's settle on this. / Let's just do this.

แล้วจะทำไม so what

แล้วด้วย made of

แล้วแต่ depending on, it depends; as you like, to be up to (someone)

แล้วแต่กรณี as the case may be, depending on circumstances

แล้วแต่อารมณ์ depending on how /you/ I/ feel

แล้วเป็นไง and then what

แล้วเสร็จ finished, completed

ก็แล้วไป Never mind., What's done is done., That's okay.

ครั้งแล้วครั้งเล่า time after time, time and again, over and over again, again and again

จบแล้ว finished, over, done with

ดีแล้ว okay, fine, good, not bad, all right; all right for you

พร้อมแล้ว all ready, all set

พอแล้ว enough, stop; Stop it!

และ and; in addition, moreover

และเล็ม to nibble, browse; to flirt (with)

โล่ shield, buckler; plaque

โล่เกียรติยศ honorary award, testimonial plaque, token of appreciation

โล้ to swing; to ride the waves; sculling

ไม่เป็นโล้เป็นพาย does not amount to much

โลก world, earth

โลกเก่า the Old World

โลกนี้ this life, this world, here and now

โลกพระอังคาร Mars

โลกมนุษย์ the world, human world, the earth

โลกเสรี the free world

โลกหน้า the next world, world to come

ชาวโลก the world

ซีกโลก hemisphere

ตลาดโลก world market

แถบขั้วโลก polar region

ลูกโลก globe

ศาลโลก World Court (International Court of Justice)

สากลโลก universe

โลกทัศน์ outlook

โลกธรรม (the eight) worldly conditions, worldly vicissitudes

โลกาภิวัตน์ globalization

โลกิยะ, โลกีย์ concerning the world, worldly, mundane

โลกียชน common man

โลกียวิสัย worldly pleasure

โลกุตตระ supramundane, transcendental

โลกุตรธรรม supramundane, transcendent

โลง coffin, casket

โล่ง open; empty, vacant; clear

โล่งใจ to feel relieved

โล่งเตียน clear (land)

โล่งอก relieved, to feel relief, What a relief!

โลด to jump, leap, spring (on)

โลดโผน adventurous, daring, daredevil, fancy, extraordinary, spectacular

โลดแล่น to speed (to)

กระโดดโลดเต้น to jump up and down excitedly

ลิงโลด to jump with joy, ecstatic

โลน[1] ribald, coarse, vulgar; rude

หยาบโลน lewd, obscene

โลน[2] crab louse

โล้น bald; with a shaven head; bare

เขาหัวโล้น bare /mountain/hill/

โลภ greed, cupidity, avarice; covetousness

โลมเล้า to caress; to be endearing

โลมา hair

โลเล indecisive, fickle, changeable, vacillating, undependable

โลหะ metal

    โลหกรรม metallurgy

    โลหกิจ mining; metal works

โลหิต blood; red

    โลหิตจาง anemia, anemic

    ความดันโลหิต blood pressure

    เม็ดโลหิตแดง red blood cell, erythrocyte

    สายโลหิต blood /relative/relation/, blood line, direct descendant, one's own flesh and blood

    เส้นโลหิต blood vessel

โละ to throw out; to unload; to lay off *(คนงาน)*

    โละทิ้ง to get rid of something

ไล่ to chase, pursue, run after; to expel, get rid of, put (someone) out, drive /off/away/; to tune (musical instruments); to test, examine

    ไล่กวด to follow on the heels (of), close in on, in hot pursuit

    ไล่ตาม to pursue

    ไล่ทัน to catch up (to, with), overtake

    ไล่ที่ to evict

    ไล่เบี้ย to have recourse (to a person for something); to be subrogated (to); to take (something) out on (someone else); to pass on liability

        ไม่มีสิทธิไล่เบี้ย without recourse

    ไล่ผี to exorcise spirits

    ไล่เลี่ย about the same, about the same time

    ไล่เลียง to cross-examine, question closely

    ไล่ออก to expel; (งาน) to dismiss, fire, sack; to turn (someone) out (of the house)

    ลูกไล่ stooge, flunky, lackey, underling

    สอบไล่ to take a final examination

ไล้ to apply, smear, rub on

ก
ข
ค
ฆ
ง
จ
ฉ
ช
ซ
ฌ
ญ
ฏ
ฏ
ฐ
ฑ
ฒ
ณ
ด
ต
ถ
ท
ธ
น
บ
ป
ผ
ฝ
พ
ฟ
ภ
ม
ย
ร
ฤ
ฤๅ
ล
ว

วก to turn (about)

วกไปวกมา winding, tortuous, circuitous, to meander; to turn this way and that

วง ring, circle, band; to put around, encircle

วงกต labyrinth

วงกบ window frame, door frame

วงกลม circle

วงการ circles, quarters, sphere, field

วงการค้า commercial circles

วงการที่เชื่อถือได้ reliable /circles/ quarters/

วงการทูต diplomatic /circles/quarters/, diplomatic sphere

วงการเมือง political circles

วงโคจร orbit

วงโคจรค้างฟ้า geostationary orbit

วงงาน field (of work); group, circle

วงเงิน amount (of)

วงจร circuit

วงจรปิด closed circuit

วงจรเปิด open circuit

วงดนตรี band, orchestra, ensemble

วงดุริยางค์ band, orchestra

วงเดือน circular saw

วงนอก outsiders, those not in the know; outside

วงใน insiders, those in the know; inside

วงไพ่ card game, circle of cardplayers

วงมโหรี Thai orchestra

วงรี ellipse, oval

วงล้อม encirclement; to be encircled, surrounded (by)

วงเล็บ parenthesis (เอก), parentheses (พหู); brackets

วงเวียน circle; compass

วงแหวน ring

ถนนวงแหวน ring road, beltway

ร่วมวง to join (in), co-, participate (in)

วงศ์ family, lineage, line, stock; family (วิทย์)

วงศ์วาน kin, family

วงศ์สกุล family

วงศาคณาญาติ relations, family, blood relatives, clan

วจนะ words, sayings

พุทธวจนะ /words/sayings/ of the Buddha

วจี word, speech

วจีกรรม speech, (by) word

วณิช merchant, trader

วณิชชา trade, commerce

วณิชย, วณิชย์ trade, commerce

วณิชยการ, พาณิชยการ commerce

วณิพก minstrel; mendicant

วน[1] to circle, go around; to circulate, revolve, whirl

วนไปเวียนมา to go in circles, go around; to mess around; winding

วนเวียน to circulate, go around; to hang around, mess around

น้ำวน eddy, whirlpool, maelstrom

วน-[2] forest, woods, jungle

วนศาสตร์ forestry

วนอุทยาน park, botanical garden

วรรค paragraph; phrase; chapter, stanza, section; space

วรรคตอน spacing

เป็นวรรคเป็นเวร inconsolably; nonstop, endlessly

เว้นวรรค to space, leave a space, spacing

วรรณ color; complexion; caste

วรรณกรรม literary work

วรรณคดี literature

วรรณนา description, narration

วรรณยุกต์ tone mark

วลี phrase

วสันต์ spring; rainy season

วอ palanquin

คางคกขึ้นวอ too big for one's britches, swellheaded

วอก the Year of the Monkey, monkey
    หน้าวอก face smeared with powder
วอกแวก unsettled, distracted, discomposed, not concentrated
ว่อง, ว่องไว quick, agile, active, nimble
วอด consumed, destroyed
    วอดวาย to die; extinguished; ruined, destroyed
วอน to beg, implore, beseech, entreat
    วอนขอ to appeal (to)
    วิงวอน to beg, plead (with someone for something), entreat, beseech, implore, supplicate
ว่อน flying about
    บินว่อน to swarm
    ปลิวว่อน flying around, to fill the air, float around in the air
วอแว to bother, annoy
วะ an emphatic word เช่น the hell, Damn!
    อะไรกันวะ What the hell is going on? What the hell do you want?
    มันเป็นใครวะ Who the hell is that?
วัก to scoop up in the hands
    วักน้ำ to scoop up water
วัง^1 palace
    พระบรมมมหาราชวัง The Grand Palace
วัง^2 clearing, open space; deep pool; deep sea
    วังวน whirlpool; deep sea
วังชา *as in* **กำลังวังชา** vitality, energy
วังเวง so lonely; eerie (feeling, sound etc), haunting
วัฏ-, วัฏฏะ cycle of birth and death
    วัฏจักร cycle, life cycle
    วัฏทุกข์ the suffering of rebirth
    วัฏสงสาร cycle of birth and death, cycle of rebirth, reincarnation
วัฒนธรรม culture
    ศิลปวัฒนธรรม art and culture
วัณโรค tuberculosis, consumption
วัด^1 monastery, wat, temple

วัด^2 to measure
    วัดแดด to tell time by the sun
    วัดตัว to take someone's measurements
    วัดที่วัดทาง to do a land survey
    วัดปรอท to take someone's temperature
    วัดผล to evaluate, assess
    วัดพื้น to fall flat on one's face
    วัดรอยเท้า to emulate, compete (with)
วัตถุ thing, object, material, substance
    วัตถุเคมี chemicals, chemical substances
    วัตถุดิบ raw material
    วัตถุนิยม materialism
    วัตถุประสงค์ object, objective, purpose, aim
    โบราณวัตถุ historical object, antique, antiquity, archeological /object/find/
วัตร *as in* **กิจวัตร** routine, regular practice
วัตรปฏิบัติ observance, practice
วัน day
    วันก่อน the day before yesterday
        วันก่อนๆ the other day, some days ago
    วันเกิด birthday
    วันโกน head-shaving day, tonsure day
    วันข้างหน้า in days to come, in the future, later on
    วันเข้าพรรษา the first day of the Buddhist lent
    วันคล้ายวันเกิด birthday
    วันเงินเดือนออก payday
    วันจักรี Chakri Day
    วันจันทร์ Monday
    วันชาติ National Day
    วันดี auspicious day, lucky day, good day
        วันดีคืนดี one fine day
    วันต่อวัน day by day
    วันที่ date
        วันที่ 3 มกราคม on the third January
        ภายในวันที่ 10 ของทุกเดือน by the tenth of each month
    วันนัด appointed day, date fixed (for

ว
ศ
ษ
ส
ห
ฬ
อ
ฮ

something)

วันพระ Buddhist sabbath

วันพฤหัสบดี Thursday

วันพุธ Wednesday

วันเพ็ญ day of the full moon

วันยังค่ำ all day long, anytime, all the time

วันแล้ววันเล่า day after day

วันศุกร์ Friday

วันเสาร์ Saturday

วันหนึ่ง one day, on a certain day

วันหยุด holiday, day off

วันออกพรรษา the end of the Buddhist lent

วันอังคาร Tuesday

วันอาทิตย์ Sunday

วันอุโบสถ observance day

วันทยหัตถ์ to salute

วันทยาวุธ Present arms!

วับ twinkle, flash

วับ ๆ, วับวาบ twinkling, flashing

วับวาม, วับแวม flashing, dazzling

หายวับไปกับตา to vanish /in a flash/in a wink

วัย age

วัยกลับ second childhood

วัยกลางคน middle age

วัยฉกรรจ์ early manhood, young adulthood, (in the) prime of life

วัยชรา old age; geriatric

วัยเด็ก childhood

วัยทารก infancy

วัยทำงาน working life

วัยรุ่น youth, adolescence; teenagers, adolescents, youngsters

วัยเรียน school age

วัยวุฒิ seniority; senior; venerable

วัยสาว girlhood, youth

วัยหนุ่ม boyhood, youth

เจริญวัย to grow up

เยาว์วัย (in one's) /youth/childhood/, young

วัลย์ *as in* **เถาวัลย์** liana, vine, creeper

วัว cow, bovine

วัวควาย cattle

วัวตัวผู้ bull

วัวตัวเมีย cow

วัวต่าง pack ox

วัวนม milk cow

วัวสันหลังหวะ to have a skeleton in the /closet/cupboard/

เนื้อลูกวัว veal

เนื้อวัว beef

ลูกวัว calf

วัสดุ material

วัสดุก่อสร้าง building materials

วา linear measure equal to two meters, wah

ตารางวา square wah, four square meters

ว่า to speak, say, state, tell; to scold, reprove, rebuke, blame, criticize, reproach, admonish; that

ว่ากล่าว to reprimand, censure, rebuke, reprove; to criticize; to lecture (someone), give a /lecture/scolding/ (to), take (someone) to task; to admonish

ว่าการ to administer; acting, in charge

ว่าขาน to protest; to blame

ว่าความ to plead (a case in court); to be the attorney (in a particular case)

ว่าง่าย good, obedient, docile, pliable, compliant, tractable, amenable

ทำการบ้านนะลูก ว่าง่ายๆ อย่าดื้อ Now be a good boy and get on with your homework son.

ว่าจ้าง to employ, engage, hire

ว่าด้วย concerning, about, on; to deal with, talk about

ว่าต่าง to represent (one's client) in court

ว่าตาม to repeat after (me); to follow

ว่าแต่ what about (you, himself etc)

ว่าแต่ว่า by the way, and the; how about,

what about

ว่าแต่ว่าเงินที่ผมจ่ายไปก่อนจะว่ายังไง And the money I advanced, how about it?

ว่านอนสอนง่าย tractable, obedient

ว่าพร้อมกัน to say in unison, say all together

ว่าไม่ฟัง to pay no attention (to), bad, disobedient

ว่ายาก stubborn, intractable, headstrong

เกรงว่า to be afraid, fear, lest, for fear that

เข้าใจว่า to understand, think

คือว่า I mean, that is to say; that is, is that, i.e.

ด่าว่า to abuse, rail (at), scold, vilify, swear (at)

ตอบว่า to reply, answer

ต่อว่า to reproach, rebuke; to complain (to someone about something)

ถ้าว่า if, in case, provided, supposing

ทราบว่า to learn, hear, understand

แบบว่า I mean, like you know, kind of

ปรากฏว่า it /appears/happens/ that

เพราะว่า because, for the reason that

รวมความว่า in short, in summary, to summarize, sum up; to conclude

เรียกว่า called, named

ว้า Oh no!, Shit!, Damn!

ว้ากเกอร์ yell leader

วาง to lay down, put down, place, set, rest (something) on

    วางกฎ to lay down a rule

    วางก้าม overbearing, insolent

    วางกำลัง to position forces

    วางขาย /be/put/ on sale, in the market

    วางไข่ to lay eggs, deposit eggs

    วางโครงการ to plan, lay plans

    วางเงิน to /leave/give/ a deposit

    วางใจ to rest easy, trust, have confidence (in)

    วางเดิมพัน to place a bet (of), make a wager

(of), put up (a thousand baht etc)

วางตน to comport oneself, conduct oneself, behave (well, badly etc)

วางโต to swagger, be arrogant

วางท่า affected, to put on airs, pompous, to pose (as); to act big

วางนโยบาย to lay down policy, formulate policy, establish policy

วางเบ็ด to lay (the) bait, lay fishing lines

วางแผน to lay plans, plan; to plot, scheme

วางเพลิง to set fire (to), commit arson

    คนวางเพลิง an incendiary, arsonist, firebug

วางมัดจำ to give a deposit, make a down payment

วางมือ to withdraw, retire, have nothing more to do with (it)

วางยา to give medicine; to poison

วางยาม to place security guards, place /guards/watchmen/

วางระเบิด to plant /a bomb/an explosive/

วางระเบียบ to prescribe rules, lay down regulations

วางรากฐาน to lay the foundation, lay the basis (for)

วางวาย to die

วางศิลาฤกษ์ to lay a foundation stone

วางหน้า to look (saddened, unaffected, etc)

วางหลัก to fix (one's) principles, lay down /principles/basic considerations/

วางหูโทรศัพท์ to hang up (the telephone)

วางอาวุธ to lay down (one's) arms, surrender

วางอำนาจ to throw one's weight around, use one's authority

ว่าง unoccupied, vacant, free, unengaged, not in use

ว่างๆ when (you are) free; to have some spare time

ว่างงาน unemployed, jobless, out of work

ว
ศ
ษ
ส
ห
ฬ
อ
ฮ

ว่างเปล่า uncultivated; vacant, unoccupied, idle

ว่างเว้น to abstain, refrain (from)

   ไม่ว่างเว้น without exception

ช่องว่าง gap

   ช่องว่างระหว่างวัย generation gap

ตำแหน่งว่าง vacant /position/post/

ที่ว่าง /unoccupied/empty/ place, empty spot, /vacant/unoccupied/ land; room, a place, space

ไม่ว่าง engaged, busy, not free

เวลาว่าง when one is free, (to have) spare time, free time, leisure

ห้องว่าง vacancy; the room is free.

อาหารว่าง snack, refreshments, light meal, hors d'oeuvres

วาจก voice (ในตำราไวยากรณ์)

   กรรตุวาจก active voice

   กรรมวาจก passive voice

วาจา word, words, speech

วาณิชย์ trade, commerce

วาด to draw, paint, sketch; to dance; to paddle a boat

   วาดเขียน to draw, paint

   วาดภาพ to /draw/paint/ a picture; to portray, depict

   วาดลวดลาย to dance, dance variations; to show some fancy /steps/footwork/

วาตภัย storm

วาท word; speech, words; creed

   วาทศาสตร์ rhetoric

   วาทศิลป์ art of speech; eloquence, rhetoric; gift of speech

วาที speaker; musician

   โต้วาที to debate, have a debate

วาน[1] to ask a favor, please

   วานส่งจดหมายหน่อย Please send this letter for me. / Do me a favor and deliver this letter.

วาน[2] yesterday

   วานซืน the day before yesterday

ว่าน medicinal plant, propitious plant

ว่านเครือ stock, line, lineage, family, relatives

วานร monkey

วาบ all of a sudden, in a flash; flashing

   ใจหายวาบ My heart sank., I nearly died.

   วูบวาบ flashing *see* **วูบวาบ** *หน้า 466*

วาโมร forest dweller; dancer

วาย to finish, end, come to an end, close down

   มะม่วงใกล้จะวายแล้ว Mangoes are coming to the end of the season.

   วายชนม์ to die, deceased

   วายปราณ to expire, pass away, breathe (one's) last

   วายวอด to be utterly destroyed, devastated, razed (by fire, bombing, etc)

ว่าย to swim

   ว่ายน้ำ to swim, go swimming

   ว่ายวน to swim around; to be involved (in), mixed up with

   แหวกว่าย to swim about

ว้าย Eek!, Oh!

วาร, วาระ day, time, period, occasion; term

   วารสาร periodical, magazine, journal

   วารดิถี occasion, day

   วาระการประชุม agenda

   วาระที่หนึ่ง the first item on the agenda

   ในวาระ on the occasion (of)

   ระเบียบวาระ agenda

   อีกวาระหนึ่ง again, once again; another occasion

วาว bright, shining, glowing

   วาววาม sparkling, flashing

ว่าว kite

   ว่าวจุฬา Chula kite, a large swallow-shaped kite

   ว่าวติดลม The kite has caught the wind.; to get rolling, get carried away (by what one is doing)

ว่าวปักเป้า Pak Pao kite, a small diamond-shaped attack kite

ชักว่าว to fly a kite

ลมว่าว kite wind (from the north)

ว้าวุ่น agitated, upset, anxious, perturbed, shaken; confused

วาสนา fortune, good luck

มีวาสนา lucky, fortunate, blessed

ว้าเหว่ lonely, lonesome, forlorn, to feel /isolated/ neglected/

วาฬ *as in* **ปลาวาฬ** whale

วิกฤต, วิกฤติ- critical, in a critical state

วิกฤตการณ์ critical period, crisis

วิกฤติกาล crisis

วิกล imperfect, defective, weak, feeble, exhausted

วิกลจริต insane, non compos mentis

วิการ lame, deformed, crippled

วิกาล *as in* **ยามวิกาล** improper time, at night

วิเคราะห์ to analyze

นักวิเคราะห์ analyst

วิ่ง to run

วิ่งกระสอบ sack race

วิ่งแข่ง to race, run a race; foot race, running race

วิ่งควบ to gallop

วิ่งแจ้น to dash (to, up to, off, away)

วิ่งตามมาทัน to run up (to); to overtake at a run

วิ่งตื๋อ to sprint, dash

วิ่งเต้น to pull strings, use /pull/influence,/; to run around, rush around (to get something done)

ผมได้ตำแหน่งมาไม่ได้วิ่งเต้นอะไรเลย I got the /post/posting/ without pulling strings

นักวิ่งเต้น a fixer

วิ่งแต้ to run gleefully; dash (off, away)

วิ่งเปี้ยว flag race

วิ่งผลัด relay race

วิ่งรอก to run a kite in; to run from place to place

วิ่งราว to snatch and run

วิ่งรี่ to rush

วิ่งเร็วจี๋ to race, speed

วิ่งวัว to race, /have/hold/run/ a race

วิ่งวุ่น to run around madly

วิ่งหนี to run away, flee

วิ่งเหยาะๆ to trot

วิงวอน to beg, plead (with someone for something) beseech, implore, supplicate, entreat

วิงเวียน dizzy, giddy, to feel faint

วิจัย to research, do research; to investigate, scrutinize

โครงการวิจัย research project

งานวิจัย research, research work

รายงานวิจัย report, do a research report

วิจาร considered thought

วิจารณ์ to criticize, comment, review

วิจารณ์หนังสือ to review a book, do a book review

คำวิจารณ์ criticism

นักวิจารณ์ critic, commentator

วิพากษ์วิจารณ์ to criticize

วิจารณญาณ intelligence, judgment, good sense

วิจิตร beautiful, wonderful

วิจิตรพิสดาร amazingly beautiful; fantastic, marvelous, elaborate, exquisite,

วิจิตรศิลป์ fine arts

วิชชา true knowledge, transcendental wisdom

วิชา knowledge; subject, branch of study, course

วิชาการ technical

ทางวิชาการ technical, theoretical; academic, scholarly

วิชาครู education

วิชาความรู้ knowledge, learning

วิชาชีพ profession, occupation

ว
ศ
ษ
ส
ห
ฬ
อ
ฮ

วิญญาณ spirit, soul; consciousness

วิญญูชน person of ordinary common sense, reasonable man

วิด to bail out (a boat), scoop water out
วิดน้ำ to bail; to scoop water out; to scoop water in
วิดพื้น to do push-ups

วิตก worried, anxious, upset, afraid; initial thought
วิตกจริต to be a worrier, fraught with anxiety; anxiety, angst
วิตกวิจาร overconcerned, full of anxiety, hypersensitive
น่าวิตก worrisome, alarming
หวั่นวิตก to be afraid, fearful

วิตถาร abnormal, kinky, deviant, perverted
คิดวิตถาร to have strange ideas

วิถี path, way, road
วิถีกระสุน trajectory
วิถีชีวิต way of life
วิถีทาง means, way
วิถีประชา folkways

วิทธะ broken

วิทย- knowledge, science
วิทยฐานะ academic /qualifications/standing/status/, educational qualifications
รับรองวิทยฐานะ to certify academic standing (of a university etc), recognize (a university etc)

วิทยา knowledge, science
วิทยากร speaker, lecturer; expert
วิทยากล a magic show
วิทยาทาน instruction, education
วิทยานิพนธ์ thesis
วิทยานิพนธ์ปริญญาเอก doctoral dissertation
วิทยาลัย college
    วิทยาลัยเทคนิค technical college
    วิทยาลัยอาชีวศึกษา vocational training college, vocational college

วิทยาศาสตร์ science
วิทยาศาสตร์ธรรมชาติ natural science
วิทยาศาสตร์บริสุทธิ์ pure science
วิทยาศาสตรบัณฑิต bachelor of science, B. Sc.
วิทยาศาสตร์ประยุกต์ applied science
นักวิทยาศาสตร์ scientist

วิทยุ radio, wireless
วิทยุกระจายเสียง (radio) broadcast
วิทยุโทรเลข telegraph; radiogram
วิทยุโทรศัพท์ radio-telephone
วิทยุสนาม walkie-talkie, field radio transmitter
วิทยุสื่อสาร a walkie-talkie; radio communication
เครื่องรับวิทยุ radio, radio receiver
เครื่องส่งวิทยุ radio transmitter
พนักงานวิทยุ radio operator

วิเทโศบาย foreign policy

วิธี method, way, means; directions, rule, regulation, practice
วิธีการ procedure
วิธีใช้ directions (for use)
วิธีดำเนินการ procedures
วิธีทำ how to do (it), directions; solution
โดยสันติวิธี by peaceful means
ยุทธวิธี tactics

วิ่น to be torn
ขาดวิ่น to be in tatters, tattered

วินัย discipline, orderly conduct; Buddhist disciplinary rules
วินัยสงฆ์ rule of discipline of the Sangha
มีวินัย disciplined, orderly
ระเบียบวินัย rules; disciplinary

วินาที second

วินาศ calamity, destruction, annihilation, ruin

วินาศกรรม sabotage
ก่อวินาศกรรม to sabotage
ผู้ก่อวินาศกรรม saboteur

วินาศภัย disaster

วินิจฉัย to judge, decide, conclude, give judgment, make a decision

    วินิจฉัยโรค to make a diagnosis, diagnose an /illness/disease/etc

        การวินิจฉัยโรค diagnosis

วิบัติ calamity, disaster, affliction, misfortune; incorrect, faulty, defective

วิบาก rough, grueling, arduous, full of obstacles; consequences of previous actions

    วิบากกรรม misfortune, result of a bad Karma; consequence of Karma

    รถวิบาก off-road vehicle; vehicle modified for obstacle racing

    วิ่งวิบาก to run an obstacle course

วิปริต abnormal, unnatural; aberrant; mad, eccentric

วิปลาส abnormal, unusual, crackpot; inaccurate, corrupt

    จิตวิปลาส demented, insane, of unsound mind

วิปัสสนา insight, intuitive vision; meditation

    วิปัสสนากรรมฐาน insight meditation

    นั่งวิปัสสนา to meditate, practice meditation, sit in meditation

วิพากษ์ to judge

    วิพากษ์วิจารณ์ to criticize

วิภาษวิธี dialectic method

วิมาน celestial abode, paradise

    วิมานทลาย shattered dreams, paradise lost

    วิมานในอากาศ castles in the air

วิมุตติ deliverance, freedom, liberation

วิริยะ perseverance

วิลันดา Dutchman, Hollander

วิลิศมาหรา ritzy

วิวัฒนาการ evolution, development

วิวาท to quarrel, have a row, have a dispute

    ทะเลาะวิวาท to have /an altercation/a fight/

วิวาห์ marriage, wedding

วิวาหมงคล wedding ceremony

    งานวิวาห์ wedding

วิเวก solitude, seclusion

วิศวกร engineer

วิศวกรรม engineering

    วิศวกรรมไฟฟ้า electrical engineering

    วิศวกรรมศาสตร์ engineering

วิสัย limit; characteristic, nature

    วิสัยทัศน์ vision

    ทัศนวิสัย visibility

    พ้นวิสัย beyond one's ability

    สุดวิสัย impossible

วิสรรชนีย์ the vowel sign "ะ"

    ประวิสรรชนีย์ to insert the vowel sign "ะ"

วิสัชนา to answer, reply

วิสัญญี unconscious

    วิสัญญีแพทย์ anesthesiologist

วิสาขบูชา Visakha Puja, Buddhist puja on the day of the full moon in the sixth lunar month to commemorate the birth, enlightenment and death of the Buddha

วิสามัญ extraordinary, special

    วิสามัญฆาตกรรม justifiable homicide

วิสาสะ familiarity, friendly terms

    ถือวิสาสะ see ถือวิสาสะ หน้า 214

วิหาร vihara, Buddhist assembly hall

วี to fan

วี้ดว้าย shrieking

วีน to fly off the handle (at someone)

วีร- brave

    วีรกรรม heroic deed, act of bravery

    วีรชน hero, heroes, courageous people

    วีรบุรุษ hero

    วีรสตรี heroine

วี่วัน day

    ทุกวี่วัน every day, every single day

วี่แวว sign, indication, clue, trace

    ไม่มีวี่แวว no sign (of), no trace, no indication, not a clue

ว
ศ
ษ
ส
ห
ฬ
อ
ฮ

วีด to slip up

วุฒิ qualifications, accomplishments, proficiency

  วุฒิภาวะ maturity

  วุฒิสภา senate

  วุฒิสมาชิก senator

  คุณวุฒิ great ability, learning

    ทรงคุณวุฒิ qualified, learned, accomplished, competent, proficient

  วัยวุฒิ seniority, senior; venerable

วุ่น troubled, troublesome, in a turmoil, upsetting

  วุ่นวาย disorganized, in a mess, chaotic, confused, in disorder, turbulent

  วิ่งวุ่น to run helter-skelter, run around nervously

วุ้น jelly, gelatin, agar

  วุ้นเส้น bean vermicelli, glass noodles, bean threads

  เละเป็นวุ้น smashed to a pulp

วูบ to flash

  วูบวาบ to flash, flashing; flashes (of heat etc); to have a hot flash; (to become) flushed, have a giddy spell; (sl) to have the hots (for someone)

  ดับวูบ to go out suddenly, extinguished in an instant

วู่วาม excitable, volatile, without thinking, hasty

เวจ water closet, toilet; excrement

  เวจกุฎี toilet for monks

  เวจมรรค anus, anal

เวช doctor, physician

  เวชกรรม medicine, medical treatment

  เวชภัณฑ์ pharmaceuticals, medical supplies, drugs

  เวชระเบียน registration (hospital)

  เวชศาสตร์ medical science, medicine

  เวชศาสตร์เขตร้อน tropical medicine

  เวชศาสตร์ด้านประสาท neuropathology

เวทนา feeling, sensation, pain, suffering; to pity

  น่าเวทนา pitiful, lamentable, sorry

เวทมนตร์ spell, magic incantation

เวที stage, ring

  เวทีมวย boxing ring, prize ring

เวน to transfer, give

  เวนคืน to expropriate; to surrender

  ค่าเวนคืน (กรมธรรม์) surrender value (of an insurance policy)

เว้น to except, skip; to give up, refrain (from), abstain (from)

  เว้นแต่ unless, except, on condition that, if not

  งดเว้น refrain from, abstain from, give up

  ยกเว้น except, excluding, not including, with the exception of; to exempt (from)

  ละเว้น to except; to give up, refrain from

เวไนยสัตว์ an educable being

เวร shift, turn; enmity, ill will; vengeance; sin

  เวรกรรม misfortune, ill fate; How awful! Jesus!; God almighty!

  จองเวร vindictive, vengeful, be bent on revenge, harbor ill feelings (towards someone)

  อยู่เวร to be on duty

เวลา time, period; when, at

  เวลากลางคืน at night, nighttime

  เวลาค่ำ in the evening

  เวลาเช้า in the morning

  เวลาตะวันตกดิน (at) sunset

  เวลาทำงาน (during) working hours, office hours

  เวลาเท่าไร What time is it?, at what time

  เวลาเที่ยง at noon, noontime

  เวลานอน bedtime, when sleeping

  เวลานัด (at the) appointed time, on time

  เวลาน้ำขึ้น at high tide

  เวลาน้ำลง at low tide

  เวลานี้ at present, now, currently, today

เวลาบ่าย in the afternoon

เวลาพระจันทร์ขึ้น at moonrise, when the moon comes up

เวลาพระอาทิตย์ขึ้น at sunrise

เวลาพลบค่ำ twilight, dusk

เวลาเล่น playtime, the time for playing

เวลาว่าง when one is free, (to have) leisure, spare time

เวลาหยุดพัก recess, (take a) break, take time out

ก่อนเวลา in advance, ahead of time, early

กินเวลา to take time

งานนี้กินเวลาเท่าไร How long will it take to finish the job? / How much time will it take?

ฆ่าเวลา to kill time (by), while away the time

เจียดเวลา to /spare/save/set aside/ some time (to, for), find time (to do something)

ช่วงเวลา during, in; time, period, interval, time span

ชั่วเวลา in (two hours, six minutes etc)

ได้เวลา it is time

ได้เวลากินข้าวแล้ว It's /mealtime/lunchtime/dinnertime/etc

ตรงเวลา on time, punctual; accurate

ตลอดเวลา the whole time, all the time, continuously, incessantly, perpetually, always

ตารางเวลา timetable, schedule

ทันเวลา in time

ในเวลา when (speaking etc), during (office hours etc), at (night etc)

บางเวลา sometimes, at times

ปลีกเวลา to find time (to), spare the time (to, for), set aside some time

เป็นเวลา regularly, at fixed times, at a certain time, at regular hours; for (six years etc)

นอนไม่เป็นเวลา to sleep at irregular hours, have no fixed time for sleeping, sleep at odd hours

ไม่มีเวลา to have no time (to)

หมดเวลา The time is up., to run out of time, have no more time

เว่อ gaping, cavernous

เว้า concave, curving inward

เว้าแหว่ง jagged, to have a bite taken out (of something)

กระจกเว้า concave /mirror/lens/

เวิ้ง open space

เวิ้งว้าง empty expanse, extensive stretch (of sea, land, forest etc)

เวียง walled town

เวียน to go around, revolve, circle

เวียนเทียน ceremony of circling a temple or chedi with lighted candles incense and flowers; ceremony of passing a lighted candle around a circle of people

เวียนวน to circle

เวียนหัว faint, dizzy, giddy

บันไดเวียน winding staircase

วกไปเวียนมา circuitous, winding, in circles

วงเวียน circle; compass

วิงเวียน to feel faint, dizzy, giddy

แวง *as in* **เส้นแวง** longitude

แว้ง to wheel /back/around/, turn suddenly

แว้งกัด to wheel back and bite

แวดล้อม surrounded (by), surrounding

สถานการณ์แวดล้อม (surrounding) circumstances

สิ่งแวดล้อม environment, surroundings

แว่น eyeglasses, glasses, spectacles; mirror

แว่นขยาย magnifying glass

แว่นตา eyeglasses, glasses

แว่นตากรอบทอง gold-rimmed glasses

แว่นตากันแดด sunglasses

แว่นตาดำ dark glasses

ว

ศ

ษ

ส

ห

ฬ

อ

ฮ

แว่นตาเดียว monocle

แว่นฟ้า decorated with bits of colored glass

แวบ flashing, glittering

ชั่วแวบ for an instant, momentarily; in a flash

ความคิดชั่วแวบ The idea came (to me) in a flash.

แวว makings; shiny, sparkling

แววตา light in one's eyes, sparkle in one's eyes, expression in one's eyes

แวววาม, แวววาว brilliant, glittering, sparkling, scintillating

มีแวว to show promise; to show signs (of), have the makings (of)

เด็กคนนี้มีแววกวี The child shows promise as a poet. / The child shows signs of /becoming a poet/poetical ability. / The child has the makings of a poet.

วี่แวว trace, indication, hint, sign

แว่ว, แว่วเสียง faint /sound/voice/, distant sound, to be heard faintly

แวะ to visit, stop (off, by, at, in)

แวะเยี่ยม to stop by, make a visit, drop /in /by/

เชิญแวะชมก่อน You're welcome to take a look around., Do come in and have a look.

โว to talk big

โวย to complain; to cry, cry out

สมัครโวยพังทั้งระบบ System Destroyed Samak Cries

โว้ย what the hell (is going on, etc), dammit, come on

มีอะไรก็พูดมาซิโว้ย Come on, speak up! / Dammit, if you have something to say, out with it!

โวยวาย to make a fuss, make a big to do (/about/ over/ something), complain

โวหาร words, language, expression; style; eloquence

ไว quickly, promptly, fast

ไวไฟ inflammable; hot, sexy

ฉับไว promptly, quick, fast

มือไว light-fingered; free with one's hands

ว่องไว active, quick, agile, nimble

หัวไว quick, smart, clever

ไว้ to place, put, keep, preserve, reserve

ไว้ใจ to trust, confide (in), have confidence (in), have faith in

ไว้ใจได้ trustworthy, reliable, dependable

ไว้ใจไม่ได้ unreliable, untrustworthy, unsound, unpredictable, not dependable

ไว้ชีวิต to spare another's life

ไว้ตัว aloof, reserved

ไว้ท่า to act dignified; to put on airs, act big

ไว้ทุกข์ to wear mourning

ไว้ผมยาว to wear one's hair long, have long hair

ไว้ลาย to do oneself justice, be as good as ever

ไว้เล็บ to have long nails, keep one's fingernail long

ไว้หนวด to grow a moustache, /wear/have/ a moustache

ไว้หน้า to spare (another's feelings, reputation etc), save (a person) from embarrassment, refrain from embarrassing someone

ไว้อาลัย to mourn (for), (to stand etc) in memory (of), in memoriam, memorial

คำไว้อาลัย eulogy

ไวยากรณ์ grammar

ไวยาวัจกร monk's lay attendant; temple affairs manager

ไวโอลิน violin

ศก year; era
ศกนี้ this era
คริสต์ศก A.D., (ย่อจาก Anno Domini), Christian era
เถลิงศกใหม่ to start the new year
พุทธศก Buddhist era, (B.E.)
วันเถลิงศกใหม่ New Year's Day

ศตวรรษ, ศตพรรษ century

ศพ corpse, body, remains, cadaver
กระบวนแห่ศพ funeral procession
เก็บศพ to keep the body; to collect the body
งานศพ funeral, cremation, obsequies
ซากศพ body, corpse, remains
เผาศพ to cremate, hold a cremation
ฝังศพ to bury the dead, hold a burial
หลุมฝังศพ grave
พระบรมศพ royal remains

ศร arrow; bow
ศรศิลป์ไม่กินกัน on bad terms
โก่งศร to /draw/bend/ a bow
คันศร bow
ลูกศร arrow

ศรัทธา belief, faith; to trust, have confidence (in), believe (in), have respect (for)
ศรัทธาในพระรัตนตรัย to have faith in the Triple Gem / believe in the Triple Gem
เสื่อมศรัทธา to lose /faith/confidence/ in, lose respect (for)

ศรี [1] fine, good; credit (to); virtuous; auspicious; glory, splendor, magnificence; goodness, virtue; wealth, prosperity; luck, fortune; success, greatness
ศรีเมือง national /pride/treasure/

ศรี [2] betel leaf

ศอ neck

ศอก elbow; cubit, a unit of length equal to half a meter
ศอกกลับ to retort, riposte; to back-elbow

ศอกกำ, ศอกกำมา short cubit
ข้อศอก elbow (joint)
ชายอกสามศอก he-man
ตีศอก to punch with the elbow

ศักดิ์ power, authority; position, rank, status
เกียรติศักดิ์ dignity, prestige, honor, reputation; distinction
บรรดาศักดิ์ rank, title, dignity

ศักดินา dignity expressed in area of land entitlement; feudal; aristocrat

ศักดิ์ศรี dignity, honor, prestige
ศักดิ์ศรีความเป็นมนุษย์ human dignity
มีศักดิ์ศรี dignified, honorable

ศักดิ์สิทธิ์ sacred, holy, hallowed, revered, sacrosanct; to be law
คำพูดของเขาศักดิ์สิทธิ์ His word is law.
ความศักดิ์สิทธิ์ sanctity
ความศักดิ์สิทธิ์ของกฎหมาย sanctity of the law

ศักย- power; tension, voltage
ศักยภาพ potential
สายไฟศักย์สูง high tension wire, high voltage line

ศักราช *see* ศก

ศัตรู enemy, foe; pest
ศัตรูพืช plant pest
ยาปราบศัตรูพืช plant pesticide

ศัพท์ sound, voice; word, term; difficult word; story; vocabulary
ศัพท์เฉพาะ technical term
ศัพท์บัญญัติ invented word, coined word
ศัพท์วิทยาศาสตร์ scientific term
ศัพท์แสง lingo, jargon; words
ศัพท์หมวด lexicon, classified /words/terms/
คุณศัพท์ adjective
ทับศัพท์ transliteration
โทรศัพท์ telephone
ฟังไม่ได้ศัพท์ unintelligible; to fail to understand

ศ
ษ
ส
ห
ฬ
อ
ฮ

ศัพทวิทยา lexicology

ศัลยกรรม surgery

 ศัลยกรรมตบแต่ง plastic surgery, cosmetic surgery

ศัลยแพทย์ surgeon

ศัลยศาสตร์ surgery

ศัสตรา weapon

ศากย- Sakya, name of the Buddha's clan

 ศากยมุนี Sakyamuni, name of the Buddha

 ศากยวงศ์ lineage of the Buddha

ศานติ peace, tranquility

 ศานติสุข happiness, tranquility, peace

ศารท autumnal, fall; autumn merit-making festival

ศาล court, tribunal; shrine, joss house

 ศาลแขวง district court

 ศาลเจ้า joss house, shrine, Chinese temple

 ศาลฎีกา Supreme Court

 ศาลเด็ก Juvenile Court, Children's Court

 ศาลทหาร military court

 ศาลเพียงตา temporary shrine

 ศาลแพ่ง civil court

 ศาลรัฐธรรมนูญ Constitutional Court

 ศาลสถิตยุติธรรม court of justice

 ศาลอาญา criminal court

 ศาลอุทธรณ์ appeal court, court of appeals

 ขึ้นศาล to go to court, be brought to court, appear in court

 จ่าศาล /clerk/registrar/ of the court

 โรงศาล courthouse

ศาลา pavilion, shelter, sala; house; temple, hall

 ศาลากลาง central government offices, (provincial) government house

 ศาลาราย cloister

 สุขศาลา public dispensary

ศาสดา exalted teacher; apostle, founder of a religion

ศาสตร์ treatise; -ology, science, art

ศาสตรา weapon

ศาสตราจารย์ professor

 ศาสตราจารย์กิตติคุณ *(จุฬา)* professor emeritus

ศาสตราจารย์กิตติเมธี *(สุโขทัย)* professor emeritus

ศาสตราจารย์เกียรติคุณ *(ธรรมศาสตร์)* professor emeritus

ผู้ช่วยศาสตราจารย์ assistant professor

รองศาสตราจารย์ associate professor

ศาสน์, ศาสนา religion

 ศาสนาคริสต์ Christianity, Christian religion

 ศาสนาพุทธ Buddhism

ศาสนูปถัมภก patron of religions

ศิโรราบ to submit (to), capitulate; to be defeated

ศิลป-, -ศิลปะ, ศิลป์ art

 ศิลปกรรม artistic work, objet d'art, work of art

  ประณีตศิลปกรรม fine artwork

 ศิลปวิทยา arts and sciences

 ศิลปศาสตร์ liberal arts

 วาทศิลป์ art of speech; eloquence, rhetoric; gift of speech

 ห้องศิลปะ art studio

 หอศิลป์ art gallery

 มีศิลปะ artistic, artful, skillful

ศิลปากร fine arts

 กรมศิลปากร Fine Arts Department

ศิลปิน, ศิลป์ artist

ศิลา stone, rock

 ศิลาจารึก stone inscription

 ศิลาฤกษ์ foundation stone

 ศิลาแลง laterite

ศิวะ Siva, Shiva

ศิวิไลซ์ civilized

 ความศิวิไลซ์ civilization

ศิษย์ student, pupil, trainee, boy; disciple

 ศิษย์ก้นกุฏิ disciple

 ศิษย์เก่า *see* นิสิตเก่า *หน้า 261*

 ศิษย์มีครู authority

 ศิษย์วัด /wat/temple/ boy

 ศิษยานุศิษย์ all pupils (of), pupils past and present, students and alumni

ลูกศิษย์ student, pupil, boy

ศีรษะ head

    กะโหลกศีรษะ cranium, skull

    ผงกศีรษะ to look up, raise one's head; to nod (at someone)

ศีล precept, code of morality, morality, moral conduct, virtue; precepts, rules for moral training, observances

    ศีลขาด to have broken a precept, have committed a transgression

    ศีลธรรม morality

    ถือศีล to /keep/observe/ the rules (of religion), observe the precepts

    ทรงศีล devout, religious, moral, virtuous

    มีศีลสัตย์ righteous, holy, upright, virtuous

ศึก war, combat, fight; conflict

    ข้าศึก enemy, foe

    ขุนศึก warlord, military chief, general

    เชลยศึก prisoner of war

    ทหารผ่านศึก war veteran

    ไส้ศึก spy, fifth column, enemy agent

    หย่าศึก to call a truce, stop fighting, /end/ break off/ hostilities

ศึกษา education; to be educated; to study

    ศึกษาธิการจังหวัด provincial education officer

    ศึกษานิเทศก์ educational supervisor

    การศึกษานำร่อง a pilot study

    ประถมศึกษา /primary/elementary/education, primary schooling

    พลศึกษา physical education

    มัธยมศึกษา /secondary/high school/education

    สามัญศึกษา general education

    อุดมศึกษา higher education, university education

ศุกร์ Friday; Venus

    ดาวพระศุกร์ Venus

    วันศุกร์ Friday

ศุภเคราะห์ lucky planet, auspicious sign

ศุภนิมิต good omen, good augury, propitious sign, good sign

ศุภมงคล auspicious

ศุภฤกษ์ auspicious /time/moment/

ศุลกากร customs duty

    กรมศุลกากร Customs Department

ศุลการักษ์ customs officer

ศูนย์ center; zero, naught; bullseye

    ศูนย์กลาง center

    ศูนย์การค้า shopping center, trade center

    ศูนย์ถ่วง center of gravity

    ศูนย์บริการสาธารณสุข public health center

    ศูนย์รวม hub

    ศูนย์สูตร equator

    ศูนย์หน้า center forward

ศูนยตา *see* สุญญตา *หน้า 501*

เศรษฐกิจ economy; finances, business

    เศรษฐกิจตกต่ำ (economic) depression; in difficult circumstances; business is bad

    เศรษฐกิจพอเพียง economy based on modest needs; economic self-sufficiency

    เศรษฐกิจฟองสบู่ bubble economy

    เศรษฐศาสตร์ economics

        เศรษฐศาสตร์จุลภาค microeconomy

        เศรษฐศาสตร์มหาภาค macroeconomy

        เศรษฐศาสตรบัณฑิต Bachelor of Economics

เศรษฐินี /rich/wealthy/affluent/ woman

เศรษฐี /rich/wealthy/affluent/ man

    มหาเศรษฐี millionaire, very rich person

เศร้า sad, depressed, sorrowful, grievous; to be a pity, deplorable

    เศร้าใจ sad

    เศร้าซึม gloomy, depressed, sorrowful, sad

    เศร้าโศก sorrowful, disconsolate

    เศร้าหมอง downcast, unhappy, gloomy, dispirited; defiled

    หน้าเศร้า to look /sad/dejected/, sad-looking, glum

เศวตฉัตร white nine-tiered umbrella being a

ศ
ษ
ส
ห
ฬ
อ
ฮ

symbol of royalty

เศษ   remainder, piece (of), what is left over; scrap(s); fraction; over, more than

เศษกระดาษ scrap of paper, piece of paper

เศษขนมปัง crumb

เศษซ้อน compound fraction

เศษผ้า remnant, piece of material

เศษไม้ leftover wood, scraps of wood

เศษโลหะ scrap metal

เศษสตางค์ small change

เศษส่วน fraction

    เศษส่วนย่อย partial fraction

เศษสิบ decimal

เศษหนึ่งส่วนสี่ one quarter

เศษเหล็ก scrap iron

เศษอาหาร leftovers, scraps

เศษอิฐหินดินทราย rubble

กินเศษกินเลย to engage in petty corruption, be slightly crooked

ห้าโมงเศษ a little after five

หาเศษหาเลย to take advantage

เศียร   head

ปวดเศียร to have a headache; to be a pain in the neck, give one a headache

โศก   sorrow, grief, sadness, suffering, distress

โศกนาฏกรรม tragedy

โศกศัลย์ to grieve, lament

โศกเศร้า sad, grieving, sorrowing

โศกา   to weep, cry

โศลก   stanza, verse

ษมา

ษ

ษมา   to apologize, beg forgiveness

ษมาลาโทษ to ask forgiveness

สกปรก dirty, unclean, soiled, filthy; underhanded, foul

   ทำสกปรก to dirty, make (something) dirty, soil

   พูดสกปรก to be foulmouthed, use dirty language

สกัด to intercept, prevent, check, block; to chisel, hew, cut with a chisel; to extract

   สกัดน้ำมัน to extract oil

   จุดสกัด checkpoint, roadblock

สกาว glowing; immaculate

สกุล family; pedigree, line, lineage, stock; genus *(วิทย์)*

   นามสกุล surname, family name

   ผู้ดีมีสกุล person of good family, person wellborn

   วงศ์สกุล family

สข. (สมาชิกสภาเขต) district council member

ส่ง to hand, deliver, send, pass, transmit; to escort, take (someone), bring; to promote, support

   ส่งกลิ่น to smell

      ส่งกลิ่นเหม็น to smell bad, stink; odoriferous

   ส่งข่าว to send news, keep (someone) informed

   ส่งจดหมาย to send a letter

   ส่งต่อ to forward (a letter, message, etc)

   ส่งต่อไป to pass (something) along

   ส่งตัว to deliver the groom

   ส่งท้าย to wind up

   ส่งโทรเลข to telegraph, cable, send a telegram, wire

   ส่งภาษา to speak in a different language, speak with a different accent

   ส่งมอบ to deliver, hand over, transfer

   ส่งส่วย to pay tribute; to service

   ส่งเสียง to make a noise, be noisy; to cry out, yell; to project the voice

   ส่งหนังสือ to deliver a letter

   ส่งออก to export

   ขนส่ง to transport, carry

      การขนส่ง transportation, carriage

   ขายส่ง to wholesale, sell wholesale

   เครื่องส่ง transmitter

   ไปส่ง to take someone, go with someone

   ผู้ส่ง sender

   เลี้ยงส่ง to give a farewell party (for someone)

สงกรานต์ Thai New Year's Celebration falling about April 14

   วันสงกรานต์ Songkran Day

สงคราม war, warfare

   สงครามกลางเมือง civil war

   สงครามปรมาณู atomic warfare

   สงครามปาก war of words

   สงครามเย็น cold war

   สงครามโลก world war

   ยามสงคราม wartime

สงเคราะห์ assistance, support, to help, aid, give /help/aid/assistance/support/

   สังคมสงเคราะห์ social welfare

สงฆ์, พระสงฆ์ Sangha, Buddhist monastic order, clergy; Buddhist monk; a chapter of (not less than four) Buddhist monks

สงบ quiet, still, calm, peaceful, composed; back to normal; to blow over

   สงบเงียบ quiet and peaceful

   สงบใจ to be at peace

   สงบปากสงบคำ to hold one's mouth

   สงบลง to abate, blow over; to cool down, be at rest

   สงบศึก truce

   สงบสติอารมณ์ to collect oneself, regain control of oneself, calm down

   สงบเสงี่ยม reserved, mild, quiet, composed

   ความสงบเรียบร้อย peace and order

สงวน to preserve, reserve, set aside

   สงวนตัว reserved; to keep one's distance

ส
ห
ฬ
อ
ฮ

สงวนท่าที noncommittal, guarded, reserved; to reserve one's /opinion/position/attitude/ etc

สงวนลิขสิทธิ์ copyright reserved

สงวนสิทธิ to reserve the right (to), rights reserved

สงวนอาชีพ to reserve an occupation

ของสงวน bosom (not to be touched)

สงสัย to doubt, suspect; to be uncertain, question, wonder (whether, if); to think, guess

สงสัยอาตมาต้องสึก I guess I'll have to leave the monkhood.

ข้อสงสัย question, doubt; doubts, suspicion

ขี้สงสัย suspicious, sceptical, doubting

ความสงสัย doubt, suspicion, scepticism

น่าสงสัย suspicious, doubtful, questionable

ผู้ต้องสงสัย suspect

สงสาร to pity, feel sorry (for); to feel sympathy (for), sympathize with

ขี้สงสาร tenderhearted, compassionate, easily moved, to feel sorry for others; over-sympathetic

น่าสงสาร What a shame!, too bad; pathetic, poor, deserving sympathy, pitiful, pitiable, unfortunate, miserable; lovable

เด็กน่าสงสาร ทั้งพี่ทั้งน้องตายหมดตอนรถชนกัน The poor boy lost his brother and sister in a car crash.

ไม่สงสารตัวเอง to have no regard for oneself, neglect oneself; to overdo it

ส่งเดช slapdash, careless

ส่งเสริม to promote, encourage, support, give support, advance

ส่งเสีย to provide for, support

สงัด quiet, tranquil, still, peaceful, serene; uncrowded

สงบสงัด peaceful, tranquil, still

สง่า dignified; elegant, grand, handsome, fine-looking

สง่างาม elegant; stately, majestic

สง่าราศี grand

สด fresh

สดคาว fresh /meat/fish/

สดชื่น fresh, refreshed, bright; refreshing

สดๆ ร้อนๆ hot, fresh

สดใส bright, fresh, radiant, cheerful

สีสดใส bright color

ของสด fresh food

เขียวสด bright green

เงินสด cash

ตลาดสด fresh-food market

นมสด fresh milk, milk

สดมภ์, สดมภ์หลัก pillar, pillar of strength; column

เลขที่สดมภ์ column number

สดับ to listen (to)

สดับตรับฟัง to listen /closely/attentively/ (to), pay attention (to)

สดุดี to praise, laud

สตรี woman; ladies

สตรีเพศ female, the fair sex

โรงเรียนสตรี girls' school

สุภาพสตรี lady

สตางค์ satang, one-hundredth of a baht

สติ consciousness, mind; conscience

สติปัญญา intelligence

สติฟั่นเฟือน deranged

สติไม่ดี simple-minded, mentally defective

สติวิปลาศ insane, crazy

สติสตัง mind

สติสัมปชัญญะ awareness

สติอารมณ์ emotions

คืนสติ to regain consciousness, come to

ได้สติ to become conscious of wrongdoing, come to one's senses; to come to, regain consciousness

ตั้งสติ to compose oneself, regain one's composure, recover one's self-possession; to be careful

มีสติ to have presence of mind; to be sensible; conscious

เสียสติ to go out of one's mind, go mad

หมดสติ (become) unconscious, lose consciousness, senseless

สตีม steam

เร่งสตีม to go full steam ahead

สตู stew

สเต็ก steak

สเตริโอ stereo

สไตร๊ค์ strike

สถาน place, locality, site; scene; way; aspect

สถานกงสุล consulate

สถานทำการทางกงสุล consular post

สถานที่ place, site, spot; building, premises, location, area

สถานที่เกิด place of birth

สถานที่เกิดเหตุ scene of /occurence /the accident/the crime/

สถานทูต embassy, legation

สถานพยาบาล clinic, nursing home

สถานภาพ status, condition

สถานเริงรมย์ entertainment area

สถานะ state, condition

สถานการณ์ situation, circumstances

สถานี station

สถานีตำรวจ police station

สถานีปลายทาง terminal, terminus; last station

สถานีรถไฟ railroad station

สถานีวิทยุ radio station, broadcasting station

สถานีอนามัย public health center, health station

สถานีอวกาศ space station

สถาบัน institution, institute

สถาปนา to establish, to promote; founded, established

สถาปนิก architect

สถาปัตยกรรม architecture

สถาพร, สถาวร perpetual, permanent, everlasting

สถิต to establish, stay, remain; to be situated, reside

สถิติ statistics, record

สถุล coarse, gross, rough; low; base; scum

สถูป stupa

สน. Metropolitan Police Station

สน[1] pine

น้ำมันสน turpentine

สน[2] to thread

สนเข็ม to thread a needle

สนใจ to be interested (in)

ความสนใจ interest

มีความสนใจ to take an interest (in), be interested (in)

สนตะพาย to put a cord through the nose of a /bull/buffalo/; to lead (a person) around by the nose *(fig)*

ส้น heel

ส้นตีน heel; You shit!

ส้นเตี้ย low-heel

ส้นเท้า heel

ส้นปืน butt (of a gun)

ส้นรองเท้า heel (of a shoe)

ส้นสูง high-heel

สนทนา to talk, converse, conversation

สนทนาปราศรัย to have a /cordial talk/ conversation/ (with)

การสนทนา talk, conversation

พบปะสนทนา to have a get-together, have a social gathering

สนเทศ information

สนเท่ห์ to have doubts, be in doubt, suspicious; puzzled, perplexed, uncertain

บัตรสนเท่ห์ anonymous letter, poison-pen letter, anonymous accusation

สนธยา dusk, twilight

สนธิ connection; combination, combined

สนธิสัญญา treaty

ส
ห
ฬ
อ
ฮ

สนนราคา the going price

สนม royal /concubine/minor wife/; a royal funeral official; prison

    สนมเอก favorite /royal concubine/minor wife/

สนอง to meet, respond, requite, return; to accept

    สนองคุณ to be grateful for a /kindness/ good turn/etc; to repay a kindness, return a favor

    สนองตอบ to respond, answer

    คำสนอง acceptance

สนั่น resounding, reverberating, thunderous, roaring

    สนั่นหวั่นไหว deafening, to make a din

สนับนิ้วมือ thimble

สนับมือ brass knuckles

สนับสนุน to support, back, be pro

    สนับสนุนโดย sponsored by

    ยิงสนับสนุน (to give) supporting fire

สนาม ground, field, lawn, yard

    สนามกอล์ฟ golf course

    สนามกีฬา stadium; playing field, athletic field

    สนามเด็กเล่น playground

    สนามเทนนิส tennis court

    สนามบิน airfield, airport

    สนามเพลาะ trench

    สนามฟุตบอล soccer field

    สนามมวย boxing stadium

    สนามม้า race course, race track

    สนามแม่เหล็ก magnetic field

    สนามยิงเป้า shooting gallery

    สนามรบ battlefield, battleground

    สนามหญ้า lawn

    สนามหลวง Pramane Ground

    ลงสนาม to enter a competition, compete, participate

สนิท tight, perfectly joined, firm, snug, close fitting; intimate, close; perfectly, completely, totally; soundly, deeply

    สนิทสนม close, very friendly; on intimate terms (with), on familiar terms

    เชื่อสนิท to be convinced, be certain, believe without reservation; to be taken in (by)

    ตีสนิท to get on familiar terms (with), get close (to someone), befriend (for ulterior motives), play up to someone

    ทหารคนสนิท aide de camp, military aide

    เพื่อนสนิท close friend, dear friend, pal

    ลืมสนิท to completely forget, be a blank

    หลับสนิท to sleep /soundly/deeply/, sound asleep, in a deep sleep

สนิม rust; corrosion

    ขึ้นสนิม to rust, rusty; corroded

    เป็นสนิม rusty; corroded

    สนิมสร้อย *see* **ถนิมสร้อย** *หน้า 208*

สนุก fun, amusing, enjoyable, happy, entertaining; to have a good time

    ไปพัทยาสนุกไหม Did you have a good time at Pataya? สนุกมาก We had a great time.

    สนุกๆ just for fun, for the fun of it

    สนุกจริง What fun!

    สนุกสนาน great fun, happy, jolly, rollicking

    สนุกสุดเหวี่ยง hilarious

    ความสนุก fun, enjoyment

สบ to meet

    สบใจ to please, satisfy

    สบตา eyes meet; to look someone in the eye

    พอสบตากัน เขาก็รู้ว่าเธอชอบเขา Their eyes met and he knew she liked him.

    เขาไม่กล้าสบตา He didn't dare look her in the eye.

    สบประมาท to belittle, disparage

    สบเหมาะ fortunately, luckily, just at the right time

    สบอารมณ์ to satisfy, please; satisfying, pleasing

สบง monk's lower garment

สบถ to swear, make an oath; to curse
สบถสาบาน to swear (to someone)

สบาย well, happy, comfortable, to feel good
สบายๆ laid-back
สบายใจ to be happy, satisfied
สบายดี well, fine, comfortable
สบายดีหรือ How do you do?
ความสบาย comfort, ease, happiness
ความสุขสบาย well-being, happiness
ตามสบาย Make yourself at home.; to relax and be comfortable; (to do) as one /pleases/ likes/, make oneself comfortable; informally; leisurely

สบึมม์ oomph

สบู่ soap
สบู่ซักผ้า laundry soap
สบู่ถูตัว toilet soap
สบู่เหลว liquid soap

สไบ shawl used as a wrap-around female upper garment, breast cloth
สไบเฉียง a shawl worn as a wrap-around upper garment with one end thrown over one shoulder

สปริง spring
เตียงสปริง spring bed

สภา council, assembly; institute
สภากาชาด Red Cross Society
สภาทนายความ Law Society
สภาเทศบาล municipal council
สภานายก president, speaker
สภานิติบัญญัติ legislature
สภาผู้แทนราษฎร National Assembly, House of People's Representatives
สภาร่าง constituent assembly
สภาสามัญ House of Commons
ประธานสภาสามัญ Speaker of the House
สภาสูง upper house, senate
เนติบัณฑิตยสภา Bar Association
ยุบสภา to dissolve the legislature

วุฒิสภา senate

สภาพ condition, state, life; nature
IMF ได้ช่วยสภาพทางพาณิชย์ของประเทศไทยจริงหรือ *Has the IMF truly sustained the commercial life of Thailand?*
สภาพการณ์ situation, circumstances
สภาพคล่อง liquidity
สินทรัพย์สภาพคล่อง liquid assets
สภาพนำ conductivity
มีสภาพดี in good condition

สภาวะ condition(s), life; nature

สม becoming; appropriate, suitable, right; together
สมการ equation
สมการกำลังสอง quadratic equation
สมคบ to conspire, plot, collude (with), be an accomplice (of), in collusion (with), in complicity (with)
สมคบคิด to conspire
สมควร should, worthy (of); proper, appropriate, fitting; good, right, just, fair; enough, reasonable
ไม่สมควร should not, inappropriate
สมควรแก่เวลา the time has come to..., to be time (to), enough said
สมควรอนุมัติ should be approved
สมคะเน as expected, as predicted
สมจริง realistic; truthful
สมใจนึก as anticipated, as expected, as thought
สมใจรัก one's heart's desire, what one loves เช่น *He married the girl who was his heart's desire. / He got the kind of work he loves.*
สมชื่อ to live up to one's name
สมทบ to add (to), contribute, join, augment
สมน้ำหน้า It serves (you) right., It's what (he) deserves.
สมประกอบ perfect; well-made

ส
ห
ฟ
อ
ฮ

ไม่สมประกอบ deformed, defective, abnormal; not all there, nutty

สมปรารถนา wished for, as desired, to be fulfilled

เธอได้ทุกสิ่งสมปรารถนา She got everything she wished for.

ท่านต้องการสิ่งใดขอให้สิ่งนั้นจงสำเร็จสมปรารถนาทุกประการ May everything you wish for be yours.

อยากได้อะไร ขอให้ได้สมปรารถนา May all your wishes be fulfilled.

สมยอม to consent, acquiesce; to connive (at, with, to)

สมรส to marry, wed

สมรู้ร่วมคิด to conspire, connive (at)

สมสู่ to cohabit, live together, have sexual relations

สมหวัง as hoped for, fulfilled

    ไม่สมหวัง disappointing

สมเหตุสมผล reasonable, logical, rational, reasoned, convincing

สมอ้าง to claim

    ให้สมกับ to befit, to be worthy of, suit

ส้ม orange; citrus fruit; sour

    ส้มโอ pomelo

    น้ำส้ม vinegar; orangeade, orange drink, orange juice

      น้ำส้มคั้น fresh orange juice

    สารส้ม alum

    สีส้ม orange

ส้มหล่น a windfall; to luck out *(US)*

สมญา name; nickname, sobriquet, epithet, cognomen

    สมญาทางการค้า tradename

สมณะ Buddhist recluse

    สมณเพศ Buddhist clergy, monkhood

    สมณศักดิ์ ecclesiastical title

สมเด็จ exalted, great, most excellent

สมถะ composed; content with what one has, modest, to lead a simple life.

เขาเป็นอยู่อย่างสมถะ He lives /simply/ modestly/. / He leads a simple life.

สมนาคุณ to return another's kindness

    ค่าสมนาคุณ honorarium

สมบัติ property; wealth; quality

    สมบัติผู้ดี qualities of a gentleman or lady, refined, good manners, fine qualities, nobility

เขาไม่มีสมบัติผู้ดี He's no gentleman. / He lacks refinement. / He is not well-bred.

    คุณสมบัติ qualifications; quality, characteristic, property; attribute; requirement

    ทรัพย์สมบัติ property, possessions, wealth

    ราชสมบัติ the throne

สมบุกสมบัน tough, rough

สมบูรณ์ complete, full; plentiful, abundant; perfect; healthy; to have put on weight

    สมบูรณ์แบบ complete, whole; exemplary; formal

สมบูรณาญาสิทธิราชย์ absolute monarchy

สมประดี, สมปฤดี, สมปฤๅดี conscious

    รู้สึกสมประดี to regain consciousness, come to

    สิ้นสมประดี unconscious

สมพงศ์ astrological compatibility

    ดวงสมพงศ์กัน to have compatible horoscopes, be well matched

สมเพช to take pity on, feel sorry for

    น่าสมเพช shameful, sad, deplorable, pitiful, shocking

สมภพ birth

    พระราชสมภพ royal birth

สมภาร abbot

สมโภช banquet, feast, celebration, festival; to celebrate

สมมต, สมมติ, สมมุติ to suppose, assume; hypothetical

    สมมติฐาน, สมมุติฐาน supposition, assumption, hypothesis

สมมุติว่า suppose, supposing, if (ตามด้วย had หรือ were เช่น *If I were you.*)

ที่สมมติขึ้น conjecture

สมรภูมิ battlefield, battleground

สมรรถภาพ ability, capability; efficiency

    ไร้สมรรถภาพ ineffective, incapable, incompetent, inefficient

    หมดสมรรถภาพ impotent

สมอ anchor

    ถอนสมอ to weigh anchor, raise an anchor

    ทอดสมอ to drop anchor, cast an anchor

สมอง brain

    สมองกล computer

    สมองดี to have a good mind, brainy

    สมองทึบ thick-headed, dim-witted

    สมองใส bright, clear-minded

    สมองไหล brain drain

สมัค, สมัคร to volunteer, enlist; to apply; to consent

    สมัครงาน to apply for a job

    สมัครใจ to be willing

        ด้วยความสมัครใจ willingly, voluntarily

        โดยสมัครใจ voluntary, voluntarily

        ไม่สมัครใจ unwilling, unconsenting, reluctant

    สมัครพรรคพวก colleagues, friends, volunteers

    สมัครเล่น amateur

    ใบสมัคร application

        ยื่นใบสมัคร to submit an application

สมัชชา meeting, assembly

    สมัชชาใหญ่ general assembly

สมัญญา see **สมญา** หน้า 478

สมัย time, period, age, era; when

    สมัยกลาง Middle Ages

    สมัยก่อน formerly, in previous times

    สมัยก่อนประวัติศาสตร์ prehistory

    สมัยเก่า old-fashioned

    สมัยเดียวกัน contemporary, contempo-

raneous

    สมัยนี้ currently, nowadays, at the present time, at present

    สมัยพระเจ้าเหา old as Adam

    สมัยหัวเลี้ยวหัวต่อ period of transition, critical time

    สมัยใหม่ modern, up-to-date

        หัวสมัยใหม่ modern, progressive (person)

    ทันสมัย up-to-date, modern, fashionable

    ร่วมสมัย contemporary

    ล้าสมัย out-dated, out of date, old-fashioned, dated, outmoded

    ล้ำสมัย advanced, radical, ahead of one's time

    หมดสมัย obsolete, antiquated, behind the times, old hat, out of date, passé

สมา to apologize, ask for forgiveness

สมาคม society, association; to associate (with)

    สมาคมลับ secret society

    สมาคมหนังสือพิมพ์ Press Association

สมาชิก member

    สมาชิกกิตติมศักดิ์ honorary member

    สมาชิกตลอดชีพ life member

    สมาชิกภาพ membership

    สมาชิกวิสามัญ extraordinary member

    สมาชิกสภาผู้แทนราษฎร member of parliament, MP

    สมาชิกสามัญ ordinary member

สมาทาน to undertake to observe

    สมาทานศีล to undertake to observe the precepts

สมาธิ concentration, meditation, one-pointedness of mind

    ขัดสมาธิ to sit cross-legged

    นั่งสมาธิ to practice a sitting meditation

    ฝึกสมาธิ to practice /concentration/meditation/

สมาน to join, connect, unite, bind; to close, heal

    สมานฉันท์ unanimous

ส
ห
ฬ
อ
ฮ

สมานผิว (an) astringent (for the skin)

สมานแผล to heal, close (ใช้กับ wound, incision, cut etc)

สมาส compound word

สม่ำเสมอ regularly, constantly, always; evenly

สมี appellation for a monk who has committed a serious offence, miscreant monk

สมุด book, notebook, pad

สมุดเงินสด cash book

สมุดฉีก note pad, scratch pad

สมุดเช็ค checkbook

สมุดไทย Thai style book, folded page book

สมุดโน้ต notebook

สมุดบัญชี account book

สมุดบันทึก diary, record book

สมุดพก report card

สมุดภาพ picture album

สมุดเยี่ยม visitors book

สมุดวาดเขียน drawing pad

หอสมุด library

ห้องสมุด study, library

สมุทร sea, ocean

คาบสมุทร peninsula

มหาสมุทร ocean

เรือเดินสมุทร oceangoing /ship/vessel/

สมุน henchman, underling; follower; lackey, flunky

สมุนไพร medicinal herb, herbal medicine

ยาสมุนไพร herbal /medicine/remedy/

สมุห์บัญชี accountant

สมุห์บัญชีใหญ่ chief accountant

สโมสร club

สโมสรทหาร army club

สโมสรสันนิบาต social function, party, reception

งานสโมสร party

สยดสยอง ghastly, terrifying, horrible, gruesome

สยบ to capitulate, bow one's head; to overpower, defeat

สยบหัวให้ to bow down (to), submit (to)

สยอง frightening

สยองขวัญ hair-raising, terrifying, horrifying, grisly; horrified

สยาม Siam, Siamese

สยาย to undo, let down

สยายผม to let one's hair down, undo one's hair

สยิว thrilling, electrifying; hair-raising

สรง to bathe; to pour water over someone ceremonially

สรงน้ำพระ to do the ritual bathing of monks

สรณะ refuge

ถือเป็นสรณะ to attach importance (to)

อย่าถือเป็นสรณะ Don't attach too much importance to that.

สรร to choose, select, pick

สรรแสร้ง to pretend, dissimulate

เลือกสรร selected

สรรค์ to create, construct, build

สรรค์สร้าง to create, construct, build

สรรพ every, entire, all, whole

สรรพคุณ qualities, qualifications, properties; indications (เฉพาะยา)

สรรพนาม pronoun

สรรพวิทยา all learning

สรรพสัตว์ sentient beings, animal kingdom

สรรพสิ่ง all things, every thing

เสร็จสรรพ finished, all done, all over

ห้างสรรพสินค้า department store

สรรพสามิต excise

สรรพากร revenue

สรรพางค์ body, physique

สรรเสริญ to praise, laud, extol

สรรเสริญเยินยอ to adulate

น่าสรรเสริญ praiseworthy, admirable, commendable

เพลงสรรเสริญพระบารมี royal anthem

สรวง sky, paradise, heaven; celestial being

สรวล, สรวลเส to laugh; mirthful

สร้อย[1] mane; ruff; necklace

    สร้อยคอ necklace, chain

สร้อย[2] *as in* **สร้อยคำ** alliterative word added for euphony or emphasis

    สร้อยเพลง refrain, chorus

    สร้อยเศร้า downcast, disconsolate, melancholy

สระ[1] pond, pool

    สระน้ำ pool, pond

    สระว่ายน้ำ swimming pool

สระ[2] sound; vowel

สระ[3] to wash, shampoo

    สระผม to /shampoo/wash/ one's hair, have a shampoo

สร่าง to lessen, abate, subside, go down

    สร่างไข้ to get over a fever, The fever has gone down.

    สร่างเมา to get sober, sober up

    เมาไม่สร่าง still drunk, still under the influence (of alcohol)

    สวยไม่สร่าง still beautiful, to have lasting beauty

สร้าง to build, construct, erect, make, create, establish

    สร้างกรรม to do what is bound to have repercussions, create karma; to be disastrous

    สร้างกุศล to do good works, perform meritorious deeds

    สร้างขึ้น to be built

    สร้างงาน to make work

    สร้างชาติ to build up the nation

    สร้างชื่อเสียง to build one's reputation

    สร้างตัว to establish oneself

    สร้างตัวเอง self-made

    สร้างโลก to create the world

    สร้างวิมานในอากาศ to build castles in the air

    สร้างศัตรู to make enemies

สร้างสรรค์ constructive

    สร้างอนาคต to build for one's future

    ก่อสร้าง to construct, build; construction, building

    โครงสร้าง structure, framework, skeleton; arrangement

    จัดสร้าง to build, establish, set up

สรีระ body

    สรีรวิทยา physiology

    สรีรศาสตร์ physiology

สรุป, สรุป to summarize, sum up, recapitulate

    สรุปข่าว news summary

    สรุปความ resume, summary

    สรุปความเห็น to conclude

    สรุปผล to summarize results, sum up

    บทสรุป conclusion

สลด saddened

    สลดใจ sad, dismayed

สลบ be unconscious, lose consciousness, pass out

    สลบไสล unconscious, dead to the world

    สลบเหมือด knocked unconscious

    ยาสลบ anesthetic

สลอน conspicuous, all seeking to be noticed

    ชูหน้าสลอน all looking expectantly

สละ to renounce, relinquish, give up, waive

    สละชีพเพื่อชาติ to sacrifice one's life for one's country

    สละราชสมบัติ to abdicate (the throne)

    สละสิทธิ์ to /give up/renounce/waive/ one's right

    เสียสละ to sacrifice, give up (something)

สละสลวย beautiful

สลัก to carve, chisel out; bolt, pin, peg

    สลักเกลียว bolt

    สลักเพชร retaining pin, linchpin; hips, buttocks

    สลักเสลา exquisite; to do beautiful carving

    สลักหลัง to endorse

ส
ห
ฬ
อ
ฮ

แกะสลัก to carve; to engrave

สลักสำคัญ significant, important

สลัด[1] salad

น้ำสลัด salad dressing

สลัด[2] pirate

สลัดอากาศ air pirate

โจรสลัด pirate; hijacker

สลัด[3] to shake off, shed, get rid of, cast off

สลัดขน to shed (its) fur

สลัดทิ้ง to cast off

สลัดใบ to shed (its) leaves

สลัดผ้า to shake out the clothes

สลัดฝุ่น to shake off the dust

สลัดรองเท้า to kick off (one's) shoes

สลัดรัก to stop loving, reject someone (who has been close)

สลับ to alternate, switch, swap, exchange, change; alternating; every other

สลับกัน alternate

สลับซับซ้อน complicated, complex

สลับไพ่ to shuffle the cards

สลับสี variegated, multicolored

ไฟสลับ alternating current

สลัว dim, indistinct, faint; hazy

แสงไฟสลัว dimly lit, dim light

สลาก label; lots, lottery ticket

สลากกินแบ่ง lottery, government lottery

สลากกินรวบ private lottery, sweepstake

จับสลาก to draw lots

สล้าง splendid, lofty, high

ดอกไม้ชูช่อสล้าง showy array of flowers, splendid flowers

อกสล้าง high ample breasts, splendid /breasts/bosom/

สลาย decay, dissolve, fall apart, disintegrate, break up, dissipate

สลายม็อบ to disperse the mob

จนฟ้าดินสลาย forever, until the end of time, eternally

แตกสลาย to go to pieces, crumble, dissolve, break (up, apart)

ฝันสลาย dreams come to nought, shattered dreams

สลึง 25 satang; a quarter of a baht

สลุต salute

ยิงสลุต to fire a salute

สวด to recite, chant; to ball (someone) out, call (someone) down (for doing something), give (someone) a dressing down

สวดมนต์ to chant; to pray

สวดยับ to be castigated, hauled over the coals

สวดศพ to do funeral chanting; perform funeral rites

สวน[1] garden, orchard, plantation; park; home-grown

สวนครัว kitchen garden

สวนดอกไม้ flower garden

สวนผลไม้ orchard

สวนผัก vegetable garden

สวนพฤกษศาสตร์ botanical garden

สวนมะม่วง mango /grove/orchard/

สวนสนุก amusement park

สวนสัตว์ zoo, zoological garden

สวนสาธารณะ public park

กล้วยสวน home-grown bananas

สวน[2] to pass in opposite directions, counter (to); to /give/have/ an enema

สวนกระแส to go counter (to), ignore

สวนทวาร to /have/give/ an enema

สวนทาง at cross-purposes, to run counter to

สวนปัสสาวะ to do a urinary catheterization

การสวนปัสสาวะ urinary catheterization

สวนสนาม to parade, pass in review

สวนหมัด to give a counter /blow/punch/

ไต่สวน to conduct a hearing, hold an inquiry, inquire into, investigate

สอบสวน to question, interrogate, examine

สืบสวน to investigate, conduct an investigation

ส่วน portion, share; section, part, piece, element; as for, as to, regarding, with regard to

ส่วนกลาง central

ส่วนกว้าง width, breadth

ส่วนกำหนด ration

ส่วนเกิน surplus, excess; additional, in addition

ส่วนเฉลี่ย average, on the whole; portion, share

ส่วนได้ส่วนเสีย interest

ส่วนตัว personal, private

ส่วนน้อย minority, a small /part/portion/

ส่วนบุคคล private

ส่วนแบ่ง share, portion, part, quota, division/

ส่วนประกอบ component

ส่วนผสม ingredient, component, constituent, contents

ส่วนภูมิภาค provincial, rural

ส่วนมาก mostly, for the most part, mainly; usually, generally, as a rule

ส่วนยาว length

ส่วนรวม common, public, general

ส่วนลด discount, reduction

ส่วนสัด shape, figure; proportions; measurements

ส่วนสูง height

ส่วนหนา thickness

ส่วนใหญ่ a majority (of), most; mostly, for the most part, mainly; bigger; important

ตามส่วน proportionately, in proportion

ปันส่วน to ration; to apportion, share

มีส่วน to take part (in), have a share (in), be partly responsible (for)

มีส่วนช่วย to contribute (to)

สัดส่วน proportions; measurements, size

หุ้นส่วน partner

สวม to put on, wear, don; to assume

สวมกอด to embrace, hug

สวมเขา to cuckold, be cuckolded

สวมตอ to pass something off (as something else)

สวมตำแหน่ง to /assume/take over/ the position

สวมนิ้ว to put on, wear (a ring)

สวมมงกุฎ to crown, wear a crown

สวมรองเท้า to wear shoes

สวมรอย to take someone's place, pretend to be someone else

สวมแว่น to wear glasses

สวมเสื้อ to put on a /shirt/blouse/, wear a shirt, have a shirt on

ไม่สวมหมวก hatless

ส้วม toilet, water closet, lavatory; outhouse

สวย pretty, attractive, good-looking, nice-looking; dry and fluffy (rice)

ส่วย tribute, tax; bribe; a people of northeastern Thailand

ส่งส่วย to pay tribute; to service

สวรรค์ heaven, paradise

สวรรค์ชั้นฟ้า heaven, celestial world

สรวงสวรรค์ heaven, paradise

สวรรคต to die (royal word)

สวะ floating weeds; trash, trashy, worthless

ปัดสวะ irresponsible

ฝีมือชั้นสวะ trashy workmanship

สวัสดิ์, สวัสดี goodness, virtue, beauty, prosperity, progress; a word of greeting เช่น Hello, Good morning, Good afternoon. Good evening. How do you do?

ความสุขสวัสดี well-being

ราตรีสวัสดิ์ good evening

อรุณสวัสดิ์ good morning

สวัสดิภาพ well-being, welfare, good; safety

โดยสวัสดิภาพ safe and sound, safely, good

ขอให้เดินทางโดยสวัสดิภาพ I hope you have a good trip.

ส
ห
ฬ
อ
ฮ

สวัสติกะ swastika

สว่าง light, bright, clear, apparent

สว่างจิต out of the closet, in the open

สว่างจ้า bright, brilliant

สว่างไสว brightly lit, all lit up, brightly illuminated; shining brightly

แสงสว่าง light

สวาท as in เล่นสวาท to make love, play around

สว่าน drill, auger, bit, gimlet

สวาปาม to wolf (down), eat greedily, devour ravenously

สวามิภักดิ์ to give one's allegiance (to)

สวิง[1] small fishnet

สวิง[2] swing

สวิงหมัด swinging punch

สวิงสวาย to feel faint, feel giddy, dizzy

ขับรถสวิงสวาย to drive wildly

เป็นลมสวิงสวาย to feel faint

ส.ส. M.P. (Member of Parliament)

สสาร matter

สสารวัตถุ material object

สหกรณ์ cooperative

สหชาติ born on the same date

สหประชาชาติ United Nations

สหพันธ์ federation

สหภาพ union

สหรัฐอเมริกา United States of America

สหราชอาณาจักร United Kingdom

สหวิทยาการ as in แบบสหวิทยาการ interdisciplinary (research)

สหศึกษา coeducation, co-ed

สหาย comrade; man, fellow, boys; associate

ส่อ to suggest, indicate, point to, hint at; to evince, show

ส่อเค้า to show signs (of), suggest, indicate

ส่อเจตนา to /evince/show/ an intention

ส่อทุจริต to /suggest/intimate/ dishonesty

ส่อนิสัย to evince one's /nature/character/

ส่อพิรุธ suspicious, questionable, to look

wrong

สอง two, double, dual

สองคม double-edged

สองครั้ง twice, two times

สองแง่สองง่าม equivocal, ambiguous; a double entendre

สองจิตสองใจ undecided, of two minds, haven't made up one's mind

ฉันยังสองจิตสองใจอยู่ I haven't made up my mind yet. / I am still undecided.

สองใจ unfaithful, two-timing

คนสองใจ two-timer

สองต่อสอง alone, in private, secretly

สองที twice

สองเท่า double, twice as much

สองนัย equivocal, ambiguous, double meaning, in two ways

สองพัน two thousand

สองล้อ bicycle; two-wheeled

สองสามนาที a few minutes

สองแสน two hundred thousand

สองหน twice, two times, over again

สองหน้า two-faced

ตีสองหน้า hypocritical, to be two-faced, double-dealing, duplicitous

ส่อง to peer, look; to shine a light (on), illuminate

ส่องกระจก to look in the mirror

ส่องกล้องทางไกล to use binoculars

ส่องดู to peer (at), observe, watch

ส่องทาง to light the way

ส่องไฟ to shine a light (on, at)

ส่องแสง to shine, glow; to illuminate

ส่องหน้า to shine (a light) in someone's eyes; to look at one's face

ส้องสุม to gather clandestinely; to amass secretly

ส้องเสพ to associate (with)

สอด to insert, penetrate, slip in; to enclose

สอดกลางคัน to butt in, interrupt, intervene

สอดคล้อง consistent (with), in line with, in

keeping (with), in conformity with, compatible (with)

ไม่สอดคล้อง inconsistent, incompatible (with), not /in keeping/in line/ with

สอดแทรก to interfere; to introduce; to permeate; pervasive

สอดรู้สอดเห็น to pry; nosy, prying, inquisitive

สอดสี in color

สอดใส่ to put on, wear

สอดไส้ stuffed, with a filling; slipped in, added surreptitiously

สอดแนม to spy (on), reconnoiter, gather intelligence

สอดส่อง to watch over, keep watch, keep an eye on

สอน to teach, instruct; to tell someone what to do

อย่ามาสอนฉันนะ Don't tell me what to do! / Don't lecture me!

สอนพูด to start to speak

สอนมวย to humble (someone), tame

สอนศาสนา to preach, engage in missionary activities, proselytize, teach religion

ส่อน (to have a) squint, cast of the eye

สอบ to verify, inquire, to compare; to examine, test, take an examination; tapered; converging

สอบเก็บคะแนน to take a quiz; formative examination

สอบข้อเขียน to take a written examination

สอบแข่งขัน to take a competitive examination

สอบเชาวน์ aptitude test

สอบซ่อม to take a re-examination, take an examination over again

สอบซ้อม to give a test, take a test

สอบได้ to pass (an exam)

สอบตก to fail (an exam)

สอบถาม to inquire, make an inquiry, ask, question

สอบทาน to verify, to proofread, collate

สอบบัญชี to audit (accounts), do an audit

สอบปากคำ to question, examine

สอบไล่ to take a final examination; /final/ summative/ examination

สอบสวน to question, interrogate, examine

สอบสัมภาษณ์ *see* **สอบสัมภาษณ์** *หน้า 492*

การสอบสัมภาษณ์ interview

การสอบเข้ามหาวิทยาลัย university entrance /exam/examination/

การสอบปากเปล่า oral examination

การสอบระหว่างเรียน test, quiz, formative examination

การสอบไล่ final examination

การสอบวัดผล final /exam/examination/

ข้อสอบ test, exam, examination, quiz, examination /questions/problems/

สอพลอ to flatter; curry favor (with), toady (to)

คนสอพลอ sycophant, flatterer, bootlicker, toady

ส้อม fork

สอย to pick with a long pole; to hem, stitch

สอยดาว with one's nose in the air

หมัดสอยดาว an uppercut to the chin

สอยผ้า to hem, sew by hand, finish by stitching

สอยมือ handstitched

ส่อเสียด to create dissension; to /slander/ discredit/ (to stir up dissension or discord)

สะกด to restrain, check, control (oneself); to suppress; to spell; to add a final voiced consonant; to put to sleep

สะกดจิต to hypnotize

สะกดใจ to /restrain/control/ oneself, suppress one's emotions

สะกดรอย to track (down), trail, trace

สะกดอกสะกดใจ *see* **สะกดใจ**

สะกิด to nudge, poke; to scratch (something) off

สะกิดใจ to remind, jog one's memory

สะเก็ด fragment, chip, splinter, shrapnel

    สะเก็ดแผล scab

    สะเก็ดระเบิด shrapnel

สะเงาะสะแงะ with a stagger

    เดินสะเงาะสะแงะ to stagger (along, down the street, etc)

สะใจ satisfied, glad; I like that !

    ไม่สะใจ disappointed

สะดม *as in* **ปล้นสะดม** to pillage, sack, plunder, commit gang robbery

สะดวก easy, convenient; smoothly

    โปรดอำนวยความสะดวกให้ด้วย Anything you can do to facilitate (the trip etc) will be appreciated. / Please render assistance.

    สะดวกสบาย comfortable; easy; with all facilities

    โดยสะดวก easily, readily, conveniently

    ไม่สะดวก inconvenient

    ขออภัยในความไม่สะดวก Sorry for the inconvenience.

สะดิ้ง affected, cutesy; vivacious, full of verve; effeminate, swishy, fay

สะดึง embroidery hoop

สะดือ navel; umbilical cord

    สะดือจุ่น protruding navel

    สะดือทะเล maelstrom

สะดุ้ง to be startled, alarmed, taken by surprise, be given a start

    สะดุ้งตื่น to wake with a start

    สะดุ้งสะเทือน to be shaken (by), taken aback (by)

        ไม่สะดุ้งสะเทือน unmoved, imperturbable, unshaken

    สะดุ้งเฮือก to be taken by surprise, startled (out of one's wits)

สะดุด to stumble, trip

    สะดุดใจ to make one think; catch one's attention; to remind someone of something

    สะดุดตา striking, eye-catching

สะดุดเท้า to trip over something, stub one's toe

สะเด็ด to dry out; super, awfully, extremely

    ข้าวสะเด็ดน้ำ boiled rice from which the excess moisture has been removed, fluffy boiled rice

สะเดาะ to unlock (something) by magic

    สะเดาะเคราะห์ to dispel ill fortune, exorcise misfortune, ward off bad luck by incantation

สะเต๊ะ satay, brochette

    หมูสะเต๊ะ pork satay, pork brochette, pork on a brochette

สะทกสะท้าน frightened, perturbed

    ไม่สะทกสะท้าน unabashed, unperturbed, composed

สะท้อน to reflect, rebound, bounce (up, back)

    สะท้อนใจ to be saddened, dismayed (by)

    ผลสะท้อน consequence, result, secondary effect, after-effect

    สีสะท้อนแสง reflective paint, luminous color

    เสียงสะท้อน echo; reverberation; repercussions

สะท้าน to tremble, shiver, quiver, quake, shake; to reverberate, thunder

    สะท้านโลก world-shaking

สะเทินน้ำสะเทินบก amphibious

    สัตว์สะเทินน้ำสะเทินบก amphibian

สะเทือน, สะเทื้อน to shake, tremble, vibrate; to affect

    สะเทือนใจ to affect, hurt (someone)

สะบักสะบอม badly bruised, given a drubbing

สะบัด to shake, flick, brush (away, off)

    สะบัดก้น to have a provocative little walk, ass wagging

        สะบัดก้นหนี to walk off in a huff, leave in a huff

        เดินสะบัดก้น to waggle along

    สะบัดร้อนสะบัดหนาว to have hot and cold flashes

สะบัดสะบิ้ง affected, artificial, pretentious; huffy

สะบัดหน้า to turn away; give one's head a toss (of annoyance, pique, etc)

สะบั้น to break, snap; an awful lot, like anything, like a house afire

สะบั้นหั่นแหลก wildly, to fever pitch, like madmen, tremendous (fight, argument etc)

ขาดสะบั้น to be severed, snap, break apart

หักสะบั้น to snap; to collapse

สะบ้า kneecap

สะพรั่ง in profusion

สะพรึงกลัว horrible

สะพรีบ en masse

สะพัด to run, flow; all over

เดินสะพัด current (account)

แพร่สะพัด to spread like wildfire, circulate, spread widely

สะพาน bridge; pier, wharf

สะพานแขวน suspension bridge

สะพานเทียบอากาศยาน aerobridge, pier, rampway

สะพานลอย overpass, flyover

ทอดสะพาน to make it easy (for someone to do something), show willingness; to /throw /build/ a bridge (over), to bridge

ราวสะพาน railing

สะพาย to wear over the shoulder

สะพายแล่ง to wear across the chest

สนสะพาย, สนตะพาย to put a cord through the nose of a /bull/buffalo/, to lead someone around by the nose

สะเพร่า careless, negligent, clumsy (of someone)

สะโพก hips, rump

สะใภ้ in-law

ลูกสะใภ้ daughter-in-law

สะลึมสะลือ half-awake

สะสม to accumulate, save, amass, save up, collect, build up

บัญชีสะสม savings account, thrift account

สะสวย pretty, nice-looking, attractive

สะสาง to clear up, finish up

สะเหร่อ like a jerk; inept

สะอาด clean, pure; innocent, guiltless; healthy

สะอาดตา nice-looking, pleasant looking, to look neat and clean; to have clean lines

สะอาดสะอ้าน clean-looking; spotless, clean

สะอาดหมดจด immaculate

สะอิดสะเอียน disgusting, sickening, revolting; revolted; to feel disgusted; to feel queasy, squeamish

สะอึก to hiccup; to catch (someone) up
คำพูดของเขาทำให้ผมสะอึก What he said caught me up.

สะอึกเข้าใส่ to rush at someone

สะอึกสะอื้น to sob

สะอื้น to sob

สะอื้นไห้ to sob, cry, weep

สะเอว waist

สะเออะ to meddle, poke one's nose into (other peoples' business etc)

สะโอดสะอง willowy

สัก[1] to spear, stab, pierce; to tattoo

สัก[2] just; about, only

สักครั้ง just once

สักแต่ mere, merely, just, only; any old way
ถ้วยชามไม่สะอาดเลยเธอ สักแต่ว่าล้าง These dishes aren't clean at all; you're doing them any old way.

สักแต่ว่าทำ for form's sake, perfunctory

สักเท่าไหร่ about how much

สักนิด just a bit

สักพัก for a while

สักหน่อย a little

สัก[3] teak

ไม้สัก teak, teakwood

สักการะ to worship

สักขีพยาน witness

สักวา a kind of poetry

สักหลาด wool, woolen

สั่ง to order, command, instruct; to /leave/ give/ a message

　สั่งการ to give instructions, leave orders

　สั่งขี้มูก to blow one's nose

　สั่งงด to cancel

　สั่งจ่าย to authorize payment

　สั่งลา to say goodbye, bid farewell

　สั่งสม see **สะสม** หน้า 487

　สั่งสอน to teach, admonish, give someone a lesson

　สั่งสินค้า to order, place an order (for)

　สั่งเสีย to give parting instructions

　ใบสั่ง ticket, police summons

　รับสั่ง to say

　หมายสั่ง court order

สังกะสี zinc; galvanized iron, corrugated iron

สังกัด to belong (to), be affiliated with, affiliation

สังเกต to notice, observe; to note, remark

　สังเกตการณ์ to observe

　สังเกตง่าย readily visible, easily seen, obvious, prominent

　สังเกตเห็น noticeable; to notice, see, observe

　ข้อสังเกต comment, observation, remarks

　ช่างสังเกต observant

　น่าสังเกต it should be noted (that)

　ผิดสังเกต noticeably, unusually, remarkably; not look right, to look funny

　พึงสังเกต it should be noted (that), note that, notice that

สังข์ conch

สังขยา egg custard

สังขาร body, self; conditioned things; body and soul

　สังขารทั้งหลายไม่เที่ยงแท้ All conditioned things are impermanent.

สังเขป concise, abridged, outline

　โดยสังเขป in brief, in short

(อธิบาย) พอเป็นสังเขป (explain) /briefly/ concisely/, to outline

สังคม society, social

　สังคมชั้นสูง high society

　สังคมนิยม socialist

　สังคมมนุษย์ human society

　สังคมโลก world social order

　สังคมวิทยา sociology

　สังคมศาสตร์ social sciences

　สังคมศึกษา social studies

　สังคมสงเคราะห์ social welfare

　สาวสังคม socialite, society girl

　ทางสังคม social

สังคายนา Buddhist Council for Collation of the Tipitaka; to review and revise; to give someone a talking to, get after someone to improve himself

สังคีต music

　สังคีตศาลา music hall

　สังคีตศิลป์ musical arts

สังเคราะห์ synthetic

สังฆ Sangha see **สงฆ์** หน้า 473

สังฆกรรม religious office performed by four or more monks within temple precincts, official Buddhist ceremony

สังฆการี Religious Affairs Department officers

สังฆทาน offerings dedicated to the Sangha

สังฆเภท schism

สังฆราช as in **สมเด็จพระสังฆราช** Supreme Patriarch

สังฆาฏิ outer robe (of a monk) folded and worn over the left shoulder

สังวร to take heed

　สังวรไว้ to bear in mind

　ข้อพึงสังวร lesson (for someone), a good lesson, something to keep in mind

สังวาล breast chain

สังวาส to make love, have sexual intercourse; to cohabit; to copulate

สังเวช to feel sorry (for), feel pity (for)

น่าสังเวช pathetic, sad, dreadful, deplorable, pitiful

สังเวย to sacrifice; to make an offering

เครื่องสังเวย offering, components of an offering

สังเวียน cockpit, enclosure for cock-fighting, arena

เจนสังเวียน veteran, old hand (at), practiced

สังสรรค์ to socialize, get together, meet informally

พบปะสังสรรค์ get together, have a social gathering, have a party

สังหรณ์ to have a premonition, foreboding

ลางสังหรณ์ omen, portent

สังหาร to kill, destroy, annihilate

สังหาริมทรัพย์ movable property, personal property

สัจ, สัจจะ truth, verity; integrity

สัจธรรม truth, reality

สัจวาจา true speech

สัญจร to travel, pass (along); to wander, roam

สัญจรไปมา to travel back and forth

ทางสัญจร passage

สัญชาตญาณ instinct

สัญชาติ nationality, citizenship

สัญญา contract, agreement, accord; to promise, undertake, agree to, give one's word, promise; perception, recognition; memory
สัญญาว่าจะไม่ทำอย่างนี้อีก Promise me you won't do it again.

สัญญาเช่า lease

สัญญาบัตร commission

สัญญาประชาคม social contract

ข้าราชการชั้นสัญญาบัตร commissioned /officer/official/

สัญญาหยุดยิง cease-fire accord

ข้อสัญญา /clause/paragraph/term/(of an agreement)

คำมั่นสัญญา promise, undertaking, pledge

เซ็นสัญญา to sign a /contract/agreement/, execute a contract

ทำสัญญา to /make/enter/ a contract

ผิดสัญญา to commit a breach of contract, violate a contract, break a /contract/ promise/

สนธิสัญญา treaty

หนังสือสัญญา written /contract/agreement/

อนุสัญญา convention

สัญญาณ signal

สัญญาณฉุกเฉิน emergency alarm

สัญญาณปลอดภัย all clear signal

สัญญาณไฟ traffic light, signal light; signal fire

สัญญาณไฟจราจร traffic light

สัญญาณภัย alarm

สัญญาณภัยทางอากาศ air raid warning

สัญญาณรบกวน disturbance, disturbed signal

ให้สัญญาณรบกวน to signal

สัญประกาศ underline

ข้อความตามที่สัญประกาศ underlined text

สัญลักษณ์ symbol, sign, token

สัญลักษณ์สาธารณสนเทศ public information symbols

สัณฐาน description, appearance, build

สัณฐานสันทัด medium build

สัดส่วน proportion(s); see **ส่วนสัด** *หน้า 483*

สัดหลวง a unit of volume equal to 20 liters

สัตย์ pledge, oath; honesty, probity; truth

ความซื่อสัตย์ fidelity, loyalty

ซื่อสัตย์ faithful, true, loyal, devoted (to); honest, upright

เสียสัตย์ to be disloyal, unfaithful; to break one's promise, be untrue (to), go back on one's /word/pledge/

สัตยาธิษฐาน vow

สัตยาบัน ratification

สัตยาบันสาร instrument of ratification

ให้สัตยาบัน to ratify

สัตว์ animal, beast

สัตว์กินนม mammal

สัตว์กินเนื้อ Carnivora, carnivore, carnivorous animal

สัตว์กินผัก Herbivora, herbivore

สัตว์กินแมลง Insectivora, insectivore

สัตว์กินหญ้า Graminivora, graminivorous animal

สัตว์ครึ่งบกครึ่งน้ำ amphibian

สัตว์เดียรัจฉาน animal

สัตว์ต่าง pack animal

สัตว์ที่มีขน fur-bearing animal, hairy animal

สัตว์น้ำ aquatic animal

สัตว์บก terrestrial animal

สัตว์ป่า wild animal

สัตว์พาหนะ riding animal, beast of burden, draft animal

สัตว์มีสันหลัง vertebrate

สัตว์ไม่มีฟัน Edentata

สัตว์ไม่มีสันหลัง invertebrate

สัตว์ร้าย predator, ferocious animal

สัตว์เลี้ยง domestic animal; pet

สัตว์เลี้ยงลูกด้วยนม mammal

สัตว์เลื้อยคลาน Reptilia, reptile

สัตว์เศรษฐกิจ economic animal

สัตว์สองเท้า biped

สัตว์สี่เท้า quadruped, four-legged animal

ขนสัตว์ fur, bristles, hair of an animal

เนื้อสัตว์ meat

ปศุสัตว์ animal husbandry; livestock, domestic animals

สัตวแพทย์ veterinarian, veterinary, doctor of veterinary medicine

สัตวแพทยศาสตร์ veterinary medicine

สัตววิทยา zoology

นักสัตววิทยา zoologist

สัน ridge, spine

สันเขา ridge of a mountain, crest

สันดอน bar

สันมีด back of a knife

สันหนังสือ spine of a book

สันหลัง spine, backbone, spinal column

สั่น to ring; to shake, vibrate; to shiver, tremble, quiver

สั่นคลอน shaky

ถูกสั่นคลอน to be undermined (by)

สั่นระฆัง to sound the bell

สั่นศีรษะ to shake one's head

ใจสั่น see ใจสั่น หน้า 126

ตัวสั่น to shiver

สั้น short

สั้นจู๋ extra short

ขาสั้น short-legged

กางเกงขาสั้น shorts

แขนสั้น short sleeves; short-armed

เสื้อแขนสั้น short sleeve shirt

คลื่นสั้น shortwave

ปืนสั้น pistol

ผ่อนสั้นผ่อนยาว adaptable, flexible, willing to make concessions

เรื่องสั้น short story

สายตาสั้น shortsighted, nearsighted, nearsightedness

สันดาน bad instincts, bad character; inborn characteristics, trait, instincts

สันดานดิบ raw instincts

ดัดสันดาน to reform, correct, train

โรงเรียนดัดสันดาน reform school, reformatory, training school

สันดาป roasting, burning; a pit of hell

สันดาปใน internal combustion

สันโดษ contentment; contented, satisfied with what one has, undemanding

สันตะปาปา pope, pontiff

สันติ peace

สันติบาล Central Bureau of Investigation

สันติภาพ peace

สันติวิธี peaceful means

สันติสุข peace and happiness

สันถวไมตรี goodwill, friendship

สันทัด to be good at something, expert (in), familiar with; of medium build, compact

สันนิบาต[1] league, congregation, assembly

สันนิบาตชาติ League of Nations

สันนิบาตอาหรับ Arab League

สันนิบาต[2] ague

สันนิวาส cohabitation

บุพเพสันนิวาส to be meant for each other, be predestined to marry, a preordained marriage; cohabitation

สันนิษฐาน to assume, presume, infer, surmise

ข้อสันนิษฐาน assumption, presumption, inference

สันสกฤต Sanskrit

สับ to chop, mince; to exchange, switch; to hook, goad

สับไก to pull the trigger

สับที่ to change places

สับเปลี่ยน to replace, substitute; to /switch/ change/ places, take turns, alternate

สับไพ่ to shuffle (cards)

สับราง to switch the tracks, throw a track switch

สับรางให้ดีเดี๋ยวรถไฟชนกัน Switch the tracks right or you'll have a collision.

สับสน to be confused, to be mixed up

สับสนอลหม่าน helter-skelter

สับหลีก to switch (by, over), by-pass; to manage to avoid (an unwanted encounter), avoid one another

หมูสับ /chopped/minced/ pork

สับปลับ to be slippery, devious

สับปหงก nodding (off to sleep), drowsy

สับปะรด pineapple

สับปะรังเค junky

สัปคับ howdah

สัปดน ribald, bawdy, suggestive, racy, risque

สัปดาห์ week

รายสัปดาห์ weekly

สัประยุทธ์ to go into battle, take up the fight

สัปหงก to doze off, be drowsy, nod

นั่งสัปหงก to sit there nodding /with drowsiness/drowsily/

สัปเหร่อ undertaker, mortician

สัพพัญญู omniscient; the Omniscient One (the Buddha)

สัพเพเหระ miscellaneous, sundry; insignificant, trivial, trifling

สัพยอก to tease, jest, pull someone's leg, be fooling

สัมปชัญญะ *as in* **สติสัมปชัญญะ** awareness

มีสติสัมปชัญญะสมบูรณ์ of sound mind

สัมปทาน concession

สัมประสิทธิ์ coefficient

สัมผัส to touch, contact; get to know, hobnob with; to rhyme

มีโอกาสสัมผัสกับชนชั้นสูง to have an opportunity to be in touch with the elite, / to have a chance to hobnob with the upper crust

สัมผัสนอก external rhyme

สัมผัสใน internal rhyme

สัมผัสสระ rhyming vowels

สัมผัสอักษร alliteration

เท่าที่ผมได้สัมผัสมา from my contacts with ..., my experience with.../shows/indicates/ etc

พิมพ์ดีดสัมผัส to touch-type

สัมพัทธ์ relative

ความจริงสัมพัทธ์ relative truth

ทฤษฎีสัมพัทธ์ theory of relativity

สัมพันธ์ relation(s), intercourse, connection(s)

สัมพันธ์ทางการทูต diplomatic relations

สัมพันธภาพ relations

สัมพันธมิตร allies

สัมพันธไมตรี /friendly/cordial/ relations, amity

มนุษยสัมพันธ์ human relations, social

ส
ห
ฬ
อ
ฮ

relations; personality

สัมภาระ baggage, things, stuff, equipment

สัมภาษณ์ to interview

    สอบสัมภาษณ์ to go for an interview, have an interview, be interviewed; to give an interview

สัมมนา seminar

สัมมาทิฐิ right /understanding/view/

สัมโมทนียกถา greeting, words of greeting

สัมฤทธิ์[1] to achieve, succeed, fulfill

    สัมฤทธิผล achievement; to achieve success

    เด็กด้อยสัมฤทธิ์ under-achiever

    ไม่สัมฤทธิผล unsuccessful, fruitless

สัมฤทธิ์[2] bronze

สัสดี recruiting officer

ส่า yeast

    ส่าเหล้า brewer's yeast

สาก[1] pestle

    สากกะเบือ kitchen pestle; a dumbbell

สาก[2] rough, coarse, raspy

    มือสาก rough hands

สากรรจ์ as in **สาหัสสากรรจ์** serious, grave

สากล international; generally accepted, universal; popular, western

    ชุดสากล coat and tie, suit, lounge suit, Western dress

    แบบสากล western; international

    เพลงสากล popular /song/music/, Western-style music

    มวยสากล international-style boxing, Western-style boxing

สาเก sake; breadfruit

สาแก่ใจ to be satisfied, do something to one's heart's content, take one's fill (of)

สาขา branch; department

    สาขาภาษาอังกฤษ English department

สาคู sago palm

สาง[1] ghost, spirit

    ผีสาง ghosts, spirits

สาง[2] to lighten, clear

    รุ่งสาง dawn

สาง[3] to clear up, sort out

    สางงาน to clear up a backlog of work, sort out what has to be done

    สางผม to comb out one's hair

สาด to throw water, splash (with water etc)

    สาดโคลน to do mudslinging

    สาดน้ำ to throw water (out, on, at)

    ฝนสาด to rain in

สาทิสลักษณ์ as in **พระบรมสาทิสลักษณ์** royal portrait

สาธก to cite as an example, illustrate

สาธยาย to recite, discourse (on, about); to chant; to relate at length

    สาธยายความผิดผมเสียยกใหญ่ She gave me a whole discourse on what I'd done wrong.

สาธารณ-, สาธารณะ public, common

    สาธารณชน the public

    สาธารณประโยชน์ (in the) public interest, (for the) public benefit

    สาธารณมติ public opinion

    สาธารณรัฐ republic

    สาธารณสุข public health

    สวนสาธารณะ park, public park

    ส้วมสาธารณะ public toilet

สาธารณ์ vile, base, depraved, Satanic

สาธารณูปโภค public utility

สาธิต to demonstrate

    โรงเรียนสาธิต demonstration school

สาธุ amen

    สาธุการ exclamation of approval, amen

    สาธุชน good man, virtuous person, upright person

        สาธุชนทั้งหลาย my good people

สาน to plait, weave

    สานต่อ to carry /on/forward/

    การจักสาน basketry, basketwork, wickerwork

    ช่างจักสาน basketmaker, matmaker, weaver

ก ข ค ฆ ง จ ฉ ช ซ ฌ ญ ฎ ฏ ฐ ฑ ฒ ณ ด ต ถ ท ธ น บ ป ผ ฝ พ ฟ ภ ม ย ร ฤ ฤๅ ล ว ศ ษ **ส**

of /mats/baskets/ etc

สานุศิษย์ students, disciples, pupils

สาบ[1] moldy smell; body odor, musky smell, animal smell

    เหม็นสาบ to have body odor, smelly

สาบ[2] *as in* ทะเลสาบ lake

สาบสูญ to disappear, to vanish

สาบาน to swear, take an oath

    ผมไม่ได้ทำ สาบานได้ I swear I didn't do it.

    สาบานตัว to be sworn in, take the oath, swear

สาป to curse, put a curse on someone, anathematize

    สาปแช่ง to curse, call down, curses upon, execrate

    ต้องคำสาป to be accursed, put under a curse

สาม three, tri-

    สามเกลอ manual pile driver

    สามขา tripod, three-legged

    สามขุม *as in* ย่างสามขุม to step forward aggressively

    สามครั้ง thrice, three times

    สามง่าม trident

    สามแฉก three-pointed, three-pronged, tridentate

    สามด้าน trilateral; three aspects

    สามตา method of fortune-telling

    สามเท่า triple, treble

    สามปี triennial

    สามพยางค์ trisyllabic

    สามภาษา trilingual, triglot

    สามล้อ trishaw, pedicab, samlor; tricycle; three-wheeled

        สามล้อเครื่อง motorized trishaw, three-wheeled taxi

    สามส่วน tripartite, in three parts

        กางเกงสามส่วน shorts

    สามสิบ thirty

    สามเส้า three-legged cooking stand; three-

note cooing; three-cornered (love affair, fight, etc)

    สามหน three times, thrice

    สามเหลี่ยมด้านเท่า equilateral triangle

    สามเหลี่ยมมุมฉาก right triangle

    สามเหลี่ยมหน้าจั่ว isoceles triangle

    ขั้นที่สาม third step

    ที่สาม third

สามเณร novice, samanera

สามหาว coarse, vulgar, boorish, offensive

สามัคคี unity, united, union; concord, harmony, community spirit

สามัญ regular, common, ordinary

    สามัญชน common /man/people/, ordinary folk

    สามัญศึกษา general education

        กรมสามัญศึกษา Department of General Education

    สามัญสำนึก common sense

สามานย์ vile, low, base

สามารถ to be able, capable, have the ability (to)

    สามารถที่จะ can, able to

    ความสามารถ ability, capability

        เต็มความสามารถ to the best of one's ability

        หย่อนความสามารถ lacking ability, inadequate, not up to standard

สามี husband

สาย[1] thread, string; line, row; wire; route; lineage; bailiwick; nominee

    สายกลาง middle way

    สายการบิน airline

    สายงาน line of activity; (within) one's competence

    สายใจ loved one, darling, beloved

    สายชนวน fuse

    สายชล current, stream

    สายซอ fiddle string

    สายโซ่ chain

ส
ห
ฬ
อ
ฮ

สายด่วน hotline

สายดิ่ง plumb line; sounding line

สายตระกูล lineage, family

สายตา vision, eyesight; (to have the) attention (of); view (of), from the viewpoint of

   สายตาไม่ดี defective vision, bad eyesight

   สายตายาว farsighted, farsightedness

   สายตาสั้น short-sighted, nearsighted, short-sightedness

   ทอดสายตา to cast one's eyes (on, over)

   อยู่ในสายตาของ under consideration by, being considered by, being looked at by; to be watched over by

สายโทรเลข telegraph wire

สายโทรศัพท์ telephone line, telephone wire

สายนาฬิกา watchband, watch strap, watch chain

สายน้ำ stream, current

สายบัว lotus stem

สายเบ็ด fishing line

สายป่าน financial staying power, the depth of one's pockets, means

   สายป่านยาว ample /staying power/ means/

   สายป่านสั้น limited /staying power/ means/

สายฝน rain, falling rain

สายพาน belt, fanbelt, conveyor belt

สายฟ้า lightning

   สายฟ้าแลบ lightning, flash of lightning

สายยาง hose

สายยู hasp

สายระยาง stay

สายระโยง stay, guy /rope/cable/wire/; long line

สายรัด strap

สายรุ้ง rainbow

สายล่อฟ้า lightning conductor, lightning rod

สายลับ spy, informer

สายโลหิต blood /relation/relative/, blood line, direct descendant, one's own flesh and blood

สายศิลปศาสตร์ arts stream

สายสร้อย chain, necklace

สายสะพาย sash; shoulder strap

สายสิญจน์ sacred thread

สายอากาศ aerial, antenna

สาย[2] late, tardy

   สายๆ (in the) late morning; late

   สายเกินไป too late (for, to)

   สายเสียแล้ว too late

ส่าย to swing back and forth, shake, sway, waggle

   ส่ายไปส่ายมา to sway back and forth, veer from side to side; to oscillate

   ส่ายศีรษะ to shake one's head

   ส่ายหน้า to shake one's head

   เดินส่ายก้น to waggle her hips (as she walks)

สายชู vinegar

สายัณห์ evening

สาร[1] message, letter, writing, instrument

   สารคดี non-fiction; feature story, article

      หน้าสารคดี feature page

   สารตรา document under seal

   สารตราตั้ง credentials, letters of credence

   สารบบ, สารบับ register

   สารบรรณ document, record

   สารบัญ, สารบาญ table of contents

   ข่าวสาร news, information

   ส่งสาร to send /word/a message/a letter/

สาร[2] substance, material

   สารเคมี chemical, chemical substance

   สารละลาย solution

   สารส้ม alum

   สารหนู arsenic

   มวลสาร mass

   ไร้สาร (ตะกั่ว) unleaded, lead-free

สาร^3 *as in* **โดยสาร** to ride (with, by), go (by); to take part in, join in

สารถี driver, chauffeur

สารทจีน a Chinese holiday

สารทิศ (from, in) every direction

สารนิเทศ information

    สารนิเทศศาสตร์ information science

สารพัด various, assorted, wide variety (of), all kinds (of), of every kind, all sorts (of), everything

    สารพัดนึก *as in* **แก้วสารพัดนึก** magic crystal ball, wishing glass

    สารพัดช่าง polytechnic; versatile, jack of all trades

        โรงเรียนสารพัดช่าง polytechnic school

สารพัน *see* **สารพัด**

สารภาพ to confess

    สารภาพผิด to admit one's /guilt/fault/

สารเลว abominable, vile, revolting

สารวัตร inspector

    สารวัตรทหาร military police

    สารวัตรนักเรียน truant officer

    สารวัตรใหญ่ chief inspector

สาระ substance, essentials, heart

    สาระของภาพ image content

    สาระสำคัญ /important/basic/ part, feature, fundamentals, gravamen

    ไร้สาระ nonsensical, empty, foolish, without substance

สาระแน to poke one's nose into (something), pry (into others' affairs), snoop

    ผมสาระแนไปเรื่อย I'm poking my nose in all sorts of things.

สาระพา, สาระพาเฮโล rhythmic chant of workers; to join the /party/crowd/

สารัตถะ substance, essence

    สารัตถประโยชน์ /substantial/essential/ benefit, real value

สาราณียกร student editor

สารานุกรม encyclopedia

สารีริกธาตุ relic of the Buddha

สาละวน to be preoccupied with, busy with

สาลิกา mynah; love amulet

สาลี wheat

    ข้าวสาลี wheat

    แป้งสาลี wheat flour

สาลี่ a Chinese pear; Thai sponge cake

สาโลหิต *see* **สายโลหิต** *หน้า 494*

สาว^1 girl, maiden, female; unmarried; young; not yet mated

    สาวแก่ old maid

    สาวใช้ maid

    สาวทึนทึก spinster

    สาวแส้ young girl

    สาวใหญ่ middle-aged woman, matron

    สาวไฮโซ socialite, high society girl

    เจ้าสาว bride

    น้องสาว younger sister

    เป็นสาว grown up, adolescent (girl), to have become a young lady

    พี่สาว older sister

    ลูกสาว daughter

    หญิงสาว young woman, girl

    หลานสาว niece, granddaughter

สาว^2 to pull (hand over hand); to step along, walk briskly

    สาวไปถึงไหน How deep will it go?

    สาวไส้ให้กากิน to wash one's dirty linen in public

    สาวเชือก to pull (up, down, out) a rope

    สาวเท้า to walk briskly, step quickly (forward, in, out, up to, into etc), quicken one's /steps/pace/

    สาวไหม to spin silk

สาวก disciple, pupil, adherent, follower

สาสม as /he/they/etc/ well deserve, as (one) so richly deserves

    จะต้องตามจับคนเหล่านั้นมาลงโทษให้สาสม

Those men must be apprehended and punished as they so richly deserve.

สาหร่าย seaweed

สาหัส seriously, severely; dire
    สาหัสจริงๆ very serious
    บาดเจ็บสาหัส /severely/seriously/ injured, badly hurt
    อาการสาหัส in /serious/critical/ condition

สาเหตุ cause, reason (for)

สาแหรก rattan carrying rack
    บ้านแตกสาแหรกขาด forced separation; families /broken up/torn asunder/
    พลอยสาแหรก star sapphire

สำคัญ important, special; significant, valuable; to understand, surmise; token, sign, mark
    สำคัญผิด to misunderstand, be mistaken, to take something for something else
    สำคัญยิ่ง to be extremely important, vital, of great significance
    สำคัญว่า to understand, take it that
    ของสำคัญ genitals, organ
    ใบสำคัญ certificate
    เอกสารสำคัญ official document

สำแดง to demonstrate, indicate

สำทับ to threaten, intimidate; to reiterate, drum (something) in

สำนวน idiom, idiomatic expression; style of writing; figure of speech, expression, wording; version; a numerical designation for counts, charges, items, or cases (in legal proceedings)
    สำนวนความ case record
    สำนวนฟ้อง case
    สำนวนสะเด่า racy style

สำนัก office, center, house, residence; school; brothel; presence
    เขาฟังธรรมอยู่ในสำนักของพระพุทธเจ้า *He listened to an exposition of the Dharma in the presence of the Buddha.*

สำนักข่าวสารอเมริกัน United States Information Service, USIS

สำนักงาน office
    สำนักงานกลาง central office, main office
    สำนักงานใหญ่ head office, main office, headquarters, principal place of business, registered office

สำนักนายกรัฐมนตรี Office of the Prime Minister

สำนักพระราชวัง Royal Household Department

สำนักพิมพ์ publishing house, publisher

สำนึก to realize, appreciate, be aware (of), know; to feel contrite
    สำนึกผิด penitent, remorseful, contrite, to realize one's fault, repent

สำเนา copy
    สำเนาความ context, gist, substance
    สำเนาถูกต้อง true copy
    สำเนาทะเบียนบ้าน copy of a house registration
    สำเนาที่รับรอง certified copy
    คัดสำเนา to make a copy
    สองสำเนา duplicates
    สามสำเนา triplicates
    สี่สำเนา quadruplicates

สำเนียง sound, intonation, accent, pronunciation

สำบัดสำนวน style of speech, locution; to play with words, smart talk; to cavil; be deceitful

สำปะหลัง sweet cassava, tapioca

สำปั้น sampan

สำเภา a Chinese junk

สำมะโนครัว census
    ทะเบียนสำมะโนครัว family register, house registration
    ใบสำมะโนครัว family registration

สำมะเลเทเมา as in **คนสำมะเลเทเมา** drunkard

สำมะหา ...so what do you expect (with, from, by)
    มือและเท้าเรายังบังคับไม่ได้ สำมะหาอะไรกะ

ลูก We can't even control our hands and feet so what do you expect with our kids?

สำรวจ to survey, inspect, examine, check

สำรวม self-controlled, restrained, composed; mixed

    สำรวมใจ to be composed, be self-possessed, calm and collected

    ความสำรวม composure

    อาหารสำรวม foods jumbled together, hodgepodge of food

สำรวย idle and extravagant, lazy spendthrift

สำรอก to vomit, regurgitate, disgorge; to bark (at), swear (at)

สำรอง to reserve (for), to have in reserve, extra, to stand-by (for), be put on a waiting list; substitute, second string; a spare

    สำรองราชการ inactive post

    ย้ายไปสำรองราชการ transferred to an inactive post

    เก็บสำรอง to keep in reserve

    ทุนสำรอง reserve fund, reserve, back-up fund

สำรับ set; complete meal, set of dishes (for a meal), foodtray, tray of food

สำราญ to be happy, have fun, to be lighthearted, to enjoy oneself

    สุขสำราญ happy, contented, to enjoy, have a good time

สำเร็จ finished, completed; accomplished, to succeed, success

    สำเร็จความใคร่ to have an orgasm, ejaculate, have a climax, obtain sexual satisfaction, have intercourse (with)

        สำเร็จความใคร่ด้วยตนเอง to masturbate

        สำเร็จความใคร่ทาง/ความคิด/ปัญญา intellectual masturbation

    สำเร็จโทษ to execute, put to death, carry out an execution

    สำเร็จรูป finished, ready-made, ready-to-wear, prepared, prefabricated

    ความสำเร็จ success, successful completion, achievement, accomplishment

    ผลสำเร็จ accomplishment, success, achievement

    อาหารสำเร็จรูป prepared food, ready-to-eat food, pre-cooked meal

สำลัก to choke (on)

    สำลักน้ำ to choke on water, swallow water down the wrong way; to sputter

สำลี cotton

สำส่อน promiscuous

    สำส่อนทางเพศ promiscuous, to have indiscriminate sexual relations, have casual sex

สำหรับ for; as for, with regard to, regarding, on, about

    สำหรับเรื่องนี้ไม่มีใครรู้ดีเท่าผม Nobody knows better than I about this. / On that subject, I know best.

    น้ำสำหรับดื่ม drinking water

สำหา *see* **สำมะหา** *หน้า 496*

สำเหนียก to take note, remember, to pay attention, take heed, listen

สำออย to wheedle

สำอาง comely, fine, nice-looking

    เครื่องสำอาง cosmetics, perfumery

สิ emphatic or imperative word

    ได้สิ sure, okay

สิกขาบท a precept for training, disciplinary rule

สิง to dwell (in), live, infest; to haunt

    สิงอยู่ทั่วไป omnipresent, ubiquitous, found everywhere, all over

    ผีสิง haunted, possessed

        บ้านผีสิง haunted house

สิ่ง thing, kind, piece, object

    สิ่งของ things, belongings

    สิ่งจำเป็นในชีวิต necessities of life

    สิ่งทอ textile

    สิ่งที่มีชีวิต living thing, animate object

    สิ่งที่ไม่มีชีวิต inanimate /thing/object/

ส ห ฬ อ ฮ

สิ่งที่ส่งมาด้วย enclosure

สิ่งปฏิกูล refuse, garbage, filth, waste

สิ่งพิมพ์ printed matter, publication

สิ่งละอันพันละน้อย nothing special, this and that, odds and ends

สิ่งแวดล้อม environment, surroundings

สิ่งสลักหักพัง wreckage, rubble

สิงโต lion

สิงโตทะเล sea lion

สิงห์ lion

    ราศีสิงห์ Leo

สิทธิ, สิทธิ์ right

    สิทธิครอบครอง right of possession, possessory rights

    สิทธิบัตร patent

    สิทธิพิเศษ privilege, prerogative, perquisite

    สิทธิฟ้องร้อง right of action

    สิทธิยับยั้ง veto

    สิทธิยึดหน่วง right of retention

    สิทธิเหนือทรัพย์สิน property right

    กรรมสิทธิ์ title (to), ownership (of)

    ลิขสิทธิ์ copyright

    มีสิทธิ์ see มีสิทธิ์ หน้า 379

สิน money, wealth

สินค้า goods, merchandise, products, commodities, wares; cargo

    สินค้าเข้า imports

    สินค้าหนีภาษี smuggled goods, contraband

    สินค้าออก exports

สินจ้าง pay, wages, remuneration

สินเชื่อ credit, facilities, loans

สินเดิม property acquired before marriage

สินไถ่ ransom; price; cost of redemption

สินทรัพย์ assets

สินน้ำใจ a present, token of appreciation, gratuity

สินบน bribe, graft, kickback

    เงินสินบน reward

สินบริคณห์ common property, community property

สินมฤดก inheritance

สินแร่ ore

สินสมรส community property acquired after marriage

สินสอด bride-price

สินไหม fine

    สินไหมทดแทน compensation

ทรัพย์สิน property

หนี้สิน liabilities, indebtedness, debts

    หนี้สินล้นพ้นตัว insolvency, to be insolvent

สิ้น to be finished, finish, end, terminate, expire

สิ้นคิด to be at a loss for what to do, at the end of one's rope; in a hopeless situation; stupid

สิ้นใจ to die, expire, breathe one's last

สิ้นชีพ, สิ้นชีวิต to die, pass away, expire

สิ้นดี totally, extremely, awfully

สิ้นแต้ม, สิ้นท่า to be frustrated; to be at one's wits' end, have no way out, be cornered

สิ้นทุกข์ to be at the end of one's troubles

สิ้นเนื้อประดาตัว penniless, ruined, to have lost everything

สิ้นบุญ to die, pass away

สิ้นปัญญา to be unable to think of anything more, unable to cope (with), run out of ideas

สิ้นแรง exhausted, worn-out

สิ้นลมหายใจ to breathe one's last

สิ้นสติ to lose consciousness, senseless, unconscious

สิ้นสุด to end, come to an end

    ไม่มีที่สิ้นสุด endless, everlasting

สิ้นหวัง hopeless, in despair

สิ้นอยาก detached, desireless, with no desire (for)

สินเธาว์ rock salt

สิบ ten

สิบตรี private first class, lance corporal

สิบโท corporal

สิบเบี้ยใกล้มือ A bird in the hand is worth two in the bush.

สิบแปดมงกุฎ godfather, archcriminal; extremely foxy

สิบเวร duty officer

สิบเอก sergeant

สิบเอ็ด eleven

สิริมงคล auspicious, lucky, happy, favorable, propitious

สิว pimple, acne, blackhead

สิวเสี้ยน blackhead

สิ่ว chisel

สี [1] color, hue; paint; dye; university; school colors; institutional pride, allegiance

สีกรมท่า navy blue

สีกา woman, laywoman

สีกากี khaki; the police

สีขาว white

สีเขียว green; blue

สีคราม indigo

สีชมพู pink

สีซอให้ควายฟัง to throw pearls before swine

สีด้าน matte /color/paint/

สีดำ black

สีแดง red

สีเทา gray

สีเทาเข้ม dark gray

สีน้ำ watercolor

สีน้ำเงิน blue

สีน้ำตาล brown

สีน้ำมัน oil paint

สีฟ้า light blue, sky blue

สีฟ้าอ่อน pale blue

สีม่วง purple, violet, lavender

สีไม่ตก fast color

สีย้อมผ้า dye

สียังไม่แห้ง wet paint

สีสด bright color, fresh color

สีส้ม orange

สีสวาด gray, fawn colored

แมวสีสวาด Siamese cat

สีหน้า (facial) expression, look, the look on (one's) face

สีหม่น dun (colored)

สีหลอด tube of paint, artists colors

สีเหลือง yellow

คนมีสี a police or military man

สี [2] to rub, brush; to mill

สีซอ to play a /violin/fiddle/

สีฟัน to brush one's teeth

แปรงสีฟัน toothbrush

ยาสีฟัน toothpaste, dentifrice, tooth powder

ขัดสี to polish

เสียดสี to be sarcastic, derisive, biting, satirical; to rub against

สี่ four, quadri-

สี่เท่า fourfold, quadruple

สี่เท้า quadruped

สี่แยก intersection, corner, crossroads

สี่ล้อ a dolly

สี่สิบ forty

สี่เหลี่ยม foursided, quadrilateral

สี่เหลี่ยมขนมเปียกปูน diamond (shaped), lozenge, rhomboid

สี่เหลี่ยมคางหมู trapezoid

สี่เหลี่ยมจัตุรัส square

สี่เหลี่ยมด้านขนาน parallelogram

สี่เหลี่ยมด้านไม่เท่า trapezium

สี่เหลี่ยมมุมฉาก rectangle

สีข้าง ribs, side

สีดอ *as in* ช้างสีดอ a short-tusked bull elephant

สีผึ้ง lipwax, lip pomade

สีห์ *as in* ราชสีห์ lion-king

ส
ห
ฬ
อ
ฮ

สึก[1] to wear away, wear down, abraded; blunt

สึกหรอ to be worn (down, away etc) deteriorate, depreciate; abraded; to wear, wear out, wasting

ค่าสึกหรอ depreciation

สึก[2] to leave the /monkhood/Sangha/

ถูกจับสึก to be defrocked

สืบ to follow, succeed, come after; to inquire about, search for, find out

สืบข่าว to find out what happened, follow up (information, news etc), investigate

สืบเชื้อสาย to descend from, be a descendant (of), be a scion (of); to have progeny, continue the line

สืบทอด to perpetuate

สืบไป from now on, henceforth

สืบพยาน to question a witness, examine a witness; to hear witnesses, have a hearing with witnesses

สืบพันธุ์ to have offspring, procreate, reproduce; to inherit

สืบมาจนทุกวันนี้ down to the present day

สืบมาแต่โบราณ handed down from ancient times

สืบราชสันตติวงศ์ to succeed to the throne

สืบสวน to investigate, conduct an investigation

สืบสันดาน to be a direct descendant

สืบสาน to carry /on/forward/, preserve, perpetuate

สืบสายโลหิต to descend from, be an off-spring (of)

สืบสาวที่มา to find out the source

สืบเสาะ to search for, seek, go in quest of

สืบให้แน่ to ascertain

นักสืบ detective, investigator

สื่อ to communicate; to conduct; to introduce

สื่อกลาง intermediary, go-between

สื่อการศึกษา educational media

สื่อไฟฟ้า conductor

สื่อมวลชน mass media

สื่อสาร to communicate

สื่อสารมวลชน mass communication

กองสื่อสาร Signal Corps

ผู้สื่อข่าว reporter, correspondent, news-paperman, journalist

สุก pure, good; to be ripe; to be ready; to be cooked; light, clear, bright

สุกงอม ripe

สุกๆ ดิบๆ half-cooked; half-baked

สุกใส bright, shining, clear, fresh

สุกเอาเผากิน slapdash, slipshod; superficial; carelessly done

ข้าวสุก cooked rice

น้ำสุก boiled water

สุกร pig, swine

เนื้อสุกร pork

สุข happiness, well-being, happy

สุขกาย healthy, physical /health/well-being/

สุขใจ happy; mental health

สุขนิยม hedonism

นักสุขนิยม hedonist

เป็นสุข happy, to have contentment

เป็นยอดแห่งความสุข blissful, absolute bliss, ecstasy

อยู่เย็นเป็นสุข to be well and happy

สุขภัณฑ์ as in **เครื่องสุขภัณฑ์** sanitary ware

สุขภาพ health

สุขภาพไม่ดี in bad health, ill, ailing

สุขลักษณะ sanitary, hygienic

สุขวิทยา hygiene

สุขศึกษา hygiene

สุขา toilet, men's room, ladies' room, W.C. (water closet), rest room

ทางไปสุขา to the /rest room/men's room/etc

สุขาภิบาล sanitation; sanitation district

สุขาวดี place of happiness, land of bliss

สุขุม subtle, careful, circumspect, deliberate,

prudent, judicious, cautious

สุคติ heaven, realms of happiness

สุงสิง to mix (with others), socialize

    คนไม่สุงสิงกับใคร introvert

สุจริต honest, upright, (of, in) good faith, law-abiding, honorable

    ซื่อสัตย์สุจริต honorable, fine, virtuous

    โดยสุจริต in good faith, honestly

    อาชีพสุจริต honest /work/job/occupation/, good honest work

สุญญตา voidness, sunyata, transcendental void, emptiness

สุด end; utmost, most, -est

    สุดกำลัง with all one's might

    สุดกู่ way off; far out, far afield; way into

    บ้านเขาอยู่สุดกู่ปลายนาโน่นแน่ะ His house is way off there at the end of the field.

    เขาคิดไปไกลสุดกู่แล้ว เราตามเขาไม่ทันหรอก His thinking is so /far out/far afield/ we can't keep up with him.

    เขาติดยาอย่างสุดกู่แล้ว ยากจะช่วยเหลือได้ He's too far into his drug habit to help him./ He's way into drugs now. Nothing is likely to help.

    สุดขีด extreme, great, enormous; frenetic

        โกรธสุดขีด enraged, infuriated, extremely angry, in a frenzy, to blow one's top

    สุดความสามารถ to the best of one's ability

    สุดคิด at one's wit's end

    สุดแค้น outraged, full of vengeance

    สุดจะพรรณนา beyond description, indescribable, ineffable

    สุดชีวิตจิตใจ with all one's heart

    สุดแต่ it depends (on), it's up to (you etc)

        สุดแต่ใจ as you like, depending on the way you feel

        สุดแต่ว่า It depends on....

    สุดโต่ง extreme, immoderate; lopsided

    สุดท้อง youngest, last

    สุดท้าย last, final, finally, to end, at the end, at the conclusion

    สุดที่จะ /in/un/...able

        สุดที่จะคิดได้ unthinkable

        สุดที่จะพรรณนา indescribable

        สุดที่จะอภัยได้ unforgivable

    สุดปัญญา over (my) head, (my) mind's a blank

    สุดยอด Tops!

        จุดสุดยอด peak; climax, orgasm

    สุดแรงเกิด with all (my) might

    สุดวิสัย impossible; unavoidable, inevitable

    สุดสายตา out of sight, beyond the range of vision

    สุดสิ้นลง to come to an end

    สุดแสนจะทนทาน intolerable, unbearable, insupportable

    สุดหล้าฟ้าเขียว to the ends of the earth, ever so far away, beyond the horizon

    สุดเหวี่ยง hard, as hard as as one /can/could/, to the utmost

    สุดเอื้อม out of reach, beyond reach

    ต่ำสุด lowest, minimum; nadir

    ร้องสุดเสียง to scream, shriek, call out at the top of one's voice

    สูงสุด highest, ultimate, maximum, supreme; tallest

สุทธิ true

    กำไรสุทธิ net profit

    ใบสุทธิ school-leaving certificate; testimonial; monk's identification card

สุนทรกถา a talk

สุนทรพจน์ address, speech, oration

สุนัข dog, canine

    สุนัขจิ้งจอก fox

    สุนัขป่า wolf

    สุนัขรับใช้ running dog

    สุนัขล่าเนื้อ hound, hunting dog

ส
ห
ฬ
อ
ฮ

กขคฆงจฉชซฌญฎฏฐฑฒณดตถทธนบปผฝพฟภมยรฤฦลวศษ

สุนิยม optimism

สุภาพ polite, courteous, well-mannered, refined, gentlemanly, ladylike

    สุภาพบุรุษ gentleman

    สุภาพสตรี lady

    สุภาพอ่อนโยน mannerly, gentle, kindly, deferential

สุภาษิต proverb, maxim, aphorism

สุม to pile up; to bank up

    สุมไฟ to bank up a fire, make a smoldering fire

    สุมอก persistent, piling up, consuming

สุ่ม[1] to /select/pick/ at random, pick out

    สุ่มตัวอย่าง to do random sampling, take a random sample

    สุ่มสี่สุ่มห้า carelessly, thoughtlessly; indiscriminately, at random

    เดาสุ่ม to make a guess

สุ่ม[2] an openwork cover-trap

    สุ่มไก่ an openwork chicken cover

สุ้มเสียง voice, tone of voice, way of speaking

สุเมรุ as in เขาพระสุเมรุ Mount Meru

สุรา spirits, liquor, distilled liquor, hard liquor, alcohol

    สุราบาน drinking; liquor

    สุราเมรัย alcoholic beverages

    คอสุรา discriminating drinker; one who likes to drink

    นักดื่มสุรา heavy drinker, alcohol fancier

    โรคพิษสุราเรื้อรัง chronic alcoholism

    เสพสุรา to drink (alcohol)

สุริย-, สุริยะ the sun

    สุริยคราส solar eclipse

    สุริยุปราคา solar eclipse

สุรุ่ยสุร่าย extravagant, lavish, wasteful

สุสาน cemetery, graveyard

สุหร่าย aspergillum

สุเหร่า mosque

สู you, my little one, sonny, little girl

สู่ to visit; to come, reach, achieve; to, towards; to live together

    สู่ขอ to ask for the hand of (someone) in marriage

    สู่ความหลุดพ้น to achieve /liberation/ freedom/release/

    สู่รู้ to be a know-it-all, boastful, flaunt one's knowledge

    สู่สม to live together, have relations with someone

    จากสูงสุดสู่สามัญ from the heights to the plebeian

    ไปมาหาสู่ to see each other, socialize

    เล่าสู่กันฟัง it is said, they say, to relate

สู้ to resist, oppose, fight, fight back; to persist, persevere, be unyielding; to /meet/ respond/ to a challenge; to face up to, deal with (people, a problem, etc)

    ติ๋มไม่สู้คน Tim /won't face up to people./ can't deal with people./

    สู้ความ to contest a legal action, fight the case

    สู้จนยิบตา to fight to the finish

    สู้ตาย to fight to the bitter end

    สู้มือ to respond

    สู้ไม่ได้ to be no match (for), cannot compare (with), unable to compete

    สู้ไม่ถอย to be unyielding

    สู้รบ to fight, battle, engage in combat

    คู่ต่อสู้ opponent, rival, antagonist

    ไม่สู้ to give up; submissive; spent, to refuse to be aroused, not up to it; cannot compare (to)

    ร้อยรู้ไม่สู้ลงมือทำ To know all about what to do cannot compare to actually doing it.

    ไม่สู้จะ not so...

    ไม่สู้ดีนัก not so good, indifferent

    ไม่สู้เป็นไร It doesn't make much difference., It does not matter.

ไม่สู้เลวนัก not too bad

สูง high, tall, lofty; high-pitched, treble; intense

สูงชัน precipitous, high and steep

สูงเด่น prominent, lofty

สูงตระหง่าน towering

สูงเทียมฟ้า sky-high

สูงระหง willowy

สูงล้ำ very high

สูงลิบลิ่ว extremely high; soaring

สูงศักดิ์ high-ranking, noble

สูงส่ง supreme, sublime, highest

สูงสุด highest, ultimate, maximum, supreme; tallest;

สูงอายุ aged, elderly, senior, advanced in years

กระโดดสูง high-jump

ใฝ่สูง ambitious, to aim high

หัวสูง pretentious

เหลื่อมล้ำต่ำสูง inequality

อักษรสูง high consonant

สูจิบัตร program

สูญ empty, void, gone; zero, naught, 0

สูญเปล่า in vain, wasted, fruitless, useless

สูญสิ้น all gone, completely disappeared

สูญเสียน้ำ dehydrated

สูญหาย lost, vanished, gone, to disappear

สูญญากาศ vacuum

สูด to inhale, breathe in

สูดกลิ่น to sniff, smell

สูดลมหายใจ to inhale, breathe in

สูตร formula; method, way

ผมมีสูตรของผมในการทำอาหาร *I have my own /formula/recipe/ for making food. / I have my own special way of cooking.*

สูตรคูณ multiplication table

สูตรเคมี chemical formula

สูตรอาหาร recipe

สูติกรรม childbirth

สูตินรีเวช obstetrics and gynecology

สูติบัตร birth certificate

สูติแพทย์ obstetrician

สูติศาสตร์ obstetrics

สูบ to pump (in, out, up, away, off); to smoke

สูบกล้อง to smoke a pipe

สูบน้ำ to pump water

สูบบุหรี่ to smoke (cigarettes)

สูบยา to smoke (tobacco, opium)

สูบลม bellows; to pump air

สูบเลือด to suck blood, bloodsucking

กระบอกสูบ cylinder

กล้องยาสูบ pipe

เตาสูบ forge

ยาสูบ tobacco

ลูกสูบ piston

สูสี[1] to be about even, close

คะแนนสูสี close vote, /close/about even/ in points

สูสี[2] to frequent, play footsie (with)

เส to diverge, stray (from), deviate

เสความ to twist words

เสพูด to be evasive, foxy

เสสรวล to giggle, guffaw

เสแสร้ง to dissemble, pretend

เสก to consecrate; to make a spell, pronounce incantations

เสกคาถา to utter /spells/incantations/

ปลุกเสก to consecrate, bless

เส็งเคร็ง lousy

เสงี่ยม modest, polite, reserved, unassuming, self-controlled

เสฉวน hermit crab; Szechuan

เสด็จ *(royal word)* to go, come, proceed

เสด็จประพาส *(royal word)* to tour, visit

เสด็จพระราชดำเนิน to go, proceed

โดยเสด็จ to attend a royalty (king, queen, prince, etc)

โดยเสด็จพระราชกุศล to contribute to a royal charity

ส
ห
ฬ
อ
ฮ

ตามเสด็จ to accompany (the royal family), be in the royal /train/retinue/

เฝ้าเสด็จ to have an audience (with)

เสถียร stable, firm, strong

เสถียรภาพ stability, security

เส้น[1] thread; line; blood vessel; a numerical designation for string or rope; a unit of length equal to 40 meters

เส้นขนาน parallel line; latitude, parallel

เส้นโค้ง curve

เส้นด้าย thread, sewing cotton

เส้นตรง linear

เส้นทแยงมุม diagonal

เส้นทาง way, route, course, road

เส้นทางหลวง highway

เส้นประ dotted line

เส้นประสาท nerve

เส้นผม strand of hair

เส้นผ่าศูนย์กลาง diameter

เส้นรุ้ง latitude

เส้นเลือด blood vessel, artery, vein

เส้นเลือดดำ vein

เส้นเลือดแดง artery

เส้นเลือดฝอย capillary

เส้นเลือดใหญ่ aorta

เส้นแวง longitude

เส้นศูนย์สูตร equator

เส้นเอ็น sinew, tendon

เส้น[2] influence, contacts, pull, backing, connections

เส้นยาแดงผ่าแปด to have a narrow escape

เส้นใหญ่ strong backing, good contacts, well connected

เด็กเส้น someone who owes his position to /pull/connections/, someone who got in by pulling strings, a fair-haired boy, someone's protegé

ไม่มีเส้น (I) don't know anyone., to have no /pull/connections/

เสน่ห์ charm, attraction, appeal; love-philter

มีเสน่ห์ charming, personable, attractive, appealing, alluring, to have charm

เสน่หา love, affection

เสนอ to submit, present, offer, propose; to move; to report, inform

เสนอข่าว to /report/present/ news

เสนอญัตติ to move, make a motion (to)

เสนอให้ลงคะแนน to call for a vote, move the previous question

ข้อเสนอ proposal, proposition, offer

คำเสนอ offer

ฝ่ายเสนอ proponent, the affirmative

นำเสนอ to hand (to), present, presented (by)

เสนาธิการ chief of staff

เสนาธิการทหาร Chief of Staff; general staff

เสนาธิการทหารบก Chief of the General Staff

เสนาธิการทหารเรือ Naval Chief of Staff

เสนาธิการทหารอากาศ Chief of Staff of the Air Force

โรงเรียนเสนาธิการทหาร General Staff College

เสนาบดี minister

เสนารักษ์ medical corps

เสนาสนะ dwelling, lodging

เสนาะ sweet, melodious, harmonious, pleasing (to the ear)

เสนียด ill-omened, calamitous, accursed

เสนียดจัญไร abomination, abominable, loathsome, execrable

เสบย happy

เสบียง provisions, food

เสบียงกรัง food that keeps, provisions

รถเสบียง restaurant car, dining car

เสพ, เสพย์ to take, consume, use, indulge (in); to associate (with)

เสพกาม to make love, have sex (with), indulge in sex

เสพย์ติด to be addicted (to), addictive

เสพยา to use drugs

เสพสุข to enjoy oneself

เสเพล irresponsible, dissolute, dissipated; bad, wild

เสภา ballad form of song

เสมหะ phlegm, mucus

เสมอ equal; like; smooth, even

เสมอกัน a draw, even, tied

เสมอต้นเสมอปลาย consistent, unchanging, steady, constant, genuine

เสมอตัว to break even

เสมอนอก to stand on the sidelines

เสมอภาค equal, equality

เสมอมา regularly

เสมอร่ำไป continually, always

เสมอหน้า equally, without discrimination

เสมอเหมือน comparable (to), equal (to)

ตีเสมอ to even the score; to behave without regard to one's (inferior) position, act insolently, be presumptuous

สม่ำเสมอ see **สม่ำเสมอ** หน้า 480

เสมา ogival merlon (บนกำแพง), boundary marker of a temple (รอบโบสถ์); boundary, area

เสมาธรรมจักร stone markers of a temple precinct

เสมียน clerk

เสมียนตรา secretary

เสมียนพิมพ์ดีด typist

เสมียนออกของ shipping clerk

เสมือน as if, like

เสย to swing up; to brush back (the hair); to collide

รถยนต์เสยรถบรรทุก The car collided with the truck.

เสยผม to brush back (one's) hair, run (one's) /fingers/comb/ through (one's) hair

เสยหมัด to give an uppercut

เสร็จ[1] finished, done, completed; ready; to end, come to an end

เสร็จเขา to be foiled

เสร็จธุระ to be free

เสร็จศึก the war is /over/ended

เสร็จสรรพ finished, all done, all over

เสร็จสิ้น over, done, completed

อาหารเสร็จแล้ว The food (breakfast, lunch, supper, dinner) is ready.

เสร็จ[2] *as in* ใบเสร็จ receipt

โดนใบเสร็จ to get a ticket

เสริม to supplement, add to, enhance, enrich, fortify; supplementary, extra

เสริมความงาม to beautify

เสริมวิตามิน /enriched/fortified/ with vitamins

เสริมส่ง, ส่งเสริม to support, back, promote, encourage

เสริมสวย to beautify

ช่างเสริมสวย beautician

ร้านเสริมสวย beauty parlor, beauty salon

เสริมอก to enhance the bosom; breast padding

เก้าอี้เสริม an extra /chair/seat/

ภาษีเสริม surtax

อาหารเสริม food supplement

เสรี free, independent

เสรีชน free people

เสรีภาพ freedom, liberty

เสรีภาพทางการหนังสือพิมพ์ freedom of the press

เสรีภาพในการพูด freedom of speech

โดยเสรี freely

เสลด phlegm, mucus

เสลา polished, pretty, fine-featured, of refined appearance, charming, clean cut, smooth-skinned

เสลี่ยง palanquin, litter

เสวนา to associate (with)

เสวย to receive, get; to enjoy, to meet with; to eat, consume; to ascend (the throne); to be

ส
ห
ฬ
อ
ฮ

ก
ข
ค
ฆ
ง
จ
ฉ
ช
ซ
ฌ
ญ
ฎ
ฏ
ฐ
ฑ
ฒ
ณ
ด
ต
ถ
ท
ธ
น
บ
ป
ผ
ฝ
พ
ฟ
ภ
ม
ย
ร
ฤ
ฤๅ
ล
ว
ศ
ษ
ส

born (as)

เสวยทุกข์ to suffer

เสวยราชย์ to ascend the throne

เสวยสุข to enjoy oneself, take pleasure (in)

เสวยอายุ to govern (a period during one's life)

เสวยอำนาจ to be in a position of power, wield power

เครื่องเสวย food

เสา post, column, pillar, stake

เสากระโดง mast

เสาเข็ม piling

เสาคอนกรีต concrete post, concrete pile

เสาโทรเลข telegraph pole

เสาธง flagstaff, flagpole

เสาเอก principal house post

เส้า pole; leg of a tripod

รักสามเส้า love triangle

เสาร์ Saturday; Saturn

เสาวนีย์ (queen's) request, command, order

เสาะ[1] to cause indigestion, give (someone) an upset stomach

เสาะท้อง to have /indigestion/an upset stomach/

ใจเสาะ fainthearted, timorous, without gumption, not a fighter, unable to take it, chickenhearted

เสาะ, เสาะหา[2] to search for, inquire after, look for, hunt for, try to find, seek

เสาะหาความรู้ to search for knowledge, seek /information/knowledge/etc

เสีย spoiled, broken, out of order, not working, damaged; to spend, pay; to lose, miss; to be dead, die

เสียการ to miss the boat, fail

เสียกำลัง to lose /strength/force/

เสียกำลังใจ to be discouraged

เสียกิริยา unmannerly, impolite, rude, to show bad manners

เสียเกียรติ undignified, demeaning

เสียขวัญ see ขวัญเสีย หน้า 48

เสียของ wasteful, to waste, spoil

เสียคน to degrade oneself, lower oneself; to get a bad name, lose one's reputation

เสียค่าเช่า to pay rent

เสียค่าใช้จ่าย to pay expenses

เสียคำพูด to break one's promise, not keep one's word, go back on one's word

เสียงาน to be wasted effort

เสียเงิน to waste money, (to be) a waste of money; to spend, pay

เสียจริต to become unbalanced, insane

เสียใจ to be sorry, regret; to be disappointed

เสียใจภายหลัง to be sorry afterwards, rue

เสียโฉม disfigured

เสียชาติเกิด to waste one's life, be unworthy of oneself, fail to make the most of one's life

เสียชีวิต to lose one's life

เสียชื่อ to get a bad name, spoil one's reputation, be discredited, look bad

เสียเชิง to be outsmarted, discomfited

เสียเชิงชาย to be put to shame, humiliated; to be unmanly

เสียดอกเบี้ย to pay interest

เสียดาย to regret, be sorry; what a shame, too bad

ที่ไม่ได้รับทำงานอีกแห่งนั้นเสียดายไหม Do you regret not having accepted the other job?

เสียเด็ก spoiled, to spoil, to be bad (for a youngster to do something)

เสียตัว to lose one's virginity, have sex for the first time; to sleep with (someone)

เสียแต่ except (for, that)

เสียทรง misshapen, out of shape; to get messed

เสียท่า, เสียที to be outdone; to fall prey (to someone); to make a mistake, be made a fool of, be a fool

เสียเที่ยว to /come/go/ for nothing; to be a waste of time, not worth the effort

เสียน้ำใจ disappointed, discouraged, disheartened, hurt

เสียเปรียบ to be at a disadvantage, lose, be prejudiced (by)

เสียภาษี to pay tax

เสียรังวัด to be discredited, be blamed for something one has not done

เสียรู้ to be outwitted, taken in (by someone), be fooled, duped

เสียรูปคดี to /affect/spoil/ the case

เสียแรง to waste effort

เสียเวลา to waste time; be a waste of time; to lose time

เสียศูนย์ to lose (one's) sense of balance; to go out of control, lose one's cool; to be off center; to veer, go off-course

เสียสละ to sacrifice, give up (something)

เสียสัญญา to break a promise

เสียสัตย์ to be disloyal, unfaithful; to break one's promise, be untrue (to), go back on one's /word/pledge/

เสียเส้น disappointed

เสียหน้า to lose face

เสียหลัก to get out of control; to /fall/tip/ topple/ over, lose one's balance; to go against /the/one's/ principle(s)

เสียหาย damaged, harmed, affected

    ค่าเสียหาย damages, compensation

เสียเหลี่ยม to be outsmarted, be shown up

ของเสีย *see* **ของเสีย** *หน้า 52*

ขาดเสียมิได้ indispensable, vital, essential

ใจเสีย alarmed; anxious, upset, apprehensive

ท้องเสีย to have indigestion, have an upset stomach

น่าเสียดาย unfortunately, too bad, regrettably, it's a shame, what a pity!

นิสัยเสีย bad, (to get into, have) bad habits

บัตรเสีย /spoiled/invalid/ ballot

เมินเสียเถอะ Not on your life!, Fat chance!

ลืมเสียเถิด Forget it! Forget about it!

สั่งเสีย to give parting instructions

สูญเสีย to lose, be deprived of

อารมณ์เสีย cranky, in a bad mood; to lose one's temper, bad-tempered

เสียง sound, tone; voice; noise; vote

เสียงกรอบแกรบ rustling, crunchy, crunching sound

เสียงก้อง loud; resonant, to resound; aspirated

เสียงกังวาล sonorous

เสียงกุกกัก clatter, noise

เสียงไก่ crowing, cackling, clucking

เสียงขรม noisy, loud, clamor, hullabaloo, din

เสียงข้างมาก majority vote

เสียงเขียว angry voice, to exclaim (angrily), snap (at)

เสียงแข็ง firmly, uncompromising, inflexible, unyielding, confidently; peremptory; (to speak in a) stern voice

เสียงค่อย (in a) soft voice, low voice, whisper

เสียงเครือ shaking voice, tremulous /sound/ voice/

เสียงจัตวา rising tone

เสียงช้าง trumpeting

เสียงดนตรี music

เสียงตรี high tone

เสียงตะกุกตะกัก faltering /speech/sound/, hesitant; stammer

เสียงโท falling tone

เสียงนกเขา cooing

เสียงปืน noise of a gun, bang

เสียงเป็ด quack

เสียงแปร่ง accent; off pitch, out of tune, not sound right

ส
ห
ฬ
อ
ฮ

เสียงฝีเท้า footsteps

เสียงพร่า husky voice, hoarse /voice/sound/; out of tune, indistinct

เสียงฟ้าร้อง thunder

เสียงแมว mewing, miaow

เสียงร้องเรียก call, shout

เสียงร้องไห้ crying, weeping, sobbing

เสียงลา braying

เสียงลือ rumor

เสียงวัว mooing

เสียงสัญญาณ siren

เสียงสั่นๆ tremulous voice, /shaking/quavering/ voice

เสียงสามัญ middle tone

เสียงหมู grunting

เสียงหลง off-key, out of tune; the voice becomes shrill

เสียงหวาน sweet /voice/sound/

เสียงห้าว deep voice; /stentorian/commanding/ voice

เสียงหัวเราะ laugh, laughter

เสียงแหบ hoarse (voice)

เสียงแหลม high-pitched, soprano, treble; shrill, /piercing/sharp/ sound

เสียงอ่อนหวาน sweet, charming, dulcet (voice, tone, sound)

เสียงอี๊ดอ๊าด creaking; squeaking; screeching

เสียงเอก low tone

เสียงฮา guffaw, coarse laughter

เสียงโฮกฮาก in a rude voice, (to speak) abruptly, harshly

ขึ้นเสียง to raise one's voice

คลื่นเสียง sound wave

จานเสียง phonograph record

ซาวเสียง to sound out, poll

ซื้อเสียง to buy votes

น้ำเสียง tone (of voice)

เป็นเสียงเดียวกัน (to speak) with a single voice, with one accord, to say the same thing, unanimously

แผดเสียง to shout, yell, scream; to trumpet

แผ่นเสียง phonograph record, platter

แว่วเสียง faint /sound/voice/, distant sound, to be heard faintly

ห้องเก็บเสียง soundproof room

หาเสียง to electioneer, campaign (for votes), look for votes

เสี่ยง[1] splinter, shard (แก้ว)

แตกเป็นเสี่ยงๆ to splinter, shatter

เสี่ยง[2] to risk, take a risk, take a chance

อย่าเสี่ยงดีกว่า *It's not worth the risk. / Better not take a chance.*

เสี่ยงชีวิต to risk one's life

เสี่ยงโชค to try one's luck, take a chance

เสี่ยงทาย to tell one's fortune by lots

เสี่ยงบุญเสี่ยงกรรม to trust to luck

เสี่ยงภัย to risk, take a risk, take a chance, adventure (into)

เสี่ยงวาสนา to trust to luck

เป็นการเสี่ยง risky

สินทรัพย์เสี่ยง risk assets

เสียด to feel a sharp pain; to push (through, up, into); to reach

เสียดท้อง to feel a sharp pain in the stomach, have a twinge of pain in the stomach, have heartburn

เสียดทาน *as in* แรงเสียดทาน friction

เสียดแทง cutting, hurtful, caustic, biting

เสียดใบ to reach

เสียดสี to be sarcastic, derisive, biting, satirical, invidious; to rub against

　　แรงเสียดสี friction

เบียดเสียด to crowd (together, against one another), crowded together, /pushing/pressing/ (against one another, through), jostling

เสี้ยน splinter

เสี้ยนตำเท้า to get a splinter in one's foot

เสี้ยนหนาม enemy (of), bane (of), scourge (of)

    เสี้ยนหนามต่อแผ่นดิน public enemy

เสียบ to insert, slip in; to pierce; to pin; to skewer; to penetrate; to stab; to impale

เสียบปลั๊ก to plug in, put the plug in

เสียม[1] a curved spade

เสียม[2] Siam

เสี้ยม to sharpen

เสี้ยมเขาควายให้ชนกัน to stir up trouble

เสี้ยมสอน to prompt, incite, instigate

เสียว to be apprehensive; hair-raising, chilling; to feel a thrill of /pain/pleasure/; painful; (sexually) exciting

เสียวกระสัน to get a sexual /thrill/tingle/; sexually exciting

เสียวซ่าน to become (sexually) excited, experience intense pleasure

เสียวฟัน to have a sensitive tooth; sensitivity of /a tooth/the teeth/

เสียวสยอง grisly, gruesome

เสียวไส้ scary, hair-raising, terrifying

เล่นเสียว to make love

เสี้ยว one quarter; fraction

เสี้ยวพระจันทร์ crescent moon

เสี้ยววินาที (in a) split second

เสือ jungle cat, tiger; bandit, gangster; wolf; clever kid

เสือกระดาษ paper tiger

เสือโคร่ง tiger

เสือซ่อนเล็บ (powerful but) unassuming

เสือดาว leopard

เสือดำ panther

เสือตกถัง a trapdoor mousetrap

เสือนอนกิน free rider; someone who makes an easy living, someone who gets something for nothing

เสือไบ a bisexual

เสือป่า scout

เสือปืนไว hotshot

เสือผู้หญิง wolf

เสือลำบาก someone fallen from grace, fallen on hard times

เสือหิว mad อย่างเช่น sex-mad, money-mad, power-mad

เขียนเสือให้วัวกลัว to make an empty threat

เสื่อ mat

เสื้อ shirt, blouse, coat, upper garment; clothes, clothing

เสื้อกล้าม undershirt

เสื้อกั๊ก vest, waistcoat

เสื้อกันฝน raincoat

เสื้อกันหนาว coat, overcoat, (winter) jacket

เสื้อกาวน์ gown

เสื้อกีฬา sport clothes

เสื้อครุย gown, academic gown

เสื้อคลุม robe, cloak, cape; bathrobe; overcoat

เสื้อชั้นใน underwear

เสื้อชูชีพ life vest, life jacket

เสื้อเชิ้ต shirt

เสื้อนอก jacket, suitcoat, coat

เสื้อนอน pyjamas, nightshirt, nightwear

เสื้อผ้า clothes, clothing, wearing apparel, garments

เสื้อผู้หญิง women's clothing; blouse, woman's jacket

เสื้อฝน raincoat

เสื้อยืด T-shirt, undershirt, jersey

เสื้อราตรี evening gown

เสื้อแสง clothing, clothes

เสื้อหนาว warm clothing, winter clothes; heavy /jacket/coat/

เสือก to meddle, intrude, interfere, be an officious intermeddler, go where one is not wanted

เสือกกระโหลก to poke one's nose into something

เสือกสน to struggle (for), strive (for)

เสือกไส to eject, kick out

   เสือกไสไล่ส่ง to throw (somebody) out

อย่าเสือก Don't interfere! Keep your nose out of it!

   อย่าเสือกดีกว่า Mind your own business.

เสื่อม to deteriorate, degenerate, wear out; to go down, be reduced, lose, decline; to lose supernatural power

เสื่อมเกียรติ disgraced, in disrepute, degrading

เสื่อมคุณภาพ not up to standard, down in quality

เสื่อมทราม degenerate, bad, immoral, degraded

เสื่อมราคา to depreciate in value

เสื่อมศีลธรรม in moral decline

เสื่อมสมรรถภาพ impotent; to work poorly, lose efficiency

เสื่อมเสีย spoiled, damaged, impaired

เสือร้องไห้ brisket

เสือหมอบ[1] stinkweed

เสือหมอบ[2] a racer, racing bike, racing

แส่ to meddle, interfere

แส่หาเรื่อง to look for trouble

แส้ fly whisk; whip; ramrod

แส้ม้า mane; whip

แสก part (แสกผม); dividing line, middle

แสกผม to part one's hair (in the middle, on the left etc)

แสกหน้า the part of the forehead between the eyebrows, middle of the forehead

กลางวันแสกๆ in broad daylight

แสง[1] light; ray, beam; jewel

แสงเงินแสงทอง silvery light of dawn, golden dawn

แสงจันทร์ moonlight, moonbeam

แสงจ้า glare, brilliant light

แสงดาว starlight

แสงเดือน moonlight

แสงแดด sun, sunlight, sunshine, sun's rays

แสงตะวัน sunlight

แสงไฟ light; firelight

แสงไม่ดี poor light, poor lighting conditions

แสงริบหรี่ dim (light)

แสงสว่าง light

แสงอรุณ dawn, daybreak

แสงอ่อนๆ /pale/soft/ light

แสงอาทิตย์ sunlight

ฉายแสง to shine; to treat with radiation, give a radiation treatment

โปร่งแสง translucent

ลำแสง beam of light

ส่องแสง to shine, glow; to illuminate

อับแสง dark, ill lit, obscure, poorly lit; in the shadows

แสง[2] weapon, arms

คลังแสง armory, arsenal, ammunition dump

ช่างแสง armorer

พระแสงดาบ royal sword

แสด orange

แสดง to show, display, appear, reveal, indicate; to explain; to act; to teach; to demonstrate; to play (a part, role, etc), perform

แสดงกิริยา to behave, act

แสดงกิริยาไม่พอใจ to act dissatisfied, be in a huff, show one's dissatisfaction

แสดงความกตัญญู to show /gratitude/ appreciation/ (for), express gratefulness

แสดงความคิดเห็น to express one's opinion

แสดงความเคารพ to show respect

แสดงความดีใจ to express happiness, be delighted

แสดงความยินดี to congratulate

แสดงความเห็นใจ to sympathize (with someone), show sympathy for, commiserate with (someone)

แสดงตน to appear, make an appearance,

show oneself

แสดงธรรม to preach, give a sermon

แสดงน้ำใจ to show spirit, show sympathy (for), (do something) as a friendly gesture

แสดงบทบาท to have a role, play a part (in)

แสดงปาฐกถา to give a /lecture/talk/

แสดงออก to show; apparent, evident, patent, obvious; to display, give oneself away, tell

    ไม่แสดงออก not to show, to /hide/ conceal/ one's feelings; not /obvious/ evident/; latent

แสดงอำนาจบาตรใหญ่ tyrannical, despotic, imperious, oppressive

การแสดง performance, show, act, exhibition

การแสดงออก action, display, expression, way, manner, appearance; manifestation

ตัวแสดง performer, actor; indicator

นักแสดง actor, professional actor; pretender

ผู้แสดง actor, performer, player, ...er เช่น lecturer, preacher

แสตมป์ stamp, duty stamp, postage stamp

    ปิดแสตมป์ to stamp (a letter), put on a stamp, affix a stamp

    สะสมแสตมป์ to collect stamps

    อากรแสตมป์ duty stamp, tax stamp

แสน exceedingly, extremely, enormously; one hundred thousand

    แสนกล super clever; infinitely tricky

    แสนโกฏิ ten billion

    แสนงอน petulant, sulky, peevish, demanding and difficult

    แสนจะ awfully, exceedingly

    แสนดี wonderful

    แสนเบื่อ to be fed up to one's ears

    แสนรู้ wonder (dog, cat, etc); a know-it-all

    แสนสาหัส extreme, dreadful, terrible (poverty, difficulty etc)

    แสนสุข extremely happy, supremely happy,

felicity, bliss

แสนยานุภาพ military might

แสบ to smart, sting, burn

เขาทำฉันแสบมาก It burns me up to think what he did to me.

    แสบไส้ to have hunger pangs, pangs of hunger

        หิวจนแสบไส้ to be starved, to feel hunger pangs

    ไอ้ตัวแสบ culprit, troublemaker, rascal, fucker

แสยง apprehensive, fearful

    แสยงขน to feel one's hair stand on end, hair-raising, terrifying

แสยะ to grin, grimace

    ยิ้มแสยะ to grin, smirk, sneer (at); give a derisive smile

แสร้ง to pretend, feign, make a pretense (of)

    แสร้งเป็นไม่เห็น to pretend not to see

    แสร้งยิ้ม to give a false smile

แสลง unwholesome, injurious, deleterious, noxious, not good for one, contraindicated

    แสลงใจ hurt, offended

    แสลงตา disagreeable to look at, offensive

    แสลงหู jarring, grating, disagreeable to the ear

    ของแสลง something which disagrees with one

แสวง to search for, seek, go looking for

    แสวงบุญ to make a pilgrimage

    แสวงหา to search for, seek, go in search of

    แสวงอำนาจ to seek power

โสโครก filthy, dirty; reef, submerged rock

    ของโสโครก filth, excrement, muck

    น้ำโสโครก sewage, polluted water

    หินโสโครก reef, submerged rock, underwater rock

โสด issue, charge, allegation; part, division; single, unmarried

ส
ห
ฬ
อ
ฮ

ชายโสด bachelor, single man

อีกโสดหนึ่ง on the other hand, moreover, in addition, apart from that

โสดาบัน the stream-enterer, one who has reached the initial step in Buddhahood

โสต ear, auditory orifice; aural meatus; stream

โสตประสาท auditory nerve

เสนาะโสต pleasant sounding, sweet, harmonious, pleasing (voice, sound, etc)

โสเภณี prostitute

ช่องโสเภณี brothel

นครโสเภณี courtesan

หญิงโสเภณี female prostitute

โสม ginseng

โสมนัส happiness, joy, delight, bliss, mental pleasure, glad-mindedness

โสมม dirty, soiled, filthy, repulsive, detestable, disgusting

โสร่ง sarong

นุ่งโสร่ง to wear a sarong

โสหุ้ย expense

ค่าโสหุ้ย expenses

ใส clear, bright, pure; unclouded

ใสแจ๋ว crystal clear, limpid

สดใส bright, fresh, radiant, cheerful

สุกใส shining, bright, clear, fresh

ใส่ to put on, wear; to load; to put in, insert

ใส่กลอน to bolt, latch, lock

ใส่กุญแจ to lock

ใส่ความ to make insinuations (about someone), insinuate (that), falsely accuse, impute (something to someone (that)); to slander, calumniate

ใส่ไคล้ slyly discredit (someone)

ใส่ใจ to pay attention, take an interest (in)

ใส่น้ำหอม to use perfume

ใส่บาตร to make a food offering (in a monk's bowl)

ใส่ไฟ see **ใส่ความ**

ใส่ยา to put medicine on, medicated

ใส่ร้าย to slander, vilify, say bad things about someone

ใส่ร้ายป้ายสี to malign

ใส่แว่นตา to wear glasses; to put on one's glasses

ใส่เสื้อ to get dressed, put clothes on, wear (a dress, shirt, coat etc)

ใส่หน้า to glare (at); to one's face

ด่าใส่หน้า to scold to one's face

ใส่ห้องขัง to jail

วิ่งเข้าใส่ to run at, rush at (someone)

ไส to push, shove

ไสกบ to plane

ไสช้าง to drive an elephant

ไสรถ to push a cart

ไสหัวไปให้พ้น Get out!, Get the hell out of here!

ผลักไส to drive someone out, get rid of, kick someone out

ไส้ bowels, intestines, innards

ไส้กรอก sausage

ไส้กรอง filter element

ไส้ไก่ spiral candy; (เครื่องใน) giblets; rubber tube-valve

ไส้ขนม a filling

ไส้เดือน earthworm

ไส้ตะเกียง wick; mantle

ไส้ติ่ง appendix

ไส้ติ่งอักเสบ appendicitis

ไส้เทียน candlewick

ไส้พุง bowels, innards; secrets

ไส้เลื่อน hernia, rupture

ไส้ศึก spy, fifth column, enemy agent

ไส้แห้ง hard up

ไสยศาสตร์ magic, sorcery, supernatural arts, thaumaturgy

ไสว *as in* **สว่างไสว** all lit up, brightly illuminated, shining brightly

หก[1] six, hexa-
    หกสิบ sixty
    ที่หก sixth

หก[2] to spill; to be upset, fall over, fall down
    หกคะเมน to /take/do/ a somersault
        หกคะเมนตีลังกา to do a somersault
    หกล้ม to fall down, take a tumble, take a fall, trip (over something)

หงส์ swan

หงอ in fear and trembling, terrified; utterly subdued

หงอก white, gray (hair), to be graying
    หัวหงอก gray-haired; hoary; a grayhead

หงอน crest, comb
    หงอนไก่ cockscomb

หง่อม aged, ancient, decrepit; overripe
    แก่หง่อม very old, hoary, ancient

หงอย dejected, depressed, downcast, down-hearted, down in the dumps, spiritless, subdued; wilted
    หงอยเหงา lonesome; glum, melancholic, depressed, low-spirited

หงาย to turn up
    หงายท้อง to roll over, turn belly up, to fall over backwards; to be defeated, fail; thwarted
    หงายไพ่ใบสุดท้าย to play one's last card
    หงายหลัง to be defeated, crushed
    เดือนหงาย moonlit night, to have moonlight
    นอนหงาย to lie on one's back, lie face upwards, supine

หง่าว to caterwaul; feeling lonely; listless

หง่ำเหง่อะ senile, in one's dotage

หงิก curled, kinky; deformed, contorted; crinkled
    ผมหงิก kinky hair, curly hair
    มือหงิก gnarled hand, contorted fingers
    หน้าหงิก contorted face, angry-looking

หงิง, หงิงๆ whimpering; to hum
    ครางหงิงๆ to whine, whimper

หงิม reserved, taciturn, reticent

หงึกๆ, หงึกหงัก nodding; bobbing
    พยักหน้าหงึกๆ to nod (in agreement or approval)

หงุงหงิง faint
    บ่นหงุงหงิง to mutter

หงุดหงิด touchy, grouchy, irritable, out of sorts cranky, moody

หญ้า grass
    หญ้าคา lalang grass, cogon
    หญ้าปากคอก easy
    หญ้าแพรก Bermuda grass
    ดายหญ้า to hoe
    ทุกหย่อมหญ้า everywhere, all over, high and low
    ทุ่งหญ้า grassland, grassy field
    ใบหญ้า blade of grass
    สนามหญ้า lawn

หญิง woman, girl, she, female, feminine
    หญิงทึนทึก old maid, spinster
    หญิงบริการ service girl
    หญิงพรหมจารี virgin
    หญิงแพศยา prostitute, harlot, streetwalker, strumpet
    หญิงม่าย widow; grass widow
    หญิงสาว young woman, girl
    เด็กหญิง (คำนำหน้าเด็กผู้หญิงอายุไม่เกิน 14 ปี ไม่มีใช้ในภาษาอังกฤษ); girl
    นักเรียนหญิง schoolgirl, female student
    ผู้หญิง woman, girl; female; women's, feminine
    เพศหญิง feminine, female; womanhood; feminine gender
    ลูกหญิง daughter

หด to shrink, contract, draw back; to get turned off
    หดตัว to contract
    หดมือ to draw back (one's hand)
    หดหู่ depressed, blue, low, despondent,

ก
ข
ค
ฆ
ง
จ
ฉ
ช
ซ
ฌ
ญ
ฎ
ฏ
ฐ
ฑ
ฒ
ณ
ด
ต
ถ
ท
ธ
น
บ
ป
ผ
ฝ
พ
ฟ
ภ
ม
ย
ร
ฤ
ฦ
ล
ว
ศ
ษ
ส
ห

dismayed

ยืดได้หดได้ elastic; changeable, shifty

หน[1] time

หนแรก the first time

หนหลัง the next time

กี่หน how many times

หลายหน several times, on /many/ several/ occasions, repeatedly

หน[2] way

หนทาง way, path, avenue, road, street

หมดหนทาง stymied, at a dead end, thwarted

ทุกหนทุกแห่ง every place, everywhere

ล่องหน to vanish, disappear, be gone

หนวก deaf

หนวกหู noisy, annoying (noise, sound etc), deafening, raucous

หูหนวก deaf

หน่วง to delay, detain, retard, hold up, hold back

หน่วงเหนี่ยว to hold up, detain, hold (some-one or something) back

หนวด moustache; tentacle

หนวดเครา beard

หนวดปลาดุก catfish /barbels/feelers/

โกนหนวด to shave

หน่วย unit, squad, corps, outfit, group

หน่วยงาน authority, authorities

หน่วยจู่โจม commando unit

หน่วยดับเพลิง fire department, fire-fighting unit

หน่วยรบ combat unit

หน่วยเลือกตั้ง polling place, polls

หลักหน่วย units

หน่วยก้าน bearing, personality

หน่วยกิต (academic) credit

หนอ an interrogative and reflective word

หน่อ shoot, sprout; son, offspring

หน่อกล้วย banana /sucker/shoot/

หน่อเนื้อเชื้อไข descendant, scion

หน่อไม้ bamboo shoot

หน่ออ่อนๆ tender shoot, young sprout

หนอก hump

หนอง pool, pond, swamp; pus

หนองใน gonorrhea

หนองบึง marsh

เป็นหนอง abscessed, suppurating

หนอน worm, maggot

หนอนข้าวโพด corn borer

หนอนคืบ looper, inchworm

หนอนบ่อนไส้ spy, infiltrator, fifth column; subversive (person, element etc)

หนอนผีเสื้อ caterpillar

หนอนฝ้าย boll weevil

หนอนหนังสือ bookworm

หน่อย a bit, little; in a moment, for a little while

หน่อยหนึ่ง small amount

ขอดูหน่อย Let me take a look.

ขอทางหน่อย Excuse me., Make way please.

ค่อยยังชั่วหน่อย slightly better, getting a little better

นิดหน่อย just a /bit/little/, small, trivial, slight

แย่หน่อย not so good

ลองหน่อย Try it.

สักหน่อย as in ไม่ได้ว่าสักหน่อย What did I say?, I didn't say a thing.

อีกหน่อย a little more

หน็อยแน่ sarcastic sound, You twit!, Look at you!

หนัก heavy, onerous, burdensome; hard; a lot, much, serious; severe, grave; to load (someone with work, etc)

หนักผมอีกแล้ว The load is on me again.

หนักข้อ, หนักมือ to excess, excessive, inordinate

หนักใจ worried, concerned, troubled, disturbed

หนักแน่น steady, stable, solid

อันหนักแน่น serious

มีเหตุผลอันหนักแน่นที่เชื่อได้ว่า serious reason to believe

หนักมาก very heavy, ponderous; very hard, arduous, backbreaking; grave

หนักหน่วง severely, strongly, violently

หนักหนา much, heavy

หนักอก terribly worried, distressed, disturbed

หนักอึ้ง extremely heavy, heavy as lead, ponderous, very weighty

กระเป๋าหนัก well-heeled, flush, well-fixed

ข้าวหนัก slow-growing rice, late rice

ความหนัก weight

ตกหนัก to get (something) in the neck; to pile up on someone, shoulder (the burden, responsibility, etc)

น้ำหนัก weight

ผ่อนหนักผ่อนเบา flexible, accommodating, conciliatory, give and take, compromise, make concessions

เพียบหนัก in critical condition, gravely ill

ภาระหนัก heavy duties, serious task, onerous responsibility

หนัง skin, leather, hide; movie, cinema, motion picture, film

หนังกลับ suede

หนังกลางแปลง open-air movie

หนังกลางวัน a kind of mango

หนังกำพร้า epidermis

หนังแกะ sheepskin

หนังไก่ onionskin (paper); chicken skin

หนังควาย buffalo hide, buffalo leather

หนังตะลุง shadow play

หนังตา eyelid

หนังแท้ genuine leather; dermis

หนังใบ้ silent picture

หนังโป๊ blue movie, X-rated film

หนังพูด talkie, talking picture

หนังเพลง musical film

หนังฟอก leather

หนังสติ๊ก rubber band

หนังสัตว์ hide, animal skin, leather

หนังหน้าไฟ to be on the firing line; scapegoat

หนังเหนียว invulnerable, tough

ฉายหนัง to show a /movie/film/motion picture/, screen a film

ดาราหนัง film star, movie star

ดูหนัง to go to the movies

ผิวหนัง skin, epidermis

ฟอกหนัง to tan leather, dress a hide

โรงหนัง cinema (*Brit*), movie theater

หนังสือ book; paper, letter, writing

หนังสือคู่มือ manual, handbook, user's guide

หนังสือชี้ชวน prospectus

หนังสือเดินทาง passport

หนังสือนำ (letter of) introduction

หนังสือนำเที่ยว guide book, tourist guide

หนังสือบริคณห์สนธิ memorandum of association

หนังสือพิมพ์ newspaper, journal

    หนังสือพิมพ์รายคาบ periodical

    หนังสือพิมพ์รายวัน daily newspaper, a daily

    หนังสือพิมพ์รายสัปดาห์ weekly newspaper, a weekly

หนังสือรับรอง letter of recommendation, certificate

หนังสือรุ่น class book

หนังสือเรียน school book, textbook

หนังสือเวียน circular letter, circular

หนังสือสวดมนต์ prayer book

หนังสือแสดงเจตจำนง letter of intent

หนังสืออ้างอิง reference (book)

หนังสืออ่านประกอบ supplementary reading

หนังสืออ่านเล่น fiction, light reading, leisure reading

เขียนหนังสือ to write

ตัวหนังสือ letter(s), lettering

ตู้หนังสือ bookcase

โต๊ะหนังสือ desk

ท่องหนังสือ to study; to learn by rote

พิมพ์หนังสือ to publish; to print a book

ภาษาหนังสือ literary language

รู้หนังสือ literate

 ไม่รู้หนังสือ illiterate

เรียนหนังสือ to study, go to school (at); to be educated

ห้องหนังสือ library, study

หนับ sticky; a gooey sound

หนา thick, fat; dense; much, many, an emphatic or supplicatory word

หนาขึ้น to thicken, become thick

หนาตา plenty (of), plentiful, all over, everywhere

หนาเตอะ thick, gross

หนาแน่น crowded, packed, congested, heavily (populated, etc), dense

 ความหนาแน่น density; congestion,

ตัว (พิมพ์) หนา boldface (type, print)

นักหนา, หนักหนา serious

หน้า[1] face; side; front; topping, icing

หน้ากระดาน abreast

หน้ากระดาษ page

หน้ากระดูก having a bony face, bony-faced; tight, miserly

หน้ากาก mask

 หน้ากากป้องกันไอพิษ gas mask

หน้ากุ้ง topping of shrimp

หน้าไก่ topping of sauted chicken, (rice) with (sauted) chicken

หน้าเขียว to be pale with anger, be blue in the face (with anger); to look green (in the face)

หน้าแข้ง shank, shin

หน้างาน work site

หน้าเง้า to scowl, pout, wear a long face

หน้าแง space between the eyebrows

หน้าจั่ว gable

หน้าจืด plain, undistinguished; shame-faced, embarrased

หน้าเจื่อน see เจื่อน หน้า 124

หน้าฉาก publicly, in public

หน้าเฉยตาเฉย unabashed, unconcerned; with a blank face

หน้าชา to be numb with embarrassment

หน้าซีด to blanch, turn pale, look pale, wan

หน้าด้าน /thick/ tough/-skinned, insensitive; shameless, brazen

หน้าดำคร่ำเครียด to look serious, look strained

หน้าดิน surface fill, topsoil

หน้าแดง flushed, red-faced, to blush

หน้าตั้ง a spicy sauce

หน้าตัวเมีย coward, spineless, wimp, sissy

หน้าตา looks, appearance, features, expression

 หน้าตาเฉย without batting an eyelash; with a straight face

 หน้าตาเฉลียวฉลาด intelligent face, bright looking, smart

 หน้าตาดี good-looking, prepossessing

 หน้าตาดุร้าย mean-looking, fierce-faced

 หน้าตายิ้มแย้ม smiling face, to look happy, cheerful (expression)

 หน้าตายู่ยี่ to have a rumpled look, look discomposed

 หน้าตาร่วงโรย exhausted, worn out, pooped

หน้าต่าง window

หน้าตาย impassive, expressionless, stony-faced

หน้าตัก the span of the knees when sitting in lotus position

หน้าตื่น to look startled, aghast, surprised, excited

หน้าแตก embarrassing, embarrassed

หน้าถอดสี to show on (one's) face

หน้าที่ job, duty, function, work, responsibility; acts

การปฏิบัติหน้าที่ทางการทูต performance of diplomatic acts

หน้าเนื้อใจเสือ wolf in sheep's clothing, dissimulator

หน้าบอกบุญไม่รับ to look dissatisfied, unfriendly, unsociable, cold

หน้าบาง too shy (to), ashamed; sensitive

หน้าบาน beaming, delighted, to look happy

หน้าบ้าน in front of the house, (at the) front door

หน้าบึ้ง sulky, sullen, to look /cross/ cranky/, grumpy-looking

หน้าบูด to look glum, in a bad mood, be in a sour mood, sour-looking

หน้าปก (front) cover

หน้าปัด face (of a /clock/watch/), dial

หน้าเป็น grinning, smirking, to wear a smile

หน้าเป็นมัน oily face

หน้าผา cliff, precipice

   หน้าผาชัน precipice

หน้าผาก forehead

หน้าไฟ before the funeral pyre

   นางหน้าไฟ someone who bears the brunt (of something)

   บวชหน้าไฟ to be ordained a monk during the cremation ceremonies of a parent or older relative

หน้าม้า a shill; a claque

หน้าม้าน abashed, discountenanced

หน้ามืด to faint, feel /dizzy/faint/, black out; to go /crazy/berserk/, lose control, be blinded by passion, crazed

   หน้ามืดตามัว blind with (love, rage, etc), besotted (by, with); to become dizzy, have a blackout

หน้ามือเป็นหลังมือ to reverse; a reversal (of)

สถานการณ์เปลี่ยนจากหน้ามือเป็นหลังมือ The situation reversed itself.

หน้ามุข balcony; porch, verandah

หน้ามุ่ย to scowl, look cross, pout, have a sour face; to look unhappy, out of sorts

หน้าไม้ crossbow; a unit of quantity for lumber

หน้าย่น wrinkled face, to have wrinkles; to frown; to wrinkle one's brow

หน้าเศร้า to look /sad/dejected/, sad-looking, glum

หน้าสลด tragic; to look shocked, crushed

หน้าสังขยา covered with egg custard

หน้าสิ่วหน้าขวาน critical situation, crisis

หน้าเสีย to look disappointed, ruffled, disconcerted; to become pale

หน้าหงาย to be balked

หน้าใหญ่ใจโต openhanded, munificent, lavish

หน้าหนา thick-skinned, insensitive, shameless, unabashed, brazen

หน้าหนาว cold season, winter

หน้าหลัง back page; reverse side

หน้าหัก flat face

หน้าแห้ง depressed, down in the mouth

หน้าใหม่ newcomer, neophyte, fresh face

หน้าไหว้หลังหลอก hypocritical

หน้าอก chest

กู้หน้า to save face, /save/retrieve/ a situation

ขายหน้า shameful, disgraceful, to be disgraced, ashamed

ดูต่างหน้า a /photograph/picture/ used as a /keepsake/memento/

ได้หน้า to get credit (for)

ต่อหน้าต่อตา before one's very eyes, right before one's eyes, in one's presence, in front of

ตั้งหน้าตั้งตา to apply oneself (to), devote oneself (to), concentrate (on)

ตีหน้า to wear an expression (of); to feign

น้อยหน้า to be outdone, feel inferior (to)

นายหน้า broker, commission agent

บากหน้า (to go to someone)/humbly/ meekly/, swallow one's pride (in going to someone for help)

บ่ายหน้า to head for; to face

เบื้องหน้า in the future; ahead (of), before, in front (of)

ใบหน้า features, face, visage

ประจันหน้า to confront, encounter

เผชิญหน้า to face, confront

พยักหน้า to nod (in assent)

พร้อมหน้า all together

ภายหน้า next time, in the future, later on

มีหน้า to look; to dare, have the effrontery (to)

มีหน้ามีตา to be a /somebody/personage/, be someone, respected, esteemed

มุ่งหน้า to head (for, to, towards)

เมินหน้า to turn away

ไม่เลือกหน้า indiscriminately, impartially, without distinction

ไม่ไว้หน้า to put to shame, not spare one's feelings, be a slap in the face (to someone), humiliating

ย่อหน้า to make a new paragraph, indent

ล้างหน้า to wash one's face, get cleaned up

วันหน้า later, next time, one day, sometime in the future

ส่ายหน้า to shake one's head

สีหน้า (facial) expression, look

เสียหน้า to lose face

หน้า[2] season

หน้านา rice-planting season

หน้าน้ำ flood season

หน้าฝน rainy season

หน้าร้อน hot season, summer

หน้าแล้ง dry season

หน้าหนาว cold season, winter

หนาม thorn, spine, barb

หนามยอกอก a torment, a thorn in the side

เป็นเสี้ยนหนาม enemy (of), scourge (of), bane (of)

ลวดหนาม barbed wire

หนามเตย prongs

หน่าย fed up, bored, tired (of), to grow cold

หน่ายหนี to take off, run out on someone

หน่ายแหนง sick of (life, marriage, work, etc), leery and fed up; exasperated (with)

เบื่อหน่าย fed up, disgusted (with), so bored (with), tired (of), to have had enough (of)

เหนื่อยหน่าย low-spirited, depressed, disheartened, sick of

หนาว cold, chilly

หนาวจัด freezing, frigid, bitter cold, very cold

หนาวใจ alone, forlorn, lonesome, to feel neglected

หนาวเหน็บ biting cold

ขี้หนาว sensitive to the cold; to feel cold all the time

ฤดูหนาว winter, cold season

หนำ[1] as in **หนำใจ** satisfied, to one's satisfaction

หนำ[2] as in **มิหนำซ้ำ** not only that, as if it weren't enough, and in addition, worse than that

หนี to flee, run away, escape, get away

หนีตามผู้ชาย to elope

หนีไม่พ้น inevitable, inescapable

หนีรอดไปได้ to make good one's escape, get away

หนีเสือปะจระเข้ out of the frying pan into the fire

หนีหาย to disappear, vanish

หนีเอาตัวรอด to flee for one's life, save one's own skin, run away

ขวัญหนี to lose heart, lose self-confidence, have a sinking feeling; scared stiff, to quail

ถอยหนี to flee, run away (from something), retreat

ผละหนี to run /off/away/, take off, skedaddle

วิ่งหนี to run away, flee

หลบหนี to evade, escape, go into hiding, abscond

หนี้ debt, obligation

หนี้บุญคุณ debt of gratitude

เป็นหนี้บุญคุณ to owe a debt of gratitude (to), be indebted (to someone for something), be beholden (to)

หนี้ที่ไม่ก่อให้เกิดรายได้ non-performing loan (NPL)

หนี้สิน debts, indebtedness, liabilities

หนี้สินรุงรัง heavily in debt, head over heels in debt

หนี้สูญ bad debt

แทงเป็นหนี้สูญ to write off a bad debt

หนี้เสีย bad debt

เจ้าหนี้ creditor; obligee

ชำระหนี้ to pay a debt, discharge one's /debt/obligation/, clear a debt; to fulfill an obligation

เป็นหนี้ to owe, be in debt, be indebted (to, by)

มีหนี้สินล้นพันตัว insolvent

ลูกหนี้ debtor, obligor

หนีบ to pinch, nip, clamp

หนีบใต้รักแร้ to carry under one's arm, clamp under one's arm

ไม้หนีบผ้า clothespin

หนึ่ง one

หนึ่งในร้อย in a hundred

หนึ่งในสาม one third; one out of three

หนึ่งไม่มีสอง unique, incomparable

ชั้นหนึ่ง first class, superb, prime

ที่หนึ่ง first, first-class

หนืด viscous, sticky; tough, cheap, stingy

หนุน to prop (up), bolster, raise up, boost; support, encourage, reinforce

หนุนเนื่อง (to come) in a steady stream, (to come) in droves, in waves

หนุนหลัง to back up, support, be behind (someone)

กองหนุน reserve corps, reserves; reinforcements

แขนหนุนหัว to rest one's head on one's arm, use one's arm for a pillow

อุดหนุน to subsidize; support, back, aid

หนุบ ๆ nibbling; throbbing pain

หนุบหนับ nibbling (at); chewy

หนุ่ม young, youthful; youth, young man, boy, adolescent, stripling

หนุ่มแน่น in the fullness of youth, virile

หนุ่มสาว young people, youngsters, young folks, boys and girls, teenagers

หนุ่มเหน้า youngster, young, teenager

พ่อหนุ่ม young man, lad, my boy

หนุ่ย rounded

หนู rat, mouse; affectionate pronoun for a child or woman

หนูตะเภา guinea pig

หนูติดกับ rat in a trap

หนูน้อย little child, kid, little shaver

คุณหนู my little one, child

ห่ม[1] to bob along

ห่ม[2] to cover oneself; to wear, put on, dress (in), clad (in)

ห่มผ้า dressed, clothed; covered, clad

เครื่องนุ่งห่ม clothing, wearing apparel, garments

ผ้านุ่งผ้าห่ม clothes

ผ้าห่ม blanket, covers

หมก buried (in, under), to bury, cover over

หมกไฟ roasted (in ashes, embers, etc), to roast

หมกมุ่น to indulge (in), be engrossed, absorbed (in); spending all one's time (in,

ห
ฬ
อ
ฮ

with, doing), to concentrate (on)

หมกเม็ด having an ulterior /motive/ purpose/ effect/; to be hiding something, tricky, have a hidden purpose; sleeper

พ.ร.บ.คลื่นหมกเม็ดบทเฉพาะกาล Waveband Bill Provisional Clause Contains Sleeper

ข้อความหมกเม็ด sleeper

หมกไหม้ to roast (in hell), suffer torment, be tormented

ห่อหมก minced /fish/chicken/ steamed in banana leaf

หมด to be finished, expire, end, terminate, be used up, have nothing left, out of

หมดกะจิตกะใจ dispirited, disheartened

หมดกำลัง to be at the end of one's strength, exhausted, all in

หมดกำลังใจ totally discouraged

หมดเกลี้ยง to run out (of something), be all gone

หมดเขต the time (for something) expires (on, at), deadline (for), final date

หมดความจำเป็น no longer /needed/ necessary/, superfluous

หมดความเชื่อถือ to have no more /confidence/faith/ in, no more respect for

หมดจด clean, spotless, unblemished, bright, impeccable, perfect

หมดจดงดงาม to perfection, perfection itself, of great beauty

หมดด้วยกัน altogether, in all, all told

หมดตัว penniless, wiped out, to lose everything

หมดตูด *see* **หมดตัว**

หมดท่า to be outdone, bested

หมดเนื้อหมดตัว wiped out, ruined, bankrupt

หมดประตูสู้ to have no way out, have one's hands tied, have no defenses

หมดปัญญา to have no further idea, be at a loss, be at one's wits' end, not be able to

think of anything; to be unable (to)

หมดปัญหา The problem is solved., that does it, to be all right

หมดเปลือก everything, holding nothing back

หมดเปลือง to cost; to spend; to consume; to waste, be wasted

หมดมลทิน to be cleared, be exonerated

หมดราคา worthless, valueless

หมดแรง exhausted, worn out

หมดแล้ว finished, all gone, nothing left

หมดเวลา The time is up., to run out of time, have no more time

หมดสติ (become) unconscious, lose consciousness, senseless

หมดหนทาง stymied, at a dead end, thwarted

หมดหนทางหากิน to have no way to earn one's living

หมดห่วง to have no more worries (about), relieved

หมดห่วงหมดใย *see* **หมดห่วง**

หมดหวัง hopeless

หมดอายุความ to be barred by the statute of limitations, barred by prescription

หมดโอกาส to miss an /opportunity/ chance/, have no chance (to), no further opportunity (to)

รวมทั้งหมด totalling, altogether

เหมือนกันหมด all the same, like peas in a pod

หม่น dull, gray; sad

หม่นหมอง glum, gloomy, dismal, melancholy

หมวก hat

หมวกกะโล่ pith helmet

หมวกกันแดด sun hat

หมวกกันน็อก crash helmet

หมวกแก๊ป cap

หมวกปริญญา academic cap, mortarboard

หมวกฟาง straw hat

หมวกสักหลาด felt hat

หมวกเหล็ก helmet

หมวด group, company, section; chapter, division

หมวดหมู่ category, group

เป็นหมวดเป็นหมู่ arranged, classified, in groups, categorized

ผู้หมวด lieutenant

หมอ doctor, physician, healer; guy

หมอกระดูก bone healer

หมอกลางบ้าน village /doctor/healer/

หมอความ lawyer

หมองู snake charmer

หมอเฉพาะโรค (medical) specialist

หมอดู fortune-teller

หมอดูลายมือ palmist

หมอเด็ก pediatrician

หมอตา oculist, ophthalmologist

หมอตำแย midwife

หมอถ้อยหมอความ glib talker, fast-talker; know-it-all

หมอเถื่อน unlicensed medical practitioner, quack doctor

หมอนวด masseur (ชาย), masseuse (หญิง)

หมอประจำตัว personal /doctor/physician/

หมอประจำบ้าน village doctor, local doctor

หมอผ่าตัด surgeon

หมอผี faith healer, exorcist, witch doctor, medicine man, shaman

หมอแผนโบราณ traditional healer, folk medicine practitioner

หมอฟัน dentist

หมอยา physician, medical doctor

หมอลำ (Lao or Northeastern) folksinger

หมอสมุนไพร herbalist, herb doctor

หมอสอนศาสนา missionary

หมอสัตว์ veterinary

หม้อ pot, pan

หม้อกรอง filter

หม้อกาแฟ coffeepot, percolator, coffee maker

หม้อแกง custard pudding; stewpan, stewpot

หม้อข้าว ricepot, rice cooker

หม้อเคลือบ enamelled /pan/pot/

หม้อดิน earthenware pot

หม้อน้ำ boiler; radiator; waterpot

หม้อแปลง transformer

หม้อไฟฟ้า storage battery

หม้อไห pots

ช่างหม้อ potter

ดินหม้อ black deposit on the bottom of a pot

ตีหม้อ to screw (sl.), go whoring; a game of blind-folded pot-smashing

หมอก mist, fog, haze; dark gray

หมอกเพลิง nebula

มีหมอก hazy, foggy, misty

เมฆหมอก cloudy and foggy, overcast; dark period, lowering /period/days/etc, a storm brewing

ก่อนเหตุการณ์พฤษภามีเมฆหมอกทางการเมือง *Before the May events, a political storm was brewing.*

ท้องฟ้าปราศจากเมฆหมอก clear and cloudless sky

หมอง tarnished, sullied

หมองใจ to be on the outs (with somebody), feel enmity (towards somebody), rancorous

หมองหมาง suspicious (of someone); estranged, alienated

มัวหมอง under a cloud, in disgrace, tainted

เศร้าหมอง downcast, unhappy, gloomy, dispirited; defiled

หม่นหมอง glum, gloomy, dismal, melancholy

หมอน pillow; ramrod; spacer

หมอนข้าง dutch wife, bolster

หมอนรถไฟ sleeper

ห
ฬ
อ
ฮ

ปลอกหมอน pillowcase
ล้มหมอนนอนเสื่อ to fall ill, become sick
หม่อน white mulberry
หมอบ to prostrate oneself; to crouch (down)
หมอบราบคาบแก้ว to give up, be utterly defeated, admit utter defeat
หมอบลง to crouch down
หมอบลงแทบเท้า to fall at one's feet, bow down (before, at)
หมอบลาน to prostrate oneself
หม่อม an honorific title for a high ranking person; title of persons related to a king
หม่อมเจ้า /His/Her/ Serene Highness, Mom Chao, grandchild of a king
หม่อมฉัน I, me
หม่อมราชวงศ์ Mom Rajawong, great-grandchild of a king
หม่อมหลวง Mom Luang, great-great-grandchild of a king
หมอย pubic hair, pubes
หมอยข้าวโพด corn silk
หมัก to soak, steep; to store; to marinate, pickle; to ferment; yeast
หมักเค็มรมควัน curing
หมักดอง fermented; pickled
หมักบ่ม to ferment, brew
หมักหมม piled up, stored up, to accumulate
เชื้อหมัก yeast
หมัด[1] flea
หมัด[2] fist, punch
หมัดเด็ด knock-out punch
เหวี่ยงหมัด to throw a punch (to the jaw etc)
กำหมัด fist
หมัน sterile, barren
ทำหมัน to sterilize, be sterilized
เป็นหมัน to be sterile; ineffectual, futile, fruitless, to come to nothing, of no avail, in vain
หมั่น diligently, make an effort (to), regularly

หมั้น to become engaged (to), betrothed (to)
ของหมั้น engagement gift, betrothal gage
คู่หมั้น fiance (ชาย), fiancée (หญิง), person engaged to be married
แหวนหมั้น engagement ring
ทองหมั้น betrothal gage of gold, gift of gold to seal an engagement to marry
หมั่นไส้ to be put off (by); to be disgusted (with); Don't be cute!
น่าหมั่นไส้ off-putting; disgusting; too cute
หมับ all of a sudden, in a flash, rapidly
คว้าหมับ to grab, snatch
ทำปากหมับๆ to work the mouth rapidly
หมา dog
หมาๆ low, base, gross
หมากลางถนน stray dog; homeless wretch
หมาขี้เรื้อน mangy dog
หมาจิ้งจอก fox; foxy, cunning
หมาจู Pekinese dog
หมาตัวเมีย bitch
หมาใน hyena, jackal
หมาบ้า mad dog, rabid dog
หมาป่า wolf
หมาไล่เนื้อ hound
หมาวัด temple dog; lowlife
หมาหนังกลับ mangy dog
หมาหมู่ pack of dogs
หมาหยอกไก่ just flirting
หมาหวงก้าง dog in the manger
หมาหอน to howl
หมาหัวเน่า pariah
หมาหางด้วน tailless dog; (fig) ignored, an outcast
หมาเห่า to bark
หมาเห่าใบตองแห้ง empty talk, all talk but no action
หมาก betel palm, areca nut, betel nut
หมากเก็บ jacks, jackstones
หมากฝรั่ง chewing gum

หมากพลู prepared betel, betel and betel nut

หมากรุก chess

กินหมาก to /chew/take/ betel

ขันหมาก traditional tray of gifts from the groom to the bride's family

ชานหมาก chewed-out betel quid

เชี่ยนหมาก betel tray, betel box

ต้นหมาก betel palm

น้ำหมาก betel juice

หมาง as in **หมางใจ** estranged, alienated; to be put off (by someone)

หมาด damp

เพิ่งเสร็จหมาดๆ hot เช่น hot out of the oven, hot off the assembly line, freshly done

หมาย warrant, writ, summons; to intend, aim mean, guess, surmise, estimate; to mark, make a sign

หมายกำหนดการ program

หมายเกณฑ์ conscription notice

หมายค้น search warrant

หมายความว่า to mean; to imply

หมายจับ arrest warrant

หมายใจ to hope, intend (to), have an intention (to)

หมายตา to take notice of, have one's eye on (someone or something)

หมายถึง to mean; to refer (to); to imply

หมายบังคับ writ of execution

หมายพยาน subpoena

หมายมั่นปั้นมือ to be ambitious (to), be determined (to), be set on (doing etc), resolved (to)

หมายเรียก summons

หมายเลข number

หมายศาล writ, summons, subpoena, court order, warrant

หมายสั่ง court order

หมายหัว to make a mental note (of someone), keep someone in mind, single (someone) out

หมายเหตุ remarks, note

กฎหมาย law, legislation, statute

คาดหมาย to expect, plan, anticipate, estimate

เครื่องหมาย sign, mark, symbol, token

เครื่องหมายการค้า trademark, trade mark

จุดหมาย aim, destination, objective, end, goal, focus

จุดหมายปลายทาง ultimate goal; destination

ที่หมาย destination, end, goal, target

นัดหมาย to date, make an appointment

เป้าหมาย purpose, object, target, aim

มอบหมาย to authorize, assign, delegate, appoint

เลขหมาย number

หม้าย see ม่าย หน้า 377

หมิ่น on the verge (of falling, defeat etc); precariously, carelessly, heedlessly; to look down (on), disparage, hold in contempt, insult

หมิ่นประมาท to libel (โดยการเขียน), slander (โดยวาจา), defame; defamatory, slanderous, libellous

ฟ้องหมิ่นประมาท to sue for /defamation /slander/libel/

หมิ่นประมาทศาล contempt of court, to be in contempt of court

หมิ่นพระบรมเดชานุภาพ (to commit) lèse majesté, lese majesty

หมิ่นเหม่ perilous, dangerous, precarious

หมี bear

หมีขาว polar bear

หมี่ vermicelli, fine noodles

หมี่กรอบ crispy vermicelli

หมี่น้ำ vermicelli in soup

หมี่แห้ง plain vermicelli

เส้นหมี่ vermicelli

หมึก ink

   หมึกพิมพ์ printing ink

   กระปุกหมึก inkpot

   ปลาหมึก squid; octopus

   ปากกาหมึกซึม fountain pen

หมิ่น[1] cheeky, impudent

หมิ่น[2] ten thousand

หมุด peg; pin; thumbtack

   เข็มหมุด pin

หมุน to turn around, rotate, spin, revolve

   หมุนเงิน to make money, turn over one's money

   หมุนติ้ว to spin

   หมุนไปตามแกน to rotate on its axis

   หมุนรอบ to rotate, revolve; spin around

     หมุนรอบดวงอาทิตย์ to revolve around the sun

   หมุนเวียน to circulate

   ม้าหมุน merry-go-round, carrousel

   หัวหมุน to spin *as in* My head is spinning.; in a state, overwhelmed (with work, things to do, etc)

หมุบ swiftly, fast, rapidly

   หมุบหมับ in a hurry, quickly

   คว้าหมุบ to snatch

หมู pig, hog, boar

   หมูๆ a snap, simple

   หมูตัวเมีย sow

   หมูทะเล porpoise

   หมูป่า wild boar

   หมูย่าง roast pork, grilled /pork/pork chop/

   หมูหยอง dried shredded pork

   หมูหัน barbecued piglet

   หมูแฮม ham

   หมูเห็ดเป็ดไก่ feast, banquet, plenty of food

   ต้มหมู to dupe, swindle, gull

   น้ำมันหมู lard

   เนื้อหมู pork

ลมบ้าหมู epilepsy

ลูกหมู piglet

หมู่[1] group, collection; those (who); friends; (police) officer

   หมู่เกาะ archipelago

   หมู่บ้าน village, hamlet; house group

   หมู่ไม้ grove (of), stand of trees

   เป็นหมวดเป็นหมู่ arranged, classified, in groups, categorized

หมู่[2] days

   หมู่นี้ these days, nowadays, lately

หยก jade

หยกๆ just, very recently

หย่ง to stand on tiptoe (หย่งตัว)

   หย่งเท้า to tiptoe

   นั่งหย่ง to squat on one's toes

หยด to drip; drop (of)

   หยดติ๋ง to drip

   หยดน้ำ drop of water

   หยดย้อย spectacularly beautiful

หยวก pith of a banana stalk

   พริกหยวก bell pepper

หยวน agreed, okay, alright

หยอก to tease, joke (with), banter; to play, be playful

   หยอกเย้า to tease, make playful remarks, be playful (with someone)

   หยอกล้อ to tease, kid around (with someone), joke (with), play a joke (on someone)

   หยอกเอิน to dally (with), spoon

หยอด to pour out drop by drop, pour slowly

   หยอดน้ำมัน to lubricate, oil, grease; to grease (one's) palm, tip

   หยอดหลุม a penny-pitching game

หย่อน slack, loose, limp, hanging; sagging; to let down, drop; to be short (of), lack, lacking

   หย่อนใจ to relax

   หย่อนบัตร to drop a ballot (in a ballotbox),

cast a ballot

หย่อนลง to lower (something)

หย่อนสมรรถภาพ impotent; incompetent, inefficient, inadequate

หย่อนอารมณ์ to relax

ลดหย่อน to bring (the price etc) down, reduce, abate, lighten; to allow a deduction

หย่อม small group, small pile, tuft

ทุกหย่อมหญ้า everywhere, all over, high and low

หยอมแหยม scanty, sparse, meager, thin

หยอย curly, frizzy

หยัก notched, indented

หยักๆ serrated, notched, zig-zag, scalloped, dentated

หยักรั้ง drawn up high

หยักศก, หยักโศก wavy

หยั่ง to fathom, sound, see, find out, discover

หยั่งความจริง to /fathom/discover/ the truth, get to the bottom of (something)

หยั่งใจ to test another's feelings, fathom (someone)

หยั่งเชิง to see what (someone) will do, spar, test (another's) reaction

หยั่งน้ำ to take a sounding, fathom the water, measure the depth of the water

หยั่งเสียง to sound out, canvass

หยัด to be firm, resolute

ยืนหยัด to stand fast, stand firm, unyielding

หยัน to belittle, hold in contempt, scoff (at), sneer (at)

หย่า to divorce, break off; to give up

หย่ากัน divorced, to get a divorce

หย่านม to wean, be weaned

หย่าร้าง divorced

ฟ้องหย่า to sue for divorce

หยากเยื่อ refuse, rubbish, waste

หยากไย่ cobwebs

หยาด drop

หยาดน้ำค้าง dewdrop; the sign " ํ " indicating the sound of "ang"

หยาดฝน raindrop

หยาดเยิ้ม ravishing, ravishingly

หยาดเหงื่อ sweat, perspiration

หยาบ rough, coarse, crude

หยาบคาย coarse, indecent, vulgar

หยาบช้า vicious

หยาบโลน obscene, dirty, ribald

หยาบหยาม to be crudely contemptuous (of, in, towards)

คำหยาบ /coarse/dirty/obscene/lewd/ word, coarse language

พูดจาหยาบโลน to use foul language

หยาม to insult, affront, disparage

หยามน้ำหน้า to regard with contempt, be contemptuous (of), be insulting

หยำเป to lead a life of dissipation, be dissipated, debauched

เมาหยำเป a drunkard, boozer, drunken sot

หยิก to pinch; kinky (ผม), crinkled (ผ้า, ใบไม้), wrinkled

ผมหยิก kinky hair, curly hair

หยิ่ง haughty, stuck up, conceited, vain, proud, aloof

หยิ่งในเกียรติ proud

หยิ่งผยอง arrogant, self-important, egocentric

หยิ่งยโส arrogant, overbearing

หยิบ to pick up, take

หยิบฉวย to snatch, grab

หยิบปากกา to pick up a pen

หยิบผิด to find fault (with), be faultfinding; to pick up something by mistake

หยิบมือเดียว a pinch (of), handful, small /number/quantity/

หยิบยกปัญหา to raise a question, /bring up/take up/ a problem

หยิบยืม to borrow

ห
ฬ
อ
ฮ

หยิบหย่ง unbusinesslike, lackadaisical

หยิม ๆ in a drizzle, drizzling

    ฝนตกหยิม ๆ to drizzle

หยี squinting, narrowed

    ตาหยี slit-eyed, narrow eyes, to squint

หยุกหยิก scrawling; to be fidgety, restless

    ลายมือหยุกหยิก scrawl; /scribbly/scrawling/ handwriting

หยุด to stop, cease; to pause

    หยุดกึก to come to a sudden stop, stop /short/abruptly/

    หยุดคิด to think about (something), take time to think, pause for reflection; to put (something) out of one's mind

    หยุดงาน to stop work

        นัดหยุดงาน to strike, walk out

    หยุดชะงัก to stop short

    หยุดเดิน to stop

    หยุดทำงาน to stop working

    หยุดนิ่ง to stand still, immobile

    หยุดพัก to take a break, stop for a rest; intermission

    หยุดยิง to cease fire

    หยุดโรงเรียน to stop school

    ไม่หยุดหย่อน tirelessly, non-stop, without letup, without slackening

    ลาหยุด to take leave

    วันหยุด holiday, day off

หยุ่น see ยืดหยุ่น หน้า 399

หยุมหยิม trivial, petty, picayune

    เรื่องหยุมหยิม /small/trifling/ matter, triviality

หยูกยา medicine

หรดี southwest

หรอ see สึกหรอ หน้า 500

หร็อมแหร็ม sparse, scanty, thin

    มีขนขึ้นหร็อมแหร็ม a /scanty/thin/ growth of hair / hair appearing sparsely / a few sparse hairs

หรา to express an emotion through a vigorous

or broad physical action

    ชูมือหรา to extend one's arm in /joy/happiness/ etc

    นอนแผ่หรา to relax with arms and legs outstretched

    ยิ้มหรา to smile broadly

หรี่ to dim, turn down, narrow

    หรี่ตา to squint, narrow one's eyes

    หรี่ไฟ to turn down the fire; to dim the light, turn down the lights

    ไฟหรี่ parking lights

    แสงหรี่ dim light

หรีด wreath

    พวงหรีด wreath

หรือ or, and; a question word

    หรือว่า or is it that, or else

    งั้นหรือ Oh?, Is that so?

    จริงหรือ Really?, Is that so?

หรุบ ๆ in a rain

    ดอกพิกุลลงหรุบ ๆ the pikul blossoms were /falling in a rain/raining down/. / There was a rain of pikul blossoms.

หรู, หรูหรา luxurious, expensive, fancy, magnificent, deluxe

    จัดงานหรูหรา to give a magnificent /party /celebration/ etc

    แต่งตัวหรูหรา to wear /fancy/expensive/ luxurious/ clothes, be all decked out, dressed /magnificently/gorgeously/

หฤทัย heart, mind

    พระหฤทัย sacred heart

หฤหรรษ์ ecstatic

หฤโหด horrible, horrendous, horrifying

    ความหฤโหด horror

หลง to be infatuated (with), fall for (someone or something), be head over heels in love (with), crazy about (someone or something), dote on; misguided, led astray; to mistake, misunderstand, take something for something else; to be left; to go astray, stray; by accident, accidental

หลงเสียจนลืมหูลืมตาไม่ขึ้น to be head over heels in love, be besotted (by)

หลงกล to be tricked, be taken in (by), be fooled (by), duped, fall for

หลงกัน to miss one another

หลงคารม to be taken in

หลงเชื่อ to be misled into believing, be deceived; fall for (something); to believe

หลงเชื่อคนง่าย to be gullible

หลงตา unnoticed, overlooked

หลงทาง to lose one's way, get lost, go astray

หลงผิด mistaken, misled, misguided; to misunderstand

หลงเมีย to be /infatuated/blindly in love/ with one's wife, be besotted by one's wife, dote on one's wife

หลงระเริง to indulge oneself (in), revel in

หลงรัก to become infatuated (with), fall for someone, be crazy about

หลงรักไม่ลืมหูลืมตา to be head over heels in love

หลงๆ ลืมๆ to be absentminded, forgetful; senile

หลงเสน่ห์ to be charmed, captivated (by someone)

หลงใหล to be mad about

ขี้หลงขี้ลืม forgetful, absentminded

ลุ่มหลง infatuated (with), intoxicated (with, by), mad about

เสียงหลง off-key; the voice becomes shrill

หล่น to fall

หลบ to avoid, evade, dodge, duck, shy away (from); to take shelter

หลบซ่อน to hide oneself

หลบมุม to find a discreet corner, stay out of sight

หลบหน้า to keep out of sight, avoid (someone)

หลบหน้าค่าตา *see* **หลบหน้า**

หลบหนี to evade, escape, go into hiding, abscond

หลบหลีก to lie low

หลุมหลบภัย air raid shelter, bunker

หล่ม quagmire, mudhole, bog, mire

หลวง great; public, state, government; royal; Luang

หลวงพ่อ venerable bhikku, elder monk

ของหลวง state property, public property

ข้าหลวง provincial/governor/commissioner/

ข้าหลวงใหญ่ high commissioner, governor-general

ถนนหลวง public road, public thoroughfare

ทะเลหลวง high seas

ทางหลวง highway, state highway, public road

นครหลวง capital

ในหลวง His Majesty, the King

เมียหลวง principal wife

เมืองหลวง capital

ยาตำราหลวง drugs listed in the pharmacopoeia

รถไฟหลวง Royal State Railways

โรงเรียนหลวง state school, government school, public school

วังหลวง royal palace

หมอหลวง royal physician

หลวม loose, ample, roomy; carelessly

หลวมๆ rough, general

หลวมตัว to get involved, compromise oneself, get mixed up (in something)

หลวมโพรก too loose, baggy, oversized; capacious

หลอ to remain, be left; worn (away, down)

ฟันหลอ broken tooth, chipped tooth

เหลือหลอ left, remaining

ห
ฬ
อ
ฮ

หล่อ[1] to cast

หล่อเทียน to pour a candle

หล่อหลอม to mold

ช่างหล่อ caster, founder

โรงหล่อ foundry

หล่อ[2] handsome, good-looking; to protect by using /water/oil/

หล่อน้ำ to protect from ants by standing something on a bowl or ant trap filled with water

หล่อลื่น lubricating

รูปหล่อ pretty as a picture, handsome

หลอก to deceive, fool, dupe, scare; to haunt

หลอกๆ sham, not for real, fooling

หลอกต้ม to dupe, swindle, cheat (someone) out of (something)

หลอกลวง to deceive, defraud, cheat, delude

หลอกเล่น to fool

หลอกหลอน to haunt

หลอกให้กลัว to scare

หลอด tube

หลอดกาแฟ (drinking) straw

หลอดแก้ว glass tube

หลอดด้าย spool (of thread, for thread)

หลอดดูด (drinking) straw

หลอดนีออน fluorescent lamp

หลอดไฟฟ้า electric lamp, light bulb, incandescent lamp

หลอดยานัตถุ์ snuff tube

หลอดลม trachea, windpipe

หลอดโลหิต blood vessel

หลอดวิทยุ radio tube

หลอดสวน catheter

หลอดเสียง larynx

หลอดเสียงอักเสบ laryngitis

หลอดอาหาร alimentary canal

หลอน to haunt; *see* **หลอก**

ภาพหลอน hallucination, illusion

หล่อน you (for a woman)

เจ้าหล่อน she, her

หลอม to smelt, melt; to forge, mold

หลอมตัว to fuse

หลอมโลหะ to smelt ore

จุดหลอม melting point

เหล็กหลอม molten iron

หละหลวม carelessly, negligently, in a slipshod manner; loose, inadequate, weak

หลัก stake, post; principle, basis, tenet, something to hold onto; main, basic, fundamental, principal; digit

หลักการ principle

ในหลักการ in principle

รับหลักการ to accept in principle

หลักเกณฑ์ standard, principles, rules, basics

หลักข้อเชื่อ creed

หลักเขตแดน boundary post

หลักชัย finishline, goal

หลักฐาน evidence; good standing

ขาดหลักฐาน lack of evidence

คนมีหลักฐาน person of good standing, responsible person

หลักทรัพย์ security, collateral; securities

หลักปฏิบัติ practices, rules of practice; principles of conduct

หลักประกัน security, assurance, guarantee

หลักไมล์ milestone

หลักลอย unsettled, of no standing

หลักวิชา theory

ตามหลักวิชา theoretically, in theory

หลักศิลาจารึก (stone) inscription

หลักสูตร syllabus, curriculum, course of study

หลักแหล่ง domicile, home, fixed abode

หลักแหลม sharp, smart, ingenious, astute, shrewd, acute

ปักหลัก to take a /stand/position/, hold firm; to settle, stay; to plant a marker

ไม่มีหลัก unprincipled, without principles

ลงหลักปักฐาน to settle (in)

เสียหลัก to get out of control; to /fall/tip/ topple/ over, lose one's balance; to go off course

หลัง back, rear; behind, after, subsequent, latter; a numerical designation for houses

หลังโกง humpbacked, hunchbacked, stooped over

หลังขดหลังแข็ง stiff, aching; backbreaking, to break one's back over (one's work etc)

หลังฉาก behind the scene

หลังบ้าน /behind/in back of/ the house, through the backdoor

หลังม้า (on) horseback

หลังมือ back of the hand

หลังยาว lazy, indolent

หลังสงคราม postwar, after the war

กระจกหลัง rear view mirror

กองหลัง back, defender

ข้างหลัง behind, in back of, to the rear (of)

ขาหลัง hind leg

คล้อยหลัง just left, to have just gone off

ช้างเท้าหลัง one's better half, helpmate

ตอนหลัง later on, subsequently

ตามหลัง to follow, behind; later

ถอยหลัง to back up, go in reverse; to regress, go backwards

ถอยหลังเข้าคลอง reactionary, retrograde, retrogressive

ทีหลัง later; next time; some other time

เบื้องหลัง inside story, more than meets the eye, one's past; behind

ภายหลัง after; subsequently, afterwards, later (on); post-

ลับหลัง behind one's back

ล้าหลัง backward, outmoded, underdeveloped, lagging behind

หลั่ง to pour (out), flow

หลั่งน้ำตา to shed tears

หลั่งน้ำอสุจิ to ejaculate

หลั่งเร็ว to have a premature ejaculation

หลั่งเลือด to bleed

หลั่งไหล to pour (in, forth)

หลังคา roof

หลังคาจาก thatch roof, attap roof

หลังคามุงกระเบื้อง tile roof

หลังคามุงสังกะสี tin roof, corrugated iron roof

หลัด ๆ very recently, a short time ago, just now

อยู่ด้วยกันหลัด ๆ *to have been together very recently*

เห็นหน้ากันหลัด ๆ *to have seen somebody just a short time ago*

หลั่น *as in* ลดหลั่น in descending order; progressively

หลับ to sleep, nap, slumber

หลับตา to close (one's) eyes, shut (one's) eyes

หลับตาทำ to be able to do something with one's eyes shut

หลับ ๆ ตื่น ๆ half asleep, drowsy

หลับนอน to cohabit (with); to go to bed

หลับใน to doze off

หลับปุ๋ย to sleep /soundly/peacefully/

หลับยาม to fall asleep while on duty, be caught napping

หลับสนิท to sleep /soundly/deeply/, sound asleep, in a deep sleep

หลับหูหลับตา to be blind (to)

หลับอุตุ to sleep/soundly/like a log/

งีบหลับ to nap, take a nap

นอนตาหลับ to feel secure (in one's own bed), be at peace

นอนไม่หลับ to be unable to get to sleep, be sleepless เช่น *to pass a sleepless night*

นอนหลับทับสิทธิ์ to fail to exercise one's right to vote

นั่งหลับ to doze off

ห
ฬ
อ
ฮ

อดตาหลับขับตานอน to go without sleep

หลัว[1] a large tall basket

หลัว[2] dimly lit, in the dim light, dark

ฟ้าหลัว overcast (sky)

หลา yard

หล้า world, earth

สุดหล้าฟ้าเขียว to the ends of the earth, ever so far away, beyond the horizon

หลาก different, various, diverse; strange, unusual, amazing; multi

หลากชนิด a variety of, different kinds (of), assorted

หลากสี variegated, multicolored, variety of colors

หลากหลาย multitude (of), various, different, diverse, a variety (of), a lot of different (things, methods, etc)

ความหลากหลาย diversity, variety

ความหลากหลายทางวัฒนธรรม multi-culturalism

น้ำไหลหลาก torrent, rushing water, sweeping flood

หลาน nephew (ชาย), niece (หญิง); grandchild

หลานเขย nephew by marriage

หลานในไส้ one's own /grandchild/nephew /niece/

หลานสะใภ้ niece by marriage

ชั่วลูกชั่วหลาน for succeeding generations

ลูกหลาน descendants, offspring, younger generation, children and grandchildren

หลาบ to be afraid to do something again; scared

หลาบจำ chastened, reformed

เข็ดหลาบ to be afraid to do something again; to have learned one's lesson, be chastened

หลาม see ล้นหลาม หน้า 436

หลาย much, many, several, multi

หลายขนาด different sizes

หลายใจ flirtatious, inconstant

หลายตลบ several times, over and over again

หลายต่อหลาย ever so many, a lot of

หลายปีดีดัก see ดีดัก หน้า 166

หลายพันปี many thousand years ago

หลายสิ่ง many things

หลายสี multicolored

หลายหลาก see หลากหลาย

หลายอย่างต่างๆ กัน many different kinds (of)

ทั้งหลายทั้งปวง /each and every/every single/ (person, thing, problem etc)

ทั้งหลายแหล่ all

มากหน้าหลายตา many, great number (of), multitude (of)

เหลือหลาย superabundance (of), infinite, surpassing

หลาว hollow spear

หลิม small and pointed

หัวหลิม pointed head

หลิ่ว as in หลิ่วตา to squint with one eye; to wink (at), give a wink (to)

เข้าเมืองตาหลิ่วต้องหลิ่วตาตาม When in Rome, do as the Romans do.

ตาหลิ่ว squinted eye

หลีก to move aside, sidestep; get out of the way; to avoid, shun

หลีกทางให้ to make way (for), step aside (for somebody)

หลีกไม่พ้น to fail to avoid; to have no room to pass

หลีกรถ to pass aside; bypass

หลีกลี้ to vanish

หลีกเลี่ยง to avoid, shirk

หลีกเลี่ยงการงาน to shirk one's /duties /responsibilities/

สับหลีก to switch (by, over), by-pass; to manage to avoid (an unwanted encounter), avoid one another

หลบหลีก to lie low

หลืบ narrow opening, passageway

หลุกหลิก restless, nervous, fidgety; uncouth, unrefined

หลุด to slip, come undone, get loose, fall off; to go free; to lose

    หลุดจำนำ forfeited

    หลุดปาก to make a slip, slip out, say something one shouldn't

    อย่าหลุดปาก Don't let it slip out. / Don't let the cat out of the bag.

    หลุดพ้น to be free (of, from), be released (from), escape (from), get out (of)

    หลุดมือ to slip out of the hand, get away

    อย่าให้หลุดมือ Don't let him get away.

    หลุดลอย in vain; to vanish in thin air

    หลุดลุ่ย to unravel, come undone; badly

    แพ้หลุดลุ่ย badly beaten

หลุนๆ to roll (down, along)

หลุบตา to lower one's eyes

หลุม pit, hole, excavation

    หลุมจอด (อากาศยาน) bay

    หลุมดำ black hole

    หลุมฝังศพ grave

    หลุมพราง pitfall, trap

        ตกหลุมพราง to fall into a trap

    หลุมหลบภัย air raid shelter, bunker

    หลุมอากาศ air pocket

    ตกหลุม to fall into a trap, be ensnared

        ตกหลุมรัก to fall in love; become a victim of love

หลู่ to insult, disparage

    หลู่เกียรติ to disparage, insult

    ลบหลู่บุญคุณ to be ungrateful

หวง jealous (of), possessive, unwilling to part with something, protective (of); reserved

    หวงก้าง *see* **หมาหวงก้าง** *หน้า 522*

    หวงห้าม taboo, forbidden, restricted, prohibited

    หวงแหน to treasure, cherish, hold dear; to

be jealous (of one's reputation, country, etc)

    หวงอำนาจ jealous of power

ห่วง[1] to be anxious, concerned, perturbed, worried

    ห่วงใย to be anxious about, worried about, concerned; to care for

    ห่วงหน้าห่วงหลัง overanxious, overcautious

    เป็นห่วง to worry (about), worried (about)

    อย่าเป็นห่วงผมเลย Don't worry about me.

        น่าเป็นห่วง worrisome

ห่วง[2] ring, link, hoop

    ห่วงโซ่อาหาร food chain

    จดหมายห่วงลูกโซ่ chain letter

ห้วง, ห้วงๆ stage, interval, period, expanse (of)

    ห้วงน้ำ expanse of water, ocean

    เสียงขาดเป็นห้วงๆ jerky speech, not smoothly spoken

หวด[1] steamer

หวด[2] to whip, lash, scourge

    หวดด้วยกระบอง to /beat/strike/ with a /club/stick/billy/

หวน[1] to turn back

    หวนกลับ to come back, return

    หวนคิด to recall, reminisce, think back

หวน[2] *as in* **โหยหวน** to moan, wail; to give an eerie call

ห้วน, ห้วนๆ short, curt, abrupt, terse, ungraceful

    พูดเสียงห้วนๆ to be brusque; unpolished speech, uncouth (talk or speech)

หวย lottery

    ใบ้หวย to give a laconic lottery tip

ห่วย, ห่วยๆ lousy, crappy *(sl)*, junky, crummy

    ของห่วยๆ junk, crap

    งานห่วยๆ lousy /job/work/

ห้วย stream, creek

    ห้วยหนองคลองบึง waters

หวอ[1] hollow, opened, exposed

    ระวังอย่าให้หวอ Be careful not to expose

ห
ฬ
อ
ฮ

ก
ข
ค
ฆ
ง
จ
ฉ
ช
ซ
ฌ
ญ
ฎ
ฏ
ฐ
ฑ
ฒ
ณ
ด
ต
ถ
ท
ธ
น
บ
ป
ผ
ฝ
พ
ฟ
ภ
ม
ย
ร
ฤ
ฤๅ
ล
ว
ศ
ษ
ส
ห

yourself.

หวอ² siren

    หวอหลบภัย warning siren

    รถหวอ police car; ambulance; fire /engine/ truck/

หวอด *see* **ก่อหวอด** *หน้า 18*

หวัง to hope, expect, look forward (to)

    หวังดี to wish another well; to mean well, well-intentioned, have goodwill (towards), with good intentions, with friendly intent

    หวังร้าย malicious, with ill will

    ความหวัง hope, expectation

    คาดหวัง to expect, anticipate, forecast, hope for

    ไม่อยากให้ใครคาดหวังกับตัวเรามากเกินไป I don't want anyone to expect too much of me.

    ผิดหวัง disappointed

    มุ่งหวัง aim, purpose, objective; to aim for, look for

    สมหวัง as hoped, (one's wish, desire etc) fulfilled

หวัด¹ in script

    เขียนหวัดอ่านไม่ออก illegible /handwriting/ script/, a scribble, scrawl

หวัด² cold, common cold

    หวัดกิน to have a cold, catch a cold

    หวัดลงคอ (to have a) sore throat

    ไข้หวัด a cold with fever

    เป็นหวัด have a cold

หวั่น to be afraid, scared, feel uneasy (about), worry (that)

    หวั่น ๆ to be anxious (about), have misgivings, apprehensive, fearful

    หวั่นเกรง to be apprehensive, fearful

    หวั่นจิต to be afraid, fear

    หวั่นวิตก frightened, worried (about)

    หวั่นหวาด to be apprehensive

    หวั่นไหว affected (by), sensitive (to), anxious, nervous

หวิว *see* **หัวเราะ** *หน้า 537*

หว่างขา crotch, groin

หวาด to fear, be afraid, scared

    หวาดเกรง to dread, tremble (at, before); with trepidation

    หวาดผวา anxious (about, over), apprehensive (about)

    หวาดระแวง to mistrust, be cautious (of), suspicious

        ความหวาดระแวง mistrust, caution

        ชอบหวาดระแวง paranoid

        โรคหวาดระแวง paranoia

    หวาดเสียว scary, frightening

    หวาดหวั่น to be scared

หวาน¹ sweet; easy

    หวานจัด sugary, too sweet

    หวานเจี๊ยบ very sweet, good and sweet

    หวานใจ sweetheart, darling, honey, sugar

    หวานฉ่ำ juicy sweet; sweet sparkling (eyes), doe-like (eyes)

    หวานหมู a snap (to), as easy as falling off a log, nothing to it

    ของหวาน dessert, sweets, pudding *(Brit)*

    ความหวาน sweetness

    น้ำหวาน sweet drink, soft drink

    เบาหวาน diabetes

    ปากหวาน *see* **ปากหวาน** *หน้า 306*

    เปรี้ยวหวาน sweet and sour

    อ่อนหวาน sweet, gentle

หวาน² to strip, stripped

    เกลียวหวาน stripped thread

หว่าน to sow, broadcast

    หว่านล้อม to cajole (a person) into (doing or agreeing to something), prevail upon someone, win someone over

    การหว่าน sowing

    นาหว่าน a broadcast ricefield

    ผู้หว่าน sower

หวาม to be seized with emotion
    หวามใจ to be gripped /by/with/ (fear, pain, passion etc), have a surge of feeling

หวาย rattan, wicker
    เก้าอี้หวาย /wicker/rattan/ chair
    ร้อยหวาย Achilles tendon

หวิด narrowly, barely, almost
    หวิดไป to narrowly miss

หวิว giddy, dizzy, faint
    ใจหวิว to skip a beat เช่น *His heart skipped a beat.*; to feel faint (with)

หวี comb
    หวีกล้วย hand of bananas
    หวีผม to comb one's hair

หวีด scream, shriek; shrill whistling sound
    นกหวีด whistle

หวือหวา showy, luxurious, fabulous, extravagant
    ไม่หวือหวา conservative, plain

หวุดหวิด narrowly, barely, almost

หวูด steam whistle

หอ tower; hall
    หอกลอง drum tower
    หอการค้า chamber of commerce
    หอคอย watchtower, lookout
        หอคอยงาช้าง ivory tower
    หอดูดาว observatory
    หอไตร library for Buddhist scriptures
    หอนาฬิกา clock tower
    หอบังคับการ control room
    หอพัก dormitory, dorm, hostel
        หอพักนักเรียน student dormitory
    หอระฆัง bell tower, belfry
    หอวิทยาศาสตร์ laboratory
    หอศิลป์ art gallery
    หอสมุด library
        หอสมุดแห่งชาติ National Library
    หอสินค้า warehouse

ห่อ to pack, package, wrap; package, parcel, packet, bale

ห่อตัว to adopt a deferential stance; to make oneself small (out of respect, against the cold etc)
    ห่อหุ้ม to envelop, cover, enclose
    หีบห่อ parcels, packages

ห้อ[1] to gallop, race
    ห้อเหยียด at full gallop, at full speed

ห้อ[2] *as in* **ห้อเลือด** bruise, contusion, black and blue (spot), subcutaneous hemorrhage

หอก spear; prick
    หอกข้างแคร่ potential enemy
    หอกซัด short-handled throwing spear
    หอกปลายปืน bayonet

ห้อง room, chamber, quarters
    ห้องเก็บของ storeroom, closet
    ห้องขัง prison cell, detention cell, jail
    ห้องขายตั๋ว booking office, box office
    ห้องคนไข้ sickroom, ward, patient's room
    ห้องคนใช้ servant's room, servants' quarters
    ห้องครัว kitchen
    ห้องเครื่อง royal kitchen; engine room
    ห้องชุด apartment, flat
    ห้องดนตรี music room
    ห้องเด็ก nursery
    ห้องแต่งตัว dressing room
    ห้องใต้ดิน cellar, basement
    ห้องใต้หลังคา attic
    ห้องแถว shophouse, row house
    ห้องโถง hall
    ห้องนอน bedroom
        ห้องนอนในรถไฟ compartment
        ห้องนอนในเรือ cabin, stateroom
    ห้องนั่งเล่น sitting room, living room, lounge, study, den
    ห้องน้ำ bathroom, lavatory, rest room, men's room, ladies' room
    ห้องปฏิบัติการ laboratory; operations room
    ห้องประชุม meeting room, assembly hall, auditorium

ห
ฬ
อ
ฮ

ห้องปาฐกถา lecture room, lecture hall

ห้องพักครู teachers' lounge

ห้องพัสดุ storeroom

ห้องภาพ studio

ห้องเย็น refrigerated room, cold storage, cold room

ห้องรับแขก parlor, living room, sitting room; reception room

ห้องรับประทานอาหาร dining room

ห้องเรียน classroom

ห้องศิลปะ art studio

ห้องสมุด library, study

    ห้องสมุดประชาชน public library

ห้องส้วม toilet, lavatory, water closet, W.C., outhouse (อยู่นอกบ้าน), men's room, ladies' room

ห้องหนังสือ study, library

ห้องอ่านหนังสือ reading room

ห้องอาหาร dining room; restaurant

กั้นห้อง to /partition/divide/ a room, put up a partition

ขึ้นห้อง to go to one's room, go upstairs

ผนังห้อง wall

ฝาห้อง wall

มุมห้อง corner (of a room)

หอน to howl, bay

เห่าหอน to bark and howl

หอบ[1] to carry, lug

   หอบของพะรุงพะรัง to carry a great load of stuff

   หอบแฟ้มเอกสาร to carry (in, out, etc) a pile of files

หอบหิ้วกันมา to live through thick and thin together

หอบ[2] to pant, breathe heavily

หอบหืด, หืดหอบ to be asthmatic, have asthma

หอบฮักๆ panting

เหนื่อยหอบ huffing and puffing, panting,

to gasp for breath

หอม[1] fragrant, aromatic, good-smelling, sweet-smelling

หอมฉุย redolent, beautiful smell

หอมหวน fragrant, sweet; gratifying

เครื่องหอม perfumery

น้ำหอม perfume, scent, lotion, toilet water, eau de Cologne

หอม[2] onion

ต้นหอม green onion, leek, shallot

หัวหอม onion

หอม[3] to kiss, give a kiss

หอมแก้ม to kiss one's cheek, give a kiss on the cheek; to nuzzle one's cheek

ห้อมล้อม /surrounded (by)/mobbed (by)/beseiged (by)/ (admirers, reporters etc)

บริวารห้อมล้อม entourage

หอย mollusc, clam, oyster

หอยโข่งทะเล abalone

หอยแครง cockle

หอยงวงช้าง nautilus

หอยทาก land snail, garden snail, slug

หอยนางรม oyster

หอยมุก pearl oyster

หอยแมลงภู่ mussel

หอยสังข์ conch

ห้อย to hang, be suspended

ห้อยโตงเตง to dangle

ห้อยท้าย to be at the end

ห้อยหัว to hang upside down

ห้อยโหน to do gymnastics

ติดสอยห้อยตาม to tag along, accompany, be part of the entourage

หัก to break, fracture, broken, fractured; to subtract, deduct

หักกลบลบหนี้ to set off (one debt against another)

หักกลับ to do a turnaround

หักคอ to break the neck; to force

หักคะแนน to take away points, reduce a grade

หักเงินเดือน to deduct from one's salary

หักใจ to put something out of one's mind; to suppress one's /emotions/feelings/, exercise self-control

หักบัญชี to put to (one's) account, debit (an account)

หักราคา to cut the price, lower the price

หักร้างถางพง to clear land for farming

หักล้าง to refute, controvert

หักศอก elbow

หักหน้า to put (someone) to shame, humiliate, mortify

หักหลัง to doublecross, betray

หักหาญ to use force, attack

หักห้ามใจ *see* **หักใจ**

หักเห to go off at a tangent, be deflected; to refract

    การหักเหของแสง refraction

หักโหม to be rough (on, with); to force; to overexert oneself, overdo (something)

    อย่าหักโหม Don't overdo it!, Don't force yourself!

แขนหัก /broken/fractured/ arm, to have /an arm fracture/a broken arm/

หัด[1] measles

เป็นหัด to have the measles

ออกหัด to come down with measles

หัด[2] to drill, train, practice, learn (to)

หัดขับรถ to practice driving, learn to drive

หัดเขียน to practice writing

หัดแถว to drill

หัดทหาร to drill soldiers

หัดพูด to learn to speak

หัดมวย to practice boxing, train as a boxer

ครูฝึกหัด apprentice teacher

เสมียนฝึกหัด apprentice clerk

หัตถ์ hand

หัตถกรรม handicraft

หัน to turn

หันกลับ to turn back

หันขวับ to turn abruptly, a quick turn (of the head etc)

หันไปทาง to turn (towards, to)

หันไปพึ่ง to resort to, turn to

หันมา to turn (towards, to)

หันมาเอาดีในทางค้าขาย He turned to trade.

หันรีหันขวาง to dither; be in a flap, flustered; to look around nervously

หันหน้า to face, turn one's head

    หันหน้าเข้าหากัน to make up, compromise, cooperate

    หันหน้าหนี to turn away

หันหลังให้ to turn one's back (on)

หันเห to deviate, diverge

หั่น to cut up, slice

หั่นงบประมาณ to cut the budget, slice off a part of the budget

หั่นเป็นฝอย to shred, mince

หั่นแหลก tremendous

ลดราคาหั่นแหลก tremendous sale

หัว head; top

หัวกบาล head

หัวกะทิ elite, the very best, cream of the crop, top people

หัวกะโหลก skull

    หัวกะโหลกไขว้ skull and cross bones

หัวเก่า of the old school, conservative, old fashioned

หัวแก้วหัวแหวน darling

หัวข้อ subject, topic; heading, caption; item

    หัวข้อการสนทนา issue, point of discussion

หัวขั้ว counterfoil, stub; stem joint; socket

หัวขาด a boil; headless

หัวข่าว headline

หัวขี้เลื่อย thick, slow-witted

ห
ฬ
อ
ฮ

หัวเข็มขัด buckle

หัวเข่า knee

หัวแข็ง obstinate, stubborn, headstrong, non-conformist

หัวโขน actor's mask; official position

หัวค่ำ early evening, dusk

หัวคะแนน canvasser, vote-getter

หัวคิด ideas, brains

หัวโค้ง bend (in the road, river, etc)

หัวเงื่อน slipknot

หัวจุก stopper; topknot

หัวโจก gang leader, big boss

หัวใจ heart; feelings; mind; cardiac

   หัวใจเต้น heartbeat, /beating/pounding/ of the heart; excited

      หัวใจเต้นแรง pounding of the heart

   หัวใจแทบขาด brokenhearted, in dispair, heartbroken

   หัวใจล้มเหลว heart failure, cardiac arrest

   หัวใจวาย heart failure

   หัวใจหยุดเต้น The heart has stopped beating.

หัวชนฝา uncompromising

หัวซุกหัวซุน to flee, fly for one's life, take to one's heels

หัวดื้อ obdurate, stubborn

หัวเดียวกระเทียมลีบ to lead a solitary existence

หัวแตก (His) head is bleeding., to be bleeding from the head, have a head wound

หัวโต๊ะ (at the) head of the table

หัวถนน end of the road, corner

หัวถอก exposed glans

หัวแถว /head/front/ of the line; leader

หัวทิ่มหัวตำ without restraint

หัวที beginning, starting point, commencement

หัวทึบ dense

หัวเทียน spark plug

หัวนม nipple

หัวนอก foreign educated, educated abroad; foreign-oriented, westernized

หัวนอน head of the bed, headboard

   หัวนอนปลายตีน origins, background, who (one) is

หัวน้ำ honey water; water source

หัวบันได /head/top/ of the stairs

หัวโบราณ old-fashioned, conservative

หัวปลี banana blossom

หัวปั่น to make (one's) head spin เช่น *There was so much to do my head was spinning.*; to be snowed under (with work), overwhelmed with work

หัวป่า cook

หัวปักหัวปำ doggedly; head over heels

   รักหัวปักหัวปำ to be head over heels in love

หัวปี eldest, firstborn

   หัวปีท้ายปี prolific

หัวผักกาด turnip

หัวพุงหัวมัน the best part

หัวมันเทศ yam

หัวมุม corner

หัวเมือง upcountry, the provinces

หัวแม่เท้า big toe

หัวแม่มือ thumb

หัวไม้ ruffian, tough, goon

หัวร่อ *see* หัวเราะ *หน้า 537*

หัวระแหง cracks in parched earth; everywhere

หัวรั้น stubborn, obdurate, obstinate, intractable

หัวร้างข้างแตก hurt, injured

หัวรุนแรง aggressive, extremist, hotheaded

หัวเรือ bow, prow

   หัวเรือใหญ่ person responsible (for), sponsor

หัวเรื่อง heading, title

หัวแรง main force, mainstay

หัวละ per head, per person, each

หัวล้าน bald

หัวเลี้ยว corner, curve, turn (in a road)

    หัวเลี้ยวหัวต่อ turning point, critical point, period of transition

หัวสมอง brains

หัวสูง pretentious

หัวเสีย in a bad mood, irritable

หัวใส bright, shrewd

หัวเก๋ากั้นขวด vastly experienced, worldly-wise

หัวหงอก grey-haired; hoary; a grayhead

หัวหน้า chief, head, leader, boss

    หัวหน้าครอบครัว head of the household

    หัวหน้าแต่ในนาม figurehead

    หัวหน้าพ่อครัว chief cook, head cook, chef

    หัวหน้าห้อง class president

    หัวหน้าใหญ่ top man, big boss

หัวหมอ a wise guy, to be smart, a smart guy; foxy, crafty

หัวหมุน to spin เช่น *My head is spinning.*; in a state, overwhelmed (with work, things to do, etc)

หัวหมู pig's head, hog's head

หัวหอก spearhead

หัวหอม onion

หัวหาด beachhead

หัวเห็ด headstrong, inflexible, intransigent, steadfast

หัวเหน่า the suprapubic region, lower belly

หัวแหลม headland; shrewd, sharp

หัวแหวน setting

หัวไหล่ shoulder

หัวอก feelings, heart

    หัวอกเดียวกัน to be in the same boat, have (some feeling or state of mind) in common

หัวอ่อน obedient, tractable, pliable, pliant

หัวเอียงซ้าย leftist

หัวเราะ to laugh

    หัวเราะคิกๆ to giggle, titter

    หัวเราะชอบใจ to laugh, chuckle, chortle

    หัวเราะท้องแข็ง to split one's sides, die with laughter

    หัวเราะในใจ to laugh to oneself

    หัวเราะในที to laugh to oneself, have a private laugh

    หัวเราะเยาะ to laugh at someone, make fun of someone, mock

    หัวเราะลั่น to roar with laughter, guffaw

    หัวเราะเอิ๊กอ๊าก to guffaw; guffawing

    น่าหัวเราะ laughable, comical, funny; ridiculous, ludicrous

หา to seek, look for; to arrange

    หากิน to make a living, do for a living; to find food

        ผู้หญิงหากิน prostitute

    หาความ to make an allegation (against, of), accuse (somebody of something)

    หาค่ามิได้ invaluable, inestimable, priceless

    หางานทำ to look for work

    หาเงิน to raise (the) money, to make (some) money

    หาเช้ากินค่ำ to live from hand to mouth

    หาตัวจับยาก peerless, incomparable

    หาทาง to find a way, look for a way (to do something)

    หาทางระบาย to seek relief (by, in)

    หาที่เปรียบมิได้ incomparable

    หามา to procure, acquire, get, obtain

    หามิได้ no, not so

    หาไม่ or else, otherwise; ends, disappears, ceases

    หา...ไม่ not

    หาไม่เจอ cannot find (it)

ห
ฟ
อ
ฮ

หาไม่แล้ว dead

หายาก rare, scarce, hard to find

หารือ to consult, talk something over (with someone)

หาเรื่อง to look for trouble, be abrasive, provocative

หาลำไพ่ to make money on the side, make something extra

หาเลือดกับปู You can't get blood out of a turnip.

หาว่า to charge, accuse (someone of doing something), allege

หาสู่ to visit

หาเสียง to electioneer, campaign (for votes), look for votes

หาเหตุ to find fault (with), stir things up, look for trouble

หาเหาใส่หัว to be looking for trouble, do something that is self-destructive, be more trouble than its worth

หาให้ to provide, get (something for someone), arrange (for it)

หาอะไร What are you looking for?; for what

หาอาหาร to prepare a meal, do the cooking

กล่าวหา to accuse, allege, charge

ข้อหา charge, accusation, allegation

ค้นหา to search for, look for, seek, hunt for something

คบหา to associate (with)

จัดหา to procure, acquire, provide, find

ซื้อหา to buy

ใฝ่หา to long (for), yearn (for), seek

รนหาที่ to do oneself in, look for trouble, ask for /trouble/it/

แสวงหา to search for, seek, go in search of

ห่า[1] a spirit held responsible for plagues

ห่ากิน to be consumed by a plague

ห่าลง outbreak of plague

โรคห่า plague

ไอ้ห่า shit, damn; bastard

ห่า[2] storm

ห่าฝน rainstorm

ห้า five, quinque., quin-, penta-

ห้าคน quintet

ห้าแต้ม (do) something foolish, (commit) a faux pas

ห้าเท่า fivefold, five times, quintuple

ห้าสิบ fifty

ห้าเหลี่ยม pentagon

ที่ห้า fifth

หาก but, however; provided

หากแต่ but, however

หากว่า provided (that), if

ต่างหาก see ต่างหาก *หน้า 194*

ถ้าหาก if, supposing, provided, providing

หาง tail; end

หางกะทิ thin coconut cream (from the second or third pressing)

หางตา corner of the eye, out of the corner of one's eye

หางแถว end of the line; underling, nobodies

หางนม skim milk

หางปลา paper fan; forked spade

หางเปีย pigtail, braid

หางเลข last numbers (of a lottery ticket)

   ถูกหางเลข to get caught up in the net, get implicated

หางว่าว kite tail; long list of names

หางเสียง intonation, tone of voice;

   พูดไม่มีหางเสียง to speak brusquely, be curt

หางเสือ rudder, helm, tiller

ห่าง distant, far from, separated

ห่างไกล far (from), far away

ห่างจาก from, far from, distant from

ห่างจากฝั่ง 5 ไมล์ five miles from shore

ห่างเหิน estranged, distant; out of touch

อยู่ห่างๆ Keep your distance.

ออกไปห่างๆ Move back.

เอาใจออกห่าง disaffected, faithless, alienated, distant

ห้าง[1] tree platform for hunting, machan

ห้าง[2] firm, company, business

ห้างร้าน businesses, commercial establishments, stores, shops, stores and shops

ห้างหุ้นส่วน partnership

ห้างหุ้นส่วนจำกัด limited partnership

นายห้าง business manager, big boss; Mr. Manager

หาญ brave, courageous, valiant, audacious

กล้าหาญ brave, courageous

อาจหาญ bold, audacious, valiant, intrepid

หาด beach

หาดทราย beach; sandy bank

ชายหาด beach

หัวหาด beachhead

ห่าน goose, gander

หาบ[1] to carry (something) on a shoulder pole, tote; shoulderload

หาบน้ำขาย to tote water for sale

หาบ[2] picul

หาบหลวง picul (a unit of weight equal to 60 kilograms)

หาม to carry

หามรุ่งหามค่ำ day and night, from morn till night, arduously

แบกหาม to carry, tote, transport, porter; porterage; unskilled labor, coolie-work

ห่าม unripe, green; gauche, untutored, crude; reckless

ห้าม to forbid, prohibit; to restrain; to separate; to warn

ห้ามเข้า No admittance., No entry., Keep out.

ห้ามเดินลัดสนาม Keep off the grass.

ห้ามประกัน to deny bail

ห้ามปราม to keep (someone) from doing,

prevent (someone) from doing; to forbid; to caution

ห้ามปิดประกาศ Post no bills., No posters.

ห้ามมวย to referee a fight

กรรมการห้ามมวย referee

ห้ามเยี่ยม No visitors.

ห้ามล้อ brake; to brake, put on the brakes

ห้ามล้อไว้บ้าง Slow down., Go easy.

ห้ามเลือด to /stanch/staunch/stop/ the bleeding

ห้ามสูบบุหรี่ No smoking.

ต้องห้าม forbidden, taboo, prohibited; untouchable

นางห้าม royal concubine

หาย to be lost, gone, disappear; to be finished, be over; to recover, get over something

หายกัน to have no further obligations; to get over (something); to make up, call (something) quits

หายขาด to be cured, fully recovered

หายเข้ากลีบเมฆ to vanish into thin air

หายไข้ to recover, get well

หายตัว to disappear, be invisible; to keep out of sight

หายป่วย to recover, get well

หายไปเสียนาน? Where have you been for so long?

หายวันหายคืน getting better

หายสนิท completely healed, completely cured

หายหน้าหายตา disappeared, gone, unseen

หายห่วง no worry about; matchless

คอยจนหายห่วง I had to wait so long I gave you up for lost. / I thought you'd never come.

หายหัว gone off, disappeared

ขวัญหาย startled; frightened, scared

คนหาย missing person; wanted

ฉิบหาย damn

ห

พ

อ

ฮ

สูญหาย lost, vanished, gone, to disappear

เสียหาย damaged, harmed, affected

หายใจ to breathe

หายใจเข้า to inhale

หายใจคล่อง to breathe /freely/easily/

หายใจไม่ทั่วท้อง to pant; anxious, to feel anxiety

หายใจไม่สะดวก to breathe with difficulty, pant

หายใจยาว to breathe deeply

หายใจโล่ง to breathe a sigh of relief

หายใจออก to exhale

หายนะ disaster, calamity, catastrophe

หาร to divide

หารร่วมมาก (หรม.) highest common factor (H.C.F.)

หารลงตัว to divide evenly (by, into)

ตัวหาร divisor

วิธีหาร division

หาว[1] open air, sky

กลางหาว in midair

หาว[2] to exhale; to yawn

หาวนอน to feel sleepy, be drowsy; to yawn

ห้าว[1] spirited, tough, daring

ห้าวหาญ daring, intrepid, fearless

เสียงห้าว deep voice, /stentorian/commanding/ voice

ห้าว[2] ripe, mature

มะพร้าวห้าว /ripe/mature/ coconut

หำ balls; boy

ห้ำ to attack, assault violently, pounce on

ห้ำหั่น to attack and cut to pieces, assail, destroy

หิ้ง shelf

หิ่งห้อย, หิ่งห้อย firefly

หิด scabies

หิดเปื่อย moist scabies

หิน stone, rock

หินแกรนิต granite

หินชนวน slate

หินปะการัง coral

หินปูน limestone, lime; tartar

หินเพชร corundum

หินไฟ flint

หินย้อย stalactite

หินแร่ ore

หินลับมีด whetstone

หินโสโครก reef, submerged rock, underwater rock

หินอ่อน marble

ถ่านหิน coal

หิมะ snow

หิริ moral shame

หิริโอตตัปปะ conscience, sense of right or wrong, scruples, moral shame and moral fear

หิว to be hungry

หิวจนแสบท้อง gnawing hunger เช่น I feel a gnawing hunger., starved, to have hunger pangs

หิวจะตาย to be famished, starved

หิวจัง to be very hungry

หิวน้ำ thirsty

หิวโหย starving, malnourished, deprived

หิ้ว to carry

หิ้วได้ portable

หิ้วท้อง to go with an empty stomach

หิ้วผู้หญิง to pick up a girl

กระเป๋าหิ้ว portable

หี vagina, cunt

หีตา tear duct

หีนยาน Hinayana

หีบ[1] box, case, chest

หีบบัตร ballot box

หีบบุหรี่ cigarette box

หีบเพลง harmonica, mouth organ; accordion

หีบศพ coffin, casket

หีบเสียง gramophone, phonograph, record player

หีบห่อ parcels, packages

หีบ[2] to crush, squeeze

  หีบฝ้าย to gin cotton

  หีบอ้อย to crush sugarcane

หึๆ to snicker; to chuckle

หึง to be jealous

  หึงหวง jealous

  ขี้หึง jealous, possessive

หึ่ง rotting (smell, odor)

หึ่งๆ buzzing; soughing

หืด, หืดหอบ asthma

  หืดขึ้นคอ with great effort

หืน rancid; base, carnal

  ขึ้นหืน to /go/be/ rancid

หื่น to lust after, crave

  หื่นกระหาย to lust after (someone or something), have a lascivious desire

  หื่นหรรษ์ ecstatic, overjoyed

หือ a questioning or challenging word, what? what! huh?

  หือไม่ขึ้น submissive, tame, under (someone's) thumb

หุง to cook

  หุงข้าว to cook /breakfast/lunch/dinner/etc; to cook rice

  หุงต้ม to cook

    เครื่องหุงต้ม cooking utensils, pots and pans

  หุงหาอาหาร to /make/fix/prepare/ a meal

  พลอยหุง cooked gem

หุน one eighth of an inch, unit of weight equal to 375 milligrams

  สองหุน a quarter of an inch

หุ่น model; dummy, mannequin (รูปตุ๊กตา); replica (หุ่นจำลอง); shape, appearance, form

  หุ่นกระบอก puppet, marionette

  หุ่นยนต์ robot; a form endued with life by incantation, zombie

  หุ่นไล่กา scarecrow

หุ่นสำอาง handsome, fine looking

หุ่นให้ to look the part, look like (a general, star, professor, farmer etc)

รัฐบาลหุ่น puppet government

หุ้น share, stock

  หุ้นกู้ debenture

    หุ้นกู้ด้อยสิทธิ์ subordinated debenture

    หุ้นกู้แปลงสภาพ convertible debenture

  หุ้นลม nominal partner; nominal share, free share; dummy stockholder, phantom stock

  หุ้นส่วน partner

    เข้าหุ้นส่วน to become a partner (in a business), enter into partnership

    หุ้นส่วนจำกัด limited partnership, limited partner

    หุ้นส่วนสามัญ ordinary partnership, ordinary partner

  หุ้นใหญ่ major /stockholder/shareholder/

  เล่นหุ้น to play the stock market

หุนหัน irascible, quick-tempered, testy; impetuous

  หุนหันพลันแล่น hot-headed; quick-tempered, splenetic

หุบ valley, vale; to close, shut; to fold

  หุบเขา valley, vale

  หุบปาก to close one's mouth, keep quiet

  หุบผา valley, ravine

หุ้ม to cover (over, by), covered (with, by, in), wrapped (in), coated (with)

  หุ้มเกราะ armored

หู ear; handle; loop

  หูกระต่าย bow tie

  หูฉี่ *as in* **แพงหูฉี่** outrageously expensive

  หูช้าง wind-wing; wood gusset; elephant-ear cookie

  หูตาสว่าง well-informed, knowledgeable, aware; to realize, know, learn, become enlightened, be enlightened

  หูตึง hard of hearing, impaired hearing

  หูบ floppy-eared, drooping ears

ห
ฬ
อ
ฮ

หูทวนลม to pay no attention (to), ignore

หูทิพย์ sharp ears; magic hearing

หูโทรศัพท์ receiver

หูเบา credulous, ready to believe anything (one) hears, suggestible, easily influenced

หูป่าตาเถื่อน a simpleton, ignorant

หูเป็นน้ำหนวก otorrhea

หูผึ่ง to prick up one's ears, become alert (to something), become interested

หูรูด drawstring; anus, anal sphincter

    ปากไม่มีหูรูด a blabbermouth

หูไว keen sense of hearing, good ears

หูหนวก deaf

หูหนาตาเล่อ leprosy

หูหิ้ว handle

กรอกหู to put something into someone's head

แก้วหู eardrum

ขัดหู jarring, to sound disagreeable, irritating

ขี้หู earwax, cerumen

คันหู itching ear, to have an itch in the ear

คู่หู as in **เพื่อนคู่หู** /intimate/close/ friend, confidant, buddy, mate, pal

เงี่ยหูฟัง to strain to hear, listen /closely/ attentively/, hearken (to)

ต่างหู earring, eardrop

ติดหูติดตา memorable, imprinted in one's mind, unforgettable

บาดหู strident, deafening, raucous, irritating

เป็นหูเป็นตาแทน to keep an eye on things (for someone), take charge (for someone), act as another's/representative/surrogate/

เปิดหูเปิดตา to open one's eyes, /learn/see/ something new; to go sightseeing, go for a change

ผิดหูผิดตา remarkably, noticeably, markedly

พูดกรอกหู to put something into someone's head, feed someone an idea, say (something) persistently

ฟังหูไว้หู to reserve judgment, be circumspect, be skeptical

หนวกหู noisy, annoying (noise, sound, etc), deafening, raucous

หูก loom

    ทอหูก to handloom, weave on a handloom

หูด wart

เห่ lullaby

    เห่เรือ chant accompanying the paddling of a boat

เหงา lonely, lonesome, low

    เหงาหงอย blue, gloomy, depressed, melancholic

    เงียบเหงา deserted, quiet and lonely; bleak

เหง้า stock, line, race; rhizome

    โคตรเหง้าเหล่ากอ stock, origins, line

เหงื่อ sweat, perspiration

    เหงื่อกาฬ cold sweat

    เหงื่อโชก dripping with perspiration

    เหงื่อตก to sweat (over something, to do something)

    เหงื่อแตก to break out in a sweat

    เหงื่อออก to perspire, sweat

    อาบเหงื่อต่างน้ำ to live by the sweat of one's brow, struggle hard (to)

เหงือก gum *(คน)*, gill *(ปลา)*

    เหงือกบวม swollen gums

เห็ด mushroom, toadstool

    ดอกเห็ด like mushrooms, to mushroom

เหตุ cause; reason, motive; event, incident; means

    เหตุกับผล cause and effect

    เหตุการณ์ event, incident, occurence, what happened, circumstance

        เหตุการณ์ตึงเครียด tense situation, crisis

    เหตุฉะนั้น therefore

    เหตุฉะนี้ for this reason

    เหตุฉุกเฉิน emergency

    เหตุไฉน why, what for, for what reason

เหตุใด why, for what reason, because of what

เหตุบังเอิญ accident, fortuitous circumstance, coincidence

เหตุผล reason, justification

เหตุไร why, for what reason

เหตุสุดวิสัย force majeure, act of God

จดหมายเหตุ chronicle, gazette, record of events

ด้วยเหตุนี้ therefore, thus, for this reason, that is why

โดยใช่เหตุ unnecessarily, for no reason, uselessly

ต้นเหตุ cause, culprit

เป็นเหตุให้ to cause, be conducive to, generate

มูลเหตุ origin, basic cause, grounds, real reason

สาเหตุ cause, reason (for)

หมายเหตุ note, remarks

หาเหตุ to find fault (with), stir things up, look for trouble

เห็น to see, regard, treat; to think; to understand

เห็นการณ์ไกล farsighted, prescient

เห็นแก่ to think of

    เห็นแก่ได้ to think only of profit, grasping, avaricious, greedy

    เห็นแก่ตัว selfish, egotistical

    เห็นแก่หน้า to be partial, biased, favor; to have consideration (for someone)

เห็นควร to approve, agree, okay; to /think/ feel/(something) should be (done etc)

เห็นจะ it looks like; to think; apparently

เห็นจะแจ้ง evident, obvious, seen so clearly

เห็นใจ to be sympathetic (with), understand, sympathize (with someone)

เห็นชอบ to approve; right understanding

เห็นด้วย to agree, assent

เห็นดีเห็นงาม to commend, favor, approve

(of), applaud

เห็นตำตา to see before one's very eyes, caught in the act (of)

เห็นถนัด to see clearly, clearly visible

เห็นท่า to seem, look like, appear

เห็นประจักษ์ clearly visible; to see; to realize

เห็นเป็น to regard as, take (someone or something) for

    เห็นเป็นการสมควร to think fit, find appropriate

    เห็นเป็นเด็ก to treat like a child, regard as a child, take someone for a youngster

    เห็นเป็นเรื่องขัน to take (something) as a joke, treat as a joke

เห็นผิดเป็นชอบ to take wrong for right

เห็นผิดสังเกต unusual, odd, to look /peculiar/wrong/funny/

เห็นพร้อมกัน to agree unanimously, be all of the same mind

เห็นพ้อง to agree, go along, subscribe to, think the same

เห็นว่า to think

เห็นสมควร to be warranted, be appropriate (to), to find it proper (to)

เห็นอกเห็นใจ to sympathize (with), be in sympathy with, understand, be understanding

ความคิดเห็น view, opinion, thought, idea

ความเห็น opinion, view, comment

ที่เห็นได้ visible

มองเห็น to see, notice, catch sight of, perceive

รู้เห็น to know, be aware

    รู้เห็นเป็นใจ to connive (with, at), abet, be in collusion (with), give encouragement (to)

ลงความเห็น to decide, conclude, come to a decision

เล็งเห็น to foresee

ห
ฟ
อ
ฮ

แลเห็น to see, sight, observe; visible

สอดรู้สอดเห็น nosy, prying, inquisitive

เหน็ดเหนื่อย weary, worn-out, fatigued

เหน็บ local loss of sensation; to tuck in; to insert a suppository; to be sarcastic

เท้าเป็นเหน็บ (My) foot has gone to sleep. / My foot /has no feeling/is devoid of sensation/.

เหน็บชา beriberi

เหน็บชากิน to go to sleep

เหน็บแนม to speak acidly, sarcastic, cutting

เหน่อ to have an accent

เหนอะหนะ sticky, to feel sticky

เหน้า young, adolescent

หนุ่มเหน้า youngster, young teenager,

เหนาะๆ easily, with ease, effortlessly

ได้มาเหนาะๆ to get (something) without trying, effortlessly, so easily

เหนียง wattles

เหนียม shy, timid, bashful, hesitant

เหนียว tough; sticky, glutinous, viscid; strong, solid; stingy, tight, parsimonious

เหนียวแน่น solid, firm, strong

เหนียวหนี้ to be a bad payer, hold back payment

เหนียวหนึบ chewy, sticky

เหนียวเหนอะหนะ gooey, sticky

เหนี่ยว to pull (down, in), draw (down, in)

เหนี่ยวนำ to induce; induction

เหนี่ยวรั้ง to delay, check, hold back

เต็มเหนี่ยว with all one's might, full blast

เหนือ north; above, over, on; upper

เหนือกว่า superior, better

เหนือลม windward

เหนือศีรษะ overhead

ชาวเหนือ northerner

ทิศเหนือ north

เหนื่อย tired

เหนื่อยใจ dispirited, discouraged

เหนื่อยแทบขาดใจ thoroughly exhausted, ready to drop

เหนื่อยแทบตาย dead tired

เหนื่อยเปล่า (to make) a wasted effort, in vain

เหนื่อยสิ้นดี terribly tired, spent, pooped

เหนื่อยหน่าย low-spirited, depressed, disheartened, sick of

เหนื่อยหอบ huffing and puffing, panting, to gasp for breath

เหนื่อยอ่อน exhausted, worn-out, tired (of), weary

เห็บ[1] tick

เห็บ[2] *as in* ลูกเห็บ hail, hailstone

เหม่ an angry sound, growl

เหม่ง glossy, shiny; sound of a gong

เหม็น to smell, stink, reek, smell bad, stinking, malodorous, fetid, foul-smelling

เหม็นกลิ่นเหล้า to reek of alcohol

เหม็นเขียว smelly, rank

เหม็นคาว fishy smell, smell of /meat/ blood/; a rank smell, smelly

เหม็นตุๆ to begin to smell

เหม็นเน่า putrid, fetid, rotten smell

เหม็นบูด rancid

เหม็นเบื่อ disgusted (with), fed up to one's ears (with, by); bored stiff (with)

เหม็นเปรี้ยว rancid, sour-smelling

เหม็นสาบ to have body odor, smelly

เหม็นอับ musty

เหม่อ abstracted, to be dreamy, gaze /vacantly /absently/, moon, stare into the distance

เหม่อลอย to gaze into space; preoccupied (with one's thoughts), vacantly, abstracted

เหมันต์ winter, cold season

เหมา to hire, contract (to do something), do for hire; to take the whole lot; to assume, presume, surmise

เหมาจ่าย flat /payment/rate/

เหมาเสร็จ to do the lot, take care of everything, all-inclusive

เหมาหมด all together, for the lot

เหมาเอาว่า to gather; presume, suppose; to take for granted

ขายเหมา to sell all together, sell in a single lot, sell the lot

รับเหมา to do contract work, contract (to do something), be hired (to), be a contractor

    ผู้รับเหมา contractor

เหมาะ, เหมาะเจาะ suitable, appropriate, fit, right, just right, well-suited (to)

    เหมาะกับกาลสมัย up-to-date, modern, right with the times

    เหมาะสม appropriate, right fitting, proper, suitable; to suit

    เหมาะเหม็ง perfect, apposite

    พอเหมาะพอเจาะ just right, perfect

เหมือง irrigation ditch; mine

    เหมืองดีบุก tin mine

    เหมืองฝาย irrigation ditch

    เหมืองแร่ mine

เหมือน similar (to), like, just like, the same as, resembling

    เหมือนกัน alike, the same (as); too, also, likewise, similarly

    เหมือนๆ กัน very similar, much the same, no different

    เหมือนกับ to be like, as if

        เหมือนกับฝัน like a dream

        เหมือนกับว่า as if, as though, the same as if

    เหมือนใจนึก just as one /thought /expected/imagined/

    เหมือนเช่นเคย as usual

    เหมือนดัง as if, as though, like

    เหมือนแต่ก่อน as before, like it used to be

    เหมือนปากว่า to be just as one said

    เหมือนมีชีวิต lifelike

    เหมือนยังกะแกะ like two peas in a pod, identical

    เหมือนหนึ่งว่า as if, as though, like, akin to

    ดูเหมือน to look as if, appear, seem like

    เปรียบเหมือน like, analogous (to)

    เสมอเหมือน comparable (to), equal (to)

เหย to make a wry face, discountenanced

    เหยเก to screw (up) one's face

เหยง excitedly, (jump) up and down

เหย่า, (วิ่ง) เหย่าๆ to jog

เหย้า house, home

    เหย้าเรือน house, home

    คืนสู่เหย้า homecoming

เหยาะ to add little by little

เหยาะๆ as in วิ่งเหยาะๆ to trot

เหยาะแหยะ halfheartedly, listlessly

เหยียด[1] to straighten; to stretch

เหยียด[2] to look down on, hold in contempt, despise, be contemptuous (of)

    เหยียดขา to stretch, take a stretch, stretch one's legs

    เหยียดผิว to be a racist

    เหยียดหยาม to look down on, hold in contempt, disparage, be contemptuous (of)

เหยียบ to step on, put one's foot on; to come close to

    เหยียบขี้ไก่ไม่ฝ่อ namby pamby

    เหยียบจมูก to slap in the face

    ถือเป็นการเหยียบจมูก It was like a slap in the face.

    เหยียบเบรค to put one's foot on the brake

    เหยียบย่าง to walk in, step in, put one's foot in

    เหยียบย่ำ to trample (on), disparage

        ถูกเหยียบย่ำ downtrodden

        ใบเหยียบย่ำ land preemption certificate

    เหยียบเรือสองแคม to play a double game, play both sides; to vacillate

เหยี่ยว hawk
  เหยี่ยวข่าว newshawk, newshound
เหยื่อ prey, victim; bait, lure (เครื่องล่อ)
  อ่อยเหยื่อ to /put out/lay/ bait, lay a trap (for); to lure, entice, tempt, offer inducements
เหยือก jug, pitcher
  เหยือกน้ำ pitcher
เหรัญญิก treasurer
เหรียญ coin, medal, medallion
  เหรียญกล้าหาญ medal for bravery
  เหรียญกษาปณ์ coins
  เหรียญเก๊ /bad/counterfeit/ coin
  เหรียญเงิน silver medal
  เหรียญตรา decoration
  เหรียญทอง gold medal
  เหรียญทองแดง bronze medal
  เหรียญที่ระลึก commemorative medal
  เหรียญบาท baht coin
เหล่ squint, crossed
  ตาเหล่ cross-eyed, to have a squint
เหล็ก iron
  เหล็กกล้า steel
  เหล็กจาร stylus
  เหล็กฉาก angle steel
  เหล็กท่อน steel bar
  เหล็กแท่ง iron bar, /iron/steel/ ingot
  เหล็กใน sting
  เหล็กแผ่น steel plate
  เหล็กไฟ flint
  เหล็กลวด wire rod
  เหล็กสว่าน auger
  เหล็กสกัด chisel
  เหล็กเส้น steel rod
  เหล็กหมาด awl
  เหล็กไหล a metal amulet said to melt at candle temperature
  ช่างตีเหล็ก blacksmith, smith
  ช่างเหล็ก blacksmith, ironsmith, ironworker
  ตีเหล็ก to forge (iron)

ถลุงเหล็ก to smelt iron
แม่เหล็ก magnet
เหลน great-grandchild
เหลว fluid, liquid, melted; watery; to fail
  เหลวทั้งเพ all nonsense
  เหลวแหลก dissolute, bad, good-for-nothing, worthless
  เหลวไหล nonsense; unreliable, undependable
  ของเหลว liquid, fluid
  ล้มเหลว to fail, be a failure
เหลอ vacuous, stupid-looking, silly, blank
เหลา[1] to sharpen
  เครื่องเหลาดินสอ pencil sharpener
เหลา[2] restaurant; old man
เหล่า group, company, band; category
  เหล่ากอ family, origins
  เหล่าทัพ armed service
  เหล่านี้ these
  เหล่าร้าย rascals, rogues, gangsters
  ผ่าเหล่า to be a mutation, mutate, be a sport; to be different
เหล้า spirits, liquor, drink, hard liquor, alcohol, booze
  เหล้าเถื่อน illicit liquor, bootleg liquor, moonshine
  เหล้าบรั่นดี brandy
  เหล้ายาปลาปิ้ง food and drink
  เหล้าโรง clear distilled spirits, cheap liquor
  เหล้าหวาน liqueur
  เหล้าองุ่น wine
  กินเหล้า to drink
  แก้วเหล้า liquor glass, whiskey glass, wine glass
  ขี้เหล้า alcoholic, drunkard, lush
  คอเหล้า a drinker, person fond of drinking, discriminating drinker, connoisseur of liquor
  นักเลงเหล้า big drinker
  เมาเหล้า drunk, intoxicated, inebriated

ก ข ค ฆ ง จ ฉ ช ซ ฌ ญ ฎ ฏ ฐ ฑ ฒ ณ ด ต ถ ท ธ น บ ป ผ ฝ พ ฟ ภ ม ย ร ฤ ฦ ล ว ศ ษ ส ห

เหลาะแหละ not serious, half-heartedly, listlessly; unreliable

เหลิง to forget oneself, overconfident, too sure of oneself, puffed up, think too much of oneself, spoiled

เหลี่ยม edge; angle

    เหลี่ยมคู cunning, craft, craftiness

    เหลี่ยมลูกบาศก์ cubic

    เล่ห์เหลี่ยม tricks, craftiness; wily, cunning, crafty, foxy; intrigue

    สามเหลี่ยม triangle

    สี่เหลี่ยม foursided, quadrilateral, quadrangle

        สี่เหลี่ยมขนมเปียกปูน rhombus, diamond (shaped), lozenge

        สี่เหลี่ยมจัตุรัส square

        สี่เหลี่ยมคางหมู trapezoid

        สี่เหลี่ยมผืนผ้า rectangle

เหลียว to turn

    เหลียวซ้ายแลขวา to be circumspect, cautious

    เหลียวดู to look around, turn to look

    เหลียวแล to pay attention (to), take an interest (in), look after someone

        ไม่เหลียวแล to be irresponsible, fail to take care (of), neglect

    เหลียวหลัง to look back

เหลือ left, remaining, left over, balance

    เหลือกำลัง too much (for someone), beyond one's capacity; terribly

    เหลือเกิน extremely, so, exceedingly, excessively; too much, awful, dreadful

    เหลือขอ incorrigible, impossible, beyond help

    เหลือเข็ญ exceedingly difficult, a killer

    เหลือคณนา countless; indescribable, immeasurable

    เหลือใจ exceedingly, surpassing, incomparable

    เหลือเชื่อ incredible, unbelievable, preposterous

    เหลือเดน rejects, dregs, leftovers, bottom of the barrel

    เหลือทน unbearable, intolerable, insupportable, insufferable, exasperating

        ผู้หญิงคนนี้ปากร้ายเหลือทน   She's insufferably bitchy.

    เหลือที่จะพรรณนา ineluctable, indescribable, beyond description, beyond words, inexpressible, ineffable

    เหลือบ่ากว่าแรง beyond one, too much (for, one), too hard, more than (one) can handle

    เหลือประมาณ inconceivably

    เหลือเฟือ ample, plenty (of) more than enough, a surplus (of)

    เหลือร้าย super, awfully, terribly

    เหลือล้น superabundance (of), infinite, surpassing

        เหลือล้นพ้นประมาณ immeasurable, boundless

    เหลือวิสัย impossible, beyond one's /power/ ability/, impracticable

    เหลือแสน extremely

    เหลือหลาย *see* **เหลือล้น**

    เหลือแหล่ an overabundance (of), a surplus (of), more than enough (for, of); a wealth of, in abundance, plentiful

    เหลืออด to lose control (of oneself), explode, fly off the handle, reach one's breaking point; intolerable, unbearable, insupportable, to be unable to put up with (something) any longer

เหลือก to roll up one's eyes

เหลือง yellow; sallow, jaundiced

    เหลืองอร่าม shining gold, glowing yellow

    เหลืองอ๋อย bright yellow

    น้ำเหลือง lymph

    นุ่งเหลืองห่มเหลือง clad in yellow robes, in monkly garb

เหลือบ horsefly, gadfly

ห
ฬ
อ
ฮ

เหลือบมอง to glance, take a look (at)

เหลือบเห็น to catch sight of

เหลื่อม overlapping, projecting

    เหลื่อมล้ำ discrimination, inequality

เหว abyss, chasm, pit

เหวย mocking sound

เหวอะหวะ *as in* **แผลเหวอะหวะ** gaping wound

เหวี่ยง to throw, fling, cast, whirl

    เหวี่ยงหมัด to throw a punch (to the jaw etc)

    เหวี่ยงแห to cast a net

    แรงเหวี่ยง centrifugal force

    สุดเหวี่ยง as hard as one /can/could/, to the utmost

เห่อ[1] to break out in a rash; to spread, erupt

เห่อ[2] to go /mad/crazy/ about something, /follow/go for/ what is in /fashion/vogue/

    เด็กวัยรุ่นเห่อเจาะเห่อสัก Teenagers are into the piercing-tattooing craze. / the tattoo-happy teenagers.

    ขี้เห่อ to be fashion-happy, fad-mad, go for whatever is in vogue

    เห่อเหิม overambitious

เหา louse, lice

เห่า to bark

เหาะ to fly, move through the air

    เหาะเหินเดินอากาศ *see* **เหาะ**

    เรือเหาะ aircraft, airplane; airship

เหิน to fly; to soar, glide

    เหินฟ้า, เหินหาว to fly, go through the air

    เหินห่าง to be estranged, grow distant, no longer close

    เดินเหิน to be up and around; to get around; to walk

เหิม high-spirited; bold; prideful

    เหิมเกริม overbold, overconfident; to take chances; to become emboldened

    เหิมหาญ courageous, brave

    เหิมห้าว inflamed (with)

เหิมฮึก energetic, lively, peppy

เหี้ย water monitor; shitty, rotten

    ไอ้เหี้ย You bastard!, You skunk!

เหี้ยน decimated, about gone, cleaned of, used up, nothing much left

    จอบนี้ใช้จนเหี้ยน This hoe has been used up. / There's nothing much left of this hoe. / The hoe has been worn down to practically nothing.

    เหี้ยนเตียน completely stripped (of), all gone

เหี้ยม ruthless, pitiless; harsh, cruel; severe, grim

    เหี้ยมเกรียม merciless, heartless

    เหี้ยมหาญ brave, valiant, valorous

    เหี้ยมโหด brutal, cruel, savage

เหี่ยว withered; wrinkled; faded; dried out; pale

    เหี่ยวแห้ง dejected, down in the mouth, in low spirits

เหือด to dry up; to be finished, disappear

    เหือดหาย to vanish, disappear

    เหือดแห้ง dried out, dried up, desiccated, parched

แห net

    ทอดแห to cast a net

    พลอยติดร่างแห to get /enmeshed/embroiled/involved/, be implicated

    ร่างแห net, mesh

แห่ procession; to go in a crowd

    แห่ตาม crowd after

    แห่ห้อม to surround

    แห่แหน to surround for protection

    กระบวนแห่ procession, parade, cortege

แหก to separate, spread apart, stretch apart

    แหกคอก eccentric; nonconformist, unorthodox, unconventional

    แหกคุก to break out of jail, pull a jailbreak

    แหกตา to fool (somebody), pull the wool over (someone's) eyes, hoodwink

    แหกปาก to yell, make a noise

แหง without doubt, definitely, sure

แหง่ calf
    ลูกแหง่ calf; mamma's boy

แห่ง place, location, spot of
    แห่งใด anywhere, where, wherever
    แห่งหนตำบลใด whereabouts
    ทุกแห่ง everywhere, at every place
    บางแห่ง some places
    สักแห่ง somewhere, someplace
    หลายแห่ง /several/many/ places

แห้ง dry
    แห้งผาก parched, arid
    แห้งแล้ง arid, very dry
    ของแห้ง dried food
    ซักแห้ง to dry-clean
    ท้องแห้ง to be starved, famished, have an empty stomach
    ปลาแห้ง dried fish
    ผอมแห้ง gaunt, scrawny; emaciated, wasted

แหงแก๋ definitely, obviously

แหง่ง sound of a bell, clanging

แหงน to look up
    แหงนคอ, แหงนหน้า to raise one's head, look up
    แหงนเต่อ, แหงนเถ่อ to be disappointed

แหน[1] duckweed

แหน[2] to treasure, keep for oneself, hold onto something, protective, possessive
    เฝ้าแหน to be in attendance, watch over
    หวงแหน to treasure, cherish

แหนง to doubt, suspect, distrust
    แหนงใจ to distrust, have a falling-out, have doubts (about somebody), suspicious

แหนบ tweezers; badge, pin; a numerical designation for rolled banana leaves
    แหนบรถยนต์ spring, leaf spring, coil spring

แหนม pickled pork

แหบ hoarse

เสียงแหบ hoarse (voice)

แหม jeez!, my goodness!

แหม่ม ma'am, madam, Western lady
    แหม่มกะปิ pseudo-Westernized Thai lady

แหมะ to stick on; sticky
    แหมะๆ dripping (sound)
    นั่งแหมะ to stick in one place

แหย spineless, weak, pusillanimous
    ยิ้มแหย see ยิ้มแหยๆ หน้า 398

แหย่ to poke, insert, stick (something) in; to tease, annoy, bother, provoke

แหยง to feel afraid (to), nervous (about), intimidated (by)

แหยม tuft of hair; to intrude, poke (into), meddle

แหยะ, แหยะๆ mushy; icky, yucky; to chew in cud-like fashion

แหล่[1] much, many
    ทั้งหลายแหล่ all, the whole lot

แหล่[2] on the verge (of), half, about to
    จะตายมิตายแหล่ half dead, about to die, on the verge of dying, in a critical state

แหล่[3] chapter; to intone (the Mahajataka stories, a prayer etc)

แหลก broken into pieces, crumbled, pulverized; destroyed
    แหลกลาญ totally destroyed
    แหลกเหลว demolished, smashed, broken up; in pieces
    สะบั้นหั่นแหลก wildly, to fever pitch, like madmen, tremendous (fight, argument etc)
    เหลวแหลก dissolute, bad, worthless, good-for-nothing

แหล่ง place, district, area, location, source (of)
    แหล่งการค้า /business/commercial/ district, market area
    แหล่งกำเนิด source, place of origin, birthplace
    แหล่งข้อมูล source
    แหล่งเงินทุน source of capital

ห
ฬ
อ
ฮ

แหล่งหล้า earth

หลักแหล่ง domicile, home, fixed abode

ตั้งหลักแหล่ง to settle (in)

แหลน javelin

แหลม pointed; sharp, clever, keen, quick, bright, intelligent; treble, high-pitched; cape, peninsula

แหลมคม critical; smart, brilliant

แหลมทอง Golden Peninsula, Thailand

แหลมเปี๊ยบ extra smart

แหลมอินโดจีน Indochina

เฉียบแหลม shrewd, sharp, astute, smart, acute

มุมแหลม acute angle

รสแหลม sharp taste, strong taste, highly flavored, tart

ล่อแหลม perilous

เสียงแหลม high-pitched, soprano, treble; shrill, /sharp/piercing/ sound

หวานแหลม very sweet

แหละ a word used for emphasis

นั่นแหละ That's it., That's the way it is., just so, indeed, yep (แทน yes); that very

พิมพ์ดีดเครื่องนั้นแหละ ใช้มา 50 ปี *That very typewriter was used for 50 years.*

นี้แหละ just like I said, you see, What did you expect?; just

ไม่ใช่น้ำส้ม ไม่ใช่น้ำหวาน น้ำร้อนนี้แหละ *...not orange juice, not a soft drink, just hot water.*

แหว to ball (someone) out

แหวเอา to scold, ball (someone) out

เสียงแหว angry voice

แห้ว [1] water chestnut

แห้ว [2] disappointed; to get zilch, miss out

แหวก to open; to push aside, make a passage (through)

แหวกช่อง to make way (for)

แหวกแนว to be original, break new ground,

novel, unconventional, radical

แหวกม่านประเพณี to flout convention, break with tradition; unorthodox

แหวกว่าย to swim about

แหว่ง to have (a piece etc) missing, have an indentation

ปากแหว่ง harelip, cleft palate

เว้าแหว่ง jagged, cut into, indented

แหวน ring

แหวนกัลเม็ด ring with a removable crown, trick ring

แหวนตรา signet ring

แหวนแต่งงาน wedding ring

แหวนเพชร diamond ring

แหวนหมั้น engagement ring

แหวนลูกสูบ piston ring

วงแหวน ring

แหวะ gaping; to vomit

แหะ ha

โห่ to boo, hoot, jeer, give catcalls; to acclaim; to shout

โห่ร้อง to cheer, hail, acclaim

ก่อนไก่โห่ at cockcrow, before dawn

โหง ghost, spirit, apparition

โหงพราย a spirit in one's power

ตายโหง to die a violent death

ผีตายโหง ghost of one who died a violent death; person who dies a violent death

โหด tough, rough, severe; unfeeling, cruel, harsh; horrendous

โหดร้าย atrocious, vicious, heartless

โหดร้ายทารุณ brutal, savage

โหดเหี้ยม inhuman, monstrous

โหน to hang, swing (from, on)

โหนรถเมล์ to ride on a bus hanging from the bar, straphang, be a straphanger

โหนก hump; protuberance; bulging, protuberant

โหนกแก้ม cheekbone

โหม to dash upon, rush on, storm

ก ข ค ฆ ง จ ฉ ช ซ ฌ ญ ฎ ฏ ฐ ฑ ฒ ณ ด ต ถ ท ธ น บ ป ผ ฝ พ ฟ ภ ม ย ร ฤ ฦ ล ว ศ ษ ส **ห**

โหมไฟ to build up a fire

โหมโรง to give a musical /prelude/over-ture/; to engage in foreplay

    เพลงโหมโรง overture

โหม่ง to butt; to dive (headfirst); sound of a gong, to gong

โหม่งลูกเข้าประตู to head the ball into the goal

โหย to be weak, exhausted, drained, worn out

โหยหวน to moan, wail; to give an eerie call

โหยหา to pine for, yearn for, long for

โหยทิว famished, weak with hunger

โหยไห้ to lament, bemoan

โหยง to be startled; to jump

สะดุ้งโหยง to start, jump (up, back, away)

โหร fortune-teller, soothsayer, astrologer

โหราจารย์ astrologer

โหราศาสตร์ astrology

โหรง, โหรงเหรง sparse, empty, few, hardly any

โหล[1] glass jar; dozen

โหล[2] hollow, sunken

ตาโหล sunken eyes, hollow eyes

โหล่ low

โหล่ในชั้น at the bottom of the class

โหลยโท่ย blah, unappealing

โหว่ having a hole, hollow; /gaping/yawning/ hole

ช่องโหว่ loophole

โหวกเหวก boisterous shouting

โหวงเหวง very light, light as a feather, weightless

โหวด steam whistle; blast of a steam whistle

โหวต to vote

ให้ to give, render, extend; make a gift (of, to); to allow, permit; to cause, have, make; for /you/her/him/them/, to

พิมพ์ต้นฉบับให้หน่อย Please type my manuscript.

พรุ่งนี้จะทำให้ I'll do it for you tomorrow.

ให้กับตัว to give to (someone) personally,

give by hand, hand (to)

ให้การ to testify

    ให้การเท็จ to perjure oneself, commit perjury, give false testimony

    คำให้การ testimony, statement

ให้กู้ to loan, lend

ให้เกิด to give rise (to), cause, create, give, make for

ให้แก่ to, for

ให้ความช่วยเหลือ to assist, /give/extend/ assistance, help, aid, give aid, lend a hand

ให้ความสะดวก to facilitate, assist, do what one can for someone

ให้คำมั่น to give one's word, undertake, promise

ให้คุณ[1] beneficial, of benefit, useful, positive

ให้คุณ[2] for you

ให้เช่า for rent, to let, rent, lease

ให้ใช้เงิน to spend, pay

ให้ดู to show

    ให้ดูดีๆ Be careful., Look carefully.

ให้ได้ without fail, definitely, must

ให้ถูก correctly, accurately

ให้ท่า to flirt (with), lead (someone) on, give encouragement (to), appear willing, give (someone) an opening, make overtures

ให้ทาน to give alms, give charity, donate

ให้ท้าย to spoil (a child, servant etc); to egg (someone) on

ให้เปล่า without charge, free, as a gift, give gratuitously, give for nothing

ให้ผล to give results, bear fruit, benefit

ให้พร to bless, give one's /blessings/good wishes/congratulations/

ให้ยืม to lend

ให้รางวัล to give a prize, reward, give a reward

ให้ร้าย to slander, malign

ให้ละเอียด in detail; finely

ห
ฟ
อ
ฮ

ให้ศีลให้พร to give one's blessing, bless

ให้สมกับ as befits, as appropriate (to) in accordance with

ให้สัญญา to promise, give one's word

ให้สิ้นชีวิต to deprive of life

ให้หา to call for, want

ให้อภัย to forgive, pardon, excuse

    ให้อภัยโทษ to pardon

ต่อให้ to give a handicap (to);

ทิ้งไว้ให้ to leave (for someone)

มีมติให้ to decide to, resolve to

ไม่ให้ to refuse, no; to keep (from), not to; not have the right (appearance, bearing, character, etc), to be against one, unsuitable *ความสามารถมีแต่หุ่นไม่ให้จึงชวดตำแหน่ง He has talent but not the right bearing so he missed out on the appointment. / Ability he has but his appearance is against him. So he missed getting the job. / Although he has ability, he did not get the job because his appearance was unsuitable.*

ยกให้ to give, present (to); to bequeath; to forgive, excuse, be excusable; to give someone credit (for something); to admit

ยอมให้ to let, permit, allow, yield

ยัดเยียดให้ to force (something) on (someone)

เสนอให้ to offer (for)

หันหลังให้ to turn one's back (on)

ใหญ่ large, big, great; main, superior, major; in charge, in command

ใหญ่โต big, huge; formidable; powerful

ใหญ่ไพศาล massive

ใหญ่หลวง immense, enormous, tremendous, huge, mammoth, gigantic

การผ่าตัดใหญ่ major surgery

กว้างใหญ่ vast, extensive, broad, spacious

ขนาดใหญ่ big, large, large size

ขนานใหญ่ (on a) large scale, in a big way

ครูใหญ่ principal, headmaster

ความเป็นใหญ่ superiority; authority; /leading/commanding/ position

พักใหญ่ /for/after/ awhile, after a time

มักใหญ่ ambitious

ยิ่งใหญ่ great, important, momentous

ใหม่ new, novel; again, anew

ใหม่ๆ fresh, new, just arrived

ใหม่ถอดด้าม brand-new, spanking new

ใหม่เอี่ยม brand-new

น้องใหม่ freshman, freshie, newcomer

มือใหม่ novice, new hand (at something)

ยุคใหม่ new era, new age

รุ่นใหม่ new model, late model, modern, new generation

สมัยใหม่ modern, up-to-date

หน้าใหม่ new face, newcomer

หัดใหม่ learning, beginner, learner

ไห jar, narrow-mouthed earthen pot

ไหปลาร้า collarbone, clavicle

ไห้ to cry, weep

ร้องไห้ to cry, weep, sob, shed tears

ร่ำไห้ to wail, sob, make lamentations

สะอื้นไห้ to sob

ไหน where, which, what

คนไหน who, which /one/person/

แค่ไหน to what extent, how much, how far

ถึงไหน How far did you get?, How far have you gone?, Where are you?

ที่ไหน where

    ที่ไหนก็ได้ anywhere

ไปไหน Where are you going?, Where are you off to?, Hi there!, How are you doing?

    ไปไหนมา Where have you been?, Hi there!

ไหนๆ anyway, just as well

ไหนๆ ก็อุตส่าห์มาถึงนี่แล้ว ทานข้าวเย็นด้วยกัน นะ You've made the effort to get here, so you might just as well stay for supper.

ไหนๆ จะไปอยู่แล้วก็แวะที่บ้านอาแถวนั้นด้วย
You're going there anyway, why not stop by your uncle's house.

ไหนๆ ก็ไหนๆ แล้ว having/ come so far/done so much/ etc
ไหนๆ ก็ไหนๆ แล้ว พวกเราไปให้ถึงยอดดอยก่อนค่ำดีกว่า Having come so far, we might as well get to the summit before nightfall.

ไหม[1] silk; silkworm
ไหมทอง silk shot with gold
ไหมเทียม rayon, artiflcial silk
ไหมพรม knitting /wool/yarn/
ผ้าไหม silk, silk /material/fabric/
เส้นไหม silk thread

ไหม[2] fine, penalty
ปรับไหม to fine, penalize

ไหม[3] positive question word
ใช่ไหม see **ใช่ไหม** หน้า 149
เชื่อไหม would you believe (it)
รู้ไหม you know; /do/did/ you know

ไหม้ to burn; to scorch; to char
เตารีดร้อนเกินไป ผ้าเช็ดหน้าจึงไหม้ The iron was hot and scorched the handkerchief.
ไหม้เกรียม charred
ไหม้ไฟ burned, burnt
ขนมปังไหม้ burnt toast
ไฟไหม้ Fire!; on fire, burning
    ไฟไหม้บ้าน The house is on fire. / The house is burning. / The house burned down. / They had a fire in the house (but not much damage was done).
ลุกไหม้ burning, flaming, blazing, in flames

ไหล to flow, run
ไหลเชี่ยวกราก torrential, to flow in a torrent
ไหลท่วม to inundate, flood
ไหลพุ่ง to gush (out, up, forth)
ไหลมาเทมา to pour /in/down/
ไหลริน to trickle; to flow gently, run (down, along)

ไหลหลั่ง to pour, stream
ไหลหลาก to flood; a flow of rushing water
น้ำลายไหล one's mouth is watering (for something); to salivate
รั่วไหล to leak out, get to be known
เลือดไหล to bleed; bloodshed

ไหล่ shoulder
ไหล่เขา mountain ridge, shoulder of a mountain
ไหล่ถนน shoulder (of a road), berm
ไหล่รวบ round-shouldered

ไหว[1] to shake, move, tremble, quake; to see through, get wind (of something) in time
เคลื่อนไหว to move
แผ่นดินไหว earthquake
หวั่นไหว sensitive (to), affected (by); anxious, nervous

ไหว[2] to be able (to do), capable (of doing), up to it (a job, task, doing something etc)
ไหวไหม Can you do it?, Are you up to it? Can you manage it?
ไม่ไหว It's too much., I give up., I'm not up to it., I don't think I can manage

ไหว้ to salute, raise the hands pressed together as a sign of respect; to pay homage (to)
ไหว้ครู to perform a ceremony to show respect for one's teachers
ไหว้เจ้า to make a spirit offering
ไหว้พระ to salute a monk; to do one's chanting (in homage to the Triple Gem)
ไหว้ละครับ please don't
ไหว้วอน to beseech
ไหว้วาน to ask for assistance, ask for a hand, request (someone's) help (in doing something)

ไหวพริบ shrewdness, acuity, quickness
มีไหวพริบ to be shrewd, sharp, intelligent, quick, quick-witted; tactful, adroit

ห
ฬ
อ
ฮ

อก breast, chest, bosom; heart

   อกกระเพื่อม bouncing bosom, bobbling breasts

   อกไก่ ridgepole

   อกขน hairy chest

   อกไข่ดาว flat-chested

   อกตรม *see* **ตรม** *หน้า 179*

   อกตั้ง at top speed

   อกแตก a place divided by a road or waterway; to /explode/blow up/ (with pent up emotions); Oh my god!

   อกผาย manly, robust

   อกสั่นขวัญหนี to have one's heart in one's mouth, terrified

   อกหัก brokenhearted, to be heartbroken

   กอดอก with arms folded across one's chest

   ชื่นอกชื่นใจ delighted, elated, pleased as punch, jubilant

   ดีอกดีใจ so happy, delighted

   ทรวงอก bosom, breast; chest

   พ้นอก to be rid (of), free (from)

   รอบอก bust

   โล่งอก relieved, to feel relief, what a relief!

   หน้าอก chest

   หัวอก feelings, heart

อกตัญญู ungrateful, thankless

อกาลิโก timeless

อกุศล bad, unwholesome, unmeritorious

   อกุศลกรรม bad action, unwholesome action

   อกุศลมูล the root causes of evil: greed, hatred and delusion

   คิดอกุศล to have bad thoughts (about, someone or something), think evil

อคติ bias, prejudice, prepossession

   ไม่มีอคติ unbiased, unprejudiced, fair-minded, just, equitable, without prepossessions, dispassionate

องค์ member, organ; body, part; characteristic

   องค์ความรู้ body of knowledge

องค์กร body, body corporate, instrumentality, organization, unit

องค์การ organization

   องค์การมหาชน public agency

องค์ชาย /Your/His/ Highness, prince

องค์ประกอบ element, composite part, constituent, factor

องค์ประชุม quorum

องค์รวม *as in* **เวชกรรมองค์รวม** holistic medicine

องค์หญิง /Your/Her/ Highness, princess

องคชาต penis, male /member/organ/, phallus

องคมนตรี privy /councillor/counsellor/

   ประธานองคมนตรี President of the Privy Council

องครักษ์ adjutant, A.D.C. (aide de camp)

องคาพยพ the constituent parts of the body

องคุลี finger; a measure equal in length to the end joint of the middle finger

องศา degree

องอาจ daring, brave, bold, with temerity; majestic, stately, dignified

องุ่น grape

   ไร่องุ่น vineyard

   เหล้าองุ่น wine

อณุ, อนุ particle

อโณทัย dawn

อด to give up, abstain from; to fast; to /do/go/ without; to go hungry

   อดกลั้น to restrain oneself, maintain self-control, resist hold back

   อดคิดไม่ได้ cannot help thinking

   อดใจ to control oneself, be patient

   อดตาย to starve to death

   อดตาหลับขับตานอน to go without sleep

   อดทน to endure, have patience, bear, put up with

      ความอดทน patience, fortitude, tenacity, stamina

   อดมื้อกินมื้อ to live from hand to mouth

อดไม่ไหว cannot help (loving, eating etc), unable to hold back (from), unable to keep from

อดอยาก poor, impoverished, starving

อดออม to economize, be frugal, use one's resources sparingly

อดอาหาร to fast, go without food

อดสู *as in* **น่าอดสู** disgraceful, shameful, execrable

อดิเรก special

อดิเรกลาภ special gift, windfall

งานอดิเรก hobby, avocation, pastime

ถวายอดิเรก to chant a prayer for long life for the king

อดีต past, former, ex-

อดีตกาล past tense; the past, former times

อดีตชาติ previous birth

อธรรม bad, evil, unjust, unfair, unrighteous

อธิกมาส intercalated month; additional month

อธิกวาร intercalated day

อธิกสุรทิน day intercalated in February

อธิกรณ์ case, matter, cause

อธิการ authority, power; abbot, chief monk, monk in charge

อธิการบดี rector, president, chancellor

พระอธิการ abbot

อธิบดี director general; chief

อธิบาย to explain

คำอธิบาย explanation

อธิปไตย sovereignty

อธิษฐาน to make a solemn wish, pray (for something), make a prayer for

อนัตตา anatta, non-self, not self

อนันต์ boundless, infinite

อเนกอนันต์ overabundant

อนันตริยกรรม the most heinous crimes: patricide, matricide, killing a saint, bruising the Buddha, causing schism in the Sangha; mortal sins

อนาคต future

อนาคตกาล future tense; (in the) future, time to come

อนาคตอันสุกใส bright future

ไม่มีอนาคต to have no future

อนาจาร /immoral/shameful/ conduct

ทำอนาจาร to molest, commit an indecent act

อนาถ pitiful

อนาถใจ heartbreaking

ตายอย่างอนาถ to die in a /dreadful/shocking/deplorable/ manner, die a ghastly death

น่าอนาถ ghastly, grisly; pitiful

อนาถา homeless; destitute

คดีอนาถา a suit in forma pauperis

คนอนาถา pauper

เด็กอนาถา waif

อนาทร unkind, uncaring

อนาธิปไตย anarchy

อนามัย health

ข้าวอนามัย unpolished rice, brown rice, healthfood rice

เจ้าหน้าที่อนามัย health /officer/official/

ถุงยางอนามัย condom

ผ้าอนามัย sanitary napkin

อนารยชน uncivilized, savage, barbarian

อนารยธรรม barbarism

อนิจกรรม death

ถึงแก่อนิจกรรม to die, pass away

อนิจจัง[1] impermanent, transient

อนิจจัง[2], **อนิจจา** Alas!

อนินทรีย์ inorganic

อนึ่ง in addition, besides, furthermore, also, moreover

อนุ sub-, micro-, minor, junior; particle; accordingly; regularly

อนุกรม series

อนุกรรมการ sub-committee

อนุชน younger generation, future generations

อนุชา younger brother

อนุปริญญา junior degree

อนุพันธ์ derivative; spin-offs, by-product

อนุภรรยา minor wife

อนุวรรค sub-paragraph

อนุศาสนาจารย์ chaplain

อนุสัญญา convention

อนุสิทธิบัตร petty patent

อนุเคราะห์ kindly, kindness; hospitality; generosity, assistance, aid

โปรดให้ความอนุเคราะห์แก่เขาด้วย Kindly render assistance. / Your assistance will be appreciated.

อนุญาต to permit, allow, authorize, consent

ห้ามเข้าโดยไม่ได้รับอนุญาต Unauthorized entry forbidden. / No entry without authorization.

ใบอนุญาต permit, license, authorization

อนุบาล to take care of, look after

โรงเรียนอนุบาล kindergarten

อนุมัติ to approve; to consent

อนุมัติบัตร exequatur

อนุมัติให้ approved

ขออนุมัติ to request approval, Approval requested.

อนุมาน to imply; to infer, surmise, deduce; inference, deduction; implication

อนุโมทนา to be glad (for someone), rejoice in another's good forture, congratulate

อนุรักษ์ to preserve

การอนุรักษ์ conservation, preservation

อนุโลม to make an exception, make allowances, be lenient, allow

โดยอนุโลม mutatis mutandis

อนุวัต pursuant (to)

อนุสติ recollection, reflection; constant mindfulness

อนุสติสิบ the Ten Reflections

อนุสนธิ with reference to, concerning, in response

to

อนุสรณ์ memorial (to, of), in remembrance of, in commemoration of

อนุสรณ์สถาน The National Memorial

เป็นอนุสรณ์ in memory of, as a token of, in remembrance of, as a memorial to

อนุสาวรีย์ monument

อนุสาวรีย์ชัยสมรภูมิ Victory Monument

อนุสาวรีย์ประชาธิปไตย Democracy Monument

อเนก multi-, many, plural

อเนกทัศน์ multivision

อเนกประสงค์ multipurpose, general purpose

อเนกอนันต์ multitude (of)

อเนจอนาถ dreadful, appalling, shocking

อบ to scent; to bake, roast; to be close, be stuffy

อบรม to train

อบอวล redolent /of/with/, perfused with

อบอ้าว sweltering, muggy, stifling, sultry; close, oppressive

อบอุ่น warm; comfortable, secure, reassured, reassuring

เตาอบ oven

น้ำอบ scented water, toilet water

อบเชย cinnamon

อบาย place of suffering; ruin, destruction

อบายภูมิ state of misery

อบายมุข vice, ruination, path to ruin

อปกติ abnormal

อปมงคล, อัปมงคล inauspicious; unpropitious, ill-omened, sinister

อปยศ, อัปยศ disgraceful, degrading, shameful, dishonorable, infamous

อปราชัย, อัปราชัย victory, triumph; defeat

อปโลกน์, อุปโลกน์ to make (someone something), call upon

ผมถูกอุปโลกน์ให้เป็นเจ้าภาพฝ่ายชาย I was made the groom's sponsor. / I was called

upon to be the groom's sponsor.

อพยพ to migrate; to evacuate; to resettle (in), take refuge

    เขมรอพยพ Cambodian refugees

อภัย to pardon, forgive

    อภัยทาน to shelter, give asylum

    อภัยโทษ amnesty, to grant amnesty, pardon

    ขออภัย to beg one's pardon, apologize, ask for forgiveness

    เขตอภัยทาน sanctuary

    ได้รับอภัยโทษ amnestied; pardoned

    สุดที่จะอภัยได้ unforgivable

    ให้อภัย to forgive, pardon, excuse

อภิชาตบุตร a child who does better than his parents, a child who surpasses his parents

อภิญญา supernatural Knowledge

อภิธรรม the Higher Doctrine, the analytic doctrine of the Buddhist canon

อภินันทนาการจาก with the compliments of, with one's compliments

อภินิหาร supernatural power, miracle

อภิบาล to protect

อภิปราย panel discussion, to speak /on/about/, discuss

    ผู้ดำเนินการอภิปราย moderator

    ผู้ร่วมอภิปราย panelist, speaker

อภิมหาอำนาจ great power(s)

อภิรมย์ happy, delighted; restful; to take a rest, repose

    น่าอภิรมย์ delightful, enjoyable, blissful

อภิลักขิตสมัย auspicious time

อภิวัฒน์ revolution

    ผู้อภิวัฒน์ revolutionary

อภิเษก water-pouring ceremony; coronation; wedding ceremony

อภิสิทธิ์ special privilege, prerogative

    อภิสิทธิ์ชน privileged person

อม to keep in the mouth, suck; to hold, absorb; to keep to oneself, conceal, harbor; to

swindle, steal, embezzle; -ish (*เช่น reddish อมแดง*)

อมควัน to smoke

อมความ to cover, include

    อมความร้อน to absorb heat

อมเงิน to embezzle, pocket the money

อมนกเขา to have oral sex, do a blow job (on someone)

อมน้ำ to absorb water, be waterlogged

อมปาก to keep one's mouth closed; to keep quiet

อมพะนำ to remain silent

อมภูมิ to hide one's lights under a bushel, modest, conceal one's abilities, keep what one knows to oneself, not forthcoming

อมมือ to suck one's thumb

    เด็กอมมือ infant; infantile, childish

อมยิ้ม to have an amused look, smile to oneself

อมโรค sickly

อมเลือดอมฝาด healthy-looking, to look healthy

อมหนอง containing pus, suppurating

    สีเขียวอมเหลือง yellowish green

อมตะ immortal, imperishable, classic, deathless; Nirvana

อมร celestial being

อมฤต divine nectar, ambrosia

    น้ำอมฤต ambrosia

อมาตย์ government officer; royal councillor

อมิตร unfriendly, inimical, hostile

อเมริกัน American

    คนอเมริกัน American

    สำนักข่าวสารอเมริกัน United States Information Service

อเมริกา America

    สหรัฐอเมริกา United States of America

อย่า don't, do not

    อย่ากิน Don't eat (it).

อย่าปริปาก Don't say a word., Keep it under your hat., Keep quiet about it.

อย่ามา don't you

อย่ามาว่าฉัน Don't you blame me!

อย่าเลย Better not., You better not., don't

อย่าแหย่เสือหลับ Let sleeping dogs lie.

อยาก to want, desire, need, require; to be /thirsty/hungry/ (for)

อยากรู้ to be curious

อย่าง kind; sort, category; thing; manner, mode; way; model; example; like, ...ly, ...ing

อย่างกันเอง informally

อย่างเก่ง at most, at best

อย่างคร่าวๆ roughly, rough

อย่างเคย as before, as usual

อย่างงั้นๆ so-so, not so good, tolerable

อย่างง่ายๆ simply; easily

อย่างเงียบๆ on the quiet

อย่างจริงจัง sincerely, wholeheartedly, really

อย่างเจ็บแสบ scathing

อย่างเจ้า like a prince, in princely fashion

อย่างใจ as expected, as hoped for, as one would like

    ไม่ได้อย่างใจ disappointing, not as expected, not up to expectations

อย่างฉับพลัน all of a sudden

อย่างเฉียบพลัน instantly

อย่างดี good quality; well

    อย่างดีที่สุด the best; at best

อย่างเด็ดขาด strictly, absolutely, without exception

อย่างเด็ดเดี่ยว resolutely; firmly

อย่างเดิม as before, the usual

อย่างเดียวกัน the same, of the same kind, in the same way

อย่างเดียวกับ like, the same as

อย่างใด what, which; at all, whatsoever

    อย่างใดอย่างหนึ่ง either, any

    แต่อย่างใด in any way, any

ไม่ได้ทำผิดแต่อย่างใด I have done nothing wrong /at all/in any way/. / I have not committed any offense whatsoever.

อย่างต่อเนื่อง sustainable; continuing, continuous, consistent, sustained, persistent, regular; regularly

อย่างธรรมดา regular, ordinary, plain

อย่างน้อยที่สุด at the very least, at least, minimum

อย่างนั้น that, like that; that's right, correct

อย่าทำอย่างนั้น Don't do that.

ฉันไม่ทำอะไรโง่ๆ อย่างนั้น I wouldn't do anything stupid like that.

    อย่างนั้นหรือ Is that so?

อย่างนี้ like this

อย่างเบาที่สุด lightest

อย่างเบาะๆ lightly, gently

อย่างเปิดเผย openly, frankly, candidly; in public

อย่างเผินๆ superficially

อย่างมาก at most, maximum

อย่างมีชีวิตชีวา lively

อย่างไม่มีปัญหา unquestionably, doubtlessly; without trouble, without any problem, easily

อย่างย่อๆ briefly, in short

อย่างย่อยยับ destructively

อย่างยิ่ง greatly, extremely, intensely, best; highly, certainly

ไม่เห็นด้วยเป็นอย่างยิ่ง I certainly do not agree.

อย่างยุติธรรม fairly, justly, equitably

อย่างรวดเร็ว rapidly, fast

อย่างรุนแรง strong, severe

อย่างไร how, anyhow; what; anything

    อย่างไรก็ดี in any event, however, anyhow, nevertheless

    อย่างไรก็ได้ whatever, anything is all right

อย่างไรก็ตาม *see* อย่างไรก็ดี

อย่างไรก็ไม่รู้ I don't know

เป็นอย่างไร Then what?

เป็นอย่างไรบ้าง How are things?

ไม่รู้จะเอาอย่างไร I don't know what to do.; I don't know what he wants.

เอาอย่างไร what do (you) want, what's the answer, what

อย่างลูกผู้ชาย like a man, manly

อย่างว่า you know what; uh-huh

อย่างเสียไม่ได้ grudgingly, unwillingly

อย่างหนึ่ง for one thing; one

อีกอย่างหนึ่ง for another thing; another

อย่างหยาบๆ roughly, approximately; coarsely, crudely

อยุติธรรม unjust, unfair

อยู่ to stay, remain; to live, dwell, be at; to be; to be alive

อยู่กับ to live with, stay with

อยู่กับตัว on one's person, with oneself

อยู่กับที่ stationary, fixed

อยู่กับบ้าน to stay home, be at home

อยู่กับเหย้าเฝ้ากับเรือน to be a homebody, live a quiet life, domestic; to be a good wife

อยู่กิน to live (together, with)

อยู่กินด้วยกัน to live together

อยู่คง to be invulnerable

อยู่งาน to serve, attend, be on duty

อยู่ง่ายกินง่าย to live simply

อยู่เฉยๆ to be quiet, keep still, keep quiet, do nothing, not do anything, be doing nothing; to pay no attention to; Don't move!

อยู่ดี ๆ without doing anything

อยู่ดี ๆ ก็เป็นนายร้อย He became a lieutenant without doing anything.

อยู่ดี ๆ ก็มีคนเอาเงินมาให้ถึงบ้าน A man came to the door and handed me some money

without my doing anything.

อยู่ดีกินดี to live well, be well-off

อยู่ตัว to be stable, stabilized; to settle in; firmly established; not stretch or shrink (ผ้า), fast (สี)

อยู่ตามลำพัง to be alone

อยู่ที่ is a matter of, is

ปัญหาอยู่ที่เงิน It's a matter of money. / The problem is money.

อยู่บ้าน to be at home, stay home

อยู่เบื้องหลัง to be behind (it, the scene, etc), be pulling the strings

อยู่เป็นเพื่อน to keep another company

อยู่ไฟ postpartum lying-in by a fire

อยู่มาวันหนึ่ง one day

อยู่มือ in one's power

อยู่ไม่เป็นสุข to have the fidgets, fidgety

อยู่เย็นเป็นสุข to be well and happy

อยู่เวร, อยู่ยาม to be on /duty/watch/guard duty/

อยู่หมัด to be under another's thumb, be in perpetual fear of someone

อยู่หลังฉาก to be behind the scene

กินอยู่ room and board

ขึ้นอยู่ to depend on, be a dependent of, belong to

ตั้งอยู่ to be located, situated (in, at, on, by)

ติดอยู่ to be stuck (at, in, on) held up (at, by); posted (on)

น่าอยู่ comfortable, cozy, livable

เป็นอยู่ alive

มีชีวิตอยู่ alive

ไม่อยู่ not in, not there, out, gone

ยังอยู่ still /in/there/; left, remaining; not dead yet, still alive, surviving

อรชร graceful

อรไท woman, girl

อรรถ term, text

อรรถกถา commentary, exegesis

อรรถกถาจารย์ commentator, exegete

อรรถกวี writer of non-fiction

อรรถคดี lawsuit, case, legal action, litigation

อรรถนิยม realism

อรรถรส flavor, feeling, aesthetic quality

อรรถาธิบาย explanation, commentary

อรรถาภิธาน thesaurus

แก้อรรถ to explain, define

คำอรรถ special term

เชิงอรรถ footnote

อรหันต์ an Arahant, the Perfected One, liberated person, Accomplished One, Worthy One

อร่อย delicious, tasty, to taste /great/good/

อร่อยเหาะ super delicious

อร่าม splendid, shining, brilliant, glowing, lustrous

เหลืองอร่าม shining gold, glowing yellow

อริ enemy

อริยะ noble , noble one

อริยบุคคล the noble ones, saints, holy persons

อริยมรรค the Eightfold Noble Path

อริยสัจ the Four Noble Truths

อรุณ dawn

อรุณสวัสดิ์ good morning

รุ่งอรุณ (at) dawn, daybreak

อรูป immaterial, formless, incorporeal

อลวน chaotic

อลเวง chaotic, in turmoil, tumultuous, in noisy confusion, uproar

อลหม่าน in chaos, in pandemonium, in great confusion, in panic

อล่องฉ่อง gorgeous

อลังการ splendiferous; resplendent; literary ornamentation, literary beauty

อลัชชี /iniquitous/shameless/immoral/ monk

อล่างฉ่าง exposed, conspicuous, in full view

อลึ่งฉึ่ง bloated, swollen, tumescent

อลูมิเนียม aluminum

อโลหะ non-metallic

อวก, อั้วก to vomit, throw up, puke

จะอั้วก going to /throw up/vomit/puke/, to feel like/throwing up/vomiting/puking/, want to throw up, etc

อวกาศ space

นักบินอวกาศ astronaut

อวด to show, display, parade, strut; to flaunt; to boast, show off

อวดเก่ง to show off

อวดดี to be vainglorious; show off, boast, put on airs, think a lot of oneself

อวดรู้ to be a know-it-all, pretentious

อวดอ้าง to boast, brag

อวตาร avatar, to be incarnated

อวน seine

อวนลอย floating seine

อวนลาก trawl

อ้วน fat, stout

อ้วนจ้ำม่ำ nice and fat, plump, chubby

อ้วนฉุ bloated

อ้วนตุ๊ต๊ะ corpulent, obese

อ้วนท้วน stout, well-fed

อ้วนพี stout, strapping

อ้วนมั่กขั้ก, อ้วนม่อต้อ pudgy, roly-poly

อวบ chubby

อ่วม (beaten) to a pulp; in bad shape

อวย[1] to grant, give, bestow

อวยชัย to invoke victory, give best wishes for success

อวยพร to give a blessing, give congratulations, congratulate, give greetings

ดื่มอวยพร to drink a toast (to), toast

อวย[2] restraining basket

หมูในอวย captive; a sure thing

อวล as in ตลบอบอวล redolent (of), pervasive

อวสาน end, doom

อวัยวะ organ, member, part of the body

อวัยวะสืบพันธุ์ reproductive organ, genitals, genital organs, loins

อวิชชา ignorance, unknowing, nescience, lack of knowledge

อเวจี hell, the lowest station of hell

อสงไขย infinite (period, number etc), innumerable, incalculable, countless; 10,000,000[20]

    นานนับอสงไขย for aeons

อสนีบาต thunderbolt

อสมการ inequality

อสรพิษ venomous snake, viper

อสังหาริมทรัพย์ immovable property, real property, landed property, real estate

อสัญกรรม death

    ถึงแก่อสัญกรรม to die, pass away

อสุจิ unclean, impure; sperm, spermatozoa

    น้ำอสุจิ semen

อสูร Asura, demon

    อสุรกาย demons

อหิงสา, อหึงสา non-violence, harmlessness; kindness

อหิวาตกโรค cholera

อโหสิกรรม forgiveness

ออ to gather (around), collect

อ้อ[1] reed

อ้อ[2] yes, uh-huh, I see, is that so

อ๋อ oh, I see

ออก[1] to /go/come/ out, exit, leave, depart; to start, begin to appear, be revealed, show; to issue, publish; to bud, sprout; to be a vassal state; to come

    ออกกฎหมาย to pass a law, legislate, enact

    ออกกะ to get off; end one's shift

    ออกกำลัง to exercise, get/take/ exercise; to exert oneself, use energy

    ออกกำลังกาย to exercise, /get/take/ exercise, do exercises

    ออกข้อสอบ to set an examination, set an examination question

    ออกแขก to entertain guests

        ชุดออกแขก dress /suit/clothes/outfit/

ออกไข่ to lay an egg; egg-laying

ออกความคิด to give an opinion, give one's thoughts (on, about)

ออกความเห็น to give one's opinion, express one's /opinion/thoughts/

    ออกความเห็นแย้ง to differ, contradict, offer a contrary opinion

ออกคำสั่ง to give an order, command, order, instruct

ออกงาน to give the first performance; to start working; to go to a /function/party/; go out in society; to /introduce/present/ to the public

ออกเงิน to pay

    ออกเงินล่วงหน้า to pay in advance, give an advance

    ออกเงินให้ to pay for someone else

ออกจะ rather, sort of, kind of

ออกจาก to leave, depart (from)

    ออกจากงาน to quit, leave (one's employment), retire

    ออกจากราชการ to retire from government service, leave government service

ออกจำหน่าย to put on sale, put on the market

ออกชื่อ to name, call (someone) by name, identify

ออกดอก to bloom, blossom; to have a venereal eruption

    ออกดอกออกผล to bear fruit, yield /interest/dividends/, be profitable

ออกเดินทาง to depart, start out, set out, leave on a trip

ออกตัว to excuse oneself, get out of (something)

    ขอออกตัว to ask to be excused

ออกทุน to put up money, invest

ออกนอกทาง to go astray; go off course

ออกปาก to ask for help; to say, speak; to

talk about

ออกไป to go out, leave; Get out!

  ออกไปข้างนอก to go out

  ออกไปจาก to leave, depart from, quit

  ออกไปให้พ้น to clear out, get out

ออกผล to bear fruit, be fruitful, produce results, bring dividends

ออกพรรษา end of the Rainy Season Retreat, end of the Buddhist Lent

ออกพันธบัตร to issue bonds

ออกภาษา to play on a foreign language

ออกมา to come out, emerge

ออกยาม to go off duty

ออกรับ to speak up for, defend (someone)

ออกร้าน to set up a stall at a fair

ออกเรือน to set up housekeeping, set up a separate household

ออกแรง to exert oneself, use one's strength

ออกโรง to give the opening performance; to make a debut

ออกลาย to show one's true colors, show one's stripe

ออกลูก to give birth, have a baby

ออกวางขาย to put on sale

ออกเวร to be off duty, go off duty

ออกเสียง to pronounce; to sound; to voice one's opinion, vote

  ออกเสียงลงคะแนน to vote

  งดออกเสียง to abstain (from)

  การออกเสียงรับรองร่างรัฐธรรมนูญ มีผู้งด ออกเสียงมากกว่าผู้ออกเสียง The votes in favor of the constitution bill were in excess of the abstentions.

ออกหน้า to put oneself forward

ออกหน้าออกตา openly; freely; publicly

ออกหมายเรียก to issue a summons

ออกหัด to have the measles

ออกห่าง to distance oneself, dissociate oneself (from); be distant, estranged

ออกอาการ to lose one's temper

ออกอีสุกอีใส to /have/get/ chicken pox

ขาออก departure, outward; export

ทางออก exit, way out

นึกออก to recollect, remember, recall, think of something

แบ่งออกเป็น to be divided into

ฟังออก to understand, follow (the meaning etc)

ลบออก minus, to subtract; to erase, expunge

เลือดออก bleeding, to bleed

ส่งออก to export

หักออก to deduct

ให้ออก to oust, ousted (from)

ออก[2] (an intensifier) very, really, great; I think it's (great, tasty etc)

  ดีออก great, really good

  สนุกออก great fun

  สวยออก I think she's pretty; really great-looking

ออกซิเจน oxygen

ออกไซด์ oxide

ออกเทน octane

ออเซาะ to wheedle (something out of somebody); to fawn (on)

ออด bell, buzzer

  กดออด to ring the /bell/buzzer/, press the buzzer

ออดแอด endlessly, chronically; feeble, weak, sickly

อ่อน mild; light (color); supple; soft; gentle, gracious; changeable; to sag; flexible, pliable; young; weak, feeble

  อ่อนกว่า younger (than); softer (than)

  อ่อนกำลัง to weaken; weakened

  อ่อนข้อ to relent, reduce one's demands

  อ่อนจิต, อ่อนใจ tired, weary, disheartened, discouraged, fed up, bored

  อ่อนน้อม deferential, respectful, gentle, unassertive, mild-mannered

อ่อนนุ่ม soft; spongy

อ่อนปวกเปียก limp

อ่อนเพลีย weary, weak, spent, worn out, pooped, tired out,

อ่อนยวบ to sag; lack of resilience

อ่อนโยน gentle, mild, courteous

อ่อนแรง to weaken, get tired, flag

อ่อนล้า weary

อ่อนหวาน sweet, gentle

อ่อนหัด inexperienced, to be a novice (at), wet behind the ears

อ่อนไหว sensitive

อ่อนแอ weak

    คนอ่อนแอ weakling

ไก่อ่อน a pushover, easy mark, chump, dupe

ขวัญอ่อน fearful, nervous, easily scared, timorous

จุดอ่อน weak point

เด็กอ่อน baby, infant; small child

ตัวอ่อน flexible, supple; pupa; young

ตัวอ่อนของจิงโจ้เรียกว่าโจอี The young of the kangaroo is called a joey.

ลูกอ่อน baby, infant

สีอ่อน light color

หน้าอ่อน young-looking, youthful

หัวอ่อน tractable, obedient

หินอ่อน marble

อ้อน to keep pleading; to be given to crying; to cry like a baby

อ้อนวอน to urge, keep on asking (for), beg (someone to do something), plead (with someone to do something), supplicate, beseech, implore

อ้อนแอ้น willowy, slender, slim

    รูปร่างอ้อนแอ้น willowy figure, /slim/ slender/ appearance

ออฟเซท offset

ออฟไซด์ off side

ออฟฟิศ office

ออม to economize, save

    ออมกำลัง to husband one's /strength/ energy/, conserve one's strength

    ออมมือ to hold back

    ออมสิน savings, savings bank

    อดออม to economize, be frugal, use one's resources sparingly

อ้อม to go around, make a detour, go a roundabout way

    อ้อมกอด embrace

    อ้อมค้อม circuitously, not forthright

        พูดอ้อมค้อม to beat around the bush, be evasive, use circumlocutions, say indirectly

    อ้อมอก care

    ทางอ้อม detour, indirect route, roundabout way; indirectly, in a roundabout way

อ้อมแอ้ม indistinctly; hesitantly, with a stammer, to equivocate

อ่อย to lay bait; to ensnare softly

    อ่อยเหยื่อ to /put out/lay/ bait, lay a trap (for); to lure, entice, tempt, offer inducements, lead someone on

อ้อย sugar cane

    อ้อยควั่น section of sugar cane

อ๋อย[1] bright, vivid

    เหลืองอ๋อย bright yellow

อ๋อย[2] moaning

    ครางอ๋อย to moan

อ้อยสร้อย to play on another's sympathy, beguile

อ้อยอิ่ง to dawdle, take one's time, linger, hang around

อ้อแอ้ to babble; to mutter; indistinct

อ๊ะ What! Oh!

อะโกโก้ a-go-go

อะตอม atom

อะมีบา amoeba

อะร้าอร่าม opulent

อะไร what; something, anything

ใน **อะไรกัน** What's going on?, What's up?; What do you mean?

มีอะไรกัน There's something between them.

อะไรก็ได้ anything is okay

อะไรต่ออะไร whatever, one thing and another, lots of things

อะไรต่อมิอะไร a slew of things, I don't know what all, lots of things, whatnots

อะไรเป็นอะไร what's what

ทำอะไร What do you think you're doing?

ทำอะไรไม่ได้ There's nothing I can do about it., Nothing can be done.

เป็นอะไรไหม Any damage or injury?

มีอะไรกินบ้าง What's for /lunch/supper/ etc?, What's on the menu?

ไม่เป็นอะไร no damage or injury, It's okay.

ไม่มีอะไร that's alright, it's okay, forget it

อะลุ่มอล่วย, อะลุ้มอล่วย to compromise; to make allowances (for), be lenient, make an exception, go easy (on someone)

อะลูมิเนียม aluminum

อะไหล่ spare part, replacement part

อักขระ letter, word, sound, alphabet

อักขรวิธี book on reading and writing

อักขรานุกรม index

อักขรานุกรมภูมิศาสตร์ gazetteer

อักขราภิธาน glossary, lexicon, dictionary

อักโข much, many

อักษร letter, character, alphabet; letters, writing

อักษรกลาง middle tone consonant

อักษรต่ำ low consonant

อักษรย่อ abbreviation

อักษรศาสตร์ arts

อักษรศาสตรบัณฑิต bachelor of arts

อักษรสูง high consonant

ทรงพระอักษร to write; to read

อักเสบ infected, inflamed

อัคคีภัย fire

อัคนี fire; lava

อัครธรรมทูต apostle

อัครมเหสี major consort, queen

อัครราชทูต minister

เอกอัครราชทูต ambassador

อัครศาสนูปถัมภก Prime Patron of Buddhism

อัครสาวก the principal disciples of the Buddha: Sariputra and Moggallana

อัง to warm (one's hands etc) before a fire

อังกฤษ England, English

คนอังกฤษ Englishman, English, British, Anglo-

จักรภพอังกฤษ British Commonwealth

ประเทศอังกฤษ England, Great Britain

ภาษาอังกฤษ English

อังคาร[1] Tuesday; Mars

วันอังคาร Tuesday

ดาวอังคาร (the planet) Mars

อังคาร[2] ashes

ลอยอังคาร to cast one's ashes on the water

อั้งเปา red envelope with a money gift

อั้งยี่ Chinese criminal association

อั้งโล่ Chinese brazier

อัจฉริยะ genius, prodigy, master

เขาเป็นคนอัจฉริยะในทางศิลปะ He is an artistic genius.

อัจฉริยบุคคล genius

อัจฉริยภาพ genius

อย่างอัจฉริยะ ingenious

อัชฌาสัย friendly disposition, pleasant /personality/ nature/

อัญชลี the hands pressed together in salutation

อัญเชิญ to invite, present, bring forth; to install

อัญประกาศ quotation mark

อัญมณี semi-precious stones, gemstones other than the nine precious gems

อัฐ money; penny

อัฐิ bones, ashes

อัฐิบรรพบุรุษ ancestor's ashes

บรรจุอัฐิ to deposit the ashes (in)

อัฒจันทร์ grandstand, stand

อัฒภาค semicolon

อัณฑะ testicles

ถุงอัณฑะ scrotum

ลูกอัณฑะ testicle

อัด to compress, pack, press, squeeze; to hold one's breath; to lay (a girl) (sl); full, front

อัดก๊อบปี้ crushed from both sides, flattened

อัดฉีด to lubricate, grease; lubrication

อัดฉีดเงิน to inject /money/funds/

อัดบุหรี่ to take a deep drag on a cigarette; to smoke

อัดแบตเตอรี่ to charge a battery

อัดแผ่นเสียง to make a (phonograph) record

อัดรูป to make a print (from a film); to develop pictures, have pictures developed

อัดลม aerated, carbonated

น้ำอัดลม aerated waters, carbonated beverage, soft drink

อัดสำเนา to make a copy

อัดเสียง to record

อัดอั้น to be at a loss (for words, ideas etc), paralyzed, stupefied

อัดอั้นตันใจ (all) choked up

อัดแอ crowded, congested

รูปหน้าอัด full-face photograph

อัตกาม masturbation

ทำอัตกาม to masturbate

อัตคัด hard-pressed, impoverished, impecunious; in penury; hard, tough

อัตคัดขัดสน in need, in want, hard up

อัตชีวประวัติ autobiography

อัตตา self, ego, personal entity; atman, soul

มีอัตตาสูง egotistical, egocentric

อัตถิภาวะนิยม existentialism

อัตตกิลมถานุโยค self-mortification

อัตโนมัติ personal opinion; automatic

โดยอัตโนมัติ automatically

อัตภาพ oneself, self; personal condition, station in life, personal /situation/status/

อัตนัย subjective

อัตนัยนิยม subjectivism

อัตรา schedule, tariff, rate; position

อัตราการเฉือน shear rate

อัตราคนเกิด birth rate

อัตราคนตาย death rate

อัตราความถี่ frequency rate

อัตราความเร็ว rate of speed

อัตราทดเฟือง gear ratio

อัตราประชากร population

อัตราปันส่วน ration

อัตราภาษีเงินได้ rate of income tax

อัตราเร่ง rate of acceleration

อัตราแลกเปลี่ยน rate of exchange

อัตราส่วน scale, ratio

อัตลักษณ์ identity

อัตวินิบาตกรรม suicide

ทำอัตวินิบาตกรรม to commit suicide

อัธยาศัย see อัชฌาสัย

อัน a common numerical designation; which, that, who, whom

อันก่อน former, that one

อันควร proper, suitable, appropriate

อันเดียว only one

อันใด whatever, what

อันที่จริง in fact, in reality, actually, as a matter of fact

อันนั้น that, that one

อันนี้ this, this one

อันละ each, per, for one

อันสมควร reasonable, right

อันหลัง latter, last one

อันเหมาะสม appropriate

อันไหน? Which one?

อันไหนๆ ก็ได้ any one, either one

อันไหนก็ตาม whichever, whatever one

อ

ฮ

เป็นชิ้นเป็นอัน substantial, serious, solid, real

เป็นอันขาด absolutely, definitely

เป็นอันมาก very much, many, a lot of, most

เป็นอันว่า it means, so

เป็นอันหนึ่งอันเดียวกัน united, to be one, as one, one and the same

มีอันจะกิน well-to-do, well-off, prosperous, well-heeled

มีอันเป็น to be struck by misfortune

สิ่งละอันพันละน้อย odds and ends, bits and pieces

อั้น to restrain oneself, hold back; to hold one's breath; to suppress, repress, (one's feelings etc); to limit, restrict

อั้นตู้ at one's wits'end; to be struck dumb

แทงไม่อั้นประตู unlimited bets

ไม่มีอั้น unlimited, unrestrained, limitless

อันดับ item; rank, ranking, rating, order, series; scale; order *(วิทย์)*

อันดับต่อไป next, next (on the program, item, etc), next number

พระอันดับ unranking monk, /ordinary/ plain/ monk

อันตรธาน to disappear, vanish

อันตราย danger, peril, harm

อันตราย ห้ามเข้า Danger. No Entry.

ได้รับอันตราย injured, harmed, hurt

ทำอันตราย to harm, hurt, be dangerous,

น่าอันตราย dangerous, perilous, risky

เป็นอันตราย dangerous

อันธพาล a roughneck, hoodlum, hooligan; scoundrel, bad guy

นักเลงอันธพาล gangster, bad character

อับ¹ small round box with a lid

อับ² close, stuffy, unventilated; stale-smelling, musty

อับจน in check; at the end of one's rope, at an impasse; hard up

อับโชค luckless, hapless, unfortunate

อับลม airless, protected from the wind

อับแสง dark, ill lit, obscure, poorly lit; in the shadows

อับอาย disgraceful, shameful, degrading; ashamed

ตกอับ to be down in one's luck, fall on hard times; to be out of favor

อับเฉา¹ dreary, bleak

อับเฉา² ballast

อับปาง to sink, go down

อัปมงคล inauspicious, unpropitious, sinister, ill-omened

อัปยศ shameful, disreputable, dishonorable, disgraceful

อัประมาณ odious, disgaceful, shameful

อัปราชัย, อปราชัย victorious

อัปรีย์ vile, despicable

อัปลักษณ์ ugly, misshapen, an eyesore, unfortunate, bad

อัปสร heavenly damsel

อัฟริกัน African

อัฟริกา Africa

อัมพฤกษ์ partially paralyzed, suffering from a minor stroke

อัมพาต paralysis; paralyzed, crippled, incapable of movement

อัยการ public prosecutor, attorney general

กรมอัยการ Public Prosecution Department

อั๊วะ I, me

อัศจรรย์ marvelous, astonishing, amazing

อัศจรรย์ใจ astonished, amazed, astounded

น่าอัศจรรย์ wonderful, amazing, incredible, astounding, miraculous

อัศเจรีย์ exclamation /point/mark/

อัศวิน knight

อัสดง sunset

อัสดงคต west

อัสดงคตประเทศ the Occident

อา¹ uncle (ชาย), aunt (หญิง)

อา[2] ah!, oh!

อ้า to open, gape, opened (up, out)

    อ้าแขน (to greet) with open arms, welcome

    อ้าซ่า sprawled out, spread apart, wide open; exposed

    อ้าปากค้าง to gape, stare open-mouthed

    อ้าปากหวอ open-mounthed, gaping

อากร duty, fee, tax, excise

    อากรมหรสพ entertainment tax

    อากรรับมรดก inheritance tax

    อากรสรรพสามิต excise tax

    อากรแสตมป์ duty stamp, tax stamp

    ภาษีอากร taxes and duties

อากัปกิริยา deportment, manner, conduct

อาการ state, condition, manner; to look (sad, happy, angry etc), show (happiness, anger etc), symptom, indication, sign (of)

    อาการ 32 the thirty-two components of the body; perfectly normal

    อาการหนัก seriously, in serious condition, in bad shape

    แสดงอาการ to show symptoms (of), give an indication (of)

    ไม่มีอาการผิดปกติ (His, its etc) condition is normal., nothing abnormal, to show nothing unusual, nothing out of the ordinary

อากาศ air; weather; sky

    อากาศดี fine weather, good weather

    อากาศเต็มที่ /bad/terrible/rotten/awful/ weather

    อากาศทะเล sea air

    อากาศธาตุ air, sky

    อากาศแปรปรวน turbulence

    อากาศไปรษณีย์ airmail

    อากาศยาน aircraft, airplane, aeroplane

    อากาศสดชื่น fresh air

    อากาศเสีย bad air, stale air

    กองทัพอากาศ air force

    ช่างอากาศ airplane mechanic

    ฐานทัพอากาศ air base

    ดินฟ้าอากาศ weather, climate

    ตากอากาศ to take the air, go to the country, take a vacation

    ทางอากาศ by air

    พยากรณ์อากาศ weather forecast

    ลมฟ้าอากาศ weather

    วิมานในอากาศ castles in the air

    ออกอากาศ to broadcast, /put/go/ on the air

อาขยาน memorized text; recitation from memory

    บทอาขยาน text to be learned by heart

อาคเนย์ southeast

อาคม spell

    คาถาอาคม incantation, spell, magic formula, mantra

อาคันตุก-, อาคันตุกะ guest, visitor

อาคาร building, structure, house, housing

    อาคารสงเคราะห์ government housing project

อาฆาต vengeful, vindictive, unforgiving

อ่าง basin, bowl, tub

    อ่างกระเบื้อง China basin, earthenware basin

    อ่างเก็บน้ำ dam, barrage, water tank, reservoir, storage pond

    อ่างเคลือบ enamelled basin

    อ่างเปล tub

    อ่างล้างมือ washbowl, washbasin, sink

    อ่างล้างหน้า washbowl, washbasin, sink

    อ่างเลี้ยงปลา fishpond; fishbowl

    อ่างอาบน้ำ bathtub

    ชามอ่าง large bowl

อ้าง to quote (as a reference or authority), refer (to), allude (to) cite, hold out

    อ้างถึง to refer (to), cite; with reference to, referring (to), ref.:

    อ้างหลักฐาน to cite evidence, offer supporting evidence

    อ้างเหตุผล to cite reasons, offer supporting reasons

    อ้างอิง to refer

อ

ฮ

ข้ออ้าง pretext, excuse; justification

หนังสืออ้างอิง reference (book)

อ้างว้าง lonely, lonesome, forlorn

อาจ[1] bold, brave; daring, audacious

อาจหาญ bold, audacious, intrepid, valiant

อาจอง brave, valiant; dignified, stately

อาจเอื้อม presumptuous, to have the effrontery (to do something)

องอาจ *see* **อาจอง**

อาจ[2], **อาจจะ** may, might, could, possibly, probably maybe, perhaps

อาจ (จะ) ใช้ได้ maybe alright, probably okay

อาจม excrement

อาจาด tart relish

อาจารย์ professor, instructor, teacher, lecturer; mentor

อาจารย์ใหญ่ headmaster, principal; cadaver

ครูบาอาจารย์ teachers

อาจิณ, เป็นอาจิณ habitual, customary, regular, routine

อาเจียน to vomit, throw up, regurgitate

อาชญา authority, power; penalty; crime

อาชญากร criminal, perpetrator

อาชญากรสงคราม war criminal

อาชญากรรม crime, penal offense

อาชญาบท provision of law

อาชญาบัตร licence

อาชญาศึก martial law

อาชญาสิทธิ์ absolute power

อาชาไนย noble, wellborn; throughbred; easily trained

บุรุษอาชาไนย well-trained person

ม้าอาชาไนย thoroughbred horse

อาชีพ, อาชีวะ occupation, vocation, career; vocational; livelihood

กงสุลอาชีพ career consul

อาญา power, authority; crime; criminal; penalty, punishment,

อาญาสิทธิ์ absolute power

กฎหมายลักษณะอาญา criminal law, penal law

รอลงอาญา to suspend a sentence, sentence suspended

ศาลอาญา criminal court

อาณัติ authority; sign

อาณัติสัญญาณ signal, sign, high sign

ไม่อยู่ใต้อาณัติของใคร to be free and independent, subject to no one, under no one's authority

อาณาเขต territory, area

สภาพนอกอาณาเขต extra-territoriality

แห่งอาณาเขต territorial

อาณาจักร world; realm, domain

อาณานิคม colony

อาณาบริเวณ area, surrounding area, territory, vicinage, bounds

อาณาประชาราษฎร์ subjects, citizens

อาด ๆ *as in* **เดินอาด ๆ** to stride (along), walk tall

อาดูร suffering; grieving, lamenting

อาตมภาพ I, me

อาตมา I, me, myself

อาถรรพณ์ ill-omened, accursed, hexed, evil

อาทร kind (to), concerned (for, about); hospitable, to give a helping hand (to)

อาทิ, อาทิเช่น for example, like, for instance

เป็นอาทิ for example, and so on, et cetera

อาทิตย์ the sun; week

อาทิตย์ละ a week, per week, weekly, once a week

อาทิตย์อุทัย rising sun

ประเทศอาทิตย์อุทัย the land of the Rising Sun

วันอาทิตย์ Sunday

อาธรรม์ wrong; unjust

ชั่วช้าอาธรรม evil, wicked

อาน[1] saddle

หมาหลังอาน saddle-backed dog

อาน[2] badly, crushingly

   ถูกตีเสียอาน badly beaten, beaten to a pulp

อ่าน to read; to know, understand

   อ่านดังๆ to read out loud, read aloud

   อ่านในใจ to read to oneself

   อ่านพร้อมกัน to read in unison

   อ่านไม่ออก illegible; not to understand; to be unable to read (a situation, motive etc), be in the dark (about, as to)

   อ่านเล่น to read for pleasure

   อ่านออก legible; understandable, apparent, discernible, to understand, read

      อ่านออกเขียนได้ literate

อานิสงส์ (to reap the) advantage, profit, good effect, benefit

อานุภาพ power, might, strength

อาบ to bathe; to wash; to coat

   อาบแดด to sunbathe, take a sunbath

      ผู้อาบแดด sunbather

   อาบน้ำ to bathe, take a bath

      อาบน้ำทะเล to bathe in the sea

      อาบน้ำศพ symbolic pouring of water over the deceased's hand

   อาบยา (ศพ) to embalm

      อาบยาพิษ dipped in poison

   อาบเหงื่อต่างน้ำ to live by the sweat of one's brow, struggle hard (to)

อาบัติ offence, offense, transgression

อาพาธ ill, sick, unwell

อาเพศ portent, harbinger

   เกิดอาเพศ to bode ill, be a bad omen, be a portent

อาภรณ์ apparel, raiment, finery, adornments

อาภัพ unfortunate, luckless, unlucky, hapless

อามิสสินจ้าง bribe

อาย[1] ashamed, embarrassed, shy, abashed

   อายใจ to feel ashamed

   อายเหนียม embarrassed; to feel shy (about doing or saying something)

ขี้อาย bashful, shy, easily embarrassed

อับอาย disgraceful, shameful, degrading; ashamed

อาย[2] as in **กลิ่นอาย** atmosphere

อ้าย[1] a familiar or derogatory masculine appellation; this, that

   อ้ายนั่น that thing, that there thing, that

   อ้ายนี่ this thing, this here thing, this

   อ้ายบ้า You must be mad!, Jerk!, You jerk!

   อ้ายสัตว์ You bastard!

   อ้ายหนู sonny; one's thing, peter (sl)

อ้าย[2] eldest brother, big brother; first

   เดือนอ้าย first month (of the lunar calendar)

อายัด to attach, garnish, freeze

   อายัดทรัพย์ to attach property

อายุ age

   อายุกลางคน middle-aged

   อายุการใช้งาน lifetime, working life

   อายุขัย life-span

   อายุคราวเดียวกัน of the same age

   อายุความ period of prescription, statute of limitations

   อายุงาน period of employment

   อายุน้อย young

   อายุมาก old, aged

   อายุยืน long-lived

   อายุวัฒนะ as in **ยาอายุวัฒนะ** elixir of life, geriatric tonic, longevity tonic

   อายุสัญญา contract term

   อายุสูง advanced in years

   เกษียณอายุ retirement age; to retire

   ช่วงอายุ lifespan, lifetime

   ต่ออายุ to renew; to extend one's life (of government service, as a musician, etc)

   มีอายุ older, elderly

   สิ้นอายุ to expire; to die

   สูงอายุ aged, elderly, senior, advanced in years

      คนสูงอายุ elderly person, senior citizen

อ

ฮ

หมดอายุ expired, to expire

อายุร- *as in*

  อายุรแพทย์ doctor of medicine, physician

  อายุรเวช physician

  อายุรเวท medicine; ayuravedic

  อายุรศาสตร์เขตร้อน tropical medicine

อารมณ์ mood, emotion, feeling, temper, temperament

  อารมณ์ขัน sense of humor

  อารมณ์ขึ้น to become emotional

  อารมณ์ดี (in a) good /mood/humor/, cheerful, happy, in a good frame of mind

  อารมณ์ไม่ดี (in a) bad mood, cranky, grouchy, out of sorts, upset

  อารมณ์ร้าย hot-tempered

  เกิดอารมณ์ to lose one's composure

  มีอารมณ์ to /get/be/ in the mood (for)

  ไม่มีอารมณ์ not in the mood (to, for)

  หมดอารมณ์ not feel like (doing something), lose one's interest (in)

อารยะ civilized, advanced; righteous; Aryan race; noble

  อารยชน civilized people, educated people

  อารยชาติ civilized nation

  อารยธรรม civilization

  นานาอารยประเทศ civilized nations, advanced countries

อารักขา protection, care

  ขอตำรวจอารักขา to ask for police protection

  คนในอารักขา protegé

  รัฐในอารักขา protectorate

อารักษ์ guardian

อารัมภกถา introduction

อารัมภบท introduction, prelude, preface, preamble, foreword

อาราธนา to invite (for monks)

อาราม[1] monastery, temple, wat

  วัดวาอาราม wats, temples

อาราม[2] in haste; intensely, over

อารามดีใจ overjoyed

อารี kind generous, friendly

  ใจอารี kind, considerate, kindhearted

  โอบอ้อมอารี kindly, warmhearted, generous, hospitable

อาละวาด to act up, become violent, go berserk, /go/be/ on a rampage, in a rage; to make trouble

อาลักษณ์ court secretary

อาลัย to miss (someone), long for someone

  ทอดอาลัย to lose hope, be in despair, despondent

  พิธีไว้อาลัย memorial service

  ไว้อาลัย to mourn (for); (to stand, etc) in memory of, in memoriam, memorial

    คำไว้อาลัย eulogy

  หมดอาลัยตายอยาก in despair, completely discouraged, without hope, dispirited

อ่าว gulf, bay

  อ่าวไทย Gulf of Thailand

อ้าว[1] hot, sultry

  อบอ้าว sweltering, muggy, stifling, sultry; close, oppressive

อ้าว[2] swiftly, quickly

  โกยอ้าว to flee, beat it

  วิ่งอ้าว to race, run at top speed

อ้าว[3] oh!, huh!, eh!

  อ้าว! ทำไมทำอย่างนั้นล่ะ Eh, what do you think you're doing?

อาวรณ์ to be worried, worry (about)

  อาลัยอาวรณ์ to be worried (about), worry (about), long for, miss

อาวาส wat

  เจ้าอาวาส abbot

อาวุธ weapon, arms

  อาวุธนิวเคลียร์ nuclear weapon

  อาวุธปืน firearms

  อาวุธยุทธภัณฑ์ armaments, munitions

  ด้วยอาวุธ armed

ติดอาวุธ armed

ปลดอาวุธ to disarm, disarmed

ปลอดอาวุธ weapon-free

อาวุโส senior, elder; precedence, seniority

อาวุโสระหว่างหัวหน้าสถานทำการกงสุล precedence as between heads of consular posts

มีอาวุโสสูงกว่า to have precedence (over)

รัฐบุรุษอาวุโส elder statesman

อาศรม ashram, hermitage

อาศัย to live, dwell, stay; to depend on, rely on; by virtue of

ผมไม่ค่อยมีเวลา ต้องอาศัยเลขาฯช่วยจัดการให้ I don't have the time so I have to rely on my secretary to handle it.

อาศัยไหว้วาน through the help (of)

อาศัยอยู่ to reside, stay (at, in)

อาศัยอำนาจ by virtue of the /power/ authority/

โดยอาศัย with the aid of, by means of

ถ้อยทีถ้อยอาศัย reciprocal

ถิ่นอาศัย local residence, hometown

ผู้อาศัย resident; a dependent

พออาศัย pretty good, not bad

สิทธิอาศัย right of residence

อาศิรพจน์, อาศิรพาท encomium, panegyric, tribute

อาสน-, อาสน์ seat

ร้อนอาสน์ on the hot seat, anxious, worried

อาสัญ death; to die, expire, pass away

อาสา to volunteer

อาสาสมัคร volunteer

ทหารอาสา volunteer

อาสาฬหบูชา Asalhabucha Day, puja of the day of the full moon of the eighth lunar month

อาหม Ahom

อาหรับ Arab, Arabian

อาหาร food; meal, dish

อาหารกลางวัน lunch, luncheon, dinner

อาหารค่ำ supper, dinner, evening meal

อาหารเจ Chinese vegetarian food, vegan food

อาหารใจ spiritual food, mental nourishment

อาหารเช้า breakfast, morning meal

อาหารตา a sight for sore eyes

อาหารเที่ยง see อาหารกลางวัน

อาหารเบา light meal, light food

อาหารประจำวัน daily meal

อาหารเย็น dinner, supper

อาหารว่าง snack, refreshments, light meal, hors d'oeuvres

อาหารสัตว์ fodder, animal food

อาหารสำเร็จรูป prepared food, ready-to-eat food, pre-cooked meal

อาหารแสลง contraindicated food, a food that /does/will/ not agree with (you, him, etc)

อาหารหนัก heavy meal, heavy food

อาหารแห้ง dried food

กินอาหาร to eat, have some food, have something to eat

เจริญอาหาร to give an appetite; to have a good appetite

ปรุงอาหาร to cook, prepare food, make a dish; to season food, make food tasty

รับประทานอาหาร to eat, take (food), dine

เชิญรับประทานอาหาร /The food/dinner/ etc/ is served.; Let us eat.

ร้านอาหาร restaurant, foodshop, eating place

รายการอาหาร menu, fare

เศษอาหาร scraps, leftovers

อำ to pull someone's leg, fool (someone)

อำนวย to provide, give, grant, bestow, yield; to direct, manage

อำนวยการ to direct /affairs/business/ etc

ผู้อำนวยการ director, administrator

อำนวยความสะดวก to facilitate, give facilities, assist

อำนวยพร to bless, give a blessing. bestow a blessing

ก
ข
ค
ฆ
ง
จ
ฉ
ช
ซ
ฌ
ญ
ฎ
ฏ
ฐ
ฑ
ฒ
ณ
ด
ต
ถ
ท
ธ
น
บ
ป
ผ
ฝ
พ
ฟ
ภ
ม
ย
ร
ฤ
ฦ
ล
ว
ศ
ษ
ส
ห
ฬ
อ

อำนาจ power, authority, control; jurisdiction

   อำนาจการปกครอง administrative power

   อำนาจคือธรรม Might is right.

   อำนาจจิต psychic power

   อำนาจเด็ดขาด absolute power

   อำนาจตุลาการ judicial power

   อำนาจทางการเมือง political power

   อำนาจนิติบัญญัติ legislative power

   อำนาจบริหาร executive /power/authority/

   อำนาจบาตรใหญ่ (to use) force, coercion, arbitrary /power/authority/

   อำนาจเผด็จการ dictatorial power

   อำนาจฝ่ายต่ำ evil power, power of darkness

   อำนาจมืด dark power

   อำนาจศาล jurisdiction of the court

   อำนาจอธิปไตย sovereignty

   ใบมอบอำนาจ power of attorney, proxy

   มหาอำนาจ /great/major/ power

   มอบอำนาจ to authorize, empower, give a power of attorney (to), delegate authority (to)

   มีอำนาจ powerful; to have the power (to), be empowered, authorized

   เรืองอำนาจ in power

   ให้อำนาจ to empower, authorize, give power (to)

อำพราง to dissemble, disguise, cover up

   นิติกรรมอำพราง spurious act, disguised act, legal subterfuge

อำพัน amber

อำไพ bright, radiant

อำเภอ amphur, amphoe, district

   นายอำเภอ district officer, Nai Amphur; sheriff

อำเภอใจ *as in* **ตามอำเภอใจ** at will, freely, as one likes, arbitrarily

อำมหิต cruel, heartless, inhuman, brutal

   ใจอำมหิต cold-blooded, merciless, vicious, inhuman

อำมาตย์ government officer; courtier; councillor

อำลา to take leave (of), say goodbye (to), bid farewell (to); to quit

อ้ำอึ้ง speechless, mute, tongue-tied

อิง to lean (on, against); to depend (on), rely (on), be based on

   อิงกลุ่ม norm referenced

   อิงเกณฑ์ criterion referenced

   อิงแอบ to press together, press up against one another

   นิยายอิงประวัติศาสตร์ story based on history, historical novel

อิจฉา to be jealous (of), envious (of), to envy

   อิจฉาตาร้อน to be green with envy

   ความอิจฉา jealousy, envy

   น่าอิจฉา enviable, How I envy you.

อิฉัน I, me

อิฐ brick

   อิฐดิบ raw brick

   อิฐหัก broken brick

   ก้อนอิฐ brick

   เตาอิฐ brick kiln

   สีอิฐ brick red

อิดโรย exhausted, weary, spent, worn out

อิดหนาระอาใจ to be fed up, sick of (life, one's work etc)

อิดออด to be half-hearted, without enthusiasm

อิดเอื้อน reluctant to say (or do) anything; to show reluctance

อิทธิ supernormal power; spiritual power; success

   อิทธิบาท basis for success, (the four) paths of accomplishment

   อิทธิพล influence, authority

   อิทธิฤทธิ์ supernatural power

อินทผลัม dates

อินทรธนู epaulets

อินทรีย์ organic

   อินทรีย์เคมี organic chemistry

   อินทรีย์สาร, สารอินทรีย์ organic substance

อินัง *as in* **ไม่อินัง** not give a damn (about)

อิ่ม to be full, have enough, replete, satisfied

อิ่มใจ contented, pleased

อิ่มตัว to be saturated; tumescent; fully

อิ่มบุญ happy at having done a good deed

อิ่มแปล้ stuffed, full

อิ่มแล้ว to be full, satisfied

อิ่มหนำ fully satisfied, satiated

อิ่มหมีพีมัน to eat to one's heart's content

อิ่มเอม fullfilled, blissful

อิ่มเอิบ to feel (or look) so happy, beaming, joyful, blissful

อิริยาบถ activity, pose

อิสตรี woman

อิสระ independent, free

อิสระเสรี free, unfettered, at liberty (to do, be etc)

นักเขียนอิสระ free-lance writer

เป็นอิสระ to be free, independent; freed, released, at liberty

อิสรภาพ freedom, independence, liberty

อิสราเอล Israel

ชาวอิสราเอล Israeli

อิสลาม Islam

อิสริยะ greatness, mastery, powerfulness

อิสริยยศ high /title/rank/

อิสริยาภรณ์ decoration, order

เครื่องราชอิสริยาภรณ์ royal orders and decorations

อิหม่าม imam

อี contemptuous prefix for a woman; familiar prefix for a person of the opposite sex; word designating a female animal; this (emphatic), now this

อีตอนนี้ now this part / now at this time

อีแก่แร้งทิ้ง old hag

อีตัว whore, chippy

อีหรอบเดียวกัน the same old /thing/way/

อี๊ ouch

อี๋อ๋อ to flirt, play footsie (with)

อีก next, more, another, additional, again re-; following; in, to; yet

อีกสิบนาทีจะสามโมงเย็น In 3 minutes it will be 3 p.m. / It's 3 minutes to 3 p.m.

น้ำตาลอีกหนึ่งกิโล another kilogram of sugar

ยังไม่มาอีกหรือ Hasn't she come yet?

อีกคนหนึ่ง another

อีกครั้งหนึ่ง again

อีกต่อหนึ่ง passed on; (to get) from someone else, in turn

อีกทอดหนึ่ง *see* **อีกต่อหนึ่ง**

อีกทีหนึ่ง again, once more

อีกนัยหนึ่ง in a sense, in another sense, in other words, on the other hand

อีกประการหนึ่ง furthermore, besides, in addition, moreover

อีกมาก much more, a lot more, plenty more

อีกไม่นาน before long, soon

อีกแล้ว not again, again

อีกวาระหนึ่ง again, once again; another period; the time has come again (when)

อีกสักหน่อย a little more; a little longer

อีกหน่อย a little more; before long, in a little while

อีกหลายอย่าง much more

อีกอย่างหนึ่ง there's something else, for another thing, once more

รุ่งขึ้นอีกวันหนึ่ง the following day, next day

อีฉัน I, me

อีนุงตุงนัง tangled, in a tangle, entangled, jumbled, (in) a mess, mess (of)

มีปัญหาอีนุงตุงนังแก้ไม่ตก I have a mess of problems I can't solve.

อีศวร Shiva

อีสาน northeast

อีสุกอีใส chicken pox

อีหลุกขลุกขลัก with great difficultly, full of obstacles, fraught with difficulty, to have difficulties

อ

ฮี

อีหลุยฉุยแฉก extravagantly, wildly

จ่ายอีหลุยฉุยแฉก to squander, be a spendthrift

อีโหน่อีเหน่ *as in* **ไม่รู้อีโหน่อีเหน่** innocent (of knowledge etc), without knowledge (of), know nothing (about something), have no inkling (of something), not know beans (about something)

เขาไม่รู้อีโหน่อีเหน่อะไรก็พลอยติดร่างแหไปด้วย *He got dragged in with the others even though he didn't know beans about what happened.*

อี to poo-poo

อึก, อึ้ก gurgling sound, swallowing sound

ดื่มน้ำอึกหนึ่ง to take a swallow of water

อึกทึก noisy, boisterous

อึกทึกครึกโครม loud and noisy, boisterous, making a clamor

อึกอัก speechless, at a loss for something to say; to stammer; pounding

อึง loud, noisy, tumultuous, cacophonous

อึงคะนึง humming with sound; noisy, to make a racket

อึงมี่ screeching; clamor

อึงอล clamorous, tumultuous, boisterous, to make a din

อึ่ง a kind of frog

อึ่งอ่าง a puffing frog having a sonorous croak

แค่หางอึ่ง nothing

มีความรู้แค่หางอึ่ง *to be a pea-brain / know nothing*

อึ้ง[1] speechless, dumb

นิ่งอึ้ง to be dumb struck, be at a loss for words

อ้าอึ้ง to stammer

อึ้ง[2] *as in* **หนักอึ้ง** heavy as lead

อึด tough, to have endurance

อึดใจ to hold one's breath; the time one's

breath can be held, a moment

อึดอัด oppressive, suffocating; uneasy, with uneasiness, uncomfortable, on edge

อึดตะปือ heaps (of)

อืดทึด swollen up, bloated

นอนอืดทึด to be a sluggard

อึมครึม threatening, dismal, murky, gloomy

อืด swollen, distended, bloated; slow, sluggish

อืดอาด inactive, slow, sluggish, slowpokey, lethargic, dilatory

ขึ้นอืด to be bloated

ท้องอืด feel gassy, to feel bloated

อื่น other

อื่นๆ others

อื่นใด whatsoever

ก่อนอื่น at the outset

เขาอื่น other people, others

ใครอื่น who else, who other than

เป็นอื่น to have changed

และอื่นๆ etc, and so on

อือ uhuh; oh boy!

อืออออ to uh-huh; to go along (with what someone says or does)

อื้อ (to have a) ringing in the ear, deaf; noisy, boisterous

อื้อฉาว /widespread/ public/ scandal, noised abroad, on everyone's lips, (something) being talked about; scandalous

อื้อซ่า lots and lots (of)

อื้ออึ้ง resounding, boisterous, tumultuous

หูอื้อ to have one's ears stopped up; to be deafened; to have a /buzzing/ringing/ in the ears

อุ rice wine

อุกกาบาต meteorite

อุกฉกรรจ์ felonious, brutal

คดีอุกฉกรรจ์ felony, serious offense

อุกฤษฏ์ highest, supreme

โทษอุกฤษฏ์ /supreme/maximum/ penalty

อุกอาจ daring, audacious; outrageous; to have the /temerity/gall/nerve/ to do something
ปล้นอย่างอุกอาจ /daring/outrageous/ robbery
อุโฆษ resounding, famous
นักเขียนนามอุโฆษ famous writer, renowned author
อุ้ง arch (of the foot)
อุ้งตีน claw
อุ้งมือ palm of the hand; in one's clutches; under one's control
อุจจาระ feces, stool, excrement
ถ่ายอุจจาระ to go to the toilet, move one's bowels, have a bowel movement, pass a stool, defecate
อุจาด obscene, filthy, ugly, shameful, disgraceful
อุจาดนัยน์ตา ugly, offensive, grotesque
อุณหภูมิ temperature
อุณหิส crown, frontlet, frontal
อุณาโลม hair between the eyebrows; the unalome (๑), a propitious device
อุด to stop up, block, cork, seal
อุดจมูก to hold one's nose
อุดตัน clogged, blocked
อุดปาก to gag
อุดฟัน to fill a tooth
อุดหู to stop up one's ears
อุดอู้ stuffy
อุดม highest; great, excellent; rich (in)
อุดมการณ์ ideal, principle
อุดมคติ ideal, principle
อุดมไปด้วย rich in, abounding in
อุดมศึกษา higher education, university education
อุดมสมบูรณ์ rich, prosperous
อุดร north, left side
อุดหนุน to support, aid, back; subsidize
อุตริ unconventional, unusual; absurd
อุตริวิตถาร abnormal, queer
อุตริมนุสธรรม highest accomplishment of man, enlightenment
อวดอุตริมนุสธรรม to claim enlightenment
อุตลุด in confusion, chaotically, in disorder, in disarray
วิ่งหนีอุตลุด to flee in disarray
สู้กันอุตลุด to battle furiously
อุตส่าห์ to take the trouble (to), make an effort (to)
ขอบคุณที่อุตส่าห์มาเยี่ยม Thank you for taking the trouble to visit.
อุตสาหกรรม industry, industrial
อุตสาหกรรมเคมี chemical industry
อุตสาหกรรมเบา light industry
อุตสาหกรรมหนัก heavy industry
อุตสาหกรรมเหมืองแร่ mining industry
เมืองอุตสาหกรรม industrial /country/area/
โรงงานอุตสาหกรรม (industrial) factory
อุตสาหะ industry, effort, perseverance, diligence
อุตุนิยม meteorology
อุตุนิยมวิทยา meteorology
กรมอุตุนิยม Meteorology Department
อุทกภัย flood, flooding
อุทกศาสตร์ hydrography
อุทธรณ์ appeal, to appeal
ศาลอุทธรณ์ Appeals Court, Court of Appeals
อุทยาน park
อุทยานประวัติศาสตร์ historical park
วนอุทยาน park, botanical garden
อุทร womb
อุทัย rising, rising sun
อุทาน interjection, exclamation, outcry
อุทาหรณ์ example, instance, illustration
อุทิศ to dedicate, devote
อุทิศแด่ dedicated to
อุทิศส่วนกุศล to dedicate merit
ทำงานอย่างอุทิศตนเต็มที่ to /devote/dedicate/ oneself to one's work
อุ่น to heat, warm; comfortable, snug

ก
ข
ค
ฆ
ง
จ
ฉ
ช
ซ
ฌ
ญ
ฎ
ฏ
ฐ
ฑ
ฒ
ณ
ด
ต
ถ
ท
ธ
น
บ
ป
ผ
ฝ
พ
ฟ
ภ
ม
ย
ร
ฤ
ล
ว
ศ
ษ
ส
ห
ฬ

อ

อุ่นแกง to warm up the curry

อุ่นขึ้น to get warmer

อุ่นเครื่อง to get warmed up

อุ่นใจ at ease, to feel comfortable

อุ่นหนาฝาคั่ง stable, solid; grand, royal
ได้รับการต้อนรับอย่างอุ่นหนาฝาคั่ง to get a royal welcome

อุ่นอาหาร to warm up the food

อบอุ่น *see* **อบอุ่น** *หน้า 556*

อุบ to keep, hold back

อุบอิบ under one's breath

ขออุบไว้ก่อน not just now

อุบล water lily

อุบ๊ะ bah!; what!

อุบัติ to occur, happen, arise

อุบัติขึ้น to happen; occur, take place; to come into existence, be born

อุบัติภัย accident, casualty

อุบัติเหตุ accident

อุบาทว์ evil, calamitous, sinister, inauspicious; grotesque

คนอุบาทว์ depraved person, wicked person, devil

วันอุบาทว์ inauspicious day, evil day

อุบาย method, way; trick, device, ploy, ruse, wiles

ออกอุบาย to find a way (to); to trick someone into doing something

อุบาสก layman, lay disciple, man lay follower, male devotee

อุบาสกอุบาสิกา the laity

อุบาสิกา laywoman, lay disciple, woman lay follower, female devotee

อุเบกขา equanimity; impartiality, neutral feeling

อุโบสถ temple, consecrated assembly hall; lay observance of the eight precepts; fortnightly recitation of the Sangha's rules of practice

อุโบสถกรรม the recitation in the temple of the rules of practice

วันอุโบสถ fortnightly day of recitation of the Sangha's rules of practice

อุปกรณ์ equipment, instrument, implement, accessories, apparatus

อุปกรณ์การสอน teaching aids, school equipment

อุปการะ to support, look after, take care (of)

อุปการคุณ gratitude

ในความอุปการะ (ของ) under the patronage of

ผู้อุปการะ patron, supporter, benefactor, person who looks after someone else

อุปัฏฐาก lay supporter, patron; attendant

อุปถัมภ์ patronage; support, to patronize, support, give patronage

อุปทาน supply

กฎแห่งอุปสงค์อุปทาน the law of supply and demand

อุปทูต chargé d'affaires

อุปนายก vice-president

อุปโภค to use, utilize, consume

เครื่องอุปโภค consumer goods; utilities

อุปมา object of comparison, comparison

อุปไมย subject of comparison

อุปรากร opera

อุปราช second king

อุปโลกน์ made-up; to make up; to invent, make, hold up as, represent as
ผมถูกอุปโลกน์ให้เป็นผู้เชี่ยวชาญทางศาสนา I've been /held up/represented/ as an expert in religion.
สมาชิกอาวุโสถูกอุปโลกน์เป็นประธานในที่ประชุม The senior member was made chairman of the meeting.

อุปสงค์ demand (*economics*)

อุปสมบท to enter the monkhood, be ordained (a monk), full admission (to the Sangha), /full/ higher/ ordination

อุปสรรค obstacle, difficulty, impediment,

hindrance, trouble, hitch

อุปัชฌาย์, อุปัชฌายะ preceptor, ordainer

อุปัฏฐาก to give support

โยมอุปัฏฐาก patron (of a monk)

อุปัทวเหตุ accident, misadventure

อุปัทวันตราย misfortune, trouble, danger

อุปาทาน clinging, grasping; fixed idea, preconceived notion; one's imagination

อุ้ม to carry, hold in one's arms

อุ้มเข้าเอว to carry on one's hip

อุ้มชู to support; back; to bring up, raise

อุ้มท้อง with child, pregnant

อุมงค์, อุโมงค์ tunnel; grotto

อุ้ย Oh!, oh my!

อุ้ยอ้าย inactive, sluggish, slow-moving, torpid

อุรา chest, breast, heart

เปรมอุรา in seventh heaven, in a state of bliss

อู *as in* ไก่อู a kind of chicken

อู่ cradle; home; drydock; boathouse; source (of)

อู่ต่อเรือ shipyard, boatyard

อู่รถ garage

อู่เรือ dock, boathouse, dry dock

เข้าอู่ (a womb or uterus) to return to normal position; (a boat) to be in a boat house, docked, in dry dock

อู้[1] coconut shell fiddle

อู้[2] sound of wind blowing

อู้อี้ indistinctly

อู้[3] to drag one's feet

อู้งาน to go slow at work, lay down on the job, do a slowdown

อูฐ camel

อูม swollen, inflated, distended

หน้าอูม fat-faced, having a full face, chubby in the face

เอก, เอกะ first, number one; single, solitary; principal, primary; special, particular; high,

great

เอกฉันท์ unanimity

โดยเอกฉันท์ unanimously

เอกชน individual, private

เอกเทศ separated part, independent

โดยเอกเทศ separately, independently

เอกบุรุษ /unique/outstanding/ man

เอกพจน์ singular

เอกภาพ unity, solidarity; uniformity

เข้าร่วมกันทำงานอย่างมีเอกภาพ They worked together in unity. / They were united in their endeavor.

เอกราช independent, free, sovereign

เอกสาร document(s), papers, printed material; records

ห้องเอกสาร record room

เอกสิทธิ์ privilege(s), special privilege

เอกอุ superb, utmost

จ่าเอก sergeant

ชั้นเอก 1st grade, first class, of the first rank

ตลาดเอก primary market

นางเอก leading actress, the leading lady, star, female lead, heroine

พระเอก leading actor, star, male lead, hero

เอ๊ก crowing

เอกเขนก at ease, sprawled out

เอกา, เอ้กา one, single, solitary

เอกาธิปไตย autocracy

ถือเอ้กา to eat only once a day

เอง oneself, by oneself; just, only; right

อยู่ตรงนี้เอง It's right here.

เอ็ง you

เอ๋ง yelp, squeal

เอ็ด one; noisy, boisterous; to yell at someone, ball (someone) out

เอ็ดตะโร to make a commotion, make a lot of noise, shouting; to yell at someone

เอ็ดอึง noisy

เสียงดังเอ็ดอึง a hubbub, racket, din

อ

ษ

ก
ข
ค
ฆ
ง
จ
ฉ
ช
ซ
ฌ
ญ
ฎ
ฏ
ฐ
ฑ
ฒ
ณ
ด
ต
ถ
ท
ธ
น
บ
ป
ผ
ฝ
พ
ฟ
ภ
ม
ย
ร
ฤ
ฦ
ล
ว
ศ
ษ
ส
ห
ฬ
อ

เอตทัคคะ expert

เอน to recline; to lean, tilt, slant; italics
เอนกาย to recline, lie down, repose
เอนตัว to lie down, recline; to lean (on, forward, backward, etc)
เอนลู่ to be flattened
เอนหลัง to recline, take a rest, relax
เอนเอียง partial, biased
ตัวเอน italics
โอนเอน swaying, bending, bowing; unsteady, shaky

เอ็น tendon, sinew, gut, catgut, string
เอ็นร้อยหวาย Achilles tendon
เส้นเอ็น tendon

เอ็นดู to be fond (of), have affection for; have tender feelings for, be kind to
น่าเอ็นดู lovely, adorable, cute, sweet

เอย a poetical closing particle; a term used in direct address, o, oh *พระจันทร์เอย O moon;* a term used to emphasize a series of things, there's
เงินค่ากินอยู่เอย ค่าเล่าเรียนเอย there's the living expenses and there's the tuition fees
ลงเอย to finish, end up, finish up (with), wind up, be concluded
ลงเอยกัน to get together in the end

เอ่ย to speak; a question word
เอ่ยขึ้น to speak (out, up)
เอ่ยถึง to mention, talk about, speak of
เอ่ยปาก to speak, mention, say something (about)
ใครเอ่ย Who is it?, Who could that be?
อะไรเอ่ย What is it?, What could it be?

เอ๊ย exclamation uttered on making a mistake, No! I mean...

เอ๋ย a sound denoting affection *เช่น* dear, my dear (boy, girl, son etc)

เอร็ดอร่อย delicious, luscious, tasty, yummy, delectable

เอว waist
เอวบางร่างน้อย tiny, petite, having a slight figure
บั้นเอว waist
ยืนเท้าเอว to stand akimbo, stand there with her hands on her hips

เออ uh-huh
เออซีวะ You bet!
เออน่ะ okay, okay!, Lay off!
เออออวย to go along (with)
เออออ to consent, join in
เออออห่อหมก to go along with someone /blindly/mindlessly/

เอ่อ to rise, well up

เอ้อระเหย to float (along, around)

เอ้อเฮอ My /gosh/god/!, Oho!

เอ๊ะ Eh!, What!

เอะใจ to suspect; suspicious, skeptical

เอะอะ to make a noise, be boisterous, noisy; to be quick to (do something)

เอา[1] to take, get, bring; to want; to receive; for, for the sake of
เอากลับบ้าน to take (something) home
เอากัน to make love, have sex; to mate
เอาการ, เอาการเอางาน serious, earnest, hardworking; unusually, really, quite
เอาความลับไปขาย to betray
เอาคืน to take (something) back, retrieve;
เอางาน to make a slight hand gesture of respect before receiving something
เอาจริงเอาจัง *see* **เอาจริง** *หน้า 112*
เอาใจ to please, make (someone) happy, humor (someone), go along with (someone)
เอาใจช่วย to support, be with (someone or something), root for
เอาใจตัวเอง to be self-willed, self-centered, self-indulgent, egotistical
เอาใจใส่ to pay attention (to), take an interest (in), care, be conscientious,

put one's mind to (something)

เอาใจออกห่าง disaffected, faithless; alienated, distant

เอาชนะ to beat, overcome, get the better of (someone)

เอาชีวิตรอด to save oneself, survive

เอาซี sure!

เอาตัวรอด to save one's own skin, come out all right, get out of (a predicament etc); to get by; to insure personal survival

เอาแต่ใจตนเอง to think only of oneself, want one's own way, willful, self-centered, inconsiderate

เอาแต่แต่งตัว to be a clotheshorse

เอาแต่สะดวกเข้าว่า take the easy way out, do it the easy way

เอาถ่าน industrious, serious

เอาเถอะ alright, okay

เอาเถิด Let's do it!, Go for it!

เอาโทษ to penalize, punish; to hold someone responsible (for)

เอาบุญเอาคุณ to want something in return, in the expectation of reward

เอาเปรียบ to take advantage (of), exploit, get the better of (someone)

เอาไป to take (away); to take along, bring

    เอาไปให้พ้น to get rid of (something), take (something) away, get (something) out of one's sight

เอามา to bring

เอามือซุกหีบ to go looking for trouble

เอามือไพล่หลัง with one's hands behind one's back

เอาเมีย to get married, take a wife

เอาเรื่อง to take up the matter; to file a complaint, press charges; aggressive, to stand up to (someone); very, decidedly

เอาละ very well; okay, now then

เอาเลย go for it; go go!

เอาหน้า to get the credit, take credit (for), make a show of (working, etc)

เอาหัวชนฝา obstinately; to fight to the end, intractable, obdurate

เอาให้ได้นะ You have got to get it!

เอาไหม Do you want it?, Shall we?

เอาอกเอาใจ to please, indulge (someone) in (something), pamper, truckle to (someone)

เอาอย่าง to imitate, to follow another's example, copy

เอาอย่างไรก็เอากัน Whatever but let's get on with it.

เอาอีกแล้ว Not again!, Here we go again., at it again

เอา[2] suffix to indicate resolute action เช่น

    กินเอา eat it

    กินเอาๆ eat and eat

    คว้าเอา grab it

    เดินเอา walk it

เอ๊าะๆ sexy teenager, nymphet

เอิกเกริก magnificent, grand, in a big way

    งานเอิกเกริก an extravaganza

เอิบอาบ contented, very pleased, elated

เอียง to tilt, slant, list (เรือ), incline, slope

    เอียงซ้าย as in **หัวเอียงซ้าย** to be a leftist, radical

    เอียงอาย shy, bashful, self-conscious; shyness

    ตาเอียง astigmatism

เอียน sickeningly sweet, cloying; to be sick of (something or someone)

    หวานจนเอียน oversweet, sickeningly sweet

เอี่ยม new, brand-new

    เอี่ยมอ่อง bright new, spanking new

เอี้ยม bib

เอี้ยมจุ๊น lighter, barge

เอี่ยมเฟี้ยม politely, deferentially

เอี่ยว interest

    เอี่ยวลม free share, complimentary share

มีเอี่ยวด้วย to have an interest (in), participate (in)

เอี้ยว to twist, turn

เอี้ยวคอ to look around, turn one's head

เอื้อ to be concerned, take an interest (in), care (about)

เอื้อเฟื้อ to be generous, bountiful, give support

ความเอื้อเฟื้อเผื่อแผ่ generosity

เอื้ออาทร solicitous (of), to have solicitude (for), be considerate (of), have consideration (for)

เอื้ออำนวย to facilitate, assist

เอื้อง [1] cud

เคี้ยวเอื้อง, บดเอื้อง to chew the cud

เอื้อง [2] a kind of orchid

เอื้อน to utter; speak sweetly, to modulate a sound to fit the rhythm, portamento, melisma

เอื้อนเสียง to make a portamento, sing in portamento style, sing a melisma, melismatic passage.

เอื้อนเอ่ย to vocalize in Thai fashion

เอือม fed up, cannot stand (something or someone); sated

เอือมระอา disgusted (with), sick of (someone or something)

เอื้อม to reach

เอื้อมมือ to reach (for something)

เอื้อมไม่ถึง out of reach, unreachable

เอื้อมอาจ impertinent, impudent

แค่เอื้อม within reach, close at hand

สุดเอื้อม out of reach, beyond reach

เอื่อย, เอื่อยๆ slowly, without haste, lazily

เอื้อย the eldest daughter

พี่เอื้อย boss

แอ๋ as in **เมาแอ๋** dead drunk

แอก yoke

ปลดแอก to unyoke; to liberate

แอ่ง depression, hollow

แอ่งน้ำ pool of water, pond

แอ้งแม้ง motionless, in a sorry state, helplessly

แอ่น to bend, back, arch one's back; to raise up; to sway

แอ่นอก to throw out one's chest

แอบ to hide; secretly, surreptitiously, on the sly

แอบจิต in the closet, dissembling

แอบดู to peep (at), peek (at), spy (on)

แอบแฝง hidden, disguised, ulterior

แอบฟัง to overhear, listen in, tap (a telephone etc)

แอบมอง see **แอบดู**

แอบอิง to lean (on, against), press against; to ride on the coattails of someone

แอบอ้าง to pass oneself off (as), claim falsely

แอฟริกัน African

แอฟริกา Africa

แอ้ม to make out

ไม่ได้แอ้ม You'll never make out., I didn't make out.

แอ่ว to visit

แอ่วสาว to go courting, go girl-visiting

แออัด congested, crowded

แออัดยัดเยียด overcrowded

ชุมชนแออัด slum

โอ [1] lacquered bowl

โอ [2] oh

โอ่ to boast, brag

โอ่โถง imposing, luxurious, grand, splendid, magnificent, majestic

โอ่อ่า splendid, grand

ขี้โอ่ a show-off, braggart; boastful, boasting, bragging

คุยโอ่ to boast, crow, brag

โอ้ oh; to shoot off one's mouth

โอ้อวด to vaunt, boast, brag; to show off

โอ๋ to pamper, mollycoddle, baby (someone)

โอ๋มาก ลูกจะเสียคนนะ Too much pampering

will spoil the child. / Mollycoddling will lead to no good.

โอ้ก   uh, ugh

    โอ้กอ้าก to retch

โอ๊ก   crowing; ouch

โอกาส   opportunity, chance, occasion, time

    โอกาสน้อยเต็มที small chance, little opportunity

    โอกาสไม่อำนวย the occasion does not permit, the time is not ripe (to), difficult (to)

    ฉวยโอกาส to seize the chance (to), take advantage (of)

        นักฉวยโอกาส opportunist

    ได้โอกาส to get the chance (to)

    ถือโอกาส to take the opportunity (to)

    ในโอกาส at this time

    บางโอกาส occasionally, at certain times, when the situation permits, when the opportunity presents itself

    เปิดโอกาส to give (someone) a /chance/ opportunity/ (to do something), open the way

    มีโอกาส to have the /opportunity/chance/ (to)

    หมดโอกาส to miss an /opportunity/ chance/, have no chance (to), no further opportunity (to)

    ให้โอกาส to give a chance (to), to offer an opportunity (to)

โอ่ง   a big water jar

โองการ   sacred word; command, order, instruction

โอช   delicious taste, delicious

    เอมโอช delicious, delectable

โอชะ, โอชา delicious, tasty, lucious, delectable, exquisite

    โอชารส fine tasting, delicious, to taste great, have a gourmet taste

โอด   sad music, dirge; to weep

    โอดครวญ to bemoan, lament, lamentation; to bewail, complain

    โอดพ้อ to bewail; to weep bitterly

    โอดโอย to cry out in pain

โอตตัปปะ fear of wrongdoing, moral fear

โอน[1] to transfer, assign

    โอนกรรมสิทธิ์ to transfer /title/ownership/

    โอนทะเบียน to transfer a /registration/ license/

    โอนบัญชี to transfer an account

    โอนสัญชาติ to become naturalized

โอน[2] to bend, bow

    โอนอ่อน to concede, acquiesce, go along (with); to respect

    โอนเอน swaying, swinging, bending, bowing; unsteady, shaky

โอบ   to hug, embrace; to surround, encircle; to flank

    โอบกอด to embrace, hug

    โอบแขนรอบ to put one's arms around

    โอบรอบ to flank

    โอบอ้อมอารี generous, kindly, hospitable, warmhearted

        ความโอบอ้อมอารี generosity, warmheartedness, hospitality

    โอบอุ้ม to support, bring up

    ตีโอบหลัง to flank from the rear

โอภาปราศรัย to warmly welcome, greet

โอม   om

โอย, โอ๊ย oh!, ouch!, groan

    โอ๊ยโย่ oh my!, my god!

โอรส   son

โอละพ่อ to the contrary, just the opposite

โอ้โลม to fondle, caress

โอวาท advice, exhortation

    ให้โอวาท to address, give a word of advice

    อยู่ในโอวาท under the tutelage of, under the influence (of), under the thumb of

        อยู่ในโอวาทของพ่อแม่ under parental control

โอษฐ์ mouth, lips

โอสถ medicine, remedy, medicinal herb

    โอสถกรรม practice of medicine; medicinal treatment

โอหนอ why oh why

โอหัง arrogant, haughty, presumptuous, insolent; stubborn

โอฬาร great, grand, majestic, magnificent

    ใหญ่โตโอฬาร monumental, stupendous, prodigious, colossal

โอ้อวด to boast, brag, vaunt, show off

โอ้เอ้ to take one's time, be sluggish (in, about), drag one's feet

ไอ vapor, steam, mist; fumes; to cough

ไอน้ำ steam, vapor

ไอพ่น jet

ไอพิษ poisonous gas, toxic fumes

ไอเสีย exhaust

ไอหอบ whooping cough

ไอ้ *see* **อ้าย**[1] *หน้า 569*

ไอ.คิว. I.Q., intelligence quotient

ไอยรา elephant

ไอ้หยา Good grief!

ไอศกรีม ice cream

    ไอศกรีมกะทิ coconut ice cream

ไอศวรรย์ sovereignty, sovereign

ไอศูรย์ *see* **ไอศวรรย์**

ฮกเกี้ยน Hokkien

ฮวงซุ้ย, ฮวงจุ้ย Chinese cemetery, Chinese tomb

ฮวบฮาบ all of a sudden

ฮ้อ good

ฮอร์โมน hormone

ฮอลิเดย์ holiday, vacation

ฮะ yes, uh huh, okay

    ฮะไฮ้, ฮะฮ้าย ha-ha

ฮักๆ panting, puffing

ฮั่น Han

ฮั่นแน่ Look at you!, How about that!

ฮัม to hum

ฮัลโหล hello

ฮั้ว to connive, collude, collusion

    การฮั้วกัน collusion

ฮา ha!; to boo, jeer (at), laugh at; to guffaw

    ฮาป่า to boo, jeer, heckle

ฮาเร็ม harem

ฮ้าไฮ้ a choral response

ฮินดี Hindi

ฮินดู Hindu

    ศาสนาฮินดู Hinduism

ฮิปปี้ hippy

ฮิปโปโปเตมัส hippo, hippopotamus

ฮิสทีเรีย hysteria

ฮีมาโตคริต hematocrit value

ฮีโมโกลบิน hemoglobin

ฮี an exclamation of surprise or displeasure, what!

ฮึกหาญ fiery, raring to go, high-spirited

ฮึกเหิม reckless, rash, impetuous

ฮึดฮัด angrily, in a rage, ready to fight

ฮือ[1] sobbing

ฮือ[2] to crowd (up, forward), mob

    ลุกฮือ to rise up, (be part of) an uprising, become inflamed; to spring up

ฮื่อ[1] to snarl; to grunt

ฮื่อ[2] uh huh

ฮุบ to swallow

ฮุบที่ดิน to swallow up the land, grab land

เฮ uproar

เฮโล to /join/follow/ the crowd, follow en masse

    เฮโลไป to get on the bandwagon

    เฮโลสาระพา to push forward en masse, press forward noisily

    เฮฮา to be boisterous; merriment, revelry, jollity

เฮกโตกรัม hectogram

เฮกโตเมตร hectometer

เฮกโตลิตร hectoliter

เฮง lucky

    เฮงซวย tough luck, bad luck

เฮ่ย What!

เฮ้ย Hey!

เฮ้ว wild

เฮอ sighing, to give a sigh

เฮีย older brother; sir, big guy

เฮี้ยน all-powerful

เฮี้ยบ strict, exacting, harsh

เฮี้ยว hooligan, roughneck

เฮือก sigh, gasp; start

    เฮือกสุดท้าย last gasp

    ถอนใจเฮือกใหญ่ to give a big sigh

    สะดุ้งเฮือก to have a start, be shocked

แฮ่ to growl

แฮ่กี๊น fried shrimp sausage

แฮม ham

แฮะ really, totally, indeed

    สวยจริงแฮะ really pretty, pretty indeed, totally beautiful

โฮ to boohoo, (weep) copiously

โฮก barking; slurping

    โฮกฮาก as in **กระโชกโฮกฮาก** see **กระโชกโฮกฮาก** หน้า 7

โฮเต็ล hotel

โฮโมเซ็กซ่วล homosexual

ไฮด์ปาร์ค Hyde Park forum

นักพูดไฮปาร์ค soapbox orator

ไฮเปอร์โบลา hyperbola

ไฮไฟ hi-fi

ไฮโล high-low craps

ภาคผนวก

APPENDICES

1
ชื่อนก - Birds

ไก่จุก	roulroul
” นวล	long-billed partridge
” ป่า	red junglefowl
” ฟ้าพญาลอ	Siamese fireback
” ฟ้าหน้าเขียว	crested fireback pheasant
” ฟ้าหลังขาว	silver pheasant
” ฟ้าหลังเทา	kalij pheasant
” ฟ้าหางลายขาว	Hume's bar-tailed pheasant
นกกก	great pied hornbill
” กระจอกชวา	Java sparrow
” กระจอกตาล	plain-backed sparrow, house sparrow
” กระจอกบ้าน	Eurasian tree sparrow
” กระจอกป่าท้องเหลือง	russet sparrow
” กระจอกใหญ่	house sparrow
” กระจ้อยกระหม่อมแดง	chestnut-crowned warbler
” กระจ้อยแก้มสีเทา	grey-cheeked warbler
” กระจ้อยเขาสูง	russet bush-warbler
” กระจ้อยคอขาว	yellow-bellied warbler
” กระจ้อยคอดำ	rufous-faced warbler
” กระจ้อยนักร้อง	Manchurian bush-warbler
นกกระจ้อยป่าโกงกาง	flyeater
” กระจ้อยพันธุ์จีน	Chinese bush-warbler
” กระจ้อยวงตาสีทอง	golden-spectacled warbler
” กระจ้อยสีน้ำตาล	brown bush-warbler
” กระจ้อยสีไพล	pale-footed bush-warbler
” กระจ้อยหัวลาย	stub-tailed bush-warbler
” กระจ้อยเหลืองไพล	aberrant bush-warbler
” กระจ้อยใหญ่	chestnut-crowned bush-warbler
” กระจ้อยอกเทา	spotted bush-warbler
” กระจาบทอง	Asian golden weaver
” กระจาบธรรมดา	baya weaver
” กระจาบอกลาย	streaked weaver, striated weaverbird

นกกระจิ๊ดขั้วโลกเหนือ	Arctic warbler
” กระจิ๊ดขาสีเนื้อ	pale-legged leaf-warbler
” กระจิ๊ดเขียวคล้ำ	greenish warbler
” กระจิ๊ดเขียวปีกสองแถบ	two-barred warbler
” กระจิ๊ดคอสีเทา	ashy-throated warbler
” กระจิ๊ดคิ้วดำท้องขาว	yellow-vented warbler
” กระจิ๊ดคิ้วดำท้องเหลือง	sulphur-breasted warbler
” กระจิ๊ดตะโพกเหลือง	lemon-rumped warbler
” กระจิ๊ดแถบปีกสีส้ม	orange-barred leaf-warbler
” กระจิ๊ดท้องสีน้ำตาล	buff-throated warbler
” กระจิ๊ดธรรมดา	inornate warbler
” กระจิ๊ดปากหนา	Radde's warbler
” กระจิ๊ดสีคล้ำ	dusky warbler
นกกระจิ๊ดหัวมงกุฎ	Eastern crowned warbler
” กระจิ๊ดหางขาวเล็ก	white-tailed leaf-warbler
” กระจิ๊ดหางขาวใหญ่	Blyth's leaf-warbler
” กระจิ๊ดอกลายเหลือง	yellow-streaked warbler
” กระจิบกระหม่อมแดง	rufous-tailed tailorbird
” กระจิบคอดำ	dark-necked tailorbird
” กระจิบธรรมดา	common tailorbird
” กระจิบภูเขา	mountain tailorbird
” กระจิบหญ้าคิ้วขาว	hill prinia
” กระจิบหญ้าท้องเหลือง	yellow-bellied prinia
” กระจิบหญ้าสีข้างแดง	rufescent prinia
” กระจิบหญ้าสีน้ำตาล	brown prinia
” กระจิบหญ้าสีเรียบ	plain prinia
นกกระจิบหญ้าอกเทา	grey-breasted prinia
” กระจิบหัวแดง	ashy tailorbird
” กระติ๊ดขี้หมู	scaly-breasted munia, spotted munia
” กระติ๊ดเขียว, นกไผ่	pin-tailed parrotfinch
” กระติ๊ดแดง	red avadavat
” กระติ๊ดตะโพกขาว	white-rumped munia
” กระติ๊ดท้องขาว	white-bellied munia
” กระติ๊ดสีอิฐ	chestnut munia
” กระติ๊ดหัวขาว	white-headed munia
” กระติ๊ดใหญ่ปากเหลือง	yellow-billed grosbeak
” กระติ๊ดใหญ่ปีกลาย	spot-winged grosbeak
” กระติ๊ดใหญ่สร้อยคอเหลือง	collared grosbeak
” กระแตแต้แว้ด	red-wattled lapwing

นกกระแตผีชายหาด	beach thick-knee
" กระแตผีเล็ก	Northern thick-knee
" กระแตผีใหญ่	great thick-knee
" กระแตหงอน	Northern lapwing
" กระแตหัวเทา	grey-headed lapwing
" กระแตหาด	river lapwing
" กระทาดงแข้งเขียว	green-legged tree partridge
" กระทาดงคอสีแสด	rufous-throated partridge
" กระทาดงจันทบูรณ์	chestnut-headed partridge
" กระทาดงปักษ์ใต้	chestnut-necklaced partridge
" กระทาดงอกสีน้ำตาล	brown-breasted tree partridge
" กระทาทุ่ง	Chinese francolin
" กระทาป่าไผ่	mountain bamboo-partridge
นกกระทาสองเดือย	ferruginous wood-partridge
" กระทุง	spot-billed pelican
" กระเบื้องคอขาว	white-throated rock-thrush
" กระเบื้องท้องแดง	chestnut-billed rock-thrush
" กระเบื้องผา	blue rock-thrush
" กระปูดเล็ก	lesser coucal
" กระปูดใหญ่	greater coucal
" กระเรียน	sarus crane
" กระสาขาว	white stork
" กระสาคอขาว	woolly-necked stork
" กระสาคอขาวปากแดง	Storm's stork
" กระสาคอดำ	black-necked stork
" กระสาดำ	black stork
นกกระสาแดง	purple heron
" กระสานวล	grey heron
" กระสาปากเหลือง	milky stork
" กระสาใหญ่	great-billed heron
" กรีดน้ำ	Indian skimmer
" กวัก	white-breasted waterhen
" กะเต็นขาวดำใหญ่	crested kingfisher
" กะเต็นแดง	ruddy kingfisher
" กะเต็นน้อยแถบอกดำ	blue-banded kingfisher
" กะเต็นน้อยธรรมดา	common kingfisher
" กะเต็นน้อยสามนิ้ว	Oriental dwarf kingfisher
" กะเต็นน้อยหลังสีน้ำเงิน	blue-eared kingfisher
" กะเต็นปักหลัก	pied kingfisher

นกกะเต็นลาย	banded kingfisher
" กะเต็นสร้อยคอสีน้ำตาล	rufous-collared kingfisher
" กะเต็นหัวดำ	black-capped kingfisher
" กะเต็นใหญ่ธรรมดา	stork-billed kingfisher
" กะเต็นใหญ่ปีกสีน้ำตาล	brown-winged kingfisher
" กะเต็นอกขาว	white-throated kingfisher
" กะเต็นเฮอคิวลิส	Blyth's kingfisher
" กะรองทองแก้มขาว	silver-eared mesia
" กะรางแก้มแดง	red-faced liocichla
" กะรางคอดำ, นกซออู้	black-throated laughing thrush
" กะรางคิ้วขาว	white-browed laughing thrush
" กะรางสร้อยคอเล็ก	lesser necklaced laughing thrush
" กะรางสร้อยคอใหญ่	greater necklaced laughing thrush
นกกะรางหัวขวาน	hoopoe
" กะรางหัวแดง	chestnut-crowned laughing thrush
" กะรางหัวหงอก	white-crested laughing thrush
" กะรางหางแดง	red-tailed laughing thrush
" กะรางอกลาย	spot-breasted laughing thrush
" กะรางอกสีน้ำตาลไหม้	white-necked laughing thrush
" กะลิง	grey-headed parakeet
" กะลิงเขียด	rufous treepie
" กะลิงเขียดสีเทา	grey treepie
" กางเขนดง	white-rumped shama
" กางเขนดงหางแดง	rufous-tailed shama
" กางเขนน้ำหลังดำ	black-backed forktail
" กางเขนน้ำหลังแดง	chestnut-naped forktail
นกกางเขนน้ำหลังเทา	slaty-backed forktail
" กางเขนน้ำหัวขาว	white-crowned forktail
" กางเขนบ้าน	Oriental magpie-robin
" กาน้อยแถบปีกขาว	black magpie
" กาน้อยหงอนยาว	crested jay
" กาน้ำปากยาว	Indian shag
" กาน้ำเล็ก	little cormorant
" กาน้ำใหญ่	great cormorant
" กาบบัว	painted stork
" กาฝากก้นเหลือง	yellow-vented flowerpecker
" กาฝากท้องสีส้ม	orange-bellied flowerpecker
" กาฝากท้องเหลือง	yellow-bellied flowerpecker
" กาฝากปากหนา	thick-billed flowerpecker

นกกาฝากสีเรียบ	plain flowerpecker
" กาฝากอกแดง	scarlet-breasted flowerpecker
" กาฝากอกเพลิง	buff-bellied flowerpecker
" กาฝากอกสีเลือดหมู	crimson-breasted flowerpecker
" กาฝากอกเหลือง	yellow-breasted flowerpecker
" กาแวน	racket-tailed treepie
" กาเหว่า	common koel
" กาฮัง	homrai, great Indian hornbill
" กิ้งโครงแกลบปีกขาว	white-shouldered starling
" กิ้งโครงแกลบหลังม่วงดำ	purple-backed starling
" กิ้งโครงแกลบหัวเทา	chestnut-tailed starling
" กิ้งโครงคอดำ	black-collared starling
" กิ้งโครงปีกลายจุด	spot-winged starling
นกกิ้งโครงพันธุ์ยุโรป	common starling
" กิ้งโครงสีกุหลาบ	rosy starling
" กิ้งโครงหัวสีนวล	vinous-breasted starling
" กินปลีแก้มสีทับทิม	ruby-cheeked sunbird
" กินปลีคอแดง	crimson sunbird
" กินปลีคอสีทองแดง	copper-throated sunbird
" กินปลีคอสีน้ำตาล	brown-throated sunbird
" กินปลีคอสีน้ำตาลแดง	red-throated sunbird
" กินปลีคอสีม่วง	purple-throated sunbird
" กินปลีดำม่วง	purple sunbird
" กินปลีแดง	scarlet sunbird
" กินปลีแดงหัวไพลิน	fire-tailed sunbird
" กินปลีท้ายทอยสีน้ำเงิน	purple-naped sunbird
นกกินปลีสีเรียบ	plain sunbird
" กินปลีหางยาวเขียว	green-tailed sunbird
" กินปลีหางยาวคอดำ	black-throated sunbird
" กินปลีหางยาวคอสีฟ้า	Dould's sunbird
" กินปลีอกเหลือง	olive-backed sunbird
" กินเปี้ยว	collared kingfisher
" กินแมลงกระหม่อมแดง	chestnut-capped babbler
" กินแมลงคอดำ	black-throated babbler
" กินแมลงคอเทา	grey-throated babbler
" กินแมลงคอลาย	spot-necked babbler
" กินแมลงเด็กแนน	Deignan's babbler
" กินแมลงตะโพกแดง	chestnut-rumped babbler
" กินแมลงตาขาว	grey-headed babbler

นกกินแมลงตาเหลือง	yellow-eyed babbler
” กินแมลงปากหนา	Horsfield's babbler
” กินแมลงป่าโกงกาง	white-chested babbler
” กินแมลงป่าฝน	Abbott's babbler
” กินแมลงป่าสีน้ำตาลแดง	ferruginous babbler
” กินแมลงป่าหางสั้น	short-tailed babbler
” กินแมลงป่าอกสีน้ำตาล	buff-breasted babbler
” กินแมลงปีกแดง	chestnut-winged babbler
” กินแมลงหน้าผากน้ำตาล	rufous-fronted babbler
” กินแมลงหลังฟู	fluffy-backed tit-babbler
” กินแมลงหัวแดงเล็ก	scaly-crowned babbler
” กินแมลงหัวแดงใหญ่	rufous-crowned babbler
” กินแมลงหัวสีคล้ำ	sooty-capped babbler
นกกินแมลงหัวสีทอง	golden babbler
” กินแมลงหัวสีน้ำตาล	moustached babbler
” กินแมลงหูขาว	white-necked babbler
” กินแมลงอกเหลือง	striped tit-babbler
” แก๊ก, นกแกง	Oriental pied hornbill
” แก้ว	parrot
” แก้วโม่ง	Alexandrine parakeet
” แก้วหัวแพร	blossom-headed parakeet
” โกงกางหัวโต	mangrove whistler
” โกโรโกโส	coral-billed ground-cuckoo
” ขมิ้นขาว	silver oriole
” ขมิ้นแดง	maroon oriole
” ขมิ้นท้ายทอยดำ	black-naped oriole
นกขมิ้นน้อยธรรมดา	common iora
” ขมิ้นน้อยปีกสีเรียบ	great iora
” ขมิ้นน้อยสีเขียว	green iora
” ขมิ้นปากเขียว	slender-billed oriole
” ขมิ้นหัวดำเล็ก	dark-throated oriole
” ขมิ้นหัวดำใหญ่	black-hooded oriole
” ขัติยา	cutia
” ขี้เถ้าลายขวาง	bar-bellied cuckoo-shrike
” ขี้เถ้าใหญ่	large cuckoo-shrike
” ขุนทอง	hill myna
” ขุนแผน	blue magpie
” ขุนแผนตะโพกแดง	scarlet-rumped trogon
” ขุนแผนตะโพกสีน้ำตาล	cinnamon-rumped trogon

นกขุนแผนท้ายทอยแดง	red-naped trogon
" ขุนแผนหัวดำ	Diard's trogon
" ขุนแผนหัวแดง	red-headed trogon
" ขุนแผนอกสีส้ม	orange-breasted trogon
" เขนท้องแดง	daurian redstart
" เขนเทาหางแดง	plumbeous redstart
" เขนน้อยข้างสีส้ม	orange-flanked bush-robin
" เขนน้อยคิ้วขาว	pied triller
" เขนน้อยไซบีเรีย	Siberian blue robin
" เขนน้อยปีกดำ	black-winged flycatcher-shrike
" เขนน้อยปีกแถบขาว	bar-winged flycatcher-shrike
" เขนน้อยพันธุ์ญี่ปุ่น	Japanese robin
" เขนน้อยสีทอง	golden bush-robin
นกเขนน้อยหัวดำ	black-throated robin
" เขนน้อยหางแดง	rufous-tailed robin
" เขนน้ำเงิน	blue-fronted robin
" เขนแปลง	white-bellied redstart
" เขนสีฟ้าท้ายสีน้ำตาล	blue-fronted redstart
" เขนสีฟ้าหางขาว	white-tailed robin
" เขนหัวขาวท้ายแดง	river chat
" เขาเขียว	emerald dove
" เขาชวา	zebra dove
" เขาเปล้าธรรมดา	thick-billed pigeon
" เขาพม่า	Oriental turtle-dove
" เขาไฟ	red turtle-dove
" เขาลายเล็ก	little cuckoo-dove
นกเขาลายใหญ่	barred cuckoo-dove
" เขาใหญ่, นกเขาหลวง	spotted dove
" เขียวก้านตองท้องสีส้ม	orange-bellied leafbird
" เขียวก้านตองปีกสีฟ้า	blue-winged leafbird
" เขียวก้านตองเล็ก	lesser green leafbird
" เขียวก้านตองหน้าผากสีทอง	golden-fronted leafbird
" เขียวก้านตองใหญ่	greater green leafbird
" เขียวคราม	Asian fairy-bluebird
" เขียวปากงุ้ม	green broadbill
" แขกเต้า	red-breasted parakeet
" แขวก	black-crowned night-heron
" คอขาวน้อย	lesser whitethroat
" คอทับทิม	Siberian rubythroat

นกคอทับทิมอกดำ	white-tailed rubythroat
” คอพัน	Eurasian wryneck
” คอมรกต	bluethroat
” คอสั้นตีนไว	sanderling
” คอสามสี	Malaysian rail-babbler
” คัคคูแซงแซว	drongo cuckoo
” คัคคูพันธุ์ยุโรป	common cuckoo
” คัคคูพันธุ์หิมาลัย	Oriental cuckoo
” คัคคูพันธุ์อินเดีย	Indian cuckoo
” คัคคูมรกต	Asian emerald cuckoo
” คัคคูลาย	banded bay cuckoo
” คัคคูเล็ก	lesser cuckoo
” คัคคูสีทองแดง	Malayan bronze cuckoo
นกคัคคูสีม่วง	violet cuckoo
” คัคคูหงอน	chestnut-winged cuckoo
” คัคคูหางแพน	rusty-breasted cuckoo
” คัคคูเหยี่ยวพันธุ์อินเดีย	common hawk-cuckoo
” คัคคูเหยี่ยวเล็ก	moustached hawk-cuckoo
” คัคคูเหยี่ยวใหญ่	large hawk-cuckoo
” คัคคูเหยี่ยวอกแดง	Hodgson's hawk-cuckoo
” คุ่มญี่ปุ่น	Japanese quail
” คุ่มสี	blue-breasted quail
” คุ่มอกดำ	rain quail
” คุ่มอกลาย	barred buttonquail
” คุ่มอืดเล็ก	small buttonquail
” คุ่มอืดใหญ่	yellow-legged buttonquail
นกคู้ท	Eurasian coot
” เค้ากู่, นกฮูก	collared scops-owl
” เค้าแคระ	collared owlet
” เค้าจุด	spotted owlet
” เค้าแดง	reddish scops-owl
” เค้าป่าสีน้ำตาล	brown wood-owl
” เค้าป่าหลังจุด	spotted wood-owl
” เค้าภูเขา	mountain scops-owl
” เค้าแมวหูสั้น	short-eared owl
” เค้าโสง, นกเค้าแมว	Asian barred owlet
” เค้าหน้าผากขาว	white-fronted scops-owl
” เค้าหูยาวเล็ก	Oriental scops-owl, common scops-owl
” เค้าเหยี่ยว	brown hawk-owl

นกเค้าใหญ่พันธุ์เนปาล	spot-bellied eagle-owl
" เค้าใหญ่พันธุ์สุมาตรา	barred eagle-owl
" เค้าใหญ่สีคล้ำ	dusky eagle-owl
" เงือกกรามช้าง	wreathed hornbill
" เงือกกรามช้างปากเรียบ	plain-pouched hornbill
" เงือกคอแดง	rufous-necked hornbill
" เงือกดำ	black hornbill
" เงือกปากดำ	bushy-crested hornbill
" เงือกปากย่น	wrinkled hornbill
" เงือกสีน้ำตาล	brown hornbill
" เงือกหัวแรด	Malayan rhinoceros hornbill
" เงือกหัวหงอก	white-crowned hornbill
" จมูกหลอดลาย	streaked shearwater
นกจมูกหลอดหางสั้น	short-tailed shearwater
" จอกป่าหัวโต	brown barbet
" จับแมลงคอขาวหน้าแดง	rufous-browed flycatcher
" จับแมลงคอแดง	red-throated flycatcher
" จับแมลงคอน้ำตาลแดง	hill blue flycatcher
" จับแมลงคอสีน้ำเงินเข้ม	blue-throated flycatcher
" จับแมลงคิ้วเหลือง	narcissus flycatcher
" จับแมลงจุกดำ	black-naped monarch
" จับแมลงดำอกสีส้ม	Mugimaki flycatcher
" จับแมลงตะโพกเหลือง	yellow-rumped flycatcher
" จับแมลงแถบคอสีส้ม	rufous-gorgetted flycatcher
" จับแมลงป่าโกงกาง	mangrove blue flycatcher
" จับแมลงปีกน้ำตาลแดง	rufous-winged flycatcher
นกจับแมลงเล็กขาวดำ	little pied flycatcher
" จับแมลงสร้อยคอขาว	white-gorgetted flycatcher
" จับแมลงสีคราม	ultramarine flycatcher
" จับแมลงสีคล้ำ	dark-sided flycatcher
" จับแมลงสีคล้ำหางแถบขาว	white-tailed flycatcher
" จับแมลงสีน้ำตาล	Asian brown flycatcher
" จับแมลงสีน้ำตาลแดง	ferruginous flycatcher
" จับแมลงสีน้ำตาลท้องลาย	brown-streaked flycatcher
" จับแมลงสีฟ้า	verditer flycatcher
" จับแมลงสีฟ้าจิ๋ว	pygmy blue flycatcher
" จับแมลงสีฟ้าท้องขาว	blue and white flycatcher
" จับแมลงสีฟ้าอ่อน	pale blue flycatcher
" จับแมลงหน้าดำคอขาว	slaty-blue flycatcher

นกจับแมลงหน้าผากขาว	snowy-browed flycatcher
" จับแมลงหลังสีเทา	slaty-backed flycatcher
" จับแมลงหัวเทา	grey-headed flycatcher
" จับแมลงหัวสีฟ้า	sapphire flycatcher
" จับแมลงอกแดง	maroon-breasted flycatcher
" จับแมลงอกเทา	grey-chested flycatcher
" จับแมลงอกส้มท้องขาว	Tickell's blue flycatcher
" จับแมลงอกสีน้ำตาล	brown-breasted flycatcher
" จับแมลงอกสีน้ำตาลอ่อน	brown-chested flycatcher
" จับแมลงอกสีเนื้อ	fulvous-chested flycatcher
" จับแมลงอกสีฟ้า	pied fantail
" จับแมลงอกสีส้ม	rufous-chested flycatcher
" จาบคาคอสีฟ้า	blue-throated bee-eater
นกจาบคาเคราแดง	red-bearded bee-eater
" จาบคาเคราน้ำเงิน	blue-bearded bee-eater
" จาบคาเล็ก	green bee-eater
" จาบคาหัวเขียว	blue-tailed bee-eater
" จาบคาหัวสีส้ม	chestnut-headed bee-eater
" จาบดินสีน้ำตาลคอลาย	spot-throated babbler
" จาบดินหัวดำ	black-capped babbler
" จาบดินอกลาย	puff-throated babbler
" จาบปีกอ่อนเขียว	black-headed greenfinch
" จาบปีกอ่อนตะโพกชมพู	pink-rumped rosefinch
" จาบปีกอ่อนเล็ก	little bunting
" จาบปีกอ่อนสีกุหลาบ	common rosefinch
" จาบปีกอ่อนสีชมพูคล้ำ	dark-breasted rosefinch
นกจาบปีกอ่อนสีแดง	scarlet finch
" จาบปีกอ่อนสีตาล	chestnut bunting
" จาบปีกอ่อนหงอน	crested bunting
" จาบปีกอ่อนหน้าดำ	black-faced bunting
" จาบปีกอ่อนหัวดำ	black-headed bunting
" จาบปีกอ่อนหัวดำขาว	Tristram's bunting
" จาบปีกอ่อนหัวเทา	chestnut-eared bunting
" จาบปีกอ่อนอกเหลือง	yellow-breasted bunting
" จาบฝนปีกแดง	rufous-winged bushlark
" จาบฝนเสียงสวรรค์	Oriental skylark
" จาบฝนเสียงใส	singing bushlark
" จุนจู๋	slaty-bellied tesia
" จุนจู๋ท้องเทา	grey-bellied tesia

นกจุนจู๋หัวสีตาล	chestnut-headed tesia
″ จู๋เต้นเขาปูน	limestone wren-babbler
″ จู๋เต้นคิ้วยาว	eye-browed wren-babbler
″ จู๋เต้นจิ๋ว	pygmy wren-babbler
″ จู๋เต้นตีนใหญ่	large wren-babbler
″ จู๋เต้นลาย	striped wren-babbler
″ จู๋เต้นหางสั้น	streaked wren-babbler
″ เจ้าฟ้าหญิงสิรินธร	white-eyed river-martin
″ โจรสลัดเกาะคริสต์มาส	Christmas Island frigatebird
″ โจรสลัดเล็ก	lesser frigatebird
″ โจรสลัดใหญ่	great frigatebird
″ เฉี่ยวดงธรรมดา	common wood-shrike
″ เฉี่ยวดงหางสีน้ำตาล	large wood-shrike
นกเฉี่ยวบุ้งกลาง	Indochinese cuckoo-shrike
″ เฉี่ยวบุ้งเล็ก	lesser cuckoo-shrike
″ เฉี่ยวบุ้งใหญ่	black-winged cuckoo-shrike
″ ชนหิน	helmeted hornbill
″ ช้อนหอยขาว, นกกุลา	black-headed ibis
″ ช้อนหอยดำ	white-shouldered ibis
″ ช้อนหอยดำเหลือบ	glossy ibis
″ ช้อนหอยใหญ่	giant ibis
″ ชาปีไหน	Nicobar pigeon
″ ชายเลนกระหม่อมแดง	sharp-tailed sandpiper
″ ชายเลนเขียว	green sandpiper
″ ชายเลนเขียวลายจุด	spotted greenshank
″ ชายเลนท้องดำ	dunlin
นกชายเลนน้ำจืด	wood sandpiper
″ ชายเลนบึง	marsh sandpiper
″ ชายเลนปากกว้าง	broad-billed sandpiper
″ ชายเลนปากโค้ง	curlew sandpiper
″ ชายเลนปากช้อน	spoon-billed sandpiper
″ ชายเลนปากแอ่น	terek sandpiper
″ ซ่อมทะเลปากยาว	long-billed dowitcher
″ ซ่อมทะเลอกแดง	Asian dowitcher
″ แซงแซวปากกา	crow-billed drongo
″ แซงแซวเล็กเหลือบ	bronzed drongo
″ แซงแซวสีเทา	ashy drongo
″ แซงแซวหงอนขน	hair-crested drongo
″ แซงแซวหางบ่วงเล็ก	lesser racket-tailed drongo

นกแซงแซวหางบ่วงใหญ่	greater racket-tailed drongo
” แซงแซวหางปลา	black drongo
” แซวสวรรค์	Asian paradise-flycatcher
” เด้าดิน	common sandpiper
” เด้าดินทุ่ง	Richard's pipit
” เด้าดินสวน	olive-backed pipit
” เด้าดินอกแดง	red-throated pipit
” เด้าดินอกสีชมพู	rosy pipit
” เด้าลมดง	forest wagtail
” เด้าลมหลังเทา	grey wagtail
” เด้าลมหัวเหลือง	citrine wagtail
” เด้าลมเหลือง	yellow wagtail
” เดินดงคอดำ	black-throated thrush
นกเดินดงคอแดง	red-throated thrush
” เดินดงดำปีกเทา	grey-winged blackbird
” เดินดงลายเสือ	scaly thrush
” เดินดงเล็กปากยาว	dark-sided thrush
” เดินดงสีคล้ำ	eyebrowed thrush
” เดินดงสีดำ	common blackbird
” เดินดงสีเทาดำ	Siberian thrush
” เดินดงสีน้ำตาลแดง	chestnut thrush
” เดินดงหลังสีไพล	long-tailed thrush
” เดินดงหัวน้ำตาลแดง	chestnut-capped thrush
” เดินดงหัวสีส้ม	orange-headed thrush
” เดินดงอกดำ	black-breasted thrush
” เดินดงอกเทา	grey-sided thrush
นกเดินดงอกลาย	dusky thrush
” ตบยุงป่าโคก	savanna nightjar
” ตบยุงพันธุ์มลายู	Malaysian eared nightjar
” ตบยุงภูเขา	grey nightjar
” ตบยุงยักษ์	great eared nightjar
” ตบยุงเล็ก	Indian nightjar
” ตบยุงหางยาว	large-tailed nightjar
” ตะกราม	greater adjutant
” ตะกรุม	lesser adjutant
” ตะขาบดง	dollarbird
” ตะขาบทุ่ง	Indian roller
” ตั้งล้อ	great barbet
” ติ๊ดแก้มเหลือง	yellow-cheeked tit

นกติ๊ดคิ้วเหลือง	yellow-browed tit
” ติ๊ดสุลต่าน	sultan tit
” ติ๊ดหน้าแดง	fire-capped tit
” ติ๊ดหัวแดง	black-throated tit
” ติ๊ดใหญ่	great tit
” ตีทอง	coppersmith barbet
” ตีนเทียน	black-winged stilt
” ตีนเหลือง	grey-tailed tattler
” แต้วแล้วเขียวเขมร	bar-bellied pitta
” แต้วแล้วแดงมลายู	garnet pitta
” แต้วแล้วท้องดำ	Gurney's pitta
” แต้วแล้วธรรมดา, นกกอหลอ	blue-winged pitta
” แต้วแล้วป่าโกงกาง	mangrove pitta
นกแต้วแล้วยักษ์, นกซุ้มหมู	giant pitta
” แต้วแล้วลาย	banded pitta
” แต้วแล้วสีน้ำเงิน	blue pitta
” แต้วแล้วหูยาว	eared pitta
” แต้วแล้วใหญ่หัวสีน้ำเงิน	blue-rumped pitta
” แต้วแล้วใหญ่หัวสีน้ำตาล	rusty-naped pitta
” แต้วแล้วอกเขียว	hooded pitta
” โต้คลื่นสีคล้ำ	Swinhoe's storm petrel
” ไต่ไม้ใต้โคนหางสีน้ำตาล	chestnut-vented nuthatch
” ไต่ไม้ท้องสีเม็ดมะขาม	chestnut-bellied nuthatch
” ไต่ไม้สีสวย	beautiful nuthatch
” ไต่ไม้หน้าผากกำมะหยี่	velvet-fronted nuthatch
” ไต่ไม้ใหญ่	giant nuthatch
นกทะเลขาเขียว	common greenshank
” ทะเลขาเขียวลายจุด	Nordmann's greenshank
” ทะเลขาแดงธรรมดา	common redshank
” ทะเลขาแดงลายจุด	spotted redshank
” ทึดทือพันธุ์เหนือ	brown fish-owl
” ทึดทือมลายู	buffy fish-owl
” น็อดดี้	brown noddy
” น็อทเล็ก	red knot
” น็อทใหญ่	great knot
” นางนวลแกลบคิ้วขาว	bridled tern
” นางนวลแกลบเคราขาว	whiskered tern
” นางนวลแกลบแคสเปียน	Caspian tern
” นางนวลแกลบจีน	Chinese crested tern

นกนางนวลแกลบดำ	sooty tern
” นางนวลแกลบดำปีกขาว	white-winged tern
” นางนวลแกลบท้องดำ	black-bellied tern
” นางนวลแกลบท้ายทอยดำ	black-naped tern
” นางนวลแกลบธรรมดา	common tern
” นางนวลแกลบน้ำเค็ม	Saunder's tern
” นางนวลแกลบปากหนา	gull-billed tern
” นางนวลแกลบแม่น้ำ	river tern
” นางนวลแกลบเล็ก	little tern
” นางนวลแกลบสีกุหลาบ	roseate tern
” นางนวลแกลบหงอนเล็ก	lesser crested tern
” นางนวลแกลบหงอนใหญ่	great crested tern
” นางนวลขอบปีกขาว	common black-headed gull
นกนางนวลธรรมดา	brown-headed gull
” นางนวลปากเรียว	slender-billed gull
” นางนวลหัวดำใหญ่	great black-headed gull
” นางนวลหางดำ	black-tailed gull
” นางนวลแฮร์ริ่ง	herring gull
” นางแอ่นตะโพกแดง	red-rumped swallow
” นางแอ่นทรายสร้อยคอดำ	sand martin
” นางแอ่นทรายสีน้ำตาล	plain martin
” นางแอ่นบ้าน	barn swallow
” นางแอ่นแปซิฟิก	Pacific swallow
” นางแอ่นผาสีคล้ำ	dusky crag-martin
” นางแอ่นมาตินพันธุ์ไซบีเรีย	common house-martin
” นางแอ่นมาตินพันธุ์เนปาล	Nepal house-martin
นกนางแอ่นมาตินพันธุ์เอเชียใต้	Asian house-martin
” นางแอ่นหางลวด	wire-tailed swallow
” นิลตวาท้องสีส้ม	vivid niltava
” นิลตวาท้องสีส้มคอดำ	rufous-bellied niltava
” นิลตวาท้องสีส้มพันธุ์จีน	Fukien niltava
” นิลตวาเล็ก	small niltava
” นิลตวาใหญ่	large niltava
” บั้งรอกเขียวอกแดง	chestnut-breasted malkoha
” บั้งรอกแดง	Raffles's malkoha
” บั้งรอกปากแดง	red-billed malkoha
” บั้งรอกเล็กท้องแดง	chestnut-bellied malkoha
” บั้งรอกเล็กท้องเทา	black-bellied malkoha
” บั้งรอกใหญ่	green-billed malkoha

นกบู๊บบี้สีน้ำตาล	brown booby
" บู๊บบี้หน้าดำ	masked booby
" ปรอดคอลาย	stripe-throated bulbul
" ปรอดจีน	Chinese bulbul
" ปรอดดำ	black bulbul
" ปรอดดำปีกขาว	black and white bulbul
" ปรอดทอง	black-headed bulbul
" ปรอดท้องสีเทา	grey-bellied bulbul
" ปรอดเทาหัวขาว	white-headed bulbul
" ปรอดภูเขา	mountain bulbul
" ปรอดแม่พะ, นกปรอดแม่ทะ	straw-headed bulbul
" ปรอดลาย	striated bulbul
" ปรอดเล็กตาขาว	grey-eyed bulbul
นกปรอดเล็กท้องเทา	spectacled bulbul
" ปรอดเล็กสีไพลตาแดง	olive bulbul
" ปรอดสวน	streak-eared bulbul
" ปรอดสีขี้เถ้า	ashy bulbul
" ปรอดสีคล้ำใต้คอเหลือง	Finsch's bulbul
" ปรอดสีน้ำตาลตาขาว	cream-vented bulbul
" ปรอดสีน้ำตาลตาแดง	red-eyed bulbul
" ปรอดสีไพลใหญ่	olive-winged bulbul
" ปรอดหงอนตาขาว	buff-vented bulbul
" ปรอดหงอนปากหนา	crested finchbill
" ปรอดหงอนหลังลาย	puff-backed bulbul
" ปรอดหน้านวล	yellow-vented bulbul
" ปรอดหลังเขียวอกลาย	streaked bulbul
นกปรอดหลังฟู	hairy-backed bulbul
" ปรอดหัวโขน	red-whiskered bulbul
" ปรอดหัวโขนก้นเหลือง	brown-breasted bulbul
" ปรอดหัวตาขาว	flavescent bulbul
" ปรอดหัวสีเขม่า	sooty-headed bulbul
" ปรอดเหลืองหัวจุก	black-crested bulbul
" ปรอดอกลายเกล็ด	scaly-breasted bulbul
" ปรอดโอ่งแก้มเทา	grey-cheeked bulbul
" ปรอดโอ่งท้องสีน้ำตาล	ochraceous bulbul
" ปรอดโอ่งเมืองเหนือ	puff-throated bulbul
" ปรอดโอ่งไร้หงอน	yellow-bellied bulbul
" ปรอดโอ่งหน้าผากเทา	white-throated bulbul
" ปลีกล้วยท้องเทา	grey-breasted spiderhunter

นกปลีกล้วยปากยาว	long-billed spiderhunter
" ปลีกล้วยปากหนา	thick-billed spiderhunter
" ปลีกล้วยลาย	streaked spiderhunter
" ปลีกล้วยเล็ก	little spiderhunter
" ปลีกล้วยหูเหลืองเล็ก	yellow-eared spiderhunter
" ปลีกล้วยหูเหลืองใหญ่	spectacled spiderhunter
" ปากกบปักษ์ใต้	Gould's frogmouth
" ปากกบพันธุ์ชวา	Javan frogmouth
" ปากกบยักษ์	large frogmouth
" ปากกบลายดำ	Hodgson's frogmouth
" ปากช้อนหน้าขาว	white spoonbill
" ปากช้อนหน้าดำ	black-faced spoonbill
" ปากซ่อมดง	Eurasian woodcock
นกปากซ่อมพง	wood snipe
" ปากซ่อมเล็ก	jack snipe
" ปากซ่อมสวินโฮ	Swinhoe's snipe
" ปากซ่อมหางเข็ม	pintail snipe
" ปากซ่อมหางพัด	common snipe
" ปากนกแก้วคิ้วดำ	lesser rufous-headed parrotbill
" ปากนกแก้วหัวเทา	grey-headed parrotbill
" ปากนกแก้วหางสั้น	short-tailed parrotbill
" ปากนกแก้วหูเทา	black-throated parrotbill
" ปากนกแก้วอกลาย	spot-breasted parrotbill
" ปากห่าง	Asian openbill
" ปากแอ่นหางดำ	black-tailed godwit
" ปากแอ่นหางลาย	bar-tailed godwit
นกปีกแพรสีเขียว	green cochoa
" ปีกแพรสีม่วง	purple cochoa
" ปีกลายตาขาว	spectacled barwing
" ปีกลายสก๊อท	Eurasian jay
" ปีกสั้นเล็ก	lesser shortwing
" ปีกสั้นสีน้ำเงิน	white-browed shortwing
" เป็ดผีเล็ก	little grebe
" เป็ดผีใหญ่	great crested grebe
" เป็ดหงส์	comb, knob-billed duck
" เปล้าขาเหลือง	yellow-footed pigeon
" เปล้าคอสีม่วง	pink-necked pigeon
" เปล้าแดง	cinnamon-headed pigeon
" เปล้าท้องขาว	white-bellied pigeon

นกเปล้าเล็กหัวเทา	little green pigeon
" เปล้าหน้าแดง	jambu fruit-dove
" เปล้าหน้าเหลือง	pompadour pigeon
" เปล้าหางเข็ม	pin-tailed pigeon
" เปล้าหางเข็มหัวปีกแดง	yellow-vented pigeon
" เปล้าหางพลั่ว	wedge-tailed pigeon
" เปล้าใหญ่	large green pigeon
" เปล้าอกสีม่วงน้ำตาล	orange-breasted pigeon
" เปลือกไม้	brown-throated treecreeper
" โป่งวิด	greater painted snipe
" พงคิ้วดำ	black-browed reed-warbler
" พงตั๊กแตนท้ายทอยสีเทา	Pallas's grasshopper-warbler
" พงตั๊กแตนอกลาย	lanceolated warbler
นกพงนาพันธุ์จีน	blunt-winged warbler
" พงนาหิมาลัย	paddyfield warbler
" พงปากหนา	thick-billed warbler
" พงหญ้า	large grass-warbler
" พงใหญ่พันธุ์ญี่ปุ่น	great reed-warbler
" พงใหญ่พันธุ์อินเดีย	clamorous reed-warbler
" พญาปากกว้างท้องแดง	black and red broadbill
" พญาปากกว้างลายเหลือง	banded broadbill
" พญาปากกว้างเล็ก	black and yellow broadbill
" พญาปากกว้างสีดำ	dusky broadbill
" พญาปากกว้างหางยาว	long-tailed broadbill
" พญาปากกว้างอกสีเงิน	silver-breasted broadbill
" พญาไฟคอเทา	grey-chinned minivet
นกพญาไฟพันธุ์เหนือ	long-tailed minivet
" พญาไฟแม่สะเรียง	short-billed minivet
" พญาไฟเล็ก	small minivet
" พญาไฟเล็กคอดำ	fiery minivet
" พญาไฟสีกุหลาบ	rosy minivet
" พญาไฟสีเทา	ashy minivet
" พญาไฟใหญ่	scarlet minivet
" พรานผึ้ง	Malaysian honeyguide
" พริก	bronze-winged jacana
" พลิกหิน	ruddy turnstone
" พิราบเขาสูง	ashy wood-pigeon
" พิราบป่า	rock pigeon
" พิราบป่าอกลาย	speckled wood-pigeon

นกโพระดกคอสีฟ้า	blue-throated barbet
" โพระดกคอสีฟ้าเคราดำ	moustached barbet
" โพระดกคางแดง	red-throated barbet
" โพระดกคางเหลือง	golden-throated barbet
" โพระดกเคราเหลือง	gold-whiskered barbet
" โพระดกธรรมดา	lineated barbet
" โพระดกหน้าผากดำ	blue-eared barbet
" โพระดกหลากสี	red-crowned barbet
" โพระดกหัวเหลือง	yellow-crowned barbet
" โพระดกหูเขียว	green-eared barbet
" ฟินฟุท	masked finfoot
" ภูหงอนท้องขาว	white-bellied yuhina
" ภูหงอนพม่า	Burmese yuhina
นกภูหงอนวงตาขาว	whiskered yuhina
" ภูหงอนหัวน้ำตาลแดง	striated yuhina
" มุดน้ำ	brown dipper
" มุ่นรกคอแดง	rufous-throated fulvetta
" มุ่นรกตาขาว	brown-cheeked fulvetta
" มุ่นรกตาแดง	grey-cheeked fulvetta
" มุ่นรกภูเขา	mountain fulvetta
" มุ่นรกสีน้ำตาล	brown fulvetta
" มุ่นรกหัวน้ำตาลแดง	rufous-winged fulvetta
" มูม	mountain imperial pigeon
" ยอดข้าวหางแพนหัวแดง	bright-capped cisticola
" ยอดหญ้าสีดำ, นกขี้หมา	pied bushchat
" ยอดหญ้าสีเทา	grey bushchat
นกยอดหญ้าหลังดำ	Jerdon's bushchat
" ยอดหญ้าหัวดำ	stonechat
" ยางกรอกพันธุ์จีน	Chinese pond-heron
" ยางกรอกพันธุ์ชวา	Javan pond-heron
" ยางเขียว	little heron
" ยางควาย	cattle egret
" ยางจีน	Chinese egret
" ยางดำ	black bittern
" ยางแดงใหญ่	great bittern
" ยางทะเล	Pacific reef-egret
" ยางโทนน้อย	intermediate egret
" ยางโทนใหญ่	great egret
" ยางเปีย	little egret

นกยางไฟธรรมดา	cinnamon bittern
" ยางไฟหัวดำ	yellow bittern
" ยางไฟหัวเทา	Schrenck's bittern
" ยางลายเสือ	Malayan night-heron
" ยูง	green peafowl
" ร่อนทะเลหางขาว	white-tailed tropicbird
" ระวังไพรแก้มสีน้ำตาล	rusty-cheeked scimitar-babbler
" ระวังไพรปากแดงยาว	red-billed scimitar-babbler
" ระวังไพรปากแดงสั้น	coral-billed scimitar-babbler
" ระวังไพรปากยาว	large scimitar babbler
" ระวังไพรปากเหลือง	white-browed scimitar-babbler
" รัฟ	ruff
" ลอยทะเลคอแดง	red-necked phalarope
นกลุมพู	green imperial pigeon
" ลุมพูขาว	pied imperial pigeon
" ลุมพูแดง	pale-capped pigeon
" แว่นตาขาวข้างแดง	chestnut-flanked white-eye
" แว่นตาขาวสีทอง	Oriental white-eye
" แว่นตาขาวสีเหลืองปักษ์ใต้	Everett's white-eye
" แว่นตาขาวหลังเขียว	Japanese white-eye
" แว่นสีเทา	grey peacock pheasant
" แว่นสีน้ำตาล	Malay peacock pheasant
" ศิวะปีกสีฟ้า	blue-winged minla
" ศิวะหางสีตาล	chestnut-tailed minla
" สกัว	pomarine skua
" สกัวขั้วโลกเหนือ	arctic skua
นกสกัวหางยาว	long-tailed skua
" สติ๊นท์คอแดง	rufous-necked stint
" สติ๊นท์นิ้วยาว	long-toed stint
" สติ๊นท์เล็ก	little stint
" สติ๊นท์อกเทา	Temminck's stint
" สาลิกาเขียว	green magpie
" สาลิกาเขียวหางสั้น	Eastern green magpie
" สีชมพูสวน	scarlet-backed flowerpecker
" เสือแมลงคอสีตาล	black-eared shrike-babbler
" เสือแมลงปีกแดง	white-browed shrike-babbler
" เสือแมลงหัวขาว	white-hooded babbler
" แสก	barn owl
" แสกแดง	bay owl

นกหกเล็กปากดำ	blue-crowned hanging lorikeet
" หกเล็กปากแดง	vernae hanging lorikeet
" หกใหญ่	blue-rumped parrot
" หนูแดง	ruddy-breasted crake
" หว้า	great argus pheasant
" หัวขวานเขียวคอเขียว	streak-breasted woodpecker
" หัวขวานเขียวตะโพกแดง	black-headed woodpecker
" หัวขวานเขียวท้องลาย	streak-throated woodpecker
" หัวขวานเขียวป่าไผ่	laced woodpecker
" หัวขวานเขียวหัวดำ	grey-headed woodpecker
" หัวขวานแคระจุดรูปหัวใจ	heart-spotted woodpecker
" หัวขวานแคระอกเทา	grey-and buff woodpecker
" หัวขวานจิ๋วคิ้วขาว	white-browed piculet
นกหัวขวานจิ๋วท้องลาย	speckled piculet
" หัวขวานจิ๋วอกแดง	rufous piculet
" หัวขวานด่างแคระ	grey-capped woodpecker
" หัวขวานด่างท้องดำ	black and buff woodpecker
" หัวขวานด่างท้องน้ำตาลแดง	rufous-bellied woodpecker
" หัวขวานด่างหน้าผากเหลือง	yellow-crowned woodpecker
" หัวขวานด่างหัวแดงอกลาย	stripe-breasted woodpecker
" หัวขวานด่างอกลายจุด	fulvous-breasted woodpecker
" หัวขวานแดง	maroon woodpecker
" หัวขวานแดงลาย	banded woodpecker
" หัวขวานแดงหลังลาย	bay woodpecker
" หัวขวานป่าไผ่	bamboo woodpecker
" หัวขวานปีกแดง	crimson-winged woodpecker
นกหัวขวานลายคอแถบขาว	buff-necked woodpecker
" หัวขวานลายตะโพกเหลือง	buff-rumped woodpecker
" หัวขวานเล็กหงอนเหลือง	lesser yellownape
" หัวขวานสามนิ้วหลังทอง	common flameback
" หัวขวานสามนิ้วหลังสีไพล	olive-backed woodpecker
" หัวขวานสีตาล	rufous woodpecker
" หัวขวานสี่นิ้วหลังทอง	greater flameback
" หัวขวานหลังสีส้ม	orange-backed woodpecker
" หัวขวานหัวเหลือง	pale-headed woodpecker
" หัวขวานใหญ่สีดำ	white-bellied woodpecker
" หัวขวานใหญ่สีเทา	great slaty woodpecker
" หัวขวานใหญ่หงอนเหลือง	greater yellownape
" หัวขวานอกแดง	crimson-breasted woodpecker

นกหัวโตกินปู	crab plover
" หัวโตขาดำ	Kentish plover
" หัวโตทรายเล็ก	lesser sand-plover
" หัวโตทรายใหญ่	greater sand-plover
" หัวโตปากยาว	long-billed plover
" หัวโตมลายู	Malaysian plover
" หัวโตเล็กขาเหลือง	little ringed plover
" หัวโตสีเทา	grey plover
" หัวโตหลังจุดสีทอง	Pacific golden plover
" หางนาค	striated warbler
" หางรำดำ	black-headed sibia
" หางรำหลังแดง	rufous-backed sibia
" หางรำหางยาว	long-tailed sibia
นกออก	white-bellied sea-eagle
" อัญชันคิ้วขาว	white-browed crake
" อัญชันจีน	band-bellied crake
" อัญชันป่าขาแดง	red-legged crake
" อัญชันป่าขาเทา	slaty-legged crake
" อัญชันเล็ก	Baillon's crake
" อัญชันเล็กลายจุด	spotted crake
" อัญชันหางดำ	black-tailed crake
" อัญชันอกเทา	slaty-breasted rail
" อัญชันอกสีไพล	water rail
" อ้ายงั่ว	Oriental darter
" อินทรีดำ	black eagle
" อินทรีแถบปีกแดง	Bonelli's eagle
นกอินทรีปีกลาย	greater spotted eagle
" อินทรีเล็ก	booted eagle
" อินทรีสีน้ำตาล	tawny eagle
" อินทรีหัวนวล	Pallas's fish-eagle
" อินทรีหัวไหล่ขาว	imperial eagle
" อินทรีหางขาว	white-tailed eagle
" อีก๋อยจิ๋ว	little curlew
" อีก๋อยตะโพกสีน้ำตาล	Eastern curlew
" อีก๋อยเล็ก	whimbrel
" อีก๋อยใหญ่	Eurasian curlew
" อีโก้ง	purple swamp hen
" อีแจว	pheasant-tailed jacana
" อีแพรดคอขาว	white-throated fantail

นกอีแพรดคิ้วขาว	white-browed fantail
" อีแพรดแถบอกดำ	pied fantail
" อีแพรดท้องเหลือง	yellow-bellied fantail
" อีแพรดอกลาย	spotted fantail
" อีล้ำ	common moorhen
" อีลุ้ม	watercock
" อีวาบตั๊กแตน	plaintive cuckoo
" อีเสือลายเสือ	tiger shrike
" อีเสือสีน้ำตาล	brown shrike
" อีเสือหลังแดง	Burmese shrike
" อีเสือหลังเทา	grey-backed shrike
" อีเสือหัวดำ	long-tailed shrike
" อุ้มบาตร์	white wagtail
นกเอี้ยงควาย	jungle myna
" เอี้ยงด่าง	Asian pied starling
" เอี้ยงดำปักษ์ใต้	Philippine glossy starling
" เอี้ยงถ้ำ	blue whistling thrush
" เอี้ยงพราหมณ์	brahminy starling
" เอี้ยงสาริกา	common myna
" เอี้ยงหงอน	white-vented myna
" เอี้ยงหัวสีทอง	golden-crested myna
" แอ่นกินรัง	edible-nest swiftlet
" แอ่นตะโพกขาวหางแฉก	Pacific swift
" แอ่นตาล	Asian palm-swift
" แอ่นท้องขาว	white-bellied swiftlet
" แอ่นท้องลาย	dark-rumped swift
นกแอ่นทุ่งเล็ก	small pratincole
" แอ่นทุ่งใหญ่	Oriental pratincole
" แอ่นบ้าน	house swift
" แอ่นพง	ashy wood-swallow
" แอ่นพันธุ์หิมาลัย	Himalayan swiftlet
" แอ่นฟ้าเคราขาว	whiskered treeswift
" แอ่นฟ้าตะโพกสีเทา	grey-rumped treeswift
" แอ่นฟ้าหงอน	crested treeswift
" แอ่นเล็กหางหนามตะโพกขาว	silver- rumped swift
" แอ่นหางสี่เหลี่ยม	black-nest swiftlet
" แอ่นใหญ่คอขาว	white-throated needletail
" แอ่นใหญ่หัวตาขาว	brown needletail
" แอ่นใหญ่หัวตาดำ	white-vented needletail

นกฮูก	collared scops-owl
เป็ดก่า	white-winged wood duck
" คับแค	cotton pygmy-goose
" เชลดัก	common shelduck
" ดำหัวดำ	Baer's pochard
" ดำหัวสีน้ำตาล	ferruginous pochard
" แดง	lesser whistling duck
" เทา	spot-billed duck
" เทาก้นดำ	gadwall
" ปากแดง	red-crested pochard
" ปากพลั่ว	Northern shoveler
" ปากสั้น	Eurasian wigeon
" ปีกเขียว	common teal
" เปีย	tufted duck
" เปียหน้าเขียว	falcated teal
" โปช๊าดหลังขาว	common pochard
" พม่า	ruddy shelduck
" แมนดาริน	mandarin duck
" ลาย	garganey
" หงส์	comb duck
" หางแหลม	Northern pintail
พญาแร้ง	red-headed vulture
ห่านหัวลาย	bar-headed goose
เหยี่ยวกิ้งก่าสีดำ	black baza
" กิ้งก่าสีน้ำตาล	Jerdon's baza
" ขาว	black-shouldered kite
" ค้างคาว	bat hawk
" ค่างดำขาว	pied harrier
" เคสเตรล	Eurasian kestrel
" ดำ	black kite
" ดำท้องขาว	Blyth's hawk-eagle
" แดง	brahminy kite
" ต่างสี	changeable hawk-eagle
" ตีนแดง	Amur falcon
" ท้องแดง	rufous-bellied eagle
" ทะเลทราย	common buzzard
" ทุ่ง	Eastern marsh-harrier
" ทุ่งแถบเหนือ	Northern harrier
" นกกระจอกเล็ก	besra

เหยี่ยวนกกระจอกใหญ่	Northern sparrowhawk
″ นกเขาชิครา	shikra
″ นกเขาท้องขาว	Northern goshawk
″ นกเขาพันธุ์จีน	Chinese goshawk
″ นกเขาพันธุ์ญี่ปุ่น	Japanese sparrowhawk
″ นกเขาหงอน	crested goshawk
″ นิ้วสั้น	short-toed eagle
″ ปลาเล็กหัวเทา	lesser fish-eagle
″ ปลาใหญ่หัวเทา	grey-headed fish-eagle
″ ปีกแดง	rufous-winged buzzard
″ ผึ้ง	crested honey-buzzard
″ เพเรกริน	peregrine falcon
″ ภูเขา	mountain hawk-eagle
″ แมลงปอขาดำ	black-thighed falconet
″ แมลงปอขาแดง	collared falconet
″ รุ้ง	crested serpent-eagle
″ เล็กตะโพกขาว	white-rumped falcon
″ หงอนสีน้ำตาลท้องขาว	Wallace's hawk-eagle
″ หน้าเทา	grey-faced buzzard
″ ออสเปร	osprey
″ ฮอบบี้	Oriental hobby
″ ฮอบบี้ยุโรป	Northern hobby
อีกา	large-billed crow
″ แก	house crow
อีแร้งดำหิมาลัย	cinereous vulture
″ เทาหลังขาว	white-rumped vulture
″ สีน้ำตาล	long-billed vulture

ชื่อเหล่านี้เป็นชื่อสามัญของนกที่พบในประเทศไทย

These are common names of birds found in Thailand.

Sources

Boonsong Lekagul and Philip D. Round. *A Guide to the Birds of Thailand.* Bangkok: Sahakarn Phaet Ltd., 1991.

Convention on International Trade in Endangered Species of Wild Fauna and Flora (CITES)

2
ชื่อสัตว์เลี้ยงลูกด้วยนม - Mammals

กระจงควาย	greater mouse deer
" เล็ก	lesser mouse deer
กระจ้อน	Indochinese ground squirrel
กระซู่	Asian two-horned rhinoceros, Sumatran rhinoceros
กระต่ายป่า	Siamese hare
กระแต	Indochinese ground squirrel
" ธรรมดา	common treeshrew
" เล็ก	pygmy treeshrew
" หางขนนก	feather-tailed treeshrew
" หางหนู	Northern smooth-tailed treeshrew
กระถิกขนปลายหูยาว	Cambodian striped tree squirrel
" ขนปลายหูสั้น	Burmese striped tree squirrel
กระทิง	gaur
กระรอกข้างลายท้องแดง	plantain squirrel
" ข้างลายท้องเทา	black-banded squirrel
" ดินแก้มแดง	red-cheeked squirrel
" ดินหลังลาย	three-striped ground squirrel
" ท้องแดง	belly-banded squirrel
" บินแก้มสีแดง	red-cheeked flying squirrel
" บินแก้มสีเทา	gray-cheeked flying squirrel
" บินจิ๋วท้องขาว	white-bellied flying squirrel
" บินเท้าขน	hairy-footed flying squirrel
" บินเล็กแก้มขาว	Phayre's flying squirrel
" บินเล็กเขาสูง	particolored flying squirrel
" ปลายหางดำ	gray-bellied squirrel
" สามสี	Prevost's squirrel
" หน้ากระแต	shrew-faced ground squirrel
" หลากสี	variable squirrel
" หางม้าจิ๋ว	Low's squirrel
" หางม้าเล็ก	slender squirrel
" หางม้าใหญ่	horse-tailed squirrel
กระเล็นขนปลายหูยาว	Cambodian striped tree squirrel

กระเล็นขนปลายหูสั้น	Burmese striped tree squirrel
กวางป่า	sambar
" ผา	goral
กูปรี	kouprey
เก้ง	common barking deer
" ดำ, เก้งหม้อ	Fea's barking deer
ควายบ้าน	Asiatic buffalo
" ป่า	wild water buffalo
ค่างดำ	banded langur
" แว่นถิ่นใต้	dusky, spectacled langur
" แว่นถิ่นเหนือ	Phayre's langur
" หงอก	silvered langur
ค้างคาวขอบหูขาวกลาง	greater short-nosed fruit bat
" ขอบหูขาวเล็ก	lesser short-nosed fruit bat
" ขอบหูขาวใหญ่	peg-toothed short-nosed fruit bat
" ขอบหูดำ	tailless fruit bat
" คุณกิติ	Kitti's hog-nosed bat
" จมูกหลอดหูยาว	Hutton's tube-nosed bat
" จมูกหลอดหูสั้น	tube-nosed bat
" ดอย	mountain fruit bat
" ดอยหลังลายขาว	harlequin bat
" ท้องสีน้ำตาลสุราษฎร์	Surat serotine
" ท้องสีน้ำตาลหูหนา	thick-eared bat
" ท้องสีน้ำตาลใหญ่	serotine
" บัวฟันกลม	Geoffroy's rousette
" บัวฟันรี	Leschenault's rousette
ค้างคาวปีกขน	hairy-winged bat
" ปีกจุด	spot-winged fruit bat
" ปีกถุงเคราดำ	black-bearded tomb bat
" ปีกถุงต่อมคาง	long-winged tomb bat
" ปีกถุงปลอม	Blyth's tomb bat
" ปีกถุงใหญ่	tomb bat
" ปีกพับกลาง	Southeast Asian bent-winged bat
" ปีกพับเล็ก	lesser bent-winged bat
" ไผ่หัวแบนเล็ก	lesser club-footed bat
" ไผ่หัวแบนใหญ่	greater club-footed bat
" ฟันหน้าซ้อนเล็ก	Blanford's bat
" ฟันหน้าซ้อนใหญ่	Tickell's bat
" มงกุฎจมูกยาวเล็ก	Pearson's horseshoe bat

ค้างคาวมงกุฎจมูกยาวใหญ่	Dobson's horseshoe bat
" มงกุฎจมูกแหลมใต้	glossy horseshoe bat
" มงกุฎจมูกแหลมเหนือ	Blyth's horseshoe bat
" มงกุฎเทาแดง	intermediate horseshoe bat
" มงกุฎปลอมเล็ก	Peters's horseshoe bat
" มงกุฎปลอมใหญ่	Shamel's horseshoe bat
" มงกุฎลาย	North Malayan horseshoe bat
" มงกุฎยอดสั้นเล็ก	Thomas's horseshoe bat
" มงกุฎยอดสั้นใหญ่	Dobson's horseshoe bat
" มงกุฎเล็ก	least horseshoe bat
" มงกุฎเลียนมลายูเล็ก	Robinson's horseshoe bat
" มงกุฎเลียนมลายูหางสั้น	lesser brown horseshoe bat
" มงกุฎสามใบพัด	trefoil horseshoe bat
ค้างคาวมงกุฎหูโตมาร์แชล	Marshall's horseshoe bat
" มงกุฎหูโตเล็ก	large-eared horseshoe bat
" มงกุฎหูโตใหญ่	Bourret's horseshoe bat
" มงกุฎใหญ่	great Eastern horseshoe bat
" มือปุ่ม	thick-thumbed pipistrelle
" แม่ไก่เกาะ	island flying fox
" แม่ไก่ป่าฝน	common flying fox
" แม่ไก่ภาคกลาง	Lyle's flying fox
" ยอดกล้วยป่า	little forest bat
" ยอดกล้วยปีกใส	Hardwicke's bat
" ยอดกล้วยผีเสื้อ	painted bat
" ยอดกล้วยเล็ก	least forest bat
" ลูกหนูกรามหน้าบนเล็ก	Thomas's pipistrelle
ค้างคาวลูกหนูจิ๋วหลังดำ	least pipistrelle
" ลูกหนูจิ๋วหลังเทา	pygmy pipistrelle
" ลูกหนูถ้ำ	Chinese pipistrelle
" ลูกหนูบ้าน	Javan pipistrelle
" เล็บกุด	cave-dwelling nectar-eating bat
" แวมไพร์แปลงเล็ก	lesser false vampire
" แวมไพร์แปลงใหญ่	greater false vampire
" สามคร	trident-nosed bat
" หน้ายักษ์กระบังหน้า	shield-faced round leaf bat
" หน้ายักษ์กุมภกรรณ	lesser great round leaf bat
" หน้ายักษ์ทศกัณฐ์	great round leaf bat
" หน้ายักษ์เล็กจมูกปุ่ม	least round leaf bat
" หน้ายักษ์เล็กสองสี	bicolored round leaf bat

ค้างคาวหน้ายักษ์เล็กหูใหญ่	fulvous round leaf bat
" หน้ายักษ์สองหลีบ	Cantor's round leaf bat
" หน้ายักษ์สามหลีบ	intermediate round leaf bat
" หน้ายักษ์หมอนโค้ง	large Malay round leaf bat
" หน้ายักษ์หมอบุญส่ง	Dr. Boonsong's round leaf bat
" หน้ายาวเล็ก	lesser long-tongued fruit bat
" หน้ายาวใหญ่	greater long-tongued fruit bat
" หน้าร่อง	hollow-faced bat
" หัวดำ	black-capped fruit bat
" หางโผล่	sheath-tailed bat
" หางหนู	free-tailed bat
ค้างคาวหูหนูตีนโตเล็ก	Deignan's bat
" หูหนูตีนโตใหญ่	large-footed bat
" หูหนูตีนเล็กเขี้ยวยาว	whiskered bat
" หูหนูตีนเล็กเขี้ยวสั้น	small-toothed whiskered bat
" หูหนูมือตีนปุ่ม	thick-thumbed myotis
" หูหนูยักษ์	large myotis
" หูหนูหน้าขน	hairy-faced bat
" อีอาอีโอ	great evening bat
" ไอ้แหว่งเล็ก	Malayan tailless round leaf bat
" ไอ้แหว่งใหญ่	East Asiatic tailless round leaf bat
ชะนีธรรมดา	white-handed gibbon
" มงกุฎ	pileated gibbon
" มือดำ	agile gibbon
ชะมดเช็ด	small Indian civet
" แปลงลายจุด, อีเห็นลายเสือ	spotted linsang, tiger civet
" แปลงลายแถบ	banded linsang
" แผงสันหางดำ	large-spotted civet
" หางสั้นหางปล้อง	large Indian civet
ช้าง	Asian elephant, Indian elephant
ติ่ง, ตุ่น	Eastern mole
นากเล็กเล็บสั้น	small-clawed otter
" ใหญ่ขนเรียบ	smooth-coated otter
" ใหญ่จมูกขน, นากใหญ่หัวปลาดุก	hairy-nosed otter
" ใหญ่ธรรมดา	common otter
" ใหญ่หัวปลาดุก	hairy-nosed otter
นางอาย	slow loris
เนื้อทราย	hog deer
" สมัน	Schomburgk's deer

บ่าง	colugo, Malayan flying lemur
บินตุรง	binturong
พญากระรอกดำ	black giant squirrel
" บินสีดำ	large black flying squirrel
" บินหูขาว	red and white giant flying squirrel
" บินหูดำ	lesser giant flying squirrel
" บินหูแดง	red giant flying squirrel
" เหลือง	cream-colored giant squirrel
พะจง	colugo, Malayan flying lemur
พังพอนกินปู	crab-eating mongoose
" ธรรมดา	Javan mongoose
พุงจง	colugo, Malayan flying lemur
เพียงพอนเล็กสีน้ำตาล	Malayan weasel
" เส้นหลังขาว	Malayan back-striped weasel
" เหลือง	Siberian weasel
เม่นหางพวง	bush-tailed porcupine
" ใหญ่แผงคอยาว	Malayan porcupine
" ใหญ่แผงคอสั้น	crestless Himalayan porcupine
แมวดาว, แมวแกว	Indian leopard cat
" ป่า, เสือกระต่าย	jungle cat
" ป่าหัวแบน	flat-headed cat
" ลายหินอ่อน	marbled cat
แรด	lesser one-horned Javan rhinoceros
ละอง, ละมั่ง	brow-antlered deer, Eld's deer
ลิงกัง	pig-tailed macaque
ลิงลม	slow loris
ลิงวอก	rhesus macaque
" เสน	stump-tailed macaque
" แสม	crab-eating macaque
" ไอ้เงี้ยะ	Assamese macaque
ลิ่น	pangolin
ลิ่นหรือนิ่มพันธุ์มลายู	Malayan pangolin
เลียงผา	Sumatran serow
วัวแดง	banteng
สมเสร็จ	Asian tapir, Malayan tapir
สาโท	moonrat
เสือกระต่าย	jungle cat
" โคร่ง	tiger
" ดาว	leopard

เสือดำ	panther
" ปลา	fishing cat
" ไฟ	Asian golden cat
" ลายเมฆ	clouded leopard
หนูเกาะ	island rat
" ขนเสี้ยนเขาหินปูน	limestone rat
" ขนเสี้ยนดอย	chestnut rat, Bonhote's rat
" ขนเสี้ยนปลายหางพู่	pencil-tailed rat
" ขนเสี้ยนสีเม็ดมะขาม	long-tailed rat
" ขนเสี้ยนหางยาว	white-bellied rat
" เขาสูง	Edward's rat
" ควาย	Muller's rat
" จี๊ด	Polynesian rat
" ถ้ำ	Neill's rat
" ท่อ	Norway rat
" ท้องขาว	roof rat
หนูท้องขาวสิงคโปร์	Singapore rat
" นาเล็ก	lesser ricefield rat
" นาใหญ่	ricefield rat
" น้ำดอยอ่างกา	Pere David's vole
" บ้านชาวเขา	Himalayan rat
" บ้านมาเลย์	Malaysian house rat
" ป่ามาเลย์	Malayan wood rat
" ผีขนยาวเหนือ	dracula shrew
" ผีจิ๋ว	dwarf shrew
" ผีเทาหางสั้น	gray shrew
" ผีนา	Southeast Asian white-toothed shrew
" ผีบ้าน	house shrew, brown musk shrew
หนูผีป่าเล็กขนเกรียน	Horsfield's shrew
" ผีป่าหางจู๋	short-tailed shrew
" ผีหางยาวฟันแดง	red-toothed shrew
" ผีหางหมู	lesser gymnure, pig-tailed shrew
" ผีอ่างกา	common European white-toothed shrew
" ไผ่เล็บแม่มือแบน	marmoset rat
" พุกเล็ก	lesser bandicoot
" พุกใหญ่	great bandicoot
" ฟันขาวกลาง	Kenneth's white-toothed rat
" ฟันขาวเล็ก	lesser white-toothed rat
" ฟันขาวใหญ่	Bower's rat

หนูฟานแดง	red spiny rat
″ ฟานเล็ก	Whitehead's rat
″ ฟานสีน้ำตาล	brown rajah rat
″ ฟานเหลือง	yellow rajah rat
″ มือลิง	long-tailed cane mouse
″ ไม้เล็บแม่มือแบน	Fea's tree rat
″ หริ่งนาหางยาว	Ryukyu mouse
″ หริ่งนาหางสั้น	sawn-colored mouse
″ หริ่งบ้าน	house mouse
″ หริ่งป่าเล็กขนเสี้ยน	Gairdner's shrew-mouse
″ หริ่งป่าใหญ่ขนเสี้ยน	Shortridge's mouse
″ หริ่งไม้หางพู่	pencil-tailed tree mouse
″ หริ่งใหญ่	Cook's mouse
″ หวาย	noisy rat
″ เหม็น	moonrat
หมาจิ้งจอก	Asiatic jackal
″ ไน	Asiatic wild dog
″ ไม้	Burmese ferret-badger; yellow-throated marten
หมีขอ, บินตุรง	binturong
″ คน, หมีหมา	Malayan sun bear
″ ควาย, หมีดำ	Asiatic black bear
หมูน้ำ	dugong, sea cow
″ ป่า	common wild pig
″ หริ่ง	hog badger
อ้นกลาง	hoary bamboo rat
″ เล็ก	bay bamboo rat
″ ใหญ่	large bamboo rat
อีเก้ง	barking deer
อีเห็นข้างลาย	common palm civet
″ เครือ	masked palm civet
″ ธรรมดา	common palm civet
″ น้ำ	otter-civet
″ ลายเสือโคร่ง, อีเห็นลายพาด	handed palm civet, Hardwick's civet
″ หน้าขาว	three-striped palm civet

ชื่อเหล่านี้เป็นชื่อสามัญของสัตว์เลี้ยงลูกด้วยนมที่พบในประเทศไทย

These are common names of mammals found in Thailand.

Sources

Boonsong Lekagul and Jeffrey A. McNeeley. **Mammals of Thailand,** 2nd ed. Bangkok, 1988.

Convention on International Trade in Endangered Species of Wild Fauna and Flora (CITES)

3

ชื่องูและสัตว์เลื้อยคลานอื่นๆ - Reptiles

กระ	hawksbill turtle
กิ้งก่า	chameleon
งูกันขบ	red-tailed pipe snake, two-headed snake
"กระ	jasper cat snake
"กระด้าง	tentacled snake
"กะปะ	Malayan pit viper
"กะปะเสือ	Wagler's pit viper, temple pit viper
"กาบหมากดำ	stripe-tailed racer
"กาบหมากหางนิล	cave dwelling snake, Malayan stripe-tailed racer
"กินทากเกล็ดสั้น	keeled slug snake
"กินทากจุดขาว	mountain slug snake
"กินทากจุดดำ	spotted slug snake
"กินทากลายขวั้น	Hampton's slug snake
"กินทากสีน้ำตาล	smooth slug snake
"กินทากหัวโหนก	blunt-headed slug snake
"ขอนไม้	xenodermine snake
"เขียวกาบหมาก	red-tailed racer
"เขียวจิ้งจกมลายู	Malayan green whip snake
งูเขียวดง	green cat-eyed snake, green cat snake
"เขียวดงลาย	banded green cat snake
"เขียวตุ๊กแก	Wagler's pit viper, temple pit viper
"เขียวปากแหนบ	long-nosed whip snake
"เขียวไผ่	bamboo pit viper, Chinese green tree viper
"เขียวพระอินทร์	golden tree snake
"เขียวร่อน	paradise tree snake
"เขียวลายดอกหมาก	golden tree snake
"เขียวหัวจิ้งจก	Oriental whip snake
"เขียวหางไหม้ตาโต	big-eyed pit viper
"เขียวหางไหม้ท้องเขียว	Pope's pit viper
"เขียวหางไหม้ท้องเหลือง	white-lipped pit viper
"ควนขนุน	Malayan brown snake
"คอขวั้นปลายหัวดำ	Malayan blackhead

งูคอขวั้นหัวดำ	common blackhead
"คออ่อนปากจะงอย	beaked sea snake
"คออ่อนหัวเข็ม	needle-headed sea snake
"คุด	brown kukri snake
"งวงช้าง	elephant trunk snake, wart snake
"งอด	striped kukri snake
"งอดเขมร	Cambodian kukri snake
"จงอาง	king cobra
"ชายธงท้องขาว	viperine sea snake
"ชายธงหลังดำ	yellow-bellied sea snake
"ชายธงหัวโต	big-headed sea snake
"ไซ	Bocourt's water snake
"ดงคาทอง	white-spotted cat snake
งูดอกหมากแดง	barred tree snake
"ดินโคราช	Khorat blind snake
"ดินฉนวยขีด	striped blind snake
"ดินตรัง	Trang blind snake
"ดินธรรมดา	common blind snake, flower pot snake
"ดินหัวขาว	white-headed blind snake
"ดินหัวเหลือง	Flower's blind snake
"ดินใหญ่มลายู	Malayan blind snake
"ดินใหญ่อินโดจีน	Indochinese blind snake
"ต้องไฟ	red cat-eyed snake
"เถา	red whip snake
"ท้องขาว	xenodermine snake
"ทะเลจุดขาว	white-spotted sea snake
งูทะเลอ่าวเปอร์เซีย	Persian Gulf sea snake
"ทับสมิงคลา	blue krait
"ทากลาย	Stoke's sea snake
"ทากลายท้องขาว	Peron's sea snake
"ทางมะพร้าวดำ	common Malayan racer
"ทางมะพร้าวแดง	red mountain racer
"ทางมะพร้าวแถบดำ	black-striped mountain racer
"ทางมะพร้าวธรรมดา	copperhead racer
"บอ	blunt headed slug snake
"บ้องไฟ	red mountain racer
"เบี้ยว	keel-bellied water snake
"ปล้องฉนวนธรรมดา	common bridle snake
"ปล้องฉนวนบอร์เนียว	slender wolf snake

งูปล้องฉนวนบ้าน	Malayan banded wolf snake
"ปล้องฉนวนภูเขา	hill wolf snake
"ปล้องฉนวนเหมืองเหนือ	banded wolf snake
"ปล้องทอง	mangrove snake
"ปล้องหวายเทา	gray coral snake
"ปล้องหวายลายขวั้นดำ	McClelland's coral snake
"ปล้องหวายหลังเส้น	stripe-backed coral snake
"ปล้องหวายหัวดำ	small-spotted coral snake
"ปล้องหวายหางแหวน	Cochran's coral snake
"ปลาตาแมว	cat-eyed fishing snake, Gerard's water snake
"ปลาหลังเทา	crab-eating water snake
"ปลาหลังม่วง	Cantor's water snake
"ปลิง	plumbeous water snake
งูปากกว้างท้องสัน	keel-bellied water snake
"ปากกว้างน้ำเค็ม	common salt water snake
"ปาล์ม	Siamese pit viper, Wirot's pit viper
"ปาล์มแดง	brown flat-nosed pit viper
"ปี่แก้วธรรมดาลายจาง	common kukri snake
"ปี่แก้วลายธรรมดา	ashy kukri snake
"ปี่แก้วสูงหลวง	Gray's kukri snake
"ปี่แก้วหลังจุดวงแหวน	Wall's kukri snake
"ปี่แก้วหัวลายหัวใจ	Basson's kukri snake
" ผ้าขี้ริ้ว	file snake, granular snake
"ฝักมะรุม	Kloss's sea snake
"พงอ้อท้องเหลือง	collared reed snake
"พงอ้อเล็ก	dwarf reed snake
งูพงอ้อหลากลาย	variable reed snake
"พงอ้อหัวขาว	white headed reed snake
"พริกท้องแดง	blue long-glanded coral snake
"พริกสีน้ำตาล	brown long-glanded coral snake
"พังกา	mangrove pit viper
"ม่านทอง	Indochinese sand snake
"แม่ตะงาวรังนก	marble cat snake, spotted cat snake
"แมวเซา	Russell's viper
"รังแหหลังศร	blue-necked keelback
"รังแหหัวแดง	orange-necked keelback
"ลายสอ	common keelback snake
"ลายสอลาวเหนือ	Angel's mountain keelback
"ลายสอสองสี	Smith's mountain keelback

งูลายสอหมอบุญส่ง	Boonsong's keelback
"ลายสอใหญ่	checkered keelback
"ลายสาบคอแดง	red-necked keelback
"ลายสาบจุดดำขาว	speckle-bellied keelback
"ลายสาบดอกหญ้า	white-striped keelback
"ลายสาบตาโต	big-eyed mountain keelback
"ลายสาบทองสามขีด	Northern keelback
"ลายสาบท่าสาร	Groundwater's keelback
"ลายสาบมลายู	Malayan mountain keelback
"ลายสาบสีจาง	Schmidt's red-necked keelback
"สมิงทะเล	black-banded sea krait
"สร้อยเหลือง	common wolf snake, house snake
"สองหัว	red-tailed pipe snake, two-headed snake
งูสามเหลี่ยม	banded krait
"สามเหลี่ยมหัวหางแดง	red-headed krait
"สายทองคอแหวน	common ringneck
"สายทองลายแถบ	striped ringneck
"สายน้ำผึ้ง	red whip snake
"สายม่านเกล็ดใต้ตาใหญ่	mountain bronzeback
"สายม่านคอขีด	Wall's bronzeback
"สายม่านแดงหลังลาย	striped bronzeback
"สายม่านธรรมดา	common bronzeback
"สายม่านลายเฉียง	Cohn's bronzeback
"สายม่านหลังทอง	elegant bronzeback
"สายรุ้งดำ	Smith's water snake
"สายรุ้งธรรมดา	rainbow water snake
งูสายรุ้งลาย	striped water snake
"สิงธรรมดา	Indochinese rat snake
"สิงหางดำ	keeled rat snake
"สิงหางลาย	Oriental rat snake
"แสงอาทิตย์	iridescent earth snake
"แส้หางม้า	dog-toothed cat snake, horse-tail whip snake
"แส้หางม้าเทา	gray cat snake
"แสมรังท้องเหลือง	Brooke's sea snake
"แสมรังลายแถบ	striped sea snake
"แสมรังลายเยื้อง	dark blue-banded sea snake
"แสมรังหางขาว	reef sea snake
"แสมรังเหลืองลายคราม	blue-banded sea snake
"หมอก	common mock viper

งูหลาม	Indian python
"หลามปากเป็ด	blood python
"หลุนชุน	common Malayan racer
"หัวกะโหลก	masked water snake, puff-faced water snake
"หัวสร	Assamese mountain snake
"หางแฮ่มกาญจน์	Kanburee pit viper
"หางแฮ่มภูเขา	mountain pit viper
"เหลือม	reticulated python
"เหลือมอ้อ	masked water snake, puff-faced water snake
"เห่า	cobra
"เห่าดวงพ่นพิษ	mottled spitting cobra
"เห่าดำพ่นพิษ	black spitting cobra
"เห่าทองพ่นพิษ	golden spitting cobra, equatorial spitting cobra
"เห่าหม้อ	monocled cobra, Siamese cobra
"เห่าสีนวล	cream colored cobra, Suphan cobra
"เห่าอีสานพ่นพิษ	Isan spitting cobra
"ไอ้งั่ว	Hardwicke's sea snake
จระเข้	crocodile, alligator, gavial
" น้ำเค็ม	saltwater crocodile, estuarine crocodile
" น้ำจืด	Siamese crocodile
" ปากกระทุงเหว	false gavial
จิ้งจก	domestic gecko, house lizard
จิ้งเหลน	skink
ตะกวด	Indian or Bengal monitor
ตะโขง	false gavial
ตะพาบ	soft-shelled turtle
ตะพาบหลังลายกะรัง	Kanburien giant soft-shelled turtle
ตุ๊กแก	tokay, large gecko
ตุ๊ดตู่	red-headed monitor
เต่า	turtle, tortoise, terrapin
" กระ	Siamese hawksbill turtle
" กระอาน	river terrapin
" กะอาน	Southern salt-water terrapin
" จักร	spiny terrapin
" จาระเม็ด	loggerhead turtle
" เดือย, เต่ากระ, เต่าเขาสูง	impression tortoise
" ตนุ	green turtle
" ทะเลลอกเกอร์เฮด	loggerhead turtle
" เทียน	yellow tortoise

เต่านา	Malayan snail-eating terrapin
" บัว	yellow-headed temple terrapin
" บึ่ง	temple terrapin
" ปูลู	Siamese big-headed turtle
" มะเฟือง	leather-backed turtle, leathery turtle
" ลายตีนเป็ด	painted Batagur terrapin
" สังกะสี, เต่าหญ้าตาแดง	Ridley's turtle
" หก	giant Asiatic tortoise
" หกดำ	black giant tortoise
" ห้วยคอลาย	stripe-necked terrapin
" หวาย	orange-headed temple terrapin
" หับ	Siamese box terrapin
" เหลือง, เต่าเทียม, เต่าขี้ผึ้ง	yellow tortoise
" อาน	green turtle
แลน	yellow tree monitor
" ดอน	yellow monitor, orange-headed monitor
เห่าช้าง	black jungle monitor
เหี้ย, เหี้ยดอก, มังกรดอก, ตัวเงินตัวทอง	water monitor

ชื่อเหล่านี้เป็นชื่อสามัญของงูและสัตว์เลื้อยคลานที่พบในประเทศไทย

These are common names of snakes and other reptiles found in Thailand.

Sources

Merel J. Cox. **The Snakes of Thailand and Their Husbandry.** Malabar, Florida: Krieger Publishing Company, 1991.

Wing Cmdr. Wirot. Nutaphand. **The Turtles of Thailand.** Bangkok: Siam Farm Zoological Garden, 1979.

Edward H. Taylor. **The Lizards of Thailand.** University of Kansas Science Bulletin, Sept. 13, 1963.

สมพร ภูริพงศ์ และสมโภชน์ อัคคะทวีวัฒน์. ***ภาพปลาและสัตว์น้ำของไทย.*** กรมประมง กระทรวงเกษตรและสหกรณ์, พิมพ์ครั้งที่ 2, องค์การค้าของคุรุสภา, กรุงเทพฯ 2535.

สุรินทร์ มัจฉาชีพ, ผศ. ***สัตว์ป่าเมืองไทย.*** แพร่พิทยา, กรุงเทพฯ

4

ชื่อแมงและแมลง - Insects

กิ้งกือ	millipede
ครั่ง	lac insect
จักจั่น	cicada
จักจั่นงวง	plant hopper
จิงโจ้น้ำ	water strider
ชีปะขาว	mayfly
ด้วง	beetle
" กว่าง	rhinoceros beetle, unicorn beetle, elephant beetle
" งวง	weevil
" งวงเจาะไม้สน	giant pine wood weevil
" งวงมะพร้าว	Asiatic palm weevil, Southern coconut weevil
" เจาะก้านกิ่ง	branch and twig borer
" เจาะเปลือกสนเขา	pine bark beetle
" เจาะไม้	wood borer
" เต่าแตง	curcubit beetle
" ถั่วเหลือง	cowpea weevil
ด้วงน้ำมัน	oil beetle, blister beetle
" ไฟ	blister beetle
" ยีราฟ	giraffe weevil
" แรด	rhinoceros beetle
" เสือ	tiger beetle
" หนวดพู่	long-horned beetle
" หนวดยาวอ้อย	stem-boring grub
" หมัดกล้วย	flea-beetle
" หมัดผัก	flea-beetle
" อกเหลือง	Gmelina defoliator
ต่อสนจุด	spotted pine sawfly
" ดำ	black pine sawfly
" ลายดำ	black-striped pine sawfly
" ลายน้ำตาล	brown-striped pine sawfly
ตะขาบ	centipede
ตั๊กแตน	grasshopper

ตั๊กแตนกิ่งไม้	stick mantis
" ตำข้าว	praying mantis
" ใบไม้	leaf mantis
" ปาทังกา	Bombay locust
" ผี	spotted grasshopper
ตัวสามง่าม	silverfish
เต่าทอง	ladybug
แตนเบียนครั่ง	lac insect parasite
บึ้ง	tarantula
บุ้งชมพู่	castor hairy caterpillar, tent caterpillar
" สะแก	castor hairy caterpillar, tent caterpillar
" หลังขาว	castor hairy caterpillar, tent caterpillar
ปลวก	termite, white ant
ผีเสื้อ	butterfly; moth
" ข้าวโพด	tropical warehouse-moth
" ปีกขาว	white butterfly
" ปีกเหลือง	sulfur-yellow butterfly
" ผี	swift moth, ghost moth
" มวนหวาน	fruit-piercing moth
" ยักษ์	giant silkmoth, atlas moth
" ไหมป่า	giant silkmoth, atlas moth, wild silkmoth
ผึ้งพันธุ์	mellifera bee
" โพรง	hive bee
" ม้าน	small dwarf bee
" มิ้ม	little bee, dwarf bee
" หลวง	giant bee, rock bee
พยาธิตัวตืด	tapeworm
พยาธิใบไม้	liver fluke
เพลี้ยกระโดดดำ	black froghopper
" กระโดดสีน้ำตาล	brown planthopper
" ไก่แจ้ทุเรียน	durian psyllid
" ไก่ฟ้ากระถิน	jumping plant louse (lice หมู่), leucaena psyllid
" จักจั่น	leafhopper
" จักจั่นฝ้าย	cotton leafhopper
" จักจั่นมะม่วง	mango leafhopper
" จักจั่นสีเขียว	green rice leafhopper
" แป้ง	mealy bug, scale insect
" แป้งลาย	striped mealybug
" ไฟ	thrips

เพลี้ยหอย	purple scale
" หอยขาว	cassava scale
" หอยอ้อย	sugarcane scale
" อ่อน	aphid
" อ่อนสำลี	wooly aphid
มดคันไฟ	fire ant
" ง่าม	harvesting ant
" ดำ	black house ant
" แดง, มดส้ม	red ant, green tree ant, large tree ant
" ตะนอย	field ant
" ตาลาน, มดตะลาน	long-legged ant
" ละเอียด	thief ant
" ลี่	Dohrn's ant
" อ้ายชื่น	carpenter ant
มวนกรรเชียง	water boatman
" ขาโต	bean bug
" เขียวข้าว	green stink bug
" นักกล้าม	squash bug
" ฝิ่น	opium bug
" พิฆาต	stink bug
" เพชฌฆาต	assassin bug
" ลำไย	longan stink bug
" โล่	stink bug
มอดข้าวเปลือก	lesser grain borer
" ขี้ขุย	powder-post beetle
" เจาะผลกาแฟ	coffee berryborer
" เจาะไม้	wood borer
" เจาะไม้ไผ่	bamboo borer
" ดิน	ground weevil
" แป้ง	flour beetle
" ฟันเลื่อย	saw-toothed grain beetle
แมงคาเรือง	luminous centipede
แมงป่อง	scorpion
" ช้าง	giant scorpion
" แซ่	whip scorpion
" เทียม	pseudoscorpion
แมงมุม	spider
แมลงกระชอน	mola cricket
" กว่าง	rhinoceros beetle, unicorn beetle

แมลงกะแท้		burrowing bug
"	กินูน	chafer, leaf chafer
"	แกลบ	cockroach
"	ค่อม, แมลงค่อมทอง	green weevil
"	คำหอม	hispid beetle
"	แคง	stink bug
"	ช้าง	antlion
"	ช้างปีกใส	lacewing
"	ช้างหนวดยาว	owlfly
แมลงชี		mayfly
"	ดานา	giant water bug
"	ตด	bombardier beetle
"	เต่าทอง	ladybird beetle
"	ทับ	metallic wood-boring beetle
"	บั่ว	rice gallmidge
"	ปอ	dragonfly
"	ปอเข็ม, แมลงประทุน	damselfly
"	ภู่	carpenter bee
"	มัน	winged ant
"	เม่า	winged termite
"	แมงป่อง	scorpionfly
แมลงวัน		fly, housefly
"	ก้นทอง	tachinid fly
"	ขายาว	long-legged fly
"	ดอกไม้	syrphid fly, flower fly
"	ดำ	black fly
"	ตัวลาย	flesh fly
"	ตายาว	stalk-eyed fly
"	วันทอง	Oriental fruitfly
"	ผลไม้	fruitfly
แมลงวันผึ้ง		bee fly
"	ลาย	soldier fly
"	สเปญ	Spanish fly
"	หลังค่อม	humpbacked fly
"	หลังลาย	flesh fly
"	หัวเขียว	blowfly, bluebottle
"	หัวโต	big-headed fly
"	หัวบุบ	robber fly
"	เหาค้างคาว	bat fly

แมลงวันเหาวัว	louse fly
แมลงสาบ	cockroach
" สิง	rice bug
" หนอนปลอกน้ำ	caddis fly
" หล่า	Malayan black rice bug
" หวี่	pomace fly, vinegar fly
" หวี่ขาว	white fly
" หวี่ทอง	moth fly
" หางมีด	springtail
" หางหนีบ	earwig
" เหนี่ยง	predacious scavenger beetle
" อี่	cicada
ยุง	mosquito
ริ้น	midge
เรือด	bedbug
ไร	mite
" กระเทียม	dry bulb mite
" กำมะหยี่ลิ้นจี่	litchi erineum mite
" ขาวพริก	broad mite, yellow mite
" แดง	red mite
" แดงกุหลาบ	rose spider mite
" แดงมะม่วง	mango red mite
" แดงส้ม	red mite
" น้ำ	water flea
" น้ำเค็ม	brine shrimp, fairy shrimp
" สองจุด	two-spotted spider mite
เสี้ยนดิน	subterranean ant
ไส้เดือน	earthworm
หนอน	caterpillar; larva, grub
" กระทู้กล้า	rice swarming caterpillar
" กระทู้ดำ	black cutworm, greasy cutworm
" กระทู้ผัก	common cutworm
" กระทู้หอม	beet armyworm
" กอ	riceborer, Asiatic riceborer
" กาแฟสีแดง	red branch borer, red coffee borer
" กินใบแดง	black rajah
" กินใบสน	leaf-eating caterpillar
" กินเปลือกลำต้น	bark-feeding borer
" ขาวกินครั่ง	white lacworm

หนอนขี้เหล็ก		sulfur yellow butterfly larva, white butterfly larva
"	คืบ	semi-looper
"	คืบกะหล่ำ	cabbage looper
"	คืบกินใบ	leaf-eating caterpillar
"	เจาะก้านลำต้นสัก	teak canker grub
"	เจาะต้นพิกุล	mimusop stem borer
"	เจาะยอดมะฮอกกานี	mahogany shoot borer
"	เจาะยอดสนเขา	pine shoot moth
"	เจาะลำต้น	stem-boring grub
"	เจาะลำต้นกัลปพฤกษ์	trunk boring caterpillar
"	เจาะลำต้นข้าวโพด	Asiatic corn borer
"	เจาะลำต้นซ้อ	Gmelina trunk borer
หนอนเจาะลำต้นพะยูง		round-headed borer
"	เจาะลำต้นมะฮอกกานี	mahogany collar borer
"	เจาะสมอฝ้าย	cotton bollworm, corn earworm
"	ชอนใบ	leaf miner
"	ตัวกลม	round worm
"	ตัวแบน	flat worm
"	ม้วนใบ	leaf roller
"	ม้วนใบถั่ว	bean leafroller
"	แมลงวันเจาะต้น	stem miner
"	แมลงวันเจาะต้นถั่ว	bean fly
"	แมลงวันเจาะยอดข้าวฟ่าง	sorghum shootfly
"	ใยผัก	diamond-back moth
"	สีชมพูกินครั่ง	pink lacworm
"	หนาม	prickly caterpillar
หมัด		flea
เหา		louse, lice *(พหู)*
เห็บ		tick
เหลือบ		horsefly, gadfly

ชื่อเหล่านี้เป็นชื่อสามัญของแมงและแมลงที่พบในประเทศไทย

These are common names of insects found in Thailand.

Sources

สุรินทร์ มิจฉาชีพ, **สัตว์ไม่มีกระดูกสันหลัง,** สนพ.โอเดียนสโตร์, 2526.

Dr. Chaweewan Hutacharoen, **แมลงป่าไม้,** 2533.

วิรัช จันทรัศมี

5

ชื่อพืช - Plants

กก	slender rush, slender sedge
" ขนาก	small-flowered umbrella sedge
" ขี้หมา	sedge
" ช้าง, ธูปฤาษี	elephant grass, narrow-leaf cattail
" ดอกเขียว	green kyllingia
" ดอกแบน	annual sedge
" ดาว	star sedge
" ตุ๊ดตู่	rice field bulrush
" ทรายดอกเหลือง	rice flatsedge
" ใบคม	compact sedge
" ยูนาน	club rush
" ลังกา	digitate sedge, umbrella plant
" เล็ก	elegant sedge
" สามเหลี่ยม	shichito matgrass
" สามเหลี่ยมเล็ก	hairy sedge
" อียิปต์	papyrus sedge
ก้นจ้ำ	beggarticks
" จ้ำขาว	hairy beggarticks
" เกรา	tembusu
กรดน้ำ, หญ้าหนวดแมว	sweet broom, Macao-tea
กรรณิการ์	night jasmine
กระจับ	Singhara nut
กระเจา	Indian elm
กระเจานา	East Indian jew's-mallow
กระเจี๊ยบแดง	roselle, Jamaican sorrel
" มอญ	lady's finger, okra
กระชับ	common cocklebur
กระซิก	blackwood, rosewood (*Dalbergia parviflora*)
กระดังงาไทย	kenanga, ylang ylang
กระดุมขน, กระดุมใบ	hairy pisswort
กระดุมใบใหญ่	broad leaved button weed
กระแตไต่ไม้	bird's nest fern

กระถินไทย	lead tree
" ณรงค์	Australian wattle
กระท่อม	**krathom** (Rubiaceae, *Mitragyna spp.* Korth)
กระทิง	Alexandrian laurel
กระทืบยอบ	sensitive sorrel
กระทุ	downy rosemyrtle
กระเทียมจีน	Chinese chives
กระบอก	trumpet flower yellow oleander
กระเบา	chaulmoogra
กระปรอกสิงห์	crested fern
กระพังไหม	skunk vine
กระวาน	cardamom, camphor seed
กร่าง	**banyan** (*Ficus bengalensis*)
กฤษณา	eaglewood, agarwood, lignum aloes
กล้วย	banana tree
กล้วยไม้	showy mistletoe
กลอย, มันกลอย	wild yam
กว้าว	haldu
ก่อเดือย	evergreen chinkapin
ก่อฝ้าย	lan oak
กะเดือยหนู	saramolla grass, wrinkled duckbeak
กะทกรก	red-fruited passion flower
กะทือ	wild ginger
กะทือ	ginger
กะปรอก	staghorn fern
กะเพรา	holy basil
กะเม็ง	eclipta
กะลา	torch ginger
กัญชาเทศ	**motherwort** (Lamiaceae, *Leonurus sibiricus* Linn.)
กันเกรา	tembusu
กัลปพฤกษ์	**pink cassia, pink shower, wishing tree** (Fabaceae, *Cassia bakeriana* Craib.)
กากหมากตาฤาษี	phallus flower
ก้านถึง	colubring
กาฝากมะม่วง	mistletoe
" ไม้ซาก	hairy mistletoe
กาแฟ	coffee
กานพลู	clove
ก้ามกุ้ง	umbrella grass

ก้ามปู	rain tree
การบูร	camphor tree
การะเกดหนู	bean pink
กาหยีเขา	tamarind plum
กาหลา	torch ginger
กำจัดต้น	prickly ash
กำมะหยี่	acuate
กุยช่าย	Chinese chive
กุหลาบ "ควีนสิริกิติ์"	"Queen Sirikit" rose
กุหลาบมอญ	damask rose
เกล็ดปลา, หญ้าเกล็ดหอย	threeflower beggarweed
เกล็ดปลาช่อน	bracted desmodium
แก้ว	orange jasmine
เก็ดแดง	blackwood, rosewood (*Dalbergia dongnaiensis*)
โกฐจุฬาลำพา	artemisia
" ชฎามังษี	jafamansi
" เชียง	lovage
" พุงปลา	myrobalan gall, terminalia gall
" หัวบัว	selinum
โกโก้	cocoa tree
ขจร (ดอกขจร)	cowslip creeper
ขนุน	jack wood
ขมิ้น	turmeric
ขมิ้นชัน	turmeric
ขมิ้นอ้อย	zedoary
ขลู่	fleabane
ขอนจีน	yellow velvet
ข่อย	Siamese rough bush, toothbrush tree (Moraceae, *Streblus asper* Lour.)
ขาเขียด	vaginal monochoria
ขานาง	Moulmein lancewood
ข่า	galangal, great galangal, jana galangal
ขางปอย	Kerr's acalypha
ข้าว	rice
" ตอก	pearly everlastings
" นก	wild rice
" ป่า	wild rice
" โพด	maize, corn, Indian corn
" เย็น	greenbriar

ข้าหลวงหลังลาย	bird's nest fern
ขิง	ginger
" แดง	red ginger
ขี้ไก่ย่าน	African mile-a-minute
ขี้ครอก	cadillo
ขี้เหล็ก	cassod tree, Thai copper pod
" เทศ	coffee senna
ขี้อ้าย	Indian almond
เข็ม	ixora
เข็มม่วง	eranthemum
เขลง	velvet tamarind
แขม	wild sugar
แขมหลวง	tassel grass
ไข่แหน	water meal
คราม	indigo
" ขน	hairy indigo
" ป่า	tephrosia
คล้าน้ำ	water canna
ควินิน	chinchona, cinchona (*Cinchona succirubra* Par.)
คอกิ่ว	winged desmodium
คอนสวรรค์	cypress vine
คาง	black siris
คำไทย	annatto tree
คำฝอย	safflower
คำมอก	Indian boxwood
คำแสด	monkey-faced tree
คูน	golden shower, Indian laburnum, purging cassia
แค	sesban (*Sesbania grandiflora* (Linn.) Pers.)
แคแดง	African tulip
แคบ้าน	vegetable humming bird, sesban
โคกกระออม	balloon vine, heart pea
โคกกระสุน	puncture vine, small caltrops, ground barnut (Zygophyllaceae, *Tribulus terrestris* L.)
ไค้นุ่น	white willow
งา	sesame
งิ้ว	kapok tree, cotton tree
เงาะ	rambutan
จมูกปลาหลด	Alpin's oxystelma
จรัสจันทร	sarassa chandhorn

จอก	water lettuce
จอกหูหนู	floating water fern
จันทน์เทศ	nutmeg tree
จันทนา	dracena
จาก	atap palm, nipa palm
จามจุรี	rain tree
จำปา	sonchampa, champak, orange champaka
จำปี	white champaka
จ้าก้อง	hen's eyes, Hilo holly
จิก	Indian oak
จุกนารี	Straits rhododendron
จูดหนู	pale yellow-spiked rush
เจตมูลเพลิงแดง	rose-colored leadwort
ฉัตรพระอินทร์	lesser roundweed
แฉลบแดง	white-barked acacia
ชงโค	orchid tree, bauhinia
ชมพู่	rose apple
ชมพูพันธุ์ทิพย์	pink tabebuia
ชมพู่สาแหรก	Malay apple
ช้องนาง	bush clock vine
ช้องนางคลี่	love vine
ช่อม่วง	purple wreath
ชะเนียง	djenkol
ชะบาร์	hibiscus
ชะมดต้น	musk mallow
ชะเอมเทศ	licorice
ชัยพฤกษ์	yellow cassia, golden shower
ชา	Singapore holly
ชาข่อย	wild tea
ช้าง	foxtail orchid
ชาพลู	pepper vine
ช้าเลือด	brasiletto
ชำมะนาด	breadflower
ชิงชัน	rosewood (*Dalbergia oliveri*)
ชิงช้าชาลี	heart-leaved moonseed
ชิงเฮา	qinghao
ชุมเห็ดเทศ	Natal plum, ringworm bush
ชุมเห็ดไทย	sicklepod, senna, foetid cassia
โซนใหญ่	bracken fern

ช้อ	gamari
ดอกแก้วเมืองจีน	sagebrush
ดอกฟ้อน	white butterfly bush
ดอกรัก	crown flower
ดองดึง	climbing lily, superb lily
ดาวกระจาย	cosmos
ดาวดึงส์	gloriosa lily
ดาวเปลาะ	brittle star, serpent star
ดาวเรือง	African marigold
ดาวเรืองพม่า	cosmos
ดาวเรืองใหญ่	Aztec marigold
ดีปลี	long pepper (*Piper retrofractum* Vahl)
ดีปลีน้ำ	pondweed
เดือย	Job's tear, adlai; barley
แดง	ironwood, pyinkado, jamba (Fabaceae, *Xylia kerrii*, *Xylia xylocarpa* (Roxb.) var. kerrii)
แดงคลอง	eugenia
โด่ไม่รู้ล้ม	elephant's fool
ตดหมูตดหมา	cat claws
ต้นกระดาษ	elephants' ears
ต้นคริสต์มาส	poinsettia
ต้นช่อครามน้ำ	pickerel weed
ตองกง	tiger grass
ต้อยติ่ง	popping pod
ตะกรับ	lax sedge
ตะโกนา	ebony (*Diospyros rhodocalyx* Kurz.)
ตะขบไทย	rukam
ตะขบป่า	ramontchi, governor's plum
ตะค้านเล็ก	pepper
ตะเคียน	Malabar ironwood, thingan (*Hopea odorata*)
ตะเคียนชัน	chingal (*Balanocarpus heimii*)
ตะเคียนทอง	iron wood (Dipterocarpaceae, *Hopea odorata* Roxb.)
ตะเคียนหนู	yon (*Anogeissus acuminata*)
ตะคร้อ	gyo, lac tree, Ceylon oak
ตะไคร้	lemon grass
ตะไคร้หอม	citronella grass
ตะลิงปลิง	cucumber tree, bilimbi
ตับเต่านา	Asian frog's bit

ตาตุ่ม	eye-blinding tree
ตาล	Palmyra palm, lontar palm, toddy palm
ตาลโตนด	Palmyra palm
ตาลทราย	American waltheria
ตำแย	stinging nettle
ตำแยช้าง	elephant nettle
ตำแยแมว	Indian acalypha
ตำลึง	ivy gonro
ตีนตุ๊กแก	tridax, coat buttons
ตีนเป็ดแดง	jelutong
เต็ง	Siamese sal
เติม	red cedar, bischofia
เตยหอม	pandanus, fragrant screwpine
เต่าเกียด	arrowhead
เต่าร้าง	fishtail palm
แตงหนู	mouse's cucumber
ถ่อน	white siris
ถั่วพุ่ม	cowpea
ถั่วพู	winged bean, Goa bean, Manila pea (Fabaceae, *Psophocarpus tetragonolobus* DC.)
ถั่วลิสง	peanut, groundnut
ถั่วหรั่ง	Congo goober, African peanut
ถั่วแระ	Angola pea, Congo pea, pigeon pea
ถั่วเหลือง	soybean
เถาคัน	treebine
เถาสะอึก	Japanese morning glory, imperial morning glory
เถาสายทองลาย	tiger's fool morning glory
เถาอรคนธ์	fire weed
ทรงกระเทียมหัวแหวน	bulrush, jointed flat sedge
ทองกวาว	bastard teak, Bengal kino tree, flame of the forest (*Butea frondosa*)
ทองหลาง	coral tree (*Erythrina indica*)
ทองโหลง	coral tree
ทองอุไร	yellow elder, yellow bell
ทับทิม	pomegranate
ทานตะวัน	common sunflower
ทานตะวันหนู	Mexican sunflower
ทุเรียน	durian
ทุเรียนเทศ	soursop, guanabana

เทา	spirogyra, pond scum
เท้ายายม่อม	Turk's turban, tube flower
เทียนกิ่ง	henna tree
″ ขาว	cumin
″ ข้าวเปลือก	fennel
″ ดำ	black cumin
″ แดง	garden cress
″ ตากบ	caraway
″ นา	water primrose
″ น้ำ	marsh henna
″ บ้าน	garden balsam
″ เยาวพาณี	parsley
″ สัตตบุษย์	anise
″ หยด	golden dewdrop
เที้ยะ	Siamese balsa
โทงเทง	gooseberry
ไทร	banyan
ไทรย้อย	weeping fig
ไทรย้อยใบแหลม	golden fig (*Ficus benjamina* Linn.)
ธรรมรักษา	Japanese canna
ธูปพราหมณ์	bulrush
นนทรี	copper pod, yellow poinciana
นุ่น	kapok tree, white cotton tree
น้อยหน่า	custard apple, sugar apple
น้อยโหน่ง	custard apple, bullock's heart
นางกวัก	yellow burhead
นางนวล	Congo jute
นางแย้ม	fragrant clerodendron
น้ำนมราชสีห์	garden spurge
″ ใบมน	graceful spurge
″ ม่วง	ground spurge
″ เล็ก	spurge
บวบงู	edible snake gourd
บวบหอม	smooth loofah
บัวจงกลนี	water lily
บัวบก	Asiatic pennywort, tiger herbal
บัวบา	water snowflake
บัวเผื่อน	waterlily
″ วิกตอเรีย	giant waterlily

บัวสาย	waterlily
" สายติ่ง	floating heart
" หลวง	lotus, Hindu lotus, sacred lotus
บานบุรี	allamanda
บานบุรีเหลือง	golden trumpet
บานไม่รู้โรย	globe amaranth, bachelor's button
บานไม่รู้โรยป่า	wild globe everlasting
บานเย็น	marvel of pern
บุกคางคก	Stanley's water-tub
บุนนาค	gangaw, Indian rose chesnut, Ceylon ironwood (*Mesua ferrea*)
เบญกานี	nutgall
เบญจมาศ	chrysanthemum
โบตั๋น	orchid cactus, Queen of the Night, nightblooming cereus
ใบเงิน	caricature plant
ใบบอน	elephant's ear
ปรง	cyad
ประ	perah
ประดู่	Burmese ebony, Burma padauk (*Pterocarpus macrocarpus*); **narra** (*Pterocarpus indicus*)
ประดู่ป่า	Burmese ebony, Burma padauk, pra duu paa (*Pterocarpus macrocarpus*)
ประทัดใหญ่	quassia
ปอกระเจา	round podded jute, potherb jute
" กระสา	paper mulberry
" แก้ว	kenaf
" เทือง	smooth crotalaria
" ปิด	screw tree, East Indian screw plant
" เส้ง	round-podded jute, potherb jute
" อีเก้ง	Indian balsa
ปอมแดง	stender euphorbia
ปันหยี	jasmine
ปาล์มขวด	royal palm
ปีแซ	spinach joint fir
ปีป	Indian cork tree
เปราะหอม	resurrection lily
เปล้าน้ำเงิน	croton
เป้าลาย	bamboo

โป๊ยกั๊ก	Chinese star anise
ผกากรอง	large-leaved lantana
ผักกระเฉด	neptunia, water mimosa
” กระเฉดบก	mimosa-leaved cassia
” กระสัง	silver bush, peperomia
” กาดนกกูด	American burnweed
” กาดน้ำ	common plantain (*Plantago major* Linn.)
” กาดส้ม	curly dock
” กาดหอม	annual sowthistle
” กูดขาว	paco
” กูดแดง	swamp fern
” กูดน้ำ	watersprite
” กวางตุ้ง	Chinese cabbage
” ขม	slender amaranth, livid amaranth
ผักขมสวน	Joseph's coat
” ขมหนาม	spiny amaranth
” ขมหัด	amaranth
” ขมหิน	red spiderling
” ขมหินต้นตั้ง	erect spiderling
” ขาเขียด	floating stag's horn fern, swamp fern
” ขี้หูด	radish
” คราดหัวแหวน	para cress
” คางไก่	old world arrowhead
” แครด	synedrella
” ชี	coriander
” ชีฝรั่ง	eryngo
ผักตบชวา	water hyacinth, water-orchid
” ตบไทย	arrow-leaved monochoria
” เต่า	European frog's bit
” บุ้ง	swamp morning glory
” บุ้งทะเล	beach morning glory, goat's foot creeper
” บุ้งฝรั่ง	morning glory
” บุ้งส้ม	buckwheat
” เบี้ย	common purslane
” เบี้ยทะเล	sea purslane
” เบี้ยหิน	horse purslane
” ปลัง	Ceylon spinach
” ปลาบ	tropical spiderwort
” ปลาบขอบใบเรียว	spreading dayflower

ผักปลาบเขียว	dry flower
" ปลาบนา	dove weed, spreading dayflower
" ปอดนา	gooseweed
" เป็ดขาว	sessile joyweed
" เป็ดเขียว	joy weed
" เป็ดน้ำ	alligator weed
" ไผ่น้ำ	marsh pepper, smartweed, slender persicaria water smartweed, knotweed
ผักแพงพวย	water primrose
" เมียก	creeping spiderling
" เลือม	elsholtzia
" แว่น	pepperwort, water clover, European pepperwort
" เสี้ยน	wild spider flower
" เสี้ยนขาว	African spider flower
" เสี้ยนผี	wide mustard, wild spider flower
" เสี้ยนม่วง	consumption weed, spider flower
" แส้ว	marsdenia
" หนาม	lasia
" หนอน	tropic croton
" อัน	water dropwort
เผือก	taro
โผงเผง	woody bean
ไผ่	bamboo
" เพ็ก	slender bamboo
ฝรั่ง	guava
ฝอยทอง	dodder
ฝาง	sappanwood, sappan tree
ฝิ่นน้ำ	water poppy
แฝก	vetiver
พญาไร้ใบ	milk bush
พญาสัตบรรณ	blackboard tree, devil tree
พยุง	blackwood, rosewood (*Dalbergia cochin-chinensis*)
พริกขี้หนู	bush red pepper, chilli pepper (*Capsicum frutescens*)
พริกไทย	pepper (*Piper nigrum*)
พฤกษ์	Indian walnut, siris, kokko (*Albizzia lebbek*)
พลวง	eng
พลับพลึง	crinum lily
พลับพลึงดอกขาว	cape lily, crinum lily

พลับพลึงดอกแดง	giant lily
พลู	betel pepper, betel vine
พวงแก้วมณี	clematis
พวงโกเมน	New Guinea creeper
พวงคราม	sandpaper vine
พวงชมพู	Honolulu creeper
พวงม่วง	golden dewdrop
พวงหยก	jade vine
พังแหรใหญ่	peach cedar
พิกุล	bullet wood
พุด	Siamese boxwood
พุทธรักษา	canna lily
พุทรา, พุดซา	monkey apple, jujuba tree (*Zizyphus spp.*)
พู่ระหง	coral hibiscus, fringed hibiscus
โพธิ์	pipal (*Ficus religiosa*)
โพธิ์เงินโพธิ์ทอง	copper leaf
โพธิ์ทะเล	portia tree, tulip tree, seaside mahoe, cork tree, umbrella tree, rosewood of Seychelles (*Thespesia populnea*)
โพธิ์ประสาท	mock bodhi tree
ฟักขาว	spring bitter cucumber
ฟักทอง	pumpkin, cushaw, winter squash
ฟ้าทะลาย	kariyat
ฟ้าแลบ	climbing raspberry
ฟีสมอส	peat moss
เฟินก้านดำ	maidenhair fern
เฟินตีนตะขาบ	fishtail fern
เฟินหางปลา	sword fern
เฟื่องฟ้า	bougainvillea
ไฟเดือนห้า	false ipecacuanha, milk weed, bloodflower (*Asclepias curassavica* Linn.)
มหาหงส์	garland flower, butterfly ginger, white ginger, ginger lily (Zingiberaceae, *Hedychium coronarium*)
มะกรูด	leech lime, kaffir lime
มะกล่ำต้น	redwood, coral wood (*Adenthera pavonina*)
มะกล่ำตาช้าง	red sandalwood tree
มะกล่ำตาหนู	crab's eye vine, precatory bean, American pea
มะกอก	hog plum

มะก่องข้าว	Chinese bell flower, country mallow
มะกาย	monkey-faced tree
มะเกลือ	ebony tree (Ebenaceae, *Diospyros mollis*)
มะขวิด	elephant apple, wood apple, kavath, gelingga, (Rutaceae, *Feronia limonia*)
มะขาม	tamarind
" แขก	senna
" เทศ	Madras thorn, Manila tamarind
" ป้อม	emblic leaf flower, emblic myrabolan
มะเขือพวง	Turkey berry, lesser eggplant
มะค่า	makhaa (*Afzelia xylocarpa*)
มะค่าแต้	ma khaa tae (*Sindora siamensis* Teijsm ex Miq. var. siamensis)
มะค่าโมง	ma khaa mong (*Afzelia xylocarpa* (Kurz) Craib)
มะคำดีควาย	soapberry, soapnut tree
มะงั่ว	acid lime, citron, sweet lime, lemon (*Citrus medica*)
มะดัน	garcinia
มะเดื่อดิน	thin-leaved fig
มะตูม	bael fruit, golden apple, Bengal quince
มะนาว	lime
มะปราง	marian fruit tree
มะผู้มะเมีย	draceria palm
มะพร้าว	coconut palm, porcupine wood
มะเฟือง	carambola
มะไฟนกคุ่ม	acrid weed
มะมุด	ambatjang mango, horse mango
มะม่วง	mango
มะม่วงหิมพานต์	cashew
มะยม	star gooseberry, otaheite gooseberry
มะระ	balsam pear, bitter cucumber
มะรุม	horse-radish tree
มะละกอ	papaya, pawpaw
มะลิ	Chinese jasmine
มะลิป่า	wild jasmine
มะลิลา	Arabian jasmine
มะลิวัลย์	climbing jasmine
มะแว้งเครือ	nightshade
มะหิ่งเม่น	showy crotalaria
มะหิ่งเม่นน้ำ	Assam rattle-box

มังคุด	mangosteen
มัน	yam
มันแกว	yam bean
มันเทศ	sweet potato
มันสำปะหลัง	cassava, manioc, tapioca
มันหมู	Hausa potato
มาเวสแดง	tree fern
แมงลัก	hairy basil
แมงลักป่า, กระเพราผี	wild spikenard, bush tea
แมลงปอ	spider orchid
โมกหลวง	kurchi
ไมยราบ	sensitive plant (*Mimosa pudica* var. hispida Bren.)
ไมยราบเครือ	giant sensitive plant, (Fabaceae, *Mimosa invisa* Mart. ex Colla)
ไมยราบยักษ์	shrubby sensitive plant, giant sensitive plant, (Fabaceae, *Mimosa invisa* Mart. ex Colla)
ไมยราบเลื้อย	sensitive vine
ไม้รวก	green bamboo
ยมหอม	Moulmein cedar, red cedar, toon
ยมหิน	Chittagong wood, chickrassy, almond-wood
ยอบ้าน	Indian mulberry
ยาสูบ	tobacco plant (Solanaceae, *Nicotiana tabacum*)
ยาง	yang, gurjun, gurjun-oil tree (*Dipterocarpus turbinatus*)
ยางขาว	yang (*Dipterocarpus alatus*)
ยางขนนนก	gutta-percha tree
ยี่เข่ง	crepe myrtle
ยี่โถ	oleander
ยูง	Burma reed; yang (*Dipterocarpus grandiflorus*)
รกฟ้า	laurel
รง	gamboge tree
รงทอง	gum gamboge tree
รัง	ingyin
รองเท้านารี	lady's slipper orchid
ร่องไม้	lilac cranthemum
ระย่อมน้อย	rauwolfia
รัก	crown flower, giant Indian milkweed; varnish tree, red zebra wood (*Melanorrhoea usitata*)
รางจืด	thunbergia

ราชพฤกษ์	pink cassia
ราตรี	lady of the night
ราตรีแกง	shrimp plant
ร่าน	spot flower
รำเพย	yellow oleander
ริบู	zebra wood
ละมุด	sapodilla
ละหุ่ง	castor oil plant, castor bean
ลัดดาวัลย์	porana
ลั่นทม	frangipani, plumeria
ลาน	fan palm
ลำโพง	Hindu datura
ลำโพงขาว	thorn apple, jimsonweed
ลำใย	longan
ลำเอียก	water coix
ลิ้นจี่	lychee
เล็บครุฑใบเฟิร์น	fernleaf aralia
เล็บมือนาง	Rangoon creeper
เลา	small wild cane
เลี่ยน	bastard cedar, bead tree, Persian lilac, neem (*Melia azedarach*)
เลียบ	fig
โล่ติ๊น	derris, tuba root
วานิลลา	**vanilla** (*Vanilla planifolia*)
ว่านกาบหอยใหญ่	oyster plant
” น้ำ	sweetflag, calamus, myrtle grass
” พระฉิม	air potato
” พังพอน	black lily
” เพชรหึง	letter plant
” หางจระเข้	aloe
” หางช้าง	blackberry lily, leopard flower
แว่นตาพระอินทร์	porpita
แววตา	blackeyed Susan
ศรีตรัง	jacaranda
สน	pine
สนุ่น	**willow, white willow, Indian willow** (*Salix tetrasperma*)
สบู่แดง	bellyache bush
ส้มป่อย	acacia, soap pod

ส้มสันดาน	treebine
สมอไทย	myrobalan wood, chebula-terminalia
สมอพิเภก	beleric myrobalan
สลอด	purging croton
สลัดได	Malayan spurge tree
สวาด	nickernut, grey nickers
สะเดา	neem tree
" ดิน	Ceylon hydrolea
" บ้าน	neem tree (*Azadirachta indica* A. Juss. var. siamensis Valeton)
" อินเดีย	nim (*Azadirachta indica* A. Juss.)
สะตอ	nitta tree, sato (Fabaceae, *Parkia spp.* Hassk.)
สะระแหน่	mint (*Mentha cordifolia* Opiz)
สะระแหน่ญี่ปุ่น	Japanese mint (*Mentha arvensis* Linn. var. piperascens Malinvaud)
สะแล	paper mulberry
สะเหรี่ยง	nitta tree
สะอึก, ชันอากาศ	morning glory
สัก	teak
สังกรณี	Philippine violet
สังวาลย์พระอินทร์	love vine
สันตะวา	ottelia
" ใบข้าว	tape weed
" ใบโปร่ง	lace-leaf, lattice-leaf
สับปะรด	pineapple
สาเก	breadfruit
สาบแร้งสาบกา	tropic ageratum
สาบเสือ	Siam weed, saap suea (Asteraceae, *Chromolaena odorata* Linn.), (*Eupatorium odoratum* Linn.)
สาบหมา	crofton weed
สามร้อยยอด	club moss
สายน้ำผึ้ง	Japanese honeysuckle
สารพัดพิษ	pink purslane, hairy purslane
สาหร่ายข้าวเหนียว	bladder wort
" ญี่ปุ่น	parrot feather
" พุงชะโด	common coontail
" ไฟ	chara
" เส้นด้าย	grassy naiad
" หางกระรอก	hydrilla, Florida elodea

สำมะงา	garden quinine
สำเหร่	Bank's melastoma
สีเสียดเปลือก	thitka
" เหนือ	catechu acacia, cutch tree
เส็งเล็ก	redweed, wire bush
เสม็ด	cajuput tree, paper bark tree, swamp tea, milk wood
เสม็ดชุน	eugenia
เสี่ยน, เกรียน	Persian lilac, chinaberry
เสี้ยว	bauhinia
แสงจันทร์	lettuce tree
แสงจันทร์นวล	moonflower
แสงใจ	nux-vomica tree, snake wood
โสน	hemp sesbania
" กินดอก	Javanese sesbania
" ขน, โสนดอก	American jointvetch
" คางคก	sesbania, jointvetch, sota plant
" หางไก่	Indian jointvetch
หงอนไก่	celosia
หญ้ากอดโขย่ง, หญ้าโขย่ง	itch grass
" กาบไผ่	palm grass
" กินี	Guinea grass
" เกล็ดหอย	heart-leaf drymary
" ขจรจบดอกเล็ก	mission grass
" ขจรจบดอกเหลือง	West Indies pennisetum
" ขจรจบดอกใหญ่	kyasuma grass
" ขน	para grass
" ขนกระต่าย	threeawn
" ขนเล็ก	arm grass, millet
หญ้าขัดใบป้อม	heart-leaf sida
" ขัดใบยาว	southern sida, broom weed
" ขัดมอน	arrow-leaf sida
" ข้าวนก	gulf cockspur, barnyard grass
" เข็ม	blue bladder wort
" เขมร	smooth button weed
" เขมรใหญ่	winged button weed
" แขม	flute reed
" โขย่ง	corn grass, itch grass
" ไข่ปู	Chinese lovegrass

หญ้าไข่แมงดา	arm grass
” ไข่เหา	seandent panic
” คา	cogon grass, lalang grass
” คิคูยู่	Kikuyu grass
” งวงช้าง	Indian heliotrope
” เจ้าชู้	lesser tassel grass, pilipiliula, love grass
” ชันกาด	torpedo grass
” ไซ	Southern cutgrass
” ดอกขน	three-lobed morning glory
” ดอกขาว	grass rush
” ดอกแดง	short-stemed sedge, Natal grass
” ดอกยาว	curved rush
” ต้มต๊อก	black nightshade
หญ้าตีนกา	goose grass
” ตีนติด	running grass
” ตีนนก	Southern crabgrass
” ตีนนกเล็ก	Indian crabgrass
” ตุ้มหู, กกดอกขาว	white kyllinga
” เต่า	beetle grass
” ใต้ใบ	piss weed
” ถอดบ้อง	horsetail
” ท่าพระ, กระดุมใบ	Brazil pusley
” นก	thread sprangletop
” นกสีชมพู	jungle rice
” นมหนอน	rice-grass paspalum
” นวลน้อย	Manila grass
หญ้านิ้วหนู	forked fringe rush
” เนเปียร์	Napier grass
” บัว	tall yellow-eyed grass
” บุ้ง	Southern sandbur
” บุ้งดอกฝอย	fine-bristled sandbur
” ใบคม	golden-beak sedge
” ใบบิด	brown rush
” ปล้อง	hymenache
” ปล้องละมาน	barnyard grass
” ปล้องหิน	Kodo millet
” ปากควาย	crowfool grass, violet crabgrass
” ปูมปาว	Kerr's sedge
” เปลือกกระเทียม	pointed fimbristylis

หญ้าเปลือกกระเทียมหัวแมลงวัน	spike rush
” แปรงหมู	sparse-flowered rush
” ผมยุ่ง	St. Paul's wort
” ฝอยเล็ก	minute bladder wort
” ไผ่	slender panic grass
” ไผ่, ไผ่จีน	bamboo grass
” พง	Johnson grass
” แพรก	Bermuda grass
” มาเลเซีย	broad-leaf carpet grass
” แม่มด	witchweed
” ยอนหู	smut grass
” ยาง	wild poinsettia
” ยางดง	Chinese sprangletop
หญ้ายุง	scented golden-beard
” รังตั๊กแตน	long-leaved paspalum
” รังนก	swollen finger grass
” รากหอม	common salomonia
” ร๊าด	diffuse panicgrass
” ละมานหางสั้น	Ridley's rice
” ละออง	little iron weed
” ลิ้นงู	old world diamond flower
” สะกาดน้ำเค็ม	knotgrass, couchgrass
” สามเหลี่ยม	triangular sedge
” แสงดำ	jaragua grass
” หนวดปลาดุก	globular fimbristylis, globe fringerush
” หนวดแมว	cat's whisker
หญ้าหวาน	stevia
” หวาย, หญ้าแพรกบัว	centipede grass, feather lovegrass
” หอม	pitted beargrass
” หัวขอ	summer rush
” หัวคอด	yellow-eyed grass
” หัวแดง	red star sedge
” หัวหงอก	pipe wort
” หางกระรอก	bristly foxtail
” หางแมว	cat's tail
” หางเสือ	threeawn
” หางหนู	three-spiked rush
” หางหมา	glossy wild sorghum
” หางหมาจิ้งจอก	knotroot foxtail

หญ้าเหนียวหมา	barbed grass
" เห็บ	sour paspalum
" แหวน	cat's tail grass
" แห้วหมู	purple nutsedge, nutgrass
" ไหวทาม	seashore grass
" อ้อน้อย	scrambling panic grass
หน้าวัว	flamino plant, anthurium
หนวดฤๅษี	common spear grass
หนาดใหญ่	camphor tree
หนามกระสุน	khaki weed (Amaranthaceae, *Atternanthera pungens* H.B.K), seeslip ground barnut, small caltrops, puncture vine (Zygophyllaceae, *Tribulus terrestris* L.)
หนามแดง	Natal plum, carunda, Christ's thorn
หมอน้อย, ผักกาดน้ำ	broad-leaf plantain
หม่อน	mulberry tree, white mulberry (Moraceae, *Morus alba* L.)
หม้อข้าวหม้อแกงลิง	pitcher plant
หมาก	betel nut, betel palm, areca palm
" แดง	sealing wax palm
" นวล	Manila palm, Merrill's palm
" ผู้หมากเมีย	good-luck plant, tree-of-kings
" เหลือง	yellow palm
หลิวดอก	bottlebrush
ห้วยชินสี	Indian toothcup
หว้า (หว้าขี้แพะ)	black plum
หวายตะมอย	pidgeon orchid
หัน	wild nutmeg
หัวใจม่วง	purple heart
หูกวาง	tropical almond
หูปลาช่อน	red tassel flower
เหงือกปลาหมอดอกขาว	sea holly
เห็ด	mushroom
" กระดุม (แชมปิญอง)	button mushroom, champignon (*Agaricus bisporus*)
	field mushroom (*A. campestris*)
	horse " (*A. arvensis*)
	wood " (*A. silvicola, A. silvestris*)
" ขมิ้น (มันปูใหญ่)	chanterelle
" ไข่ไก่	hen's egg mushroom

เห็ดไข่นก	grisette
" ไข่ห่าน	goose egg mushroom (*Amanita princeps*)
" โคน	termite mushroom (*Termitomyces sp.*)
" ชานหมาก	horse mushroom, field mushroom, wood mushroom
" แดง (น้ำหมาก)	red russula (*Russula rosacea*), **the sickener** (*Russula emetica*)
" ตับเต่า	cep, cepe, edible boletus
" ตีนตุ๊กแก	split gill mushroom
" ปะการังขาว (หูหนูขาว)	white coral mushroom (*Tremella fuciformis*)
" เป๋าฮื้อ	abalone mushroom
" เผาะ (เป๊าะ, เผาะ)	earth star (*Astracus hygrometricus*)
เห็ดฟาง	straw mushroom
" เม่น	wood hedgehog
" รังนกกระจิบ	bird's nest fungus (*Cyathus sp.*)
" รังแห	netted stinkhorn (*Dictyophora sp.*)
" ลม	lentinus
" หล่มกระเขียว	green russula (*Russula virescens*)
" หล่มขาว	milk white russula (*Russula delica*)
" หลินจื่อ	ganoderma, ling
" หอม	Shitake mushroom (*Lentinus edodes*)
" หอยนางรม	oyster mushroom
" หูหนู	Jew's ear, tree ear
เหลืองอินเดีย	yellow tabebuia
แหน	curly leaf pondweed
" แดง	giant duckweed, pinnate mosquito fern
" เป็ดเล็ก	duck meal
" เป็ดใหญ่	greater duckweed
" เล็ก	common duckweed
แห้วกระดาน	bulrush
" จีน	water chestnut
" ทรงกระเทียม	water chestnut
" ทรงกระเทียมเล็ก	needle spikerush
" หมู	nutgrass
โหระพา	sweet basil
องุ่น	grape
อบเชย	cinnamon tree
ออมเงิน	syngonium
อ้อ	giant reed
อ้อเล็ก	common reed

อ้อยแดง	sugar cane
อัญชัน	water morning glory, blue pea, butterfly pea
อันกะเหรี่ยง	hairy triumfetta
อินทนิล	pride of India
" น้ำ	queen's flower, queen's crape myrtle, pride of India
อีเหนียว	silverleaf desmodium
เอื้อง	denrobium
" ดิน	crepe ginger, spiral flag
" แมงมุม	scorpion orchid, spider orchid
" หมายนา	crepe ginger, spiral flag, Malay ginger (*Costus spp.* (Koen.) J.E. Smith)
ฮอมป่า	wild hops

ชื่อเหล่านี้เป็นชื่อสามัญของพืชที่พบในประเทศไทย

These are common names of plants found in Thailand. In special cases, scientific names have been added to aid identification.

Sources

กองบรรณาธิการวารสารบ้านและสวน. *สารานุกรมไม้ประดับในประเทศไทย.* หจก. วารสารบ้านและสวน, 2524.

ไม้และของป่าบางชนิดในประเทศไทย (หมวดชื่อในทางการค้า), กรมป่าไม้, 2491.

Pimsai Amaranand. *Gardening in Thailand.* Bangkok: The Siam Society.

กิตติกรณ์, ภูวิภาดาวรรธน์, รุจิเรขเสรีกุล, เชาวนปรีชา, วงวานิช, สรชาต. *รายชื่อพืชทั่วไป*, กองพืชไร่ กรมวิชาการเกษตร. กรุงเทพฯ, 2523.

Christiane Jacquat. *Plants from the Markets of Thailand.* Bangkok: Editions Duang Kamol, 1990.

Faculty of Pharmacy, Mahidol University. *Medicinal Plants in Siri Ruckhachati Garden.* Bangkok, 1992.

Tavatchai Radanachale and James F. Maxwell, Multiple Cropping Center. *List of Weeds Reported in Thailand.* Faculty of Agriculture, Chiang Mai University, 1992.

Chuakul, Saralamp, Paonil, Temsiri, Rirkkul, Clayton. *Medicinal Plants in Thailand.* Faculty of Pharmacy, Mahidol University, Bangkok, 1997.

M.R. Smansnid Svasti.

6
ชื่อปลาและสิ่งมีชีวิตใต้น้ำ อื่นๆ - Aquatic Life

กุ้งกระดาน	oriental flathead lobster (*Thenus orientalis*)
" จักจั่น	Spanish lobster (*Parribacus* spp.)
" ตั๊กแตน	mantis shrimp (fam. Squillidae)
กัลปังหา	sea fan, gorgonian (*Octocorallia*)
กุ้ง	shrimp, prawn (*Natantia*)
" กะต่อม	dwarf prawn (*Macrobrachium equidens*)
" ก้ามกราม	giant freshwater prawn (*Macrobrachium rosenbergii*)
" กุลาดำ	giant tiger prawn (*Penaeus monodon*)
" กุลาลาย	green tiger prawn (*Penaeus semisulcatus*)
" เคย	mysid shrimp (*Mysis* spp., *Acetes* spp.)
" แชบ๊วย	banana prawn (*Penaeus merguiensis*)
" ดีดขัน	snapping shrimp (fam. Alphaeidae)
" ตะกาด	greasy-back shrimp (*Metapenaeus ensis*)
" ฝอย	Lanchester's freshwater prawn (*Macrobrachium lanchesteri*)
" มังกร	spiny lobster (*Panulirus* spp.)
" มังกรประขาว	purplish brown spiny lobster (*Panulirus longipes*)
" มังกรหัวเขียว	painted spiny lobster (*Panulirus versicolor*)
" เหลืองหางฟ้า	bluetail yellow prawn (*Penaeus latisulcatus*)
จักจั่นทะเล	mole crab (*Emerita* spp., *Hippa* spp.)
ดอกไม้ทะเล	sea anemone (*Actininaria*)
" ทะเลครก	radianthus (*Radianthus* spp.)
" พรม	sea mat, zoanthid (*Zoanthus* spp.)
ดาวขนนก	feather star (*Crinoidea*)
" ทะเล	sea star, starfish (*Asteroidea*)
" เปราะ	brittle star, serpent star (*Ophiuroidea*)
" มงกุฎหนาม	crown-of-thorns starfish (*Acanthaster planci*)
" หมอนปักเข็ม	cushion star (*Culcita* spp.)
ตัวสงกรานต์	bristle worm (*Eunice* spp.)
เต่ากระ	hawksbill turtle (*Eretmochelys imbricata*)
" ตนุ	green turtle (*Chelonia mydas*)

เต่ามะเฟือง	**leatherback turtle** (*Dermochelys coriacea*)
" หญ้า	**olive ridley turtle** (*Lepidochelys olivacea*)
" หัวฆ้อน / เต่าตาแดง	**loggerhead turtle** (*Caretta caretta*)
ทากทะเล	**sea slug** (*Nudibranch*)
บุ้งทะเล	**fireworm** (fam. Amphinomidae)
ปลากด	**bagrid catfish** (fam. Bagridae)
" กดเกราะ	**sucker catfish** (*Hypostomus* spp., *Pterigoplichthys* spp.)
" กดแก้ว	**redtail catfish** (*Hemibagrus wickioides*)
" กดดำ	**whitetail catfish** (*Hemibagrus wickii*)
" กดทะเล	**sea catfish** (*Arius* spp.)
" กดเหลือง	**yellow bagrid catfish** (*Hemibagrus nemurus*)
" กดอเมริกัน	**channel catfish** (*Ictalurus punctatus*)
" กดอุก	**froghead sea-catfish** (*Hemipimelodus* spp.)
" กบ	**frogfish** (*Antennarius* spp.)
" กระดี่นาง	**moonbeam gourami** (*Trichogaster microlepis*)
ปลากระดี่มุก	**pearl gourami** (*Trichogaster leeri*)
" กระดี่หม้อ	**three-spot gourami** (*Trichogaster trichopterus*)
" กระดูกแข็ง	**bony fish**
" กระดูกอ่อน	**cartilaginous fish**
" กระบอก	**mullet** (fam. Mugilidae)
" กระบอกดำ	**greenback mullet** (*Chelon subviridis*)
" กระบอกท่อนไต้	**diamond-scale mullet** (*Ellochelon vaigiensis*)
" กระบอกยน	**ladyfish** (*Albula* spp.)
" กระบอกหางเขียว	**bluespot mullet** (*Moolgarda pedaraki*)
" กระบี่	**hairtail blenny** (*Xiphasia setifer*)
" กระเบนค้างคาว	**eagle ray** (*Aetomyleus* spp.)
ปลากระเบนจมูกโต	**cownose ray** (*Dasyatis kahlii*)
" กระเบนจุด	**Gerrad's stingray** (*Himantura gerradi*)
" กระเบนทอง	**blue-spot fantail stingray** (*Taeniura lymna*)
" กระเบนธง	**cowtail stingray** (*Pastinachus sephen*)
" กระเบนนก	**eagle ray** (*Aetomyleus* spp.)
" กระเบนไฟฟ้า	**numbfish, electric ray** (*Narcine* spp.)
" กระเบนราหู	**manta ray** (*Mobula* spp., *Manta birostris*)
" กระเบนลายแมลงวัน	**darkspotted stingray** (*Himantura uarnak*)
" กระโห้	**giant carp** (*Catlocarpio siamensis*)
" กราย	**clown featherback** (*Chitala ornata*)
" กริมควาย	**croaking gourami** (*Trichopsis vittatus*)
" กะตัก	**anchovy** (*Stolephorus* spp.)

ปลากะทิง	tire-track spiny eel (*Mastacembelus armatus*)
" กะทิงไฟ	spotted fire eel (*Mastacembelus erythrotaenia*)
" กะทุงเหว	needlefish (*Xenentodon cancila*)
" กะทุงเหวทะเล	hound needlefish (*Tylosurus crocodylus*)
" กะทุงเหวแบน	barred long tom (*Ablennes hians*)
" กะโทงแทง	marlin (*Makaira* spp.)
" กะโทงแทงดาบ	swordfish (*Xiphias gladius*)
" กะโทงแทงดำ	black marlin (*Makaira indica*)
" กะโทงร่ม	sailfish (*Istiophorus platypterus*)
" กะบาง	scaletail stingray (*Dasyatis imbricatus*)
" กะพง	snapper (fam. Lutjanidae)
" กะพงขาว	giant seaperch (*Lates calcarifer*)
" กะพงเขียว	green jobfish (*Aprion virescens*)
ปลากะพงแดง	red snapper (*Lutjanus malabaricus*)
" กะพงลาย	barred tigerfish (*Coius quadrifasciatus*)
" กะมัง	Smith's barb (*Puntioplites* spp.)
" กะเมาะ	wedgesnout mullet (*Moolgarda perusii*)
" กะแมะ	angler catfish (*Chaca bankanensis*)
" กะรังแดง	coral cod (*Cephalopholis miniatus*)
" กะรังลายน้ำเงิน	blue-lined rockcod (*Cephalopholis boenak*)
" กะรังหน้างอน	baramundi cod (*Cromileptes altivelis*)
" กะรังหัวโขน	stonefish (*Synanceia* spp.)
" กะรังหัวโขนดำ	stinger (*Inimicus* spp.)
" กะสง	eye-spot cheek snakehead (*Channa lucius*)
" กะสูบขีด	barred barb (*Hampala macrolepidota*)
" กะสูบจุด	eye-spot barb (*Hampala dispar*)
ปลากะแห	tinfoil barb (*Barbodes schwanenfeldi*)
" กัด	Siamese fighting fish (*Betta splendens*)
" กาดำ	sailfin carp, black sharkminnow (*Morulius chrysophekadion*)
" กาแดง	redfin shark (*Epalzeorhynchos frenatus*)
" ก้าง	dwarf snakehead (*Channa limbata*)
" ก้างพระร่วง	glass catfish (*Kryptopterus bicirrhis*)
" การ์ตูน	clownfish, anemonefish (*Amphiprion* spp.)
" การ์ตูนดำ	Clark's anemonefish (*Amphiprion clarki*)
" การ์ตูนส้ม	tomato anemonefish (*Amphiprion ephippium*)
" กินยุง	mosquito fish (*Gambusia holbrookii*)
" กุเรา	threadfin (fam. Polynemidae)
" กุแร	sardine (*Sardinella* spp.)

ปลาแก้มช้ำ	red-cheek barb (*Systomus orphroides*)
" ข่า	Irrawaddy dolphin (*Orcaella brevirostris*)
" ข้างตะเภา	crescent grunter (*Terapon jarboa*)
" ข้างใส	razor fish (*Aeoliscus* spp.)
" ข้างเหลือง	smoothed tail trevally (*Selaroides leptolepis*)
" ข้าวเม่า	glassfish (fam. Ambassidae)
" ข้าวเม่าน้ำลึก	squirrel fish (*Sargocentron* spp.)
" ขี้ตังเบ็ด	surgeonfish (fam. Acanthuridae)
" เข็ม	halfbeak (*Dermogenys* spp.)
" เขือ	blind goby (*Trypauchen* spp.)
" แขยงข้างลาย	striped catfish (*Mystus mysticetus*)
" แขยงธง	Bocourt's river catfish (*Heterobagrus bocourti*)
" แขยงนวล	estuarine mystus (*Mystus wolffii*)
ปลาแขยงใบข้าว	long-fin mystus (*Mystus singaringan*)
" แขยงหิน	bumblebee catfish (*Leiocassis siamensis*)
" ไข่มุก	pearl fish (*Carapus* spp.)
" ครีดคราด	javelin grunt (*Pomadasys* spp.)
" ค้อ	hillstream loach (fam. Balitoridae)
" คางเบือน	twisted-jaw sheatfish (*Belodontichthys dinema*)
" เค้าขาว	great white sheatfish (*Wallago atta*)
" เค้าดำ	black giant sheatfish (*Wallago leerii*)
" แค้ควาย	giant goonch (*Bagarius yarrelli*)
" โคก	gizzard shad (*Nematalosa* spp.)
" ไหลงู	snake eel (*Ophichthus* spp.)
" จวด	croaker, drumfish (fam. Scieanidae)
" จวดเทียน	tigertooth croaker (*Otolithoides ruber*)
ปลาจักรผาน	Indian halibut (*Psettodes erumei*)
" จาด	stream barb (*Poropuntius* spp.)
" จาน	spadefish (fam. Sparidae)
" จาระเม็ดขาว	silver pomfret (*Pampus argenteus*)
" จาระเม็ดดำ	black pomfret (*Parastromateus niger*)
" จาระเม็ดเทา	Chinese silver pomfret (*Pampus chinensis*)
" จิ้งจก	butterfly loach (*Balitora* spp.)
" จิ้งจอก	Siamese flying fox (*Epalzeorhynchos kalopterus*)
" จิ้มฟันจระเข้	pipefish (fam. Syngnathidae)
" จืด	stinging catfish (*Heteropneustes fossilis*)
" จุมพรวด	giant mudskipper (*Periophthalmodon schlosseri*)
" จูบ	albino kissing guarami (*Helostoma temmincki*)
" ฉนาก	sawfish (*Pristis* spp.)

ปลาฉลาม	**shark**
" ฉลามกบ	**nurseshark** (*Chiloscyllium* spp.)
" ฉลามวาฬ	**whale shark** (*Rhyncodon typus*)
" ฉลามเสือ	**tiger shark** (*Galeocerdo cuvier*)
" ฉลามหัวค้อน	**hammerhead shark** (*Sphyrna* spp.)
" ฉลามหัวบาตร	**bull shark** (*Carcharhinus leucus*)
" ฉลามหูดำ	**black-tip shark** (*Carcharhinus melanopterus*)
" เฉา	**grass carp** (*Ctenopharyngodon idellus*)
" โฉมงาม	**diamond trevally** (*Aleclis* spp.)
" ช่อน	**snakehead** (*Channa* spp.)
" ช่อนงูเห่า	**cobra snakehead** (*Channa marulia*)
" ช่อนทะเล	**cobia** (*Rachycentron canadum*)
" ชะโด	**giant snakehead** (*Channa micropeltes*)
ปลาชะโอน	**one-spot catfish** (*Ompok bimaculatus*)
" ช้างเหยียบ	**flathead** (fam. Platycephalidae)
" ซ่ง	**bighead carp** (*Hypophthalmichthys nobilis*)
" ซับขนุน	**false trevally** (*Lactarius lactarius*)
" ซาละเปา	**Indian drift** (*Ariomma indicum*)
" ซิว	**rasbora minnow** (*Rasbora* spp.)
" ซิวแก้ว	**Thai river sprat** (*Clupeichthys aesarnensis*)
" ซิวข้างขวาน	**harlequin fish** (*Rasbora heteromorpha*)
" ซิวข้าวสาร	**ricefish, medaka** (*Oryzius* spp.)
" ซิวควาย	**yellowtail rasbora** (*Rasbora tornieri*)
" ซิวใบไผ่	**pearl danio** (*Danio* spp.)
" ซิวหนวดยาว	**flying barb** (*Esomus* spp.)
" ซิวหางแดง	**redtail rasbora** (*Rasbora borapetensis*)
ปลาซิวอ้าว	**shark minnow** (*Luciosoma* spp.)
" ซีกเดียว	**flounder** (fam. Pleuronectidae)
" ญวน	**false trevally** (*Lactarius lactarius*)
" ดอกหมาก	**silverbiddy, mojarra** (*Gerres* spp.)
" ดัก	**torrent catfish** (*Amblyceps* spp.)
" ดาบเงิน	**hairtail** (*Trichiurus* spp.)
" ดาบลาว	**wolf herring** (*Chirocentrus dorab*)
" ดุกด้าน	**walking catfish**
" ดุกทะเล	**eel catfish** (fam. Plotosidae)
" ดุกอุย	**bighead walking catfish** (*Clarias macrocephalus*)
" ดุมซี	**leaffish** (*Nandus* spp.)
" แดง	**sheatfish** (*Micronema bleekeri*)
" ตองลาย	**royal featherback** (*Chitala blanci*)

ปลาตะกรับ	**spotted scat** (*Scatophagus argus*)
" ตะกรับลาย	**sergeant major** (*Abudefduf* spp.)
" ตะโกก	**soldier barb** (*Cyclocheilichthys enoplos*)
" ตะคองเหลือง	**golden trevally** (*Gnathanodon speciosus*)
" ตะพัด	**bonytongue** (*Scleropages formosus*)
" ตะพาก	**orange fin barb** (*Hypsibarbus wetmorei*)
" ตะเพียนขาว	**silver barb** (*Barbodes gonionotus*)
" ตะเพียนทอง	**red-fin barb** (*Barbodes altus*)
" ตะเพียนเทศ	**crucian carp** (*Carassius auratus*)
" ตะเพียนน้ำเค็ม	**gizzaro shad, kelee shad** (*Tenualosa kelee*)
" ตะลุมพุก	**toli shad** (*Tenualosa toli*)
" ตั๊กแตนหิน	**blenny** (fam. Blenniidae)
ปลาตับเต่า	**halfbeak** (fam. Hemiramphidae)
" ตาโต	**bigeye** (*Priacanrhus* spp.)
" ตาใส	**Greenway's barb** (*Mystacoleucus greenwayi*)
" ตาหวาน	**bigeye** (*Priacanrhus* spp.)
" ตาเหลือกสั้น	**Indo-Pacific tarpon** (*Megalops cyprinoides*)
" ตาแหงน	**grubfish** (*Parapercis* spp.)
" ตีน	**mudskipper** (*Boleophthalmus* spp.)
" ตุ๊ดตู่	**jewfish** (*Opistognathus* spp.)
" ตูหนา	**eel, true eel** (*Anguilla bicolor*)
" ทรงเครื่อง	**red-tail shark** (*Epalzeorhynchos bicolor*)
" ทรายขาว	**monocle bream** (*Scolopsis* spp.)
" ทรายแดง	**threadfin bream** (*Nemipterus* spp.)
" ทอง	**goldfish** (*Carassius auratus*)
ปลาท้องพลุ	**leaping barb** (*Chela laubuca*)
" ทะเล	**marine fish**
" ทู	**chub mackerel, short mackerel** (*Rastelliger brachysoma*)
" ทูแขก	**round scad** (*Decapterus* spp.)
" ทูน่า	**tuna** (*Thunnas* spp.)
" ทูน่าปากกว้าง	**dogtooth tuna** (*Gymnosarda unicolor*)
" เทพา	**Chaophraya giant catfish** (*Pangasius sanitwongsei*)
" เทโพ	**black-eared catfish** (*Pangasius larnaudi*)
" เทวดา	**angelfish** (*Pterophyllum scalare*)
" นกกระจอก	**flying fish** (fam. Exocoetidae)
" นกแก้ว	**parrot fish** (fam. Scaridae)
" นกขุนทอง	**wrasse** (fam. Labridae)
" นกขุนทองเขี้ยว	**tuskfish** (*Choerodon* spp.)

ปลานกขุนทองพยาบาล	cleaner wrasse (*Labroides dimidiatus*)
" นกขุนทองหัวโหนก	humphead wrasse (*Cheilinus undulatus*)
" นกฮูกปีกจุด	helmet gurnard (*Dactyloptena orientalis*)
" นวลจันทร์ทะเล	milkfish (*Chanos chanos*)
" นวลจันทร์น้ำจืด	mrigal (*Cirrhinus mrigala*)
" นางอ้าว	salmon carp (*Raiamas guttatus*)
" น้ำกร่อย	estuarine fish
" น้ำเงิน	silver sheatfish (*Micronema apogon*)
" น้ำจืด	freshwater fish
" น้ำหมึก	stream barillius (*Opsarius* spp.)
" นิล	Nile tilapia (*Orechromis miloticus*)
" เนื้ออ่อน	sheatfish (fam. Siluridae)
" โนรี	bannerfish (*Heniochus* spp.)
ปลาไน	common carp (*Cyprinus carpio*)
" ไนแฟนซี	fancy carp, Nishigi koi (*Cyprinus carpio*)
" บ้า	sultanfish (*Leptobarbus hoeveni*)
" บึก	Mekong giant catfish (*Pangasianodon gigas*)
" บู่	goby (fam. Gobiidae)
" บู่เกล็ดแข็ง	flathead sleeper (fam. Eleotrididae)
" บู่ทราย	marbled sleeper (*Oxyeleotris marmoratus*)
" บู่เสือ	bumblebee goby (*Brachygobius* spp.)
" บู่ใส	dwarf goby (*Gobiopterus* spp.)
" บู่หมาจู	bumblebee goby (*Brachygobius doriae*)
" ใบขนุน	spinefoot (*Siganus* spp.)
" ใบไม้	sole (fam. Soleidae)
" ปล้องอ้อย	Kuhli's loach (*Pangio kuhlii*)
ปลาปอมปาดัวร์	discus (*Symphysodon* spp.)
" ปักเป้า	blowfish, puffer
" ปักเป้าจุดดำ	star puffer (*Arothron stellatus*)
" ปักเป้าซีลอน	Ceylon number-eight puffer (*Monotreta biocellarus*)
" ปักเป้าหนาม	porcupinefish (*Diodon* spp.)
" ปากคม	lizardfish (*Saurida* spp.)
" ปิรันย่า	piranha (*Serrasalmus* spp.)
" แป้น	ponyfish (*Leiognathus* spp.)
" แป้นแก้ว	glassfish (fam. Ambassidae)
" แปบ	abramine (*Paralaubuca* spp.)
" ผมนาง	longfin trevally (*Carangoides armatus*)
" ผีเสื้อ	butterflyfish (fam. Chaetodontidae)
" ผีเสื้อกลางคืน	sea moth (fam. Pegasidae)

ปลาผีเสื้อติดหิน	**sucker loach** (*Homaloptera* spp.)
″ ผีเสื้อเทวรูป	**moorish idol** (*Zanclus cornutus*)
″ ผีเสื้อปากยาว	**longnose butterflyfish** (*Chelmon rostratus*)
″ ผีเสื้อลายแปดเส้น	**eight-banded butterflyfish** (*Chaetodon octofasciatus*)
″ ฝักพร้า	**greater abramine** (*Macrochirichthys macrochirus*)
″ พรม	**giant bonylip carp** (*Osteochilus melanopleura*)
″ พลวง	**brook carp** (*Neolissochilus* spp.)
″ พาคู	**pacu** (*Colossoma* spp.)
″ แพะ	**goatfish** (fam. Mullidae)
″ มังกรน้อย	**dragonet** (fam. Callionymidae)
″ ม้า	**smallscale croaker** (*Boesemania microlepis*)
″ ม้าน้ำ	**seahorse** (*Hippocampus* spp.)
ปลาแมงป่อง	**scorpionfish** (fam. Scorpaenidae)
″ แมว	**sabertooth thryssa** (*Setipinna* spp.)
″ แมวหูดำ	**hairfin anchovy** (*Setipinna melanochir*)
″ ยอดม่วง	**tongue sole** (*Cynoglossus* spp.)
″ ยี่สกทอง	**golden giant carp** (*Probarbus jullieni*)
″ ยี่สกเทศ	**rohu** (*Labeo rohita*)
″ ร่องไม้ตับ	**striped bonylip carp, bonylip barb** (*Osteochilus microcephalus*)
″ รากกล้วย	**horseface loach** (*Acanthopsis* spp.)
″ ราหูน้ำจืด	**Chaophraya giant stingray** (*Himantura chaophraya*)
″ ริวกิว	**sea catfish** (*Arius thalassinus*)
″ แรด	**giant gourami** (*Osphronemus goramy*)
ปลาโรนัน	**guitar fish, shovelnose ray** (*Rhynchobatus* spp.)
″ โรนิน	**sharkray** (*Rhina ancylostoma*)
″ ลัง	**Indian mackerel** (*Rastelliger kanagurta*)
″ ลิ่น	**silver carp** (*Hypophthalmichthys molitrix*)
″ ลิ้นควาย	**flounder** (fam. Pleuronectidae)
″ ลิ้นหมา	**tongue sole, tonguefish** (fam. Cynoglossidae, Soleidae)
″ เล็บมือนาง	**flying fox** (*Crossocheilus reticulatus*)
″ เลียหิน	**stoneroller** (*Garra* spp.)
″ วัว	**triggerfish** (fam. Balistidae)
″ วัวสามเงี่ยง	**tripodfish** (fam. Triacanthidae)
″ วัวหางติด	**leatherjacket** (fam. Monacanthidae)
″ เวียน	**greater brook carp, marsheer** (*Tor* spp.)

ปลาสยุมพร	**one-spot catfish** (*Ompok bimaculatus*)
" สร้อยขาว	**mud carp** (*Henicorhynchus* spp.)
" สร้อยนกเขา	**bony-lipped barb** (*Osteochilus* spp.)
" สร้อยนกเขาทะเล	**sweetlip** (*Plectorhynchus* spp.)
" สร้อยน้ำผึ้ง / ปลาอีดูด	**honey sucker** (*Gyrinocheilus aymonieri*)
" สละ	**queenfish** (*Scomberoides commersoniana*)
" สลาด	**brown featherback** (*Notopterus notopterus*)
" สลิด	**snakeskin gourami, sepat Siam** (*Trichogaster pectoralis*)
" สลิดทะเล	**damselfish** (fam. Pomacentridae)
" สลิดหิน	**rabbitfish** (*Siganus* spp.)
" สวาย	**irridescent shark-catfish** (*Pangasianodon hypophthalmus*)
ปลาสอด	**swordtail** (*Xiphophorus* spp.)
" สะตือ	**giant featherback** (*Chitala lopis*)
" สังกะวาด	**yellow Siamese catfish** (*Pangasius macronema*)
" สาก / ปลาน้ำดอกไม้	**baracuda** (*Sphyraena* spp.)
" สำลี	**black-banded kingfish** (*Seriolina nigrofasciata*)
" สิงห์โต	**lionfish** (*Pterois* spp.)
" สินสมุทร	**angelfish** (*Pomacanthus* spp.)
" สีกุน	**trevally, jack** (fam. Carangidae)
" สีกุนกลม	**smallmouth scad** (*Alepes* spp.)
" สีขน	**giant trevally** (*Caranx* spp.)
" เสือข้างลาย	**banded barb** (*Systomus partipentazona*)
" เสือดำ	**leaf fish** (*Nandus* spp.)
" เสือตอ	**tiger perch** (*Coius microlepis*)
ปลาเสือพ่นน้ำ	**archer fish** (*Toxotes* spp.)
" เสือสุมาตรา	**tiger barb** (*Systomus tetrazona*)
" ไส้ตันตาขาว	**apogon** (*Cyclocheilichthys repasson*)
" ไส้ตันตาแดง	**redeye apogon** (*Cyclocheilichthys apogon*)
" หนวดพราหมณ์	**paradise threadfin** (*Polynemus longipectoralis*)
" หนามหลัง	**spiny barb** (*Mystacoleucus* spp.)
" หน้าหงส์	**Indian threadfin** (*Polynemus indicus*)
" หมอ	**climbing perch** (*Anabas testudineus*)
" หมอช้างเหยียบ	**catopra** (*Pristolepis fasciatus*)
" หมอตาล	**kissing gourami** (*Helostoma temmincki*)
" หมอเทศ	**Mozambique tilapia** (*Oreochromis mossambicus*)
" หมู	**botia loach, spiny loach** (*Botia* spp.)
" หมูคอก	**skunk loach** (*Botia morleti*)

ปลาหมูสี	emperor (fam. Lethrinidae)
" หลด	spiny eel (*Macrognathus* spp.)
" หลังเขียว	sardine (*Sardinella* spp.)
" หลังเขียวกลม	rainbow sardine (*Amblygaster* spp.)
" หัวแข็ง	silverside (fam. Atherinidae)
" หัวตะกั่ว	blue panchax (*Aploicheilus panchax*)
" หางไก่	grenadier anchovy (*Coilia* spp.)
" หางแข็ง	jack, trevally (fam. Carangidae)
" หางธง	flagtail (*Kuhlia* spp.)
" หางนกยูง	guppy (*Poecilia reticulata*)
ปลาหางบ่วง	golden carp (*Barbicthys nitidus*)
" หางไหม้	bala shark (*Balantiocheilos melanopterus*)
" หูช้าง	batfish (*Platax* spp.)
" เห็ดโคน	sand whiting (*Sillago* spp.)
" เหาฉลาม	shark sucker, remora (*Echeneis naucrates*)
" เหลืองปล้อง	fusilier (fam. Caesionidae)
" ไหลนา	swamp eel (*Monopterus albus*)
" อมไข่	cardinal fish (fam. Apogonidae)
" ออสการ์	oscar (*Astronotus ocellatus*)
" อ้าว	salmon carp (*Raiamas guttatus*)
" อินทรีจุด	spotted Spanish mackerel (*Scomberomorus guttatus*)
ปลาอินทรีช้าง	wahoo (*Acanthocybium solandri*)
" อินทรีบั้ง	Spanish mackerel (*Scomberomorus commerson*)
" อีกง	estuarine mystus (*Mystus gulio*)
" อีคุด	porgy, sea bream (fam. Sparidae)
" อีด	eel loach (*Pangio* spp.)
" อีโต้มอญ	dolphinfish (*Coryphaenus hippurus*)
" อีปุด	ilisha (*Ilisha* spp.)
" อีมุด	cownose guitarfish (*Rhinobatos thouini*)
" อุก	toadfish (fam. Batrachoididae)
" อุนรุทธ์	coral grouper (*Plectopomus* spp.)
" โอกล้วย	frigate tuna (*Auxis thazard*)
" โอดำ	longtail tuna (*Thunnus tonggol*)
" โอแถบ	skipjack (*Katsuwonis pelamis*)
" โอลาย	mackerel tuna (*Euthynnus affinis*)
ปลิงควาย	leech (*Hirudo* spp.)
" ทะเล	sea cucumber (*Holothuria* spp.)
ปะการัง	stony coral (*Scleractinian*)

ปะการังเขากวาง	**staghorn coral** (*Acropora* spp.)
" โขดหิน	**hump coral** (*Porites* spp.)
" ช่อง	**pore coral** (*Favites* spp.)
" ดอกไม้	**anemone coral** (*Euphyllia* spp.)
" ดาว	**starflower coral** (*Diploastrea* spp.)
" ผักกาด	**leaf coral** (*Montipora* spp.)
" ไฟ	**fire coral** (*Millepora* spp.)
" หินส้ม	**red tube coral** (*Tubastrea coccinea*)
" เห็ด	**mushroom coral** (*Fungia* spp.)
" อ่อน	**soft coral** (*Stoloniferan*)
ปากกาทะเล	**sea pen** (*Pteroeides* spp.)
ปูไก่	**land crab** (fam. Gecarcinidae)
" จั๊กจั่น	**spanner crab** (*Ranina ranina*)
" เจ้าฟ้า	**panda crab** (*Phricothelphusa sirindhorn*)
" ดาว	**three-spot swimming crab** (*Portunus sanguino-lentus*)
" ทะเล	**mud crab, blue crab** (*Scylla* spp.)
" ทูลกระหม่อม	**mealy crab** (*Thaipotamon chulabhorn*)
" นา	**paddy-field crab** (fam. Paratelphusidae)
" น้ำตก	**waterfall crab** (fam. Potamidae)
" ใบ้	**rock crab, spooner** (fam. Xanthidae)
" เปี้ยว	**fiddler crab** (*Uca* spp.)
" มะพร้าว	**coconut crab, robber carb** (*Birgus latro*)
" ม้า	**blue swimming crab** (*Portunus pelagicus*)
ปูแมงมุม	**spider crab** (fam. Majidae)
" ราชินี	**tricolor crab** (*Thaiphusa sirikit*)
" ฤาษี	**box crab** (*Calappa* spp.)
" ลม	**ghost crab** (*Ocypode ceratophthalma*)
" ลาย	**crucifix crab** (*Charybdis cruciata*)
" เสฉวน	**hermit crab** (fam. Paguridae, Coenobitidae)
" แสม	**mangrove crab, vinegar crab** (*Episesarma* spp.)
" แสมหิน	**sally light-foot crab** (*Grapsus* spp.)
" หนุมาน	**moon crab** (*Matuta* spp.)
" หิน	**ridge swimming crab** (*Charybdis natator*)
เป๋าฮื้อ	**abalone** (*Haliotis* spp.)
พรมทะเล	**sea mat, zoanthid** (*Polythoa* spp.)
พะยูน	**dugong, sea cow** (*Dugong dugong*)
เพรียง	**barnacle** (*Balanus* spp.)
" คอห่าน	**goose barnacle** (*Lepas* spp.)

เพรียงเจาะไม้	ship worm (*Teredo* spp.)
" หัวหอม	sea squirt (*Ascidians*)
ฟองน้ำ	sponge (*Phylum Porifera*)
" ครก	barrel sponge (*Xestospongia* spp.)
" ถูตัว	commercial sponge (*Spongia* spp.)
ม้าน้ำ	seahorse (*Hippocampus* spp.)
เม่นทะเล	sea urchin (*Echinoidea*)
" แท่งดินสอ	slate pencil urchin (*Phyllacanthus* spp.)
" หัวใจ	heart urchin (*Lovenia* spp.)
แมงกะพรุน	jellyfish (*Scyphozoa*)
" ไฟ	stinging jellyfish (*Cyanea* spp.)
" ไฟขวดเขียว	Portugese man-of-war (*Physalia physalis*)
" หนัง	commercial jellyfish (*Rhopilema* spp.)
" เหรียญ	porpita (*Porpita porpita*)
" ลอดช่อง	commercial jellyfish (*Lobonema* sp.)
แมงดาทะเล	horseshoe crab (*Carcinoscorpius rotundicanda*)
แมงดาหางเหลี่ยม	giant king crab (*Tachypleus gigas*)
แม่เพรียง	bristle worm, king ragworm (*Eunice* spp., *Polychaete*)
แมลงสาบทะเล	sea slater (*Lygia* spp.)
ลิ้นทะเล	chiton (*Polyplacophora*)
โลมาแกลบ	spinner dolphin (*Stenella longirostris*)
" จุด	spotted dolphin (*Stenella attenuata*)
" แถบ	striped dolphin (*Stenella coeruleoalba*)
" ทะเลลึก	common dolphin (*Delphinus delphis*)
" ปากขวด	bottlenose dolphin (*Tursiops aduncus*)
" เผือก	Indo-Pacific humpback dolphin (*Sousa chinensis*)
" หัวบาตรหลังเรียบ	finless porpoise (*Neophocaena phocaenoides*)
" อิระวดี	Irrawaddy dolphin (*Orcaella brevinostris*)
วาฬแกลบ	Bryde's whale (*Balaenoptera edeni*)
" เพชฌฆาต	killer whale (*Orcinus orca*)
" เพชฌฆาตแปลง	false killer whale (*Pseudorca crassidens*)
" หัวทุย	sperm whale (*Physeter macrocephalus*)
" หัวทุยแคระ	Pigmy sperm whale (*Kogia breviceps*)
ไส้เดือนทะเล	clamworm , king ragworm (*Polychaete*)
หนอนฉัตร	Christmas tree worm (*Spirobranchus giganteus*)
" ถั่ว	pea worm (*Sipunculid*)
" ริบบิ้น	flatworm (*Polyclad*)
" สายพาน	ribbon worm (*Nemertea*)

หมึกกระดอง	**cuttlefish** (*Sepia* spp.)
หมึกยักษ์	**octopus** (fam. Octopidae)
หวีวุ้น	**comb jelly** (*Ctenophora*)
หอยกระดุม	**olive shell** (*Oliva* spp.)
″ กระต่าย	**bonnet shell** (*Phalium* spp.)
″ กระปุก	**troughshell** (*Mactra* spp.)
″ กะพง	**horse mussel** (*Modiolus* spp.)
″ ก้างปลา	**murex** (*Murex* spp.)
″ กาบ	**clam** (*Bivalvia*)
″ ขม	**pond snail, viviparous snail** (*Filopaludina* spp.)
″ ขวาน / หอยกีบม้า	**marsh clam** (*Corbicula* spp.)
″ ขี้ค้อน	**telescope snail** (*Telescopium telescopium*)
″ ขี้นก	**periwinkle** (*Littorina* spp.)
″ โข่ง	**apple snail** (*Pila* spp.)
หอยไข่นกกระทา	**bubble** (*Bulla* spp.)
″ ครองแครง	**marginella** (*Marginella* spp.)
″ คันธนู	**spindle cowry** (fam. Ovulidae)
″ แครง	**granular ark, blood cockle** (*Anadara granosa*)
″ แครงน้ำลึก	**hooked ark** (*Cucullaea labiata*)
″ งวงช้าง	**pearly nautilus** (*Nautilus pompilius*)
″ งวงช้างกระดาษ	**paper nautilus** (*Argonauta* spp.)
″ งาช้าง	**tusk shell** (*Dentalium* spp.)
″ เงาะ	**ramose murex** (*Chiconeus romusus*)
″ จอบ	**flag penshell** (*Atrina vexillum*)
″ จำปี	**miter** (*Mitra* spp., *Vexillum* spp.)
″ จุ๊บแจง	**cerith** (*Cerithium* spp.)
″ ชักตีน	**conch** (*Strombus* spp.)
หอยเชลล์	**moon scallop** (*Amusium pleuronctes*)
″ เชลล์สี	**scallops** (fam. Pectinidae)
″ ซองพลู	**pen shell** (*Pinna* spp.)
″ ตลับ	**Venus clam** (*Meretrix* spp.)
″ ตลับลาย	**Asiatic hard clam** (*Meretrix meretrix*)
″ ตะโกรม	**cup oyster** (*Saccostrea cucullata*)
″ ตาล	**baler shell** (*Melo melo*)
″ ตาวัว	**turban shell** (*Turbo* spp.)
″ ตุ๊กแก	**maculated ivory whelk** (*Babylonia areolata*)
″ เต้าปูน	**cone shell** (*Conus* spp.)
″ เต้าปูนไทย	**glory-of-Thailand cone** (*Conus thailandis*)
″ เต้าปูนเบงกอล	**glory-of-Bengal cone** (*Conus bengalensis*)

หอยเต้าปูนลายผ้า	textile cone (*Conus textile*)
" เต้าปูนลายแผนที่	geographic cone (*Conus geographus*)
" ทะนาน	tun shell (*Tonna* spp.)
" ทากลาย	African giant snail (*Achatina fulica*)
" เท้าช้าง	horned helmet (*Cassis cornata*)
" นมสาว	commercial top shell (*Trochus niloticus*)
" นางรม	oyster, hooded oyster (*Saccostrea cuccullata*)
" นางรมลอย	pearl oyster (*Pteria* spp.)
" นางรมหนาม	spiny oyster (*Spondylus* spp.)
" น้ำพริก	nerite (fam. Neritidae)
" เบี้ย	cowry (*Cypraea* spp.)
" เบี้ยแก้	serpent's head cowry (*Cypraea caputserpentis*)
" เบี้ยควาย	Arabian cowry (*Cypraea arabica*)
หอยเบี้ยจั่น	money cowry (*Cypraea moneta*)
" เบี้ยโป่งเสือ	tiger cowry (*Cypraea tigris*)
" ปากเป็ด	tongue shell (*Lingula* spp.)
" ปิ่น	spindle shell (*Fusinus* spp.)
" ปีกนางฟ้า	Lister's conch (*Strombus listeri*)
" แปดเกล็ด	chiton (*Polyplacophora*)
" ฝากลม	gastropods
" ฝาคู่	bivalve
" พัด	scallop (fam. Pectinidae)
" ม่วง	violet snail (*Janthina prolongata*)
" มวนพลู	turret shell (*Territella terebra*)
" มะเฟือง	harp shell (*Harpa* spp.)
" มะระ	drupe shell (*Drupa* spp.)
หอยมือเสือ	giant clam (*Tridacna* spp.)
" มือหมี	horsehoof, giant clam (*Hippopus hippopus*)
" มุก	mother-of-pearl oyster (*Pinctada margaritifera*)
" มุกไฟ	green turban (*Turbo marmorata*)
" แมงป่อง	scorpion conch (*Lambis scorpius*)
" แมลงภู่	green mussel (*Perna viridis*)
" ร้อยรู	abalone (*Haliotis* spp.)
" ลาย	baby clam (*Paphia undulata*)
" ลูกข่าง	top shell (*Trochus maculatus*)
" เล็บมือนาง	spider conch (*Lambis* spp.)
" สังข์	Indian chank, sacred chank (*Turbinella pyrum*)
" สังข์จุกพราหมณ์	noble volute (*Cymbiola nobilis*)
" สังข์แตร	triton trumpet (*Charonia tritonis*)

หอยสังข์หนาม	murex shell (*Murex* spp.)
" สังข์หอม	horse conch (*Pleuroploca* spp.)
" เสียบ	wedge shell, bean shell (*Donax* spp.)
" หมวกเจ๊ก	limpet (fam. Patellidae)
หอยหลอด	razor clam (fam. Solenidae)
" เหล็กมาด	auger shell (*Terebra* spp.)
เห็ดทะเล	mushroom anemone (*Heteractis* spp.)
อีแปะทะเล	sand dollar (*Peronella* spp.)

ชื่อเหล่านี้เป็นชื่อสามัญตามองค์การอาหารและเกษตรแห่งสหประชาชาติ และชื่อทางการค้าและวิทยาศาสตร์ของปลาและสัตว์น้ำอื่นๆ ที่พบในประเทศไทย

These are the FAO-listed common names and commercial and scientific names of notable fish, molluscs, coral and other aquatic animals (fauna) found in Thailand.

Sources

ชวลิต วิทยานนท์, **สถาบันพิพิธภัณฑ์สัตว์น้ำ**, กรมประมง

Vidthayanon, C., Karnasuta, K. and Nabhitabhata, J. ***Diversity of Freshwater Fishes in Thailand.*** Museum & Aquarium Div. Techn. Paper No. 5 Dept. Fisheries/Office of Environmental Policy and Planning, Bangkok, 102 p., 1997.

Allen, G.R. ***Marine Fishes of South-East Asia.*** Periplus Editions, 1997.

Carpenter, K.E. and Niem, V.H.(eds) ***FAO Species Identification Guide for Fishery Purposes.*** The living marine resources of the Western Central Pacific. Vol. 1; Seaweeds, corals, bivalves and gastropods and Vol. 2; Cephalopods, crustaceans, holothurians and sharks, 1998.

7

ชื่อภูมิศาสตร์ - Geographical Names

ก

กรณาฏกะ	Karnataka
กระบี่	Krabi
กรีซ, สาธารณรัฐเฮลเลนิก	Greece, Hellenic Republic
กรีนแลนด์, กะลาลลิตนูนาต	Greenland, Kalaallit Nunaat
กรุงเทพมหานคร	Bangkok, Krung Thep Maha Nakhon, Bangkok Metropolis
กลันตัน	Kelantan
กลารัส	Glarus
กลุ่มเกาะซูลู	Sulu Archipelago
" ติแอร์ราเดลฟูเอโก	Tierra del Fuego
" มะริด	Mergui Archipelago
" รีอู	Riouw Archipelago
" ลุยซิแอด	Louisiade Archipelago
กวนตัน	Kuantan
กวม	Guam
กว่างตง, กวางตุ้ง	Guangdong, Kwangtung
กวาเดอลูป	Guadeloupe
กว่างซีจ้วง	Guangxi Zhuang, Kwangsi Chuang
กอตฮอบ, นุก	Godthab, Nuk
กะฉิ่น	Kachin
กะยา	Kayah
กะเหรี่ยง	Karen
กังการ์	Kangar
กังต็อก	Gangtok
กัมปาลา	Kampala
กัมพูชา : ราชอาณาจักรกัมพูชา	Cambodia, Kingdom of Cambodia
กัลกัตตา	Calcutta
กัว	Goa
กัวเตมาลา, สาธารณรัฐกัวเตมาลา	Guatemala, Republic of Guatemala
กัวเตมาลาซิตี	Guatemala City
กัวลาตรังกานู	Kuala Trengganu
กัวลาลัมเปอร์	Kuala Lumpur

ก

กัวลาลิปิส	Kuala Lipis
กาญจนบุรี	Kanchanaburi
กาฐมาณฑุ	Kathmandu
กาตาร์, รัฐกาตาร์	Qatar, State of Qatar
กานา, สาธารณรัฐกานา	Ghana, Republic of Ghana
กานซู	Gansu, Kansu
กาบอง, สาธารณรัฐกาบอง	Gabon, Gabonese Republic
กาโบโรเน	Gaborone
กาเยน	Cayenne
กายอานา, สาธารณรัฐสหกรณ์กายอานา	Guyana, Cooperative Republic of Guyana
กาฬสินธุ์	Kalasin
กำแพงเพชร	Kamphaeng Phet
กินชาซา	Kinshasa
กินี, สาธารณรัฐกินี	Guinea, Republic of Guinea
กินีบิสเซา, สาธารณรัฐกินีบิสเซา	Guinea Bissau, Republic of Guinea Bissau
กุ้ยหยาง	Guiyang, Kuei-yang
กุ้ยโจว	Guizhou, Kweichow
กูชิง	Kuching
เกรเนดา	Grenada
เกรละ	Kerala
เกาหลีใต้, สาธารณรัฐเกาหลี	South Korea, Republic of Korea
เกาหลีเหนือ, สาธารณรัฐ ประชาธิปไตยประชาชนเกาหลี	North Korea, Democratic People's Republic of Korea
เกาะกวม	Guam
” กวาเดอลูป	Guadeloupe
” กอตแลนด์	Gotland
” กัวดัลคะแนล	Guadalcanal
” เกรเนดา	Grenada
” เกอร์นซี	Guernsey
” แกรนด์คานารี	Grand Canary
” แกรนด์บาฮามา	Grand Bahama
” คริสต์มาส	Christmas Island
” ครีต	Crete
” คอร์ซิกา	Corsica
” คอร์ฟู	Corfu
” คาปรี	Capri
” คิวชู	Kyushu
” คิวบา	Cuba
” คูราเซา	Curacao

ก

เกาะเคปเบรตัน	Cape Breton
" เคาไอ	Kauai
" จาเมกา	Jamaica
" เจอร์ซี	Jersey
" ชวา	Java
" ชัวเซิล	Choiseul
" ชิโกกุ	Shikoku
" ซามอส	Samos
" ซามาร์	Samar
" ซาโมทรากิ	Samothraki
" ซาร์ดิเนีย	Sardinia
" ซิซิลี	Sicily
" ซีแลนด์	Zealand
เกาะซุมบา	Soemba
" ซุมบาวา	Soembawa
" เซนต์คริสโตเฟอร์	St. Christopher
" เซนต์โธมัส	St. Thomas
" เซนต์แมตธิว	St. Matthew
" เซนต์ลูเซีย	St. Lucia
" เซนต์วินเซนต์	St. Vincent
" เซนต์เฮเลนา	St. Helena
" เซบู	Cebu
" เซลีเบส	Celebes
" แซคาลิน	Sakhalin
" แซนซิบาร์	Zanzibar
" ไซปรัส	Cyprus
เกาะไซปัน	Saipan
" โดมินิกา	Dominica
" ตรินิแดด	Trinidad
" ตริสตานดาคุนยา	Tristan da Cunha
" ตรุก	Truk
" ตาฮีตี	Tahiti
" ติมอร์	Timor
" เตเนรีฟ	Tenerife
" โตเบโก	Tobago
" ไต้หวัน, เกาะฟอร์โมซา	Taiwan, Formosa
" ทาซอส	Thasos
" แทสเมเนีย	Tasmania
" นอร์ฟอล์ก	Norfolk Island

ก

เกาะนาอูรู	Nauru
” นิวกินี, เกาะปาปัว	New Guinea, Papua
” นิวบริเตน	New Britain
” นิวฟันด์แลนด์	Newfoundland
” เนกรอส	Negros
” แนกซอส	Naxos
” บอร์เนียว	Borneo
” บาซิลัน	Basilan
” บาร์บูดา	Barbuda
” บาร์เบโดส	Barbados
” บาห์เรน	Bahrain, Bahrein
” บาหลี	Bali
” บิลลิตัน	Billiton
เกาะบูแกงวิล	Bougainville
” ปัตมอส	Patmos
” ปันเตลลาเรีย	Pantellaria
” ปีนัง	Penang
” ปูลูกองดอร์	Poulo Condore
” แพลไมรา	Palmyra
” ฟลอเรส	Flores
” มอริเชียส, เกาะมอโรไต	Mauritius, Morotai
” มอลตา	Malta
” มาจอร์กา	Majorca
” มาดากัสการ์	Madagascar
” มาดูรา	Madoera
” มาร์ตินีก	Martinique
เกาะมินดาเนา	Mindanao
” มินโดโร	Mindoro
” มินอร์กา	Minorca
” มิลอส	Milos
” เมาอี	Maui
” แมน	Isle of Man
” โมโลไค	Molokai
” ไมโกนอส	Mykonos
” แย็ป	Yap
” ราโรตองกา	Rarotonga
” ริวกิว, เกาะลูชู	Ryukyu, Luchu Islands
” เรอูเนียง	Réunion
” โรดส์	Rhodes

ก

เกาะโรตา	Rota
" ลังกา	Ceylon
" ลังเกแลนด์	Langeland
" ลันซาโรเต	Lanzarote
" ลาไน	Lanai
" ลาบวน	Labuan
" ลูซอน	Luzon
" เลเต	Leyte
" เลมนอส	Lemnos
" เลรอส	Leros
" เลสบอส, เกาะมิติลินี	Lesbos, Mitylene
" เวก	Wake Island
" ไวท์	Isle of Wight
" สโกปีลอส	Skopelos
" สแปรตลี	Spratly
" สาร์ก	Sark
เกาะสุมาตรา	Sumatra
" อันดรอส	Andros
" อันติกัว	Antigua
" อัสเซนชัน	Ascension
" อิทะกา	Ithaca
" อิวีซา	Iviza
" อีลิวเธอรา	Eleuthera
" เอลบา	Elba
" เออแลนด์	Öland
" แอนดรอส	Andros
" แอมบอยนา	Amboina
" โอแลนด์	Åland
" โออาฮู	Oahu
" ฮอกไกโด	Hokkaido
" ฮอนชู, เกาะฮอนโด	Honshu, Hondo
" ฮิสแปนิโอลา, เกาะเฮติ	Hispaniola, Haiti
แกมเบีย, สาธารณรัฐแกมเบีย	Gambia, Republic of Gambia
โกตดิวัวร์, สาธารณรัฐโกตดิวัวร์	Cote D'Ivoire, Republic of Cote D'Ivoire
โกตากินะบะลู	Kota Kinabalu
โกตาบารู	Kota Bharu
โกนากรี	Conakry
โกหิมา	Kohima

ข

ขอนแก่น	Khon Kaen

ค

คลองสาน	Khlong San
ควิเบก	Quebec
ควีนส์แลนด์	Queensland
คองคอร์ด	Concord
คองโก, สาธารณรัฐคองโก	Congo, Republic of the Congo
คอโมโรส, สหพันธ์สาธารณรัฐ อิสลามคอโมโรส	Comoros, Federal Islamic Republic of the Comoros
คอรอร์	Koror
คอสตาริกา, สาธารณรัฐคอสตาริกา	Costa Rica, Republic of Costa Rica
คาซัคสถาน, สาธารณรัฐคาซัคสถาน	Kazakhstan, Republic of Kazakhstan
คานธีนคร	Gandhinagar
คาบูล	Kabul
คาร์ดิฟฟ์	Cardiff
คาร์ทูม	Khartoum
คารากัส	Caracas
คาร์นาวอน	Carnavon
คาร์สันซิตี	Carson City
คาสตรีส์	Castries
คิกาลี	Kigali
คิชิเนฟ	Kishinev
คิงส์ตัน	Kingston
คิงส์ทาวน์	Kingstown
คิโต	Quito
คิริบาส, สาธารณรัฐคิริบาส	Kiribati, Republic of Kiribati
คิวบา, สาธารณรัฐคิวบา	Cuba, Republic of Cuba
คีร์กิซ, สาธารณรัฐคีร์กิซ	Kyrgyz, Republic of Kyrgyz
คีล	Kiel
คุชราต	Gujarat
คุนหมิง	Kunming, K'un-ming
คูชิง	Kuching
คูร์	Chur
คูเวต, รัฐคูเวต	Kuwait, State of Kuwait
คูเวตซิตี	Kuwait City
เคนยา, สาธารณรัฐเคนยา	Kenya, Republic of Kenya
เคปเวิร์ด, สาธารณรัฐเคปเวิร์ด	Cape Verde, Republic of Cape Verde
เคานาส	Kaunas
เคียฟ	Kiev
แคนเบอร์รา	Canberra
แคนาดา	Canada

ค

แคเมอรูน, สาธารณรัฐแคเมอรูน	Cameroon, Republic of Cameroon
แคสตรีส์	Castries
โคเปนเฮเกน	Copenhagen
โครเอเชีย, สาธารณรัฐโครเอเชีย	Croatia, Republic of Croatia
โคลัมบัส	Columbus
โคโซโว	Kosovo
โคลัมเบีย, สาธารณรัฐโคลัมเบีย	Colombia, Republic of Colombia
โคโลเนีย	Kolonia
ไคโร	Cairo

จ

จอร์จทาวน์	Georgetown
จอร์เจีย, สาธารณรัฐจอร์เจีย	Georgia, Republic of Georgia
จอร์แดน, ราชอาณาจักรฮัชไมต์จอร์แดน	Jordan, Hashemite Kingdom of Jordan
จอห์นสตัน อะทอลล์	Johnston Atoll
จันทบุรี	Chanthaburi
จัณฑีครห์	Chandigarh
จัมมู (see ชัมมู)	
จิบูตี, สาธารณรัฐจิบูตี	Djibouti, Republic of Djibouti
จีน, สาธารณรัฐประชาชนจีน	China, People's Republic of China
จี้หนาน	Jinan, Tsinan
จี๋หลิน	Jilin, Kirin
จุงกิง	Chongqing, Chungking
จูโน	Juneau
เจนีวา	Geneva
เจฟเฟอร์สันซิตี	Jefferson City
เจมส์ทาวน์	Jamestown
เจสเซลตัน	Jesselton
เจ้อเจียง	Zhejiang
เจิ้งโจว	Zhengzhou, Cheng-chou
เจียงซี	Jiangxi, Kiangsi
เจียงซู	Jiangsu, Kiangsu

ฉ

ฉงชิ่ง	Chongqing, Chungking
ฉะเชิงเทรา	Chachoengsao
ฉือเจียจวง	Shijiazhuang, Shih-chia-chuang
ฉางชา	Changsha, Ch'ang-sha
เฉิงตู	Chengdu, Ch'eng-tu

ช

ชลบุรี	Chon Buri
ชัมมูและแคชเมียร์, ชัมมูและกัศมีร์	Jammu and Kashmir
ชัยนาท	Chai Nat
ชัยปุระ	Jaipur

ช	ชัยภูมิ	Chaiyaphum
	ช่างไฮ่	Shanghai
	ชาด, สาธารณรัฐชาด	Chad, Republic of Chad
	ชานซี	Shanxi, Shansi
	ชานตง	Shandong, Shantung
	ชาร์ลอตต์อะมาลี	Charlotte Amalie
	ชิงไห่	Qinghai, Tsinghai
	ชิน	Chin
	ชิลี, สาธารณรัฐชิลี	Chile, Republic of Chile
	ชุมพร	Chumphon
	เชนไน (มาดราส *เดิม*)	Chennai (*formerly* Madras)
	เชียงราย	Chiang Rai
	เชียงใหม่	Chiang Mai
	ไชเอน	Cheyenne
ซ	ซันตาเฟ	Santa Fé
	ซัสแคตเชวัน	Saskatchewan
	ซาเกร็บ	Zagreb
	ซานา	Sanaa, San'a
	ซานซัลวาดอร์	San Salvador
	ซานติอาโก	Santiago
	ซานโตโดมิงโก	Santo Domingo
	ซานมารีโน, สาธารณรัฐซานมารีโน	San Marino, Republic of San Marino
	ซานฮวน	San Juan
	ซานโฮเซ	San Jose
	ซาบาห์	Sabah
	ซามัว, รัฐอิสระซามัว	Samoa, Independent State of Samoa
	ซาร์บรึคเคิน	Saarbrücken
	ซาราเยโว	Sarajevo
	ซาราวัก	Sarawak
	ซาลซ์บูร์ก	Salzburg
	ซาเลม	Salem
	ซาอีร์ (*เปลี่ยนชื่อเป็นสาธารณรัฐ ประชาธิปไตยคองโก*)	**Zaire** (*now* Democratic Republic of Congo)
	ซาอุดีอาระเบีย, ราชอาณาจักร ซาอุดีอาระเบีย	Saudi Arabia, Kingdom of Saudi Arabia
	ซิดนีย์	Sydney
	ซิตเว	Sittwe
	ซินเจียงอุยกูร์	Xinjiang Uygur, Sinkiang Uighur
	ซิมบับเว, สาธารณรัฐซิมบับเว	Zimbabwe, Republic of Zimbabwe

ซ

ซิสไก	Ciskei
ซีเรีย, สาธารณรัฐอาหรับซีเรีย	Syria, Syrian Arab Republic
ซีหนิง	Xining, Hsi-ning
ซีอาน	Xian, Sian
ซูดาน, สาธารณรัฐประชาธิปไตยซูดาน	Sudan, Democratic Republic of the Sudan
ซูริก	Zurich
ซูรินาเม, สาธารณรัฐซูรินาเม	Suriname, Republic of Suriname
ซูวา	Suva
เซเชลส์, สาธารณรัฐเซเชลส์	Seychelles, Republic of Seychelles
เซนต์กอลล์	Saint Gall
เซนต์คิตส์และเนวิส	St. Kitts and Nevis
เซนต์จอนส์	Saint Johns
เซนต์จอร์เจส	Saint George's
เซนต์ลูเซีย	Saint Lucia
เซนต์วินเซนต์และเกรนาดีนส์	Saint Vincent and the Grenadines
เซนต์เฮเลียร์	St. Helier
เซเนกัล, สาธารณรัฐเซเนกัล	Senegal, Republic of Senegal
เซอร์เบีย	Serbia
เซาโตเม	Sao Tome
เซาโตเมและปรินซิเป, สาธารณรัฐ ประชาธิปไตยเซาโตเมและปรินซิเป	Sao Tome and Principe, Democratic Republic of Sao Tome and Principe
เซาเปาลู	São Paulo
เซี่ยงไฮ้	Shanghai
เซียร์ราลีโอน, สาธารณรัฐ เซียร์ราลีโอน	Sierra Leone, Republic of Sierra Leone
แซคราเมนโต	Sacramento
แซง-เดอนี	Saint-Denis
แซงปิแอร์	Saint Pierre
แซมเบีย, สาธารณรัฐแซมเบีย	Zambia, Republic of Zambia
โซเฟีย	Sofia
โซมาเลีย, สาธารณรัฐประชาธิปไตย โซมาลี	Somalia, Somali Democratic Republic
โซล	Seoul
โซโลทูร์น	Solothurn
ไซปรัส, สาธารณรัฐไซปรัส	Cyprus, Republic of Cyprus

ด

ดักลาส	Douglas
ดับลิน	Dublin
ดาการ์	Dakar
ดามัสกัส	Damascus

ด

ดาร์วิน	Darwin
ดาร์เอสซาลาม	Dar es Salaam
ดึสเซลดอร์ฟ	Düsseldorf
ดุสิต	Dusit
ดูชานเบ	Dushanbe
ดูไบ	Dubai
เดนมาร์ก, ราชอาณาจักรเดนมาร์ก	Denmark, Kingdom of Denmark
เดนเวอร์	Denver
เดมอยน์	Des Moines
เดรสเดิน	Dresden
แดลเมเชีย	Dalmatia
โดมินิกา, เครือรัฐโดมินิกา	Dominica, Commonwealth of Dominica
โดมินิกัน, สาธารณรัฐโดมินิกัน	Dominican Republic
โดเวอร์	Dover
โดฮา	Doha

ต

ตรัง	Trang
ตรังกานู	Trengganu
ตราด	Trat
ตรินิแดดและโตเบโก, สาธารณรัฐ ตรินิแดดและโตเบโก	Trinidad and Tobago, Republic of Trinidad and Tobago
ตริปุระ	Tripura
ตริโปลี	Tripoli
ตริวันดรัม	Trivandrum
ตลิ่งชัน	Taling Chan
ตองกา, ราชอาณาจักรตองกา	Tonga, Kingdom of Tonga
ตองยี	Taunggyi
ตะนาวศรี	Tenasserim
ตาก	Tak
ตาระวา	Tarawa
ติฟลิส	Tiflis
ติรานา	Tirana
ตุรกี, สาธารณรัฐตุรกี	Turkey, Republic of Turkey
ตูนิเชีย, สาธารณรัฐตูนิเชีย	Tunisia, Republic of Tunisia
ตูนิส	Tunis
ตูวาลู	Tuvalu
เตกูซิกัลปา	Tegucigalpa
เตรนตัน	Trenton
เตหะราน	Tehran, Teheran
เติร์กเมนิสถาน	Turkmenistan

ต	แตลลาแฮสซี	Tallahasse
	แตลลิน	Tallin
	โตเกียว	Tokyo
	โตโก, สาธารณรัฐโตโก	Togo, Republic of Togo
	โตปิกา	Topeka
	โตรอนโต	Toronto
	ไต้หวัน	Taiwan
ท	ทบิลิซิ	Tbilisi
	ทมิฬนาฑู	Tamil Nadu
	ทรานส์ไก	Transkei
	ทวาย	Tavoy
	ทะเลกรีนแลนด์	Greenland Sea
	" ขาว	White Sea
	" คอรัล	Coral Sea
	" คารา	Kara Sea
	" แคริบเบียน	Caribbean Sea
	" แคสเปียน	Caspian Sea
	" จีน	China Sea
	" จีนตะวันออก	East China Sea, Eastern Sea
	" จีนใต้, ทะเลนานไฮ	South China Sea, Nan Hai
	ทะเลชวา	Java Sea
	" ชุกชี	Chuckchee Sea
	" ซิซิเลียน	Sicilian Sea
	" ซูลู	Sulu Sea
	" เซราม	Ceram Sea
	" เซลีเบส	Celebes Sea
	" ไซบีเรียนตะวันออก	East Siberian Sea
	" ญี่ปุ่น	Sea of Japan
	" ดำ	Black Sea
	" เดดซี	Dead Sea
	ทะเลแดง	Red Sea
	" ติมอร์	Timor Sea
	" ตีร์เรเนียน	Tyrrhenian Sea
	" ตุงไฮ	Tung Hai
	" แทสมัน	Tasman Sea
	" ไทเบริแอส	Sea of Tiberias
	" นอร์วีเจียน	Norwegian Sea
	" บอลติก	Baltic Sea
	" บันดา	Banda Sea

ฑ

ทะเลเบริง	Bering Sea
" แบเรนต์ส	Barents Sea
" โบฟอร์ต	Beaufort Sea
" ฟลอเรส	Flores Sea
" ฟิลิปปินส์	Philippine Sea
" มาร์มะรา	Sea of Marmara
" มินดาเนา	Mindanao Sea
" เมดิเตอร์เรเนียน	Mediterranean Sea
" โมลุกกะ	Molucca Sea
" รอสซี	Ross Sea
" ลัฟเตฟ	Lavtev Sea
" ลิกูเรียน	Ligurian Sea
" เวดเดล	Weddell Sea
ทะเลสโกเชีย	Scotia Sea
" เหนือ	North Sea
" เหลือง, หรือทะเลฮวงไฮ	Yellow Sea, Hwang Hai
" อันดามัน	Andaman Sea
" อาซอฟ	Sea of Azov
" อาราฟูรา	Arafura Sea
" อารัล	Aral Sea
" อาหรับ	Arabian Sea
" อินแลนด์	Inland Sea
" อีเจียน, เอเจียน	Aegean Sea
" เอเดรียติก	Adriatic Sea
" โอคอตสก์	Sea of Okhotsk
" ไอริช	Irish Sea
" ไอโอเนียน	Ionian Sea
ทาจิกิสถาน, สาธารณรัฐทาจิกิสถาน	Tajikistan, Republic of Tajikistan
ทาลลินน์	Tallinn
ทิเบต	Tibet
ทิมพู	Thimphu
ทิสปุระ	Dispur
เทียนจิน, เทียนสิน	Tianjin, Tientsin
เทลอาวีฟ	Tel Aviv
แทชเคนต์, ทาชเคนต์	Tashkent
แทนซาเนีย, สหสาธารณรัฐแทนซาเนีย	Tanzania, United Republic of Tanzania
แทสเมเนีย	Tasmania
โทรอนโต	Toronto
โทฮอยอานดู	Thohoyandou

ฑ	ไทเป	Taipei
	ไทย, ราชอาณาจักรไทย	Thailand, Kingdom of Thailand
	ไทรบุรี, เกดะห์	Kedah
	ไท่หยวน	Taiyuan, T'ai-yuan
ธ	ธนบุรี	Thonburi
	ธากา	Dhaka
น	นครนายก	Nakhon Nayok
	นครปฐม	Nakhon Pathom
	นครพนม	Nakhon Phanom
	นครราชสีมา	Nakhon Ratchasima
	นครศรีธรรมราช	Nakhon Si Thammarat
	นครสวรรค์	Nakhon Sawan
	นนทบุรี	Nonthaburi
	นราธิวาส	Narathiwat
	นอร์เวย์, ราชอาณาจักรนอร์เวย์	Norway, Kingdom of Norway
	นัสซอ	Nassau
	นาคาแลนด์	Nagaland
	น่าน	Nan
	นามิเบีย, สาธารณรัฐนามิเบีย	Namibia, Republic of Namibia
	นาอูรู, สาธารณรัฐนาอูรู	Nauru, Republic of Nauru
	นิการากัว, สาธารณรัฐนิการากัว	Nicaragua, Republic of Nicaragua
	นิโกเซีย	Nicosia
	นิวแคลิโดเนีย	New Caledonia
	นิวซีแลนด์	New Zealand
	นิวเซาท์เวลส์	New South Wales
	นิวเดลี	New Delhi
	นิวบรันสวิก	New Brunswick
	นิวฟันด์แลนด์	New Foundland
	นีอาเม	Niamey
	นีอูเอ	Niue
	นูกูอะโลฟา	Nuku'alofa, Nukualofa
	นูเมอา	Noumea
	นูแอกซอต	Nouakchott
	เนกรีเซมบิลัน	Negri Sembilan
	เนเธอร์แลนด์, ราชอาณาจักร เนเธอร์แลนด์	Netherlands, Kingdom of the Netherlands
	เนเธอร์แลนด์แอนทิลลิส	Netherlands Antilles
	เนปาล, ราชอาณาจักรเนปาล	Nepal, Kingdom of Nepal
	เนอชาแตล	Neuchatel

น	โนวาสโกเชีย	Nova Scotia
	ไนจีเรีย, สหพันธ์สาธารณรัฐไนจีเรีย	Nigeria, Federal Republic of Nigeria
	ไนเจอร์, สาธารณรัฐไนเจอร์	Niger, Republic of Niger
	ไนโรบี	Nairobi
บ	บรัสเซลส์	Brussels
	บราซชาวิล	Brazzaville
	บราซิล, สหพันธ์สาธารณรัฐบราซิล	Brazil, Federative Republic of Brazil
	บราซิเลีย	Brasilia
	บราทิสลาวา	Bratislava
	บริดจ์ทาวน์	Bridgetown
	บริติชโคลัมเบีย	British Columbia
	บริเตนใหญ่	Great Britain
	บริสเบน	Brisbane
	บรูไน, เนการาบรูไนดารุสซาลาม	Brunei, Negara Brunei Darussalam
	บอตสวานา, สาธารณรัฐบอตสวานา	Botswana, Republic of Botswana
	บอนน์	Bonn
	บอยซี	Boise
	บอร์เนียวเหนือ, หรือซาบาห์	North Borneo, Sabah
	บอสตัน	Boston
	บอสเนียและเฮอร์เซโกวีนา, สาธารณรัฐ บอสเนียและเฮอร์เซโกวีนา	Bosnia and Herzegovina, Republic of Bosnia and Herzegovina
	บังกลาเทศ, สาธารณรัฐ ประชาชนบังกลาเทศ	Bangladesh, People's Republic of Bangladesh
	บังกี	Bungui
	บังคาลอร์	Bangalore
	บันจูล	Banjul
	บันดาร์เสรีเบกาวัน	Bandar Seri Begawan
	บัลแกเรีย, สาธารณรัฐบัลแกเรีย	Bulgaria, Republic of Bulgaria
	บากู	Baku
	บางกอกน้อย	Bangkok Noi
	บางกอกใหญ่	Bangkok Yai
	บางกะปิ	Bang Kapi
	บางขุนเทียน	Bang Khun Thian
	บางเขน	Bang Khen
	บางรัก	Bang Rak
	บาเซิล	Basel
	บามาโก	Bamako
	บาร์เบโดส	Barbados
	บาสแตร์	Basseterre

บ

บาห์เรน, รัฐบาห์เรน	Bahrain, Bahrein, State of Bahrain
บาฮามาส, เครือรัฐบาฮามาส	Bahamas, Commonwealth of the Bahamas
บิชเคก	Bishkek
บิสเซา	Bissau
บิสมาร์ก	Bismarck
บีโช	Bisho
บุรุนดี, สาธารณรัฐบุรุนดี	Burundi, Republic of Burundi
บูคาเรสต์	Bucharest
บูจุมบูรา	Bujumbura
บูดาเปสต์	Budapest
บูร์กินาฟาโซ, สาธารณรัฐบูร์กินาฟาโซ	Burkina Faso, Republic of Burkina Faso
บูเอโนสไอเรส	Buenos Aires
เบนิน, สาธารณรัฐเบนิน	Benin, Republic of Benin
เบรเกนซ์	Bregenz
เบิร์น	Bern, Berne
เบลเกรด	Belgrade
เบลฟัสต์	Belfast
เบลารุส, สาธารณรัฐเบลารุส	Belarus, Republic of Belarus
เบลีซ	Belize
เบอร์ลิน	Berlin
แบกแดด	Baghdad
โบพูทัตสวานา	Bophuthatswana

ป

ปทุมวัน	Pathum Wan
ปราก	Prague
ปราจีนบุรี	Prachin Buri
ปรินซ์เอดเวิร์ดไอแลนด์	Prince Edward Island
ป้อมปราบศัตรูพ่าย	Pom Prap Sattru Phai
ปอร์โต-โนโว	Porto-Novo
ปอร์โตแปรงซ์	Port-au-Prince
ปะนัน	Panan
ปะลิส	Perlis
ปะหัง	Pahang
ปักกิ่ง	Beijing, Peking
ปัญจาบ	Punjab
ปัฏนา	Patna
ปากีสถาน	Pakistan
ปาโกปาโก	Pago Pago
ปานามา, สาธารณรัฐปานามา	Panama, Republic of Panama
ปานามาซิตี	Panama City

ป

ปาปัวนิวกินี	Papua New Guinea
ปาปีเอตี	Papeete
ปารากวัย, สาธารณรัฐปารากวัย	Paraguay, Republic of Paraguay
ปารามาริโบ	Paramaribo
ปารีส	Paris
ปาเลา, สาธารณรัฐปาเลา	Palau, Republic of Palau
ปีนัง	Penang
ปีแอร์	Pierre
เปโตรซาวอดสก์	Petrozavodsk
เประ	Perak
เปรู, สาธารณรัฐเปรู	Peru, Republic of Peru
เปอร์โตริโก (เครือรัฐ)	Puerto Rico, Commonwealth of
เปียงยาง	Pyongyang
โปรตุเกส, สาธารณรัฐโปรตุเกส	Portugal, Republic of Portugal
โปรวิเดนซ์	Providence
โปแลนด์, สาธารณรัฐประชาชนโปแลนด์	Poland, Polish People's Republic
ไปรอา	Praia

ฝ
พ

ฝรั่งเศส, สาธารณรัฐฝรั่งเศส	France, French Republic
พญาไท	Phaya Thai, Phya Tai
พนมเปญ	Phnom Penh
พระโขนง	Phra Khanong
พระนครศรีอยุธยา	Phra Nakhon Si Ayuthaya
พริทอเรีย	Pretoria
พม่า, สหภาพพม่า	Myanmar, Union of Myanmar (เดิมชื่อ Burma)
พอนดิเชอร์รี	Pondicherry
พอทสดัม	Potsdam
พอร์ตมอร์สบี	Port Moresby
พอร์ตวิลา	Port Vila
พอร์ตหลุยส์	Port Louis
พอร์ต-ออฟ-สเปน	Port-of-Spain
พะโค, หงสาวดี	Pegu
พะเยา	Phayao
พะสิม	Bassein
พังงา	Phangnga
พัทยา, เมืองพัทยา	Pataya City
พัทลุง	Phatthalung
พิจิตร	Phichit
พิษณุโลก	Phitsanulok

พ

พิหาร	Bihar
เพชรบุรี	Phetchaburi
เพชรบูรณ์	Phetchabun
เพอร์ท	Perth
แพร่	Phrae

ฟ

ฟรุนเซ	Frunze
ฟรีบูร์ก	Fribourg
ฟอร์-เดอ-ฟรองซ์	Fort-de-France
ฟะลัม	Falam
ฟิจิ	Fiji, Republic of Fiji
ฟิลิปปินส์, สาธารณรัฐฟิลิปปินส์	Philippines, Republic of the Philippines
ฟีนิกซ์	Phoenix
ฟูไจราห์	Fujairah
ฟูนชาล	Funchal
ฟูนะฟูตี	Funafuti
เฟรนช์เกียนา	French Guiana
เฟรนช์โปลีนีเซีย	French Polynesia
แฟรงก์เฟอร์ต	Frankfurt

ภ

ภาษีเจริญ	Phasi Charoen
ภุพเนศวร	Bhubaneswar
ภูฏาน, ราชอาณาจักรภูฏาน	Bhutan, Kingdom of Bhutan
โภปาล	Bhopal

ม

มณีปุระ	Manipur
มหาราษฏระ	Maharashtra
มหาสารคาม	Maha Sarakham
มองโกเลีย	Mongolia
มองโกเลียใน	Inner Mongolia
มอญ	Mon
มอนต์โกเมอรี	Montgomery
มอนต์เซอร์รัต	Montserrat
มอนต์เปเลียร์	Montpelier
มอนเตนิโกร	Montenegro
มอนเตวิเดโอ	Montevideo
มอริเชียส, สาธารณรัฐมอริเชียส	Mauritius, Republic of Mauritius
มอริเตเนีย, สาธารณรัฐ อิสลามมอริเตเนีย	Mauritania, Islamic Republic of Mauritania
มอลโดวา, สาธารณรัฐมอลโดวา	Moldova, Republic of Moldova
มอลตา, สาธารณรัฐมอลตา	Malta, Republic of Malta
มอสโก	Moscow

ม	มะละกา	Malacca
	มะละแหม่ง, เมาะลำเลิง	Moulmein
	มักเดบูร์ก	Magdeburg
	มัณฑะเลย์	Mandalay
	มัทราส	Madras
	มัธยประเทศ	Madhya Pradesh
	มันโรเวีย	Monrovia
	มัลดีฟส์, สาธารณรัฐมัลดีฟส์	Maldives, Republic of Maldives
	มัสกัต	Masqat, Muscat
	มาเกว	Magwe
	มาเก๊า	Macao
	มาจูโร	Majuro
	มาซิโดเนีย, สาธารณรัฐมาซิโดเนีย	Macedonia, Republic of Macedonia
	มาเซรู	Maseru
	มาดริด	Madrid
	มาดากัสการ์, สาธารณรัฐมาดากัสการ์	Madagascar, Republic of Madagascar
	มาตา-อูตู	Mata-Utu
	มานากัว	Managua
	มานามา	Manama
	มาบาโท	Mmabatho
	มาปูโต	Maputo
	มาร์ตินีก	Martinique
	มาลาวี, สาธารณรัฐมาลาวี	Malawi, Republic of Malawi
	มาลี, สาธารณรัฐมาลี	Mali, Republic of Mali
	มาเล	Malé
	มาเลเซีย	Malaysia
	มิโซรัม	Mizoram
	มิตจีนา	Myitkyina
	มินสก์	Minsk
	มิวนิก	Munich
	มุกดาหาร	Mukdahan
	มุกเดน	Mukden
	มุมไบ	Mumbai
	เมกกะ, ริยาด	Mecca, Riyadh
	เม็กซิโก, สหรัฐเม็กซิโก	Mexico, United Mexican States
	เมนสก์	Mensk
	เมลเบิร์น	Melbourne
	เมียนม่าร์	Myanmar
	แมดิสัน	Madison

ม	แมนิโทบา	Manitoba
	แม่ฮ่องสอน	Mae Hong Son
	โมกาดิชู	Mogadishu
	ไมโครนีเซีย, สหพันธรัฐไมโครนีเซีย	Micronesia, Federated States of Micronesia
	โมซัมบิก, สาธารณรัฐโมซัมบิก	Mozambique, Republic of Mozambique
	โมนาโก, ราชรัฐโมนาโก	Monaco, Principality of Monaco
	โมโรนี	Moroni
	ไมนซ์	Mainz
ย	ยโสธร	Yasothon
	ยะไข่	Arakan (Rakhine)
	ยะลา	Yala
	ยะโฮร์	Johore
	ยะโฮร์บาห์รู	Johore Bahru
	ย่างกุ้ง	Yangon (*เดิมชื่อ* Rangoon)
	ยานนาวา	Yan Nawa
	ยามุสซุโกร	Yamoussoukro
	ยาอุนเด	Yaoundé
	ยุโรป	Europe
	ยูกันดา, สาธารณรัฐยูกันดา	Uganda, Republic of Uganda
	ยูโกสลาเวีย, สหพันธ์สาธารณรัฐ ยูโกสลาเวีย	Yugoslavia, Federal Republic of Yugoslavia
	ยูคอน	Yukon
	ยูเครน	Ukraine
	ยิบรอลตาร์	Gibraltar
	เยนันยอง	Yenangyaung
	เยเมน, สาธารณรัฐเยเมน	Yemen, Republic of Yemen
	เยรูซาเลม	Jerusalem
	เยเรวาน	Yerevan
	เยอรมนี, สหพันธ์สาธารณรัฐเยอรมนี	Germany, Federal Republic of Germany
ร	รวันดา, สาธารณรัฐรวันดา	Rwanda, Republic of Rwanda
	รอสส์ดีเพนเดนซี	Ross Dependency
	รอลี	Raleigh
	ร้อยเอ็ด	Roi Et
	ระนอง	Ranong
	ระยอง	Rayong
	รัสเซีย, สหพันธรัฐรัสเซีย	Russia, Russian Federation
	ราชบุรี	Ratchaburi
	ราชสถาน	Rajasthan
	ราษฎร์บูรณะ	Rat Burana

ร

ราบาต	Rabat
ราสอัลไคมาห์	Ras al-Khaimah
ราวัลปินดี	Rawalpindi
ราโรตองกา	Rarotonga
ริกา	Riga
ริชมอนด์	Richmond
ริยาด	Riyadh
ริวเดจาเนโร	Rio de Janeiro
เรกยะวิก	Reykjavik
เรอูนียง	Reunion
โรโซ	Roseau
โรดทาวน์	Road Town
โรม	Rome
โรมาเนีย	Romania

ล

ลพบุรี	Lop Buri
ลอนดอน	London
ลักเซมเบิร์ก, ราชรัฐลักเซมเบิร์ก	Luxembourg, Grand Duchy of Luxembourg
ลักษทวีป	Lakshdweep
ลัคเนา	Lucknow
ลัตเวีย, สาธารณรัฐลัตเวีย	Latvia, Republic of Latvia
ลากอส	Lagos
ลาซา	Lhasa
ลาดกระบัง	Lat Krabang
ลาบวน	Labuan
ลาปาซ	La Paz
ลาว, สาธารณรัฐประชาธิปไตย ประชาชนลาว	Laos, Lao People's Democratic Republic
ลิกเตนสไตน์, ราชรัฐลิกเตนสไตน์	Liechtenstein, Principality of Liechtenstein
ลิงคอล์น	Lincoln
ลิทัวเนีย, สาธารณรัฐลิทัวเนีย	Lithuania, Republic of Lithuania
ลิตเติลร็อก	Little Rock
ลินซ์	Linz
ลิเบรอวิล	Libreville

ลิเบีย, สาธารณรัฐสังคมนิยม
    ประชาชนอาหรับลิเบีย
	Libya, The Great Socialist People's Libyan
	      Arab Jamahiriya

ลิมา	Lima
ลิลองเว	Lilongwe
ลิสบอน	Lisbon
ลือบลือานา	Ljubljana

ล	ลูซากา	Lusaka
	ลูเซิร์น	Lucerne
	ลูอันดา	Luanda
	เลโซโท, ราชอาณาจักรเลโซโท	Lesotho, Kingdom of Lesotho
	เลบานอน, สาธารณรัฐเลบานอน	Lebanon, Republic of Lebanon
	แลนซิง	Lansing
	โลซาน	Lausanne
	โลเม	Lome
	ไลบีเรีย, สาธารณรัฐไลบีเรีย	Liberia, Republic of Liberia
ว	วอชิงตัน ดี.ซี.	Washington, D.C.
	วอร์ซอ	Warsaw
	วัลเลตตา	Valletta
	วาดุซ	Vaduz
	วาติกัน, นครรัฐวาติกัน	Vatican, Vatican City State, The Holy See
	วานูอาตู, สาธารณรัฐวานูอาตู	Vanuatu, Republic of Vanuatu
	วิกตอเรีย	Victoria
	วินนิเปก	Winnipeg
	วินด์ฮุก	Windhoek
	วิลนีอุส	Vilnius
	วิลเลมสตัด	Willemstad
	วีสบาเดิน	Wiesbaden
	เว้	Hue
	เวนดา	Venda
	เวเนซุเอลา, สาธารณรัฐเวเนซุเอลา	Venezuela, Republic of Venezuela
	เวลลิงตัน	Wellington
	เวลส์	Wales
	เวียงจันทน์	Vientiane
	เวียดนาม, สาธารณรัฐสังคมนิยม เวียดนาม	Vietnam, Socialist Republic of Vietnam
	เวียนนา	Vienna
ศ	ศรีนคร	Srinagar
	ศรีลังกา, สาธารณรัฐสังคมนิยม ประชาธิปไตยศรีลังกา	Sri Lanka
	ศรีสะเกษ	Si Sa Ket
	ศิมลา	Simla
ส	สกลนคร	Sakon Nakhon
	สกอตแลนด์	Scotland
	สโกเปีย	Skopje
	สงขลา	Songkhla

ส		
	สตอกโฮล์ม	Stockholm
	สตูล	Satun
	สปลิต	Split
	สเปน, ราชอาณาจักรสเปน	Spain, Kingdom of Spain
	สมุทรปราการ	Samut Prakan
	สมุทรสงคราม	Samut Songkhram
	สมุทรสาคร	Samut Sakhon
	สระแก้ว	Sa Kaeo
	สระบุรี	Saraburi
	สเรมบัน	Seremban
	สลังงอร์	Selangor
	สโลวะเกีย, สาธารณรัฐสโลวัก	Slovakia, Slovak Republic
	สโลวีเนีย, สาธารณรัฐสโลวีเนีย	Slovenia, Republic of Slovenia
	สวาซิแลนด์, ราชอาณาจักรสวาซิแลนด์	Swaziland, Kingdom of Swaziland
	สวิตเซอร์แลนด์, สมาพันธรัฐสวิส	Switzerland, Swiss Confederation
	สวีเดน, ราชอาณาจักรสวีเดน	Sweden, Kingdom of Sweden
	สหภาพโซเวียต, สหภาพสาธารณรัฐ สังคมนิยมโซเวียต *(ชื่อในอดีต)*	Soviet Union, Union of Soviet Socialist Republics
	สหรัฐอเมริกา	United States of America
	สหรัฐอาหรับเอมิเรตส์	United Arab Emirates
	สหราชอาณาจักรบริเตนใหญ่ และไอร์แลนด์เหนือ	United Kingdom of Great Britain and Northern Ireland
	สะกาย	Sagaing
	สาธารณรัฐเช็ก	Czech Republic
	สาธารณรัฐโดมินิกัน	Dominican Republic
	สาธารณรัฐประชาธิปไตยคองโก	Democratic Republic of Congo
	สาธารณรัฐแอฟริกากลาง	Central African Republic
	ส่านซี	Shaanxi, Shensi
	สิกขิม	Sikkim
	สิงคโปร์, สาธารณรัฐสิงคโปร์	Singapore, Republic of Singapore
	สิงห์บุรี	Sing Buri
	สุโขทัย	Sukhothai
	สุพรรณบุรี	Suphan Buri
	สุราษฎร์ธานี	Surat Thani
	สุรินทร์	Surin
	เสิ่นหยาง	Shenyang
ห		
	หงสาวดี	Pegu
	หนองแขม	Nong Khaem
	หนองจอก	Nong Chok

ห

หนองบัวลำภู	Nong Bua Lamphu, Nhong Bua Lumpoo
หนานจิง	Nanjing, Nanking
หนานฉาง	Nanchang, Nan-chang
หนานหนิง	Nanning, Nan-ning
หนิงเซี่ยหุย	Ningxia Hui, Ningsia Hui
หมู่เกาะกาลาปากอส	Galapagos
" กิลเบอร์ต	Gilbert Islands
" ควีนชาร์ล็อต	Queen Charlotte Islands
" คอโมโร	Comoro Islands
" คอรัลซี	Coral Sea Islands
" คะเนรี	Canary Islands
" คุก	Cook Islands
" คุริล	Kurile Islands
" เคคอส	Caicos Islands
" เคปเวิร์ด	Cape Verde Islands
" เคย์แมน	Cayman Islands
หมู่เกาะโคโกส	Cocos, Kelling Islands
" เชตแลนด์	Shetland Islands
" แชนเนล	Channel Islands
" ซามัว	Samoa
" ซุนดาน้อย	Lesser Sunda Islands
" ซุนดาใหญ่	Greater Sunda Islands
" เซเชลส์	Seychelles
" แซนตาครูซ	Santa Cruz Islands
" โซไซเอตี	Society Islands
" โซโลมอน	Solomon Islands
" ไซคลาดิส	Cyclades
หมู่เกาะญี่ปุ่น	Japanese Islands
" โดเดกานิส	Dodecanese
" ตองกา	Tonga
" เติกส์และเคคอส	Turks and Caicos Islands
" นิโคบาร์	Nicobar Islands
" นิวแคลิโดเนีย	New Caledonia
" นิวเฮบริดีส	New Hebrides Islands
" บริติช	British Isles
" บริติชเวอร์จิน	British Virgin Islands
" บันดา	Banda Islands
" บาบาร์	Babar Islands
" บาวน์ตี	Bounty Islands

ห

หมู่เกาะบาฮามาส	Bahamas
" เบอร์มิวดาส์	Bermudas
" แบลิแอริก	Balearic Islands
" โบนิน	Bonin Islands
" พริบิลอฟ	Pribilof Islands
" พิตแคร์น	Pitcairn Islands
" ฟรีเซียน	Frisian Islands
" ฟอล์กแลนด์	Falkland Islands
" ฟิจิ	Fiji
" ฟิลิปปิน	Philippine Islands
" แฟโร	Faroe Islands
" มาร์เคซัส	Marquesas Islands
" มัลดีฟ	Maldive Islands
" มาเดรา	Madeira Islands
หมู่เกาะมาร์แชล, สาธารณรัฐ	Marshall Islands, Republic of the Marshall
หมู่เกาะมาร์แชลล์	Islands
" มาเรียนา	Mariana Islands
" มิดเวย์	Midway Islands
" โมลุกกะ	Molucca Islands
" รัสเซลล์	Russell Islands
" ลักกาดีฟ	Laccadive Islands
" ลีวาร์ด	Leeward Islands
" โลโฟเตน	Lofoten
" วาลลิสและฟุตูนา	Wallis and Futuna Islands
" วินด์วาร์ด	Windward Islands
" วิสายัน	Visayan Islands
" เวอร์จินของสหรัฐอเมริกา	Virgin Islands of the United States
" สปิตสเบอร์เกน	Spitsbergen
หมู่เกาะแสปรตลี	Spratly Islands
" ออร์กนี	Orkney Islands
" อะซอร์ส	Azores
" อันดามัน	Andaman Islands
" อาลิวเชียน	Aleutian Islands
" อีเจียน	Aegean Islands
" แอดมิรัลตี	Admiralty Islands
" แอนติลลิสน้อย, หรือ	Lesser Antilles, Caribbees
หมู่เกาะแคริบบีส์	
" แอนติลลิสใหญ่	Greater Antilles
" ไอโอเนียน	Ionian Islands

ห	หมู่เกาะเฮบรีดีส	Hebrides
	หยุนหนาน	Yunnan
	หลานโจว	Lanzhou, Lan-chou
	ห้วยขวาง	Huai Khwang
	หางโจว	Hangzhou, Hangchow
	หูเป่ย์	Hubei, Hupeh
	หูหนาน	Hunan
	เหลียวหนิง	Liaoning
	เหอเป่ย์	Hebei, Hopeh
	เหอเฟย์	Hefei, Ho-fei
	เหอหนาน	Henan, Honan
	ไหโข่ว	Haikou
	ไหหนาน, ไหหลำ	Hainan
อ	อเมริกันซามัว	American Samoa
	อเมริกาใต้	South America
	อเมริกาเหนือ	North America
	อรุณาจัลประเทศ	Arunachal Pradesh
	อลอร์สตาร์	Alor Star
	ออกัสตา	Augusta
	ออตตาวา	Ottawa
	ออนแทรีโอ	Ontario
	ออรีกอน	Oregon
	ออลบานี	Albany
	ออสเตรเลีย	Australia
	ออสเตรเลีย, เครือรัฐออสเตรเลีย	Australia, Commonwealth of Australia
	ออสเตรีย, สาธารณรัฐออสเตรีย	Austria, Republic of Austria
	ออสโล	Oslo
	อะกาญา	Agana
	อะซอร์ส	Azores
	อะซุนซิโอน	Asuncion
	อะโลฟี	Alofi
	อักกรา	Accra
	อังกฤษ	England
	อัครตละ	Agartala
	อังการา	Ankara
	อังโกลา, สาธารณรัฐประชาชน อังโกลา	Angola, People's Republic of Angola
	อัจมาน	Ajman
	อันดอร์รา, ราชรัฐอันดอร์รา	Andorra, Principality of Andorra

 อ

อันดอร์ราลาเวลลา	Andorra la Vella
อันติกัวและบาร์บูดา	Antigua and Barbuda
อัฟกานิสถาน	Afghanistan
อัมมาน	Amman
อัมสเตอร์ดัม	Amsterdam
อัล-คูเวต, คูเวต	Al-Kuwait, Kuwait
อัลมาอาตา	Alma Ata
อัสสัม	Assam
อัสตานา	Astana
อาชคาบัด	Ashkhabad
อ่างทอง	Ang Thong
อาเซอร์ไบจาน, สาธารณรัฐ อาเซอร์ไบจาน	Azerbaijan Republic of Azerbaijan
อานธรประเทศ	Andhra Pradesh
อานฮุย	Anhui, Anhwei
อาบิดจัน	Abidjan
อาบูดาบี	Abu Dhabi
อาปีอา	Apia
อาร์เจนตินา, สาธารณรัฐอาร์เจนตินา	Argentina, Argentina Republic
อาร์เมเนีย, สาธารณรัฐอาร์เมเนีย	Armenia, Republic of Armenia
อารูบา	Aruba
อำนาจเจริญ	Amnat Charoen, Umnajjaroen
อิเควทอเรียลกินี, สาธารณรัฐ อิเควทอเรียลกินี	Equatorial Guinea, Republic of Equatorial Guinea
อิตาลี, สาธารณรัฐอิตาลี	Italy, Republic of Italy
อินฉวน	Yinchuan, Yin-ch'uan
อินเดีย, สาธารณรัฐอินเดีย	India, Republic of India
อินเดียนา	Indiana
อินเดียนาโปลิส	Indianapolis
อินโดนีเซีย, สาธารณรัฐอินโดนีเซีย	Indonesia, Republic of Indonesia
อินส์บรุค	Innsbruck
อิมผาล	Imphal
อิรวดี	Irrawaddy
อิรัก, สาธารณรัฐอิรัก	Iraq, Republic of Iraq
อิสราเอล, รัฐอิสราเอล	Israel, State of Israel
อิสลามาบัด	Islamabad
อิหร่าน, สาธารณรัฐอิสลามอิหร่าน	Iran, Islamic Republic of Iran
อีโปห์	Ipoh
อียิปต์, สาธารณรัฐอาหรับอียิปต์	Egypt, Arab Republic of Egypt

อ

อึมบาบาน	Mbabane
อุซเบกิสถาน, สาธารณรัฐอุซเบกิสถาน	Uzbekistan, Republic of Uzbekistan
อุดรธานี	Udon Thani
อุตรดิตถ์	Uttaradit
อุตตรประเทศ	Uttar Pradesh
อุทัยธานี	Uthai Thani
อุบลราชธานี	Ubon Ratchathani
อุมตาตา	Umtata
อุมม์อัลไกไวน์	Umm al-Qaiwain
อุรุกวัย, สาธารณรัฐอุรุกวัย	Uruguay, Oriental Republic of Uruguay
อุรุมชี	Urumqi, Urumchi
อูลานบาตอร์	Ulan Bator, Ulaanbaatar
อูวากาดูกู	Ouagadougou
อู่ฮั่น	Wuhan
เอกวาดอร์, สาธารณรัฐเอกวาดอร์	Ecuador, Republic of Ecuador
เอเชีย	Asia
เอดมันตัน	Edmonton
เอดินบะระ	Edinburgh
เอเดน	Aden
เอธิโอเปีย, สหพันธ์สาธารณรัฐ ประชาธิปไตยเอธิโอเปีย	Ethiopia, Federal Democratic Republic of Ethiopia
เอเธนส์	Athens
เอ็นจาเมนา	N'Djamena
เอริเทรีย, รัฐเอริเทรีย	Eritrea, State of Eritrea
เอลซัลวาดอร์, สาธารณรัฐเอลซัลวาดอร์	El Salvador, Republic of El Salvador
เอสโตเนีย, สาธารณรัฐเอสโตเนีย	Estonia, Republic of Estonia
แองโกลา, สาธารณรัฐแองโกลา	Angola, Republic of Angola
แอดดิสอาบาบา	Addis Ababa
แอดิเลด	Adelaide
แอตแลนตา	Atlanta
แอนตาร์กติกา	Antarctica
แอนติกาและบาร์บูดา	Antigua and Barbuda
แอนแนโปลิส	Annapolis
แอฟริกา	Africa
แอฟริกาใต้, สาธารณรัฐ แอฟริกาใต้	South Africa, Republic of South Africa
แอลจีเรีย, สาธารณรัฐประชาธิปไตย ประชาชนแอลจีเรีย	Algeria, Democratic and Popular Republic of Algeria
แอเดเลด	Adelaide

อ	แอร์ฟูร์ท	Erfurt
	แอลเบเนีย, สาธารณรัฐประชาชน	Albania, People's Republic of Albania
	แอลเบเนีย	
	แอลเบอร์ตา	Alberta
	โอกลาโฮมาซิตี	Oklahoma City
	โอมาน, รัฐสุลต่านโอมาน	Oman, Sultanate of Oman
	โอริสสา	Orissa
	โอไฮโอ	Ohio
	ไอซ์แลนด์, สาธารณรัฐไอซ์แลนด์	Iceland, Republic of Iceland
	ไอซอล	Aizawl
	ไอดาโฮ	Idaho
	ไอร์แลนด์, สาธารณรัฐไอร์แลนด์	Ireland, Republic of Ireland
	ไอร์แลนด์เหนือ	Northern Ireland
	ไอโอวา	Iowa
ฮ	ฮ่องกง	Hong Kong
	ฮอนดูรัส, สาธารณรัฐฮอนดูรัส	Honduras, Republic of Honduras
	ฮันโนเวอร์	Hannover
	ฮัมบูร์ก	Hamburg
	ฮานอย	Hanoi
	ฮาร์ตฟอร์ด	Hartford
	ฮาร์บิน	Harbin
	ฮาราเร	Harare
	ฮาวานา	Havana
	ฮาวาย	Hawaii
	ฮูฮอต	Huhhot
	เฮติ, สาธารณรัฐเฮติ	Haiti, Republic of Haiti
	เฮย์หลงเจียง	Heilongjiang, Heilungkiang
	เฮลซิงกิ	Helsinki
	เฮเลนา	Helena
	แฮร์ริสเบอร์ก	Harrisburgh
	แฮลิแฟกซ์	Halifax
	โฮนีอารา	Honiara
	โฮโนลูลู	Honolulu
	โฮบาร์ต	Hobart
	ไฮเดอราบาด	Hyderabad

ชื่อประเทศ เมืองหลวงทั้งหมด เมือง รัฐ แขวง เกาะ และทะเลที่สำคัญๆ เหล่านี้ สะกดตัวภาษาไทยตามหลักของ ราชบัณฑิตยสถาน

These are transliterations of the names of all countries, their capitals and also principal states, provinces, cities, seas and islands. They are the spellings recommended by the Royal Institute but other spellings may be found in use.

Sources

ประกาศสำนักนายกรัฐมนตรีและประกาศราชบัณฑิตยสถาน

    เรื่อง กำหนดชื่อทวีป ประเทศ เมืองหลวง มหาสมุทร ทะเล และเกาะ และเรื่อง การเขียนชื่อจังหวัด เขต อำเภอ และกิ่งอำเภอ. ราชบัณฑิตยสถาน, กรุงเทพฯ, 2533

    เรื่อง กำหนดชื่อประเทศ ดินแดน เขตการปกครอง และเมืองหลวง. ราชบัณฑิตยสถาน, กรุงเทพฯ 2541

8
ชื่ออาหารไทยและส่วนประกอบ
Thai Dishes and Ingredients

กบผัดเผ็ด	spicy-fried frogs
กระชาย	lesser ginger
กระทงทอง	golden baskets / crispy cups filled with minced pork and peanuts
กระท้อน	santol
กระเทียม	garlic
กระเทียมดอง	pickled garlic / garlic pickle
กระเพาะปลา	dried fish maw soup
กล้วย	banana
″ กวน	sugar-boiled banana puree
″ แขก	deep fried bananas
″ ฉาบ	sweet banana crisps
″ ตาก	sun-dried bananas
″ บวชชี	bananas in coconut sauce / bananas cooked in coconut milk
ก๋วยเตี๋ยว	rice noodles
″ น้ำ	noodle soup
″ เนื้อตุ๋น	aromatic beef and aniseed soup with rice noodles/
″ เนื้อสับ	noodles with ground beef / flat rice noodles with sauted curried minced beef
″ ผัดขี้เมาทะเล, หมู, กุ้ง, ไก่, เนื้อ	noodles fried with spicy seafood, pork, shrimps, chicken or beef
″ ผัดซีอิ๊ว	stir-fried wide noodles / noodles fried in soy sauce
″ ผัดไทย	fried small rice noodles with shrimp, bean curd, bean sprouts, preserved radish and ground peanuts
″ ผัดราดหน้าทะเล, หมู, กุ้ง, ไก่, เนื้อ	fried rice noodles and oyster sauce with your choice of seafood, pork, shrimp, chicken or beef
″ ราดหน้าไก่	fried noodles with chicken, vegetables and gravy

กะทิ	coconut cream
กะปิ	shrimp paste
กะหรี่ปั๊บ	curry puff
กานพลู	cloves
กุ้งกระเทียมพริกไทย	shrimp fried with garlic and black pepper
" นึ่งกระเทียม	steamed garlic shrimp
" ผัดพริก	chili prawns
" เผาน้ำปลาหวาน	broiled shrimp with sweet sauce
" มะขาม	grilled prawns topped with tamarind sauce
" หรือหมู ทอดกระเทียมพริกไทย	stir-fried prawns or pork with garlic, black pepper and coriander root
" แห้ง	dried shrimps
" แห้งยำ	sun-dried shrimp salad
" อบวุ้นเส้น	casseroled prawns (shrimps) with glass noodles /
เกี๊ยวกรอบ	crispy parcels / crispy wonton
" น้ำ	wonton soup / minced pork and prawn wonton soup
" น้ำหรือแห้ง	pork dumplings in chicken broth or dry shrimp dumplings with red pork, shrimp and crab meat
แกงกะหรี่เนื้อหรือไก่	beef or chicken yellow curry
" กะหรี่ผัก	yellow vegetable curry
" ไก่	red chicken curry
" เขียวหวานกุ้งยอดมะพร้าวอ่อน	prawns in green curry with coconut palm tips
" เขียวหวานไก่	green chicken curry
" เขียวหวานเนื้อ	green beef curry
" เขียวหวานเนื้อหรือไก่	beef or chicken green curry
" เขียวหวานผักเต้าหู้	green curry with fresh vegetables and bean curd
" เขียวหวานหมู, กุ้ง, ไก่, เนื้อ และทะเล	green curry of pork, prawns, chicken, beef or seafood
" คั่วสับปะรด	pineapple curry
" คั่วสับปะรดกุ้ง	sweet curry with pineapple and shrimps
" คั่วสับปะรดหอยแมลงภู่	mussels and pineapple curry
" คั่วหมูป่า	wild boar curry
" จืดแตงกวายัดไส้	stuffed cucumber soup
" จืดปลาหมึกยัดไส้	stuffed squid soup
" จืดผักกาดดอง	Chinese mustard pickle soup
" จืดลูกรอก	egg sausage, shrimp, pork and spring onion in broth

แกงต้มส้ม	sweet-sour soup
" บวดถั่วดำ	black beans stewed in coconut milk
" บวดฟักทอง	squash in coconut sauce
" ป่าเนื้อ	spicy beef curry
" ป่าปลาดุก	spicy catfish clear curry
" ป่าหมูป่า	wild boar country curry
" เผ็ดไก่	red chicken curry
" เผ็ดเนื้อ	spicy beef curry / red beef curry
" เผ็ดเป็ดย่าง	roast duck with red curry / red duck curry / duck curry with cherry tomatoes / red curry with roasted duck
" เผ็ดหมู	red pork curry
" พะแนงไก่	chicken and peanut curry
" มัสมั่นเนื้อ	Muslim beef curry
แกงมัสมั่นเนื้อหรือไก่	beef or chicken Mussaman curry
" เลียง	spicy mixed vegetable soup without coconut / vegetable and prawn soup
" ส้ม	tamarind-flavored soup / hot and sour mixed vegetables and fish soup
" ส้มแป๊ะซะ	crispy fish with tamarind sauce
" หน่อไม้	bamboo shoot soup
" หมูเทโพ	pork curry
" เหลือง	light yellow curry
" อ่อมมะระ	bitter cucumber curry
" ฮังเล	Chiang Mai pork curry / a Northern style pork curry
" โฮ๊ะ	Northern mixed curry
ไก่ต้มข่า	chicken and galangal in coconut milk soup / chicken in mild coconut and galangal soup / chicken coconut soup
" ทอด	fried chicken
ไก่ผัดขิง	ginger chicken / chicken fried with ginger
" ผัดใบกะเพรา	spicy-fried chicken with basil
" ผัดเม็ดมะม่วงหิมพานต์	stir-fried chicken with cashew nuts / chicken with chilis and cashews / fried chicken with cashew nuts
" ย่าง	barbecued chicken / grilled chicken
" ย่างอีสาน	Northeast barbecued chicken
" ห่อใบเตย	fried marinated chicken wrapped in pandanus leaf

ขนมกล้วยหอม	banana pancakes
” ข้าวแกง	custard squares
” จีน	Thai rice-flour noodles / lighty fermented rice noodles
” จีนน้ำเงี้ยว	rice noodles with spicy meat sauce
” จีนน้ำพริก	noodles in sweet curry sauce
” จีนน้ำยา	rice noodles with sauce / noodles in fish curry sauce
” ด้วง	short noodles rolled in coconut
” ถั่วแปบ	mung bean stuffing
” เบื้องญวน	stuffed crispy egg-crepe / Vietnamese stuffed crispy omelette
” ปิ้งหน้ากุ้ง	shrimp toast
” เปียกปูน	sweet blackened jelly
” เม็ดขนุน	jackfruit seeds
” หม้อแกง	custard squares / baked bean and custard pudding
” เหนียว	sweet rice with syrup
” ปิ้งหน้าหมู	fried minced pork canape
ขมิ้น	turmeric
ข่า	Siamese ginger / galangal
ข้าวเกรียบปากหม้อ	steamed rice-skin dumplings
” ขาหมู	pork leg with rice
” คลุกกะปิ	shrimp paste fried rice
” ซอย	Chiang Mai noodles / curried noodles soup
” ต้มกุ้ง	rice porridge with shrimp / softboiled rice with shrimp / rice congee with shrimp
” ต้มไก่	rice porridge with chicken
” ต้มหมู	rice porridge with pork / softboiled rice with pork / pork congee
ข้าวตัง	crispy rice / rice crackers
” ตังหน้าตั้ง	rice crackers with a minced shrimp and pork dip / rice crackers with pork and coconut sauce / crispy rice crackers with ground pork dip
” ผัด	fried rice
” ผัดกะเพรา	fried rice with basil
” ผัดกะเพราตามสั่ง	fried rice with hot basil to order
” ผัดกุ้ง, ไก่, หมู หรือเนื้อปู	fried rice with shrimp, chicken, pork or crabmeat
” ผัดคะน้าปลาเค็ม	fried rice with kale and salty fish
” ผัดตามสั่งหมู, กุ้ง, ไก่, เนื้อ	fried rice with your choice of pork, shrimp, chicken or beef

ข้าวผัดน้ำพริก	fried rice with spicy sauce
” ผัดปู	crab fried rice / fried rice with crabmeat
” ผัดมันกุ้ง	fried rice with prawn fat
” ผัดสับปะรด	fried rice with shrimps, chicken and pineapple served in a pineapple shell
” ผัดหมู	pork fried rice
” ผัดหมูใบกะเพรา	pork-fried rice with basil leaf
” มัน	coconut rice
” มันไก่	steamed chicken rice / chicken rice
” เม่าราง	roasted flattened sticky rice
” ยำ	rice salad
” สวย	steamed rice
” หน้าเป็ด	duck with rice
ข้าวหลาม	sweet rice in bamboo
” หมูแดง	barbecued pork with rice / barbecued red pork with rice
” เหนียว	sticky rice / steamed sticky rice
” เหนียวแก้ว	sweet sticky rice
” เหนียวดำ	black sticky rice
” เหนียวดำเปียก	black sticky rice pudding
” เหนียวดำหน้ากระฉีก	black rice with coconut
” เหนียวตัด	sticky rice squares
” เหนียวเปียกลำใย	sweet rice pudding with longan
” เหนียวมะม่วง	sweet sticky rice with mango / ripe mango with glutinous rice
” เหนียวมูล	sweet sticky rice
” เหนียวหน้ากุ้ง	sweet yellow rice with shrimp topping
” อบสับปะรด	baked rice in a pineapple
ขิง	ginger
ขิงดอง	pickled ginger / ginger pickle
ขึ้นฉ่าย	Asian celery
ไข่เค็ม	salted eggs
” เจียวเนื้อปู	Thai omelette (*Brit*) with crabmeat
” เจียวหมูสับ	minced pork omelet (*US*)
” ตุ๋นทรงเครื่อง	steamed seafood with egg
” ยัดไส้	stuffed omelet
” ยัดไส้หมูสับ	pork stuffed omelet
” ยัดไส้อาหารทะเล	seafood stuffed omelet
” ลูกเขย	boiled egg fried with tamarind sauce

ครองแครงกรอบ	sweet clams in the shell
” กะทิ	clam shell delight
คอหมูย่าง	charcoal-broiled pork neck
คะน้า	kale / Chinese spinach
” น้ำมันหอย	Chinese spinach fried in oyster sauce
” ปลาเค็ม	stir-fried Chinese spinach with sun-dried salted fish
เครื่องแกงเขียวหวาน	green curry paste
” เผ็ด / เครื่องแกงแดง	red curry paste
” มัสมั่น	Mussaman (Muslim) curry paste
แคบหมู	fried pork skin
งบ	grilled minced fish and vegetable curry
งา	sesame
เงาะ	rambutan
แจ่วบอง	Northeastern spicy dip
ฉู่ฉี่กุ้ง	curry-fried prawns (shrimps) / prawns (shrimps) with coconut milk and chili paste
” กุ้งนาง	large prawns fried in red curry sauce
” ปลา	curry-fried fish
เฉาก๊วย	grass jelly
ชมพู่	rose apple
ซี่โครงหมูทอดกระเทียมพริกไทย	fried pork spare ribs with garlic and pepper
” อบ	five spice pork spare ribs
ซีอิ๊ว	soy sauce
” ขาว	clear soy sauce
” ดำ	black soy sauce
ซุปหน่อไม้	shredded bamboo shoot
ดอกข้าวโพด	baby corn
ดอกจันทน์	mace
ต้นหอม	spring onions / scallions
ต้มข่าไก่	spicy chicken, coconut and galangal soup / spring chicken and galangal in coconut milk soup / chicken in coconut milk with galangal
” โคล้งปลากรอบ	smoked fish soup / sour and spicy smoked-dry fish soup
” จับฉ่าย	ten vegetable stew
” จืดเต้าหู้หมูสับ	clear soup with bean curd and minced pork
” จืดสาหร่ายทะเล	clear soup with seaweed and minced pork
” แซบ	Northeast-style spicy soup

ต้มยำกุ้ง	hot and sour shrimp soup / spicy lemongrass soup with shrimp
" กุ้งใหญ่	hot and sour prawn soup
" ไก่	spicy chicken soup
" ไก่, หมู, กุ้ง, เนื้อ	hot and sour soup with chicken, pork, prawns or beef
" ทะเล	sour and spicy seafood soup
" ปลากรอบ	tom yam with smoked fish / spicy lemon grass soup with smoked fish
" โป๊ะแตก	hot and sour soup with seafood
" เห็ดกับเต้าหู้	spicy fresh mushrooms and bean curd soup
ต้มส้มปลาช่อน	herbed snakefish in sweet and sour soup
" ปลาทู	mackerel in tamarind flavored soup
ต้มหางวัว / ซุปหางวัว	oxtail soup
ตะโก้	pudding with coconut topping
ตะไคร้	lemon grass
ตับหวาน	spicy liver salad
เตย	pandanus leaf
เต้าเจี้ยว	salted soya beans
เต้าหู้	bean curd / tofu
" ขาว	white bean curd / white tofu
" ยี้	pickled bean curd
" หลอด	soft white bean curd
" เหลือง	yellow bean curd / yellow tofu
ถั่วเขียว	mung beans
ถั่วงอก	bean sprouts
" ฝักยาว	long beans
" พลู	winged beans
ทองหยอด	golden balls
ทองเอก	wheat flour dumpling with egg yolk
ทอดมันกุ้ง	shrimp cakes / fried light curried shrimp cakes / deep fried shrimp cakes with condiments
" ข้าวโพด	fried corn cakes
" ปลา	spicy deep-fried fish cakes
" ปลากราย	fried curried fish cakes
ทับทิมกรอบ	crispy water chestnuts / coated water chestnut pieces in coconut milk
ทุเรียน	durian
น้ำแกงจืด	Thai soup stock
น้ำจิ้มสะเต๊ะ	peanut sauce

น้ำซีอิ๊ว	Chinese soy sauce
” ญี่ปุ่น	Japanese soy sauce
น้ำตก	sliced beef salad
น้ำต้มกระดูกวัว	beef stock
น้ำตาลทราย	sugar / granulated sugar / castor sugar
” ทรายแดง	brown sugar
” ป่น	icing sugar
” ปึก / น้ำตาลปีบ	palm sugar
” อ้อย	lump / cube / sugar
น้ำปลา	fish sauce
” พริก	fish sauce with chili
” มะนาว	sour fish sauce
” ร้า	fermented fish sauce
น้ำพริกกะปิ	spicy dried shrimp sauce / raw vegetables with spicy shrimp paste dip
” กะปิ ปลาทูทอด	shrimp paste sauce served with fried mackerel and vegetables
” กุ้งสด	shrimp with shrimp paste mixture served with fresh, spicy hot sauce with fresh prawn pieces
” แกงเขียวหวาน	green curry paste
” แกงเผ็ด	red curry paste
” แกงมัสมั่น	Mussaman curry paste
” ขี้กา	hot and sour chili sauce
” ตาแดง	flaked fish and tamarind sauce
” ปลาทู	fried mackerel with shrimp paste sauce / fried fish with vegetable and spicy dip
น้ำพริกเผา	roasted chili paste / black chili paste
” พะแนง	panaeng curry paste / dry curry paste
” มะขาม	spicy young tamarind paste
” มะม่วง	green mango dip
” มะม่วงปลาสลิดทอด	spicy chopped green mango served with fried dried fish
” ลงเรือ	spicy chili sauce and shrimp paste served with sweetened pork, fluffy catfish, salted egg and fresh vegetables
” หนุ่ม	green chili dip / Northern style spicy dip with vegetables
” อ่อง	spicy meat and tomato dip / vegetables with Chiang Mai dipping sauce / spicy meat and tomato dip

น้ำมะขาม	tamarind water / tamarind juice
น้ำมันพืช	vegetable oil
น้ำส้มสายชู	vinegar
เนื้อเค็ม	salty sun-dried beef
" น้ำตก	sliced beef salad
" ผัดน้ำมันหอย	beef with oyster sauce
" ผัดพริก	chili fried beef / beef fried with chili
" ย่าง	charcoal beef / grilled beef / barbecued beef broiled beef
" ย่างน้ำตก	charcoal beef Northeastern style
" สะเต๊ะ	beef satay
" หมู, กุ้ง, ไก่, ผัดน้ำมันหอย หรือผัดขิงสด	fried beef, pork, prawns, or chicken with oyster sauce or fresh ginger
เนื้ออบ	marinated braised beef with cucumber
บะหมี่	egg noodles
" กรอบราดหน้าไก่	crispy egg-noodles with chicken topping
" น้ำหมู	pork and noodle soup
" น้ำหรือแห้ง หมูแดง, ปู, กุ้ง, ไก่, เนื้อ	egg noodle soup or dry noodles with red pork, crab meat, shrimp and beef
" หมูแดง	egg noodles with barbecued pork
บัวลอย	rice dumplings in coconut milk / taro, pumpkin and rice flour balls in coconut milk
แบะแซ	a rice flour thickener
ใบกระวาน	bay leaf
" กะเพรา	sweet basil / holy basil
" ตอง	banana leaf
" มะกรูด	wild lime leaf
" แมงลัก	basil
" โหระพา	sweet basil
ปลากะพงขาวพริกขิง	fried baby white snapper topped with various spices, kaffir lime and string beans
" กะพงขี้เมา	snapper with spicy garlic sauce
" เก๋าสามรส	fried grouper topped with sweet, sour and hot sauce
" เค็ม	sun-dried salted fish
" เค็มทอด	fried salted fish
" จะละเม็ดทรงเครื่อง	deep-fried pomfret garnished with shredded pork and mushrooms
" เจี๋ยน	whole fish with ginger sauce

ปลาช่อนแป๊ะซะ	steamed whole fish in sauce
” ดุกทอดกรอบผัดเผ็ด	fried crispy catfish with chili paste
” ดุกฟูน้ำพริกมะม่วง	puff-fried catfish with mango sauce
” นึ่ง	steamed fish
” นึ่งเกี้ยมบ๊วย	steamed whole fish with plum pickles
” นึ่งมะนาวพริกสด	steamed fish with lemon and chili
“ เผา	grilled (broiled) whole fish
” ร้าทรงเครื่อง	fermented dip for vegetables
” ราดพริก	fried fish topped with chili sauce
ปลาหมึกทอด	crisp fried calamari / fried squid
” กระเทียมพริกไทย	stir-fried calamari with black pepper and garlic
” ผัดเผ็ด	spicy fried calamari
” ยัดไส้	stir-fried stuffed calamari
” ย่าง	charcoal broiled squid
” แห้ง	dried fish
ปีกไก่ย่าง	barbecued chicken wings
ปูจ๋า	deep-fried crabmeat and minced pork in the shell / stuffed crabshells / deep fried crabmeat and minced pork
ปูนึ่ง	steamed crab with hot sauce
” ผัดผงกะหรี่	stir-fried crab curry / crab with curry powder
” หลน	crab dip
เป็ดตุ๋นมะนาวดอง	duck steamed with Chinese melon and pickled limes
” พะโล้	steamed duck / golden brown duck
” ย่างน้ำผึ้ง	honey roast duck
เปรี้ยวหวานกระดูกหมู	sweet and sour pork spare ribs
เปาะเปี๊ยะทอด	spring rolls
” สด	steamed spring rolls / fresh spring rolls
แป้งข้าวเจ้า	rice flour
” ข้าวโพด	cornflour
” ข้าวเหนียว	sticky rice flour
” ท้าวยายม่อม	arrowroot
” มัน	tapioca flour
” สาลี	wheat flour
โป๊ยกั๊ก	star anise
โป๊ะแตก	seafood combination soup / seafood soup
ผงฟู	baking powder
ผลไม้ในน้ำเชื่อม	tropical fruits in jasmine or lime syrup

ผลไม้รวม	fresh fruits in season
ผักกาดเค็ม	salted Chinese cabbage
” ชี	coriander / cilantro / Chinese parsley
” ดอง	picked vegetables
” ต้มกะทิ	mixed vegetables in coconut sauce
” ทอด	crisp deep-fried vegetables
” บุ้ง	water spinach / water morning glory
” ลวกน้ำพริก	vegetables with dipping sauce
ผัดกะเพรา	stir fried meat with basil
” กะเพราไก่, เนื้อ หรืออาหารทะเล	fried minced chicken, minced beef or seafood with chilis and basil
” กะเพราตามสั่ง	your choice of meats spicy-fried with basil
” กุ้งมังกร	stir-fried lobster with ginger sauce
” ขิงไก่	stir-fried ginger chicken
” ขิงเนื้อ	stir-fried beef with ginger, onion, capsicum and shallots
” คะน้าเนื้อ	fried kale with beef
” คะน้าปลาเค็ม	fried kale with salty fish
” คะน้าหมูกรอบ	fried kale with crispy pork
” ไทย	stir-fried Thai noodles / fried Thai noodle omelette
” ไทยชาววัง	thin rice noodles with dry shrimp, beansprouts and beancurd wrapped with egg
ผัดใบกะเพราเขียวหวานไก่	stir-fried chicken with basil and green curry
” เปรี้ยวหวานกุ้ง	sweet and sour prawns
” เปรี้ยวหวานหมู, ไก่, กุ้ง	sweet and sour pork, chicken, or shrimp with vegetables
” โป๊ะแตก	lemon grass seafood combination
” ผัก	stir-fried vegetable
” ผักเต้าหู้	tofu fried with vegetables
” ผักบุ้งไฟแดง	quick-fried water morning glory
” ผักรวม	stir-fried mixed vegetables
” ผักรวมมิตรกุ้ง	fried mixed vegetables with shrimps
” ผักรวมมิตรน้ำมันหอย	fried mixed vegetables in oyster sauce
” เผ็ดเนื้อ	spicy fried beef
” เผ็ดปลาดุก	spicy catfish
” เผ็ดปลาไหล	spicy fried eel
” เผ็ดหมูป่า	wild boar spice-fried
” พริกขิงไก่หรือหมู	fried chicken or pork with various spices, kaffir lime and string beans

ผัดพริกสดตามสั่ง	fried bell pepper with your choice of meat
" พริกสดหมู, ไก่หรือเนื้อ	fried young fresh chili with pork, chicken or beef
" ฟักทอง	stir-fried squash
" วุ้นเส้น	stir-fried glass noodles with vegetables
" สะตอ	beans fried with shrimp paste / fried flat beans with pork
" หอยแมลงภู่	stir-fried mussels with chili, garlic and basil
" หอยลายน้ำพริกเผา	fried clams with chili paste sauce
เผือก	taro
" ฉาบ	sweet taro crisps
ฝอยทอง	golden threads
พริกขี้หนู	small hot / red green / chili
" ชี้ฟ้า	small /red/green/yellow/ chili
" ไทยขาว	white pepper
" ไทยดำ	black pepper
" ไทยอ่อน	green peppercorns
" น้ำปลา	fish sauce with chilis
" ป่น	roasted chili /powder/flakes/
" หยวก	large mild chili
" แห้ง	dried chilis
พล่ากุ้ง	shrimp salad Northeast style / shrimp salad with lemon grass and mint / lightly grilled prawns seasoned with fresh herbs
" เนื้อ	lighty grilled seasoned beef
" เนื้อมะเขืออ่อน	spicy grilled beef salad with shredded egg plant
" หอย	clam salad
" หอยนางรม	oysters marinated with curry paste
พะแนงเนื้อ	stir-fried beef curry / coconut beef curry
" เนื้อ, ไก่ หรือกุ้ง	beef, chicken or prawns in thick red curry
" ปีกไก่ยัดไส้	dry curry of stuffed chicken wings
" สามรส	dry curry of beef, chicken or pork with sweet basil and palm sugar sauce
ฟัก	winter melon / wax gourd
ฟักทอง	pumpkin / squash
มะกรูด	kaffir lime
มะขาม	tamarind
มะเขือ	eggplant
มะเขือพวง	pea aubergine / eggplant

มะเขือยาว	aubergines
มะนาว	lime
มะนาวดอง	pickled lime / pickled lemon
มะปราง	plum mango
มะพร้าว	coconut
มะพร้าวแก้ว	coconut balls
มะเฟือง	carambola
มะม่วงดอง	pickled mango
มะละกอ	papaya / pawpaw
มังคุด	mangosteen
มันกุ้ง	shrimp fat
มันแกว	yam bean root
มันสำปะหลัง	tapioca
มัสมั่นน่องไก่	chicken drumstick curry and potato
" เนื้อ	Mussaman steak
เม็ดขนุน	jackfruit seeds
เม็ดผักชี	coriander seeds
เมล็ดพริกไทยแห้ง	peppercorn
เมี่ยงกุ้ง	shrimps, fresh ginger, shallots, coriander, mint leaves with mieng sauce
" คำ	a combination of lime, shallot, ginger, roasted coconut, dried shrimp, peanuts and "cha-plu" leaves with mieng sauce / a combination of finely-chopped crispy coconut, cubed lemon, shallot, ginger, dried shrimp and crispy peanuts, to be wrapped in "cha-plu" leaves and "thong-lang" leaves and topped with mieng sauce
" ปลาทู	herbs and mackerel wrapped in "cha-plu" leaves / fresh herbs and fresh minced mackerel, to be wrapped in "cha-plu" leaves
แมงลัก	sweet basil seeds
ยอดข้าวโพดผัดกุ้ง	fried baby corn with shrimp
ยอดผักชี	coriander sprigs
ยำกุนเชียง	Chinese sausage salad
" ขโมย	mixed salad with boiled chicken, pork, egg and vegetable
" แตงกวา	cucumber salad
" ถั่วพู	spicy salad of winged beans and shrimps

ยำทวาย	boiled vegetables, chicken with peanut and cocount milk sauce / boiled vegetables and bean curd topped with peanut sauce
” ทะเล	spicy seafood salad
” เนื้อ	spicy beef salad
” ปลาดุกฟู	spicy deep-fried catfish salad
” ปลาหมึก	calamari salad with mint, onion and lemon grass / squid salad / calamari salad
” โป๊ะแตก	spiced seafood salad
” มะเขือยาว	roasted /aubergine/eggplant/ salad
” มะม่วง	green mango salad
” วุ้นเส้น	glass noodle salad / vermicelli with minced pork and prawns / spicy vermicelli salad with various meats and shrimps
” ส้มโอ	pomelo salad with shrimp and coconut flakes
” หนังหมู	pork rind with lemon grass salad
” หอยแมลงภู่	spicy mussel salad
” หัวปลีทรงเครื่อง	spicy fermented pork salad
” ใหญ่	Thai chef salad / great salad
ยี่หร่า	cumin
รากผักชี	coriander root
โรตี	Southern flat bread
ลวก	blanched
ละมุด	sapodilla
ลาบไก่	chicken salad with mint, onion and lemon grass / spicy chicken salad / spicy minced chicken with raw vegetables
” ดิบ	raw beef salad
” เนื้อ	spicy minced beef salad
” ปลาดุก	spicy catfish salad
” หมู	spicy minced pork salad
” หมู ไก่ หรือเนื้อ	ground pork chicken or beef salad
ลูกกระวาน	cardamom
ลูกจันทน์	nutmeg
ลูกชุบ	delectable imitation fruits
ลูกตาล	palmyra fruit
ลูกมะพร้าว (เนื้อหน้าอก)	brisket
วุ้นเส้น	glass noodles / bean vermicelli / bean threads / cellophane noodles

ส้มเขียวหวาน	mandarin, tangerine orange
” ซ่า	citron
” ตำ	spicy papaya salad / green papaya salad / papaya pok pok
” โอ	pomelo
สังขยา	Thai custard
” เผือก	coconut cream custard in taro
” ฟักทอง	steamed whole pumpkin with coconut custard / Thai custard in a squash / coconut custard in young pumpkin
” มะพร้าว	Thai custard in a coconut
สาคู	tapioca pearls
” เปียก	tapioca pudding
” ไส้หมู	tapioca pork
เส้นหมี่	rice vermicelli
แสร้งว่ากุ้ง	blanched shrimps seasoned with chili, onion and lemon grass served with fresh vegetables and fluffy catfish
” ปลาดุกฟู (ยำปลาดุกฟู)	crispy fluff catfish served with spicy prawn dip
ไส้กรอกอีสาน	Northeast sausage
ไส้อั่ว	Chiang Mai sausage / northern Thai spicy sausage
หน่อไม้	bamboo shoot
หมี่	noodles
” กรอบ	crispy noodles, sweet and sour crisp-fried noodles, sweet crisp-fried noodles
” กะทิ	coconut noodles
หมูกรอบ	crispy fried pork
” กระเทียมพริกไทย	pork fried with garlic and peppercorns, pork fried with garlic and black pepper
” แดง	roast red pork
” ต้มเค็ม	pork casserole
” ต้มเค็มพะโล้	steamed five spice pork
” ผัดถั่วงอก	bean sprouts fried with pork
” ผัดถั่วฝักยาว	stir-fried pork and green beans
” ย่าง	barbecued pork, grilled pork
” หวาน	sweet pork
ห่อหมก	minced fish steamed in a banana leaf
” ทะเล	steamed curried seafood in coconut shell
” ปลา	steamed fish curry

ห่อหมกหมู	steamed pork and vegetable curry
หอมเล็ก	shallots
หอยแครงลวก	steamed blanched clams with dipping sauce
" ทอด	fried mussel pancakes
" ผัดน้ำพริกเผา	clams with chili sauce
" แมลงภู่เผา	broiled mussels with chili sauce
" แมลงภู่อบ	pan-steamed mussels
" แมลงภู่อบหม้อดิน	steamed mussels with lime leaves and galangal
" ลายผัดน้ำพริกเผา	stir-fried baby clams with roasted chili paste and basil
หัวไชโป๊ว	preserved radish
หัวผักกาด	white radish
เห็ดฟาง	straw mushrooms
" หอม	dried Chinese mushrooms
" หูหนู	wood fungus
แหนม	sausage in banana leaf
" สด	fresh sausage / pork salad with mint peanuts and ginger
แห้ว	Chinese water chestnuts
อบเชย	cinnamon
อินทผลัม	dates
ไอศกรีมกะทิ	coconut ice cream
แฮ่กึ๊น	seafood rolls

ชื่อเหล่านี้เป็นชื่ออาหารไทย ตามที่ใช้กันทั่วไปในตำราทำกับข้าวและรายการอาหารตามภัตตาคาร ตามปกติชื่อภาษา
อังกฤษจะเขียนทับศัพท์เพื่อความสะดวกในการสั่งอาหาร การทับศัพท์ควรสะกดตามเสียงอ่าน

These are the names of some Thai dishes as used in a variety of cookbooks and restaurant menus. They are usually accompanied by transliterations of the Thai names for identification when ordering. Any system of transliteration may be used which is likely to elicit helpful sounds.

Sources

Somi Anuntra Miller and Patricia Lake. *Thai Cooking Class.* Sydney: Bay Books, 1992.

Krissnee Ruangkritya and Tim Martsching. *Adventures in Thai Food and Culture.* Bangkok: Jongjit Ruangkritya, 1991.

Panurat Poladitmontri, Judy Law and William Warren. *Thailand the Beautiful Cookbook.* Bangkok: Asia Books, 1992.

M.L. Taw Kritakara and M.R. Pimsai Amranand. *Modern Thai Cooking.* Bangkok: Duang Kamol, 1977.

9

ยศทางการทหารและตำรวจ
Military and Police Ranks

ทหารบก - Army

กองทัพบกไทย **Royal Thai Army**	กองทัพบกสหรัฐอเมริกา **U.S. Army**	กองทัพบกอังกฤษ **British Army**
จอมพล	General of the Army	Field-Marshal
พลเอก	General	General
พลโท	Lieutenant General	Lieutenant-General
พลตรี	Major General	Major-General
	Brigadier General	Brigadier
พันเอก	Colonel	Colonel
พันโท	Lieutenant Colonel	Lieutenant-Colonel
พันตรี	Major	Major
ร้อยเอก	Captain	Captain
ร้อยโท	1st Lieutenant	Lieutenant
ร้อยตรี	2nd Lieutenant	2nd Lieutenant
นายดาบ	Chief Warrant Officer	–
–	Warrant Officer	Warrant Officer 1st Class
		Warrant Officer 2nd Class
–	Sergeant Major of the Army	–
จ่าสิบเอก	Command Sergeant Major	Staff Sergeant
จ่าสิบโท	Master Sergeant	Sergeant
	1st Sergeant	–
จ่าสิบตรี	Sergeant 1st Class	–
	Staff Sergeant	–
	Specialist 6	–
สิบเอก	Sergeant	–
	Specialist 5	–
สิบโท	Corporal	Corporal
	Specialist 4	–
สิบตรี	Private 1st Class	Lance Corporal
พลทหาร	Private	Private

ทหารเรือ - Navy

กองทัพเรือไทย	กองทัพเรือสหรัฐอเมริกา	กองทัพเรืออังกฤษ
Royal Thai Navy	**U.S. Navy**	**Royal Navy**
จอมพลเรือ	Fleet Admiral	Admiral of the Fleet
พลเรือเอก	Admiral	Admiral
พลเรือโท	Vice Admiral	Vice-Admiral
พลเรือตรี	Rear Admiral	Rear-Admiral
นาวาเอก	Commodore	Commodore
นาวาโท	Captain	Captain
นาวาตรี	Commander	Commander
เรือเอก	Lieutenant Commander	Lieutenant Commander
เรือโท	Lieutenant	Lieutenant
–	Lieutenant Junior Grade	Sub-Lieutenant
เรือตรี	Ensign	Midshipman
พันจ่าเอก	Chief Warrant Officer	–
พันจ่าโท	Warrant Officer	Fleet Chief Petty Officer
–	Master Chief Petty Officer of the Navy	–
พันจ่าตรี	Master Chief Petty Officer	–
–	Senior Chief Petty Officer	–
–	Chief Petty Officer	Chief Petty Officer
จ่าเอก	Petty Officer 1st Class	Petty Officer
จ่าโท	Petty Officer 2nd Class	–
จ่าตรี	Petty Officer 3rd Class	Leading Seaman
พลเรือ	Seaman	Able Seaman
–	Seaman Apprentice	Ordinary Seaman
–	Seaman Recruit	Junior Seaman

ทหารอากาศ - Air Force

กองทัพอากาศไทย Royal Thai Air Force	กองทัพอากาศสหรัฐอเมริกา U.S. Air Force	กองทัพอากาศอังกฤษ Royal Air Force
จอมพลอากาศ	General of the Air Force	Marshal of the Royal Air Force
พลอากาศเอก	General	Air Chief Marshal
พลอากาศโท	Lieutenant General	Air Marshal
พลอากาศตรี	Major General	Air Vice Marshal
–	Brigadier General	Air Commodore
นาวาอากาศเอก	Colonel	Group Captain
นาวาอากาศโท	Lieutenant Colonel	Wing Commander
นาวาอากาศตรี	Major	Squadron Leader
เรืออากาศเอก	Captain	Flight Lieutenant
เรืออากาศตรี	2nd Lieutenant	Flying Officer
เรืออากาศโท	1st Lieutenant	Pilot Officer
พันจ่าอากาศเอก	Chief Warrant Officer	–
–	Chief Master Sergeant of the Air Force	–
พันจ่าอากาศโท	Chief Master Sergeant	Warrant Officer
พันจ่าอากาศตรี	Senior Master Sergeant	–
จ่าอากาศเอก	Master Sergeant	Flight Sergeant
–	Technical Sergeant	Chief Technician
–	Staff Sergeant	Sergeant
จ่าอากาศโท	Sergeant	–
จ่าอากาศโท	Airman 1st Class	Corporal
จ่าอากาศตรี	Airman	Senior Aircraftman
-	–	Leading Aircraftman
พลทหารอากาศ	Airman Basic	Aircraftman

ตำรวจไทย - Thai Police

ตำแหน่ง	Position
ผู้บัญชาการตำรวจแห่งชาติ (ผบ.ตร.)	Commissioner-General
รองผู้บัญชาการตำรวจแห่งชาติ (รอง ผบ.ตร.)	Deputy Commissioner-General
ผู้ช่วยผู้บัญชาการตำรวจแห่งชาติ (ผู้ช่วย ผบ.ตร.)	Assistant Commissioner-General
ผู้บัญชาการ (ผบช.)	Commissioner
ผู้บัญชาการตำรวจภูธรภาค 1-9 (ผบช.ภ.1-9)	Commissioner of Provincial Police Region 1-9
รองผู้บัญชาการ (รอง ผบช.)	Deputy Commissioner
ผู้ช่วยผู้บัญชาการ (ผู้ช่วย ผบช.)	Assistant Commissioner
ผู้บังคับการ (ผบก.)	Commander
ผู้บังคับการอำนวยการ (ผบก.อก.)	Commander of General Staff Division
ผู้บังคับการตำรวจภูธรจังหวัด...(ผบก.ภ.จว.)	Commander of...Provincial Police
รองผู้บังคับการ (รอง ผบก.)	Deputy Commander
ผู้กำกับการ (ผกก.)	Superintendent
รองผู้กำกับการ (รอง ผกก.)	Deputy Superintendent
สารวัตรใหญ่ (สวญ.) (ปัจจุบันเลิกใช้)	Chief Inspector *(out of use)*
สารวัตร (สว.)	Inspector
รองสารวัตร (รอง สว.)	Sub-Inspector
ผู้บังคับหมู่ (ผบ.หมู่)	Squad Leader
ลูกแถว	Serviceman

ยศ	Rank
พลตำรวจเอก (พล.ต.อ.)	Police General (Pol. Gen.)
พลตำรวจโท (พล.ต.ท.)	Police Lieutenant General (Pol. Lt. Gen.)
พลตำรวจตรี (พล.ต.ต.)	Police Major General (Pol. Maj. Gen.)
พันตำรวจเอก (พ.ต.อ.)	Police Colonel (Pol. Col.)
พันตำรวจโท (พ.ต.ท.)	Police Lieutenant Colonel (Pol. Lt. Col.)
พันตำรวจตรี (พ.ต.ต.)	Police Major (Pol. Maj.)
ร้อยตำรวจเอก (ร.ต.อ.)	Police Captain (Pol. Capt.)
ร้อยตำรวจโท (ร.ต.ท.)	Police Lieutenant (Pol. Lt.)
ร้อยตำรวจตรี (ร.ต.ต.)	Police Sub-Lieutenant (Pol. Sub-Lt.)
ดาบตำรวจ (ด.ต.)	Police Senior Sergeant Major (Pol. Sen. Sgt. Maj.)
จ่าสิบตำรวจ (จ.ส.ต.)	Police Sergeant Major (Pol. Sgt. Maj.)
สิบตำรวจเอก (ส.ต.อ.)	Police Sergeant (Pol. Sgt.)
สิบตำรวจโท (ส.ต.ท.)	Police Corporal (Pol. Cpl.)
สิบตำรวจตรี (ส.ต.ต.)	Police Lance Corporal (Pol. L/C.)
พลตำรวจ (พลฯ)	Police Constable (Pol. Const.)

10

ชื่อส่วนราชการและธนาคารไทย
Thai Government Organs and Banks

กระทรวงกลาโหม - Ministry of Defence

กรมราชองครักษ์	Royal Aide de Camp Department
กองทัพบก	Royal Thai Army
กองทัพเรือ	Royal Thai Navy
กองทัพอากาศ	Royal Thai Air Force
กองบัญชาการทหารสูงสุด	The Supreme Command Headquarters
สำนักงานเลขานุการรัฐมนตรี	Office of the Secretary to the Minister
สำนักงานปลัดกระทรวงกลาโหม	Office of the Permanent Secretary for Defence
องค์การสงเคราะห์ทหารผ่านศึก	The War Veterans Organization of Thailand

รัฐวิสาหกิจ	**State Enterprises**
องค์การแก้ว	The Glass Organization
องค์การทอผ้า	The Textile Organization
องค์การแบตเตอรี่	The Battery Organization
องค์การผลิตอาหารสำเร็จรูป	The Preserved Food Organization
องค์การฟอกหนัง	The Tanning Organization

กระทรวงการคลัง - Ministry of Finance

กรมธนารักษ์	The Treasury Department
กรมบัญชีกลาง	The Comptroller-General's Department
กรมศุลกากร	The Customs Department
กรมสรรพสามิต	The Excise Department
กรมสรรพากร	The Revenue Department
สำนักงานเลขานุการรัฐมนตรี	Office of the Secretary to the Minister
สำนักงานปลัดกระทรวงการคลัง	Office of the Permanent Secretary for Finance
สำนักงานเศรษฐกิจการคลัง	The Fiscal Policy Office

รัฐวิสาหกิจ	**State Enterprises**
ธนาคารกรุงไทย จำกัด (มหาชน)	Krung Thai Bank Public Company Ltd.
ธนาคารเพื่อการเกษตรและสหกรณ์การเกษตร	Bank for Agriculture and Agricultural Cooperatives

ธนาคารเพื่อการส่งออกและนำเข้าแห่งประเทศไทย	Export-Import Bank of Thailand (EXIM)
ธนาคารออมสิน	The Government Savings Bank
ธนาคารอาคารสงเคราะห์	The Government Housing Bank
โรงงานไพ่	Playing Card Factory
โรงงานยาสูบ	Thailand Tobacco Monopoly
สำนักงานสลากกินแบ่งรัฐบาล	The Government Lottery Office
องค์การสุรา (กรมสรรพสามิต)	Liquor Distillery Organization, (Excise Department)
(ดูสถาบันการเงินอื่นๆ หน้า 725)	*(see Other Financial Institutions p. 725)*

กระทรวงการต่างประเทศ - Ministry of Foreign Affairs

กรมพิธีการทูต	Department of Protocol
กรมยุโรป	Department of European Affairs
กรมเศรษฐกิจ	Department of Economic Affairs
กรมสนธิสัญญาและกฎหมาย	Department of Treaties and Legal Affairs
กรมสารนิเทศ	Department of Information
กรมองค์การระหว่างประเทศ	International Organization Department
กรมอาเซียน	Department of ASEAN Affairs
กรมอเมริกาและแปซิฟิกใต้	Department of American and South Pacific Affairs
กรมเอเชียตะวันออก	Department of East Asian Affairs
กรมเอเชียใต้ ตะวันออกกลาง และแอฟริกา	Department of South Asian, Middle East and African Affairs
สำนักงานเลขานุการรัฐมนตรี	Office of the Secretary to the Minister
สำนักงานปลัดกระทรวงการต่างประเทศ	Office of the Permanent Secretary for Foreign Affairs

กระทรวงเกษตรและสหกรณ์ - Ministry of Agriculture and Cooperatives

กรมชลประทาน	The Royal Irrigation Department
กรมตรวจบัญชีสหกรณ์	Department of Cooperative Auditing
กรมประมง	Department of Fisheries
กรมปศุสัตว์	Department of Livestock Development
กรมป่าไม้	Royal Forest Department
กรมพัฒนาที่ดิน	Land Development Department
กรมวิชาการเกษตร	Department of Agriculture
กรมส่งเสริมการเกษตร	Department of Agricultural Extension
กรมส่งเสริมสหกรณ์	The Cooperative Promotion Department
สำนักงานการปฏิรูปที่ดินเพื่อเกษตรกรรม	Agricultural Land Reform Office

สำนักงานเลขานุการรัฐมนตรี	Office of the Secretary to the Minister
สำนักงานปลัดกระทรวงเกษตรและสหกรณ์	Office of the Permanent Secretary for Agriculture and Cooperatives
สำนักงานเศรษฐกิจการเกษตร	Office of Agricultural Economics

รัฐวิสาหกิจ — State Enterprises

บริษัท ไม้อัดไทย จำกัด	The Thai Plywood Company Limited
สำนักงานกองทุนสงเคราะห์การทำสวนยาง	Office of the Rubber Replanting Aid Fund
องค์การตลาดเพื่อเกษตรกร	The Marketing Organization for Farmers
องค์การส่งเสริมกิจการโคนมแห่งประเทศไทย	Dairy Farming Promotion Organization of Thailand
องค์การสวนยาง	Rubber Estate Organization
องค์การสะพานปลา	Fish Marketing Organization
องค์การอุตสาหกรรมป่าไม้	The Forest Industry Organization
องค์การอุตสาหกรรมห้องเย็น	The Government Cold Storage Organization

กระทรวงคมนาคม - Ministry of Transport and Communications

กรมการขนส่งทางบก	The Department of Land Transport
กรมการบินพาณิชย์	The Department of Aviation
กรมเจ้าท่า	The Harbour Department
กรมทางหลวง	The Department of Highways
กรมไปรษณีย์โทรเลข	The Post and Telegraph Department
กรมอุตุนิยมวิทยา	The Meteorological Department
สำนักงานคณะกรรมการส่งเสริมการพาณิชย์นาวี	Office of the Maritime Promotion Commission
สำนักงานปลัดกระทรวงคมนาคม	Office of the Permanent Secretary for Transport and Communications
สำนักงานเลขานุการรัฐมนตรี	Office of the Secretary to the Minister

รัฐวิสาหกิจ — State Enterprises

การท่าเรือแห่งประเทศไทย	The Port Authority of Thailand
การท่าอากาศยานแห่งประเทศไทย	The Airports Authority of Thailand
การรถไฟแห่งประเทศไทย	The State Railway of Thailand
การสื่อสารแห่งประเทศไทย	The Communications Authority of Thailand
บริษัท การบินไทย จำกัด	Thai Airways International Ltd.
บริษัท ขนส่ง จำกัด	The Transport Company Limited
บริษัท ไทยเดินเรือทะเล จำกัด	Thai Maritime Navigation Co., Ltd.
บริษัท วิทยุการบินแห่งประเทศไทย จำกัด	Aeronautical Radio of Thailand Ltd.
องค์การขนส่งมวลชนกรุงเทพฯ	The Bangkok Mass Transit Authority

องค์การโทรศัพท์แห่งประเทศไทย   The Telephone Organization of Thailand

องค์การรับส่งสินค้าและพัสดุภัณฑ์   The Express Transportation Organization of Thailand

กระทรวงพาณิชย์ - Ministry of Commerce

กรมการค้าต่างประเทศ	Department of Foreign Trade
กรมการค้าภายใน	Department of Internal Trade
กรมการประกันภัย	The Insurance Department
กรมทรัพย์สินทางปัญญา	Department of Intellectual Property
กรมทะเบียนการค้า	Department of Commercial Registration
กรมเศรษฐกิจการพาณิชย์	Department of Business Economics
กรมส่งเสริมการส่งออก	Department of Export Promotion
สำนักงานเลขานุการรัฐมนตรี	Office of the Secretary to the Minister
สำนักงานปลัดกระทรวงพาณิชย์	Office of the Permanent Secretary for Commerce
องค์การคลังสินค้า	The Public Warehouse Organization

กระทรวงมหาดไทย - Ministry of Interior

กรมการปกครอง	Department of Local Administration
กรมการผังเมือง	Department of Town and Country Planning
กรมการพัฒนาชุมชน	The Community Development Department
กรมที่ดิน	Department of Lands
กรมโยธาธิการ	The Public Works Department
กรมราชทัณฑ์	Department of Corrections
สำนักงานเร่งรัดพัฒนาชนบท	Office of Accelerated Rural Development
สำนักงานเลขานุการรัฐมนตรี	Office of the Secretary to the Minister
สำนักงานปลัดกระทรวงมหาดไทย	Office of the Permanent Secretary for Interior

รัฐวิสาหกิจ	**State Enterprises**
การเคหะแห่งชาติ	The National Housing Authority
การทางพิเศษแห่งประเทศไทย	The Expressway and Rapid Transit Authority of Thailand
การประปานครหลวง	The Metropolitan Waterworks Authority
การประปาส่วนภูมิภาค	The Provincial Waterworks Authority
การไฟฟ้านครหลวง	The Metropolitan Electricity Authority
การไฟฟ้าส่วนภูมิภาค	The Provincial Electricity Authority
องค์การตลาด	The Marketing Organization

กระทรวงยุติธรรม - Ministry of Justice

กรมคุมประพฤติ	Department of Probation
กรมบังคับคดี	Legal Execution Department
ศาลฎีกา	The Supreme Court
ศาลทรัพย์สินทางปัญญาและการค้าระหว่างประเทศ	The Intellectual Property and International Trade Court
ศาลแพ่ง	The Civil Court
ศาลแพ่งกรุงเทพใต้	The Civil Court of Southern Bangkok
ศาลภาษีอากรกลาง	The Central Tax Court
ศาลเยาวชนและครอบครัวกลาง	The Central Juvenile and Family Court
ศาลแรงงานกลาง	The Central Labour Court
ศาลล้มละลาย	The Bankruptcy Court
ศาลอุทธรณ์	The Court of Appeals
ศาลอุทธรณ์ภาค 1	The Court of Appeals Region 1
ศาลอาญา	The Criminal Court
สำนักงานเลขานุการรัฐมนตรี	Office of the Secretary to the Minister
สำนักงานปลัดกระทรวงยุติธรรม	Office of the Permanent Secretary for Justice
สำนักงานส่งเสริมงานตุลาการ	Office of the Judicial Affairs

กระทรวงแรงงานและสวัสดิการสังคม - Ministry of Labour and Social Welfare

กรมการจัดหางาน	Department of Employment
กรมประชาสงเคราะห์	Department of Public Welfare
กรมพัฒนาฝีมือแรงงาน	Department of Skill Development
กรมสวัสดิการและคุ้มครองแรงงาน	Department of Labour Protection and Welfare
สำนักงานประกันสังคม	Social Security Office
สำนักงานปลัดกระทรวงแรงงานและสวัสดิการสังคม	Office of the Permanent Secretary for Labour and Social Welfare
สำนักงานเลขานุการรัฐมนตรี	Office of the Secretary to the Minister

กระทรวงวิทยาศาสตร์ เทคโนโลยี และสิ่งแวดล้อม - Ministry of Science, Technology and Environment

กรมควบคุมมลพิษ	Pollution Control Department
กรมพัฒนาและส่งเสริมพลังงาน	Department of Energy Affairs

กรมวิทยาศาสตร์บริการ	Department of Science Service
กรมส่งเสริมคุณภาพสิ่งแวดล้อม	Department of Environmental Quality Promotion
สำนักงานเลขานุการรัฐมนตรี	Office of the Secretary to the Minister
สำนักงานคณะกรรมการวิจัยแห่งชาติ	The National Research Council of Thailand
สำนักงานนโยบายและแผนสิ่งแวดล้อม	Office of Environmental Policy and Planning
สำนักงานพลังงานปรมาณูเพื่อสันติ	Office of Atomic Energy for Peace
สำนักงานปลัดกระทรวงวิทยาศาสตร์ เทคโนโลยี และ สิ่งแวดล้อม	Office of the Permanent Secretary for Science, Technology and Environment

รัฐวิสาหกิจ — State Enterprises

| สำนักงานพัฒนาวิทยาศาสตร์และเทคโนโลยีแห่งชาติ | National Science and Technology Development Agency |
| สถาบันวิจัยวิทยาศาสตร์และเทคโนโลยีแห่งประเทศไทย | Thailand Institute of Scientific and Technological Research |

กระทรวงศึกษาธิการ - Ministry of Education

กรมการศาสนา	The Religious Affairs Department
กรมการศึกษานอกโรงเรียน	Department of Non-formal Education
กรมพลศึกษา	Department of Physical Education
กรมวิชาการ	Department of Curriculum and Instruction Development
กรมศิลปากร	The Fine Arts Department
กรมสามัญศึกษา	Department of General Education
กรมอาชีวศึกษา	Department of Vocational Education
สถาบันเทคโนโลยีราชมงคล	Rajamangala Institute of Technology
สำนักงานคณะกรรมการการประถมศึกษาแห่งชาติ	Office of the National Primary Education Commission
สำนักงานคณะกรรมการการศึกษาเอกชน	Office of the Private Education Commission
สำนักงานคณะกรรมการข้าราชการครู	Office of the Teacher Civil Service Commission
สำนักงานคณะกรรมการวัฒนธรรมแห่งชาติ	Office of the National Culture Commission
สำนักงานปลัดกระทรวงศึกษาธิการ	Office of the Permanent Secretary for Education
สำนักงานเลขานุการรัฐมนตรี	Office of the Secretary to the Minister
สำนักงานสภาสถาบันราชภัฏ	The Office of Rajabhat Institutes Council

รัฐวิสาหกิจ — State Enterprises

| คุรุสภา | The Teachers Council of Thailand |
| องค์การค้าของคุรุสภา | Kurusapa Business Organization |

กระทรวงสาธารณสุข - Ministry of Public Health

กรมการแพทย์	Department of Medical Services
กรมควบคุมโรคติดต่อ	Department of Communicable Disease Control
กรมวิทยาศาสตร์การแพทย์	Department of Medical Sciences
กรมสุขภาพจิต	Department of Mental Health
กรมอนามัย	Department of Health
สำนักงานเลขานุการรัฐมนตรี	Office of the Secretary to the Minister
สำนักงานคณะกรรมการอาหารและยา	The Food and Drug Administration
สำนักงานปลัดกระทรวงสาธารณสุข	Office of the Permanent Secretary for Public Health
รัฐวิสาหกิจ	**State Enterprise**
องค์การเภสัชกรรม	The Government Pharmaceutical Organization

กระทรวงอุตสาหกรรม - Ministry of Industry

กรมทรัพยากรธรณี	Department of Mineral Resources
กรมโรงงานอุตสาหกรรม	Department of Industrial Works
กรมส่งเสริมอุตสาหกรรม	Department of Industrial Promotion
สำนักงานเลขานุการรัฐมนตรี	Office of the Secretary to the Minister
สำนักงานปลัดกระทรวงอุตสาหกรรม	Office of the Permanent Secretary for Industry
สำนักงานมาตรฐานผลิตภัณฑ์อุตสาหกรรม	The Thai Industrial Standards Institute
รัฐวิสาหกิจ	**State Enterprises**
การนิคมอุตสาหกรรมแห่งประเทศไทย	The Industrial Estate Authority of Thailand
การปิโตรเลียมแห่งประเทศไทย	The Petroleum Authority of Thailand
บริษัท นารายณ์ภัณฑ์ จำกัด	Narayana Phand Co., Ltd. (a joint venture with the Ministry of Industry)
โรงงานน้ำตาล กรมโรงงานอุตสาหกรรม	Sugar Factories Inc., Department of Industrial Works
สำนักงานเศรษฐกิจอุตสาหกรรม	The Office of Industrial Economics
องค์การเหมืองแร่ในทะเล	The Offshore Mining Organization

ทบวงมหาวิทยาลัย - Ministry of University Affairs

จุฬาลงกรณ์มหาวิทยาลัย	Chulalongkorn University
มหาวิทยาลัยเกษตรศาสตร์	Kasetsart University
มหาวิทยาลัยขอนแก่น	Khon Kaen University
มหาวิทยาลัยเชียงใหม่	Chiang Mai University

มหาวิทยาลัยธรรมศาสตร์	Thammasat University
มหาวิทยาลัยนเรศวร	Naresuan University
มหาวิทยาลัยบูรพา	Burapa University
มหาวิทยาลัยมหิดล	Mahidol University
มหาวิทยาลัยรามคำแหง	Ramkhamhaeng University
มหาวิทยาลัยศรีนครินทรวิโรฒ	Srinakharinwirot University
มหาวิทยาลัยศิลปากร	Silpakorn University
มหาวิทยาลัยสงขลานครินทร์	Prince of Songkla University
มหาวิทยาลัยสุโขทัยธรรมาธิราช	Sukhothaithammathirat Open University
มหาวิทยาลัยอุบลราชธานี	Ubon Ratchathani University
สถาบันเทคโนโลยีการเกษตรแม่โจ้	Maejo Institute of Agricultural Technology
สถาบันเทคโนโลยีพระจอมเกล้า ธนบุรี	King Mongkut's Institute of Technology, Thonburi
สถาบันเทคโนโลยีพระจอมเกล้า พระนครเหนือ	King Mongkut's Institute of Technology, North Bangkok
สถาบันเทคโนโลยีพระจอมเกล้า วิทยาเขตเจ้าคุณทหาร ลาดกระบัง	King Mongkut's Institute of Technology, Lat Krabang
สถาบันบัณฑิตพัฒนบริหารศาสตร์	National Institute of Development Administration
สำนักงานปลัดทบวงมหาวิทยาลัย	Office of the Permanent Secretary for University Affairs
สำนักงานเลขานุการรัฐมนตรี	Office of the Secretary to the Minister

สำนักนายกรัฐมนตรี - Office of the Prime Minister

กรมประชาสัมพันธ์	The Public Relations Department
กรมวิเทศสหการ	Department of Technical and Economic Cooperation
คณะกรรมการส่งเสริมการลงทุน	Board of Investment (BOI)
สำนักข่าวกรองแห่งชาติ	National Intelligence Agency
สำนักเลขาธิการนายกรัฐมนตรี	The Secretariat of the Prime Minister
สำนักงบประมาณ	The Bureau of the Budget
สำนักงานคณะกรรมการกฤษฎีกา	Office of the Juridical Council, Office of the Council of State
สำนักงานคณะกรรมการการศึกษาแห่งชาติ	Office of the National Education Commission
สำนักงานคณะกรรมการข้าราชการพลเรือน	Office of the Civil Service Commission
สำนักงานคณะกรรมการจัดระบบการจราจรทางบก	Office of the Commission for the Management of Road Traffic
สำนักงานคณะกรรมการนโยบายพลังงานแห่งชาติ	National Energy Policy Office
สำนักงานคณะกรรมการป้องกันและปราบปรามการทุจริตและประพฤติมิชอบในวงราชการ	Office of the Commission of Counter Corruption

สำนักงานคณะกรรมการป้องกันและปราบปรามยาเสพติด	Office of the Narcotics Control Board
สำนักงานคณะกรรมการพัฒนาการเศรษฐกิจและสังคมแห่งชาติ	Office of the National Economic and Social Development Board
สำนักงานคณะกรรมการพิเศษเพื่อประสานงานโครงการอันเนื่องมาจากพระราชดำริ	Office of the Royal Development Projects Board
สำนักงานคณะกรรมการส่งเสริมการลงทุน	Office of the Board of Investment
สำนักงานคณะกรรมการส่งเสริมและประสานงานเยาวชนแห่งชาติ	National Youth Bureau
สำนักงานตำรวจแห่งชาติ	Office of the National Police
สำนักงานเลขาธิการคณะรัฐมนตรี	The Secretariat of the Cabinet
สำนักงานปลัดสำนักนายกรัฐมนตรี	Office of the Permanent Secretary, the Prime Minister's Office
สำนักงานสถิติแห่งชาติ	National Statistical Office
สำนักงานสภาความมั่นคงแห่งชาติ	Office of the National Security Council

รัฐวิสาหกิจ	**State Enterprises**
การกีฬาแห่งประเทศไทย	Sports Authority of Thailand
การท่องเที่ยวแห่งประเทศไทย (ททท.)	The Tourism Authority of Thailand (TAT)
การไฟฟ้าฝ่ายผลิตแห่งประเทศไทย (กฟผ.)	The Electricity Generating Authority of Thailand (EGAT)
องค์การรถไฟฟ้ามหานคร	Metropolitan Rapid Transit Authority (MRA)
องค์การสวนสัตว์	The Zoological Park Organization
องค์การสื่อสารมวลชนแห่งประเทศไทย (อสมท.)	Mass Communication Organization of Thailand (MCOT)

หน่วยราชการอิสระ - Independent Public Agencies

ธนาคารแห่งประเทศไทย	Bank of Thailand
ราชบัณฑิตยสถาน	The Royal Institute
ศาลรัฐธรรมนูญ	The Constitutional Court
ศาลาว่าการกรุงเทพมหานคร	Bangkok Metropolitan Administration
สำนักงานตรวจเงินแผ่นดิน	Office of the Auditor-General of Thailand
สำนักงานทรัพย์สินส่วนพระมหากษัตริย์	Bureau of the Crown Property
สำนักงานเลขาธิการวุฒิสภา	The Secretariat of the Senate
สำนักงานเลขาธิการสภาผู้แทนราษฎร	The Secretariat of the House of Representatives
สำนักงานอัยการสูงสุด	Office of the Attorney-General
สำนักพระราชวัง	Bureau of the Royal Household
สำนักราชเลขาธิการ	The Office of His Majesty's Principal Private Secretary

สถาบันการเงินอื่นๆ - Other Financial Institutions

คณะกรรมการกำกับหลักทรัพย์และตลาดหลักทรัพย์ (ก.ล.ต.)	Securities and Exchange Commission (SEC)
คณะกรรมการเพื่อส่งเสริมการปรับปรุงโครงสร้างหนี้ (คปน.)	The Corporate Debt Restructuring Advisory Committee (CDRAC)
ตลาดหลักทรัพย์แห่งประเทศไทย	The Stock Exchange of Thailand (SET)
บรรษัทเงินทุนอุตสาหกรรมขนาดย่อม	Small Industrial Finance Corporation (SIFC)
บรรษัทเงินทุนอุตสาหกรรมแห่งประเทศไทย	The Industrial Finance Corporation of Thailand (IFCT)
บรรษัทตลาดรองสินเชื่อที่อยู่อาศัย (บตท.)	Secondary Mortgage Corporation (SMC)
บรรษัทบริหารสินทรัพย์สถาบันการเงิน (บบส.)	Asset Management Corporation (AMC)
องค์การบริหารสินเชื่ออสังหาริมทรัพย์ (อบส.)	Property Loan Management Organization (PLMO)
องค์การเพื่อการปฏิรูประบบสถาบันการเงิน (ปรส)	Financial Sector Restructuring Authority (FRA)

ธนาคารไทย

Thai Banks

ไทยธนาคาร จำกัด (มหาชน)	Bankthai Public Company Ltd.
ธนาคารกรุงเทพ จำกัด (มหาชน)	Bankok Bank Public Company Ltd.
ธนาคารกรุงไทย จำกัด (มหาชน)	Krung Thai Bank Public Company Ltd.
ธนาคารกรุงศรีอยุธยา จำกัด (มหาชน)	Bank of Ayudhya Public Company Ltd.
ธนาคารกสิกรไทย จำกัด (มหาชน)	Thai Farmers Bank Public Company Ltd.
ธนาคารดี บี เอส ไทยทนุ จำกัด (มหาชน)	DBS Thai Danu Bank Public Company Ltd.
ธนาคารทหารไทย จำกัด (มหาชน)	The Thai Military Bank Public Company Ltd.
ธนาคารไทยพาณิชย์ จำกัด (มหาชน)	The Siam Commercial Bank Public Company Ltd.
ธนาคารนครหลวงไทย จำกัด (มหาชน)	Siam City Bank Public Company Ltd.
ธนาคารเพื่อการเกษตรและสหกรณ์การเกษตร	Bank for Agriculture and Agricultural Cooperatives
ธนาคารเพื่อการส่งออกและนำเข้าแห่งประเทศไทย	Export-Import Bank of Thailand (EXIM)
ธนาคารรัตนสิน จำกัด (มหาชน)	Radhanasin Bank Public Company Ltd.
ธนาคารศรีนคร จำกัด (มหาชน)	Bangkok Metropolitan Bank Public Company Ltd.
ธนาคารสแตนดาร์ดชาร์เตอร์ดนครธน จำกัด (มหาชน)	Standard Chartered Nakornthon Bank Public Company Ltd.
ธนาคารออมสิน	The Government Savings Bank
ธนาคารอาคารสงเคราะห์	The Government Housing Bank
ธนาคารเอเชีย จำกัด (มหาชน)	Bank of Asia Public Company Ltd.

Sources

กองข่าวต่างประเทศ, กรมประชาสัมพันธ์, *นามสงเคราะห์ส่วนราชการไทย* (ฉบับที่ 12), 2540

หน่วยราชการ, ธนาคารแห่งประเทศไทย

เกี่ยวกับผู้รวบรวม

ดำเนิน การเด่น

ได้รับปริญญาอักษรศาสตรบัณฑิตเกียรตินิยมด้าน
รัฐศาสตร์ จากเคนยันคอลเลจ ที่มลรัฐโอไฮโอ และ
นิติศาสตรดุษฎีบัณฑิตจากคณะนิติศาสตร์ แห่ง
มหาวิทยาลัยฮาร์วาร์ด เป็นสมาชิกสภาทนายความ
นอกจากจะมีอาชีพทางด้านกฎหมายแล้ว ยังได้แปล
กฎหมาย ระเบียบข้อบังคับ และประกาศต่างๆ
ในราชกิจจานุเบกษาเป็นภาษาอังกฤษ แปลเรื่องสั้นชุด
ฟ้าบ่กั้น ของ ลาว คำหอม เป็นภาษาอังกฤษ ซึ่งตีพิมพ์
โดยสำนักพิมพ์มหาวิทยาลัยอ๊อกฟอร์ด ในชื่อว่า *The
Politician and Other Stories*

Domnern Garden

JD (Harvard), admitted to practice law
in Thailand, translator of laws, decrees,
regulations, translator of
*The Politician and Other Stories
(Fah Baw Kan)* by the National Artist in
Literature, Khamsing Srinawk, for
Oxford University Press.

เสฐียรพงษ์ วรรณปก

สำเร็จเปรียญเก้าประโยคตั้งแต่ยังเป็นสามเณร ได้รับ
ปริญญาอักษรศาสตรบัณฑิตเกียรตินิยม และปริญญาโท
ทางด้านภาษาตะวันออกโบราณ (บาลี-สันสกฤต)
จากมหาวิทยาลัยเคมบริดจ์ เป็นศาสตราจารย์แห่ง
มหาวิทยาลัยศิลปากร และเป็นผู้บรรยายพิเศษในสาขา
วิชาพุทธศาสตร์ ณ มหาจุฬาลงกรณราชวิทยาลัย เป็น
ราชบัณฑิตประเภทปรัชญา สาขาศาสนศาสตร์ และเป็น
นักเขียนที่มีผลงานเด่นๆ อีกหลายเรื่อง เช่น *พุทธวจนะ
ในธรรมบท พุทธจริยาวัตร พุทธศาสนาทัศนะและ
วิจารณ์* ฯลฯ รวมทั้งบทความทางหน้าหนังสือพิมพ์และ
นิตยสารฉบับต่างๆ อยู่เป็นประจำ

Sathienpong Wannapok

MA (Cambridge) in Oriental Studies,
fellow of the Royal Institute, professor at
Silpakorn University, special lecturer in
Buddhism at Mahachulalongkorn
Buddhist University, author of works in
Thai and English including *Buddha's
Words in the Dhammapada* and *Life of
the Buddha*, and a regular contributor to
newspapers and periodicals.

Second edition cover redesigned by Nuachin Kantaputra